Firearms Law and the Second Amendment

ASPEN CASEBOOK SERIES

Firearms Law and the Second Amendment
Regulation, Rights, and Policy

Nicholas J. Johnson
Professor of Law
Fordham University

David B. Kopel
Adjunct Professor of Law
University of Denver

George A. Mocsary
Visiting Assistant Professor of Law
University of Connecticut

Michael P. O'Shea
Associate Professor of Law
Oklahoma City University

Wolters Kluwer
Law & Business

Printed in the United States of America.

1 2 3 4 5 6 7 8 9 0

ISBN 978-1-4548-0511-3

Library of Congress Cataloging-in-Publication Data

Firearms law and the Second Amendment regulation : rights, and
   policy / Nicholas J. Johnson . . . [et al.].
     p. cm.
   Includes index.
   ISBN 978-1-4548-0511-3
1. Firearms — Law and legislation — United States — History. 2. United States. Constitution.
2nd Amendment. 3. Gun control — United States. I. Johnson, Nicholas J.
   KF3941.F57 2011
   344.7305'33–dc23

2011049656

About Wolters Kluwer Law & Business

Wolters Kluwer Law & Business is a leading global provider of intelligent information and digital solutions for legal and business professionals in key specialty areas, and respected educational resources for professors and law students. Wolters Kluwer Law & Business connects legal and business professionals as well as those in the education market with timely, specialized authoritative content and information-enabled solutions to support success through productivity, accuracy and mobility.

Serving customers worldwide, Wolters Kluwer Law & Business products include those under the Aspen Publishers, CCH, Kluwer Law International, Loislaw, Best Case, ftwilliam.com and MediRegs family of products.

CCH products have been a trusted resource since 1913, and are highly regarded resources for legal, securities, antitrust and trade regulation, government contracting, banking, pension, payroll, employment and labor, and healthcare reimbursement and compliance professionals.

Aspen Publishers products provide essential information to attorneys, business professionals and law students. Written by preeminent authorities, the product line offers analytical and practical information in a range of specialty practice areas from securities law and intellectual property to mergers and acquisitions and pension/benefits. Aspen's trusted legal education resources provide professors and students with high-quality, up-to-date and effective resources for successful instruction and study in all areas of the law.

Kluwer Law International products provide the global business community with reliable international legal information in English. Legal practitioners, corporate counsel and business executives around the world rely on Kluwer Law journals, looseleafs, books, and electronic products for comprehensive information in many areas of international legal practice.

Loislaw is a comprehensive online legal research product providing legal content to law firm practitioners of various specializations. Loislaw provides attorneys with the ability to quickly and efficiently find the necessary legal information they need, when and where they need it, by facilitating access to primary law as well as state-specific law, records, forms and treatises.

Best Case Solutions is the leading bankruptcy software product to the bankruptcy industry. It provides software and workflow tools to flawlessly streamline petition preparation and the electronic filing process, while timely incorporating ever-changing court requirements.

ftwilliam.com offers employee benefits professionals the highest quality plan documents (retirement, welfare and non-qualified) and government forms (5500/PBGC, 1099 and IRS) software at highly competitive prices.

MediRegs products provide integrated health care compliance content and software solutions for professionals in healthcare, higher education and life sciences, including professionals in accounting, law and consulting.

Wolters Kluwer Law & Business, a division of Wolters Kluwer, is headquartered in New York. Wolters Kluwer is a market-leading global information services company focused on professionals.

To my family, near and far, here and gone
—Nicholas J. Johnson

To my father, Jerry Kopel, who devoted his career as a State Representative, an attorney, and a journalist to standing up for the rights of the underdog
—David B. Kopel

To Vicki, my family, and my loyal friends
—George A. Mocsary

To J.M.O. and to Honest John Martin (1812-1875)
—Michael P. O'Shea

Summary of Contents

||ONLINE||

Contents

‖ 2 ‖

Antecedents of the Second Amendment 37

|| 3 ||

The Colonies and the Revolution   101

‖ 4 ‖

The New Constitution   185

‖ 5 ‖

The Right to Arms, Militias, and Slavery in the Early
Republic and Antebellum Periods   243

II 6 II

Reconstruction and Beyond   289

‖ PART TWO ‖
THE RIGHT TO ARMS IN THE MODERN WORLD

‖ 7 ‖

A New and Dangerous Century

‖ 8 ‖

Between *Miller* and *Heller*: The Second Amendment
in the Modern Era

‖ 9 ‖

The Supreme Court Affirms an Individual Right to Arms

‖ 10 ‖

Firearms Policy and Status:
Race, Gender, Age, Disability, and Sexual Orientation

‖ 11 ‖

Applying the Affirmed Right to Arms   783

‖ ONLINE ‖

‖ 12 ‖

Social Science

‖ 13 ‖

International Law

‖ 14 ‖

Comparative Law

‖ 15 ‖

In-Depth Explanation of Firearms and Ammunition

Preface

While this book proceeds chronologically, we expect that many users will approach the material out of sequence. Indeed, we have done so in our own classes. For example, it can be very effective to launch right into contemporary gun-law issues by starting with the Supreme Court's major cases on the Second Amendment, *District of Columbia v. Heller*, and *McDonald v. Chicago* in Chapter 9, followed by Chapter 11 for post-*Heller* issues. It is also effective to assign the chapters covering the 17th and 18th century in conjunction with coverage of *Heller* and *McDonald*. This approach illuminates the originalist historical analysis in both cases. The most relevant original materials for *Heller* (from English origins to the first decades of American independence) appear in Chapters 2 through 5. The original materials relevant to the Fourteenth Amendment are in Chapter 6.

The book is sufficiently modular to accommodate instructors who wish to use particular chapters as part of more general courses, e.g., criminal law, constitutional law, or jurisprudence. For example, someone teaching criminal law might use Chapters 7 and 8 (covering the main federal gun control statutes) for a discrete segment on firearms violations. The treatments of *Heller* and *McDonald* in Chapter 9, and the material on standards of review in Chapter 11, are a nice vehicle for examining various general modes of constitutional decision-making. The material in Chapter 10 is a good choice for showing how the perspectives of divergent communities can affect the assessment of legal and constitutional issues. Online Chapter 13, on international law, could be used as a unit in a general course on international law, a seminar on arms control, or a class on the laws of warfare.

Instructors interested in particular policy topics, such as gun shows, import restrictions, handgun carry permits, or "assault weapons," will find sections covering them. Of course, the index highlights discrete treatments of such topics.

The Notes & Questions in the book frequently raise forward-looking issues and core questions that relate to current controversies. Some of the Notes & Questions are designated "Connection Questions" (CQ) to indicate their relevance to cases or topics in other chapters.

While the U.S. debate on gun rights typically uses "the Second Amendment" as a shorthand for those rights, much of the legal history, and many of the contemporary legal battles, involves state constitutions. Today, 44 state constitutions have right-to-arms provisions. The book covers state right-to-arms issues in depth, both for their intrinsic importance and because the state cases sometimes provide guidance or background for understanding the Second Amendment. Because state issues appear throughout the book, readers should use the Table of Statutes, Constitutions, and Regulations, and the Index, to find all the material on any particular state.

Overview of the Book

Chapter 1 explains how firearms function and describes the major types of firearms. Chapter 1 also outlines the general scope of modern American gun laws, including variations among the states. The Chapter includes an Appendix of state constitutional provisions on the right to arms. The next nine chapters tell, in generally chronological order, the story of the development of gun regulation and gun rights in the United States.

The Second Amendment right to arms is widely viewed as a historical successor to the English right to arms, which was codified in the English Declaration of Right of 1689. Chapter 2 examines the historical and political background of the English right and English gun laws. It also explores the religious and philosophical background of the ideas of armed self-defense and a citizen militia. The chapter begins with early Chinese philosophy, then covers ancient Greece and Rome, Judeo-Christian perspectives, medieval thought, and the Renaissance.

Chapter 3 examines the American colonial experience and the American Revolution. Colonial militias were important military and political institutions, and the militia regulations provide insight into the early understanding of the public and private roles of arms possession. The chapter then describes the British efforts to confiscate American firearms and gunpowder that helped precipitate the American Revolution. Finally, the chapter covers the War of Independence, and the U.S. and state governments before 1789.

Chapter 4 discusses the framing of the U.S. Constitution and its Bill of Rights. Ratification of the U.S. Constitution in 1789 created a more active and powerful federal government; among its new powers were direct federal control over the militia. The Bill of Rights was added to the Constitution in 1791, including a Second Amendment that affirmed the necessity of a well regulated militia, and recognized the right of the people to keep and bear arms. Chapter 4 examines the debates over the Constitution's ratification, the drafting history of the Second Amendment, and the ways in which the American right to arms was viewed by the earliest constitutional commentators.

Chapter 5 surveys the first seven decades of the new republic. This period saw an evolution of the American understanding of both the role of militias and of the individual right to arms. The chapter starts with the political crisis of 1798-1800 that brought several states to the brink of armed resistance. The War of 1812 displayed the strengths and weaknesses of American militias. Chapter 5 also chronicles a significant transition in the direction of gun regulation in America. While colonial- and revolutionary-era gun control laws were mainly concerned with forcing people to own and carry guns, by the 1820s laws prohibiting people from carrying concealed guns and knives began to emerge, particularly in the South. These laws gave rise to the first judicial opinions addressing the scope of permitted regulation under the right to arms guarantees in the federal and state constitutions. The predominant view of the courts of this period was that the constitutional right to arms included an individual right to carry common weapons for self-defense, and that legislatures could regulate the right. Many courts held that legislatures could prohibit the concealed carrying of weapons. The Southern states continued the colonial practice of enacting highly restrictive laws prohibiting the ownership or carrying of guns by slaves and, sometimes, by free Blacks, setting the precedent for broader restrictions after the Civil War. Abolitionists invoked the Second Amendment to complain about the disarmament of Free Soil settlers in Kansas in the 1850s, and to argue that slavery and the Second Amendment were incompatible.

Chapter 6 begins with the period following the Civil War, proceeds through Reconstruction, and ends at the turn of the 19th century. In this period, the Fourteenth Amendment was adopted to protect individual civil liberties against state interference — and especially to combat the violations of rights of newly freed slaves and their supporters. The chapter includes some of the many sources suggesting that the Amendment was intended to secure the individual liberties guaranteed in the federal bill of rights (including an individual right to arms for self-defense) against state infringement by state and local governments. The chapter also tracks the decline of Reconstruction, and the failure of the initial promise of the Fourteenth Amendment. Materials include decisions by the U.S. Supreme Court narrowly interpreting the Fourteenth Amendment, rendering it of little value as a guarantor of individual liberties; adoption by the Southern states of Jim Crow laws; and affirmation by Southern courts of increasingly restrictive (and often racially discriminatory) regulation of firearms — particularly the carrying and ownership of inexpensive handguns. As labor unrest grew in the North, some states prohibited mass armed parades, and the Supreme Court upheld such bans in *Presser v. Illinois*. The Court was, however, quite protective of armed self-defense by individuals, in "The Self-Defense Cases" which arose in federal territories.

Chapter 7 examines the early twentieth century. In this period, gun control for individuals expanded beyond the South, as Northern states, concerned about the labor movement and unassimilated immigrants, adopted a variety of handgun control laws. The chapter also marks the emergence of the first federal gun control laws. In the 1930s, the federal government imposed regulations on commercial gun sales. The most significant of these was National Firearms Act of 1934 (NFA), which severely restricted ownership of a few classes of firearms viewed as unusually dangerous, such as machine guns and short shotguns. Chapter 7 is anchored by the Supreme Court's treatment of a Second Amendment challenge to the NFA in *United States v. Miller*. *Miller* is a short and ambiguous opinion that declared that exercises of the Second Amendment right had to have a "reasonable relationship" to the maintenance of a well regulated militia. For decades afterward, there was argument about whether *Miller* meant that the type of gun had to be suitable for a militia in order for it to be protected by the Second Amendment, or whether the individual had to be in a militia in order to have Second Amendment rights. After *Miller*, lower federal courts began to develop a state-government-focused conception of the Second Amendment that gave little or no credence to individual challenges to federal or state gun regulations.

Chapter 8 is the longest chapter in this book. It covers the balance of the 20th century. The scope of federal firearms regulation grew dramatically in this period, with the passage of several major statutes, including the federal Gun Control Act of 1968, the Firearms Owners Protection Act of 1986, and the federal "assault weapon" ban that was enacted in 1994 and which sunset in 2004. The chapter offers a detailed treatment of the various issues that arise under the modern statutes and accompanying regulations, the vast majority of which remain valid even after the Supreme Court's 2008 affirmation of the individual right to keep and bear arms in *District of Columbia v. Heller*. During the late 20th century, lower federal courts rejected any version of a Second Amendment right that would impose meaningful limits on gun regulation. However, the tenor of judicial treatments of the issue began to change towards the end of the century, as scholarly and political debates bolstered the individual-rights theory. The chapter includes a section on social and political history that elucidates the most important bills, statutes, controversies, and political battles of the period. This history provides important context for the Supreme Court's ultimate affirmation of the individual right to arms.

Chapter 9 is dedicated to the landmark decisions in *District of Columbia v. Heller* and *McDonald v. Chicago*. In these decisions, a five-Justice majority of the Supreme Court held that the Second Amendment protects an individual right to keep and bear arms for self-defense; that the Second Amendment right is a fundamental right made fully applicable against the states by the Fourteenth Amendment; and that handgun bans violate the Second Amendment.

Chapter 10 examines issues of gun rights and gun regulation from the special perspectives of race, gender, sexual orientation, and disability. The materials are mainly drawn from the amicus briefs filed in *Heller* by a variety of interest groups.

Chapter 11 addresses the aftermath of *Heller* and *McDonald*. This chapter covers several of the most important constitutional questions left unanswered by the two Supreme Court decisions, and how these topics are being addressed by state and federal courts. While, as Chapters 5 through 7 showed, state court case law on state right to arms provisions has been developing for almost two centuries, serious doctrinal development of the Second Amendment itself began only after *Heller*. Courts today are grappling with issue such as the standard of review, what types of arms are protected, and the right to "bear" arms in public places. Students and professors who want to explore gray areas in emerging legal doctrine will find Chapter 11 of particular interest.

Online Chapters

The printed casebook ends with Chapter 11, but online chapters are available through a password protected website at http://www.aspenlawschool.com/books/johnson_firearms/ maintained by Aspen Publishers. Owners of the printed book have free access to these four additional online chapters:

Chapter 12. Social science about the benefits and harms of firearms possession and use.

Chapter 13. International gun control law, from sources such as the United Nations, the Organization of American States, and other treaties and international law documents. The chapter also covers the "Classical" period of international law, in which philosophers such as Grotius, Puffendorf, Vattel, Victoria, and Suárez built the foundations of international law partly by extrapolating from general principles of the rights and the limits of personal self-defense.

Chapter 14. Comparative gun control laws. Examining the gun laws of several nations, including Canada, the United Kingdom, Japan, Nazi Germany, and Switzerland.

Chapter 15. While Chapter 1 provides an introduction to the different types of firearms and ammunition, and how they function, this chapter covers the same topic in greater depth and detail. It includes many illustrations and diagrams.

There is also a free website at http://www.firearmsregulation.org. This public website provides additional resources, including suggested topics for student research papers, a comprehensive list of published law review articles and ALR Annotations on arms-law topics, and links to numerous Internet resources on firearms law and policy.

Publishing Student Research

Many students will use this book in upper-level classes in which they will write research papers. The public website offers some ideas for paper topics, as well as bibliographical and resource guides to help you get started.

Because Second Amendment doctrine is still in an early stage of development — especially in comparison to its closest analogue, the First Amendment, in which doctrinal development began in the 1930s — there are many opportunities for law student papers to make a genuine contribution to legal knowledge and analysis. If you write a good paper for your class, send it to us for consideration for publication on the public website.

Nicholas J. Johnson
David B. Kopel
George A. Mocsary
Michael P. O'Shea

January 2012

Acknowledgments

A great many people contributed to this book, but special mention must go to Nick Johnson's research assistants John Hunt and Tameem Zainulbhai; Dave Kopel's research interns Milena Boasherlieva, James Heinbaugh, Jonathan Shaw, and Margot Van Loon; and George Mocsary's research assistant Michael J. Kaczynski.

We are also grateful to copyright holders for permission to reprint excerpts from the following items:

Robert H. Churchill, *Popular Nullification, Fries's Rebellion, and the Waning of Radical Republicanism, 1798-1801*, 67 Penn. Hist. 105, 107 (Winter 2000). Permission granted by Pennsylvania History.

Robert J. Cottrol & Raymond T. Diamond, *"Never Intended to Be Applied to the White Population": Firearms Regulation and Racial Disparity — The Redeemed South's Legacy to a National Jurisprudence?*, 70 Chi.-Kent L. Rev. 1307, 1318-23 (1995). Reprinted with permission of Chicago-Kent Law Review.

"Sheffield Bowie" knife made in England for the American market. Permission to use photo granted by the Permanent Collection of the Historic Arkansas Museum, Little Rock, Arkansas.

J. Harvie Wilkinson, III, *Of Guns, Abortions, and the Unraveling Rule of Law*, 95 Va. L. Rev. 253 (2009). Reprinted with permission of Virginia Law Review.

Firearms Law and the Second Amendment

PART ONE
THE ORIGINS OF THE
RIGHT TO ARMS

A Brief Introduction to Firearms and Their Regulation

Why are debates about gun policy so contentious? One reason is that the debates involve fundamental, often conflicting beliefs about politics, morality, and philosophy. They also involve complex questions about the causes of crime, and arguments about social science. This book will explore all of those variables. A further reason for the difficulty of gun-policy debates is that decision makers and members of the general public sometimes lack basic knowledge about firearms and how they function. Therefore, this book begins with a brief introduction to how guns work and common firearms terminology. This chapter also includes an introduction to current laws governing firearms ownership and use in America.

Finally, an appendix to this chapter provides the full text of all American state constitutional guarantees of the right to arms, past and present. While the federal constitution's Second Amendment has gotten most of the public attention in the right to arms debate, state constitutional provisions have been the source of most of the case law over the past two centuries. The U.S. Supreme Court, in *District of Columbia v. Heller*, 554 U.S. 570 (2008) (Chapter 9) and in other cases, has used the state cases for guidance. Accordingly, anyone who wants to understand American gun laws needs to understand the state constitutions.

Many readers may benefit from a more detailed presentation of the "technical" firearms material in this chapter. Therefore, we strongly encourage you to refer to online Chapter 15, available at http://firearmregulation.org. The online chapter features photographs, drawings, and more detailed explanations of the firearms types and technologies discussed here.

A. The Parts of a Firearm and Ammunition

Firearms use the energy created by rapid burning of a chemical compound (*gunpowder*) to launch one or more projectiles out of a metal tube called a *barrel*. The firearm is fired by pressing the *trigger* with a finger. Typically, the trigger's movement causes a spring-loaded hammer to fall. The *hammer* impacts the *firing pin*, and the firing pin strikes the *ammunition cartridge* that sits in the gun's *firing chamber*. The impact of the firing pin will ignite the cartridge (as explained further below) and the gun will fire.

Modern rifle and handgun ammunition takes the form of individual *cartridges* (sometimes called *rounds*). Each cartridge holds a bullet, gunpowder, and a primer — all the materials needed to fire one shot — together in a metallic *case*.

Some people refer loosely to cartridges as *bullets* ("How many bullets were in the gun?"), but this usage is incorrect. A *bullet* is simply the projectile part of the cartridge, a shaped piece of metal. The bullet is usually made of lead and/or copper, and is launched from the cartridge out of the barrel of a gun.

A modern gun cannot fire unless it is loaded with properly sized cartridges (not just bullets). Cartridges are generally designated in ways that indicate the diameter of the bullet — either in millimeters, or in parts of an inch in the English system. The number of digits used varies. For example, .223, .30, .305, .458, and .50 are all rifle calibers measured in inches. They are listed in order of increasing diameter. Among the metric rifle calibers are 5.56 mm, 7 mm, 7.62 mm, and 12.7 mm (again, in increasing diameter).

Almost always caliber designation for particular ammunition will include a second item of information. For the metric calibers, it is common, but not universal, to also indicate the case length. Thus, the 7.62 × 39 cartridge has a bullet diameter of 7.62 millimeters and a case length of 39 millimeters. In the English system, a name or letters are commonly added. For example, for .32 caliber handguns, there is the .32 NAA, .32 ACP, and .32 S&W Long. Their bullet diameters are the same, but their cases are different. A handgun made to use one of these varieties of .32 caliber cartridges generally could not use one of the others.

The *primer* and gunpowder inside the cartridge case provide the chemical energy that launches the bullet from the gun. The primer is like a chemical spark plug. It is located at the base of the cartridge. When the primer is struck by the firing pin, it ignites with a sudden hot flash. The primer's flash ignites the gunpowder, which then burns rapidly inside the case, creating an expanding mass of hot gas that pushes the bullet out of the cartridge case, and down the barrel of the gun, to the target.

The kinetic energy of the bullet is mainly function of its mass and its velocity. It is important to realize that the same size bullet (e.g., .30 caliber diameter) can sit atop cartridge cases of various sizes. The larger the cartridge case (to accommodate more gunpowder), the greater the bullet velocity. The same bullet at greater velocity will carry more energy. Because rifle cases are typically longer than handgun cases, rifle ammunition usually has greater energy than handgun ammunition. (For any cartridge, the addition of the word "magnum" means that it has more gunpowder, hence more energy, than a standard round of that caliber. The .222 Remington Magnum cartridge has more gunpowder than the .222 Remington.)

Some cartridges can be used in both rifles and handguns. (A good example is the small, inexpensive .22 Long Rifle, by far the most popular cartridge in the world.) When fired from a rifle, the bullet will have greater energy than when fired from a handgun. Because the rifle barrel is much longer than the handgun barrel, almost all of the gunpowder gas expansion is used to push the bullet faster and faster down the barrel. In the handgun, however, the bullet exits the barrel after a few inches; once the bullet has left the barrel, the gunpowder gas just expands into the air outside the front of the barrel (the *muzzle*), and does not contribute more energy to the bullet's flight.

Billions of cartridges are produced commercially in the United States each year. While a serious competitive shooter may expend tens of thousands of rounds of ammunition every year in practice and competition, most gun owners consume ammunition at a much lower rate.

Ammunition is commonly sold at retail in boxes of 20 to 50, or 100 cartridges, as well as in cases of 500 or 1,000 cartridges. In the United States, ammunition is sold at gun stores, sporting goods stores, large retail stores, and gun shows. A large volume of ammunition is also sold and shipped using the Internet or mail-order catalogs.

Like manufacturers of firearms, individuals or companies who wish to manufacture ammunition for sale must obtain a Federal Firearms License (FFL) from the federal Bureau of Alcohol, Tobacco, Firearms, and Explosives (ATF). No federal license is required to manufacture ordinary firearms or ammunition for personal use.

B. *Firearm Features*

Beyond the basic details discussed above, there are aspects of firearm functionality that sometimes feed important regulatory distinctions.

1. Firing Mechanism

A firearm is normally fired by pressing the trigger, which releases a spring-loaded hammer (or in some designs a similar mechanism called a *striker*). The hammer falls, and its force causes a firing pin to strike the primer in an ammunition cartridge; the primer flash ignites the gunpowder; the gunpowder burns, and the expanding gas from the gunpowder pushes the bullet out the barrel of the gun.

In a modern handgun or rifle, the barrel is *rifled*. That means that its inside surface has been cut with a pattern of spiral grooves that cause the bullet to spin around its long axis as it travels through the barrel. This spin makes the bullet fly in a straighter path when it emerges from the muzzle (the open end of the barrel) of the gun.

2. Ammunition Feeding

Most modern firearms are *repeating arms*, or *repeaters*. In other words, they can be fired multiple times before it is necessary to manually insert more ammunition into the gun. "Repeater" means simply that the gun holds more than one round of ammunition. It does not mean that it fires multiple times per trigger pull. A gun that shoots more than once per trigger pull is called a "fully automatic" gun or a machine gun. The mechanism where a repeating arm stores its ammunition, and from which the ammunition is fed during use, is called a *magazine*. With some guns, the magazine is a hollow compartment or tube that is permanently attached to the gun. A *revolver* handgun uses an integral revolving cylinder to store several rounds of ammunition in the gun. Other guns, especially semi-automatic and fully automatic firearms (see below), use *detachable magazines*: metal or plastic rectangular boxes that can be filled with ammunition, temporarily attached to the gun during use, then removed when empty and reloaded with fresh ammunition.

3.　Safety Devices

A modern firearm will fire only when the trigger is pressed, though defects in some older firearm designs could result in the gun firing when dropped. Accordingly, the most elementary safety device on modern firearms is the trigger guard, which protects the trigger from accidental motion, such as when a gun is being pulled out of a holster. The trigger guard also makes it easier for the gun user to obey one of the fundamental rules of gun safety: "Keep your finger off the trigger until you are ready to shoot."

Modern firearms typically include additional safety features. The most common of these is an *external safety*, a mechanical device that prevents the trigger or hammer from moving. The safety is typically activated by pressing a button or lever on the outside of the gun. When the safety is activated, the gun will not fire, even if the trigger is pressed.

Virtually all modern rifles and shotguns, and most semi-automatic handguns, have external safeties. On the other hand, most revolver style handguns and a few semi-automatics lack an external safety. (Some of these semi-automatics instead have a safety in the trigger itself, which prevents the gun from firing if dropped, but does not block the gun from firing if the trigger is deliberately pressed.)

Other safety devices operate when the gun is *not* in use, in order to prevent access or use by an unauthorized person. The most obvious of these is a gun safe. Likewise, a small key-activated trigger lock or cable lock (meant to be threaded through the *action*, the part of the gun where the firing and loading takes place) can be attached to the gun itself to prevent unauthorized use. New handguns sold in the United States are required to come with a locking device. Since the 1990s, researchers have pursued more sophisticated safety mechanisms, such as palm-print readers built into the grip of a handgun. Sometimes these are called *smart guns*. Thus far, no smart-gun technology has become sufficiently reliable to be commercially viable.

All locking devices involve tradeoffs. A gun that is locked is more secure from an unauthorized user, but harder to deploy against an imminent threat. Locking devices are imperfect, and some low-quality trigger locks are easily defeated.

4.　Firearm User Safety

Firearm safety education stresses the importance of careful adherence to gun handling rules to avoid accidents. While the user must know how to operate mechanical safety devices, safety training emphasizes that reliance on mechanical devices is never a substitute for following all safety rules.

A common formulation of the elementary rules of gun safety is:

1. *Treat every gun as if it is loaded.* So even if you are certain that a gun is unloaded, you must still obey all other safety rules.
2. *Always point the gun in a safe direction.* This is sometimes called the rule of *muzzle discipline.* It means that under no circumstances should a gun ever be pointed at a person, unless in legitimate self-defense. A "safe direction" means that the user must positively identify her target, and know what is behind the target. For example, a hunter at the bottom of a hill should not shoot an animal on the crest of the hill, because the hunter would not know what was beyond the target.
3. *Keep your finger off the trigger until you are ready to shoot.* This is the rule of *trigger discipline,* and it is critical to avoid unintentionally firing the gun. Even when a gun is being drawn for immediate self-defense, the proper motion is to keep the index finger outside the trigger guard until the gun is pointed at the target.

C. *The Major Types of Firearms*

A large-scale survey conducted in 1994 estimated that there were approximately 192 million functional firearms in private hands in the United States. Philip J. Cook & Jens Ludwig, Guns in America: Results of a Comprehensive National Survey on Firearms Ownership and Use (1996). Since then, tens of millions more guns have been added to the supply. In fact, in 2009 alone, roughly five million new guns were produced for sale in the United States. The total number of privately owned guns in the United States today is likely at least equal to the entire adult population of the country (approximately 230 million adults). Some recent estimates put the number closer to 300 million firearms in the civilian inventory. In 2006, the Small Arms Survey, an independent research project of the Graduate Institute of International Studies in Geneva, Switzerland, estimated the U.S. inventory at between 250 million and 290 million. Small Arms Survey, Small Arms Survey 2007: Guns and the City 47, tbl. 2.3 (2007).

Current surveys indicate that about 34 percent of American adults own a gun. Lydia Saad, Gallup, Self-Reported Gun Ownership Is Highest Since 1993, *available at* http://www.gallup.com/poll/150353/self-reported-gun-ownership-highest-1993.aspx. (Oct. 26, 2011). Polling-based estimates of individual or household gun ownership may be underestimates, because some gun owners refuse to disclose themselves to a stranger on the telephone. If one estimates gun ownership by household rather than by individual, it would be roughly accurate to say that about half of American households contain a firearm. Id.

The vast majority of privately owned firearms fall into the three basic categories of *handguns,* *rifles,* and *shotguns.*

1. Handguns

The handgun is generally the most controversial category of firearm, primarily because its portability and concealability make it the most common type of gun used in crime. Approximately 70 percent of all firearms murders in the United States in 2008 were perpetrated with handguns. Across the board, handguns are employed more often in violent crimes than are rifles or shotguns. Unlike *long guns* (rifles and shotguns), a handgun (especially in smaller models) can be carried concealed from detection by others, whereas long guns are virtually impossible to carry concealed. Handguns can also be conveniently carried for long periods of time.

The handgun's characteristics — ease of storage, access, and manipulation — also make it, in the words of the Supreme Court, the firearm that "is overwhelmingly chosen by American society for th[e] lawful purpose" of self-defense, and "the most preferred firearm in the nation to 'keep' and use for protection of one's home and family." *Heller*, 554 U.S. at 628-29 (Chapter 9) (invalidating a ban of handguns as a violation of the Second Amendment). Millions of Americans are licensed to carry handguns for personal protection outside the home.

In 2009, the most recent year for which final production figures exist, American manufacturers produced about 2.3 million handguns for domestic sale. In addition, more than two million more handguns were commercially imported into the United States from other nations.

a. Semi-Automatic Pistols

About four-fifths of new handguns produced in the United States are *semi-automatic pistols*, also frequently referred to simply as *pistols*. Handguns of this type feed ammunition from a detachable magazine that is usually inserted in the gun's grip.

It is important to understand the distinction between *semi-automatic* operation, which is found in many types of common pistols, rifles, and shotguns, and *fully automatic* operation, which is found in machine guns and is subject to especially strict regulation.

Semi-automatic guns fire only one round of ammunition per each pull of the trigger. Each time the gun is fired, the semi-automatic action uses part of the energy of the combusting gunpowder to automatically eject the spent case, re-cock the firing mechanism, and load a fresh cartridge into the firing chamber. Thus, the user of a semi-automatic firearm does not need to manipulate the gun in order to load the next round. The gun loads itself. This is why semi-automatic guns are also often referred to as *self-loading* or *auto-loading* guns.

In contrast, a *fully automatic* firearm (commonly called a "machine gun"[1]) fires multiple times with a single pull of the trigger. A fully automatic firearm

---

1. Strictly speaking, there are some machine guns (such as the hand-cranked Gatling Gun from the nineteenth century) that are not automatics. The online Introduction to Firearms explains the issue in more detail. However, the federal National Firearms Act of 1934 (detailed in Chapter 7) uses "machine gun" to mean "automatic."

automatically loads new cartridges into the chamber, fires them, then ejects the empty case and loads and fires another cartridge continuously until the trigger is released. Some of these guns also have a burst-fire function that fires two or three rounds per trigger pull. Under federal law, any firearm that can fire more than one round per trigger pull is deemed a machine gun.

(Semi-automatic pistols are sometimes colloquially called "automatics." For example, one might hear: "He owns a Colt model 1911 automatic, a Glock 9mm automatic, and a Ruger .22 automatic." This person owns three semi-automatic pistols, not true automatics.)

Detachable magazines allow efficient reloading of semi-automatic handguns. The user pushes a button to release the magazine, and pulls it out of the gun. The user can then insert a new, loaded magazine into the gun, and resume firing. The typical magazine capacity for today's semi-automatic pistols is 10 to 17 rounds, although some models have smaller and larger capacities.

The semi-automatic pistol has become the dominant type used for military issue, law enforcement, self-defense, competitions, and informal target shooting. As with revolvers, semi-automatic pistols range in size from quite large and heavy to as small as a wallet.

b. Revolvers

The first commercially successful *revolvers* were produced by Samuel Colt in the 1830s, and revolvers are still popular for many purposes. These handguns carry their ammunition in chambers cut into a revolving cylinder that is located behind the barrel of the gun. Pressing the trigger rotates the cylinder and causes the next chamber to come into line with the barrel and hammer. As the trigger reaches the final point of its rearward travel, the next chamber has locked into place in alignment with the barrel. The basic design has changed little since the late nineteenth century. Modern revolvers typically hold five or six rounds of ammunition, although some smaller caliber revolvers can hold ten or more rounds.

Revolvers are generally simpler to operate than semi-automatic pistols, and many users prefer the simplicity. On the other hand, revolvers are slower to reload and hold fewer rounds of ammunition than most pistols. Some of the best-selling revolvers today are small, lightweight guns with short "snubnose" barrels, often used for concealed carry. Larger revolvers with long barrels are popular for target shooting.

In addition, revolvers are generally preferred to semi-automatic pistols for use in medium to large game hunting with handguns, because revolvers better accommodate larger calibers and customized ammunition. These hunting revolvers generally are long-barreled, bulky, and relatively heavy. They are frequently mounted with a telescopic sight. Some hunters will use smaller lower-powered handguns for small game.

In earlier generations, revolvers were the most common type of handgun produced in America, and were standard sidearms for police. However, a major shift to semi-automatic pistols occurred in the 1980s. While semi-automatic pistols comprised only 28 percent of new handguns produced in the United States in 1973, their share had grown to 80 percent by 1993. American police officers today mostly carry semi-automatic pistols as sidearms, although a few still prefer revolvers.

c. *Legitimate Uses of Handguns*

Handguns are commonly owned and used for home defense, concealed carry, recreational target shooting, competition, and hunting. Handguns are more likely to be acquired for the purpose of self-defense than are long guns. Surveys consistently report that the majority of handgun purchasers are motivated at least in part by personal-protection concerns. Cook & Ludwig, *supra.* In a 1998 National Gun Policy Survey conducted by the National Opinion Research Center, 65 percent of handgun owners reported that protection against crime was one of their reasons for owning a gun.

Approximately six million Americans hold a state-issued license to carry a handgun for self-defense outside their homes. Mike Stuckey, MSNBC.com, Record numbers licensed to pack heat: Millions obtain permits to carry concealed guns, *available at* http://www.msnbc.msn.com/id/34714389/ns/us_news-life/t/record-numbers-licensed-pack-heat/#.Tn1ueGpsOyw (June 24, 2010). Most states today issue a concealed handgun carry permit to an adult who passes a fingerprint-based background check and a safety class. (These laws are detailed below.)

Another popular use for handguns is target shooting. Informal target shooting or "plinking" can be conducted at commercial shooting ranges and clubs, public ranges, undeveloped public lands, or on private property. Organized target shooting with handguns takes many forms. Target pistol shooting is an Olympic sport and indeed was one of the original sports of the modern Olympics. Hunting with handguns is allowed in all states, generally as part of the general firearms hunting season for the relevant game.

d. *Criminal Uses of Handguns*

Gun crime is predominantly committed with handguns. Of 14,180 murders in the United States in 2008, 9,484 (roughly two-thirds) were committed with firearms, and of those, at least 6,755 (70 percent of firearms murders) were committed with handguns. Similarly, in 1997 interviews of prison inmates who were armed with a firearm during their offense of conviction, over 80 percent reported that they were armed with a handgun. While handguns comprise a large minority of privately owned firearms, they are used in the majority of gun crimes.

Annual firearms deaths are often reported in the range of 30,000 per year. That figure combines homicides, as indicated above, with suicides, which comprise the majority of those deaths.

2. Rifles

In 2009, American manufacturers produced slightly over 2.1 million rifles for sale in the United States, making the rifle the second most widely produced category of firearm in America. In addition, over 600,000 rifles were imported to the United States from foreign countries in that year.

Federal law defines a rifle as:

> a weapon designed . . . and intended to be fired from the shoulder and . . . to use the energy of the explosive in a fixed cartridge to fire only a single projectile through a rifled bore for each single pull of the trigger.

28 U.S.C. §5845(c). Thus, a rifle is defined by two traits: (1) it is a long gun, and (2) its barrel, or *bore*, is rifled. Most rifles today fall into a few common types.

a.   Bolt-Action

Bolt-action rifles, introduced as military weapons in the late nineteenth century, are now the type of rifle most commonly used for hunting. Approximately 44 percent of the rifles purchased in the United States in the first four months of 2010 were bolt-action rifles. A bolt-action rifle may be either a single-shot or magazine type. The magazine type typically holds several cartridges in an integral magazine or a detachable magazine. By manually lifting a handle attached to the bolt, pulling the handle back, and then returning the bolt to its starting place, the user can eject an empty case from the firing chamber, and load a fresh round into the chamber from the magazine. With fewer moving parts, bolt-action rifles are usually among the most reliable and accurate rifle types.

b.   Semi-Automatic

The other leading type of rifle is the semi-automatic (or self-loading) rifle. In recent years, sales of semi-automatic rifles have been comparable to bolt-action rifle sales. About 42 percent of the rifles sold in early 2010 were semi-automatic.

A semi-automatic rifle functions in a manner similar to a semi-automatic pistol, discussed above. When the rifle is fired, some of the energy from the burning gunpowder also cycles the rifle's action. This automatically ejects the empty cartridge case, re-cocks the hammer or other firing mechanism, and loads a fresh cartridge into the firing chamber.

Semi-automatic rifles store and feed their ammunition from a magazine. Some use fixed magazines integral to the rifle. These are loaded by inserting ammunition through the top of the gun or into a tube that runs underneath the rifle's barrel. Many semi-automatic rifles use detachable magazines, similar to those of semi-automatic pistols.

Semi-automatics are easier for many people to use because their recoil is less than that from other guns in the same caliber. This lower recoil is a basic function of the gun, which — just like a semi-automatic handgun — diverts some of the firing energy to achieve automatic reloading and re-cocking. In addition, firearms with detachable magazines can usually be reloaded more quickly than other firearms. Although most defensive gun use involves just a few shots, many police and private citizens prefer the ability to reload quickly if necessary. Of course, as is always the case, these same advantages can be exploited by violent criminals.

An increasingly prominent and controversial category of semi-automatic rifle has an appearance similar to fully automatic military rifles. For example, to most observers, the semi-automatic AR-15 rifle appears identical to the automatic M-16 rifle, which became a standard U.S. military rifle in the 1960s. The important place where they differ is the firing mechanism. While the AR-15 can only fire semi-automatically, the M-16 can fire automatically, in three round bursts, *or* semi-automatically.

AR-15-style semi-automatic rifles are made by many manufacturers, and often deployed by police. These rifles are also widely owned by private citizens for personal defense, and for all of the other purposes for which rifles are used. Although they generally are marginally less accurate than bolt-actions, especially accurate versions are the primary type of rifle used in organized target shooting competitions. *See generally* Andrew Park, *A Hot-Selling Weapon, an Inviting Target,* N.Y. Times, June 3, 2007, at B1 (describing the AR-15 and similar rifles as becoming "the guns of choice for many hunters, target shooters and would-be home defenders"). Official records indicate that almost half a million AR-15 type rifles were produced for sale in the United States in 2009.

Semi-automatic rifles with a military or futuristic appearance, such as the AR-15, have been dubbed "assault rifles" by gun control advocates, and "modern sporting rifles" by the National Shooting Sports Foundation, the trade association for the American firearms industry. Several states have outlawed "assault rifles." For example, New Jersey prohibits the possession, by most private citizens, of over 50 different named semi-automatic firearms models, including the AR-15, and "substantially identical" copies of those guns. N.J. Rev. Stat. §§2C:39-1(w), 2C:39-5(f). California prohibits the possession of a list of specific "assault weapons." Other guns are designated "assault weapons" by a general definition that captures any semi-automatic centerfire[2] rifle that has one or more of a list of features, such as a pistol grip, a folding or collapsible stock, a flash suppressor attached to the muzzle, and other features. Cal. Penal Code §12276.1. In addition, New York, Massachusetts, and the District of Columbia outlaw "assault weapons." Bans of this type apply mostly to rifles, but also include some handguns and shotguns. Maryland and Hawaii outlaw "assault pistols" a class of semi-automatic pistols with a military or futuristic appearance.

From 1994 to 2004, federal law contained a similar set of restrictions. The Public Safety and Recreational Firearms Use Protection Act, formerly at 18 U.S.C. §922(v) (1994), prohibited the manufacture for sale to private individuals of defined "assault weapons," including the AR-15. The federal ban also prohibited the manufacture for sale to private individuals of detachable rifle

---

2. Online Chapter 15 explains the difference between *centerfire* and *rimfire* ammunition, which refers to two different ways of putting the primer compound into a cartridge. Today, rimfire ammunition is confined to small cartridges, such as the .22 Long Rifle, while centerfire ammunition includes both small and large cartridges.

or handgun magazines holding more than ten rounds. *Id.* §922(w). However, the federal ban included a ten-year sunset provision and required a study of its effectiveness. Congress chose not to reenact the ban, and it expired on September 13, 2004. Consequently, under federal law, everything formerly restricted under the "assault weapons" ban is now treated the same as other firearms, regulated by the federal Gun Control Act of 1968 (Chapter 8). Most states likewise do not impose special restrictions on these guns.

Chapter 8 explains "assault weapons" prohibitions in detail.

c.   Lever-Action

Lever-action rifles, the first repeating rifles, were developed in the nineteenth century. They allow the user to manually eject a spent round and chamber a fresh round by manipulating a lever attached to the rifle's trigger guard. Lever-action rifles, such as replicas of the famed Winchester 1873 rifle, are still fairly popular today for hunting and target shooting, and are serviceable for self-defense. They are widely used in the self-consciously nostalgic sport of cowboy action shooting, in which participants wear Western clothing and shoot cowboy-themed target courses using firearms of nineteenth-century design.

d.   Single-Shot

The oldest rifle style is the *single-shot.* These rifles are still produced. Many are simple and economically priced. Others are expensive exacting renditions of early forms. After firing, the cartridge must be removed or ejected from the breech of the rifle and replaced by hand. These guns are often highly accurate. Like single-shot handguns, single-shot rifles are popular at two extremes of shooting: for training beginners, and for long-distance shooting by experts.

e.   Characteristics of Rifles

Rifles have greater range and accuracy than either handguns or shotguns. Rifles can be fired more accurately than handguns because they have longer barrels and are braced against the shoulder and both hands for firing. Also, the longer barrel allows for more gunpowder energy to be imparted to the bullet, thus helping the bullet resist the effects of air friction and gravity. Using a typical police or self-defense handgun, on a 25-yard target range, a skilled pistol shooter would face a tough challenge in placing several consecutive shots on the paper target into a one-inch "group." Conversely, a rifle shooter can achieve this kind of accuracy with relative ease. Rifles are also generally more powerful than handguns because rifle cartridges tend to be larger, accommodating more gunpowder, which launches bullets at higher velocities.

Rifles are also more accurate than shotguns because shotguns (as described below) usually fire numerous pellets, which disperse in a conical pattern. The round pellets are much less aerodynamically stable than rifle or handgun bullets, so a shotgun is not a long-range firearm.

The ammunition capacity of rifles varies widely. Bolt-action rifles commonly hold from 4 to 6 cartridges. Lever-action rifles can range from 6 rounds up to a dozen or more. Semi-automatic rifles use magazines that can range from 5 rounds capacity up to 20 or 30 rounds. Magazines holding more than 30 rounds are available, but are less common in actual use.

f. Legitimate Uses of Rifles

As noted above, rifles are standard equipment for hunting. They are also increasingly popular for police work and self-defense. Target shooting with rifles takes a wide range of forms, with the apex being the National Matches held every year at Camp Perry, Ohio. According to one industry survey, an estimated 10.6 percent of American adults engaged in target shooting with a rifle in 2009.

g. Crime with Rifles

Of all firearms types, rifles are least commonly used in violent crime. In 1997 interviews of prison inmates, only 1.3 percent of state and federal prisoners reported being armed with a rifle during their offense of conviction. U.S. Department of Justice, Bureau of Justice Statistics, Firearm Use by Offenders, NCJ 189369 (Nov. 2001). However, the generally greater power of rifles means that rifle wounds are more likely to be fatal than handgun wounds. Because a rifle allows accurate firing from a much greater distance than handguns or shotguns, criminals equipped with rifles can pose a grave threat to potential victims and even to well-equipped law enforcement officers.

Rifles have also figured prominently in political assassinations. In the 1960s, President John F. Kennedy and civil-rights leader Rev. Martin Luther King, Jr., were both killed by assassins firing rifles from concealment. Today, one challenge of safeguarding dignitaries stems from the threat posed by potential assassins armed with rifles.

3. Shotguns

Shotguns comprise the third major category of common firearms. As of 1993, the ATF estimated that Americans owned 66 million shotguns. In 2008, 752,389 shotguns were manufactured in the United States for sale. Federal law defines a shotgun as a gun that is

> intended to be fired from the shoulder . . . [and uses] the energy of the explosive in a fixed shotgun to fire through a smooth bore either a number of projectiles (ball shot) or a single projectile for each pull of the trigger.

28 U.S.C. §5845(d). Thus, a shotgun is a long gun with a smooth bore, that is, a barrel whose interior lacks the spiral rifling grooves found in rifles and handguns.

a. Shotgun Shells

Shotgun ammunition differs in several respects from handgun or rifle ammunition. Shotgun ammunition takes the form of cylindrical *shot shells* with plastic cases, instead of the metallic cases characteristic of handgun and rifle cartridges. A typical shot shell is filled with round, metal *shot pellets* that are released when the shell is fired. Payloads of shot range from *birdshot* loads, which fit hundreds of tiny pellets into a single shell, to *buckshot* loads, which use much larger and heavier pellets, sometimes as few as eight or nine pellets per shell. In other respects (e.g., primer and powder), shotgun ammunition is similar to rifle and handgun ammunition.

Shotguns are commonly used for the hunting of birds and small land animals. Larger loads with fewer pellets would be used for large waterfowl, while loads containing tiny pellets would be standard for small birds and game. The largest pellets (buckshot) are used for hunting deer or for police work and self-defense.

Not all shotgun shells contain multiple pellets; they also can be loaded with a single, large projectile, a *shotgun slug*. Shooting slugs lets the shotgun function similarly to a powerful rifle at shorter ranges. The typical use for a shotgun slug would be deer hunting.

b. Types of Shotguns

Like rifles and handguns, shotguns are available in a variety of action types from single-shot to repeaters. The most common repeating shotgun in the United States is the *pump action*. The pump shotgun stores ammunition in a tubular magazine underneath the barrel. To eject a fired shell from the firing chamber and load a fresh one into the chamber from the shotgun's tubular magazine, the user pumps the shotgun's *fore-end* back and forth. Pump shotguns are rugged and generally less expensive to manufacture than semi-automatic or double-barreled shotguns. They are widely used for police work, home defense, hunting, and rural control of pests and predators.

Semi-automatic shotguns function like other semi-automatic guns. When the shotgun is fired, the recoil energy or gas released by firing causes the action to eject the spent shell and load a fresh shell into the firing chamber. Unlike semi-automatic pistols and rifles, semi-automatic shotguns rarely use detachable ammunition magazines. As with pump-action shotguns, their ammunition supply is typically stored in a fixed magazine tube that runs underneath the shotgun's barrel.

Double-barreled shotguns, popular for competition and bird hunting, have no magazine, but feature two adjacent barrels that allow two shots before reloading. Double-barreled shotguns can be relatively inexpensive but high-quality models sell for tens of thousands of dollars. Many countries with very restrictive firearms laws impose relatively fewer regulations on the ownership of double-barreled shotguns, compared to semi-automatics.

c. Legitimate Uses of Shotguns

Shotguns are used for hunting, especially bird and small-game hunting; for shooting sports such as trap shooting, skeet shooting, and sporting clays; for self-defense; for police work; and for protection from threatening or pest animals in rural areas. They also play a limited role in military operations, especially for security duty and for fighting in buildings or other close quarters. Some densely populated states, such as Massachusetts, disallow rifles for hunting deer. In these areas, it is common for deer hunters to use shotguns loaded with buckshot or slugs.

The shotgun sports of trap, skeet, and sporting clays are the most popular organized shooting sports in the United States. In these sports, the shooter tries to hit flying clay disks. An estimated 8.4 million Americans participate in the shotgun sport of sporting clays. Comparable numbers participate in trap shooting (7.58 million) and skeet shooting (6.98 million). National Shooting Sports Foundation Survey, Sport Shooting Participation in the United States 2009. One survey estimated that almost 5 million Americans participate annually in waterfowl hunting, which employs shotguns. 1999-2002 National Survey on Recreation and the Environment, USDA Forest Service and U. of Tennessee.

Some firearms trainers recommend the use of a shotgun instead of a handgun for home defense. They emphasize that the shotgun is much more powerful than the handgun, and that the use of a shoulder stock enables the shotgun to be aimed more accurately under stress than a handgun. Further, because the shot pellets spread out as they fly, it is easier to hit an aggressor at close range with a shotgun. However, the weight of a shotgun (typically seven to nine pounds, compared to perhaps two pounds for a handgun) and its heavy recoil can make it difficult for small-statured shooters, or those with limited upper-body strength, to use a shotgun effectively for self-defense.

d. Crime with Shotguns

Behind handguns, shotguns are the second most commonly used in crime. In 1997 interviews of prison inmates who were armed with a firearm during their offense of conviction, approximately 13 percent reported that they were armed with a shotgun. In addition, 7.4 percent of police officers fatally shot between 1982 and 1993 (with guns other than their own duty weapons) were killed by perpetrators using shotguns.

Often, criminals carrying shotguns will saw off much of the barrel (an act that is illegal under federal law, see Chapter 7). The sawed-off shotgun is not very accurate, but like all shotguns can be devastatingly powerful at close range, if loaded with large-diameter shot pellets.

D. *Modern Gun-Control Laws*

Although the remainder of this book will examine past and present gun-control laws in detail, we offer here a brief summary of U.S. gun-control laws in the twenty-first century along with some state variations.

1. Purchasing a Gun from a Commercial Dealer

Suppose you wish to buy a firearm. How do you do it? Typically, you go to a retail storefront, or other location used by a vendor who sells guns as a business. The seller must have a Federal Firearms License. (The term "FFL" is used interchangeably to refer to the license itself and to the individual or business entity that holds the license.) In order to purchase the gun, you must first fill out a federal transfer record (ATF Form 4473) in which you provide your address, date of birth, race, height, and so on. You answer a series of yes-or-no questions to affirm that you do not fall into one of the several categories of "prohibited persons" who are barred by federal law from purchasing or possessing a firearm — for example, whether you are a convicted felon, adjudicated mentally ill, a habitual user of narcotics, or an illegal alien. You show the vendor a photo identification, which he records. You must be at least 18 years old to purchase a rifle or shotgun, and 21 to purchase any other type of gun, such as a handgun.

Next, by telephone or Internet, the vendor contacts the National Instant Check System (NICS, a federal program run by the Federal Bureau of Investigation from an office in West Virginia), or a state counterpart, run by a state police agency. The "instant" check may take seconds, minutes, or hours. Once the system verifies that you are not on any list of prohibited persons, the vendor records an authorization number for the sale, and you may take the gun home. Typically, the entire purchase process can be completed within an hour or so, although sometimes longer delays are created by the instant check procedure.

A minority of states and localities impose additional requirements before you can legally purchase a firearm. These could include a waiting period of several days before you can take possession of the gun; acquiring a special license that allows you to possess firearms; a requirement to obtain the approval of state or local law enforcement officials for each purchase; or a requirement to pass a safety class. In a few highly restrictive places — such as New York City or Washington, D.C. — the process can take months. In some states, the extra requirements might apply only to handguns, or only to certain long guns, such as semi-automatic rifles deemed "assault weapons."

2. Purchasing a Gun from Private Sellers

Pursuant to the federal Gun Control Act of 1968 (GCA), any person (or corporation) "engaged in the business" of selling firearms must have a Federal Firearms License. "Engaged in the business" means someone who makes repetitive transactions in firearms as a regular course of trade or business with the principal objective of livelihood and profit. Any person who claims to be an "unlicensed dealer" in guns is, in effect, admitting to being a felon.

However, a person who is *not* "engaged in the business" may make occasional sales of firearms *to another resident of the same state* without having to go through any of the federal paperwork or formal customer background checks required for licensees. So in most states, you can lawfully buy or trade a firearm from a neighbor, a friend, or so on, on whatever terms are agreeable to the two of you. However, if the seller has reason to believe that the buyer is a prohibited person, then the sale is a federal crime. Likewise, it is normally a federal crime to sell or give a firearm to another person (even a family member) who does not reside in the same state as you do. Finally, if you engage in too many sales of this type in a short period of time, and derive significant income from it, you risk being deemed to be "engaged in the business" of selling firearms — which, again, is a federal felony if you do not have an FFL.

Sales between two non-FFL gun owners in the same state are often referred to as *private sales.* A minority of states prohibit private sales, and require that all transactions in firearms be routed through an FFL, and comply with whatever extra rules apply in that state to FFL sales.

3.   Purchases in Various Locations

You cannot lawfully buy a handgun outside your state of residence, not even from an FFL. If you were on vacation and saw a handgun you wished to buy, the only lawful way to complete the transaction would be for the seller to ship the handgun to an FFL in your home state. You could then pick up the gun from your home-state FFL, after compliance with the requirements of the GCA described above and any other requirements of your home state. Long guns may be purchased across state lines, provided that all the laws of both states are complied with. (A few restrict out-of-state purchases by their residents.)

Gun shows are events usually held at a fairground building, convention center, or similar place, on a weekend, where buyers and sellers congregate. FFLs are allowed to sell firearms at their official place of business and at gun shows. Most sellers at a typical gun show are FFLs. But there are also usually private sellers in attendance. The non-FFLs may purchase a table at the gun show and try to negotiate sales or purchases with passersby. In most states, the laws for selling private guns at a gun show are exactly the same as for sales anywhere else. A few states, such as Colorado and Oregon, require private sellers to conduct background checks at gun shows (with the assistance of a cooperating FFL). Of course, in those states where all firearms transactions must go through an FFL, private sellers would also have to route the gun show transaction through a cooperating FFL.

4.   Gun Registration

The Form 4473 that you filled out when buying the gun must be retained by the dealer for at least 20 years. The form is available for inspection by the ATF during annual compliance inspections of the dealer, and whenever needed in the course of a bona fide law enforcement investigation. When an FFL dealer goes out of business, he must forward to the ATF his business records, including records of firearms sold.

Federal law forbids the federal government from creating a centralized registration list of guns or gun owners. However, a minority of states do register all gun owners, all guns, or all handguns. The registration list is often created by harvesting data from the paperwork required for gun purchases.

5. Keeping a Gun at Home

As with any potentially lethal instrument, the general rules of criminal and civil negligence apply to your use and storage of a firearm. A minority of states have adopted special storage laws for firearms, such as requirements that the firearm be stored in such a way as to make them inaccessible to minors.

6. Target Shooting

Target ranges may be open to the public, or may be private clubs. Many private clubs are open to the public on some days of the year, especially before hunting season. Public ranges may be operated by the government or by private organizations. Public lands (e.g., those managed by the National Forest Service or Bureau of Land Management) are generally open to the public for target shooting; such lands may also have designated places for target shooting.

When driving to the target range, you will be required in many states to keep the gun unloaded and locked away, unless you have a concealed carry permit (see below). In a handful of jurisdictions, such as New York or New Jersey (for handguns), you will need a specific permit to transport even an unloaded gun to and from the target range.

7. Hunting with a Gun

State game laws vary widely. Some require a hunting license for all hunting, some only for hunting on public land, and some have exemptions for hunting on one's own land. In all states, the laws and regulations specify with particularity the lawful hunting seasons for various species. States may also limit the types of guns you can use to hunt — for example, by requiring rifle hunters to use a cartridge at or above a minimum power level sufficient for humanely taking a particular species of game. If you need a hunting license, you will very likely need a hunter safety card, which can be earned by taking and passing a special hunter safety class.

Once you have the hunter safety card, you can obtain a hunting license. Again, licenses vary greatly from state to state. A "small game" permit might authorize the hunting of game such as fox, rabbits, and squirrels within the state, during the relevant seasons, for an entire year. A deer or elk permit might authorize hunting only during a particular week, and only within a particular part of the state.

In the "North American model" of hunting management, permits are issued and hunting seasons are specified so that species are maintained at a healthy level. Thus, for some species (e.g., coyotes in Colorado), year-round hunting might be allowed. For others (e.g., elk), the state would be divided into game management units, and the number of permits issued for a particular unit would depend on animal population that particular year. If the population is down, the number of hunting permits issued for the next year in that unit would be reduced.

The North American model has been in use since the early twentieth century, and has been very successful at maintaining and growing populations of game animals. Fishing in the United States is also managed pursuant to this model.

If you travel to another state to hunt, you will almost certainly pay much more for an out-of-state hunting license than you would for a license from your home state. Indeed, out-of-state hunters are a major economic resource for most state wildlife departments. *Cf. Baldwin v. Fish and Game Commission of Montana*, 436 U.S. 371 (1978) (differential fees for non-residents do not violate the Constitution's Article IV "privileges and immunities" clause).

Except for obviously nonedible species (e.g., prairie dogs), the hunting laws will require that you harvest the meat from whatever you shoot and take it home for consumption. You will probably be allowed to give away some of the meat, but not to sell it.

8.   Carrying a Gun for Protection

a.   At Home or in Your Place of Business

Except in a few jurisdictions, no permit is required to carry a gun at home or at your place of business. Your "place of business" generally means one that you own or operate, not a place where you are merely an employee. In some jurisdictions, an employer is allowed to authorize his or her employees to carry a firearm at the place of business.

b.   In Your Automobile

Some states require a permit for carrying a gun in an automobile, and some do not. States may have particular rules about how the gun must be transported in the car, such as in the console or glove compartment, or open and visible.

c.   In Public Places

About half the states allow open carry of a handgun (e.g., in a visibly exposed belt holster) without a permit, but the practice is rare in most places. Open carry has long been a norm in Arizona, and "open carry" advocates in many other states are seeking to re-normalize the practice.

By far the most common method of defensive carry is concealed carry, with the gun in a holster that is concealed from view under clothing, or concealed in some other manner (e.g., a purse with a special compartment). If you can lawfully possess a handgun, you can lawfully carry it concealed, without a permit, in Alaska, Arizona, Vermont, Wyoming, and the rural parts of Montana.

The American norm, however, is for concealed carry to require a license. All the aforesaid states (except Vermont) plus 34 other states grant "shall issue" carry permits to adults who meet certain objective criteria. Typically, these require a fingerprint-based background check and passing a safety class. A few of these states do not require fingerprints, or do not require a class. Some of these states also have what is called "the naked man" rule; the issuing authority may deny a permit to a person who has a clean record but for whom the licensing authority can point to specific evidence showing that the person could be a danger to himself or others. Two states, Alabama and Connecticut, by statute allow considerable police discretion but, in practice, commonly issue permits to applicants who meet the same standards as in shall-issue states.

In total, there are 41 states where concealed carry in public either needs no license, or is permitted pursuant to a licensing system whereby almost all law-abiding adult applicants can obtain a permit if they choose.

In eight states, carry permits are issued only on a "may issue" basis, under which local issuing authorities exercise far more discretion in deciding who will, and will not, be allowed to obtain a permit. These states are California, Hawaii, Massachusetts, Rhode Island, New York, New Jersey, Delaware, and Maryland, plus the District of Columbia. Local practices vary quite a bit in these jurisdictions. In some counties, such as upstate New York, carry permits are issued fairly readily, under criteria typical of a shall-issue state. In others, permits may be issued only to individuals who can document a special threat to their safety, such as obtaining a restraining order against a stalker, or transporting diamonds, prescription drugs, or large sums of cash for business. Other locales appear to issue permits readily to celebrities or other well connected individuals, and hardly ever to anyone else. Some jurisdictions deny permits to almost everyone.

One state, Illinois, has no process to issue handgun carry licenses to private citizens. However, Illinois statutorily allows a limited degree of firearms-carrying by persons in certain occupations (e.g., security guards, elected officials), or in certain circumstances (e.g., at home, while hunting or fishing). The law in the District of Columbia is similar.

9. Local Laws

What if the city or county where you live attempted to enact some new gun control laws that were more restrictive than the laws of your state? In most states, additional local gun-control laws are forbidden by a state *preemption* statute. The statute is based on the state legislature's determination that the firearms laws should be uniform throughout the state.

A minority of states have only *limited preemption.* This means that localities can enact laws only on certain topics (e.g., they can restrict the discharge of firearms within city limits), or are prohibited from addressing certain subjects (e.g., they cannot create additional requirements for the purchase of firearms). Several states have preemption through judicial rulings rather than by statute. Only one state, Hawaii, has no preemption at all.

10. Using a Gun for Self-Defense

Any defensive use of a firearm is automatically considered to be a use of deadly force. Forget any movies you may have seen about shooting an assailant in the hand. If you shoot at someone, you have used deadly force, regardless of the results or your intention.

Every American jurisdiction allows the use of deadly force when you are reasonably in fear of imminent death or serious bodily injury, or are the victim of an in-progress crime (e.g., arson, armed robbery) that necessarily creates such danger, and you reasonably believe that no lesser force would suffice. Defense of family members is widely allowed, and in most states, so is defense of any victim.

The laws of some states require retreat, if safe retreat is possible, before the use of deadly force. The late-nineteenth-century general rule denied that there was a duty to retreat. Retreat was imposed in many states in the latter part of the twentieth century under the influence of the Model Penal Code. Today the trend is again toward legislative abolition of a duty to retreat.

Another modern trend is to expand the circumstances when self-defense by firearm is allowed. Over 20 states have recently enacted laws that temper the prerequisite of determining that a lesser force would not be sufficient. Some of these "castle doctrine" or "stand your ground" laws may broaden the lawfulness of the use of deadly force only in the home. Others also designate one's place of business or one's automobile as permissible zones. Still others allow deadly force against a violent felonious assailant in any public place where the victim has the right to be.

E.   Gun Control Controversies Today

The modern gun control debates in the United States involve both philosophical and empirical issues. Chapter 2 introduces many of the philosophical issues, and we return to them throughout the book. The empirical, social science assessments are treated in the most depth in online Chapter 12, but they also appear in many places throughout the printed book. If you do not have access to that online chapter, read *District of Columbia v. Heller* (Chapter 9), amicus briefs from the International Law Enforcement Educators and Trainers Association (pro-gun) and the American Public Health Association (anti-gun) for concise overviews of the leading research. All the *Heller* amicus briefs are available at DCGunCase.com, Case Filings, *available at* http://dcguncase.com/blog/case-filings/, and collectively, they present excellent summaries of the key pro and con arguments in the modern American gun debate.

A core philosophical issue is what legitimate purpose, if any, there is to citizen possession of arms in general, or firearms in particular. The German philosopher Max Weber expressed the belief that, as a basic requirement of organized government, the state must have a monopoly on the use of force. The most famous antecedent of Weber was Plato. Under the Weber/Plato view, citizen possession of arms is permissible, at most, for recreational purposes, or while serving in military forces under direct government control. Likewise, armed resistance to government oppression, or even to government tyranny, must be prevented, and personal self-defense may be contrary to good order. In the last hundred years, prohibitions on collective or personal self-defense have also been informed by religious pacifism.

The contrary view often springs from the belief that self-defense is a natural, inherent, and unalienable right. To put the issue in the terms of seventeenth-century political philosophy, the argument is that people in a state of nature do not, and cannot, surrender their right of self-defense when they leave the state of nature to enter into a social contract. *See* John Locke, Second Treatise of Government §16 (1690); Thomas Hobbes, Leviathan 199 (C.B. Macpherson ed., Penguin Books 1968) (1651). Going further, using force in self-defense may be seen not only as a personal right, but also as a *duty*, especially the duty to defend persons to whom one has a special obligation of care, such as one's family or students.

Some people support a right of personal self-defense, but are leery of validating collective acts of defense against tyrannical government. One concern is that the potential evils of civil war and anarchy are so horrible that they preclude armed rebellion against the state. A different view is that the two forms of self-defense (private and collective) are part of a continuum, the main difference being the greater dangers and power of the criminal tyrant.

Even assuming that forcible resistance to government could be legitimate, there is the question of who may do the resisting. In the predominant Anglo-American view, defense against government tyranny is not left up to the discretion of the individual, but requires the leadership of "intermediate magistrates" (e.g., state or local governments).[3] For example, in *Federalist* 46 (Chapter 4), James Madison argued that in the unlikely event that the proposed federal government became tyrannical, it would easily be overwhelmed by American citizens serving in militias, and led by state governments.

Some theorists, however, argue that the decision to take up arms against an oppressive government may legitimately be made by individual citizens in some circumstances — especially when "intermediate magistrates" have been eliminated or taken over by the central government (as in Nazi Germany).

Putting aside political theory, an important question is whether firearms are actually effective for self-defense. In one view, using a firearm under stress is too difficult for a person without extensive training; a would-be defender with a gun is more likely to have the gun taken away by the assailant than to be able to use the gun effectively. The other side cites research showing that take-aways are quite rare, that most armed self-defense does not even involve firing a shot (the attacker flees as soon as the defensive gun is displayed), and that

---

3. The use of "intermediate magistrates" as a term of art in resistance theory was created by persecuted Protestants (especially Calvinists) in continental Europe during the sixteenth and seventeenth centuries, but the principle is much older.

successful armed self-defense is common. Chapter 11 details the conflicting research on the frequency of self-defense; the lowest research estimate is about 100,000 instances of defensive gun use (which need not include a shot being fired) annually in the United States, while the high estimate is several million.

Even if guns are effective for self-defense, there is still the issue of whether owning a gun is more dangerous than not, either to the possessor or to others who might be harmed as a result of the presence and misuse of privately owned firearms. After all, most people are not at high risk of being criminally assaulted, especially in the home. And a gun in the home might be involved in an accident. There are about 700 fatal gun accidents in the United States each year. Of these, about 70 involve children under 14.

The gun also might be used in a suicide. In fact, most gun deaths in the United States are from suicide. Researchers disagree as to whether the absence of guns would simply lead to the substitution of other means. However, because attempts at suicide by firearm are especially likely to be fatal, and require little planning, firearms may pose particular dangers to those who might have a strong, but impulsively short, suicidal intent, such as young people or the mentally ill.

Another potential danger of firearms in the home is that they might impulsively be used to perpetrate a domestic homicide. The National Coalition to Ban Handguns (now known as the Coalition to Stop Gun Violence) wrote that every year thousands of "gun murders [are committed] by law-abiding citizens who might have stayed law-abiding if they had not possessed firearms." National Coalition to Ban Handguns, A Shooting Gallery Called America (n.d.). Or as the Violence Policy Center, another handgun-prohibition group, puts it, "[T]he majority of homicide victims die not as a result of criminal activity, but because of arguments between people who know each other . . . not from 'guns in the wrong hands,' but from the virtually unregulated distribution of an inherently dangerous consumer product. . . ." Violence Policy Center, About the Violence Policy Center (n.d.).

Pro-gun advocates counter that most murderers already have a criminal record, and that ordinary citizens are not "seething cauldrons of homicidal rage, ready to kill to avenge any slight to their dignity, eager to seek out and summarily execute the lawless," for whom "[o]nly lack of immediate access to a gun restrains them and prevents the blood from flowing in the streets." Jeffrey R. Snyder, A Nation of Cowards, 113 Pub. Int. 40, 49 (1993).

Self-defense advocates also cite research showing that many murders that occur among people who know each other do not spring from family arguments, but from drug-dealer disputes, gang warfare, and so on. The research unanimously shows that in the home of a domestic abuser, the presence of a firearm greatly increases the risk of homicide.

"Guns don't kill people. People kill people" is a common saying of pro-gun advocates. They argue that if guns were not available, murderers and other criminals would simply use other means. This is undoubtedly true in some cases, but not in all cases. The very features that make guns so effective for self-defense — their ease of use and ability to project force at a distance — also make them effective for criminals. Three gangsters who wish to kill a woman may be able to beat her to death with fists, feet, and clubs. But a scrawny

17-year-old intent on mass murder can kill several bigger, more athletic people quickly with a gun or with an automobile, but not with much else. And if the 17-year-old just wants to rob a liquor store, nothing will facilitate his crime like a firearm.

A lesser controversy is whether, on balance, recreational firearms uses are justifiable. Lawful guns owned for any purpose, including recreational ones, can be stolen, and thus supply the large black market in firearms. Historically, a wide variety of activities (such as gambling, prostitution, or homosexual sex) have been outlawed or restricted simply because the majority find them to be immoral and disgusting. Many people feel the same way about guns.

If one accepts the premise that gun ownership and use is not *per se* illegitimate, then traditional target shooting is probably its most uncontroversial form. Yet some people do object to newer types of target shooting events that test shooters' armed self-defense skills, in *practical shooting* or *action pistol* competitions. In these sports, participants move through a course set up to simulate defensive shooting scenarios, scoring points for hitting "bad guy" targets, and with large penalties for shooting the wrong target. Many thousands of Americans participate in these activities each year. Target ranges are also noisy, and people who move into new housing developments near target ranges often object to the noise and file nuisance lawsuits. They resent the *range protection acts* in many states, which shut down such suits.

What about hunting? Millions of Americans hunt for recreation, while some hunt partially as a source of livelihood, deriving from wild game a valuable supply of meat for their families. Some animal-rights advocates argue that hunting is immoral, a violent and unnecessary exploitation of animals. Hunting advocates argue in response that legal, regulated hunting is designed to promote the health of species, and that annual hunting limits are carefully managed to do so. They point out that regulated hunting and the fees from it have been the primary cause of the thriving recovery of many once-rare species, such as the Wapiti (elk) and the wild turkey. Today, there are more deer in America than when Columbus landed. On the other hand, hunters often align with farmers to oppose the reintroduction or uncontrolled spread of top-of-the-food-chain predator species, such as wolves, which have decimated elk herds in the northern Rockies. Hunting is an important source of government revenue: taxes paid by hunters and other gun owners fund conservation programs that benefit all species. The 1937 federal Pittman-Robertson Wildlife Restoration Act established a 10 or 11 percent excise tax on the sale of firearms and ammunition, and was later extended to bows and arrows. Some of the hundreds of millions of dollars that it generates pay for target range construction, but most of it goes to state wildlife agencies.

Hunters argue that outdoorsmanship builds good character, and that hunting is a valuable tradition passed from parents to children. Some animal-rights advocates respond that killing a living animal cannot possibly engender good character. Hunters suggest that the people in the strongest position to make the argument are vegans who do not wear leather or other animal products. Nonhunters who do consume or wear animals simply delegate the killing to someone else; and animals raised in factory farms may experience much worse lives than do wild animals, who, if they were not killed by a hunter, would eventually be torn to bits and eaten by other predators.

A broad source of controversy is gun culture. Few observers would deny that the debate over the gun issue implies profound differences in cultural views among Americans. What effect does widespread gun ownership have on the civic character of American life? Does it promote a culture of self-reliance, and reinforce a social norm that political power should be decentralized and widely distributed? Or are the effects on the citizenry atavistic or worse, leading to a coarsening of manners and an atmosphere of suspicion and simmering violence?

Finally, there are the questions about firearms and certain groups that have often been victimized, such as racial minorities, women, the disabled, and homosexuals. Would these groups be better off under laws that outlaw gun possession, or do they especially need guns for protection? Chapter 10 provides the arguments on both sides of the issue for various groups. Gun control laws aimed at Blacks are an inextricable part of the general history of American gun regulation, and so are presented throughout the book.

While the rest of this book is mainly about firearms law and policy, there are some related subjects that have been under-studied by scholars, and that would be excellent subjects for student research. These include hunting law and policy, and the law and policy of arms *other* than firearms — particularly air guns, knives and other edged weapons, bows, and blunt weapons. The website for this book, http://firearmregulation.org, provides suggestions for research papers on many different topics related to arms rights and arms control, suitable for law students writing their first or second in-depth research paper.

Appendix: *The Right to Arms in State Constitutions*

Today, 44 of the 50 states have a constitutional right to arms. Over time, the general trend has been in favor of such provisions. For example, since 1875, 13 new states have joined the union, and 12 of them had right to arms provisions in their statehood constitutions. Since 1978, 12 states have added or strengthened an arms rights guarantee.

The evolution of state arms rights from 1776 to the present provides an overview of national and regional moods about the right to bear arms. For more information on the material in this section, see Eugene Volokh, *State Constitutional Rights to Keep and Bear Arms*, 11 Tex. Rev. L. & Pol. 191 (2006) (cataloguing all state right to arms provisions). The online supplement to this book, http://firearmregulation.org, contains a complete list of law review articles surveying state constitutional rights to arms, or studying the right in a particular state.

Thirty-seven state constitutions explicitly guarantee a right of self-defense, and some also guarantee the right to defend property. Sometimes self-defense is part of the "right to arms" provision, but it is often separately enumerated. A standard form of separate enumeration is from Article I of the 1788 Massachusetts Constitution, a classic and widely copied statement of natural rights:

"All people are born free and equal and have certain natural, essential and unalienable rights; among which may be reckoned the right of enjoying and defending their lives and liberties; that of acquiring, possessing and protecting property; in fine, that of seeking and obtaining their safety and happiness." Colorado's 1876 Constitution exemplifies the wording changes that were typical as English usage changed: "All persons have certain natural, essential and inalienable rights, among which may be reckoned the right of enjoying and defending their lives and liberties; of acquiring, possessing and protecting property; and of seeking and obtaining their safety and happiness." Colo. Const., Art. II, §3.

The table below provides the full text of all the state constitutional right to arms guarantees, but not all the self-defense guarantees. For the full text of the separate provisions on self-defense, see Eugene Volokh, *State Constitutional Rights of Self-Defense and Defense of Property*, 11 Tex. Rev. L. & Pol. 399 (2007).

Many state constitutions have separate, and extensive, provisions regarding the militia, often consuming an entire Article. They may also have language about conscientious objectors, standing armies, or other military forces. Such provisions are not reproduced below, except for militia language that appears within the right to arms guarantee.

Date of Statehood	State	Constitutional Provision and Year of Enactment
1787	**DE**	**Del. Const. of 1897, art. I, §20 (as amended in 1987): "A person has the right to keep and bear arms for the defense of self, family, home and State, and for hunting and recreational use."**
1787	**PA**	**Pa. Const. of 1968, art. I, §21: "The right of the citizens to bear arms in defense of themselves and the State shall not be questioned."** Pa. Const. of 1874, art. I, §21: Retained 1790 provision. Pa. Const. of 1838, art. IX, §21: Retained 1790 provision. Pa. Const. of 1790, art. IX, §21: "That the right of the citizens to bear arms in defence of themselves, and the State shall not be questioned." Pa. Const. of 1776, art. XIII: "[T]he people have a right to bear arms for the defence of themselves and the state; and as standing armies in the time of peace are dangerous to liberty, they ought not to be kept up; And that the military should be kept under strict subordination to, and governed by, the civil power."
1787	**NJ**	No right to arms guarantee.
1788	**GA**[*]	Ga. Const. of 1983, art. I, §I, ¶VIII: Retained 1877 provision; unaffected by subsequent amendments. Ga. Const. of 1976, art. I, §I, ¶V: Retained 1877 provision. Ga. Const. of 1945, art. I, §I, ¶XXII: Retained 1877 provision. **Ga. Const. of 1877, art. I, §I, ¶XXII: "The right of the people to keep and bear arms shall not be infringed, but the General Assembly shall have power to prescribe the manner in which arms may be borne."** Ga. Const. of 1868, art. I, §14: "A well-regulated militia being necessary to the security of a free people, the right of the people to keep and bear arms shall not be infringed; but the general

Date of Statehood	*State*	*Constitutional Provision and Year of Enactment*
		assembly shall have power to prescribe by law the manner in which arms may be borne."
		Ga. Const. of 1865, art. I, §4: "A well-regulated militia, being necessary to the security of a free State, the right of the people to keep and bear arms shall not be infringed."
1788	**CT**	**Conn. Const. of 1818, art. I, §17: "Every citizen has a right to bear arms in defense of himself and the State."**
1788	**MA**	**Mass. Const. of 1780, pt. 1, art. XVII: "The people have a right to keep and to bear arms for the common defence. And as in time of peace, armies are dangerous to liberty, they ought not to be maintained without the consent of the legislature; and the military power shall always be held in an exact subordination to the civil authority, and be governed by it."**
1788	**MD**	No right to arms guarantee.
1788	**SC**[*]	**S.C. Const. of 1895, art. I, §20: "A well regulated militia being necessary to the security of a free State, the right of the people to keep and bear arms shall not be infringed. As in times of peace armies are dangerous to liberty, they shall not be maintained without the consent of the General Assembly. The military power of the State shall always be held in subordination to the civil authority and be governed by it."**
		S.C. Const. of 1868, art. I, §28: "The people have a right to keep and bear arms for the common defence. As, in times of peace, armies are dangerous to liberty, they ought not to be maintained without the consent of the general assembly. The military power ought always to be held in an exact subordination to the civil authority, and be governed by it."
1788	**NH**	**N.H. Const. of 1784, art. 2-a (as amended in 1982): "All persons have the right to keep and bear arms in defense of themselves, their families, their property and the state."**
1788	**VA**[*]	**Va. Const. of 1971, art. I, §13: "[A] well regulated militia, composed of the body of the people, trained to arms, is the proper, natural, and safe defense of a free state, therefore, the right of the people to keep and bear arms shall not be infringed; that standing armies, in time of peace, should be avoided as dangerous to liberty; and that in all cases the military should be under strict subordination to, and governed by, the civil power."**
		Va. Const. of 1902, art. I, §13: Retained 1776 provision.
		Va. Const. of 1870, art. I, §15: Retained 1776 provision.
		Va. Const. of 1864, art. I, §13: Retained 1776 provision.
		Va. Const. of 1850, art. I, §13: Retained 1776 provision.
		Va. Const. of 1830, art. I, §13: Retained 1776 provision.
		Va. Const. of 1776, Bill of Rights, §13: "[A] well-regulated militia, composed of the body of the people, trained to arms, is the proper, natural, and safe defence of a free State; that standing armies, in time of peace, should be avoided, as dangerous to liberty; and that in all cases the military should be under strict subordination to, and governed by, the civil power."

Date of Statehood	State	Constitutional Provision and Year of Enactment
1788	NY	No right to arms guarantee in the Constitution. However, the Civil Right Law, a statute enacted in 1909, includes a verbatim copy of the Second Amendment. N.Y. Civ. Rights L., §4.
1789	NC*	**N.C. Const. of 1971, art. I, §30: "A well regulated militia being necessary to the security of a free State, the right of the people to keep and bear arms shall not be infringed; and, as standing armies in time of peace are dangerous to liberty, they shall not be maintained, and the military shall be kept under strict subordination to, and governed by, the civil power. Nothing herein shall justify the practice of carrying concealed weapons, or prevent the General Assembly from enacting penal statutes against that practice."** N.C. Const. of 1876, art. I, §24: "A well-regulated militia being necessary to the security of a free State, the right of the people to keep and bear arms shall not be infringed; and, as standing armies in time of peace are dangerous to liberty, they ought not to be kept up, and the military should be kept under strict subordination to, and governed by, the civil power. Nothing herein contained shall justify the practice of carrying concealed weapons, or prevent the Legislature from enacting penal statutes against said practice." N.C. Const. of 1868, art. I, §24: "A well-regulated militia being necessary to the security of a free State, the right of the people to keep and bear arms shall not be infringed; and as standing armies in time of peace are dangerous to liberty, they ought not to be kept up, and the military should be kept under strict subordination to and governed by the civil power." N.C. Const. of 1776, A Declaration of Rights, art. XVII: "[T]he people have a right to bear arms, for the defence of the State; and, as standing armies, in time of peace, are dangerous to liberty, they ought not to be kept up; and that the military should be kept under strict subordination to, and governed by, the civil power."
1790	**RI**	R.I. Const. of 1987, art. I, §22: Retained 1842 provision. **R.I. Const. of 1842, art. I, §22: "The right of the people to keep and bear arms shall not be infringed."**
1791	**VT**	Vt. Const. of 1793, ch. I, art. 16: Retained 1786 provision. **Vt. Const. of 1786, ch. I, art. XVIII: "[T]he people have a right to bear arms for the defence of themselves and the State — and as standing armies in time of peace are dangerous to liberty, they ought not to be kept up; and that the military should be kept under strict subordination to and governed by the civil power."** Vt. Const. of 1777, ch. I, art. XV (adopted while Vermont was an independent republic): "That the people have a right to bear arms for the defence of themselves and the State; and, as standing armies, in time of peace, are dangerous to liberty, they ought not to be kept up; and that the military should be kept under strict subordination to and governed by the civil power."

Date of Statehood	State	Constitutional Provision and Year of Enactment
1792	KY	Ky. Const. of 1891, §1: "All men are, by nature, free and equal, and have certain inherent and inalienable rights, among which may be reckoned: . . . The right to bear arms in defense of themselves and of the State, subject to the power of the General Assembly to enact laws to prevent persons from carrying concealed weapons." Ky. Const. of 1850, art. XIII, §25: "[T]he rights of the citizens to bear arms in defence of themselves and the State shall not be questioned; but the general assembly may pass laws to prevent persons from carrying concealed arms." Ky. Const. of 1799, art. X, §23: Retained 1792 provision. Ky. Const. of 1792, art. XII, §23: "[T]he right of the citizens to bear arms in defence of themselves and the State shall not be questioned."
1796	TN*	Tenn. Const. of 1870, art. I, §26: "[T]he citizens of this State have a right to keep and to bear arms for their common defense; but the Legislature shall have power, by law, to regulate the wearing of arms with a view to prevent crime." Tenn. Const. of 1834, art. I, §26: "[T]he free white men of this State have a right to keep and to bear arms for their common defence." Tenn. Const. of 1796, art. XI, §26: "[T]he freemen of this State have a right to keep and to bear arms for their common defence."
1803	OH	Ohio Const. of 1851, art. I, §4: "The people have the right to bear arms for their defense and security; but standing armies, in time of peace, are dangerous to liberty, and shall not be kept up; and the military shall be in strict subordination to the civil power." Ohio Const. of 1802, art. VIII, §20: "[T]he people have a right to bear arms for the defence of themselves and the State; and as standing armies, in time of peace, are dangerous to liberty, they shall not be kept up, and that the military shall be kept under strict subordination to the civil power."
1812	LA*	La. Const. of 1974, art. I, §11: "The right of each citizen to keep and bear arms shall not be abridged, but this provision shall not prevent the passage of laws to prohibit the carrying of weapons concealed on the person." La. Const. of 1879, art. 3: "A well regulated militia being necessary to the security of a free State, the right of the people to keep and bear arms shall not be abridged. This shall not prevent the passage of laws to punish those who carry weapons concealed."
1816	IN	Ind. Const. of 1851, art. I, §32: "The people shall have a right to bear arms, for the defense of themselves and the State." Ind. Const. of 1816, Art. I, §20: "[T]he people have a right to bear arms for the defense of themselves and the State, and that the military shall be kept in strict subordination to the civil power."
1817	MS*	Miss. Const. of 1890, art. 3, §12: "The right of every citizen to keep and bear arms in defense of his home, person or property, or in aid of the civil power when thereto legally summoned, shall not be called in question, but the legislature may regulate or forbid carrying concealed weapons."

Date of Statehood	State	Constitutional Provision and Year of Enactment
		Miss. Const. of 1868, art. I, §15: "All persons shall have a right to keep and bear arms for their defence."
		Miss. Const. of 1832, art. I, §23: Retained 1817 provision.
		Miss. Const. of 1817, art. I, §23: "Every citizen has a right to bear arms, in defence of himself and the State."
1818	IL	**Ill. Const. of 1970, art. I, §22: "Subject only to the police power, the right of the individual citizen to keep and bear arms shall not be infringed."**
1819	AL*	Ala. Const. of 1901, art. I, §26: Retained the 1865 provision.
		Ala. Const. of 1875, art. I, §27: Retained the 1865 provision.
		Ala. Const. of 1865, art. I, §27: "That every citizen has a right to bear arms in defence of himself and the State."
		Ala. Const. of 1861, art. I, §23: Retained 1819 provision.
		Ala. Const. of 1819, art. I, §23: "Every citizen has a right to bear arms in defence of himself and the State."
1820	ME	**Me. Const. of 1819, art. I, §16 (as amended in 1987): "Every citizen has a right to keep and bear arms and this right shall never be questioned."**
		Me. Const. of 1819, art. I, §16: "Every citizen has a right to keep and bear arms for the common defence; and this right shall never be questioned."
1821	MO	**Mo. Const. of 1945, art. I, §23: "[T]he right of every citizen to keep and bear arms in defense of his home, person and property, or when lawfully summoned in aid of the civil power, shall not be questioned; but this shall not justify the wearing of concealed weapons."**
		Mo. Const. of 1875, art. II, §17: "[T]he right of no citizen to keep and bear arms in defense of his home, person and property, or in aid of the civil power, when thereto legally summoned, shall be called in question; but nothing herein contained is intended to justify the practice of wearing concealed weapons."
		Mo. Const. of 1865, art. I, §8: "[T]he people have the right peaceably to assemble for their common good, and to apply to those vested with the powers of government for redress of grievances by petition or remonstrance; and that their right to bear arms in defence of themselves and of the lawful authority of the State cannot be questioned."
		Mo. Const. of 1820, art. XIII, §3: "[T]he people have the right peaceably to assemble for their common good, and to apply to those vested with the powers of government for redress of grievances by petition or remonstrance; and that their right to bear arms in defence of themselves and of the State cannot be questioned."
1836	AR*	Ark. Const. of 1874, art. I, §5: Retained 1868 provision.
		Ark. Const. of 1868, art. I, §5: "The citizens of this State shall have the right to keep and bear arms for their common defence."
		Ark. Const. of 1864, art. II, §21: Retained 1836 provision.
		Ark. Const. of 1861, art. II, §21: Retained 1836 provision.

Date of Statehood	State	Constitutional Provision and Year of Enactment
		Ark. Const. of 1836, art. II, §21: "[T]he free white men of this State shall have a right to keep and to bear arms for their common defence."
1837	**MI**	Mich. Const. of 1968, art. I, §6: Retained 1835 provision. Mich. Const. of 1908, art. II, §5: Retained 1835 provision. Mich. Const. of 1850, art. VXIII, §7: Retained 1835 provision. **Mich. Const. of 1835, art. I, §13: "Every person has a right to bear arms for the defence of himself and the State."**
1845	**FL**[*]	**Fla. Const. of 1968, art. I, §8 (subsections (b)-(d) added in 1990):** **"(a) The right of the people to keep and bear arms in defense of themselves and of the lawful authority of the state shall not be infringed, except that the manner of bearing arms may be regulated by law.** **(b) There shall be a mandatory period of three days, excluding weekends and legal holidays, between the purchase and delivery at retail of any handgun. For the purposes of this section, 'purchase' means the transfer of money or other valuable consideration to the retailer, and 'handgun' means a firearm capable of being carried and used by one hand, such as a pistol or revolver. Holders of a concealed weapon permit as prescribed in Florida law shall not be subject to the provisions of this paragraph.** **(c) The legislature shall enact legislation implementing subsection (b) of this section, effective no later than December 31, 1991, which shall provide that anyone violating the provisions of subsection (b) shall be guilty of a felony.** **(d) This restriction shall not apply to a trade in of another handgun."** Fla. Const. of 1968, art. I, §8: "The right of the people to keep and bear arms in defense of themselves and of the lawful authority of the state shall not be infringed, except that the manner of bearing arms may be regulated by law." Fla. Const. of 1885, art. I, §20: "The right of the people to bear arms in defence of themselves and the lawful authority of the State, shall not be infringed, but the Legislature may prescribe the manner in which they may be borne." Fla. Const. of 1868, art. I, §22: "The people shall have the right to bear arms in defence of themselves and of the lawful authority of the State." (In 1865, a postbellum convention drew up a constitution in 1865 that did not include an arms-bearing provision. This constitution was never submitted to the people for ratification, and it was rejected by the reconstruction U.S. Congress, which put Florida under military rule. It was replaced by the fully effective 1868 constitution.) Fla. Const. of 1838, art. I, §21: "[T]he free white men of this State shall have a right to keep and to bear arms for their common defence."
1845	**TX**[*]	**Tex. Const. of 1876, art. I, §23: "Every citizen shall have the right to keep and bear arms in the lawful defence of himself or the State; but the legislature shall have power by law to regulate the wearing of arms with a view to prevent crime."**

Date of Statehood	State	Constitutional Provision and Year of Enactment
		Tex. Const. of 1868, art. I, §13: "Every person shall have the right to keep and bear arms, in the lawful defence of himself or the State, under such regulations as the legislature may prescribe." Tex. Const. of 1866, art. I, §13: Retained 1845 provision. Tex. Const. of 1845, art. I, §13: "Every citizen shall have the right to keep and bear arms in the lawful defence of himself or the State." Tex. Const. of 1836, Declaration of Rights, §14 (adopted while Texas was an independent republic): "Every citizen shall have the right to bear arms in defence of himself and the republic. The military shall at all times and in all cases be subordinate to the civil power."
1846	IA	No right to arms guarantee.
1848	WI	**Wis. Const. of 1848, art. I, §25 (as amended in 1998): "The people have the right to keep and bear arms for security, defense, hunting, recreation or any other lawful purpose."**
1850	CA	No right to arms guarantee.
1858	MN	No right to arms guarantee.
1859	OR	**Or. Const. of 1857, art. I, §8 (amended so that provision is presently in §27): "The people shall have the right to bear arms for the defence of themselves and the State, but the military shall be kept in strict subordination to the civil power."**
1861	KS	**Kan. Const. of 1859, Bill of Rights, §4 (as amended in 2010): "A person has the right to keep and bear arms for the defense of self, family, home and state, for lawful hunting and recreational use, and for any other lawful purpose."** Kan. Const. of 1859, Bill of Rights, §4: "The people have the right to bear arms for their defense and security; but standing armies, in time of peace, are dangerous to liberty, and shall not be tolerated, and the military shall be in strict subordination to the civil power." Kan. Const. of 1858, art. I, §4: Retained/reinstated 1855 provision. Kan. Const. of 1857, Bill of Rights, §19: "[T]he citizens of this State shall have a right to keep and bear arms for their common defence." (There is a debate over whether this "Lecompton Constitution," which contained pro-slavery language, and was intended to replace the anti-slavery 1855 Topeka Constitution, was ever legally in effect. There was no controversy related to the arms-bearing provision.) Kan. Const. of 1855, art. I, §4: "The people have the right to bear arms for their defence and security; but standing armies in time of peace are dangerous to liberty and shall not be kept up; and the military shall be kept in strict subordination to the civil power."
1863	WV	**W. Va. Const. of 1872, art. III, §22 (as amended in 1986): "A person has the right to keep and bear arms for the defense of self, family, home and state, and for lawful hunting and recreational use."**
1864	NV	**Nev. Const. of 1864, §11(1) (as amended in 1982) "Every citizen has the right to keep and bear arms for security and defense, for lawful hunting and recreational use and for other lawful purposes."**

Date of Statehood	State	Constitutional Provision and Year of Enactment
1867	NE	Neb. Const. of 1875, art. I, §1 (as amended in 1988): "All persons are by nature free and independent, and have certain inherent and inalienable rights; among these are life, liberty, the pursuit of happiness, and the right to keep and bear arms for security or defense of self, family, home, and others, and for lawful common defense, hunting, recreational use, and all other lawful purposes, and such rights shall not be denied or infringed by the state or any subdivision thereof. To secure these rights, and the protection of property, governments are instituted among people, deriving their just powers from the consent of the governed."
1876	CO	Colo. Const. of 1876, art. II, §13: "[T]he right of no person to keep and bear arms in defence of his home, person, and property, or in aid of the civil power when thereto legally summoned, shall be called in question; but nothing herein contained shall be construed to justify the practice of carrying concealed weapons."
1889	ND	N.D. Const. of 1889, art. I, §1 (as amended in 1984): "All individuals are by nature equally free and independent and have certain inalienable rights, among which are those of enjoying and defending life and liberty; acquiring, possessing and protecting property and reputation; pursuing and obtaining safety and happiness; and to keep and bear arms for the defense of their person, family, property, and the state, and for lawful hunting, recreational, and other lawful purposes, which shall not be infringed."
1889	SD	S.D. Const. of 1889, art. VI, §24: "The right of the citizens to bear arms in defense of themselves and the state shall not be denied."
1889	MT	Mont. Const. of 1972, art. II, §12: Retained 1889 provision. Mont. Const. of 1889, art. III, §13: "The right of any person to keep or bear arms in defense of his own home, person and property, or in aid of the civil power when thereto legally summoned, shall not be called in question, but nothing herein contained shall be held to permit the carrying of concealed weapons."
1889	WA	Wash. Const. of 1889, art. I, §24: "The right of the individual citizen to bear arms in defense of himself, or the state, shall not be impaired, but nothing in this section shall be construed as authorizing individuals or corporations to organize, maintain or employ an armed body of men."
1890	ID	Idaho Const. of 1889, art. I, §11 (as amended in 1978): "The people have the right to keep and bear arms, which right shall not be abridged; but this provision shall not prevent the passage of laws to govern the carrying of weapons concealed on the person nor prevent passage of legislation providing minimum sentences for crimes committed while in possession of a firearm, nor prevent the passage of legislation providing penalties for the possession of firearms by a convicted felon, nor prevent the passage of any legislation punishing the use of a firearm. No law shall impose licensure, registration or special taxation on the ownership or

Date of Statehood	State	Constitutional Provision and Year of Enactment
		possession of firearms or ammunition. Nor shall any law permit the confiscation of firearms, except those actually used in the commission of a felony." Idaho Const. of 1889, art. I, §11: "The people have the right to bear arms for their security and defense; but the Legislature shall regulate the exercise of this right by law."
1890	WY	Wyo. Const. of 1889, art. I, §24: "The right of citizens to bear arms in defense of themselves and of the State shall not be denied."
1896	UT	Utah Const. of 1896, art. I, §6 (as amended in 1984): "The individual right of the people to keep and bear arms for security and defense of self, family, others, property, or the state, as well as for other lawful purposes shall not be infringed; but nothing herein shall prevent the Legislature from defining the lawful use of arms." Utah Const. of 1896, art. I, §6: "The people have the right to bear arms for their security and defense, but the legislature may regulate the exercise of this right by law."
1907	OK	Okla. Const. of 1907, art. II, §26: "The right of a citizen to keep and bear arms in defense of his home, person, or property, or in aid of the civil power, when thereunto legally summoned, shall never be prohibited; but nothing herein contained shall prevent the Legislature from regulating the carrying of weapons."
1912	NM	N.M. Const. of 1912, art. II, §6 (as amended in 1986): "No law shall abridge the right of the citizen to keep and bear arms for security and defense, for lawful hunting and recreational use and for other lawful purposes, but nothing herein shall be held to permit the carrying of concealed weapons. No municipality or county shall regulate, in any way, an incident of the right to keep and bear arms." N.M. Const. of 1912, art. II, §6 (as amended in 1971): "No law shall abridge the right of the citizen to keep and bear arms for security and defense, for lawful hunting and recreational use and for other lawful purposes, but nothing herein shall be held to permit the carrying of concealed weapons." N.M. Const. of 1912, art. II, §6: "The people have the right to bear arms for their security and defense, but nothing herein shall be held to permit the carrying of concealed weapons."
1912	AZ	Ariz. Const. of 1912, art. II, §26: "The right of the individual citizen to bear arms in defense of himself or the state shall not be impaired, but nothing in this section shall be construed as authorizing individuals or corporations to organize, maintain, or employ an armed body of men."
1959	AK	Alaska Const. of 1959, art. II, §19 (as amended in 1994; the amendment also changed the section title from "Right to Bear Arms" to "Right to Keep and Bear Arms"): "A well-regulated militia being necessary to the security of a free state, the right of the people to keep and bear arms shall not be infringed. The individual right to keep and bear arms shall not be denied or infringed by the State or a political subdivision of the State."

Date of Statehood	State	Constitutional Provision and Year of Enactment
		Alaska Const. of 1959, art. II, §19: "A well-regulated militia being necessary to the security of a free state, the right of the people to keep and bear arms shall not be infringed."
1959	**HI**	**Haw. Const. of 1959, art. I, §17: "A well regulated militia being necessary to the security of a free state, the right of the people to keep and bear arms shall not be infringed."**

Notes: (1) Provisions in effect today are in **bold**. (2) States marked with an asterisk ("*") were once members of the Confederate States of America. All but one of these states were required by Congress to create new constitutions before being re-admitted to the Union. (Tennessee was re-admitted before this mandate was imposed.) (3) States' constitutions that were in effect before the enactment of the first constitution containing an arms-bearing provision are not listed. (4) Nonsubstantive changes solely to punctuation, spelling, and typeface between versions of a constitution are not separately noted. (5) *Date of Statehood* is the date that one of the original 13 states ratified the Constitution, or the date that one of the other 37 states was admitted to the Union.

‖2‖

Antecedents of the Second Amendment

Debates about the legitimate use of arms long predate the invention of firearms or the existence of the United States of America. This chapter provides a sample of the arguments that various social philosophers have offered for or against arms possession, and about appropriate constraints on the use of arms. Most of the readings in this chapter are part of the intellectual background of the Second Amendment. For a broader perspective, we also provide some sources that were unfamiliar to the American Framers. As you read this chapter, you will find that many of the debates about arms and arms control have been going on for millennia.

One theme of this chapter is the benefits and dangers of militias versus standing armies. So, for background: Standing armies consist of full-time soldiers armed and paid by the state. In contrast, a militia consists of soldiers who only serve for part of the year or in situations of necessity. The rest of the time, they maintain their civilian occupations as farmers, merchants, and so on. Typically, they supply their own arms. (For material on the modern status of militias, standing armies, and other organized and unorganized forces in the United States, see Chapter 4.)

A. The Early Far East

1. Confucianism

There is no evidence that Framers of the Second Amendment were familiar with the Confucians or Taoists. Nevertheless, we begin our study here because it is often claimed that self-defense is part of "natural law" — that is, part of a universally shared set of common human intuitions and understandings. Examining the Chinese philosophers is one step in considering the issue.

Second, among the justifications that people have offered for arms possession are sporting purposes (particularly hunting), resistance to tyrannical government, and the benefits of a militia-centric system of national defense. All of these issues were addressed by Confucian and Taoist philosophers.

The most important collection of Confucian sayings is the *Analects*.

The Analects of Confucius
Simon Leys trans. (1997)

"To govern a state of middle size," the ruler should "mobilize the people only at the right times." (Analects 1:5). The Master said: "The people need to be taught by good men for seven years before they can take arms." The Master said: "To send a people to war that has not been properly taught is wasting them." (13:29-30).

The Master said: "A gentleman avoids competition. Still, if he must compete let it be at archery. There, as he bows and exchanges civilities both before the contest and over drinks afterward, he remains a gentleman, even in competition." (3:7).

In archery, it does not matter whether one pierces the target, for archers may be of uneven strengths. Such was the view of the ancients. (3:16).

The Master fished with a line, not with a net. When hunting, he never shot a roosting bird. (7:27).

The Head of the Ji Family was richer than a king, and yet Ran Qiu kept pressuring the peasants to make him richer still. The Master said: "He is my disciple no more. Beat the drum, my little ones, and attack him: you have my permission." (11:17).

Mencius[1]

"Confucius" is an imperfect translation of "K'ung-tzu," or, in English, "Master K'ung." Mencius was the most influential developer of Master K'ung's thought. He lived from about 371 to 289 B.C., a period when rival Chinese states were adopting the principles of the Legalist philosophers. The Legalists favored extremely centralized governments with rigidly applied laws. The Legalist states were very militaristic, aiming to regiment the peasants into armies made for wars of conquest. Eventually, the state of Ch'in, which had gone further than any other in adopting Legalism, conquered all of China, ruling it from 221 to 207 B.C. The Legalists, like the Utilitarian philosophers of nineteenth-century Britain, viewed humans as egocentrics whose only motivation was reward or punishment. D.C. Lau, "Introduction," in Mencius 10-11 (D.C. Lau trans., 1970).

Mencius viewed rapacious governors as equivalent to ordinary robbers: "Now the way feudal lords take from the people is no different from robbery." Accordingly, accepting a gift from a feudal lord was like accepting stolen property from a robber. *Id.* at 154 (book 5, part B). Mencius told King Hsüan of Ch'i that royal ministers should remove a king who repeatedly ignored their warnings

---

1. [Most of what we know about the thought of Mencius is in a book that is simply called "The Mencius." For the benefit of readers who may use a different edition of this often-republished work, we provide information about the subdivision which we are citing, in addition to the page number of the particular edition we used. We likewise provide subdivisions for some other ancient sources cited in this chapter. —EDS.]

and made serious mistakes. *Id.* at 66-67 (book 1, part B, item 6); 121-22 (book 4, part A, item 9). Further, said Mencius, a good subject could banish a bad ruler, if the subject had good motives. *Id.* at 188-89 (book 7, part A, item 31).

In a discussion of two previous emperors who had been overthrown, Mencius was asked, "Is regicide permissible?"

He replied:

> A man who mutilates benevolence is a mutilator, while one who cripples rightness is a crippler. He who is both a mutilator and a crippler is an "outcast." I have heard of the punishment of the "outcast Tchou," but I have not heard of any regicide.

Id. at 68 (book 1, part B, item 8).

The common Chinese understanding was that the ruler had the "mandate of heaven." Mencius added an important qualification: "Heaven sees as the people see; Heaven hears as the people hear." Michael Nylan, The Five "Confucian" Classics 155 (2001). In other words, a ruler who lost the support of the people had necessarily lost the mandate of heaven, and hence was no longer a legitimate ruler.

Like Confucius (and the Taoists, see below), Mencius strictly insisted that hunting be according to the rules. One day, a charioteer drove all morning for an archer who failed to shoot any birds; the charioteer had obeyed all the rules, and the archer blamed the charioteer for the archer's lack of success. The charioteer asked for another chance; after the second hunt, the charioteer explained, "I used underhanded methods, and we caught ten birds in one morning." Mencius rebuked the charioteer for bending himself to please others. Mencius 106-07 (book 3, part B, item 1). Conversely, Mencius praised a gamekeeper who refused to answer a summons from his master, because the master had given an improper signal, by raising a pennon (a thin triangular flag) rather than by raising a cap. *Id.* at 157-58 (book 5, part B, item 7).

Personal protection was uncontroversial for Confucians. In a story illustrating that one should only accept gifts when there is justification, Mencius seemed to accept the legitimacy of arms for personal protection:

> In Hsüeh, I had to take precautions for my safety. The message accompanying the gift said, "I hear you are taking precautions for your safety. This is a contribution towards the expense of acquiring arms." Again, why should have I refused? But in the case of Ch'i, I had no justification for accepting a gift. To accept a gift without justification is tantamount to being bought.

Id. at 88 (book 2, part B, item 3).

NOTES & QUESTIONS

1. In contrast to a standing professional army, a militia consists of soldiers who only serve for a limited time in situations of necessity. The rest of the time, they maintain their civilian occupations as farmers, merchants, etc. In Confucian theory, a state of "middle size" was ideal because it could

manifest the characteristics of moderation that Confucianism extolled. How might a militia system, as opposed to a full-time professional standing army, foster moderation?

2. Why might Confucius have favored such extensive training before militiamen were sent into combat?

3. One of the modern martial arts is a form of archery called *kyudo* (pronounced "cue-dough"). In *kyudo*, marksmanship is much less important than good form and a proper mental state. What virtues might be cultivated by noncompetitive, highly ritualized sports, such as the archery favored by Confucius?

4. Thomas Jefferson advised his nephew: "Games played with a bat and ball are too violent, and stamp no character on the mind." Letter from Thomas Jefferson to Peter Carr (1785) *in* John Foley, The Jeffersonian Cyclopedia 318 (1900). "As to the species of exercise, I advise the gun." *Id.* Do you see any parallels between the Jeffersonian and Confucian attitudes? Does either make sense today?

5. What is the conservation basis for Confucius's fishing and hunting practices? Are there rationales in addition to species protection?

6. Confucius authorized the beating of the war drum to summon people to overthrow a king who was extorting money from them. How could a philosopher who extolled moderation in all things support the violent overthrow of a ruler?

7. Of what significance is the statement that one should not shoot a roosting bird? Note that personal and family honor was — and still is — important in Eastern traditions. CQ: In what ways has the concept of honorable usage of arms been relevant at different periods in the United States' history? *See* Chapter 5; *Andrews v. State,* 50 Tenn. (3 Heisk.) 165 (1871) (Nelson, J., concurring) (Chapter 6); *Wilson v. State,* 33 Ark. 557 (1878) (Chapter 6).

8. How could Mencius plausibly claim that killing a wicked king was not "regicide"?

9. Mencius was not unique in claiming that unjust and oppressive rulers were simply a type of criminal. The fifth-century Christian theologian Augustine of Hippo wrote:

Indeed, that was an apt and true reply which was given to Alexander the Great by a pirate who had been seized. For when that king had asked the man what he meant by keeping hostile possession of the sea, he answered with bold pride, "What thou meanest by seizing the whole earth; but because I do it with a petty ship, I am called a robber, whilst thou who dost it with a great fleet art styled emperor."

Augustine, Concerning the City of God Against the Pagans 139 (Henry Bettenson trans., Penguin Books, 1984) book 4 (translation of 1467 edition; original edition approx. 410). Or as the fourth-century B.C. Taoist philosopher Chuang Tzu put it: "He who steals a belt buckle pays with his life; he who steals a state gets to be a feudal lord." The Complete Works of Chuang Tzu 11 (Burton Watson trans., 1968). The seventeenth-century English political writer Algernon Sidney agreed that being subjected to a tyrant is little different from being under the power of a pirate. Algernon Sidney, Discourses Concerning Government 574 (Thomas G. West ed., Liberty Fund 1996) (ch. 3, §46) (1698, published posthumously). Sidney was executed for treason in 1683, and later venerated by the English and Americans as one of the greatest martyrs of liberty.

The same view was prominent among the American Founders. Don B. Kates, *The Second Amendment and the Ideology of Self-Protection*, 9 Const. Comment. 87 (1992). What is your assessment of the claim by Mencius and the rest that the only difference between an ordinary mugger and a criminal government is one of scale? If forcible resistance to the former is legitimate, does it follow that forcible resistance to the latter is also legitimate? Compare the views of Thomas Hobbes and John Locke, *infra*.

10. If the etiquette rules for hunting are so rigid that raising a hat as a signal is improper, does this suggest that one purpose of hunting is something other than catching game? If so, what might the purpose be?

2.   Taoism

The second great world religion to emerge from China was Taoism. As with Confucianism, Taoism's historical roots are obscure; the foundation is usually attributed to a sage named Lao Tzu, although some people argue that the Lao Tzu material is a collection of earlier material. In legend, Lao Tzu is said to have been renowned as a swordsman. Deng Ming-Dao, Scholar Warrior: An Introduction to the Tao in Everyday Life 11 (1990).

"The Tao" literally means "the way." Over the centuries, various versions of Taoism have developed; in some of these versions, Taoism is a philosophy, or a way of life, but it is not what Westerners would usually call a religion. In other versions, Taoism does have the characteristics of a religion. Over Chinese history, many people have followed various blends of Confucianism and Taoism. Taoism has also mixed with Buddhism, especially Zen Buddhism.

a.   Tao Te Ching

The foundation of Taoism is the *Tao Te Ching*, ascribed to Lao Tzu, and probably written around the sixth century B.C. The *Tao Te Ching* (Book of the Way and Its Power) is a collection of poems, prose, and proverbs. It is second only to the Bible in the number of worldwide translations. Regarding arms, it reads:

> Now arms, however beautiful, are instruments of evil omen, hateful, it may be said, to all creatures. Therefore they who have the Tao do not like to employ them.

> The superior man . . . uses them only on the compulsion of necessity. Calm and repose are what he prizes; victory (by force of arms) is to him undesirable.

Lao-tzu, Tao Te Ching, no. 31 (J. Legge trans., 1891), *available at* http://www.sacred-texts.com/tao/taote.htm (parenthetical in original).

> In a little state with a small population, I would so order it, that, though there were individuals with the abilities of ten or a hundred men, there should be no employment of them; . . .
>   Though they had boats and carriages, they should have no occasion to ride in them; though they had buff coats and sharp weapons, they should have no occasion to don or use them.

Id. no. 80.

NOTES & QUESTIONS

1. The attitude toward arms and violence expressed in the first poem above are also common in Christian thought, and in other religions as well, such as certain strains of Buddhism. As we will see later, there are many who disagree. Some wish to outlaw arms, and to prohibit or severely restrict armed self-defense. Others celebrate arms and self-defense. Do you agree or disagree with the views expressed in the first poem? Why?

2. In the second poem, why does the state have people keep arms but not use them?

3. CQ: Compare the description of the state described in the second poem to the description of Switzerland in online Chapter 14. Switzerland has not been involved in a war since a civil war over 150 years ago.

b. Wen-Tzu

The *Wen-Tzu*, also known as "Understanding the Mysteries," is attributed to disciples of Lao Tzu who wrote down his discourses. A major theme of the *Wen-Tzu* is the virtue of moderation, both in the individual and the state. It warned: "If you allow small groups to infringe upon the right of large masses and allow the weak to be oppressed by the strong, then weapons will kill you." Thomas Cleary, The Taoist Classics: The Collected Translations of Thomas Cleary 192 (1999) (no. 49). It further states:

> What makes a country strong is willingness to die. What makes people willing to die is justice. What makes justice possible to carry out is power. So give people direction by means of culture, make them equal by arming them, and they may be said to be sure of victory. When power and justice are exercised together, this may be said to be certain strength. . . .

... When there is a day set for battle, if they [the people] look upon death as like going home, it is because of the benevolence [that] has been bestowed upon them.

Id. at 289-90 (no. 171).

c. The Master of the Hidden Storehouse

Lao Tzu's disciple Keng Sang-tzu has been credited with writing *The Master of the Hidden Storehouse*, a collection of advice for rulers. However, the history of the work is obscure until the T'ang Dynasty in the eighth century A.D., where it was honored as part of a revival of Taoist studies. The Emperor Hsuan-tsung, who reigned from 713 to 755, liked it so much that he called it the "Scripture of Open Awareness." Regarding militias, it reads:

When warfare is truly just, it is used to eliminate brutal rulers and rescue those in misery. . . .
. . . [W]hen a just militia enters enemy territory, the people know they are being protected. When the militia comes to the outskirts of cities, it does not trample the crops, does not loot the tombs, does not plunder the treasures, and does not burn the houses. . . .
. . . [A] just militia safeguards the lives of individual human beings many times over, why would people not like it?
Therefore, when a just militia arrives, people of the neighboring countries join it like flowing water; the people of an oppressed country look to it in hope as if it were their parents. The further it travels, the more people it wins.

Id. at 126-27, 141-42 (2000).

d. Huainanzi

Sometime before the first millennium A.D., the *Huainanzi* (The Masters of Huainan) was composed. The *Huainanzi* extolled a free, diverse society, in which individuals lived in a balanced way, including in balance with nature. It includes the following observations:

- "The reason why leaders are set up is to eliminate violence and quell disorder. Now they take advantage of the power of the people to become plunderers themselves. They're like winged tigers — why shouldn't they be eliminated? If you want to raise fish in the pond, you have to get rid of otters; if you want to raise domestic animals, you have to get rid of wolves — how much the more so when governing people!"
- "When water is polluted, fish choke; when government is harsh, people rebel."
- "So you cannot fight against an army of parents, children, and siblings, because of how much they have already done for one another." "When people serve as militia in the same spirit as children doing something for their parents or older siblings, then the force of their power is like an avalanche — who can withstand it?"

- "What makes warriors strong is readiness to fight to the death. What makes people ready to fight to death is justice. . . . Therefore, when people are united by culture and equalized by martial training, they are called sure winners."
- The people expect "three things from the rulers: that the hungry can be fed, the weary can be given rest, and the worthy can be rewarded." If the government neglects them, "then even if the country is large and its people many, the militia will still be weak."
- "The basis of military victory or defeat is in government." If the people "cleave to those above, then the militia is strong." But when "those below turn against those above, then the militia is weak."
- "When you use arms well, you employ people to work for their own benefit. When you use arms badly, you employ people to work for your own benefit. When you employ people to work for their own benefit, anyone in the world can be employed. When you employ people to work for your own benefit, then you will find few."
- "A degenerate society is characterized by expansionism and imperialism, starting unjust military operations against innocent countries, killing innocent people, cutting off the heritage of ancient sages. . . . This is not what armies are really for. A militia is supposed to put down violence, not cause violence."
- "Sages' use of arms is like combing hair or thinning sprouts: a few are removed for the benefit of many. There is no greater harm than killing innocent people in supporting unjust rulers." Likewise, "In ancient wars, they did not kill young or capture the old. . . ."

Id. at 313, 316-18, 330, 357, 360-61, 367.

The *Wen-Tzu* had praised certain restraints on hunting:

> There were laws of ancient kings not to surround the herds to take the full-grown animals, not to drain the ponds to catch fish, and not to burn the woods to hunt for game. Before the proper seasons, traps were not to be set in the wild and nets were not to be set in the water. . . . Pregnant animals were not to be killed, birds' eggs were not to be sought out, fish less than a foot long were not to be taken. . . .

Id. at 270-71 (no. 151). The *Huainanzi* contained very similar language, and added some more rules for how hunting takes place in a society in harmony with the Way: "In early spring . . . pregnant animals are not to be killed. . . . In late autumn, hunters practice with their weapons, and ceremonies propitiating animals are carried out." In contrast to the harmonious hunting of the idealized past, "[i]n latter-day government, there are heavy taxes on hunting, fishing, and commerce. Hatcheries are closed off; there is nowhere to string nets, nowhere to plow." *Id.* at 325, 329, 352-53. "So to obtain sharp swords is not as good as mastering the art of the swordsmith." *Id.* at 314.

> In human nature, nothing is more valuable than benevolence; nothing is more urgent than wisdom. Therefore, if one has courage and daring without benevolence, one is like a madman wielding a sharp sword. . . . So the ambitious should not be lent convenient power; the foolish should not be given sharp instruments.

Id. at 326.

In the space of one generation, the cultural and the martial may shift in relative significance, insofar as there are times when each is useful. Nowadays, however, martialists repudiate culture and the cultured repudiate the martial. Adherents of cultural and martial arts reject each other, not knowing their functions according to the time.

Id. at 369.

NOTES & QUESTIONS

1. What role does arms possession play in political order and civil equality, according to the *Wen-Tzu*?

2. Why might a militia be better or worse at liberating foreign countries than a standing army?

3. The *Huainanzi* (like many other Taoists, and many Confucians) analogized the government and the people to a benevolent family, with government playing the role of parents. How did the militia fit into this vision?

4. According to the *Huainanzi,* under what circumstances is it legitimate to use violence to overthrow the government?

5. The Taoists and the American Founders both thought that large armies and wars of aggressive expansion were an abomination that would destroy a good society. Conversely, a harmonious and ideal state was one that simply defended itself with a well-trained and well-armed citizen militia. As far as we know, the American Founders had no knowledge of Taoism, but instead drew their vision of a militia from knowledge of the history of Greece, Rome, Switzerland, England, and other parts of Europe. Yet the Taoists and the Americans arrived at similar conclusions. What might account for this?

6. The Taoists seems to have envisioned a more active welfare state than did the American Founders. In what ways might a more activist government contribute to the effective functioning of a militia in a balanced, harmonious society? In making a society more balanced and harmonious?

7. In what ways might a larger state reduce the need for a militia as a deterrent or protection against tyranny? In what ways might a large state have greater needs for checks against tyranny?

8. Besides ensuring the long-term health of game species, in what other ways do the Taoist hunting and fishing rules help a society live in harmony with nature?

9. For what practical or other reasons could being a swordsmith be considered better than owning many swords?

10. How might one prevent the foolish from obtaining sharp instruments, and the ambitious from obtaining inordinate power? Under what conditions might such efforts succeed or fail?

11. Can you think of times in American history, or instances today, in which martialists and the cultured have failed to respect the proper contributions of each other?

B.　Ancient Greece and Rome

1.　Greece

While the Framers of the Second Amendment knew almost nothing about Chinese political philosophy, they were thoroughly familiar with the history of ancient Greece and Rome. The Framers studied classical history very carefully in order to understand how liberty had been defended, advanced, and lost.

a.　Greek Law

In a famous oration in a criminal case, Demosthenes explicated an Athenian statute that provided: "If any man while violently and illegally seizing another shall be slain straightway in self-defence, there shall be no penalty for his death." Demosthenes explained that "straightway" meant that the victim had slain the aggressor in immediate self-defense, rather than after "long premeditation." The words "in self-defence" made it clear that the law was "giving indulgence to the actual sufferer, and to no other man." Demosthenes explained, "[T]here is such a thing as justifiable homicide," for some kinds of homicide can "be accounted righteous." "Against Aristocrates" in 3 Demosthenes, Orations (1935) (originally delivered in 352 B.C.).

According to the historian Xenophon, Athenian law presumed that the citizen militia would possess their own arms, which they would use when called to military service. Arms-carrying was allowed in the countryside, but not in the city unless there was a particular need. Xenophon, Hellenica, book 1.

The following is Plato's view of the ideal law of self-defense, although we do not know if any Greek government followed this particular law.

> But if a brother kills brother in a civil broil or under other like circumstances, if the other has begun, and he only defends himself, let him be free from guilt as he would be if he had slain an enemy; and the same rule will apply if a citizen kills a citizen, or a stranger a stranger. Or if a stranger kill a citizen or a citizen a stranger in self-defence, let him be free from guilt in like manner; and so in the case of a slave who has killed a slave; but if a slave have killed a freeman in self-defence, let him be subject to the same law as he who has killed his father. . . . If a man catch a thief coming into his house by night to steal, and he take and kill him, of if he slay a footpad in self-defence, he shall be guiltless. And any one who does violence to a free woman or a youth, shall be slain with impunity by the injured person, or by his

or her father or brother or sons. If a man find his wife suffering violence, he may kill the violator and be guiltless in the eye of the law; or if a person kill another in warding off death from his father or mother or children or brethren or wife who are doing no wrong, he shall assuredly be guiltless.

Plato, Laws, book 9, at 209, 213 (Benjamin Jowett trans., 2009).

NOTES & QUESTIONS

1. Plato placed an important limitation on self-defense: It was forbidden against certain social superiors. Generally speaking, this has not been the rule in the West. The political philosophers who conceived international law (such as Francisco Suarez, Christine de Pisan, and Hugo Grotius, discussed in online Chapter 13) explicitly approved of personal self-defense against one's superior, in case of necessity. Even in the American South on the eve of the Civil War, a court ruled that the natural right of self-defense guaranteed the right to a free Black to use violence against a white law enforcement officer:

> The conviction of the defendant may involve the proposition that a free negro is not justified, under any circumstances, in striking a white man. To this, we cannot yield our assent. . . . An officer of the town having a *notice to serve on the defendant*, without any authority whatever, *arrests him and attempts to tie him!!* Is not this gross oppression? For what purpose was he to be tied? What degree of cruelty might not the defendant reasonably apprehend after he should be entirely in the power of one who had set upon him in so highhanded and lawless a manner? Was he to submit tamely? — Or, was he not excusable for resorting to the natural right of self-defense? Upon the facts stated, we think his Honor ought to have instructed the jury to find the defendant not guilty. There is error. *Venire de novo.*

State v. Davis, 52 N.C. (7 Jones) 52, 53, 55 (1859).

On the other hand, under Sharia law certain people under Islamic rule (typically Jews and Christians, and sometimes Buddhists or Hindus) are classified as *dhimmi*: To be allowed to continue to practice their religion, they must accept a second class status that includes a prohibition on the possession of arms, and a prohibition on any use of force against a Muslim, including in self-defense. This prohibition can be traced to the Covenant of 'Umar, which traditionally was said to have been a seventh-century treaty between the Caliph Umar I and Syrian Christians. Although the true historical origins of the Covenant are unclear, the Covenant was universally accepted by Muslim legal scholars as setting forth the basic standards for Muslim rule over conquered monotheists. The Covenant requires that the conquered people agree "not to ride on saddles; not to keep arms nor put them in our houses nor to wear swords . . . he who strikes a Muslim has forfeited his rights." A.S. Tritton, The Caliphs and Their Non-Muslim Subjects: A Critical Study of the Covenant of 'Umar 5-9 (1970); *see also* David B. Kopel, *Dhimmitude and Disarmament*, 18 George Mason U. Civ. Rts. L.J. 305 (2008); Bat Ye'or, Miriam Cochan & David Littman, *Islam and Dhimmitude: Where Civilizations Collide*, 56 Middle East J. 733 (2002); Bat Ye'or, The Decline of Eastern Christianity under Islam: From Jihad to Dhimmitude (1996); Bat Ye'or, The Dhimmi: Jews and Christians under Islam (1985).

Similar standards have sometimes been applied by Christian nations. For example, the Visigothic Code, which was used in Spain after the fall of the Western Roman Empire, provided: "All Christians are Forbidden to Defend or Protect a Jew, by Either Force or Favor. . . . No one shall attempt, under any pretext, to defend such persons in the continuance of their depravity, even should they be under his patronage. No one, for any reason, or in any manner, shall attempt by word or deed, to aid or protect such persons, either openly or secretly, in their opposition to the Holy Faith and the Christian religion." The Visigothic Code (Forum judicum) (S.P. Scott ed., 1910), *available at* http://libro.uca.edu/vcode/visigoths.htm, book 12, tit. 2, law 15.

Likewise, in Japan during the Tokugawa Shogunate (1603-1868) self-defense against a social superior was forbidden, whereas the Samurai could kill disrespectful commoners at will, under *kiri-sute gomen* (permission to kill and depart). David B. Kopel, *Japanese Gun Control*, 1993 Asia-Pac. L. Rev. 26, 33.

2. Are there non-invidious reasons for a prohibition on "upward" self-defense? How might the allowance or prohibition of upward self-defense affect social relations? What are the advantages and disadvantages of laws that allow arms-carrying in rural areas but not in urban ones?

b. *Plato vs. Aristotle*

It has often been suggested that most of the major debates in 2,500 years of Western philosophy can be found in the contrasting views of Plato and his student Aristotle. Plato and Aristotle both agreed that arms possession and political power were inseparable. Or as Mao Zedong, founder of the People's Republic of China, would later put it, "political power grows out of the barrel of a gun." However, Plato and Aristotle drew very different lessons from this shared insight.

i. Plato

The Republic is Plato's most important work of political philosophy. In it he describes how the possession of arms plays an essential role in what he considers the inevitable development of society from oligarchy to democracy to despotism:

> [The oligarchs] next proceed to make a law which fixes a sum of money as the qualification of citizenship; the sum is higher in one place and lower in another, as the oligarchy is more or less exclusive; and they allow no one whose property falls below the amount fixed to have any share in the government. These changes in the constitution they effect by force of arms, if intimidation has not already done their work. . . .
>
> Another discreditable feature [of oligarchy] is, that, for a like reason, they are incapable of carrying on any war. Either they arm the multitude, and then they are more afraid of them than of the enemy; or, if they do not call them out in the hour of battle, they are oligarchs indeed, few to fight as they are few to rule. . . .

[The people eventually displace the oligarchs,] whether the revolution has been effected by arms, or whether fear [of an imminent armed revolution] has caused the opposite party to withdraw.

[Later, the democratic people fall under the sway of a demagogic tyrant. The tyrant does not fully reveal himself until he has disarmed the people:]

Teacher: "Then the parent [the people] will discover what a monster he has been fostering in his bosom; and, when he wants to drive him out, he will find that he is weak and his son [the tyrant] strong."

Student: "Why, you do not mean to say that the tyrant will use violence? What! Beat his father if he opposes him?"

Teacher: "Yes, he will, having first disarmed him."

Plato, The Republic, 353 (book VIII) (Benjamin Jowett trans., 1928). In *The Laws*, Plato set out his vision of an ideal state, which was ruled by a philosopher-king. The king uses a standing professional army, "the Guardians," to police the society and keep everyone else under control. Arms would be stored at central armories, and could only be used by the people once a month, during state-supervised training. The military would have full control of all arms imports, and independent retail sale of arms would be forbidden. Plato, Laws, Books VII-VIII (A.E. Taylor ed., 1966). *Laws* was the platonic ideal of the totalitarian society, that "no man, and no woman, be ever suffered to live without an officer set over them, and no soul of man to learn the trick of the doing one single thing of its own sole motion, in play or in earnest, but, in peace as in war, ever to live with the commander in sight. . . ." *Id.* at Book IX, p. 335.

NOTES & QUESTIONS

1. What is the difference between a philosopher-king and a tyrant? Is there a danger that a philosopher-king could become a tyrant? Is there a way to enjoy the benefits of the philosopher-king without risking tyranny?

2. Some critics of Plato have cast him as the philosophical founding father of totalitarianism. Do his views about arms and self-defense support this criticism?

3. Karl Marx and Plato agreed that societies must move through stages of development in a particular order, and that material conditions greatly influence this evolution. How might the presence or absence of arms affect these developments?

4. Are *The Republic* and *The Laws* inconsistent with each other? How might they be reconciled?

5. After Athens was defeated by Sparta in the Peloponnesian War, Sparta appointed the Thirty Tyrants to rule Athens in 404 B.C. Consolidating power, the Tyrants disarmed the entire Athenian population, except for 3,000 supporters of the tyrants. The tyrants murdered approximately 8 percent of the Athenians. In *The Open Society and Its Enemies*, the very influential twentieth-century philosopher Karl Popper devoted considerable

energy to arguing that Plato was an ally of the Thirty Tyrants. (There is no historical consensus on whether this charge has been proven.)

As Popper wrote, "[T]he democrats fought on. At first only seventy strong, they prepared under the leadership of Thrasybulus [an Athenian general] and Antyus [an Athenian politician] the liberation of Athens, where Critias [leader of the Thirty Tyrants] was meanwhile killing scores of citizens...." Karl Popper, 1 The Open Society and Its Enemies 192 (Princeton Univ. Press 1971) (1945). After months of warfare, the democrats destabilized the tyrants, who lost their support from Sparta, and democracy was restored to Athens.

According to Popper, there are two circumstances under which violence against the government is permissible:

> [First,] under a tyranny which makes reforms without violence impossible, and it should have only one aim, that is, to bring about a state of affairs which makes reforms without violence possible.
>
> [Second,] resistance, once democracy has been attained, to any attack (whether from within or without the state) against the democratic constitution and the use of democratic methods. Any such attack, especially if it comes from the government in power, or if it is tolerated by it, should be resisted by all loyal citizens, even to the use of violence. In fact, the working of democracy rests largely on the understanding that a government which attempts to misuse its powers and to establish itself as a tyranny (or which tolerates the establishment of a tyranny by anybody else) outlaws itself, and that citizens have not only a right but also a duty to consider the action of such a government as a crime, and its members as a dangerous gang of criminals.

Id. at 151-52.

Do you agree with Popper's rules for resistance? CQ: Chapter 4, on the American Revolution, will address related issues. Consider the claims that the Declaration of Independence makes, arguing that the armed assertion of independence is a last resort, all other means of redress having failed.

ii. Aristotle

In *Politics*, Aristotle maintained that each citizen should work to earn his own living, should participate in political or legislative affairs, and should bear arms. Aristotle criticized the theory of the philosopher Hippodamus, who wanted a strict division of roles between skilled labor, agriculture, and defense. Aristotle found Hippodamus's division defective, because such a division would lead to the armed ruling the unarmed: "But the husbandmen have no arms, and the artisans neither arms nor land, and therefore they become all but slaves of the warrior class." 1 The Politics of Aristotle 48 (B. Jowett trans. & ed., 1885). He repeatedly explained the connection between arms and self-government:

- "[W]hen the citizens at large administer the state for the common interest, the government is called by the generic name,—a constitution. . . . And there is a reason for this use of language. One man or a few may excel in virtue; but of virtue there are many kinds: and as the number increases it becomes more difficult for them to attain perfection in every kind, though they may in military virtue, for this is found in the masses. Hence, in a constitutional government the fighting-men have the supreme power, and those who possess arms are the citizens." *Id.* at 80.

- "The devices by which oligarchies deceive the people are five in number: . . . (4) concerning the possession of arms, and (5) gymnastic exercises, they legislate in a similar spirit. For the poor are not obliged to have arms, but the rich are fined for not having them; and in like manner no penalty is inflicted on the poor for non-attendance at the gymnasium, and consequently, having nothing to fear, they do not attend, whereas the rich are liable to a fine, and therefore they take care to attend. . . ." *Id.* at 131.

- "[W]ithout discipline, infantry are useless, and in ancient times there was no military knowledge or tactics, and therefore the strength of armies lay in their cavalry. But when cities increased and the heavy armed grew in strength, more had a share in the government; and this is the reason why the states, which we call constitutional governments, have been hitherto called democracies." *Id.* at 73.

- "As of oligarchy so of tyranny . . . both mistrust the people, and therefore deprive them of their arms." *Id.* at 171.

- "Let us then enumerate the functions of a state . . . there must be arms, for the members of a community have need of them in order to maintain authority both against disobedient subjects and against external assailants." *Id.* at 220.

- "Again, there is in a state a class of warriors, and another of councillors, who advise about the expedient and determine matters of law, and these seem in an especial manner parts of a state. Now, should these two classes be distinguished, or are both functions to be assigned to the same persons? Here again there is no difficulty in seeing that both functions will in one way belong to the same, in another, to different persons. To different persons in so far as their employments are suited to different ages of life, for the one requires wisdom, and the other strength. But on the other hand, since it is an impossible thing that those who are able to use or to resist force should be willing to remain always in subjection, from this point of view the persons are the same; for those who carry arms can always determine the fate of the constitution. It remains therefore that both functions of government should be entrusted to the same persons, not, however, at the same time, but in the order prescribed by nature, who has given to young men strength and to older men wisdom." *Id.* at 221-22.

In *The Athenian Constitution,* Aristotle wrote a political history of the city-state of Athens. Rediscovered in the late nineteenth century, *The Athenian Constitution* provided validation of Aristotle's theory that tyrants aim to disarm the people. In the sixth century B.C., the tyrant Peisistratus took over Athens. Aristotle explained how the tyrant obtained absolute power by disarmament:

> Now, he stripped the people of their arms after the following fashion: Ordering a review under arms in the Anakeum, he pretended to make an attempt to harangue them, but spoke in a low voice; and when they said they could not hear, he bade them go up to the propylæa of the Acropolis, that he might be heard the better. Whilst he continued addressing them, those who had been appointed for the purpose took away the arms of the people, and shut them up in the neighbouring buildings of the Thesæum. They then came and informed Peisistratus. After finishing his speech, he told the people what had been done about their arms, saying that they had no need to be surprised or out of heart, but bade them go home and attend to their own affairs, adding that all public matters would now be his concern.

Aristotle, Constitution of Athens, ch. XV (Thomas J. Dymes trans., 1891).

NOTES & QUESTIONS

1. By about 1830, the United States reflected Aristotle's view about the scope of the voting franchise. Property requirements for voting had been abolished in almost every state, so that the class of eligible voters was very similar to the class of persons liable to perform militia duty—namely, free white adult males. (Of course, the United States also allowed voting by males over the age of 45, which was the typical upper limit for militia service.) What are the arguments for and against Aristotle's view that the people with the responsibility for defending the state should be the ones who control the state?

2. Imagine you are founding a new nation, and you have carefully studied Plato and Aristotle. What lessons about arms control policy would you draw from your studies?

3. CQ: Thomas Jefferson described Aristotle, Cicero, John Locke, and Algernon Sidney as the four major sources of the American consensus on rights and liberty, which Jefferson distilled into the Declaration of Independence. Letter from Thomas Jefferson to Henry Lee (May 8, 1825), *in* 16 The Writings of Thomas Jefferson 117-19 (Andrew A. Lipscomb ed., 1903). What elements of Aristotle's political philosophy can you find in the Declaration of Independence, and in the political structure of the American Early Republic?

2. Rome

The law of the Roman Republic and Empire was the dominant legal system in the Western world for many centuries. Even after the Western Roman Empire fell in the fifth century A.D., Roman law remained a foundation of European law. Thus, Roman law later became part of the laws of much of Latin America, Africa, and Asia, through the process of colonization. Roman law continued to be a major element of the European legal system during the Napoleonic era. Although post-colonial nations have developed their legal systems in diverse ways, Roman law still comes closer than anything else to the legal common heritage of developed societies.

The foundation of Roman law was the Twelve Tables (*Lex Duodecim Tabularum,* or *Duodecim Tabulae*). The Twelve Tables were, literally, twelve bronze tablets containing some of the basic legal rules, published in final form in 449 B.C. They were placed in the Forum, so that every citizen could easily read them. After extensive public debate and discussion, they were created by a committee of ten (*decemvirs*), which relied in part on Greek law, and which made further revisions based on public comment by citizens. Titus Livius, The Early History of Rome 192-248 (book 3, 8-59) (Aubrey de Sélincourt trans., 1971) (first published sometime during the reign of Augustus Caesar).

The very creation of the Twelve Tables was a monumental development in due process. The laws were published, readily accessible, and written to be readily understood by an ordinary citizen. Previously, the laws had been closely guarded by an élite that secretly manipulated the laws to its own benefit. Unfortunately, the Twelve Tables themselves were later destroyed, so what we know of them comes from secondary sources. Self-defense rules were in Table VIII:

12. If a theft be committed at night, and the thief be killed, let his death be deemed lawful.
13. If in the daytime (only if he defend himself with weapons).

Id. at Table VIII, items 12-13 (parenthetical addition by translator).[2] An alternate version reads:

12. If a thief commits a theft by night, if the owner kills the thief, the thief shall be killed lawfully.
13. By daylight . . . if a thief defends himself with a weapon . . . and the owner shall shout.
14. In the case of all other . . . thieves caught in the act freemen shall be scourged and shall be adjudged as bondsmen to the person against whom the theft has been committed provided that they have done this by daylight and have not defended themselves with a weapon. . . .

The Twelve Tables, Table VIII: Torts or Delicts, items 12-14, *available* at http://avalon.law.yale.edu/ancient/twelve_tables.asp. For a thousand years, the Twelve Tables were venerated as the embodiment of Roman law.

---

2. *See also* Allan Chester Johnson et al., Ancient Roman Statutes 11 (2003) (alternate translation, to the same effect). Another scholar puts this law in Table VIII, law 3: "If one is slain while committing theft by night, he is rightly slain." Fordham University, Ancient History Sourcebook: The Twelve Tables, Table VIII, *available at* http://www.fordham.edu/HALSALL/ancient/12tables.html. Still another scholar puts the law in Table II, law 4. "Where anyone commits a theft by night, and having been caught in the act is killed, he is legally killed." S.P. Scott, 1 The Civil Law Including The Twelve Tables, The Institutes of Gaius, The Rules of Ulpian, The Opinions of Paulus, The Enactments of Justinian, and The Constitutions of Leo 59 (1932).

After the people of Rome overthrew the Tarquin kings in 509 B.C., Rome's growing military might was based on a militia. When needed, some or many free men were required to serve in the militia for several months a year, and to supply all their own equipment. In 107 B.C., Gaius Marius, who seized and held near-absolute power for several years, began to supplant the militia with a professional standing army, using a mixture of volunteers and conscripts. There were short-term benefits, in that soldiers were now supplied with equipment; previously, some militiamen lacked the resources even to buy shoes for themselves. The increased training and drilling made possible by a standing army made the Roman army more effective in combat.

However, the shift of the military balance in Rome from militia to army ultimately shifted the political balance. Ambitious politicians, including Julius Caesar, began to use the troops under their command, either directly or through the implicit threat of force, to achieve near-absolute rule. After a series of civil wars, Julius's great-nephew Octavian completed the destruction of the Republic by using the military to install himself as absolute ruler. For the next five centuries, control of Rome would hinge on who commanded the support of the most powerful faction of the army.

The lesson drawn by the Enlightenment in Europe was aptly summarized by Edward Gibbon: "A martial nobility and stubborn commons, possessed of arms, tenacious of property, and collected into constitutional assemblies, form the only balance capable of preserving a free constitution against enterprises of an aspiring prince." Edward Gibbon, 1 Decline and Fall of the Roman Empire 78 (1787).

Among the most influential political philosophers of the Renaissance was Niccolo Machiavelli. He detailed how the first two emperors of Rome (Octavius, who re-named himself "Augustus," and his successor Tiberius) used weapons control and a standing army to hold absolute power. According to Machiavelli, a king would be more secure in the long term if he were defended by a militia rather than by a standing army:

> ... Ottavianus first, and then Tiberius, thinking more of their own power than the public usefulness, in order to rule over the Roman people more easily, begun to disarm them and to keep the same armies continually at the frontiers of the Empire. And because they did not think it sufficient to hold the Roman People and the Senate in check, they instituted an army called the Praetorian (Guard), which was kept near the walls of Rome in a fort adjacent to that City. And as they now begun freely to permit men assigned to the army to practice military matters as their profession, there soon resulted that these men became insolent, and they became formidable to the Senate and damaging to the Emperor. Whence there resulted that many men were killed because of their insolence, for they gave the Empire and took it away from anyone they wished, and it often occurred that at one time there were many Emperors created by the several armies. From which state of affairs proceeded first the division of the Empire and finally its ruin. Kings ought, therefore, if they want to live securely, have their infantry composed of men, who, when it is necessary for him to wage war, will willingly go forth to it for love of him, and afterwards when peace comes, more willingly return to their homes; which will always happen if he selects men who know how to live by a profession other than this. And thus he ought to desire, with the coming of peace, that his Princes return to governing their people, gentlemen to the

cultivation of their possessions, and the infantry to their particular arts (trades or professions); and everyone of these will willingly make war in order to have peace, and will not seek to disturb the peace to have war.

Niccolo Machiavelli, The Art of War 16-17 (Christopher Lynch trans., Wilder Publications 2008) (1521).

Cicero was a great Roman lawyer and orator of the first century B.C. Historically, he has been viewed as one of the noblest of all Romans, and as a hero who did his best to prevent the degenerating Republic from destroying itself and transforming into the Empire.

During the Dark Ages, knowledge of many of the Greek and Roman writers (including Aristotle) was lost in the West, but Cicero never disappeared from view. Recovery of knowledge of Antiquity began in the Little Renaissance of the twelfth century, and continued with enthusiasm in the Renaissance in the fourteenth through seventeenth centuries and then the Enlightenment in the eighteenth century. Cicero's prestige continued to grow. By the 1600s, he was perhaps the most influential and admired political theorist in the West.

If you studied law a century ago, you might well have mastered Latin by the time you finished your secondary education, and in the course of that education, you would have studied the following speech by Cicero, in defense of Titus Annius Milo:

> What is the meaning of our retinues, what of our swords? Surely it would never be permitted to us to have them if we might never use them. This, therefore, is a law, O judges, not written, but born with us — which we have not learned, or received by tradition, or read, but which we have taken and sucked in and imbibed from nature herself; a law which we were not taught, but to which we were made — which we were not trained in, but which is ingrained in us — namely, that if our life be in danger from plots, or from open violence, or from the weapons of robbers or enemies, every means of securing our safety is honorable. For laws are silent when arms are raised, and do not expect themselves to be waited for, when he who waits will have to suffer an undeserved penalty before he can exact a merited punishment.
>
> The law very wisely, and in a manner silently, gives a man a right to defend himself . . . the man who had used a weapon with the object of defending himself would be decided not to have had his weapon about him with the object of killing a man.

Cicero, Speech in Defence of Titus Annius Milo, *in* Orations of Marcus Tullius Cicero 204-05 (Charles Duke Yonge trans., rev. ed. 1899) (originally delivered 52 B.C.). Ironically, Cicero never delivered the speech as written, because Milo's enemy, Pompey, surrounded the court with troops. However, the speech was preserved and studied by many generations of Latin students and scholars.

Cicero was an explicit advocate of tyrannicide:

> What can be greater wickedness than to slay not only a man, but even an intimate friend? Has he then involved himself in guilt, who slays a tyrant, however, intimate? He does not appear so to the Roman people at least, who of all great exploits deems that the most honorable. Has expediency, then, overcome virtue? Nay, rather, expediency has followed virtue.

Cicero, On Duties [*De Officiis*], *in* Cicero's Three Books of Offices and Other Moral Works 120-21 (Cyrus R. Edmonds trans., 1871) (in original, Book III of *De Officiis*, ch. 4).

> Now as to what relates to Phalaris,[3] the decision is very easy; for we have no society with tyrants, but rather the broadest separation from them; nor is it contrary to nature to despoil, if you can, him whom it is a virtue to slay—and this pestilential and impious class of men ought to be entirely exterminated from the community of mankind. For as certain limbs are amputated, both if they themselves have begun to be destitute of blood, and, as it were, of life, and if they injure the other parts of the body, so the brutality and ferocity of a beast in the figure of a man, ought to be cut off from the common body, as it were, of humanity.
>
> Of this sort are all those questions in which our duty is sought out of the circumstances of the case.

Id. at 126-27 (in original, Book III of *De Officiis*, ch. 6). Cicero's principles were put into action in 44 B.C. when Marcus Junius Brutus the Younger and other Senators assassinated Julius Caesar. The assassination failed to restore the Republic, however, and over the next five centuries, assassination was usually the sole means of removing an especially bad Emperor.

Similarly, the Roman philosopher Seneca (4 B.C.-65 A.D.) wrote, "No offering is more acceptable to God than the blood of a tyrant." Seneca, *De Beneficiis* 8, 20 (A. Golding trans., 1974).

Under Roman law, citizens had a right to carry personal arms, although the right was not always respected. Conquered peoples had no legal right to arms. In 212 A.D., Roman citizenship was extended to all free subjects of the Empire. Emperor Caracalla, *Constitutio Antoniniana De Civitate, in* Paul Robinson Coleman-Norton, Frank Card Bourne, Allan Chester Johnson & Clyde Pharr, Ancient Roman Statutes: A Translation with Introduction, Commentary, Glossary, and Index 212, 225-26 (2003). Consequently, they all enjoyed the right to arms. The right to arms was abolished in 364, at least for persons who did not have advance approval from the government: "No person whatever, without Our knowledge and advice, shall be granted the right to employ any weapons whatsoever." Clyde Pharr, The Theodosian Code and Novels §XV.15.1, at 439 (2001) (Emperors Valentian (Valentinianus I) and Valens Augustuses to Bulphorus, Governor of Campia, Decree of Oct. 5, 364). ("Novels" was a legal term of art for new laws.)

Inability to protect their subjects led to a restoration of the right in 440 in both the Western and the Eastern Roman Empires. The restoration was reconfirmed several years later by the Western Emperor Majorian Augustus:

> [B]ecause it is not sufficiently certain, under summertime opportunities for navigation, to what shore the ships of the enemy can come, We admonish each and all by this edict that, with confidence in the Roman strength and the courage with which they ought to defend their own, with their own men against the enemy . . . they shall use those arms which they can, but they shall preserve the public discipline and the moderation of free birth unimpaired.

---

3. [Tyrant of Acragas, Sicily, alleged to have engaged in torture and cannibalism, and who ruled from approximately 570 to 554 B.C.—EDS.]

Restoration of the Right to Use Weapons (De Reddito Jure Amrorum) (June 24, 440), *in id.*, at tit. 9, p. 524.

NOTES & QUESTIONS

1. Why do the Twelve Tables vary how much force may be used against night-time vs. day-time robbers?

2. Cicero's line "laws are silent when arms are raised" (*inter arma enim silent leges*, also translated as "For laws are silent amid arms") became a famous embodiment of legal principle. It is sometimes invoked as a justification that "anything goes" during wartime—and even that governments may ignore their own constitutions. But consider it in the personal self-defense context of Cicero's speech. Under what circumstances can the law legitimately forbid self-defense by a person who at a moment of peril is left unprotected by the state? Can the government forbid self-defense under positive law? Or does natural law, as Cicero suggests, place limits on positive law? What about positive constitutional law?

3. If assassination is the only way to depose a ruler like Julius Caesar, Caligula, Nero, Commodus, or Hitler, is it legitimate? How can any theory that authorizes tyrannicide prevent self-appointed rescuers from threatening any ruler with assassination?

4. Does the fact that tyranny and despotism remained alive and well in the Roman Empire after Julius Caesar's assassination show that tyrannicide is not a justifiable reason for arming a population? Recall that Roman citizens had the right to possess personal arms at the time of the assassination.

a. Corpus Juris

The Western Roman Empire fell in 476, when the last emperor, Romulus Augustulus, was deposed. The Eastern Roman Empire, also known as the Byzantine[4] Empire, lasted until the middle of the fifteenth century. Around 534, the Byzantine Emperor Justinian ordered the creation of a compilation of all Roman law, which became known as the *Corpus Juris Civilis*. The *Corpus Juris*, by preserving for posterity the work of Rome's legal scholars, transmitted to the world the memory of Rome's historic culture of liberty and the rule of law. The Emperor Justinian's *Corpus Juris* formally replaced the Twelve Tables as the embodiment of Roman law, and the self-defense principles of the Twelve Tables were incorporated into the *Corpus Juris*.

---

4. The Byzantines never called themselves "Byzantines." Instead, they considered themselves "Romans"—a continuation of the state that had, according to tradition, been founded in 753 B.C.

The *Corpus Juris* was not meant to create new law, but to provide a comprehensive collection of existing law. Accordingly, it contains rules from many different Roman legal commentators from previous centuries. These rules are not necessarily mutually consistent. However, the general principle was that the use of deadly force was permissible when no lesser force would suffice.

The famous formulation of the self-defense rule was "Cassius writes that it is permissible to repel force by force, and this right is conferred by nature. From this it appears, he says, that arms may be repelled by arms."[5] Dig. 43.16.1.27 (Ulpian, Edict 69).

The *Digest* (in Latin, *Digesta*) was by far the lengthiest part of the *Corpus Juris*, and consisted of 50 books that compiled the surviving fragments from cases decided by Roman judges, and opinions written by legal scholars. The Bluebook citations for the *Digest* provide the volume, title, law, and part numbers. The parenthetical after the numbers indicates the author and the document quoted and cited by the *Digest*—here the eminent Roman lawyer Gnaeus Domitius Annius Ulpianus, who wrote in the early third century A.D.; fragments from his 83-book legal commentary *Ad edictum* comprise about a fifth of the *Digest*.

A near-identical formulation is embodied in the self-defense provision of the modern Italian criminal code (*è lecito respingere la violenza con la violenza*), which recognizes self-defense as a justification. Codice Penale [C.p.] art. 52 (It.); *see also id.* art. 53 (legitimate use of arms as a justification).

Some other statements of self-defense law are found in the Digest, the Code (*Codex Justinianus*, which is the laws and decisions made by Roman Emperors before Justinian), and the Institutes (a summary of key laws), which collectively comprise the original *Corpus Juris*. The *Novels* (statutes promulgated by Justinian after the 534 A.D. publication of the second edition of the *Corpus Juris*) were considered by later generations to be part of the *Corpus Juris*. For detailed analysis of Code provisions on self-defense and arms, see Will Tysse, *The Roman Legal Treatment of Self-Defense and the Private Possession of Weapons in the* Codex Justinianus, 16 J. Firearms & Pub. Pol'y 163 (2004).

b. Corpus Juris *Provisions on Self-Defense*[6]

- "The right to repel violent injuries. You see, it emerges from this law that whatever a person does for his bodily security he can be held to have done rightfully; and since nature has established among us a relationship of sorts, it follows that it is a grave wrong for one human being to encompass the life of another." Dig. 1.1.3 (Florentinus, Institutes 1).
- "If someone kills anyone else who is trying to go for him with a sword, he will not be deemed to have killed unlawfully; and if for fear of death someone kills a thief, there is no doubt he should not be liable under the *lex Aquila*. But if,

---

5. "Cassius" here is the first-century A.D. Roman jurist Gaius Cassius Longinus, author of *Libri juris civilis*. He is not the Senator of the exact same name who participated in the assassination of Julius Caesar.

6. The Corpus Juris translations are from The Digest of Justinian (Phil.: U. of Penn. Pr., 1998) (Alan Watson ed.). The bracketed inserts were added by the translator.

although he could have arrested him, he preferred to kill him, the better opinion is that he should be deemed to have acted unlawfully." Dig. 9.2.5 (Ulpian, Edict 18).

- "A person lawfully in possession has the right to use a moderate degree of force to repel any violence exerted for the purpose of depriving him of possession, if he holds it under a title which is not defective." Code Just. 8.4.1 (Emperors Diocletian and Maximian).
- "But anyone who uses force to retain his possession is not, Labeo says, possessing it by [illegitimate] force." Dig. 43.16.1.28 (Ulpian, Edict 69).
- "Someone who recovers by force in the same conflict a possession of which he has been forcibly deprived is to be understood as reverting to his original condition rather than possessing it by force. So if I eject you and you immediately eject me, and I then eject you, the interdict "where by force" will lie effectively in your favor."[7] Dig. 43.16.17 (Julian, Digest 48).
- "[I]t is not always lawful to kill an adulterer or thief, unless he defends himself with a weapon. . . ." Dig. 4.2.7 (Ulpian, Edict 11).
- "If anyone kills a thief by night, he shall do so unpunished if and only if he could not have spared the man['s life] without risk to his own." Dig. 48.8.9 (Ulpian, Edict 37).
- "The Law of the *Twelve Tables* permits one to kill a thief caught in the night, provided one gives evidence of the fact by shouting aloud, but someone may only kill a person caught in such circumstances at any other time if he defends himself with a weapon, though only if he provides evidence by shouting." Dig. 9.1.4 (Gaius, Provincial Edict 7).
- "[I]f I kill your slave who is lying in ambush to rob me, I shall go free; for natural reason permits a person to defend himself against danger." Dig. 9.2.4 (Gaius, Provincial Edict 7).
- "Where parties commit damage because they could not otherwise protect themselves, they are guiltless; for all laws and all legal principles permit persons to repel force by force. But if I throw a stone at an adversary for the purpose of defending myself, and I do not hit him but do hit a passer-by, I will be liable under the *Lex Aquilia*; for you are only permitted to strike a person who is attacking you, and this solely where you do so in defending yourself, and not where it is done for the purpose of revenge." Dig. 9.2.45 (Paul, Sabinus 10).

The *Corpus Juris* authorized the possession of arms for lawful defense or hunting, while forbidding the accumulation of arms for seditious purposes:

- "Persons who bear weapons for the purpose of protecting their own safety are not regarded as carrying them for the purpose of homicide." Dig. 48.6.11 (Paul, Views 5).
- "A man is liable under the *lex Julia* on *vis publica* on the grounds that he collects arms or weapons at his home or on his farm or at his country house beyond those customary for hunting or a journey by land or sea. But those arms are excepted which someone has by way of trade or which come to him by inheritance. Under the same heading come those who have

---

7. In other words, the original rightful owner who forcefully reclaimed his own property would not lose a lawsuit claiming that the owner's possession of the land was based merely on force.

entered into a conspiracy to raise a mob or a sedition or who keep either slaves or freemen under arms. 1. A man is also liable under the same statute if, being of full age, he appears in public with a missile weapon." Dig. 48.6.1-3 (Marcian, Institutes 14 & Scaevola).

The *Corpus Juris* served as a source — and often as the primary source — for local laws, and was regarded as the authoritative source of international law. Indeed, the *jus gentium* (the *Corpus Juris* term for laws that apply everywhere) became synonymous with what we today call international law.

Notwithstanding the *Corpus Juris*'s apparent legal protection of self-defense and the possession of arms, the Emperor Justinian himself made arms manufacture a government monopoly, and forbade all arms sales to civilians:

> Therefore, desiring to prevent men from killing each other, We have thought it proper to decree that no private person shall engage in the manufacture of weapons, and that only those shall be authorized to do so who are employed in the public arsenals, or are called armorers; and also that manufacturers of arms should not sell them to any private individual. . . . We prohibit private individuals from either making or buying bows, arrows, double-edged swords, ordinary swords, weapons usually called hunting knives, those styled *zabes*, breast-plates, javelins, lances and spears of every shape whatever, arms called by the Isaurians *monocopia*, others called *sitinnes*, or missiles, shields, and helmets; for We do not permit anything of this kind to be manufactured, except by those who are appointed for that purpose in Our arsenals, and only small knives which no one uses in fighting shall be allowed to be made and sold by private persons.

Novels, tit. 14. Nevertheless, Justinian affirmed the lawfulness of self-defense: "Someone who kills a robber is not liable, at least if he could not otherwise escape danger." J. Inst. 4.3 (enactment of Justinian).

During the Middle Ages and thereafter, the portions of the *Corpus Juris* dealing with the proper authority of the king were analyzed to show that the king was granted his authority by the people, and that a king who broke his agreement with the people — by exercising un-granted powers, or by using his powers tyrannically — was a traitor, and could be resisted with force, as could any traitor. Kathleen A. Parrow, *From Defense to Resistance*, 83 Transactions of the Am. Phil. Soc. 18, 54 (1993).

For example, the provision (Code 8.4.1) affirming the lawfulness of use of force against robbers was cited by the French Huguenots (Calvinists persecuted by the Catholic government) in the sixteenth century as justification for armed resistance to France's central government, which was attempting to wipe them out. They argued that the undisputed right of self-defense in "the case of a Christian assaulted by brigands in the forest" could be applied to national self-defense against an invader or a domestic tyrant. Parrow, *supra*, at 45-46 (citing Peirre Fabre, *Traitte Du Quel on peut apprendre en quel cas il est permis à l'homme Chrestien de porter les armes et par lequel est respondu à Peirre Charpentier, tendant à la fine d'empescher la paix, & nous laisser la guerre* (trans. from Latin to French 1576), *in* French Political Pamphlets collection in Newberry Library (Lindsay and Neu, no. 877)).

NOTES & QUESTIONS

1. What sorts of modern gun controls are prefigured by the weapons restrictions in the *Corpus Juris?*

2. How similar are modern statutory and common law self-defense rules to those of the *Corpus Juris?*

3. Do you agree with the Huguenots' view that legal rules about resistance to ordinary criminals can be applied to resistance to rulers?

4. Note the special condemnation given to the possession of "missile weapons." Why might such weapons be given such special negative treatment? Are modern guns the equivalent of the missile weapons referred to by the *Corpus Juris?*

C. *Judeo-Christian Thought*

1. Jewish Thought

Besides studying Greece and Rome, the American Framers looked closely to the history of ancient Israel and the Jewish people, which they knew from studying the Old Testament. According to the Book of Exodus, after the Egyptians suffered ten plagues because Pharaoh refused Moses's repeated commands to "let my people go," the Hebrew slaves were permitted to leave. Before departing Egypt, the Hebrews were allowed to take whatever they wanted from the Egyptians, because God made the Egyptians favorably disposed to the Hebrews. *Exodus* 12:35-36. The Hebrew slaves thus received partial reparations for hundreds of years of slavery. "And God took the people toward the way of the Wilderness to the Sea of Reeds. And the Children of Israel were armed when they went up from Egypt." *Exodus* 13:18.[8] Presumably, the weapons were obtained from the Egyptians.[9]

---

8. Here, we quote a standard Jewish Bible translation. Rashi, 2 The Torah: With Rashi's Commentary Translated, Annotated, and Elucidated: Shemos/Exodus 145 (Yisrael Isser Zvi Herczeg et al. trans. & eds., 4th ed. 1997). Rashi is the foremost of all Jewish Bible commentators.

Instead of "armed," the King James Version uses the word "harnessed" (a word typically used for horses) as an awkward way of expressing that the Hebrews marched out in military order. Other translations better express the passage's sense that the Hebrews marched out free in battle array: "And the people of Israel went up . . . equipped for battle" (Revised Standard Version); "and the children of Israel went up armed" (American Standard Version); "And the sons of Israel went up in military order" (American Baptist Publication Society). The Hebrew word is *chamushim,* probably related to the Egyptian *chams,* meaning "lance." The Pentateuch and Haftorahs 265 n.18 (Joseph H. Hertz ed., 1967).

9. This is the view set forth in Rashi, *supra,* at 145 (explaining that *Exodus* 13:18 was written so that readers would not wonder where the Israelites got the arms with which they fought the Amalekites a short while later).

Later, according to the Old Testament, God gave the Jewish people a detailed legal code, which today is called the Mosaic Law. Under that law, the nearest relative of a person who was murdered was obliged to kill the murderer, providing blood restitution for the death of the innocent. However, there was an exception for some killings of robbers. Edward J. White, The Law in Scriptures 77 (2000). If the deceased were not a real burglar, but someone who was mistaken for a burglar, there was no criminal offense. Samuel Mendelsohn, The Criminal Jurisprudence of the Ancient Hebrews 33 n.55 (The Lawbook Exchange 2001) (1891). For further analysis of Jewish law, see David B. Kopel, *The Torah and Self-Defense*, 109 Penn. St. L. Rev. 17 (2004).

The key law for self-defense was: "If a thief be found breaking up, and be smitten that he die, there shall no blood be shed for him. If the sun be risen upon him, there shall be blood shed for him." *Exodus* 22:2. In other words, killing a night-time burglar was lawful, and killing a day-time burglar was not. However, as we shall see, the day/night distinction was not applied literally.

The *Talmud* is a multi-layered commentary on Jewish law, and is itself a source of Jewish law. Regarding the passages in *Exodus*, the *Talmud* explains:

> The reason why the Scripture freed the detector if he killed the burglar, is because it is certain that a man cannot control himself when he sees his property taken. And as the burglar must have had the intention to kill anyone, in such a case, who should oppose him, the Scripture dictates that if one comes to kill you, hasten to kill him first.

The Babylonian Talmud: Tract Sanhedrin 214 (Michael L. Rodkinson trans., 1918) (public domain version available at http://www.sacred-texts.com/jud/talmud.htm#t08). The final sentence is not an option; it is a positive command: There is a duty to use deadly force to defend oneself against murderous attack.

The *Talmud* also imposes an affirmative duty for bystanders to kill if necessary to prevent a murder, the rape of a betrothed woman, or pederasty. 2 Talmud Bavli; The Gemara: The Classic Vilna Edition with an Annotated, Interpretive Elucidation, as an Aid to Talmud Study, Tractate Sanhedrin folio 73a[1] (Michael Wiener & Asher Dicker elucidators, Mesorah Pubs., 2d ed. 2002). The commentators agree that a person is required to hire a rescuer if necessary to save the victim from the "pursuer" (the *rodef*). *Id.* at folio 73a[3]. Likewise, "if one sees a wild beast ravaging [a fellow] or bandits coming to attack him . . . he is obligated to save [the fellow]." *Id.* at folio 73a[1] (brackets in original).

The duty to use force to defend an innocent is based on two Bible passages. The first is *Leviticus* 19:16, "you shall not stand up against the life of your neighbor." Or in the modern New American Bible translation, "nor shall you stand idly by when your neighbor's life is at stake."

The second passage comes from *Deuteronomy* 22:23-27 and explains that if a man and a betrothed (engaged) woman have illicit sex in the city, it would be initially (but not conclusively) presumed that she consented because she could have cried out for help. But if the sexual act occurred in the country, she would be presumed to have been the victim of a forcible rape: "For he found her in the field, and the betrothed damsel cried, and there was none to save her." The passage implies that bystanders must heed a woman's cries and come to her rescue. 2(a) The Mishneh, Sefer Nezekin 150-51 (Matis Roberts trans. & commentary, 1987).

The Biblical history of the Jewish people included many stories that, to some readers, justified forcible resistance to tyranny. For example, the seventeenth-century English patriot and political philosopher Algernon Sidney advocated revolution against the oppressive Stuart kings of England. In support of his advocacy, he reeled off a list of well-known Jewish heroes who used violence against tyrants: "Moses, Othniel, Ehud, Barak, Gideon, Samson, Jephthah, Samuel, David, Jehu, the Maccabees, and others." Algernon Sidney, Discourses Concerning Government 228 (Thomas G. West ed., Liberty Fund 1996) (1698).

Here is how Sidney (and other advocates of forcible resistance to tyranny) would have understood the above stories: Moses, while a prince of Egypt, killed a slave driver who was beating a Hebrew slave. Othniel led the Hebrews in a war of national liberation against a Mesopotamian king. Ehud assassinated a foreign king who had conquered the Hebrews. Barak, along with General Deborah, liberated the Hebrews from Canaanite rule. Gideon liberated the Hebrews from the Midianites. Samson fought the Philistines. Jephthah led the war of liberation against the Ammonites. Samuel was the spiritual leader in a war of national liberation against the Philistines, who had forbidden the Hebrews to possess arms and had outlawed swordsmiths. David overthrew King Saul at Samuel's orders. Jehu overthrew the Israelite King Jehoram, who was leading Israel to participate in a nature religion involving human sacrifice. The Maccabees led a successful war of national liberation against Graeco-Syrian rulers who wanted to eliminate the Jewish religion.

NOTES & QUESTIONS

1. Like the ancient Hebrews, many other societies have believed that a distinctive feature of a free man is possession of arms, and a distinctive feature of a slave is to be disarmed. What accounts for this view? Does this distinction make sense today?

2. In a common English translation, the Sixth Commandment states: "Thou shalt not kill." Many scholars, however, argue that "Thou shalt not murder" much more closely matches the original Hebrew. How can either version be reconciled with provisions of the law, discussed above, that mandate or permit killing, including the establishment of dozens of capital offenses in the Mosaic law?

3. One of the greatest Jewish legal scholars of antiquity was Philo of Alexandria (approx. 20 B.C.-50 A.D.), who wrote about the Jewish law in Alexandria, Egypt, during the period when Egypt and Israel were both under Roman rule. Much of Philo's treatise aimed to show that Jewish law from the Bible was consistent with Roman law. Philo argued that the Mosaic provision about killing robbers conformed to the Roman law of the Twelve Tables (*supra*), because every night robber was a potential murderer. The burglar would be armed, at the least, with iron house-breaking tools, which could be used as weapons. Because assistance from the police or neighbors would be unlikely at night-time, the victim was allowed immediate resort to deadly force. Philo of Alexandria, "The Special Laws, IV," *in* The Works of Philo 616-17 (C.D. Yonge trans., 1993) ("Concerning Housebreakers"). Modern

scholarship about the practices at Philo's time suggests that use of deadly force during a day-time burglary would be legal if a victim in mortal peril called for help and none arrived. Edwin R. Goodenough, The Jurisprudence of the Jewish Courts of Egypt: Legal Administration by the Jews under the Early Roman Empire as Described by Philo Judeaus 154-55, 231-32 (The Lawbook Exchange 2002) (1929).

Jewish legal scholars have unanimously interpreted the "sun" language metaphorically: If the circumstances indicated that the burglar posed a violent threat to the victims in the home, the burglar could be slain regardless of the time of day; conversely, if it were clear that the burglar was only taking property, and would not attack the people in the home, even if they interfered with the burglary, the burglar could not be slain. In modern legal theory, this form of interpretation is called "purposivism." That is, the interpreter seeks to fulfill the purpose behind the particular statute or constitutional provision. This mode of interpretation is obviously quite different from reading the statute literally, which would make the legality of killing a burglar depend on the hour of the day, not on the home-owner's perception of the burglar's intentions. Is purposivism is a legitimate interpretive method for the burglary laws in *Exodus*? For modern American statutes and constitutions?

4. The great Jewish legal scholar Maimonides (Rabbi Moshe Ben Maimon, a/k/a "Rambam") (1153-1204) elaborated on when it was permissible to kill a burglar:

    > 8. [The license mentioned above] "applies to a thief caught breaking in or one caught on a person's roof, courtyard or enclosed area, whether during the day or during the night. . . .

    > 12. Similarly, a person who breaks into a garden, a field, a pen or a corral may not be killed, for the prevailing assumption is that he came merely [to steal] money, for generally the owners are not found in such places."

    James Townley, The Reasons of the Laws of Moses from the "More Nevochim" of Maimonides 226-28 (The Lawbook Exchange 2001) (1827). Are Maimonides's spatial distinctions sensible? Many American states recognize greater self-defense rights (such as a stronger presumption in favor of the use of deadly force in self-defense) in the home than in other places, including one's yard, porch, or outbuildings. Are these distinctions compelling?

5. A 1998 law in Israel, derived from the Levitical law, mandates that a person aid another who is in immediate danger if aid can be rendered without danger to the rescuer. A few American states have similar laws, often called Good Samaritan laws. Daniel Friedman, To Kill and Take Possession: Law, Morality, and Society in Bible Stories 90-91 (2002). Is it appropriate to mandate that a person come to the aid of others? That she defend herself against certain types of attacks? Does it depend on the particular type of society?

6. Shortly after the Israelites began their invasion of Canaan by crossing the Jordan River from the east, Canaan came under assault from the west as well. The sea-faring Philistines, who may have come from Crete, had failed in an attempt to conquer Egypt, so they set their sights on Canaan. Technologically superior to the Israelites, the Philistines were outstanding ironsmiths who equipped their soldiers with high-quality iron weapons. Chaim Herzog & Mordechai Gichon, Battles of the Bible 81-82 (Greenhill Books, 2002) (1978); William G. Dever, Who Were the Early Israelites and Where Did They Come From? 69 (2003). The Philistine invasion of Canaan was partially successful, for they established secure control over the territory of Gaza.

In the final chapters of *Judges*, some of the Israelites came under a degree of Philistine control; Samson fought them single-handedly, over the objections of the other Israelites. By the beginning of the *First Book of Samuel*, the Philistines had captured extensive territories from the disunited Israelite tribes. After conquering Judah, which controlled the southern part of modern-day Israel, the Philistines imposed one of the first weapons-control laws in recorded history: "Now there was no smith found throughout the land of Israel: for the Philistines said, Lest the Hebrews make them swords or spears." *1 Samuel* 13:19. In order to sharpen agricultural tools such as plows, the Israelites had to pay for services from a Philistine ironsmith. *Id.* 13:20-21.

Because of the weapons control law, the Israelites had few good weapons to use against the Philistines, although the future Israeli king Saul and his son Jonathan apparently had some of their own: "So it came to pass on the day of battle, that there was neither sword nor spear found in the hand of any of the people that were with Saul and Jonathan: but with Saul and with Jonathan his son was there found." *Id.* 13:22.

As the above passages illustrate, governments intending to prevent subjects from possessing arms must do more than outlaw arms themselves; they must also find a way to prevent people from making their own arms. The Philistine ban on ironsmithing appears to have been mostly effective in accomplishing its goal. Similarly, during the Tokugawa period in Japan, starting in the seventeenth century, the government was able to impose very restrictive controls on the small number of gunsmiths in the nation, thereby ensuring that the almost total prohibition on firearms would be effective. David B. Kopel, The Samurai, the Mountie, and the Cowboy: Should America Adopt the Gun Controls of Other Democracies? 29-33 (1992).

Today, the manufacture of a working firearm is not particularly difficult. People with access to the machine tools found in many homes can make firearms, as do West African villagers with considerably inferior tools. *See, e.g.,* Charles Chandler, *Gun-Making as a Cottage Industry,* 3 J. Firearms & Pub. Pol'y 155 (1990); Emanuel Addo Sowatey, *Small Arms Proliferation and Regional Security in West Africa: The Ghanian Case, in* 1 News from the Nordic Afr. Inst. 6 (2005) (despite colonial and post-colonial arms bans, a gunsmith in Ghana can make several guns per day; some make working copies of the AK-47). Under what circumstances could a government attempting to impose arms prohibition have as much success at constricting arms manufacture as the Philistines did?

2.   Early Christian Thought

The New Testament, which is the story of early Christianity, covers a much shorter period of time than does the Old Testament, and pays much less attention to political history. However, two passages are often cited in discussions about the legitimacy of weapons, and another has been important to Western political thinking about the legitimacy of resistance to government.

a.   *The Sermon on the Mount*

These are excerpts from the most famous sermon by Jesus.

Think not that I am come to destroy the law, or the prophets: I am not come to destroy, but to fulfill. For truthfully I say unto you, Till heaven and earth pass, one jot or one small mark shall in no way pass from the law, till all be fulfilled. Whosoever therefore shall break one of these least commandments, and shall teach men so, he shall be called the least in the kingdom of heaven: but whosoever shall do and teach them, the same shall be called great in the kingdom of heaven. For I say unto you, That unless your righteousness shall exceed the righteousness of the scribes and Pharisees, you shall in no case enter into the kingdom of heaven.

You have heard that it was said of them of old time, You shall not kill; and whosoever shall kill shall be in danger of the judgment: But I say unto you, That whosoever is angry with his brother without a cause shall be in danger of the judgment: and whosoever shall say to his brother, Raca, shall be in danger of the council: but whosoever shall say, You fool, shall be in danger of hell fire. . . .

You have heard that it was said by them of old time, You shall not commit adultery: But I say unto you, That whosoever looks on a woman to lust after her has committed adultery with her already in his heart. And if your right eye offend you, pluck it out, and cast it from you: for it is profitable for you that one of your members should perish, and not that your whole body should be cast into hell. And if your right hand offend you, cut it off, and cast it from you: for it is profitable for you that one of your members should perish, and not that your whole body should be cast into hell. . . .

You have heard that it has been said, An eye for an eye, and a tooth for a tooth: But I say unto you, That you resist not evil: but whosoever shall smite you on your right cheek, turn to him the other also. And if any man will sue you at the law, and take away your coat, let him have your cloak also. And whosoever shall compel you to go a mile, go with him two. Give to him that asks you, and from him that would borrow of you turn you not away. You have heard that it has been said, You shall love your neighbor, and hate your enemy. But I say unto you, Love your enemies, bless them that curse you, do good to them that hate you, and pray for those who despitefully use you, and persecute you. . . . Be you therefore perfect, just as your Father which is in heaven is perfect. . . .

Matthew 5:17-22, 27-30, 38-44, 48, 6:5-6 (King James Version).

b.   *The Final Instructions to the Apostles*

According to the New Testament, at the Last Supper, Jesus gave his final instructions to the apostles, and revoked a previous order about not carrying useful items. He asked, "When I sent you out with no moneybag or knapsack or sandals, did you lack anything?" "Nothing," the apostles replied. Jesus continued:

> But now, let the one who has a moneybag take it, and likewise a knapsack. And let the one who has no sword sell his cloak and buy one. For I tell you that this scripture must be fulfilled in me: And he was numbered with the transgressors. For what is written about me has its fulfillment.

The apostles responded, "Look, Lord, here are two swords." Jesus said to them, "It is enough." Luke 22:35-38 (English Standard Version).

Although the New Testament does not explicitly say so, the sword-carrying by 2 of the 12 apostles was apparently illegal under Roman law, since very few Jews at the time were Roman citizens.[10]

c. The Arrest of Jesus

Just a few hours after Jesus had given the above instructions, Roman soldiers came to arrest him in the Garden of Gethsemane. Peter, whom Jesus had appointed as the leader of the disciples, rushed to defend Jesus, took a sword, and cut off the ear of a Roman soldier. Jesus healed the soldier's ear by touching it. He said to Peter: "Put up again thy sword into its place: for all they that take the sword shall perish with the sword," or "Put up thy sword into the sheath: the cup which my Father has given me, shall I not drink it?" Matthew 26:52, John 18:11 (King James Version).

d. Paul's Letter to the Romans

Next to the Gospels (four biographies of Jesus), the most influential book of the New Testament is Paul's letter to the Christians in Rome. Regarding submission to government, Paul wrote in Romans 13:1-7 (King James Version):

> Let every soul be subject unto the higher powers. For there is no power but of God: the powers that be are ordained of God. Whosoever therefore resisteth the power, resisteth the ordinance of God: and they that resist shall receive to themselves damnation. For rulers are not a terror to good works, but to the evil. Wilt thou then not be afraid of the power? do that which is good, and thou shalt have praise of the same: For he is the minister of God to thee for good. But if thou do that which is evil, be afraid; for he beareth not the sword in vain: for he is the minister of

---

10. The Apostle Matthew was a tax collector (Matthew 10:3). He might therefore have been allowed legally to carry a sword. It is possible that Matthew walked around carrying *two* swords, although it was unusual for one person to carry two swords. The sword(s) might have been carried concealed in a bag or knapsack, although Luke 22 suggests that the apostles did not carry bags or knapsacks before the Last Supper. The typical Roman sword of the Republic was the *gladius Hispaniensis*, whose blade was approximately 30 inches long. In the first century A.D., the *gladius* was replaced by the Pompeii-type sword, whose blade was only 16 inches. The latter type of sword would have been relatively easy to carry concealed, especially under loose flowing garments.

God, a revenger to execute wrath upon him that doeth evil. Wherefore ye must needs be subject, not only for wrath, but also for conscience sake. For this cause pay ye tribute also: for they are God's ministers, attending continually upon this very thing. Render therefore to all their dues: tribute to whom tribute is due; custom to whom custom; fear to whom fear; honour to whom honour.

To the same effect is 1 Peter 2:11-25.

e. Other Early Christian Writings

It is sometimes asserted that early Christians were uniformly pacifist. But there is extensive evidence of Christians serving in the Roman army, especially after Roman citizenship was extended empire-wide in 212 A.D. Moreover, the Biblical history of the earliest church, the *Book of Acts*, contains stories of Roman soldiers who converted to Christianity, and who continued to serve as soldiers.

Many early Christians were indeed complete pacifists. *The Didache*, also known as *Teaching of the Twelve Apostles*, is an early set of instructions for gentile converts, perhaps dating from the latter part of the first century or the first half of early second century. Near the beginning of a restatement of the Sermon on the Mount, *The Didache* instructs: "[W]hen anyone robs you of your property, demand no return. You really cannot do it. Give to anyone that asks you, and demand no return." *The Didache, in* 6 Ancient Christian Writers: The Didache 15 (James A. Kleist trans. & annot., 1948).

Writing in the latter part of second century, Athenagoras was one of the first Christian writers to blend Christian doctrine with the ideas of the Greek philosopher Plato. He wrote: "[W]e have learned, not only not to return blow for blow, nor to go to law with those who plunder and rob us, but to those who smite us on one side of the face to offer the other side also, and to those who take away our coat to give likewise our cloak." Athenagoras, A Plea for the Christians, ch. 1, *available at* http://www.ccel.org/fathers2/ANF-02/anf02-46.htm#P2521_682256.

NOTES & QUESTIONS

1. Which of the sayings in the Sermon on the Mount appear to be meant to be taken literally? In the context of the times, a slap on the cheek was a serious personal insult. Can the example be extrapolated to a general admonition against self-defense? Does "resist not evil" mean that a person should not resist evil? In what ways, if any, might resistance to evil be legitimate, based the New Testament passages above?

2. What point(s) should be drawn from Jesus's instruction that the apostles should carry swords?

3. The instruction to Peter to put his sword in its sheath is one of the most common proof-texts for Christian pacifists. Nonpacifists argue that when

Peter put his sword back in its place, he was no more disarmed than a man who puts his handgun back into its holster. Which interpretation do you think is more persuasive?

4. The Athenagoras quote appears to extend the New Testament injunction, 1 Corinthians 6:1-8, that Christians should not use secular lawsuits to settle their disputes with each other. To what extent, if any, is asking a court to criminally prosecute someone, or asking a court to settle a civil dispute, akin to participation in violence?

3. Medieval Christian Thought

The general Christian view during the Dark Ages in the West (commonly dated from the fall of the Western Roman Empire until the early second millennium) was that, pursuant to Romans 13, everyone must submit to government, no matter how oppressive.

One of the first contrary voices was Manegold of Lautenbach, a scholar at a monastery destroyed by the German Emperor Henry IV. Manegold analogized a cruel tyrant to a disobedient swineherd who stole his master's pigs, and who could be removed from his job by the master. A.J. Carlyle & R.W. Carlyle, Medieval Political Theory in the West 164 (1950) (translating and paraphrasing Manegold's Latin text in *Liber ad Gebehardum* (1085)). For more on medieval Christian thought, see David B. Kopel, *The Catholic Second Amendment*, 29 Hamline L. Rev. 519 (2006). According to Manegold:

> [I]f the king ceases to govern the kingdom, and begins to act as a tyrant, to destroy justice, to overthrow peace, and to break his faith, the man who has taken the oath is free from it, and the people are entitled to depose the king and to set up another, inasmuch as he has broken the principle upon which their mutual obligation depended.

In "the Little Renaissance" that began in the twelfth century, one of the most important events was the Western rediscovery of Aristotle and of the *Corpus Juris*. The University of Bologna, Italy, was the first Western academic institution to study the *Corpus*. Almost as soon as the *Corpus Juris* was rediscovered, and for centuries afterward, the greatest activity of legal scholars was studying the *Corpus Juris*, and writing commentaries on it; the commentaries were usually written *Talmud*-style, in the form of marginal annotations. The *Corpus Juris* led to the University of Bologna creating the first law school that the Western world had known since the fall of Rome.

Because the authors of the *Corpus Juris* had written down all the legal rules and decisions they could find, and merely organized the rules and decisions by subject matter, there appeared to be many legal standards that were contradicted by other legal standards. Using techniques that are the intellectual tools of every good lawyer, legal scholars at the University of Bologna and elsewhere looked for ways to reconcile the seemingly inconsistent statements in Justinian's text. "Glossolators" provided a gloss, which was an explanatory commentary in the wide margins of the printed edition of Justinian's *Corpus Juris*, and that sought to explicate and reconcile the various rules. This method of scholarship was known as Scholasticism.

Around 1140 A.D., Gratian of Bologna was first scholar to bring the Scholastic approach to canon law (church law). The subtitle of his treatise showed his objective of harmonizing "Discordant Canons." The *Decretum* (including later commentaries) was the definitive consolidation, harmonization, and analysis of all church laws since the time of the apostles. The *Decretum* was taught in law schools, and until 1917 served as the first volume of the *Corpus Juris Canonici,* the law of the Roman Catholic Church.

Gratian began with a concise expression of natural law:

> Natural law is common to all nations because it exists everywhere through natural instinct, not because of any enactment.
>
> For example: the union of men and women, the succession and rearing of children, the common possession of all things, the identical liberty of all, or the acquisition of things which are taken from the heavens, earth, or sea, as well as the return of a thing deposited or of money entrusted to one, and the repelling of violence by force. This, and everything similar, is never regarded as unjust but is held to be natural and equitable.

Gratian, The Treatise on Law (Decretum Dd. 1-20) with the Ordinary Gloss Pt. 1 D.1 p.2 c.7 (Augustine Thompson & James Gordley trans., 1993).

a. *John of Salisbury's* Policraticus

A cosmopolitan and well-educated English bishop, John of Salisbury wrote the first serious new book of political science published in the West since the fourth century. It was perhaps the most influential book written since the Byzantine Emperor Justinian's legal treatise *Corpus Juris* had been compiled six centuries before, and it remained influential throughout the Middle Ages. *Policraticus* (Statesman's Book), published in 1159, was for the next hundred years considered the most important book on government. Thomas Aquinas, whose work later displaced Salisbury's, consciously built on Salisbury's foundation.

Policraticus argued that intermediate magistrates, such as local governors, had a duty to lead forcible resistance, if necessary, against serious abuses by the highest magistrate, such as the king. Not since the Cicero had any Western writer provided a detailed theory of tyrannicide. Salisbury wrote:

> [I]t is not only permitted, but it is also equitable and just to slay tyrants. For he who receives the sword deserves to perish by the sword.
>
> But "receives" is to be understood to pertain to he who has rashly usurped that which is not his, not to he who receives what he uses from the power of God. He who receives power from God serves the laws and is the slave of justice and right. He who usurps power suppresses justice and places the laws beneath his will. Therefore, justice is deservedly armed against those who disarm the law, and the public power treats harshly those who endeavour to put aside the public hand. And, although there are many forms of high treason, none of them is so serious as that which is executed against the body of justice itself. Tyranny is,

therefore, not only a public crime, but if this can happen, it is more than public. For if all prosecutors may be allowed in the case of high treason, how much more are they allowed when there is oppression of laws which should themselves command emperors? Surely no one will avenge a public enemy, and whoever does not prosecute him transgresses against himself and against the whole body of the earthly republic. . . .

John of Salisbury, Policraticus 25 (Cary J. Nederman ed. & trans., Cambridge Univ. Press 1990) (circa 1159).

As the image of the deity, the prince is to be loved, venerated and respected; the tyrant, as the image of depravity, is for the most part even to be killed. . . .

Id. at 191.

[I]t is just for public tyrants to be killed and the people to be liberated for obedience to God.

Id. at 207.

b. *Thomas Aquinas*

The apex of medieval thought was Saint Thomas Aquinas's *Summa Theologica*, a massive treatise on numerous matters of ethics and theology.

Question 64, "Of Murder" "Whether it is lawful to kill a man in self-defense?"
    It is written (Ex. 22:2): "If a thief be found breaking into a house or undermining it, and be wounded so as to die; he that slew him shall not be guilty of blood." Now it is much more lawful to defend one's life than one's house. Therefore neither is a man guilty of murder if he kill another in defense of his own life. . . .
    I answer that, Nothing hinders one act from having two effects, only one of which is intended, while the other is beside the intention. Now moral acts take their species according to what is intended, and not according to what is beside the intention, since this is accidental as explained above. . . . Accordingly the act of self-defense may have two effects, one is the saving of one's life, the other is the slaying of the aggressor. Therefore this act, since one's intention is to save one's own life, is not unlawful, seeing that it is natural to everything to keep itself in "being," as far as possible. And yet, though proceeding from a good intention, an act may be rendered unlawful, if it be out of proportion to the end. Wherefore if a man, in self-defense, uses more than necessary violence, it will be unlawful: whereas if he repel force with moderation his defense will be lawful, because according to the jurists, "it is lawful to repel force by force, provided one does not exceed the limits of a blameless defense." Nor is it necessary for salvation that a man omit the act of moderate self-defense in order to avoid killing the other man, since one is bound to take more care of one's own life than of another's. But as it is unlawful to take a man's life, except for the public authority acting for the common good, as stated above [Article 3], it is not lawful for a man to intend killing a man in self-defense, except for such as have public authority, who while intending to kill a man in self-defense, refer this to the public good, as in the case of a soldier fighting

against the foe, and in the minister of the judge struggling with robbers, although even these sin if they be moved by private animosity.

Aquinas, Summa Theologica, Second Part of the Second Part 195 (Fathers of the English Dominican Province trans., Burns Oates & Washborne 1929) (1265-74) (public domain version available at http://www.ccel.org/ccel/aquinas/summa.html).

Another topic was resistance to government:

"Whether sedition is always a mortal sin?" . . . [S]edition is contrary to the unity of the multitude, viz. the people of a city or kingdom. . . . [S]edition is opposed to the unity of law and common good: whence it follows manifestly that sedition is opposed to justice and the common good. Therefore by reason of its genus it is a mortal sin, and its gravity will be all the greater according as the common good which it assails surpasses the private good which is assailed by strife.

Accordingly the sin of sedition is first and chiefly in its authors, who sin most grievously; and secondly it is in those who are led by them to disturb the common good. Those, however, who defend the common good, and withstand the seditious party, are not themselves seditious, even as neither is a man to be called quarrelsome because he defends himself. . . .

. . . A tyrannical government is not just, because it is directed, not to the common good, but to the private good of the ruler, as the Philosopher [Aristotle] states (Polit. iii, 5; Ethic. viii, 10). Consequently there is no sedition in disturbing a government of this kind, unless indeed the tyrant's rule be disturbed so inordinately, that his subjects suffer greater harm from the consequent disturbance than from the tyrant's government. Indeed it is the tyrant rather that is guilty of sedition, since he encourages discord and sedition among his subjects, that he may lord over them more securely; for this is tyranny, being conducive to the private good of the ruler, and to the injury of the multitude.

Thomas Aquinas, Summa Theologica, Second Part of Second Part 583-84 (Fathers of the English Dominican Province trans., William Benton & Encyclopedia Britannica Inc. 1952) (1265-74).

NOTES & QUESTIONS

1. Do you think there is a "natural law," in the sense that Gratian used the term? If so, is self-defense part of it?

2. CQ: Compare Manegold's views with the American Declaration of Independence: "That to secure these rights, Governments are instituted among Men. . . . That whenever any Form of Government becomes destructive of these ends, it is the Right of the People to alter or to abolish it, and to institute new Government. . . ." What is your assessment of claims by Manegold and Thomas Jefferson that any legitimate ruler is necessarily contractually bound to protect the public good? That the people necessarily have a right to remove their rulers, by force if necessary?

3. CQ: Compare Salisbury's views with the motto that Thomas Jefferson and Benjamin Franklin proposed placing on the Great Seal of the United States:

"Rebellion to tyrants is obedience to God." The words were the motto of John Bradshaw (1602-1659), the lawyer who served as President of the Parliamentary Commission that sentenced British King Charles I to death.

4. The theory in *Policraticus* of "intermediate magistrates" is a check on the use of forcible resistance. It means that self-appointed individuals (in the worst case, people like Timothy McVeigh or Charles Manson) have no authority to try to start a revolution. Rather, a revolution may only be initiated by "intermediate magistrates," such as local governments. CQ: Was the American Revolution consistent with this theory? In Chapter 4, you will read *Federalist* 46, in which James Madison describes resistance to a hypothetical tyrannical federal government as being led by the states. Is Salisbury's view merely an invitation for *coup d'ètats*?

5. Note how Aquinas's theory of double effect resembles Cicero's speech in defense of Milo: "[T]he man who had used a weapon with the object of defending himself would be decided not to have had his weapon about him with the object of killing a man." The Aquinas theory of double effect has been used to analyze many ethical issues. Is it persuasive?

6. CQ: Like Thomas Aquinas and John of Salisbury, U.S. Supreme Court Justice Joseph Story (Chapter 5) suggested that the forceful removal of a tyrant would be a legitimate way to restore of constitutional law and order: "The militia is the natural defence of a free country against sudden foreign invasions, domestic insurrections, and domestic usurpations of power by rulers. . . . The right of the citizens to keep and bear arms has justly been considered, as the palladium of the liberties of a republic; since it offers a strong moral check against the usurpation and arbitrary power of rulers; and it will generally, even if these are successful in the first instance, enable the people to resist and triumph over them. . . ." Joseph Story, A Familiar Exposition of the Constitution of the United States 264-65 (1842). What is your assessment of the claims by Salisbury, Aquinas, and Story that overthrowing a perceived tyrant by force can lead to the restoration of a society of ordered liberty?

D. Second-Millennium Europe

1. Italian Influence

From time immemorial, the Swiss cantons maintained a citizen militia. The crossbow was the symbolic national weapon, and William Tell the exemplar of civic virtue. With the militia, the Swiss cantons won and secured their independence from nearby empires. Because the Swiss conducted much of their self-government in outdoor town assemblies, similar to the New England town meetings, they were much admired by the American Founders.

However, the events that reinvigorated the militia in Western political thought occurred in Italy. During the Renaissance and thereafter, Italian city-states mobilized their militias and won independence from various empires.

The pro-militia Italian writers were heavily influenced by Aristotle, *supra*, who believed that citizenship and the possession of arms were coextensive. During the seventeenth century, militia advocates in England and Scotland carefully studied the Italian writers. The foundation of militia ideology was belief in active citizenship: that free states should be defended by the armed citizens of those states, that participation in the militia was the embodiment of virtuous active citizenship, and that reliance on professionals and mercenaries to defend a state was expensive, dangerous, and degrading to the character of the citizenry. In Italy, reliance on militias was sometimes successful, and sometimes not. It was always in tension with the aristocracy's fear of the people being armed. *See* J.G.A. Pocock, The Machiavellian Moment: Florentine Political Thought and the Atlantic Republican Tradition (2d ed. 2003).

Many authors extolled the militia. For example, Leonardo Bruni, writing in the early fifteenth century, praised the city whose inhabitants "acted by themselves without the help of any foreign auxiliaries, fighting on their own behalf and contending as much as possible for glory and dignity." Unlike foreign mercenaries, native militia, who were "fighting for the love of their city," would fight fearlessly. Quentin Skinner, 1 The Foundations of Modern Political Thought: The Renaissance 76-77 (2002).

Among the Italian authors, the one who is best known in the twenty-first century, and who was by far the most influential in Great Britain, was Niccolo Machiavelli. Here, he tells the story of how the ancient Roman Republic used the militia for self-defense, and argues that modern Italian city-states should do the same:

Niccolo Machiavelli, Discourses on the First Decade of Titus Livius
ch. 30 (Ninian Hill Thomson trans., 1883)

Now, one of the tests whereby to gauge the strength of any State, is to observe on what terms it lives with its neighbours: for when it so carries itself that, to secure its friendship, its neighbours pay it tribute, this is a sure sign of its strength, but when its neighbours, though of less reputation, receive payments from it, this is a clear proof of its weakness. . . . And, to begin with our own republic of Florence, we know that in times past, when she was at the height of her renown, there was never a lordling of Romagna who had not a subsidy from her, to say nothing of what she paid to the Perugians, to the Castellans, and to all her other neighbours. But had our city been armed and strong, the direct contrary would have been the case, for, to obtain her protection, all would have poured money into her lap, not seeking to sell their friendship but to purchase hers.

Nor are the Florentines the only people who have lived on this dishonourable footing. The Venetians have done the same, nay, the King of France himself, for all his great dominions, lives tributary to the Swiss and to the King of England; and this because the French king and the others named, with a view to escape dangers rather imaginary than real, have disarmed their subjects; seeking to reap a present gain by wringing money from them, rather than follow a course which would secure their own safety and the lasting welfare of their country.

Which ill-practices of theirs, though they quiet things for a time, must in the end exhaust their resources, and give rise in seasons of danger to incurable mischief and disorder. It would be tedious to count up how often in the course of their wars, the Florentines, the Venetians, and the kingdom of France have had to ransom themselves from their enemies, and to submit to an ignominy to which, once only, the Romans were very near being subjected. It would be tedious, too, to recite how many towns have been bought by the Florentines and by the Venetians, which, afterwards, have only been a trouble to them, from their not knowing how to defend with iron what they had won with gold. While the Romans continued free they adhered to this more generous and noble method, but when they came under the emperors, and these, again, began to deteriorate, and to love the shade rather than the sunshine, they also took to purchasing peace, now from the Parthians, now from the Germans, and at other times from other neighbouring nations. And this was the beginning of the decline of their great empire.

Such are the evils that befall when you withhold arms from your subjects; and this course is attended by the still greater disadvantage, that the closer an enemy presses you the weaker he finds you. For any one who follows the evil methods of which I speak, must, in order to support troops whom he thinks can be trusted to keep off his enemies, be very exacting in his dealings with those of his subjects who dwell in the heart of his dominions; since, to widen the interval between himself and his enemies, he must subsidize those princes and peoples who adjoin his frontiers. States maintained on this footing may make a little resistance on their confines; but when these are passed by the enemy no further defence remains. Those who pursue such methods as these seem not to perceive that they are opposed to reason and common sense. For the heart and vital parts of the body, not the extremities, are those which we should keep guarded, since we may live on without the latter, but must die if the former be hurt. But the States of which I speak, leaving the heart undefended, defend only the hands and feet. The mischief which has thus been, and is at this day wrought in Florence is plain enough to see. For so soon as an enemy penetrates within her frontiers, and approaches her heart, all is over with her. . . .

But with the Romans the reverse of all this took place. For the nearer an enemy approached Rome, the more completely he found her armed for resistance; and accordingly we see that on the occasion of Hannibal's invasion of Italy, the Romans, after three defeats, and after the slaughter of so many of their captains and soldiers, were still able, not merely to withstand the invader, but even, in the end, to come off victorious. This we may ascribe to the heart being well guarded, while the extremities were but little heeded. For the strength of Rome rested on the Roman people themselves, on the Latin league, on the confederate towns of Italy, and on her colonies, from all of which sources she drew so numerous an army, as enabled her to subdue the whole world and to keep it in subjection.

The Italian Cesare Beccaria (1738-94) is the founder of the social science of criminology. His masterpiece *On Crimes and Punishments* (*Dei Delitti e Delle Pene*) proposed humanizing reforms of criminal justice, such as the abolition of torture and of secret trials. As soon as the book appeared in English, it was snapped up by John Adams, Thomas Jefferson, and other influential Americans.

Jefferson liked Beccaria's passage on gun control so much that he copied it into his "commonplace book" of favorite sayings. Two and a half centuries later, the passage is still oft-quoted in the American gun control debate:

Cesare Beccaria, An Essay on Crimes and Punishments
ch. 40, Edward D. Ingraham trans., 1819 (1764)

A principal source of errors and injustice are false ideas of utility. For example: that legislator has false ideas of utility who considers particular more than general conveniencies, . . . who would sacrifice a thousand real advantages to the fear of an imaginary or trifling inconvenience; who would deprive men of the use of fire for fear of their being burnt, and of water for fear of their being drowned; and who knows of no means of preventing evil but by destroying it.

The laws of this nature are those which forbid to wear arms, disarming those only who are not disposed to commit the crime which the laws mean to prevent. Can it be supposed, that those who have the courage to violate the most sacred laws of humanity, and the most important of the code, will respect the less considerable and arbitrary injunctions, the violation of which is so easy, and of so little comparative importance? Does not the execution of this law deprive the subject of that personal liberty, so dear to mankind and to the wise legislator? And does it not subject the innocent to all the disagreeable circumstances that should only fall on the guilty? It certainly makes the situation of the assaulted worse, and of the assailants better, and rather encourages than prevents murder, as it requires less courage to attack unarmed than armed persons.

NOTES & QUESTIONS

1. Even if Machiavelli were right about the value of a well-armed militia for Italian city-states, does that mean militias are *necessarily* the best defense of the state? Does the answer depend on the circumstances of the time and place, including the kind of tools and technology available?

2. Is Beccaria's analysis sound? Can one accept Beccaria's analysis and still support some gun controls, such as laws forbidding convicted criminals from possessing guns, or to attempt to prevent convicted criminals from acquiring guns?

2. England

So far, we have examined some sources that were unknown to the American Framers (the Confucians and the Taoists), some that were intimately known (Greeks, Romans, and the Bible), and some of that were indirectly known (the medieval Catholics were indirectly known to the Americans as their ideas were later restated by Western European Protestants). Nothing, however, was as influential to the Americans in general, and to the Second Amendment in particular, as the history of England. For the Americans, this was their own history, and when the American Revolution began, the Americans were demanding nothing more than respect for "the rights of Englishmen."

English gun laws were a natural and obvious influence on early understandings of the Second Amendment. Some Americans, such as St. George Tucker (author of the first American constitutional law treatise, see Chapter 4), pointed to English restrictions as precisely what the Second Amendment was intended to prevent. Others pointed to English restrictions, including the 1328 Statute of Northampton, as showing that the English right to arms was quite limited, and therefore so is the derivative American right. In *District of Columbia v. Heller*, 554 U.S. 570 (2008) (Chapter 9), Justice Scalia's majority and Justice Stevens's dissent argue at great length about what English law really implies about the Second Amendment.

a. *Magna Charta*

King John I signed "the Great Charter" at Runnymeade in 1215. His harsh, abusive, and autocratic rule had sparked a national revolt led by the barons, and his acceptance of Magna Charta was the price for his being allowed to retain his throne. Many of the rights specified in Magna Charta were believed to be affirmations of long-established rights and customs, including laws that had come from King Edward the Confessor (reigned 1042-66). Magna Charta contains numerous provisions about feudal law that are not directly relevant today, but the overall purpose of Magna Charta is to protect property against arbitrary seizure or control by the king, to prevent royal interference in families (such as the king ordering baronial daughters to marry someone picked by the king), to require parliamentary approval for taxes, and to provide for orderly, nonarbitrary enforcement and creation of law. The "jury of his peers" provision is the direct ancestor of modern jury rights in Anglo-American law. The "law of the land" provision is the father of the "due process of law" guarantees of the Fifth and Fourteenth Amendments. One of the final provisions of Magna Charta was the enforcement mechanism:

‖ Magna Charta
1215[11]

61. Since, moreover, for God and the amendment of our kingdom and for the better allaying of the quarrel that has arisen between us and our barons, we have granted all these concessions, desirous that they should enjoy them in complete and firm endurance for ever, we give and grant to them the underwritten security, namely, that the barons choose five-and-twenty barons of the kingdom, whomsoever they will, who shall be bound with all their might, to observe and hold, and cause to be observed, the peace and liberties we have granted

---

11. Like other English statutes of the time, Magna Charta was originally written in Latin. The above translation is from Project Gutenberg, http://www.gutenberg.org/cache/epub/10000/pg10000.html.

and confirmed to them by this our present Charter, so that if we, or our justiciar, or our bailiffs or any one of our officers, shall in anything be at fault toward any one, or shall have broken any one of the articles of the peace or of this security, and the offense be notified to four barons of the foresaid five-and-twenty, the said four barons shall repair to us (or our justiciar, if we are out of the realm) and, laying the transgression before us, petition to have that transgression redressed without delay. And if we shall not have corrected the transgression (or, in the event of our being out of the realm, if our justiciar shall not have corrected it) within forty days, reckoning from the time it has been intimated to us (or to our justiciar, if we should be out of the realm), the four barons afore-said shall refer that matter to the rest of the five-and-twenty barons, and those five-and-twenty barons shall, together with the community of the whole land, distrain and distress us in all possible ways, namely, by seizing our castles, lands, possessions, and in any other way they can, until redress has been obtained as they deem fit, saving harmless our own person, and the persons of our queen and children; and when redress has been obtained, they shall resume their old relations toward us. And let whoever in the country desires it, swear to obey the orders of the said five-and-twenty barons for the execution of all the aforesaid matters, and along with them, to molest us to the utmost of his power; and we publicly and freely grant leave to every one who wishes to swear, and we shall never forbid any one to swear. All those, moreover, in the land who of themselves and of their own accord are unwilling to swear to the twenty-five to help them in constraining and molesting us, we shall by our command compel the same to swear to the effect aforesaid. And if any one of the five-and-twenty barons shall have died or departed from the land, or be incapacitated in any other manner which would prevent the foresaid provisions being carried out, those of the said twenty-five barons who are left shall choose another in his place according to their own judgment, and he shall be sworn in the same way as the others. Further, in all matters, the execution of which is intrusted to these twenty-five barons, if perchance these twenty-five are present, that which the majority of those present ordain or command shall be held as fixed and established, exactly as if the whole twenty-five had concurred in this; and the said twenty-five shall swear that they will faithfully observe all that is aforesaid, and cause it to be observed with all their might. And we shall procure nothing from any one, directly or indirectly, whereby any part of these concessions and liberties might be revoked or diminished; and if any such thing has been procured, let it be void and null, and we shall never use it personally or by another.

The English kings hated Magna Charta. King John repudiated it shortly before his death, but subsequent monarchs succumbed to pressure to reaffirm and repub-lish it. However, in the republications, the successors did not include Article 61.

NOTES & QUESTIONS

1. Taking into account the theory of "intermediate magistrates," can you imagine ways in which Article 61 might inform the Framers' understanding of the proper forms of resistance to the federal government, should that government become tyrannical?

2. Could the Second Amendment and its state analogues be seen as modernized versions of Article 61?

3. Article 61 of Magna Charta was not unique. In Hungary in 1222, the nobles forced King Andrew II to promulgate a "Golden Bull," in which legal process was regularized and the government made subject to law; taxation without consent was prohibited; a legislature (the Diet) was created; and abusive officials were required to forfeit their office. Just as Magna Charta recognized the right to the use of force to enforce the great charter against future kings, so did the Golden Bull:

> We also ordain that if We or any of Our Successors shall at any time contravene the terms of this statute, the bishops and the higher and lower nobles of Our realm, one and all, both present and future, shall by virtue thereof have the uncontrolled right in perpetuity of resistance both by word and deed without thereby incurring any charge of treason.

Notably, while Magna Charta allowed force only after a majority decision of the nobles, the Golden Bull allowed any single noble to make the decision.

Likewise, the crusader kingdom of Jerusalem acknowledged that the king's vassals had a right to renounce fealty and to rebel in certain cases of abuse of justice by the king. J.C. Holt, Magna Charta and the Idea of Liberty 124 (1972). In Castile (a kingdom comprising much of modern Spain), the Pact of 1282 recognized that towns had a right of insurrection if the king violated the Pact. R. Altamira, *Magna Charta and Spanish Medieval Jurisprudence, in* Magna Charta Commemoration Essays (E.H. Malden ed., 1917). Aragon, Spain's other major kingdom, likewise acknowledged the right of nobles to depose a king who violated judicial procedures or other legal rights. *Id.* at 137; Geronimo Zurita, Anales de la Corona de Aragón 323 (1610), *available at* http://ifc.dpz.es/publicaciones/ebooks/id/2448. The formula was famously summarized as "*si non, non*" ("if not, not"); that is, if the king obeyed the laws and respected the rights of the people, then the people owed him allegiance; and if not, not. Víctor Balaguer, Instituciones y Reyes de Aragón 128 (1969) (1890). (The original phrase is in Catalan, but the words are the same in French, which perhaps accounts for their becoming so well known.)

If a ruler agrees to conditions under which he may be forcibly overthrown, has he made political conditions more stable or less stable?

4. The agreements in note 3, like Magna Charta, took the form of bilateral contracts. As such, they reinforced the principle that the monarch's sovereignty was limited. Antonio Marongiu, *The Contractual Nature of Parliamentary Agreements* (1968), *in* J.C. Holt, *supra*, at 139-40. As opposed to the philosophical notion of a "social contract," Magna Charta and its cousins were actual written contracts. The contractual theory of government became quite important in Europe, and was the counterpoint to the claim that kings enjoyed unlimited power by divine right. CQ: In the American colonies, the contractual nature of government was an oft-repeated theme of political sermons, and the Declaration of Independence explicitly adopts the contractual theory (Chapter 3). In what ways are American state and federal constitutions similar to and dissimilar from Magna Charta–type contracts?

b. English Statutes

i. Assize of Arms

Under the old Saxon tradition of the *fyrd*, every male aged 16 to 60 bore arms to defend the nation. The American Founders idealized pre-Saxon England, and considered the Norman Conquest of 1066 to be the root of much evil in English law.

In 1181, the Norman King Henry II promulgated the Statute of Assize of Arms. It ordered the surrender of coats of mail and breastplates owned by Jews. Christian freemen were required to acquire arms appropriate to their social rank (the higher one's rank, the more extensive and expensive the required arms).

Statute of Assize of Arms
27 Henry II, art. 3 (1181)[12]

1. Whoever possesses one knight's fee shall have a shirt of mail, a helmet, a shield, and a lance; and every knight shall have as many shirts of mail, helmets, shields, and lances as he possesses knight's fees in demesne.
2. Moreover, every free layman who possesses chattels or rents to the value of 16m[arks] shall have a shirt of mail, a helmet, a shield, and a lance; and every free layman possessing chattels or rents to the value of 10m[arks] shall have a hauberk, an iron cap, and a lance.
3. Item, all burgesses and the whole community of freemen shall have [each] a gambeson, an iron cap, and a lance.
4. Besides, each of them shall swear to have these arms before the feast of St. Hilary, to be faithful to the lord king Henry — namely, the son of the Empress Matilda — and to bear these arms in his service according to his command and in fealty to the lord king and his kingdom. And henceforth no one having these arms shall sell them or pledge them or lend them or alienate them in any other way; nor shall a lord in any way alienate them from his men, either through forfeiture or through gift or through pledge or in any other way.
5. If any one having these arms dies, his arms shall remain to his heir. If, however, the heir is not of age to use arms in time of need, that person who has wardship over him shall also have custody of the arms and shall find a man who can use the arms in the service of the lord king until the heir is of age to bear arms, and then he shall have them.
6. Any burgess who has more arms than he ought to have by this assize shall sell them, or give them away, or in some way alienate them to such a man as will keep them for the service of the lord king of England. And none of them shall keep more arms than he ought to have by this assize.

---

12. Historically, English statutes are cited according to the regnal year (e.g., "5" is the fifth year that the particular king was reigning), then the king's name (e.g., "Henry III"), and then the sequence of lawmaking that year (e.g., "ch. 25," "c. 25," or "art. 25" is the twenty-fifth statute enacted that particular regnal year). After that, the calendar year follows in parentheses. English statutes from 1235 to 1713 are authoritatively collected in the multi-volume *Statutes of the Realm*, which is available in the English Reports sublibrary of Hein Online.

7. Item, no Jew shall keep in his possession a shirt of mail or a hauberk, but he shall sell it or give it away or alienate it in some other way, so that it shall remain in the king's service.

8. Item, no one shall carry arms out of England except by the command of the lord king: no one is to sell arms to another to carry out of England; nor shall a merchant or any other man carry them out of England.

9. [The justices shall compile reports from the knights about all the men in each knight's jurisdiction, reporting on which men are in the above classes, and what arms they own, based on sworn oaths.]

10. Item, the justices shall have proclamation made in the counties through which they are to go that, with respect to those who do not have such arms as have been specified above, the lord king will take vengeance, not merely on their lands or chattels, but on their limbs.

11. Item, no one who does not possess 16m[arks] or 10m[arks] in chattels is to swear concerning free and lawful men.

12. Item, the justices shall command through all the counties that no one, as he loves his life and all that he has, shall buy or sell any ship to be taken away from England, and that no one shall carry any timber or cause it to be carried out of England. And the lord king commands that no one shall be received for the oath concerning arms unless he is a freeman.

ii. Statute of Northampton

The 1328 Statute of Northampton imposed a very broad restriction on arms-carrying, although there appears to be little evidence of it actually having been much enforced. In practice, nearly everyone carried knives as tools for daily use.

> Item, it is enacted, that no man great nor small, of what condition soever he be, except the king's servants in his presence, and his ministers in executing of the king's precepts, or of their office, and such as be in their company assisting them, and also [upon a cry made for arms to keep the peace, and the same in such places where such acts happen,] be so hardy to come before the King's justices, or other of the King's ministers doing their office, with force and arms, nor bring no force in affray of the peace, nor to go nor ride armed by night nor by day, in fairs, markets, nor in the presence of the justices or other ministers, nor in no part elsewhere, upon pain to forfeit their armour to the King, and their bodies to prison at the King's pleasure. And that the King's justices in their presence, sheriffs, and other ministers in their bailiwicks, lords of franchises, and their bailiffs in the same, and mayors and bailiffs of cities and boroughs, within the same cities and boroughs, and borough-holders, constables, and wardens of the peace within their wards, shall have power to execute this act. And that the justices assigned, at their coming down into the country, shall have power to enquire how such officers and lords have exercised their offices in this case, and to punish them whom they find that have not done that which pertained to their office.

2 Edward III, ch. 3 (1328) (brackets added by translators for *Statutes of the Realm*).

Over three centuries later, a charge under the statute was brought against a notable political opponent of the despotic King James II. The opponent had gone to church armed, and was acquitted by the jury. The case was reported twice, with summaries of the interpretation of the Chief Justice of the King's Bench. The Chief Justice explained that the statute applies only to persons "who go armed to terrify the King's subjects." *Sir John Knight's Case*, 87 Eng. Rep. 75, 76 (K.B.). While the statute "is almost in desuetudinem," it would apply "when the crime shall appear to be malo animo" (with evil intent). The Chief Justice noted "a general connivance to gentlemen to ride armed for their security." *Rex v. Sir John Knight*, 90 Eng. Rep. 330, 330 (K.B. 1686). The limiting construction of the case was treated as the authoritative rule thereafter. 4 Blackstone, Commentaries *149.

Two weeks after Knight's acquittal, the king, finding the Statute of Northampton an insufficient tool to enforce general disarmament, ordered full enforcement of the Game Act of 1671, which is discussed below.

iii. Gun and Crossbow Control

Longbows were considered the ideal weapon of the English yeoman, who had used them in England's great victories against the French at Crecy in 1346 and Agincourt in 1415. The crossbow, which is easier to use at very short range, was considered a nefarious weapon of highwaymen. In contrast, the Swiss put the crossbow on the same cultural pedestal as the English did the longbow, treating it as their iconic weapon of national independence.

King Henry VII observed that the proliferation of crossbows was leading people to neglect longbow practice, and also leading them to shoot "the king's deer." Accordingly, crossbow possession was banned except for persons who had an annual income from land of at least 200 Marks; those persons could obtain a crossbow license. Even then, the crossbow was only supposed to be used for home defense, not for target practice. Any person who saw any other person shooting a crossbow was authorized to confiscate it. 19 Henry VII, ch. 4 (1503-04).

The first arms control of King Henry VIII was a 1511 statute forbidding servants and apprentices from playing table games, "tennis, cosh, dice, cards, bowls, nor any other unlawful games in no wise," except during the 12 days of Christmas. The stated reason was that gambling sometimes led servants to rob their masters, and that the game distracted people from a better activity: "that the most defensible and natural feat of shooting should in no wise decay but increase." Every able-bodied male aged 60 or under was required to have his own bow and arrows; fathers were required to teach their sons how to shoot. 3 Henry VIII, ch. 25 (1511).[13]

Not long afterward, another statute tightened the anti-crossbow laws of the king's late father, Henry VII. The new statute complained that crossbow licenses had been issued to people who did not meet the income qualifications, and the people were practicing with crossbows all over the kingdom. Accordingly, all extant licenses were cancelled, and the minimum income was raised to 300 Marks. Again, crossbow possession was allowed only for home defense, not for practice. 3 Henry VIII, ch. 32 (1511-12).

A 1514 statute consolidated the above mandates for longbows and income restrictions on crossbows. Handguns were also restricted under the same terms as crossbows. Again the statute ordered the King's subjects to possess longbows, to practice with them, and to provide longbows to their children. 6 Henry VIII,

---

13. The proclamations in this section can be found in 1-3 Tudor Royal Proclamations (Paul L. Hughes & James F. Larkin eds., 1964), providing modern English translations of many proclamations from 1485 (ascension of Henry VII) until 1603 (death of Elizabeth I).

ch. 13 (1514-15). Wars with France forced Henry VIII to lower the property qualification for handguns and crossbows to 100 pounds. 14 & 15 Henry VIII, ch. 7 (1523).

A 1526 proclamation told the mayors and sherifs of London to stop being "negligent, slack, or remiss" in enforcing the arms restrictions. 1 Tudor Royal Proclamations 151 (Apr. 10, 1526).

A few weeks later, another proclamation affirmed the ban on bowling, tennis, cards, and other games, complained that games distracted people from "the exercising of longbows and archery," and ordered all justices of the peace to tell all households to make sure that the householders, their servants, and their children "hereafter have in their houses bows and arrow." 1 Tudor Royal Proclamations 152 (May 5, 1526).

Two years later, Henry complained that archery had decayed because of "the newfangles and wanton pleasure that men now have in using crossbows and handguns." Moreover, handguns and crossbows were being used in crimes, and for hunting by non-nobles. So the king authorized any person to confiscate any unlawful crossbow or handgun from any person, and further authorized any person who shall "probably suppose" that a home contained an illegal crossbow or handgun to enter that home and take it. 1 Tudor Royal Proclamations 177 (Dec. 4, 1528).

Then, in 1533, all licenses were cancelled by a new statute. But the new law was much like the old laws, limiting handguns and crossbows to persons with an annual income of 100 pounds. There was an exception allowing possession by persons living in walled towns within seven miles of the sea, or in the four counties near the Scottish border, for defense of towns, goods, and houses. The statute affirmed the lawfulness of manufacturing handguns and crossbows. The king reserved for his government the unlimited power to give anyone a crossbow or handgun license, exempting them from the law. 25 Henry VIII, ch. 17 (1533).

While the king earlier expressed his "displeasure and indignation" about non-enforcement of arms bans, 1 Tudor Royal Proclamations 249 (Jan. 24, 1537), Parliament repealed the bans in 1539, so that anyone aged 16 or more could own and shoot handguns and hackbuts, "considering how expedient it is at this present time to have some number of his subjects skilled and exercised in the feat of shooting handguns and hackbuts" for defending the realm and "annoying" its enemies. 31 Henry VIII, ch. 8 (1539). ("Hackbut," "hagubut," and "haquebutt" are archaic spellings for "harquebus," a type of short musket.)

The next year, public safety concerns about people carelessly shooting in cities, towns, and boroughs led to a requirement that in London, handgun and hackbut shooting only take place at appropriate target ranges. 1 Tudor Royal Proclamations 288 (July 27, 1540).

In 1541, a new statute setting property qualifications for handguns, hackbuts, and crossbows was enacted:

> [T]hat no person . . . except he have landes tents fees annuyties or Offices to the yerely value of one hundred pounds . . . shall shote in any Crosbowe handgun hagbutt or demyhake. . . .
>   . . . [N]o person . . . shall shote in cayre kepe use or have in his own house or els where any handgun other than suche as shal be in the stock and gonne of the

lenghe of one hole Yarde. [K]eep in his or their houses or elsewhere, any cross-bow, hand-guns, hagbut or demi-hake.

An Acte concerninge Crosbowes and Handguns, 33 Henry VIII, ch. 6 (1541). Again, Henry wished to promote "the good and laudable excise of the longe bowe, whiche alwaye heretofore hathe bene the suertie, savegarde and contynuall defence of this Realme of Englande." The 1541 law added detail to the 1540 law about appropriate places to shoot. The scope of this ban was substantially miti-gated by provisions allowing any inhabitant of market towns or boroughs, and anyone with a house more than two furlongs outside of town, to possess and use handguns (at least a yard long) for self-defense and for shooting at earthen embankments. Further, the act declared that it did not apply within 5 miles of the coasts, within 12 miles of the Scottish border, or on various small islands. *Id.* Note that in the 1541 statute, a "handgun" is a firearm less than one yard in length. This encompasses some firearms that are today considered long guns.

A 1546 proclamation revoked the 1539 statute legalizing handguns in general, while still allowing possession by persons authorized under the 1541 law. 1 Tudor Royal Proclamations 372 (July 8, 1546). During the brief reign of Henry's only son, Edward, a ban on shooting "hayle shott" was applied to persons who did not have the income qualifications for handguns and hackbuts. 2 & 3 Edward VI ch. 14 (1548). "Hail shot" is what we would today call "shotgun ammunition" — a round of ammunition containing several small pellets, rather than a single large bullet.

During the reign of Henry's eldest daughter Mary (1553-58), new mandates for arms possession were enacted. Like the old Assize of Arms, the new laws required persons in various categories of wealth to possess various kinds of weapons, horses, or armor. Notably, haquebutts (short muskets) were now mandatory for those with annual estates of as low as ten pounds. 4 & 5 Phil. & M. ch. 2 (1557-58).

In 1600, a proclamation of Queen Elizabeth I complained about the "slack execution" of the gun control laws, and "the common carrying and use of guns contrary to said statutes," such as by bird hunters, "common and ordinary persons traveling the highway to carry pistols and other kinds of pieces," and by "ruffians and other lewd and dissolute men." 3 Tudor Royal Proclamations 218 (Dec. 21, 1600).

The English monarchs were fond of creating monopolies for all sorts of goods, such as soap or playing cards, and giving production or import rights to their friends in exchange for kickbacks. Under the Tudors and early Stuarts, gunpowder was royal monopoly. The continuing inability of the monopolists to produce sufficient gunpowder helped lead to the repeal of the monopoly in 1641. Lindsay Boynton, The Elizabethan Militia 1558-1638 260-61 (1967).

The Tudor gun control laws were hardly enforced in the seventeenth cen-tury, and even in the sixteenth, enforcement was only sporadic. It appears that the Tudor monarchs had generally failed to convince local sheriffs and justices of the peace to enforce those laws. A key problem was that the system relied on paid informants, but the informants apparently had little enthusiasm for report-ing illegal gun possession. *See* M.W. Beresford, *The Common Informer, the Penal Statutes, and Economic Regulation,* 10 Econ. Hist. Rev. (2d series) 221, 226 (1957) (of 26,243 information cases brought before the Court of the Exchequer from

1519-1659, only 220 involved "guns, archery, horses"). The hail shot ban was formally repealed in 1694. 6 & 7 Wm. & Mary, ch. 13 (1694) (noting that the ban "hath not for many yeares last past been putt in execution but became uselesse and unnecessary yett neverthelesse several malicious persons have of late prosecuted several Gentlemen qualified to keep and use Guns").[14]

The income restrictions for handguns were never formally repealed, but under the English practice of the time, statutes could be repealed by implication without being formally named. The handgun ban was thus arguably repealed in the first year of Elizabeth's successor, James I. 1 Jas. I, ch. 27 (1603-04) (comprehensive anti-poaching law, repealing all related "former statutes," but not naming them individually). One also might view the handgun statute as implicitly repealed by statutes from 1692 onward listing forbidden hunting equipment that commoners could not possess (e.g., traps, snares) and omitting firearms. In any case, it seems that during the seventeenth century, anyone who could afford a handgun was able to buy one, at least until a general crackdown on gun ownership in 1671. As detailed below, a very aggressive gun control program was implemented by the Stuart monarchs in the latter part of the seventeenth century, eventually leading to the overthrow of King James II, and to the enactment of a Bill of Rights, which guaranteed the right to arms.

NOTES & QUESTIONS

1. In order to promote practice with modern militia weapons (e.g., high-powered rifles), would it be legitimate for an American state government, or the national government, to ban forms of recreation that distract people from rifle practice? According to the Constitution, states have "the Authority of training the militia according to the discipline prescribed by Congress." U.S. Const. Art. I, §8. Could state or federal bans on non-rifle forms of recreation be justified under this power? Under the congressional power over interstate commerce? Under the Necessary and Proper Clause? Under the states' police power?

2. Like alcohol prohibition in the United States in the early twentieth century, the Tudor bans on handguns, crossbows, shotguns, tennis, playing cards, and so on were hampered by the reluctance of local law enforcement officials to enforce these restrictions. Does local control of law enforcement generally produce this sort of lenient enforcement? Is this kind of leniency a good thing? Does it matter whether this leniency is dispensed uniformly?

---

14. Following modern practice in the U.K., we use the modern English abbreviations of the regnal names. Thus, "James" is "Jas." and "William" is "Wm." Readers who look up the original statutes in Statutes of the Realm will see that the publication was still under the influence of "Law French." (Law French was a result of the 1066 Norman Conquest, when French became the official language of English law; even for centuries after English was restored as the official language, legal discourse still included many French words.) Thus, in Statutes of the Realm, "James" is abbreviated "Jac." (for the French "Jacques,") and "William" is "Gm." (for the French "Guillaume").

3. If the government allows possession of a weapon, is it wise for the government to forbid practice with the weapon?

4. Should governments have the authority to restrict ownership of weapons to
people of a certain economic class? Do laws that impose heavy licensing fees
(e.g., hundreds of dollars) amount to class-based arms restrictions? What
about laws banning inexpensive firearms ("Saturday Night Specials") but
allowing more expensive handguns?

c. Castle Doctrine Cases

The adage that "a man's house is his castle," comes from a pair of English
cases that affirmed the right of home defense:

> If one is in his house, and hears that such a one will come to his house to beat him,
> he may assemble folk of his friends and neighbors to help him, and aid in the
> safeguard of his person; but if one were threatened that if he should come to such a
> market, or into such a place, he should there be beaten, in that case he could not
> assemble persons to help him go there in personal safety, for he need not go there,
> and he may have a remedy by surety of the peace. But a man's house is his castle
> and defense, and where he has a peculiar right to stay.

Y.B. Trin. 14 Henry 7 (1499), *reported in* Y.B. 21 Henry 7, fol. 39, Mich., pl. 50
(1506) ("Anonymous." No case name).

> That the house of everyone is to him as his castle and fortress, as well for his
> defence against injury and violence, as for his repose; and although the life of
> man is a thing precious and favored in law; so that although a man kills another
> his defence, or kills one *per infortun'*, without any intent, yet it is felony, and in
> such case he shall forfeit his goods and chattels, for the great regard which the
> law has to a man's life; but if thieves come to a man's house to rob him, or
> murder, and the owner of his servants kill any of the thieves in defence of
> himself and his house, it is not felony, and he shall lose nothing, and therewith
> agree . . . every one may assemble his friends and neighbours to defend his
> house against violence: but he cannot assemble them to go with him to the
> market, or elsewhere for his safeguard against violence: and the reason of all
> this is, because *domus sua cuique est tutissimum refugium.* ["To everyone his house
> is his surest refuge."]

Semayne's Case, 77 Eng. Rep. 194, 195 (K.B. 1603). For more on these cases, and
their antecedents back to 1330, see David I. Caplan & Sue Wimmershoff-Caplan,
*Postmodernism and the Model Penal Code v. The Fourth, Fifth, and Fourteenth
Amendments — and the Castle Privacy Doctrine in the Twenty-First Century*, 73
UMKC L. Rev. 1073 (2005).

The castle doctrine would become a philosophical cornerstone of the
American right to privacy and the right to freedom from searches without
probable cause. *See* Samuel D. Warren & Louis D. Brandeis, *The Right to Privacy*,
4 Harv. L. Rev. 193, 220 (1890) ("The common law has always recognized a
man's house as his castle, impregnable. . . .").

The arguments of Boston lawyer James Otis in 1761 against the Writs of Assistance (searches by British customs officials with neither probable cause nor a particularized warrant) are widely considered the foundation of the American Fourth Amendment, which protects "the right of the people to be secure in their persons, houses, papers, and effects" from unreasonable and warrantless searches. Otis grounded his argument to the court on the castle doctrine: "Now one of the most essential branches of English liberty is the freedom of one's house. A man's house is his castle; and whilst he is quiet, he is as well guarded as a prince in his castle. This writ, if it should be declared legal, would totally annihilate this privilege." Charles Francis Adams, 2 The Works of John Adams 524 (1856) (John Adams's notes recording Otis's speech), *see also* William Cuddihy & B. Carmon Hardy, *A Man's House Was Not His Castle: Origins of the Fourth Amendment to the United States Constitution*, 37 Wm. & Mary Q. 3d 371 (1980).

NOTES & QUESTIONS

1. CQ: The castle doctrine cases and the saying "a man's house is his castle," were cited in the U.S. Supreme Court decision holding that, absent special circumstances, a person may not be arrested in his home without a warrant. *Payton v. New York*, 445 U.S. 573 (1980). The Court observed that "in the Colonies 'the freedom of one's house' was one of the most vital elements of English liberty." Does this special solicitude for the home still make sense today? Consider this point when you read the *Heller* decision (Chapter 9). Does *Heller* continue the tradition of the castle doctrine cases by upholding the right to own, carry, and use guns for self-defense in the home?

2. It has been argued that the Second, Third, and Fourth Amendments all have roots in the castle doctrine, as a cluster of home security protections. Caplan & Caplan, *supra*, at 1075; David I. Caplan, *The Right to Have Arms and Use Deadly Force Under the Second and Third Amendments*, 2 J. Firearms & Pub. Pol'y 165 (1989) (arguing that the Third Amendment protected the home against the oppression of housing enlisted soldiers drawn from the dregs of society; men who enlisted as an alternative to prison or execution). The Fourth Amendment guards the home against irregular intrusions, or intrusions not supported by probable cause. The Second Amendment ensures that citizens will have the practical means to stop (and deter) home invasions. Is it fair to understand the Second, Third, and Fourth Amendments as collectively creating a zone of safety and protection in the home? Do any other constitutional provisions protect the home?

3. *Semayne's Case* appears in case reports by Sir Edward Coke, the Attorney General of England who was much admired as a defender of civil liberty under law, and as an opponent of monarchical absolutism. Regarding the court's statements about killings outside the home, a footnote added by a modern annotator in the 1907 edition states: "This position is taken down much too broadly, there are many cases in which the killing another *se defendendo* [in self-defense] or *per infortunium* [an accidental killing while performing a lawful act], will not be considered by the law to be a felony,

and it is doubted by Foster, J., whether in case of homicide *per infortunium* or *se defendendo*, a forfeiture of all the party's chattels was ever incurred." 2 Coke Rep. at 574 (1907). In *Institutes of the Laws of England*, a major legal treatise, Coke wrote that "one is allowed to repel force with force" and "the laws permit the taking up of arms against armed persons." 1 Edward Coke, Institutes of the Laws of England 162a (Johnson & Warner eds., 1812). Legal historians continue to argue about the scope of lawful self-defense outside the home in England during the medieval period and the sixteenth century. Does it make sense for the law to create separate rules for self-defense inside the home versus in public places? What about in one's yard or driveway?

4. Over the last quarter-century, the National Rifle Association (NRA) has been successful in promoting the passage of "castle doctrine" laws in many states. Although the laws vary from state to state, the general approach is to eliminate a duty to retreat from an attacker, and to allow the use of deadly force in self-defense against violent felony attacks even when lesser force might suffice. Some states apply the castle doctrine to any place where the defender has a legal right to be. Some apply the doctrine only in the home. Others add one's automobile or one's own business premises as special places where the doctrine applies. One justification for the castle doctrine is that it prevents overzealous prosecutors from bringing criminal cases against legitimate defenders. Is this a sufficient reason? Why do you think the NRA picked "castle doctrine" as its name for expanded self-defense rights, even outside the home?

d. Hue and Cry, the Militia, the Glorious Revolution, and the Declaration of Right[15]

Under English law originating long before the Norman Conquest of 1066, all able-bodied men from the age of 16 to 60 were obliged to join in the *hutesium et clamor* (hue and cry) to pursue fleeing criminals. Death being the usual judicial punishment for felons, pursuing citizens were allowed to use deadly force if necessary to prevent escape. For details about the hue and cry, see Frederick Pollock & Frederic W. Maitland, 2 The History of English Law Before the Time of Edward I 575-81 (1895) (and also elsewhere in this treatise); 4 Blackstone *290-91 (describing hue and cry system as still in effect); Statute of Winchester, 13 Edward I, chs. 4-6 (1285) (formalizing hue and cry system; requiring all men aged 15 to 60 to possess arms and armor according to their wealth; lowest category, having "less than Twenty Marks in Goods," must have swords, knives, bows, and other small arms).

Able-bodied males 16 to 60 were likewise required to participate in the militia. The men-at-arms were freeholders, craftsmen, or other middle-class citizens, under the command of upper-class men of the community. The highest

---

15. This section is adapted from David B. Kopel, Gun Control in Great Britain (1992) and David B. Kopel, The Samurai, the Mountie, and the Cowboy: Should America Adopt the Gun Controls of Other Democracies? (1992). For more background, see Joyce Lee Malcolm, To Keep and Bear Arms: The Origins of an Anglo-American Right (1994).

militia commanders were wealthy and well-born men of the county, appointed by the monarch, and known as Lords-Lieutenant. About once a year, all the militiamen in an area would have to assemble for a formal inspection, to make sure that they had the appropriate equipment as required by law. (See below for the statutes creating the requirements.) "To pass muster" was to pass this inspection. Muster days were welcome relief from agricultural drudgery, and after the inspection, there often would be a festive dinner. While the musters were mostly for equipment inspection, not training, starting in 1573 a subset of the militia, known as "trained bands," were provided with training. Militia musters and training were carried out by county officials. The militia could not be required to serve outside its own county, except in case of actual or threatened invasion. Lindsay Boynton, The Elizabethan Militia 1558-1638 (1967); Richard Burn, A Digest of the Militia Laws (Biblio Bazaar 2010) (1779).

The seventeenth century saw continual struggle between the king, the Parliament, and the rest of society over who should control the tools of violence in Great Britain. This crucial century was studied intensely by the creators of the American republic.

From the Royalist perspective, the King of England had the authority to raise and maintain a standing army of professional soldiers. If necessary, the king could command that soldiers be quartered in his subjects' houses, at his subjects' expense. The militia was also to be under the king's command.

The competing view was best articulated by James Harrington's 1656 treatise *The Commonwealth of Oceana.* Harrington, speaking for both radical libertarians and for country squires, expressed the conventional wisdom of the opponents of a standing army. Widely read even a century later, Harrington expressed what became the conventional wisdom of the Founders of the American republic: A free society rests upon the foundation of small farmers who own their own land. The virtuous yeoman farmer, bringing his own arms to duty in a popular militia, is the best security of a free state. Unlike a standing army, a militia would never tyrannize its native land. Indeed, a militia could overthrow a despot. And unlike hired mercenaries or professional soldiers, the militiaman had his own country to fight for, and was therefore the best defense of a free state against foreign invasion. Other influential pro-militia writings included Algernon Sidney, Discourses Concerning Government (1698); John Toland, The Militia Reformed (1698); Anonymous (probably John Toland, Walter Moyle, and John Trenchard), An Argument Showing that a Standing Army is inconsistent with a Free Government, and absolutely destructive to the Constitution of the English Monarchy (1697), and A Short History of Standing Armies (1698). For a more skeptical view of militias, see Andrew Fletcher, Discourse Concerning Militias (1697).

Parliament usually represented the views of the rural, landed aristocracy that opposed monarchical efforts to centralize state power in London. In the "country versus court" battle, many of the small landholders, tenant farmers, and artisans sided with the rural aristocracy opposed to central control from London. Although many viewed militia service as an annoyance, and did what they could to avoid it, there was a great fear of the king's standing army, since the army was often composed of the dregs of society and did as much to terrify and abuse British towns as to protect them.

In 1642, Parliament asserted the right to regulate the militia. "By God, not for an hour!" the king thundered back. King Charles I thought that "Kingly power is but a shadow," without command of the militia. He considered the militia question the "fittest subject for a King's Quarrel," and challenged the Parliament's alleged usurpation of the power of the sword.

A crisis of government ensued. In 1642, a Royalist army marched on London, but retreated without a shot when faced down by a 20,000-man militia loyal to Parliament. John Milton wrote the poem "When the Assault was Intended to the City" in tribute. Civil war began that year, with the militia issue as important as any other question.

After two decades of conflict and military rule, monarchy triumphed, and in 1660 the Restoration placed the English people once again under the authority of a king. Within weeks of taking power, King Charles II ordered gunsmiths to report all gun sales, and banned imports. By the Militia Act of 1662, a Parliament loyal to King Charles II confirmed the king's sole authority over the militia. The Act authorized the king's agents "to search for and seize all arms in the custody or possession of any person or persons who the said lieutenants or any two or more of their deputies shall judge dangerous to the peace of the kingdom." 14 Charles II, ch. 3 (1662).

For the most part, the militia disobeyed orders to suppress Dissenters (Protestants who did not submit to the Anglican Church). Many militiamen called out to intimidate the king's political opponents deserted at the first opportunity.

Under Charles II, Parliament initiated the strictest gun control program England had ever known. The 1671 Game Act forbade 95 percent of the population (those not owning lands worth at least 100 pounds in annual rentals) from hunting, and barred non-hunters from owning guns or bows. The law further authorized day-time searches of any home suspected of holding an illegal gun. 22 & 23 Charles II, ch. 25 (1671).

Some in Parliament wrestled with the king for control of the militia. They argued that in contrast to the standing army, the militia could secure a free state. As Sir Henry Capel put it: "Our security is the militia: that will defend us and never conquer us." 2 Grey's Debates of the House of Commons 218 (1769) (debates of Nov. 3, 1673).

Despite the severe laws, as the Catholic convert King James II observed in 1686, "a great many persons not qualified by law" kept weapons in their homes. The new king commanded "strict search to be made for such muskets or guns and to seize and safely keep them till further order." 2 Calendar of State Papers (Domestic), James II, no. 1212, at 316 (Dec. 6, 1686). The king attempted to build up his standing army, with Catholic officers in charge. By neglecting the militia, he hoped it would wither as a threat to his power.

In the Glorious Revolution of 1688-89, James II was driven out of the country by the professional army raised in the Netherlands under the command of the Protestant William of Orange. James's army deserted at the first opportunity, and not a single life was lost. William and his English wife Mary then established a system of limited monarchy, operating under an informal constitution. In response to the abuses of absolute monarchs, Parliament enacted the 1689 Declaration of Right. The first part of the statute listed the abuses of James II and his father Charles II:

> 5. By raising and keeping a standing army within this kingdom in time of peace, without the consent of parliament, and quartering soldiers contrary to law.

6. By causing several good subjects, being protestants, to be disarmed at the same time when papists were both armed and employed contrary to law.

The second part of the Declaration created positive laws to preserve what Parliament said were ancient rights:

> And thereupon the said Lords Spiritual and Temporal and Commons . . . do in the first place (as their ancestors in like case have usually done) for the vindicating and asserting their ancient rights and liberties declare: . . .
>
> 6. That the raising or keeping a standing army within the kingdom in time of peace, unless it be with consent of parliament, is against the law.
> 7. The subjects which are protestants may have arms for their defence suitable to their conditions as and allowed by law.

1 Wm. & Mary, sess. 2, ch. 2 (1689).

The Declaration of Right excluded Catholics because they were considered potentially disloyal and dangerous, especially in light of the frequent efforts of the Pope and of the Catholic monarchs in France and Spain to overthrow the English kings and replace them with a Catholic. However, a separate statute allowed a Catholic to keep firearms with permission from a local justice of the peace "for the defence of his House or person." 1 Wm. & Mary, ch. 15 (1689). The militia in Great Britain was of little importance in the early eighteenth century, but was reinvigorated in 1757, during the Seven Years War with France. J.R. Western, The English Militia in the Eighteenth Century (1965).

For more on the seventeenth-century conflict, see Joyce Lee Malcolm, To Keep and Bear Arms: The Origins of an Anglo-American Right (1994); Lois G. Schwoerer, "No Standing Armies!" The Antiarmy Ideology in Seventeenth-Century England (1974).

e. Blackstone

William Blackstone's *Commentaries* is perhaps the most influential legal treatise ever written in English. It carries enormous authority in every nation that has adopted the common law. In detailing common law protection of human rights, Blackstone first set forth the three primary rights: personal security, personal liberty, and private property. William Blackstone, 1 Commentaries *142. Blackstone then turned to the auxiliary rights—such as the right to petition the government for redress of grievances—that protect the primary rights:

> The fifth and last auxiliary right of the subject, that I shall at present mention, is that of having arms for their defence suitable to their condition and degree, and such as are allowed by law. Which is also declared by the same statute 1 W. and M. st. 2 c. 2 and it is indeed a public allowance under due restrictions, of the natural right of resistance and self preservation, when the sanctions of society and laws are found insufficient to restrain the violence of oppression.

Id. at *143.

Much later in the four-volume treatise, Blackstone reiterated his point about armed resistance: "[I]n cases of national oppression, the nation has very justifiably risen as one man, to vindicate the original contract subsisting between the king and his people." 4 William Blackstone, Commentaries *82.

He affirmed the lawfulness of self-defense against criminals:

> ... HOMICIDES, committed for the advancement of public justice, are; ... 2. If an officer, or any private person, attempts to take a man charged with felony, and is resisted; and, in the endeavour to take him, kills him. .... 3. IN the next place, such homicide, as is committed for the prevention of any forcible and atrocious crime, is justifiable by the law of nature; and also by the law of England, as it stood so early as the time of Bracton,[16] and as it is since declared by statute 24 Hen. VIII. c. 5. ... This reaches not to any crime unaccompanied with force, as picking of pockets, or to the breaking open of any house in the day time, unless it carries with it an attempt of robbery also. So the Jewish law, which punished no theft with death, makes homicide only justifiable, in cafe of nocturnal house-breaking: "if a thief be found breaking up, and he be smitten that he die, no blood shall be shed for him: but if the fun be risen upon him, there shall blood be shed for him; for he should have made full restitution." At Athens, if any theft was committed by night, it was lawful to kill the criminal, if taken in the fact: and, by the Roman law of the twelve tables, a thief might be slain by night with impunity; or even by day, if he armed himself with any dangerous weapon: which amounts very nearly to the fame as is permitted by our own constitutions.
>
> THE Roman law also justifies homicide, when committed in defence of the chastity either of oneself or relations: and so also, according to Selden,[17] stood the law in the Jewish republic. The English law likewise justifies a woman, killing one who attempts to ravish her: and so too the husband or father may justify killing a man, who attempts a rape upon his wife or daughter; but not if he takes them in adultery by consent, for the one is forcible and felonious, but not the other. And I make no doubt but the forcibly attempting a crime, of a still more detestable nature, may be equally resisted by the death of the unnatural aggressor. For the one uniform principle that runs through our own, and all other laws, seems to be this: that where a crime, in itself capital, is endeavoured to be committed by force, it is lawful to repel that force by the death of the party attempting. But we must not carry this doctrine to the same visionary length that Mr. Locke does; who holds "that all manner of force without right upon a man's person," puts him in a "state of war with the aggressor;" and, of consequence, that, "being in such a state of war, he may lawfully kill him" that conclusion may be in a state of uncivilized nature, yet the law of England, like that of every other well-regulated community, is too tender of the public peace, too careful of the lives of the subjects, to adopt so contentious a system; nor will suffer with impunity any crime to be prevented by death, unless the fame, if committed, would also be punished by death.
>
> IN these instances of justifiable homicide, you will observe that the slayer is in no kind of fault whatsoever, not even in the minutest degree; and is therefore to be totally acquitted and discharged, with commendation rather than blame.

Id. *179-82.

---

16. Henry de Bracton (ca. 1210-68), author of De Legibus et Consuetudinibus Angliae (On the Laws and Customs of England).

17. John Selden (1584-1654), scholar of ancient English and Jewish law.

Blackstone warned against standing armies:

In a land of liberty, it is extremely dangerous to make a distinct order of the profession of arms. . . . Nothing then . . . ought to be more guarded against in a free state than making the military power . . . a body too distinct from the people.

1 Blackstone, *supra*, *408, 414. Blackstone also noted that game laws sometimes had ulterior motives: "for prevention of popular insurrection and resistance to the government, by disarming the bulk of the people . . . [a] reason often meant rather than allowed by the makers of forest and game laws." *Id.* at *412.

NOTES & QUESTIONS

1. CQ: As detailed in Chapter 8, in the United States, the Gun Control Act of 1968 (GCA) approximated some aspects of Charles II's gun control laws. Charles II banned all gun imports, while the GCA prohibited the import of inexpensive firearms (mainly, surplus European army rifles from WWII, and inexpensive handguns), which were competing with the products of American manufacturers. The GCA did not require the reporting of all gun sales, but it did require dealers to keep detailed sales records subject to government inspection. Some American states track the laws of Charles II more closely by requiring comprehensive reporting to the government of all firearms sales.

2. CQ: As part of the modern debate about the Second Amendment, there is vigorous argument about the meaning of the Declaration of Right's clause 7, guaranteeing "protestants . . . arms for their defence." Some, including historian Joyce Malcolm, and Justice Scalia in *Heller* (Chapter 9), see the English clause as a progenitor of the Second Amendment, guaranteeing a personal right to arms for self-defense. Justice Stevens, on the other hand, dismissed the British Declaration as not useful in interpreting the Second Amendment. Still others, including Justice Breyer, dissenting in *McDonald v. Chicago*, 130 S. Ct. 3020 (2010) (Chapter 9), argue that the clause means that a militia is to be preferred to a standing army. Based on the text and context of the Declaration of Right, which interpretation do you find persuasive? What interpretation does Blackstone support? For more, see Joyce Lee Malcolm, To Keep and Bear Arms: The Origins of an Anglo-American Right (1994) (right was for personal defense); Patrick J. Charles, *The Right of Self-Preservation and Resistance: A True Legal and Historical Understanding of the Anglo-American Right to Arms*, 2010 Cardozo L. Rev. De Novo 18 (2010) (the right was for Parliament to arm the militia).

3. Contrary to what the Declaration of Right preamble claimed, a personal right to defensive arms was "ancient" in English law only inasmuch as it was a widespread cultural assumption. From the viewpoint of proponents of a new right, what are the advantages of declaring that the right is ancient or traditional? Can you think of parallels in American law?

4. James Madison's notes for his speech to Congress introducing the Bill of Rights explained that the proposals were to deal with the "omission of guards in favr. of rights & libertys." He wrote that his amendments "relate 1st. to private rights." A Bill of Rights was "useful — not essential." There was a "fallacy on both sides — especy as to English Decln. of Rts." First, the Declaration was a "mere act of parlt." In other words, because the Declaration of Right is merely a statute, it could be over-ridden, explicitly or implicitly, by any future Parliament. The Declaration would constrain the king, but did not restrain future Parliaments.

   Second, according to Madison, the English Declaration was too narrow; it omitted certain rights and protected others too narrowly. In particular, there was "no freedom of press — Conscience." There was no prohibition on "Gl. Warrants" and no protection for "Habs. corpus." Nor was there a guarantee of "jury in Civil Causes" or a ban on "criml. attainders." Lastly, the Declaration protected only "arms to Protestts." James Madison, Notes for Speech in Congress Supporting Amendments, June 8, 1789, *in* The Origin of the Second Amendment 645 (David E. Young ed., 1991).

   Based on these concerns, can you tell if Madison viewed the English right as including a personal right of armed self-defense, or as an assertion of Parliamentary supremacy over the militia? How does the text of the Second Amendment address Madison's concerns about an overly restrictive definition of the right? How does the general structure of the Constitution address Madison's concerns about what future legislatures might do?

5. At least in France, the Norman cry of *haro*, used to call out citizens to pursue a thief, was applicable against magistrates who flagrantly abused their power or exceeded their jurisdiction; Norman jurists regarded such government criminals as *larrons* [robbers]). Kathleen A. Parrow, *From Defense to Resistance*, 83 Transactions of the American Philosophical Society 18 (pt. 6, 1993) (citing Hippolyte Pissard, Le Clamer de Haro dans le Droit Normand 118-19 (1911). This is reminiscent of views quoted earlier in this chapter (by Cicero, Augustine, Manegold, John of Salisbury, and others) that unjust government is a large-scale form of organized crime. To what extent, if any, can institutions like the hue and cry, the militia, or a personal right to arms provide deterrence or redress from such crime?

6. Theodore Schroeder was leader of the Free Speech League, the first group in American history to defend the rights of all speakers on all subjects based on the principles of the First Amendment. Schroeder's 1916 book *Free Speech for Radicals* used the Glorious Revolution of 1688 to argue for protection of speech urging the overthrow of the government:

   > If we are to erect this complaint against disarming part of the people into a general principle, it must be that in order to maintain freedom we must keep alive both the spirit and the means of resistance to government whenever "government is in rebellion against the people," that being a phrase of the time. This of course included the right to advocate the timeliness and right of resistance.

The reformers of that period were more or less consciously aiming toward the destruction of government from over the people in favor of government from out of the people, or as Lincoln put it, "government of, for and by the people." Those who saw this clearest were working towards the democratization of the army by abolishing standing armies and replacing them by an armed populace defending themselves, not being defended and repressed by those in whose name the defence is made.

Upon these precedents, others like them, and upon general principles reformers like DeLolme and John Cartwright[18] made it plain that the right to resist government was one protected by the English Constitution.

Theodore Schroeder, Free Speech for Radicals 105-06 (1916). Is Schroeder correct that the Declaration of Right implicitly recognizes a right of the people to take up arms against a government that is "in rebellion against the people"? Is the argument stronger when coupled with Blackstone's interpretation of the right to arms? How can Schroeder's views be reconciled with the fact that *after* the Declaration of Right, England still had laws against sedition, and that Blackstone wrote about such laws with apparent approval?

7. In 1780, after a spate of rioting, the Recorder of London — the city attorney — was asked if the right to arms protected armed groups, such as those which had helped suppress the riots. He wrote:

The right of his majesty's Protestant subjects, to have arms for their own defense, and to use them for lawful purposes, is most clear and undeniable. It seems, indeed, to be considered, by the ancient laws of this kingdom, not only as a *right*, but as a *duty*; for all the subjects of the realm, who are able to bear arms, are bound to be ready, at all times, to assist the sheriff, and other civil magistrates, in the execution of the laws and the preservation of the public peace. And that right, which every Protestant most unquestionably possesses, *individually*, may, and in many cases *must*, be exercised collectively, is likewise a point which I conceive to be most clearly established by the authority of judicial decisions and ancient acts of parliament, as well as by reason and common sense.

Quoted in William Blizard, Desultory Reflections on Police: With an Essay on the Means of Preventing Crime and Amending Criminals 59-60 (1785). In the view of the Recorder of London, who possesses the right to arms? For what purposes does the right exist?

---

18. [British aristocrat John Cartwright was an early supporter of the American Revolution, and an advocate of radical reform in Great Britain, including a Parliament elected by universal suffrage. The Swiss Jean Louis de Lolme, while living in England, authored The Constitution of England, in 1775. De Lolme praised the right of Englishmen to be "provided with arms for their own defence," and noted that violent resistance to tyranny "gave birth to the Great Charter." While "resistance is . . . the ultimate and lawful resource against the violences of power," an armed citizenry would rarely need to resist, for "[t]he power of the people is not when they strike, but when they keep in awe: it is when they can overthrow every thing, that they never need to move." J.L. de Lolme, The Constitution of England 219 (John MacGregor ed., J. Cuthell 1853) (1775). — Eds.]

f. John Locke

The English philosopher John Locke (1632-1704) is known as the "Father of Liberalism." Some historians consider him the preeminent political philosopher for the American Revolution, while others rank him as one of several leading influences.

John Locke, Second Treatise of Government
1690

§16 The *State of War* is a State and Enmity and Destruction; And therefore declaring by Word or Action . . . a sedate setled Design, upon another Mans Life, *puts him in a State of War* with him against whom he has declared such an Intention, and so has exposed his Life to the others Power to be taken away by him, or any one that joyns with him in his Defence, and espouses his Quarrel: it being reasonable and just I should have a Right to destroy that which threatens me with Destruction. For *by the Fundamental Law of Nature* . . . one may destroy a Man who makes War upon him . . . for the same Reason, that he may kill a *Wolf* or a *Lyon*; because such Men are not under the ties of the Common Law of Reason, have no other Rule, but that of Force and Violence, and so may be treated as Beasts of Prey . . . .

§17 And hence it is, that he who attempts to get another Man into his Absolute Power, does thereby *put himself into a State of War* with him; It being . . . a Declaration of a Design upon his Life. For . . . he who would get me into his Power without my consent, would use me as he pleased, when he had got me there, and destroy me to when he had fancy to it: for no body can desire to *have me in his Absolute Power*, unless it be to compel me by force to that which is against the Right of my Freedom, *i.e.,* make me a Slave. To be free from such force is the only security of my Preservation. . . . He that in the State of Nature, *would take away the Freedom,* that belongs to any one in that State must necessarily be supposed to have a design to take away every thing else, that *Freedom* being the Foundation of all the rest: As he that in the State of Society would take away the *Freedom* belonging to those of that Society or Common-wealth, must be supposed to design to take away from them every thing else, and so to be looked on as *in a State of War.*

§18 This makes it Lawful for a Man to *kill a Thief,* who has not in the least hurt him, nor declared any design upon his Life, any farther then by the use of Force, so to get him in his Power, as to take away his Money, or what he pleases from him: because using force, where he has no Right, to get me in his Power, let his pretence be what it will, I have no reason to suppose, that he, who would *take away my Liberty,* would not when he had me in his Power, take away everything else. And therefore it is Lawful for me to treat him, as one who has put *himself into a State of War* with me, *i.e.* kill him if I can; for to that hazard does he justly expose himself, whoever introduces a State of War, and is *aggressor* in it. . . .

§23 . . . For a Man, not having the Power of his own Life [because life is a gift in trust from God], *cannot,* by Compact, or his own Consent, *enslave* himself to any one, nor put himself under the Absolute, Arbitrary Power of another, to take away his Life, when he pleases. . . .

§220 To tell *people* they *may provide for themselves*, by erecting a new Legislature, when by Oppression, Artifice, or being delivered over to a Foreign Power, their old one is gone, is only to tell them they may expect Relief, when it is too late, and the evil is past Cure. This is in effect no more than to bid them first to be Slaves, and then to take care of their Liberty; and when their Chains are on, tell them, they may act like Freemen. . . . Men can never be secure from Tyranny, if there be no means to escape it, till they are perfectly under it: And therefore it is, that they have not only a Right to get out of it, but to prevent it. . . .

§228 . . . If the innocent honest Man must quietly quit all he has for Peace sake, to him who will lay violent hands upon it, I desire it may be consider'd, what a kind of Peace there will be in the World, which consists only in Violence and Rapine; and which is to be maintain'd only for the benefit of the Robbers and Oppressors. Who would not think it an admirable Peace betwixt the Mighty and the Mean, when the Lamb, without resistance, yielded his Throat to be torn by the imperious Wolf?

g. *Novanglus*

In "Novanglus," a series of 1775 newspaper essays, John Adams set forth the most sophisticated legal and philosophical arguments for the colonists' right of resistance. In essay number six, Adams cited the preeminent international law theorist Hugo Grotius for the point that it was not seditious to resist a ruler who was assuming powers that had never been granted:

> The same course is justly used against a legal magistrate who takes upon him to exercise a power which the law does not give; for in that respect he is a private man, — "*Quia*," as Grotius says, "*eatenus non habet imperium*," [Because he does not have the authority to that extent.] — and may be restrained as well as any other; because he is not set up to do what he lists, but what the law appoints for the good of the people; and as he has no other power than what the law allows, so the same law limits and directs the exercise of that which he has.

John Adams, *Novanglus*, essay 6, *in* Charles Francis Adams, 4 The Works of John Adams 82 (1856) (internal quotation marks omitted).

Adams quoted verbatim a massive footnote by Jean de Barbeyrac, author of an extensively annotated edition of Samuel von Pufendorf's treatise (discussed in online Chapter 13) on international law and political philosophy. In the footnote, Barbeyrac wove together Grotius (the primary founder of classical international law, and a preeminent political philosopher), Samuel von Pufendorf (the first professor of international law, and author of a treatise that was second only to Grotius), Jean LeClerc (a liberal Swiss Protestant philosopher and theologian), John Locke, and Algernon Sidney. Barbeyrac, with Adams in agreement, had argued that revolution against tyranny was a means to restore civil society, that resistance was justified before the tyranny become omnipotent, and that armed resistance would not lead to mob rule. The Barbeyrac quote is a proper end for this chapter, for it synthesizes some of the key European sources on which Americans relied to justify their armed revolt against the British Empire.

John Adams, Novanglus
4 The Works of John Adams 82-84 (Charles Francis Adams ed., 1856)

When we speak of a tyrant that may lawfully be dethroned by the people, we do not mean by the word *people,* the vile populace or rabble of the country, nor the cabal of a small number of factious persons, but the greater and more judicious part of the subjects, of all ranks. Besides, the tyranny must be so notorious, and evidently clear, as to leave nobody any room to doubt of it, & c. Now, a prince may easily avoid making himself so universally suspected and odious to his subjects; for, as Mr. Locke says in his Treatise of Civil Government, c. 18, §209, — "It is as impossible for a governor, if he really means the good of the people, and the preservation of them and the laws together, not to make them see and feel it, as it is for the father of a family not to let his children see he loves and takes care of them." And therefore the general insurrection of a whole nation does not deserve the name of a rebellion. We may see what Mr. Sidney says upon this subject in his Discourse concerning Government: — "Neither are subjects bound to stay till the prince has entirely finished the chains which he is preparing for them, and put it out of their power to oppose. It is sufficient that all the advances which he makes are manifestly tending to their oppression, that he is marching boldly on to the ruin of the State." In such a case, says Mr. Locke, admirably well, — "How can a man any more hinder himself from believing, in his own mind, which way things are going, or from casting about to save himself, than he could from believing the captain of the ship he was in was carrying him and the rest of his company to Algiers, when he found him always steering that course, though cross winds, leaks in his ship, and want of men and provisions, did often force him to turn his course another way for some time, which he steadily returned to again, as soon as the winds, weather, and other circumstances would let him?" This chiefly takes place with respect to kings, whose power is limited by fundamental laws.

If it is objected that the people, being ignorant and always discontented, to lay the foundation of government in the unsteady opinion and the uncertain humor of the people, is to expose it to certain ruin; the same author will answer you, that "on the contrary, people are not so easily got out of their old forms as some are apt to suggest. England, for instance, notwithstanding the many revolutions that have been seen in that kingdom, has always kept to its old legislative of king, lords, and commons; and whatever provocations have made the crown to be taken from some of their princes' heads, they never carried the people so far as to place it in another line." But it will be said, this hypothesis lays a ferment for frequent rebellion. "No more," says Mr. Locke, "than any other hypothesis. For when the people are made miserable, and find themselves exposed to the ill usage of arbitrary power, cry up their governors as you will for sons of Jupiter; let them be sacred and divine, descended or authorized from heaven; give them out for whom or what you please, the same will happen. The people generally ill treated, and contrary to right, will be ready upon any occasion to ease themselves of a burden that sits heavy upon them. 2. Such revolutions happen not upon every little mismanagement in public affairs. Great mistakes in the ruling part, many wrong and inconvenient laws, and all the slips of human frailty will be borne by the people without mutiny and murmur. 3. This power in the people of providing for their safety anew by a legislative, when their legislators have acted contrary to their trust by invading their property, is the best fence against rebellion, and the probablest means to hinder it; for rebellion being an opposition, not to persons, but authority, which is founded only in the constitutions and laws of the government; those, whoever they be, *who by force break through, and by force justify the violation of them, are truly and properly rebels.* For when men, by entering into society and civil government, have excluded force, and introduced laws for the preservation of property, peace, and unity, among themselves; those who set up force again, in opposition to the laws, do *rebellare,* that is, do bring back again the state of war, and are properly, rebels," as the author shows. In the last place, he demonstrates that there are also greater inconveniences in allowing all to those that govern, than in granting something to the people. But it will be said, that ill affected and factious men may spread among the people, and make them believe that the prince or legislative act contrary to their trust, when they only make use of their due prerogative. To this Mr. Locke answers, that the people, however, is to judge of all that; because nobody can better judge whether his trustee or deputy acts well, and according to the trust reposed in him, than he who deputed him. "He might make the like query," (says Mr. Le Clerc, from whom this extract is taken) "and ask, whether the people being oppressed by an authority which they set up, but for their own good, it is just that those who are vested with this authority, and of which they are complaining, should themselves be judges of the complaints made against them." The greatest flatterers of kings dare not say, that the people are obliged to suffer absolutely all their humors, how irregular soever they be; and therefore must confess, that when no regard is had to their complaints, the very foundations of society are destroyed; the prince and people are in a state of war with each other, like two independent states, that are doing themselves justice, and acknowledge no person upon earth, who, in a sovereign manner, can determine the disputes between them.

NOTES & QUESTIONS

1. CQ: As noted above, Thomas Jefferson described the Declaration of Independence as a synthesis of widely shared beliefs based on Aristotle, Cicero, Sidney, and Locke. Can you identify passages in the Declaration similar to the Locke excerpt?

2. If you were writing a constitution and you agreed with the views expressed above by Locke, what type of provisions would you include?

3. Timothy McVeigh was a neo-Nazi who perpetrated the worst act of domestic terrorism in American history, blowing up the Alfred Murrah federal building in Oklahoma City in 1995, murdering 168 people. McVeigh was captured while fleeing in his automobile. In the car was Locke's Second Treatise on Government. McVeigh was wearing a t-shirt with the words *sic semper tyrannis* ("thus always to tyrants"). This is the state motto of Virginia, whose state flag portrays personified Liberty holding a spear and standing with one foot on the chest of a dead king whom she has just slain. The phrase was attributed to Brutus when he killed Julius Caesar, and it was uttered by

John Wilkes Booth when he murdered Abraham Lincoln. There was a picture of Lincoln on McVeigh's t-shirt. Are crimes like McVeigh's and Booth's predictable outgrowths of a society allowing access to tools of violence and the publication of books like Locke's, or of works praising the assassination of Caesar?

4. Locke's theory of resistance to tyranny is an extrapolation from the right of self-defense. But is Locke's premise correct? Herbert Wechsler, one of the most influential criminal law scholars of the twentieth century, wrote that laws regarding self-defense reflect the "universal judgment that there is no social interest in preserving the lives of the aggressors at the cost of those of their victims." Herbert Wechsler & Jerome Michael, *A Rationale of the Law of Homicide*, 37 Colum. L. Rev. 701, 736 (1937). Is such a judgment really universal today? Was it ever? Personal self-defense is part of the law of every legal system in the world today. Schlomit Wallerstein, *Justifying the Right to Self-Defense: A Theory of Forced Consequences*, 91 Va. L. Rev. 999, 999 (2005) ("the right to self-defense is recognized in all jurisdictions"). The scope of the right, however, varies from nation to nation.

5. Locke's theories incorporated arguments by Thomas Hobbes, who wrote that people create governments to free themselves from a state of nature in which life is "nasty, brutish, and short" because there exists constant competition that leads to a constant "condition of warre." Thomas Hobbes, Leviathan 84-85 (A.R. Waller ed., Cambridge Univ. Press 1904) (1651). In Hobbes's view, individuals covenant to cede all natural rights (including the ability to do whatever one wanted in the state of nature) to the government, including the right to change their government, no matter how bad it is. *Id.* at 120. However, Hobbes made an exception, noting that "[a] Covenant not to defend my selfe from force, by force, is always voyd. . . . For man by nature chooseth the . . . danger of death in resisting . . . than . . . certain and present death in not resisting." *Id.* at 94-95. A right that can be surrendered or delegated to the government is an "alienable" right. CQ: The Declaration of Independence affirms that certain rights are "inalienable," and thus could never have been surrendered to Parliament or the king. Do you agree with Hobbes that self-defense is inalienable? If so, what are the legal implications?

‖3‖

The Colonies and the Revolution

This chapter discusses American firearms possession and regulation in the Colonial and Revolutionary Era. Section A discusses the early colonial period; Section B the pre-Revolutionary period; Section C the British gun-control program that provoked armed resistance; Section D the Revolution; Section E the Articles of Confederation; and Section F the new state constitutions and state statutes.

A. Firearms Control in the Colonies

This section presents the arms-control laws of the 13 American colonies. The typical law required the ownership of arms, and sometimes required carrying of arms, or the training of dependents in the use of arms. Providing guns to suspect groups — Indians, slaves, the politically disloyal, and sometimes, free Blacks — was often forbidden. A few states imposed safety laws against shooting firearms in crowded public places.

1. Early Arms Mandates

a. Colonial Statutes Mandating Arms Possession

The laws described in this subsection are presented in chronological order, based on the colony's first known arms mandate.

i. Massachusetts

The first successful settlement in the Massachusetts Bay Colony was established in 1628. On March 22, 1631, the Colony adopted a law mandating that all adult males be armed.[1] Nathaniel B. Shurtleff, 1 Records of the Governor and Company of the Massachusetts Bay in New England 84 (1853) [hereinafter 1 Shurtleff].

The arms mandate was not limited to the militia. A 1645 order declared that "all inhabitants" must "have armes in their howses fitt for service, with pouder, bullets, match, as other souldiers." Nathaniel B. Shurtleff, 3 Records of the Governor and Company of the Massachusetts Bay in New England 84 (1853) [hereinafter 3 Shurtleff].

The law also established "trained bands," who were an elite unit of the militia and trained more frequently than the general militia. The trained bands were required to have "ether full musket boare, or basterd musket at the least, & that none should be under three foote 9 inches." Nathaniel B. Shurtleff, 2 Records of the Governor and Company of the Massachusetts Bay in New England 134 (1853) (enacted 1645) [hereinafter 2 Shurtleff]; *id.* at 222 (enacted 1647).

In 1652, the colony ordered that all "Scotsmen, Negers, & Indians inhabiting with or servants to the English" who were between the ages of 16 and 60 participate in militia training. 3 Shurtleff, *supra*, at 268. But in 1656, the law was changed, so that "no Negroes or Indians . . . shal be armed or permitted to trayne." *Id.* at 397.

ii. Maryland

In 1639, Maryland required "that every housekeeper or housekeepers within this Province shall have ready continually upon all occasions within his her or their house for him or themselves and for every person within his her or their house able to bear armes[,] one Serviceable fixed gunne of bastard muskett boare" along with a pound of gunpowder, four pounds of pistol or musket shot, "match for matchlocks and of flints for firelocks." "An Act for Military Discipline" (enacted 1639) *in* 1 Archives of Maryland 77 (William Hand Browne ed., 1885) [hereinafter Archives of Maryland].

A 1642 revision declared, "That all housekeepers provide fixed gunn and Sufficient powder and Shott for each person able to bear arms." 3 Archives of Maryland at 103 (William Hand Browne ed., 1885). In 1658, the law was revised to specify minimum quantities: "[E]very househoulder provide himselfe speedily with Armes & Ammunition according to a former Act of Assembly viz 2 [pounds] of powder and 5 [pounds] of shott & one good Gun well fixed for every man able to bear Armes in his house." 3 Archives of Maryland, *supra*, at 345.

---

1. For dates in this chapter, readers should be aware that in the English-speaking countries, the calendar changed from "Old Style" (Julian) to "New Style" (Gregorian) in 1752. Under the Old Style, the New Year began on March 25 (the traditional date of the Annunciation to the Virgin Mary), not January 1. So the people of Massachusetts considered the above March 22 date to be 1630, not 1631. We have generally rendered dates in New Style, but researchers using Western European date citations between 1582 (when France adopted the New Style calendar) and 1752 should be aware that the days between January 1 and March 24 may be assigned to a different year, depending on the country. The shift can also move the calendar date as far forward as 11 days (e.g., July 1 Old Style can become July 12 New Style) because the New Style corrected the incorrect number of leap year days that had appeared in the Old Style calendar. (New Style omits leap years every 100 years, except for the 400th year. So, under New Style, there was no leap year day in 1800 or 1900, but there was one in 2000.)

The Maryland requirement that all householders have guns for themselves and for any man living in their house was supplemented by a statute that any person wishing to acquire title to Maryland land must bring "Armes and Ammunition as are intended & required by the Conditions above said to be provided & carried into the said Province of Maryland for every man betweene the ages of sixteene & fifty years w[hi]ch shalbe transported thether." The arms minimum was "one musket or bastard musket with a snaphance lock," ten pounds of gunpowder, forty pounds of "Lead, Bullets, Pistoll, and Goose shot." 3 Archives of Maryland, *supra,* at 100-01 (enacted 1641).

Maryland imposed additional arms mandates on militiamen. A 1715 statutory compilation includes a requirement that every militiaman "appear and bring with him one good serviceable Gun, fixed, with Six Charges of Powder." Militia cavalrymen were to "find themselves with Swords, Carbines, Pistols, Holsters and Ammunition." The Laws of the Province of Maryland 115 (Evan Jones 1718) [hereinafter *Maryland Laws*].

iii. Connecticut

A 1650 Connecticut law required "[t]hat all persons that are above the age of sixteene yeares, except magistrates and church officers, shall beare arms . . . ; and every male person within this jurisdiction, above the said age, shall have in continuall readines, a good muskitt or other gunn, fitt for service, and allowed by the clark of the band." Code of 1650, Being a Compilation of the Earliest Laws and Orders of the General Court of Connecticut 72-73 (Silas Andrus ed., 1822); J. Hammond Trumbull (vol. 1-3) & Charles J. Hoadly (vol. 4-15), 1 The Public Records of the Colony of Connecticut, Prior to the Union with New Haven Colony 542-43 (1850) (hereinafter *Public Records of Connecticut*).

iv. New York

In 1664, the Dutch colony of New Amsterdam surrendered when a fleet of English warships arrived in the harbor. England's King Charles II gave the new colony to his brother, the Duke of York, who renamed it "New York." The Duke promptly mandated: "Besides the Generall stock of each Town Every Male within this government from Sixteen to Sixty years of age, or not freed by public Allowance, shall if freeholders at their own, if sons or Servants at their Parents and Masters Charge and Cost, be furnished from time to time and so Continue well furnished with Arms and other Suitable Provition hereafter mentioned: under the penalty of five Shillings for the least default therein Namely a good Serviceable Gun, allowed Sufficient by his Military Officer to be kept in Constant fitness for present Service." 1 The Colonial Laws of New York from the Year 1664 to the Revolution 49-50 (1894).

v. Virginia

In 1684, Virginia required that all free Virginians must "provide and furnish themselves with a sword, musquet and other furniture fitt for a soldier . . .

two pounds of powder, and eight pounds of shott." William Waller Hening, 3 The Statutes at Large; Being a Collection of all the Laws of Virginia, from the First Session of the Legislature, in the Year 1619, at 13 (1823) (enacted 1684) [hereinafter 3 Hening]. A 1705 statute ordered every foot soldier to acquire "a firelock, muskett, or fusee well fixed." 3 Hening, *supra*, at 338. In 1748, all militiamen were required to have "arms and ammunition." William Waller Hening, 6 The Statutes at Large; Being a Collection of all the Laws of Virginia, from the First Session of the Legislature, in the Year 1619, at 116 (1823). Militiamen who did not have enough money to provide their own arms would be given arms "out of his majesty's magazine." *Id.* at 116-18. Cavalry officers had to buy themselves "holsters and pistols well fixed." *Id.* at 537 (enacted 1755).

vi. New Jersey

The arms mandate in New Jersey was narrower than in most other colonies. It only applied to militiamen. New Jersey enrolled all men aged 16 to 50 in the militia, exempting ministers, doctors, schoolmasters, legislators, slaves, and "Civil Officers of the Government." The law mandated that militiamen "shall be sufficiently armed with one good sufficient Musquet or Fusee well fixed, a Sword or [Bayonet], a Cartouch box or Powder-horn, a pound of Powder, and twelve sizeable Bullets, who shall appear in the Field, so armed, twice every year." The Laws and Acts of the General Assembly of Her Majesties Province of Nova Caesarea or New-Jersey 12-13 (1709) (enacted 1703).

vii. New Hampshire

New Hampshire required "That all Male Persons from Sixteen Years of Age to Sixty, (other than such as are herein after excepted) shall bear Arms . . . allowing Three Months time to every Son after his coming to Sixteen Years of Age, and every Servant so long, after his time is out, to provide themselves with Arms and Ammunition. . . . That every Listed Souldier and Housholder, (except Troopers) shall be always provided with a well fix'd, Firelock Musket, of Musket or Bastard-Musket bore, . . . or other good Fire-Arms, to the satisfaction of the Commission Officers of the Company . . . on penalty of *Six Shillings* for want of Such Arms, as is hereby required." Acts and Laws, Passed by the General Court or Assembly of the Province of New-Hampshire in New-England 91-92 (from a 1716 statutory compilation, perhaps enacted earlier).

viii. North Carolina

As early as 1715 and perhaps before, North Carolina enacted a militia statute, and then reenacted a similar statute in 1746. The first statute defined the militia as all freemen between 16 and 60. The militiamen were obligated to appear at militia musters "with a good Gun well-fixed Sword & at least Six

Charges of Powder & Ball" or pay a fine. The 1746 statute broadened the militia to include servants. Militiamen had to "be well provided with a Gun, fit for Service, ... and at least Twelve Charges of Powder and Ball, or Swan Shot, and Six spare Flints." *Laws of North Carolina–1715*, ch. 25, *in* 2 The Earliest Printed Laws of North Carolina, 1669-1751, at 29-31 (John D. Cushing ed., 1977).

The North Carolina militia did not exclude free Blacks. A Collection of all the Public Acts of Assembly, of the Province of North-Carolina: Now in Force and Use 215-16 (1751). Thus, "free Negroes served in the militia of North Carolina with no apparent discrimination against them." John Hope Franklin, The Free Negro in North Carolina, 1790-1860, at 101-02 (1995).

ix. Delaware

Delaware imposed a broad requirement "[t]hat every *Freeholder* and taxable Person residing in this Government (except such as are hereafter excepted) shall, on or before the First Day of March next, provide himself with the following Arms and Ammunition, viz. One well fixed Musket or Firelock, one Cartouch-Box, with Twelve Charges of Gun-Powder and Ball therein, and Three good Flints, to be approved of by the Commanding Officer of the respective Company to which he belongs, and shall be obliged to keep such Arms and Ammunition by him, during the Continuance of this Act." Laws of the Government of New-Castle, Kent and Sussex Upon Delaware 171 (1741) (enacted 1742; the "1741" on the title page apparently indicates the first of an annual series).

Delaware militiamen were a subclass of "Freeholder[s] and taxable Person[s]," all of whom were required to have arms. The militia comprised all males older than 18 and younger than 50. Exemptions from militia service were given to "all Justices of the Peace, Physicians, Lawyers, and Millers, and Persons incapable through Infirmities of Sickness or Lameness, shall be exempted and excused from appearing to muster, except in Case of an Alarm: They being nevertheless obliged, by this Act, to provide and keep by them Arms and Ammunition as aforesaid, as well as others. And if an Alarm happen, then all those, who by this Act are obliged to keep Arms as aforesaid ... shall join the General Militia." *Id.* at 176-77.

Quakers, who by this period were mostly but not entirely pacifists, did not have to own guns, serve in the militia, or perform the nightly watch duties required in some towns. To obtain the exemption, Quakers had to pay a fee of two shillings six pence each day that "others are obliged to attend the said Muster, Exercise, or Watch." *Id.* at 176. Ministers were exempt from all arms-related requirements, and were not required to pay a fee. *Id.* at 177.

x. Pennsylvania

Unlike her sister colonies, Pennsylvania did not create a militia during the colonial period, nor did it require the broader class of adult males or householders to own guns. The colony was founded by the Quaker William Penn, in settlement of the enormous debts that the Duke of York (the future King James II) owed Penn's father. ("Pennsylvania" means "Penn's woods.") Quakers had political control of the colony until 1755-56. Thereafter, there were intense political battles over the creation of a militia. *See, e.g.*, 1 Pennsylvania Archives, 4th series, 706-08; 2 Pennsylvania Archives, 4th series, 441, 548, 555. Some local governments did create militias, but it was not until 1776 that a statewide militia obligation was created under the new Pennsylvania Constitution. *See* Chapter 4.

b. *Colonial Statutes Mandating Arms-Carrying*

In addition to the requirement of possessing arms, about half the colonies had laws requiring arms-carrying in certain circumstances.

i. Virginia

The first American law to require gun-carrying was enacted in Virginia in 1619. It applied to those attending church on Sundays: "and all suche as beare armes shall bring their pieces, swords, pouder and shotte." "Proceedings of the Virginia Assembly, 1619," *in* Lyon Gardiner Tyler, Narratives of Early Virginia, 1606-25, at 273 (Barnes & Noble 1959) (1907). In 1632, the law was revised to require: "All men that are fittinge to beare arms, shall bring their pieces to the church." William Waller Hening, 1 The Statutes at Large; Being a Collection of all the Laws of Virginia, from the First Session of the Legislature, in the Year 1619, at 198 (1823).

A separate statute applied to travelers. "That no man go or send abroad without a sufficient parte will armed. . . . That go not to worke in the ground without their arms (and a centinell upon them.) . . . That the commander of every plantation take care that there be sufficient of powder and am[m]unition within the plantation under his command and their pieces fixt and their arms complete. *Id.* at 127, 198 (enacted 1623, and revised in 1632).

ii. Connecticut

Like Virginia, Connecticut mandated carrying of arms to church. The statute included language explaining the purpose of the mandate. "To prevent or withstand such sudden assaults as may be made by Indeans upon the Sabboth or lecture dayes, It is Ordered, that one person in every several howse wherein is any souldear or souldears, shall bring a musket, pystoll or some peece, with powder and shott to e[a]ch meeting." 1 *Public Records of Connecticut* 95-96 (enacted 1643).

The New Haven Colony, which was separate from Connecticut until 1662, enacted its own mandatory carry statute in 1644. Records of the Colony and Plantation of New Haven, From 1638 to 1649, at 131-32 (Charles J. Hoadly ed., 1857).

iii.   Massachusetts

In Massachusetts, a statute from 1637 required all persons over 18, except for magistrates and church elders, "come to the publike assemblies with their muskets, or other peeces fit for servise, furnished with match, powder, & bullets." 1 Shurtleff *supra*, at 190. The statute was repealed the next year. 2 Shurtleff, *supra*, at 38 (enacted 1637). But in 1643, the military officer of each town was ordered to "appoint what armes to bee brought to the meeting houses on the Lords dayes, & other times of meeting." Records of the Governor and Company of the Massachusetts Bay in New England: 1642-1649, at 38 (1853) 1 Shurtleff, *supra*, at 190.

Like Virginia, Massachusetts imposed obligations on travelers. Beginning in 1631, Massachusetts required those traveling to the adjacent Plymouth Colony not go "without some armes, though 2 or 3 togeathr." 1 Shurtleff, *supra*, at 85. The mandate was expanded in 1636 to require that "no person shall travel above one mile from his dwelling house, except in places wheare other houses are neare together, without some armes, upon paine of 12*d.* for every default."

iv.   Rhode Island

In 1639, Rhode Island directed that "noe man shall go two miles from the Towne unarmed, eyther with Gunn or Sword; and that none shall come to any public Meeting without his weapon." 1 Records of the Colony of Rhode Island and Providence Plantations, in New England 94 (John Russell Bartlett ed., 1856). Portsmouth, Rhode Island, has a law to similar effect. *Id.* at 79 (enacted 1643).

v.   Maryland

Maryland mandated arms for church meetings and travel, requiring that "Noe man able to bear arms to goe to church or Chappell . . . without fixed gunn and 1 Charge at least of powder and Shott." Further, "Noe man able to bear arms to goe . . . any considerable distance from home without fixed gunn and 1 Charge at least of powder and Shott." 3 *Archives of Maryland* 103, *supra*, at (enacted 1642).

vi.   South Carolina

Beginning in 1743, South Carolina imposed a fine on "every white male inhabitant of this Province, (except travelers and such persons as shall be above sixty years of age,) who [are] liable to bear arms in the militia of this Province . . . shall, on any Sunday or Christmas day in the year, go and resort to any church or any other public place of divine worship within this Province, and shall not carry with him a gun or a pair of horse-pistols . . . with at least six charges of gun-powder and ball, and shall not carry the same into the church or other place of divine worship as aforesaid." The law also ordered that church officials check each man entering the church, to ensure that he was carrying a gun. The stated motive of the law was "for the better security of this Province against the insurrections and other wicked attempts of Negroes and other Slaves." David J. McCord, 7 Statutes at Large of South Carolina 417-19 (1840).

vii. Georgia

Georgia had some of the same concerns as her northern neighbor. A 1770 Georgia law adopted the South Carolina model, imposing fines on those in the general militia who came to church unarmed. 19 (part 1) The Colonial Records of the State of Georgia 137-40 (Allen D. Candler ed., 1904) [hereinafter *Georgia Records*].

c. *Statutory Requirements for Arming Free Servants and Children*

The colonies generally required that when an indentured servant or apprentice finished his or her term of labor, the master provide some goods, known as "freedom dues," so that the person could begin independent life. Farley Grubb, *The Statutory Regulation of Colonial Servitude: An Incomplete-Contract Approach,* 37 Explorations in Econ. Hist. 69 (2000). Three colonies, Maryland, Virginia, and North Carolina, specifically required that when a servant had fulfilled his obligation, the former master must provide him with arms.

Some colonial statutes imposed a further obligation on heads of households to ensure that their servants and children were armed. As noted above, Maryland required householders to arm their adult male servants.

Maryland required masters to give discharged male servants, "One Gun of Twenty Shillings Price, not above Four Foot by the barrel, nor less than Three and a Half; which said Gun shall, by the Master or Mistress, in the Presence of the next Justice of the Peace, be delivered to such Free-man, under the Penalty of Five Hundred Pounds of Tobacco on such Master or Mistress omitting so to do. . . ." The law fined a former servant who sold his gun within the ensuring 12 months. 22 Archives of Maryland 548 (William Hand Browne ed., 1902) (enacted 1699); 26 Archives of Maryland 256 (William Hand Browne ed., 1906) (enacted 1704).

In North Carolina, the master could discharge his obligation by giving the freed servant three barrels of Indian corn and two suits of clothes, or one suit of clothes and "a good well-fixed Gun, if he be a Manservant." The Earliest Printed Laws of North Carolina, 1669-1751, at 63 (John D. Cushing ed., 1977) (enacted 1715). A 1741 statutory revised the "freedom dues," and ended the arms requirement. *Id.* at 165.

Virginia required, for males, various items, including "one well fixed musket or fuzee, of the value of twenty shillings, at least." 3 The Statutes at Large of Virginia 451 (1836).

The Massachusetts Bay Colony appears to have been the only colony with a formal program for training children, both boys and girls, in weapons use.

A 1645 law provided that "all youth within this jurisdiction, from ten yeares ould to the age of sixteen yeares, shalbe instructed, by some one of the officers of the band, or some other experienced souldier . . . upon the usuall training dayes, in the exercise of armes, as small guns, halfe pikes, bowes & arrows." 2 Shurtleff, *supra,* at 99 (enacted 1645).

NOTES & QUESTIONS

1. CQ: The discussion following the U.S. Supreme Court's decisions in *District of Columbia v. Heller,* 554 U.S. 570 (2008) (Chapter 9), and *McDonald v. Chicago,* 130 S. Ct. 3020 (2010) (Chapter 9), addresses the variety of methodologies judges have used to interpret the Constitution. One of those, originalism, was deployed to some degree by all of the opinions in *Heller* and *McDonald.* What, if any, impact do these early arms mandates have on your originalist assessment of the modern right to arms? Does the distinction between a command to possess arms and a right to possess arms diminish the significance of these laws? Later in this chapter, we will see a distinction between the duty to serve in the militia and a right to possess arms. See if your assessment of the command versus right distinction is the same in both contexts.

2. One commentator argued that the notion of a constitutional right to arms is a creature of the twentieth century, invented by the gun lobby; he claimed that before the Civil War, Americans never had very many guns nor a robust gun culture. Michael A. Belleslies, Arming America: The Origins of a National Gun Culture (2000). How would one square the early arms possession statutes with Bellesiles' argument?

    Bellisiles' book was eventually exposed as a fraud. The book was withdrawn and pulped by the publisher. Bellisiles resigned from Emory University in 2002, and a prize awarded for the book was rescinded. Nearly every page of the book contained errors and misstatements of fact. The quantitative core of the book was Bellesiles' claim that probate records proved that functional firearms were rarely mentioned in wills, and therefore must have been rare. However, examination of those records by other scholars revealed the opposite of what Bellesiles had claimed. In some cases, the records clearly had not been examined by Bellesiles. For example, he claimed to have examined nineteenth century San Francisco probate records that had burned during the Great San Francisco Earthquake of 1906. Likewise, he had made claims about the "wills" of people from Providence, Rhode Island, who died intestate.

    For scholarship addressing the Bellesiles controversy, see Clayton Cramer, Armed America: The Remarkable Story of How and Why Guns Became as American as Apple Pie (2009); Peter Charles Hoffer, Past Imperfect: Facts, Fictions, Fraud—American History from Bancroft and Parkman to Ambrose, Bellesiles, Ellis, and Goodwin (2007). Jon Wiener, Historians in Trouble: Plagiarism, Fraud and Politics in the Ivory Tower (2005) (arguing that the power of interested constituencies explains the different consequences following discoveries of academic fraud); Clayton E. Cramer, *Why Footnotes Matter: Checking Arming America's Claims,* 1 Plagiary 149 (2006); James Lindgren, *Fall from Grace: Arming America and the Bellesiles Scandal,* 111 Yale L.J. 2195 (2002) (at the time, the most-read law review ever, with over a hundred thousand downloads); James Lindgren & Justin L. Heather, *Counting Guns in Early America,* 43 Wm. & Mary L. Rev. 1777 (2002); 59 William & Mary Q. 3d ser. (Jan. 2002) (symposium of articles by Gloria L. Main, Randolph Roth, Ira D. Gruber, and Jack Rakove, the first three finding major problems with Bellesiles' scholarship, with Rakove defending Bellesiles).

3. Is there any plausible modern analogue to the early statutory obligation to carry guns to church? If not, is this early requirement in any way relevant to our modern understanding about the right to arms? CQ: In Chapters 9 and 11, we will see that the scope of the right to bear arms (a right to carry guns in public?) remains subject to debate.

4. As discussed in Chapter 8, current federal law prohibits minors from possessing handguns (with some exceptions). Some states also prohibit those under a certain age from possessing handguns or all guns, and some of these laws date to the early twentieth century. While affirming the individual right to keep and bear arms, the Supreme Court also has said that "long-standing" restrictions on access to firearms by minors are presumptively valid. *See Heller* (Chapter 9). Compare this treatment to the early firearms mandate to train children on the use of arms. Was *Heller* an originalist decision in this regard?

2. Early Firearms Regulation and Prohibition

a. *Safety Regulations*

Various colonial laws prohibited unsafe behavior with guns. Virginia banned shooting "any guns at drinkeing (marriages and funerals onely excepted)." The reason was that guns were fired to sound the alarm about Indian attacks, "of which no certainty can be had in respect of the frequent shooting of gunns in drinking. . . ." 1 Hening, *supra,* at 401-02 (enacted 1656). Preventing false alarms also seems to have been the motive for a Maryland law that, "No man to discharge 3 guns within the space of ¼ hour . . . except to give or answer alarm." 3 Archives of Maryland, *supra,* at 103 (enacted 1642). In 1713-14, the Massachusetts legislature determined that "by the indiscreet firing of guns laden with shot and ball within the town and harbour of Boston, the lives and limbs of many persons have been lost, and others have been in great danger, as well as other damage has been sustained." As a consequence, the legislature outlawed shooting any "gun or pistol" in Boston ("the islands thereto belonging excepted"). The Act expired by its own terms in three years, and had an exception of militia training under the supervision of an officer, and any other target shooting authorized by a militia, but there was no explicit exception for self-defense. 3 Acts and Resolves, Public and Private, of the Province of the Massachusetts Bay 305-06 (1878).

In Pennsylvania, colonial legislation, which remained after Independence, fined anyone who "shall fire any gun or other fire arms . . . within the city of Philadelphia." An Abridgment of the Laws of Pennsylvania, 1700-1811, at 173 (John Purdon ed., 1811). Likewise, it was illegal to "wantonly, and without reasonable occasion, discharge and fire off any hand-gun, pistol or other firearms" in inhabited areas on New Year's night. Violators were fined. *Id.* at 174.

Pennsylvania also punished anyone who "shall presume to carry any gun, or hunt" on the land of others without permission, or who "shall presume to fire a gun on or near any of the king's highways." *Id.* at 208.

b.   *Limits on Gun Sales to Indians*

As European settlement of America commenced, there were diverse views about whether to trade guns with the indigenous population. Dutch settlers in New Netherlands (now lower New York State) came from one of history's greatest trading empires. The Dutch in the Hudson River Valley bartered guns to the Mohawk tribes. In 1643, some of the Mohawk launched a two-year war against Dutch settlements, but spared the Hudson River Valley.

The Dutch attempted to license gun traders in 1650, with the aim of stopping the supply of guns to Indians. The West India Company, a giant mercantile trading concern, protested, arguing that Indians would pay a black market price so high that controls were impossible. In 1656, the government decreed that settlers themselves could possess only matchlock rifles. Modern flintlock rifles, which were more reliable, and easier and faster to fire, were banned. A death penalty for selling guns to the Indians was enacted, but gun trading with the Indians continued. Carl P. Russell, Guns on the Early Frontiers 10-13 (1957).

In 1648, the directors of the Dutch East India Company observed that the Indians were so determined to obtain firearms that they would go to war if the trade were cut off. Their solution was to ban private firearms trade with the Indians, but allow the Dutch East India Company to sell small quantities of guns directly to the Indians. Francis Jennings, The Ambiguous Iroquois Empire: The Covenant Chain Confederation of Indian Tribes with English Colonies 84 (1984).

Notwithstanding Dutch restrictions, natives had a ready supply of guns from the French. Based in Canada, the French penetrated deep into the continent and traded firearms as they went. Building an empire of commerce that stretched deep into what would become the Louisiana Territory, the Governor of New France, the *Comte de Frontenac*, provided an unrestricted supply of guns to the Indians. The gun's value in tribal wars and for hunting made it one of the most enticing commodities the Europeans could offer in trade to the Indians. The French explorer Robert de La Salle observed: "The savages take better care of us French than of their own children. From us only can they get guns and goods." Bill Gilbert, God Gave Us This Country: Tekamthi and the First American Civil War 40 (1989); Frederick Jackson Turner, The Character and Influence of the Indian Trade in Wisconsin: A Study of the Trading Post as an Institution 32 (Ayer Publishing, 1991) (Ph.D. dissertation Johns Hopkins University, 1891) (La Salle quote); Russell, *supra*, at 19.

Frontenac's policy was a sound approach for France. Unlike the English (and later the Americans), the French were not settling the land with waves of immigrant farmers. The French wanted trade, and the sparse population needed to sustain that trade would not provoke the Indians into wars over land. On a wave of successful commerce with the Indians, the French progressed through Canada into western Pennsylvania and the Ohio Valley before English settlers from the Atlantic coast found their way through the gaps in the Appalachian mountains.

But with the victory of Britain and its colonies in the French and Indian War of 1754-63, the French were expelled from North America. French trading posts closed, and the French gun trade with the Indians ceased. In the course of 100 years, France had sold the Indians roughly 200,000 guns. Russell, *supra*, at 16-23. Although imports ceased, French traders within formerly French territory (Mid-western North America) kept trading their existing stocks of guns to the Indians.

France gained the Louisiana Territory from Spain in 1800 through the treaty of San Ildefonso, and sold it to the United States in 1803. The Spanish approached arms-trading with the Indians differently.

Exploring the southern part of North America, the Spaniards enslaved Indians. In 1501, only nine years after the discovery of the New World by Spain's navigator Christopher Columbus, King Ferdinand and Queen Isabella banned the sale of guns to Indians. Still, Indians in Florida and the Southwest stole guns from the Spanish, or bought them from trading networks linked to the French. The enslaved Pueblo Indians of New Mexico acquired and hoarded guns one at a time. They revolted in 1680. Pueblo attacks over the next 16 years killed hundreds of Spanish immigrants, and pushed white settlement out of Santa Fe, all the way back to El Paso. In the 1750s, Comanche raiders, using guns supplied by the French, forced Spain to abandon north Texas. Russell, *supra*, at 26-34; The Pueblo Indian Revolt of 1696 (J. Manual Espinosa ed., 1988).

As long as Indians were not armed inside Spanish territory, the Spanish calculated that gun trade with Indians could be in Spain's interest. For example, Spanish Florida supplied firearms to the Indians of the Gulf Plain, for use against American settlers in Georgia and Alabama. Russell, *supra*, at 38-39.

Initially, the English approach to the Indian arms trade was similar to Spain's. By law, arms-trading with the Indians was prohibited. In 1641, the Crown ordered that no person should give the Indians "any weapons of war, either guns or gunpowder, nor sword, nor any other Munition, which might come to be used against ourselves." Despite this order, many merchants in the colonies pursued the profitable trade with the Indians.

Soon, the British government itself was trading guns with tribes in Illinois and the rest of what would become the Northwest Territory. As trouble with the American colonists worsened, the British saw the advantage of arming Indians to attack American farmers and backwoodsmen on the frontier. Russell, *supra*, at 41-50.

While the American colonial legislatures of the early seventeenth century often mandated that white colonists own and carry guns, they aimed to prevent Indians from acquiring guns. E.g., 1 Archives of Maryland, *supra*, at 71 (1639 statute making it a felony "to sell give or deliver to any Indian or to any other declared or professed enemie of the Province any gunne pistol powder or shott without the knowledge or lycence of the Leiutenant Generall"); *id*. at 250

(1649 statute, "noe Inhabitant of this Province shall deliver any Gunne or
Gunnes or Ammunicon or other kind of martiall Armes, to any Indian borne
of Indian Parentage."); 3 Archives of Maryland, *supra,* at 103 (1642 statute
against selling arms to Indians, with potential capital punishment); 1 Shurtleff,
supra, at 196 (1642 Massachusetts Bay Colony law outlawing sale to Indians of
guns, gunpowder, shot, lead, or shot molds, and also outlawing white repair of
Indian guns); 1 *Public Records of Connecticut, supra,* at 79-80 (forbidding gun sales
to Indians); *id.* at 113-14, 138, 145-46, 197-98 (banning the sale of guns outside of
Connecticut; forbidding foreign merchants from doing in business in Connecticut, in retaliation for Dutch and French gun sales to the Indians). The legislation usually failed to prevent colonists from selling guns to Indians.

In New England, laws became less restrictive as the Indian threat receded.
In 1688, the Massachusetts General Court (the legislature) authorized gun and
ammunition sales to Indians "not in hostility with us or any of the English in New
England. . . ." Nathaniel B. Shurtleff, 4 Records of the Governor and Company
of the Massachusetts Bay in New England 365 (1853). In 1661, Connecticut
allowed the friendly Tunxis Indians to "have free liberty to carry their guns,
through the English towns, provided they are not above 10 men in company."
1 *Public Records of Connecticut, supra,* at 351, 375.

Virginia went through a similar cycle. A harsh 1658 statute declared "what
person or persons so ever shall barter or sell with any Indian or Indians for piece,
powder or shot, and being lawfully convicted, shall forfeit his whole estate."
Further, anyone who discovered an Indian in possession of gun, powder, or
shot, could confiscate it. 1 Hening, *supra,* at 441. The next year, the legislature
admitted the futility of the ban and repealed it, recognizing, "it is manifest that
the neighboring plantations both of English and [foreigners] do plentifully
furnish the Indians with guns, powder & shot, and do thereby draw from us
the trade of beaver to our great loss and their profit, and besides the Indians
being furnished with as much of both guns and ammunition as they are able to
purchase, It is enacted, That every man may freely trade for guns, powder and
shot: It derogating nothing from our safety and adding much to our advantage."
1 Hening, *supra,* at 525.

In 1665, the Virginia legislature renewed its restrictive approach. The impetus was the English conquest of New Amsterdam (modern New York), which
halted the Dutch gun trade with the Indians. With Dutch supply eliminated,
Virginia reinstated its ban on gun sales to Indians, but Virginians defied the law.
1 Hening, *supra,* at 525. This prompted passage of an even more severe law in
1676 declaring that "the traders with Indians by their [avarice] have so armed
the Indians with powder, shot and guns, that they have been thereby emboldened," and providing capital punishment for violations. Further, any Virginian
found "within any Indian town or three miles without the English plantations"
and carrying more than one gun or more than "ten charges of powder and shot
for his necessary use" was presumed to have been in illegal trade with the
Indians. William Waller Hening, 2 The Statutes at Large; Being a Collection
of all the Laws of Virginia, from the First Session of the Legislature, in the Year
1619, at 336-37 (1823).

By 1763, Maryland felt safe enough to allow limited sales to Indian men.
Still, the law made it illegal for "any Person or Persons within this Province to
Sell or give to any Indian Woman or Child any Gun Powder Shot or lead

Whatsoever[,] nor to any Indian Man within this Province more than the Quantitys of one Pound of Gun Powder and six Pounds of Shot or lead at any one Time[,] and not those or lesser Quantitys of Powder or Lead oftener than once in Six Months." 58 Archives of Maryland 420 (J. Hall Pleasants ed., 1941).

As the frontier moved westward, concern in the original colonies about armed Indians declined. However, parts of the frontier were in a state of white-Indian war from the seventeenth century until the late nineteenth century. Accordingly, many states enacted bans on gun possession by Indians. Some of these statutes lingered for decades after the wars had ended. For example, Colorado's nineteenth-century ban on selling guns to Indians remained on the statute books until a comprehensive revision of the state criminal code in 1971.

c. Gun Restrictions on Blacks

Early restrictions on Blacks' access to firearms reflected the shifting status of subordinate populations. In 1680, Virginia forbade "any negroe or other slave to carry or arme himselfe with any club, staffe, gunn, sword or any other weapon of defence or offence." 2 Hening, *supra,* at 481. But by 1723, Blacks and Indians were allowed into the militia. Even those who were not militiamen, but who lived in their own houses, could have arms; specifically, "every free negro, mulatto, or indian, being a house-keeper, or listed in the militia, may be permitted to keep one gun, powder, and shot." William Waller Hening, 4 The Statutes at Large; Being a Collection of all the Laws of Virginia, from the First Session of the Legislature, in the Year 1619, at 131 (1823). Blacks and Indians who were "not house-keepers, nor listed in the militia" were prohibited arms. But even non-militia, non-householder Blacks and Indians living on frontier plantations could possess arms if they were granted a license "to keep and use guns, powder, and shot." *Id.* Virginia's brief period of *armed* Black and Indian militiamen ended in 1738. Although Blacks were still required to serve in the militia, the law demanded that they "shall appear without arms." Id., 5 at 17.

During the American Revolution, military necessity pressed Virginia to allow free Blacks in the state's military. L.P. Jackson, *Virginia Negro Soldiers and Seamen in the American Revolution,* 27 J. Negro Hist. 247 (1942).

Maryland adopted a licensing law that became typical in slave states during the nineteenth century. It mandated "[t]hat no Negro or other slave, within this Province, shall be permitted to carry any Gun or any other offensive Weapon, from off their Master's Land, without Licence from their said Master." *Maryland Laws, supra,* at 125.

Georgia enacted a similar, but more elaborate law in 1755, and then reenacted it in 1768. The statute, "for the Establishing and Regulating Patrols," forbade slave possession or carrying of "Fire Arms or any Offensive Weapon whatsoever, unless such Slave shall have a Ticket or License in Writing from his Master Mistress or Overseer to Hunt and Kill Game Cattle or Mischievous Birds or Birds of Prey." The law allowed slaves to have guns when accompanied by a white of at least 16 years old, or while defending crops from birds. From the setting of the sun on Saturday until sunrise on Monday, no slave could carry "any Gun Cutlass Pistol or other Offensive Weapon." The Georgia slave patrol, referenced in the statutory title, had the power and duty of "Searching and examining any Negroe house for Offensive Weapons Fire Arms and Ammunition." 19 (part 1) *Georgia Records, supra*, at 76-78, 117-18. Many states with large slave populations had similar slave patrols, aimed at catching slaves who were off their masters' property without permission, or who had illegal arms.

In general, colonial policy was to keep Blacks disarmed. But there were formal shifts in this policy when manpower was needed. This occurred during the French and Indian War (1754-63) and during the Revolutionary War. Enforcement of formal prohibitions also was relaxed under certain circumstances. When the need was great enough, even slaves were sometimes armed and enrolled in state militias. Benjamin Quarles, *The Colonial Militia and Negro Manpower*, 45 Miss. Valley Hist. Rev. 643 (1959).

d. Sporadic Disarmament of Dissidents

The American colonies never experienced anything like the pervasive attempts to disarm the free population that took place in England during the seventeenth-century reign of the Stuart Kings. *See* Chapter 2. But there were instances in which religious or political dissidents, or those suspected of disloyalty were disarmed.

In the 1630s in the Massachusetts Bay Colony, Anne Hutchinson criticized the Puritan government for its legalistic interpretation of the Bible, and asserted that the Old Testament was no longer binding law. In 1637, Hutchinson and some of her supporters were tried for spreading "antinomian" ideas, and then banished. Seventy-seven of her supporters were disarmed. Bradley Chapin, Criminals Justice in Colonial America, 1606-1660, at 103-04 (1983); Edward Johnson, Johnson's Wonder-Working Providence: 1628-1651, at 175 (J. Franklin Jameson ed., 1959) (listing numbers of persons disarmed in each town); 1 Shurtleff, *supra*, 211-12 (disarming orders).

A 1676 Virginia's statute directed "that all persons have hereby liberty to sell armes and ammunition to any of his majesties loyall subjects inhabiting this colony." 2 Hening, *supra*, at 403, suggesting that it was illegal to sell arms or ammunition to disloyal persons.

Alone among the colonies, Maryland was heavily populated by Catholics. During much of the seventeenth century, England, which had broken from the Roman Catholic Church in the sixteenth century, was under threat from Catholic powers who sought, by invasion or intrigue, to reassert Catholic control. *See* Chapter 2. Although much diminished, that threat persisted into the eighteenth century. Catholic France remained England's primary foreign rival, and religious hostility exacerbated tensions.

In 1754, a global war broke out between France and England. It was called the "French and Indian War" in the American colonies. Colonial militias participated extensively in the fighting, often alongside British regulars. In 1756, Maryland removed Catholics from the state militia, and as setoff, doubled their real estate taxes. 52 Archives of Maryland, 450 (J. Hall Pleasants ed., 1935) (exempting from militia service "Papists, the Persons commonly called Neutralls, Servants, and Slaves"), 598 (forbidding military enlistment of any

"Roman Catholic or Deserter, knowing them to be such"). Marylanders who refused to swear loyalty to King George also were forbidden to possess arms or ammunition. *Id.* at 451-52. Further, "all Arms Gunpowder and Ammunition of what kind soever any Papist or reputed Papist within this Province hath or shall have in his House or Houses" were to be confiscated. *Id.* at 454.

When the French and Indian War began, the British insisted that the French people of Nova Scotia swear allegiance to King George III. Some of these Acadians (as the Nova Scotia French called themselves) moved to French Louisiana. Many who refused the oath were deported to other British colonies. Some were sent to Georgia as indentured servants; there they were restricted from possessing firearms. A 1756 Georgia law forbade the indentured Acadian "to have or use any fire Arms or other Offensive Weapons otherwise than in his Masters Plantation or immediately under his Inspection. . . ." 18 *Georgia Records, supra,* at 190-91.

Revolt and revolution against British rule also generated episodes of disarmament. During the Revolution, a large minority of the American population (called "Tories") remained loyal to the Crown. Some states, such as Maryland, confiscated the guns of Tories and gave them to militiamen. Maryland did, however, compensate the Tories for the value of their confiscated firearms. 5 American Archives, 4th series, 1509 (Peter Force ed., 1843) (enacted 1776).

NOTES & QUESTIONS

1. CQ: In *Heller*, dissenting Justice Breyer referenced municipal gun laws restricting the carrying of loaded guns into buildings in Boston, and restricting the discharge of firearms in Boston, Philadelphia, and New York as evidence that the District of Columbia's ban on handguns was not much more severe than historical American practice. Similarly, in *Ezell v. Chicago*, 651 F.3d 684 (7th Cir. 2011) (Chapter 11), some historians who supported Chicago's prohibition on target ranges referenced seventeenth- or eighteenth-century regulations on target shooting in cities. How common should a particular restriction be in order to be considered to demonstrate a consensus that a particular restriction does not violate the right to arms (as guaranteed in state constitutions, and as arguably analogous to the Second Amendment)? Can similar reasoning be used for the First Amendment? Many states in the Early Republic had state constitutional protections of speech and the press, but still enforced laws against blasphemy and seditious libel (bringing the government into disrepute), and allowed criminal and civil prosecution for libel cases where truth of the statement was no defense.

2. Some of the restrictions on firing guns have no express exception for self-defense. Can a self-defense exception be presumed? Can it be presumed for other laws without such an express exemption, such as statutes against assault or homicide?

3. In many states today, hunting laws specifically forbid firing a gun across a road while hunting (or in any other circumstance, except self-defense).

Hunter safety training also teaches hunters never to shoot across a road. Should it be constitutional to prohibit arms possession by a person who has violated such a law? What about prohibiting that person from carrying arms? Are such laws justifiable under originalist methodology as analogies to the safety laws detailed above?

4. For more detail on the material presented in this section, see Clayton E. Cramer, Armed America: The Remarkable Story of How and Why Guns Became as American as Apple Pie (2009), and Clayton E. Cramer, *Colonial Firearm Regulation*, 16 J. Firearms & Pub. Pol'y 1 (2004).

5. CQ: The issue of racial conflict is present from the very beginning of the story of guns in America. As we will see in subsequent chapters, disarmament of Blacks, both slave and free, has been a frequent issue in American firearms policy. In the early twentieth century, concerns about immigrants also became important in gun control. If modern gun laws are not obviously motivated by racism, and do not make explicit racial distinctions, should the racial history of gun control be of modern relevance?

B. Firearms, Self-Defense, and Militias in Pre-Revolutionary America

From 1763 until the 1776 Declaration of Independence, colonists accumulated many grievances against the British. The discrete spark of actual hostilities was gun confiscation. The stage was set by British seizure of American gunpowder and a ban on importation of firearms and gunpowder to the colonies. Boston was under military occupation and the British had confiscated Bostonians' firearms. The war began at nearby Lexington and Concord, when British troops marched out to confiscate firearms there.

Individual Americans brought their own firearms to serve in the Continental Army, in the state militias, and in the independent militias that began forming before independence was declared. American Patriots saw themselves as virtuously armed in the cause of liberty. Their ideas of the civic-republican virtue of an armed and free people would eventually shape the Second Amendment.

This section traces pre-war American views about the right to arms, resistance against tyranny, and British gun prohibition.

1. The Boston Massacre Trial

The most famous American trial of the eighteenth century was the Boston Massacre prosecution. On the night of March 5, 1770, British Redcoats fired on a threatening crowd that was pelting them with iceballs. Five members of the crowd died. The British government selected the noted American attorney Robert Treat Paine to prosecute the soldiers for murder. John Adams was among the counsel for the defense. Although the facts were disputed, the law was not. Both sides presumed the legal right of both soldiers and civilians to defend themselves from violent attacks.

According to Paine, because of the well-known abuses by the Redcoats against the citizens of Boston, "the most peaceable among us had . . . found it necessary to arm themselves with heavy Walking Sticks or Weapons of Defense when they went abroad." Prosecutor Samuel Quincy argued that the soldiers were outside their barracks and armed "with clubs, cutlasses, and other weapons of death; this occasioned a general alarm; every man therefore had a right, and very prudent it was to endeavor to defend himself if attacked; this accounts for the reason of Dr. *Young* or any one inhabitant of the town having a sword that evening." John Adams, 3 Legal Papers of John Adams 149, 274 (L. Kinvin Wroth & Hiller B. Zobel eds., 1965).

Defense counsel John Adams invoked "Self Defence, the primary Canon of the Law of Nature." Citing the treatise of William Hawkins, a leading authority on the common law, Adams agreed that the Bostonians had a right to be armed for self-defense against the soldiers: "Here every private person is authorized to arm himself, and on the strength of this authority, I do not deny the inhabitants had a right to arm themselves at that time, for their defence, not for offence." *Id.* at 248.

The jury charge explicitly directed that citizens were sometimes required to carry arms: "It is the duty of all persons (except women, decrepit persons, and infants under fifteen) to aid and assist the peace officers to suppress riots & c. when called upon to do it. They may take with them such weapons as are necessary to enable them effectually to do it." *Id.* at 285.

Outside the court room, John Adams's cousin Samuel Adams penned an essay that focused on the death of Crispus Attucks, a free Black man who had been killed during the Massacre. Mr. Attucks "was leaning upon his stick when he fell, which certainly was not a threatening posture: It may be supposed that he had as good right, by the law of the land, to carry a stick for his own and his neighbor's defence, in a time of danger, as the Soldier who shot him had, to be arm'd with musket and ball, for the defence of himself and his friend the Centinel." 2 The Writings of Samuel Adams 119 (Harry Alonzo Cushing ed., 1904).

The soldier who killed Crispus Attucks was convicted of manslaughter. All the others were acquitted. Bernhard Knollenberg, Growth of the American Revolution: 1766-1775, at 87-88 (rev. ed. 2003). Annual orations on the "Massacre Day" anniversary continued to promote ill feelings toward the standing army of Redcoats in Boston.

NOTES & QUESTIONS

1. In another Massachusetts trial, in 1771, James Otis, Samuel Quincy, and John Adams teamed up as defense counsel. Otis expounded the right of self-defense, quoting from the speech that the revered ancient Roman lawyer Cicero had prepared for his defense of Titus Annius Milo: "When arms speak, the laws are silent; they bid none to await their word. . . . And yet most wisely, and, in a way, tacitly, the law authorizes self-defense. . . . The man

who had employed a weapon in self-defence was not held to have carried that weapon with a view to homicide." John Adams, 1 Legal Papers of John Adams 160 (L. Kinvin Wroth & Hiller B. Zobel eds., 1965). (For more on Cicero and the Milo case, see Chapter 2.)

2.   A Colonial View of the English Right to Arms

The 1689 English Declaration of Right affirmed Englishmen's right to arms, and the right was elaborated in William Blackstone's treatise. *See* Chapter 2. The American colonists believed they had the same entitlement to "the rights of Englishmen" as those who lived in England. The most extensive pre-war American analysis of the right to arms was a newspaper essay by Samuel Adams. Adams, writing as "E.A.," begins with a criticism of the seventeenth-century Stuart monarchs, and then defends a Boston town meeting (in the midst of an intense political dispute with England) urging all Bostonians to acquire arms.

E.A., Boston Gazette, Feb. 27, 1769, at 3
1 The Writings of Samuel Adams 317-18
(Harry Alonzo Cushing ed., 1904)

In the days of the STUARTS, it was look'd upon by some men as a high degree of prophaness, for any subject to enquire into what was called the *mysteries* of government: *James* the first thundered his anathema against Dr. *Cowel,* for his daring presumption in treating of—those *mysteries*; and forbad his subjects to read his books, or even to keep them in their houses. In those days *passive obedience, non-resistance,* the *divine hereditary right* of kings, and their being accountable to God *alone,* were doctrines generally taught, believ'd and practiced: But behold the sudden transition of human affairs! In the very next reign the people assum'd the right of *free enquiry,* into the nature and end of government, and the conduct of those who were entrusted with it: *Laud* and *Strafford* were bro't to the block; and after the horrors of a civil war, in which some of the best blood of the nation was spilt as water upon the ground, they finally called to account, arraign'd, adjudg'd, condemn'd and even executed the monarch himself! . . . The two sons of *Charles* the first . . . reigned in their turns; but by copying after their father, their administration of government was *grievous* to their subjects, and *infamous* abroad. *Charles* the second indeed reign'd till he died; but his brother *James* was oblig'd to abdicate the throne, which made room for *William* the third, and his royal consort *Mary,* the daughter of the unfortunate *James*— This was the fate of a race of kings, bigoted to the greatest degree to the doctrines of *slavery* and regardless of the *natural, inherent, divinely hereditary* and *indefeasible* rights of their subjects. —At the revolution, the British Constitution was again restor'd to its original principles, declared in the bill of rights; which was afterwards pass'd into a law, and stands as a bulwark to the natural rights of subjects. "To vindicate these rights, says Mr. *Blackstone,* when actually violated or attack'd, the subjects of England are entitled first to the regular administration and *free course of justice* in the courts of law—next to the right of *petitioning the King* and parliament for redress of grievances—and lastly, to the right of *having and using arms for self-preservation and defence.*" These he calls "auxiliary subordinate rights, which serve principally as *barriers* to protect and maintain inviolate the three great and primary rights of *personal security, personal liberty* and *private property*": And that of *having arms for their defense* he tells us is "a public allowance, under due restrictions, of the *natural right of resistance and self-preservation,* when the sanctions of society and laws are found *insufficient* to restrain the *violence of oppression.*" — How little do those persons attend to the rights of the constitution, if they know anything about them, who find fault with a late vote of this town, calling upon the inhabitants to *provide themselves with arms for their defence* at any time; but more especially, when they had reason to fear, there would be a necessity of the means of self preservation against the *violence of oppression.*

Everyone knows that the exercise of the military power is forever *dangerous* to civil rights. . . . But there are some persons, who would, if possibly they could, perswade the people *never to make use* of their *constitutional* rights or terrify them from doing it. No wonder that a resolution of this town to *keep arms* for its own defence, should be represented as having at bottom a *secret intention* to oppose the landing of the King's troops: when those very persons, who gave it this colouring, had before represented the peoples petitioning their Sovereign, as proceeding from a *factious* and *rebellious* spirit. . . .

NOTES & QUESTIONS

1. Future President John Adams described Scottish Whig James Burgh's *Political Disquisitions* as "a book which ought to be in the hands of every American who has learned to read," John Adams, *Novanglus,* essay 2 n.*, *in* Charles Francis Adams, 4 The Works of John Adams 21 (1856). Burgh agreed with the American Revolutionaries about the practical impact of concentrating arms in the hands of standing armies rather than the people:

   > The confidence, which a standing *army* gives a minister, puts him upon carrying things with a higher hand, than he would attempt to do, if the people were armed, and the court unarmed, that is, if there were no land-force in the nation, but a militia. Had we at this time no standing army, we should not think of *forcing* money out of the pockets of three millions of our subjects [the Americans]. . . . There is no end to observations on the difference between the measures likely to be pursued by a minister backed by a standing *army,* and those of a court awed by the fear of an *armed people.*

   James Burgh, 2 Political Disquisitions 475-76 (1774). The quote appeared, for example, in the New York Journal, Feb. 9, 1775, at 1.

3. Religion, Arms, and Resistance

Many colonial Americans came to see gun ownership as not only a personal right, but also a civic duty and a religious obligation, particularly for the militia defense of the religious liberty and self-government of their communities.

The Congregationalists (concentrated in New England) and the Presbyterians (all over the country, and including the many Scotch-Irish immigrants) were particularly strong in their views on the issue, while the Anglicans (tied to the Church of England) were less so.

Among the American elite, there were a few, most notably Benjamin Franklin and Thomas Jefferson, who admired the moral philosophy of Jesus, but who put little stock in the Bible stories of Christian miracles. Even Jefferson and Franklin, however, agreed that the forcible defense of God-given liberty was an inescapable moral obligation.

The large body of the American people — those who would fill the ranks of the militia and the Continental Army — held to fairly conventional religious beliefs, by American standards. Those beliefs were at the core of Americans' audacity to start a war against the greatest empire in the world, and help explain why personal possession of arms became so important to their identity.

The modern gun control debate has many arguments about whether seventeenth- and eighteenth-century Americans saw arms-bearing as a "right" or a "duty." Americans in those centuries exhibited less interest than modern Americans in parsing the distinction. In this section, we will see some of the reasons why the Bill of Rights amendment about liberty of conscience and religion would be followed by the amendment about arms rights and civic duty.

American Revolutionaries had many grievances that were not directly about religion — taxation without representation, unwarranted searches and seizures, firearms confiscation. Nevertheless, it was American religion, especially New England religion, that provided Americans with an intellectual framework for pressing their disputes with England. Black-robed American clergymen were described as the "black regiment" for their role in building popular support for war against England.

King George III reportedly denounced the American Revolution as "a Presbyterian rebellion." Douglas F. Kelly, The Emergence of Liberty in the Modern World: The Influence of Calvin on Five Governments from the 16th Through 18th Centuries 131 (1992). Many British sympathizers in America blamed the Presbyterians for the war. Spread widely over the American colonies, Presbyterians were in frequent contact with their brethren in other colonies. A young Presbyterian man from North Carolina might be trained for the ministry at Princeton, New Jersey, and then called to minister to a congregation in New Hampshire. Presbyterians were thus the first to develop and promote the idea of *American* rights rather than the rights of a particular state or region.

In 1775, the great Anglo-Irish statesman Edmund Burke tried to warn the British Parliament that the Americans could not be subjugated: "[T]he people are Protestants, and of that kind which is the most adverse to all implicit submission of mind and opinion." While the Catholic and Anglican Churches were supported by the government, and were inclined to support the state, the American sects were based on "dissenting interests." They had "sprung up in direct opposition to the ordinary powers of the world, and could justify that opposition only on a strong claim of natural liberty. Their very existence depended on the powerful and unremitted assertion of that claim. All Protestantism, even the most cold and passive, is a sort of dissent. But the religion most prevalent in our northern colonies is a refinement of the principle of resistance: it is the dissidence of dissent, and the protestantism of the Protestant religion." Edmund Burke, Speech on Moving His Resolutions for Conciliation with the Colonies (Mar. 22, 1775), *in* Edmund Burke: Selected Writings and Speeches 159-60 (Peter J. Stanlis ed., 1963) [hereinafter *Selected Burke*].

Much of the best land belonged to the Anglicans, but the Church of England had no bishop in America. As a result, American Anglican churches were controlled by wealthy land owners who enjoyed independence from British oversight. Rumors that the king was preparing to send bishops to America, to administer both the Anglican and other Protestant churches, sent the Americans into an ecumenical rage. John Adams said that no issue was more important in making the American people question the authority of Parliament than the controversy over American bishops. "The objection was not merely to the office of a bishop, even though that was to be dreaded, but to the authority of Parliament, on which it could be founded." John Adams, 10 The Works of John Adams 185 (Charles Frances Adams ed., 1850-56). If Parliament had the authority to appoint a bishop for America, Parliament would also have the authority to "introduce the whole hierarchy, establish tithes, forbid marriages and funerals, establish religions, forbid dissenters, make schism heresy." *Id.*

The New England Puritans, who by the time of the Revolution were known as "Congregationalists," had set out to build a "City upon a Hill," as John Winthrop put it in a 1630 shipboard sermon to settlers on their way to the Massachusetts Bay Colony. European philosophers such as Jean-Jacques Rousseau theorized about an abstract "social contract." In the Mayflower Compact, Puritans created a real one. Before setting foot in the New World, Puritans made a contract defining the terms of their relationship with each other and with God. The colonies of Massachusetts, Connecticut, and Rhode Island were all created by voluntary compacts.

The Puritans believed that when God made a covenant with his people, he would maintain the covenant, and protect them. Perry Miller, Nature's Nation 19 (1967). "They conceived the universe to be a great kingdom whose sovereign was God, whose relations with His Son and with men were determined by covenant or compact, 'covenant-constitutions,' which were always conditional and implied strict obedience on each side." Alice M. Baldwin, The New England Clergy and the American Revolution 13 (F. Ungar Pub. Co. 1958) (1928). Among the laws of nature that were binding on God and man were Christ's "law of liberty." *Id.* at 18.

According to historian Alice Baldwin this view was

> fundamental to any understanding of American constitutional thought. God's government is founded on and limited by law and therefore all human governments must be so founded and limited, if patterned after His. A government, therefore, which exercises its authority unconstitutionally acts illegally. Here is one great source of the American doctrine of government by law.

Id. at 19.

In other words, "God ruled over men by a divine constitution. Natural law and Christian rights were legal rights because a part of the law of God. . . . Any act contrary to the constitution was illegal therefore null and void." *Id.* at 168. God constrained all rulers through the requirement that they govern the people for their own good, as did God the father and Jesus. *Id.* at 34-35. Life, liberty, and property—in fact all civil rights—came from God. They were therefore guarded by divine law against any violation by government. *Id.* at 38-39.

Revolutionary sentiment would be grounded in the idea that King George was violating the compact by which God had allowed him the throne. Acquiescence in his violation of that compact was participation in defying God. Submission to tyranny was a crime against God. *Id.* at 90 (Andrew Eliot's 1765 election sermon to the North Church[2] in Boston; the election sermon, preached shortly before an election, was considered an especially appropriate time for pastors to address civic issues). Ending the king's rule in America would not be seditious or disorderly. Rather, it would constitute the restoration of true civil order, a restoration of God's contract with his American people. "Resistance to a madman is not a revolution; it is, in obedience to God, an exercise of the police power." Miller, *supra*, at 104.

One of the most important of all the sermons undergirding the American case for revolution was delivered on January 30, 1750, by leading Congregationalist minister Jonathan Mayhew. January 30 was the anniversary of the execution of England's absolutist King Charles I whose "martyrdom" was venerated by Anglican ministers propounding the duty of submission to government. Mayhew's sermon argued that such blind submission was abhorrent.

Historian Bernard Bailyn called it the "most famous sermon preached in pre-Revolutionary America." 1 Pamphlets of the American Revolution: 1750-1776, at 204 (Bernard Bailyn ed., 1965). John Adams called it his personal "Catechism" of revolution. Letter from John Adams to Thomas Jefferson (July 18, 1818), *in* The Adams-Jefferson Letters: The Complete Correspondence Between Thomas Jefferson and Abigail and John Adams 527 (Lester J. Cappon ed., 1987) (1957). According to Adams, "It was read by everybody; celebrated by friends, and abused by enemies. . . . It spread an universal alarm against the authority of Parliament. It excited a general and just apprehension, that bishops, and dioceses, and churches, and priests, and tithes, were to be imposed on us by Parliament." Letter from John Adams to Hezekiah Niles, Feb. 13, 1818.

Jonathan Mayhew, A Discourse Concerning Unlimited Submission and Non-Resistance to the Higher Powers: With Some Reflections on the Resistance Made to King Charles I and on the Anniversary of His Death
Hall & Goss, 1818 (Jan. 30, 1750)

Rom; xiii. 1, 8.

1. Let every soul be subject unto the higher powers. For there is no power but of God: the powers that be, are ordained of God.

---

2. The North Church is the one from which the signal lanterns were lit on the night of April 18, 1775, to alert Paul Revere and William Dawes that the British were coming.

2. Whosoever therefore resisteth the power, resisteth the ordinance of God: and they that resist, shall receive to themselves damnation.

3. For rulers are not a terror to good works, but to the evil. Wilt thou then not be afraid of the power? do that which is good, and thou shalt have praise of the same:

4. For he is the minister of God to thee for good. But if thou do that which is evil, be afraid; for he beareth not the sword in vain: for he is the minister of God, a revenger to execute wrath upon him that doth evil.

5. Wherefore ye must needs be subject, not only for wrath, but also for conscience sake.

6. For, for this cause pay you tribute also: for they are God's ministers, attending continually upon this very thing.

6. Render therefore to all their dues: tribute to whom tribute is due; custom, to whom custom; fear, to whom fear; honour, to whom honour. . . .

There is one very important and interesting point which remains to be inquired into; namely, the *extent* of that subjection *to the higher powers,*[3] which is here enjoined as a duty upon all christians. Some have thought it warrantable and glorious, to disobey the civil powers in certain circumstances; and, in cases of very great and general oppression, when humble remonstrances fail of having any effect; and when the publick welfare cannot be otherwise provided for and secured, to rise unanimously even against the sovereign himself, in order to redress their grievances; to vindicate their natural and legal rights: to break the yoke of tyranny, and free themselves and posterity from inglorious servitude and ruin. It is upon this principle that many royal oppressors have been driven from their thrones into banishment; and many slain by the hands of their subjects. . . . And upon this principle was that revolution brought about, which has been so fruitful of happy consequences to *Great-Britain.* But, in opposition to this principle, it has often been asserted, that the scripture in general (and the passage under consideration in particular) makes all resistance to princes a crime, in any case whatever. . . . Now whether we are obliged to yield such an absolute submission to our prince; or whether disobedience and resistance may not be justifiable in some cases, notwithstanding any thing in the passage before us, is an inquiry in which we are all concerned; and this is the inquiry which is the main design of the present discourse. . . .

[I]f we attend to the nature of the argument with which the apostle here inforces the duty of submission to *the higher powers,* we shall find it to be such an one as concludes not in favor of submission to all who bear the *title* of rulers, in common; but only, to those who *actually* perform the duty of rulers, by exercising a reasonable and just authority, for the good of human society. . . . It is obvious, then, in general, that the civil rulers whom the apostle here speaks of, and obedience to whom he presses upon christians as a duty, are *good rulers,* such as are, in the exercise of their office and power, benefactors to society. Such they are described to be, thro'out this passage. Thus it is said, that they are not *a terror to good works, but to the evil;* that they are *God's ministers for good; revengers to execute wrath upon him that doth evil;* and that *they attend continually upon this very thing.* St. Peter gives the same account of rulers: . . . It is manifest that this character

---

3. [Refers to civil rulers. — Eds].

and description of rulers, agrees only to such as are rulers in fact, as well as in name: to such as govern well, and act agreeably to their office. . . . [I]f they are not *ministers for good to society*, but for evil and distress, by violence and oppression; if they execute wrath upon sober, peaceable persons, who do their duty as members of society; and suffer rich and honourable knaves to escape with impunity; if, instead of the good work of advancing the publick welfare, they *attend* only upon the gratification of their own lust and pride and ambition, to the destruction of the public welfare; if this be the case, it is plain that the apostle's argument for submission does not reach them; they are not the same, but different persons from those whom he characterizes; and who must be obeyed according to his reasoning. . . .

. . . It is blasphemy to call tyrants and oppressors, *God's ministers.* They are more properly *the messengers of satan to buffet us.* . . . [S]uch rulers as do not perform the pleasure of God, by doing good; but the pleasure of the devil, by doing evil . . . are not, therefore, *God's ministers*, but the devil's! . . . [W]hat reason is there for submitting to that government, which does by no means answer the design of government? . . . [S]uch persons as (although they bear the title of rulers) use all their power to hurt and injure the public . . . are not *God's ministers*, but *satan's.* . . .

THUS, upon a careful review of the apostle's reasoning in this passage, it appears that his arguments to enforce submission, are of such a nature, as to conclude only in favour of submission to *such rulers as he himself describes*; i.e. such as rule for the good of society, which is the only end of their institution. Common tyrants, and public oppressors, are not intitled to obedience from their subjects, by virtue of any thing here laid down by the inspired apostle. . . .

. . . Suppose God requires a family of children, to obey their father and not to resist him; and inforces his command with this argument; that the superintendence and care and authority of a just and kind parent, will contribute to the happiness of the whole family; so that they ought to obey him for their own sakes more than for his: Suppose this parent at length runs distracted, and attempts, in his mad fit, to cut all his children's throats: Now, in this case, is not the reason before assigned, why these children should obey their parent while he continued of a sound mind, namely, *their common good*, a reason equally conclusive for disobeying and resisting him, since he is become delirious, and attempts their ruin? It makes no alteration in the argument, whether this parent . . . loses his reason[] or . . . retains his understanding. . . .

IF we calmly consider the nature of the thing itself, nothing can well be imagined more directly contrary to common sense, than to suppose that *millions* of people should be subjected to the arbitrary, precarious pleasure of *one single man*; (who has *naturally* no superiority over them in point of authority) so that their estates, and every thing that is valuable in life, and even their lives also, shall be absolutely at his disposal, if he happens to be wanton and capricious enough to demand them. . . .

. . . [A] nation thus abused to arise unanimously, and to resist their prince, even to the dethroning him, is not criminal; but a reasonable way of vindicating their liberties and just rights; it is making use of the means, and the only means, which God has put into their power, for mutual and self-defence. And it would be highly criminal in them, not to make use of this means. It would be stupid tameness, and unaccountable folly, for whole nations to suffer *one* unreasonable, ambitious and cruel man, to wanton and riot in their misery. And in such a case it would, of the two, be more rational to suppose, that they did NOT resist, than that they who did, would *receive to themselves damnation.*

[Mayhew then exhorted his audience to understand that Charles I was a "corrupt" and merciless tyrant with a "lust for power" whom his subjects justifiably "beheaded [because he] was not, properly speaking, *their king;* but a *lawless tyrant.*" "The power of this Almighty King . . . is limited by law; not, indeed, by acts of parliament, but by the eternal laws of truth, wisdom and equity; and the everlasting tables of right reason."]

From the beginning of English settlement in New England, the relationship between the ministry and the militia was close and symbiotic. New England ministers often gave special sermons and offered prayers on Election Day (when a sermon was preached to the legislature and governor), Artillery Day (when new militia artillery officers were elected), and militia muster days. These sermons often spoke of the duty of Christian men to fight for liberty against tyranny.

The following sermon, by Rev. Simeon Howard, is a typical example. The sermon addresses many of the common themes in New England preaching in the years shortly before the beginning of the Revolution in 1775. While Mayhew's sermon would change the way that many people thought about resistance to government, the Howard sermon expresses the conventional wisdom of 1773.

Simeon Howard, A Sermon Preached to the Ancient and Honorable Artillery Company in Boston
June 7, 1773

"Stand fast therefore in the liberty wherewith Christ hath made us free." (Galatians V:I). . . .

This liberty has always been accounted one of the greatest natural blessings which mankind can enjoy. Accordingly, the benevolent and impartial Father of the human race, has given to all men a right, and to all naturally an equal right to this blessing. . . .

[T]he liberty which men have is all that natural liberty which [they possess in a state of nature], excepting what they have expressly given up for the good of the whole society; a liberty of pursuing their own happiness, governing their actions, and disposing of their property and persons as they think fit, providing they transgress no law of nature, and keep those restrictions which they have consented to come under. . . .

When a society commits to one or a few a power to govern them, the general practice is to limit this power by certain prescribed rules and restrictions. . . .

There are some natural liberties or rights which no person can divest himself of, without transgressing the law of nature. A man cannot for instance, give up the liberty of private judgement in matters of religion, or convey to others a right to determine of what religion he shall be, and in what way he shall worship

God. A grant of this nature would destroy the foundation of all religion in the man who made it, and must therefore be a violation of the law of nature; nor would he be obliged to abide by it, if in consequence of it, he should be required to act contrary to the dictates of his conscience. Or should a man pretend to grant to others a power to order and govern all his actions, that were not of a religious nature, so that in all cases he must act agreeable to their direction; this would be inconsistent with that submission which he owes to the authority of God, and his own conscience. The grant would be in itself void, and he would, notwithstanding, be at liberty to act according to his own conscience, though contrary to the command of those to whom he had made so extravagant a donation. . . .

Now for men to stand fast in their liberty means, in general, resisting the attempts that are made against it, in the best and most effectual manner they can.

When any one's liberty is attacked or threatened, he is first to try gentle methods for his safety; to reason with, and persuade the adversary to desist, if there be opportunity for it; or get out of his way, if he can; and if by such means he can prevent the injury, he is to use no other.

But the experience of all ages has shewn that those, who are so unreasonable as to form designs of injuring others, are seldom to be diverted from their purpose by argument and persuasion alone; Notwithstanding all that can be said to shew the injustice and inhumanity of their attempt, they persist in they have gratified the unruly passion which set them to work. And in this case, what is to be done by the sufferer! Is he to use no other means for his safety, but remonstrance or flight, when these will not secure him? Is he patiently to take the injury and suffer himself to be robbed of his liberty or his life, if the adversary sees fit to take it? Nature certainly forbids this tame submission, and loudly calls to a more vigorous defence. Self-preservation is one of the strongest, and a universal principle of the human mind:

And this principle allows of every thing necessary to self-defence, opposing force to force, and violence to violence. This is so universally allowed that I need not attempt to prove it. . . .

And there are, if I mistake not, several passages in the new testament, which shew, that, it was not the design of this divine institution to take away from mankind the natural right of defending their liberty, even by the sword. . . . [See Chapter 2 for discussion of some of the New Testament passages that Howard addressed.]

Defending ourselves by force of arms against injurious attacks, is a quite different thing from rendering evil for evil. The latter implies doing hurt to another, because he has done hurt to us; the former implies doing hurt to another, if he is hurt in the conflict only because there is no other way of avoiding the mischief he endeavours to do us: the one proceeds from malice and revenge; the other merely from self-love, and a just concern for our own happiness, and argues no ill will against any man.

And therefore it is to be observed,

That necessary self-defence, however fatal it may prove to those who unjustly attack us, implies no principle inconsistent with that love to our enemies which Christ enjoins. For, at the same time that we are defending ourselves against their assaults, we may bear good-will towards them, wish them well, and pray God to befriend them: All which we doubtless ought to do in respect of our bitterest enemies.

But it is only defensive war that can be justified in the sight of God. When no injury is offered us, we have no right to molest others.

And christian meekness, patience and forbearance, are duties that ought to be practised both by kingdoms and individuals. . . . If these endeavours are unsuccessful, it then becomes proper, to use more forceable means of resistance.

A people may err by too long neglecting such means, and shamefully suffer the sword to rust in its scabberd, when it ought to be employed in defending their liberty. The most grasping and oppressive power will commonly let its neighbours remain in peace, if they will submit to its unjust demands. And an incautious people may submit to these demands, one after another, till its liberty is irrecoverably gone, before they saw the danger. Injuries small in themselves, may in their consequences be fatal to those who submit to them; especially if they are persisted in. And, with respect to such injuries, we should ever act upon that ancient maxim of prudence; obsta principiis.[4] The first unjust demands of an encroaching power should be firmly withstood, when there appears a disposition to repeat and encrease such demands. And oftentimes it may be both the right and duty of a people to engage in war, rather than give up to the demands of such a power, what they could, without any incoveniency, spare in the way of charity. War, though a great evil, is ever preferable to such concessions, as are likely to be fatal to public liberty. And when such concessions are required and insisted upon, as the conditions of peace, the only consideration to be attended to by the abused state, is that which our Saviour intimates common prudence will always suggest in such cases: . . .

After a people have been forced into a war for their own security, they ought to set reasonable bounds to their resentment, or they may become as guilty as the first aggressors. They should aim at nothing more than repelling the injury, obtaining reparation for damages sustained, and security against future injuries.

They should endeavor to be united and at peace among themselves. The strength of a society, as well as its honour and happiness, depends much upon its union. Our Saviour's maxim is founded in reason, and has been confirmed by the experience of all ages: "Every kingdom divided against itself is brought to desolation." (Matt. 12:25) When the body politic is divided into parties, and the members make a business of opposing each other, it is in a fair way to ruin. They are not likely to unite in measures of defence against a common enemy, and will therefore lie open to the encroachments of violence and oppression, and become an easy prey to every invader. The tyrants of the earth, sensible of this, have commonly acted upon this maxim, divide et impera:[5] let us first divide the people, whom we mean to enslave, into parties, and we shall then easily bring them under our power.

They should endeavor to maintain among themselves a general disposition to submit to government. Society cannot subsist without government; and there can be no government without laws, and a submission to laws. If a licentious

---

4. [Resist the first advances. — Eds.]
5. [Divide and conquer. — Eds.]

spirit prevails among a people, a general disposition to trample upon laws and despise government, they will probably make but a poor figure in defending themselves against a common enemy; for, in making this defence, there must be leaders and followers, some to command and some to obey: And, other things being equal, the more a disposition to submit to rule and order prevails among a people, the more likely will they be to defend their liberty against foreign invasions. Indeed without any enemy from abroad, the general prevalence of a licentious spirit may as effectually destroy the liberty of a people, as the most despotic government; for civil "liberty is something as really different from that licentiousness which supposeth no government, as from that slavery which supposeth tyranny: it is a freedom restrained by beneficial laws, and living and dying with public happiness." (Bp. Hoadly.[6]) . . .

That people that would be in a capacity to defend themselves successfully against encroachments, should take care that their internal government be free and easy; allowing all that liberty to every one which is consistent with the necessary restraints of government; laying no burdens upon any, but what are for the good of the whole, and to which the whole society has actually or virtually consented.

A people who would stand fast in their liberty, should furnish themselves with weapons proper for their defence, and learn the use of them.

It is indeed an hard case, that those who are happy in the blessings of providence, and disposed to live peaceably with all men, should be obliged to keep up the idea of blood and slaughter, and expend their time and treasure to acquire the arts and instruments of death. But this is a necessity which the depravity of human nature has laid upon every state. Nor was there ever a people that continued, for any considerable time, in the enjoyment of liberty, who were not in a capacity to defend themselves against invaders, unless they were too poor and inconsiderable to tempt an enemy.

So much depends upon the military art, in the present day, that no people can reasonably expect to defend themselves successfully without it. However numerous they may be, if they are unskilled in arms, their number will tend little more to their security, than that of a flock of sheep does to preserve them from the depredations of the wolf: accordingly it is looked upon as a point of wisdom, in every state, to be furnished with this skill, though it is not to be obtained without great labor and expence.

In some nations the method has been to trust for defence and security to what is called a STANDING ARMY; a number of men paid by the public, to devote themselves wholly to the military profession; while the body of the people followed their peaceable employments, without paying any attention to the art of war.

---

6.   [Church of England Bishop Benjamin Hoadly (1676-1761) was an advocate for Whig principles and defender of the Glorious Revolution of 1688. He was also the author of a famous 1705 sermon that made many of the same points that Mayhew would later make. *See* Reed Browning, Political and Constitutional Ideas of the Court Whigs 67-88 (1982); Benjamin Hoadly, A Defence of the Foregoing Sermon 26 (John Hoadly ed., 1773) (both the sermon and the defense thereof argued for a right of individual self-defense, and extrapolated from that a national right of self-defense against a tyrant such as James II). — EDS.]

But this has ever been thought, by the wise and prudent, a precarious defence.

Such armies are, as to the greater part of them, generally composed of men who have no real estate in the dominions which they are to defend; their pay is their living, and the main thing that attaches them to their employers; their manner of life tends to corrupt their morals, and, though they are naturally of the same temper with other men, they seldom continue long in this profession, before they become distinguished by their vices: So that neither their temporal interest, nor their regard to virtue can be supposed to attach them so strongly to the country that employs them, but that there will always be danger of their being tempted by the promise of larger pay to betray their trust, and turn their arms against it. No people therefore, can with safety trust intirely to a standing army, even for defence against foreign enemies.

But without any such enemy, a standing army may be fatal to the happiness and liberty of a community. They generally propagate corruption and vice where they reside, they frequently insult and abuse the unarmed and defenceless people: When there is any difference between rulers and subjects, they will generally be on the side of the former, and ready to assist them in oppressing and enslaving the latter.

For though they are really servants of the people, and paid by them; yet this is not commonly done in their name; but in the name of the supreme magistrate. The KING's BREAD, and the KING'S SERVICE, are familiar expressions among soldiers, and tend to make them consider him as their only master, and prefer his personal interest to that of the people. So that an army may be the means, in the hands of a wicked and oppressive sovereign, of overturning the constitution of a country, and establishing the most intolerable despotism. It would be easy to shew from history, that this measure has been fatal to the liberties of many nations. And indeed, it has seldom been approved by the body of a people.

A safer way, and which has always been esteemed the wisest and best, by impartial men, is to have the power of defence in the body of the people, to have a well-regulated and well-disciplined militia. ("Our trained bands are the trustiest and most proper strength of a free nation." Milton's Eikon.[7]) This is placing the sword in hands that will not be likely to betray their trust, and who will have the strongest motives to act their part well, in defence of their country, whenever they shall be called for. An army composed of men and property, who have been all their days inured to labour, will generally equal the best veteran troops, in point of strength of body and firmness of mind, and when fighting in defence of their religion, their estates, their liberty, and families, will have stronger motives to exert themselves, and may, if they have been properly disciplined, be not much inferior to them in the skill of arms. . . .

Caution however ought to be used in constituting a militia, that it may answer the end for which it is designed, and not be liable to be made an instrument of tyranny and oppression. It should be subject to discipline and order,

---

7. [John Milton, Eikonoklastes (1649) ("The Icon-Breaker"). Commissioned by Parliament, the book argued that reverence for the executed absolutist King Charles I, and for absolute monarchy in general, was a form of idolatry. "Trained bands" were a subset of the militia that received extra training. — Eds.]

and somewhere in the state should be lodged a power of calling it forth to action, whenever the safety of the people requires it. But this power should be so limited and restrained, as that it cannot call it unnecessarily, or oblige it to commit violence or oppression upon any of the subjects.

Once more, it is necessary for a people who would preserve their liberty, to maintain the general practice of religion and virtue. This will tend to make them courageous: The truest fortitude is ever to be found where the passions and affections are in subjection to the laws of God. Religion conciliates the favor of God, upon whom success in war essentially depends, and the hope of this favour will naturally inspire a brave and undaunted resolution. Not to mention that the unity, riches, and bodily strength of a people are greatly favoured by virtue. On the other hand; vice naturally makes men timerous, and fills the breast with baseness and cowardise. What is here said is agreable to the observation of that wise King and inspired writer, who tells us, "the wicked flee, when no man pursueth; but the righteous are bold as a lion." (Proverbs 28:1)

Let me now offer a few considerations to shew the obligations men are under to defend that liberty which providence has conferred upon them. This is a trust committed to us by heaven: we are accountable for the use we make of it, and ought therefore, to the best of our power to defend it. . . .

Men are bound to preserve their own lives, as long as they can, consistently with their duty in other respects. Would not he, who should lose his life by neglecting to resist a wild beast, be criminal in the sight of God? And can he be innocent who loses it by neglecting to oppose the violent attacks of wicked men, oftentimes as fierce and cruel as the most savage beast?

. . . Every man is bound both by the law of nature and revelation, to provide in the best manner he can, for the temporal happiness of his family, and he that neglects this, has, according to the declaration of an inspired apostle, denied the faith, and is worse than an infidel. . . . But in what way can a man be more justly chargeable with this neglect, than by suffering himself to be deprived of his life, liberty or property, when he might lawfully have preserved them?

Reason, humanity and religion, all conspire to teach us, that we ought in the best manner we can, to provide for the happiness of posterity. . . . And who that has the bowels of a father, or even the common feelings of humanity, can think without horror, of being the means of subjecting unborn millions to the iron scepter of tyranny? But further: a regard to the happiness of mankind in general, makes it a duty to resist great injuries. . . . It is therefore an act of benevolence to oppose and destroy that power which is employed in injuring others; and as much, when it is that of a tyrant, as of a wild beast.

Once more; from a regard to religion men are obliged to defend their liberty against encroachments, though the attack should not immediately affect religion. Slavery exposes to many temptations to vice, and by debasing and weakening the mind, destroying its fortitude and magnimity renders it less capable of resisting them, and creates a dependance upon, and subjection to wicked men, highly prejudicial to virtue. Hence it has been often observed, and is confirmed by experience, that the loss of liberty is soon followed by the loss of all virtue and religion. . . .

All that now remains is to offer some reflections, and apply the subject to the present occasion.

Oppressors may indeed for a time, be successful and overcome all opposition, yet it seldom happens that they persevere in their injurious practice, without meeting with such resistance as causes their mischief to return upon their own heads, and their violent dealings to come down upon their own pates: It is an old observation, that few tyrants descend in peace to the grave. . . .

. . . Our greatest security, under God, will be our being in a capacity to defend ourselves. Were we, indeed, sure that Great-Britain would always be both able and willing to protect us in our liberty, which from present appearances, we have little reason to expect, it would be shameful for so numerous a people as this, and a people of so much natural strength and fortitude, to be, thro' inattention to the art of war, incapable of bearing a part in their own defence. . . . Nothing is wanting but our own care and application to make us, with the neighbouring colonies, a formidable people. And religion, honor, patriotism, and even self-love, all unite in demanding from us this application and care. This people, it may be presumed, will never of choice, keep among them a standing army in time of peace:

Virtue, domestic peace, the insulted walls of our State-House, and even the once crimsoned stones of the street, all loudly cry out against this measure. But every well-wisher to the public, should countenance and encourage a military spirit among our militia through the province.

Our political Fathers have it in their power to do much for this end; and we have a right to expect that, out of faithfulness to God and this people, they will not neglect it. . . .

Whereas when gentlemen of fortune, notwithstanding the allurements of pleasure on the one hand, and the fatiguing exercise of a soldier on the other, exert themselves to acquire and promote the military art, they are an honor to their circumstances, and a blessing to the public. . . .

NOTES & QUESTIONS

1. What is the dominant theme of the materials in this section? Is it individual self-defense or is it a military, community defense theme? Are they mutually exclusive?

2. According to Mayhew and Howard, under what conditions is obedience to government religiously required? When is violent resistance to government a religious duty? Are Mayhew and Howard's refutations of the absolute duty to obey government convincing?

3. Why was community self-defense by a militia considered more virtuous and safer than relying on a standing army?

4. In the views of Mayhew and Howard, what are the characteristics of a good citizen? Do you see any ways in which the U.S. Constitution attempts to promote this vision of good citizenship?

5. Mayhew and Howard were very mainstream in their view that self-defense was a moral duty. The natural rights philosophers — such as Thomas

Hobbes, John Locke, William Blackstone, and Montesquieu — who provided the intellectual foundation of the American Revolution saw self-defense as the "fundamental law of nature" from which many other legal principles could be deduced. John Locke, Second Treatise of Government §16 (C.B. Macpherson ed., Hackett Publ'g Co. 1980) (1690).

Locke argued that a man's life belonged to God. Accordingly, life was inalienable property. A man could not legitimately destroy his life by suicide, or submit to slavery. As a sermon by the famous Presbyterian Rev. Gilbert Tennent put it:

> He that suffers his life to be taken from him by one that hath no Authority for that Purpose, when he might preserve it by Defence, incurs the Guilt of self-murder since God hath enjoined him to seek the continuance of his Life, and Nature Itself teaches every creature to defend itself. . . .

Gilbert Tennent, The Late Association for Defence (Dec. 24, 1747) (Philadelphia) *quoted in* Charles Asbury, The Right to Keep and Bear Arms in America: The Origins and Application of the Second Amendment to the Constitution 40 (1974) (unpublished doctoral thesis in history, U. of Mich.) (available at U. of Mich. Grad. Library; pamphlet for original sermon in William Clements Library, U. of Mich.).

The Declaration of Independence, *infra*, is premised on the same principle, that certain rights are "inalienable." That is, it was impossible they could have been voluntarily surrendered to Parliament in a social compact. Do you agree that the right to life is inalienable? Other rights? Why? Tennent argued that an inalienable right to life means that failure to defend oneself is the moral equivalent of suicide. Do you find the analogy sound?

6. According to Howard and Mayhew, the loss of political freedom creates a condition of moral degradation and servile dependence. Therefore, civil liberty, which is necessary for proper cultivation of the Christian soul according to God's natural law, is sacred. Civil liberty being sacred, God would fight on behalf of a nation that fought for its civil liberty. (See Patrick Henry's speech, *infra*, for a forceful expression of this theory.) The American ministers bolstered this idea by pointing to numerous stories in the Old Testament where obeying God's will enabled the Hebrews to triumph militarily over numerically superior forces. The religious self-confidence that God would fight for them was a crucial reason why the American public dared to start a war against the most powerful empire in the world. Can you think of instances where similar beliefs influenced American actions?

7. The America-Israel analogy was very common in New England religious thought. From the earliest days of English settlement, sermons compared the Americans' situation to the ancient Israelites. At first, the Americans were seen as analogous to Israel in the Wilderness, when the Hebrew tribes wandered the desert for 40 years after escaping from Egyptian slavery. *See, e.g.,* Marie L. Ahern, The Rhetoric of War: Training Day, the Militia, and

the Military Sermon (1989); Miller, *supra*. After New England became well settled and the Wilderness analogy was no longer compelling, ministers invoked the governance of ancient Israel, finding good examples (e.g., a militia system) and bad ones (oppressive taxation by monarchs).

As New England sought to draw the other nine colonies into revolution, the dominant theme was the story of the "Jewish Republic." Israel had governed itself during the period of Judges, but had sinned against God by becoming a monarchy. America needed to throw off monarchy, and adopt self-government, which was the only system of government approved by God. Congregationalist minister Peter Whitney's 1776 sermon *American Independence Vindicated*, captured current attitudes well when he argued that the thirteen "tribes" of Americans had been patient in their suffering under oppression, like the tribes of Israel under the tyrannical King Rehoboam, until they, like the Israelis, had no choice but to revolt.

America-Israelite imagery was advanced even by people who did not take the Bible literally. Thomas Jefferson's proposed design of the Great Seal featured the Israelites in the wilderness after the Exodus, being led by the pillar of cloud and fire. Benjamin Franklin favored a Great Seal of Moses parting the Red Sea, and Pharaoh's chariots being drowned in the waters.

Can you find in the later history of the United States, and in modern times, echoes of America's early self-identification with Israel? Do you share it? Do you think it is a helpful or an unhelpful idea?

8. CQ: In *United States v. Miller*, 307 U.S. 174 (1939) (Chapter 7) and *Heller* (Chapter 9), the Supreme Court took the view that the "militia" referred to in the Second Amendment constituted the body of the people bearing their private arms. Does that seem consistent with the references in this section?

9. Are privately owned firearms essential to the functioning of the militia as it was understood in colonial America?

10. For more on the black regiment and its role in inciting the Revolution, see, in addition to the sources cited elsewhere in this section, Political Sermons of the American Founding Era, 1730-1805 (Ellis Sandoz ed., 2010) (2 vols.); Dale S. Kuehne, Massachusetts Congregationalist Political Thought 1760-1790: The Design of Heaven (1996); Harry S. Stout, The New England Soul: Preaching and Religious Culture in Colonial New England (1988); The Pulpit of the American Revolution (John Wingate Thornton ed., 1970) (1860) (reprinting some important sermons).

Important sermons were printed, and read widely throughout the colonies. Indeed, by 1776, Congregationalist pamphlets from New England exceeded the number of secular pamphlets from all the other colonies combined by more than four to one. For some examples of leading sermons, in addition to the ones cited in this section, see John Lathrop, Innocent Blood Crying to God (1771); Eli Forbes, The Dignity and Importance of the Military Character Illustrated (1771 Artillery Day); William Gordon, A Discourse Preached December 15th, 1774, Being the Day Recommended by the Provincial Congress; And Afterwards at the Boston Lecture; William Emerson, Sermon on 2 Chronicles 13:12 (Mar. 13, 1775); Samuel Langdon, Government Corrupted by Vice, and Recovered by Righteousness (May 31, 1775).

C. The British Crackdown

1. The Coercive (Intolerable) Acts and the Powder Alarm

Parliament's 1773 Tea Act re-affirmed a tax that the Americans considered flagrantly unlawful. They believed that taxation without consent was simply theft, for only through a representative legislature could the people consent to taxation. Accordingly, the British Parliament had no authority to tax the Americans. The colonists' principle was "no taxation without representation." On December 16, 1773, some Bostonians disguised themselves with war paint and Indian clothing, boarded three ships of the East India Company (a joint-stock company that enjoyed monopolies created by Parliament for certain forms of trade), and dumped three shiploads of tea into the water. Furious about the Boston Tea Party, Parliament in 1774 passed the Coercive Acts, known in the Colonies as the Intolerable Acts. The Acts included numerous harsh measures:

- The Boston Port Act shut the port of Boston until the damages from the Tea Party were repaid.
- The Massachusetts Government Act put most of the state government under the direct control of the royal governor appointed by the king. The Act also forbade town meetings (a common form of municipal self-government) more than once a year.
- The Administration of Justice Act authorized the royal governor to move trials of royal officials outside of Massachusetts — a law that George Washington denounced as the "Murder Act" because he feared it would allow British officials to commit crimes with impunity.
- The Quartering Act authorized the governors of every colony to designate unoccupied buildings and public accommodations (such as inns) for quartering British soldiers. This responded to the colonial legislatures' general neglect of their obligation (imposed by a 1765 Act of Parliament) to provide quarters for British soldiers in North America. Once the French had been driven out of North America by the 1763 Anglo-American victory in the French and Indian War, the Americans expected the British troops that had been sent to fight the war to return home. Parliament decided to keep the troops in North America after the war ended, and many Americans regarded this as a nefarious plot to oppress and threaten the colonists.
- The Quebec Act defined the Quebec colony as extending far down into the Allegheny Mountains, and thereby negated many American land claims in the West.

The Intolerable Acts were offensive, but it was the possibility that the British might deploy the army to enforce them that primed many colonists for armed resistance. The Patriots of Lancaster County, Pennsylvania, resolved: "That in the event of Great Britain attempting to force unjust laws upon us by the strength of arms, our cause we leave to heaven and our rifles." Resolution at an Assembly of the Inhabitants of Hanover, Lancaster County (June 4, 1774), *quoted in* Joe D. Huddleston, Colonial Riflemen in the American Revolution 15 (1978).

A South Carolina newspaper essay, reprinted in Virginia, urged that any law that had to be enforced by the military was necessarily illegitimate:

> With all the plausible Pretences to Protection and Defense, a standing Army is the most dangerous Enemy to the Liberties of a Nation that can be thought of. . . . It is much better, with a well regulated Militia, to run the Risk of a foreign Invasion, than, with a Standing Army, to run the Risk of Slavery. . . . When an Army is sent to enforce Laws, it is always an Evidence that either the Law makers are conscious that they had no clear and indisputable Right to make those Laws, or that they are bad and oppressive. Wherever the People themselves have had a Hand in making Laws, according to the first Principles of our constitution, there is no Danger of Non-submission, nor can there be Need of an Army to enforce them.

A Carolinian (pseudonym), *Some of the Blessings of military Law, or the Insolence of* GOVERNOR GAGE: *From the South Carolina Gazette, of August 23, 1774*, Virginia Gazette, Sept. 27, 1774, at 1.

The Royal Governor of Massachusetts, General Thomas Gage, dispatched the Redcoats to break up an illegal town meeting in Salem. But when large numbers of armed Americans appeared in response, the British retreated. Gage's aide John Andrews explained that

> there was upwards of three thousand men assembled there from the adjacent towns, with full determination to rescue the Committee if they should be sent to prison, even if they were oblig'd to repel force by force, being sufficiently provided for such a purpose; as indeed they are all through the country — every male above the age of 16 possessing a firelock with double the quantity of powder and ball enjoin'd by law.

Ray Raphael, A People's History of the American Revolution: How Common People Shaped the Fight for Independence 55 (2002).

Military rule would be difficult to impose on an armed populace. Gage had only 2,000 troops in Boston. There were thousands of armed men in Boston, and more in the surrounding area. Robert P. Richmond, Powder Alarm 82-83, 86-87 (1971). One response to the problem was to deprive the Americans of gunpowder.

As noted in online Chapter 15, modern "smokeless" gunpowder is stable under most conditions. The "black powder" of the eighteenth century was far more volatile. Accordingly, large quantities of black powder were often stored in a town's "powder house," typically a reinforced brick building. The powder house would hold merchants' reserves, large quantities stored by individuals, as well as powder for use by the local militia. Although colonial laws generally required militiamen (and sometimes all householders, too) to supply their own firearms and a minimum quantity of powder, not everyone could afford it. Consequently, the government sometimes supplied "public arms" and powder to individual militiamen. Practice varied on whether militiamen who had been given public arms would keep them at home. Public arms would often be stored in a special armory, which might also be the powder house.

The British were concerned that Massachusetts towns had been withdrawing their gunpowder from the powder houses. Before dawn on September 1, 1774, 260 Redcoats acting on General Gage's order sailed up the Mystic River and seized all the barrels of powder from the Charlestown powder house (next to the present site of Tufts University, in what is now Somerville). The only powder that was left to take belonged to the colonial government, so Gage was within his legal rights to seize it. But the seizure still incensed the public. *See* David Hackett Fischer, Paul Revere's Ride 44-51 (1994).

The "Powder Alarm," as it became known, was a serious provocation. The people of Suffolk County (which includes Boston) assembled and adopted the Suffolk Resolves on September 6, 1774. The 19 points of political principle, grievance, and plans for action included:

> 9. That the Fortifications begun and now carrying upon Boston Neck are justly alarming to this County, and give us reason to apprehend some hostile intention against that town, more especially as the Commander in Chief has in a very extraordinary manner removed the powder from the magazine at Charleston, and has also forbidden the keeper of the magazine at Boston to deliver out to the owners the powder which they had lodged in said magazine. . . .
>
> 11. That whereas our enemies have flattered themselves that they shall make an easy prey of this numerous, brave and hardy people, from an apprehension that they are unacquainted with military discipline; we, therefore, for the honour, defence and security of this county and province, advise, as it has been recommended to take away all commissions from the officers of the militia, that those who now hold commissions, or such other persons, be elected in each town as officers in the militia, as shall be judged of sufficient capacity for that purpose, and who have evidenced themselves the inflexible friends to the rights of the people; and that the inhabitants of those towns and districts, who are qualified, do use their utmost diligence to acquaint themselves with the art of war as soon as possible, and do, for that purpose, appear under arms at least once every week.

The Suffolk Resolves were distributed across the colonies; Paul Revere rode them down to the First Continental Congress, which had just assembled in Philadelphia. The Congress unanimously condemned Britain's "wicked ministerial measures," endorsed the course of action that had been adopted by the Suffolk Resolves, and urged all the other colonies to send supplies to help the Bostonians. 1 Journals of the American Congress from 1774-1788, at 14 (1823) (adopted Sept. 10, 1774). (The full text of the Suffolk Resolves was entered in the Congress's official journal. *Id.* at 9-14.)

Governor Gage directed the Redcoats to begin general, warrantless searches for arms and ammunition. Many of these searches were conducted when people tried to enter Boston by ship, or by the land "neck" that led to the old part of the city. Nearby Worcester County sent a complaint to General Gage:

> This County are constrained to observe, they apprehend the People justified in providing for their own Defense, while they understood there was no passing the Neck without Examination, the Cannon at the North-Battery spiked up, & many places searched, where Arms and Ammunition were suspected to be; and if found seized; yet as the People have never acted offensively, nor discovered any disposition so to do, as above related, the County apprehend this can never justify the seizure of private Property.

Boston Gazette, Oct. 17, 1774, at 2. According to the *Boston Gazette*, of all General Gage's offenses, "what most irritated the People" was "seizing their Arms and Ammunition." Boston Gazette, Dec. 5, 1774, at 4.

When the Massachusetts Assembly convened, General Gage declared it illegal, so the representatives re-assembled as the "Provincial Congress," with the wealthy merchant John Hancock presiding. On October 26, 1774, the Massachusetts Provincial Congress adopted a resolution condemning military rule, and criticizing Gage for "unlawfully seizing and retaining large quantities of ammunition in the arsenal at Boston, and sundry pieces of ordnance in the same town — committed to the custody of [Gage's] troops the arms, ammunition, ordnance and warlike stores of all sorts, provided at the public expense for the use of the province." The Provincial Congress urged all militia companies to organize and elect officers. The new elections would mean removal of officers who had been appointed by the royal governor. At least a quarter of the militia (the famous Minutemen) were directed to "equip and hold themselves in readiness to march at the shortest notice." The Provincial Congress further declared:

> That as the security of the lives, liberties and properties of the inhabitants of this province depends under providence on their knowledge and skill in the art military, and in their being properly and effectually armed and equipt; if any of said inhabitants are not provided with arms and ammunition according to law, they immediately provide themselves forthwith; and that they use their utmost diligence to perfect themselves in military skill.

Boston Gazette, Oct. 31, 1774, at 3.

In flagrant defiance of royal authority, the Provincial Congress appointed a Committee of Safety and vested it with the power to call forth the militia. Knollenberg, *supra*, at 219-21. The militia of Massachusetts no longer answered to the British government. It was now the instrument of what was becoming an independent government of Massachusetts.

2. Disarmament Orders from London

Information traveled across the Atlantic at the speed of a sailing ship. The average trip was two months, so it is unknown precisely when the British government learned of the Powder Alarm. But we do know that the British government generally approved of Gage's policies. Lord Dartmouth, the royal

Secretary of State for America, sent Gage a letter on October 17, 1774, urging him to disarm New England, to the extent reasonably possible:

> Amongst other things which have occurred on the present occasion as likely to prevent the fatal consequence of having recourse to the sword, that of disarming the Inhabitants of the Massachusetts Bay, Connecticut and Rhode Island, have been suggested. Whether such a Measure was ever practicable, or whether it can be attempted in the present state of things you must be the best judge; but it certainly is a Measure of such a nature as ought not to be adopted without almost a certainty of success, and therefore I only throw it out for your consideration.

Letter from Lord Dartmouth to General Thomas Gage (Oct. 17, 1774), *in* 2 The Correspondence of General Thomas Gage with the Secretaries of State, and with the War Office and the Treasury, 1763-1775, at 175 (Clarence E. Carter ed., 1933).

Gage received Dartmouth's letter on December 3. His reply explained the impediment: "Your Lordship's Idea of disarming certain Provinces would doubtless be consistent with Prudence and Safety, but it neither is nor has been practicable without having Recourse to Force, and being Masters of the Country." Letter from Lord Dartmouth to General Thomas Gage (Dec. 15, 1774), *in* 1 The Correspondence of General Thomas Gage with the Secretaries of State, and with the War Office and the Treasury, 1763-1775, at 387 (Clarence E. Carter ed., 1931-33).

Gage's letter was made public by a reading in the British House of Commons. William Cobbett, 18 Parliamentary History of England 106. It was then picked up and publicized in America as proof of Britain's malign intentions. Mercy Otis Warren, History of the rise, progress, and termination of the American Revolution; interspersed with biographical, political and moral observations (2011) (1805).

3. The Import Ban

Two days after Lord Dartmouth dispatched his disarmament recommendation to General Gage, King George III and his ministers blocked importation of arms and ammunition to America:

> WHEREAS an Act of Parliament has passed in the Twenty Ninth Year of the Reign of his late Majesty King George the Second, intitled, "An Act to empower his Majesty to prohibit the Exportation of Saltpetre, and to enforce the Law for impowering his Majesty to prohibit the Exportation of Gunpowder, or any sort of Arms or Ammunition, and also to empower his Majesty to restrain the carrying coastways of Saltpetre, Gunpowder, or any sort of Ammunition."
>
> And His Majesty judging it necessary to prohibit the Exportation of Gunpowder, or any sort of Arms or Ammunition, out of this Kingdom, doth therefore, with the advice of his Privy Council, hereby order, require, prohibit and command that no Person or Persons Whatsoever (except the Master General of the Ordnance for his Majesty's Service) do, at any time during the space of Six Months from the date of this Order in Council, presume to transport into any parts out of this Kingdom,

or carry coastways any Gunpowder, or any sort of Arms or Ammunition, on board any Ship or Vessel, in order to transporting the same to any part beyond the Seas or carrying the same coastways, without Leave and Permission in that behalf, first obtained from his Majesty or his Privy Council, upon Pain of incurring and suffering the respective Forfeitures and Penalties inflicted by the aforementioned Act. . . .

5 Acts Privy Council 401. The six-month decree was repeatedly renewed, remaining in effect until the Anglo-American peace treaty in 1783. James Truslow Adams, Revolutionary New England 1691-1776, at 412 (1923).

Read literally, the order only required a government permit to export arms or ammunition from Great Britain to America. In practice, no permits were granted. The Crown sent orders to the colonial governors (via Gage, for distribution), and to the British navy, to immediately block all arms and ammunition shipments into the 13 colonies. Knollenberg, *supra*, at 204-05.

Letters from other British officials sent along with the orders raised concerns about the thriving illegal (from the British perspective) arms trade between North America and the Netherlands. *E.g.*, Letter from Lord Dartmouth to General Thomas Gage (Oct. 19, 1774), *in* 2 The Correspondence of General Thomas Gage, *supra*, at 176-77. The concerns were well founded. Benjamin Franklin was masterminding the import of arms and ammunition from the Netherlands, France, and Spain. Richmond, *supra*, at 95.

The Boston Committee of Correspondence learned of the arms embargo, and promptly dispatched Paul Revere to New Hampshire, with the warning that two British ships were headed to Fort William and Mary, in Portsmouth, to seize firearms, cannons, gunpowder. On December 14, 1774, 400 New Hampshire patriots captured all the material at the fort. James Truslow Adams, *supra*, at 412. A New Hampshire newspaper argued that the seizure was prudent and proper, reminding readers that the ancient Carthaginians had consented to "deliver up all their Arms to the Romans," and were decimated by the Romans soon after. The parallels with America seemed plain:

Could they [the Ministry] not have given up their Plan for enslaving America without seizing . . . all the Arms and Ammunition? and without soliciting and finally obtaining an Order to prohibit the Importation of warlike Stores in the Colonies? . . . And shall we like the Carthaginians, peaceably surrender our Arms to our Enemies, in Hopes of obtaining in Return the Liberties we have so long been contending for? . . .

I . . . hope that no Person will, at this important Crisis, be unprepared to act in his own Defence, should he by Necessity be driven thereto. And I must here beg Leave to recommend to the Confederation of the People of this Continent, Whether, when we are by an arbitrary Decree prohibited *the having* Arms and Ammunition by Importation, we have not by the Law of Self Preservation, a Right to seize upon all those within our Power, in order to *defend the* LIBERTIES which GOD and Nature have given us . . . ?

A Watchman, New Hampshire Gazette and Historical Chronicle, Jan. 13, 1775, at 1, *in* 1 American Archives, Fourth Series, 1065 (Peter Force ed., 1843).

Edmund Burke, the intellectual founder of conservative political thought, was among the minority of Members of Parliament who urged accommodation of American concerns. He introduced the "Resolutions for Conciliation with America," which proposed to stop British taxation of domestic commerce in the 13 colonies. Speaking in support of the Resolutions, Burke compared the attempt to disarm America with the previous disarmament of the Welsh:

> Sir, during that state of things, Parliament was not idle. They attempted to subdue the fierce spirit of the Welsh by all sorts of rigorous laws. They prohibited by statute the sending all sorts of arms into Wales, as you prohibit by proclamation (with something more of doubt on the legality) the sending arms to America. They disarmed the Welsh by statute, as you attempted, (but still with more question on the legality) to disarm New England by an instruction. They made an Act to drag offenders from Wales into England for trial, as you have done (but with more hardship) with regard to America.

Speech on Moving His Resolutions for Conciliation with the Colonies (Mar. 22, 1775), in Selected Burke, supra, at 208.[8]

Another moderate, the Duke of Manchester, "cautioned the House to proceed with deliberation, as America had now three millions of people, and most of them were trained to arms, and he was certain they could now produce a stronger army than Great-Britain." Pennsylvania Reporter, Apr. 17, 1775, at 2.

The Massachusetts Provincial Congress took steps to accelerate domestic arms manufacture. The Congress offered to purchase "so many effective arms and bayonets as can be delivered in a reasonable time upon notice given to this congress at its next session." It also urged American gunsmiths and other "such persons, as are skilled in the manufacturing of fire arms and bayonets, diligently to apply themselves thereto, for supplying such of the inhabitants as shall be deficient." The Journals of each Provincial Congress of Massachusetts in 1774 and 1775, at 103 (1838). A few weeks earlier, the Congress resolved: "That it be strongly recommended, to all the inhabitants of this colony, to be diligently attentive to learning the use of arms." New-Hampshire Gazette, Jan. 27, 1775, at 1.

4. Calls for Defiance: Patrick Henry and the South

The troubles in New England inflamed the other colonies. The day after Burke proposed his "Resolutions for Conciliation with America," to Parliament, the Convention of Delegates of Virginia in Richmond witnessed one of the most famous speeches of the Revolution. The Virginia House of Burgesses was

---

8. Burke was probably referring to the Penal Laws against Wales, which were enacted by Parliament in response to the Welsh Revolt (1400-15), led by Owain Glyndŵr (in English, Owen Glendower). The laws were little enforced after 1440, and are widely thought to have been repealed by the Laws in Wales Acts (1535 and 1542). However, formal repeal was not accomplished until the early seventeenth century. 4 & 5 Jas. I, ch. 1(1607); 21 Jas. I, chs. 10, 28 (1624). Similar laws were imposed at various times on Ireland and on Scotland, for the purpose of suppressing national independence movements.

meeting as a special convention in Richmond, because the Royal Governor, Lord Dunmore, had suspended the Virginia Assembly.

Patrick Henry's great speech to the assembly on March 23, 1775, used an escalating series of rhetorical questions, climaxed by a call to arms. Although there is no extant text of Henry's speech, the version that became well known to succeeding generations was compiled by U.S. Attorney General (1817-29) William Wirt in his 1817 biography, *Sketches of the Life and Character of Patrick Henry*. His speech is most famous for its closing line.

Patrick Henry, The War Inevitable, Speech at the Second Revolutionary Convention of Virginia
March 23, 1775

. . . I have but one lamp by which my feet are guided, and that is the lamp of experience. I know of no way of judging of the future but by the past. And judging by the past, I wish to know what there has been in the conduct of the British ministry for the last ten years to justify those hopes with which gentlemen have been pleased to solace themselves and the House.

Is it that insidious smile with which our petition has been lately received? Trust it not, sir; it will prove a snare to your feet. Suffer not yourselves to be betrayed with a kiss.

Ask yourselves how this gracious reception of our petition comports with those warlike preparations which cover our waters and darken our land. Are fleets and armies necessary to a work of love and reconciliation? Have we shown ourselves so unwilling to be reconciled that force must be called in to win back our love? Let us not deceive ourselves, sir. These are the implements of war and subjugation; the last arguments to which kings resort.

I ask gentlemen, sir, what means this martial array, if its purpose be not to force us to submission? Can gentlemen assign any other possible motive for it? Has Great Britain any enemy, in this quarter of the world, to call for all this accumulation of navies and armies? No, sir, she has none. They are meant for us: they can be meant for no other. They are sent over to bind and rivet upon us those chains which the British ministry have been so long forging.

And what have we to oppose to them? Shall we try argument? Sir, we have been trying that for the last ten years. Have we anything new to offer upon the subject? Nothing. We have held the subject up in every light of which it is capable; but it has been all in vain. Shall we resort to entreaty and humble supplication? What terms shall we find which have not been already exhausted? Let us not, I beseech you, sir, deceive ourselves.

Sir, we have done everything that could be done to avert the storm which is now coming on. We have petitioned; we have remonstrated; we have supplicated; we have prostrated ourselves before the throne, and have implored its interposition to arrest the tyrannical hands of the ministry and Parliament. Our petitions have been slighted; our remonstrances have produced additional violence and insult; our supplications have been disregarded; and we have been spurned, with contempt, from the foot of the throne! In vain, after these things, may we indulge the fond hope of peace and reconciliation. There is no longer any room for hope.

If we wish to be free — if we mean to preserve inviolate those inestimable privileges for which we have been so long contending — if we mean not basely to abandon the noble struggle in which we have been so long engaged, and which we have pledged ourselves never to abandon until the glorious object of our contest shall be obtained — we must fight! I repeat it, sir, we must fight! An appeal to arms and to the God of hosts is all that is left us!

They tell us, sir, that we are weak; unable to cope with so formidable an adversary. But when shall we be stronger? Will it be the next week, or the next year? Will it be when we are totally disarmed, and when a British guard shall be stationed in every house? Shall we gather strength by irresolution and inaction? Shall we acquire the means of effectual resistance by lying supinely on our backs and hugging the delusive phantom of hope, until our enemies shall have bound us hand and foot?

Sir, we are not weak if we make a proper use of those means which the God of nature hath placed in our power. The millions of people, armed in the holy cause of liberty, and in such a country as that which we possess, are invincible by any force which our enemy can send against us.

Besides, sir, we shall not fight our battles alone. There is a just God who presides over the destinies of nations, and who will raise up friends to fight our battles for us. The battle, sir, is not to the strong alone; it is to the vigilant, the active, the brave. Besides, sir, we have no election. If we were base enough to desire it, it is now too late to retire from the contest. There is no retreat but in submission and slavery! Our chains are forged! Their clanking may be heard on the plains of Boston! The war is inevitable — and let it come! I repeat it, sir, let it come.

It is in vain, sir, to extenuate the matter. Gentlemen may cry, Peace, Peace — but there is no peace. The war is actually begun! The next gale that sweeps from the north will bring to our ears the clash of resounding arms! Our brethren are already in the field! Why stand we here idle? What is it that gentlemen wish? What would they have? Is life so dear, or peace so sweet, as to be purchased at the price of chains and slavery? Forbid it, Almighty God! I know not what course others may take; but as for me, give me liberty or give me death!

The Convention adopted various resolutions proposed by Henry, including: "That a well regulated Militia, composed of Gentlemen and Yeomen, is the natural Strength, and only Security, of a free Government." In contrast, a standing army is "always subversive of the quiet, and dangerous to the liberties of the people." A well-regulated militia would "secure our inestimable rights and liberties from those further violations with which they are threatened." Journal of Proceedings of Convention Held at Richmond 10-11 (1775).

The Convention formed a committee — including Patrick Henry, Richard Henry Lee, George Washington, and Thomas Jefferson — "to prepare a plan for the embodying, arming, and disciplining such a number of men as may be sufficient" to defend the commonwealth. *Id.* at 11. The Convention urged "that every Man be provided with a good Rifle" and "that every Horseman be provided . . . with Pistols and Holsters, a Carbine, or other Firelock." *Id.* at 17.

When the Virginia militiamen assembled a few weeks later, many wore canvas hunting shirts adorned with the motto "Liberty or Death." Henry Mayer, A Son of Thunder: Patrick Henry and the American Revolution 251 (1991).

In South Carolina, Patriots established a government, headed by the "General Committee." According to the Committee:

> [B]y the late prohibition of exporting arms and ammunition from England, it too clearly appears a design of disarming the people of America, in order the more speedily to dragoon and enslave them; it was therefore recommended, to all persons, to provide themselves immediately, with at least twelve and a half pounds of powder, with a proportionate quantity of bullets.

John Drayton, 1 Memoirs of the American Revolution: So Far As It Related to the States of North and South Carolina, and Georgia 166 (1821).

NOTES & QUESTIONS

1. Patrick Henry was an Anglican, but his Presbyterian mother often took him to hear the brilliant Virginia Presbyterian minister Samuel Davies, who directly influenced Henry on the necessity of manly resistance to tyranny, and whose evangelical, emotional, dramatic, and direct style of preaching greatly influenced Henry's oratory as a lawyer and then as a politician. Mayer, *supra*, at 36-39. For example, during the French and Indian War, Davies had preached:

   > Must peace then be maintained? Maintained with our perfidious and cruel invaders? Maintained at the expense of property, liberty, life, and everything dear and valuable? Maintained when it is in our power to vindicate our right and do ourselves justice? Is the word of peace then our only business? No; in such a time even the God of Peace proclaims by His providence, "To arms!"

   Samuel Davies, The Curse of Cowardice (May 8, 1758) (preached to the militia of Hanover County, Virginia) *in* On Faith and Free Government 93-98 (Daniel C. Palm ed., 1997).

   In what ways did Henry express views similar to those of the New England Congregationalists discussed above?

2. How does Henry's liberty or death ethos square with the fact of African slavery in America? Did Henry expect that American slaves, including those he owned, would eventually opt for liberty or death?

   At the height of his wealth, Henry owned over three dozen adult slaves, plus their children. He denounced slavery as an "Abominable" Practice and "a Species of Violence & Tyranny, which our more rude & barbarous, but more honest Ancestors detested." So, "I will not, I cannot justify it." Acknowledging that Virtue and "her Precepts" were contrary to slavery, he had to "lament my want of conforming to them." Mayer, *supra*, at 168-69. Henry worked earnestly to abolish the international slave trade, using the troubles with England as a pretext for shutting down the import of slaves. Of course, fighting the slave trade is not exactly the same as fighting against domestic slavery. Cf. Michael Tadman, *Debates on Slave Societies and Natural Increase in the Americas*, 105 Am. Hist. Rev. 1534 (Dec. 2000) (In the antebellum period, U.S. slaves showed a natural population growth of about 25 percent per decade. While 427,000 Africans were imported into North America, by 1865 the population was over 4 million.)

5. Defiance in Practice and the Independent Militias

Americans no longer recognized the royal governors as the legitimate commanders of the state militias, and they planned to resist any militia units that remained loyal to the king. When the First Continental Congress convened in September 1774, shortly after the Powder Alarm, the plan was to urge a complete economic boycott of trade with Great Britain. But what if the boycott failed to solve the problem? Virginia's Patrick Henry and Richard Henry Lee introduced a resolution urging mobilization of the militias and preparation for war, for "America is not Now in a State of Peace." With some changes in wording to soften the language (such as putting it in the subjunctive tense, thereby making it less direct), the resolution was adopted by the unanimous vote of all the state delegations. However, the message that Congress sent to the American people in October did not mention militias, but simply set forth the details of the boycott, and announced the formation of the Continental Association (comprised of the state governments) to coordinate the boycott. Mayer, *supra*, at 223-27; Continental Association, 1 Journals of the American Congress from 1774 to 1788, at 23-26 (1823).

Without formal legal authorization, even from the Continental Congress, Americans began to form independent militias, outside the traditional chain of command of the royal governors. In Virginia, George Washington and George Mason organized the Fairfax Independent Militia Company. Other independent militias embodied in Virginia along the same model. E.M. Sanchez-Saavedra, A Guide to Virginia Military Organizations in the American Revolution (1978). The volunteer militiamen pledged that "we will, each of us, constantly keep by us" a firelock, six pounds of gunpowder, and twenty pounds of lead. George Mason, 1 The Papers of George Mason 210-11 (Robert A. Rutland ed., 1970).

In 1775, George Mason drafted the *Fairfax County Militia Plan for Embodying the People*. The Plan affirmed that "a well regulated Militia, composed of the Gentlemen, Freeholders, and other Freemen" was needed to defend "our ancient Laws & Liberty" from the Redcoats. "And we do each of us, for ourselves respectively, promise and engage to keep a good Fire-lock in proper Order, & to furnish Ourselves as soon as possible with, & always keep by us, one Pound of Gunpowder, four Pounds of Lead, one Dozen Gun Flints, & a pair of Bullet-Moulds, with a Cartouch Box, or powder-horn, and Bag for Balls." *Id.* at 215-16.

Later, in "Remarks on Annual Elections for the Fairfax Independent Company," Mason explained that "all men are by nature born equally free and independent." Because government creates "the most arbitrary and despotic powers this day upon earth," liberty can only be protected by "frequently appealing to the body of the people." Roman history, argued Mason, showed that freedom could not be maintained if the government relied on mercenaries.

Rather, the people must be taught "the use of arms and discipline" so they can "act in defence of their invaded liberty." *Id.* at 229-30.

Independent militias also formed in Connecticut, Rhode Island, New Hampshire, Maryland, and South Carolina. They chose their own officers and rejected the authority of officers who had been appointed by the royal governors. Knollenberg, *supra*, at 214-16.

John Adams firmly defended the newly constituted Massachusetts militia.

> "The new-fangled militia," as the specious Massachusettensis[9] calls it, is such a militia as he never saw. They are commanded through the province, not by men who procured their commissions from a governor as a reward for making themselves pimps to his tools, and by discovering a hatred of the people, but by gentlemen, whose estates, abilities, and benevolence have rendered them the delight of the soldiers. . . . [I]n a land war, this continent might defend itself against all the world.

John Adams, Novanglus and Massachusettensis: Political Essays, Published in the Years 1774 and 1775, at 32 (Applewood Books 2009) (1819) (Novanglus 3, Feb. 6, 1775).

NOTES & QUESTIONS

1. Independent, or semi-independent, militias were an accepted feature of early American life. The federal Militia Act of 1792 (see Chapter 4.E) recognized independent militias, and incorporated them into the federal militia: "And whereas sundry corps of artillery, cavalry and infantry now exist in several of the said states, which by the laws, customs, or usages thereof, have not been incorporated with, or subject to the general regulations of the militia. . . . *Be it further enacted,* That such corps retain their accustomed privileges subject, nevertheless, to all other duties required by this Act, in like manner with the other militia." 1 Stat. 271 (1792).

   Between 1815 (the end of the War of 1812) and 1860 (the beginning of mobilization for the Civil War), most states did little to train their militias. (The major exception was Massachusetts, which by the late 1850s had built a quite good select militia of 5,000.) Accordingly, some civic-minded men founded volunteer militia organizations. The movement started in the 1830s. By 1850, it had expanded nationwide. Typically, these independent militias would receive a corporate charter from the state, and the governor would issue commissions to the officers. Some of the militia organizations were purely local, while others had chapters in several states. The quality of training varied widely. Some companies sported fancy uniforms and

---

9. [The young Loyalist lawyer Daniel Leonard, who wrote a series of anti-Revolution essays in the *Massachusetts Gazette* and *Boston Post-Boy* in 1774-75. In this chapter, we have not attempted to give "equal time" to the American Loyalists who opposed the Revolution. The Loyalists are certainly important to the history of the Revolution, but they are of little, if any, significance to the development of the American ideology of guns and militias and, ultimately, of the Second Amendment, which is, after all, the subject of this particular book. — EDS.]

excelled in complicated marches. But few developed much skill in combat shooting or tactics. Mass enlistments from the volunteer militias filled the ranks of the U.S. Army during the Mexican-American War (1846-48), and these volunteers at least had more military training than raw recruits. In the chaotic early days of the American Civil War (1861-65), volunteer militias saved Washington, D.C., from Confederate conquest. The National Guard, which first arose in some states near the end of the Civil War, was in its earliest incarnations an independent militia. However, as detailed in Chapter 4.F, the Guard eventually traded independence for state and then federal funding, and today is almost entirely under the control of the federal Department of Defense. *See* Jerry M. Cooper, The Rise of the National Guard: The Evolution of the American Militia, 1865-1920, at 11-22 (2002); Marcus Cunliffe, Soldiers and Civilians: The Martial Spirit in America, 1775-1865, at 5-7 (1968).

2. Small groups of modern Americans sometimes assemble themselves under the label "militia." What is the difference between these groups and the independent militias of Washington, Mason, and other Revolutionaries?

3. CQ: In *Heller,* the Court describes the militia as the body of the people bearing arms provided by themselves in common use at the time. This idea has other important implications for the scope of the right to keep and bear arms. It is grounded in the original, late-eighteenth-century conception of militia. To what degree should original usage and understanding dictate our modern decision making? Assuming it is legitimate to use original understanding as the basis for establishing an individual right to arms under the Second Amendment, is it also necessary that we credit the legitimacy of independent militias?

D. Arms and the American Revolution

1. Gun Confiscation at Lexington and Concord

The American War of Independence — as it was commonly called at the time — began on April 19, 1775, when 700 Redcoats under the command of Major John Pitcairn left Boston to seize American arms at Lexington and Concord. The events and themes that grow out of this conflict fuel much of our modern debate and understanding about the right to keep and bear arms.

The militias that assembled at the Lexington Green and the Concord Bridge consisted of able-bodied men aged 16 to 60. They supplied their own firearms, although a few poor men had to borrow a gun. Robert A. Gross, The Minutemen and Their World 61, 69-70 (1976). The Lexington militia included at least one Black man. Essex Gazette, Apr. 25, 1775, at 3; Alice Hinkle, Prince Estabrook: Slave and Soldier (2001) (he was freed after serving in the Continental Army). Warned of the British advance, the young women of Lexington assembled cartridges late into the evening of April 18.

At dawn, 700 British regulars confronted 200 militiamen at Lexington. "Disperse you Rebels — Damn you, throw down your Arms and disperse!" ordered Major Pitcairn. Although eyewitness accounts conflict about who fired first, American folklore remembers the perhaps apocryphal words of militia commander Captain John Parker: "Don't fire unless fired upon, but if they mean to have a war, let it begin here."[10] It does seem to have been the established American policy to put the onus of firing first on the British.

The British, supported by cannon fire, routed the Americans at Lexington. They then marched to Concord. Ralph Waldo Emerson later recounted the events at Concord's North Bridge:

> By the rude bridge that arched the flood,
> Their flag to April's breeze unfurled,
> Here once the embattled farmers stood,
> And fired the shot heard round the world.

Ralph Waldo Emerson, Hymn: Sung at the Completion of the Concord Monument, *in* Collected Poems and Translations 125 (1994). After a few minutes of fighting at the bridge, the Concord militia drove off a British detachment, However, the Concord militia was not large enough to attempt to engage the full Redcoat force. So at both Concord and Lexington, the British could conduct house-to-house searches for firearms and powder, concentrating on locations previously identified by spies. (Thanks to the alarm that had been spread the night before by Paul Revere and William Dawes, the militia's main powder reserves, at Concord, had been moved out of town before the British arrived.) The morning's events confirmed the British conviction that the American militia were a rabble in arms who could not stand up to the well-disciplined British regulars.

When the British began to withdraw back to Boston, things got much worse for them. Armed Americans were swarming in from nearby towns. Although some of the Americans cohered in militia units operating under a unified command, a great many of them fought on their own, taking sniper positions at whatever opportunity presented itself. Rather than fight in open fields, like European soldiers, the Americans hid behind natural barriers, fired from ambush positions, and harried the Redcoats all the way back to Boston.

One British officer complained that the Americans acted like "rascals" and fought as "concealed villans" with "the cowardly disposition . . . to murder us all." One British officer reported: "These fellows were generally good marksmen, and many of them used long guns made for Duck-Shooting." Frederick MacKenzie, A British Fusilier in Revolutionary Boston, Being the Diary of Lieutenant Frederick Mackenzie, Adjutant of the Royal Welch Fusiliers, January 5–April 30, 1775, at 67 (Allen French ed., 1926; reprinted 1969) (quoting an unnamed officer).

---

10. Parker's musket today hangs in the chamber of the Massachusetts Senate. A trigger lock was attached to the musket in 1998 under a gun control law enacted that year. The next year, the legislature removed the trigger lock mandate for antique firearms, and the trigger lock was removed. Mass. Acts 1998, ch. 180, amended by Acts 1999, ch. 1, §4.

To save the British expedition from complete annihilation on the road, the British had to dispatch a rescue force from Boston. Lord Percy, commander of the rescue force, recounted:

> They have men amongst them who know very well what they are about, having been employed as Rangers against the Indians & Canadians, & this country being much covered with woods, and hilly, is very advantageous for their method of fighting.
>
> Nor are several of their men void of a spirit of enthusiasm, as we experienced yesterday, for many of them concealed themselves in houses, & advanced within 10 yards to fire at me & other officers, tho' they were morally certain of being put to death themselves in an instant.

Letter from Earl Percy to General Edward Harvey (Apr. 20, 1775), *in* Hugh Percy, Letters of Hugh Earl Percy from Boston and New York 1774-1776, at 52-53 (1902).

Among the American fighters along the road that day were several women as well as a group of men who were too old for the militia, led by David Lamson, a "mulatto." Peter Oliver's Origin & Progress of the American Rebellion: A Tory View 118, 120 (Douglass Adair & John A. Schutz eds., 1961) (written in 1781); J.E. Tyler, *An Account of Lexington in the Rockingham Mss. at Sheffield*, 10 Wm. & Mary Q. (3d ser.) 99, 106 (1953) (letter to Lord Rockingham from Massachusetts, probably written by a high-ranking naval officer; "even Weamin had firelocks"); Fischer, *supra*, at 170-71, 243-44. For a detailed survey of Black participation in the Revolution, see William Cooper Nell, The Colored Patriots of the American Revolution (2010) (1855).

At day's end, there were 50 Americans killed, 39 wounded, and 5 missing. Among the British, 65 were killed, 180 wounded, and 27 missing. *Id.* at 321. On a per-shot basis, the Americans inflicted higher casualties than did the British regulars. *Id.* at 408 n.61.

Meanwhile, in Virginia, Britain also moved to disarm the Americans. On April 21, 1775, royal authorities confiscated 20 barrels of gunpowder from the public magazine in the capital city of Williamsburg, and destroyed the public firearms there by removing their firing mechanisms. Virginia Gazette (Williamsburg), Aug. 5, 1775, at 2, col. 1. In response to complaints, manifested most visibly by the mustering of a large independent militia led by Patrick Henry, Governor Dunmore explained that "he was surprised to hear the people were under arms on this occasion, and that he should not think it prudent to put powder into their hands in such a situation." Pennsylvania Reporter, May 8, 1775, at 4. The confrontation ended peacefully when emissaries of the governor delivered a legal note promising to pay restitution. Mayer, *supra*, at 256-57.

2. Gun Confiscation in Boston

At Lexington and Concord, coercive disarmament had not worked out for the British. Back in Boston, General Gage recognized that British troops there were heavily outnumbered by armed Bostonians. "[K]nowing that many of the Boston householders had arms, [Gage] was afraid the town would rise at his back." Allen French, The Day of Lexington and Concord, the Nineteenth of April,

1775, at 56 (1925). Gage set out to disarm the Bostonians but though a strategy that avoided direct force.

On April 23, 1775, Gage offered the Bostonians the opportunity to leave town, if they surrendered their arms, directing "that upon the inhabitants in general lodging their arms in Faneuil Hall, or any other convenient place, under the care of the selectmen, marked with the names of the respective owners, that all such inhabitants as are inclined, may depart from the town. . . . And that the arms aforesaid at a suitable time would be return'd to the owners." *Attested Copy of Proceedings Between Gage and Selectmen, April 23, 1775,* Connecticut Courant, July 17, 1775, at 4.

The Boston selectmen voted to accept the offer, and a massive surrender of arms began. Connecticut Courant, May 8, 1775, at 3. Within days, 2,674 guns were deposited. John Rowe, Anne Rowe Cunningham & Edward Lillie Pierce, Letters and Diary of John Rowe: Boston Merchant, 1759-1762, 1764-1779, at 293-94 (2008) (1903). They consisted, according to one historian, of "1778 firearms" (muskets or rifles), "634 pistols, 973 bayonets" (bayonets attached to the long guns), and "38 blunderbusses" (short-barreled shotguns). Richard Frothingham, History of the Siege of Boston 95 (1903).

Based on an estimate of 15,000 Bostonians, Douglas Southall Freeman, 3 George Washington: A Biography 576 (1948-57), there was one gun surrendered for every 5.6 residents. Historian Page Smith estimates the Boston population to have been somewhat higher. Still, he concludes that the surrendered guns "were a very substantial armory for a city of some 16,000, many of whom were women and children. If we take into account those weapons that had already been taken out of the city by patriots, it is probably not far off the mark to say that every other male Bostonian over the age of eighteen possessed some type of firearm." Page Smith, 1 A New Age Now Begins: A People's History of the American Revolution 506 (1976). These estimates do not, of course, take into account any firearms that the Bostonians secreted away, smuggled out of town, or otherwise refused to surrender.

Having collected their arms, Gage then refused to allow the Bostonians to leave. Connecticut Courant, May 8, 1775, at 3. He claimed that many more arms had been concealed than surrendered. This was suggested by the fact that a large proportion of the surrendered guns were "training arms" — large muskets with bayonets, that would be difficult to hide. Eventually, a system of passes was set up, allowing Bostonians to leave town. But the passes were difficult to obtain, and even then, Bostonians were often prohibited from taking their household goods or food. After several months, food shortages in Boston convinced Gage to allow easier emigration from the city.

Gage's Boston disarmament program incited other Americans to take up arms. Benjamin Franklin, returning to Philadelphia after an unsuccessful diplomatic trip to London, "was highly pleased to find the Americans arming and preparing for the worst events, against which he thinks our spirited exertions will be the only means under God to secure us." Massachusetts Spy, May 17, 1775, at 3.

A letter on behalf of the Massachusetts Provincial Congress warned the Provincial Congress of New York of

the breach of a most solemn treaty with respect to the inhabitants of Boston when they had surrendered their arms and put themselves wholly in the power of a military commander. [New Yorkers should avail] yourselves of every article which our enemies can improve with the least advantage to themselves for effecting the like desolation, horrors and insults on the inhabitants of your city and Colony, or which might enable you to make the most effectual defence. . . . If you should delay securing them until they should be out of your power, and within a few days you should behold these very materials improved in murdering you, and yourselves perishing for the want of them, will not the chagrin and regret be intolerable.

2 Journals of the Provincial Congress, Provincial Convention, Committee of Safety and Council of Safety of the State of New York: 1775-1776-1777, at 10 (1842) (letter of May 26, 1775).

The government in London dispatched more troops and three more generals to America: William Howe, Henry Clinton, and John Burgoyne. The generals arrived on May 25, 1775, with orders from Lord Dartmouth:

That all Cannon, Small Arms, and other military Stores of every kind that may be either in any public Magazine, or secretly collected together for the purpose of aiding Rebellions, should also be seized and secured, and that the persons of all such as, according to the Opinions of His Majesty's Attorney and Solicitor General, have committed themselves in Acts of Treason & Rebellion, should be arrested & imprisoned.

Letter from Lord Dartmouth to Thomas Gage (Apr. 15, 1775), *in* 2 Correspondence of General Thomas Gage, *supra*, at 191.

Per Dartmouth's orders, Gage imposed martial law on June 12, and offered a general pardon to all rebels (except for Samuel Adams and John Hancock) provided they would immediately desist and submit. The Americans declined.

The war underway, Americans continued to show their skill at arms. They captured Fort Ticonderoga in upstate New York. At the June 17, 1775, Battle of Bunker Hill, outside Boston the militias held their ground against the British regulars and inflicted heavy casualties, until they ran out of ammunition, and were finally driven back. (If not for Gage's powder confiscation the previous September, Bunker Hill likely would have resulted in an outright British defeat.) General Gage acknowledged that the Americans were not mere rabble. He asked London for more troops and mercenaries.

On June 19, Gage renewed his demand that the Bostonians surrender their arms, and he declared that anyone found in possession of arms would be deemed guilty of treason:

Whereas notwithstanding the repeated assurances of the selectmen and others, that all the inhabitants of the town of Boston had *bona fide* delivered their fire arms unto the persons appointed to receive them, though I had advices at the same time of the contrary, and whereas I have since had full proof that many had been perfidious in this respect, and have secreted great numbers: I have thought fit to issue this proclamation, to require of all persons who have yet fire arms in their possession immediately to surrender them at the court house, to such persons as shall be authorized to receive them; and hereby declare that all persons in whose possession any fire arms may hereafter be found, will be deemed enemies to his majesty's government.

New York Journal, Aug. 31, 1775, at 1.

Meanwhile, the Continental Congress had voted to send ten companies of riflemen from Pennsylvania, Maryland, and Virginia to aid the Massachusetts militia. 1 Journals of the American Congress from 1774 to 1788, at 82-83 (June 15, 1775) (1823).

3. Declaration of Causes and Necessity of Taking Up Arms

On July 6, 1775, the Continental Congress adopted the Declaration of Causes and Necessity of Taking Up Arms. The Declaration was written by Thomas Jefferson and the great Pennsylvania lawyer John Dickinson. Among the grievances were General Gage's efforts to disarm the people of Lexington, Concord, and Boston.

The Declaration by the Representatives of the United Colonies of North America, July 6, 1775
2 The Political Writings of John Dickinson, Esquire, Late President of the State of Delaware, and of The Commonwealth of Pennsylvania 38-43 (1801)

Soon after intelligence of these proceedings [a new British tax plan] arrived on this Continent, General *Gage*, who, in the course of the last year had taken possession of the Town of Boston, in the Province of *Massachusetts-Bay*, and still occupied it as a garrison, on the 19th day of *April* sent out from that place a large detachment of his army, who made an unprovoked assault on the inhabitants of the said Province, at the Town of *Lexington*, as appears by the affidavits of a great number of persons, some of whom were officers and soldiers of that detachment, murdered eight of the inhabitants, and wounded many others. From thence the troops proceeded in warlike array to the Town of *Concord*, where they set upon another party of the inhabitants of the same Province, killing several and wounding more, until compelled to retreat by the country people suddenly assembled to repel this cruel aggression. Hostilities, thus commenced by the *British* Troops, have been since prosecuted by them without regard to faith or reputation. — The inhabitants of *Boston*, being confined within that Town by the General, their Governour, and having, in order to procure their dismission, entered into a treaty with him, it was stipulated that the said inhabitants, having deposited their arms with their own Magistrates, should have liberty to depart, taking with them their other effects. They accordingly delivered up their arms; but in open violation of honour, in defiance of the obligation of treaties, which even savage nations esteemed sacred, the Governour ordered the arms deposited as aforesaid, that they might be preserved for their owners, to be seized by a body of soldiers; detained the greatest part of the inhabitants in the Town, and compelled the few who were permitted to retire, to leave their most valuable effects behind.

By this perfidy, wives are separated from their husbands, children from their parents, the aged and the sick from their relations and friends, who wish to attend and comfort them; and those who have been used to live in plenty, and even elegance, are reduced to deplorable distress. . . .

Our cause is just. Our union is perfect. Our internal resources are great, and, if necessary, foreign assistance is undoubtedly attainable. — We gratefully acknowledge, as signal instances of the Divine favour towards us, that His providence would not permit us to be called into this severe controversy until we were grown up to our present strength, had been previously exercised in warlike operations, and possessed of the means of defending ourselves. With hearts fortified with these animating reflections, we most solemnly, before God and the world, DECLARE, that, exerting the utmost energy of those powers which our beneficent Creator hath graciously bestowed upon us, the arms we have been compelled by our enemies to assume, we will, in defiance of every hazard, with unabating firmness and perseverance, employ for the preservation of our liberties; being, with one mind, resolved to die freemen rather than live slaves.

Lest this declaration should disquiet the minds of our friends and fellow-subjects in any part of the Empire, we assure them that we mean not to dissolve that union which has so long and so happily subsisted between us, and which we sincerely wish to see *restored.* — Necessity has not yet driven us into that desperate measure, or induced us to excite any other nation to war against them. — We have not raised armies with ambitious designs of separating from *Great Britain,* and establishing independent states. We fight not for glory or for conquest. We exhibit to mankind the remarkable spectacle of a people attacked by unprovoked enemies, without any imputation or even suspicion of offence. — *They* boast of their privileges and civilization, and yet proffer no milder conditions than servitude or death.

In our own native land, in defence of the freedom that is our birth-right, and which we ever enjoyed till the late violation of it — for the protection of our property, acquired solely by the honest industry of our forefathers and ourselves, against violence actually offered, we have taken up arms. We shall lay them down when hostilities shall cease on the part of the aggressors, and all danger of their being renewed shall be removed, and not before.

With an humble confidence in the mercies of the supreme and impartial Judge and Ruler of the Universe, we most devoutly implore his divine goodness to protect us happily through this great conflict, to dispose our adversaries to reconciliation on reasonable terms, and thereby to relieve the Empire from the calamities of civil war.

On July 8, the Continental Congress followed up with an open letter to the people of Great Britain complaining that "your Ministers (equal Foes to British and American freedom) have added to their former Oppressions an Attempt to reduce us by the Sword to a base and abject submission." As a result:

On the sword, therefore, we are compelled to rely for protection. Should victory declare in your favor, yet men trained to arms from their Infancy, and animated by the Love of Liberty, will afford neither a cheap or easy conquest. Of this at least we are assured, that our Struggle will be glorious, our success certain; since even in death we shall find that freedom which in life you forbid us to enjoy.

1 Journals of the American Congress from 1774-1788, *supra*, at 106-11 (adopted July 8, 1775).

One observer, new to the American tradition, pressed the patriots' cause in a publication that commented on the American gun culture. John Zubly, an immigrant from Switzerland who was serving as a Georgia delegate to the Continental Congress, wrote a pamphlet entitled *Great Britain's Right to Tax . . . By a Swiss*, which was published in London and Philadelphia. It excoriated Gage for "detaining the inhabitants of Boston, after they had, in dependence on the General's word of honour, given up their arms, to be starved and ruined. . . ." He warned that "in a strong sense of liberty, and the use of firearms almost from the cradle, the Americans have vastly the advantage over men of their rank almost everywhere else." Indeed, children were "shouldering the resemblance of a gun before they are well able to walk." "The Americans will fight like men, who have everything at stake," and their motto was "DEATH OR FREEDOM." John Joachim Zubly, Great Britain's Right to Tax . . . By a Swiss (1775).

Some feared that the Massachusetts gun confiscation was the prototype for confiscation throughout America. For example, according to a newspaper article published in three states, "It is reported, that on the landing of the General Officers, who have sailed for America, a proclamation will be published throughout the provinces inviting the Americans to deliver up their arms by a certain stipulated day; and that such of the colonists as are afterwards proved to carry arms shall be deemed rebels, and be punished accordingly." Virginia Gazette, June 24, 1775, at 1 (also published in New York Journal on the same date, and in the Maryland Gazette on July 20).

Independent militias had been forming before Lexington and Concord, but the events of that day convinced many more Americans to arm themselves and to embody militias independent of royal control. A report from New York City observed that "the inhabitants there are arming themselves, have shut up the port, and got the keys of the Custom-House." Pennsylvania Reporter, May 1, 1775, at 3. Further, "the whole city and province are subscribing an association, forming companies, and taking every method to defend our rights. The like spirit prevails in the province of New Jersey, where a large and well disciplined militia are now fit for action." The New York General Committee (a patriot organization) resolved "that it be Recommended to every Inhabitant, to perfect himself in Military Discipline, and be provided with Arms, Accoutrements, and Ammunition, as by Law directed." New York Journal, May 4, 1775, at 2.

General Gage sent the news to London: "[Massachusetts], Connecticut, and Rhode Island are in open Rebellion and I expect the same Accounts of New-Hampshire. They are arming at New-York and as we are told, in Philadelphia, and all the Southern Provinces." Letter from General Thomas Gage to Lord Dartmouth (May 25, 1775), *in* 1 The Correspondence of General Thomas Gage, *supra*, at 401.

In Virginia, Lord Dunmore already knew the trouble that Patrick Henry's independent militia, discussed above, could cause. Henry's example was being copied everywhere: "Every County is now Arming a Company of men whom they call an independent Company for the avowed purpose of protecting their Committee, and to be employed against Government if occasion require." John

Carter Matthews, Richard Henry Lee 30 (1978). Henry's militia seized the public arms in Williamsburg. Virginia Gazette, May 6, 1775, at 3.

North Carolina's Royal Governor Josiah Martin issued a proclamation against "endeavoring to engage the People to subscribe papers obliging themselves to be prepared with Arms, to array themselves in companies, and to submit to the illegal and usurped authorities of Committees." R.D.W. Conner, 1 History of North Carolina: The Colonial and Revolutionary Periods, 1584-1783, 360 (1919). Martin complained that "The Inhabitants of this County on the Sea Coast are . . . arming men, electing officers and so forth. In this little town [New Bern] they are now actually endeavoring to form what they call independent Companies under my nose." *Id.* at 362.

North Carolina's three delegates to the Continental Congress (Richard Caswell, William Hooper, and Joseph Hewes) sent a message to the Committees of Safety (local patriot organizations) declaring:

> It is the Right of every English Subject to be prepared with Weapons for his Defense. We conjure you . . . to form yourselves into a Militia. . . . Carefully preserve the small quantity of Gunpowder which you have amongst you, it will be the last Resource when every other Means of Safety fails you; Great-Britain has cut you off from further supplies. . . . We cannot conclude without urging again to you the necessity of arming and instructing yourselves, to be in Readiness to defend yourselves against any Violence that may be exerted against your Persons and Properties.

North Carolina Gazette (New Bern), July 7, 1775, at 2.

Furious, Governor Martin issued a "Fiery Proclamation" condemning the attempt "to excite the people of North Carolina to usurp the prerogative of the Crown by forming a Militia and appointing officers thereto and finally to take up arms against the King and His Government." Independent militia were banned, and Martin declared that "persons who hath or have presumed to array the Militia and to assemble men in Arms within this Province without my Commission or Authority have invaded His Majesty's just and Royal Prerogative and violated the Laws of their Country to which they will be answerable for the same." 10 Colonial Records of North Carolina 144-45, 150 (William L. Saunders ed., 1890).

A Virginia gentleman wrote a letter to a Scottish friend explaining what was happening in America:

> We are all in arms, exercising and training old and young to the use of the gun. No person goes abroad without his sword, or gun, or pistols. . . . Every plain is full of armed men, who all wear a hunting shirt, on the left breast of which are sewed, in very legible letters, "*Liberty or Death.*"

3 American Archives, 4th series, 621 (Peter Force ed., 1843) (Sept. 1, 1775).

4. Falmouth Destroyed

In the summer of 1775, Lord Dartmouth relieved General Gage of his American command, replacing him with General William Howe. This was no gesture of conciliation. The Americans' refusal to surrender their firearms now prompted a different response. Royal Admiral Samuel Graves ordered that all seaports north of Boston be burned. Fischer, *supra*, at 284.

When the British navy showed up at Falmouth, Massachusetts (today's Portland, Maine), the town attempted to negotiate. British "Captain Henry Mowat informed the Committee at Falmouth, there had arrived orders from England about ten days since, to burn all the sea port towns on the continent, that would not lay down and deliver up their arms, and give hostages for their future good behavior. . . ." Falmouth would avoid destruction only if "we would send off our carriage guns,[11] deliver up our small arms, ammunition, & c. and send four gentleman of the town as hostages, which the town could not do." The townspeople gave up eight muskets, which was hardly sufficient, and so Falmouth was destroyed by naval bombardment. George Washington (whom the Continental Congress had just appointed Major General and Commander-in-Chief of the just-created Continental Army on June 14) urged colonial newspapers to print stories on the destruction, highlighting British brutality. *See* New York Journal, Nov. 2, 1775, at 3; Letter from George Washington to Esek Hopkins (Oct. 21, 1775) (no signature), *in* 6 Revolutionary Correspondence from 1775 to 1782, at 132 (1867).

NOTES & QUESTIONS

1. Do the details of Revolutionary conflicts have any precedential value for understanding the modern right to keep and bear arms? Consider the American's harassment of British troops as they retreated back to Boston, where many American patriots were their own commanders. How does this translate into the modern conversation about the right to keep and bear arms? Is there any modern context in which you would support armed Americans acting as their own commanders?

2. Consider James Madison's statement that Americans' familiarity with private arms produced a significant advantage over the British. Is this kind of familiarity with firearms of any value in the modern era? Does Madison's statement indicate whether the right of the people in the Second Amendment is a reference to individual citizens?

3. Is the imposition of martial law a reliable signal that armed resistance is legitimate? Is the risk of martial law a reason why citizens should possess their own arms?

4. Do the warrantless seizures of firearms by the British Army suggest any connection between the Second and Fourth Amendments?

5. General Gage promised to return the Bostonians' guns if they gave him temporary custody of them. In 1972, the Provisional Irish Republican

---

11. [Cannons mounted on a wheeled carriage, so that they can be moved from place to place. — EDs.]

Army (PIRA) was waging a terrorist campaign in Northern Ireland (which was, and still is, part of the United Kingdom). The PIRA was arming itself in part by stealing guns from registered gun owners in the independent Republic of Ireland. The Republic's legislature enacted a temporary custody order, which required the surrender of certain types of firearms for a 30-day period when a person's license for that gun expired. (Licenses were for a term of years, not lifetime.) The police then kept the guns, and refused to renew the license. The guns remained in police custody for 34 years, until a High Court lawsuit forced their return. If the government were collecting firearms en masse, would you surrender a firearm into promised temporary custody? If no, is there anything else you would refuse to surrender when ordered? If yes, is there any item you would refuse to surrender?

5. The Declaration of Independence

In July 1776, the states assembled at Philadelphia in the Continental Congress unanimously adopted the Declaration of Independence. The Declaration first set forth fundamental principles of government. As Thomas Jefferson later explained, these principles restated the American consensus, derived from Aristotle, Cicero, John Locke, and Algernon Sidney. *See* Letter from Thomas Jefferson to Henry Lee (May 8, 1825), *in* 16 The Writings of Thomas Jefferson 117-19 (Andrew A. Lipscomb ed., 1903). Those writers are discussed in Chapter 2.

The Declaration of Independence
United States 1776

When in the course of human events, it becomes necessary for one people to dissolve the political bands which have connected them with another, and to assume among the powers of the earth, the separate and equal station to which the laws of nature and of nature's God entitle them, a decent respect to the opinions of mankind requires that they should declare the causes which impel them to the separation.

We hold these truths to be self-evident: that all men are created equal; that they are endowed by their Creator with certain unalienable rights; that among these are life, liberty, and the pursuit of happiness. That, to secure these rights, governments are instituted among men, deriving their just powers from the consent of the governed; that whenever any form of government becomes destructive of these ends, it is the right of the people to alter or to abolish it, and to institute new government, laying its foundation on such principles, and organizing its powers in such form, as to them shall seem most likely to effect their safety and happiness. Prudence, indeed, will dictate that governments long established should not be changed for light and transient causes; and accordingly all experience hath shown that mankind are more disposed to suffer, while evils are sufferable than to right themselves by abolishing the forms to which they are accustomed. But when a long train of abuses and usurpations, pursuing invariably the same object, evinces a design to reduce them under absolute despotism, it is their right, it is their duty, to throw off such government, and to provide new guards for their future security. Such has been the patient sufferance of these colonies; and such is now the necessity which constrains them to alter their former systems of government. The history of the present King of Great Britain is a history of repeated injuries and usurpations, all having in direct object the establishment of an absolute tyranny over these states. To prove this, let facts be submitted to a candid world. . . .

He has refused to pass other laws for the accommodation of large districts of people, unless those people would relinquish the right of representation in the legislature, a right inestimable to them, and formidable to tyranny only. He has called together legislative bodies at places unusual, uncomfortable, and distant from the depository of their public records, for the sole purpose of fatiguing them into compliance with his measures.

He has dissolved representative houses repeatedly, for opposing with manly firmness his invasions on the rights of the people. . . .

He has kept among us, in times of peace, standing armies, without the consent of our legislatures.

He has affected to render the military independent of, and superior to, the civil power.

He has combined with others to subject us to a jurisdiction foreign to our Constitution and unacknowledged by our laws, giving his assent to their acts of pretended legislation:

For quartering large bodies of armed troops among us;

For protecting them, by a mock trial, from punishment for any murders which they should commit on the inhabitants of these States;

For cutting off our trade with all parts of the world;

For imposing taxes on us without our Consent;

For depriving us, in many cases, of the benefits of trial by jury;

For transporting us beyond seas to be tried for pretended offences;

For abolishing the free system of English laws in a neighbouring province [Quebec], establishing therein an arbitrary Government, and enlarging its boundaries, so as to render it at once an example and fit instrument for introducing the same absolute rule into these colonies;

For taking away our charters, abolishing our most valuable laws, and altering fundamentally the forms of our governments;

For suspending our own legislatures, and declaring themselves invested with power to legislate for us in all cases whatsoever.

He has abdicated government here, by declaring us out of his protection, and waging war against us.

He has plundered our seas, ravaged our coasts, burned our towns, and destroyed the lives of our people.

He is at this time transporting large armies of foreign mercenaries to complete the works of death, desolation, and tyranny already begun with circumstances of cruelty and perfidy scarcely paralleled in the most barbarous ages, and totally unworthy the head of a civilized nation.

He has constrained our fellow-citizens, taken captive on the high seas, to bear arms against their country, to become the executioners of their friends and brethren, or to fall themselves by their hands.

He has excited domestic insurrection among us, and has endeavored to bring on the inhabitants of our frontiers the merciless Indian savages, whose known rule of warfare is an undistinguished destruction of all ages, sexes, and conditions.

In every stage of these oppressions we have petitioned for redress in the most humble terms; our repeated petitions have been answered only by repeated injury. A prince, whose character is thus marked by every act which may define a tyrant, is unfit to be the ruler of a free people.

Nor have we been wanting in our attentions to our British brethren. We have warned them, from time to time, of attempts by their legislature to extend an unwarrantable jurisdiction over us. We have reminded them of the circumstances of our emigration and settlement here. We have appealed to their native justice and magnanimity; and we have conjured them, by the ties of our common kindred, to disavow these usurpations which would inevitably interrupt our connections and correspondence. They too, have been deaf to the voice of justice and of consanguinity. We must, therefore, acquiesce in the necessity which denounces our separation, and hold them as we hold the rest of mankind, enemies in war, in peace friends.

We, therefore, the representatives of the UNITED STATES OF AMERICA, in General Congress assembled, appealing to the Supreme Judge of the world for the rectitude of our intentions, do, in the name and by the authority of the good people of these colonies solemnly publish and declare, That these United Colonies are, and of right ought to be, FREE and INDEPENDENT STATES; that they are absolved from all allegiance to the British crown and that all political connexion between them and the state of Great Britain is, and ought to be, totally dissolved; and that, as FREE and INDEPENDENT STATES, they have full power to levy war, conclude peace, contract alliances, establish commerce, and do all other acts and things which INDEPENDENT STATES may of right do. And for the support of this Declaration, with a firm reliance on the protection of DIVINE PROVIDENCE, we mutually pledge to each other our lives, our fortunes, and our sacred honor.

NOTES & QUESTIONS

1. The Declaration does not specifically mention gun confiscation in its litany of King George's abuses. Why not? Do any items in the litany relate to the British gun control program?

2. The litany directly addresses only two items that later appear in the Bill of Rights: the quartering of soldiers and the right to jury trial. Why is unreasonable search and seizure missing? Freedom of conscience, assembly, petition, and expression?

3. Earlier in this chapter, the material prompted questions about what constituted legitimate violent resistance to tyranny, including acts of resistance by a single individual, small groups, or private militias. The Declaration of Independence asserts the right to resist tyranny. The Declaration is the

product of a legislative body representing the people of the several colonies, which assumed all the powers of independent states. Does this support the argument that any legitimate resistance to tyranny anticipated by the Second Amendment must proceed in a similar way? What would constitute sufficient widespread support for violent resistance against federal "tyranny" in the modern era? What if such support was manifested by a coalition of three highly populated cities? A ballot referendum in a single sparsely populated state? Legislation passed in a group of states spanning more than one large region of the country?

4. Among the items in the Declaration's indictment of King George's acts of tyranny are that "[h]e has combined with others to subject us to a jurisdiction foreign to our Constitution and unacknowledged by our laws, giving his assent to their acts of pretended legislation." In other words, the British Parliament in London had no lawful authority to impose domestic legislation in the 13 colonies. Accordingly, parliamentary acts purporting to enact domestic American laws were merely acts of "pretended legislation" — illegitimate usurpations not entitled to the respect of a real law. For other expressions of a similar principle, see, e.g., *Calder v. Bull,* 3 U.S. 386 (1798) (seriatim opinion of Justice Chase) ("An ACT of the Legislature (for I cannot call it a law) contrary to the great first principles of the social compact, cannot be considered a rightful exercise of legislative authority.").

Likewise, the French sometimes referred to the enactments of the pro-Nazi Vichy government (1940-44) as "pretend laws" or "decrees said to be law." *See* Pierre Lemieux, Confessions d'un Courer des Bois Hors-la-Loi 42 (2001); Les Acquisitions Immobilières de la Ville de Paris Entre 1940 et 1944 Sont-Elles le Produit de Spoliations? Rapport établi par le Conseil du Patrimoine Privé de la Ville de Paris avec le concours de son Groupe d'experts (Nov. 16, 1998), *available at* http://www.v1.paris.fr/FR/La_Mairie/executif/communiques/ancienne_mandature/mandature_1995_2001/patrimoine. ASP (describing certain Vichy laws as "les Actes dits 'lois,'" or as "prétendus lois, décrets et arrêtés, règlements ou décisions," that is, "the acts said to be 'law,'" and "pretend laws, decrees, orders, regulations, or decisions").

The appellations of "pretend laws" or "said-to-be laws" imply that purported acts of a government, while following the standard form of law, may be manifestly unjust and thus illegitimate. The pretend laws do not merit the presumption of obedience that is accorded to real laws.

The contrary view, known as legal positivism, is that "law" is simply a sovereign's command that is habitually obeyed, and that law has no moral constraint. Leading proponents of this view include the nineteenth-century English legal philosopher John Austin, and U.S. Supreme Court Justice Oliver Wendell Holmes.

Can you imagine a government command so unjust that you would classify it as a pretend law? Are there any current laws that you think fit that category? Would you classify a law that forbids self-defense against genocide, homicide, rape, or tyranny a pretend law?

Of the 27 paragraphs listing the specific abuses of King George, 9 concerned militarism. Can any general principles of proper government be discerned from the military grievances?

6.   Thomas Paine on Self-Defense, Resistance, and Militias

Thomas Paine was perhaps the most influential writer on behalf of American independence. His pamphlet *Common Sense*, first published January 10, 1776, urged the American public not only that their cause was righteous, but that the probability of their success was great. On the issue of preparedness, Paine exhorted, "Our small arms [are] equal to any in the world. . . . Saltpeter and gunpowder we are every day producing." Common Sense, *in* 1 The Complete Writings of Thomas Paine 35 (Philip S. Foner ed., 1969).

Paine had warned earlier about the dangers of disarmament:

> The supposed quietude of a good man allures the ruffian; while on the other hand, arms like laws discourage and keep the invader and the plunderer in awe, and preserve order in the world as well as property. The balance of power is the scale of peace. The same balance would be preserved were all the world destitute of arms, for all would be alike; but since some *will not*, others *dare not* lay them aside. . . . Horrid mischief would ensue were one half the world deprived of the use of them; . . . the weak will become a prey to the strong.

Thomas Paine, *Thoughts on Defensive War*, Pennsylvania Magazine, July 1775, *in* 2 The Complete Writings of Thomas Paine 35 (Philip S. Foner ed., 1969).

Despite the excitement and optimism that had followed the Declaration of Independence, the next several months of war went badly for the Americans. The British defeated George Washington's Army in Brooklyn and chased them off Manhattan. The Continental Army was fortunate to survive as an effective fighting force. It was in this context that Paine penned a new series of essays, *The American Crisis*, the first of which was published on December 23, 1776. He began:

> These are the times that try men's souls. The summer soldier and the sunshine patriot will, in this crisis, shrink from the service of their country; but he that stands it *now*, deserves the love and thanks of man and woman. Tyranny, like hell, is not easily conquered; yet we have this consolation with us, that the harder the conflict, the more glorious the triumph.

1 The Complete Writings of Thomas Paine, *supra*, at 50.

Paine observed that "the temporary defence of a well-meaning militia" had "set bounds to the progress of the enemy. . . ." But Paine concluded that the militia alone could not win the war, arguing, "I always considered militia as the best troops in the world for a sudden exertion, but they will not do for a long campaign." *Id.* at 54.

Reflecting the common view, Paine drew no distinction between self-defense against individual criminals and collective self-defense against a criminal government. In 1766, when Parliament repealed the much hated Stamp Act, it simultaneously passed the Declaratory Act. The Declaratory Act asserted that Parliament had "full power and authority to make laws and statutes of sufficient force and validity to bind the colonies and people of America, subjects of the crown of Great Britain, in all cases whatsoever." Paine analogized this assertion of power, and the right to resist such power, to resistance against a robber:

> If a thief breaks into my house, burns and destroys my property, and kills or threatens to kill me, or those that are in it, and to "*bind me in all cases whatsoever*" to his absolute will, am I to suffer it? What signifies it to me, whether he who does it is a king or a common man; my countryman or not my countryman; whether it be done by an individual villain, or an army of them?

Id. at 55-56.

Paine also warned against capitulation to Britain's continued gun confiscation program, now pressed by General Howe:

> Howe's first object is, partly by threats and partly by promises, to terrify or seduce the people to deliver up their arms and receive mercy. The ministry recommended the same plan to Gage, and this is what the Tories call making their peace. . . . Were the back counties to give up their arms, they would fall an easy prey to the Indians, who are all armed: this perhaps is what some Tories would not be sorry for. Were the home counties to deliver up their arms, they would be exposed to the resentment of the back counties, who would then have it in their power to chastise their defection at pleasure. And were any one state to give up its arms, *that* state must be garrisoned by all Howe's army of Britons and Hessians to preserve it from the anger of the rest.

Id. at 56.

A subsequent installment of Paine's *The American Crisis* criticized the British order that "all inhabitants who shall be found with arms, not having an officer with them, shall be immediately taken and hung up." This meant that any American not under the immediate command of an American officer would be considered a guerilla, and not entitled to a soldier's treatment as a prisoner of war upon capture. *The American Crisis II*, Jan. 13, 1777, *in* 1 The Complete Writings of Thomas Paine, *supra*, at 65.

In another installment, Paine reminded Americans of Gage's letter to London "in which he informs his masters, 'That though their idea of his disarming certain counties was a right one, yet it required him to be master of the country, in order to enable him to execute it.'" *The American Crisis III*, Apr. 19, 1777, *in* 1 The Complete Writings of Thomas Paine, *supra*, at 85.

7. Gun Confiscation and Smuggling Reprised

Dutch traders continued to evade the British arms embargo, even though the Dutch government had formally agreed to respect it. Traders secreted gunpowder in tea chests and rice barrels, and then shipped the contraband to the Dutch Caribbean island of St. Eustatia (a/k/a Saint Eustacius) for delivery to America. 2 American Archives, 4th series, 276; Daniel Miller, Sir Joseph Yorke and Anglo-Dutch Relations, 1774-1780, at 40-41 (1970). Until British capture in 1781, St. Eustatia would be a prime hub for America's trade with the outside world.

Throughout the war, the Patriots continued their pre-war trade with smugglers. Measures to disarm political foes emerged on both sides. British victories had preserved the authority of Royal Governor William Tryon, at least in the vicinity of New York City. On December 2, 1776, Tryon decreed "[t]hat all offensive arms, indiscriminately, be forthwith collected, in each manor, township and precinct, as soon as possible, to deliver them up at head-quarters, to the Commander-in-chief of the King's troops." Henry Onderdonk, Jr., Revolutionary Incidents of Suffolk and Kings Counties; With an Account of the Battle of Long Island, and the British Prisons and Prison-ships at New York 59 (1849).

In 1777, with British victory seeming likely, Colonial Undersecretary William Knox drafted a plan entitled "What Is Fit to Be Done with America?" The plan aimed to ensure that there would be no future rebellions. It provided that the Church of England would be established in every one of the 13 colonies as the state church. Parliament would have power to tax within America. A hereditary aristocracy would be established. There would be a permanent standing army, and "[t]he Militia Laws should be repealed and none suffered to be re-enacted, & the Arms of all the People should be taken away, . . . nor should any Foundery or manufactuary of Arms, Gunpowder, or Warlike Stores, be ever suffered in America, nor should any Gunpowder, Lead, Arms or Ordnance be imported into it without Licence." 1 Sources of American Independence 176 (Howard H. Peckman ed., 1978).

American authorities imposed their own disarmament measures against the Loyalists. About half of white Americans supported independence (Patriots), 15-20 percent were opposed (Tories), and the rest were undecided or indifferent. Robert M. Calhoon, *Loyalism and Neutrality, in* A Companion to the American Revolution 230 (Jack P. Greene & J.R. Pole eds., 2004). In New York and other states, the new state and local governments sometimes attempted to disarm the Tories, usually by ordering them to surrender their firearms, and often offering financial compensation for the surrendered guns. *E.g.,* 1 Journals of the Provincial Congress, Provincial Convention, Committee of Safety and Council of Safety of the State of New-York: 1775-1776-1777, *supra,* at 149-50. American Tories, just like their Patriot brethren, resisted surrendering their arms. *E.g.,* 1 Calendar of Historical Manuscripts, Relating to the War of the Revolution 201 (1868) (in the Office of the Secretary of State, Albany, N.Y.).

NOTES & QUESTIONS

1. To what degree are rhetoric and practices of arms regulation and ownership during the Revolutionary period relevant to our understanding of the modern Second Amendment? Does the seemingly widespread ownership of arms mean that the militia is inevitably defined as the body of the people bearing their own private arms? CQ: Following *Heller* (Chapter 9), some have questioned whether a lifetime ban on owning firearms can be sustained for people who have been convicted of minor criminal offenses. Does the Revolutionary experience speak to the legitimacy of government rules that disarm untrustworthy people? Permanent disarmament?

2. Much of the discussion about arms in the pre-constitutional period occurs in the context of open violent revolt. How should one incorporate that context into an analysis of the modern Second Amendment? For the argument that

the Revolution's principles arc too dangerous for modern times, see David C. Williams, *Civic Republicanism and the Citizen Militia: The Terrifying Second Amendment*, 101 Yale L.J. 551 (1991).

3. The U.S. Constitution included protections against some of the excesses of state government that had taken place during the Revolution. For example, Article I, Sections 9 and 10 prohibit bills of attainder and ex post facto laws. Does this mean that attempts to disarm the Tories, for example, should have no bearing on our understanding of the boundaries of the modern Second Amendment, which *Heller* (Chapter 9) explains is a codification of a preexisting right? Is it relevant whether American Patriots believed that efforts to disarm Tories were legitimate or just a wartime excess?

4. *Heller* presents a detailed examination of the original intent of the Constitution and Bill of Rights. Is Thomas Paine a fair source of that original understanding? What, if anything, do the excerpts from Paine suggest about the meaning of the Second Amendment?

5. Colonial Undersecretary William Knox's 1777 proposal, "What is to be Done with America," appears to acknowledge that the state militias and the arms of the people are different, though connected, things. CQ: See if you recognize this theme when you read *Heller* in Chapter 9.

8. The Militia, the Continental Army, and American Marksmanship

"First and foremost, patriot militia ensured that rebellious Americans gained control of state and local governments early in the war." Cooper, *supra*, at 7. The benefits of Patriot control of all 13 state governments during the war cannot be overestimated. Had the British maintained control of even a single important state government, such as New York, the Revolution might have failed.

In 1775, the Massachusetts militia acquitted itself well when fighting to defend its own territory. But American citizen-soldiers were reluctant to follow the discipline required of professional European soldiers and performed poorly on extended campaigns. As in the French and Indian War (1754-63), militias of the Revolution resisted traveling far from home for very long. Even Americans who formally enlisted in the Continental Army resisted signing up for more than a year. At the end of their year, they would leave for home, even mid-campaign.

The inadequacy of the Continental Army was made painfully clear during the first winter of the war, when an American force led by Benedict Arnold headed north to seize Canada. The late 1775 expedition was a disaster. In January 1776, half the American enlistments were set to expire, prompting a desperate and failed late December attack on Montreal, before the "army" melted away.

The Americans' insistence on returning to their homes at least once a year, and resistance to distant deployments, impeded military effectiveness. But it also had benefits. As part time soldiers, militiamen not only fought the British, but their work on frequent returns home helped keep the economy afloat.

The militia offered at least one tactical advantage. British control of the water meant they could move faster and usually could choose when to engage the Continental Army. But the British had no such advantage over the American militia. Comprised of almost every able-bodied adult male, the militia could rise wherever the British deployed. As historian Daniel Boorstin put it, "[t]he American center was everywhere and nowhere — in each man himself." Daniel Boorstin, The Americans: The Colonial Experience 370 (1965).

The Americans could better afford losses in battle because a large fraction of the adult white male population was available to fight. British soldiers imported from across the Atlantic were more difficult to replace. The British could capture major coastal cities such as Boston and New York City, but control of the vast interior proved impossible. Many militiamen had learned warfare from Indian fighting. In the mountains, swamps, and forests, they denied use of the country to the British. The militiamen had the advantages of intimate knowledge of the terrain, support from much of the local population, and the incentive that comes with defending one's home territory.

Following a British defeat in one of their campaigns, the great British statesman William Pitt (an advocate of reconciliation with America) told the British House of Lords, "If I were an American, as I am an Englishman, while a foreign troop was landed in my country, I would never lay down my arms — never — never — NEVER! You cannot conquer America." Speech in the House of Lords, Nov. 18, 1777.

Whether in the militia or the Continental Army, the guns deployed were mostly personal firearms. As late as 1781, George Washington insisted that enlistees in the Continental Army provide their own guns. Letter from George Washington to Joseph Reed (June 24, 1781), *in* 22 The Writings of George Washington 258 (Jared Sparks ed., 1834); Letter from George Washington to Thomas Parr (July 28, 1781), *in* 22 Writings of George Washington 427 (Jared Sparks ed., 1834). And as early as 1776, when the Pennsylvania militia was formed, the state mandated that the militiamen supply their own weapons. March 12, 1776, 5 American Archives, *supra*, at 681.

Some Americans fought with Pennsylvania- and Kentucky-style rifles, which were far more accurate than the smooth bore British muskets. These high quality rifles were mainly built by German immigrant gunsmiths. Redcoats firing from formation were expected to "level" rather than aim their smooth bore muskets. Success depended on the cumulative effect of volley fire. American guerrillas, though, did not typically engage in formal set battles. They hid behind rocks and trees and sniped at the enemy. American riflemen were known to hit a target the size of a man's head from 200 yards away. The rifling of the gun's bore gave the projectile a stabilizing spin that vastly improved accuracy at extended ranges. (See Chapter 1 and online Chapter 15 for an explanation of how rifling works.)

The American riflemen specialized in sniping at the British officers, causing them considerable apprehension and distracting them from command. The British officers, in turn, denied the American riflemen quarter, considering them executioners rather than honorable soldiers.

In 1789, historian David Ramsay commented about the Battle of Bunker Hill that "[n]one of the provincials in this engagement were riflemen, but they were all good marksmen. The whole of their previous military knowledge had been derived from hunting, and the ordinary amusements of sportsmen. The dexterity which by long habit they had acquired in hitting beasts, birds, and marks, was fatally applied to the destruction of British officers." David Ramsay, 1 A History of the American Revolution 190 (Applewood Books 2011) (1789).

The Americans bragged that, thanks to their rich gun culture, Patriot fighters could outshoot the British regulars. For example, James Madison wrote in a letter to William Bradford (a future U.S. Senator from Rhode Island, and also the namesake and great-great-grandson of the first governor of Plymouth Colony) that Virginia's riflemen could defeat the British before the British muskets were even within range to fire on the Virginians:

> The strength of this Colony will lie chiefly in the rifle-men of the Upland Counties, of whom we shall have great numbers. You would be astonished at the perfection this art is brought to. The most inexpert hands rec[k]on it an indifferent shot to miss the bigness of a man's face at the distance of 100 Yards. I am far from being among the best & should not often miss it on a fair trial at that distance. If we come into an engagement, I make no doubt but the officers of the enemy will fall at the distance before they get within 150 or 200 Yards. Indeed I believe we have men that would very often hit such a mark 250 Yds.

Letter from James Madison to William Bradford (June 19, 1775), *in* 1 The Papers of James Madison 153 (William T. Hutchinson et al. eds., 1962).

Thomas Jefferson, in a letter to his Italian friend Giovanni Fabbroni, detailed British casualties from April 1775 to November 1777. As for American casualties, Jefferson did not have precise data, but he estimated that

> it has been about one half the number lost by [the British]. . . . This difference is ascribed to our superiority in taking aim when we fire; every soldier in our army having been intimate with his gun from his infancy.

Letter from Thomas Jefferson to Giovanni Fabbroni (June 8, 1778), *in* Thomas Jefferson, Writings 760 (1984).

George Washington expressed the same sentiment: "Our Scouts, and the Enemy's Foraging Parties, have frequent skirmishes; in which they always sustain the greatest loss in killed and Wounded, owing to our Superior skill in Fire arms." Letter from George Washington to John A. Washington (Feb. 24, 1777), *in* 7 The Writings of George Washington 198 (Jared Sparks ed., 1834). Washington also concluded that the militia could rarely hold its own against regular troops, complaining that the militia's "want of discipline and refusal, of almost every kind of restraint and Government, have produced . . . an entire disregard of that order and subordination necessary to the well doing of an army." Letter from George Washington to the President of the Continental Congress (Sept. 2, 1776).

A modern study of Washington's use of the militia in Connecticut, New York, and New Jersey concludes that, while the militia could not, by itself, defeat the Redcoats in a pitched battle, it was essential to American success:

> Washington learned to recognize both the strengths and the weaknesses of the militia. As regular soldiers, militiamen were deficient. . . . He therefore

increasingly detached Continentals to support them when operating against the British army. . . . Militiamen were available everywhere and could respond to sudden attacks and invasions often faster than the army could. Washington therefore used the militia units in the states to provide local defense, to suppress Loyalists, and to rally to the army in case of an invasion. . . .

Washington made full use of the partisan qualities of the militia forces around him. He used them in small parties to harass and raid the army, and to guard all the places he could not send Continentals. . . . Rather than try to turn the militia into a regular fighting force, he used and exploited its irregular qualities in a partisan war against the British and Tories.

Mark W. Kwasny, Washington's Partisan War: 1775-1783, at 337-38 (1996).

With every patriotic able American male a militiaman, the British could triumph only by occupying the entire United States, and that was far beyond their manpower and resources. After seven years of winning most of the battles but getting no closer to winning the war, the British gave up.

Historian Don Higginbotham summarized the militia's contribution: "Seldom has an armed force done so much with so little — providing a vast reservoir of manpower for a multiplicity of military needs, fighting (often unaided by Continentals) in the great majority of the 1,331 land engagements of the war." Don Higginbotham, *The American Militia: A Traditional Institution with Revolutionary Responsibilities, in* Reconsiderations on the Revolutionary War 103 (Don Higginbotham ed., 1978).

David Ramsay observed that "[f]or the defence of the colonies, the inhabitants had been, from their early years, enrolled in companies, and taught the use of arms." Ramsay, *supra*, at 178. "Europeans, from their being generally unacquainted with fire arms are less easily taught the use of them than Americans, who are from their youth familiar with these instruments of war." Ramsay also concluded that Americans were less fit for long-term military service than Europeans, because they were often reluctant to take orders. *Id.* at 181-82, 207. (Ramsay was a physician in the South Carolina militia, a delegate to the Continental Congress, a South Carolina state legislator during and after the war, and eventually President of the South Carolina Senate.)

Finally, the militia provided the only practical means for mobilizing most of America's manpower. The Continental Congress had neither the money, the administrative competence, nor the political legitimacy to create a huge Continental Army. In contrast, the state militias had existed for a century and a half, and the states did have the experience, the administrative competence, and the financial means to put much of the adult male population into military service via the militias. Cooper, *supra*, at 7.

E.   *The Articles of Confederation*

The Declaration of Independence rejected British sovereignty in the 13 colonies. The new nation was first governed by the state governments, and for national and international matters, by the Continental Congress — the latter operating on an ad hoc basis. To establish the structure of true national government, the Articles of Confederation, formally naming the new nation "The United States of America," were drafted by the Continental Congress, and sent to the states for ratification in 1777. They went into effect in 1781, when Maryland became the last of the 13 states to ratify.

The Congress established by the Articles of Confederation had no direct power to tax, and thus there was no need for a bill of rights. Like the new Constitution that would be adopted in 1789, the Articles of Confederation forbade states from keeping armies or naval ships in peacetime, unless Congress consented. The Articles did require that "every State shall always keep up a well regulated and disciplined militia, sufficiently armed and accoutered, and shall provide and constantly have ready for use, in public stores, a due number of field pieces and tents, and a proper quantity of arms, ammunition and camp equipage." Articles of Confederation, Art. VI. The "public stores" were for public arms, which were to be supplied to militiamen who could not afford their own guns.

The militias were a state responsibility. But the Continental Congress could requisition the state to supply land forces "for the common defense," and Congress could appoint officers above the rank of colonel while those forces were in national service. Art. VII. Under a federal requisition, the state legislature had the duty to "raise the men and cloath, arm and equip them in a soldier like manner," with the Continental Congress paying the expense. *Id.* Art. IX.

A 1783 report by a Continental Congress committee explained how the militia system should operate:

> [I]n considering the means of national defence, Congress ought not to overlook that of a well regulated militia; that as the keeping up such a militia and proper arsenals and magazines by each State is made a part of the Confederation, the attention of Congress to this object becomes a constitutional duty; that as great advantages would result from uniformity in this article in every State, and from the militia establishment being as similar as the nature of the case will admit to that of the Continental forces, it will be proper for Congress to adopt and recommend a plan for this purpose.

The militia were "all the free male inhabitants in each state from 20 to fifty." "Those who are willing to be at the expence of equipping themselves for Dragoon [cavalry] service to be permitted to enter into that corps, the residue to be formed into Infantry. . . ." Everyone was responsible for bringing his own arms and equipment:

> Each officer of the Dragoons to provide himself with a horse, saddle &c. pistols and sabre, and each non-commissioned officer and private with the preceding articles and these in addition, a carbine and cartouch [cartridge] box, with twelve rounds of powder and ball for his carbine, and six for each pistol.
>
> Each officer of the Infantry to have a sword, and each non-commissioned officer and private, a musket, bayonet and cartouch box, with twelve rounds of powder and ball.

25 Journals of the Continental Congress 1774-1789, 741-42 (1922) (adopted Oct. 23, 1783).

F. The Right to Arms, Standing Armies, and Militias in the Early State Constitutions and Statutes

Even before Declaration of Independence formally terminated English sovereignty, American states began throwing over royal charters, and adopting new principles of self-government. The state constitutional provisions related to arms, the military, the right of forcible resistance to preserve liberty, and self-government are presented below in order of adoption. For a comprehensive survey of arms-bearing and militia provisions in state constitutions, from 1776 to the present day, refer to the state constitution appendix to Chapter 1.

1. South Carolina

The first new state constitution was adopted on March 26, 1776, by the South Carolina assembly. The Preamble expressed the necessity of armed self-defense:

> Hostilities having been commenced in the Massachusetts Bay, by the troops under command of General Gage, whereby a number of peaceable, helpless, and unarmed people were wantonly robbed and murdered, and there being just reason to apprehend that like hostilities would be committed in all the other colonies, the colonists were therefore driven to the necessity of taking up arms, to repel force by force, and to defend themselves and their properties against lawless invasions and depredations.

S.C. Const. of 1776, pmbl.

The South Carolina Constitution had no bill of rights because, as Charles Pinckney put it, "we might perhaps have omitted the enumeration of some of our rights, it might hereafter be said we had delegated to the general government a power to take away such of our rights as we had not enumerated." 4 The Debates in the Several State Conventions on the Adoption of the Federal Constitution 316 (Jonathan Elliot ed., 1836).

2. Virginia

Adopted by a special convention on June 12, 1776, the Virginia Declaration of Rights set forth fundamental principles of government:

> I. That all Men are by Nature equally free and independent, and have certain inherent Rights . . . ; namely, the Enjoyment of Life and Liberty, with the Means of . . . pursuing and obtaining . . . Safety.
>
> II. That all Power is vested in, and consequently derived from, the People. . . .
>
> XIII. That a well regulated Militia, composed of the Body of the People, trained to Arms, is the proper, natural, and safe Defense of a free State; that standing Armies, in Time of Peace, should be avoided, as dangerous to Liberty.

Va. Const. of 1776, Bill of Rights, §§I, II, XIII.

The Virginia Convention then began drafting a constitution. Thomas Jefferson was in Philadelphia, serving in the Continental Congress. He penned a proposal providing among other things that: "No freeman shall ever be debarred the use of arms. . . . There shall be no standing army but in time of . . . actual war." Thomas Jefferson, 1 The Papers of Thomas Jefferson 344-45 (Julian P. Boyd ed., 1950). In a second draft, he added a bracketed section, to designate optional language: "No freeman shall be debarred the use of arms [within his own lands or tenements]." *Id.* at 347, 353.

The reference to use of arms on one's own lands and tenements may have been a rebuke to English game laws, which prohibited commoners from hunting on their own land. It also would have allowed legislation to establish a deer hunting season and thus to prevent taking of deer when off one's own property, which Jefferson proposed to the Virginia assembly not long after. 2 The Papers of Thomas Jefferson 443-44 (Julian P. Boyd ed., 1950). The Virginia Convention adopted a Constitution on June 29, 1776, without including Jefferson's proposed Bill of Rights.

As a member of the Virginia House of Burgesses, Jefferson also introduced a bill to expand the militia system, eliminating the racial restrictions, and providing militiamen who were too poor to afford their own arms with arms at public expense. *Id.* at 251.

Jefferson, only 33 at the time, was well acquainted with the "use of arms." When Jefferson was age 10, his father, Colonel Peter Jefferson, gave him a gun and sent him into the forest to promote his self-reliance. Dumas Malone, Jefferson the Virginian 46-47 (1948) (Vol. 1 of Dumas Malone, Jefferson and His Time (1948)). By the time Jefferson was 14, his father "had already taught him to sit his horse, fire his gun, boldly stem the Rivanna when the swollen river was 'Rolling red from brae to brae,' and press his way with unflagging foot through the rocky summits of the contiguous hills in pursuit of deer and wild turkeys." Henry S. Randall, 1 The Life of Thomas Jefferson 14-15 (1865).

3. New Jersey

The New Jersey Provincial Congress assembled into a special convention and adopted a constitution on July 2, 1776. The New Jersey Convention met under imminent military peril, with the British fleet offshore. There was little opportunity for philosophical discussions of liberty, or for the drafting of a bill of rights. The New Jersey framers instead relied on common law protections of rights. Charles R. Erdman, Jr., The New Jersey Constitution of 1776, 37 (1929). As Judge William Griffith explained two decades later, "public sentiment in New Jersey in 1776 dwelt with slight regard upon the *forms* of constitution. Engaged in a desperate conflict for freedom itself, it was thought of more consequence to exert courage in repelling foreign tyranny, than to sit canvassing the comparative merits of *theories*, which were to secure internal liberty, not yet won from our oppressors." William Griffith, Eumenes: Being a Collection of Papers Written for the Purpose of Exhibiting Some of the More Prominent Errors and Omissions of the Constitution of New Jersey 9 (1799).

In 1775, after the fighting at Lexington and Concord, the New Jersey Provincial Congress organized a militia. 3 Documentary History of the Ratification of the Constitution 130 (1978). With a new constitution established in 1776, Governor William Livingston urged the Council and Assembly of New Jersey to adopt "some further regulations respecting the better ordering the Militia." New-York Gazette and the Weekly Mercury, Oct. 5, 1776, at 2. The Assembly proclaimed of "the necessity of a well regulated militia for the defence of a free State." New York Gazzette and the Weekly Mercury, Oct. 26, 1776, at 1.

By 1777, British victories had brought the land war into New Jersey. General George Washington implored the New Jersey county militias "by all you hold dear, to rise up as one Man, and rid your Country of its cruel invaders. . . . [T]his can be done by a general appearance of all its Freemen armed and ready to give them opposition. . . . I am convinced every Man who can bear a Musket, will take it up." 10 The Writings of George Washington 90 (Jared Sparks ed., 1834).

By 1781, New Jersey elaborated its militia laws. The militia were "all effective Men between the Ages of sixteen and fifty Years," without racial restrictions. Every militiaman was commanded to "constantly keep himself furnished with a good Musket . . . [or] a good Rifle-Gun," except that every horseman "shall at all Time keep himself provided with a good Horse, a Saddle properly furnished with a Pair of Pistols and Holsters." Acts of the Council and General Assembly of the State of New Jersey 168-69, 180, 235 (1784); Robert J. Gough, *Black Men and the Early New Jersey Militia*, 37 N.J. Hist. 227 (1970) (Blacks served in New Jersey militia during the Revolution, but were later excluded.).

4. Pennsylvania

While the Americans had claimed that their right to arms was guaranteed by common law, as affirmed by the 1689 English Declaration of Right, Pennsylvania was the first state to explicitly protect the right to arms in its state constitution.

With Benjamin Franklin presiding, the Pennsylvania Constitutional Convention met from July 15 until September 28, 1776. In comparison to other states during the early Revolution, the Pennsylvania Convention took a long time to deliberate, for the delegates enjoyed the luxury of no immediate threat from the British. The majority of the Pennsylvania delegates were "Associators" — that is, members of armed associations. J. Paul Selsam, The Pennsylvania Constitution of 1776: A Study in Revolutionary Democracy 148 (1936). Because of the still substantial influence of Pennsylvania's Quaker minority, the state had never created a formal militia, so armed defense of the state had become the responsibility of voluntary associations.

The 1776 Constitution provided:

> That the people have a right to bear arms for the defense of themselves, and the state; and as standing armies in the time of peace, are dangerous to liberty, they ought not to be kept up; and that the military should be kept under strict subordination to, and governed by the civil power.

Pa. Const. of 1776, art. XIII.

A separate section finally created a state militia: "The freemen of this commonwealth and their sons shall be trained and armed for its defense, under such regulations, restrictions and exceptions as the general assembly shall by law direct." *Id.* §5. Another article guaranteed hunting and fishing rights: "The inhabitants of this state shall have liberty to fowl and hunt in seasonable times on the lands they hold, and on all other lands not inclosed." *Id.* §43.

But the issue underlying this provision went beyond merely hunting. As an essay in the *Pennsylvania Evening Post* explained, English law presumed that all game is the property of the king, who gives hunting privileges to the aristocracy, while withholding such privileges from commoners. Pennsylvania, urged the writer, must take a different path:

> In order to prevent poachers, as they are called, from invading this aristocratical prerogative, the possession of hunting dogs, snares, nets, and other engines by unprivileged persons, has been forbidden, and, under pretence of the last words, guns have been seized. And though this was not legal, as guns are not engines appropriated to kill game, yet if a witness can be found to attest before a Justice that a gun has been thus used, the penalty is five pounds, or three months imprisonment fall on the accused.
>
> The prosecutors are generally fox-hunters,[12] and if the Justices are such, alas, the culprit has no chance of escaping punishment though the evidence be slander! Thus penal laws, and trial without juries, are multiplied on a trivial subject, and the freeholders of moderate estates deprived of a natural right. Nor is this all; the body of the people kept from the use of guns are utterly ignorant of the arms of modern war, and the kingdom effectually disarmed, except of the standing force. . . . Is any thing like this desired in Pennsylvania?

Remarks on the Resolves, Pennsylvania Evening Post, Nov. 5, 1776, at 554.

5. Delaware

Though the Delaware Constitution of 1776 did not contain an arms-bearing or militia provision, a separate Declaration of Rights provided "[t]hat a well regulated Militia is the proper, natural and safe Defense of a free Government." Del. Declaration of Rights of 1776, §18. Like Pennsylvania, Delaware declared that standing armies are dangerous to liberty, and that the military should be kept subordinate to the civil power. *Id.* §§19-20.

Like Virginia and South Carolina, Delaware would eventually (in 1987) add a right to arms to its state constitution.

6. Maryland

Maryland's 1776 Declaration of Rights is generally considered to be part of its Constitution of the same year. It affirmed "[t]hat a well-regulated militia is the

---

12. [That is, they are aristocrats who ride on horseback following trained dogs who pursue foxes. — EDS.]

proper and natural defence of a free government." Md. Constitution of 1776, A Declaration of Rights, art. XXV. The next two articles denounced standing armies and provided that the military ought to be subservient to the civil power. *Id.* arts. XXVI-XXVII.

Maryland's present-day constitution contains no right to arms.

7. North Carolina

North Carolina's 1776 Declaration of Rights, also generally considered to be part of its constitution of the same year, guaranteed two rights of "the People": "[t]hat the People have a right to bear Arms for the Defense of the State; and as standing Armies in Time of Peace are dangerous to Liberty, they ought not to be kept up" and "[t]hat the People have a Right to assemble together." N.C. Const. of 1776, A Declaration of Rights, arts. XVII-XVIII.

North Carolina also demonstrated one way to recognize an explicitly collective right: "The Property of the Soil in a free Government being one of the essential Rights of the collective Body of the People, it is necessary . . . that the Limits of the State should be ascertained with Precision." *Id.*, art. XXV.

While the militia was not constitutionally recognized, the North Carolina Provincial Congress did implement a militia system. In April 1776, it mandated "that each Militia Soldier shall be furnished with a good Gun, Bayonet, Cartouch Box, Shot Bay and Powder Horn, a Cutlass or Tomahawk; and where any person shall appear to the Field Officers not possessed of sufficient Property to afford such Arms and Accoutrements, the same shall be provided at Public Expense." Journal of Proceedings of the Provincial Congress of North Carolina 32 (1776).

In 1791, the North Carolina legislature required "that all Freemen and indentured Servants within this State, from 15 to 50 years of age, shall compose the militia thereof," and that militia privates would supply their own muskets and rifles, and cavalrymen their own pistols. Statutes of the State of North Carolina 519, 592 (1791). The new state of North Carolina retained the old colony's obligation that all men follow the hue and cry in pursuit of fleeing felons. A Collection of the Statutes of the Parliament of England in Force in the State of North Carolina 6, 398 (1792). (For more on the hue and cry, see Chapter 2.)

8. Georgia

The Georgia Constitution, adopted February 5, 1777, had no bill of rights. It did impose a military duty on local governments that "Every County in this State that has, or hereafter may have, two hundred and fifty men upwards, liable to bear arms, shall be formed into a battalion." Ga. Const. of 1777, art. XXXV.

The British held most of the settled areas of Georgia from 1778 through the end of the Revolution. Guerrilla bands of self-armed, independent Americans harassed the invaders. British expeditions burned homes and destroyed property as they marched, sparing only those who surrendered their arms on demand. Kenneth Coleman, The American Revolution in Georgia, 1763-1789, 119 (1958); 3 Documentary History of the Ratification of the Constitution 204 (Merrill Jensen ed., 2d ed. 1978).

Georgia's delegates at the Continental Congress in 1778 sought to deny citizenship rights to those who refused to take up arms in defense of the Revolution. Article IV of the Articles of Confederation excluded paupers, vagabonds, and fugitives from the guarantee that "the free inhabitants of each of those states . . . shall be entitled to all privileges and immunities of free citizens in the several states." Georgia proposed that "all persons who refuse to bear Arms in defense of the State to which they belong," and persons convicted of treason, should also be excluded from the privileges and immunities of free citizens. Coleman, *supra*, at 94. Congress rejected the provision.

9. New York

In September 1776, the British drove George Washington off Long Island and captured New York City. New York's Constitutional Convention of 1776-77 took nine months to produce a constitution, in large part because the convention was frequently on the run from the British. As Theodore Roosevelt later wrote, "[T]he members were obliged to go armed, so as to protect themselves from stray marauding parties." Theodore Roosevelt, Gouverneur Morris 51 (1898).

There was no right to arms, but there was a duty:

> [I]t is the duty of every man who enjoys the protection of society to be prepared and willing to defend it; this convention therefore . . . doth ordain, determine, and declare that the militia of this State, at all times hereafter, as well in peace as in war, shall be armed and disciplined, and in readiness for service. That all such of the inhabitants of this State being of the people called Quakers as, from scruples of conscience, may be adverse to the bearing of arms, be therefrom excused by the legislature; and do pay to the State such sums of money, in lieu of their personal service, as the same may, in the judgment of the legislature, be worth.

N.Y. Const. of 1777, art. XL.

The English common law hue and cry duty (Chapter 2) was reaffirmed by legislating "that all men generally be ready, and armed and accoutered, . . . and at the cry of the country, to pursue and arrest felons." 1 Laws of the State of New York, Comprising the Constitution, and the Acts of the Legislature, Since the Revolution, from the First to the Fifteenth Session, Inclusive 336 (1792).

A 1787 statute provided that "that no citizen of this state shall be constrained to arm himself, or to go out of this state" unless approved by the legislature. *Id.* at 491. (For more on the debate over federal militia powers, see Chapter 4.) This directly conflicted with the federal militia powers proposed by the Philadelphia Constitutional Convention the same year.

10. Vermont

Ethan and Ira Allen led the Green Mountain Boys in seeking American independence from Britain, and Vermont's independence from New York. Ira Allen's memoirs extolled the skills of Vermonters in hunting and target shooting, and the importance of those skills in achieving independence for the United States and for Vermont. Ira Allen, Autobiography (1799).

In September 1776, a seven-member convention, comprised of Ira Allen and six other men, set Vermont's objectives: "To regulate the Militia; To furnish troops according to our ability, for the defence of the Liberties of the United States of America." Toward this goal, the convention urged "that each non-commissioned officer and soldier immediately furnish himself with a good gun with a Bayonet, sword or tomahawk." *Id.* at 85, 87.

Vermont declared its independence from New York in January 1777, and a constitutional convention met in July. Following Pennsylvania's lead, Vermont adopted a broad guarantee of the right to arms: "That the people have a right to bear arms for the defence of themselves and the State; and, as standing armies, in the time of peace, are dangerous to liberty, they ought not to be kept up." Vt. Const. of 1777, ch. I, art. XV. And, "that the inhabitants of this State, shall have liberty to hunt and fowl, in seasonable times, on the lands they hold, and on other lands (not enclosed)." *Id.* ch. II, art. XXXIX.

Also tracking Pennsylvania, another article affirmed the duty of militia service on the principle that everyone has "a right to be protected in the enjoyment of life, liberty and property," and therefore everyone must "yield his personal service, when necessary," except that "any man who is conscientiously scrupulous of bearing arms" would not "be justly compelled thereto" if he paid an equivalent. *Id.* ch. II, art. IX.

The Vermont militia statute was typical. All men aged 16 to 50 "shall bear arms, and duly attend all musters," and that "every listed soldier and other householder, shall always be provided with, and have in constant readiness, a well fixed firelock . . . or other good fire-arms." The Laws from the Year 1779 to 1786, Inclusive, *in* Vermont State Papers 307 (1823). Further, every man must "provide himself, at his own expense, with a good musket or firelock," and horsemen "shall always be provided with . . . holsters with bear-skin caps, a case of good pistols, a sword or cutlass." Statutes of the State of Vermont, Passed February and March 1789, at 95-97 (1789).

A new state constitution reiterated the right to arms, as did the 1796 constitution. Vt. Const. of 1786, ch. I, art. XVIII (arms-bearing); *id.* ch. II, art. XXXVIII (hunting and fishing); *see also* Vt. Const. of 1793, ch. I, art. 16 (arms-bearing), ch. II, §40 (hunting and fishing).[13]

11.   Massachusetts

In 1778, the people of Massachusetts rejected a proposed constitution that lacked a bill of rights. A 1779 convention drafted a new proposal, which was adopted in 1780. The new constitution was drafted by a committee including James Bowdoin, Samuel Adams, and John Adams.

---

13. Vermont was formally admitted to the Union in 1791, although it had been a functioning state for many years. However, the New York state government had asserted that Vermont was legally part of New York. For Vermont's unusual, quasi-independent status in 1777-91, see Frederic Franklyn Van der Water, The Reluctant Republic Vermont, 1724-1791 (1974).

Pursuant to the principle, articulated in the Declaration of Independence, that the purpose of government is the protection of natural rights, the Massachusetts Constitution began with a Declaration of Rights. The first article of the Declaration of Rights stated:

> All men are born free and equal, and have certain natural, essential, and unalienable rights; among which may be reckoned the right of enjoying and defending their lives and liberties; that of acquiring, possessing, and protecting property; in fine, that of seeking and obtaining their safety and happiness.

Mass. Const. of 1780, pt. I, art. I. Massachusetts's article I epitomizes the American understanding of natural rights. It was copied by many subsequent state constitutions.

The Declaration of Rights also provided that:

> The people have a right to keep and bear arms for the common defence. And as, in time of peace armies are dangerous to liberty, they ought not to be maintained without the consent of the legislature; and the military power shall always be held in an exact subordination to the civil authority, and be governed by it.

Id. art. XVII. This was the first time that an American state constitution had used the word "keep" in connection with the right to arms.

Also significant is the Declaration's denunciation of peacetime armies in the same article as its right to arms. This tracks the Pennsylvania approach and would be followed by Ohio and several other states. The Massachusetts Convention, after much debate, had deleted the word "standing" before "armies." Thus, the Convention made the point that armies of all types, not only standing armies, are "dangerous to liberty." Journal of the Convention for Framing a Constitution of Government for the State of Massachusetts Bay 41 (1779-1780) (1832); John Adams, Diary and Autobiography 401 (L.H. Butterfield ed., 1961).

Separately, the Declaration of Rights reiterated the duty of individuals to perform military service, as the necessary counterpart of society's duty to citizens. Thus, every able-bodied man was "obliged, consequently, . . . to give his personal service, or an equivalent, when necessary. . . ." Mass. Const. of 1780, pt. I, art. X.

In 1786, six years after enactment of Massachusetts's Constitution, Shays's Rebellion broke out in western Massachusetts. The Massachusetts legislature responded with two new laws requiring armed citizens to participate in suppressing lawless disorder. The first law was a milder version of England's 1714 Riot Act (1 Geo. I, ch. 5): If 12 or more people "armed with clubs, or other weapons" assembled, they could be ordered to disperse by a justice of the peace. The justice of the peace could "require the aid of a sufficient number of persons in arms" to enforce his order. 1 The Perpetual Laws of the Commonwealth of Massachusetts, From the Establishment of Its Constitution in the Year 1780, To the End of the Year 1800, at 346 (1801).

The second law stated that:

> Whereas in a free government, where the people have a right to bear arms for the common defence, and the military power is held in subordination to the civil

authority, it is necessary for the safety of the State that the virtuous citizens thereof should hold themselves in readiness, and when called upon, should exert their efforts to support the civil government, and oppose the attempts of factious and wicked men who may wish to subvert the laws and Constitution of Their country.

Id. at 366.

Another arms-related law appeared in 1792, requiring prior approval from the fire warden for transportation of gunpowder on Boston streets "in any quantity, exceeding twenty five pounds, being the quantity allowed by law to be kept in shops for sale." 2 Perpetual Laws of the Commonwealth of Massachusetts 144 (1801).

12.   New Hampshire

In 1776, the Granite State adopted a terse constitution objecting to the British "depriving us of our national and constitutional rights and privileges." N.H. Const. of 1776, para. 2. A more complete constitution was adopted in 1784. The Bill of Rights of the 1784 Constitution stated:

> II. All men have certain natural, essential, and inherent rights; among which are — the enjoying and defending life and liberty — acquiring, possessing and protecting property — and in a word, of seeking and obtaining happiness. . . .
> X. . . . The doctrine of non-resistance against arbitrary power, and oppression, is absurd, slavish, and destructive of the good and happiness of mankind. . . .
> XII. Every member of the community has a right to be protected by it in the enjoyment of his life, liberty and property; he is therefore bound to contribute his share in the expense of such protection, and to yield his personal service when necessary.
> XIII. No person who is conscientiously scrupulous about the lawfulness of bearing arms, shall be compelled thereto, provided he will pay an equivalent.
> XXIV. A well regulated militia is the proper, natural, and sure defence of a state.
> XXV. Standing armies are dangerous to liberty, and ought not to be raised or kept up without the consent of the legislature.

N.H. Const. of 1784.

The lone gun control law of early New Hampshire aimed to prevent fires in the large town of Portsmouth. The law was based on the legislative finding that "the keeping of large quantities of gun-powder in private houses in Portsmouth . . . [w]ould greatly endanger the lives and properties of the inhabitants thereof, in case of fire; which danger might be prevented, by obliging the owners of such powder, to deposit the same in the magazine provided by said town for that purpose." Therefore, no person "shall keep in any dwelling-house, store or other building . . . more than ten pounds of gun-powder." Instead, large quantities of powder would be stored in a central magazine (a fireproof building). The voters would annually choose "a keeper of said magazine, all the powder so deposited, and to account therefore." The Perpetual Laws of the State of New Hampshire 184-85 (Portsmouth 1789).

13.   Connecticut

Connecticut did not adopt a constitution until 1818. Instead, in 1776, the General Assembly reaffirmed the state's 1662 corporate charter. David M. Roth & Freeman Meyer, From Revolution to Constitution: Connecticut 1763 to 1818, at 25 (1975); Melbert B. Cary, The Connecticut Constitution 2-3 (1900).

As of 1775, the militia consisted of all able-bodied males aged 16 to 50. R.R. Hinman, A General View of Connecticut at the Commencement of the Revolutionary War (1842), *in* Chronology and Documentary Handbook to the State of Connecticut 40-50 (Mary L. French ed., 1973). The Connecticut response to the British disarming of Boston was legislation encouraging the manufacture of firearms and gunpowder. Connecticut also set up a system of minutemen — militiamen prepared for quick action. Public Records of the Colony of Connecticut, From May, 1775, to June, 1776, at 17, 291, 451 ff. (Charles Hoadley ed. 1890); David M. Roth, Connecticut: A Bicentennial History 101 (1979).

The 1784 code of Connecticut required that citizens supply their own arms to serve in the watch and ward, and also to participate in the hue and cry. David M. Roth, Connecticut: A Bicentennial History 22, 156 (1979).

The 1784 Militia Act enrolled males 16 to 45 in the militia, but mandated gun ownership among a broader group: all militia infantry as well as all "Householders under fifty-five Years of Age, shall, at all times be furnished at their own Expense, with a well fixed Musket." Militia horsemen had to have "a Case of good Pistols, a Sword or Cutlass." The state militia's commander was responsible for annual arms inspections of "Householders and others by Law obliged to keep Arms." The statutory rationale for the militia duties was that "the Defence and Security of all free States depends (under God) upon the Exertions of a well regulated and Disciplined Militia." Acts and Laws of the State of Connecticut 144, 150-51 (1784).

Joel Barlow was a leading diplomat and writer during 1780s and 1790s. He was one of the "Connecticut Wits," a group of writers centered around Yale. Barlow noted that in Europe, an armed populace would be regarded "as a mark of an uncivilized people, extremely dangerous to a well-ordered society." He contended that because the American system was built on popular sovereignty, which brought out the best in man's character, the people could be trusted with guns: "It is *because the people are civilized that they are with safety armed.*" Joel Barlow, Advice to the Privileged Orders in the Several States of Europe: Resulting From the Necessity and Propriety of a General Revolution in the Principle of Government 16 (Cornell University Press, 1956) (1792). *Advice to the Privileged Orders,* written at the suggestion of Barlow's friend Tom Paine, argued that if the state represented the people as a whole, not just one class, society would be more stable.

Another Connecticut Wit, Timothy Dwight, future President of Yale, wrote, "The people of New-England have always had, and have by law always been required to have, arms in their hands. Every man is, or ought to be, in the possession of a musket." Dwight wrote that he did not know of "a single instance, in which arms have been the instruments of carrying on a private quarrel." The reason, he said, was that "if proper attention be paid to the education of the children in knowledge and religion, few men will be disposed to use arms, unless for their amusement, and for the defense of themselves and their country." Timothy Dwight, 4 Travels in New England and New York 335 (1823).

14. Rhode Island

Rhode Island used its colonial charter as the basis of government until it adopted a constitution in 1842. Various Rhode Island statutes prohibited misuse of firearms. These included a ban on dueling. Public Laws of the State of Rhode Island 593 (1798). Also, sheriffs could order the dispersal of assemblies of 12 or more people "armed with clubs or other weapons," or of 30 or more persons who were assembled riotously. As in Massachusetts, a sheriff who required assistance could "require the aid of a sufficient number of persons in arms." *Id.* at 583.

There were, however, no restrictions on arms possession by Indians or slaves, even though they were subject to a 9:00 P.M. curfew and forbidden from purchasing alcohol. *Id.* at 612-14.

The 1842 constitution, still in effect, stated that, "The right of the people to keep and bear arms shall not be infringed." In 2004, the majority of the Rhode Island Supreme Court ruled that the state constitution guarantees the right to own guns, but not to carry them. *Mosby v. Devine*, 851 A.2d 1031 (R.I. 2004).

NOTES & QUESTIONS

1. Does Article I of the Massachusetts Declaration of Rights establish a right of self-defense? If so, does it necessarily include a right to have a firearm for self-defense? Does the answer depend on whether there are equally effective substitutes? CQ: In *McDonald* (Chapter 9), Justice Stevens's dissent argues that the "liberty" protected by the Fifth and Fourteenth Amendments includes the right of self-defense, but can be constrained by local firearms prohibitions like Chicago's handgun ban even if substitute arms are less effective for self-defense.

2. The Massachusetts Declaration of Rights used the phrase "the people have a right" for both the right to arms and for the rights of assembly and petition:

    > The people have a right, in an orderly and peaceable manner, to assemble to consult upon the common good; give instructions to their representatives, and to request of the legislative body, by the way of addresses, petitions, or remonstrances, redress of the wrongs done them, and of the grievances they suffer.

    Mass. Const. of 1780, pt. I, art. XIX. John Adams also used the phrase "the people have a right," which was approved by the drafting committee, for the freedom of speech and of the press: "The people have a right to the freedom of speaking, writing, and publishing their sentiments. The liberty of the press, therefore, ought not to be restrained." Journal of the Convention for Framing a Constitution of Government for the State of Massachusetts Bay (1779-1780), at 41 (1832). However, the convention ultimately adopted different language: "The liberty of the press is essential to the security of freedom in a State; it ought not, therefore, to be restrained in this commonwealth." Mass. Const. of 1780, pt. I, art. XVI.

When the Declaration of Rights says "the people have a right," what kind of right does it mean? A right belonging to individuals? A right belonging to the community, but not to individuals? Something else?

3. What is the significance of the language "for the common defence" in the Massachusetts right to arms declaration? CQ: The phrase also appears in some early nineteenth-century state constitutions, for example, Tennessee and Arkansas. *See* Chapter 5. The U.S. Senate rejected a proposal to add the phrase to the Second Amendment. *See* Chapter 4. Does the term connote a militia purpose? Might the term connote participation in non-militia community defense, such as a hue and cry? (See Chapter 2 for this common law communal protection against criminals.) Is personal self-defense against criminals a form of aiding "the common defence"? Is it up to the legislature to answer these questions? Can the legislature prohibit arms that are lawfully possessed "for the common defence" from being used for recreation? What about for subsistence hunting? What about for self-defense?

4. The Massachusetts right to assemble also has a purpose clause: "to consult upon the common good." Should this allow the legislature or the executive to ban assemblies that they consider incompatible with the common good? Does the Massachusetts Constitution of 1780 only protect assemblies aimed at the common good? Does it deny protection to assemblies that only benefit a discrete group or a few individuals?

5. The town of Northampton, which is today the home of Smith College, complained in a resolution that the Massachusetts constitution's right to arms was too narrow:

> We also judge that the people's right to keep and bear arms, declared in the seventeenth article of the same declaration is not expressed with that ample and manly openness and latitude which the importance of the right merits; and therefore propose that it should run in this or some like manner, to wit, The people have a right to keep and bear arms as well for their own as the common defence. Which mode of expression we are of opinion would harmonize much better with the first article than the form of expression used in the said seventeenth article.

The Popular Sources of Political Authority: Documents on the Massachusetts Constitution of 1780, at 574 (Oscar & Mary Handlin eds., 1966).

Williamsburg also urged "that the people have a right to keep and to bear Arms for their Own and the Common defence." The town explained:

> Voted Nemine Contradic.[14] Our reasons gentleman for making the Addition Are these. 1st that we esteem it an essential privilege to keep Arms in Our houses for Our Own Defense and while we Continue honest and Lawful subjects of Government we Ought Never to be deprived of them.

---

14. [Short for "nemine contradicente," meaning, "with no one speaking against." — EDS.]

Reas. 2 That the legislature in some future period may confine all the fire Arms to some publick Magazine and thereby deprive the people of the benefit of the use of them.

Id. at 624.

Newspaper articles in 1786-87 addressed the ambiguities of the Massachusetts right to arms. "Scribble Scrabble" wrote that "the constitution does not directly say the people have a right to keep & bear arms for squibing at pigeons and other game," so "the legislature have a power to control it in all cases, except the one mentioned in the bill of rights." Scribble Scrabble, Cumberland Gazette (Portland, Me.), Dec. 8, 1786, at 1. (At the time, Maine was part of Massachusetts.) "Senex" disagreed with "Scribble Scrabble's" narrow reading, for "[t]he idea that Great Britain meant to take away their arms, was fresh in the minds of the people; therefore in forming a new government, they wisely guarded against it." "Senex," Cumberland Gazette (Portland, Me.), Jan. 12, 1787, at 1.

"Scribble Scrabble" wrote that defensive arms were a natural right: "How different [from voting] is the case of keeping and bearing arms. This is a right almost coeval with man." Indeed, Adam himself "had a right, in Paradise, to have grasped a club and smashed the old Serpent," and similarly all men have had "a right to keep and bear arms for their common defense, to kill game, fowl, &c." However, "The Bill of Rights secures to the people the use of arms in common defense; so that, if it be an alienable right, one use of arms is secured to the people against any law of the legislature." While the Constitution did not prevent infringement of the natural right, the Massachusetts legislature thus far had not interfered, so "whatever right people had to use arms in a state of nature, they retain at the present time." Scribble-Scrabble, Cumberland Gazette (Portland, Me.), Jan. 26, 1787, at 1.

6. Judicial interpretations of the Massachusetts right to arms raise interesting questions. In *Commonwealth v. Blanding*, 3 Pick. (20 Mass.) 304 (1825), Massachusetts's Chief Justice Parker explained, "The liberty of the press was to be unrestrained, but he who used it was to be responsible in case of its abuse; like the right to keep fire arms, which does not protect him who uses them for annoyance or destruction." Does *Blanding*'s analogy anticipate a general right to arms or only a right to have firearms for militia service?

In *Commonwealth v. Murphy*, 166 Mass. 171 (1896), the Massachusetts Supreme Judicial Court upheld a ban on unlicensed armed parades. The defendant claimed that the ban violated the state's right to arms. The court disagreed because "[t]he protection of a similar constitutional provision has often been sought by persons charged with carrying concealed weapons, and it has been almost universally held that the legislature may regulate and limit the mode of carrying arms." The court supplied a string cite to cases from Tennessee, Texas, Alabama, Arkansas, Indiana, and Missouri (plus one contrary case from Kentucky). The "similar constitutional provision" in each of these cases was a state right to arms clause that protected the right of everyone (not just militiamen) to have firearms in their home for self-defense and other purposes.

In 1976, the Massachusetts court rejected a criminal defendant's challenge to a state law restricting the possession of sawed-off shotguns. The court declared that the state constitutional arms right was only for militiamen, and that it no longer existed for any practical purpose since the National Guard now had its own guns. The decision did seem to acknowledge that the earlier view might have been different:

> [T]here is nothing to suggest that, even in early times, due regulation of possession or carrying of firearms, short of some sweeping prohibition, would have been thought to be an improper curtailment of individual liberty or to undercut the militia system.

Commonwealth v. Davis, 343 N.E.2d 847, 849 (Mass. 1976).

Justice Breyer recognized that the original view of the Massachusetts constitution appears to have been a general (not militia-only) right to arms:

> Samuel Adams, who lived in Boston, advocated a constitutional amendment that would have precluded the Constitution from ever being "construed" to "prevent the people of the United States, who are peaceable citizens, from keeping their own arms." Samuel Adams doubtless knew that the Massachusetts Constitution contained somewhat similar protection.

Heller, supra, at 716 (Breyer, J., dissenting) (internal citations omitted; Chapter 9).

Language nearly identical to the Massachusetts provision ("common defence," with no explicit mention of any other purpose) appears in the state constitutions of Arkansas, Florida, South Carolina, and Tennessee, and has been interpreted in all those states to include the right of individuals who are not in the militia to have guns in their home for personal defense. (A contrary 1986 decision from the Supreme Court of Maine was overturned by the voters with a 1987 constitutional amendment.)

One justification for recognizing a right to individual home defense as guaranteed by "common defense" language has been that families that protect themselves against violent criminals are contributing to the common defense of society.

7. CQ: A central issue of the *Heller* (Chapter 9) decision is how to reconcile the militia language with the right to arms language. Is this language best understood by thinking of the militia as a duty or as a right? The New York constitution characterized defense of society as a duty. How do the other early constitutions characterize the militia, as a right or as a duty? If service in the militia is a right, what would be the parameters of that right?

8. What is your interpretation of the Pennsylvania right to arms provision? Do you read it as an individual or collective/state right?

9. Compare the Pennsylvania right to arms guarantee with the language of the Second Amendment. Note that the federal guarantee is a right to keep and bear while Pennsylvania speaks simply of a right to bear arms. Later we

will see arguments that the Second Amendment reference to bearing arms has an exclusively military connotation. Do you read the Pennsylvania usage that way?

10. Pennsylvania's guarantee of the right to hunt and fish reflects an interest and tradition that continues to this day, in the form of very high per capita sales of hunting and fishing licenses. Even the Quakers, most of whom were reticent about using arms for personal defense, had no objection to hunting, and some of them were avid outdoorsmen.

For more on Pennsylvania in the late colonial period, Revolution, and Early Republic, see David B. Kopel & Clayton Cramer, *Credentials Are No Substitute for Accuracy: Nathan Kozuskanich, Stephen Halbrook and the Role of the Historian*, 19 Widener L.J. 343 (2010); Nathan Kozuskanich, *History or Ideology? A Response to David B. Kopel and Clayton E. Cramer*, 19 Widener L.J. 321 (2010); David B. Kopel & Clayton Cramer, *The Keystone of the Second Amendment: The Quakers, the Pennsylvania Constitution, and the Questionable Scholarship of Nathan Kozuskanich*, 19 Widener L.J. 277 (2010); Nathan Kozuskanich, *Defending Themselves: The Original Understanding of the Right to Bear Arms*, 38 Rutgers L.J. 1041, 1070 (2008); Nathan Kozuskanich, *Originalism, History, and the Second Amendment: What Did Bearing Arms Really Mean to the Founders?*, 10 U. Pa. J. Const. L. 413 (2008).

11. Rhode Island's 1842 Constitution was adopted after an uprising known as the Dorr War. In *Luther v. Borden*, 48 U.S. 1 (1849), the U.S. Supreme Court used a Dorr War case to explain that the U.S. Constitution's guarantee to each state of a republican form of government is a political, non-justiciable question. Enforcement of the Guarantee Clause is up to Congress, not the courts, according to *Luther*.

The dissenters in *Mosby, supra*, argued for a right to carry, and criticized the majority for relying on *Aymette v. State*, 2 Humph. 154 (Tenn. 1840) (Chapter 5) and other antebellum Southern cases interpreting state constitutions that had narrower (arguably) language. The *Mosby* case also interpreted Rhode Island's two separate statutes for licensing the carrying of handguns, and concluded that one of the statutes mandated non-discretionary issuance to applicants who met particular criteria. However, relief was not granted to the plaintiffs because of procedural flaws in their claims. For more on *Mosby*, see David B. Kopel, *The Licensing of Concealed Handguns for Lawful Protection: Support from Five State Supreme Courts*, 62 Alb. L. Rev. 101 (2005). For a thorough discussion of the modern evolution of state constitutional arms-bearing guarantees, see Nicholas J. Johnson, *A Second Amendment Moment: The Constitutional Politics of Gun Control*, 71 Brook. L. Rev. 715 (2005).

||4||

The New Constitution

By 1787, many Americans believed that the Articles of Confederation had created an unacceptably weak national government. Some felt that the nation was inadequately defended. The Articles required that "every State shall always keep up a well-regulated and disciplined militia, sufficiently armed and accoutered, and shall provide and constantly have ready for use, in public stores, a due number of field pieces and tents, and a proper quantity of arms, ammunition and camp equipage." Articles of Confederation, art. VI. However, the national government had no means of compelling states to keep up their militias, nor did the national government have the authority to force state militias into national service. Shays's Rebellion intensified the feeling that the lack of a strong national authority left the nation in serious danger. As George Washington put it, "That something is necessary, none will deny; for the situation of the general government, if it can be called a government, is shaken to its foundation, and liable to be overturned by every blast. In a word, it is at an end; and, unless a remedy is soon applied, anarchy and confusion will inevitably ensue." Letter from George Washington to Thomas Jefferson (May 30, 1787), *in* 3 The Records of the Federal Convention of 1787, at 31 (Max Farrand ed., 1911).

A Constitutional Convention therefore convened on May 25, 1787. The Confederation Congress had called for a convention to revise the Articles of Confederation, but 11 states sent delegations that had been given much broader authority. The latter approach prevailed, and the Convention began work on creating a new governing document.

For more detail on the material presented in this chapter, see David Young, The Origin of the Second Amendment: A Documentary History of the Bill of Rights (2d ed. 1995) (reprinting virtually every relevant primary document) and Stephen P. Halbrook, The Founders' Second Amendment: Origins of the Right to Bear Arms (2008) (the most complete narrative of the development of the right to arms from the pre-Revolutionary period through the late eighteenth century, with the author's own interpretation). Together, these two books present virtually all of the known relevant documents from the period. Readers may, of course, differ regarding interpretation of those documents.

A. Standing Armies, Militias, and Individual Rights — The Constitutional Convention of 1787

The nation had not forgotten that it separated from England in part because the king had kept, "in times of peace, standing armies without the consent of our legislatures." And "He affected to render the military independent of, and superior to the civil power." The Declaration of Independence ¶¶ 12-13 (1776). Thus, while the Framers sought a stronger national government, they determined that its powers should be limited so as not to risk the tyranny that had necessitated the Revolution. They sought to ensure that a federal standing army would be under strict civilian control, and that state militias would remain vital and effective, while available for federal service when needed, thus reducing the need for a large standing army.

Article I, Section 8 of the proposed Constitution gave Congress the power

> To raise and support Armies, but no Appropriation of Money to that Use shall be for a longer Term than two Years; . . .
>
> To provide for calling forth the Militia to execute the Laws of the Union, suppress Insurrections and repel Invasions;
>
> To provide for organizing, arming, and disciplining, the Militia, and for governing such Part of them as may be employed in the Service of the United States, reserving to the States respectively, the Appointment of the Officers, and the Authority of training the Militia according to the discipline prescribed by Congress; . . .
>
> To make all Laws which shall be necessary and proper for carrying into Execution the foregoing Powers, and all other Powers vested by this Constitution in the Government of the United States. . . .

Unless the states obtained "the consent of Congress," they were forbidden to "keep troops . . . or engage in war, unless actually invaded, or in such imminent danger as will not admit of delay." U.S. Const. art. I, §10, cl. 3. Militiamen were not considered "troops" in this sense, because they served part time, not as full-time professionals.

The proposed Constitution was sent to the states for ratification, with the approval of nine states being the minimum necessary to bring the Constitution into force. Proponents of the Constitution called themselves "Federalists" and dubbed their opponents "Anti-Federalists." The names stuck, although it was the "Anti-Federalists" who were more concerned about ensuring that the country retained a federal system of government, as opposed to a consolidated national government. The Anti-Federalists were wary of the new powers granted to the federal government regarding militias, and of the federal powers to create a standing army.

Some Anti-Federalists worried that Congress could destroy the militia by failing to arm it, by disarming it, by otherwise neglecting it, or by creating a *select militia*. In contrast to a popular militia of the people, a select militia consists of only a small segment of the people. The American public knew that when the

Stuart kings of Great Britain had tried to impose autocratic rule during the seventeenth century, they had attempted to replace the popular militia with a select militia. Select militias were considered dangerous in part because of their similarity to standing armies; rather than comprising the People as a whole, they constituted only a narrow segment of the People who were favored by the particular faction that controlled the government.

Anti-Federalists were also concerned that, even though Congress did not have exclusive control over the militia, federal power would trump state control. The Anti-Federalists feared that if the federal government could dominate the militia, or weaken it, the states and their citizens would be vulnerable to a federal standing army that might impose tyranny, or that a malicious federal government might neglect the militia and thereby leave the states practically defenseless against attacks by Indians or a foreign power.

While the proposed federal government was supposed to be one of limited, enumerated powers, the Constitution included several broad-seeming provisions, such as the Necessary and Proper Clause, U.S. Const., art. I, §8, cl. 18, which the Anti-Federalists warned could be misused to create a government of nearly unlimited power. The Anti-Federalists therefore wanted a bill of rights enumerating fundamental individual rights that could not be infringed, much like the 1689 English Declaration of Right and the bills of rights already present in most state constitutions. A federal bill of rights was considered especially necessary because the Articles of Confederation had given Congress power only over the states, but the new Constitution would give Congress direct power over individuals.

At the Constitutional Convention in Philadelphia, some delegates had proposed a bill of rights. However, the proposal came late in the Convention, and the majority of delegates were unwilling to commence a long debate on precisely what to include. However, the absence of a bill of rights became a key Anti-Federalist objection during the state ratification debates. As we shall see, one response to the Anti-Federalists' concerns about potential federal tyranny was that, if the federal government became tyrannical, the state militias, consisting of the entire able-bodied free male population, would easily overwhelm the much smaller federal standing army (since the federal government would not able to afford a huge standing army).

The Federalists also argued that a bill of rights was unnecessary because the proposed Constitution was one of enumerated powers. According to the Federalists, nothing in the enumerated powers gave Congress the power to establish a national religion, censor the press, disarm the people, or do anything else that the Anti-Federalists worried about.

Another argument against a bill of rights was that enumerating certain rights might imply a lack of protection for other rights that were not enumerated. James Madison eventually addressed this concern with the Ninth Amendment, affirming that "[t]he enumeration in the Constitution of certain rights shall not be construed to deny or disparage others retained by the people."

For more detail on what transpired during the Convention, see Robert Yates, John Lansing & Luther Martin, Secret Proceedings and Debates of the Convention Assembled at Philadelphia, in the Year 1787, for the Purpose of Forming the Constitution of the United States of America (1821); The Avalon Project at Yale Law School, The Debates in the Federal Convention of 1787

Reported by James Madison, *available at* http://www.yale.edu/lawweb/avalon/ debates/605.htm (imaged from The Debates in the Federal Convention in 1787, Which Framed the Constitution of the United States of America, Reported by James Madison, A Delegate from the State of Virginia (Gaillard Hund & James Brown Scott eds., 1920). For analyses of the Convention's work on the militia clauses, see Stephen P. Halbrook, *The Right of the People or the Power of the State: Bearing Arms, Arming Militias, and the Second Amendment*, 26 Val. U. L. Rev. 131, 135-39 (1991), and Keith A. Ehrman & Dennis A. Henigan, *The Second Amendment in the Twentieth Century: Have You Seen Your Militia Lately?*, 15 U. Dayton L. Rev. 5, 18-25 (1989).

NOTES & QUESTIONS

1. The Federalist Papers were a pseudonymous series of newspaper essays written in defense of the proposed Constitution. The authors were James Madison, Alexander Hamilton, and John Jay. In *Federalist* 26, Alexander Hamilton argued that the population need not fear a federal standing army because it could only be maintained with the consent of Congress — unlike in Great Britain, where the kings had attempted to raise standing armies themselves. Whereas the English monarchs had evaded Parliament by using their own wealth to pay the standing armies, Hamilton argued that a federal standing army could not be dangerous because it would be dependent on funding from Congress, and any particular appropriations to fund the army could only last for two years. Do you agree with Hamilton?

2. Were the Anti-Federalists' fears of a select militia sensible? Would it be appropriate to describe modern state and municipal police forces as a form of select militia? Such organizations were largely unknown in late eighteenth-century America. Today, there are over 700,000 full-time law enforcement officers in the United States. *See* U.S. Department of Justice, Federal Bureau of Investigation, Crime in the United States 2009, tbl. 74 (Sept. 2010). Police organizations today often include elite, highly militarized units such as SWAT teams. Does this pose a threat to liberty? Ensure liberty and public safety? A mixture of both?

3. Were the Anti-Federalists justified in fearing that Congress would exceed its enumerated powers? That it would destroy the militia?

4. During the Constitutional Convention, the delegates considered a "clause giving the national legislature a negative on such laws of the states as might be contrary to the Articles of the Union, or treaties with foreign nations." 5 Debates on the Adoption of the Federal Constitution 170 (Jonathan Elliot ed. 1845) [hereinafter 5 Elliot's Debates]. Charles Cotesworth Pinckney of South Carolina supported the motion, believing "'that the national legislature should have authority to negative all laws which they should judge to be improper.' He urged that such universality of power was indispensably

necessary to render it effectual; that the states must be kept in due subordination to the nation. . . ." *Id.* at 170-71. James Madison, of Virginia, agreed: "He could not but regard an indefinite power to negative legislative acts of the states as absolutely necessary to a perfect system." *Id.* at 171. Elbridge Gerry, of Massachusetts, disagreed, believing the proposed power was too broad and "that the proposed negative would extend to the regulations of the militia — a matter on which the existence of the state might depend. The national legislature, with such a power, may enslave the states. Such an idea . . . has never been suggested or conceived among the people." *Id.* at 172. The proposed provision was rejected. What do you make of these statements, both on their own and with respect to the proposed clause about which they were made? Keep them in mind as you read about the Constitution's ratification history.

5. The initial version of the militia clause to emerge from committee would have authorized Congress

> [t]o make laws for organizing, arming, and disciplining the militia, and for governing such parts of them as may be employed in the service of the United States; reserving to the states, respectively, the appointment of the officers, and authority of training the militia according to the discipline prescribed[.]

5 Elliot's Debates, *supra,* at 464. This prompted the following debate:

> Mr. [Roger] SHERMAN [of Connecticut] moved to strike out the last member, "and authority of training," &c. He thought it unnecessary. The states will have this authority, of course, if not given up.

> Mr. [Oliver] ELLSWORTH [of Connecticut] doubted the propriety of striking out the sentence. The reason assigned applies as well to the other reservation, of the appointment of officers. He remarked, at the same time, that the term "discipline," was of vast extent, and might be so expounded as to include all power on the subject.

> Mr. [Rufus] KING [of Massachusetts], by way of explanation, said, that by *organizing,* the committee meant, proportioning the officers and men — by *arming,* specifying the kind, size, and calibre of arms — and by *disciplining,* prescribing the manual exercise, evolutions, &c.

> Mr. SHERMAN withdrew his motion.

> Mr. [Elbridge] GERRY [of Massachusetts]. This power in the United States, as explained, is making the states drill-sergeants. He had as lief let the citizens of Massachusetts be disarmed, as to take the command from the states, and subject them to the general legislature. It would be regarded as a system of despotism.

> Mr. [James] MADISON [of Virginia] observed, the "*arming,*" as explained, did not extend to furnishing arms; nor the term "*disciplining,*" to penalties, and courts martial for enforcing them.

> Mr. KING added to his former explanation, that arming meant not only to provide for uniformity of arms, but included the authority to regulate the modes of furnishing, either by the militia themselves, the state governments,

or the national treasury; that *laws* for disciplining must involve penalties, and
everything necessary for enforcing penalties.

Id. at 464-65. Based on this exchange, what powers over the militia did the
delegates decide to give to Congress?

6. George Mason of Virginia proposed that a phrase reading "that the liberties
    of the people may be better secured against the danger of standing armies in
    time of peace" be inserted into Article I, Section 8, before the phrase
    "To provide for organizing, arming, and disciplining, the Militia." Would
    the addition of this phrase have made any legal difference? Any other
    difference? Mason was offering what modern scholars call a "justification
    clause," which was common in state constitutions at the time. The Second
    Amendment has its own justification clause, and there is considerable
    debate about its legal effect.

B. State Ratification Conventions

After the Constitutional Convention sent the proposed Constitution to the state
ratification conventions, Federalists and Anti-Federalists commenced public
debate. The Delaware, New Jersey, Georgia, and Connecticut state conventions
ratified the Constitution without proposing any amendments or making any
statements relevant to standing armies, militias, or arms-bearing. There was,
however, revealing debate on these issues in Pennsylvania, Massachusetts, Maryland, South Carolina, New Hampshire, Virginia, New York, North Carolina,
and Rhode Island.

1. Pennsylvania

Pennsylvania was second, after Delaware, to ratify the Constitution. There was
serious debate in the Pennsylvania Convention over the need for a bill of rights
and the balance of military power between the federal government and the
states. These themes would gain momentum as the other states considered
ratification.

Pennsylvania's Anti-Federalists, who wanted a bill of rights, feared that the
people would be disarmed and that other rights would be violated. Federalists
countered that a bill of rights was unnecessary because the federal government
was one of enumerated powers and, as Federalist delegate and future Supreme
Court Justice James Wilson put it, "[i]f we attempt an enumeration, every thing
that is not enumerated is presumed to be given. The consequence is, that an
imperfect enumeration would throw all implied power into the scale of the
government, and the rights of the people would be rendered incomplete." 2
Debates on the Adoption of the Federal Constitution 436 (Jonathan Elliot ed.,

1836) [hereinafter 2 Elliot's Debates]. Any right not given up was retained, the Federalist argument went.

The Anti-Federalists also feared that Congress could use its militia powers to abolish or disarm the militia, or to create a select militia. They expressed concern that Congress might use the militia of one state to cause mischief in another state. The Federalists responded that Congress's power to arm the militia would promote standardization but not lead to disarmament. James Wilson contended that a standing army would be largely unnecessary because "[t]he militia formed under this system, and trained by the several states, will be such a bulwark of internal strength, as to prevent the attacks of foreign enemies. I have been told that, about the year 1744, an attack was intended by France upon Massachusetts Bay, but was given up on reading the militia law of the province." *Id.* at 522. (For the Massachusetts militia law, see Chapter 3.)

The Anti-Federalists proposed the following amendments to the Constitution:

7. That the people have a right to bear arms for the defence of themselves and their own State or the United States for the purpose of killing game; and no law shall be for disarming the people or any of them unless for crimes committed, or real danger of public injury from individuals; and as standing armies in the time of peace are dangerous liberty, they ought not to be kept up; and that they shall be kept under strict subordination to and be by the civil power.
8. The inhabitants of the several States shall have liberty to fowl and hunt in seasonable times on the lands they hold, and on all other lands in the United States not inclosed, in like manner to fish in all navigable waters, and other private property without being restrained therein by any laws to be passed by the legislature of the United States. . . .
11. That the power of organizing arming and disciplining the militia, (the manner of disciplining the militia to be prescribed by Congress) remain with the individual States and that Congress shall not have authority to call or march any of the militia out of their own State, without the consent of such State and for such length of time only as such State shall agree.

Pennsylvania and the Federal Constitution 1787-1788, at 422 (John Bach McMaster & Frederick D. Stone eds., 1888). The Pennsylvania Convention had been convened hastily, so that Federalists from Philadelphia could dominate before Anti-Federalists from the rest of the state could organize. Thus, the proposed amendments were defeated and the Constitution ratified. The Anti-Federalists then published the famous *Dissent of the Minority*, which reiterated the above demands for a bill of rights, and which was circulated throughout the country.

NOTES & QUESTIONS

1. Was James Wilson right to worry that the enumeration of some rights would be treated as an implication of federal powers over all rights that were not enumerated? Would unenumerated rights have been more secure if the Bill of Rights had never been adopted? What effect does the Ninth Amendment have on the analysis of these questions? What about the Fifth Amendment's

rule that "[n]o person shall . . . be deprived of life, liberty, or property, without due process of law"?

2. Was Wilson right that a strong militia law would continue, as it had in 1744, to deter foreign aggression?

3. The Pennsylvania dissenters' call for a right to arms included a general ban on disarming any person "unless for crimes committed, or real danger of public injury from individuals." How would you apply such a standard? Should any crime or endangerment qualify, or only certain types?

4. The dissenters also urged constitutional protection of the right to hunt and to have arms for hunting. As detailed in Chapter 2, in Great Britain laws to prevent commoners from hunting had often been used as pretext for disarming them. The Vermont and Pennsylvania constitutions were the first American constitutions to include an explicit right to hunt and fish. Today, 13 state constitutions have such a guarantee, most of them adopted within the last two decades. *E.g.*, Wis. Const., art. I, §26 (2003) ("The people have the right to fish, hunt, trap, and take game subject only to reasonable restrictions as prescribed by law."); *see* Stephen P. Halbrook, *The Constitutional Right to Hunt: New Recognition of an Old Liberty in Virginia*, 19 Wm. & Mary Bill Rts. J. 197 (2010). All hunting- and fishing-rights clauses explicitly affirm the government's authority to regulate hunting and fishing, such as to protect the long-term health of species. Could a right to hunt be viewed as implicit in the Second Amendment? Could it be an unenumerated right protected by the Fifth, Ninth, or Fourteenth Amendment?

2. Massachusetts

Massachusetts was the sixth state to ratify. As in Pennsylvania, the debates featured many warnings about standing armies. Theodore Sedgwick (who later became a U.S. Representative, Senator, and Justice of the Massachusetts Supreme Judicial Court) responded by asking whether "an army could be raised for the purpose of enslaving themselves and their brethren? [O]r, if raised, whether they could subdue a nation of freemen, who know how to prize liberty; and who have arms in their hands? He said it was a deception . . . to say that this power could be thus used." 2 Elliot's Debates, *supra*, at 97.

Samuel Adams proposed an amendment to the Constitution requiring

> that the said Constitution be never construed to authorize Congress, to infringe the just liberty of the press, or the rights of conscience; or to prevent the people of the United States, who are peaceable citizens, from keeping their own arms; or to raise standing armies, unless when necessary for the defence of the United States, or of some one or more of them; or to prevent the people from petitioning in a peaceable and orderly manner, the federal legislature, for a redress of grievances; or to subject the people to unreasonable searches & seizures of their persons, papers, or possessions.

6 Documentary History of the Ratification of the Constitution 1453 (John P. Kaminski & Gaspare J. Saladino eds., 2000). The convention rejected Adams's proposal, but included in its ratification message proposed amendments recommended by Governor John Hancock, including one stating "[t]hat it be expressly declared that all powers not explicitly delegated by the aforesaid Constitution are reserved to the several states, to be by them exercised." 1 Debates on the Adoption of the Federal Constitution 322 (Jonathan Elliot ed., 1836) [hereinafter 1 Elliot's Debates].

NOTES & QUESTIONS

1. Imagine that Samuel Adams's proposed amendment had been adopted. What would be the characteristics of the right to arms that it protected? In what ways would it be different from the Second Amendment?

2. How should we interpret the convention's rejection of Adams's proposed amendment? Does it suggest that the convention was complacent about individual rights? That the rights he mentioned were taken for granted, and that Congress had no ability to infringe them? That the majority of delegates did not want to burden the ratification process with the complications of proposed amendments?

3. Maryland

In the Maryland Convention, the Constitution's supporters knew they had a majority. The majority allowed the Constitution's opponents to speak, but then voted to ratify the Constitution without amendments.

After ratification, however, a committee was appointed to consider amendments to the Constitution. The following amendments were proposed and unanimously agreed to by the committee, but were not attached to the state's ratification message:

> 1. That Congress shall exercise no power but what is expressly delegated by this Constitution. . . .
> 9. That no soldier be enlisted for a longer time than four years, except in time of war, and then only during the war. . . .
> 13. That the militia shall not be subject to martial law, except in time of war, invasion, or rebellion.

2 Elliot's Debates, *supra*, at 550, 552. The following amendments were rejected by the committee:

> 1. That the militia, unless selected by lot, or voluntarily enlisted, shall not be marched beyond the limits of an adjoining state, without the consent of their legislature or executive. . . .

    4. That no standing army shall be kept up in time of peace, unless with the consent of two thirds of the members present of each branch of Congress.

    5. That the President shall not command the army in person, without the consent of Congress. . . .

    10. That no person conscientiously scrupulous of bearing arms, in any case, shall be compelled personally to serve as a soldier. . . .

    15. That it be declared, that all persons intrusted with the legislative or executive powers of government are the trustees and servants of the public; and, as such, accountable for their conduct. Wherefore, whenever the ends of government are perverted, and public liberty manifestly endangered, and all other means of redress are ineffectual, the people may, and of right ought to, reform the old, or establish a new government. The doctrine of non-resistance against arbitrary power and oppression is absurd, slavish, and destructive of the good and happiness of mankind.

Id. at 552-54.

NOTES & QUESTIONS

1. When James Madison began drafting the Bill of Rights, he distilled what he considered to be the best and most widely supported of the proposals for amendments. As you will see, the (rejected) Maryland protection of the religiously scrupulous against compulsory military service appeared in Madison's first draft of what would become the Second Amendment.

2. Rejected clause 15 restates some of the principles of the second paragraph of the Declaration of Independence. With some variation in wording, similar language is contained in the New Hampshire Constitution, and was also included in Tennessee's Constitution a few years later. N.H. Const., Bill of Rights, art. X, Tenn. Const. of 1796, art. 11, §2. Does this type of statement of principle provide useful constitutional guidance? What does it mean to say that "[t]he doctrine of non-resistance against arbitrary power and oppression is absurd, slavish, and destructive of the good and happiness of mankind"? What kind of resistance does this invite? How would a person, or the People, decide when there has been an exercise of arbitrary power or oppression that demands resistance?

4. New Hampshire

New Hampshire was the ninth state to ratify, thus making the Constitution, by its own terms, the governing charter for all nine ratifying states. U.S. Const., art. VII. The Anti-Federalists had relatively strong influence in New Hampshire, and had a list of amendments prepared for the convention. The Anti-Federalists moved that the Constitution be ratified on the condition that it not be effective in the state until the proposed amendments were also ratified. Federalists moved to ratify the Constitution and merely recommend the amendments.

The Federalists prevailed and New Hampshire transmitted the following language as part of its ratification message:

> [I]t is the opinion of this Convention, that certain amendments and alterations in the said Constitution would remove the fears and quiet the apprehensions of many of the good people of this state, and more effectually guard against an undue administration of the federal government, — The Convention do therefore recommend that the following alterations and provisions be introduced in the said Constitution: —
>
> I. That it be explicitly declared that all powers not expressly and particularly delegated by the aforesaid Constitution are reserved to the several states, to be by them exercised. . . .
>
> X. That no standing army shall be kept up in time of peace, unless with the consent of three fourths of the members of each branch of Congress; nor shall soldiers, in time of peace, be quartered upon private houses, without the consent of the owners. . . .
>
> XII. Congress shall never disarm any citizen, unless such as are or have been in actual rebellion.

1 Elliot's Debates, *supra*, at 326.

NOTES & QUESTIONS

1. Compare the New Hampshire proposal against disarming "any citizen" except in cases of "actual rebellion" with the right to arms proposals considered in Pennsylvania and Massachusetts. Do these three proposals anticipate the same type of right to arms?

2. How would you, over 200 years after the fact, apply three provisions that protected respectively, (a) a citizen's right to arms except in cases of actual rebellion, (b) a right to arms that excluded convicted criminals and persons dangerous to public safety, and (c) a right to arms for everyone who is a peaceable citizen? As counsel for a plaintiff claiming an individual right to arms, which of these three versions of the right to arms would you prefer?

5. Virginia

The Virginia Ratification Convention was well documented. By the time it commenced, public debates over standing armies, militias, and arms-bearing had intensified. New Hampshire's ratification was completed during the Virginia Convention, although the Virginians did not know this. Had either Virginia (tenth to ratify) or New York (eleventh) rejected the Constitution, it is questionable whether the nine ratifying states could have formed a successful new government without them.

Former Governor Patrick Henry set the tone: "Guard with jealous attention the public liberty. Suspect every one who approaches that jewel. Unfortunately, nothing will preserve it but downright force. Whenever you give up that force, you are inevitably ruined." 3 Debates on the Adoption of the Federal Constitution 45 (Jonathan Elliot ed., 1836) [hereinafter 3 Elliot's Debates]. Responding to a Federalist assertion that a bill of rights was unnecessary because abuses of power could be remedied by convening a new constitutional convention that would rescind the delegated powers, he continued:

> O sir, we should have fine times, indeed, if, to punish tyrants, it were only sufficient to assemble the people! Your arms, wherewith you could defend yourselves, are gone. . . . Did you ever read of any revolution in a nation . . . inflicted by those who had no power at all? You read of a riot act[1] in a country which is called one of the freest in the world, where a few neighbors cannot assemble without the risk of being shot by a hired soldiery, the engines of despotism. We may see such an act in America.
>
> A standing army we shall have, also, to execute the execrable commands of tyranny; and how are you to punish them? Will you order them to be punished? Who shall obey these orders? Will your mace-bearer[2] be a match for a disciplined regiment? In what situation are we to be? The clause before you gives a power of direct taxation, unbounded and unlimited, exclusive power of legislation, in all cases whatsoever, for ten miles square, and over all places purchased for the erection of forts, magazines, arsenals, dockyards, &c. What resistance could be made? The attempt would be madness. You will find all the strength of this country in the hands of your enemies; their garrisons will naturally be the strongest places in the country. Your militia is given up to Congress, also, in another part of this plan: they will therefore act as they think proper: all power will be in their own possession. You cannot force them to receive their punishment: of what service would militia be to you. [W]hen, most probably, you will not have a single musket in the state? [F]or, as arms are to be provided by Congress, they may or may not furnish them.
>
> Let me here call your attention to that part which gives the Congress power "to provide for organizing, arming, and disciplining the militia, and for governing such part of them as may be employed in the service of the United States—reserving to the states, respectively, the appointment of the officers, and the authority of training the militia according to the discipline prescribed by Congress." By this, sir, you see that their control over our last and best defence is unlimited. If they neglect or refuse to discipline or arm our militia, they will be useless: the states can do neither—this power being exclusively given to Congress. The power of appointing officers over men not disciplined or armed is ridiculous; so that this pretended little remains of power left to the states may, at the pleasure of Congress, be rendered nugatory.

Id. at 51-52.

---

1. [English statute enacted in 1714, and in effect until 1973. 1 Geo. I, ch. 5: "That if any persons to the number of twelve or more, being unlawfully, riotously, and tumultuously assembled together, to the disturbance of the publick peace" are ordered to disperse by a law enforcement officer reading the requisite language from the Riot Act, and rioters then fail to disperse, the rioters shall be guilty of a felony punishable by death.

A much narrower analogue to the Riot Act was included in Section 3 of the federal Militia Act of 1792. The provision is discussed later in this chapter. As codified in current federal law: "Whenever the President considers it necessary to use the militia or the armed forces under this chapter, he shall, by proclamation, immediately order the insurgents to disperse and retire peaceably to their abodes within a limited time." 15 U.S.C. §334. The provision only applies when "there is an insurrection in any State against its government." 15 U.S.C. §331. — Eds.]

2. [Literally, the carrier of a mace, a medieval weapon for close combat. Here it is used in the ceremonial sense, in which being the mace-bearer is a role of honor for guarding an institution, such as a college. The literal meaning of "mace" reminds listeners that a poor-armed assembly could be crushed by a standing army. — Eds.]

Federalists retorted that strengthening the national military was one of the reasons that the Constitutional Convention had been called. Governor Edmund Randolph opined that, despite the militia's admirable performance against the British, "it is dangerous to look to them as our sole protectors" against other countries. *Id.* at 77. (At the same time, presciently, he feared potential conflicts with other states and did not want Virginia to be without a militia should it be "struck off from the Union." *Id.* at 75.) Richard Henry Lee (who in the Continental Congress had introduced the resolution to declare U.S. independence) agreed with Randolph's point about overreliance on the militia, stating, "I have seen incontrovertible evidence that militia cannot always be relied upon. I could enumerate many instances, but one will suffice. Let the gentleman recollect the action of Guildford.[3] The American regular troops behaved there with the most gallant intrepidity. What did the militia do? The greatest number of them fled." In any event, held Lee, "The states are, by no part of the plan before you, precluded from arming and disciplining the militia, should Congress neglect it." *Id.* at 178.

James Madison, referring to the "inadequate, unsafe, and pernicious Confederation," *id.* at 88, addressed what the Anti-Federalists perceived as a

> great danger in the provision concerning the militia. This I conceive to be an additional security to our liberty, without diminishing the power of the states in any considerable degree. . . . The authority of training the militia, and appointing the officers, is reserved to the states. Congress ought to have the power to establish a uniform discipline throughout the states, and to provide for the execution of the laws, suppress insurrections, and repel invasions: these are the only cases wherein they can interfere with the militia; and the obvious necessity of their having power over them in these cases must convince any reflecting mind. Without uniformity of discipline, military bodies would be incapable of action: without a general controlling power to call forth the strength of the union to repel invasions, the country might be overrun and conquered by foreign enemies: without such a power to suppress insurrections, our liberties might be destroyed by domestic faction, and domestic tyranny be established.

Id. at 90. Delegate Francis Corbin asked, with respect to the theory that the federal government may use the militia to tyrannize, "Who are the militia? Are we not militia? Shall we fight against ourselves? No, sir; the idea is absurd." *Id.* at 112.

Patrick Henry answered Federalist arguments that Congress's enumerated powers deprived neither the states of their implied power to arm their militias nor the people of their individual rights:

> If they can use implication for us, they can also use implication against us. We are giving power; they are getting power; judge, then, on which side the implication will be used! When we once put it in their option to assume constructive power, danger will follow. Trial by jury, and liberty of the press, are also on this foundation of implication. If they encroach on these rights, and you give your implication for a plea, you are cast; for they will be justified by the last part of it, which gives them full

---

3. [The Battle of Guilford Court House took place March 15, 1781 in Greensboro, North Carolina. — Eds.]

power "to make, all laws which shall be necessary and proper to carry their power into execution." Implication is dangerous, because it is unbounded: if it be admitted at all, and no limits be prescribed, it admits of the utmost extension. They say that every thing that is not given is retained. The reverse of the proposition is true by implication. . . .

Mr. Henry then declared a bill of rights indispensably necessary; that a general positive provision should be inserted in the new system, securing to the states and the people every right which was not conceded to the general government; and that every implication should be done away.

Id. at 149-50 (Notes of James Madison). Henry addressed the problem of implication in the specific context of the militia:

The clause which says that Congress shall "provide for arming, organizing, and disciplining the militia, and for governing such part of them as may be employed in the service of the United States, reserving to the states respectively the appointment of the officers," seemed to put the states in the power of Congress. I wished to be informed, if Congress neglected to discipline them, whether the states were not precluded from doing it. Not being favored with a particular answer, I am confirmed in my opinion, that the states have not the power of disciplining them, without recurring to the doctrine of constructive implied powers. If, by implication, the states may discipline them, by implication, also, Congress may officer them; because, in a partition of power, each has a right to come in for part; and because implication is to operate in favor of Congress on all occasions, where their object is the extension of power, as well as in favor of the states. We have not one fourth of the arms that would be sufficient to defend ourselves. The power of arming the militia, and the means of purchasing arms, are taken from the states by the paramount powers of Congress. If Congress will not arm them, they will not be armed at all.

There have been no instances shown of a voluntary cession of power, sufficient to induce me to grant the most dangerous power; a possibility of their future relinquishment will not persuade me to yield such powers.

Id. at 169.

Edmund Randolph[4] responded:

I am astonished how this idea could enter into the gentleman's mind, whose acuteness no man doubts. How can this be fairly deduced from the following clause?: — "To provide for the organizing, arming, and disciplining the militia, and for governing such part of them as may be employed in the service of the United States, reserving to the states respectively the appointment of the officers, and the authority of training the militia, according to the discipline prescribed by Congress." He complains much of implication; but in this case he has made use of it himself, for his construction of this clause cannot possibly be supported without

---

4. As a delegate to the Philadelphia Convention, Randolph had refused to sign the proposed Constitution because he deemed the checks and balances insufficient. At the Virginia Convention, however, Randolph supported ratification, because he knew that eight states had already ratified (news of New Hampshire ratification having not yet reached Virginia) and he did not want Virginia to be left out of the new Union. Having already served as Governor of Virginia, Randolph would become the first U.S. Attorney General, and the second Secretary of State.

it. It is clear and self-evident that the pretended danger cannot result from the clause. Should Congress neglect to arm or discipline the militia, the states are fully possessed of the power of doing it; for they are restrained from it by no part of the Constitution.

Id. at 206.

George Mason had served as a delegate at the Philadelphia Convention and played a major role in drafting the Constitution. But he refused to sign it, and was adamant that it should not be ratified without a bill of rights. Among the guarantees he wanted was an explicit concurrent power of the states to arm their militias, for federal neglect or oppression of the militia could lead to tyranny:

Forty years ago, when the resolution of enslaving America was formed in Great Britain, the British Parliament was advised by an artful man, who was governor of Pennsylvania, to disarm the people; that it was the best and most effectual way to enslave them; but that they should not do it openly, but weaken them, and let them sink gradually, by totally disusing and neglecting the militia. [Here Mr. Mason quoted sundry passages to this effect.] This was a most iniquitous project. Why should we not provide against the danger of having our militia, our real and natural strength, destroyed? The general government ought, at the same time, to have some such power. But we need not give them power to abolish our militia. If they neglect to arm them, and prescribe proper discipline, they will be of no use. . . . I wish that, in case the general government should neglect to arm and discipline the militia, *there should be an express declaration that the state governments might arm and discipline them.* . . .

They may effect the destruction of the militia, by rendering the service odious to the people themselves, by harassing them from one end of the continent to the other, and by keeping them under martial law. . . .

If, at any time, our rulers should have unjust and iniquitous designs against our liberties, and should wish to establish a standing army, the first attempt would be to render the service and use of militia odious to the people themselves—subjecting them to unnecessary severity of discipline in time of peace, confining them under martial law, and disgusting them so much as to make them cry out, "Give us a standing army!" I would wish to have some check to exclude this danger; as, that the militia should never be subject to martial law but in time of war. I consider and fear the natural propensity of rulers to oppress the people. I wish only to prevent them from doing evil. By these amendments I would give necessary powers, but no unnecessary power. *If the clause stands as it is now, it will take from the state legislatures what divine Providence has given to every individual—the means of self-defence.*

Id. at 380-81 (emphases added; brackets in original).

Madison immediately rejoined:

I most cordially agree, with the honorable member last up, that a standing army is one of the greatest mischiefs that can possibly happen. It is a great recommendation for this system, that it provides against this evil more than any other system known to us, and, particularly, more than the old system of confederation. The most effectual way to guard against a standing army, is to render it unnecessary. The most effectual way to render it unnecessary, is to give the general government full power to call forth the militia, and exert the whole natural strength of the Union, when necessary. . . . Can we believe that a government of a federal nature, consisting of many coequal sovereignties, and particularly having one branch chosen from the people, would drag the militia unnecessarily to an immense distance? . . .

I cannot conceive that this Constitution, by giving the general government the power of arming the militia, takes it away from the state governments. The power is concurrent, and not exclusive. Have we not found, from experience, that, while the power of arming and governing the militia has been solely vested in the state legislatures, they were neglected and rendered unfit for immediate service? Every state neglected too much this most essential object. But the general government can do it more effectually.

Id. at 381-82.

Patrick Henry famously replied:

[T]here is a positive partition of power between the two governments. To Congress is given the power of "arming, organizing, and disciplining the militia, and governing such part of them as may be employed in the service of the United States." To the state legislators is given the power of "appointing the officers and training the militia according to the discipline prescribed by Congress." I observed before, that, if the power be concurrent as to arming them, it is concurrent in other respects. . . . Let me put it in another light.

May we not discipline and arm them, as well as Congress, if the power be concurrent? So that our militia shall have two sets of arms, double sets of regimentals, &c.; and thus, at a very great cost, we shall be doubly armed. *The great object is, that every man be armed.* But can the people afford to pay for double sets of arms, &c.? *Every one who is able may have a gun.* But we have learned, by experience, that, necessary as it is to have arms, and though our Assembly has, by a succession of laws for many years, endeavored to have the militia completely armed, it is still far from being the case. When this power is given up to Congress without limitation or bounds, how will your militia be armed? You trust to chance; for sure I am that nation which shall trust its liberties in other hands cannot long exist. If gentlemen are serious when they suppose a concurrent power, where can be the impolicy to amend it? Or, in other words, to say that Congress shall not arm or discipline them, till the states shall have refused or neglected to do it?

Id. at 386 (emphasis added).

Others joined the debate. Future Chief Justice John Marshall argued that states retain the power to arm the militia because they have not explicitly ceded it away. *Id.* at 419-21.

George Mason, in an oft-quoted exposition of the nature of a true militia, warned that federal powers could pervert the popular militia into a select militia:

"Who are the militia? They consist now of the whole people, except a few public officers. But I cannot say who will be the militia of a future day. If that paper on the table gets no alteration, the militia of the future day may not consist of all classes, high and low, and rich and poor; but they may be confined to the lower and middle classes of the people, granting exclusion to the higher classes of the people. If we should ever see that day, the most ignominious punishments and heavy fines may be expected. Under the present government, all ranks of people are subject to militia duty. Under such a full and equal representation as ours, there can be no ignominious punishment inflicted. But under this national, or rather consolidated government, the case will be different. The representation being so small and inadequate, they will have no fellow-feeling for the people.

Id. at 425-26 (emphasis added).

Recognizing that the Virginia Convention would not approve the Constitution without at least some limiting language, the Federalists moved for a vote on resolution ratifying the Constitution and declaring that "among other essential rights, the liberty of conscience and of the press cannot be cancelled, abridged, restrained or modified by any authority of the United States." *Id.* at 653. The resolution further recommended that the amendment process be taken up after ratification via the mechanism provided in the Constitution.

The Anti-Federalists objected because, in the words of Patrick Henry, "the necessity of securing our *personal rights* seems not to have pervaded the minds of men." *Id.* at 588. Henry thought that the mention of press and conscience rights along with "other essential rights" was too limited and vague to provide much protection. He proposed a resolution to refer a declaration of rights he had prepared (which was nearly identical to the declaration of rights ultimately included with Virginia's ratification message, *infra*) to the other states for their consideration before ratification.

Debate about the potential dangers of an incomplete enumeration of rights and the inability of the federal government to act outside the scope of its enumerated powers ensued. Henry insisted that he was not proposing any amendments that did "not stand on the broad basis of human rights." *Id.* at 625. James Madison relented and agreed that "such amendments, as seemed, in his judgment, to be without danger, he would readily admit." *Id.* at 627.

The following day, James Madison restated his commitment to work toward securing amendments after ratification. Before the delegates would consider ratification, Zachariah Johnston, who would vote for ratification, stated that under the Constitution, "The people are not to be disarmed of their weapons. They are left in full possession of them." *Id.* at 646.

The delegates then ratified the Constitution in two stages. First, they passed a ratification message with some general statements about the nature of the Constitution and the desire for future amendments. Second, they passed a resolution enjoining Virginia's congressmen to seek various amendments.

Virginia Ratification Message
1 Debates on the Adoption of the Federal Constitution 327
(Jonathan Elliot ed., 1836)

We the Delegates of the people of Virginia, duly elected in pursuance of a recommendation from the General Assembly, and now met in Convention, having fully and freely investigated and discussed the proceedings of the Federal Convention, and being prepared as well as the most mature deliberation hath enabled us, to decide thereon, — Do in the name and in behalf of the people of Virginia, declare and make known that the powers granted under the Constitution, being derived from the people of the United States may be resumed by them whensoever the same shall be perverted to their injury or oppression, and that every power not granted thereby remains with them and at their will; that therefore no right of any denomination, can be cancelled, abridged, restrained or modified, by the Congress, by the Senate or House of Representatives acting in any capacity, by the President or any department or officer of the United States, except in those instances in which power is given by the Constitution for those purposes; and that among other essential rights, the liberty of conscience and of the press cannot be cancelled, abridged, restrained or modified by any authority of the United States. With these impressions, with a solemn appeal to the Searcher of hearts for the purity of our intentions, and under the conviction, that, whatsoever imperfections may exist in the Constitution, ought rather to be examined in the mode prescribed therein, than to bring the Union into danger by a delay, with a hope of obtaining amendments previous to the ratifications. . . .

Resolution of Virginia's Proposed Amendments
3 Debates on the Adoption of the Federal Constitution 657-61
(Jonathan Elliot ed., 1836)

. . . [R]eported, from the Committee appointed, such *amendments* to the proposed Constitution of Government for the United States, as were by them deemed necessary to be recommended to the consideration of the Congress which shall first assemble under the said Constitution, to be acted upon according to the mode prescribed in the 5th article thereof; and he read the same in his place, and afterwards delivered them in at the clerk's table, where the same were again read, and are as follows:

That there be a declaration or bill of rights asserting and securing from encroachment the essential and unalienable rights of the people in some such manner as the following:

1st. That there are certain natural rights, of which men, when they form a social compact, cannot deprive or divest their posterity; among which are the enjoyment of life, and liberty, with the means of acquiring, possessing, and protecting property, and pursuing and obtaining happiness and safety.

2d. That all power is naturally invested in, and consequently derived from, the people; that magistrates therefore are their *trustees* and agents, and at all times amenable to them.

3d. That the Government ought to be instituted for the common benefit, protection, and security of the people; and that the doctrine of non-resistance against arbitrary power and oppression, is absurd, slavish, and destructive to the good and happiness of mankind. . . .

17th. That the people have a right to keep and bear arms; that a well regulated militia composed of the body of the people trained to arms, is the proper, natural, and safe defence of a free state. That standing armies in time of peace are dangerous to liberty, and therefore ought to be avoided, as far as the circumstances and protection of the community will admit; and that in all cases, the military should be under strict subordination to, and governed by the civil power. . . .

19th. That any person religiously scrupulous of bearing arms ought to be exempted, upon payment of an equivalent to employ another to bear arms in his stead. . . .

AMENDMENTS TO THE CONSTITUTION.

1st. That each state in the union shall respectively retain every power, jurisdiction and right, which is not by this constitution delegated to the Congress of the United States, or to the departments of the federal government. . . .

9th. That no standing army, or regular troops shall be raised, or kept up, in time of peace, without the consent of two thirds of the members present, in both houses.

10th. That no soldier shall be enlisted for any longer term than four years, except in time of war, and then for no longer term than the continuance of the war.

11th. That each state respectively shall have the power to provide for organizing, arming, and disciplining its own militia, whensoever Congress shall omit or neglect to provide for the same. That the militia shall not be subject to martial law, except when in actual service, in time of war, invasion or rebellion; and when not in the actual service of the United States, shall be subject only to such fines, penalties, and punishments as shall be directed or inflicted by the laws of its own state.

12th. That the exclusive power of legislation given to Congress over the federal town and its adjacent district, and other places, purchased or to be purchased by Congress of any of the states, shall extend only to such regulations as respect the police and good government thereof. . . .

17th. That those clauses which declare that Congress shall not exercise certain powers, be not interpreted in any manner whatsoever, to extend the powers of Congress; but that they be construed either as making exceptions to the specified powers where this shall be the case, or otherwise, as inserted merely for greater caution. . . .

AND the Convention do, in the name and behalf of the people of this Commonwealth, enjoin it upon their representatives in Congress to exert all their influence, and use all reasonable and legal methods, to obtain a ratification of the foregoing alterations and provisions, in the manner provided by the 5th article of the said Constitution; and in all Congressional laws to be passed in the mean time, to conform to the spirit of these amendments, as far as the said Constitution will admit.

NOTES & QUESTIONS

1. The Virginia and Maryland debates expressed fears of the militia being oppressed by martial law. So Fifth Amendment's grand jury guarantee specifically applies to "the Militia," except "when in actual service in time of War or public danger."

2. The Federalists asserted that the Constitution was one of enumerated powers and that the federal government could not exercise unenumerated powers. They also argued that the states had the implied concurrent powers to raise militias. The Anti-Federalists worried that the federal government might exercise implied power over things not specifically forbidden. Which view was more accurate at the Founding? Are things different today?

3. Do you agree with the arguments of Theodore Sedgwick from Massachusetts and Francis Corbin of Virginia that the members of a militia under federal control would not tyrannize their fellow citizens? Shays's Rebellion was suppressed by the Massachusetts militia in 1787 despite the belief by some of the rebels that the militia not would engage them. The militia fired a cannon at the rebels, killing four of them and dispersing the rest. At least some militia members of the army that suppressed Fries's Rebellion in 1800 (Chapter 5) were reluctant to do so, but they ultimately obeyed orders. This time, no one was killed because the militia and rebels struck a deal to resolve the conflict.

4. Other than the Second Amendment, does any part of the Bill of Rights address Mason's concerns? What is the implication of George Mason's statement that "*[i]f the clause stands as it is now, it will take from the state legislatures what divine Providence has given to every individual — the means of self-defence*"? What kind of right was he trying to protect: an individual right, a collective right, or a state's right? Are the three entirely distinct? What about Patrick Henry's statement that "*[t]he great object is, that every man be armed. . . . Every one who is able may have a gun*"? What do you think Henry envisioned?

5. Do you read Article I, Section 8, as leaving the states with the concurrent power to arm the militia? In what areas of the Constitution is there a "positive partition of power" between state and federal governments, and where are there concurrent powers? Can you think of instances in which federal constitutional powers have been held by implication to extinguish concurrent state powers? Instances in which state powers held by implication have been protected?

6. New York

By the time the New York ratification debates had commenced, the concerns raised in the other conventions were widely known. In an exchange about the federal government's power over the states, John Williams, former New York state legislator and future U.S. Representative, asked:

> [I]f the Congress should judge it a proper provision, for the common defence and general welfare, that the state governments should be essentially destroyed, what, in the name of common sense, will prevent them? . . . Are not the terms, *common defence and general welfare*, indefinite, undefinable terms? What checks have the state governments against such encroachments? . . . And what restraint have they against tyranny in their head? Do they rely on any thing but arms, the *ultima ratio*?[5] . . . But have they the means necessary for the purpose? Are they not deprived of the command of the purse and the sword of their citizens? Is not the power, both over taxation and the militia, wrested from their hands by this Constitution, and bestowed upon the general government?

2 Elliot's Debates, *supra*, at 338.

Robert Livingston (Member of the Committee of Five that drafted the Declaration of Independence; Secretary of Foreign Affairs under the Articles of Confederation; at the time, Chancellor (the highest judicial office) of New York; and future U.S. Ambassador to France, who in that capacity negotiated the Louisiana Purchase) replied:

> They tell us that the state governments will be destroyed, because they will have no powers left them. This is new. Is the power over property nothing? Is the power over life and death no power? Let me ask what powers this Constitution would take from the states. Have the state governments the power of war and peace, of raising troops, and making treaties? The power of regulating commerce we possess; but

---

5. [The last resort. — Eds.]

the gentlemen admit that we improperly possess it. What, then, is taken away? Have not the states the right of *raising money*, and *regulating the militia?*

Id. at 384.

Thomas Tredwell, New York state legislator and future U.S. Representative, beginning a speech criticizing the absence of a bill of rights, referred to the "misery" caused by the tyranny of the Hapsburg King Philip II over the Netherlands "before the people took up arms in their own defence" to rebuff "all the armies of that haughty monarch."[6] *Id.* at 397. He went on:

> The first and grand leading, or rather misleading, principle in this debate, and on which the advocates for this system of unrestricted powers must chiefly depend for its support, is that, in forming a constitution, whatever powers are not expressly granted or given the government, are reserved to the people, or that rulers cannot exercise any powers but those expressly given to them by the Constitution. . . . Why is it said that the privilege of the writ of *habeas corpus* shall not be suspended, unless, in cases of rebellion or invasion, the public safety may require it? What clause in the Constitution, except this very clause itself gives the general government a power to deprive us of that great privilege, so sacredly secured to us by our state constitutions? Why is it provided that no bill of attainder shall be passed, or that no title of nobility shall be granted? Are there any clauses in the Constitution extending the powers of the general government to these objects? Some gentlemen say that these, though not necessary, were inserted for greater caution. . . .
>
> . . . It is ardently to be wished, sir, that these and other invaluable rights of freemen had been as cautiously secured. . . .
>
> In this Constitution, sir, we have departed widely from the principles and political faith of '76, when the spirit of liberty ran high, and danger put a curb on ambition. Here we find no security for the rights of individuals, no security for the existence of our state governments; here is no bill of rights, no proper restriction of power; our lives, our property, and our consciences, are left wholly at the mercy of the legislature and the powers of the judiciary may be extended to any degree short of almighty.

Id. at 398, 399, 401.

The convention ultimately ratified the Constitution, and included the following first principles in its ratification message:

> That all power is originally vested in, and consequently derived from, the people, and that government is instituted by them for their common interest, protection, and security. . . .
>
> That the powers of government may be reassumed by the people whensoever it shall become necessary to their happiness; that every power, jurisdiction, and right, which is not by the said Constitution clearly delegated to the Congress of the United States, or the departments of the government thereof, remains to the people of the several states, or to their respective state governments, to whom they may have granted the same; and that those clauses in the said Constitution, which declare that Congress shall not have or exercise certain powers, do not imply that Congress is entitled to any powers not given by the said Constitution; but such

---

6. The Netherlands War of Independence began in 1568 against Philip II, and achieved final success in 1648.

clauses are to be construed either as exceptions to certain specified powers, or as inserted merely for greater caution. . . .

That the people have a right to keep and bear arms; that a well regulated militia, including the body of the people *capable of bearing arms*, is the proper, natural, and safe defence of a free state.

That the militia should not be subject to martial law, except in time of war, rebellion, or insurrection.

That standing armies, in time of peace, are dangerous to liberty, and ought not to be kept up, except in cases of necessity; and that at all times the military should be under strict subordination to the civil power. . . .

Under these impressions, and declaring that the rights aforesaid cannot be abridged or violated, and that the explanations aforesaid are consistent with the said Constitution, and in confidence that the amendments which shall have been proposed to the said Constitution will receive an early and mature consideration, — We, the said delegates, in the name and in the behalf of the people of the state of New York, do, by these presents, assent to and ratify the said Constitution. In full confidence, nevertheless, that, until a convention shall be called and convened for proposing amendments to the said Constitution, the militia of this state will not be continued in service out of this state for a longer term than six weeks. . . .

1 Elliot's Debates, *supra*, at 327-29. Like Virginia, the New York Convention also adopted a separate resolution enjoining the state's congressmen "to exert all their influence, and use all reasonable means" to seek certain amendments to the Constitution. *Id.* at 329.

7. North Carolina

The North Carolina Convention included the usual debates over the federal-state balance of military power and the concurrent need and danger of enumerating rights. North Carolina was the first state to refuse to ratify the Constitution until amendments were proposed.

Resolution of North Carolina's Proposed Amendments
4 Debates on the Adoption of the Federal Constitution 242-47
(Jonathan Elliot ed., 1836)

Resolved, That a declaration of rights asserting and securing from encroachment the great principle of civil and religious liberty, and the unalienable rights of the people, together with amendments to the most ambiguous and exceptionable parts of the said Constitution of government, ought to be laid before Congress, and the convention of the states that shall or may be called for the purpose of amending the said Constitution, for their consideration, previous to the ratification of the Constitution aforesaid on the part of the state of North Carolina.

DECLARATION OF RIGHTS.

1. That there are certain natural rights, of which men, when they form a social compact, cannot deprive or divest their posterity, among which are the

enjoyment of life and liberty, with the means of acquiring, possessing, and protecting property, and pursuing and obtaining happiness and safety.

2. That all power is naturally vested in, and consequently derived from, the people; that magistrates, therefore, are their trustees and agents, and at all times amenable to them.

3. That government ought to be instituted for the common benefit, protection, and security, of the people; and that the doctrine of nonresistance against arbitrary power and oppression is absurd, slavish, and destructive to the good and happiness of mankind. . . .

17. That the people have a right to keep and bear arms; that a well regulated militia, composed of the body of the people, trained to arms, is the proper, natural, and safe defence of a free state; that standing armies, in time of peace, are dangerous to liberty, and therefore ought to be avoided, as far as the circumstances and protection of the community will admit; and that, in all cases, the military should be under strict subordination to, and governed by, the civil power. . . .

19. That any person religiously scrupulous of bearing arms ought to be exempted, upon payment of an equivalent to employ another to bear arms in his stead. . . .

AMENDMENTS TO THE CONSTITUTION.

1. That each state in the Union shall respectively retain every power, jurisdiction, and right, which is not by this Constitution delegated to the Congress of the United States, or to the departments of the federal government. . . .

9. That no standing army or regular troops shall be raised or kept up in time of peace, without the consent of two thirds of the members present in both houses.

10. That no soldier shall be enlisted for any longer term than four years, except in time of war, and then for no longer term than the continuance of the war.

11. That each state respectively shall have the power to provide for organizing, arming, and disciplining its own militia, whensoever Congress shall omit or neglect to provide for the same; that the militia shall not be subject to martial law, except when in actual service in time of war, invasion, or rebellion; and when not in the actual service of the United States, shall be subject only to such fines, penalties, and punishments, as shall be directed or inflicted by the laws of its own state.

12. That Congress shall not declare any state to be in rebellion, without the consent of at least two thirds of all the members present in both houses.

13. That the exclusive power of legislation given to Congress over the federal town and its adjacent district, and other places purchased or to be purchased by Congress of any of the states, shall extend only to such regulations as respect the police and good government thereof. . . .

26. That Congress shall not introduce foreign troops into the United States without the consent of two thirds of the members present of both houses.

North Carolina ratified the Constitution several weeks after James Madison proposed, in the first session of Congress, the amendments that would become the Bill of Rights.

8. Rhode Island

Rhode Island, the last of the original 13 states to ratify the Constitution, would not do so until May 1790, several months after the proposed Bill of Rights was sent to the states. Rhode Island's ratification message first declared some essential principles of government, and then listed amendments for Congress to consider.

> **Rhode Island Ratification Message**
> 1 Debates on the Adoption of the Federal Constitution 334-36
> (Jonathan Elliot ed., 1836)

I. That there are certain natural rights of which men, when they form a social compact, cannot deprive or divest their posterity, — among which are the enjoyment of life and liberty, with the means of acquiring, possessing, and protecting property, and pursuing and obtaining happiness and safety.

II. That all power is naturally vested in, and consequently derived from, the people; that magistrates, therefore, are their trustees and agents, and at all times amenable to them.

III. That the powers of government may be reassumed by the people whensoever it shall become necessary to their happiness. That the rights of the states respectively to nominate and appoint all state officers, and every other power, jurisdiction, and right, which is not by the said Constitution clearly delegated to the Congress of the United States, or to the departments of government thereof, remain to the people of the several states, or their respective state governments, to whom they may have granted the same; and that those clauses in the Constitution which declare that Congress shall not have or exercise certain powers, do not imply that Congress is entitled to any powers not given by the said Constitution; but such clauses are to be construed as exceptions to certain specified powers, or as inserted merely for greater caution.

XVII. That the people have a right to keep and bear arms; that a well-regulated militia, including the body of the people capable of bearing arms, is the proper, natural, and safe defence of a free state; that the militia shall not be subject to martial law, except in time of war, rebellion, or insurrection; that standing armies, in time of peace, are dangerous to liberty, and ought not to be kept up, except in cases of necessity; and that, at all times, the military should be under strict subordination to the civil power. . . .

XVIII. That any person religiously scrupulous of bearing arms ought to be exempted upon payment of an equivalent to employ another to bear arms in his stead.

Under these impressions, and declaring that the rights aforesaid cannot be abridged or violated, and that the explanations aforesaid are consistent with the said Constitution, and in confidence that the amendments hereafter mentioned will receive an early and mature consideration, and, conformably to the fifth article of said Constitution, speedily become a part thereof,—We, the said delegates, in the name and in the behalf of the people of the state of Rhode Island and Providence Plantations, do, by these presents, assent to and ratify the said Constitution. In full confidence, nevertheless, that, until the amendments hereafter proposed and undermentioned shall be agreed to and ratified. . . .

AMENDMENTS

VI. That no person shall be compelled to do military duty otherwise than by voluntary enlistment, except in cases of general invasion; any thing in the second paragraph of the sixth article of the Constitution, or any law made under the Constitution, to the contrary notwithstanding. . . .

XII. As standing armies, in time of peace, are dangerous to liberty, and ought not to be kept up, except in cases of necessity, and as, at all times, the military should be under strict subordination to the civil power, that, therefore, no standing army or regular troops shall be raised or kept up in time of peace. . . .

XIV. That the Congress shall not declare war without the concurrence of two thirds of the senators and representatives present in each house.

NOTES & QUESTIONS

1. New York proposed standing army and militia amendments, but not an arms-bearing amendment. However, its ratification message presumed that the right to bear arms was unaffected by the new Constitution. What, if anything, does this imply about New Yorkers' views on the right to bear arms? Similarly, Virginia, North Carolina, and Rhode Island sent general declarations of rights separately from desired amendments. Is this distinction significant?

C. *Commentary During the Ratification Period*

1. The Federalist Papers

▌▌ **The Federalist No. 29 (Alexander Hamilton)**
▌▌ **January 9, 1788**

. . . Little more can reasonably be aimed at, with respect to the people at large, than to have them properly armed and equipped; and in order to see that this be not neglected, it will be necessary to assemble them once or twice in the course of a year.

But though the scheme of disciplining the whole nation must be abandoned as mischievous or impracticable; yet it is a matter of the utmost importance that a well-digested plan should, as soon as possible, be adopted for the proper establishment of the militia. The attention of the government ought particularly to be directed to the formation of a select corps of moderate extent, upon such principles as will really fit them for service in case of need. By thus circumscribing the plan, it will be possible to have an excellent body of well-trained militia, ready to take the field whenever the defense of the State shall require it. This will not only lessen the call for military establishments, but if circumstances should at any time oblige the government to form an army of any magnitude that army can never be formidable to the liberties of the people while there is a large body of citizens, little, if at all, inferior to them in discipline and the use of arms, who stand ready to defend their own rights and those of their fellow-citizens. This appears to me the only substitute that can be devised for a standing army, and the best possible security against it, if it should exist.

The Federalist No. 46 (James Madison)
January 29, 1788

... The only refuge left for those who prophesy the downfall of the State governments is the visionary supposition that the federal government may previously accumulate a military force for the projects of ambition. ... Extravagant as the supposition is, let it however be made. Let a regular army, fully equal to the resources of the country, be formed; and let it be entirely at the devotion of the federal government; still it would not be going too far to say, that the State governments, with the people on their side, would be able to repel the danger. The highest number to which, according to the best computation, a standing army can be carried in any country, does not exceed one hundredth part of the whole number of souls; or one twenty-fifth part of the number able to bear arms. This proportion would not yield, in the United States, an army of more than twenty-five or thirty thousand men. To these would be opposed a militia amounting to near half a million of citizens with arms in their hands, officered by men chosen from among themselves, fighting for their common liberties, and united and conducted by governments possessing their affections and confidence. It may well be doubted, whether a militia thus circumstanced could ever be conquered by such a proportion of regular troops. Those who are best acquainted with the last successful resistance of this country against the British, will be most inclined to deny the possibility of it. Besides the advantage of being armed, which the Americans possess over the people of almost every other nation, the existence of subordinate governments, to which the people are attached, and by which the militia officers are appointed, forms a barrier against the enterprises of ambition, more insurmountable than any which a simple government of any form can admit of. Notwithstanding the military establishments in the several kingdoms of Europe, which are carried as far as the public resources will bear, the governments are afraid to trust the people with arms. And it is not certain, that with this aid alone they would not be able to shake off their yokes. But were the people to possess the additional advantages of local governments chosen by themselves, who could collect the national will and direct the national force, and of officers appointed out of the militia, by these governments, and attached both to them and to the militia, it may be affirmed with the greatest assurance, that the throne of every tyranny in Europe would be speedily over-turned in spite of the legions which surround it. Let us not insult the free and gallant citizens of America with the suspicion, that they would be less able to defend the rights of which they would be in actual possession, than the debased subjects of arbitrary power would be to rescue theirs from the hands of their oppressors. Let us rather no longer insult them with the supposition that they can ever reduce themselves to the necessity of making the experiment, by a blind and tame submission to the long train of insidious measures which must precede and produce it. . . .

2. Tench Coxe

Tench Coxe, a Philadelphian, wrote numerous widely circulated articles in favor of the proposed Constitution and Bill of Rights. This section is derived from Stephen P. Halbrook & David B. Kopel, *Tench Coxe and the Right to Keep and Bear Arms in the Early Republic*, 7 Wm. & Mary Bill Rts. J. 347 (1999). Many of the Coxe materials quoted here are available in Documentary History of the Ratification of the Constitution (Merrill Jensen ed., 1976).

Coxe was appointed to subcabinet positions (one step below a Cabinet Secretary) by Presidents Washington, Adams, Jefferson, and Madison. In the Jefferson administration, his duties included running a federal program to provide firearms to militiamen who could not afford to purchase their own weapons. From Coxe's appearance on the national stage in the late 1780s, until his death in 1824, he wrote prolifically. His work includes essays in major newspapers, lengthy reports for Presidents, and personal correspondence with leading political figures.

Less than ten days after the Constitutional Convention in Philadelphia ended, Tench Coxe began defending the Constitution, in a series of essays published in the Philadelphia *Independent Gazeteer*, and then reprinted throughout the United States. Coxe sent the first two essays to James Madison in New York. Madison responded, "I have received & perused with much pleasure the remarks on the proposed Constitution for the U.S. which you have been so good as to favor me with," and promised to see that they were published in Virginia.

Two centuries later, Justice William Brennan, citing one of Coxe's essays about the jurisdiction of federal courts, noted that Coxe had been "widely reprinted" during the ratification debates. *Atascadero State Hospital v. Scanlon*, 473 U.S. 234, 273 n.24 (1985) (Brennan, J., dissenting). Justice Byron White described Coxe's essays as "the first major defense of the Constitution published in the United States." *Nixon v. Fitzgerald*, 457 U.S. 731, 773 n.14 (1982) (White, J., dissenting).

While some have looked only to the authors of *The Federalist* (James Madison, Alexander Hamilton, and John Jay) to understand the arguments made for ratification of the Constitution, modern historians have a broader view. Tench Coxe — along with writers such as James Wilson, John Dickinson,

Noah Webster, and others — is recognized as a "leading defender" of the Constitution, one of the influential "Other Federalists" who played a major role in shaping the debate over the Constitution. Friends of the Constitution: Writings of the "Other" Federalists 1787-1788 88 (Colleen A. Sheehan & Gary L. McDowell eds., 1998).

In No. IV of the pro-ratification series of newspaper essays, Coxe reassured readers that in case of federal tyranny, the "friends of liberty . . . using those arms which Providence has put into their hands, will make a solemn appeal to 'the power above.'" *An American Citizen IV*, (Phil.) Indep. Gazeteer, Oct. 21, 1787. The new Constitution, said Coxe, no more needed a declaration of rights than did the Articles of Confederation: "*Neither* of them have a bill of rights, *nor does either* notice the liberty of the press, because they are already provided for by *the State Constitutions*; and relating only to personal rights, they could not be mentioned in a contract among *sovereign states*." As for the alleged danger of a standing army: "The militia, who are in fact the effective part of the people at large, will render many troops quite unnecessary. They will form a powerful check upon the regular troops, and will generally be sufficient to over-awe them. . . . " *Id.* (Interestingly, an original edition of *An Examination of the Constitution*, containing all installments of Coxe's ratification essays, in the Jefferson Collection of the Library of Congress, has this passage and no other marked at the margin, perhaps by the original reader.)

Regarding essay No. IV, Coxe wrote Madison: "At the request of Mr. Wilson, Dr. Rush and another friend or two I added a 4th paper, calculated to shew the general advantages & obviate some of the Objections to the System. . . . I . . . wish that you and Col. H[amilton] may make any use of them, which you think will serve the cause." Madison replied that he had distributed of the papers as directed, and had given copies to Alexander Hamilton: "I have no doubt that he will make the best use of them. . . . The 4th is a valuable continuation, and I shall be equally desirous of seeing it in the Virginia Gazettes; and indeed in those of every State." Essay No. IV was widely published. According to James Madison, all of Coxe's essays "had a very valuable effect," in Virginia. Letter from James Madison to Tench Coxe (Jan. 3, 1788), *in* 10 The Papers of James Madison 349 (Robert A. Rutland ed., 1977).

In response to the dissenters at the Pennsylvania ratifying convention, Coxe insisted that the new Constitution did not give Congress excessive control over the militia. Writing as "A Pennsylvanian," Coxe contended:

> The power of the sword, say the minority of Pennsylvania, is in the hands of Congress. My friends and countrymen, it is not so, for THE POWERS OF THE SWORD ARE IN THE HANDS OF THE YEOMANRY OF AMERICA FROM SIXTEEN TO SIXTY. The militia of these free commonwealths, entitled and accustomed to their arms, when compared with any possible army, must be *tremendous and irresistible*. Who are the militia? *are they not ourselves*. Is it feared, then that we shall turn our arms *each man against his own bosom*. Congress have no power to disarm the militia. Their swords, and every other terrible implement of the soldier, are *the birth-right of an American*. What clause in the state or federal constitution hath *given away* that important right. . . . [T]he unlimited power of the sword is not in the hands of either the *federal or state governments*, but where I trust in God it will ever remain, *in the hands of the people*.

A Pennsylvanian, *To The People of the United States*, (Phil.) Indep. Gazeteer, Feb. 20, 1788, at 2.

It is possible that Coxe influenced the writers of *The Federalist*, and vice versa. Madison and Hamilton had read and disseminated his publications before composing their own essays, and there is some similarity between treatments. For instance, after reading "An American Citizen, IV," Hamilton argued in *Federalist* 29 that an "army can never be formidable to the liberties of the people while there is a large body of citizens, little if at all inferior to them in discipline and the use of arms, who stand ready to defend their rights and those of their fellow-citizens." Conversely, a Coxe essay (partially reprinted in the block quote above) was written after Madison sent him *Federalist* 46. The two essays make essentially the same point.

Among the other advantages Coxe saw in the new Constitution was that ex post facto laws "are exploded by the new system." (*See* U.S. Const., art. I, §§9-10. The explicit prohibition on ex post facto laws would raise peoples' consciousness of their rights, and encourage them to armed revolt against any future government that attempted to impose ex post facto laws:

> If a time of public contention shall hereafter arrive, the firm and ardent friends to liberty may know the length to which they can push their noble opposition, on the foundation of the laws. Should their country's cause impel them further, they will be acquainted with the hazard, and using those arms which Providence has put into their hands, will make a solemn appeal to "the power above."

Tench Coxe, An Examination of the Constitution for the United States of America, 18-19, *in* Pamphlets on the Constitution of the United States, Published During its Discussion by the People, 1787-1788, at 147-48 (Paul L. Ford ed., Da Capo Press 1968) (1788).

In other essays written in response to the objections of the Pennsylvania minority, Coxe argued that the new federal government would not be able to interfere with the state militias, because the Constitution provided that states would train their own militia and choose the officers for the state militia.

3. Other Federalists

The point made by James Madison and Tench Coxe — that armed citizens would be an absolute defense in the unlikely occurrence of federal tyranny — was also made by other Federalist commentators. Noah Webster, who today is best known for creating the first dictionary of American English, wrote: "Before a standing army can rule, the people must be disarmed; as they are in almost every kingdom in Europe. The supreme power in America cannot enforce unjust laws by the sword; because the whole body of the people are armed, and constitute a force superior to any band of regular troops that can be, on any pretence, raised in the United States." Noah Webster, *An Examination into the Leading Principles of the Federal Constitution* (Oct. 16, 1787), *in* Pamphlets on the Constitution of the United States, Published During its Discussion by the People, 1787-1788, *supra*, at 56.

Similar points were made by two pseudonymous writers: "[E]ven the power of a veteran army could not subdue a patriotic militia ten times its number. . . ." "Foreign Spectator," (Phil.) Indep. Gazeteer, Sept. 21, 1787. Likewise, "The whole personal influence of the Congress, and their parricide army could never prevail over a hundred thousand men armed and disciplined, owners of the country. . . ." "A Supplement to the Essay on Federal Sentiments," (Phil.) Indep. Gazeteer, Oct. 23, 1787.

NOTES & QUESTIONS

1. Do you find Alexander Hamilton's argument in *Federalist* 29 in favor of a select militia compelling? Hamilton was much more supportive of concentrated national power than were many of his fellow Federalists.

2. Even before the Bill of Rights was adopted, the Constitution included some protections of individual rights. *See* U.S. Const., art. I, §§9-10 (guaranteeing right of habeas corpus, prohibiting federal and state governments from enacting bills of attainder and ex post facto laws, and prohibiting state laws impairing the obligation of contracts). How do these protections affect arguments about the need for a bill of rights?

3. What was the nature of the federal tyranny feared by the Anti-Federalists? Do those or similar fears make sense today, or are the Anti-Federalists' fears of federal tyranny anachronistic?

4. Consider whether other provisions of the Constitution have been construed to grant Congress exclusive powers, or only concurrent powers. In *Houston v. Moore*, 18 U.S. (5 Wheat.) 1 (1820) (discussed in Chapter 5), a divided Supreme Court ruled that federal powers to discipline the militia are exclusive, at least when a state militia has been called into federal service. Keep this issue in mind as you read the history of the Second Amendment in Congress.

5. Was Coxe right that swords and every other terrible implement of the soldier "are the birthright of an American"? Are they still? If not, what has changed?

D.   The Second Amendment

Out of the state ratifying conventions emerged a bargain between Federalists and Anti-Federalists to ratify the Constitution in exchange for the adoption of a bill of rights. James Madison made the agreement at the Virginia ratification convention, and won a seat in the House of Representatives on a platform promising a bill of rights. When the First Congress convened, many Federalists were anxious to get the new federal government underway, and so resisted calls to work on a bill of rights. However, Madison persisted. He intended that the amendments would leave the "structure & stamina of the Govt. as little touched as possible." Letter from James Madison to Edmund Randolph (June 15, 1789), *in* 12 The Papers of James Madison 219 (Charles F. Hobson & Robert A. Rutland eds., 1979). His purpose was not to reduce the powers that had been granted to the new government. Rather, he aimed to make explicit what the Federalists had argued was already implicit in a constitution enumerated and of limited powers: that the new federal government had no power to establish a national religion, censor the press, abolish trial by jury, and so on.

Madison drew many of his ideas for the proposed Bill of Rights from the state ratification conventions. Some things though, were not drawn from the conventions. For example, not one state had called for an amendment requiring just compensation for the taking of private property, but Madison included it in the provision that became the Fifth Amendment.

1. The Second Amendment's Path Through Congress

On June 8, 1789, Madison offered amendments to the Constitution, which he proposed be interlineated into the text of the Constitution, rather than be appended to the end of the document, as they ultimately were. Madison began by proposing that

> . . . there be prefixed to the constitution a declaration, that all power is originally vested in, and consequently derived from, the people.
>
> That government is intended and ought to be exercised for the benefit of the people. . . .
>
> That the people have an indubitable, unalienable, and indefeasible right to reform or change their Government, whenever it be found adverse or inadequate to the purposes of its institution.

1 Annals of Cong. 451 (Joseph Gales ed., 1834). His original proposal to the House of Representatives of the text that would become the Second Amendment read:

> The right of the people to keep and bear arms shall not be infringed; a well armed and well regulated militia being the best security of a free country: but no person religiously scrupulous of bearing arms shall be compelled to render military service in person.

Id. at 451.

Madison proposed that the right to arms language be inserted into Article I, Section 9, after Clause 3. Clauses 2 and 3 protect individuals against suspension of the writ of habeas corpus, bills of attainder, and ex post facto laws.

He also suggested that what were to become the First, Third, Fourth, Eighth, and Ninth Amendments, portions of the Fifth Amendment (double jeopardy, self-incrimination, due process, just compensation), and portions of the Sixth Amendment (speedy public trial, right to confront witnesses, right to be informed of charges, right to favorable witnesses, right to counsel) also be inserted there.

Madison proposed that the remainder of the Fifth (grand jury), Sixth (jury trial, in the form of a declaration that "trial by jury is one of the best securities to the rights of the people, ought to remain inviolate"), and the Seventh Amendment (civil jury trial) be inserted into Article III, which deals with the judiciary. He recommended that what would become the Tenth Amendment be inserted as a new article between Articles VI and VII. His proposed limitation on congressional pay raises was to be inserted into Article I, Section 6, which governs congressional pay. (This was eventually ratified as the Twenty-seventh Amendment in 1992.)

After Article I, Section 10, Clause 1, which prohibits states from violating some individual rights, such as by passing bills of attainder and ex post facto laws, Madison would have inserted: "No State shall violate the equal rights of conscience, or the freedom of the press, or the trial by jury in criminal cases." *Id.* at 451-53.

For the speech introducing the Bill of Rights into the House of Representatives, Madison's notes contain the following: "They relate first to private rights — fallacy on both sides — espec as to English Decln. Of Rights — 1. mere act of parl[iamen]t. 2. no freedom of press — Conscience . . . attaineders — arms to protest[an]ts." James Madison, "Notes for Speech in Congress Supporting Amendments," June 8, 1789, in 12 Madison Papers 193-94 (Robert Rutland ed., 1979) (bracketed letters not in original).

In other words, the English Declaration of Right was defective because it was a mere act of Parliament, and thus could be overridden by a future Parliament. Further, the English Declaration of Right did not go far enough, because it did not protect freedom of the press and the rights of conscience, because it did not outlaw bills of attainder, and because its arms guarantee protected Protestants only.

Madison characterized the overall nature of the Bill of Rights amendments this way:

> In some instances they assert those rights which are exercised by the people in forming and establishing a plan of Government. In other instances, they specify those rights which are retained when particular powers are given up to be exercised by the Legislature. In other instances, they specify those positive rights, which may seem to result from the nature of the compact. Trial by jury cannot be considered as a natural right, but a right resulting from a social compact which regulates the action of the community, but is as essential to secure the liberty of the people as any one of the pre-existent rights of nature. In other instances, they lay down dogmatic maxims with respect to the construction of the Government; declaring that the legislative, executive, and judicial branches shall be kept separate and distinct. . . .
>
> But whatever may be the form which the several States have adopted in making declarations in favor of particular rights, the great object in view is to limit and qualify the powers of Government, by excepting out of the grant of power those cases in which the Government ought not to act, or to act only in a particular mode. They point these exceptions sometimes against the abuse of executive power, sometimes against the legislative, and in some cases, against the community itself; or, in other words, against the majority in favor of the minority.

1 Annals of Cong., *supra*, at 454. Addressing objections that a bill of rights was unnecessary because the federal government was one of explicitly enumerated powers, Madison warned that delegated powers could allow Congress to infringe

on rights, especially if the Necessary and Proper clause were construed with excessive laxity.

Madison's proposal was referred to a special House committee, which rejected his idea to interlineate the amendments into the body of the Constitution. The committee felt that the changes would make it appear that the original Constitution had been defective. The committee insisted that the changes be appended to the end of the Constitution, as Amendments.

The Committee revised Madison's arms right amendment to read:

> A well regulated militia, composed of the body of the people, being the best security of a free state, the right of the people to keep and bear arms shall not be infringed; but no person religiously scrupulous shall be compelled to bear arms.

Id. at 778.

The committee reported the proposed Amendments to the House on July 28, and the entire House began to debate the Amendments on August 13. On August 17, the House began discussion of the future Second Amendment. Representative Elbridge Gerry of Massachusetts objected to the "religiously scrupulous" clause on the grounds that Congress could use it as an excuse to disarm anyone it deemed to have "religious scruples." He further contended that "[a] well-regulated militia being the best security of a free State, admitted an idea that a standing army was a secondary one. It ought to read, 'a well regulated militia, trained to arms.'" Nonetheless, the House adopted the language without changes. *Id.* at 779-80.

Representative Aedanus Burke of South Carolina proposed adding this clause:

> A standing army of regular troops in time of peace is dangerous to public liberty, and such shall not be raised or kept up in time of peace but from necessity, and for the security of the people, nor then without the consent of two-thirds of the members present of both Houses; and in all cases the military shall be subordinate to the civil authority.

Id. at 780. This proposal was rejected.

The House did not discuss the future Second Amendment for another three days, when Representative Thomas Scott of Pennsylvania objected to the "religiously scrupulous" clause, echoing Rep. Gerry's concerns and adding that the clause "would lead to the violation of another article in the constitution, which secures to the people the right of keeping arms, and in this case recourse must be had to a standing army." *Id.* at 796. After some discussion, the House added the phrase "in person" to the end of the clause. *Id.* (In other words, a religious pacifist could not be compelled to personally serve in the militia, but he could be compelled to pay a substitute to serve in his place.) The House made no other changes before sending the Amendment to the Senate four days later.

In the early years of the Republic, the Senate (like England's Parliament) met behind closed doors, so precise details of the Senate's debate are unavailable. What is known is that the Senate (1) removed the religiously scrupulous clause and the phrase "composed of the body of the people," (2) replaced "the best" with "necessary to the," and (3) rejected a proposal to add the words "for the common defence" after "the right of the people to keep and bear arms." 1 Journal of the First Session of the Senate 71, 77 (1820).

The Senate also rejected two proposals for separate amendments on military matters. The first would have required congressional supermajorities to maintain a standing army during peacetime:

> That standing armies, in time of peace, being dangerous to liberty, should be avoided, as far as the circumstances and protection of the community will admit; and that in all cases the military should be under strict subordination to, and governed by, the civil power; that no standing army or regular troops shall be raised in time of peace, without the consent of two-thirds of the members present in both Houses; and that no soldier shall be enlisted for any longer term than the continuance of the war.

Id. at 71. The second rejected proposal, sponsored by Connecticut Senator Roger Sherman, would have explicitly protected states' powers to arm and train their militias:

> That each state, respectively, shall have the power to provide for organizing, arming, and disciplining its own militia, whensoever Congress shall omit or neglect to provide for the same; that the militia shall not be subject to martial law, except when in actual service, in time of war, invasion, or rebellion; and when not in the actual service of the United States, shall be subject only to such fines, penalties, and punishments, as shall be directed or inflicted by the laws of its own state.

Id. at 75.

The Second Amendment now appeared in its present form, to which the House consented:

> A well regulated Militia, being necessary for the security of a free State, the right of the people to keep and bear Arms, shall not be infringed.

On September 25, 1789, Congress sent the Bill of Rights to the states. On December 15, 1791, ratified by three-quarters of the states, the Second Amendment and 10 of the 12 proposed amendments became the law of the land.

2. Commentary on the Second Amendment

The Bill of Rights was far less controversial than the Constitution had been. It was ratified, pursuant to the Constitution, by state legislatures, rather than by special state conventions. Except for congressional records, there are very few surviving commentaries from the period (1789-91) when the Second Amendment was adopted by Congress and the states. The only extensive analysis came from Tench Coxe, who had recently completed his service as one of Pennsylvania's last delegates to Congress under the Articles of Confederation.

Ten days after James Madison introduced the Bill of Rights in the U.S. House of Representatives, and two days after they were published in the Philadelphia press, Coxe penned the most comprehensive section-by-section exposition on the Bill of Rights published during its ratification period. Regarding Madison's proposed right to arms amendment, Coxe wrote: "As civil rulers, not having their duty to the people duly before them, may attempt to tyrannize, and as the military forces which must be occasionally raised to defend our country, might pervert their power to the injury of their fellow-citizens, the people are confirmed by the next article in their right to keep and bear their private arms." Federal Gazette, and Phil. Evening Post, June 18, 1789, at 2.

Coxe sent a copy of his article to Madison. Letter from Tench Coxe to James Madison (June 18, 1789), *in* 12 The Papers of James Madison, *supra*, at 239-40. Madison wrote back acknowledging "Your favor of the 18th instant. The printed remarks inclosed in it are already I find in the Gazettes here [New York]." Madison added that ratification of the amendments "will however be greatly favored by explanatory strictures of a healing tendency, and is therefore already indebted to the co-operation of your pen." Letter from James Madison to Tench Coxe (June 24, 1789), *in* 12 The Papers of James Madison, *supra*, at 257. Madison had apparently seen Coxe's defense of the amendments in the *New York Packet* the day before he wrote to Coxe. New York Packet, June 23, 1789, at 2. The article was also prominently displayed on the first page of the July 4 celebration issue of the *Massachusetts Centennial.*

NOTES & QUESTIONS

Almost all of the issues raised in the questions below became important in the legal debate over the meaning of the Second Amendment in the latter part of the twentieth century and the early part of the twenty-first. The majority and dissenting opinions in *District of Columbia v. Heller*, 554 U.S. 570 (2008) (Chapter 9), address them at length. As you study subsequent chapters of this book, you will see how some of the answers have varied over the course of American history.

1. Notwithstanding the varied disputes created by the syntax of the Second Amendment, it is generally agreed that the comma after "Arms" has no legal or grammatical significance. In eighteenth-century writing, it was common to insert a comma where the reader would pause to breathe.

2. The ten amendments constituting what we now call the Bill of Rights were ratified by the requisite number of state legislatures within two years. These amendments were actually the Third through Twelfth Amendments, originally. The first two amendments (barring a sitting Congress from raising its own pay, and requiring that House of Representatives districts contain no more than 50,000 people) did not gain sufficient state votes to become part of the Constitution. As noted above, the pay-raise provision was ratified in 1992 as the Twenty-seventh Amendment.

3. Recall two of Madison's criticisms of the English Declaration of Right (discussed in Chapter 2). First, the Declaration was a "mere act" of Parliament, and therefore binding on the king and the judiciary, but could be undone by any future Parliament. Second, the English Declaration only guaranteed

arms to Protestants. Does the Second Amendment overcome these "defects"?

4. What is the meaning of the first half of the Second Amendment, "A well regulated militia, being necessary to the security of a free state"? Does the first half indicate that state governments are the intended beneficiaries of the right? The phrase "necessary to the security of a free State" echoes the 1720 English newspaper essays, collectively known as "Cato's Letters," which described freedom of speech and of the press as "essential to the security of a free state." Collected into a book in 1723, and widely reprinted in newspapers all over America, "*Cato's Letters* were the most popular and esteemed source of political ideas in colonial America." Michael Kent Curtis, Free Speech, "The People's Darling Privilege" 37 (2000).

5. Suppose that instead of a single-sentence Second Amendment, the Constitution contained two separate stand-alone amendments: "The right of the people to keep and bear Arms, shall not be infringed." and "A well regulated Militia is necessary to the security of a Free State." Would the legal meaning be different? If so, how?

6. Eugene Volokh argues that the first half of the amendment is a "justification clause"—a common feature in late eighteenth- and early nineteenth-century constitutions. For example, Rhode Island's 1842 constitution: "The liberty of the press being essential to the security of freedom in a state, any person may publish his sentiments on any subject, being responsible for the abuse of that liberty. . . ." Eugene Volokh, *The Commonplace Second Amendment*, 73 N.Y.U. L. Rev. 793 (1998). According to Volokh, the operative clause continues to exist with full force regardless of whether later generations agree with the theory expressed in the justification clause (e.g., that a free press or a militia are essential to a free state, that thrift in government spending is necessary and so state legislators may not raise their own pay, or that holding a criminal trial in the vicinage where an alleged crime was committed is necessary for fairness).

    The contrary viewpoint is presented in H. Richard Uviller & William G. Merkel, The Militia and the Right to Arms, or, How the Second Amendment Fell Silent (2002). They argue that the Second Amendment, controlled by the first clause, was intended solely for the civic republican purpose of enabling a citizen militia. That militia no longer existing in any practical sense, the Second Amendment has little if any modern legal relevance.

    Nelson Lund, echoing a point made by Judge Thomas Cooley's influential nineteenth-century treatises (Chapter 6), retorts that a constitutional right is meant to be a protection against government abuse, and cannot be extinguished by government's failure to perform its own duties related to the right (i.e., failing to maintain a citizen militia). Nelson Lund, *Putting the Second Amendment to Sleep*, 8 Green Bag 2d 101 (2004) (book review). For other reviews of Uviller and Merkel, see Randy E. Barnett, *Was the Right to Keep and Bear Arms Conditioned on Service in an Organized Militia?*, 83 Tex. L. Rev. 237 (2004); Sanford Levinson, *Superb History, Dubious Constitutional and Political Theory: Comments on Uviller and*

Merkel, The Militia and the Right to Arms, 12 Wm. & Mary Bill Rts. J. 315 (2004) (arguing that Uviller and Merkel pay insufficient attention to doctrinal development of the Second Amendment after 1791, and the Fourteenth Amendment's treatment of the Second Amendment as a right of personal self-defense); Jonathan Simon, *Gun Rights and the Constitutional Significance of Violent Crime,* 12 Wm. & Mary Bill Rts. J. 335 (2004) (applying Bruce Ackerman's theory of "Constitutional Moments" to the Second Amendment, and arguing that beginning in the 1960s, the American public, and their legislative representatives, have affirmed a Second Amendment centered on defensive gun use against criminals); H. Richard Uviller & William G. Merkel, *The Authors Reply to Commentaries on, and Criticisms of the Militia and the Right to Arms, Or, How the Second Amendment Fell Silent,* 12 Wm. & Mary Bill Rts. J. 357 (2004) (the Fourteenth Amendment did not change the militia-only text of the Second Amendment; changes in public attitudes about self-defense are of no constitutional significance).

Which of the above approaches is the best method to interpret a constitutional provision that includes an express justification?

7. Imagine a constitutional guarantee: "A well informed electorate, being necessary to the security of a free State, the right of the people to keep and read Books, shall not be infringed." Who has the right to keep and read books? Voters? Everyone? Books for all purposes, or only books relevant to voting?

8. David C. Williams argues that the primary original purpose of the Second Amendment was for the People to be able to overthrow a tyrannical government. The Second Amendment thus presumed that "the People" would be virtuous and united, and would use their arms to protect ordered liberty, rather than to engage in factional violence against each other. In modern times, the Second Amendment is no longer operative, because "the People" — the virtuous and unified people presumed in the Amendment — no longer exist. *See* David C. Williams, The Mythic Meanings of the Second Amendment (2003); David C. Williams, *Civic Constitutionalism, The Second Amendment, and the Right of Revolution,* 79 Ind. L.J. 379 (2004); David C. Williams, *The Constitutional Right to "Conservative" Revolution,* 32 Harv. C.R.-C.L. L. Rev. 413 (1997); David C. Williams, *Civic Republicanism and the Citizen Militia: The Terrifying Second Amendment,* 101 Yale L.J. 551 (1991); *see also* David C. Williams, *Death to Tyrants:* District of Columbia v. Heller *and the Uses of Guns,* 69 Ohio St. L.J. 641 (2008) (criticizing the Scalia majority in *Heller* (Chapter 9), for paying lip service to the right to resist tyranny, but inventing an implausible theory to uphold machine gun bans, even though such guns are the most useful in resisting tyranny).

Are the American people so much less unified and virtuous today than they were in 1791 that Williams's thesis is persuasive? If so, is it the government's fault, and is the solution to reconstitute the militia? Consider this essay by Glenn Reynolds:

I have no doubt that if all able-bodied citizens were required to put in a few days per year walking the streets of their neighborhoods, crime would drop substantially. Citizens could be called together for training and equipment inspection ("mustered") and could be required to provide themselves with the necessary equipment, whether that included firearms or not. This would produce direct results — in terms of law enforcement on the streets — light-years beyond current proposals to add additional professional police, and at far lower cost. However, I wonder whether politicians will be willing to endorse such a requirement, in a society that struggles to get people to show up for jury duty.

This difficulty in securing public service is one reason why the militia system initially declined. Everyone wants to be a free rider, and I have no illusions about the enthusiasm of the average citizen for tramping about the streets in midwinter in search of crime. But the burden is not that great, and the statutory authority for imposing it is already on the books, both at the state and federal levels. . . .

We have spent the last hundred years or so expecting steadily less from citizens in terms of public involvement and citizen responsibilities. Not surprisingly, most citizens have managed to live down to these expectations. Instead of trying to find new ways to protect people, and society, from irresponsibility through regulation, perhaps it is time to start expecting more from people: more involvement, more responsibility, more simple goodness. We might find that people will live up to these expectations, as they have lived down to the current ones. The framers of our constitutions, at both the state and federal levels, certainly thought so, and the state of our society today suggests that they may have known something that we have forgotten.

Glenn Harlan Reynolds, *The Right to Keep and Bear Arms Under the Tennessee Constitution: A Case Study in Civic Republican Thought*, 61 Tenn. L. Rev. 647, 670-73 (1994). Can Congress or the states impose the Reynolds plan via their militia powers? Does the first clause of the Second Amendment indicate that federal or state powers to actually use the militia for civic purposes should be interpreted generously?

9. "[T]he right . . . shall not be infringed." Does the Second Amendment create a new legal right or safeguard an existing one? CQ: *United States v. Cruikshank*, 92 U.S. 542 (1876) (Chapter 6), *Heller* (Chapter 9), and *McDonald v. Chicago*, 130 S. Ct. 3020 (2010) (Chapter 9), address this question in depth. If it is a preexisting right, what was that right? A natural right? The right from the 1689 English Declaration of Right? A right to have arms for service in the militia? A right of states to have effective militias? A combination of some or all of these, as adapted to American understanding of the late eighteenth century?

10. Much of the modern debate about the Second Amendment has focused on the meaning of the phrase "bear arms." There is general agreement that in the Founding Era, "bear arms" was used most often in a militia or military sense. There is disagreement about whether the Second Amendment embraces only this meaning. The Scalia majority and the Stevens dissent in *Heller* (Chapter 9) argue the issue at length.

In the early 1780s, the Virginia General Assembly appointed a Committee of Revisors to recodify the statutes that had accumulated during the previous two centuries of the Commonwealth. Among the revisors were Thomas Jefferson, George Wythe (signer of the Declaration of Independence and the Constitution; Chancellor of Virginia; distinguished law professor who taught Jefferson, John Marshall, and St. George Tucker), and Edmund Pendleton (Speaker of the House of Delegates during the Revolution, and later the first President of the Virginia Supreme Court of Appeals).

Among the many proposed statutes drafted by the Committee of Revisors was a "Bill for Preservation of Deer." Thomas Jefferson, 2 The Papers of Thomas Jefferson 444 (Julian P. Boyd ed., 1950).

James Madison introduced that bill into the House of Burgesses in 1785. While allowing unlimited hunting on one's own enclosed lands, the bill established seasons for hunting deer in other locations. Anyone who violated the law would be temporarily forbidden to carry a long gun outside his own property:

> Whosoever shall offend against this act, shall forfeit and pay, for every deer by him unlawfully killed, twenty shillings, one half thereof to the use of the commonwealth, and the other half to the informer; and moreover, shall be bound to their good behavior; and, if within twelve months after the date of the recognizance *he shall bear a gun out of his inclosed ground, unless whilst performing military duty,* shall be deemed a breach of the recognizance, and be good cause to bind him anew, and *every such bearing of a gun* shall be a breach of the new recognizance and cause to bind him again.

Id. vol. 2, at 443-44 (emphasis added).

In early American usage, "gun" meant a long gun. In the linguistic usage of the time, "guns" were different from "pistols." Noah Webster, *An American Dictionary of the English Language* (1828) (defining gun, and explaining, "But one species of firearms, the pistol, is never called a gun"). Under this usage, the Madison bill would temporarily prohibit a hunting law violator from carrying the firearms most useful for hunting, while still allowing the violator to carry a handgun for defense. The bill advanced to second reading in the Virginia legislature, but no further action was taken. *Id.* at 444.

Is the Bill for Preservation of Deer convincing evidence of the meaning that James Madison and the Committee Revisors attached to the phrase "bear arms"?

11. There is less modern debate over the eighteenth-century meaning of "keep" arms. Most commentators agree that "keep" included the general possession and storage of arms. An example of this usage is a 1785 statute that the Virginia legislature *did* adopt: "No slave shall keep any arms whatever nor pass unless with written orders from his master or employer, or in his company with arms from one place to another." A Bill Concerning Slaves, Chapter 51, Virginia Assembly, 1779; *in* The Essential Jefferson 140 (Albert Fried ed., 1963). In the nineteenth century, one line of cases (launched by Tennessee's *Aymette v. State*, 21 Tenn. (2 Hump.) 154 (1840) (Chapter 5), read "keep arms" as including a right of every free person to keep guns at home, but "bear arms" as only a right of militiamen in actual service. (*Heller* (Chapter 9), discusses this case, and rejects *Aymette's* narrow reading of "bear.") The dominant line of nineteenth-century cases (Chapters 5 and 6) read "keep and bear arms" more broadly, as a right of all

individuals to own and carry arms, but even then only the types of arms suitable for militia service (e.g., rifles, swords, and large handguns, but not arms considered useful mainly for brawls and affrays, such the Bowie knife). Some scholars argue that although "keep," in isolation, does not have a military connotation, the phrase "keep and bear arms" was meant as a unitary term of art to comprise only the militia. *See, e.g.,* Michael C. Dorf, *What Does the Second Amendment Mean Today?*, 76 Chi.-Kent L. Rev. 291, 317 (2000) (arguing for this interpretation, but acknowledging that the plain meaning of "keep" could also plausibly support an individual right).

12. Does the Second Amendment solve the Anti-Federalist objections to the federal militia power? Did it attempt to? After the ratification of the Second Amendment, was the federal militia power in Article I reduced? If so, how? Were state militia powers any more secure against federal abuse?

A pair of amicus briefs in *Heller* (Chapter 9), offer sophisticated, contrasting views of intended effect of the Second Amendment in regard to state militias.

According to Academics for the Second Amendment, the Second Amendment was carefully written to avoid diminishing federal militia power. James Madison wrote the Second Amendment to conciliate Anti-Federalists by extolling the militia and providing a general protection against federal interference with gun ownership; this was easy to do, since the Federalists never had any desire to interfere with gun ownership, just as they never had any desire to establish a national religion, and so were more than willing to guarantee, in the First Amendment, the nonestablishment of religion. In short, the Second Amendment was "a tub to the whale."

A whaling vessel is sometimes "so surrounded with whales, that the situation of the crew becomes dangerous. When this is the case, it is usual to throw out a tub in order to divert their attention; when the marine monsters amuse themselves in tossing this singular sort of a plaything into the air, to and fro, as children do a shuttlecock. Their attention being drawn, every sail is hoisted, and the vessel pursues its course to its destination. Hence came the saying, 'Throwing a Tub to the Whale!'" William Pulleyn, Etymological Compendium 321 (2010) (1853). The phrase was commonly used to mean a political distraction. For the view that the entire Bill of Rights was a tub to the whale — that is, a guarantee that the Federalists would not do things they never wanted to do anyway, and a successful political distraction from calls to constrict the powers that the Federalists did want to exercise — see Kenneth R. Bowling, *"A Tub to the Whale": The Founding Fathers and the Adoption of the Federal Bill of Rights*, 8 J. Early Republic 223 (1988).

In contrast, the amicus brief of the Brady Center argues that the sole intended beneficiary of the Second Amendment was the state governments. For the benefit of state governments, the Second Amendment conferred an individual right to arms, only for state militia service, and only if Congress failed to exercise its Article I power to arm the militia.

The amicus briefs in *Heller* are available at DCGunCase.com, Case Filings, *available at* http://dcguncase.com/blog/case-filings, those in *McDonald* (Chapter 9), at ChicagoGunCase.com, Case Filings, *available at* http://www.chicagoguncase.com/case-filings, and both on Westlaw and Lexis. The best amicus briefs, on both sides of the cases, provide succinct and well-written analyses and evidence regarding many of the Second and Fourteenth Amendment issues, and general policy questions, discussed throughout this text.

13. The right to arms guarantee of the 1875 Missouri Constitution (still in force) provides in part: "That the right of no citizen to keep and bear arms in defense of his home, person and property, or in aid of the civil power, when thereto legally summoned, shall be called into question. . . ." In this text, the right to arms is explicitly guaranteed for two purposes: personal defense (home, person, and property), and civil defense (in aid of the civil power). Can the Second Amendment be read as guaranteeing a right to arms for *both* purposes?

David Hardy argues that Madison used the Second Amendment to meld two related but distinct ideologies of arms-bearing: The first clause embodies the civic virtue, civic republicanism, citizen militia ideology of the seventeenth-century English Radical Whigs, and their Renaissance Italian predecessors. The second clause embodies a natural law and human rights tradition of ancient roots, most prominently associated with Thomas Jefferson. David T. Hardy, *The Second Amendment and the Historiography of the Bill of Rights*, 4 J.L & Pol. 4 (1987). The article argues that the Second Amendment should therefore be read to protect individual gun ownership for self-defense and for militia use, *and* to protect state militia powers. Do you agree, or does the text of the Second Amendment force a binary choice?

E. Post-Ratification

1. The Militia Acts

In 1790, Secretary of War Henry Knox offered a plan to create a national select militia, founded on intensive training of males aged 18 to 20. 1 Annals of Cong. app. 2141-61. Even in a Federalist-dominated Congress, the idea was anathema. Moreover, it is questionable whether the nascent federal government would have had the administrative capability to establish an effective national militia. Instead of the Knox plan, Congress enacted the Militia Act of 1792, and revised it later that year. The 1792 law was the main governing statute for the United States militia until 1903.

First Militia Act of 1792
1 Stat. 264 (1792)

. . . An Act to provide for calling forth the Militia to execute the laws of the Union, suppress insurrections and repel invasions.

SECTION 1. *Be it enacted by the Senate and House of Representatives of the United States of America in Congress assembled,* That whenever the United States shall be invaded, or be in imminent danger of invasion from any foreign nation or Indian tribe, it shall be lawful for the President of the United States, to call forth such number of the militia of the state or states most convenient to the place of danger or scene of action as he may judge necessary to repel such invasion, and to issue his orders for that purpose, to such officer or officers of the militia as he shall think proper; and in case of an insurrection in any state, against the government thereof, it shall be lawful for the President of the United States, on application of the legislature of such state, or of the executive (when the legislature cannot be convened) to call forth such number of the militia of any other state or states, as may be applied for, or as he may judge sufficient to suppress such insurrection.

SEC. 2. And be it further enacted, That whenever the laws of the United States shall be opposed or the execution thereof obstructed, in any state, by combinations too powerful to be suppressed by the ordinary course of judicial proceedings, . . . the same being notified to the President of the United States, by an associate justice or the district judge, it shall be lawful for the President of the United States to call forth the militia of such state to suppress such combinations, and to cause the laws to be duly executed. And if the militia of a state, where such combinations may happen, shall refuse, or be insufficient to suppress the same, it shall be lawful for the President, if the legislature of the United States be not in session, to call forth and employ such numbers of the militia of any other state or states most convenient thereto, as may be necessary, and the use of militia, so to be called forth, may be continued, if necessary, until the expiration of thirty days after the commencement of the ensuing session.

SEC. 3. Provided always, and be it further enacted, That whenever it may be necessary, in the judgment of the President, to use the military force hereby directed to be called forth, the President shall forthwith, and previous thereto, by proclamation, command such insurgents to disperse, and retire peaceably to their respective abodes, within a limited time.

SEC. 4. And be it further enacted, That the militia employed in the service of the United States, shall receive the same pay and allowances, as the troops of the United States, who may be in service at the same time, or who were last in service, and shall be subject to the same rules and articles of war: And that no officer, non-commissioned officer or private of the militia shall be compelled to serve more than three months in any one year, nor more than in due rotation with every other able-bodied man of the same rank in the battalion to which he belongs. . . .

SEC. 10. And be it further enacted, That this act shall continue and be in force, for and during the term of two years, and from thence to the end of the next session of Congress thereafter, and no longer.

Second Militia Act of 1792
1 Stat. 271 (1792)

. . . An Act more effectually to provide for the National Defence by establishing an Uniform Militia throughout the United States.

SECTION 1. *Be it enacted by the Senate and House of Representatives of the United States of America in Congress assembled,* That each and every free able-bodied white

male citizen of the respective states, resident therein, who is or shall be of the age
of eighteen years, and under the age of forty-five years (except as is herein after
excepted) shall severally and respectively be enrolled in the militia by the
captain or commanding officer of the company, within whose bounds such
citizen shall reside, and that within twelve months after the passing of this
act. And it shall at all times hereafter be the duty of every such captain or
commanding officer of a company to enrol every such citizen, as aforesaid,
and also those who shall, from time to time, arrive at the age of eighteen
years, or being of the age of eighteen years and under the age of forty-five
years (except as before excepted) shall come to reside within his bounds; and
shall without delay notify such citizen of the said enrolment, by a proper non-
commissioned officer of the company, by whom such notice may be proved.
That every citizen so enrolled and notified, shall, within six months thereafter,
provide himself with a good musket or firelock, a sufficient bayonet and belt, two
spare flints, and a knapsack, a pouch with a box therein to contain not less than
twenty-four cartridges, suited to the bore of his musket or firelock, each cartridge to contain a proper quantity of powder and ball: or with a good rifle,
knapsack, shot-pouch and powder-horn, twenty balls suited to the bore of his
rifle, and a quarter of a pound of powder; and shall appear, so armed, accoutred
and provided, when called out to exercise, or into service, except, that when
called out on company days to exercise only, he may appear without a knapsack.
That the commissioned officers shall severally be armed with a sword or hanger
and espontoon, and that from and after five years from the passing of this act, all
muskets for arming the militia as herein required, shall be of bores sufficient for
balls of the eighteenth part of a pound. And every citizen so enrolled, and
providing himself with the arms, ammunition and accoutrements required as
aforesaid, shall hold the same exempted from all suits, distresses, executions or
sales, for debt or for the payment of taxes. . . .

SEC. 3. *And be it further enacted,* That within one year after the passing of this
act, the militia of the respective states shall be arranged into divisions, brigades,
regiments, battalions and companies, as the legislature of each state shall
direct. . . .

SEC. 4. *And be it further enacted,* That out of the militia enrolled, as is herein
directed, there shall be formed [certain units.]

NOTES & QUESTIONS

1. The First Militia Act was repealed and reenacted, with revisions, in 1795. The
    "Calling Forth Act" removed the language (in section 2 of the First Militia
    Act) requiring judicial notification before the President could call forth the
    militia. There were also some small revisions in sections 4 and 5. 1 Stat. 424
    (1795).

2. Compare the 1792 Militia Acts to the Second Amendment, whose ratifica-
    tion had just been completed by the states in 1791. Assume the 1792 Con-
    gress did not intend the Militia Acts to violate the Second Amendment.
    What, if anything, do the Militia Acts imply about the nature of the right

protected by the Second Amendment? About firearms ownership in
general? About federal militia powers?

3. President George Washington's first address to a joint session of Congress
urged that "A free people ought not only to be armed but disciplined; to
which end a uniform and well digested plan is requisite." 1 Journal of the
Second Session of the Senate 103 (1820).

During the ensuing debates on what would become the Militia Acts of
1792, many statements were made about arms-bearing. Representative
Thomas Fitzsimons of Pennsylvania (a signer of the Constitution) stated
that "[a]s far as the whole body of the people are necessary to the general
defence, they ought to be armed." 2 Annals of Cong. 1852 (Joseph Gales ed.,
1834).

Representative James "Left Eye" Jackson of Georgia argued that "the
people of America would never consent to be deprived of the privilege of
carrying arms. Though it may prove burdensome to some individuals to be
obliged to arm themselves, yet it would not be so considered when the
advantages were justly estimated," *id.*, and that "that every citizen was not
only entitled to carry arms, but also in duty bound to perfect himself in
the use of them, and thus become capable of defending his country," 14
Documentary History of the First Federal Congress: Debates in the House of
Representatives: Third Session, December 1790-March 1791, at 64 (1996).

Representative Hugh Williamson of North Carolina (a signer of the
Constitution) asked rhetorically, "Congress are to provide for arming and
disciplining the militia; but who are the militia? . . . [T]he militia ought to
consist of the whole body of citizens without exception." 2 Annals of Cong.,
supra, at 1868-69.

Connecticut Senator Roger Sherman also spoke. Sherman was the only
man to sign all four of the great state papers of the American Founding:
the Continental Association (created by the First Continental Congress on
October 20, 1774, the Continental Association's purpose was to organize a
boycott of British goods in all 13 colonies), the Declaration of Independence, the Articles of Confederation, and the Constitution. Sherman served
on the Committee of Five, which drafted the Declaration of Independence;
proposed at the Constitutional Convention the Connecticut Compromise
(that representation be by population in the House, equal state representation in the Senate) that made agreement on the Constitution possible; and
served on the U.S. House Committee that created the Bill of Rights. As noted
above, he also offered a proposed amendment, not adopted by the House
Committee, to affirm concurrent state powers to arm the militia. His excel-
lence was universally recognized by his contemporaries. Patrick Henry called
him one of the three greatest men at the Constitutional Convention. Thomas
Jefferson wrote that Sherman "never said a foolish thing in his life." 3 The
New England Farmer 334 (S.W. Cole & Simon Brown eds., 1851).

Regarding the Militia Acts, Sherman "conceived it to be the privilege
of every citizen, and one of his most essential rights, to bear arms, and to
resist every attack upon his liberty or property, by whomsoever made.
The particular states, like private citizens, have a right to be armed, and
to defend, by force of arms, their rights, when invaded." 14 Debates in

the House of Representatives 92-93 (William Charles DiGiacomantonio et al. eds., 1995).

Do the Militia Acts establish individual rights or individual duties? Do the statements from the debates speak of rights or duties or both?

4. Why would Congress require the President to give insurgents an opportunity to abandon their insurgency before using the militia to suppress it? CQ: Chapter 5 discusses Fries's Rebellion (under President John Adams). In 1794, President George Washington called forth the state militias to suppress the Whiskey Rebellion in western Pennsylvania, the only instance in American history in which a President has personally commanded the military in the field. Both Presidents followed the statutory command to first order the insurgents to end their rebellions.

5. The Constitution gave the Congress, not the President, the power to call forth the militia. U.S. Const. art. I., §8, cl. 15. The First Militia Act delegated this power to the President. This delegation was, in some situations, contingent on action by the third branch of the government, namely a federal judge. (The judicial provision was removed in 1795.)

Is everything the First or Second Congresses did presumptively or irre-futably consistent with the original meaning of the Constitution? Is it constitutional for one branch of government to delegate its enumerated powers to another? Can Congress properly delegate to the President other congressional military powers, such as the power to declare war? The power to appropriate funds for the military? Could the President delegate to Congress his power to command the military? Could Congress make the President's exercise of a delegated military power contingent on a determination by a federal judge? If some of powers are delegable, and others are not, what are the differences?

6. Is there any significance to the fact that the militia, when federalized, was to receive the same pay as troops in the federal army?

7. John Adams served two terms as Vice-President under President George Washington (1789-97), before serving as President (1797-1801). He was no stranger to gun-carrying, having taken a pocket pistol with him when he departed for France in 1778 to serve as America's Ambassador. David McCullough, John Adams 177 (2001).

In 1787, Adams completed a three-volume book defending the American form of government in general, and the state constitutions in particular, against a European-based critique. The book included this passage:

> It must be made a sacred maxim, that the militia obey the executive power, which represents the whole people, in the execution of laws. To suppose arms in the hands of citizens, to be used at individual discretion, *except in private self-defence*, or by partial orders of towns, counties, or districts of a state, is to demolish every constitution, and lay the laws prostrate, so that liberty can be enjoyed by no man — it is a dissolution of the government. The

fundamental law of the militia is, that it be created, directed, and commanded by the laws, and ever for the support of the laws. This truth is acknowledged by our author, when he says, "The arms of the commonwealth should be lodged in the hands of that part of the people which are firm to its establishment."

3 John Adams, A Defence of the Constitutions of Government of the United States of America, Against the Attack of M. Turgot in His Letter to Dr. Price, Dated the Twenty-Second Day of March, 1778, at 475 (1787). Adams was not discussing the Second Amendment, which had not yet been proposed, but he was setting forth general principles of good government.

What is Adams's view on whether people can form legitimate militias without government authorization? Recall that, as detailed in Chapter 3, in 1774-76, Americans such as George Washington, Patrick Henry, John Marshall, and many others, formed militias in flagrant defiance of the royal governors. As detailed in question 1 in Chapter 3.C.5, the Militia, Act of 1792 explicitly recognized independent militias, and provided for their being called into federal service when needed. Is Adams's support for the independent militias in 1774-76 consistent with his views in 1787?

In 1787, Adams is speaking as a representative of the established order. In 1775, he is a nascent Revolutionary. Is it inevitable that the political establishment will take a conservative view about the boundaries of legitimate political violence?

Adams's 1787 commentary explicitly allowed for individual discretion in the use of arms for private self-defense. Are the interests and concerns of a ruling establishment different on the questions of political versus personal violence? Does political violence threaten the established order in a way that violent self-defense does not?

8. The Second Militia Act of 1792 enrolled only free whites, a point to which Chief Justice Roger Taney pointed in *Dred Scott v. Sandford*, 60 U.S. 393 (1857), to argue that while a state might make free Black citizens, they were not citizens of the United States. After the Louisiana Purchase, Territorial Governor William C.C. Claiborne ignored the federal statute and allowed free blacks to remain in the volunteer militia that had been organized under the French. Some of these volunteers participated in the War of 1812, including the 1815 Battle of New Orleans. Roland C. McConnell, Negro Troops of Antebellum Louisiana: A History of the Battalion of Free Men of Color (1968); Donald E. Everett, *Emigres and Militiamen: Free Persons of Color in New Orleans, 1803-15*, 38 J. Negro Hist. 377 (1953). In New Jersey, blacks had served in the state militia alongside whites during the Revolution, but after the war, state law forbade them from militia service. Robert J. Gough, *Black Men and the Early New Jersey Militia*, 37 N.J. Hist. 227 (1970).

9. The Second Militia Act provided that the militiaman "shall hold the same [his mandatory equipment] exempted from all suits, distresses, executions or sales, for debt or for the payment of taxes." The language appears to protect the individual's militia equipment from creditors, including state governments, *and* to forbid the militiaman from pledging his equipment as

security for any debt. Does this suggest that militia arms are a unique form of property, in which there is a public interest in protecting the ownership of the property — both from third parties, and from alienation by the militia-man himself? CQ: As early as the seventh century, England's militia laws (Chapter 2) had specified that regarding an individual's mandated arms, a man "might neither sell, lend, nor pledge, nor even alienate them from his heirs." Francis Grose, Military Antiquities Respecting a History of the English Army 2 (2010) (1812).

2. St. George Tucker

a. *Tucker's* Blackstone

The most influential and widely used law textbook of the early Republic was the five-volume, 1803 American edition of William Blackstone's *Commentaries on the Common Law of England*, edited and annotated by the Virginia jurist St. George Tucker (1752-1827). Tucker was a militia colonel during the Revolutionary War, a Virginia Court of Appeals judge, a federal district judge, and professor of law at the College of William and Mary. Tucker's *Blackstone* was not merely a repro-duction of the famous English text. It contained numerous annotations and other material suggesting that the English legal tradition had undergone devel-opment in its transmission across the Atlantic, generally in the direction of greater individual liberty. Tucker's treatment of Blackstone's discussion of the right to arms was typical. Blackstone classified the right to arms as one of five "auxiliary right[s] of the subject."

Tucker used two footnotes (numbers 40 and 41 in the original, reproduced below) to contrast Blackstone's summary of the English right to arms with the broader American right recognized by the Second Amendment.

> The fifth and last auxiliary right of the subject, that I shall at present mention, is that of having arms for their defence[40] suitable to their condition and degree, and such as are allowed by law.[41] Which is also declared by the . . . statute 1 W. & M. st. 2 c. 2, and it is indeed, a public allowance under due restrictions, of the natural rights of resistance and self-preservation, when the sanctions of society and laws are found insufficient to restrain the violence of oppression.

William Blackstone, 1 Commentaries 143-44 (St. George Tucker ed., Lawbook Exchange, Ltd. 1996) (1803).

---

40. The right of the people to keep and bear arms shall not be infringed. Amendments to C.U.S. Art. 4, and this without any qualification as to their condition or degree, as is the case in the British government. [See question 2 in Section D.2, above, for an explanation of why Tucker cited the arms right this way.]

41. Whoever examines the forest and game laws in the British code, will readily perceive that the right of keeping arms is effectually taken away from the people of England. The commentator himself [Blackstone] informs us, Vol. II, p. 412, "that the prevention of popular insurrections and resistance to government by disarming the bulk of the people, is a reason oftener meant than avowed by the makers of the forest and game laws."

Tucker's *Blackstone* also included a lengthy appendix on the new American Constitution. This appendix was the first scholarly treatise on American constitutional law and has been frequently relied upon by the United States Supreme Court and scholars. Tucker's primary treatment of the Second Amendment appeared in the appendix's discussion of the Bill of Rights:

> A well regulated militia being necessary to the security of a free state, the right of the people to keep, and bear arms, shall not be infringed. Amendments to the C.U.S. Art. 4.
>
> This may be considered as the true palladium of liberty. . . . The right of self defence is the first law of nature: in most governments it has been the study of rulers to confine this right within the narrowest limits possible. Wherever standing armies are kept up, and the right of the people to keep and bear arms is, under any colour or pretext whatsoever, prohibited, liberty, if not already annihilated, is on the brink of destruction. In England, the people have been disarmed, generally, under the specious pretext of preserving the game: a never failing lure to bring over the landed aristocracy to support any measure, under that mask, though calculated for very different purposes. True it is, their bill of rights seems at first view to counteract this policy: but the right of bearing arms is confined to protestants, and the words suitable to their condition and degree, have been interpreted to authorise the prohibition of keeping a gun or other engine for the destruction of game, to any farmer, or inferior tradesman, or other person not qualified to kill game. So that not one man in five hundred can keep a gun in his house without being subject to a penalty.

Appendix to Vol. 1, Part D, p. 300 (ellipsis in original).

Tucker's appendix also mentioned the right to arms in the context of congressional power over the militia. Noting that the Constitution gives Congress the power of organizing, arming, and disciplining the militia, while reserving to the states the power to train the militia and appoint its officers, U.S. Const., art. I, §8, cl. 16, Tucker asked whether the states could act to arm and organize the militia if Congress did not. He argued that the language of the Second Amendment supported the states' claim to concurrent authority over the militia:

> The objects of [the Militia Clauses in Article I] of the constitution, . . . were thought to be dangerous to the state governments. The convention of Virginia, therefore, proposed the following amendment to the constitution; "that each state respectively should have the power to provide for organizing, arming, and disciplining it's own militia, whenever congress should neglect to provide for the same." . . . [A]ll room for doubt, or uneasiness upon the subject, seems to be completely removed, by the [second] article of amendments to the constitution, since ratified, viz. "That a militia being necessary to the security of a free state, the right of the people to keep, and bear arms, shall not be infringed." To which we may add, that the power of arming the militia, not being prohibited to the states, respectively, by the constitution, is, consequently, reserved to them, concurrently with the federal government.

Id. at 272-73.

Tucker's treatise was studded with other references to the right to arms. For example, Tucker contended that Congress's power to enact statutes that are "necessary and proper" for carrying into effect its other enumerated powers, U.S. Const. art. I, §8, cl. 18, did not include the power to make laws that violated important individual liberties. Such laws could not be deemed "necessary and proper" in the constitutional sense, argued Tucker; therefore, they were invalid and could be struck down by a federal court. Tucker chose as an illustration a hypothetical law prohibiting the bearing of arms:

> If, for example, congress were to pass a law prohibiting any person from bearing arms, as a means of preventing insurrections, the judicial courts, under the construction of the words necessary and proper, here contended for, would be able to pronounce decidedly upon the constitutionality of those means.

Id. at 289.

Similarly, Tucker observed that the English law of treason applied a rebuttable presumption that a gathering of men was motivated by treason and insurrection if weapons were present at the gathering. Tucker, however, was skeptical that the simple fact of being armed "ought . . . of itself, to create any such presumption in America, where the right to bear arms is recognized and secured in the constitution itself." Vol. 5 Appendix, at 9, note B. He added: "In many parts of the United States, a man no more thinks, of going out of his house on any occasion, without his rifle or musket in his hand, than a European fine gentleman without his sword by his side." *Id.*

Tucker's prominence and his proximity to the framing of the Bill of Rights have made him an important source for the original understanding of the Second Amendment. His writings have mostly been interpreted as reflecting a broad view of the Second Amendment right to arms, one that includes the keeping and use of private arms for individual self-defense. *See, e.g., Heller,* 554 U.S. at 594-95, 606-07 (Chapter 9); Stephen P. Halbrook, *St. George Tucker's Second Amendment: Deconstructing the True Palladium of Liberty,* 3 Tenn. J.L. & Pol'y 114 (2007).

b. Tucker's Early Lecture Notes

Historian Saul Cornell argues that Tucker changed his mind about the Second Amendment. According to Cornell, Tucker's 1791-92 lecture notes for the class he taught at William & Mary described the Second Amendment in a more militia-centric way than did Tucker's 1803 book. Saul Cornell, *St. George Tucker and the Second Amendment: Original Understandings and Modern Misunderstandings,* 47 Wm. & Mary L. Rev. 1123 (2006). Since all ten amendments in the Bill of Rights were declared ratified on December 15, 1791, the 1791-92 lecture notes would, presumably, be a better source of the original meaning of the Second Amendment than would Tucker's 1803 book. Cornell quotes Tucker as stressing the concurrent authority of states to arm their citizens:

> If a State chooses to incur the expence of putting arms into the Hands of its own Citizens for their defense, it would require no small ingenuity to prove that they have no right to do it, or that it could by any means contravene the Authority

of the federal Govt. It may be alleged indeed that this might be done for the purpose of resisting the Laws of the federal Government, or of shaking off the Union: to which the plainest answer seems to be, that whenever the States think proper to adopt either of these measures, they will not be with-held by the fear of infringing any of the powers of the federal Government. But to contend that such a power would be dangerous for the reasons above-mentioned, would be subversive of every principle of Freedom in our Government; of which the first Congress appears to have been sensible by proposing an Amendment to the Constitution, which has since been ratified and has become a part of it, viz. "That a well regulated militia being necessary to the Security of a free State, the right of the people to keep & bear Arms shall not be infringed." To this we may add that this power of arming the militia, is not one of those prohibited to the States by the Constitution, and, consequently, is reserved to them under the [Tenth Amendment].

Id. at 1130. Justice Stevens's dissenting opinion in the *Heller* decision cited Cornell's critique of Tucker. *Heller*, 554 U.S. at 666 n.32 (Stevens, J., dissenting) (citing Cornell's article for the claim that, Tucker once thought the Second Amendment was militia-only) (Chapter 9). Writing for the majority, Justice Scalia countered that the passage above is chiefly about the meaning of the Militia Clauses and the Tenth Amendment, not the Second Amendment. *Id.* at 606 n.19.

After *Heller* was decided, attorney David Hardy traveled to Williamsburg, Virginia, to study Tucker's handwritten lecture notes himself, at William & Mary's library. Hardy found that, in the lecture notes, Tucker described the Second Amendment in language quite similar to what Tucker would write in the 1803 book:

> The right of self defense is the first law of nature. In most governments it has been the study of rulers to abridge this right with the narrowest limits. Where ever standing armies are kept up & the right of the people to bear arms is by any means or under any colour whatsoever prohibited, liberty, if not already annihilated is in danger of being so. — In England the people have been disarmed under the specious pretext of preserving the game. By the alluring idea, the landed aristocracy have been brought to side with the Court in a measure evidently calculated to check the effect of any ferment which the measures of government may produce in the minds of the people. — The Game laws are a [consolation?] for the government, a rattle for the gentry, and a rack for the nation.
>
> [Tucker added a marginal note:] In England the right of the people to bear arms is confined to protestants — and by the terms suitable to their condition & degree, the effect of the Declaration is entirely done away. Vi: Stat. 1 W & M l:2 c. 2 [the English Declaration of Right].

David T. Hardy, *The Lecture Notes of St. George Tucker: A Framing Era View of the Bill of Rights,* 103 Nw. U. L. Rev. Colloquy 1527, 1533-34 (2009).

For more on the Tucker debate, see Saul Cornell, *Originalist Methodology: A Critical Comment,* 103 Nw. U. L. Rev. Colloquy 1541 (2009) (responding to Hardy's article in the same issue); Saul Cornell, Heller, *New Originalism, and Law Office History: "Meet the New Boss, Same as the Old Boss,"* 56 UCLA L. Rev. 1095 (2009); David T. Hardy, *Originalism and Its Tools: A Few Caveats,* 1 Akron J. Const.

L. & Pol'y 40 (2009), *available at* http://www.akronconlawjournal.com/articles/originalism-and-its-tools-a-few-caveats.pdf.

F.   Federal and State Military Forces of Today

As we have seen, many Anti-Federalists feared that the Militia Clauses of the proposed Constitution gave the new federal government too much power over the militia, especially when combined with the power granted to the federal government to raise a standing army. This controversy strengthened calls from the states to have a Bill of Rights added to the new Constitution. Reflecting these concerns, the Second Amendment begins with a clause affirming that "a well regulated militia" is "necessary to the security of a free State." What, if anything, do such terms correspond to today? This section briefly explains what types of "militia" are recognized by federal law today, and how they differ from the United States Army and other regular military forces. Today, legally recognized military forces in the United States fall into four groups:

1.   The United States Armed Forces

The United States Armed Forces include the five major military service branches: the United States Army, Navy, Marine Corps, Air Force, and Coast Guard. These are created and maintained pursuant to Congress's powers to "raise and support Armies," to "provide and maintain a Navy," and to "make Rules for the Government and Regulation of the land and naval Forces." U.S. Const., art. I, §8, cls. 12-14. (The first of these provisions is sometimes referred to as the Armies Clause.) The armed forces' Commander in Chief is the President of the United States. U.S. Const., art. II, §2, cl. 1. The armed forces may be freely deployed overseas.

The Posse Comitatus Act, 18 U.S.C. §1385, enacted in 1878 and as amended later, places limitations on the use of Army and Air Force units for domestic law enforcement purposes. The Posse Comitatus Act reinforces limits on military enforcement of domestic laws that date from the Insurrection Act of 1807, which for the first time authorized use of the army (not just the militia) to enforce federal law. 10 U.S.C. §§331-335. In 2006, the Insurrection Act limits on presidential use of the military for domestic law enforcement were greatly weakened, but these changes were repealed in 2008. Starting in 1981, "drug war" exceptions have been added to the Posse Comitatus Act, resulting in a now substantial use of the military for domestic law enforcement.

The United States Armed Forces are currently all-volunteer services. However, enforced conscription (the draft) was first used to raise troops during the Civil War, and then again in World War I. Peacetime conscription was imposed in 1940. Conscription continued until 1972, covering World War II, the Korean War, the Vietnam War, and peacetime years. In the *Selective Draft Law*

Cases, 245 U.S. 366 (1918), the Supreme Court unanimously held that the Armies Clause, in conjunction with the other provisions of Article I, gives Congress the constitutional authority to conscript individual citizens into the regular armed forces. This power, the Court held, is separate from and additional to Congress's power under the Constitution's Militia Clauses. Thus, while Congress can "call forth the militia" only "to execute the Laws of the Union, suppress Insurrections and repel Invasions," U.S. Const., art. I, §8, cl. 15, these limitations do not apply to forces raised under the Armies Clause.

The *Selective Draft Law Cases* rejected the argument that a federal military draft violates the state militia powers that are recognized in Article I, Section 8, in that a federal draft can essentially destroy a state militia by inducting all the militiamen into the federal army. The Second Amendment played no role on either side of this argument. For a theory that federal military conscription violates the Second Amendment, see Akhil Reed Amar, The Bill of Rights: Creation and Reconstruction 53-61 (1998).

2. The National Guard

Especially after 1815, most states, with the notable exception of Massachusetts, were desultory about training their militias. Partly in response, civic-minded men around the nation created volunteer militia units, the most famous of which were the Zouaves. Founded a few decades before the Civil War, these groups met for military practice and camaraderie. They would typically receive a charter from the state, and their officers would be granted state military commissions by the governor. During wartime, such as during the Mexican War and especially the Civil War, the units would volunteer en masse, and their units usually entered federal service intact. *See* Jerry Cooper, The Rise of the National Guard: The Evolution of the American Militia, 1865-1920 (2002); Jerry M. Cooper, The Militia and the National Guard in America Since Colonial Times: A Research Guide (1993); Marcus Cunliffe, Soldiers and Civilians: The Martial Spirit in America 1775-1865, 177-254 (1968). Volunteer militias in New York and Massachusetts played an important role in protecting Washington, D.C., from Confederate invasion during the chaotic period after the firing on Fort Sumter. Cunliffe, *supra*, at 252-54. The volunteer system was less formal than in England, where statutes expressly provided a formal system for the recognition and use of volunteer militia companies. (For the English statutes on volunteer companies, see 2 Geo. III, ch. 20; 18 Geo. III, ch. 59; 19 Geo. III, ch. 76.)

Toward the end of the Civil War, a new sort of state volunteer force began to arise. These militias usually called themselves the "National Guard," and during the latter decades of the nineteenth century, they received official state recognition, financial support, and training.

The National Guard soon developed a symbiotic relationship with another organization — the National Rifle Association (NRA), which was founded in 1871. The NRA was created by former Union officers and New York National Guardsmen who were appalled by the poor marksmanship of Union soldiers during the Civil War. Aiming to restore the historically revered status of the American citizen-marksman, the NRA rejected the then common idea that in modern warfare the soldier was simply cannon fodder, and did not need individual skill at arms. The NRA's corporate charter from New York State included the purpose "to promote the introduction of a system of aiming drill and target firing among the National Guard of New York and the militia of other states." James B. Trefethen, Americans and Their Guns 10 (1967).

Seven of the first eight NRA presidents were leading Union officers, including retired President Ulysses S. Grant, and General Winfield Scott Hancock, "the hero of Gettysburg," who had been the 1880 Democratic presidential nominee. Emulating the National Rifle Association of Great Britain, the American NRA introduced long-range rifle shooting as a formal American sport with national matches, and soon became the standard-setter for many of the shooting sports; the NRA targets and marksmanship training manuals were adopted by the army and navy. *Id.* at 103. The National Guard Association, an organization dedicated to promoting the interests of the National Guard, held its first convention in 1879, and elected NRA co-founder George Wingate as its first president. Jerry M. Cooper, The Rise of the National Guard: The Evolution of the American Militia, 1865-1920 85-88 (2002). The NRA and the National Guard were intertwined, and during the first two decades of the twentieth century, the leadership of the two organizations closely overlapped. Russell S. Gilmore, Crackshots and Patriots: The National Rifle Association and America's Military-Sporting Tradition, 1871-1929 (Ph.D. dissertation, University of Wisconsin, 1974).

National Guard units participated in the 1898 Spanish-American War, and although they performed better than had volunteer independent militias in the wars of 1846 or 1861, the deficiencies in the quality of their training became apparent. So Congress repealed the Militia Act of 1792, and enacted the Militia Act of 1903, 32 Stat. 775, commonly known as the "Dick Act" for its sponsor Representative Charles W.F. Dick, a Major General in the Ohio National Guard. With some important revisions five years later, 35 Stat. 399, the Dick Act remains the foundation of current federal law on the militia.

The Dick Act gave formal federal recognition — and financial support — to the National Guard. According to the Act, the "organized militia" of the United States *is* the National Guard, plus Naval Militias maintained by some states. 10 U.S.C. §311(b)(1). (The Dick Act also defines the "unorganized militia." See *infra.*)

Units of the National Guard are organized by state, and when not called into active federal service, Guard members remain under the command of their state's governor. In this sense, the Guard is part of the state militia. Over the past century, however, both congressional legislation and judicial decisions have narrowed the distinctions between the National Guard and the regular federal armed forces.

The National Defense Act of 1916, 39 Stat. 166 (1916), substantially increased federal control over the National Guard, giving it much more the character of a reserve unit of the standing army than a state-controlled militia. The 1916 Act gave the federal government veto power over the appointment of National Guard officers, notwithstanding the language in Article I, Section 8, "reserving to the States respectively the Appointment of the Officers." Proponents said that they were doing no more than what Patrick Henry, at the Virginia ratifying convention, had warned that they would be able to do. H.R. Rep. No. 297, 64th Cong., 1st Sess. (1916).

Since 1933, federal law has mandated a system of "dual enlistment," whereby each person who enlists in a state National Guard unit must simultaneously enlist in the National Guard of the United States, which is a part of the United States Army. Any Guard unit can be called up into federal service as a part of the regular armed forces. When this happens, the Guard unit temporarily ceases to be part of the state National Guard until it is released from federal service. Notably, the new assertion of power over the National Guard was explicitly not enacted under Congress's militia power, but under the Armies Clause. 48 Stat. 153 (1933); U.S. Const. art. I, §8, cl. 12 (granting Congress the power "To raise and support Armies").

The congressional decision to rely on the army power, and to stop treating the National Guard as a militia, was based in part on constitutional objections that the Constitution gives the federal government no authority to deploy the militia outside the United States, except in very limited circumstances. *See, e.g.*, Authority of President to Send Militia into a Foreign Country, 29 U.S. Op. Atty. Gen. 322 (1912) (Calling Forth Clause authorizes federal militia only to suppress insurrections (which are necessarily domestic), execute the laws of the union (same), and repel invasions (which might, at most, involve a border crossing to attack a foreign force massed in a neighboring country)).

At first, the federalization power was limited. Federal law provided that the President could only order the National Guard to active duty in periods of national emergency. In 1952, Congress eliminated the requirement of a national emergency, but provided that Guard units could not be ordered to active duty without the consent of the governor of the relevant state. However, in 1986, Congress acted again, eliminating a governor's power to prevent deployment outside of the United States if the refusal were simply because the governor "object[ed] to the location, purpose, type, or schedule of such active duty." 10 U.S.C. §12301(f).

In *Perpich v. Department of Defense*, 496 U.S. 334 (1990), the Supreme Court unanimously upheld this legislation against a constitutional challenge by Minnesota Governor Rudy Perpich, who claimed that sending the Minnesota Guard to training in Honduras violated the states' prerogatives under the Militia Clauses. Writing for the Court, Justice Stevens emphasized that "[t]he congressional power to call forth the militia may in appropriate cases supplement its broader power to raise armies and provide for the common defense and general welfare, but it does not limit those powers." *Id.* at 350. Moreover, even under the Militia Clauses, Congress could validly choose to use its constitutional power to "discipline the Militia" to send National Guard units to places outside of the United States for training. *Id.* at 350-51.

Thus, according to *Perpich* and the *Selective Draft Law Cases*, the Armies Clause gives Congress power to freely draft National Guard units into the regular federal armed forces, at which point they may be deployed abroad to foreign countries and used for any otherwise valid purpose, not merely for the limited purposes listed in the Militia Clauses. In addition, even under the Militia Clauses, Congress has power, if it chooses, to require states to send their National Guard units abroad for training, even over the objection of the state's governor. While the Second Amendment stresses the importance of a "well regulated Militia" to "the security of a free State," *Perpich* does not cite or discuss the Second Amendment.

For more on the National Guard, and the history of the militia, see Michael D. Doubler, The National Guard and Reserve: A Reference Handbook (2008); Jerry M. Cooper, The Rise of the National Guard: The Evolution of the American Militia, 1865-1920 (2002); Jerry Cooper, The Militia and National Guard in America Since Colonial Times: A Research Guide (1993).

3. State Defense Forces

The Constitution prohibits any state from "keep[ing] Troops, or Ships of War in time of Peace," without "the consent of Congress." U.S. Const., art. I, §10, cl. 3. However, Congress has provided its consent through a federal statute that authorizes each state, the District of Columbia, as well as the Commonwealth of Puerto Rico and some other U.S. territories, to "organize and maintain defense forces" separate from the National Guard. 32 U.S.C. §109(c). Approximately 20 states and Puerto Rico maintain active forces of this type. By law, the units of these "state defense forces" (SDFs) may not be "called, ordered, or drafted into the [United States] armed forces," although their individual members are not exempt from being drafted or otherwise called into federal military service. 32 U.S.C. §109(c), (d). The size of state defense forces varies, though each is smaller than a single brigade (3000 to 5000 troops) of the United States Armed Forces or National Guard. Many SDFs focus more upon disaster relief and emergency services than military arms training.

4. The Unorganized Militia

Federal law provides that all able-bodied men between 17 and 44 years of age who are United States citizens (or "have made a declaration of intention to become citizens"), and who do not belong to the organized militia, are members of "the unorganized militia" of the United States. 10 U.S.C. §311(a), (b)(2). They are subject to call-up by the federal government in order to "execute the Laws of the Union, suppress Insurrections [or] repel Invasions," under the Constitution's Militia Clauses. In addition, if Congress so provides, citizens can be drafted into the regular armed forces, as affirmed in the *Selective Draft Law Cases.*

Many state statutes and constitutions likewise define the state militia as comprising all able-bodied males between particular ages, and sometimes making exceptions for persons in certain occupations, such as the ministry.

Congress in 1798 had appropriated funds to purchase 30,000 stands of arms[7] for the militia. 1 Stat. 576 (1798). Congress also provided for training of volunteer militia, and for the sale of federal arms to them. 1 Stat. 569 (1798). In 1808, under President Thomas Jefferson, Congress created a permanent program, appropriating $200,000 annually for distributing "public arms" to militiamen who could not afford their own. The distribution of arms (and eventually, clothing and camp equipment) to state militias continued throughout

---

7. A stand of arms is a firearm (typically, a rifle or musket) with its usual appurtenances, such as bayonet, cartridge box, etc.

the nineteenth century. At the beginning, the program was a substantial boon to the nascent American firearms industry, and helped promote the development of interchangeable parts. Halbrook & Kopel, *supra*, at 374-89 (Tench Coxe as the originator and first administrator of the permanent program, under Presidents Thomas Jefferson and James Madison).

In 1903, the same year that Congress established the modern organized militia as the National Guard, Congress also acted to bolster training for the unorganized militia. Congress created the National Board for the Promotion of Rifle Practice (NBPRP) to set up and oversee official National Matches in riflery; by statute, the 21-member board included all 8 trustees of the NRA. In 1905, Congress authorized the sale of surplus military rifles to gun clubs; the NBPRP selected the NRA as its agent for the distribution of arms. Pub. L. No. 149; Gilmore, *supra*, at 155-57. In 1916 (the same year that Congress took over the National Guard, via the National Defense Act), the Office of the Director of Civilian Marksmanship (DCM) was created by Congress to administer the civilian marksmanship program, and the NRA was named by statute as the liaison between the army and civilians. Trefethen, *supra*, at 307. A 1924 statute required membership in a NRA-affiliated gun club as a condition of purchasing a DCM rifle. 10 U.S.C. §4308(a)(5). The requirement of NRA membership was later invalidated as a violation of the equal protection principles implicit in the Fifth Amendment. *Gavett v. Alexander*, 477 F. Supp. 1035 (D.D.C. 1979).

The DCM program was privatized in 1996, and turned into the federally chartered, but private, Corporation for the Promotion of Rifle Practice and Firearms Safety (CPRPFS). 36 U.S.C. §§40701 et seq. There is no longer any federal funding for the program, other than providing it with surplus .22 and .30 caliber rifles.

NOTES & QUESTIONS

1. Recall the fears of the Anti-Federalists and others that the Constitution gave Congress virtually plenary power over the militia, which could enable it to eliminate any possibility of the states maintaining a credible military deterrent against federal overreaching. Would you say that the history of federal regulation of the militia and the National Guard suggests that those fears were accurate? If so, do you view this as a negative development, a positive one, or a neutral one?

   Is any protection for state-controlled forces undermined by the federal government's Armies Clause power to simply draft the individual members of the SDFs directly into the United States Armed Forces? Does it sound like the federal government's power over state militias is effectively plenary? Is it even clear what the "militia" is at this point? *See Perpich*, 496 U.S. at 352-54 (holding that state militias may be called into federal service and deployed overseas despite the state governor's objection); *Selective Draft Law Cases*, 245 U.S. at 374-83 (Congress has the authority to destroy a state militia by bodily conscripting all its members into the federal standing army); *Martin v. Mott*, 25 U.S. 19, 28-33 (1827) (state governors may not dispute a federal determination that conditions exist that allow a state militia to be called into federal service); *Houston v. Moore*, 18 U.S. at 1 (1820) (Chapter 5) (holding that federal militia legislation preempts state legislation, even if the state legislation merely duplicates the federal statute); J. Norman Heath, *Exposing the Second Amendment: Federal Preemption of State Militia Legislation*, 79 U. Det. Mercy L. Rev. 39 (2001) (detailing case law history of federal-state conflicts over militia control, and pointing out the almost complete absence of the Second Amendment from legal arguments about that conflict). What does your answer imply about the nature of the right guaranteed by the Second Amendment?

2. Would it violate the Militia Clauses, or the Second Amendment, for Congress to withdraw its consent to State Defense Forces? What if Congress simultaneously withdrew authorization for the SDFs and activated all state National Guard units into federal service and deployed them outside of U.S. territory? The Court in *Perpich* seemed to be aware of this issue and left open the possibility that, if it occurred, a constitutional objection might have merit:

> Congress has provided by statute that in addition to its National Guard, a State may provide and maintain at its own expense a defense force that is exempt from being drafted into the Armed Forces of the United States. . . . As long as that provision remains in effect, there is no basis for an argument that [federal statutes allowing the National Guard to be deployed without the state governor's consent] depriv[e] Minnesota of any constitutional entitlement to a separate militia of its own.

> *Perpich*, 496 U.S. at 352. Could Justice Stevens, who authored *Perpich*, *supra*, have been alluding to such a possibility in the passage of his *Heller* (Chapter 9) dissent, concluding that "the Second Amendment was adopted to protect the right of the people of each of the several States to maintain a well regulated militia"? 554 U.S. at 637 (2008) (Stevens, J., dissenting); *see also id.* at 654 n.20 ("The Court assumes . . . incorrectly . . . that even when a state militia was not called into service, Congress would have had the power to exclude individuals from enlistment in that state militia. That assumption . . . [is] flatly inconsistent with the Second Amendment.").

3. CQ: Presuming that the Second Amendment applies only to the organized militia, and that this means the National Guard, does a person have a constitutional right to serve in the National Guard? Putting aside the Fourteenth Amendment guarantee of equal protection, if the Guard refused to enroll women (as it did in the past) or homosexuals (as it did until recently), would that violate the *Second* Amendment? *See* Uviller & Merkel, *supra*, at 152, 274 n.147 (suggesting that Second Amendment could be so read). If so, were the Militia Acts of 1792, *supra*, obviously unconstitutional, since they excluded women and Blacks? Why didn't Congress notice the constitutional problem, and why did no one even mention it during passage of the Acts? Can the National Guard refuse to enroll persons above a certain age?

In *Heller* (Chapter 9), Justice Scalia addresses the theory that the Second Amendment guarantees a right to serve in the militia.

4. Is the National Guard a select militia, as defined, and feared, by the Founders? Undeniably, the National Guard has sometimes been used for malignant purposes, such as its participation in the massacre of the families of striking coal workers in southern Colorado on Orthodox Easter Sunday, 1914. *See* Alvin R. Sunseri, The Ludlow Massacre: A Study in the Mis-Employment of the National Guard (1972). The Guard was also used elsewhere to break strikes, but historian Jerry Cooper finds that more often, the Guard was used to prevent violence between strikers and corporations, and that in the South, it was frequently and successfully used to protect black prisoners from lynch mobs. *See* Cooper, The Rise of the National Guard 44-64; Cooper, Research Guide (annotated bibliography of scholarship on both sides of the issue).

   Is today's National Guard a militia at all, given its integration into the U.S. Army during the twentieth century?

5. How would you characterize the U.S. Air Force and the Air National Guard? Like the army, navy, or militia contemplated by the Constitution, or something else entirely?

6. During the late nineteenth and early twentieth century, the promotion of citizen rifle practice was very popular in many quarters. Many public schools and churches built indoor rifle ranges on their premises. President Theodore Roosevelt called for firearms training in his Dec. 6, 1906, Annual Message to Congress ("We should establish shooting galleries in all the large public and military schools, should maintain national target ranges in different parts of the country, and should in every way encourage the formation of rifle clubs throughout all parts of the land.") and his December 3, 1907, Annual Message ("we should encourage rifle practice among schoolboys, and indeed among all classes"). Roosevelt was a life member of the NRA, as were his Secretary of War Elihu Root; Gifford Pinchot, the first head of United States Forest Service, and later the Governor of Pennsylvania; and William Howard Taft, who succeeded Root as Secretary of War, succeeded Roosevelt as President, and later served as Chief Justice. (As President, Taft wrote in 1909, "I approve the teaching under proper regulations of rifle shooting to the boys in the advanced grades," thus providing the impetus for the Washington School Rifle Tournament.) Gilmore, *supra,* at 160; Trefethen, *supra,* at 156. Do schools have a civic obligation to offer marksmanship training?

||5||

The Right to Arms, Militias, and Slavery in the Early Republic and Antebellum Periods

The young Republic expanded dramatically in its first seven decades. Between 1790 and 1860, the population of the United States increased from just under 4 million to over 31 million. While 4 out of 5 Americans were still rural dwellers, the percentage of the population living in urban areas had quadrupled. U.S. Census Bureau, Selected Historical Decennial Census, Urban and Rural Definitions and Data, *available at* http://www.census.gov/population/www/censusdata/files/table-4.pdf. During this period, 20 new states joined the original 13, more than tripling the Union's geographic size. This period of national growth witnessed significant practical and judicial developments in the nature and extent of the right to bear arms.

A. Militias as a Military and Political Force in the Post-Revolutionary Period

1. The Crisis of 1798-99

The Federalist Program

The conceptions of popular resistance and republican governance that the United States had inherited from the successful Revolution were tested by a severe internal political crisis in the late 1790s. In 1778, the French had intervened in support of the American Revolution partly because it presented an opportunity to initiate a global war against England. Two decades later, the French monarchy had been overthrown and replaced by a radical dictatorship. Although there had been some occasional cessations of hostilities, the global war between France and England was still going strong. Neither the French nor the English respected the trade rights of neutrals, including the United States.

By the late eighteenth century, internal United States politics were burdened by extreme hostility and paranoia. One faction, centered on Thomas Jefferson and James Madison, favored a pro-French policy. They formed the nucleus of the Democratic-Republican party. The other faction coalesced around Alexander Hamilton and favored Britain. They became known as the Federalists. While President John Adams (1797-1801) worked assiduously to keep the United States out of war, other Federalists, including Hamilton, saw war with France as an opportunity to build a large standing army and expand the new federal government. To the Republicans, Hamilton and his congressional allies were crypto-monarchists intent on pushing the new nation toward a European model that the American Revolution and the Constitution had rejected. Meanwhile, French seizures of American merchant ships escalated into an undeclared naval quasi-war.

These hostilities prompted the Federalist majority in Congress (with some support from Democratic-Republicans) to raise and equip a standing army of 13,000 and to build up the navy. To fund this military expansion, Congress enacted in 1798 a direct tax on privately owned houses, land, and slaves.

This so-called House Tax was followed by the Federalist-sponsored Alien and Sedition Acts of 1798, which aimed to control internal unrest. The Alien Friends Act gave the President virtually plenary power to expel from the country any foreign citizen whom he "judge[d] dangerous to the peace and safety of the United States." 1 Stat. 570, 571 (1798). The Sedition Act criminalized the publication of "false, scandalous and malicious writing[s]" that tended to bring the federal government, the President, or either House of Congress into "contempt or disrepute." 1 Stat. 596 (1798). The defendant bore the burden of proving the truth of a seditious writing prosecuted under the Act.

The Alien Act was never enforced, but its passage did lead to self-deportations by many noncitizens who had been prominent pro-French agitators. The Sedition Act, in contrast, was vigorously enforced, and significantly chilled political speech. Several speakers and writers sympathetic to the Democratic-Republican Party, including newspaper editors and even U.S. Representative Matthew Lyon, were successfully prosecuted under the Sedition Act in 1798 and 1799 for statements critical of Federalist officials.

These measures provoked bitter opposition from Democratic-Republicans, including Vice-President Thomas Jefferson, who tended to favor a diplomatic resolution of the French crisis. Some opponents viewed the expansion of the military, the Sedition Act's restrictions on political dissent, and the new tax as movement toward federal tyranny. Federalists, in contrast, looked with suspicion on Democratic-Republicans, viewing them as covert sympathizers with the radical ideals of the French Revolution, which had created the first modern totalitarian dictatorship.

2. The Kentucky and Virginia Resolutions

In 1798, as legislatures in Republican-leaning states debated how to oppose the Alien and Sedition Acts, Vice-President Jefferson and James Madison secretly authored proposals for state resistance that were enacted, in modified forms, by the legislatures of Kentucky and Virginia. Madison's Virginia Resolution proclaimed that the states were bound to "interpose" to block the effects of unconstitutional federal laws:

> [T]his Assembly . . . doth explicitly . . . declare, that it views the powers of the federal government, as resulting from the compact, to which the states are parties [i.e., the Constitution]; . . . as no further valid that they are authorized by the grants enumerated in that compact; and that in case of a deliberate, palpable, and dangerous exercise of other powers, not granted by the said compact, the states who are parties thereto, have the right, and are in duty bound, to interpose for arresting the progress of the evil, and for maintaining within their respective limits, the authorities, rights and liberties appertaining to them.

Virginia Resolution of Dec. 24, 1798, §3. The Kentucky Resolution of 1798 went further. As originally drafted by Jefferson, it acknowledged that the ordinary remedy for oppressive laws was elective democracy, but it also asserted the authority of the states to nullify, or declare void, federal laws that they believed exceeded the federal government's powers under the Constitution:

> . . . [I]n cases of an abuse of the delegated powers [of the federal government], the members of the general government, being chosen by the people, a change by the people would be the constitutional remedy; but, where powers are assumed which have not been delegated, a nullification of the act is the rightful remedy; that every State has a natural right in cases not within the compact, . . . to nullify of their own authority all assumptions of power by others within their limits.

Thomas Jefferson, Draft of the Kentucky Resolution of 1798, *in* 17 Papers of James Madison 179. The Kentucky legislature omitted Jefferson's "nullification" language from the Resolution it passed, but it included language that was as strong:

> . . . [T]hat the several states composing the United States of America, are not united on the principle of unlimited submission to their general government; but that, by a compact under the style and title of a Constitution for the United States, and of amendments thereto, they constituted a general government for special purposes — delegated to that government certain definite powers, reserving, each state to itself, the residuary mass of right to their own self-government; and that whensoever the general government assumes undelegated powers, its acts are unauthoritative, void, and of no force: . . . [and] that, as in all other cases of compact among parties having no common judge, each party has an equal right to judge for itself, as well of infractions, as of the mode and measure of redress. . . .

Kentucky Resolution of Nov. 10, 1798, §§1, 8, *in* 4 The Debates in the Several State Conventions on the Adoption of the Federal Constitution 540, 543 (Jonathan Elliot ed., 1891) [hereinafter 4 Elliot's Debates]. Both the Kentucky Resolution of 1798 and the Virginia Resolution specifically decried the Sedition Act as unconstitutional because Congress had no power to restrict speech. *See* William J. Watkins, Jr., Reclaiming the American Revolution: The Kentucky and Virginia Resolutions and Their Legacy 55-75 (2004).

While urging nullification, Jefferson also tried to calm his political allies who thought that secession from the Union was a remedy for the Federalists' acts. He wrote to Virginia Senator John Taylor,

A little patience, and we shall see the reign of witches pass over, their spells dissolve, and the people, recovering their true sight, restore their government to its true principles. It is true that in the meantime we are suffering deeply in spirit, and incurring the horrors of a war and long oppressions of enormous public debt. . . . If the game runs sometimes against us at home we must have patience till luck turns, and then we shall have an opportunity of winning back the principles we have lost. . . .

Letter from Thomas Jefferson to John Taylor (June 1, 1798), *in* 7 The Writings of Thomas Jefferson, at 265-66 (G.P. Putnam & Sons, 1895).

3. Fries's Rebellion

While the Kentucky and Virginia Resolutions contemplated that state governments would serve as centers of resistance to unconstitutional federal assertions of power, events that reflected a more radical view erupted in southeastern Pennsylvania in early 1799. The federal "House Tax" was resented with particular bitterness in this region, which was dominated by German-American immigrant communities known as the Pennsylvania Dutch. When federal tax assessors began visiting houses in the local townships to measure them for purposes of assessment, they met resistance that ranged from thrown pots of hot water to armed intimidation. John Fries, a traveling auctioneer and Revolutionary War veteran, was one of several leaders who roused armed groups, including state militia companies, to prevent the enforcement of the tax. A federal marshal was sent to arrest militia leaders, but in Bethlehem, Pennsylvania, a large crowd of armed militiamen and other insurgents freed the prisoners by force. Apparently, the "breakout" took place in response to a deal offered by the marshal, in which he told Fries that "I cannot give [the prisoners] up willingly, but if you take them by force, I cannot help it." Robert H. Churchill, To Shake Their Guns in the Tyrant's Face: Libertarian Political Violence and the Origins of the Militia Movement 83 (2008). No shots were fired during the incident.

The insurgency sputtered out when Federalist President John Adams declared the resisting townships to be in a state of insurrection and began organizing a detachment of the militia to quell it. By the spring of 1799, the Pennsylvania insurgents had dispersed and agreed to submit to the tax. Nevertheless, in April, 2,000 federal troops marched through Pennsylvania, capturing Fries and many other insurgents. The soldiers engaged in numerous house-to-house searches of private dwellings at night, and burned the "liberty poles" that had been erected in protest by the citizens in the rebellious counties. Fries was tried for treason, convicted, and sentenced to death, but was later pardoned by President Adams.

The Kentucky legislature met in 1799, in the aftermath of the rebellion and its suppression, and approved a second Kentucky Resolution, which again condemned the Alien and Sedition Acts as "palpable violations of the . . . constitution," and declared that "a nullification," by the States, "of all unauthorized acts done under color of that instrument is the rightful remedy." Kentucky Resolution of Nov. 22, 1799, *in* 4 Elliot's Debates, *supra*, at 545. Yet Kentucky in 1799 also declared that it would "bow to the laws of the Union," and refrained from again declaring the Alien and Sedition Acts null and void. *Id.* As prosecutions proceeded under the Sedition Act, critics of the Federalist program looked to the election of 1800 for a remedy.

That democratic mechanism, however, disclosed its own problems in the presidential election of 1800. The Republicans won new majorities in both the House and the Senate, but the Electoral College vote for President produced a deadlock between Jefferson and Aaron Burr, nominally Jefferson's ally. (Under the original Constitution, the electors cast two votes, and the vice-presidency was awarded to the candidate who received the second greatest number of electoral votes. The South Carolina electors forgot to omit one vote for Burr, as they had orginally planned, resulting in the deadlock.) The tie had to be broken by ballot of the state delegations to the House of Representatives, a body that was still dominated by a (now lame duck) Federalist majority. Each state had one vote, determined by a majority of its Representatives. The House cast 35 ballots without obtaining a majority of the states. The risk arose that the Federalists would invoke a federal statutory provision to temporarily install the (Federalist) President pro tempore of the Senate as President until the newly elected Congress was seated in December 1801.

At this point, the specter of armed resistance arose anew. Republican Governors James Monroe of Virginia and Thomas McKean of Pennsylvania started planning to mobilize their state militias if the House violated the Constitution maneuvering anyone other than Jefferson or Burr into the Presidency. Dumas Malone, Jefferson the President: First Term, 1801-1805 6-11 (1970). While the House was deadlocked, Jefferson wrote to Governor Monroe, "We thought it best to declare openly and firmly, one and all, that the day such an act passed, the middle states would arm, and that no such usurpation, even for a single day, should be submitted to." Letter from Thomas Jefferson to James Monroe (Feb. 15, 1801), *in* 7 The Writings of Thomas Jefferson, *supra*, at 491.

Partly because arch-Federalist Alexander Hamilton threw his support to Jefferson (whom Hamilton accepted as a good man with bad ideas, versus Burr, whom Hamilton believed was driven solely by the acquisition of power), several House Federalists abstained, allowing their states' votes to swing to Jefferson. On February 17, 1801, on the 36th ballot, Jefferson won 10 of the 16 states in the House ballot, and thus won the election. On what was then the constitutionally scheduled inauguration day of March 4, 1801, Thomas Jefferson was peacefully sworn in as President of the United States. The mood of crisis subsided. The Sedition Act expired by its own terms. The unpopular federal direct taxes were repealed by the new Republican Congress.

After retiring from the presidency, Jefferson continued to believe that the state militias were the final security against dictatorship. So, while the force of a demagogue

> may paralyze the single State in which it happens to be encamped, sixteen other, spread over a country of two thousand miles diameter, rise up on every side, ready organized for deliberation by a constitutional legislature, and for action by their governor, constitutionally, the commander of the militia of the State, that is to say, of every man in it able to bear arms; and that militia, too, regularly formed into regiments and battalions, into infantry, cavalry and artillery, trained under officers general and subordinate, legally appointed, always in readiness, and to whom they are already in habits of obedience.

Letter from Thomas Jefferson to Destutt de Tracy (Jan. 26, 1816), *in* 9 The Writings of Thomas Jefferson 305, 309 (Paul L. Ford Bergh ed., 1898).

In France, thought Jefferson, the revolutionary republic had been replaced by a Parisian dictatorship because there were no local centers of resistance.

> But with us, sixteen out of seventeen States rising in mass, under regular organization, and legal commanders, united in object and action by their Congress, or, if that be in *duresse*, by a special convention, presents such obstacles to an usurper as forever to stifle ambition the first conception of that object.

Id.

Later in this chapter, you will see Supreme Court Justice Joseph Story—who was an ardent supporter of a strong federal government—expressing similar views in his treatises of 1833 and 1840. Even though the idea of state militias resisting perceived tyranny remained intellectually respectable, it became less of a practical political reality. After the tumult of 1798-1801, the specter of military conflict between state and federal governments would not arise again until the Civil War. In the next excerpt, Robert Churchill explains how 1798-1801 itself led to reduced willingness to resort to the militia.

Robert H. Churchill, Popular Nullification, Fries's Rebellion, and the Waning of Radical Republicanism, 1798-1801
67 Penn. Hist. 105, 107 (Winter 2000)

[T]he period of 1798-1800 was one of ideological as well as political struggle. A fierce debate raged in the nation and within the Democratic Republican Party. Moderate Republicans insisted that the party should resist the Alien and Sedition Acts and other war measures in a constitutional manner. They defined constitutional resistance as encompassing only popular petitioning and electoral organization. A more radical group of Republicans believed that the war measures were an intolerable infringement of liberty and the Constitution. Some articulated the doctrine of state nullification as a constitutional middle ground between politics and revolution. Jefferson, John Breckenridge, and John Taylor belong in this more radical camp. Nevertheless, theirs were not the only radical voices in 1798. Other radicals in 1798 emphasized the sovereignty of the people over the sovereignty of the states. Radical Republicans in New York, New Jersey, and Pennsylvania as well as Virginia and Kentucky openly discussed the propriety of popular nullification, armed resistance, and revolution in response to the Federalist program of 1798. . . .

[Fries's Rebellion] . . . played a crucial role in shaping the conclusion of this debate. The resort to overt armed resistance forced radical Republicans to recognize that the language of nullification would inevitably encourage spontaneous and uncontrollable popular rebellion. This stark reality strengthened the hand of moderates and contributed to the formation of a consensus within the party that armed resistance to the acts of Congress was impermissible. The new consensus emphasized obedience to the laws and the reliance on petitioning and elections as the proper means of resisting oppressive laws. Only interference in the electoral process, Republicans concluded, could justify the resort to armed resistance. This evolution in Republican ideology redefined the meaning of popular sovereignty in America and marked a repudiation of the most radical legacy of the American Revolution.

As a practical matter, nullification and its milder cousin interposition became part of the practice of popular constitutionalism. They next appeared during the second term of President Jefferson, when New Englanders invoked them to defy Jefferson's complete embargo on all foreign trade (which was an attempt to coerce the English to stop seizing American ships). They were invoked again in the late 1820s and early 1830s by South Carolinians and other Southerners outraged over the "Tariff of Abominations," which protected Northern manufacturers while provoking foreign retaliation in the form of harsh tariffs against Southern agricultural exports. After that, interposition and nullification became buzzwords of anti-slavery advocates, especially in New England and the upper Midwest. These advocates contended that the federal Fugitive Slave Act of 1850, which ordered state governments and private citizens to assist in the capture of fugitive slaves, grotesquely exceeded Congress's constitutional powers. Much later, interposition and nullification were proclaimed by Southerners resisting federal court orders for school desegregation, following *Brown v. Board of Education*, 347 U.S. 483 (1954).

As of 2011, 16 states have defied the federal 1970 Controlled Substances Act by passing laws to re-legalize the use of medical marijuana. Nine have challenged the federal Gun Control Act of 1968 by enacting "Firearms Freedom Acts" declaring (contrary to the terms of the Gun Control Act) that firearms made within the state, and that never leave the state, are not subject to federal control under Congress's power to regulate interstate commerce. *See, e.g.*, Montana Firearms Freedom Act, Mont. Code Ann. §30-20-104 (2009) ("A personal firearm, a firearm accessory, or ammunition that is manufactured commercially or privately in Montana and that remains within the borders of Montana is not subject to federal law or federal regulation, including registration, under the authority of congress to regulate interstate commerce. It is declared by the legislature that those items have not traveled in interstate commerce."). (For more on the Firearms Freedom Acts, see Chapter 8.)

Interposition and nullification have never been endorsed as legally valid by federal courts. However, they have often been successful politically, impeding the exercise of federal power on an unwilling state, and sometimes convincing the federal government to change the law or to relent from vigorous enforcement of the law.

4. The War of 1812

The comparative strengths and weaknesses of militias and standing armies were tested in the United States' second war with Great Britain. The War of 1812 arose against the backdrop of the war between the British Empire and Napoleonic France. The United States felt aggrieved by British restrictions on neutral trade and the impressments (capture for forced military service) of American sailors by British Navy ships on the high seas. At the outset of the war, the United States had only a small regular army of approximately 12,000 men, in conformity with the Republican ethos of a small, thrifty federal government and hostility to standing armies. At the beginning of the war, the "War Hawks," led by Representatives Henry Clay and John Calhoun, were confident that state militias would be able to achieve American military goals, including conquest and annexation of the British colony of Canada.

Militia units served in several major battles, often with disappointing results. American efforts to invade British holdings in Canada with armies composed largely of militia failed repeatedly. Indeed, historians suggest that the failure played an important role in Canada's development of a distinctive political culture that is much more deferential to central authority than America's. *See generally* Pierre Berton, The Invasion of Canada: 1812-1813 (2001).

British regulars routed the Maryland militia at the Battle of Bladensburg in August 1814, opening the way to the British invasion of Washington, D.C., and the burning of the White House and other public buildings in the American capital. President James Madison and his Cabinet were forced to flee to Virginia before the advancing British.

But in the American mind, all that was erased on January 8, 1815, at the Battle of New Orleans. Led by General Andrew Jackson, a combination of professional soldiers, militia, irregulars, free Blacks, Creoles, Cajuns, Spaniards, Frenchmen, Portuguese, Germans, Italians, Indians, Anglos, lawyers, privateers, farmers, and shop-keepers confronted the best units of the best army in the world. The outnumbered Americans, fighting from defensive positions, demolished the British while suffering hardly any casualties themselves. The Tennessee militia arrived in raccoon caps, while the Kentucky militia was clad in rags. Militiamen brought their own hunting guns, because the federal government lacked the resources to supply them with military weapons. Many were skilled marksmen accustomed to shooting squirrels and other small targets from distant trees.

Unbeknownst to the combatants, a U.S.-British peace treaty had already been signed between the combatants in Ghent, Kingdom of the Netherlands. However, given that the British had violated the 1783 Treaty of Paris (which had settled the American War of Independence) by refusing to evacuate their forts in the western United States, it is possible that if the British had won at New Orleans, they would have kept the city and port, thereby choking off international commerce for most of the western United States.

The victory in the Battle of New Orleans became a touchstone of American patriotism. Robert Remini, The Battle of New Orleans: Andrew Jackson and America's First Military Victory (2001). "The Hunters of Kentucky" was the most popular song in the nation, exulting: "For Jackson he was wide awake, he was not scared of trifles. Full well he knew what aim we'd take with our Kentucky rifles," Ted Franklin Belve, The Hunters of Kentucky 213 (2011) (quoting Samuel Woodward's famous ballad).

On the whole, the militia had at best a mixed record during the War of 1812, performing miserably in some battles, and much better when it had effective leadership, as at New Orleans. In the post-war public mind, the great success at New Orleans far overshadowed the militia failures. C. Edward Skeen, Citizen Soldiers in the War of 1812 (1999).

Two decades later, at the Alamo, in San Antonio, a small band of Texans held off the enormous army of the Mexican general Santa Ana. The Alamo's defenders, at the cost of their lives, stalled Santa Ana for weeks, giving General Sam Houston time to gather an army of Texans. At the Battle of San Jacinto a few weeks later, Texan forces, outnumbered two to one, destroyed the Mexican Army, captured Santa Ana, and established the independent Republic of Texas. In 1845, Texas joined the United States of America.

Like Lexington, Concord, and Bunker Hill, the Battle of New Orleans and the defense of the Alamo became iconic American stories. As with any national mythos, what is left out is also revealing. For example, the inept American invasions of Canada in 1775-76 and 1812-13, as well as Fries's Rebellion, became at most minor episodes in American history textbooks.

As the nineteenth century progressed, Americans retained much of the founding ethos. They were convinced that the United States was an exceptional nation—freer and more virtuous than any other place on earth. One foundation of this happy condition, in the popular understanding, was the virtuous citizen-soldier with his rifle, ready to spring to the defense of liberty. But as the controversy over slavery began to divide Americans against each other, Southerners and Northerners increasingly thought that *their* region was the true heir of the Revolution, and that the *other* was hostile and depraved.

NOTES & QUESTIONS

1. Do you agree with the premises of the Kentucky and Virginia Resolutions? If Congress passed laws next year attempting to criminalize political dissent, in what measures of opposition would it be appropriate for citizens to engage? What measures of opposition by state governments would be appropriate?

2. What lessons can be drawn about the value and role of the militias from the crises of 1798-1801? Did state militias in early America make a positive or negative contribution to the development of political stability? To political liberty? To American effectiveness in war?

B.   Antebellum Case Law on the Right to Arms Under State and Federal Constitutions

Of the 20 new states that joined the Union between 1790 and 1860, 14 included provisions in their state constitutions recognizing a right to arms. *See* Eugene Volokh, *State Constitutional Rights to Keep and Bear Arms*, 11 Tex. Rev. L. & Pol. 191 (2006). (You can trace the development of state constitutional provisions using the table found in the appendix to Chapter 1.)

Ten of the new guarantees broadly followed the model of the Pennsylvania Declaration of Rights, which protected the right of the people "to bear arms for the defense of themselves and the state." *See* Pa. Declaration of Rights, art. XIII (1776)

("That the people have a right to bear arms for the defense of themselves and the state; and as standing armies in the time of peace are dangerous to liberty, they ought not to be kept up; And that the military should be kept under strict subordination to, and governed by, the civil power."). In 1790, Pennsylvania adopted a new constitution that simply stated: "The right of citizens to bear arms, in defence of themselves and the State, shall not be questioned." Pa. Const. of 1790, art. I, §21. Antebellum state constitutions with similar "defense of themselves and the state" language included (in chronological order): Vt. Const. of 1777, ch. I, art. 15; Ky. Const. of 1799, art. XII, §23; see also Ky. Const. of 1850, art. XIII, §25 (retaining 1799 language but adding a final clause: ". . . but the general assembly may pass laws to prevent persons from carrying concealed arms."); Ohio Const. of 1802, art. VIII, §20; Ind. Const. of 1816, art. I, §20; Miss. Const. of 1817, art. I, §23; Ala. Const. of 1819, art. I, §23; Mo. Const. of 1820, art. XIII, §3; Mich. Const. of 1835, art. I, §13; Tex. Const. of 1845, art. I, §13; Or. Const. of 1857, art. I, §27. In addition, Connecticut, one of the original 13 states, added a guarantee of this type in 1818. Conn. Const., art. I, §17 (1818). Rhode Island, another of the original 13, did not adopt a state constitution until 1842; when it did, it provided that "[t]he right of the people to keep and bear arms shall not be infringed." R.I. Const., art. I, §22. On the other hand, the constitutions of four of the new states followed the model of the Massachusetts Constitution, which described the right to arms as being simply "for the common defense." See Mass. Const., pt. I, art. 17 (1780) ("The people have a right to keep and to bear arms for the common defence. And as, in time of peace, armies are dangerous to liberty, they ought not to be maintained without the consent of the legislature; and the military power shall always be held in an exact subordination to the civil authority, and be governed by it."). See also Tenn. Const. of 1796, art. XI, §26; Tenn. Const. of 1834, art. I, §26; Me. Const. of 1819, art. I, §16; Ark. Const. of 1836, art. II, §21; Fla. Const. of 1838, art. I, §21.

Several of the new state constitutional provisions identified the holder of the right as "the people." Others spoke of "the citizens," "every citizen," or "every person" as the right's holder. Finally, a few Southern constitutions adopted or revised in the 1830s limited the right to "free white men." Tenn. Const. of 1834, art. I, §26; Ark. Const. of 1836, art. II, §21; Fla. Const. of 1838, art. I, §21.

Throughout the nineteenth century, the South was the gun control center of the United States. The most common restriction was a ban on carrying concealed weapons. The bans may have been intended to prevent dueling. See Clayton E. Cramer, Concealed Weapon Laws of the Early Republic: Dueling, Southern Violence, and Moral Reform (1999).

Most of these statutes — the first important American gun control laws — were challenged on the theory that they infringed the guarantees of the right to arms in the state constitutions. In some cases, it was also claimed that these laws violated the federal Second Amendment. These challenges generated a series of state court decisions that often upheld particular restrictions on bearing arms, but also established constitutional boundaries for weapons control legislation. As you read the different opinions below, you may be surprised at the similarities between the arguments in early nineteenth-century cases and those in the modern gun control debate.

Most antebellum courts and scholars concluded that the liberty rights found in the first ten amendments to the United States Constitution did not, of their own force, restrict state or local governments. The United States

Supreme Court ratified this view in its landmark decision of *Barron v. City of Baltimore*, 32 U.S. (7 Pet.) 243, 250-51 (1833), holding that the Bill of Rights was "intended solely as a limitation on the exercise of power by the government of the United States, and is not applicable to the legislation of the states."[1]

Most state courts followed suit. *See, e.g., State v. Newsom*, 27 N.C. (5 Ired.) 250, 251 (1844) (rejecting a Second Amendment challenge to a state law requiring free Blacks to obtain a license in order to possess a gun, because "[i]t is now the settled construction" of the federal Constitution "that no limitation upon the power of government extends to, or embraces the different States, unless they are mentioned, or it is expressed to be so intended," and the Second Amendment does not expressly mention the states). *Newsom* is excerpted later in this chapter.

But even after *Barron*, not all courts agreed. At a time when the scope of the U.S. Supreme Court's authority over state courts was highly contested, many state judges considered *Barron* to be authoritative only in federal courts. State supreme courts, on this view, were still free to enforce the Bill of Rights. Significantly, under the federal Judiciary Act of 1789, the U.S. Supreme Court had the authority to review cases in which a state court had found a state law to be constitutional, but *not* to review cases in which a state court found a state law to violate the U.S. Constitution. The Supreme Court was not granted power over the latter classes of cases until the early twentieth century. *See* Jason Mazzone, *The Bill of Rights in Early State Courts*, 92 Minn. L. Rev. 1 (2007); *cf.* Akhil Reed Amar, The Bill of Rights 145-56 (1998) (discussing "the *Barron* contrarians").

There were dozens of state cases applying parts of the federal Bill of Rights to states, and the leading case was Georgia's 1846 *Nunn v. State*, enforcing the Second Amendment. The case struck down both a ban on most handguns (the only such ban enacted in the United States before the Civil War) and a ban on the open carrying of weapons, while upholding the ban as applied to the concealed carrying of weapons. The *Nunn* opinion contains good summaries of many of the significant pre-1846 decisions on concealed carry.

1.   A Right to Carry Weapons Openly for Self-Defense

Nunn v. State
1 Ga. 243 (1846)

LUMPKIN, Judge.

This was an indictment for a high misdemeanor. . . .

The defendant . . . moved to quash the proceeding . . . because the act of 1837, under which he was prosecuted, was contrary to the Constitution of the United States and of the State of Georgia. . . .

The act of 1837 was passed to guard and protect the citizens of the State against the unwarrantable and too prevalent use of *deadly weapons*.

---

1.   Chapter 6 will begin the story of the use of the Fourteenth Amendment to make the Bill of Rights, including the Second Amendment, applicable to the states. That story concludes in Chapter 9, with the 2010 Supreme Court case *McDonald v. City of Chicago*, 130 S. Ct. 3020 (2010).

Section 1st enacts, "that it shall not be lawful for any merchant or vender of wares or merchandize in this State, or any other person or persons whatever, to sell, or to offer to sell, or to keep or to have about their persons, or elsewhere, any of the herein-after-described weapons, to wit: Bowie or any other kinds of knives, manufactured and sold for the purpose of wearing or carrying the same as arms of offence or defence; pistols, dirks, sword-canes, spears, &c., shall also be contemplated in this act, save such pistols as are known and used as horseman's pistols," &c. . . . .

Section 4th, disposes of the fines arising under the act, and exempts sheriffs and other officers, therein named, from its provisions while in the actual discharge of their respective duties. It then declares, *that no person or persons shall be found guilty of violating the before-recited act, who shall openly wear, externally, bowie-knives, dirks, tooth-picks, spears, and which shall be exposed plainly to view.* It allows venders or any other persons to sell any of the aforesaid weapons, which they then owned or had on hand, "till the first day of March next ensuing its date."

[The court here discusses the potential vagueness of the statute, and possible inconsistencies between its section 1 and section 4, and holds that the statute is not vague and that its sections are not inconsistent.]

What, then, is the obvious purpose of the Assembly, to be deduced from the whole act, deviating a little, as we are at liberty to do, from the literal meaning of its language, and looking to the *subject matter*, to which the words are always supposed to have regard, and the reason and spirit of the act? It *prohibits bowie-knives, dirks, spears, (and it may be, tooth-picks,[2]) from being sold, or secretly kept about the person, or elsewhere; and it forbids, altogether, the use, or sale, or keeping, of sword-canes, and pistols, save such pistols as are known and used as horseman's pistols,* &c. Now, the defendant, Hawkins H. Nunn, was indicted and convicted of a high misdemeanor, "for *having and keeping about his person, and elsewhere, a pistol, the same not being such a pistol as is known and used as a horseman's pistol.*"

It is not pretended that he carried his weapon *secretly*, but it is charged as a crime, that he had and kept it about his person, and elsewhere. And this presents for our decision the broad question, is it competent for the Legislature to deny to one of its citizens this privilege? *We think not.*

This question has occasionally come before the courts of the Union for adjudication.

In *Bliss v. The Commonwealth*, [12 Ky. (2 Litt.) 90 (1822),] the defendant was indicted, on the act of the [Kentucky] Legislature "to prevent persons from wearing concealed arms." It provides that any person in the Commonwealth, who shall, after its passage, "wear a pocket-pistol, dirk, large knife, or sword in a cane, concealed as a weapon, unless when traveling on a journey, shall be fined in any sum not less than one hundred dollars; which may be recovered in any court having jurisdiction of like sums, by action of debt, or on presentment of a grand jury."

The indictment, in the words of the act, charge[d] Bliss with having *worn, concealed as a weapon, a sword in a cane.*

---

2. [The "Arkansas toothpick," a large and capable knife. *See* Note 6 following *Aymette v. State*, in Section 2. — EDS.]

Bliss was found guilty of the charge, and . . . appealed to the [Court of Appeals of Kentucky, at that time the state's highest court], by a majority of which (Judge Mills dissenting) the judgment was reversed.

The argument . . . turned mainly on the 23d section of the 10th article of the [1799] Constitution of Kentucky, which provides "that the right of the citizens to bear arms in defence of themselves and the State, shall not be questioned."

The attorney-general did not contend that it would be competent for the Legislature, by the enactment of any law, to prevent the citizens from bearing arms; but a distinction was taken between a law prohibiting the exercise of the right, and a law merely regulating the manner of exercising that right. [The Attorney General argued that banning concealed carry was a permissible regulation of the right to bear arms.]

But the court says,

That the provisions of the act in question do not import an entire destruction of the right, will not be controverted; for though the citizens are forbid wearing weapons, concealed in the manner described in the act, they may nevertheless bear arms in any admissible form. *But to be in conflict with the Constitution, it is not essential that the act should contain a prohibition against bearing arms, in every possible form. It is the right to bear arms, that is secured by the Constitution, and whatever restrains the full and complete exercise of that right, though not an entire destruction of it, is forbidden by the explicit language of the Constitution.*

> If, therefore, the act in question imposes any restraint on the right, immaterial what appellation may be given to the act, whether it be an act regulating the manner of bearing arms, or any other, the consequence in reference to the Constitution is precisely the same, and its collision with that instrument equally obvious.
>
> And can there be entertained a reasonable doubt, but the provisions of the act import a restraint on the right of the citizens to bear arms? The court apprehends not. The right has no limits, short of the moral power of the citizens to exercise it, and in *fact consists of nothing else but the liberty*. Diminish that liberty, therefore, and you necessarily restrain the right; and such is the diminution and restraint which the act in question most indisputably imports, by prohibiting the citizens bearing weapons. In truth, the right of the citizens to bear arms has been as directly assailed by the provisions of this act, as though they were forbid carrying guns on their shoulders, swords in scabbards, or when in conflict with an enemy, were not allowed the use of bayonets. And, if the act be consistent with the Constitution, it cannot be incompatible with that instrument for the Legislature by successive enactments to entirely cut off the exercise of the right of the citizens to bear arms. For in principle there is no difference between a law prohibiting the wearing [of] concealed arms, and a law forbidding the wearing of such as are exposed; and, if the former be unconstitutional, the latter must be so likewise.

[12 Ky. (2 Litt.) at 91-92.]

The conclusion at which the court arrived was, *that an act to prevent persons from wearing even concealed weapons is unconstitutional and void.*

In the *State v. Reid*, 1 Ala. 612 [(1840)], the same question came up, but was differently adjudged; thus verifying the old truth, "*tot homines, quot sententiae*," — so many men, so many opinions!

By the first section of the act of Alabama (passed 1838-1839) it is declared, "that if any person shall carry concealed about his person any species of fire-arms, or any bowie knife, Arkansas tooth-pick, or any other knife of the like kind, dirk, or any other deadly weapon, the person so offending shall, on conviction thereof before any court having competent jurisdiction, pay a fine not less than fifty, nor more than five hundred dollars, to be assessed by the jury trying the case; and be imprisoned for a term not exceeding three months, at the discretion of the judge of said court."

Under this section, the defendant was indicted . . . for carrying concealed about his person a certain species of fire-arms, called a pistol, contrary to the form of the statute. The defendant . . . insisted, that the law under which he was prosecuted, was contrary to the [1819] constitution of Alabama, which declares, "that every citizen has a right to bear arms in defence of himself and the State." — 23d sect. 1st art. of the Constitution.

Collier, Chief Justice, says:

> The question recurs, does the act "to suppress the evil practice of carrying weapons secretly," trench upon the constitutional rights of the citizen? *We think not.*
>
> The Constitution, in declaring that every citizen has the right to bear arms, in defence of himself and the State, has neither expressly nor by implication denied to the Legislature the right to enact laws in regard to *the manner* in which arms shall be borne.
>
> We do not desire to be understood as maintaining, that in regulating the manner of bearing arms, the authority of the Legislature has no other limit than its own discretion. A statute which, under the pretence of *regulating*, amounts to a *destruction* of the right, or which requires arms to be so borne as to render them wholly useless for the purpose of defence, would be clearly unconstitutional. But a law which is merely intended to promote personal security, and to put down lawless aggression and violence, and to this end prohibits the wearing of certain weapons in such a manner as is calculated to exert an unhappy influence upon the moral feelings of the wearer, by making him less regardful of the personal security of others, does not come in collision with the Constitution.

[1 Ala. at 616-17.]

The same point arose in the case of *The State v. Mitchell.* — [3 Blackf. 229 (Ind. 1833)]. There the defendant was indicted under [an 1831] statute of Indiana, which is as follows: "Every person, not being a traveler, who shall wear or carry a dirk, pistol, sword in a cane, or other dangerous weapon, *concealed*, shall, upon conviction thereof, be fined in any sum not exceeding one hundred dollars." The court decided that this act was not contrary to the Constitution of that State, which declares that "the people have a right to bear arms for the defence of themselves and the State."[3]

It is true, that these adjudications are all made on clauses in the State Constitutions; but these instruments confer no *new rights* on the people which

---

3. [The one-sentence *Mitchell* opinion simply announces this result. — EDS.]

did not belong to them before. When, I would ask, did any legislative body in the Union have the right to deny to its citizens the privilege of keeping and bearing arms in defence of themselves and their country?

If this right, "inestimable to freemen," has been guaranteed to British subjects, since the abdication and flight of the last of the Stuarts and the ascension of the Prince of Orange, did it not belong to our colonial ancestors in this western hemisphere? Has it been a part of the *English* Constitution ever since the bill of rights and act of settlement? and been forfeited here by the substitution and adoption of our own Constitution? No notion can be more fallacious than this! On the contrary, this is one of the fundamental principles, upon which rests the great fabric of civil liberty, reared by the fathers of the Revolution and of the country. And the Constitution of the United States, in declaring that the right of the people to keep and bear arms, should not be infringed, only reiterated a truth announced a century before, in the act of 1689, "to extend and secure the rights and liberties of English subjects" — whether living 3,000 or 300 miles from the royal palace. And it is worthy of observation, that both charters or compacts look to the same *motive,* for the irrespective enactments. The act of 1 William and Mary, declares that it is against law to raise or keep a standing army in the kingdom, in time of peace without the consent of Parliament, and therefore places arms in the hands of the people; and our Constitution assigns as a reason why this right shall not be interfered with, or in any manner abridged, that the free enjoyment of it will prepare and qualify *a well-regulated militia,* which are necessary to the security of a free State.

I am aware that it has been decided, that this, like other amendments adopted at the same time, is a restriction upon the government of the United States, and does not extend to the individual States. The court held otherwise, however, in the case of the *People v. Goodwin,* [1 Wheeler C.C. 470, 18 Johns. 187 (N.Y. Sup. 1820),] and Chief Justice Spencer, who delivered its opinion, says:

> The defendant's counsel rely principally on the fifth article of the amendments to the Constitution of the *United States,* which contains this provision: "*Nor shall any person be subject, for the same offence, to be twice put in jeopardy of life or limb.*" It has been urged by the prisoner's counsel, that this constitutional provision operates upon State courts [as well as federal]. This has been denied on the other side. I *am inclined* to the opinion, that the article in question does extend *to all judicial tribunals,* whether constituted by the Congress of the United States or the States individually. The provision is general in its nature and unrestricted in its terms; and the sixth article of the Constitution declares, that that Constitution shall be the supreme law of the land, and the judges in every State shall be bound thereby, any thing in the constitution or laws of any State to the contrary notwithstanding. *These general and comprehensive expressions extend the provisions of the Constitution of the United States, to every article which is not confined by the subject matter to the national government, and is equally applicable to the States. . . .*

The language of the *second* amendment is broad enough to embrace both Federal and State governments — nor is there anything in its terms which restricts its meaning. The preamble which was prefixed to these amendments shows, that they originated in the fear that the powers of the general government were not sufficiently limited. . . . But admitting all this, does it follow that because the people refused to delegate to the general government the power to take from them the right to keep and bear arms, that they designed to rest it in the State governments? Is this a right reserved to the *States* or to *themselves*? Is it not an unalienable right, which lies at the bottom of every free government? . . . This right is too dear to be confided to a republican legislature. . . .

In solemnly affirming that a well-regulated militia is necessary to the *security* of a *free State*, and that, in order to train properly that militia, the unlimited right of the *people* to *keep* and *bear* arms shall not be impaired, are not the sovereign people of the State committed by this pledge to preserve this right inviolate? . . .

The right of the people peaceably to assemble and petition the government for a redress of grievances; to be secure in their persons, houses, papers, and effects, against unreasonable searches and seizures; in all criminal prosecutions, to be confronted with the witness against them; to be publicly tried by an impartial jury; and to have the assistance of counsel for their defence, *is as perfect under the State as the national legislature, and cannot be violated by either.*

Nor is the *right* involved in this discussion less comprehensive or valuable: "The right of the people to bear arms shall not be infringed." The right of the whole people, old and young, men, women and boys, and not militia only, to keep and bear *arms* of every description, and not *such* merely as are used by the *militia*, shall not be *infringed*, curtailed, or broken in upon, in the smallest degree; and all this for the important end to be attained: the rearing up and qualifying a well-regulated militia, so vitally necessary to the security of a free State. Our opinion is, that any law, State or Federal, is repugnant to the Constitution, and void, which contravenes this *right*, originally belonging to our forefathers, trampled under foot by Charles I. and his two wicked sons and successors, re-established by the revolution of 1688, conveyed to this land of liberty by the colonists, and finally incorporated conspicuously in our own *Magna Charta!* And Lexington, Concord, Camden,[4] River Raisin,[5] Sandusky,[6] and the laurel-crowned field of New Orleans, plead eloquently for this interpretation! And the acquisition of Texas may be considered the full fruits of this great constitutional right.

We are of the opinion, then, that so far as the act of 1837 seeks to suppress the practice of carrying certain weapons *secretly*, that it is valid, inasmuch as it does not deprive the citizen of his *natural* right of self-defence, or of his constitutional right to keep and bear arms. But that so much of it, as contains a prohibition against bearing arms *openly*, is in conflict with the Constitution, and *void;* and that, as the defendant has been indicted and convicted for carrying a pistol, without charging that it was done in a concealed manner . . . the judgment of the court below must be reversed, and the proceeding quashed.

---

4. [South Carolina site of a 1780 battle in the Revolutionary War. The local militia performed terribly, and the British won a major victory. — Eds.]

5. [Michigan site of an 1813 battle in the War of 1812. The Indian allies of the British massacred American prisoners. — Eds.]

6. [Ohio site of a 1782 battle in the American Revolution, and an 1813 battle in the War of 1812. The latter was an American victory. — Eds.]

NOTES & QUESTIONS

1. Note the court's statement that state constitutions "confer no *new rights* on the people which did not belong to them before," the rhetorical question about legislatures having the ability to deny their citizens these rights, and the court's conclusion that the right to bear arms is "too dear to be confined to a republican legislature." On this view, the Second Amendment recognizes and protects a natural right to arms but does not create that right. A similar view about the Second Amendment was expressed by the U.S. Supreme Court in *United States v. Cruikshank*, 92 U.S. 542 (1875) (Chapter 6). Do you agree? What about the other rights enumerated in the Bill of Rights? Does the court's holding imply that carrying concealed weapons is not a natural right, but that carrying weapons openly is? How did it reach such a conclusion? Are legislatures better suited to make such determinations?

2. *A right to carry arms for self-defense. Nunn v. State*'s interpretation of the Second Amendment to protect a right to carry arms openly, but not concealed, is consistent with a majority of pre–Civil War decisions of state courts applying state or federal constitutional provisions to state laws restricting the carrying of weapons.

   As you have read, *Nunn* discussed prior decisions by the supreme courts of Kentucky, Indiana, and Alabama. The first American right-to-arms case, *Bliss v. Commonwealth*, 12 Ky. (2 Litt.) 90 (1822), held that even concealed carry was protected under the Kentucky Constitution. However, later cases such as *State v. Mitchell*, 3 Blackf. 229 (Ind. 1833), *State v. Reid*, 1 Ala. 612 (1840), and *Nunn* all took a different view of the right, upholding prohibitions on concealed carry. Another notable case, *State v. Chandler*, 5 La. Ann. 489 (1850), held that a ban on concealed carrying of weapons did not violate the Second Amendment, because that Amendment protected the "right to carry arms . . . in full open view." The court said that open carry and concealed carry were both part of the right to bear arms, but that either could be banned as long as the other were allowed. *Cockrum v. State*, 24 Tex. 394, 401 (1859), upheld a statute enhancing the penalty for unlawful killings committed with a Bowie knife, while acknowledging that "the right to carry a bowie-knife for defense [was] secured" by the Texas Constitution.

   Do these cases suggest that judicial understanding of the right to arms was changing, so that it included personal self-defense, and not just the militia? Do they mean that personal self-defense was always part of the right? *District of Columbia v. Heller*, 554 U.S. 570 (2008) (Chapter 9) involves stark disagreement between Justices Antonin Scalia and John Paul Stevens about whether cases like *Nunn* or *Chandler* are legitimate sources for understanding the original meaning of the Second Amendment.

3. *Open carry.* The right recognized in *Nunn* (and similar state cases of the era) protected the open carrying of arms. Legislatures could not prohibit peaceable citizens from carrying in public common types of firearms and bladed weapons for self-defense. Yet most courts agreed that the legislature retained authority to regulate the exercise of the right in certain ways, such as by prohibiting concealed carry.

Is open carry more desirable than carrying weapons concealed? Less desirable? Or is it a wash? The antebellum courts tended to draw a moral distinction between open and concealed carry, viewing the former as appropriate for honest citizens, while concealed carry was seen as a dubious practice characteristic only of thugs, robbers, and other disreputable types. As the Louisiana Supreme Court put it, the constitutional right to arms was a right

> to carry arms . . . in full open view, which places men upon an equality. This is the right guaranteed by the Constitution of the United States, and which is calculated to incite men to a manly and noble defence of themselves, if necessary, and of their country, without any tendency to secret advantages and unmanly assassinations.

State v. Chandler, 5 La. Ann. 489, 489 (1850) (upholding ban on concealed carry of deadly weapons; reversing manslaughter conviction due to faulty jury instructions); *see also Reid*, 1 Ala. at 617 (carrying weapons in a concealed manner "is calculated to exert an unhappy influence upon the moral feelings of the wearer, by making him less regardful of the personal security of others"). Does this reflect an antiquated view of "manly and noble" conduct? Do you agree with the claims made in the antebellum opinions about the social impropriety of concealed carry? What about the propriety of carrying weapons in general? If different norms apply in your community today, what causes do you think explain those differences?

4. *Open carry today.* The majority of American states now allow the open carry of loaded handguns under at least some circumstances. However, state and local laws vary greatly. In some states, the right to open carry is a protected right under the state constitution. This is more frequently the case in states whose constitutional right to arms guarantees a right to bear arms for self-defense, while stating that the legislature retains authority to restrict the carrying of "concealed weapons" — thereby arguably *excluding* the ability to prohibit open carry of weapons. *See, e.g., City of Las Vegas v. Moberg*, 485 P.2d 737, 738 (N.M. App. 1971) (holding that municipal prohibition on gun-carrying, "as it is applied to carrying arms openly and in plain view," violates state constitutional right to bear arms); N.M. Const. of 1971, art. II, §6 ("No law shall abridge the right of the citizen to keep and bear arms for security and defense, . . . but nothing herein shall be held to permit the carrying of concealed weapons."); *Holland v. Commonwealth*, 294 S.W.2d 83, 85 (Ky. 1956) (declaring that under Kentucky Constitution, "the legislature is empowered only to deny to citizens the right to carry concealed weapons. . . . If the gun is worn outside the jacket or shirt in full view, no one may question the wearer's right so to do; but, if it is carried under the jacket or shirt, the violator is subject to imprisonment for not less than two nor more than five years."); Ky. Const. of 1891, §1, cl. 7 (recognizing individuals' "right to bear arms in defense of themselves and of the State, subject to the power of the General Assembly to enact laws to prevent persons from carrying concealed weapons"); *see also* Wisconsin Department of Justice Advisory Memorandum, *available at* http://www.doj.state.wi.us/news/files/FinalOpenCarryMemo.pdf (Apr. 20, 2009) (concluding that Wisconsin

Constitution's right to arms provision, adopted in 1998, protects "the right to openly carry a firearm" for self-defense and other purposes); Wis. Const. art. I, §25 ("The people have the right to keep and bear arms for security, defense, hunting, recreation or any other lawful purpose.").

Some states do not consider open carry to be constitutionally protected, but do not prohibit it. Still others require residents to have a valid carry permit in order to carry a handgun, but do not require permit holders to conceal their guns. *E.g.*, Ind. Code §35-47-2-1 (2008) ("carry a handgun . . . on or about the person's body"). A number of states prohibit the open carrying of handguns by private citizens in almost all cases, while allowing licensed concealed carry. *E.g.*, Tex. Penal Code §§46.02; 46.035(a). Finally, Illinois prohibits both concealed and open carry of handguns, except on private property with permission of the property owner. 720 Ill. Comp. Stat. 5/24-1(a)(4), (a)(10).

Whether open or concealed, lawful carry is frequently subject to location restrictions, such as bans on carrying on K-12 school property and in certain government buildings. Today, in 41 of the 50 states, adults who want to carry a gun for protection can readily obtain a concealed carry license, or can carry concealed without need for a license. In most of these states, the applicant must pass a fingerprint-based background check and a safety class. The practice of open carry, in contrast, is relatively rare in most parts of the United States today, although it is more common in rural areas and the West, especially Arizona. There is also a grassroots political movement for open carry; the movement seeks to re-normalize the open, lawful presence of firearms in public. Thus, in many jurisdictions where open carry is lawful, it has lately become more visible.

In practice, however, open carriers sometimes encounter more obstacles than the letter of the applicable weapons carry laws might predict. Broadly worded criminal statutes prohibiting disturbing the peace or disorderly conduct have sometimes been invoked to detain or arrest open carriers. *See, e.g.*, Edmund H. Mahoney, Hartford Courant, courant.com, *Support Is Growing for Openly Carried Permitted Weapons*, Apr. 18, 2010, http://articles.courant.com/2010-04-18/news/hc-open-carry-gun-owners-gun-laws-permits (reporting judge's dismissal of charges against a Connecticut man with a gun carry permit who openly carried in restaurant; police officers arrested him for breach of the peace); Linda Spice, Milwaukee Journal Sentinel, JSOnline *West Allis Man Not Guilty in Open Carry Gun Case*, Feb. 17, 2009, http://www.jsonline.com/news/crime/39722082.html (reporting dismissal of charges against a Wisconsin man who carried a handgun openly while planting a tree in his yard; police officers entered the man's property, arrested him for disorderly conduct, and confiscated his gun).

5. "Categoricalism" is a modern term for deciding constitutional cases based on whether something is "inside" or "outside" the right. For example, in a First Amendment context, a speech in favor of lower taxes is "inside" the right and may not be banned. In contrast, words uttered in furtherance of a criminal conspiracy to evade taxes are "outside" the right, and may be criminally punished. Another method of constitutional adjudication is "balancing," wherein the court weighs the burden of the restriction on a right

against the benefits of that restriction. *See* Joseph Blocher, *Categoricalism and Balancing in First and Second Amendment Analysis*, 84 N.Y.U. L. Rev. 375 (2009). Observe the categorical jurisprudence in *Nunn* (open carry is part of the right, but concealed carry is not; therefore, the former is protected, while the latter may be banned) and in *Bliss* (both open and concealed carry are inside the right, and neither may be banned). In contrast, *Reid* seemed to treat both open and concealed carry as part of the right, but concluded that concealed carry could be banned because this was only a "regulation" of the right, not a "destruction" of it, since open carry was still allowed. *Chandler* takes a similar approach. Which approach do you think is better?

6. The *Bliss* standard of review is "whatever restrains the full and complete exercise of that right, though not an entire destruction of it, is forbidden by the explicit language of the Constitution." What gun controls, if any, might pass this standard of review? Is the *Bliss* standard of review appropriate for assessing gun rights? For other rights?

2. The "Civilized Warfare" Test: Militia Weapons Only?

A different approach prevailed in Tennessee, where the state constitution guaranteed a right of "free white men . . . to keep and to bear arms for their common defense." Tenn. Const. of 1834, art. I, §26.

Aymette v. State
21 Tenn. (2 Humph.) 154 (1840)

GREEN, J., delivered the opinion of the court.

[The evidence at trial was that on the night of June 26, 1839, William Aymette went searching at a hotel for a man named Hamilton, "swearing that he would have his heart's blood." Aymette had a Bowie knife concealed under his vest, which he took out occasionally and brandished. He then "proceeded from place to place in search of Hamilton, and occasionally exhibited his knife."]

The plaintiff in error was convicted in the . . . circuit court, for wearing a bowie knife concealed under his clothes, under the act of 1837-8, ch. 137, sec. 2, which provides, "That if any person shall wear any bowie knife, or Arkansas tooth-pick, or other knife or weapon, that shall in form, shape or size resemble a bowie knife or Arkansas tooth-pick, under his clothes, or keep the same concealed about his person, such person shall be guilty of a misdemeanor, and upon conviction thereof, shall be fined in a sum not less than two hundred dollars, and shall be imprisoned in the county jail, not less than three months and not more than six months."

It is now insisted that the above act of the legislature is unconstitutional, and therefore the judgment in this case should have been arrested.

In the first article of the [1834] Constitution of this State, containing a declaration of rights, sec. 26, it is declared, "That the free white men of this State, have a right to keep and bear arms for their common defence."

This declaration, it is insisted, gives to every man the right to arm himself in any manner he may choose, however unusual or dangerous the weapons he may employ; and thus armed, to appear wherever he may think proper, without molestation or hindrance, and that any law regulating his social conduct, by restraining the use of any weapon or regulating the manner in which it shall be carried, is beyond the legislative competency to enact, and is void.

In order to have a just and precise idea of the meaning of the clause of the constitution under consideration, it will be useful to look at the state of things in the history of our ancestors, and thus comprehend the reason of its introduction into our constitution.

[In England, the] act of 22 and 23, Car. 2d, ch. 25, sec. 3, . . . provided that no person who has not lands of the yearly value of £100, other than the son and heir apparent of an esquire, or other person of higher degree, &c., shall be allowed to keep a gun, &c. By this act, persons of a certain condition in life were allowed to keep arms, while a large proportion of the people were entirely disarmed. But King James the 2d, by his own arbitrary power, and contrary to law, disarmed the Protestant population, and quartered his Catholic soldiers among the people. This, together with other abuses, produced the revolution by which he was compelled to abdicate the throne of England. William and Mary succeeded him, and in the first year of their reign, Parliament passed an act recapitulating the abuses which existed during the former reign, and declared the existence of certain rights which they insisted upon as their undoubted privileges. Among these abuses, they say, in sec. 5, that he had kept a "standing army within the kingdom in time of peace without consent of Parliament, and quartered soldiers contrary to law." Sec. 6. "By causing several good subjects, being Protestants, to be disarmed, at the same time when Papists were both armed and employed contrary to law."

In the declaration of rights that follows, sec. 7 declares, that "the subjects which are Protestants may have arms for their defence, suitable to their condition and as allowed by law." This declaration, although it asserts the right of the Protestants to have arms, does not extend the privilege beyond the terms provided in the act of Charles 2d, before referred to. . . . It was in reference to these facts, and to this state of the English law, that the second section of the amendments to the Constitution of the United States was incorporated into that instrument. It declares that "a well regulated militia being necessary to the security of a free state, the right of the people to keep and bear arms shall not be infringed."

In the same view, the section under consideration of [the Tennessee] bill of rights was adopted.

The evil that was produced by disarming the people in the time of James the second, was, that the King, by means of a standing army, quartered among the people, was able to overawe them, and compel them to submit to the most arbitrary, cruel and illegal measures. Whereas, if the people had retained their arms, they would have been able, by a just and proper resistance to those oppressive measures, either to have caused the King to respect their rights, or surrender (as he was eventually compelled to do) the government into other hands. No private defence was contemplated or would have availed anything. . . . The complaint was against the government. The grievances to which they were thus forced to submit, were for the most part of a public character, and could have been redressed only by the people rising up for their common defence to vindicate their rights.

The section under consideration, in our bill of rights, was adopted in reference to these historical facts, and in this point of view its language is most appropriate and expressive. Its words are, "The free white men of this state have a right to keep and bear arms for their common defence." It, to be sure, asserts the right much more broadly than the statute of first William and Mary. For the right there asserted, is subject to the disabilities contained in the act of Charles the second. [Only] lords and esquires, and their sons and persons, whose yearly income from land amounted to one hundred pounds, were of suitable condition to keep arms. But, with us, every free white man is of suitable condition; and, therefore, every free white man may keep and bear arms. But to keep and bear arms for what? If the history of the subject had left in doubt the object for which the right is secured, the words that are employed must completely remove that doubt. It is declared that they may keep and bear arms for their common defence. The word "common" here used, means according to Webster; 1. Belonging equally to more than one, or to many indefinitely. 2. Belonging to the public. 3. General. 4. Universal. 5. Public. The object then, for which the right of keeping and bearing arms is secured, is the defence of the public. The free white men may keep arms to protect the public liberty, to keep in awe those who are in power, and to maintain the supremacy of the laws and the constitution. The words "bear arms" too, have reference to their military use, and were not employed to mean wearing them about the person as part of the dress.

As the object for which the right to keep and bear arms is secured, is of general and public nature, to be exercised by the people in a body, for their common defence, so the arms, the right to keep which is secured, are such as are usually employed in civilized warfare, and that constitute the ordinary military equipment. If the citizens have these arms in their hands, they are prepared in the best possible manner to repel any encroachments upon their rights by those in authority. They need not, for such a purpose, the use of those weapons which are usually employed in private broils, and which are efficient only in the hands of the robber and the assassin. These weapons would be useless in war. They could not be employed advantageously in the common defence of the citizens. The right to keep and bear them, is not, therefore, secured by the constitution. . . .

The citizens have the unqualified right to keep the weapon, it being of the character before described. . . . But the right to bear arms is not of that unqualified character. The citizens may bear them for the common defence; but it does not follow, that they may be borne by an individual, merely to terrify the people, or for purposes of private assassination. And as the manner in which they are worn, and circumstances under which they are carried, indicate to every man, the purpose of the wearer, the legislature may prohibit such manner of wearing as would never be resorted to by persons engaged in the common defence.

We are aware that the court of appeals of Kentucky, in the case of *Bliss v. The Commonwealth,* 2 Littel's Rep. 90 (1822), has decided that an act of their legislature, similar to the one now under consideration, is unconstitutional and void. We have great respect for the court by whom that decision was made, but we cannot concur in their reasoning.

We think the view of the subject which the opinion of the court in that case takes, is far too limited for a just construction of the meaning of the clause of the [Kentucky] constitution they had under consideration. It is not precisely in the words of our constitution, nevertheless, it is of the same general import. The words are, that "the right of the citizens to bear arms in defence of themselves, and the State, shall not be questioned." [Ky. Const. of 1799, art. 10, sec. 23.]

In the former part of this opinion, we have recurred to the circumstances under which a similar provision was adopted in England, and have thence deduced the reason of its adoption, and consequently have seen the object in view, when the right to keep and bear arms was secured. All these considerations are left out of view, in [*Bliss*], and the court confine themselves entirely to the consideration of the distinction between a law prohibiting the right, and a law merely regulating the manner in which arms may be worn. They say, there can be no difference between a law prohibiting the wearing concealed weapons, and one prohibiting the wearing them openly.

We think there is a manifest distinction. In the nature of things, if they were not allowed to bear arms openly, they could not bear them in their defence of the State at all. To bear arms in defence of the State, is to employ them in war, as arms are usually employed by civilized nations. The arms, consisting of swords, muskets, rifles, &c., must necessarily be borne openly; so that a prohibition to bear them openly, would be a denial of the right altogether. And as in their constitution, the right to bear arms in defence of themselves, is coupled with the right to bear them in defence of the State, we must understand the expressions as meaning the same thing, and as relating to public, and not private; to the common, and not the individual defence.

. . . The 28th section of our bill of rights provides, "that no citizen of this State shall be compelled to bear arms, provided he will pay in equivalent, to be ascertained by law." Here we know that the phrase has a military sense, and no other; and we must infer that it is used in the same sense in the 26th section, which secures to the citizen the right to bear arms. A man in the pursuit of deer, elk and buffaloes, might carry his rifle every day, for forty years, and, yet, it would never be said of him, that he had borne arms, much less could it be said, that a private citizen bears arms, because he has a dirk or pistol concealed under his clothes, or a spear in a cane. So that, with deference, we think the argument of the court in the case referred to, even upon the question it has debated, is defective and inconclusive.

In the case of *Simpson v. State*, 5th Yer. Rep. 356 (Tenn. 1833), Judge White, in delivering the opinion of the court, makes use of the general expression, that "by this clause in the constitution [art. 26], an express power is given, and secured to all the free citizens in the State to keep and bear arms for their defence, without any qualification whatever, as to their kind and nature."

But in that case, no question as to the meaning of this provision in the constitution arose, or was decided by the court, and the expression is only an incidental remark of the judge who delivered the opinion, and, therefore, is entitled to no weight.

We think, therefore, that upon either of the grounds assumed in this opinion, the legislature had the right to pass the law under which the plaintiff in error was convicted. Let the judgment be affirmed.

NOTES & QUESTIONS

1. *The civilized warfare test. Aymette*'s conclusion that the right to arms only protects those weapons that are appropriate for organized military use in civilized warfare — which modern commentators have called the "civilized warfare test" — was a minority view in the antebellum era. Outside of Tennessee, only one judge seems to have adopted it. *See State v. Buzzard*, 4 Ark. (2 Pike) 18, 32 (1842) (Dickinson, J., concurring) (rejecting Second Amendment challenge to ban on concealed carry of pistols, dirks, large knives, and sword canes because, among other reasons, "[t]he enactment in question . . . ha[s] reference to weapons and arms of a wholly different character from such as are ordinarily used for warlike purposes"). However, as you will read in Chapter 6, this test gained greater acceptance by courts in the latter decades of the nineteenth century. *See* David B. Kopel, *The Second Amendment in the Nineteenth Century*, 1998 BYU L. Rev. 1359, 1415-32. Michael P. O'Shea, *Modeling the Second Amendment Right to Carry Arms (I): Judicial Tradition and the Scope of 'Bearing Arms' for Self-Defense*, 61 Am. U. L. Rev. (forthcoming 2012), *available at* http://ssrn.com/abstract = 1949477.

    Aymette indicates that the arms protected by this test include swords, muskets, and rifles, but did not include "a spear concealed in a cane," nor, apparently, Aymette's Bowie knife. *Id.* at 160-61. In both the First and Second World Wars, United States military units frequently issued large, double-bladed "trench knives" to infantrymen as standard fighting equipment. Some of these knives, such as the famous "Ka-Bar" of the United States Marine Corps, were little different from some Bowie knives of the nineteenth century, and would likely have fallen within the prohibition in the Tennessee concealed weapons statute at issue in *Aymette*. Bowie knives themselves were widely used in the Mexican War (1846-48), and Jim Bowie himself had died defending the Alamo in 1836. Is any of this relevant to an appraisal of *Aymette*'s holding?

    If, pursuant to *Aymette* and its progeny, suitability for militia use is the test of whether a given weapon is within the scope of the right, then what types of "arms" are protected? Only the precise types of arms possessed by the National Guard? (The Guard is defined by federal statute as the "organized militia" of the United States. The rest of the United States' militia is defined as all able-bodied males aged 18 to 45, with a few exceptions for religious ministers and the like. 10 U.S.C. §§310-11. *See* Chapter 4.E) Or does this test encompass any weapon that might be useful for militia service — even including sporting guns, which were not made for combat, but which could be used in combat?

2. The *Aymette* court acknowledges an "unqualified" right to "keep" protected arms, but states that public carrying can be restricted to militia-style carrying: "[T]he legislature may prohibit such manner of wearing as would never be resorted to by persons engaged in the common defence." Is *Aymette* defining a general individual right, a militia-only right, or a hybrid of the two? Or is *Aymette* just a decision about which types of arms are protected? As we will see in Chapter 7, similar questions have been asked about the Supreme Court's opinion in *United States v. Miller*, 307 U.S. 174 (1939), a case that upheld strict registration and taxation requirements for short-barreled shotguns, in part by relying on *Aymette*.

3. *Keeping arms vs. bearing arms.* Like the Second Amendment, the Tennessee Constitution's right to arms refers to a right both to "keep" arms and to "bear" arms. *Aymette* treats these as two different rights, declaring that "citizens have the unqualified right to keep . . . weapon[s]" that satisfy the civilized warfare test, but that "the right to bear arms is not of that unqualified character." What distinction is drawn here between the right to keep and the right to bear? Is it justified? If so, does that mean that state constitutions that refer only to a right to "bear arms" do not protect a right to acquire arms and keep them at home?

4. The *Aymette* court distinguishes *Bliss* partly on the ground that the Tennessee constitution contains a provision allowing a citizen to "pay an equivalent" to avoid bearing arms, and notes that this implies a military meaning of the arms-bearing provision in question. But the Kentucky constitution interpreted in *Bliss* also contained similar language allowing one to "pay an equivalent" to avoid bearing arms. Ky. Const. of 1799, art. III, §28. Many other state constitutions of the late eighteenth and early nineteenth century contain some clauses or sections that are clearly military-only — such as affirmations of the supremacy of civil government over the military, or rules for conscientious objectors. Do these military provisions imply that the arms right referred to in the same section of the constitution must be militia-only? Compare the First and Fifth Amendments, which agglomerate several topics. Could "bear arms" be used in a militia sense in one part of a constitution and in a general sense in another part?

5. *Distinguishing a prior case. Aymette* ends with a brief reference to an earlier case, *Simpson v. State*, 13 Tenn. (5 Yer.) 356 (1833). In *Simpson*, the Tennessee Supreme Court dismissed an indictment for the common law crime of affray. The indictment alleged only that Simpson had appeared on a public street, "arrayed in a warlike manner" with arms, thereby causing "great terror and disturbance" to other citizens. The court concluded that the required elements of an affray included "fighting or actual violence" involving two or more persons. Thus, since the indictment against Simpson did not allege any violent acts, he could not be prosecuted for affray.

   A leading English treatise, which was influential in the United States even after independence, suggested that "there may be an affray where there is no actual violence, as where a man arms himself with dangerous and unusual weapons, in such a manner as will naturally cause terror to the people. . . ." William Hawkins, Treatise on Pleas of the Crown 358 (1716). However, the *Simpson* court rejected this broad view of the offense. The court reasoned, in part, that indictment for appearing in public armed with dangerous weapons would conflict with the Tennessee Constitution's right to bear arms:

   > But suppos[ing] it to be assumed on any ground, that our ancestors adopted and brought over with them this . . . portion of the common law, our constitution has completely abrogated it; it says, "that the freemen of this state have a right to keep and to bear arms for their common defence." Art. II, sec. 26. . . . [T]his clause of our constitution fully meets and opposes the passage or clause in Hawkins, of "a man's arming himself with dangerous and unusual weapons," as being an independent ground of affray. . . . By this clause of the constitution, an express power is given and secured to all the free citizens of the state to keep and bear arms for their defence, without any qualification

whatever as to their kind or nature . . . ; neither, after so solemn an instrument hath said the people may carry arms, can we be permitted to impute to the acts thus licensed such a necessarily consequent operation as terror to the people to be incurred thereby; we must attribute to the framers of it the absence of such a view.

Id. at 359-60. Did *Aymette* correctly characterize *Simpson* when it stated that "no question as to the meaning of this provision in the constitution . . . was decided by the court," so that the passage from *Simpson* was "only an incidental remark of the judge who delivered the opinion, which is entitled to no weight"? *See Aymette, supra.* Treatment of precedent aside, which view of the Tennessee Constitution do you find more persuasive? Does it ultimately make any difference to *Aymette*'s result, given that Aymette did not merely appear in public with a weapon, but also brandished it and uttered threats to kill Hamilton? To *Aymette*'s rationale?

On what grounds did *Aymette* distinguish the Kentucky decision in *Bliss v. Commonwealth*? Do you agree that Kentucky's right to arms provision ("The right of the citizens to bear arms in defence of themselves, and the State, shall not be questioned") meant the same thing as Tennessee's provision ("[T]he free white men of this State have a right to keep and bear arms for their common defence.")? Is this conclusion necessary to *Aymette*'s result? If you were a judge on the Tennessee Supreme Court in 1840, how would you have analyzed William Aymette's claim?

6. *Bowie knives and Arkansas toothpicks: Knife carry laws.* The weapons control statutes of the early nineteenth century extended well beyond the carrying of firearms. As you have seen, some restricted the carrying of knives, especially large-bladed fighting knives such as the Bowie knife and the long, pointed "Arkansas toothpick."

From a twenty-first-century vantage, the meaning of "Bowie knife" and "Arkansas toothpick" is rather vague. Indeed, historians of weaponry still do not know exactly what kind of knife Colonel Jim Bowie used in the famous 1827 fight by a riverside in Louisiana. However, the term "Bowie knife" came to be used to refer to a large-bladed knife, often with a clip-pointed blade, which was effective for both slashing and piercing. By the 1840s, such blades were produced by both domestic and English knifesmiths for the American market. *See* Raymond W. Thorpe, Bowie Knife (1948).

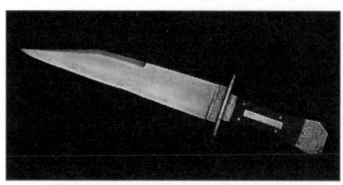

Permanent collection of the Historic Arkansas Museum, Little Rock, Arkansas

ENGLISH-MADE BOWIE-TYPE KNIFE, CIRCA 1847-48

Newspapers of the period pointed out the threat posed by the Bowie knife. One praised Tennessee's 1838 ban on concealed carry of Bowie knives as a "salutary act" that would "effectively stop the use and sale of one of the most bloody instruments of death known to the present age . . . every friend of humanity and good order must rejoice that the practice of wearing this barbarous weapon" had been criminalized — at least if carried concealed. *Chronicle*, 53 Niles' National Register 400, Feb. 17, 1838 (reprinting an article from the Nashville *Whig*). As late as 1859, a time when advances in firearms technology had made effective, repeating handguns, such as the six-shot Colt revolver, a practical reality, the Texas Supreme Court emphasized the unusually fearsome character of the Bowie knife:

> It is an exceedingly destructive weapon. It is difficult to defend against it, by any degree of bravery, or any amount of skill. The gun or pistol may miss its aim, and when discharged, its dangerous character is lost, or diminished at least. The sword may be parried. With these weapons men fight for the sake of the combat, to satisfy the laws of honor, not necessarily with the intention to kill, or with a certainty of killing, when the intention exists. The bowie-knife differs from these in its device and design; it is the instrument of almost certain death. He who carries such a weapon, for lawful defence, as he may, makes himself more dangerous to the rights of others, considering the frailties of human nature, than if he carried a less dangerous weapon.

Cockrum v. State, 24 Tex. 394, 402-03 (1859) (upholding a statute providing that all unlawful killings committed with a Bowie knife would be treated as murder, the most serious degree of homicide, while acknowledging that lawful use, carrying, and possession of Bowie knives could not constitutionally be banned).

Today the carrying of Bowie knives, and other blades viewed as offensive weapons, remains illegal in many states — even in some where the lawful carrying of firearms for defense is common. Oklahoma's statute is fairly typical:

> A. It shall be unlawful for any person to carry upon or about his or her person, or in a purse or other container belonging to the person, . . . any dagger, bowie knife, dirk knife, switchblade knife, spring-type knife, sword cane, knife having a blade which opens automatically by hand pressure applied to a button, spring, or other device in the handle of the knife, . . . or any other offensive weapon, whether such weapon be concealed or unconcealed, except this section shall not prohibit:
>
> 1. The proper use of . . . knives for hunting, fishing, educational or recreational purposes;
>
> 2. The carrying or use of [firearms] in a manner otherwise permitted by statute or authorized by the Oklahoma Self-Defense Act [a "shall issue" concealed handgun carry permitting statute];
>
> 3. The carrying, possession and use of any weapon by a peace officer or other person authorized by law to carry a weapon in the performance of official duties and in compliance with the rules of the employing agency. . . .

21 Okla. Stat. §1272 (2010). California law takes a similar approach, prohibiting the concealed carrying of any "dirk or dagger," and defining a "dirk" or "dagger" as "a knife or other instrument with or without a handguard

that is capable of ready use as a stabbing weapon that may inflict great bodily injury or death," with the proviso that "a nonlocking folding knife, a folding knife that [does not open automatically], or a pocketknife" is not illegal to carry unless "the blade of the knife is exposed and locked into position." Cal. Penal Code §§12020(a)(4), (a)(32)(e)(4). Florida, by contrast, allows concealed carry licensees to carry "a handgun, electronic weapon or device, tear gas gun, knife, or billie." Fla. Stat. §790.06(1).

Are these statutes sufficiently clear about what knives are allowed? State knife law is a complicated subject whose details are beyond the scope of this text. Broadly speaking, the carrying of blades with two cutting edges — such as daggers, dirks, and swords — is heavily restricted in many states, while fixed or folding knives that have a single edge are more likely to be viewed as non-weapons (although some of them can be used effectively for fighting), and are frequently owned and carried by citizens for chores, hunting, fishing, and similar purposes. State knife laws often restrict the carry of knives with blades beyond a specified length. *See, e.g.*, Conn. Gen. Stat. §53-206(a) (providing that "Any person who carries upon his or her person . . . any dirk knife, or any switch knife, . . . or stiletto, or any knife the edged portion of the blade of which is four inches or over in length, . . . or any other dangerous or deadly weapon or instrument, shall be fined not more than five hundred dollars or imprisoned not more than three years or both"); Tex. Penal Code §46.01(6) (defining "illegal knives," prohibited from being carried, to include "daggers," "bowie knives," and any "knife with a blade over five and one-half inches"). Most Bowie-type knives would fail these length requirements as well.

7. What do you make of the *Aymette* court's discussion of King James's abuses of Protestants by Catholics, followed by its recitation of the Tennessee constitution's racist arms-bearing provision, and then the statement and subsequent defense of the position that "with us, every free white man is of suitable condition"? Compare this analysis with both postbellum decisions on the right to bear arms and postbellum changes to state constitutions in Chapter 6.

3. A Collective "Right of Sovereignty" Subject to Legislative Discretion?

One more antebellum approach merits examination. Arkansas, the birthplace of the Arkansas toothpick (a variant of the Bowie knife), saw its full share of armed violence in the early nineteenth century. The most notorious episode transpired on the very floor of the Arkansas Legislature in December 1837. During debate on a minor bill, Representative J.J. Anthony delivered an insulting remark about Speaker of the House John Wilson. The Speaker immediately confronted Anthony, and both men drew concealed Bowie knives. Anthony cut Wilson in the arm; Wilson stabbed Anthony in the torso, instantly killing him, and then passed out from loss of blood. Wilson was expelled from the legislature, and the brawl drew condemnation from newspapers across the state, but Wilson was later acquitted of a murder charge on the ground that the killing was excusable. Cramer, *supra*, 92-94 (1999).

In that same session, the state legislature approved a ban on the concealed carrying of "any pistol, dirk, butcher or large knife, or a sword in a cane," except when carried by a traveler. Violation was punished by one to six months' imprisonment and a fine of $25 to $100, which was to be split evenly between the government and any "informer" who assisted in the conviction. Div. VIII, art. I, sec. 13, Revised Statutes of the State of Arkansas, Adopted at the October Session of the General Assembly of Said State, A.D. 1837, at 280 (1838).

In *State v. Buzzard*, 4 Ark. (2 Pike) 18 (1842), a divided Arkansas Supreme Court held that this prohibition did not violate either the Second Amendment or the Arkansas Constitution, which (like Tennessee's) stated that "the free white men of this State shall have a right to keep and to bear arms for their common defense." Ark. Const. of 1836, art. II, sec. 21.

Unlike *Aymette, supra*, and *Nunn, supra, Buzzard* had scant influence outside the state. However, *Buzzard* is worth studying because the three separate opinions by the three judges express such different views of the right to arms. Indeed, *Buzzard* foreshadowed much of the right to arms debate of the twentieth and twenty-first centuries.

Chief Justice Ringo argued that recognizing an individual right to keep and bear arms for self-defense would lead to unacceptable consequences, such as invalidation of laws permitting arrested persons to be temporarily disarmed, or prohibiting the storage of dangerous quantities of gunpowder. *Id.* at 21. Like Justice Stevens dissenting in *Heller* (Chapter 9), Ringo denied that the Second Amendment protected private rights unrelated to service in the state militia:

> [I]t may not be without utility to inquire for what object the right to keep and bear arms is retained exempt from all legal regulation or control, if in fact it has been so retained. . . . Is it to enable each member of the community to protect and defend by individual force his private rights against every illegal invasion, or to obtain redress in like manner for injuries thereto committed by persons acting contrary to law? Certainly not; because, according to the fundamental principles of government, such rights are created, limited, and defined by law, or retained subject to be regulated and controlled thereby; and the laws alone are and must be regarded as securing to every individual the quiet enjoyment of every right with which he is invested. . . . And to these authorities every person is, in most cases, bound to resort, for the security of his private rights, as well as the redress of all injuries thereto. . . . And therefore . . . the right in question could not have been so retained and secured with any view to the protection or vindication of such rights of individuals as are merely private.

Id. at 23-24; *see also id.* at 27 (concluding that the "common defense" language of the Arkansas right to arms provision meant that it had "the sole object of . . . provid[ing] . . . adequate means for the preservation and defense of the State and her republican institutions"). Since the ban on concealed carrying of weapons did not "detract anything from the power of the people to defend their free state and the established institutions of the country," it was, in Chief Justice Ringo's view, constitutionally valid. *Id.*

Justice Dickinson concurred. His opinion constitutes the first appearance of the collective right view that gained so many adherents in the following century: that the Second Amendment protects a right of governments rather than individuals.

> The class of cases to which the constitutional provision applies is widely different from the right of a private citizen to bear, concealed about his person, deadly weapons or arms. . . . [W]hen arms are not kept or used for the defense of the State or Federal government, the manner of carrying and mode of using them are subject to the control and authority of the State Legislature. . . . The provision of the Federal Constitution, under which the appellee claims his discharge, is but an assertion of that general right of sovereignty belonging to independent nations to regulate their military force.

Id. at 29, 32 (Dickinson, J., concurring). Justice Dickinson rejected as incoherent the idea that individuals should retain a right to use arms independent of regulation by the government. "To assert that a citizen is entitled to protection from his government, the means of securing [protection], is a contradiction in terms difficult if not impossible to be reconciled." *Id.* at 32. In his view, as long as state weapons laws did not conflict with federal laws disciplining and regulating the militia, those laws were valid under the Second Amendment. *Id.* at 32-33. Justice Dickinson closed by commenting that the ban on concealed weapons was not only constitutional, it was "the exercise of a power loudly called for by our citizens, and which, if strictly enforced by the public authorities, would add greatly to the peace and good order of society, the security of our citizens, . . . and the reputation of the State abroad." *Id.* at 33. The Dickinson opinion is the only known expression of the pure collective right idea in nineteenth-century judicial opinions or legal scholarship.

Finally, Justice Lacy dissented. Taking the *Barron*-contrarian view that the Second Amendment applied directly to the states, he concluded that it protected a right of individuals to keep and carry weapons for self-defense. *Id.* at 38-39. Justice Lacy argued that confining the right to keep and bear arms to the organized militia would make the inclusion of the right in the constitution pointless:

> The security of the state is the constitutional reason for the guaranty. But when was it contended before that the reason given for the establishment of the right or its uninterrupted enjoyment not only limited the right itself, but restrained it to a single specific object? According to this construction, the right itself is not only abridged, but literally destroyed; and the security of the free State is made to depend exclusively and alone upon the force of the militia. . . . According to the rule laid down in [the concurrence's] interpretation of this clause, I deem the right to be valueless and not worth preserving, for the State unquestionably possesses the power, without the grant, to arm the militia and direct how they shall be employed in cases of invasion or domestic insurrection. . . . [W]hy give that which is no right in itself and guarantees a privilege that is useless?

Id. at 35 (Lacy, J., dissenting).

Justice Lacy also criticized Justice Dickinson's argument that, since governments were instituted to protect individuals, it was inappropriate to place limits on government control of arms and their use. In Lacy's view, government actors themselves might be a threat to individual rights: "To suppose that public liberty cannot be in danger, except from a foreign foe or internal disorder, is virtually to deny the importance and necessity of written constitutions. If there was no fear of our own rulers, why impose restraints on them . . . ?" *Id.* at 43. He concluded by adopting a broad interpretation of the right to arms similar to the Kentucky court in *Bliss*. The Second Amendment protected a natural right of the individual "to carry his own private arms about his person, in any manner that he may think proper for his security or safety," whether openly or concealed. *Id.* at 43.

4. The Use of Antebellum State Court Decisions to Interpret the Second Amendment

The opinions in this chapter cast long shadows. The United States Supreme Court cited *Aymette v. State* more prominently than any other case in its brief Second Amendment opinion in *United States v. Miller* (Chapter 7). Indeed, some of *Miller*'s analysis appeared to follow *Aymette*'s civilized warfare test. The Supreme Court concluded that the defendant's possession of an unregistered sawed-off shotgun was not protected by the Second Amendment, no evidence had been presented "that this weapon is any part of the ordinary military equipment, or that its use could contribute to the common defense." *Id.* at 178.

Decades later, however, in *Heller* (Chapter 9), a majority of the Supreme Court rejected *Aymette* as a guide to the Second Amendment:

> *Aymette* . . . recognized that both the state right and the federal right were descendants of the 1689 English right, but (erroneously, and contrary to virtually all other authorities) read that right to refer only to "protect[ion of] the public liberty" and "keep[ing] in awe those in power." . . . [It] then adopted a sort of middle position, whereby citizens were permitted to carry arms openly, unconnected with any service in a formal militia, but were given the right to use them only for the military purpose of banding together to oppose tyranny. This odd reading of the right is . . . not the one we adopt. . . .

Heller, 554 U.S. at 613. Instead, the *Heller* Court drew on the *Reid-Nunn-Chandler* line of cases to interpret the Second Amendment, and concluded that the Second Amendment protects a personal right to keep and bear arms for self-defense. The five-Justice majority quoted at length *Nunn v. State*'s emphatic description of the Second Amendment as protecting:

> [t]he right of the whole people, old and young, men, women and boys, and not militia only, to keep and bear *arms* of every description, and not *such* merely as are used by the *militia*, [which] shall not be *infringed*, curtailed, or broken in upon, in the smallest degree; and all this for the important end to be attained: the rearing up and qualifying a well-regulated militia, so vitally necessary to the security of a free State. Our opinion is, that any law, State or Federal, is repugnant to the Constitution, and void, which contravenes this *right*, originally belonging to our forefathers, trampled under foot by Charles I. and his two wicked sons and successors, re-established by the revolution of 1688, conveyed to this land of liberty by the colonists, and finally incorporated conspicuously in our own Magna Charta!

Id. at 612-13, (quoting *Nunn, supra*). *Heller* declared that the Georgia Supreme Court had "perfectly captured the way in which the operative clause of the Second Amendment furthers the purpose announced in the prefatory clause, in continuity with the English right [to arms]." *Id.*

Finally, *Buzzard* too had some important, if distant, relatives. Although the opinion was only occasionally cited outside Arkansas, the collective right vision of the Second Amendment that first saw light in Justice Dickinson's *Buzzard* concurrence was embraced by many lower federal courts in the twentieth century, albeit never with a citation to *Buzzard. See* Chapter 8.

NOTES & QUESTIONS

1. How relevant are these early nineteenth-century state court decisions to interpreting and applying the Second Amendment today? Which early cases are the most instructive? For example, does the fact that the Second Amendment includes language about the importance of "a well-regulated militia" suggest that the Amendment pertains only to civic purposes such as deterring tyranny through a strong militia, like the right recognized in *Aymette*? If you think so, do you also agree with *Aymette* that the right to "keep arms" is a separate right that has a broader scope than the right to "bear arms"?

2. During the drafting of the federal Bill of Rights in 1791, a proposal was made to add four words to the text of (what would become) the Second Amendment so that it would refer to "the right of the people to keep and bear arms *for the common defence*" — the same language as the state constitutional provisions at issue in *Aymette* and *Buzzard.* However, this proposal was rejected by Congress, and the Second Amendment was ratified without including the "common defence" language. Is this drafting history relevant to interpreting the Amendment? What about the rejection of clause three of James Madison's original draft of the Second Amendment: "The right of the people to keep and bear arms shall not be infringed; a well armed and well regulated militia being the best security of a free country; but no person religiously scrupulous of bearing arms shall be compelled to render military service in person"? What about the rejection of Senator Roger Sherman's proposal for a separate amendment authorizing states to provide for arming the militia if the federal government failed to do so — a power that some persons have said is the sole legal effect of the Second Amendment, and that others have said is among the legal effects?

C. Weapons Control and Southern Culture

The early judicial decisions interpreting the right to arms issued mainly from Southern state courts because the legislatures in those states enacted the first significant gun-control laws in the United States. Why were the gun control laws of this period concentrated in the South? Evidence suggests that violence, both armed and unarmed, was especially frequent in the antebellum South. In one Virginia county in the first decade of the nineteenth century, indictments for violent crimes outnumbered those for property crimes by a factor of five. Edward M. Steel, *Criminality in Jeffersonian America — A Sample*, 18 Crime & Delinq. 154 (1972). Travelers often remarked upon the violence of the region and its inhabitants.

Scottish traveler Thomas Cather, who visited the American South and West in 1836, reported that "[e]veryone goes armed with dagger, Bo[wie] knife, or pistols, and sometimes with all three, and in a society where the passions are so little under control it is not to be wondered . . . that murderous affrays should so often take place in the streets." Thomas Cather, Voyage to America: The Journals of Thomas Cather 143-44 (1973). Alexis de Tocqueville, the famous French observer of American democracy, found in his travels through the backcountry regions that "[t]he inhabitants of Kentucky and Tennessee are well known throughout the Union for their violent habits; . . . they say that quarrels often lead to bloodshed, and that elections seldom pass off without knife-blows given and received." Likewise, in Alabama, a local lawyer assured de Tocqueville that there was "no one here but carries arms under his clothes. At the slightest quarrel, knife or pistol comes to hand." Alexis de Tocqueville, Journey to America 103, 284 (1981). The practice of dueling in order to redress an insult was a more formal expression of a similar impulse, and "though confined to a segment of the upper classes, dueling served essentially the same purpose as the lowliest eye-gouging battle among Tennessee hog-drivers" — namely to affirm and defend one's standing and social position. Bertram Wyatt-Brown, Honor and Violence in the Old South 142 (1986).

Southern culture was ambivalent about the issue. On one hand, personal violence was recognized as a serious social problem. Many contemporary sources echoed the Georgia legislature's concern about "the unwarrantable and too prevalent use of *deadly weapons*." *See* Cramer, *supra*, at 111-12, 120-22 (reproducing editorials from Alabama and Tennessee newspapers in the 1830s deploring violence, especially when committed with concealed weapons). On the other hand, both judges and juries embraced the norms of an honor culture that excused some of this violence. Jurors were reluctant to convict defendants who were embroiled in violent quarrels. And while indictments for violent crimes often outnumbered property crimes such as theft, the penalties inflicted for property crimes were typically more severe. Edward L. Ayers, Vengeance and Justice: Crime and Punishment in the Nineteenth-Century American South 17-18, 74-75, 111 (1984).

Historians identify several possible causes of violence in the early South, while disagreeing about their relative importance. The popularity of cheap distilled liquor increased drunkenness and disinhibitted violence. The South's traditional culture of honor (in which an individual cannot maintain his place in society if he lets a public insult pass unchallenged) is another frequently identified cause. Southerners of all classes placed value upon resisting with violence, insult or injury. Wyatt-Brown, *supra*, at 142-53. Another theory was that slavery, which because of gradual Northern abolition became an exclusively Southern institution, degraded the character of both the master and the slave. A slaveholder himself, Thomas Jefferson wrote that "the whole commerce between master and slave is a perpetual exercise of the most boisterous passions, the most unremitting despotism on the one part, and degrading submissions on the other." Jefferson was convinced that such a master, "nursed, educated, and daily exercised in tyranny," would naturally "be stamped by it with odious peculiarities." Thomas Jefferson, Notes on the State of Virginia, Query XVIII (1781).

Other scholars point out that much of the poorer land in the South (e.g., Appalachia, the South Carolina back country) was settled by Scots-Irish immigrants—a group of poor whites from war-torn northern border regions in the United Kingdom. People from this culture had a well developed reputation for fighting long before they crossed the Atlantic. *See* David Hackett Fischer, Albion's Seed: Four British Folkways in America 650-51, 769-71 (1989) Even today, Southern states tend to have higher rates of homicide and other violent crime than most other states. *See* Crime Rates by State, 2006 and 2007, and by Type, 2007, U.S. Census Bureau, 2010 Statistical Abstract, table 297, *available at* http://www.census.gov/compendia/statab/2010/tables/10s0297.pdf.

Do you think there is a connection between Southern culture and the development of the right to arms in the nineteenth century?

D.   The Right to Arms and Slavery

Nunn, supra, was decided by the Georgia Supreme Court, which one commentator describes as an "emphatically proslavery" court during the 1840s and 1850s. Akhil Reed Amar, *The Bill of Rights and the Fourteenth Amendment,* 101 Yale L.J. 1193, 1217 n.112 (1992). The same court that recognized the right to arms and applied it to state laws in *Nunn* (and later held that slaves were entitled to the Fifth Amendment's constitutional protection against double jeopardy, see *State ex rel. Tucker v. Lavinia,* 25 Ga. 311 (1858)) also conferred extensive legal protection on the institution of slavery.

From the earliest days of the republic, popular and legal conceptions of the right to arms and the role of the militia intersected with the problems of slavery and racial division, particularly in the South. One traditional role of armed whites in the Southern states was to prevent and suppress slave insurrections. *See* Carl T. Bogus, *The Hidden History of the Second Amendment,* 31 U.C. Davis L. Rev. 309, 331-37 (1998). In the mid-eighteenth century, Georgia and the Carolinas developed organized slave patrols of able-bodied white men, who played an important role in maintaining slavery.

In the debates surrounding the ratification of the Constitution, Anti-Federalist delegates repeatedly expressed the fear that the new Constitution gave Congress too much control over the militia. They worried that Congress could disarm the militia or destroy it through neglect. Some of these objections appeared to reflect Southern concern about the militia's importance in controlling slaves. At Virginia's ratifying convention, Patrick Henry, an opponent of ratification, argued that the provision in the proposed Constitution denying the states the authority to "engage in war, unless actually invaded," U.S. Const., art. I, §10, cl. 3, would entail that the Southern states could not use their militia to suppress slave revolts. "If there should happen an insurrection of slaves, the country cannot be said to be invaded. [The states] cannot, therefore, suppress it without the interposition of Congress. . . . Congress, and Congress only, can call forth the militia." 3 Debates of the Several State Conventions, on the Adoption of the Federal Constitution 42 (Jonathan Elliot ed., 2d ed. 1836). Emphasizing these references, some scholars have argued that a major purpose of the adoption of the Second Amendment, with its reference to the importance of a "well-regulated militia," was to reassure the Southern states that Congress would not interfere with an institution central to maintaining the slave system. *See* Bogus, *supra*, at 369. However, both Northern and Southern delegates also expressed concern that federal control would undermine the militia's role in deterring or resisting federal government tyranny.

The second federal Militia Act adopted in 1792 contained an express racial exclusion, defining the militia of the United States as comprising all "free able-bodied white male citizen[s]" from the ages of 18 to 44. Some Southern states restricted the right of not only of slaves but also of free Blacks to keep and bear arms, and these restrictions tended to grow more stringent as the century passed. They rested upon white fears that armed Blacks, especially freemen, were likely to conspire and ultimately to plan insurrection. *See* Robert J. Cottrol & Raymond T. Diamond, *The Second Amendment: Toward an Afro-Americanist Reconsideration*, 80 Geo. L.J. 309 (1991).

Recall the Georgia Supreme Court's opinion in *Nunn, supra*, which held that the Second Amendment protected a "right of the whole people, old and young, men, women and boys, . . . to keep and bear arms of every description," and invalidated part of Georgia's 1837 statute banning most handguns and prohibiting the carrying of weapons. This decision did not affect another gun control statute that had been enacted less than two years after Nat Turner's 1831 slave revolt. Georgia's 1833 gun control statute prohibited "any free person of colour in this state, to own, use, or carry fire arms of any description whatever." Act of Dec. 23, 1833, sec. 7, 1833 Ga. Laws 226, 228. No evidence suggests that *Nunn*'s broad affirmation of a right to arms for "the whole people," including women and boys, was thought to include Blacks. The 1833 law disarming Blacks was contemporaneous with three new or revised racially restrictive right to arms provisions (limited to "free white men" only) that were adopted in Southern state constitutions in the aftermath of Turner's Rebellion. *See* Tenn. Const. of 1834, art. I, §26; Ark. Const. of 1836, art. II, §21; Fla. Const. of 1838, art. I, §21.

The prospect of a meaningful right to arms for Blacks was so unsettling to many that the United States Supreme Court invoked this possibility in its notorious opinion in the *Dred Scott* case. The claim was part of a parade of horribles that would result if black Americans were deemed to be citizens. Slaves, and their free descendants, could not be part of "the People" protected by the Constitution, Chief Justice Roger Taney argued, because then they would have the rights of Article IV, Section 2: "The Citizens of each State shall be entitled to all Privileges and Immunities of Citizens in the several States." This

> would give to persons of the negro race . . . the right to enter every other State whenever they pleased . . . the full liberty of speech in public and in private upon all subjects upon which [a state's] own citizens might speak; to hold public meetings upon political affairs, and to keep and carry arms wherever they went.

Dred Scott v. Sandford, 60 U.S. (19 How.) 393, 417 (1856). For Second Amendment purposes, *Dred Scott* is also notable for its statement that Congress's power to regulate the federal territories did not authorize it to "deny to the people the right to keep and bear arms" or other constitutional rights. *Id.* at 450.

Ironically, Northern abolitionists made similar arguments about the connection between the right to arms and political status, but used them to support diametrically opposed conclusions. *Because* the Constitution guaranteed all persons the right to keep and bear arms, they argued, it thereby implicitly forbade slavery: The condition of servitude and the condition of being entitled to keep and bear arms for personal self-defense were logically incompatible. Joel Tiffany, A Treatise on the Unconstitutionality of American Slavery 117-18 (1849); Lysander Spooner, The Unconstitutionality of Slavery 98 (Burt Franklin 1965) (1860).

Abolitionist constitutionalism started off as a fringe theory, but over time, it won important adherents, including Frederick Douglass. While the more cautious of the abolitionists argued that slavery was unconstitutional in federal territories, the bolder argument claimed that slavery was unconstitutional everywhere. A core of the argument, wherever applied, was that slavery violated the Fifth Amendment's prohibition on the deprivation of liberty without due process of law. Abolitionist constitutional theory eventually became the mainstream legal theory of the Republican Party. Its most prestigious advocate, Salmon P. Chase (Governor of Ohio, U.S. Senator, Secretary of the Treasury) was appointed Chief Justice of the Supreme Court by President Abraham Lincoln in 1864. With the Thirteenth, Fourteenth, and Fifteenth Amendments in 1865-70, the triumph of abolitionist constitutionalism appeared complete. *See* Randy E. Barnett, *Whence Comes Section One? The Abolitionist Origins of the Fourteenth Amendment,* 3 J. Legal Analysis (2011).

The next case conveys a sense of the many legal disabilities imposed upon free Blacks in the South before the ratification of the Fourteenth Amendment (Chapter 6).

State v. Newsom
27 N.C. (5 Ired.) 250 (1844)

[An 1840 North Carolina statute made it a misdemeanor for any "free negro, mulatto, or free person of color" to "wear or carry about his or her person, or keep in his or her house, any shot gun, musket, rifle, pistol, sword, dagger or bowie-knife," unless he or she had previously obtained a license from the local county Court of Pleas. The license was issued at the discretion of the court, and had to be renewed every year. Elijah Newsom, a "free person of color," was convicted by a jury for carrying a shotgun without the required license. Newsom challenged the licensing statute as unconstitutional; the trial court agreed and set aside the jury's verdict. The state appealed.]

NASH, J.

We are of opinion there was error in the judgment pronounced by the presiding Judge. . . . It has been urged, that the act of 1840, under which the defendant was prosecuted, is unconstitutional, being in violation of the 2d article of the amended Constitution of the United States, and also of the 3d and 17th articles of the Bill of Rights of this State.[7] We do not agree to the correctness of either of these objections.

The Constitution of the United States was ordained and established by the people of the United States, for their own government, and not for that of the different States. The limitations of power, contained in it and expressed in general terms, are necessarily confined to the General Government. It is now the settled construction of that instrument, that no limitation upon the power of government extends to, or embraces the different States, unless they are mentioned, or it is expressed to be so intended. *Barro[n] v. The Mayor, &c. of Baltimore, 7 Peter's Rep. 240.* ... In the 2d article of the amended Constitution, the States are neither mentioned nor referred to. It is therefore only restrictive of the powers of the Federal Government.

Nor do we perceive that the act of 1840 is in violation of either of the articles of our Bill of Rights, which have been referred to. The 3d article forbids the granting of exclusive privileges or separate emoluments, but in consideration of public services. ... The act of 1840 imposes upon free men of color, a restriction in the carrying of fire arms, from which the white men of the country are exempt. Is this a violation of the 3d article in spirit, or is it such a palpable violation as will authorize the court to declare it void? If so, then is the whole of our legislation upon the subject of free negroes void. From the earliest period of our history, free people of color have been among us, as a separate and distinct class, requiring, from necessity, in many cases, separate and distinct legislation.

The relation of master and servant, of free and bond, of white and colored, excluded the idea that the latter ought or could be safely admitted to testify against the former. Accordingly, in the year 1762 an act was passed, which excludes all colored persons within the fourth degree [i.e., with at least one-sixteenth nonwhite ancestry] from being heard as witnesses against a white man. And in 1777 it is, in almost so many words, re-enacted, and still remains upon our statute book unrepealed. This was the code at the time our Constitution was formed, and the statute of 1777 was framed by many of the men, who aided in forming the Constitution. From the time of the first enactment to the present, innumerable cases have been tried in our various courts, in which white persons and colored have been parties litigant ... and yet, in no instance, has the constitutionality of the act of 1777 been questioned. It is admitted that, if the act of 1840 does violate the spirit and meaning of the 3d article, it cannot be sustained because the Legislature have passed other acts equally infringing it; but it is

---

7. [Article 3 of the North Carolina Bill of Rights stated:

[N]o men, or set of men, are entitled to exclusive or separate emoluments or privileges from the community, but [i.e., except] in consideration of public services.

N.C. Const. of 1776, Decl. of Rights, §3. The right to arms provision, Article 17, stated:

[T]he people have a right to bear arms, for the defense of the State; and as standing armies, in time of peace, are dangerous to liberty, they ought not to be kept up; and ... the military should be kept under strict subordination to, and governed by, the civil power.

Id. §17. — Eds.]

believed that the long acquiescence under the act of 1777 by all classes of society — legislative, judicial, and private — has given an exposition to the 3d article of the Bill of Rights, which is obligatory on the courts.

In the year 1831, the Legislature passed an act, providing, that when a free person of color was convicted by due course of law of a misdemeanor, and was unable to pay the fine imposed on him, the Court should direct the sheriff to hire him out at public auction, to any person who would pay the fine for his services for the shortest space of time. Manuel was a free man of color, and, being convicted of an assault and battery, and unable to pay his fine, was ordered by the court to be hired out. The case [*State v. Manuel,* 20 N.C. (4 Dev. & Bat.) 20 (1838),] was brought here by appeal, and was felt to be one of great importance in principle. . . . The act of 1831, it was urged, was unconstitutional, as violating, among others, this 3d article of the Bill of Rights. The court decided, that it did not conflict with that article; yet it cannot be denied, that it introduced a different mode of punishment, in the case of a colored man and a white man for the same offence. If the law in that case, in which one class of citizens is condemned to lose their liberty, by being hired out as slaves, while another class is exempt from that ignominious mode of punishment, and subjected to one much less revolting to the feelings of a freeman, is not a violation of the 3d article under consideration, much less can the act of 1840 be so. . . .

The act of 1840 is one of police regulation. It does not deprive the free man of color of the right to carry arms about his person, but subjects it to the control of the County Court, giving them the power to say, in the exercise of a sound discretion, who, of this class of persons, shall have a right to the license, or whether any shall.

This brings us to the consideration of the 17th article of the Bill of Rights. We cannot see that the act of 1840 is in conflict with it. That article declares "that the people have a right to bear arms for the defence of the State." The defendant is not indicted for carrying arms in defence of the State, nor does the act of 1840 prohibit him from so doing. Its only object is to preserve the peace and safety of the community from being disturbed by an indiscriminate use, on ordinary occasions, by free men of color, of fire arms or other arms of an offensive character. Self preservation is the first law of nations, as it is of individuals. And, while we acknowledge the solemn obligations to obey the Constitution, as well in spirit as in letter, we at the same time hold, that nothing should be interpolated into that instrument, which the people did not will. We are not at liberty to give an artificial and constrained interpretation to the language used, beyond its ordinary, popular and obvious meaning.

Before, and at the time our Constitution was framed, there was among us this class of people, and they were subjected to various disabilities, from which the white population was exempt. It is impossible to suppose, that the framers of the Bill of Rights did not have an eye to the existing state of things, and did not act with a full knowledge of the mixed population, for whom they were legislating. They must have felt the absolute necessity of the existence of a power somewhere, to adopt such rules and regulations, as the safety of the community might, from time to time, require. . . . As a further illustration of the will of the people, as to the light in which free people of color are to be considered as citizens, the present Constitution of the State entirely excludes them from the exercise of the elective franchise.[8] Nor does the new constitution, in any of its provisions, overrule or contravene the preceding legislation on the subject we are considering.

We *must*, therefore, regard it as a principle, settled by the highest authority, the organic law of the country, that the free people of color cannot be considered as citizens, in the largest sense of the term, or, if they are, they occupy such a position in society, as justifies the Legislature in adopting a course of policy in its acts peculiar to them; so that they do not violate those great principles of justice, which ought to lie at the foundation of all laws.

Upon full consideration of all the objections, urged by the prisoner's counsel, we do not find such clear repugnancy between the constitution and the act of 1840, as to warrant us in declaring that act unconstitutional and void. We are therefore of opinion, there was error in rendering judgment against the State.

Ordered accordingly.

NOTES & QUESTIONS

1. Did the outcome in *Newsom* depend on the defendant's race? Did the court suggest that the requirement for an annual license could not constitutionally be applied to the white population?

2. *Discretionary licensing. Newsom* states that the gun licensing law for Blacks did not "deprive the free man of color of the right to carry arms about his person," but merely "subject[ed] it to the control of the County Court," which, apparently, was free to use its discretion to conclude that no nonwhite persons ought to be issued gun licenses. Is this a meaningful "right to carry arms"? Is it sometimes appropriate to allow local officials to decide on a case-by-case basis who should own or carry guns? What if all citizens, without regard to race, were subject to the same discretionary requirement? A few states, such as Massachusetts, give local officials, such as town police chiefs or county sheriffs, great discretion to decide who may possess firearms. Eight states (California, Delaware, Hawaii, Maryland, Massachusetts, New Jersey, New York, and Rhode Island) give similar officials very broad discretion in deciding who may obtain a permit to carry a handgun in public. Because of *Heller* (Chapter 9) and *McDonald* (Chapter 9), many of these "may issue" permit laws are currently being challenged in court on the ground that they are allegedly inconsistent with the Second and Fourteenth Amendments. Under what circumstances is it appropriate to give law enforcement officials discretion about who may exercise a constitutional right? What kind of guidelines about the use of discretion might make the discretion constitutionally legitimate?

---

8. [An 1835 constitutional convention had extensively amended the North Carolina Constitution, especially with respect to voting. One set of amendments lowered the property requirements for free whites to vote, but also abolished the right of nonwhites to vote. — Eds.]

3. *Using historical practice to interpret constitutional language.* According to *Newsom*, North Carolina's long history of laws treating blacks differently from whites showed that the state constitution's ban on creating "separate privileges" for any "set of men" did not prohibit laws that discriminated on the basis of race. Are such arguments ever valid? Should long historical practice be able to outweigh the apparent meaning of constitutional text? In what circumstances?

Robert J. Cottrol & Raymond T. Diamond, "Never Intended to Be Applied to the White Population": Firearms Regulation and Racial Disparity — The Redeemed South's Legacy to a National Jurisprudence?
70 Chi.-Kent L. Rev. 1307, 1318-23 (1995)

... C. JUDICIAL INTERPRETATION IN A REGION AT ARMS

It was in the South as a region that state courts first began the effort to reconcile the right to arms with restrictions designed to promote public safety. This effort began the still largely unrealized project of transforming the notion of a right to arms from an object of Whiggish political theory to a matter of workable jurisprudence. In many ways it was natural that the South would play this pioneering role. If guns and a right to arms have been a peculiar part of American culture, they have been perhaps even more distinctively a part of the lawways and folkways of the South. Almost from the beginning, the unique need to maintain white domination in the nation's first truly multi-racial society led the South to a greater vigor with respect to the private possession of arms and to the universal deputization of the white population as a means of insuring racial control. This pattern would begin long before the American [R]evolution and the subsequent adoption of the Second Amendment.

And it would continue and be strengthened well into the nineteenth century. After the War of 1812, at a time when national commentators came to decry the decreased willingness of the population as a whole to participate in militia training and to fear that neglect might erode either the right to arms or the effectiveness of private arms in resisting potential tyranny, the practice of widespread active militia participation would remain a vigorous part of Southern culture.

Southern culture would also come to sanction the use of arms in contexts that went far beyond either personal or communal defense. For white men, the use of arms to resolve personal disputes and the frequent preference for dueling instead of use of the courts to redress insults and other slights, real or perceived, helped lend a different flavor to the Southern experience with arms — a flavor that was remarkable even in a nation distinguished by widespread firearms ownership and use.

It was in this Southern atmosphere that in so many ways encouraged the use of arms, that legislative bodies first came to consider, on a widespread level, limits on the right to arms. The first set of limits were widespread throughout the South and generally agreed upon, that Blacks whether slave or free would have severely limited access to firearms. ... But it was the attempt of some

Southern legislatures to regulate the behavior of whites, to set limits on the manner in which white people could carry arms, that brought about controversy and an attempt to develop a jurisprudence that balanced the right to arms with legislation done in the interest of public safety. . . . [The authors then discuss three judicial decisions that "bear enduring significance" for today's gun rights debate: *Aymette v. State, Nunn v. State*, and *Bliss v. Commonwealth*, describing the last case as representing "the road not taken."]

The evidence from the antebellum era complicates our efforts to determine the motives of those who passed restrictive firearms legislation later in the century. The antebellum South was a society with a robust tradition of bearing arms, calling on the citizen to maintain social order and a tolerance for extra-legal violence. Southern constitutional law recognized the importance of the right to bear arms with perhaps even greater vigor than the nation as a whole. At the same time even, in the antebellum era, Southern legislators and jurists began to recognize the desirability of placing limits, and given the cultural milieu, we are forced to wonder whether these were more honored in the breach than by the observance of that right. The mixed legal and cultural legacy of the antebellum South suggests no easy answers in determining motive in the decades that would follow.

NOTES & QUESTIONS

1. Are antebellum Southern sources on constitutional rights irredeemably tainted by the legacy of slavery? Or do they point the way to a broadening of their concept of liberty, originally for free whites only, to a multiracial polity?

E.   Antebellum Legal Commentary on the Right to Arms[9]

Several early American constitutional commentators discussed the Second Amendment. St. George Tucker, whose 1792 lecture notes from William & Mary were the foundation for his 1803 American version of Blackstone, is discussed in Chapter 4. For a generation, Tucker's Blackstone was the leading treatise on American law, including constitutional law.

1.   William Rawle

The next major American constitutional treatise after Tucker's *Blackstone* was William Rawle's 1825 *A View of the Constitution of the United States of America*.

Rawle, a prominent Pennsylvania attorney, declined President George Washington's offer to become the first Attorney General of the United States,

---

9. Much of the discussion of the commentators that follow is adapted from Kopel, *supra.*

but did serve as United States Attorney from 1792 to 1800. His treatise described the Second Amendment at length, beginning with a praise of the *well-regulated* militia:

> The Bill of Rights declares, that a well regulated militia is necessary to the security of a free state, a proposition from which few will dissent. Although in actual war the services of regular troops are confessedly more valuable, yet while peace prevails, and in the commencement of a war before a regular force can be raised, the militia form the palladium of the country. They are ready to repel invasion, to suppress insurrection, and preserve the good order and peace of government. That they should be well regulated, is judiciously added. A disorderly militia is disgraceful to itself, and dangerous not to the enemy, but to its own country. The duty of the state government is, to adopt such regulations as will tend to make good soldiers with the least interruptions of the ordinary and useful occupations of civil life. In this all the Union has a strong and visible interest.
>
> The corollary, from the first position, is, that the right of the people to keep and bear arms shall not be infringed.
>
> The prohibition is general. No clause in the Constitution could by any rule of construction be conceived to give to congress a power to disarm the people. Such a flagitious attempt could only be made under some general pretence by a state legislature. But if by any blind pursuit of inordinate power, either should attempt it, this amendment may be appealed to as a restraint on both.
>
> In most of the countries of Europe, this right does not seem to be denied, although it is allowed more or less sparingly, according to circumstances. In England, a country which boasts so much of its freedom, the right was secured to protestant subjects only, on the revolution of 1688; and it is cautiously described to be that of bearing arms for their defence "suitable to their conditions, and as allowed by law." . . . An arbitrary code for the preservation of game in that country has long disgraced them. A very small proportion of the people being permitted to kill it, though for their own subsistence, a gun or other instrument, used for that purpose by an unqualified person, may be seized or forfeited. Blackstone, in whom we regret that we cannot always trace the expanded principles of rational liberty, observes however, on this subject, that the prevention of popular insurrections and resistance to government by disarming the people, is oftener meant than avowed by makers of forest and game laws.

William Rawle, A View of the Constitution of the United States of America 121-23 (1825). Rawle also recognized limitations on the right:

> This right ought not, however, in any government, to be abused to the disturbance of the public peace.
>
> An assemblage of persons with arms, for an unlawful purpose, is an indictable offense, and even the carrying of arms abroad by an individual, attended with circumstances giving just reason to fear that he purposes to make an unlawful use of them, would be sufficient cause to require him to give surety of the peace.

Id. at 126.

2.   Joseph Story

The next major American constitutional treatise was the 1833 *Commentaries on the Constitution of the United States*, written by Supreme Court Justice Joseph Story, who taught at Harvard Law School while serving on the Court. Story, a native of Massachusetts, was perhaps the dominant legal figure of pre–Civil War America.

> No man ever was more steeped in the law, intellectually and interpersonally. Professional study, the common element for bench and bar, attained new levels with Story. He wrote nine important treatises, and taught at — virtually created — the Harvard Law School. . . .

Robert Cover, Justice Accused: Antislavery and the Judicial Process 238 (1975). President James Madison appointed Joseph Story to the Supreme Court in 1811; at age 32, he was the youngest man ever nominated. He served on the United States Supreme Court until 1845, the year of his death.

In 1840, Story published an expanded version of his *Commentaries*, as well as a popularized version of the work, entitled *Familiar Exposition of the Constitution of the United States*. Story's constitutional treatises differed in important ways from their predecessors; he was far more enthusiastic about broad federal powers than Rawle or Tucker had been. Indeed, Rawle had argued for the authority of states to secede from the Union. But Story almost single-handedly created the doctrine of an indissoluble Union, a doctrine that would carry the day intellectually in the North. Some of Story's treatises were still in use in the twentieth century.

Story's *Commentaries* discussed the Second Amendment primarily as a guarantee of free government:

> §1890. . . . The right of the citizens to keep and bear arms has justly been considered as the palladium of the liberties of a republic [in a footnote, Story cited Tucker's *Blackstone*]; since it offers a strong moral check against the usurpation and arbitrary power of rulers; and will generally, even if these are successful in the first instance, enable the people to resist and triumph over them [citing Tucker and Rawle]. And yet, though this truth would seem so clear, and the importance of a well regulated militia would seem so undeniable, it cannot be disguised that, among the American people, there is a growing indifference to any system of militia discipline, and a strong disposition, from a sense of its burdens, to be rid of all regulations. How it is practicable to keep the people duly armed, without some organization, it is difficult to see. There is certainly no small danger that indifference may lead to disgust, and disgust to contempt; and thus gradually undermine all the protection intended by this clause of our national bill of rights.

3 Joseph Story, Commentaries on the Constitution of the United States 746-47 (1833). Story concluded by contrasting the American right to arms with the narrower one in England:

> §1891. A similar provision in favour of protestants (for to them it is confined) is to be found in the bill of rights of 1688, it being declared, "that the subjects, which are

protestants, may have arms for their defence suitable to their condition, and as allowed by law." But under various pretences the effect of this provision has been greatly narrowed; and it is at present in England more nominal than real, as a defensive privilege [citing Tucker].

Id. at 747. Here, Story tracked Madison's brief notes on the Second Amendment, in which Madison contrasted the Second Amendment with the narrower English right, the latter being unsatisfactory because it was confined to Protestants. *See* Chapter 4.

a.　*The Second Amendment in Story's* Familiar Exposition

Story's 1840 work for a popular audience, *Familiar Exposition of the Constitution of the United States,* contains some Second Amendment material not found in the *Commentaries.* The *Familiar Exposition* discusses both the militia system and the keeping of arms by the people, in connection with the Second Amendment:

§450. The next amendment is, "A well-regulated militia being necessary to the security of a free state, the right of the people to keep and bear arms shall not be infringed." One of the ordinary modes, by which tyrants accomplish their purposes without resistance, is, by disarming the people, and making it an offence to keep arms, and by substituting a regular army in the stead of a resort to the militia. The friends of a free government cannot be too watchful, to overcome the dangerous tendency of the public mind to sacrifice, for the sake of mere private convenience, this powerful check upon the designs of ambitious men.

§451. The importance of this article will scarcely be doubted by any persons, who have duly reflected upon the subject. The militia is the natural defence of a free country against sudden foreign invasions, domestic insurrections, and domestic usurpations of power by rulers. It is against sound policy for a free people to keep up large military establishments and standing armies in time of peace, both from the enormous expenses, with which they are attended, and the facile means, which they afford to ambitious and unprincipled rulers, to subvert the government, or trample upon the rights of the people. The right of the citizens to keep and bear arms has justly been considered, as the palladium of the liberties of a republic; since it offers a strong moral check against the usurpation and arbitrary power of rulers; and it will generally, even if these are successful in the first instance, enable the people to resist and triumph over them. And yet, though this truth would seem so clear, and the importance of a well-regulated militia would seem so undeniable, it cannot be disguised, that among the American people there is a growing indifference to any system of militia discipline, and a strong disposition, from a sense of its burdens, to be rid of all regulations. How it is practicable to keep the people duly armed without some organization, it is difficult to see. There is certainly no small danger, that indifference may lead to disgust, and disgust to contempt; and thus gradually undermine all the protection intended by this clause of our National Bill of Rights.

Joseph Story, A Familiar Exposition of the Constitution of the United States 264-65 (1840).

b.   Houston v. Moore

Joseph Story had one occasion to discuss the Second Amendment during his years as a Supreme Court Justice, in his dissenting opinion in *Houston v. Moore*, 18 U.S. (5 Wheat.) 1 (1820). This convoluted case arose from state and federal efforts to call up the militia during the War of 1812. In 1814, as the war dragged on, the state of Pennsylvania enacted a statute that provided that "every non-commissioned officer and private of the militia who shall have neglected or refused to serve when called into actual service" by the President should be punished according to the terms of the federal militia law of 1795. The Pennsylvania law specified that persons accused of violating the law would be tried by a state court-martial.

When Houston refused to obey a federal order calling up the Pennsylvania militia to defend Baltimore from the British Army, he was tried by a Pennsylvania court-martial and fined. He challenged the fine in court, arguing that the Constitution did not authorize a state to regulate the militia apart from the specific forms of authority enumerated in Article I's Militia Clauses. A majority of the Supreme Court rejected Houston's challenge, reasoning that, although the states could not enact their own, distinctive punishments for militia resisters, the Pennsylvania law was constitutional because it simply authorized a state court-martial to apply existing federal law.

Justice Story dissented. In his view, once the federal government enacted extensive legislation governing the militia, its authority was plenary, excluding any role for the states; thus, he would have held the state court-martial scheme invalid ("pre-empted" by federal law, in contemporary legal terminology). But what if Congress failed to enact laws governing the militia, and neglected it entirely? In that case, Story acknowledged, the states could probably act. Although neither of the parties to the case had mentioned the Second Amendment, Story discussed it in passing as possibly relevant to the issues before the Court:

> If . . . the present case turned upon the question, whether a State might organize, arm, and discipline its own militia in the absence of, or subordinate to, the regulations of Congress, I am certainly not prepared to deny the legitimacy of such an exercise of authority. It does not seem repugnant in its nature to the grant of a like paramount authority to Congress; and if not, then it is retained by the States [by the terms of the Tenth Amendment]. The [second] amendment to the constitution, declaring that "a well regulated militia being necessary to the security of a free State, the right of the people to keep and bear arms shall not be infringed," may not, perhaps, be thought to have any important bearing on this point. If it have, it confirms and illustrates, rather than impugns the reasoning already suggested.

Id. at 52-53 (Story, J., dissenting).

NOTES & QUESTIONS

1. How would you characterize the major early nineteenth-century commentators' view of the right to keep and bear arms? What purpose(s) does the

right serve? Can it be exercised individually? Does it include the keeping or carrying of weapons for personal defense?

2.   Tucker, whom you read in Chapter 4, lived his entire professional life in Virginia. Rawle hailed from a middle state, Pennsylvania. Story was a native of Massachusetts. Do you notice differences in emphasis in their respective views of the Second Amendment right? If so, is there a regional character to these differences?

3.   *Houston v. Moore* involves the boundaries between state and federal militia powers. What conclusion do you draw from the fact that neither the parties nor six out of seven Supreme Court Justices appear to have thought that the Second Amendment had anything to do with the issue? From the fact that Justice Story's dissent thought that the Second Amendment might support his view that states could exercise federal militia powers that the federal government neglected?

‖6‖

Reconstruction and Beyond

On March 3, 1865, a month before the Civil War ended, Congress acted on President Abraham Lincoln's request to establish the Bureau of Refugees, Freedmen, and Abandoned Lands—popularly called the "Freedmen's Bureau." The Bureau was given "control of all subjects relating to refugees and freedmen from rebel states." 13 Stat. 507 (1865). Originally expected to last for one year after the end of the Civil War, the Bureau remained in service until 1872. The Bureau's immediate focus was providing food, clothing, and shelter to the freedmen, and then helping former slaves become truly free.

The defeated South aimed to preserve as much of the pre-War, white-dominated social order as possible. The Emancipation Proclamation and the Thirteenth Amendment abolished chattel slavery, but many Southerners were unwilling to afford to the freedmen basic civil rights. Through the enactment of Black Codes and by private terror, the South attempted to impose a social order that amounted to *de facto* servitude. Freedmen were legally required to sign long-term contracts binding them to white employers. They were denied the right to assemble, access to courts, property and contract rights, and were prohibited from possessing firearms.

For additional reading on the material in this chapter, see Stephen Halbrook, Securing Civil Rights: Freedmen, the 14th Amendment, and the Right to Bear Arms (2010); Douglas A. Blackmon, Slavery by Another Name: The Re-Enslavement of Black Americans from the Civil War to World War II (2008); Akhil Reed Amar, The Bill of Rights: Creation and Reconstruction (1998); Clayton E. Cramer, Nicholas J. Johnson & George A. Mocsary, *"This Right Is Not Allowed by Governments That Are Afraid of the People": The Public Meaning of the Second Amendment When the Fourteenth Amendment Was Ratified,* 17 Geo. Mason L. Rev. 823 (2010); David Yassky, *The Second Amendment: Structure, History, and Constitutional Change,* 99 Mich. L. Rev. 651 (2000); David B. Kopel, *The Second Amendment in the Nineteenth Century,* 1998 B.Y.U. L. Rev. 1359 (1998); and Robert J. Cottrol & Raymond P. Diamond, *The Second Amendment: Toward an Afro-Americanist Reconsideration,* 80 Geo. L.J. 309 (1991).

A. The Initial Southern Response to Black Freedom

Two developments directly curtailed the promise of liberty for the freedmen: enactment of the Black Codes and the birth of terrorist organizations such as the Ku Klux Klan.

1. The Black Codes

One impulse for the Black Codes was Southern whites' fear of Black retribution for slavery. Rumors of Black secret societies and planned mass rebellions spread through the white Southern population. Although no actual evidence was found of Black secret societies or planned uprisings, by November 1865 panic had spread through the former Confederacy and in particular through those states with the largest Black populations. Determined to maintain white control over the freedmen, Southern legislatures enacted legislation exclusively targeted at freedmen. The Black Codes required freedmen to submit to long-term labor "contracts" with white employers; prevented them from traveling without permission; and restricted the right to assemble, to contract, to own property, and to testify in court. They also banned arms possession by Blacks, or required them to obtain permits, which were generally denied. The permit requirements did not apply to whites.

An Act Prescribing Additional Penalties for the Commission of Offenses Against the State and for Other Purposes
Laws of Fla., Dec. 18, 1865, ch. 1,466, no. 3 §12

SEC 12. . . . [I]t shall not be lawful for any negro, mulatto, or other person of color, to own, use, or keep in his possession or under his control, any bowie-knife, dirk, sword, fire-arms, or ammunition of any kind, unless he first obtain a license to do so from the judge of probate of the county in which he may be a resident for the time being; and the said judge of probate is hereby authorized to issue such license, upon the recommendation of two respectable citizens of the county, certifying to the peaceful and orderly character of the applicant; and any negro, mulatto, or other person of color, so offending, shall be deemed to be guilty of a misdemeanor, and upon conviction shall forfeit to the use of the informer all such fire-arms and ammunition, and in addition thereto, shall be sentenced to stand in the pillory for one hour, or be whipped, not exceeding thirty-nine stripes, or both, at the discretion of the jury.

An Act to Punish Certain Offences Therein Named, and for Other Purposes
1865 Miss. Laws 166 (Nov. 29, 1865)

SEC. 1. *Be it enacted,* . . . That no freedman, free negro or mulatto, not in the military service of the United States government, and not licensed so to do by the board of police of his or her county, shall keep or carry fire-arms of any kind, or any ammunition, dirk or bowie knife, and on conviction thereof in the county court shall be punished by fine, not exceeding ten dollars, and pay the costs of such proceedings, and all such arms or ammunition shall be forfeited to the informer; and it shall be the duty of every civil and military officer to arrest any freedman, free negro, or mulatto found with any such arms or ammunition, and cause him or her to be committed to trial in default of bail. . . .

SEC. 3. If any white person shall sell, lend, or give to any freedman, free negro, or mulatto any fire-arms, dirk or bowie knife, or ammunition, or any spirituous or intoxicating liquors, such person or persons so offending, upon conviction thereof in the county court of his or her county, shall be fined not exceeding fifty dollars, and may be imprisoned, at the discretion of the court, not exceeding thirty days. . . .

SEC. 5. If any freedman, free negro, or mulatto, convicted of any of the misdemeanors provided against in this act, shall fail or refuse for the space of five days, after conviction, to pay the fine and costs imposed, such person shall be hired out by the sheriff or other officer, at public outcry, to any white person who will pay said fine and all costs, and take said convict for the shortest time.

Landry Parish, Louisiana, Ordinance of 1865
Senate Exec. Doc. No. 2., *in* **1 Documentary History of Reconstruction: Political, Military, Social, Religious, Educational and Industrial, 1865 to the Present Time 280, at 93-94 (Walter L. Flemming ed., 1906) (1865)**

Sec. 5 . . . No public meetings or congregations of negroes shall be allowed within said parish after sunset; but such public meetings and congregations may be held between the hours of sunrise and sunset, by the special permission in writing of the captain of patrol, within whose beat such meetings shall take place. This prohibition, however, is not to prevent negroes from attending the usual church services, conducted by white ministers and priests. Every negro violating the provisions of this section shall pay a fine of five dollars, or in default thereof shall be compelled to work five days on the public road, or suffer corporeal punishment as hereinafter provided.

Sec. 6 . . . No negro shall be permitted to preach, exhort, or otherwise declaim to congregations of colored people, without a special permission in writing from the president of the police jury. Any negro violating the provisions of this section shall pay a fine of ten dollars, or in default shall be forced to work ten days on the public road, or suffer corporeal punishment as hereinafter provided.

Sec. 7 . . . No negro who is not in the military service shall be allowed to carry fire-arms, or any kind of weapons, within the parish, without the special written permission of his employers, approved and indorsed by the nearest and most convenient chief of patrol. Any one violating the provisions of this section shall forfeit his weapons and pay a fine of five dollars, or in default of the payment of said fine, shall be forced to work five days on the public road, or suffer corporeal punishment as hereinafter provided.

Alabama Black Code Passed in 1865
Cong. Globe, 39th Cong., 1st Sess. 1838 (April 7, 1866)

1. That it shall not be lawful for any freedman, mulatto, or free person of color in this State, to own fire-arms, or carry about his person a pistol or other deadly weapon.

2. That after the 20th day of January, 1866, any person thus offending may be arrested upon the warrant of any acting justice of the peace, and upon conviction fined any sum not exceeding $100 or imprisoned in the county jail, or put to labor on the public works of any county, incorporated town, city, or village, for any term not exceeding three months.

3. That if any gun, pistol or other deadly weapon be found in the possession of any freedman, mulatto or free person of color, the same may by any justice of the peace, sheriff, or constable be taken from such freedman, mulatto, or free person of color; and if such person is proved to be the owner thereof, the same shall, upon an order of any justice of the peace, be sold, and the proceeds thereof paid over to such freedman, mulatto, or person of color owning the same.

4. That it shall not be lawful for any person to sell, give, or lend fire-arms or ammunition of any description whatever, to any freedman, free negro or mulatto; and any person so violating the provisions of this act shall be guilty of a misdemeanor, and upon conviction thereof, shall be fined in the sum of not less than fifty nor more than one hundred dollars, at the discretion of the jury trying the case.

2. The Ku Klux Klan and Other Extralegal Suppression of Freedmen

Post-war white supremacists across the South participated in unorganized mobs, in organized terror groups such as the Ku Klux Klan, and sometimes in private militias. The Ku Klux Klan was formed in 1866 in Tennessee as an organization of white Confederate Army veterans. It soon began terrorizing Blacks who exercised their rights and also terrorized white Republicans and unionists. A variety of similar white terrorist organizations operated under names such as the Knights of the White Camellia, the Pale Faces, the White Brotherhood, and the Society of the White Rose. Often, the Klan's initial tactic was to forcibly disarm Blacks and white political opponents. This made it easier to intimidate them through subsequent threats and violence. Federal criminal prosecutions, under the May 1870 Enforcement Act (which reenacted and strengthened the Civil Rights Act of 1866) and the 1871 Force Act, eventually eroded the KKK in a formal sense. But "Klan-like activities would continue and contribute to the outcome of the federal election of 1876 that ended Reconstruction." Cottrol & Diamond, *supra*, at 351.

The Republicans who controlled Congress were disturbed by reports of the Klan and similar organizations confiscating the freedmen's firearms and perpetrating other crimes. In response, Congress enacted a series of counter-measures, some of them over the veto of President Andrew Johnson. These statutes remain the foundation of federal civil rights law today. The most important countermeasure was the Fourteenth Amendment. The countermeasures are discussed below.

Some state-sponsored militias were a separate threat to freedmen. These militias only disarmed Blacks and enforced Black Codes, but also engaged in Klan-style attacks on Blacks. Congress eventually disbanded the state militias, but not before they engaged in significant mischief. Freedmen did use fire-arms to defend themselves from private terrorists and state militias. But the militias and the Klan generally employed superior arms, tactics, and the element of surprise.

NOTES & QUESTIONS

1. Fear of Black resistance and revolt were an inherent feature of slavery in America. Walter Rucker chronicles the long history of slave resistance and the fear and reaction it sparked. Revolts by Gabriel Prosser in 1800, Denmark Vesey in 1822, and Nat Turner in 1831 are well known. But small-scale revolts and "conspiracies" date to the seventeenth century. *See, e.g.*, Walter C. Rucker, The River Flows on: Black Resistance, Culture and Identity Formation in Early America (2006) (describing the hunting-down of revolting "maroons" (mixed-race) and bans on public slave funerals out of fear that they facilitated conspiracies). One of the most ambitious efforts was John Brown's abortive 1859 uprising, with his attempt to capture firearms from the federal armory at Harper's Ferry, Virginia, and distribute them to the slaves. From the perspective of the time, were fears of an armed Black uprising plausible in 1865? In 1870 or 1875? As detailed below, Southern state governments continued to disarm Blacks into the late nineteenth century, long after federal support for reconstruction had dissolved and risk of mass Black retribution for slavery had faded. What might account for the continuing fear of armed Blacks?

2. While the Black Codes blatantly violated Black civil rights, they were only peripherally concerned with enforcing social segregation. Segregation laws were more characteristic of the late nineteenth and early twentieth centuries—the height of "Jim Crow." However, the Florida Black Codes did provide an early example of mandated segregation, prohibiting blacks and whites from entering the other groups' churches, railroad cars, or other public accommodations. 1865 Fla. Laws 23, 25. Can you see any relationship between these early segregation laws and the Black Code firearms prohibitions?

3. Granting that the federal government was unable to provide full protection against violent imposition of white supremacy (as was often the case during Reconstruction) or unwilling to do so (as was the case after the end of Reconstruction in 1877), what options were left to the freedmen and their white allies?

B.   The Congressional Response: The Fourteenth Amendment, the Freedmen's Bureau Acts, and the Civil Rights Act

By late 1865, it was clear that the former Confederate states were aiming to maintain the Slave Power in a different form. Many in the North (as well as some Southerners) decried the legal and extralegal limitations on the rights of freedmen. Among other things, the criticism focused explicitly on deprivations of the right to keep and bear arms. Philosophically, firearms were seen as a badge and incident of civil freedom. More practically, they were tools for resisting violent oppression.

In December 1865, Congress began to consider laws to ensure the rights of freedmen. From among these, three are especially important. First, the move toward a constitutional amendment "to empower Congress to pass all necessary and proper laws to secure to all persons in every State of the Union equal protection of their rights, life, liberty, and property," Cong. Globe, 39th Cong., 1st Sess. 14 (1865). Eventually, this became the Fourteenth Amendment.

Next was the Second Freedmen's Bureau Act, enacted in 1866. This continued the work of its predecessor in providing assistance to freedmen and to refugees of whatever color. In all areas under martial law, which is to say most of former Confederate States of America, the Second Freedmen's Bureau Act authorized federal "military protection and . . . jurisdiction" whenever "any of the civil rights belonging to white persons, [including] full and equal benefit of all laws and proceedings for the security of person and estate . . . are refused or denied to negroes, mulattoes, freedmen or any other persons, on account of race, color, or any previous condition of slavery or involuntary servitude." 14 Stat. 176-77 (1866)

Third was the Civil Rights Act of 1866. This was a national law, applying not just in the portions of the South subject to federal military governance. It nationally guaranteed the "full and equal benefit of all laws and proceedings for the security of person and property," and provided that individuals could vindicate their rights in federal court.

These three initiatives progressed through Congress almost simultaneously. So, much of the debate on one is often relevant to understanding the others. While the proposals were being debated, committees heard testimony from large numbers of witnesses, and read written reports, including those submitted by the Union commanders who were governing districts in the South. Congress also received petitions from people who had seen the new social order developing in the South. Witnesses gave oral and written accounts of discrimination against and mistreatment of freedmen and their sympathizers. The accounts chronicled everything from inequality under Black Codes to murders and other acts of violence against freedmen and their white allies. One such memorial presented to the Senate in January 1866 was from "the colored citizens of the State of South Carolina in convention assembled" asking "that colored men . . . should have the constitutional protection in keeping arms." Cong. Globe, 39th Cong., 1st Sess., *supra*, at 337. From that point on, throughout the discussion of the three proposals, the right to keep and bear arms was invoked frequently as one of the elementary civil rights and rights of citizenship that freedmen were entitled to enjoy to along with whites. Some opponents of the bills, apparently viewing the right to arms as a right of citizenship, asserted that some groups, including people of color, Indians, and Chinese, should not be considered full-fledged citizens and should therefore not be entitled to the right.

Some of the most ardent of the Radical Republicans contended that section 2 of the Thirteenth Amendment had granted Congress plenary power to remedy every civil disability suffered by the former slaves. But many others in Congress doubted that an amendment abolishing slavery had included the implicit congressional power to protect every civil right. Broad powers exercised under the Freedmen's Bureau Act, applicable to areas under military rule, might be justified by reference to Congress's War Powers under Article I. But no one expected federal military rule in the South to last forever. Once civil government was restored to the South, the federal military power would no longer apply. The Civil Rights Act of 1866, already in force nationally, seemed to be on tenuous constitutional footing. A crucial purpose of the Fourteenth Amendment was to give the Civil Rights Act a firm constitutional foundation.

In February 1866, the House of Representatives amended the Senate's proposed version of the Freedmen's Bureau Act, to guarantee the "full and equal benefit of all laws and proceedings for the security of person and estate *including the constitutional right to bear arms,*" *id.* at 654 (language added by amendment emphasized), and passed it with that language the following day. The Senate approved this exact language, and in a few days the final version of the bill was passed by both houses of Congress. Ten days later, President Andrew Johnson vetoed the bill claiming that it relied too heavily on military rule and infringed on the right to trial by jury because it provided for trials by military court. President Johnson stated no objection to the bill's constitutional right to bear arms provision. The next day the Senate tried but failed to override the veto.

In the meantime, the first draft of what would become the Fourteenth Amendment emerged from Joint Committee on Reconstruction. It read:

> The Congress shall have power to make all laws which shall be necessary and proper to secure to the citizens of each State all privileges and immunities of citizens in the several States; and to all persons in the several States equal protection in the rights of life, liberty, and property.

Id. at 806. In March 1866, the Second Freedmen's Bureau Act (still containing the language protecting the right to bear arms) was reintroduced in the Senate. A few days later, Congress passed the Civil Rights bill, but President Johnson vetoed it. The following month, Congress overrode the veto and the Civil Rights Act became law. Attention then focused on the Second Freedmen's Bureau Act and the proposed Fourteenth Amendment. The debates made clear that the two remaining proposals had the same objectives as the newly enacted Civil Rights Act.

In June 1866, Congress passed the proposed Fourteenth Amendment by the requisite margins, and it was transmitted to the legislatures of the 37 states. The following month, Congress passed the Second Freedmen's Bureau Act, which President Johnson again vetoed. This time, Congress overrode the veto the very day it received Johnson's veto message. The final version of the Act protected the "constitutional right to bear arms," classifying it among "immunities and rights." 14 Stat. 176-77 (1866).

The original intent of the Fourteenth Amendment has long been debated by scholars. In brief, the view that predominated in the early to mid-twentieth century (when many people argued that Reconstruction was an ignoble and corrupt oppression of the South) was that the Privileges or Immunities Clause of the Fourteenth Amendment guaranteed little more than the rights that are necessary for existence as a legal person, such as the right to form contracts, the right to own and convey property, and the right to testify in court. This view is particularly associated with legal scholars Charles Fairman and Raoul Berger. *See, e.g.*, Charles Fairman, *Does the Fourteenth Amendment Incorporate the Bill of Rights?*, 2 Stan. L. Rev. 5 (1949); Raoul Berger, Incorporation of the Bill of Rights in the Fourteenth Amendment: A Nine-Lived Cat, 42 Ohio St. L.J. 435 (1981).

The Fairman/Berger view was famously challenged by Supreme Court Justices Hugo Black and William O. Douglas, in their joint dissent in *Adamson v. California*, 332 U.S. 46, 68 (1948), which included a lengthy appendix of congressional debates on the Fourteenth Amendment. Black and Douglas argued that the Fourteenth Amendment was intended to make every one of the first eight amendments to the Constitution enforceable against the states. In recent decades, the view has become generally accepted (but not unanimously so) among legal scholars across a very broad ideological spectrum that the Privileges or Immunities Clause was intended to protect all of the first eight amendments, including a personal right to arms for self-defense. *See, e.g.*, Michael Kent Curtis, No State Shall Abridge: The Fourteenth Amendment and the Bill of Rights (1990); Richard L. Aynes, *On Misreading John Bingham and the Fourteenth Amendment*, 103 Yale L.J. 57 (1993). While most modern Fourteenth Amendment scholars agree that the Privileges or Immunities Clause was intended to protect all of the first eight amendments, including a personal right to arms for self-defense, they do not agree on whether the Privileges or Immunities Clause protects unenumerated rights, or what those unenumerated rights might be. Justice Washington's list cover a broader range than does the Fairman/Berger view.

In 1867, Congress exercised its powers of military rule over the defeated Confederacy to abolish the state militias in all ex-Confederate states except Tennessee. Congress rejected proposals to disarm the militiamen themselves, for fear of violating the Second Amendment. Racially integrated state militias were then created, and were deployed to defend the freedmen and Republican state governments. However, the Republican governors were generally reluctant to fully utilize the derided "Negro militias" for fear of sparking a race war. *See* Otis A. Singletary, Negro Militia and Reconstruction (1957).

Thirteenth Amendment
13 Stat. 567 (1865) (Proposed for Ratification by Congress)
13 Stat. 774 (1865) (Ratified by Three-fourths of the States)

Section 1. Neither slavery nor involuntary servitude, except as a punishment for crime whereof the party shall have been duly convicted, shall exist within the United States, or any place subject to their jurisdiction.

SECTION 2. Congress shall have power to enforce this article by appropriate legislation.

Civil Rights Act of 1866
14 Stat. 27 (1866)

. . . An Act to protect all Persons in the United States in their Civil Rights, and furnish the Means of their Vindication.

Be it enacted by the Senate and House of Representatives of the United States of America in Congress assembled, That all persons born in the United States and not subject to any foreign power, excluding Indians not taxed, are hereby declared to be citizens of the United States; and such citizens, of every race and color, without regard to any previous condition of slavery or involuntary servitude, except as a punishment for crime whereof the party shall have been duly convicted, shall have the same right, in every State and Territory in the United States, to make and enforce contracts, to sue, be parties, and give evidence, to inherit, purchase, lease, sell, hold, and convey real and personal property, and to full and equal benefit of all laws and proceedings for the security of person and property, as is enjoyed by white citizens, and shall be subject to like punishment, pains, and penalties, and to none other, any law, statute, ordinance, regulation, or custom, to the contrary notwithstanding.

SEC. 2. . . . That any person who, under color of any law, statute, ordinance, regulation, or custom, shall subject, or cause to be subjected, any inhabitant of any State or Territory to the deprivation of any right secured or protected by this act, or to different punishment, pains, or penalties on account of such person having at any time been held in a condition of slavery or involuntary servitude, except as a punishment for crime whereof the party shall have been duly convicted, or by reason of his color or race, than is prescribed for the punishment of white persons, shall be deemed guilty of a misdemeanor, and, on conviction, shall be punished by fine not exceeding one thousand dollars, or imprisonment not exceeding one year, or both, in the discretion of the court.

SEC. 3. [Federal courts have jurisdiction to hear suits brought under this Act.]

SEC. 4. [Federal prosecutors and police officials are empowered to prosecute and make arrests for violations of this Act.]

SEC. 5. [Federal police officials are required to enforce warrants issued under this Act under penalty of fine payable to the victim of the civil rights violation.]

SEC. 6. [Anyone interfering with the enforcement of this Act is subject to fine and imprisonment.]

SEC. 9. *And be it further enacted,* that it shall be lawful for the President of the United States, or such person as he may empower for that purpose, to employ such part of the land or naval forces of the United States, or of the militia, as shall be necessary to prevent the violation and enforce the due execution of this act. . . .

Second Freedmen's Bureau Act
14 Stat. 173 (1866)

. . . *An Act to continue in force and to amend "An Act to establish a Bureau for the Relief of Freedmen and Refugees," and for other Purposes.*

Be it enacted by the Senate and House of Representatives of the United States of America in Congress assembled, That the act to establish a bureau for the relief of freedmen and refugees, approved March third, eighteen hundred and sixty-five, shall continue in force for the term of two years from and after the passage of this act.

Sec. 2. . . . That the supervision and care of said bureau shall extend to all loyal refugees and freedmen, so far as the same shall be necessary to enable them as speedily as practicable to become self-supporting citizens of the United States, and to aid them in making the freedom conferred by proclamation of the commander-in-chief, by emancipation under the laws of States, and by constitutional amendment, available to them and beneficial to the republic.

Sec. 3. . . . Military officers or enlisted men may be detailed for service and assigned to duty under this act; and the President may, if in his judgment safe and judicious so to do, detail from the army all the officers and agents of this bureau. . . . And all persons appointed to service under this act and the act to which this is an amendment, shall be so far deemed in the military service of the United States as to be under the military jurisdiction, and entitled to the military protection of the government while in discharge of the duties of their office. . . .

Sec. 14. . . . That in every State or district where the ordinary course of judicial proceedings has been interrupted by the rebellion, and until the same shall be fully restored, and in every State or district whose constitutional relations to the government have been practically discontinued by the rebellion, and until such State shall have been restored in such relations, and shall be duly represented in the Congress of the United States, the right to make and enforce contracts, to sue, be parties, and give evidence, to inherit, purchase, lease, sell, hold, and convey real and personal property, and to have full and equal benefit of all laws and proceedings concerning personal liberty, personal security, and the acquisition, enjoyment, and disposition of estate, real and personal, including the constitutional right to bear arms, shall be secured to and enjoyed by all the citizens of such State or district without respect to race or color, or previous condition of slavery. And whenever in either of said States or districts the ordinary course of judicial proceedings has been interrupted by the rebellion, and until the same shall be fully restored, and until such State shall have been restored in its constitutional relations to the government, and shall be duly represented in the Congress of the United States, the President shall, through the commissioners and the officers of the bureau, and under such rules and regulations as the President, through the Secretary of War, shall prescribe, extend military protection and have military jurisdiction over all cases and questions concerning the free enjoyment of such immunities and rights, and no penalty or punishment for any violation of law shall be imposed or permitted because of race or color, or previous condition of slavery, other or greater than the penalty or punishment to which white persons may be liable by law for the like offence. But the jurisdiction conferred by this section upon the officers of the bureau shall not exist in any State where the ordinary course of judicial proceedings has not been interrupted by the rebellion, and shall cease in every State when the courts of the State and the United States are not disturbed in the peaceable course of justice, and after such State shall be fully restored in its constitutional relations to the government, and shall be duly represented in the Congress of the United States. . . .

Fourteenth Amendment
14 Stat. 358 (1866) (Proposed for Ratification by Congress)
15 Stat. 708 (1868) (Ratified by Three-fourths of the States)

SEC 1. All persons born or naturalized in the United States, and subject to the jurisdiction thereof, are citizens of the United States and of the State wherein they reside. No State shall make or enforce any law which shall abridge the privileges or immunities of citizens of the United States; nor shall any State deprive any person of life, liberty, or property, without due process of law; nor deny to any person within its jurisdiction the equal protection of the laws. . . .

SEC 5. The Congress shall have power to enforce, by appropriate legislation, the provisions of this article.

The legislative acts and constitutional debates described above provide the context for the case excerpted below. The case arose as a result of the infamous Colfax Massacre on Easter Sunday, April 13, 1873. As detailed in Charles Lane's book *The Day Freedom Died* (2008), William Cruikshank was among the leaders of a group of whites who attacked and slaughtered scores of Blacks at the county courthouse in Colfax, Louisiana (provocatively named for Schuyler Colfax, Republican President Ulysses S. Grant's first Vice-President). The massacre arose over a dispute about whether the white supremacist Democrats allied with Cruikshank or the black and white Republicans who barricaded themselves in the courthouse would control the county government. The white Republicans were allowed to flee before the massacre began. The barricaded Blacks were armed, but mostly with low-quality short-range shotguns. Cruikshank and his followers attacked with high-quality, longer-range rifles. Among the stellar defense team in *Cruikshank* were former U.S. Supreme Court Justice John Campbell, and U.S. Senator Reverdy Johnson (D-Md.), an ardent opponent of Reconstruction and the Fourteenth Amendment.

The *Cruikshank* decision was announced the same day as *United States v. Reese*, 92 U.S. 214 (1875), which seriously weakened federal protection of voting rights for Blacks. In tandem, *Reese* and *Cruikshank* significantly curtailed congressional power under the Fourteenth Amendment. *See* Robert M. Goldman, Reconstruction and Black Suffrage: Losing the Vote in *Reese & Cruikshank* (2001).

United States v. Cruikshank
92 U.S. 542 (1875)

Mr. Chief Justice Waite delivered the opinion of the court.

[The federal government brought charges against William Cruikshank for violating the rights of two Black men to peaceably assemble and to bear arms under section 6 of the Enforcement Act of May 31, 1870, which reads:

> That if two or more persons shall band or conspire together, or go in disguise upon the public highway, or upon the premises of another, with intent to violate any provision of this act, or to injure, oppress, threaten, or intimidate any citizen, with intent to prevent or hinder his free exercise and enjoyment of any right or privilege granted or secured to him by the constitution or laws of the United States, or because of his having exercised the same, such persons shall be held guilty of felony, and, on conviction thereof, shall be fined or imprisoned, or both, at the discretion of the court, — the fine not to exceed $5,000, and the imprisonment not to exceed ten years; and shall, moreover, be thereafter ineligible to, and disabled from holding, any office or place of honor, profit, or trust created by the constitution or laws of the United States.] . . .

The offences provided for by the statute in question do not consist in the mere "banding" or "conspiring" of two or more persons together, but in their banding or conspiring with the intent, or for any of the purposes, specified. To bring this case under the operation of the statute, therefore, it must appear that the right, the enjoyment of which the conspirators intended to hinder or prevent, was one granted or secured by the constitution or laws of the United States. If it does not so appear, the criminal matter charged has not been made indictable by any act of Congress.

We have in our political system a government of the United States and a government of each of the several States. Each one of these governments is distinct from the others, and each has citizens of its own who owe it allegiance, and whose rights, within its jurisdiction, it must protect. The same person may be at the same time a citizen of the United States and a citizen of a State, but his rights of citizenship under one of these governments will be different from those he has under the other. *Slaughter-House Cases*, 83 U.S. 36 (1872). . . .

The government of the United States is one of delegated powers alone. Its authority is defined and limited by the Constitution. All powers not granted to it by that instrument are reserved to the States or the people. No rights can be acquired under the constitution or laws of the United States, except such as the government of the United States has the authority to grant or secure. All that cannot be so granted or secured are left under the protection of the States.

We now proceed to an examination of the indictment, to ascertain whether the several rights, which it is alleged the defendants intended to interfere with, are such as had been in law and in fact granted or secured by the constitution or laws of the United States.

The first and ninth counts state the intent of the defendants to have been to hinder and prevent the citizens named in the free exercise and enjoyment of their "lawful right and privilege to peaceably assemble together with each other and with other citizens of the United States for a peaceful and lawful purpose."

The right of the people peaceably to assemble for lawful purposes existed long before the adoption of the Constitution of the United States. In fact, it is, and always has been, one of the attributes of citizenship under a free government. It "derives its source," to use the language of Chief Justice Marshall, in *Gibbons v. Ogden*, 22 U.S. 1 (1824), "from those laws whose authority is acknowledged by civilized man throughout the world." It is found wherever civilization exists. It was not, therefore, a right granted to the people by the Constitution. The government of the United States when established found it in existence, with the obligation on the part of the States to afford it protection. As no direct power over it was granted to Congress, it remains, according to the ruling in *Gibbons v. Ogden, id.* 203, subject to State jurisdiction. Only such existing rights were committed by the people to the protection of Congress as came within the general scope of the authority granted to the national government.

The first amendment to the Constitution prohibits Congress from abridging "the right of the people to assemble and to petition the government for a redress of grievances." This, like the other amendments proposed and adopted at the same time, was not intended to limit the powers of the State governments in respect to their own citizens, but to operate upon the National government alone. *Barron v. The City of Baltimore*, 32 U.S. 243 (1833). . . . It is now too late to question the correctness of this construction. As was said by the late Chief Justice, in *Twitchell v. The Commonwealth*, 74 U.S. 321 (1868), "the scope and application of these amendments are no longer subjects of discussion here." They left the authority of the States just where they found it, and added nothing to the already existing powers of the United States.

The particular amendment now under consideration assumes the existence of the right of the people to assemble for lawful purposes, and protects it against encroachment by Congress. The right was not created by the amendment; neither was its continuance guaranteed, except as against congressional interference. For their protection in its enjoyment, therefore, the people must look to the States. The power for that purpose was originally placed there, and it has never been surrendered to the United States.

The right of the people peaceably to assemble for the purpose of petitioning Congress for a redress of grievances, or for any thing else connected with the powers or the duties of the national government, is an attribute of national citizenship, and, as such, under the protection of, and guaranteed by, the United States. The very idea of a government, republican in form, implies a right on the part of its citizens to meet peaceably for consultation in respect to public affairs and to petition for a redress of grievances. If it had been alleged in these counts that the object of the defendants was to prevent a meeting for such a purpose, the case would have been within the statute, and within the scope of the sovereignty of the United States. Such, however, is not the case. The offence, as stated in the indictment, will be made out, if it be shown that the object of the conspiracy was to prevent a meeting for any lawful purpose whatever.

The second and tenth counts are equally defective. The right there specified is that of "bearing arms for a lawful purpose." This is not a right granted by the Constitution. Neither is it in any manner dependent upon that instrument for its existence. The second amendment declares that it shall not be infringed; but this, as has been seen, means no more than that it shall not be infringed by Congress. This is one of the amendments that has no other effect than to restrict the powers of the national government, leaving the people to look for their protection against any violation by their fellow-citizens of the rights it recognizes, to what is called, in *The City of New York v. Miln*, 36 U.S. 102 (1837), the "powers which relate to merely municipal legislation, or what was, perhaps, more properly called internal police," "not surrendered or restrained" by the Constitution of the United States. . . .

The fourteenth amendment prohibits a State from depriving any person of life, liberty, or property, without due process of law; but this adds nothing to the rights of one citizen as against another. It simply furnishes an additional guaranty against any encroachment by the States upon the fundamental rights which belong to every citizen as a member of society. As was said . . . in *Bank of Columbia v. Okely*, 17 U.S. 235 (1819), [due process] secures "the individual from the arbitrary exercise of the powers of government, unrestrained by the established principles of private rights and distributive justice." These counts in the indictment do not call for the exercise of any of the powers conferred by this provision in the amendment. . . .

The fourteenth amendment . . . does not . . . add anything to the rights which one citizen has under the Constitution against another. The equality of the rights of citizens is a principle of republicanism. Every republican government is in duty bound to protect all its citizens in the enjoyment of this principle, if within its power. That duty was originally assumed by the States; and it still remains there. The only obligation resting upon the United States is to see that the States do not deny the right. This the amendment guarantees, but no more. The power of the national government is limited to the enforcement of this guaranty. . . .

The order of the Circuit Court arresting the judgment upon the verdict is, therefore, affirmed; and the cause remanded, with instructions to discharge the defendants. . . .

NOTES & QUESTIONS

1. Did the Framers of the Fourteenth Amendment have a different vision of federalism than did the Framers of the original Constitution and the Bill of Rights? In which vision does *Cruikshank* fit?

2. Would a state or local government be compliant with the Freedmen's Bureau Act, the Civil Rights Act, or the Fourteenth Amendment if it disarmed everyone equally, without regard to race? What if the state allowed all races to serve in the state organized militia, but prohibited firearms ownership by everyone else? Does the Civil Rights Act's use of the phrase "full and equal" as opposed to just "equal" affect the answer?

3. What do you make of the fact that the Second Freedmen's Bureau Act included explicit protection of the right to bear arms while the Civil Rights Act did not?

4. What is the holding in *Cruikshank*? What is its effect on the Second Amendment and the Bill of Rights? The Court relies on *Barron v. Baltimore* for the proposition that the Bill of Rights applies only to the federal government.

Does this make the adoption of the Fourteenth Amendment a futile exercise? CQ: Decades later, the Supreme Court began to use the Due Process Clause of the Fourteenth Amendment to make some but not all provisions of the Bill of Rights enforceable against the states, via the doctrine of "incorporation." We will return to the incorporation issue, as applied to the Second Amendment, in discussion of *McDonald v. Chicago*, 130 S. Ct. 3020 (2010), in Chapter 9.

5. Can you frame the argument that the *Thirteenth* Amendment gave Congress authority to pass the Enforcement Act? The Civil Rights Act? In the 1968 case *Jones v. Alfred H. Mayer Co.*, 392 U.S. 409 (1968), the Supreme Court held that Congress was empowered by the Thirteenth Amendment to eradicate all "badges and incidents" of slavery and could therefore prohibit private racial discrimination in the sale or rental of real property. What, if any, congressional actions to protect Second Amendment rights could be justified by the *Jones* precedent?

6. What do you make of the statement in *Cruikshank* that the rights enumerated in the First and Second Amendments predated the Constitution and do not depend on it for their existence? CQ: As we will see in Chapter 9, the majority in *District of Columbia v. Heller*, 554 U.S. 570 (2008), cited *Cruikshank* for the proposition that the right to arms is a natural right that is protected by, but not created by, the Second Amendment. For more on natural rights theory regarding arms and self-defense, see Chapter 2.

7. The Constitution provides that "[t]he United States shall guarantee to every State in this Union a Republican Form of Government, and shall protect each of them against Invasion; and on Application of the Legislature, or of the Executive (when the Legislature cannot be convened) against domestic Violence." U.S. Const., art. IV, §4. What does a republican form of government entail? Could Congress have used this authority to act against the Black Codes of the post-war South? Against the private confiscation of arms from freedmen?

8. *Cruikshank* is often read as foreshadowing the "state action" doctrine of the Fourteenth Amendment, which was announced in the *Civil Rights Cases*, 109 U.S. 3 (1883). There, the Court, over the dissent of Justice John Marshall Harlan, struck down provisions of the Civil Rights Act of 1875, which had prohibited racial discrimination by private businesses such as hotels, theaters, and passenger railroads. The majority relied on the language of the Fourteenth Amendment that "No state shall. . . ." to hold that the Amendment only reaches state action, and accordingly Congress has no power under Section 5 of the Amendment to reach purely private discrimination. Justice Harlan's dissent argued that all of the entities in question had some connection to state power — an argument that was most convincing for highly regulated entities such as hotels or railroads, which had a legal duty to serve the general public. Does the post-Reconstruction experience suggest any practical problems with the state action doctrine? Consider that terrorism drove many Blacks and white republicans out of

the political arena, allowing white supremacists to take control of every Southern government. Should the Fourteenth Amendment have been written differently? Did the Supreme Court appropriately solve the problem starting in the mid-twentieth century by interpreting the interstate Commerce Clause so broadly that Congress was given a power to enact legislation on almost every subject?

9. *The Civil Rights Act of 1871* a/k/a *The Anti-KKK Act.* In 1871, under the power granted to it by Section 5 of the Fourteenth Amendment, Congress passed the original version of what is now codified as the well-known 42 U.S.C. §1983, allowing civil suits against anyone who has violated a claimant's civil rights while acting under the color of law. 17 Stat. 13 (1871). The Act's legislative history explicitly suggests that one of its goals was to protect the right to bear arms:

> Section eight is intended to enforce the well-known constitutional provision guaranteeing the right of the citizen to "keep and bear arms," and provides that whoever shall take away, by force or violence, or by threats and intimidation, the arms and weapons which any person may have for his defense, shall be deemed guilty of larceny of the same.

H.R. Rep. No. 41-37, at 3 (1871) (Rep. Benjamin Butler). What does Congressman Butler's statement imply about the nature of the Second Amendment? Taking into account the still-valid precedent of the *Civil Rights Cases,* and the well-established validity of 42 U.S.C. §1983 (with its "under color of law" limitation) what, if any, congressional actions to protect Second Amendment rights might be permissible under Section 5 of the Fourteenth Amendment?

10. During the latter part of the nineteenth century, and, in some quarters, for much of the first half of the twentieth, the Court's decisions in *Cruikshank* and *Slaughter-House* were lauded for wisely negating much of Section 1 and Section 5 of the Fourteenth Amendment, which were seen as the products of a temporary national hysteria. For example, according to a laudatory biography of Chief Justice Morrison Waite, "[t]he radical plan to protect the Negro by subjection of the states was thus 'demolished' by Waite and his associates. . . . This marked the overthrow of the congressional plan of reconstruction within seven years after the adoption of the Fourteenth Amendment." Bruce R. Trimble, Chief Justice Waite: Defender of the Public Interest (1938). Some advocates of a living Constitution argue that the Court should have the power to negate provisions that are obsolete or ill-advised, such as the Contracts Clause, the limitation of Congress to only exercising enumerated powers, the prohibition on direct taxes that are not apportioned by population, the prohibition on states entering into compacts and agreements with each other without congressional consent, or the Second Amendment.

    If such judicial nullification is ever legitimate, what, if anything, was illegitimate about what *Cruikshank* and *Slaughter-House* did to the Privileges or Immunities Clause? If the Constitution must evolve with the times, is the general public acceptance of the results in those cases proof that the Court acted correctly? *See generally* Nicholas J. Johnson, *Plenary Power and Constitutional Outcasts: Federal Power, Critical Race Theory, and the Second, Ninth, and Tenth Amendments*, 57 Ohio St. L.J. 1555 (1996).

11. One practical result of *Cruikshank* was that white violence against Blacks who exercised constitutional rights could usually occur with impunity. The federal government had great difficulty prosecuting cases, while state and local governments were not interested in such prosecutions, or were themselves intimidated. *See generally* George Rable, But There Was No Peace: The Role of Violence in the Politics of Reconstruction (1984). Should the Framers of the Fourteenth Amendment have explicitly empowered Congress to act against all private infringements of constitutional rights? Would the grant of such authority have effectively given Congress almost limitless power?

C. Labor Agitation and the Repressive Response

Throughout the nineteenth century, the growing nation became home to large numbers of immigrants. Industrial plants in the cities relied on immigrant labor, but efforts of the workers to unionize or strike often met with violent resistance. In 1876, the centennial year of U.S. independence was characterized not only by parades and fireworks, but by a wave of strikes, riots, and urban violence. During first century of American independence, gun control had been mainly a Southern enterprise targeted at Blacks. In the final decades of the nineteenth century, Southern gun control became even more aggressive, as detailed in Section E. During the same period, gun control legislation also began to emerge in some Northern states, often as a response to violence associated with labor tensions. Experience had alerted strikers and picketers to the risk of attack by armed squads employed by management. Participants in mass labor demonstrations often went armed and several states passed laws banning armed public parades.

The major Second Amendment case from the Supreme Court in the nineteenth century involved a challenge to an Illinois statute prohibiting the display of arms while on parade. The statute was challenged by a socialist labor group of German immigrants that had formed a private militia to defend its members. The group set up a challenge to the Illinois law by conducting a parade while carrying unloaded rifles.

‖ **Presser v. Illinois**
‖ **116 U.S. 252 (1886)**

WOODS, J.

[Herman Presser was indicted for violating the Military Code of Illinois, which prohibited "any body of men whatever, other than the regular organized volunteer militia of this state, and the troops of the United States, to associate themselves together as a military company or organization, or to drill or parade with arms in any city or town of this state, without the license of the governor thereof." He was convicted and fined $10, about the equivalent of $235 today.]

[Presser] belonged to a society called the "Lehr und Wehr Verein," [roughly, "Education and Resistance Society"] a corporation organized . . . "for the purpose," as expressed by its certificate of association, "of improving the mental and bodily condition of its members so as to qualify them for the duties of citizens of a republic. Its members shall, therefore, obtain, in the meetings of the association, a knowledge of our laws and political economy, and shall also be instructed in military and gymnastic exercises[.]" [I]n December, 1879, [he] marched at the head of said company, about 400 in number, in the streets of the city of Chicago, he riding on horseback and in command; . . . the company was armed with rifles, and Presser with a cavalry sword; . . . the company had no license from the governor of Illinois to drill or parade as a part of the militia of the state, and was not a part of the regular organized militia of the state, nor a part of troops of the United States, and had no organization under the militia law of the United States. . . . The case was taken to the supreme court of Illinois, where the judgment was affirmed. Thereupon Presser brought the present writ of error for a review of the judgment of affirmance.

The position of the plaintiff in error in this court was that the entire statute under which he was convicted was invalid and void because its enactment was the exercise of a power by the legislature of Illinois forbidden to the states by the constitution of the United States. The clauses of the constitution of the United States referred to in the assignments of error were as follows:

"Article 1, §8. The congress shall have power . . . to raise and support armies; . . . to provide for calling forth the militia to execute the laws of the Union, suppress insurrections, and repel invasions; to provide for organizing, arming, and disciplining the militia, and for governing such part of them as may be employed in the service of the United States, reserving to the states, respectively, the appointment of the officers, and the authority of training the militia, according to the discipline prescribed by congress; . . . to make all laws which shall be necessary and proper, for carrying into execution the foregoing powers," etc.

"Article 1, §10. No state shall, without the consent of congress, keep troops . . . in time of peace."

"Art. 2 of Amendments. A well regulated militia being necessary to the security of a free state, the right of the people to keep and bear arms shall not be infringed."

The plaintiff in error also contended that the enactment of the fifth and sixth sections of article 11 of the Military Code was forbidden by . . . article 14 of Amendments, which provides that "no state shall make or enforce any law which shall abridge the privileges or immunities of citizens of the United States, nor shall any state deprive any person of life, liberty, or property without due process of law."

The first contention of counsel for plaintiff in error is that the congress of the United States having, by virtue of the provisions of article 1 of section 8, above quoted, passed the act of May 8, 1792, entitled "An act more effectually to provide for the national defense by establishing an uniform militia throughout the United States," (1 St. 271,) the act of February 28, 1795, "to provide for calling forth the militia to execute the laws of the Union, suppress insurrections, and repel invasions," (1 St. 424,) and the act of July 22, 1861, "to authorize the employment of volunteers to aid in enforcing the laws and protecting public property," (12 St. 268,) and other subsequent acts, now forming "Title 16, The Militia," of the Revised Statutes of the United States, the legislature of Illinois had no power to pass the [portions of the Military Code of Illinois under which Presser was indicted].

The argument in support of this contention is, that the power of organizing, arming, and disciplining the militia being confided by the constitution to congress, when it acts upon the subject, and passes a law to carry into effect the constitutional provision, such action excludes the power of legislation by the state on the same subject. . . .

We have not found it necessary to consider or decide the question thus raised as to the validity of the entire Military Code of Illinois, for, in our opinion, the sections under which the plaintiff in error was convicted may be valid, even if the other sections of the act were invalid. For it is a settled rule "that statutes that are constitutional in part only will be upheld so far as they are not in conflict with the constitution, provided the allowed and prohibited parts are separable." *Packet Co. v. Keokuk*, 95 U.S. 80 [1877]. . . .

We are of opinion that this rule is applicable in this case. The first two sections of article 1 of the Military Code provide that all able-bodied male citizens of the state between the ages of 18 and 45 years, except those exempted, shall be subject to military duty, and be designated the "Illinois State Militia," and declare how they shall be enrolled and under what circumstances. The residue of the Code, except the two sections on which the indictment against the plaintiff in error is based, provides for a volunteer active militia, to consist of not more than 8,000 officers and men, declares how it shall be enlisted and brigaded, and the term of service of its officers and men; provides for brigade generals and their staffs, for the organization of the requisite battalions and companies and the election of company officers; provides for inspections, parades, and encampments, arms and armories, rifle practice, and courts-martial; provides for the pay of the officers and men, for medical service, regimental bands, books of instructions and maps; contains provisions for levying and collecting a military fund by taxation, and directs how it shall be expended; and appropriates $25,000 out of the treasury, in advance of the collection of the military fund, to be used for the purposes specified in the Military Code.

It is plain from this statement of the substance of the Military Code that the two sections upon which the indictment against the plaintiff in error is based may be separated from the residue of the Code, and stand upon their own independent provisions. . . .

. . . [T]he legislation on which the indictment is based is not invalid by reason of the provisions of the constitution of the United States which vest congress with power to raise and support armies, and to provide for calling out, organizing, arming, and disciplining the militia, and governing such part of them as may be employed in the service of the United States, [or] that provision which declares that "no state shall, without the consent of congress, . . . keep troops . . . in time of peace."

We are next to inquire whether the fifth and sixth sections of article 11 of the Military Code are in violation of the other provisions of the constitution of the United States relied on by the plaintiff in error. The first of these is the second amendment, which declares: "A well regulated militia being necessary to the security of a free state, the right of the people to keep and bear arms shall not be infringed."

We think it clear that the sections under consideration, which only forbid bodies of men to associate together as military organizations, or to drill or parade with arms in cities and towns unless authorized by law, do not infringe the right of the people to keep and bear arms. But a conclusive answer to the contention that this amendment prohibits the legislation in question lies in the fact that the amendment is a limitation only upon the power of congress and the national government, and not upon that of the state. It was so held by this court in the case of *U.S. v. Cruikshank*, 92 U.S. 542, 553 [(1875)], in which the chief justice, in delivering the judgment of the court, said that the right of the people to keep and bear arms "is not a right granted by the constitution. Neither is it in any manner dependent upon that instrument for its existence. The second amendment declares that it shall not be infringed, but this, as has been seen, means no more than that it shall not be infringed by congress. This is one of the amendments that has no other effect than to restrict the powers of the national government, leaving the people to look for their protection against any violation by their fellow-citizens of the rights it recognizes to what is called in *City of New York v. Miln*, 36 U.S. 102, 139 [1837], the 'powers which relate to merely municipal legislation, or what was perhaps more properly called internal police,' 'not surrendered or restrained' by the constitution of the United States." See, also, *Barron v. Baltimore*, 7 Pet. 243 [1833]. . . .

It is undoubtedly true that all citizens capable of bearing arms constitute the reserved military force or reserve militia of the United States as well as of the states, and, in view of this prerogative of the general government, as well as of its general powers, the states cannot, even laying the constitutional provision in question out of view, prohibit the people from keeping and bearing arms, so as to deprive the United States of their rightful resource for maintaining the public security, and disable the people from performing their duty to the general government. But, as already stated, we think it clear that the sections under consideration do not have this effect.

The plaintiff in error next insists that the sections of the Military Code of Illinois under which he was indicted are an invasion of that clause of the first section of the fourteenth amendment to the constitution of the United States which declares: "No state shall make or enforce any law which shall abridge the privileges or immunities of citizens of the United States." It is only the privileges and immunities of citizens of the United States that the clause relied on was intended to protect. A state may pass laws to regulate the privileges and immunities of its own citizens, provided that in so doing it does not abridge their privileges and immunities as citizens of the United States. The inquiry is therefore pertinent, what privilege or immunity of a citizen of the United States is abridged by sections 5 and 6 of article 11 of the Military Code of Illinois? The plaintiff in error was not a member of the organized volunteer militia of the state of Illinois, nor did he belong to the troops of the United States or to any organization under the militia law of the United States. On the contrary, the fact that he did not belong to the organized militia or the troops of the United States was an ingredient in the offense for which he was convicted and sentenced. The question is, therefore, had he a right as a citizen of the United States, in disobedience of the state law, to associate with others as a military company, and to drill and parade with arms in the towns and cities of the state? If the plaintiff in error has any such privilege, he must be able to point to the provision of the constitution or statutes of the United States by which it is conferred. For, as was said by this court in *U.S. v. Cruikshank* 92 U.S. 542 (1875), the government of the United States, although it is "within the scope of its powers supreme and above the states," "can neither grant nor secure to its citizens any right or privilege not expressly or by implication placed under its jurisdiction." "All that cannot be so granted or so secured are left to the exclusive protection of the state."

We have not been referred to any statute of the United States which confers upon the plaintiff in error the privilege which he asserts. . . . The right voluntarily to associate together as a military company or organization, or to drill or parade with arms, without, and independent of, an act of congress or law of the state authorizing the same, is not an attribute of national citizenship. Military organization and military drill and parade under arms are subjects especially under the control of the government of every country. They cannot be claimed as a right independent of law. Under our political system they are subject to the regulation and control of the state and federal governments, acting in due regard to their respective prerogatives and powers. . . .

It cannot be successfully questioned that the state governments, unless restrained by their own constitutions, have the power to regulate or prohibit associations and meetings of the people, except in the case of peaceable assemblies to perform the duties or exercise the privileges of citizens of the United States, and have also the power to control and regulate the organization, drilling, and parading of military bodies and associations, except when such bodies or associations, are authorized by the militia laws of the United States. The exercise of this power by the states is necessary to the public peace, safety, and good order. To deny the power would be to deny the right of the state to disperse assemblages organized for sedition and treason, and the right to suppress armed mobs bent on riot and rapine. . . .

It is next contended by the plaintiff in error that sections 5 and 6 of article 11 of the Military Code, under which he was indicted, are in conflict with the acts of congress for the organization of the militia. But this position is based on what seems to us to be an unwarranted construction of the sections referred to. It is clear that their object was to forbid voluntary military associations, unauthorized by law, from organizing or drilling and parading with arms in the cities or towns of the state, and not to interfere with the organization, arming and drilling of the militia under the authority of the acts of congress. If the object and effect of the sections were in irreconcilable conflict with the acts of congress, they would of course be invalid. But it is a rule of construction that a statute must be interpreted so as, if possible, to make it consistent with the constitution and the paramount law. *Parsons v. Bedford*, 28 U.S. 433 (1830); *Grenada Co. Sup'rs v. Brogden*, 112 U.S. 261 (1884); S.C. 5 Sup. Ct. Rep. 125; *Marshall v. Grimes*, 41 Miss. 27 [1866]. If we yielded to this contention of the plaintiff in error, we should render the sections invalid by giving them a strained construction, which would make them antagonistic to the law of congress. We cannot attribute to the legislature, unless compelled to do so by its plain words, a purpose to pass an act in conflict with an act of congress on a subject over which congress is given authority by the constitution of the United States. We are, therefore, of opinion that, fairly construed, the sections of the Military Code referred to do not conflict with the laws of congress on the subject of the militia. . . .

All the federal questions presented by the record were rightly decided by the supreme court of Illinois. Judgment affirmed.

NOTES & QUESTIONS

1. What is the holding in *Presser*? That the Second Amendment is not violated by the state ban on group military exercises? That the Second Amendment does not apply directly to the states? That the Second Amendment is not a right of individuals? That the Fourteenth Amendment does not make the Second Amendment applicable to the states?

   In the twentieth and twenty-first centuries, scholars and lawyers have propounded each of the above interpretations. For example, Nelson Lund argues that "*Cruikshank* and *Presser* correctly held that the Second Amendment itself does not apply to the states. Both cases should also be read by the inferior courts to hold that the right to keep and bear arms is not among the rights covered by the Privileges or Immunities Clause of the Fourteenth Amendment." Nelson Lund, *Anticipating the Second Amendment Incorporation: The Role of the Inferior Courts*, 59 Syracuse L. Rev. 185 (2008).

   Dennis Henigan argues that *Presser* is "wholly inconsistent" with the view that the Second Amendment preserves a right of individuals to engage in armed resistance against government tyranny—what some writers term the "insurrectionary theory" of the Amendment. *See* Dennis A. Henigan, *Arms, Anarchy, and the Second Amendment*, 26 Val. U. L. Rev. 107, 125 (1991). Henigan reasons that "if the people are to be an effective armed force against tyranny, then the Second Amendment also must guarantee their right to join together in resisting the government." *Id.* at 124. This he says is inconsistent with the statement in *Presser* that

   > [m]ilitary organization and military drill and parade under arms are subjects especially under the control of the government of every country. . . . Under our political system they are subject to the regulation and control of the State and Federal governments, acting in due regard to their respective prerogatives and powers.

   Id. at 125 (quoting *Presser*, 116 U.S. at 267). Is Henigan right about the implications of *Presser*? Today, many commercial shooting academies offer formal training in armed fighting to private citizens. Some even provide military-style training in coordinated "team tactics" to such students. Should such meetings be regulated or forbidden by the government? Would there be any constitutional limits on such regulation?

2. Assume that *Presser* held that the Fourteenth Amendment's Privileges or Immunities Clause did not make the Second Amendment binding on the states. Note that decades later the doctrine of "selective incorporation" began to use the Due Process Clause of the Fourteenth Amendment to make portions of the Bill of Rights enforceable against the states. CQ: Did *Presser* bar lower federal courts from applying Due Process selective incorporation to the Fourteenth Amendment? The U.S. Court of Appeals for the Second Circuit, in a three-judge *per curiam* opinion joined by future Supreme Court Justice Sonia Sotomayor, held that *Presser* did in fact prohibit due process incorporation. *Maloney v. Cuomo*, 554 F.3d 56, 58 (2d Cir. 2009), *cert. granted and judgment vacated sub nom. Maloney v. Rice*, 130 S. Ct. 3541 (2010) (as a result of *McDonald* (Chapter 9)). The Seventh Circuit, in an opinion by Chief Judge Easterbrook, came to the same conclusion — though when the case reached the Supreme Court, a plurality of the Justices voted to incorporate the right to arms under the Due Process Clause. *National Rifle Association of Am. v. City of Chicago*, 567 F.3d 856, 857-58 (7th Cir. 2009), *rev'd and remanded, McDonald v. City of Chicago*, 130 S. Ct. 3020 (2010) (Chapter 9).

    Put aside the Second Amendment for a moment to consider whether the federal government's powers over the militia, set out in Article I of the Constitution, imply some limits on state gun control laws. What part of the *Presser* opinion implies that the Court thought so? What kind of state laws might interfere with federal militia powers? CQ: In *McDonald*, (Chapter 9), majorities of both Houses of Congress signed an amicus brief claiming that the Chicago handgun ban interfered with congressional militia powers (since Congress could choose to require some militiamen to bring their own handguns to militia service), and therefore the Chicago ban was unconstitutional under *Presser*. Do you agree? Should an individual have standing to challenge alleged state infringements of Congress's Article I powers?

3. Does Congress have plenary power over the organized militia? Does the Second Amendment limit this power? *See Perpich v. Dep't of Defense*, 496 U.S. 334, 352-54 (1990) (holding that state militias may be called into federal service and deployed overseas despite the state governor's objection); *Selective Draft Law Cases*, 245 U.S. 366, 374-83 (1918) (holding that Congress has the authority to abolish a state militia by bodily conscripting all its members into the federal standing army); *Martin v. Mott*, 25 U.S. 19, 28-33 (1827) (holding that the President has the power to call the militia from state control into federal service); *Houston v. Moore*, 18 U.S. 1, 24 (1820) (holding that federal militia legislation preempts state legislation, even if the state legislation merely duplicates the federal statute). What does your answer imply about the nature of the right guaranteed by the Second Amendment?

4. What is the combined effect of *Cruikshank* and *Presser*? One pair of commentators had this to say:

    > With its view that the statute restricting armed parading did not interfere with the right to keep and bear arms, and its view that Congress's militia power

prevented the states from disarming its citizens, the *Presser* Court had gone out of its way in dicta to reaffirm the old federalism and to reject the framers' view of the Fourteenth Amendment that the Bill of Rights applied to the states.

The rest of the story is all too well known. The Court's denial of an expanded role for the federal government in enforcing civil rights played a crucial role in redeeming white rule. The doctrine in *Cruikshank*, that blacks would have to look to state government for protection against criminal conspiracies, gave the green light to private forces, often with the assistance of state and local governments, that sought to subjugate the former slaves and their descendants. Private violence was instrumental in driving blacks from the ranks of voters. It helped force many blacks into peonage, a virtual return to slavery, and was used to force many blacks into a state of ritualized subservience. With the protective arm of the federal government withdrawn, protection of black lives and property was left to largely hostile state governments.

Cottrol & Diamond, *supra*, at 348-49.

5. Presser's attorney was Lyman Trumbull, who as a Republican Senator had co-authored the Thirteenth Amendment. After retiring from Congress, Trumbull became a Democrat and an eminent Illinois lawyer who also defended the 1894 Chicago railroad strikers. Trumbull's primary argument was that the entire Illinois Militia Act of 1879 was preempted by federal statute. The Illinois law said that the state militia consisted of no more than 8,000 men, but the federal Militia Acts of 1792 said that all white males aged 18 to 45 were part of the federal militia. 116 U.S. at 256-59. The *Presser* Court sidestepped the issue, holding that because Presser was prosecuted under a constitutionally valid provision (the ban on armed parades without a permit), the Court need not consider the rest of the Illinois law. If the Court had ruled on Trumbull's preemption claim, how should it have ruled? As long as Illinois did nothing to interfere with a person's federal service, did Illinois have the concurrent power under Article I, Section 8, Clause 16 to define its state militia however it pleased? Was such a right reinforced (or created) by the Second Amendment?

6. Two Supreme Court cases near the end of the century involve the Second Amendment as a secondary issue, and have been cited by the Supreme Court recently in *Heller* (Chapter 9) and *McDonald* (Chapter 9). The first, *Miller v. Texas*, 153 U.S. 535 (1894), involved a white man, Miller, who fell in love with a Black woman and became a target of harassment. The Dallas City Police heard that Miller was carrying a handgun without a license. The law of the time did not require that a warrant be obtained in order to arrest a person for unlicensed gun-carrying. A group of police officers assembled in a local tavern, enjoyed a good session of whiskey-drinking, headed over to Miller's store, snuck through a side alley, and then burst into Miller's store with guns drawn. The evidence is conflicting as to whether Miller thought that the men were assaulting criminals or government officials. The evidence is also conflicting about who fired first. In any case, Miller got off the first good shot, killing one of the intruders, but was outnumbered and ultimately captured.

The episode infuriated the white people of Dallas. Newspapers raged that a white man who loved a "greasy negress" had shot a police officer. At the trial, where defendant Miller was charged with murder, the prosecutor told the jury that Miller had been illegally carrying a gun. Miller was convicted of murdering a police officer. Miller's appeal to the Supreme Court claimed that his Second, Fourth, Fifth, and Fourteenth Amendment rights had been violated. Miller argued that (1) the Texas statute against concealed carry was invalid; (2) the statute allowing arrest without a warrant was invalid; and (3) his alleged violation of the carry law should not have been used as an argument by the prosecutor.

The Supreme Court disagreed and wrote that a "state law forbidding the carrying of dangerous weapons on the person . . . does not abridge the privileges or immunities of citizens of the United States." Further, "the restrictions of these amendments [Second and Fourth] operate only upon the Federal power." *Miller v. Texas*, 153 U.S. 535, 538 (1894). The Court added that "[i]f the Fourteenth Amendment limited the power of the States as to such rights, as pertaining to the citizens of the United States, we think it was fatal to this claim that it was not set up in the trial court." *Id.* Miller's death sentence was upheld, but he was eventually released from prison. For details on the case, see Cynthia Leonardatos, David B. Kopel & Stephen P. Halbrook, Miller versus Texas*: Police Violence, Race Relations, Capital Punishment, and Gun-toting in Texas in the Nineteenth Century — and Today*, 9 J.L. & Pol'y 737 (2001).

Three years after *Miller v. Texas*, the Supreme Court heard *Robertson v. Baldwin*, a case involving merchant seamen who had jumped ship. After being captured, the seamen were impressed back into maritime service without due process. The seamen argued that the terms of their service contract amounted to "involuntary servitude" in violation of the Thirteenth Amendment. *Robertson v. Baldwin*, 165 U.S. 275 (1897). The Court disagreed, explaining that all constitutional rights (including the right to be free from involuntary servitude) include certain exceptions. These exceptions did not need to be specifically noted in the Constitution, since they were obvious and traditional:

> The law is perfectly well settled that the first ten amendments to the Constitution, commonly known as the Bill of Rights, were not intended to lay down any novel principles of government, but simply to embody certain guaranties and immunities which we had inherited from our English ancestors, and which had from time immemorial been subject to certain well-recognized exceptions arising from the necessities of the case. In incorporating these principles into the fundamental law, there was no intention of disregarding the exceptions, which continued to be recognized as if they had been formally expressed. Thus, the freedom of speech and of the press (Art. I) does not permit the publication of libels, blasphemous or indecent articles, or other publications injurious to public morals or private reputation; the right of the people to keep and bear arms (Art. II) is not infringed by laws prohibiting the carrying of concealed weapons; the provision that no person shall be twice put in jeopardy (Art. V) does not prevent a second trial if upon the first trial the jury failed to agree or if the verdict was set aside upon the defendant's motion. . . .

Id. at 281-82.

How do the *Miller* and *Robertson* Courts appear to view the Second Amendment right? As one for the militia only? As a private right extending to the general population? Does *Miller v. Texas* stand against application of the Second Amendment to the states via the Fourteenth Amendment's Privileges or Immunities Clause? Via the Due Process Clause?

The idea that the Bill of Rights incorporates all the rights "inherited from our English ancestors" is not universally accepted. For example, Justice Douglas wrote: "[T]o assume that English common law in this field became ours is to deny the generally accepted historical belief that 'one of the objects of the Revolution was to get rid of the English common law on liberty of speech and of the press.'" *A Book Named "John Cleland's Memoirs of a Woman of Pleasure" v. Attorney General of Mass.*, 383 U.S. 413, 429 (1966) (Douglas, J., concurring). Early nineteenth-century American legal commentator St. George Tucker (Chapter 4) strongly urged that First and Second Amendment rights, among others, were much broader than their British counterparts. Which position has stronger historical support? Which position is better policy?

D. Nineteenth-Century Commentary

1. Chief Justice Thomas M. Cooley

Chapters 4 and 5 presented assessments of the Second Amendment by America's first generation of great constitutional commentators: St. George Tucker, William Rawle, and Joseph Story. The preeminent legal commentator of the second half of the nineteenth century was Thomas M. Cooley. He served as Dean of the University of Michigan Law School from 1871-83, and as Chief Justice of the Michigan Supreme Court from 1864-85. He was almost universally regarded as the preeminent authority on American constitutional law, and is still considered among the most important lawyers in American history.

Cooley authored two treatises on Constitutional Law. His *A Treatise on the Constitutional Limitations Which Rest Upon the Legislative Power of the States of the American Union* first appeared in 1868. As one commentator noted several years later, the treatise is "cited in every argument and opinion on the subjects which it treats, and not only is the book authoritative as a digest of law, but its author's opinions are regarded as almost conclusive." *Cooley's Constitutional Limitations*, 27 Alb. L.J. 300 (1883) (book note). Cooley's *The General Principles of Constitutional Law in the United States of America* first appeared in 1880. It was based on his earlier treatise and styled as a student's and practitioner's manual. It contained an expanded discussion of the right to bear arms. Both works went through numerous editions, which were published both before and after Cooley's death in 1898. Excerpted below are passages from the first editions of each work.

Thomas M. Cooley, A Treatise on the Constitutional Limitations Which Rest upon the Legislative Power of the States of the American Union
350 (1868)

RIGHT TO BEAR ARMS.

Among the other defenses to personal liberty should be mentioned the right of the people to keep and bear arms. A standing army is peculiarly obnoxious in any free government, and the jealousy of one has at times been demonstrated so strongly in England as almost to lead to the belief that a standing army recruited from among themselves was more dreaded as an instrument of oppression than a tyrannical king, or any foreign power. So impatient did the English people become of the very army which liberated them from the tyranny of James II., that they demanded its reduction, even before the liberation could be felt to be complete; and to this day, the British Parliament render a standing army practically impossible by only passing a mutiny bill from session to session. The alternative to a standing army is "a well-regulated militia," but this cannot exist unless the people are trained to bearing arms. How far it is in the power of the legislature to regulate this right, we shall not undertake to say, as happily there has been very little occasion to discuss that subject by the courts.[1]

Thomas M. Cooley, The General Principles of Constitutional Law in the United States of America
270-72 (1880)

SECTION IV. — THE RIGHT TO KEEP AND BEAR ARMS

The Constitution. — By the second amendment to the Constitution it is declared that, "a well-regulated militia being necessary to the security of a free State, the right of the people to keep and bear arms shall not be infringed."

The amendment, like most other provisions in the Constitution, has a history. It was adopted with some modification and enlargement from the English Bill of Rights of 1688, where it stood as a protest against arbitrary action of the overturned dynasty in disarming the people, and as a pledge of the new rulers that this tyrannical action should cease. The right declared was meant to be a strong moral check against the usurpation and arbitrary power of rulers, and as a necessary and efficient means of regaining rights when temporarily overturned

---

1. In [*Bliss v. Commonwealth* (Ky. 1822; Chapter 5)], the statute "to prevent persons bearing concealed arms" was held unconstitutional, as infringing on the right of the people to bear arms in defence of themselves and of the State. But see [*Nunn v. State* (Ga. 1846; holding that the Second Amendment protected open but not concealed carry; Chapter 5)]. As bearing also upon the right of self-defence, see [*Ely v. Thompson* (Ky. 1820)], where it was held that the statute subjecting free persons of color to corporal punishment for "lifting their hands in opposition" to a white person was held unconstitutional.

by usurpation. [Here Justice Cooley cites to St. George Tucker's Blackstone (Chapter 4).]

The Right is General. — It may be supposed from the phraseology of this provision that the right to keep and bear arms was only guaranteed to the militia; but this would be an interpretation not warranted by the intent. The militia, as has been elsewhere explained, consists of those persons who, under the law, are liable to the performance of military duty, and are officered and enrolled for service when called upon. But the law may make provision for the enrolment of all who are fit to perform military duty, or of a small number only, or it may wholly omit to make any provision at all; and if the right were limited to those enrolled, the purpose of this guaranty might be defeated altogether by the action or neglect to act of the government it was meant to hold in check. The meaning of the provision undoubtedly is, that the people, from whom the militia must be taken, shall have the right to keep and bear arms; and they need no permission or regulation of law for the purpose. But this enables the government to have a well-regulated militia; for to bear arms implies something more than the mere keeping; it implies the learning to handle and use them in a way that makes those who keep them ready for their efficient use; in other words, it implies the right to meet for voluntary discipline in arms, observing in doing so the laws of public order.

Standing Army. — A further purpose of this amendment is, to preclude any necessity or reasonable excuse for keeping up a standing army. A standing army is condemned by the traditions and sentiments of the people, as being as dangerous to the liberties of the people as the general preparation of the people for the defence of their institutions with arms is preservative of them.

What Arms may be kept. — The arms intended by the Constitution are such as are suitable for the general defence of the community against invasion or oppression, and the secret carrying of those suited merely to deadly individual encounters may be prohibited. [Here Justice Cooley cites to *Andrews v. State, infra.*]

NOTES & QUESTIONS

1. Is Justice Cooley describing a collective, individual, or hybrid right to bear arms? CQ: The modern U.S. Supreme Court disagrees about the answer. *Compare Heller*, 554 U.S. at 616-18, *with id.* at 707 (Breyer, J., dissenting) (Chapter 9). In a recent case, the United States Court of Appeals for the Seventh Circuit drew upon Cooley as historical support for the conclusion that the Second Amendment right to own firearms also implies a right to practice with them in order to develop skill at their use. *Ezell v. City of Chicago*, 651 F.3d 684, 704 (7th Cir. 2011) (ordering the entry of a preliminary injunction against a municipal ban on operating firing ranges within city limits).

2. In *Ely v. Thompson*, 10 Ky. 70 (1820), cited by Justice Cooley in the footnote in *Constitutional Limitations*, the court validated an act of self-defense by a free

Black man against a white constable in spite of a statute prohibiting Blacks' violence against whites. *Cf. State v. Davis*, 52 N.C. (7 Jones) 52, 53, 55 (1859):

> The conviction of the defendant may involve the proposition that a free negro is not justified, under any circumstances, in striking a white man. To this, we cannot yield our assent. . . .
>   An officer of the town having a notice to serve on the defendant, without any authority whatever, arrests him and attempts to tie him!! Is not this gross oppression? For what purpose was he to be tied? What degree of cruelty might not the defendant reasonably apprehend after he should be entirely in the power of one who had set upon him in so highhanded and lawless a manner? Was he to submit tamely? — Or, was he not excusable for resorting to the natural right of self-defense? Upon the facts stated, we think his Honor ought to have instructed the jury to find the defendant not guilty. There is error. *Venire de novo*.

Should people have the right to use violence against unlawful force inflicted by law enforcement officers? Does the Second Amendment imply such a right? *See* Darrell A.H. Miller, *Retail Rebellion and the Second Amendment*, 86 Ind. L.J. 939 (2011).

3.   What is Justice Cooley "happy" about in *Constitutional Limitations*?

4.   Earlier in *Constitutional Limitations*, Justice Cooley notes:

> The Constitution of the United States assumes the existence of . . . distinct State governments . . . exercising the powers of government under some form of written constitution, and that instrument would remain unaffected by the adoption of the national Constitution, except in those particulars in which the two would come in conflict, and then the latter would modify and control the former.

Thomas M. Cooley, A Treatise on the Constitutional Limitations Which Rest Upon the Legislative Power of the States of the American Union 21 (1868). Later in the work, he added that

> Certain things are to be looked for in all these [state constitutions]; though even as to these there is great variety, not only of substance, but also in the minuteness of their provisions to meet particular cases, [including] . . . a declaration of rights for the protection of individuals and minorities. This declaration usually contains the following classes of provisions: —
>   1. Those declaratory of the general principles of republican government; such as, [including equality for all, including freedmen, the] indefeasible right to alter, reform, or abolish their government in such manner as they may think proper; . . . that standing armies are not to be maintained in time of peace. . . .
>   2. Those declaratory of the fundamental rights of the citizen; as that all men are by nature free and independent, and have certain inalienable rights, among which are those of enjoying and defending life and liberty, . . . that every man may bear arms for the defence of himself and of the State. . . .

Id. at 34-35.

Cooley notes later that "the right to keep fire-arms . . . does not protect him who uses them for annoyance or destruction." *Id.* at 421 (comparing the right to arms to liberty of the press in Massachusetts, noting that the abuse of neither is protected).

The excerpted language used by Justice Cooley in the first edition of *General Principles* was repeated verbatim in the second (1891) and third (1898) editions. These two subsequent editions were updated by other editors because Justice Cooley for health and other reasons could not do the work. A fourth edition was published in 1931, some 33 years after Cooley's death. It cited *Presser, supra,* for the proposition that the "Second Amendment is a limitation upon Congress and not upon the legislatures of the several states" and that "the State could prohibit altogether the carrying or selling of arms by private citizens." Thomas M. Cooley, The General Principles of Constitutional Law in the United States of America 341 (Andrew Alexander Bruce ed., 4th ed. 1931). The reviser of the fourth edition was Andrew Alexander Bruce, a Northwestern law professor and a Justice of the North Dakota Supreme Court. Compare the vision of the Second Amendment in Bruce's twentieth-century edition of Cooley's text with the one that Cooley penned 50 years earlier.

2.   Other Commentary

Many other late nineteenth-century legal commentators discussed the right to bear arms in the context of both the federal and state constitutions. The original meaning, resistance to tyranny, standing armies, militias, and self-defense are common themes in the commentary of the post-war era.

Joel Bishop presented the most restrictive view from this period. His criminal law commentaries remained influential well into the twentieth century. Bishop viewed the right to bear arms mainly in the context of the criminal law of the carrying of weapons. His views changed between the first and second editions of his work. *See* Commentaries on the Law of Statutory Crimes, published in 1873 and 1883, respectively.

Joel Prentiss Bishop, Commentaries on the Law of Statutory Crimes
§§792-93 (1873)

[After discussing a number of statutes criminalizing the carrying of weapons under different circumstances, Bishop writes:]

§792. CONSTITUTIONALITY OF THESE STATUTES: —

The right to keep and bear arms. — The Constitution of the United States provides, that, "a well-regulated militia being necessary to the security of a free state, the right of the people to keep and bear arms shall not be infringed." This provision is found among amendments; and, though most of the amendments are restrictions on the General Government alone, not on the States, this one seems to be of a nature to bind both the State and National legislatures; and doubtless it does. As to its interpretation, if we look to this question in the light of juridical reason, without the aid of specific authority, we shall be led to the conclusion that the provision protects only the right to "keep" such "arms" as are used for purposes of war, in distinction from those which are employed in quarrels, brawls, and fights between maddened individuals; since such, only, are properly known by the name of "arms;" and such, only, are adapted to promote "the security of a free State." In like manner, the right to "bear" arms refers merely to the military way of using them, not to their use in bravado and affray. Still, the Georgia tribunal seems to have held, that a statute prohibiting the open wearing of arms upon the person violates this provision of the Constitution, though a statute against wearing of the arms concealed does not.[5] And, in accord with the latter branch of this Georgia doctrine, the Louisiana court has laid it down, that the statute against carrying concealed weapons does not infringe the constitutional right of the people to keep and bear arms; for this statute is a measure of police, prohibiting only a particular mode of bearing arms, found dangerous to the community.[1]

§793.

Continued. — Of a similar nature to this provision in the Constitution of the United States, are provisions found in the constitutions of several of the states. And the Alabama court has held, that the statute against carrying concealed weapons is not in violation of the constitutional guarantee, to every citizen, of the right "to bear arms in defence of himself and the State."[2] The Constitution of Kentucky declares, that "the rights of the citizens to bear arms in defence of themselves and the State shall not be questioned"; and a majority of the court held the statutory provision against carrying concealed weapons, to be in violation of this constitutional guaranty. The learned judge who delivered the opinion said "To be in conflict with the constitution, it is not essential that the act should contain a prohibition against bearing arms in every possible form; it is the *right* to bear arms in defense and the State that is secured by the constitution, and whatever restrains the full and complete exercise of that right, though not an entire destruction of it, is forbidden by the explicit language of the constitution."[3] On the other hand, a similar clause in the Arkansas Constitution was declared by the Arkansas court not to be violated by this enactment, — the object of which is, the court considered, not to prevent the carrying of weapons in self-defence, but only to regulate the manner of carrying them.[4] And the Arkansas doctrine is the one approved generally by the American tribunals.[5]

---

5. *Nunn v. The State*, 1 Kelly 243 [Ga. 1846; Chapter 5]; *Stockdale v. The State*, 32 Ga. 225 [1861].

1. *The State v. Jumel*, 13 La. An. 399 [1858].

2. *Owen v. The State*, 31 Ala. 387 [1858]. . . .

3. *Bliss v. Commonwealth*, 2 Litt. 90 [Ky. 1822; Chapter 5].

4. *The State v. Buzzard*, 4 Ark. 18 [1842; Chapter 5].

5. *Aymette v. The State*, 2 Humph. 154 [(1840; see Chapter 5)]; *The State v. Reid*, 1 Ala. 612 [Ala. 1840; Chapter 5]; *The State v. Mitchell*, 3 Blackf. 229 [Ind. 1833; Chapter 5]. The North Carolina court held, that the "act to prevent free people of color from carrying fire-arms" does not violate this constitutional provision; for, first, these people are not in the fullest sense citizens; or, secondly, if that are, they "occupy such a position in society as justifies the legislature in adopting a course of policy in its acts peculiar to them." *The State v. Newsom*, 5 Ire. 250 [N.C. 1844]. This was the doctrine laid down before the late changes in our National and State constitutions places all persons, who are native-born, on equal footing among us, whatever may have been their former status.

Joel Prentiss Bishop, Commentaries on the Law of Statutory Crimes
§§792-93 (2d ed. 1883)

§792. CONSTITUTIONALITY OF THESE STATUTES: —

Under United States Constitution. — The provision which, if any in the United States Constitution, governs this question, is, that "a well-regulated militia being necessary to the security of a free State, the right of the people to keep and bear arms shall not be infringed." It is among the older amendments, most of which are held to be restrictions on the national power, and not to bind the States. This one is declaratory of personal rights, so also are some of the others which are adjudged not to extend to the States; and, contrary perhaps to some former views, it is now settled in authority that this provision has no relevancy to State legislation.[1] Still, —

§793.

Under State Constitutions. — The same guaranty to the people of the right "to keep and bear arms" is largely found in our State constitutions; in some of them, in these words alone, and in others more or less qualified. In reason, the keeping and bearing of arms has reference only to war, and possibly also to insurrections wherein the forms of war are as far as practicable observed; yet certainly not to broils, bravado, and tumult, disturbing the public repose, or to private assassination and secret revenge. Nor are these, in the language of the constitutional provision now under consideration, "necessary to the security of a free State." Nor yet are dirks, bludgeons, revolvers, and other weapons which are not used in war, "arms." Moreover, there is no species of property, and no private right, the "keeping" and "bearing" of which may not be *regulated*[3] by legislation for the public good. Hence, in reason, statutes like those explained in the foregoing sections do not violate any of our constitutions; and so, with some differences in the form of the argument and limitations of the doctrine, our courts generally hold; though there are opinions in dissent.

NOTES & QUESTIONS

1. What do you make of the differences between the two editions of Bishop's work? *Cruikshank* had been decided when Bishop published his second edition, but *Presser* had not.

---

1. *United States v. Cruikshank*, 92 U.S. 542 [1875, *supra*]; *Andrews v. The State*, 3 Heisk. 165 [Tenn. 1871, *infra*]; *Fife v. The State*, 31 Ark. 455 [Ark. 1876, *infra*]. See *Nunn v. The State*, 1 Kelly, 243 [Ga. 1846; see Chapter 5]; *Stockdale v. The State*, 32 Ga. 225 [1861]; *The State v. Jumel*, 13 La. An. 399 [1858].

3. . . . *Lewis v. The State*, 2 Texas Ap. 26 [1877]; *Wilson v. The State*, 33 Ark. 557 [1878, *infra*]; *The State v. Buzzard*, 4 Pike. 18 [1842; see Chapter 5]; *The State v. Speller*, 86 N.C. 697 [1882]; *Edmonds v. Baubury*, 28 Iowa 267 [1869].

2. What kinds of gun controls would Cooley and Bishop agree are constitutional? On what controls would they disagree?

E. Late Nineteenth-Century State Laws and Cases

In the postbellum era, state courts issued many decisions addressing state constitutional rights to arms. Some of them also examined the Second Amendment. As you read the cases below keep in mind the treatment of the Reconstruction Era, earlier in this chapter, and also the pre-war state cases in Chapter 5.

The following two opinions were issued by the Tennessee Supreme Court in consecutive years.

Andrews v. State
50 Tenn. (3 Heisk.) 165 (1871)

FREEMAN, J., delivered the opinion of the Court.

The questions presented for our decision in these cases, involve an adjudication of the constitutionality of the act of the Legislature of Tennessee [providing] . . . "that it shall not be lawful for any person to publicly or privately carry a dirk, swordcane, Spanish stiletto, belt or pocket pistol or revolver[. . .]."

[The court relied on *Barron v. Baltimore*, 32 U.S. 243 (1833), to hold that there was no merit to the argument that the Tennessee statute was unconstitutional under the federal Second Amendment.]

We come now to the Constitution of the State of Tennessee, and endeavor to see what restrictions or limitations the sovereign people of Tennessee have chosen to place upon themselves, in reference to this subject, for the general good. . . .

The [1870] Constitution of Tennessee [provides in] Art. 1, s. 24, of the Bill of Rights, [that]: "That the sure and certain defense of a free people is a well regulated militia; and as standing armies in time of peace are dangerous to freedom, they ought to be avoided, as far as the circumstances and safety of the community will admit; and that in all cases, the military shall be kept in strict subordination to the civil authority." . . .

Section 26 is: "That the citizens of this State have a right to keep and bear arms for their common defense. But the Legislature shall have power by law, to regulate the wearing of arms, with a view to prevent crime." . . .

What rights are guaranteed by the first clause of this sec., 26, "that the citizens have a right to keep and to bear arms for their common defense?" We may well look at any other clause of the same Constitution, or of the Constitution of the United States, that will serve to throw any light on the meaning of this clause. The first clause of section 24 says, "that the sure defense of a free people is a well-regulated militia." We then turn to Art. 2, of amendments to the

Constitution of the United States, where we find the same principle laid down in this language: "A well-regulated militia being necessary to the security of a free state, the right of the people to keep and bear arms shall not be abridged." We find that, necessarily, the same rights, and for similar reasons, were being provided for and protected in both the Federal and State Constitutions; in the one, as we have shown, against infringement by the Federal Legislature, and in the other, by the Legislature of the State.

What was the object held to be so desirable as to require that its attainment should be guaranteed by being inserted in the fundamental law of the land? It was the efficiency of the people as soldiers, when called into actual service for the security of the State, as one end; and in order to this, they were to be allowed to keep arms. What, then, is involved in this right of keeping arms? It necessarily involves the right to purchase and use them in such a way as is usual, or to keep them for the ordinary purposes to which they are adapted; and as they are to be kept, evidently with a view that the citizens making up the yeomanry of the land, the body of the militia, shall become familiar with their use in times of peace, that they may the more efficiently use them in times of war; then the right to keep arms for this purpose involves the right to practice their use, in order to attain to this efficiency. The right and use are guaranteed to the citizen, to be exercised and enjoyed in time of peace, in subordination to the general ends of civil society; but, as a right, to be maintained in all its fullness. . . .

But farther than this, it must be held, that the right to keep arms involves, necessarily, the right to use such arms for all the ordinary purposes, and in all the ordinary modes usual in the country, and to which arms are adapted, limited by the duties of a good citizen in times of peace; that in such use, he shall not use them for violation of the rights of others, or the paramount rights of the community of which he makes a part.

Again, in order to arrive at what is meant by this clause of the State Constitution, we must look at the nature of the thing itself, the right to keep which is guaranteed. It is "arms"; that is, such weapons as are properly designated as such, as the term is understood in the popular language of the country, and such as are adapted to the ends indicated above; that is, the efficiency of the citizen as a soldier, when called on to make good "the defence of a free people"; and these arms he may use as a citizen, in all the usual modes to which they are adapted, and common to the country.

What, then, is he protected in the right to keep and thus use? Not every thing that may be useful for offense or defense; but what may properly be included or understood under the title of arms, taken in connection with the fact that the citizen is to keep them, as a citizen. Such, then, as are found to make up the usual arms of the citizen of the country, and the use of which will properly train and render him efficient in defense of his own liberties, as well as of the State. Under this head, with a knowledge of the habits of our people, and of the arms in the use of which a soldier should be trained, we would hold, that the rifle of all descriptions, the shot gun, the musket, and repeater, are such arms; and that under the Constitution the right to keep such arms, can not be infringed or forbidden by the Legislature. Their use, however, to be subordinated to such regulations and limitations as are or may be authorized by the law of the land, passed to subserve the general good, so as not to infringe the right secured and the necessary incidents to the exercise of such right.

What limitations, then, may the Legislature impose on the use of such arms, under the second clause of the 26th section, providing: "But the Legislature shall have power, by law, to regulate the wearing of arms, with a view to prevent crime?" . . .

It is insisted . . . that this clause confers power on the Legislature to prohibit absolutely the wearing of all and every kind of arms, under all circumstances. To this we can not give our assent. The power to regulate, does not fairly mean the power to prohibit; on the contrary, to regulate, necessarily involves the existence of the thing or act to be regulated. . . .

But the power is given to regulate, with a view to prevent crime. The enactment of the Legislature on this subject, must be guided by, and restrained to this end, and bear some well defined relation to the prevention of crime, or else it is unauthorized by this clause of the Constitution.

It is insisted, however, by the Attorney General, that, if we hold the Legislature has no power to prohibit the wearing of arms absolutely . . . then the citizen may carry them at all times and under all circumstances. This does not follow by any means, as we think. . . .

Therefore, a man may well be prohibited from carrying his arms to church, or other public assemblage, as the carrying them to such places is not an appropriate use of them, nor necessary in order to his familiarity with them, and his training and efficiency in their use. As to arms worn, or which are carried about the person, not being such arms as we have indicated as arms that may be kept and used, the wearing of such arms may be prohibited if the Legislature deems proper, absolutely, at all times, and under all circumstances.

It is insisted by the Attorney General, that the right to keep and bear arms is a political, not a civil right. In this we think he fails to distinguish between the nature of the right to keep, and its necessary incidents, and the right to bear arms for the common defense. Bearing arms for the common defense may well be held to be a political right, or for protection and maintenance of such rights, intended to be guaranteed; but the right to *keep* them, with all that is implied fairly as an incident to this right, is a private individual right, guaranteed to the citizen, not the soldier. . . .

[T]he idea of the Constitution is, the keeping and use of such arms as are useful either in warfare, or in preparing the citizen for their use in warfare, by training him as a citizen, to their use in times of peace. In reference to the second article of the Amendments to the Constitution of the United States, Mr. Story says, vol. 2, s. 1897: [The court then quotes from Story's *Familiar Exposition of the Constitution of the United States*, where Story writes that "[t]he militia is the natural defense of a free country against sudden foreign invasion, domestic insurrection and domestic usurpations of power by rulers," and that "[t]he right of the citizen to keep and bear arms, has justly been considered as the palladium of the liberties of the republic, since it offers a strong moral check against usurpation and arbitrary power of rulers. . . ."]

We cite this passage as throwing light upon what was intended to be guaranteed to the people of the States, against the power of the Federal Legislature, and at the same time, as showing clearly what is the meaning of our own Constitution on this subject, as it is evident the State Constitution was intended to guard the same right, and with the same ends in view. So that, the meaning of the one, will give us an understanding of the purpose of the other.

The passage from Story, shows clearly that this right was intended, as we have maintained in this opinion, and was guaranteed to, and to be exercised and enjoyed by the citizen as such, and not by him as a soldier, or in defense solely of his political rights.

Mr. Story adds, in this section: "Yet though this truth would seem to be so clear, (the importance of a militia,) it can not be disguised that among the American people, there is a growing indifference to any system of militia discipline, and a strong disposition, from a sense of its burdens, to be rid of all regulations. How is it practicable," he asks, "to keep the people duly armed without some organization, it is difficult to see. There is certainly no small danger that indifference may lead to disgust, and disgust to contempt, and thus gradually undermine all the protection intended by this clause of our national bill of rights."

We may for a moment, pause to reflect on the fact, that what was once deemed a stable and essential bulwark of freedom, "a well regulated militia," though the clause still remains in our Constitutions, both State and Federal, has, as an organization, passed away in almost every State of the Union, and only remains to us as a memory of the past, probably never to be revived. . . .

The principle on which all right to regulate the use in public of these articles of property, is, that no man can so use his own as to violate the rights of others, or of the community of which he is a member.

So we may say, with reference to such arms, as we have held, he may keep and use in the ordinary mode known to the country, no law can punish him for so doing, while he uses such arms at home or on his own premises. . . . Yet, when he carries his property abroad, goes among the people in public assemblages where others are to be affected by his conduct, then he brings himself within the pale of public regulation, and must submit to such restriction on the mode of using or carrying his property as the people through their Legislature, shall see fit to impose for the general good.

We may here refer to the cases of *Bliss v. Commonwealth*, 12 Ky. (2 Litt.) 90 (1822) [Chapter 5]; *State v. Reid*, 1 Ala. 612 (1840) [Chapter 5], and case of *Nunn v. State*, 1 Ga. 243 (1846) [Chapter 5], as containing much of interesting and able discussion of these questions; in the two last of which the general line of argument found in this opinion is maintained. The Kentucky opinion takes a different view, with which we can not agree. We have not followed precisely either of these cases, but have laid down our own views on the questions presented, aided, however, greatly by the reasoning of these enlightened courts.

We hold, then, that the Act of the Legislature in question, so far as it prohibits the citizen "either publicly or privately to carry a dirk, sword cane, Spanish stiletto, belt or pocket pistol," is constitutional. As to the pistol designated as a revolver, we hold this may or may not be such a weapon as is adapted to the usual equipment of the soldier, or the use of which may render him more efficient as such, and therefore hold this to be a matter to be settled by evidence as to what character of weapon is included in the designation "revolver." We know there is a pistol of that name which is not adapted to the equipment of the soldier, yet we also know that the pistol known as the repeater is a soldier's weapon — skill in the use of which will add to the efficiency of the soldier. If such is the character of the weapon here designated, then the prohibition of the statute is too broad to be allowed to stand, consistently with the views herein expressed. It will be seen the statute forbids by its terms the carrying of the weapon publicly or privately, without regard to time or place, or circumstances, and in effect is an absolute prohibition against keeping such a weapon, and not a regulation of the use of it. Under this statute, if a man should carry such a weapon about his own home, or on his own premises, or should take it from his home to a gunsmith to be repaired, or return with it, should take it from his room into the street to shoot a rabid dog that threatened his child, he would be subjected to the severe penalties of fine and imprisonment prescribed in the statute.

In a word, as we have said, the statute amounts to a prohibition to keep and use such weapon for any and all purposes. It therefore, in this respect, violates the constitutional right to keep arms, and the incidental right to use them in the ordinary mode of using such arms and is inoperative.

If the Legislature think proper, they may by a proper law regulate the carrying of this weapon publicly, or abroad, in such a manner as may be deemed most conducive to the public peace, and the protection and safety of the community from lawless violence. We only hold that, as to this weapon, the prohibition is too broad to be sustained.

The question as to whether a man can defend himself against an indictment for carrying arms forbidden to be carried by law, by showing that he carried them in self-defense, or in anticipation of an attack of a dangerous character upon his person, is one of some little difficulty.

The real question in such case, however, is not the right of self-defense, as seems to be supposed, (for that is conceded by our law to its fullest extent,) but the right to use weapons, or select weapons for such defense, which the law forbids him to keep or carry about his person. If this plea could be allowed as to weapons thus forbidden, it would amount to a denial of the right of the Legislature to prohibit the keeping of such weapons; for, if he may lawfully use them in self-defense, he may certainly provide them, and keep them, for such purpose; and thus the plea of right of self-defense will draw with it, necessarily, the right to keep and use everything for such purpose, however pernicious to the general interest or peace or quiet of the community. Admitting the right of self-defense in its broadest sense, still on sound principle every good citizen is bound to yield his preference as to the means to be used, to the demands of the public good. . . . The law allows ample means of self-defense, without the use of the weapons which we have held may be rightfully prescribed by this statute. The object being to banish these weapons from the community by an absolute prohibition for the prevention of crime, no man's particular safety, if such case could exist, ought to be allowed to defeat this end. Mutual sacrifice of individual rights is the bond of all social organizations, and prompt and willing obedience to all laws passed for the general good, is not only the duty, but the highest interest of every man in the land. . . .

In this view of the case, the question of what circumstances will justify a party in carrying arms, such as the Constitution permits him to keep, in legitimate self-defense, is hardly fairly before us. We may say, that the clause of the Constitution authorizing the Legislature to regulate the wearing of arms with a view to prevent crime, could scarcely be construed to authorize the Legislature to prohibit such wearing, where it was clearly shown they were worn bona fide to ward off or meet imminent and threatened danger to life or limb, or great bodily harm, circumstances essential to make out a case of self-defense. . . .

[The indictment in each case only charges that the parties carried a pistol, without specifying the character of the weapon, whether belt or pocket pistol, or revolver.] For this error the cases will be reversed; the indictments quashed, and remanded to the Circuit Courts to be further proceeded in.

NICHOLSON, C.J., and DEADERICK, J., concurred in the general views of the opinion.

SNEED, J., dissented from so much of the opinion as questioned the right of the Legislature to prohibit the wearing of arms of any description, or sought to limit the operation of the act of 1870.

NELSON, J., delivered the following opinion[, joined by TURNEY, J.]:

Concurring, as I do, in much of the reasoning of the majority of the Court, and believing that the object of the Legislature, in passing the act of 1870, was to promote the public peace, I am, nevertheless constrained by a sense of duty to observe, that, in my opinion, that statute is in violation of one of the most sacred rights known to the Constitution. . . . The expression in [*Aymette v. State* 21 Tenn. (2 Humph) 154 (1840) (Chapter 5); see Chapter 5] that the citizens do not need for the purpose of repelling encroachments upon their rights, "the use of those weapons which are usually employed in private broils, and are efficient only in the hands of the robber and assassin," is, in my view, an unwarrantable aspersion upon the conduct of many honorable men who were well justified in using them in self-defense. . . . The word "bear" was not used alone in the military sense of carrying arms, but in the popular sense of wearing them in war or in peace. The word "arms," means "instruments or weapons of offense or defense," and is not restricted, by any means, to public warfare.

. . . The word "bear" was manifestly employed in the Constitution of 1870, to convey the idea of carrying arms either for public or private defense; otherwise, it was unnecessary to add the provision that the Legislature shall have power "to regulate the wearing of arms with the view to prevent crime." The habit, or custom, intended to be regulated, was not that of bearing arms fit only to be used in war, and which, from the publicity with which such arms are carried, needed but little, if any, regulation. It was well known to the Convention, that a very large number of citizens had become accustomed, during the late civil war, to carry pistols and other weapons not ordinarily used in warfare, and had retained this habit after the close of the war, and that dangerous wounds, as well as frequent homicides, were the result of its universal prevalence; and the object of conferring express power to regulate the mode of wearing them, was not to destroy the right, but so to control it that the Legislature, by declaring that such arms should be worn publicly and not secretly upon the person, might prevent those crimes which are often committed by armed men in taking the lives of their unarmed adversaries. To "regulate" does not mean to destroy, but "to adjust by rule," "to put in good order," to produce uniformity of motion or of action; and, under this provision, there can be no question that, while the Legislature has no power to prohibit the wearing of arms, it has the right to declare that, if worn upon the person, they shall be worn in a public manner. The act of 1870, instead of regulating, prohibits the wearing of arms, and is, therefore, in my opinion, unconstitutional and void. . . .

"... Self-defense, therefore, as it is justly called the primary law of nature, so it is not, neither can it be, in fact, taken away by the law of society": 3 Black. Com.,

34, m. In accordance with this view, I hold that when a man is really and truly endangered by a lawless assault, and the fierceness of the attack is such as to require immediate resistance in order to save his own life, he may defend himself with any weapon whatever, whether seized in the heat of the conflict, or carried for the purpose of self-defense. He is not bound to humiliate or, perchance, to perjure himself, in the slow and often ineffectual process of "swearing the peace,"[1] or to encourage the onslaught of his adversary by an acknowledgment of timidity or cowardice. . . .

Regretting, as I do, that the nobler objects of bearing and wearing arms are too often and too horribly perverted, I can not approve legislation which seems to foster and encourage a craven spirit on the part of those who are disposed to obey the laws, and leaves them to the tender mercies of those who set all law at defiance.

The Tennessee legislature responded to *Andrews* by passing a new weapons-carrying statute in 1871 that seemed to restrict handgun-carrying within narrow bounds. The revised statute again prohibited the carrying of any "dirk, sword-cane, Spanish stiletto, belt or pocket pistol," and then added the following proviso: "or [any] revolver, other than an army pistol, or such as are commonly carried and used in the United States army, and in no case shall it be lawful for any person to carry such army pistol publicly or privately about his person in any other manner than openly in his hands."

A case challenging the new statute came before the Tennessee Supreme Court in the following year. Justice Thomas Nelson, who wrote the partially concurring opinion in *Andrews*, had by then resigned from the court.

State v. Wilburn
66 Tenn. (7 Bax.) 57 (1872)

[Robert Wilburn was indicted for carrying two handguns, one of which was a full-sized military revolver, a/k/a an "army pistol," while the other was not. He was charged with two violations of the 1871 weapons carry statute: first, carrying a handgun that was not an army pistol; second, carrying an army pistol "concealed, and not openly in his hands." Wilburn was tried on the first count, but was acquitted by the jury. The trial court dismissed the second count, relating to the army pistol, before trial. The Attorney General appealed the dismissal of the second count to the Tennessee Supreme Court. Wilburn filed no brief on appeal.]

NICHOLSON, C.J., delivered the opinion of the court.

The record furnishes us no information as to the ground on which the second count was quashed. . . . We presume, however, that the Circuit Judge must either have held that the offense charged is not indicted, or that it is not sufficiently described under the law.

By sec. 26 of the Declaration of Rights, art. 1 of the [Tennessee] Constitution of 1870, "the citizens of this State have a right to keep and bear arms for

---

1. [A common law procedure to require a person who posed a serious risk of future attack to post bond. — EDS.]

their common defense; but the Legislature shall have power, by law, to regulate the wearing of arms, with a view to prevent crime."

The first act passed after the adoption of the Constitution of 1870, was as follows: "It shall not be lawful for any person to publicly or privately carry a dirk, sword cane, Spanish stiletto, belt or pocket pistol, or revolver." But this act was not to apply to an officer or policeman engaged in his official duties . . . or to any person on a journey out of his county or State. . . .

The power of the Legislature to make the carrying of weapons not adapted to the common defense, unlawful, admits of no controversy. This power existed before as well as since the adoption of the Constitution of 1870. None of the weapons enumerated in the act of 1870 fall under the denomination of arms for the common defense, except it may be the "revolver." This term is sometimes applied to a pistol not recognized as an army weapon, and sometimes to the well-known army weapon usually called a "repeater."

Hence this court, in the case of *Andrews v. The State,* 3 Heis. 165, held that the carrying of all the weapons enumerated in the act of 1870, was constitutionally declared unlawful by that act, including the revolver. When it should appear by the proof that it was properly an army weapon, then it was held that the prohibition of the statute was too broad; as, in effect, it is an absolute prohibition against keeping such a weapon, and not a regulation of the use of it. In this respect, the act was regarded as violating the constitutional right to keep arms. But the court further held that the Legislature might, "by a proper law, regulate the carrying of this weapon publicly and abroad, in such a manner as may be deemed most conducive to the public peace, and the protection and safety of the community from lawless violence." It was not intended by this declaration to hold that the power of the Legislature was restricted to the enactment of proper laws for "carrying this weapon publicly or abroad." On the contrary, it is fairly to be inferred from the reasoning in the opinion, that the power of the Legislature to regulate the carrying or wearing of the army pistol, privately or publicly, was conceded, except that a doubt was indicated as to whether the Legislature could constitutionally prohibit such wearing or carrying of this weapon, when it was clearly shown it was worn *bona fide* to ward off or meet imminent and threatened danger to life or limb, or great bodily harm. But this question was not decided, but reserved until it should properly arise.

After . . . *Andrews v. The State* . . . the Legislature passed the act of 1871, ch. 90, under which the defendant in the present case was indicted. The title of the act is, "to preserve the peace and to prevent homicide." It enacts, "that it shall not be lawful for any person to publicly or privately carry a dirk, sword-cane, Spanish stiletto, belt or pocket pistol, or revolver, other than an army pistol, or such as are commonly carried and used in the United States army, and in no case shall it be lawful for any person to carry such army pistol publicly or privately about his person in any other manner than openly in his hands," etc. The same exceptions as to officers, policemen, and persons on a journey, are then made, as in the act of 1870. . . .

[T]he difference in the provision as to the carrying of the army pistol was, therefore, manifestly intended to remedy the defect held to exist in the act of 1870, by the decision of this court. In other words, it was intended to regulate the wearing of the army pistol, by prohibiting its wearing or carrying publicly or privately about the person, in any other manner than openly in the hands. It was not an absolute prohibition of the carrying or wearing of this weapon, as it recognizes the right to carry it openly in the hands, and it concedes to public officers and travelers the right to carry or wear the army pistol, or any of the other weapons enumerated in the act, under the circumstances specified in the act.

We are not called upon, in the present case, to determine what the Legislature meant by the "carrying of the army pistol openly in the hands," or why such an exception was made. The only questions now before us are, first, whether the act of 1871, prohibiting the carrying of an army pistol about the person publicly or privately, is authorized by the clause in the Constitution which empowers the Legislature, by law, to regulate the wearing of arms, with a view to prevent crime. As already indicated, we have no doubt on this question, and hold the act to be clearly constitutional. The Constitution of 1834 contained only the provision securing to the citizen "the right to keep or bear arms for the common defense." The additional clause in the Constitution of 1870 was adopted to remove all doubt as to the power of the Legislature to regulate the use of the arms which the citizens had a right to keep. It was not intended that the keeping or using of such arms should be prohibited, but that the use thereof by wearing or carrying about the person might be so regulated by law as to prevent crime. It was crime resulting from the habit of wearing arms, or of going armed, which the Convention sought to prevent, by expressly conferring this power of the Legislature. The Legislature has deemed it a proper prevention of crime to regulate the use of this arm by prohibiting the wearing of it or carrying it about the person, privately or publicly, unless it be carried openly in the hands. . . . This was a legitimate exercise of the power to regulate the wearing of the weapon, and is authorized by the Constitution, and does not interfere with the right of keeping the arm, or of bearing it for the common defense. . . .

We are therefore of opinion that the offense is charged with sufficient certainty in the indictment to authorize a conviction if the same should be sustained by proof on a trial.

The judgment is reversed and the cause remanded.

NOTES & QUESTIONS

1. Does *Wilburn* follow the reasoning in *Andrews*? Clarify it? Reject it? Or something else?

2. A handgun can be carried for long periods of time in a proper holster (either openly or concealed) without risk of accident. However, the Tennessee statute in *Wilburn* declared that the only legal way to carry an army pistol was unholstered, "openly in the hands." This method is not only inconvenient, but is far more likely to cause an accidental discharge of the firearm, especially if it is carried for a long period of time.

   On the other hand, "in the hands" carry might be appropriate for a short period of time, in response to an imminent and serious threat. Moreover, such a method may have been somewhat less dangerous in the late nineteenth century than it would be today. In the 1870s and 1880s, military handguns were single-action revolvers (online Chapter 15), which, when loaded properly, cannot discharge unless the hammer is first cocked back by hand. Today, many common types of military and police handguns will fire if the chamber is loaded and the trigger is pulled. Why do you think the Tennessee legislature chose to require this mode of carry? Do precise controls on the exact method of carry (e.g., mandating "in the hand," or, hypothetically, mandating "in a holster" or "not in a purse or briefcase") violate the right to arms?

3. *Andrews* concludes that "the same rights, and for similar reasons, were . . . provided for and protected in both the Federal and [Tennessee] Constitutions." Do you agree? Is it relevant that the Tennessee Constitution says the right to keep and bear arms is "for the common defense," while the Framers of the Bill of Rights specifically rejected a proposal to include "for the common defense" in the Second Amendment? Does the prefatory language about a "well regulated militia" in the Second Amendment amount to the same thing?

4. *Andrews* says that the right "to keep and to bear arms for the common defense" only extends to those weapons that "make up the usual arms of the citizen of the country, and the use of which will properly train and render him efficient in defense of his own liberties, as well as of the State." This is the civilized warfare test used by the same court three decades earlier in *Aymette* (Chapter 5). Other types of weapons, *Andrews* indicates, could lawfully be banned. Next, *Andrews* appears to view the right to "bear arms for the common defense" as a collective political right rather than an individual one. But *Andrews* then claims that the right to "keep arms" is different; it is a broad individual right that implies, "necessarily, the right to use such arms for all the ordinary purposes, and in all the ordinary modes usual in the country, and to which arms are adapted, limited by the duties of a good citizen in times of peace." Do those ordinary purposes include the right to carry one's (military) arms for self-defense? What does *Andrews* suggest about the answer to this question? How about *Wilburn*? Is there a reason why "bear" might be a political right when "keep" is personal?

5. What do you make of Justice Nelson's discussion of "honor" in his *Andrews* concurrence? Nelson complains that court decisions dismissing nonmilitary weapons such as Bowie knives and small pistols as tools only of robbers and thugs cast "an unwarrantable aspersion upon the conduct of many honorable men who were well justified in using them in self-defense." Nelson was a Unionist who strongly opposed secession in the volatile years leading to Tennessee's joining the Confederacy in 1861. Might he have spoken from personal experience? We know that Nelson's experiences collided with the issue of armed self-defense, in startling fashion, shortly after he penned his *Andrews* concurrence. Nelson resigned from the Tennessee Supreme Court in the fall of 1871 in order to assist in the legal defense of his son, David, who had used a shotgun to kill former Confederate General James H. Clanton, in a gunfight that erupted in the middle of downtown Knoxville. Some media reports claimed that David started the fight while drunk, and he was indicted and charged with first degree murder. But David was acquitted by a local jury, which accepted his claim that he killed Clanton in self-defense. *See* Thomas B. Alexander, Thomas A.R. Nelson of East Tennessee 152-55,

166 (1956). Should judges' personal experiences with weapons and/
or with self-defense be relevant to their interpretation of constitutional
guarantees?

In general, state courts during late nineteenth and early twentieth centuries tended to reject the notion of a legal duty to retreat before acting in
self-defense. *See* Richard Maxwell Brown, No Duty to Retreat: Violence and
Values in American History and Society (1994). Below, in Section G of this
chapter, we will discuss the Supreme Court's rejection of a retreat requirement. Other than honor, are there any reasons to oppose a retreat rule?

Tennessee's 1870 constitution and its right to keep and bear arms
provision remain in force today. Neither *Andrews* nor *Wilburn* has been overruled. *Andrews* is the more influential case, having been cited several times by
the Tennessee Supreme Court in the late nineteenth and twentieth centuries,
as well as by the courts of several other states, and three times by the U.S.
Supreme Court in *Heller* (Chapter 9). *Wilburn* also has been cited a few times,
but never by a Tennessee court. For a general discussion of the
Tennessee right to arms cases, and their possible relevance to applying the
Second Amendment, see Glenn Harlan Reynolds, *The Right to Keep and Bear
Arms Under the Tennessee Constitution: A Case Study in Civic Republican Thought*,
61 Tenn. L. Rev. 647 (1994). As you read subsequent cases in this book,
consider how various judges select which cases to use as precedents.

Few observers in 1871 would have disputed the conclusion in *Andrews*
that full-sized, repeating handguns such as the Colt Army and Navy revolvers
were important military small arms. They had been used extensively in the
Civil War, mainly by cavalry troopers, whose fast-moving, often chaotic
skirmishes put a premium on rapid firepower. Repeating rifles such as
the Henry and Spencer lever-action carbines were also introduced during
the war, but were scarce in the Confederacy. Revolvers were the only type of
repeating guns that were relatively plentiful in the in South and prevalent
among Southern troops. *See generally* William B. Edwards, Civil War Guns
(1978).

In the late nineteenth century, very high-speed printing presses prolif-
erated, leading to the birth of the "penny press" (newspapers sold for one
cent), which tended to focus on sensational and lurid stories. The high-speed
presses were seen as solidly within the First Amendment. In contrast, until
the last quarter of the twentieth century, there was a substantial body of
First Amendment thought that considered television and radio outside
the protection of the First Amendment. Compare the proliferation of repeating firearms. How did courts and commentators in the nineteenth
century view the high-quality repeating arms — as within the right to arms,
or not?

6. *Andrews* states that the militia as the Framers had known it had "passed
    away." In the court's view, what significance does that disappearance have
    for the constitutional right to arms?

7. During the nineteenth century, not only did arms change, so did ammuni-
    tion. The 1870s saw the emergence of metallic cartridges for repeating hand-
    guns like the S&W Model 3 Schofield and the Colt SAA. The metallic

cartridge made possible new revolvers that were more reliable and quicker to reload than either the muzzleloaders or cap-and-ball revolvers (loaded from the front of the cylinder and capped with wax) that preceded them. The metallic cartridge from this period is essentially the type of ammunition that is now used in all modern firearms. The main difference is that early metallic cartridge ammunition used black powder instead of smokeless powder. Black powder produced lower pressures and produced large clouds of white smoke when fired. (See online Chapters 1 and 15 for details on the metallic cartridge.)

Do you think these technological developments had an impact on the case law on handgun-carrying in this chapter? What do you think of the argument that the right to arms should only protect the types of arms that were in existence when the right was placed in a constitution?

The Postbellum Experience in Arkansas

Like the courts of Tennessee, the Arkansas Supreme Court struggled with the constitutional right to arms in the aftermath of Reconstruction. The Arkansas Constitution had formerly provided that the "free white men" had "the right to keep and bear arms for their common defense." Recall that in *State v. Buzzard*, 4 Ark. 18 (1842) (Chapter 5), a majority took a narrow view of this provision. Arkansas's post-war constitutions eliminated the racially exclusive language, but retained the focus on the common defense. *See* Ark. Const. of 1868, art. I, §5, and Ark. Const. of 1874, art. I, §5: "The citizens of this State shall have the right to keep and bear arms for their common defence."

A series of four cases in the 1870s and 1880s applied this language to prohibitions on carrying guns, as the legislature toughened the state's already restrictive antebellum weapons laws.

In *Carroll v. State*, 28 Ark. 99 (1872), the defendant challenged his conviction and $25 fine for carrying "a pistol in the breast pocket of his coat." The trial court had rejected his request for jury instructions requiring acquittal if (1) he had the pistol concealed only on his own property, or (2) was carrying the concealed pistol out of a legitimate fear that his life was in danger. The state supreme court, affirmed the conviction, ruling:

> . . . There is no provision in the statute excusing a party when carrying a pistol concealed as a weapon on his own premises, nor would it constitute any excuse for so wearing a weapon, to show that the accused was in fear or even in danger of being attacked.
>
> As held by this court in the case of *Buzzard v. The State*, 4 Ark. 18 (1842) [Chapter 5], a constitutional right to bear arms in defense of person and property does not prohibit the legislature from making such police regulations . . . as to the manner in which such arms shall be borne. Neither natural nor constitutional right authorizes a citizen to use his own property or bear his own arms in such way as to injure the property or endanger the life of his fellow citizen, and these regulations must be left to the wisdom of the legislature, so long as their discretion is kept within reasonable bounds. And it is not unreasonable for the legislature to enact that deadly weapons shall not be worn concealed, that those associating with the bearer may guard against injury by accident or otherwise.

In *Fife v. State*, 31 Ark. 455 (1876), the defendant was convicted of carrying a "pocket revolver," in violation of a state statute prohibiting the carrying of "any pistol of any kind whatever, or any dirk, butcher or Bowie knife, or sword or spear in a cane, brass or metal knucks, or razor, as a weapon." He challenged the conviction under the Second Amendment and the arms-bearing provision of Arkansas's constitution. The court held that the Second Amendment does not apply to states. Then, citing *Aymette* (Chapter 5), *Andrews, supra*, and Bishop's *Commentaries on the Law of Statutory Crimes, supra*, the court held that the state constitution protected only military weapons. The court also cited *Buzzard* (Chapter 5) for the proposition that a law prohibiting carrying concealed weapons did not offend either the state or federal constitutions. Because a pocket pistol was a concealable, nonmilitary weapon, carrying it was not protected, and the conviction was affirmed.

The Court refined its statement about military weapons in *Wilson v. State*, 33 Ark. 557 (1878), which reversed the conviction of a defendant for carrying concealed "a large army size" pistol. The opinion made no mention of *Buzzard*. The court ruled that "to prohibit the citizen from wearing or carrying a war arm . . . [was] an unwarranted restriction upon [the defendant's] constitutional right to keep and bear arms. . . . If cowardly and dishonorable men sometimes shoot unarmed men with army pistols or guns, the evil must be prevented by the penitentiary and gallows, and not by a general deprivation of a constitutional privilege." *Wilson* cited the Tennessee decision in *Andrews*, and suggested that some limits on carrying army pistols were permissible, such as prohibiting wearing them to "places of public worship, elections, etc."

Wilson's affirmation of a right to carry a military handgun was narrowed in *Haile v. State*, 38 Ark. 564 (1882). The Arkansas legislature responded to *Wilson* much as the Tennessee legislature had responded to the similar decision in *Andrews*. An 1881 Arkansas statute prohibited the carrying of all handguns except for army pistols, and declared that army pistols could only be carried "uncovered and in the hand." Haile was convicted for carrying a Colt military revolver openly, but on his belt, not in the hand. The supreme court upheld the conviction, citing *State v. Wilburn, supra*. It emphasized the "common defense" language of the Arkansas right to arms provision:

> It must be confessed that [carrying one's pistol openly in the hand] is a very inconvenient mode of carrying [it] habitually, but the habitual carrying does not seem essential to "common defense." The inconvenience is a slight matter compared with the danger to the whole community, which would result from the common practice of going about with pistols in a belt, ready to be used on every outbreak of ungovernable passion. It is a police regulation, adjusted as wisely as the Legislature thought possible, with all essential constitutional rights.

Id. at 566. The court concluded that as long as "every citizen may keep arms in readiness upon his place, may render himself skillful in their use by practice, and carry them upon a journey without . . . hindrance, it seems to us, the essential objects of this particular clause of the bill of rights will be preserved, although the citizen be required to carry them uncovered, and in the hand, off his own premises, if he should deem it necessary to carry them at all." *Id.* at 567.

State v. Duke
42 Tex. 455 (1875)

GOULD, J.

This is an appeal by the State from the judgment of the District Court sustaining a motion to set aside, as insufficient, an indictment, charging that George Duke did, on the 23d day of December, 1871, in said Caldwell county, "unlawfully carry on his person one pistol, known as a six-shooter." The first and second Sections of the "Act to regulate the keeping and bearing of deadly weapons," passed April 11, 1871, are as follows:

> "Any person carrying on or about his person, saddle, or in his saddle-bags, any pistol, dirk, dagger, slung-shot, swordcane, spear, brass knuckles, bowie knife, or any other kind of knife, manufactured or sold, for the purpose of offense or defense, unless he has reasonable grounds for fearing an unlawful attack on his person, and that such ground of attack shall be immediate and pressing; or unless having or carrying the same on or about his person for the lawful defense of the State, as a militiaman in actual service, or as a peace officer or policeman, shall be guilty of a misdemeanor. . . ."
>
> "SECTION 2. Any person charged under the first Section of this Act, who may offer to prove by way of defense, that he was in danger of an attack on his person, or unlawful interference with his property, shall be required to show that such danger was immediate and pressing, and was of such a nature as to alarm a person of ordinary courage; and that the arms so carried were borne openly, and not concealed beneath the clothing; and if it shall appear that this danger had its origin in a difficulty first commenced by the accused, it shall not be considered a legal defense."

The objection made to the indictment was that it charged no offense known to the laws of the State, bringing up the question of the constitutionality of this Act, and also of the sufficiency of the indictment under the statute, if held valid.

[The court here relied on *Barron v. Baltimore*, 32 U.S. (7 Pet.) 243 (1833), to hold that there was no merit to the argument that the statute was unconstitutional under the federal Second Amendment.]

[W]e pass to the consideration of the 13th Section of the Bill of Rights in the Constitution of the State; which is as follows: "Every person shall have the right to keep and bear arms in the lawful defense of himself or the State, under such regulations as the Legislature may prescribe." The question presented by the case before us is, does that part of the Act making it an offense to carry a pistol, except in the cases therein specified, violate this section of the Bill of Rights?

In *English v. The State*, 35 Tex. 478 (1872), this court held that it did not. We acquiesce in the decision, but do not adopt the opinion expressed that the word "arms," in the Bill of Rights, refers only to the arms of a militiaman or soldier. Similar clauses in the Constitutions of other States have generally been construed by the courts as using the word arms in a more comprehensive sense. (. . . *The State v. Reid*, 1 Ala., 612 (1840) [Chapter 5]; *The State v. Mitchell*, 3 Blackf. 229 (Ind. 1833) [Chapter 5]; Nunn v. The State, 1 Kelly 243 (Ga. 1846) [Chapter 5]; *The State v. Buzzard*, 4 Ark. 18 (1842) [Chapter 5]. . . .)

There is no recital of the necessity of a well-regulated militia [in the Texas Constitution], as there is in the corresponding clause in the Constitution of the

United States. The arms which every person is secured the right to keep and bear (in the defense of himself or the State, subject to legislative regulation), must be such arms as are commonly kept, according to the customs of the people, and are appropriate for open and manly use in self-defense, as well as such as are proper for the defense of the State. If this does not include the double-barreled shot-gun, the huntsman's rifle, and such pistols at least as are not adapted to being carried concealed, then the only arms which the great mass of the people of the State have, are not under constitutional protection. . . .

The question for our decision is the constitutionality of the Act under which this indictment was proved. It undertakes to regulate the place where, and the circumstances under which, a pistol may be carried; and in doing so, it appears to have respected the right to carry a pistol openly when needed for self-defense or in the public service, and the right to have one at the home or place of business. We hold that the statute under consideration is valid, and that to carry a pistol under circumstances where it is forbidden by the statute, is a violation of the criminal law of the State. . . .

Affirmed.

NOTES & QUESTIONS

1. *Duke* rejects the civilized warfare test, and holds that all guns commonly kept by the people for self-defense qualify as "arms" within the Texas Constitution, as long as they are suited to open, rather than concealed carry. The post-war Tennessee and Arkansas courts, on the other hand, accepted the civilized warfare test and in those states, the only handguns whose ownership was constitutionally protected were full-sized military revolvers. In light of the "common defense" language of the Tennessee and Arkansas Constitutions (Chapter 1, appendix), did the state legislatures have the proper authority to limit handgun ownership only to those models most suitable for militia use? Was the limitation good policy?

   Some commentators argue that the "civilized warfare" restrictions served the pernicious purpose of preventing Blacks from acquiring handguns, while "render[ing] safe the high quality, expensive, military issue handguns that many former Confederate soldiers still maintained but that were often out of financial reach for cash poor freedmen." Robert J. Cottrol & Raymond T. Diamond, *"Never Intended to Be Applied to the White Population": Firearms Regulation and Racial Disparity — The Redeemed South's Legacy to a National Jurisprudence?*, 70 Chi.-Kent L. Rev. 1307, 1334 (1995). Similar arguments have been raised about modern laws that ban "Saturday Night Specials" (small inexpensive handguns). T. Markus Funk, *Gun Control and Economic Discrimination: The Melting-Point Case-in-Point*, 85 J. Crim. L. & and Criminology 764 (1995). For either the nineteenth-century laws, or their modern descendants, should courts consider legislative intent in evaluating constitutionality? What if it is determined that some legislators had discriminatory motives, while others had innocent ones? Should courts or legislatures consider whether laws that significantly raise the economic cost of owning or carrying guns have disparate impact on racial minorities or the poor?

2. *Wilburn, Haile,* and *Duke* all end up in roughly the same place with respect to the right to carry arms outside the home. In *Duke,* the court upheld a limitation on handgun-carrying similar to the necessity doctrine in the criminal law of self-defense: no carrying a handgun "unless [one] has reasonable grounds for fearing an unlawful attack on his person, and that such ground of attack shall be immediate and pressing." In practice, the statutes in *Wilburn* and *Haile,* requiring weapons to be carried "open in the hand" would tend to limit the practice of carrying handguns to situations of imminent necessity. Such laws technically allowed a person to walk about with his Colt in hand even absent an imminent threat. But in practice, the "open in hand" requirement would tend to limit handgun-carrying to situations of immediate danger. The end result, thus, may have been very similar to the carry-ban-with-self-defense exception in *Duke.*

    What do these cases suggest about the application of the right to bear arms to public spaces today? Do they reflect a restrictive Jim Crow–era atmosphere of the Southern states from which they arose, or are they a principled attempt to uphold public safety by confining handgun-carrying to clear cases of self-defense?

3. In 1890, Tennessee and Arkansas had the toughest gun control laws in the United States. Those laws were much more restrictive than the toughest rules at the time. Today, the most restrictive jurisdictions include New York, New Jersey, Massachusetts, the District of Columbia, and California. Why do you think that the locus of gun control changed over the intervening 120 years?

4. The Ohio case of *State v. Nieto,* 130 N.E. 663 (Ohio 1920), involving a Mexican employee of a railroad, upheld a complete ban on concealed carry, even in one's own home. A dissenting judge wrote:

    > I desire to give some special attention to some of the authorities cited, supreme court decisions from Alabama, Georgia, Arkansas, Kentucky, and one or two inferior court decisions from New York, which are given in support of the doctrines upheld by this court. The southern states have very largely furnished the precedents. It is only necessary to observe that the race issue there has extremely intensified a decisive purpose to entirely disarm the negro, and this policy is evident upon reading the opinions.

    Id. at 669 (Wanamaker, J., dissenting). Do you agree that the Southern cases are racist? Even though the decisions themselves say nothing about race?

The case that follows is technically a twentieth-century case, and it would exercise a wide influence among many state and federal courts in the course of that century. Consider to what extent it reflects a culmination of the late nineteenth-century cases, and to what extent it is a new departure.

City of Salina v. Blaksley
83 P. 619 (Kan. 1905)

GREENE, J.

James Blaksley was convicted in the police court of the city of Salina, a city of the second class, of carrying a revolving pistol within the city while under the influence of intoxicating liquor. . . .

The question presented is the constitutionality of section 1003 of the General Statutes of 1901, which reads: "The council may prohibit and punish the carrying of fire arms or other deadly weapons, concealed or otherwise, and may arrest and imprison, fine or set at work all vagrants and persons found in said city without visible means of support, or some legitimate business."

Section 4 of the Bill of Rights is as follows: "The people have the right to bear arms for their defense and security; but standing armies, in time of peace, are dangerous to liberty, and shall not be tolerated, and the military shall be in strict subordination to the civil power." The contention is that this section of the Bill of Rights is a constitutional inhibition upon the power of the Legislature to prohibit the individual from having and carrying arms, and that section 1003 of the General Statutes of 1901 is an attempt to deprive him of the right guarantied by the Bill of Rights, and is therefore unconstitutional and void. The power of the Legislature to prohibit or regulate the carrying of deadly weapons has been the subject of much dispute in the courts. The views expressed in the decisions are not uniform, and the reasonings of the different courts vary. It has, however, been generally held that the Legislatures can regulate the mode of carrying deadly weapons, provided they are not such as are ordinarily used in civilized warfare. To this view, there is a notable exception in the early case of *Bliss v. Commonwealth*, 2 Litt. (Ky.) 90 [1822; Chapter 5], where it was held, under a constitutional provision similar to ours, that the act of the Legislature prohibiting the carrying of concealed deadly weapons was void, and that the right of the citizen to own and carry arms was protected by the Constitution, and could not be taken away or regulated. While this decision has frequently been referred to by the courts of other states, it has never been followed. The same principle was announced in Idaho in [*In re Brickey*, 70 P. 609 (Idaho 1902)], but no reference is made to *Bliss v. Commonwealth* [Chapter 5], nor to any other authority in support of the decision. In view of the disagreements in the reasonings of the different courts by which they reached conflicting conclusions, we prefer to treat the question as an original one.

The provision in section 4 of the Bill of Rights "that the people have the right to bear arms for their defense and security" refers to the people as a collective body. It was the safety and security of society that was being considered when this provision was put into our Constitution. It is followed immediately by the declaration that standing armies in time of peace are dangerous to liberty and should not be tolerated and that "the military shall be in strict subordination to the civil power." It deals exclusively with the military. Individual rights are not considered in this section. The manner in which the people shall exercise this right of bearing arms for the defense and security of the people is found in article 8 of the Constitution, which authorizes the organizing, equipping, and disciplining of the militia, which shall be composed of "able-bodied male citizens between the ages of twenty-one and forty-five years." The militia is essentially the people's army, and their defense and security in time of peace. There are no other provisions made for the military protection and security of the people in time of peace. In the absence of constitutional or legislative authority, no person has the right to assume such duty. In some of the states where it has been held, under similar provisions, that the citizen has the right preserved by the Constitution to carry such arms as are ordinarily used in civilized warfare, it is placed on the ground that it was intended that the people would thereby become accustomed to handling and using such arms, so that in case of an emergency they would be more or less prepared for the duties of a soldier. The weakness of this argument lies in the fact that in nearly every state in the Union there are provisions for organizing and drilling state militia in sufficient numbers to meet any such emergency.

That the provision in question applies only to the right to bear arms as a member of the state militia, or some other military organization provided for by law, is also apparent from the second amendment to the federal Constitution, which says: "A well regulated militia, being necessary to the security of a free state, the right of the people to keep and bear arms shall not be infringed." Here, also, the right of the people to keep and bear arms for their security is preserved, and the manner of bearing them for such purpose is clearly indicated to be as a member of a well-regulated militia, or some other military organization provided for by law. Mr. Bishop, in his work on Statutory Crimes, in treating of this provision, which is found in almost every state Constitution, says, in section 793: "In reason, the keeping and bearing of arms has reference only to war and possibly also to insurrections wherein the forms of war are, as far as practicable observed." . . .

The judgment is affirmed. All the Justices concurring.

NOTES & QUESTIONS

1. What is the holding in *Blaksley*?

2. *Blaksley* is the first case in which the collective right interpretation of an arms-bearing provision appeared in a court's *holding*. The first time such an interpretation was ever *mentioned* in a judicial decision (*Buzzard*, see Chapter 5) was more than 60 years before *Blaksley*, and more than 50 years after the Second Amendment was adopted. Does this diminish the credibility of the collective-right interpretation, or is this merely the normal progression of the law in a common law system? Does the answer say anything about the role of high courts in adhering to *stare decisis*?

3. *Blaksley* declined to follow the Idaho Supreme Court decision in *In re Brickey*, 70 P. 609 (Idaho 1902). *Brickey* was a handgun carry case that interpreted a state constitutional guarantee similar to the Kansas provision: "The people have the right to bear arms for their security and defense; but the Legislature shall regulate the exercise of this right by law." Idaho Const. of 1889, art. I, §11. The *Brickey* court reversed the defendant's conviction for carrying a loaded revolver in the city of Lewiston. It concluded that under the Second Amendment and the Idaho Constitution, "the legislature has no power to

prohibit a citizen from bearing arms in any portion of the state of Idaho," though it could regulate the exercise of the right by prohibiting concealed carry. *Id.* at 609. Why might the Kansas and Idaho courts have reached such different interpretations of similar language?

4. If the arms-bearing provision in the Kansas Constitution merely states one of the powers of state government, as *Blaksley* holds, why does the provision appear in the Bill of Rights of the Kansas Constitution?

5. *Blaksley* states that the militia is responsible for the people's "defense and security in time of peace." Does the combination of this language and the court's holding mean that the Kansas legislature could explicitly ban self-defense? Is the answer to this question affected by the well-established rule that governments have no responsibility for protecting individuals from crime? *DeShaney v. Winnebago County,* 489 U.S. 189 (1989) (government inaction in rescuing child who was known to be severely abused, and was later murdered); *Riss v. New York,* 240 N.E.2d 806 (N.Y. 1958) (stalker who attacked and disfigured his victim; dissent notes that Miss Riss was prevented from carrying a gun in public by New York law).

F.   *State Constitutions at the Turn of the Century*

Of the 45 states to have joined the union by the twentieth century, 32 had arms-bearing and related provisions in their state constitutions. Many of these provisions underwent change, especially after the Civil War. A survey of the history of these provisions provides an overview of the national mood about the right to bear arms, and perhaps some instruction about the factors motivating that mood.

The chart in the appendix to Chapter 1 summarizes the changes to state constitutional right to arms provisions. Review the history of those provisions from the Founding through 1900 now, before proceeding.

Many of the new provisions affirm a right to arms, but also tend to provide some explicit limitations on the right. Broadly speaking, there were two causes for the proliferation of new state constitutions in the second half of nineteenth century. First, many new Western states joined the Union and adopted their first constitutions. Second, all the former Confederate states were required to write new constitutions as a condition of readmission to the Union.

NOTES & QUESTIONS

1. Do you notice any patterns in how the constitutions were altered over time? Compare the ante- and postbellum provisions in the Chapter 1 appendix. What do these patterns imply?

2. South Carolina's 1868 constitution, all of Tennessee's constitutions, and Missouri's 1820 constitution contain Declarations of Rights allowing individuals to pay an "equivalent" to avoid having to bear arms and an exemption for conscientious objectors. Each of these constitutions also has a separate article dealing exclusively with the state's militia. The South Carolina Constitution mentions exemptions in *both* its Declaration of Rights and its militia article. Tennessee's (which, unlike the others, allows anyone, not just conscientious objectors, to pay an equivalent) *splits* these provisions between its Declaration of Rights and militia articles. Missouri's mentions its exemptions *only* in its Declaration of Rights.

   If these constitutions guaranteed an individual right to bear arms, why would they contain provisions allowing one to pay an equivalent to avoid bearing arms, and why would they connect them with their arms-bearing guarantees instead of discussing them only in their militia articles? Is there any significance to the places in which each constitution establishes the right to arms, the payment of an equivalent, and militia service?

   Many other state constitutions provide for conscientious-objector exemptions. Those provisions are often located in the sections delineating the powers of the state, including the state's militia powers. Those constitutions do not mention conscientious-objector exemptions in the declarations of rights sections that guarantee the right to arms. E.g., Colo. Const. of 1876, art. II, §13 (right to arms), art. XVII, §5 (conscientious objectors).

3. Do the post-1860 Southern constitutional right to arms provisions differ from the provisions in the new Western states? If so, what might explain the differences?

4. Some arms-bearing provisions were connected to requirements that the military be subordinate to the "civil authority" or "civil power." Every constitution in effect at the turn of the century except those of Georgia, New Hampshire, and New York had such provisions in their constitutions, either directly connected to its arms-bearing guarantee or listed separately. In some cases, as in Pennsylvania's 1790 and Indiana's 1851 constitutions, the civil power provisions were split off from the arms-bearing provisions of earlier constitutions into separate guarantees. Pa. Const. of 1790, art. IX, §22; Ind. Const. of 1851, art. I, §33.

   Why might such provisions have been prevalent after the Civil War? Might states have had a more palpable fear of tyranny after the war than before? To what military organizations do the provisions refer? Many of these constitutions had prohibitions on the keeping of standing armies, either connected with or separate from their arms-bearing provisions. *Compare* N.C. Const. of 1868, art. I, §24 (Chapter 1 appendix), *supra, with* Ala. Const. of 1875, art. I, §28. Can states have armies? *See* U.S. Const., art. I, §10, cl. 3. Is a state ban on armies a prudent measure, in case the federal ban is not enforced?

5. What do you make of the fact that right-to-arms clauses in a state constitution section that also contained clauses limiting standing armies and affirming the subordination of the military to the civil power were regularly

interpreted by state courts as protecting an individual right? *See, e.g.,* *Andrews, supra; State v. Speller,* 86 N.C. 697, 700-01 (1882); *State v. Huntley,* 25 N.C. (3 Ired.) 418, 422-23 (1843). Recall the Founders' views on select militias (Chapters 3 and 4).

6. Compare the 1865-99 state constitutional arms guarantees with those from 1776-96. Which ones emphasize a militia purpose more? Which ones seem closer to the way that we articulate personal rights in the twenty-first century? Are there regional differences in either period?

7. What does Utah's 1896 constitution Utah Const. of 1896, art. I, §6, guarantee? CQ: See the dissents in *Heller* (Chapter 9).

8. Some states guaranteed their citizens the right to arms even before they were states. Vermont and Texas were not territories, but independent republics before joining the Union. (Texas was plainly an independent nation, while Vermont's status was somewhat unclear.) Does this imply anything about the meaning of the right to arms in their constitutions? About the right to arms in other state constitutions?

9. The many constitutions that contain explicit allowance for regulation of concealed carry avoid the result in *Bliss v. Commonwealth* (Chapter 5), where concealed carry was held to be protected by the state constitutional right to arms. Why did the nineteenth-century courts remain relatively tolerant of open carry, but hostile to concealed carry? Are the same reasons applicable today, when licensed concealed carry is the norm in most of the United States, while open carry is socially controversial?

10. For more on the evolution of state constitutional arms-bearing provisions, including up through the present day, see Nicholas J. Johnson, *A Second Amendment Moment: The Constitutional Politics of Gun Control,* 71 Brook. L. Rev. 715, 728-44. For detailed analysis of state cases interpreting state constitutional right to arms provisions, from the early nineteenth century to present, see David B. Kopel & Clayton Cramer, *State Court Standards of Review for the Right to Arms,* 50 Santa Clara L. Rev. 1113 (2010). Michael P. O'Shea, *Modeling the Second Amendment Right to Carry Arms (I): Judicial Tradition and the Scope of 'Bearing Arms' for Self-Defense,* 61 Am. U. L. Rev. (forthcoming 2012), *available at* http://ssrn.com/abstract = 1949477.

G.   *The Self-Defense Cases*

Between 1893 and 1896, the Supreme Court decided a series of cases implicating the right of self-defense. The Court decided one more major self-defense case in 1921. Because the alleged crimes involved in the 1893-96 cases took place in Indian territory over which the federal government had primary jurisdiction, the

Court had the opportunity to create federal common law on the criminal law of self-defense. None of the cases have been overruled.

A brief summary of each case provides a useful overview of American self-defense law. Of course, none of these cases are directly binding on state courts. However, to the extent that *Heller* (Chapter 9) and its progeny (Chapter 11) recognize a federal constitutional right of self-defense, the following cases may be of value in determining the parameters of that right.

Gourko v. United States, 153 U.S. 183 (1894), held that it was error for the trial court to instruct the jury that the mere carrying of a pistol was evidence of premeditated intent to kill, and that the defendant could therefore not be found guilty of manslaughter rather than murder.

Starr v. United States, 153 U.S. 614 (1894), held that it was error for the trial court to instruct the jury that a bond-jumper who shot a civilian deputized as a peace officer could not claim self-defense because he was an outlaw. Rather, the bond-jumper was entitled to claim self-defense if he did not know that he was defending against a peace officer.

In *Thompson v. United States*, 155 U.S. 271 (1894), a man was threatened with being shot when taking the only road to a remote area. Before heading back home, he borrowed a rifle from the woman whom he visited, and shot the person who again threatened him. The Court held that it was error for the trial court to instruct the jury that in arming himself, the defendant evinced either an intent to provoke trouble or to kill.

Beard v. United States, 158 U.S. 550 (1895), held that it was error for the trial court to instruct the jury that (1) Beard's taking a gun to confront thieves on his property was provocation that barred the claim of self-defense, and (2) one must attempt to retreat from attackers on one's own property (as opposed to inside one's home, for it was already established law that there was no duty to retreat).

Allison v. United States, 160 U.S. 203 (1895), held that it was error for the trial court to instruct the jury that (1) fear of deadly attack based on prior attacks by the same person was insufficient justification for claiming self-defense, and (2) carrying a gun showed an intent to provoke and kill.

Wallace v. United States, 162 U.S. 466 (1896), held that it was error for the trial court to (1) exclude testimony proffered by the defendant to support his self-defense claim, that would have shown that he was threatened by someone he shot (and who first stabbed him), and (2) prevent the defendant from testifying about his fear of imminent attack. The Court added that (3) the defendant was entitled to defend himself from deadly attack even if he was legally wrong in using a gun to oust trespassers from his property, and (4) the fact that the defendant was armed was not a reason to disallow the defendant's reliance on the threats made against him.

Alberty v. United States, 162 U.S. 499 (1896), held that it was error for the trial court to instruct the jury that a man who confronted his wife's adulterous paramour off of the family property could only resort to self-defense if he could not retreat safely.

Acres v. United States, 164 U.S. 388 (1896), held that it was *not* error for the trial court to instruct the jury that, among other things, (1) a rock can be a "deadly weapon" depending on how it is used, and (2) self-defense must be based on a "reasonable" belief in "present danger . . . of great injury."

Allen v. United States actually consists of three cases, 150 U.S. 551 (1893), 157 U.S. 675 (1895), and 164 U.S. 493 (1896). Together, the first two iterations of this case held that it was error for the trial court to (1) *imply* to the jury that the defendant could not claim self-defense because he did not deliberate long enough over whether it was warranted, (2) instruct that sticks (which with some whites attacked the Black defendant Allen) could not be deadly weapons, (3) instruct that carrying a gun was evidence of a premeditated intent to kill. The third iteration held that (4) it was correct to instruct the jury that self-defense could only be used to repel an attack endangering life or causing "great bodily harm," and (5) that there was a duty to retreat where one was attacked on public property if the confrontation did not involve special circumstances (such as confronting one's wife's lover). These cases also gave birth to the "*Allen* charge," which is still used today as a standard instruction by judges to encourage deadlocked juries to continue to deliberate and to resolve their differences.

Rowe v. United States, 164 U.S. 546 (1896), held that an attacker's right to self-defense is restored upon withdrawing from the fight he started. The court also held that it was error for the trial court to instruct the jury that, when attacked, one must first attempt to "step[] to one side" or use nondeadly force before resorting to deadly force.

In *Brown v. United States*, 256 U.S. 335 (1921), a man was pursued in a federal naval yard by a knife-wielding attacker who had previously threatened to kill him. Justice Oliver Wendell Holmes famously wrote for the Court that (1) "[d]etached reflection cannot be demanded in the presence of an uplifted knife," (2) a victim need not attempt to disable his attacker to claim self-defense, and (3) the defendant had no duty to retreat from "a place where he was called to be, in the discharge of his duty."

A number of principles can be gleaned from these cases:

(1) The mere possession of a weapon, absent a law prohibiting it, is in and of itself an innocent act. *Gourko; Thompson; Beard; Allison; Wallace; Allen.*

(2) Everyone is entitled to resort to self-defense. *Starr; Thompson; Allison; Wallace; Rowe.*

(3) There is no duty to retreat before resorting to deadly force in self-defense. *Beard; Alberty; Rowe; Brown.* Note: Current state laws differ widely on the duty to retreat. The trend in the early twenty-first century has been toward removing the duty to retreat, or limiting the places where the duty might apply. The removal of the duty to retreat — either in the home, in the automobile, or in any public place where a person has a legal right to be — has been promoted by the National Rifle Association under the name "castle doctrine." *See* Chapter 2.D.2.c.

(4) One may only resort to self-defense if he holds a reasonable belief that he is in imminent danger of great bodily harm. *Acres; Allen.*

(5) The past conduct of the one against whom self-defense is claimed is relevant to determining whether the defender had a legitimate belief that self-defense was warranted. *Allison; Wallace.*

(6) A spur-of-the-moment decision to resort to self-defense is legitimate because of the very nature of situations in which self-defense is warranted. *Allen; Brown.*

(7) It is not just the nature of the weapon in question, but how it is used, that determines whether it is "deadly," and thus justifies the use of self-defense. *Allen; Acres.*

For more information about these cases, see David B. Kopel, *The Self-Defense Cases: How the United States Supreme Court Confronted a Hanging Judge in the Nineteenth Century and Taught Some Lessons for Jurisprudence in the Twenty-First,* 27 Am. J. Crim. L. 293 (2000). For assessments of a constitutional right to self-defense pre-*Heller,* see Nicholas J. Johnson, *Self Defense?,* 2 J.L. Econ. & Pol'y 187 (2006); John Cerone, *Is There a Human Right of Self Defense?,* 2 J.L. Econ. & Pol'y 319 (2006).

NOTES & QUESTIONS

1. Compare the materials on natural law and self-defense in Chapter 2 to the material in this section. Do *The Self-Defense Cases* represent a continuation of the self-defense traditions of Western civilization and English law? Or do they represent something peculiarly American?

2. If you were a state supreme court justice charged with interpreting the common law, would you reject any of the rules from *The Self-Defense Cases?* Why or why not?

3. Do you think that the constitutional principle of Due Process necessarily includes a right of self-defense? CQ: Justice Stevens's dissenting opinion in *McDonald v. City of Chicago,* 130 S. Ct. 3020 (2010) (Chapter 9), suggests that it might.

PART TWO
THE RIGHT TO ARMS IN
THE MODERN WORLD

||7||

A New and Dangerous Century

Part I of this book presented foundational material underpinning a contemporary discussion of firearms policy, regulation, and rights. We started with a basic description of firearms technology. Next we examined the philosophical and ideological questions and debates surrounding armed self-defense and community defense against tyranny. We then examined the keeping and bearing of arms in practice during the early development of the nation. As the nation grew, its early notions about citizenship, individuality, arms ownership, and the legitimacy of armed resistance were tested.

The historical material in Part I chronicled facts, ideas, and attitudes spanning millennia. Part II focuses on the present. By the turn of the twentieth century, the United States had grown into a politically stable world power. America was the "land of opportunity" where the poor and ambitious from around the world came to build better lives. As the century progressed and the nation faced new challenges, many diverse views about private firearms ownership emerged.

A. Immigration, Labor Unrest, and Alcohol Prohibition

The early part of the twentieth century witnessed severe hostility toward aliens. *See, e.g.*, Charles H. Watson, *Need of Federal Legislation in Respect to Mob Violence in Cases of Lynching of Aliens*, 25 Yale L.J. 561 (1916). Huge waves of immigration from Eastern and Southern Europe were destabilizing America socially — to an even greater degree than earlier waves of Irish and German immigrants in antebellum America had once done. Many of the new immigrants clustered in large cities, and contributed to the labor unrest that characterized the late nineteenth and early twentieth centuries. Immigrants were also disproportionately likely to belong to violent extremist political organizations such as the communists or anarchists.

The 1901 assassination of President William McKinley by anarchist Leon Czolgosz, an American-born son of Polish immigrants, resulted in South Carolina banning the sale of handguns. That ban stayed on the books from 1902 until 1965, although it did not prevent South Carolinians from acquiring handguns by mail or buying them in other states and bringing them into South Carolina.

The statutes discussed in the next two cases were ostensibly passed to conserve wild game for use by American citizens, but they did more than just prevent aliens from hunting.

Patsone v. Pennsylvania
232 U.S. 138 (1914)

[On October 19, 1909, Joseph Patsone was arrested in his home for possessing a shotgun in violation of a Pennsylvania law prohibiting aliens from possessing shotguns and rifles. The statute was framed as a protection of the state's wild game, but it absolutely banned aliens from having long guns even in their homes.

A commentator described the trial.

> A Justice of the Peace summarily tried Patsone, without counsel or an interpreter. The Justice fined Patsone $25, and ordered the shotgun confiscated. Patsone was clueless as to what had transpired, except that his shotgun and money had been taken as a condition of his release. That communication is not difficult to imagine in gestural sign language.
>
> . . . Patsone was not allowed the services of legal counsel for a defense, nor an interpreter so that he might be heard and have some notion of what was going on. He could hardly put on evidence or present a defense in his native Italian language. The Magistrate might not have understood a word. There was clearly, however, no evidence presented that Patsone had ever hunted game in the Commonwealth, or intended to do so, or that he possessed the now confiscated shotgun for nefarious purposes, nor that he had ever "brandished" same to frighten man, beast, or fowl.

Roy Lucas, *From* Patsone *and* Miller *to* Silveira v. Lockyer: *To Keep and Bear Arms*, 26 T. Jefferson L. Rev. 257, 282 (2004) (discussing *Commonwealth v. Papsone*,[1] 19 Pa. D. 311; 1909 WL 4596, at *2 and noting that the law in question prohibited possession of long guns inside aliens' homes).]

MR. JUSTICE HOLMES delivered the opinion of the court:

The plaintiff in error was an unnaturalized foreign-born resident of Pennsylvania, and was complained of for owning or having in his possession a shotgun, contrary to [Pennsylvania law]. This statute makes it unlawful for any unnaturalized foreign-born resident to kill any wild bird or animal except in defense of person or property, and "to that end" makes it unlawful for such foreign-born person to own or be possessed of a shotgun or rifle; with a penalty of $25 and a forfeiture of the gun or guns. The plaintiff in error was found guilty and was sentenced to pay the above-mentioned fine. . . . He brings the case to this court on the ground that the statute is contrary to the 14th Amendment and also is in contravention of the treaty between the United States and Italy, to which latter country the plaintiff in error belongs.

---

1. The defendant's name was spelled "Papsone" in the lower courts.

Under the 14th Amendment the objection is two fold; unjustifiably depriving the alien of property, and discrimination against such aliens as a class. But the former really depends upon the latter, since it hardly can be disputed that if the lawful object, the protection of wild life (*Geer v. Connecticut*, 161 U.S. 519 (1896)), warrants the discrimination, the means adopted for making it effective also might be adopted. The possession of rifles and shotguns is not necessary for other purposes not within the statute. It is so peculiarly appropriated to the forbidden use that if such a use may be denied to this class, the possession of the instruments desired chiefly for that end also may be. The prohibition does not extend to weapons such as pistols that may be supposed to be needed occasionally for self-defense. . . .

The discrimination undoubtedly presents a more difficult question. But we start with the general consideration that a state may classify with reference to the evil to be prevented, and that if the class discriminated against is or reasonably might be considered to define those from whom the evil mainly is to be feared, it properly may be picked out. A lack of abstract symmetry does not matter. The question is a practical one, dependent upon experience. The demand for symmetry ignores the specific difference that experience is supposed to have shown to mark the class. It is not enough to invalidate the law that others may do the same thing and go unpunished, if, as a matter of fact, it is found that the danger is characteristic of the class named. *Lindsley v. National Carbonic Gas Co.*, 220 U.S. 61 (1911). The state "may direct its law against what it deems the evil as it actually exists without covering the whole field of possible abuses." *Central Lumber Co. v. South Dakota*, 226 U.S. 157 (1912); *Rosenthal v. New York*, 226 U.S. 260 (1912); *L'Hote v. New Orleans*, 177 U.S. 587 (1900). . . . The question therefore narrows itself to whether this court can say that the legislature of Pennsylvania was not warranted in assuming as its premise for the law that resident unnaturalized aliens were the peculiar source of the evil that it desired to prevent. *Barrett v. Indiana*, 229 U.S. 26 (1913).

Obviously the question, so stated, is one of local experience, on which this court ought to be very slow to declare that the state legislature was wrong in its facts. *Adams v. Milwaukee*, 228 U.S. 572 (1913). If we might trust popular speech in some states it was right; but it is enough that this court has no such knowledge of local conditions as to be able to say that it was manifestly wrong. See *Trageser v. Gray*, 73 Md. 250 (Md. 1890); *Com. v. Hana*, 195 Mass. 262 (1907). . . .

CHIEF JUSTICE [WHITE] dissents [without opinion].

People v. Nakamura
62 P.2d 246 (Colo. 1936)

MR. JUSTICE HOLLAND:
. . . Nakamura, an unnaturalized foreign-born resident [was charged with unlawful possession of three pheasants and a shotgun, "for the purpose of hunting wild game." He pleaded guilty to the first count, and the second count was quashed on the ground that the law under which he was convicted was unconstitutional under sections 13 and 27 of article 2 of the Constitution of the state of Colorado. The state appealed].

Section 6882, Compiled Laws of 1921, is as follows: "That from and after the passage of this act, it shall be unlawful for any unnaturalized foreign-born resident to hunt for or capture or kill, in this state, any wild bird or animal, either game or otherwise, of any description, excepting in defense of persons or property; and to that end it shall be unlawful for any unnaturalized foreign-born resident, within this state, to either own or be possessed of a shotgun or rifle of any make, or a pistol or firearm of any kind. Each and every person violating any provisions of this section shall be guilty of a misdemeanor, and, upon conviction thereof, shall be punished by a fine of not less than twenty-five dollars ($25) nor more than two hundred and fifty dollars ($250), or by imprisonment in the county jail not less than ten (10) days or more than three (3) months, or by both such fine and imprisonment; Provided, That in addition to the before-named penalty all guns of the above-mentioned kinds found in possession or under control of an unnaturalized foreign-born resident shall, upon conviction of such person, be declared forfeited to the state of Colorado, and shall be sold by the fish and game commissioner as hereinafter directed."

Sections 13 and 27 of article 2 of the Constitution are as follows:

"Sec. 13. That the right of no person to keep and bear arms in defense of his home, person and property, or in aid of the civil power when thereto legally summoned, shall be called in question; but nothing herein contained shall be construed to justify the practice of carrying concealed weapons."

"Sec. 27. Aliens, who are or may hereafter become bona fide residents of this state, may acquire, inherit, possess, enjoy and dispose of property, real and personal, as native born citizens."

The people contend that the "right" referred to in section 13 of the Constitution is not a personal right, but one of collective enjoyment for common defense, and that the act in question is a proper exercise of the police power.

It is apparent that the statute above quoted was designed to prevent possession of firearms by aliens, as much, if not more, than the protection of wild game within the state. It is equally clear that the act wholly disarms aliens for all purposes. The state may preserve its wild game for its citizens, may prevent the hunting and killing of same by aliens, and for that purpose may enact appropriate laws, but in so doing, it cannot disarm any class of persons or deprive them of the right guaranteed under section 13, article 2 of the Constitution, to bear arms in defense of home, person, and property. The guaranty thus extended is meaningless if any person is denied the right to possess arms for such protection. Under this constitutional guaranty, there is no distinction between unnaturalized foreign-born residents and citizens.

The act permits the alien to "hunt for or capture or kill" any wild bird or animal "in defense of persons or property," but it does not, and of course cannot, fix the day or hour when such occasion might arise, therefore, if the statutes prevent the means of the enjoyment of the constitutional right and guaranty thus given, by prohibiting the alien to own or possess a gun, or the means ordinarily employed, then it clearly defeats its stated exception. It is a valid exercise of the police power for the Legislature to prohibit unnaturalized foreign-born residents from hunting or killing wild game of the state, and in the exercise of such power it may distinguish between citizens of the state and aliens, and it follows that such portion of the act in question as is directed to this end is constitutional, but in so far as it denies the right of the unnaturalized foreign-born resident to keep and bear arms that may be used in defense of person or property, it contravenes the constitutional guaranty and therefore is void. "The police power of a state cannot transcend the fundamental law, and cannot be exercised in such manner as to work a practical abrogation of its provisions." *Smith v. Farr*, 46 Colo. 364 (1909), citing with approval *Hannibal & St. J. Railroad Co. v. Husen*, 95 U.S. 465 (1877).

The defendant's motion to quash the second count of the information was properly sustained, and the resulting judgment therefore is affirmed.

MR. JUSTICE BOUCK, dissenting.

The trial court sustained the defendant's motion and quashed the questioned count. In doing so, it apparently assumed that the defendant's shotgun is necessarily included among arms which, under section 13 of article 2, he has "the right . . . to keep and bear . . . in defense of his home, person and property." Whether the shotgun in this particular case was such a weapon, depends upon the facts. If the possession was solely "for the purpose of hunting wild game," as the information alleges, it was manifestly not in defense of home, person, or property. If, on the other hand, such was not the sole purpose, but the purpose was also to keep and bear the arms for defense within the meaning of our Constitution, then this fact might entitle the defendant to an acquittal. The fact might be, however, that an alien is possessed of a veritable armory of weapons, or at least of an ample supply for defense, and that a shotgun might be kept and used by him merely as a convenient means of violating the game statute under consideration, or even for the purpose of subverting the government itself.

A court ought not to presume that the Legislature intended to interfere with the constitutional rights of the defendant. The Legislature recognized the importance of avoiding such interference, as is shown by the express exception inserted in the act itself ("excepting in defense of persons or property"). A presumption exists, as usual, that the act of the Legislature is constitutional, and such presumption continues until the statute is proved unconstitutional beyond a reasonable doubt.

It is earnestly contended by the defendant that the count is bad because it does not negative the exception referred to. An exception need not be pleaded. It is a matter of defense. The defendant's remedy is to introduce evidence, if he has any, tending to establish either that he is within the express statutory exception or that the circumstances disclose he is within the protection of the constitutional provision, which must of course be read into, and in connection with, the statute. See *People v. Williams*, 61 Colo. 11 (1916), and cases there cited. . . .

NOTES & QUESTIONS

1. In evaluating some restraints on First Amendment expression, the Supreme Court has developed the "less restrictive means" test. The test is part of strict scrutiny, and says that a particular speech restriction is unconstitutional if the government's goal could be accomplished by less restrictive means. Some state courts have applied the less restrictive means test to gun rights

cases. (The leading case is *City of Lakewood v. Pillow*, 501 P.2d 744 (Colo. 1972).) The stated purpose of the laws in *Patsone* and *Nakamura* was to conserve wild game for the benefit of citizens. Could the goal have been accomplished simply by prohibiting all hunting by aliens? Was the gun ban an essential measure to prevent aliens from hunting illegally? Was it a reasonable one?

2. Analyzing the English laws restricting hunting and possession of hunting tools, William Blackstone (Chapter 2) observed that among the purposes of the restrictions was "preventing of popular insurrections and resistance to the government, by disarming the bulk of the people: which last is a reason oftener meant, than avowed, by the makers of forest or game laws." William Blackstone, 2 Commentaries on the Laws of England *412 (1768). Does Blackstone's critique have any relevance to *Patsone* and *Nakamura*?

3. What do you make of Justice Holmes's statement, "The prohibition does not extend to weapons such as pistols that may be supposed to be needed occasionally for self-defense"? Note that the *Nakamura* decision explicitly references the individual right to arms for self-defense contained in section 13 of the Colorado Constitution. Justice Holmes's statement about self-defense makes no reference to any constitutional or statutory provision. Did Justice Holmes think the aliens' right of armed self-defense was so obvious that he did not need to provide a citation? What is the root of Holmes's self-defense claim? The U.S. Constitution? The Pennsylvania Constitution? Federal common law? The intent of the Pennsylvania Legislature? Natural rights? Or is the self-defense language just dicta? *See* Nicholas J. Johnson, *Self-Defense*, 2 J.L. Econ. & Pol'y 187 (2006).

4. In *Takahashi v. Fish & Game Comm'n*, 334 U.S. 410 (1948), the U.S. Supreme Court ruled that California could not prohibit legally resident aliens from acquiring commercial fishing licenses. The Court said that even though federal law (at the time) prohibited Japanese aliens from becoming U.S. citizens, California could not discriminate against them in occupational licensing. While the majority opinion presumed to believe California's stated motive of conserving fish, the concurrence charged that the statute was transparently motivated by prejudice. Would *Takahashi* change the analysis of *Patsone* or *Nakamura*? To what extent should courts look into legislative motivation?

5. The Supreme Court did not mention the right to arms in *Patsone*, but it was discussed by the courts below. The Pennsylvania Quarter Sessions court, which upheld Patsone's conviction on appeal, said: "The act clearly does not violate the terms of the Bill of Rights, because the prohibition of the possession of a shot-gun or a rifle is not a prohibition to bear arms. Arms of defence, such as revolvers and knives, are left to the foreigners for their use." *Papsone*, 19 Pa. D. 311; 1909 WL 4596, at *1 (1909). The court found that "there are two separate and distinct offenses created by this act; the first is the hunting of game by the alien, and the second is his possession of a shot-gun or rifle." *Id.* at 2. It upheld the law on both counts. *Id.* at 4. What do you make of the Quarter Sessions Court's hypothetical about a ban on aliens'

possession of "revolvers and knives"? Based on this ruling, what arguments would you make about the validity of a law that banned some types of revolvers, but still allowed aliens to possess other types of revolvers?

6. On appeal from the Quarter Sessions court, the Pennsylvania Superior Court cited *United States v. Cruikshank*, 92 U.S. 542 (1876) (Chapter 6) and *Presser v. Illinois*, 116 U.S. 252 (1886) (Chapter 6), for the proposition that the regulation of hunting game falls within the state's police power. *Commonwealth v. Papsone*, 44 Pa. Super. 128, 1910 WL 4175, at *3 (1910). The Supreme Court of Pennsylvania affirmed, quoting in its entirety the opinion of the Pennsylvania Superior Court. *Commonwealth v. Patsone*, 79 A. 928 (Penn. 1911). Was this correct?

7. What are the similarities and differences between *Dred Scott v. Sandford*, 60 U.S. 393 (1857) (Chapter 5), *Patsone*, and *Nakamura* regarding the arms rights of citizens and non-citizens?

8. In 1911, the Sullivan Act was passed in New York, making it a misdemeanor to possess or carry a pistol without a permit. Possession permits were readily obtainable, but carry licenses were not. They were issued at the discretion of the police, many of whom were Irish. Some advocates of the law commended it as a way to crack down on the lawlessness of newly arrived immigrants, particularly Italians and Jews. For example, a 1905 editorial in the *New York Times* praised the then-proposed measure, stating that it would "prove corrective and salutary in a city filled with immigrants and evil communications, floating from the shores of Italy and Austria-Hungary." Editorial, *Concealed Pistols*, N.Y. Times, Jan. 27, 1905, at 6.

The Act was named after Tim Sullivan, a notoriously corrupt gangster turned politician. Since the Sullivan Act applied to everyone, did it raise any constitutional problems? In *People ex Rel. Darling v. Warden of City Prison*, 139 N.Y.S. 277 (App. Div. 1st Dept. 1913), a majority of New York's intermediate appeals court upheld the Act because it regulated guns rather than banning them. The dissenters thought the regulation conflicted with New York's Civil Rights Law — a statute that includes a verbatim copy of the Second Amendment. Who was right, the majority or the dissent?

B.   The Federal Government Begins to Act

Recall that in *Presser v. Illinois* (Chapter 6), the Supreme Court held that the Second Amendment did not bar state laws prohibiting individuals from assembling and marching in armed groups. At least one motivation for the law was protection of business interests from the burgeoning labor movement. The strike was labor's most powerful tool. Strike breaking often escalated into violent confrontation between workers and armed private police forces hired by management. Local laws like the one upheld in *Presser* aimed to maintain management's advantage when violence erupted. *See* Stephen P. Halbrook,

The Right of Workers to Assemble and to Bear Arms: Presser v. Illinois, *One of the Last Holdouts Against Application of the Bill of Rights to the States,* 76 U. Det. Mercy L. Rev. 943 (1999).

The pattern continued in the early twentieth century, as the organized labor movement gained momentum and industrial interests tried to maintain control over their workforces. During the same period, communist and anarchist groups often attempted to provoke violence. In November 1917, the Bolsheviks (a communist sect) overthrew the democratic Russian government, which itself had overthrown the czar a half-year earlier. The Bolsheviks moved quickly to seize the moment in history and promote global communist revolution. Frightened governments in the United Kingdom, Canada, and New Zealand, among others, responded by enacting gun-licensing laws. *See* David B. Kopel, The Samurai, the Mountie, and the Cowboy: Should America Adopt the Gun Controls of Other Democracies? (1992). Fear of Bolshevism and similar revolutionary movements also led to a variety of state and local gun controls in the United States in the early decades of the twentieth century.

In the United States, a large segment of the urban working class were immigrants, as were coal miners — a fact that intensified the desire for tighter gun controls. In 1929, the Great Depression threw the nation into economic turmoil.

National alcohol prohibition under the Eighteenth Amendment in 1919 spurred an increase in murders and other firearms crimes. Particularly notorious and fearsome was the use of machine guns by gangsters to fight turf battles with their rivals. One such incident, the 1929 St. Valentine's Day massacre in Chicago, horrified the nation. The general increase in crime resulting from Prohibition led to the first national calls for handgun prohibition. Having been almost exclusively a Southern and race-based issue in the nineteenth century, gun control now appeared on the national stage. Nationally, the leading voices for handgun prohibition were conservative, Northeastern, urban, and upper-class businessmen and attorneys. Pacifists who wanted to end war by getting rid of all weapons, including firearms, also played a role, but they were much less powerful than the business elite, which was used to getting its way.

In response, the National Rifle Association (NRA), which had been promoting marksmanship since its founding in 1871, first became involved in politics during the 1920s. The NRA used its member magazine, *The American Rifleman,* to inform members about handgun prohibition proposals, mobilizing them to contact elected officials. Russell S. Gilmore, Crackshots and Patriots: The National Rifle Association and America's Military-Sporting Tradition, 1871-1929 at 236-58 (Ph.D. dissertation, University of Wisconsin, 1974); James B. Trefethen, Americans and Their Guns (1967).

The NRA defeated handgun prohibition in every jurisdiction, sometimes by promoting, as an alternative, a model law known as the Uniform Pistol and Revolver Act. The Act prohibited the carrying of concealed handguns unless the person had a license.

On the federal level, a 1927 statute prohibited concealable firearms from being shipped through the mail. 44 Stat. 1059-60 (currently codified at 18 U.S.C. §1715(o)). However, the statute did not apply to delivery by package carriers, so its effect was limited.

The repeal of Prohibition by the Twenty-first Amendment in 1933 removed gangsters from the alcohol business and was followed by a precipitous drop in gun crimes. By this time, however, the Roosevelt administration had already planned federal firearms control, and Congress eventually passed the first major federal gun control statute, the National Firearms Act of 1934 (NFA).

National Firearms Act of 1934
48 Stat. 1236 (1934)

AN ACT

To provide for the taxation of manufacturers, importers, and dealers in certain firearms and machine guns, to tax the sale or other disposal of such weapons, and to restrict importation and regulate interstate transportation thereof. . . .

(a) The term "firearm" means a shotgun or rifle having a barrel of less than eighteen inches in length, or any other weapon, except a pistol or revolver, from which a shot is discharged by an explosive if such weapon is capable of being concealed on the person, or a machine gun, and includes a muffler or silencer for any firearm whether or not such firearm is included within the foregoing definition.[2]

(b) The term "machine gun" means any weapon which shoots, or is designed to shoot, automatically or semiautomatically, more than one shot, without manual reloading, by a single function of the trigger. . . .

Sec. 2. [Importers, manufacturers, and dealers in firearms must register with the Internal Revenue Service (IRS) and pay a tax at the following rates: importers or manufacturers, $500 a year; dealers, other than pawnbrokers, $200 a year; pawnbrokers, $300 a year.]

Sec. 3. [A tax of $200 per firearm must be paid to transfer a firearm, by sale or otherwise.]

Sec. 4. [When a firearm is transferred, an IRS registration form must be completed, and the transferee must be photographed and fingerprinted.]

Sec. 5. [Anyone who owns a firearm must register it within 60 days of the Act's passage.]

Sec. 6. It shall be unlawful for any person to receive or possess any firearm which has at any time been transferred in violation of section 3 or 4 of this Act.

Sec. 7. (a) Any firearm which has at any time been transferred in violation of the provisions of this act shall be subject to seizure and forfeiture. . . .

Sec. 8. (a) Each manufacturer and importer of a firearm shall identify it with a number or other identification mark approved by the Commissioner, such number or mark to be stamped or other placed thereon in a manner approved by the Commissioner.

(b) It shall be unlawful for anyone to obliterate, remove, change, or alter such number or other identification mark. . . .

---

2. [Note this unusual definition of "firearm." As used in the NFA, a "firearm" does not include most weapons that are normally called firearms, such as most rifles, shotguns, and handguns. Instead, the category of NFA "firearms" includes only some particular weapons that were thought to be gangster weapons. By NFA definition, "firearm" also includes accessories such as sound suppressors ("silencers"). As originally proposed, the NFA would have applied to handguns. This provision was removed after the National Rifle Association objected. In exchange, the NRA dropped its opposition to the NFA. — Eds.]

SEC. 9. Importers, manufacturers, and dealers shall keep such books and records and render such returns in relation to the transactions in firearms specified in this Act as the Commissioner, with the approval of the Secretary, may by regulations require.

SEC. 10. [Importation restrictions]

SEC. 11. It shall be unlawful for any person who is required to register as provided in section 5 hereof and who shall not have so registered, or any other person who has not in his possession a stamp-affixed order as provided in section 4 hereof, to ship, carry, or deliver any firearm in interstate commerce.

SEC. 12. The Commissioner with the approval of the Secretary, shall prescribe such rules and regulations as may be necessary for carrying the provisions of this Act into effect.

SEC. 13. This Act shall not apply to the transfer of firearms (1) to the United States Government, any State, Territory, or possession of the United States, or to any political subdivision thereof, or to the District of Columbia; (2) to any peace officer or any Federal officer designated by regulations of the Commissioner; (3) to the transfer of any firearm which is unserviceable and which is transferred as a curiosity or ornament.

SEC. 14. Any person who violates or fails to comply with any of the requirement of this Act shall, upon conviction, be fined not more than $2,000 or be imprisoned for not more than five years, or both, in the discretion of the court.

Federal Firearms Act of 1938
52 Stat. 1250

[The Federal Firearms Act (FFA) is the first federal law to regulate the interstate commerce in ordinary firearms (rifles, shotguns, and handguns). The FFA requires a federal license for persons engaged in the business of interstate commerce in firearms. The FFA was later superseded by the much more extensive Gun Control Act of 1968, but the FFA is important historically as laying the foundation for wide-ranging federal control over firearms commerce.]

AN ACT

To regulate commerce in firearms. . . .

(3) The term "firearm" means any weapon, by whatever name known, which is designed to expel a projectile or projectiles by the action of an explosive and a firearm muffler or firearm silencer, or any part or parts of such weapon. . . .

(6) The term "crime of violence" means murder, manslaughter, rape, mayhem, kidnapping, burglary, housebreaking; assault with intent to kill, commit rape, or rob; assault with a dangerous weapon, or assault with intent to commit any offense punishable by imprisonment for more than one year. . . .

(8) The term "ammunition" shall include all pistol or revolver ammunition except .22-caliber rim-fire ammunition.

SEC. 2. (a) [Only] a manufacturer or dealer having a license issued under the provisions of this Act, [may] transport, ship, or receive any firearm or ammunition in interstate or foreign commerce.

[It shall be unlawful: (b) to receive a firearm that has been shipped or transported in interstate or foreign commerce in violation of (a); (c) for any licensed manufacturer or dealer to transport or ship in interstate or foreign commerce a firearm to a consumer in a State which requires consumers to have a license, unless the manufacturer or dealer has seen the consumer's license; (d) to transport or ship in interstate or foreign commerce a firearm or ammunition to anyone under indictment, convicted of a crime of violence, or a fugitive; (e) for such individuals to transport or ship firearms in interstate or foreign commerce; (f) for persons in category (e) to possess firearms which have been shipped or transported in interstate or foreign commerce; possession of a firearm by such individuals is presumptive evidence of violation of this Act; (g-h) to transport or ship in interstate or foreign commerce stolen firearms; (i) to transport or ship in interstate or foreign commerce a firearm that has had the serial number removed or altered; the possession of any such firearm is presumptive evidence of violation of this Act.]

Sec. 3. (a-b) [Manufacturers or dealers desiring to transfer a firearm in interstate or foreign commerce must apply to the Secretary of the Treasury and pay a fee of $25 per year or $1 per year, respectively, for a license.]

(c) [If a licensee is convicted of a violation of this Act, his license shall be revoked.]

(d) Licensed dealers shall maintain such permanent records of importation shipment, and other disposal of firearms and ammunition as the Secretary of the Treasury shall prescribe. . . .

Sec. 5. Any person violating any of the provisions of this Act or any rules and regulations promulgated hereunder, or who makes any statement in applying for the license or exemption provided for in this Act, knowing such statement to be false, shall, upon conviction thereof, be fined not more than $2,000, or imprisoned for not more than five years, or both. . . .

Sec. 7. The Secretary of the Treasury may prescribe such rules and regulations as he deems necessary to carry out the provisions of this Act.

Sonzinsky v. United States
300 U.S. 506 (1937)

[*Sonzinsky* tested the NFA's tax mechanism. The key question for the Court was whether Congress could use its tax power as a roundabout way of enacting a criminal law, even though the Constitution gave Congress no general power to make criminal laws.]

Mr. Justice Stone delivered the opinion of the Court.

The question for decision is whether section 2 of the National Firearms Act of June 26, 1934, . . . which imposes a $200 annual license tax on dealers in firearms, is a constitutional exercise of the legislative power of Congress. . . .

In the exercise of its constitutional power to lay taxes, Congress may select the subjects of taxation, choosing some and omitting others. See *Flint v. Stone Tracy Co.*, 220 U.S. 107, 158 (1911); *Nicol v. Ames*, 173 U.S. 509, 516 (1899); *Bromley v. McCaughn*, 280 U.S. 124 (1929). Its power extends to the imposition of exercise taxes upon the doing of business. See *License Tax Cases*, 72 U.S. 462 (1866); *Spreckles Sugar Refining Co. v. McClain*, 192 U.S. 397, 412 (1904); *United States v. Doremus*, 294 U.S. 86, 94 (1919). Petitioner does not deny that Congress may tax his business as a dealer in firearms. He insists that the present levy is not a true tax, but a penalty imposed for the purpose of suppressing traffic in a certain noxious type of firearms, the local regulation of which is reserved to the states because not granted to the national government. To establish its penal and prohibitive character, he relies on the amounts of the tax imposed by section 2 on dealers, manufacturers, and importers, and of the tax imposed by section 3 on each transfer of a "firearm," payable by the transferor. The cumulative effect on the distribution of a limited class of firearms, of relatively small value, by the successive imposition of different taxes, one on the business of the importer or manufacturer, another on that of the dealer, and a third on the transfer to a buyer, is said to be prohibitive in effect and to disclose unmistakably the legislative purpose to regulate rather than to tax.

The case is not one where the statute contains regulatory provisions related to a purported tax in such a way as has enabled this Court to say in other cases that the latter is a penalty resorted to as a means of enforcing the regulations. See *Child Labor Tax Cases*, 259 U.S. 20, 35 (1922); *Hill v. Wallace*, 259 U.S. 44 (1922); *Carter v. Carter Coal Co.*, 298 U.S. 238 (1936). Nor is the subject of the tax described or treated as criminal by the taxing statute. Compare *United States v. Constantine*, 296 U.S. 287 (1935). Here section 2 contains no regulation other than the mere registration provisions, which are obviously supportable as in aid of a revenue purpose. On its face it is only a taxing measure, and we are asked to say that the tax, by virtue of its deterrent effect on the activities taxed, operates as a regulation which is beyond the congressional power.

Every tax is in some measure regulatory. To some extent it interposes an economic impediment to the activity taxed as compared with others not taxed. But a tax is not any the less a tax because it has a regulatory effect, *United States v. Doremus, Nigro v. United States*, 276 U.S. 372, 353, 354 (1928); *License Tax Cases*, supra; see *Child Labor Tax Cases*, supra; and it has long been established that an Act of Congress which on its face purports to be an exercise of the taxing power is not any the less so because the tax is burdensome or tends to restrict or suppress the thing taxed. *Veazie Bank v. Fenno*, 75 U.S. 533, 548 (1869); *McCray v. United States*, 195 U.S. 27, 60-61 (1904); cf. *Alaska Fish Company v. Smith*, 255 U.S. 44, 48 (1921).

Inquiry into the hidden motives which may move Congress to exercise a power constitutionally conferred upon it is beyond the competency of courts. *Veazie Bank v. Fenno*, supra; *McCray v. United States*, supra; *United States v. Doremus*, supra; see *Magnano Co. v. Hamilton*, 292 U.S. 40, 44, 45 (1934); cf. *Arizona v. California*, 283 U.S. 423, 455 (1931); *Smith v. Kansas City Title Co.*, 255 U.S. 180, 210 (1921); *Weber v. Freed*, 239 U.S. 325, 329, 330 (1915); *Fletcher v. Peck*, 6 Cranch 87, 130 (1810). They will not undertake, by collateral inquiry as to the measure of the regulatory effect of a tax, to ascribe to Congress an attempt, under the guise of taxation, to exercise another power denied by the Federal Constitution. *McCray v. United States*, supra; cf. *Magnano Co. v. Hamilton*, supra.

Here the annual tax of $200 is productive of some revenue. [The $200 tax was paid by 27 dealers in 1934, and by 22 dealers in 1935.] We are not free to speculate as to the motives which moved Congress to impose it, or as to the extent to which it may operate to restrict the activities taxed. As it is not attended by an offensive regulation, and since it operates as a tax, it is within the national taxing power. *Alston v. United States*, 274 U.S. 289, 294 (1927); *Nigro v. United States*, supra; *Hampton & Co. v. United States*, 276 U.S. 394, 411, 413 (1928). . . .

Affirmed.

NOTES & QUESTIONS

1. The new federal gun control laws were part of a larger expansion of federal authority into U.S. criminal law. A commentator at the time explained:

> The transition of crime from a chiefly local problem to one of interstate and even international proportion has been taking place since the World War. This gradual change, necessarily resulting in a partial disability of local law enforcement, engendered the clamor for federal crime control. Accordingly, in 1933, the Senate directed the Committee on Commerce to investigate the subjects of kidnapping, "racketeering," and other forms of crime, and to recommend the necessary remedial legislation. To the layman it might seem that the only authority required for the passage of such laws would be the police power but actually, the United States Government is, in this respect, under the very burdensome restraint of the Tenth Amendment. The national government has no police power except that expressly or impliedly granted it by the Constitution.
>
> The important powers through which Congress may try to curb . . . crimes are the power to tax, the power over interstate and foreign commerce, and the power "to make all laws which shall be necessary and proper for carrying into execution the foregoing powers." The power to tax has been responsible for the control of narcotics and machine guns, while the power over interstate and foreign commerce has resulted in the control over kidnapping, white slavery [forced prostitution], stolen motor vehicles, and opium for smoking purposes.
>
> Although it was common knowledge that many crimes occurred through the use of dangerous and deadly weapons, such as pistols and revolvers, control of these articles by the federal government was hampered by the Second Amendment and by various groups favoring state control. Finally, the Committee on Commerce, through a subcommittee headed by Senator Murphy of Iowa, Senator Vandenberg of Michigan, and the late Senator Copeland of New York, proposed the Federal Firearms Act which met with the approval of the National Rifle Association and the National Pistol Association.[3] . . .

Alfred M. Ascione, *The Federal Firearms Act*, 13 St. John's L. Rev. 437, 437-38 (1939).

What do you make of the author's reference to the Second Amendment? Does the author understand the Second Amendment as an individual right or protection of a state prerogative? He explains that both the Second and Tenth Amendments were seen as obstacles to creating federal criminal laws. Did the NFA and FFA employ appropriate solutions to these limitations?

While strongly endorsing the 1938 FFA, the National Rifle Association also worked to stop a proposal from Attorney General Homer Cummings for national gun registration. The registration bill was never granted a vote in Congress. Does the NRA's support for the FFA confirm the criticism of more absolutist gun-rights advocates that the NRA is the largest gun control organization in the United States?

2. Testifying before the House Ways and Means Committee, Attorney General Cummings explained that the NFA did not ban outright the affected firearms because a ban would violate the Second Amendment. But he said that a heavy

---

3.   [At the time, a leading organizer of handgun sports. — EDS.]

tax would be permissible. *The National Firearms Act of 1934: Hearings on H.R. 9066 Before the House Comm. on Ways and Means*, 73rd Cong. 6, 13, 19 (1934). In inflation-adjusted dollars, $200 in 1934 was equivalent to $3,255 in 2010. In *Grosjean v. American Press Co.*, the Court ruled that a 2 percent gross receipts tax on large-circulation newspapers violated the First Amendment, because the circumstances showed that the tax was not for the purpose of raising revenue, but was "a deliberate and calculated device in the guise of a tax to limit the circulation of information to which the public is entitled in virtue of the constitutional guaranties." 297 U.S. 233, 250 (1936). In contrast, *Sonzinsky* rejected the argument that the NFA tax was a sham because it was not intended to raise revenue. Would (or should) the result in *Sonzinsky* be different if a court decided that the highly taxed arms were protected by the Second Amendment?

3. Justice Stone noted that the NFA tax did actually produce some revenue. The $200 transfer tax on the "firearms" designated by the NFA has not been increased since its enactment, making the tax's deterrent power weaker as inflation depreciated the value of the dollar. Why do you think that Congress has never increased the NFA tax? As detailed in Chapter 8, in 1986, Congress banned the sale of new machine guns to the public.

4. CQ: James Madison, during the debates over the amendments that were to become the Bill of Rights, stated that "there is more danger of . . . powers being abused by the State Governments than by the Government of the United States." 1 Annals of Cong. 458 (1789) (Joseph Gales ed., 1834). In light of what you have learned so far about the U.S. experience through 1938, was Madison's prediction accurate? Keep the prediction in mind as you read subsequent chapters to see if your opinion changes.

5. During the debates on the Bill of Rights, Madison argued that specific guarantees of liberty would be necessary because the new federal powers would provide Congress with a pretext to illegitimately infringe on state powers. 1 Annals of Cong. 455-56 (1789) (Joseph Gales ed., 1834) (referring specifically to the Necessary and Proper Clause). Sonzinsky's brief made Tenth Amendment arguments. Did Justice Stone properly address these arguments? Is it plausible to conclude that the NFA and FFA are usurpations of powers reserved to the states? Are they clearly legitimate exercises of congressional power?

6. The NFA was modeled on the 1914 Harrison Narcotics Act, which used the federal tax power to impose stringent controls on the possession or sale of cocaine and opiates. 38 Stat. 785 (1914). The Supreme Court had upheld such use of the tax power. *United States v. Jim Fuey Moy*, 241 U.S. 394 (1916); *United States v. Doremus*, 494 U.S. 86 (1919). In the late 1980s and early 1990s, efforts to outlaw "assault weapons" were substantially bolstered by claims that the guns were the "weapon of choice" of drug dealers. Can you think of other ways, in law or in policy, in which drug control and gun control have been mutually reinforcing?

7. In 1937, Attorney General Cummings, when promoting a national gun registration law (which was successfully blocked by the NRA) said, "Show

me the man who does not want his gun registered, and I will show you a man who should not have a gun." Selected Papers of Homer Cummings 86 (Carl Brent Swisher ed., 1939). Do you agree?

United States v. Miller
307 U.S. 174 (1939)

MR. JUSTICE MCREYNOLDS delivered the opinion of the Court.

[A pair of bootleggers, Jack Miller and Frank Layton, were caught in possession of a sawed-off shotgun. The district court dismissed the indictment on the grounds that the National Firearms Act of 1934 (NFA) violated the Second Amendment to the U.S. Constitution. The federal government appealed, but Miller and Layton disappeared before the Supreme Court heard the case. Only the government filed a brief and presented at oral argument.]

An indictment in the District Court Western District Arkansas, charged that Jack Miller and Frank Layton "did unlawfully, knowingly, wilfully, and feloniously transport in interstate commerce from the town of Claremore in the State of Oklahoma to the town of Siloam Springs in the State of Arkansas . . . a double barrel 12-gauge Stevens shotgun having a barrel less than 18 inches in length, . . . not having registered said firearm . . . and not having in their possession a stamp-affixed written order for said firearm as provided by . . . the 'National Firearms Act' [and regulations promulgated thereunder] . . . , and against the peace and dignity of the United States."

A duly interposed demurrer alleged: The National Firearms Act is not a revenue measure but an attempt to usurp police power reserved to the States, and is therefore unconstitutional. Also, it offends the inhibition of the Second Amendment to the Constitution[] — "A well regulated Militia, being necessary to the security of a free State, the right of people to keep and bear Arms, shall not be infringed."

The District Court held that section eleven of the Act violates the Second Amendment. It accordingly sustained the demurrer and quashed the indictment.

The cause is here by direct appeal.

[The Court first reaffirmed *Sonzinsky, supra,* and held that the NFA did not unconstitutionally usurp the police powers reserved to the states by the Tenth Amendment.]

In the absence of any evidence tending to show that possession or use of a "shotgun having a barrel of less than eighteen inches in length" at this time has some reasonable relationship to the preservation or efficiency of a well regulated militia, we cannot say that the Second Amendment guarantees the right to keep and bear such an instrument. Certainly it is not within judicial notice that this weapon is any part of the ordinary military equipment or that its use could contribute to the common defense. *Aymette v. State,* 2 Humph. 154, 158 [Tenn. 1840].

The Constitution as originally adopted granted to the Congress power — "To provide for calling forth the Militia to execute the Laws of the Union, suppress Insurrections and repel Invasions; To provide for organizing, arming, and disciplining, the Militia, and for governing such Part of them as may be employed in the Service of the United States, reserving to the States respectively, the Appointment of the Officers, and the Authority of training the Militia according to the discipline prescribed by Congress." [U.S. Const., art. I, §8.] With obvious purpose to assure the continuation and render possible the effectiveness of such forces the declaration and guarantee of the Second Amendment were made. It must be interpreted and applied with that end in view.

The Militia which the States were expected to maintain and train is set in contrast with Troops which they were forbidden to keep without the consent of Congress. The sentiment of the time strongly disfavored standing armies; the common view was that adequate defense of country and laws could be secured through the Militia—civilians primarily, soldiers on occasion.

The signification attributed to the term Militia appears from the debates in the Convention, the history and legislation of Colonies and States, and the writings of approved commentators. These show plainly enough that the Militia comprised all males physically capable of acting in concert for the common defense. "A body of citizens enrolled for military discipline." And further, that ordinarily when called for service these men were expected to appear bearing arms supplied by themselves and of the kind in common use at the time.

Blackstone's Commentaries . . . points out "that king Alfred first settled a national militia in this kingdom," and traces the subsequent development and use of such forces.

Adam Smith's Wealth of Nations, Book V, Ch. 1, contains an extended account of the Militia. It is there said: "Men of republican principles have been jealous of a standing army as dangerous to liberty." "In a militia, the character of the labourer, artificer, or tradesman, predominates over that of the soldier: in a standing army, that of the soldier predominates over every other character; and in this distinction seems to consist the essential difference between those two different species of military force."

"The American Colonies In The 17th Century," Osgood, Vol. 1, ch. XIII, affirms in reference to the early system of defense in New England—

"In all the colonies, as in England, the militia system was based on the principle of the assize of arms. This implied the general obligation of all adult male inhabitants to possess arms, and, with certain exceptions, to cooperate in the work of defence." "The possession of arms also implied the possession of ammunition, and the authorities paid quite as much attention to the latter as to the former." "A year later [1632] it was ordered that any single man who had not furnished himself with arms might be put out to service, and this became a permanent part of the legislation of the colony [Massachusetts]."

Also "Clauses intended to insure the possession of arms and ammunition by all who were subject to military service appear in all the important enactments concerning military affairs. Fines were the penalty for delinquency, whether of towns or individuals. According to the usage of the times, the infantry of Massachusetts consisted of pikemen and musketeers. The law, as enacted in 1649 and thereafter, provided that each of the former should be armed with a pike, corselet, head-piece, sword, and knapsack. The musketeer should carry a 'good fixed musket', not under bastard musket bore, not less than three feet, nine inches, nor more than four feet three inches in length, a priming wire, scourer, and mould, a sword, rest, bandoleers, one pound of powder, twenty bullets, and two fathoms of match. The law also required that two-thirds of each company should be musketeers."

The General Court of Massachusetts, January Session 1784, provided for the organization and government of the Militia. It directed that the Train Band should "contain all able bodied men, from sixteen to forty years of age, and the Alarm List, all other men under sixty years of age. . . ." Also, "That every non-commissioned officer and private soldier of the said militia not under the controul of parents, masters or guardians, and being of sufficient ability therefor in the judgment of the Selectmen of the town in which he shall dwell, shall equip himself, and be constantly provided with a good fire arm," &c.

By an Act passed April 4, 1786 the New York Legislature directed: "That every able-bodied Male Person, being a Citizen of this State, or of any of the United States, and residing in this State, (except such Persons as are hereinafter excepted) and who are of the Age of Sixteen, and under the Age of Forty-five Years, shall, by the Captain or commanding Officer of the Beat in which such Citizens shall reside, within four Months after the passing of this Act, be enrolled in the Company of such Beat . . . That every Citizen so enrolled and notified, shall, within three Months thereafter, provide himself, at his own Expense, with a good Musket or Firelock, a sufficient Bayonet and Belt, a Pouch with a Box therein to contain not less than Twenty-four Cartridges suited to the Bore of his Musket or Firelock, each Cartridge containing a proper Quantity of Powder and Ball, two spare Flints, a Blanket and Knapsack. . . ."

The General Assembly of Virginia, October, 1785, (12 Hening's Statutes) declared, "The defense and safety of the commonwealth depend upon having its citizens properly armed and taught the knowledge of military duty."

It further provided for organization and control of the Militia and directed that "All free male persons between the ages of eighteen and fifty years," with certain exceptions, "shall be inrolled or formed into companies." "There shall be a private muster of every company once in two months."

Also that "Every officer and soldier shall appear at his respective muster-field on the day appointed, by eleven o'clock in the forenoon, armed, equipped, and accoutred, as follows: . . . every non-commissioned officer and private with a good, clean musket carrying an ounce ball, and three feet eight inches long in the barrel, with a good bayonet and iron ramrod well fitted thereto, a cartridge box properly made, to contain and secure twenty cartridges fitted to his musket, a good knapsack and canteen, and moreover, each non-commissioned officer and private shall have at every muster one pound of good powder, and four pounds of lead, including twenty blind cartridges; and each serjeant shall have a pair of moulds fit to cast balls for their respective companies, to be purchased by the commanding officer out of the monies arising on delinquencies. Provided, That the militia of the counties westward of the Blue Ridge, and the counties below adjoining thereto, shall not be obliged to be armed with muskets, but may have good rifles with proper accoutrements, in lieu thereof. And every of the said officers, non-commissioned officers, and privates, shall constantly keep the aforesaid arms, accoutrements, and ammunition, ready to be produced whenever called for by his commanding officer. If any private shall make it appear to the satisfaction of the court hereafter to be appointed for trying delinquencies under this act that he is so poor that he cannot purchase the arms herein required, such court shall cause them to be purchased out of the money arising from delinquents."

Most if not all of the States have adopted provisions touching the right to keep and bear arms. Differences in the language employed in these have naturally led to somewhat variant conclusions concerning the scope of the right guaranteed. But none of them seem to afford any material support for the challenged ruling of the court below.

In the margin some of the more important opinions and comments by writers are cited.[3]

We are unable to accept the conclusion of the court below and the challenged judgment must be reversed. The cause will be remanded for further proceedings.

MR. JUSTICE DOUGLAS took no part in the consideration or decision of this cause.

NOTES & QUESTIONS

1. What is *Miller*'s holding? Is the opinion ambiguous? If so, do you think the ambiguities were inadvertent or deliberate? Is *Miller* "deficient," as Justice Kennedy suggested during oral arguments for *District of Columbia v. Heller*, 554 U.S. 570 (2008) (Chapter 9)?

2. *Miller* said that the Second Amendment was adopted in order "to assure the continuation and render possible the effectiveness of" the militia, and that it "must be interpreted and applied with that end in view." The Supreme Court concluded that Miller's possession of a sawed-off shotgun lacked a "reasonable relationship to the preservation or efficiency of a well regulated militia." In your view of the case, would any of the following examples of arms possession be constitutionally protected under *Miller*?

   a. Carrying a high-quality handgun, such as a police officer or soldier might use? *Compare Andrews v. State*, 50 Tenn. 165 (1871) (concluding that "repeaters" (large revolvers) are militia weapons, and so citizens are entitled to keep them under state constitutional right to arms, and perhaps to carry them for self-defense) *with Ex parte Thomas*, 97 P. 260 (Okla. 1908) (concluding that handguns are not militia weapons, and thus are not protected by the state constitutional right to arms).

   b. Keeping a rifle at home? *Cf.* Robert H. Churchill, *Gun Regulation, the Police Power, and the Right to Keep Arms in Early America: The Legal Context of the Second Amendment*, 25 Law & Hist. Rev. 139 (2007) (discussing the American colonists' understanding that they were entitled to keep guns to preserve liberty that was different from the earlier English understanding; a long gun is arguably the archtypical type of gun kept at home to defend one's liberties).

   c. Keeping a machine gun at home, in a state whose constitution provides that "all able-bodied male citizens between the ages of 21 and 45 years" are members of the state militia? *See United States v. Oakes*, 564 F.2d 384 (10th Cir. 1977) (citing *Miller* and rejecting the argument that just

---

3. Concerning The Militia — *Presser v. Illinois*, 116 U.S. 252; *Robertson v. Baldwin*, 165 U.S. 275; *Fife v. State*, 31 Ark. 455; *Jeffers v. Fair*, 33 Ga. 347; *Salina v. Blaksley*, 83 P. 619; *People v. Brown*, 235 N.W. 245; *Aymette v. State*, 2 Humph., Tenn., 154; *State v. Duke*, 42 Tex. 455; *State v. Workman*, 14 S.E. 9; Cooley's Constitutional Limitations, Vol. 1, p. 729; Story on The Constitution, 5th Ed., Vol. 2, p. 646; Encyclopaedia of the Social Sciences, Vol. X, p. 471, 474.

because a person falls within a state's constitutional and statutory definition of the state militia, he has a personal right to own firearms). What if a state enacted a statute stating that all adult males (or all adults) are part of the state militia and that every one of them is required to acquire his or her own machine gun?

3. Decades later, a majority of the Supreme Court would revisit *Miller*'s treatment of the Second Amendment, criticizing *Miller* as a "virtually unreasoned" opinion that "discusses none of the history of the Second Amendment." *Heller*, 554 U.S. at 624 n.24 (Chapter 9). Is that a fair description?

4. What do you make of *Miller*'s definition of the early militia as "all males physically capable of acting in concert for the common defense"? Does this imply that the right to possess arms inures to a broad segment of the population? Does this statement combined with modern equal protection doctrines turn the right into an individual one that is also possessed by females or by those who are not physically capable of acting in concert in the common defense?

5. How do you interpret the following passage?

> In the absence of any evidence tending to show that possession or use of a "shotgun having a barrel of less than eighteen inches in length" at this time has some reasonable relationship to the preservation or efficiency of a well regulated militia, we cannot say that the Second Amendment guarantees the right to keep and bear such an instrument. Certainly it is not within judicial notice that this weapon is any part of the ordinary military equipment or that its use could contribute to the common defense.

This passage is often stressed by persons who believe that the Second Amendment secures only a collective or state right to arms. How would you describe the parameters of such a right? Under this view, could the government prevent citizens from having firearms in their homes? Compare your response here to your answers to question 7 below.

Now consider the quoted passage in the context of the procedural posture of the case. The district court dismissed the indictment, writing nothing more than a conclusory assertion that the law violated the Second Amendment. So there were no findings about the suitability of Miller's gun for militia purposes. The Supreme Court was unwilling to take judicial notice of the militia utility of Miller's gun and remanded the case to the district court. If you were counsel for Miller on remand, would you view the Supreme Court's decision as an invitation to introduce evidence about the militia utility of Miller's gun? If you could prove that Miller's gun was "part of the ordinary military equipment" or "could contribute to the common defense," would Miller then have a right to possess it even if he were not a part of a state-organized militia? Of the militia as defined by *Miller*? These questions were not pressed on remand because Mr. Miller disappeared. Indeed, he had already gone missing before the Supreme Court heard his case. (He later turned up in Oklahoma, shot dead, evidently as revenge for testifying against fellow gang members in another case.) Miller was not even represented by counsel in the Supreme Court. Instead, the Solicitor General briefed and argued the case unopposed. Miller's attorney filed no brief, but wrote the Court and told them to rely on the government's brief. *See* Nelson Lund, Heller *and Second Amendment Precedent*, 13 Lewis & Clark L. Rev. 335, 336-39 (2009). Recent research suggests that *Miller* was a collusive prosecution, involving a U.S. Attorney, a federal district judge who had strongly supported federal gun control in his former role as a member of Congress, and a compliant defense attorney, working to set up a Supreme Court test case to affirm the National Firearms Act. *See* Brian L. Frye, *The Peculiar Story of* United States v. Miller, 3 N.Y.U. J.L. & Liberty 48 (2008). Supposing that a later court accepted Frye's account of the *Miller* litigation, should the court give less precedential value to *Miller*?

6. Does *Miller* focus on the arm or on the individual? The government made two arguments for the NFA's constitutionality under the Second Amendment: First, the government argued that the Amendment "gave sanction only to the arming of the people as a body to defend their rights against tyrannical and unprincipled rulers" and "did not permit the keeping of arms for purposes of private defense." Brief of the United States at 12, *United States v. Miller*, 307 U.S. 174 (1939) (No. 38-696). Thus, the right was "only one which exists where the arms are borne in the militia or some other military organization provided for by law and intended for the protection of the state." *Id.* at 4-5. Second, the government argued that "the term 'arms' . . . refers only to those weapons which are ordinarily used for military or public defense purposes and does not relate to those weapons which are commonly used by criminals." *Id.* at 15. Did Justice McReynolds adopt the government's first argument, so that only individuals involved with a state-run militia could bear arms? Or did he adopt the government's second argument, under which the type of weapon involved determines which is protected? Consider these questions in the context of the Court's definition of "militia" discussed in the next note.

7. One source of disputes about the meaning of *Miller* is the following paragraph:

> The signification attributed to the term Militia appears from the debates in the Convention, the history and legislation of Colonies and States, and the writings of approved commentators. These show plainly enough that the Militia comprised all males physically capable of acting in concert for the common defense. "A body of citizens enrolled for military discipline." And further, that ordinarily when called for service these men were expected to appear bearing arms supplied by themselves and of the kind in common use at the time.

Can you construct an argument that reconciles the claim that *Miller* recognizes only a right of state governments with the description of the militia as men expected to appear bearing arms "supplied by themselves of the kind in common use at the time"? Can you construct an argument that the reference to "arms supplied by themselves" acknowledges an individual right to arms? Compare the strengths and weaknesses of these two arguments. For a detailed analysis of the various possible readings of

Miller, and of how *Heller* (Chapter 9) interpreted *Miller*, see Michael P. O'Shea, *The Right to Defensive Arms After* District of Columbia v. Heller, 111 W. Va. L. Rev. 349 (2009).

8. What is the significance of *Miller*'s discussion of weapons "of the kind in common use at the time"? Is Justice McReynolds saying that weapons are protected if they are commonly used? What are the implications of common use — either on its own or combined with the "reasonable relationship" passage? Under the common use standard, are governments forbidden from banning new firearms technologies once they have become commonly used? *Heller* (Chapter 9), also uses a version of the common use test. For analysis of the implications of the test, see *Heller*, 554 U.S. at 720-21 (Breyer, J., dissenting) (criticizing the test for preventing bans on common arms); Craig S. Lerner & Nelson Lund, Heller *and Nonlethal Weapons*, 60 Hastings L.J. 1387 (2009) (criticizing the common use test as insufficiently protective of the right to arms).

9. What are the implications if military weapons are protected? Would weapons such as swords, knives, and bayonets be protected? At the time of *Miller*, and during the Second World War, the standard infantry rifle was semi-automatic. During the Korean War, however, the military began to transition to fully automatic rifles as the typical military firearm. Does *Miller*'s rule mean that the arms most protected by the Second Amendment are battlefield guns such as the U.S. Army's M-16 rifle? Or does it mean that *Miller*'s rule was made unworkable by technological change?

10. The Constitution grants Congress the power to arm the militia. U.S. Const. art. I, §8, cl. 16. It also forbids states to "keep Troops, or Ships of War in time of Peace." *Id.* §10, cl. 3. How do you interpret *Miller*'s declaration that the Second Amendment "must be interpreted and applied" consistent with "assur[ing] the continuation and . . . effectiveness" of the militia? If the Second Amendment gave the states, rather than Congress, the power to arm militias, would this imply that it partially repealed Article I, Section 8, Clause 16, and/or Article I, Section 10, Clause 3? *See* George A. Mocsary, *Explaining Away the Obvious: The Infeasibility of Characterizing the Second Amendment as a Nonindividual Right*, 76 Fordham L. Rev. 2113, 2154-55 (2008) (arguing that interpreting *Miller* to hold that the Second Amendment guarantees a state power creates a conflict with Article I).

11. By now you have read many of the sources cited in *Miller*'s third footnote. See Chapters 5 and 6. What do you make of this footnote? Review the cited sources if needed.

12. Justice McReynolds was notoriously lazy. This extended to his opinion-writing. *See, e.g.*, Barry Cushman, *Clerking for Scrooge*, 70 U. Chi. L. Rev. 721 (2003). During the *Heller* oral argument, Justice Kennedy observed that "*Miller* kind of ends abruptly as an opinion." Can *Miller*'s ambiguities be partly explained as the product of a Justice who wanted to get the opinion finished with the least effort possible?

C. National Firearms Act Regulation Today

Miller did not squarely engage whether the Second Amendment limits federal restrictions on the types of ordinary handguns, rifles, and shotguns commonly sold at retail gun stores today. These guns are not "firearms" in the specialized sense used in the National Firearms Act, so they are not subject to NFA regulation. Instead, these common arms are regulated by the provisions of the federal Gun Control Act of 1968 (GCA) (Chapter 8) and state law.

National Firearms Act regulation today represents a relatively small and specialized area of firearms law, in comparison with the vast number of firearms, transactions, and traders that are regulated under the GCA of 1968. Nevertheless, a basic grasp of how the NFA works is important to an understanding of the broader network of federal firearms regulation. The boundaries of NFA categories also influence the design of common commercial firearms, as manufacturers seek to satisfy consumer preferences while avoiding features that would cause their products to be subjected to the strict NFA requirements.

The items controlled by the 1934 NFA are subject to additional controls by the 1968 GCA. For example, the NFA sets up a tax and registration system for silencers; the GCA outlaws silencer possession by the same classes of people the GCA prohibits from possessing ordinary firearms.

Under current law, six categories of arms and accessories are subject to NFA requirements.

Machine Guns.[4] Defined as "any weapon which shoots, is designed to shoot, or can be readily restored to shoot, automatically more than one shot, without manual reloading, by a single function of the trigger." 26 U.S.C. §5845(a)(6), (b). Thus, the key criterion for a machine gun is whether the gun can fire more than one shot with a single pull of a trigger. Some machine guns are designed to fire "bursts" of two or three shots per trigger pull, while some will simply keep firing automatically as long as the trigger is held back, until the gun runs out of ammunition.

---

4. This text generally employs the colloquial, two-word term "machine gun," but the term found in the United States Code is actually a single word: "machinegun." What the statute (and this chapter) calls a "machine gun" or "machinegun" is properly called an "automatic." In an automatic, when the trigger stays pressed, round after round is automatically loaded and fired, and the spent shell casings are ejected. Technically speaking (although not in common parlance), there is a difference between an automatic and a machine gun. For example, the Gatling Gun, which was invented during the Civil War, is a machine gun but not an automatic. In a Gatling Gun, the rapid load/eject/reload operation is performed by manually turning a hand crank. Accordingly, the Gatling Gun is not covered by the National Firearms Act, which defines "machinegun" to be automatics only.

Chapter 1 explains the difference between automatic and semi-automatic guns. The "machinegun" provisions apply only to true automatics. Confusingly, many gun users refer to semi-automatic pistols as "automatics." For example, the 1911 Colt semi-automatic pistol might be called "the Colt automatic." Do not be misled by this nomenclature. The machinegun provisions have nothing to do with semi-automatic pistols or any other semi-automatics.

Machine guns are subject to additional federal restrictions not applicable to other types of NFA firearms. A 1986 law criminalizes the possession by private citizens of any machine gun that was not properly registered under the NFA as of May 19, 1986. *See* 18 U.S.C. §922(o). Thus, with the exception of licensed dealers in NFA firearms, only law enforcement, military, or other governmental entities may lawfully possess machine guns manufactured after the 1986 date. This prohibition effectively created a fixed pool of machine guns, registered prior to the cutoff date, that can be lawfully owned by private citizens (after going through all the NFA requirements), but to which no new machine guns can be added. Prices for these "transferable" weapons have increased steadily over time, and currently begin at $3,000 for the most basic models, and range up to $20,000 or more for rare or collectible guns.

In late 2006, the Bureau of Alcohol, Tobacco, Firearms and Explosives (ATF) reported to the Justice Department that a total of 391,532 machine guns were registered in the National Firearms Registration and Transfer Record (NFRTR), the centralized registry created by the NFA. *See* U.S. Dep't of Justice, Office of the Inspector General, *National Firearms Registration and Transfer Record I-2007-006* (2007). However, most of those are non-transferable, post-1986 machine guns registered to law enforcement agencies and other government entities. In 1986, the Bureau's director testified to Congress that an estimated 118,000 machine guns were registered. Proposed Legislation to Modify the 1968 Gun Control Act: Hearings Before the House Judiciary Committee, 99th Cong., 1165 (1987). This number likely marks an upper boundary on the number of transferable registered machine guns.

Short Barreled Rifles. Any "rifle having a barrel or barrels of less than 16 inches in length," and any "weapon made from a rifle if such weapon as modified has an overall length of less than 26 inches or a barrel or barrels of less than 16 inches in length." 26 U.S.C. §5845(a)(3), (a)(4). Thus, in order to avoid being subject to NFA requirements, a rifle must have a barrel length of at least 16 inches[5] and must also be at least 26 inches in overall length. Cutting down an existing rifle below either of these dimensions is considered "making" a short barreled rifle, and is illegal without prior registration and payment of the NFA tax.

In late 2006, the ATF reported that 33,518 short barreled rifles were registered in the NFRTR.

Short Barreled Shotguns. Any "shotgun having a barrel or barrels of less than 18 inches in length," and any "weapon made from a shotgun if such weapon as modified has an overall length of less than 26 inches or a barrel or barrels of less than 18 inches in length." 26 U.S.C. §5645(a)(1), (a)(2). Thus, in order to avoid being subject to NFA requirements, a shotgun must have a barrel length of at least 18 inches and must also be at least 26 inches in overall length. Cutting down an existing shotgun below either of these dimensions is considered "making" a short barreled shotgun, and is illegal without prior registration and payment of the NFA tax.

---

5. When originally enacted, the NFA applied to all rifles with barrels less than 18 inches long (as is still true for shotguns), but in 1960 Congress lowered the requirement to 16 inches. Pub. L. No. 86-478, §3, 74 Stat. 149 (1960). Today many types of rifles are sold with barrels of between 16 and 18 inches in length.

In late 2006, ATF reported that 95,699 short barreled shotguns were registered in the NFRTR.

Silencers. Though they are a type of gun accessory rather than a gun, silencers are classified as "firearms" regulated by the NFA. They are also often referred to as *sound suppressors,* since the devices reduce the noise produced by shooting a firearm but do not ordinarily eliminate it.

> The terms "firearm silencer" and "firearm muffler" mean any device for silencing, muffling, or diminishing the report of a portable firearm, including any combination of parts, designed or redesigned, and intended for use in assembling or fabricating a firearm silencer or firearm muffler, and any part intended only for use in such assembly or fabrication.

18 U.S.C. §921(a)(24); 26 U.S.C. §5845(a)(7). Notice that individual silencer parts are treated the same as complete silencers.

In late 2006, ATF reported that 150,364 silencers were registered in the NFRTR.

Destructive Devices. Added to the NFA's coverage in 1968, the category of destructive devices includes two major types of weapon:

> any explosive, incendiary, or poison gas bomb, grenade, rocket having a propellant charge of more than four ounces, missile having an explosive or incendiary charge of more than one-quarter ounce, mine, or similar device; [and]

> any type of weapon by whatever name known which will, or which may be readily converted to, expel a projectile by the action of an explosive or other propellant, the barrel or barrels of which have a bore of more than one-half inch in diameter, except a shotgun or shotgun shell which the Secretary finds is generally recognized as particularly suitable for sporting purposes. . . .

26 U.S.C. §5645(f)(1), (f)(2) (punctuation omitted). Thus, explosive devices such as bombs and large-bore firearms such as cannon are deemed destructive devices. Any gun with a bore larger than half an inch (.50 caliber) is presumptively an NFA-regulated destructive device, unless it falls within an exception.

Notice the reference to shotguns in the statutory text above. Because all 10, 12, 16, and 20 gauge shotguns have a bore diameter larger than half an inch, any such shotgun that does not fall within the "generally recognized as particularly suitable for sporting purposes" exception is considered a destructive device! (.410 shotguns which have bore diameters of 41/100 of an inch, are not presumptively destructive devices. *See* Chapter 1.A for a discussion of caliber designations.) The shotgun models commonly sold at gun stores are considered to satisfy the "sporting purposes" exception and thus are not NFA firearms. Additional exceptions are found in §5645(f)(3):

> The term "destructive device" shall not include any device which is neither designed nor redesigned for use as a weapon; any device . . . which is redesigned for use as a signaling, pyrotechnic, line throwing, safety, or similar device; . . . or any other device which the Secretary finds is not likely to be used as a weapon, or is an antique or is a rifle which the owner intends to use solely for sporting purposes.

As of late 2006, the ATF reported that 1,186,138 destructive devices were registered in the NFRTR. Over three-quarters of these (totaling 918,517) were "flash bang" grenades, nonlethal explosive devices used by military and law enforcement organizations. When detonated, flash bang grenades disorient targets by emitting an intense blast of sound and light.

"Any Other Weapons." Often informally abbreviated AOW, this perplexing category does not really encompass *any* other weapon besides the ones listed in the foregoing five categories. To the contrary, it excludes all ordinary pistols, revolvers, rifles, and shotguns. The category includes:

> any weapon or device capable of being concealed on the person from which a shot can be discharged through the energy of an explosive, a pistol or revolver having a barrel with a smooth bore designed or redesigned to fire a fixed shotgun shell, weapons with combination shotgun and rifle barrels 12 inches or more, less than 18 inches in length, from which only a single discharge can be made from either barrel without manual reloading, and shall include any such weapon which may be readily restored to fire. Such term shall not include a pistol or a revolver having a rifled bore, or rifled bores, or weapons designed, made, or intended to be fired from the shoulder and not capable of firing fixed ammunition.

26 U.S.C. §5845(e). The entire definition must be read in order to decide what counts as an AOW. The category includes, by ATF regulatory interpretation, many types of concealable firearms that do not qualify as ordinary pistols and revolvers, such as: (1) guns disguised to resemble another item (pen guns, briefcase guns, etc.); (2) handguns that have a smooth bore, shotgun barrel instead of the usual rifled barrel; (3) short barreled shotguns made with only a pistol grip, not a shoulder stock, and which have never been outfitted with a shoulder stock; (4) pistols with a second, protruding vertical grip attached in front of the trigger guard; and (5) a few types of early twentieth-century firearms, such as the Marble's Game Getter, which combined a short shotgun barrel and a short rifle barrel, each of which could be fired once before reloading. Because this last type of firearm was seen as useful for farmers and outdoorsmen, Congress soon amended the statute to lower the tax for transferring an AOW from $200 to $5. It remains so today. For more on the scope of the AOW category, see Stephen P. Halbrook, Firearms Law Deskbook §6.14 (2011). The *Deskbook* is very useful for all NFA issues.

When the NFA was first enacted, the $200 tax payment that it requires for making or transferring a covered "firearm" was equivalent to more than $3,000 today — a prohibitive amount for most would-be owners, and usually several times more than the retail price of the firearm itself. Thus, the statute originally functioned as a near prohibition on the manufacture or sale of NFA items for ownership by private citizens. However, as decades passed and inflation reduced the value of the $200 tax, NFA ownership became somewhat more feasible.

States remain free to impose their own additional restrictions on NFA-regulated items, and some completely prohibit categories of NFA weapons. *See, e.g.*, 11 Del. C. §1444 (making it a felony to possess any "firearm silencer, sawed-off shotgun, [or] machine gun," regardless of whether it is federally registered). Most states allow them to be lawfully possessed if federal NFA requirements are met. *See, e.g.*, S.C. Code 1976 §16-23-250 (exempting, from state ban on possession of machine guns, "any person authorized to possess these weapons by the United States . . . Bureau of Alcohol, Tobacco and Firearms. . . .").

The NFA Transfer Procedure. Today the procedure for a lawful transfer of an NFA item to an individual transferee often takes several months to complete. The transferor (the manufacturer or seller) must file with the ATF a form that includes the identity of the transferor, the transferee, a description and serial number of the firearm, the photograph and fingerprints of the transferee, and a validly paid and cancelled federal NFA tax stamp. 27 C.F.R. §479.85. In addition, when the transferee is an individual, ATF regulations require that the transferee obtain:

> A certificate of the local chief of police, sheriff of the county, head of the State police, State or local district attorney or prosecutor, or such other person whose certificate may in a particular case be acceptable to the Director, . . . stat[ing] that the certifying official is satisfied that the fingerprints and photograph accompanying the application are those of the applicant and that the certifying official has no information indicating that the receipt or possession of the firearm would place the transferee in violation of State or local law or that the transferee will use the firearm for other than lawful purposes.

Id. If the requirements are not satisfied, the transfer will not be approved by ATF and the individual cannot lawfully obtain the NFA item. In practice, this regulation vests local law enforcement officials with considerable discretion as to whether individuals can make or obtain NFA weapons in their jurisdiction. In some areas, sheriffs and police chiefs will routinely sign the certification to allow transfers to individuals who have clean records. In others, the certifications are never or virtually never approved.

NOTES & QUESTIONS

1. The National Firearms Act imposes heavy taxes and regulations on the manufacture, transfer, and sale of covered firearms. Dealers must also pay special taxes in order to deal in NFA firearms. Thus, the NFA effectively excludes the types of weapons within its coverage from the mainstream commercial firearms trade. The United States Supreme Court suggested in *Heller* (Chapter 9), that certain kinds of "dangerous and unusual weapons" lie entirely outside of the category of "arms" whose possession is protected by the Second Amendment. *Heller* also strongly suggested that machine guns and short barreled shotguns — both categories of weapons covered by the NFA — qualify as dangerous and unusual weapons.

    Do you think the weapons covered by the NFA should be deemed constitutionally unprotected? Should the statute be expanded? Proposals are sometimes made to add new categories of guns, such as long range .50 BMG caliber rifles, to the NFA.

2. Sound suppressors (commonly known as "silencers") are widely used by firearms owners in European nations such as Finland, France, Sweden, and the United Kingdom. Sound suppressors protect the neighbors of target ranges or of farmers (engaged in pest control) from loud sounds. On a per-gun owner basis, sound suppressors are much less common in the United

States, thanks to the NFA's $200 tax and strict registration requirements. Although most U.S. gun laws are less stringent than their European counterparts, the U.S. regulation of "silencers" is much more severe. One motive for the NFA's hefty tax on sound suppressors may have been fear that sound suppressors could facilitate poaching (at a time when hunger and malnutrition were widespread). Under current federal regulations, any device that reduces the sound of a firearm by at least 3 decibels is considered a "silencer." Sound suppressors typically reduce a gunshot sound by about 15-20 decibels. The suppressed sound is not really "silent"; it can still be more than four times louder than a chainsaw. However, with a heavily silenced firearm, the sound of the bullet flight may be louder than the sound of the gunshot, thereby making it more difficult for a witness to identify the origin of the gunshot. Most states allow silencer possession, as long as the possessor complies with the NFA. Should silencer controls be changed to a more lenient, European-style system? Should silencers be prohibited entirely? Or should the law be left as is?

D. Miller's Aftermath: The Shrinking Second Amendment

As the previous section discussed, *Miller* can be interpreted in several ways. Some have suggested that the understanding of *Miller* was substantially impacted by subsequent lower court constructions. The next two cases followed quickly on the heels of *Miller*.

Cases v. United States
131 F.2d 916 (1st Cir. 1942)

WOODBURY, Circuit Judge.

This is an appeal from a judgment of the District Court of the United States for Puerto Rico sentencing the defendant to a term of imprisonment after he had been found guilty by a jury on all four counts of an indictment charging him with violating §2(e) and (f) of the [FFA], by transporting and receiving a firearm and ammunition. The grounds upon which the defendant bases his appeal are that the statute under which he was indicted is unconstitutional. . . .

The defendant contends that the Federal Firearms Act is unconstitutional because . . . (b) it violates the Second Amendment by infringing the right of the people to keep and bear arms; [and] (c) it is an undue extension of the commerce clause . . . In our view none of these contentions are sound. . . .

The Federal Firearms Act undoubtedly curtails to some extent the right of individuals to keep and bear arms but it does not follow from this as a necessary consequence that it is bad under the Second Amendment which reads "A well regulated Militia, being necessary to the security of a free State, the right of the people to keep and bear Arms, shall not be infringed."

The right to keep and bear arms is not a right conferred upon the people by the federal constitution. Whatever rights in this respect the people may have depend upon local legislation; the only function of the Second Amendment being to prevent the federal government and the federal government only from infringing that right. *United States v. Cruikshank*, 92 U.S. 542 (1875); *Presser v. Illinois*, 116 U.S. 252 (1886). But the Supreme Court in a dictum in *Robertson v. Baldwin*, 165 U.S. 275, 282 (1897), indicated that the limitation imposed upon the federal government by the Second Amendment was not absolute and this dictum received the sanction of the court in the recent case of *United States v. Miller*, 307 U.S. 174 (1939).

In the case last cited the Supreme Court, after discussing the history of militia organizations in the United States, upheld the validity under the Second Amendment of the National Firearms Act . . . in so far as it imposed limitations upon the use of a shotgun having a barrel less than eighteen inches long. It states the reason for its result . . . as follows: "In the absence of any evidence tending to show that possession or use of a 'shotgun having a barrel of less than eighteen inches in length' at this time has some reasonable relationship to the preservation or efficiency of a well regulated militia, we cannot say that the Second Amendment guarantees the right to keep and bear such an instrument. Certainly it is not within judicial notice that this weapon is any part of the ordinary military equipment or that its use could contribute to the common defense."

Apparently, then, under the Second Amendment, the federal government can limit the keeping and bearing of arms by a single individual as well as by a group of individuals, but it cannot prohibit the possession or use of any weapon which has any reasonable relationship to the preservation or efficiency of a well regulated militia. However, we do not feel that the Supreme Court in this case was attempting to formulate a general rule applicable to all cases. The rule which it laid down was adequate to dispose of the case before it and that we think was as far as the Supreme Court intended to go. At any rate the rule of the *Miller* case, if intended to be comprehensive and complete would seem to be already outdated, in spite of the fact that it was formulated only three and a half years ago, because of the well known fact that in the so called "Commando Units" some sort of military use seems to have been found for almost any modern lethal weapon. In view of this, if the rule of the *Miller* case is general and complete, the result would follow that, under present day conditions, the federal government would be empowered only to regulate the possession or use of weapons such as a flintlock musket or a matchlock harquebus. But to hold that the Second Amendment limits the federal government to regulations concerning only weapons which can be classed as antiques or curiosities, — almost any other might bear some reasonable relationship to the preservation or efficiency of a well regulated militia unit of the present day, — is in effect to hold that the limitation of the Second Amendment is absolute. Another objection to the rule of the *Miller* case as a full and general statement is that according to it Congress would be prevented by the Second Amendment from regulating the possession or use by private persons not present or prospective members of any military unit, of distinctly military arms, such as machine guns, trench mortars, anti-tank or anti-aircraft guns, even though under the circumstances surrounding such possession or use it would be inconceivable that a private person could have any legitimate reason for having such a weapon. It seems to us unlikely that the framers of the Amendment intended any such result.

Considering the many variable factors bearing upon the question it seems to us impossible to formulate any general test by which to determine the limits imposed by the Second Amendment but that each case under it, like cases under the due process clause, must be decided on its own facts and the line between what is and what is not a valid federal restriction pricked out by decided cases falling on one side or the other of the line.

[The defendant-appellant shot someone with a .38 caliber revolver in a Puerto Rico night club.] While the weapon may be capable of military use, or while at least familiarity with it might be regarded as of value in training a person to use a comparable weapon of military type and caliber, still there is no evidence that the appellant was or ever had been a member of any military organization or that his use of the weapon under the circumstances disclosed was in preparation for a military career. In fact, the only inference possible is that the appellant at the time charged in the indictment was in possession of, transporting, and using the firearm and ammunition purely and simply on a frolic of his own and without any thought or intention of contributing to the efficiency of the well regulated militia which the Second Amendment was designed to foster as necessary to the security of a free state. We are of the view that, as applied to the appellant, the Federal Firearms Act does not conflict with the Second Amendment to the Constitution of the United States.

It is clear that in enacting the Federal Firearms Act Congress was exercising the power conferred upon it by the commerce clause, but it is equally clear that Congress meant to deal comprehensively with the subject and to exert all the power which it had in respect thereto. See *Atlantic Cleansers & Dyers v. United States*, 286 U.S. 427, 434 (1932); *People of Puerto Rico v. Shell Co.*, 302 U.S. 253, 259 (1937). Since its power as we have seen, as to a territory like Puerto Rico is plenary, except as limited by express constitutional restrictions, Congress is not fettered by the commerce clause, Const. art. 1, Sec. 8, cl. 3, in its power to legislate for Puerto Rico. See *Lugo v. Suazo*, 59 F.2d 386, 390 (1st Cir. 1932); and *Sancho v. Bacardi Corp.*, 109 F.2d 57, 62, 63 (1st Cir. 1940), reversed on another point sub nom., *Bacardi Corp. v. Domenech*, 311 U.S. 150 (1940). . . . The question of whether or not Congress would have the power to regulate such conduct if it had occurred in a state is not raised. Since the appellant's argument on this constitutional question assumes that the situation presented is governed by the rules which would be applicable if his acts had been done in a state, it is beside the point and need not be considered. . . .

The judgment of the District Court is affirmed.

United States v. Tot
131 F.2d 261 (3d Cir. 1942)

GOODRICH, Circuit Judge.

[Defendant Tot was convicted under the FFA for having received a firearm that has been shipped in interstate commerce after having been convicted of a crime of violence as defined in the Act. A .32 caliber Colt pistol was in his home when he was arrested on other charges.]

The Second Amendment to the Constitution of the United States provides: "A well regulated Militia, being necessary to the security of a free State, the right of the people to keep and bear Arms, shall not be infringed."

The appellant's contention is that if the statute under which this prosecution was brought is to be applied to a weapon of the type he had in his possession, then the statute violates the Second Amendment.

It is abundantly clear both from the discussions of this amendment contemporaneous with its proposal and adoption and those of learned writers since that this amendment, unlike those providing for protection of free speech and freedom of religion, was not adopted with individual rights in mind, but as a protection for the States in the maintenance of their militia organizations against possible encroachments by the federal power. The experiences in England under James II of an armed royal force quartered upon a defenseless citizenry was fresh in the minds of the Colonists. They wanted no repetition of that experience in their newly formed government. The almost uniform course of decision in this country, where provisions similar in language are found in many of the State Constitutions, bears out this concept of the constitutional guarantee. A notable instance is the refusal to extend its application to weapons thought incapable of military use.

The contention of the appellant in this case could, we think, be denied without more under the authority of *United States v. Miller*, 307 U.S. 174 (1939). This was a prosecution under the National Firearms Act of 1934 and the weapon, the possession of which had occasioned the prosecution of the accused, was a shotgun of less than 18 inch barrel. The Court said that in the absence of evidence tending to show that possession of such a gun at the time has some reasonable relationship to the preservation or efficiency of a well regulated militia, it could not be said that the Second Amendment guarantees the right to keep such an instrument. The appellant here having failed to show such a relationship, the same thing may be said as applied to the pistol found in his possession. It is not material on this point that the 1934 statute was bottomed on the taxing power while the statute in question here was based on a regulation of interstate commerce.

But, further, the same result is definitely indicated on a broader ground and on this we should prefer to rest the matter. Weapon bearing was never treated as anything like an absolute right by the common law. It was regulated by statute as to time and place as far back as the Statute of Northampton in 1328 and on many occasions since. The decisions under the State Constitutions show the upholding of regulations prohibiting the carrying of concealed weapons, prohibiting persons from going armed in certain public places and other restrictions, in the nature of police regulations, but which do not go so far as substantially to interfere with the public interest protected by the constitutional mandates. The Federal statute here involved is one of that general type. One could hardly argue seriously that a limitation upon the privilege of possessing weapons was unconstitutional when applied to a mental patient of the maniac type. The same would be true if the possessor were a child of immature years. In the situation at bar Congress has prohibited the receipt of weapons from interstate transactions by persons who have previously, by due process of law, been shown to be aggressors against society. Such a classification is entirely reasonable and does not infringe upon the preservation of the well regulated militia protected by the Second Amendment. . . .

The social end sought to be achieved by this legislation, the protection of society against violent men armed with dangerous weapons, all would concede to be fundamental in organized government. The entry of the federal authority in the field to help accomplish this purpose has not been challenged. It has been taken for granted by both sides in the discussion of this case. We also think it may be assumed. In accomplishing the admittedly constitutional object we do not think the means taken by this statute, while stringent, have become so oppressive and arbitrary that we are entitled to say that Congress has exceeded its authority in acting without due process of law.

The judgment is affirmed.

NOTES & QUESTIONS

1. The Supreme Court denied *certiorari* for *Cases, Velazquez v. United States*, 319 U.S. 770 (1943), and reversed *Tot* on the ground that the FFA's presumption that the firearm was received by a defendant in interstate commerce was a violation of the Due Process Clause. *Tot v. United States*, 319 U.S. 463 (1943). Later, in the Gun Control Act of 1968, Congress included a specific jurisdictional requirement that a particular gun must have been "in commerce or affecting commerce." *United States v. Bass*, 404 U.S. 336 (1971) (applying statute to any gun which ever moved in interstate commerce). In neither *Tot* nor *Bass* did the Supreme Court address the Second Amendment or the constitutional scope of the interstate commerce power. If *Miller* is as ambiguous as we have suggested, why did the Court not clarify it when given the chance in *Tot*, instead of reversing on other grounds?

2. Did *Cases* and *Tot* follow the ruling in *Miller*? Make the argument that these decisions were consistent with *Miller*. Make the argument that the decisions embellished or depart from the ruling in *Miller*. As you develop these arguments, consider whether *Miller* focused on the firearm or the individual. Consider also how *Miller* defined "militia."

3. What do you make of the originalist analysis in *Cases* and *Tot* in light of the material in Chapters 2 through 4?

4. Compare the enumerated powers discussion in *Cases* with that in *Sonzinzky, supra*. Given that *Cases* and *Tot* dealt with the Second Amendment while *Sonzinzky* did not, should it matter that the Second Amendment was adopted after the Commerce Clause and taxing power in Article I?

E. Armed Citizens and the Second World War

1. The United States

In 1941, on the eve of American entry into the Second World War, Congress enacted the Property Requisition Act, which gave the President sweeping powers to requisition privately owned "machinery, tools, or materials" that were immediately needed for the national defense, in return for compensation to be paid to the former owners of the property. The Act stated that it was not to be construed "to impair or infringe in any manner the right of any individual to keep and bear arms." It specifically prohibited the President from "requisitioning or requiring the registration of any firearms [otherwise lawfully] possessed by any individual for his personal protection or sport." 55 Stat. 742.

The accompanying legislative committee report of the U.S. House of Representatives stated that these exceptions to the President's authority were included "[i]n view of the fact that certain totalitarian and dictatorial nations are now engaged in the willful and wholesale destruction of personal rights and liberties"; accordingly, the committee "deem[ed] it appropriate for the Congress to expressly state that the proposed legislation shall not be construed to impair or infringe the constitutional right of the people to bear arms." For more information on the history of the Property Requisition Act's Second Amendment provision, see Stephen P. Halbrook, *Congress Interprets the Second Amendment: Declarations by a Co-Equal Branch on the Individual Right to Keep and Bear Arms,* 62 Tenn. L. Rev. 597, 618-31 (1995).

After America entered the war, the National Guard was called up by the federal government and activated for overseas duty. Several states and territories, including Maryland, raised state guard militia units to protect their coastlines, bridges, and other vital areas. In the radio address announcing the creation of the Maryland State Guard and calling for volunteers, Governor Herbert O'Conor explained: "For the present the hard-pressed Ordinance Department of the United States Army cannot be expected to furnish sufficient arms, ammunition, or equipment. Hence, the volunteers, for the most part, will be expected to furnish their own weapons. For this reason, gunners (of whom there are 60,000 licensed in Maryland), members of Rod and Gun Clubs, of Trap Shooting and similar organizations, will be expected to constitute a part of this new military organization." *Maryland Minute Men* (Radio Station WFBR and Maryland Coverage Network Mar. 10, 1942), *in* 3 State Papers and Addresses of Governor Herbert L. O'Conor 618 (n.d.), *available at* Archives of Maryland Online, http://www. aomol.net/html/volumes5.html (click on volume 409, then enter "618" into "page" field and then click the "Go" link). Volunteers in other states, and in the territories of Hawaii and Alaska, also performed militia duties with their personally owned rifles and pistols. *See* Robert Dowlut & Janet A. Knoop, *State Constitutions and the Right to Keep and Bear Arms,* 7 Okla. City U. L. Rev. 177, 197-98 (1982).

2. The United Kingdom

The fall of France in 1940 left most of Western Europe under the control of the Third Reich or other fascist powers, except for the United Kingdom and Switzerland. Facing an imminent threat of German invasion, Britain found itself severely short of small arms needed for defense, and sought them abroad. The U.S. government sold surplus military rifles to Britain, and U.S publications carried advertisements urging readers to donate "pistols — revolvers — rifles — shotguns — binoculars" to "Defend a British Home." American Rifleman, Nov. 1940. Numerous shipments of American small arms crossed the Atlantic Ocean and helped to equip British military and Home Guard units. After the war, the government collected donated firearms from Home Guard units and then destroyed them. The development of British gun laws is discussed further in online Chapter 14.

SEND
A GUN
TO DEFEND
A BRITISH HOME

British civilians, faced with threat of invasion, desperately need arms for the defense of their homes.

THE AMERICAN COMMITTEE FOR DEFENSE OF BRITISH HOMES

has organized to collect gifts of

PISTOLS—RIFLES—REVOLVERS
SHOTGUNS—BINOCULARS

from American civilians who wish to answer the call and aid in defense of British homes.

These arms are being shipped, with the consent of the British Government, to CIVILIAN COMMITTEE FOR PROTECTION OF HOMES BIRMINGHAM, ENGLAND

The members of which are Wickham Steed, Edward Hulton, and Lord Davies

YOU CAN AID

by sending any arms or binoculars you can spare to

AMERICAN COMMITTEE FOR DEFENSE OF BRITISH HOMES

C. Suydam Cutting, *Chairman*
ROOM 100
10 WARREN STREET, NEW YORK, N. Y.

NOTES & QUESTIONS

1. How did the wartime Congress understand the Second Amendment right to arms when passing the Property Requisition Act? How does this understanding compare with the view adopted at nearly the same time by the courts in *Cases* and *Tot*?

2. In the 2010 Supreme Court case of *McDonald v. Chicago*, 130 S. Ct. 3020 (2010) (Chapter 9), 58 Senators (including 19 Democrats) and 251 U.S. Representatives (including 78 Democrats) filed an amicus brief pointing to America's use of individually armed citizens during World War II, and arguing that today, an armed citizenry could provide defense against

Mumbai-style terrorism in which terrorists in a single or multiple locations carry out gun or bomb attacks against civilians in public places. They also argued that our constitutional structure demands that Congress must always have the choice to use the militia. Is the congressional argument persuasive?

‖8‖

Between *Miller* and *Heller*:
The Second Amendment
in the Modern Era

Second Amendment doctrine in the modern era is intriguing because so much time — nearly seven decades — separates the Supreme Court's direct treatments of the Second Amendment in *United States v. Miller*, 307 U.S. 174 (1939) (Chapter 7) and the landmark decision of *District of Columbia v. Heller*, 554 U.S. 570 (2008) (Chapter 9). This period is not doctrinal wasteland. Indeed, this is the period where the modern gun control movement and the national debate about firearms rights and regulation developed. As the length of this chapter attests, legislatures, lower courts and, indirectly, the Supreme Court were quite active during this period on questions of gun regulation and gun rights.

This modern era witnessed development of a nearly unanimous view in the lower federal courts that the Second Amendment did not protect a private right to keep and bear arms. However, there were periodic injections of uncertainty into the Second Amendment debate from cryptic references in Supreme Court decisions; enactment of federal legislation imposing important new limitations on the purchase, sale, or possession of firearms; and the emergence of a robust scholarly debate about the meaning of the Second Amendment, leading to in-depth re-examination that prefigured the Supreme Court's decision in *Heller* recognizing an individual right to keep and bear arms.

This chapter examines the developments of the modern era in four parts. This division reflects substantive distinctions, but they also are connected in the sense that the developments they describe all occur in the context of the political and social developments of the last half-century.

Section A presents lower federal court rulings from the 1960s through the 1990s. Drawing on the *Miller, Cases,* 131 F.2d 916 (1st Cir. 1942), and *Tot,* 131 F.2d 261 (3d Cir. 1942), decisions from Chapter 7, these cases illustrate the near-unanimous rejection of the private-right interpretation of the Second Amendment. When Justice Stevens states in dissent in *Heller* that hundreds of judges have taken or relied on the view that the Second Amendment does not protect a right beyond the organized militia, he is talking about these decisions. Many of these decisions presented only cursory analysis to dispose of arguably frivolous Second Amendment claims by criminal defendants.

Section B illustrates that the Supreme Court was not entirely silent about the Second Amendment between *Miller* and *Heller*. At various points, statements by dissenters and majorities sent signals that complicated impressions about the meaning of the Second Amendment. Some of these references raise questions that remain unresolved even after *Heller*.

Section C describes the social and political history of gun rights and gun control between *Miller* and *Heller*. This narrative section explains the growth and changes of the gun rights and gun control movements, developments in social views about gun rights and gun control, the influence of legal scholarship about the Second Amendment, and how all the changes in the world outside of case law finally converged to set the stage for *Heller*.

Section D, consuming most of the chapter, covers the regulation of firearms in the modern era. It focuses on restrictions imposed by the 1968 Gun Control Act, as amended and supplemented by legislation including the Firearms Owners Protection Act of 1986, the 1993 Brady Act, the 1994 assault weapons ban, and the 2005 Protection of Lawful Commerce in Arms Act, as well as administrative interpretation of these provisions by the Bureau of Alcohol, Tobacco, Firearms and Explosives (ATF). This section also covers several gun control measures that have been prominent in state and federal policy debates, including restrictions on gun shows, limits on secondary sales, and "assault weapon" bans.

Section E is dedicated to two Circuit Court decisions, *United States v. Emerson*, 270 F.3d 203 (5th Cir. 2001), and *Silveira v. Lockyer*, 312 F.3d 1052 (9th Cir. 2002). These decisions from the Fifth and Ninth Circuits, respectively, broke the mold of lower federal court treatment of the Second Amendment. Unlike earlier decisions, they were extensively researched and reasoned. They also came to opposite conclusions about the meaning of the Second Amendment. In combination with the D.C. Circuit case, *Parker v. District of Columbia*, 478 F.3d 370 (D.C. Cir. 2007) (designated *District of Columbia v. Heller* on certiorari to the Supreme Court), these decisions underscored a new and profound disagreement between circuits about the meaning of the Second Amendment. The views and disputes they frame are a preview of the issues the Supreme Court engaged in *Heller*.

A.   The Second Amendment in the Lower Federal Courts

This section examines lower federal court treatments of the Second Amendment during the nearly seven decades that passed between *Miller* (Chapter 7) and *Heller* (Chapter 9). Chapter 7 showed how the early circuit court decisions in *Cases* and *Tot* stripped the ambiguity out of the Supreme Court's treatment of the Second Amendment in *Miller*.

Subsequent federal court decisions followed this lead. Until the Fifth Circuit's 2001 decision in *United States v. Emerson*, *infra*, most lower federal courts gave little credit to the idea that the Second Amendment or *Miller* protected any sort of non-militia, individual right to private firearms. Many of those decisions involved Second Amendment claims by criminal defendants that were rejected with very little analysis.

The Ninth Circuit's detailed critique in *Silveira v. Lockyer, infra,* followed earlier decisions in rejecting the individual rights view of the Second Amendment but characterized them this way: "Like other courts, we reached our [earlier] conclusion regarding the Second Amendment's scope largely on the basis of the rather cursory discussion in *Miller,* and touched only briefly on the merits of the debate. . . . *Miller,* like most other cases that address the Second Amendment, fails to provide much reasoning in support of its conclusion." Notwithstanding such criticisms, there is no disputing the point pressed by Justice Stevens's dissent in *Heller* that numerous judges had read *Miller* as rejecting the general individual right. The next four cases are typical of those decisions.

United States v. McCutcheon
446 F.2d 133 (7th Cir. 1971)

[Defendant was convicted of possession of an unregistered short barreled shotgun in violation of the National Firearms Act of 1934. This was the same offense that prompted the decision in *United States v. Miller* (Chapter 7).]

HASTINGS, Senior Circuit Judge. . . .

We do not feel required to cite the legislative history of analogous legislation and cases deciding kindred questions relating thereto, or the century and a half of federal legislation providing for an organized militia, now the National Guard. We deem it sufficient to rely upon the landmark decision of *United States v. Miller,* 307 U.S. 174 (1939), and its progeny. *Miller* was concerned with an alleged violation of the National Firearms Act by one indicted for transporting in interstate commerce for 12 gauge sawed-off shotgun without having registered it or paid the tax required by the Act. The Court first held that the Act was not unconstitutional as an invasion of police powers reserved to the States. In rejecting a holding by the lower court that the Act was violative of the Second Amendment, the Court said at page 178:

> "In the absence of any evidence tending to show that possession or use of a 'shotgun having a barrel of less than eighteen inches in length' at this time has some reasonable relationship to the preservation or efficiency of a well regulated militia, we cannot say that the Second Amendment guarantees the right to keep and bear such an instrument. Certainly it is not within judicial notice that this weapon is any part of the ordinary military equipment or that its use could contribute to the common defense. *Aymette v. State,* 2 Humphreys (Tenn.) 154, 158."

There then followed a consideration of the constitutional and legislative history of the Second Amendment and the Act. The Court concluded that there was no material support for the challenged ruling of the court below.

In like manner, we find no merit in the Second Amendment issue raised in the case at bar.

Stevens v. United States
440 F.2d 144 (6th Cir. 1971)

[Defendant was convicted of violating provisions of the 1968 Gun Control Act that prohibited felons from possessing firearms.]

PHILLIPS, Chief Judge. . . .

We turn now to the consideration of whether Congress has the power to prohibit the possession of a firearm by a convicted felon. Since the Second Amendment right "to keep and bear Arms" applies only to the right of the State to maintain a militia and not to the individual's right to bear arms, there can be no serious claim to any express constitutional right of an individual to possess a firearm. *United States v. Miller*, 307 U.S. 174 (1939). Stevens asserts, however, that Congress is without constitutional power to deny him this privilege. We hold that Congress has this authority under the commerce clause.

Cody v. United States
460 F.2d 34 (8th Cir. 1972)

[Cody was convicted of making false statements to a licensed firearms dealer in connection with the purchase of a firearm in violation of the Gun Control Act of 1968.]

BRIGHT, Circuit Judge. . . .

We find no merit in the contention that §922(a)(6) violates appellant's Second Amendment right to bear arms. Since *United States v. Miller*, 307 U.S. 174 (1939), it has been settled that the Second Amendment is not an absolute bar to congressional regulation of the use or possession of firearms. The Second Amendment's guarantee extends only to use or possession which "has some reasonable relationship to the preservation or efficiency of a well regulated militia." *Id.* at 178. *See United States v. Synnes*, 438 F.2d 764, 772 (8th Cir. 1971), vacated on other grounds, 404 U.S. 1009 (1972); *Cases v. United States*, 131 F.2d 916, 922 (1st Cir. 1942), cert. denied sub nom., *Cases Velazquez v. United States*, 319 U.S. 770 (1943). We find no evidence that the prohibition of §922(a)(6) obstructs the maintenance of a well regulated militia. . . .

The judgment of conviction is affirmed.

United States v. Brimley
529 F.2d 103 (6th Cir. 1976)

[Defendant appealed his conviction for possession of an unregistered short barreled firearm in violation of the National Firearms Act of 1934.]

HARVEY, District Judge.

Next, the appellants assert that the statute under which they were convicted is itself unconstitutional as not being authorized by the Necessary and Proper

Clause of Article I of the Constitution and/or as an exercise of a power expressly denied Congress by the Second Amendment to the Constitution.

Congress could have prohibited the transfer of firearms altogether. Instead, it chose to permit transfer subject to well-defined regulation. *Varitimos v. United States*, 404 F.2d 1030, 1032 & n.4 (1st Cir. 1968), *cert. denied*, 395 U.S. 976 (1969).

The taxing power of Congress provides the authority to validate the provisions of 26 USC §5861(d), *Sonzinsky v. United States*, 300 U.S. 506, 514 (1937). Citing the above authority, the basic issue of validity was previously considered by the Fifth Circuit.

> "Test of validity is whether on its face the tax operates as a revenue generating measure and the attendant regulations are in aid of a revenue purpose . . . (citations omitted). . . . Furthermore, that an act accomplishes another purpose than raising revenue does not invalidate it. (citation omitted) Section 5861(d) making possession of an unregistered weapon unlawful is part of the web of regulation aiding enforcement of the transfer tax provision in §5811. Having required payment of a transfer tax and registration as an aid in collection of that tax, Congress under the taxing power may reasonably impose a penalty on possession of unregistered weapons. Such a penalty imposed on transferees ultimately discourages the transferor on whom the tax is levied from transferring a firearm without paying the tax."

United States v. Ross, 458 F.2d 1144, 1145 (5th Cir. 1972), *cert. denied*, 409 U.S. 868 (1972). See also *United States v. Matthews*, 438 F.2d 715, 716-17 (5th Cir. 1971); *United States v. Smith*, 341 F. Supp. 687, 688-89 (N.D. Ga. 1972).

As for the appellants' contention that the statutes under which they are charged are violative of their right to bear arms as guaranteed by the Second Amendment to the Constitution, this Court must agree with the Supreme Court and the Ninth and Fifth Circuit Courts that have reviewed this question and have answered it adversely to appellants' contention. *United States v. Miller*, 307 U.S. 174, 178 (1939), *United States v. Tomlin*, 454 F.2d 176 (9th Cir. 1972), *United States v. Williams*, 446 F.2d 1401 (5th Cir. 1971).

NOTES & QUESTIONS

1. The excerpts from the four cases above comprise the entire Second Amendment analyses offered by the respective courts. Beyond their conclusion that it does not support the various individual rights claims raised, are these decisions in agreement about the meaning of the Second Amendment? What explains the relatively cursory treatment of these Second Amendment claims? Are the Second Amendment claims raised by the criminal defendants in these cases frivolous? Professor Brannon Denning has argued that the twentieth-century lower federal court cases consistently read *Miller* to stand for propositions that were not clearly established by that decision. *See* Brannon P. Denning, *Can the Simple Cite Be Trusted?: Lower Court Interpretations of* United States v. Miller *and the Second Amendment*, 26 Cumb. L. Rev. 961 (1996). CQ: Keep these cases in mind as you read Justice Breyer's dissent in *McDonald v. Chicago*, 130 S. Ct. 3020 (2010)(Chapter 9). Would it have been appropriate

for these decisions to elaborate the positive content of the Second Amendment, or would that have ranged beyond the question presented to the courts?

2. CQ: After you have read the *Heller* decision in the next chapter, consider whether the Supreme Court's recognition of a private right to arms for self-defense should change the results in the four cases in this segment. Notice the assessment in *McCutcheon* that the protected militia is the modern National Guard. Does this interpretation respect the interest of states in maintaining militias? The Supreme Court has repeatedly affirmed that the federal government has plenary authority over the National Guard. *See Perpich v. Dep't of Defense*, 496 U.S. 334, 352-54 (1990) (holding that state militias may be called into federal service and deployed in foreign countries over state objections); *Selective Draft Law Cases*, 245 U.S. 366, 374-83 (1918) (holding that Congress has the authority to abolish a state militia by bodily incorporating it into the federal army); *Martin v. Mott*, 25 U.S. (12 Wheat.) 19, 28-33 (1827) (holding that the President has the unreviewable power to call the militia from state control into federal service); *Houston v. Moore*, 18 U.S. (5 Wheat.) 1, 24 (1820) (holding that federal militia legislation preempts state legislation). If the Second Amendment is solely a state's right, what is the content of that right, given federal plenary authority? Is the organized militia referred to in Chapter 4 the only protected one? *Cf.* 10 U.S.C. §311 (2000) (defining "organized" militia as the National Guard and Naval Militia, and "unorganized militia" as all other able-bodied males at least 17 years old and less than 45 years old). For the long and nearly unbroken history of judicial rejection of state claims opposing assertions of federal militia powers, see J. Norman Heath, *Exposing the Second Amendment: Federal Preemption of State Militia Legislation*, 79 U. Det. Mercy L. Rev. 39 (2001).

3. Notice the *Brimley* court's explanation that the 1934 National Firearms Act (NFA) was grounded on the taxing power. The purpose of the NFA was to regulate "gangster weapons" such as machine guns. U.S. Attorney General Homer S. Cummings testified to the House Ways and Means Committee that firearms could not be banned outright under the Second Amendment, so he proposed restrictive regulation in the form of a high tax and federal registration. *See* Chapter 7.B. CQ: When you read *Heller* in the next chapter, pay attention to the Court's assessment of whether a machine gun ban would survive a Second Amendment challenge.

Some decisions from this era offer more than cursory analysis of the Second Amendment. Generally, the analysis in these cases is less a direct application of *Miller* and more an elaboration of *Miller* informed by subsequent lower court decisions. So, in a sense, these cases helped build a jurisprudence of the Second Amendment with little assistance from the Supreme Court. Over the decades, the Court's relative silence on the Second Amendment arguably suggested approval of that jurisprudence. The next case is one of the most cited circuit court treatments of the Second Amendment in the early modern era. Many other federal courts relied on it. As you read it, keep in mind your assessments of *Miller*, *Cases*, and *Tot* from the previous chapter.

United States v. Warin
530 F.2d 103 (6th Cir. 1976)

LIVELY, Circuit Judge.

This case requires a determination of whether certain provisions of the National Firearms Act as amended by the Gun Control Act of 1968, 26 U.S.C. §5801 et seq., are an invalid infringement on the right to keep and bear arms guaranteed by the Second Amendment to the Constitution. . . .

The defendant appeals from his conviction of the charge that he "willfully and knowingly possessed a firearm, that is a 9 mm prototype submachine gun measuring approximately 21 inches overall length, with a barrel length of approximately 7 1/2 inches, which had not been registered to him in the National Firearms Registration and Transfer Record as required by Chapter 53, Title 26, United States Code" in violation of 26 U.S.C. §§5861(d) and 5871.

At trial before the court, the following facts were stipulated to be true:

> That on or about the 19th day of March, 1974, in the Northern District of Ohio, Western Division, Francis J. Warin willfully and knowingly possessed a firearm, that is, a 9-millimeter prototype submachine gun measuring approximately twenty-one inches overall length, with a barrel length of approximately seven and a half inches, which had not been registered to him in the National Firearms Registration and Transfer Record, . . . that submachine guns are used by the armed forces of the United States, and that submachine guns contribute to the efficient operation of the armed forces of the United States in their function of defending the country. . . . That the weapon involved in this case is a submachine gun. . . . That 9-millimeter submachine guns have been used by at least one Special Forces Unit of the Army in the Vietnam, . . . although they are not in general use. 9-millimeter submachine guns have been used by the military forces of the United States on at least one occasion during the Vietnam war. . . . That submachine guns are part of the military equipment of the United States military — . . . and that firearms of this general type, that is, submachine guns, do bear some relationship, some reasonable relationship, to the preservation or efficiency of the military forces.

The district court found that the defendant, as an adult male resident and citizen of Ohio, is a member of the "sedentary militia" of the State.[1] It was not contended that Warin was a member of the active militia. The court also found

---

1. The source of the term "sedentary militia" is unclear. The district court's finding was based in part upon Ohio Constitution, Art. IX §1, which does not by its own force make adult citizens of Ohio members of the organized or active militia, but merely subjects them to enrollment in that body:

> ARTICLE IX: MILITIA
> §1 Who shall perform military duty.
> All citizens, resident of this state, being seventeen years of age, and under the age of sixty-seven years, shall be subject to enrollment in the militia and the performance of military duty, in such manner, not incompatible with the Constitution and laws of the United States, as may be prescribed by law. (As amended Nov. 7, 1961.)

that the defendant was an engineer and designer of firearms whose employer develops weapons for the government and —

> that the defendant had made the weapon in question, which is indeed a firearm as described in the Act. It is also clear from the evidence that the weapon was of a type which is standard for military use, and fires the ammunition which is in common military use for the weapons used by individual soldiers in combat. The defendant testified that he had designed and built the weapon for the purpose of testing and refining it so that it could be offered to the Government as an improvement on the military weapons presently in use. The weapon was not registered to him as required by law.

These findings are not disputed. . . .

Warin argues that . . . a member of the "sedentary militia" may possess any weapon having military capability and that application of 26 U.S.C. §5861(d) to such a person violates the Second Amendment. We disagree. In *Miller* the Supreme Court did not reach the question of the extent to which a weapon which is "part of the ordinary military equipment" or whose "use could contribute to the common defense" may be regulated. In holding that the absence of evidence placing the weapon involved in the charges against Miller in one of these categories precluded the trial court from quashing the indictment on Second Amendment grounds, the Court did not hold the converse — that the Second Amendment is an absolute prohibition against all regulation of the manufacture, transfer and possession of any instrument capable of being used in military action.

Within a few years after *Miller* . . . was announced the First Circuit dealt with arguments similar to those made by Warin in the present case. In *Cases v. United States,* 131 F.2d 916 (1st Cir. 1942), cert. denied sub nom. *Velazquez v. United States,* 319 U.S. 770 (1943), the court held that the Supreme Court did not intend to formulate a general rule in *Miller,* but merely dealt with the facts of that case. The court of appeals noted the development of new weaponry during the early years of World War II and concluded that it was not the intention of the Supreme Court to hold that the Second Amendment prohibits Congress from regulating any weapons except antiques "such as a flintlock musket or a matchlock harquebus." 131 F.2d at 922. If the logical extension of the defendant's argument for the holding of *Miller* was inconceivable in 1942, it is completely irrational in this time of nuclear weapons.

Agreeing as we do with the conclusion in *Cases v. United States,* supra, that the Supreme Court did not lay down a general rule in *Miller,* we consider the present case on its own facts and in light of applicable authoritative decisions. It is clear that the Second Amendment guarantees a collective rather than an individual right. In *Stevens v. United States,* 440 F.2d 144, 149 (6th Cir. 1971), this court held, in a case challenging the constitutionality of 18 U.S.C. App. §1202(a)(1):

> Since the Second Amendment right "to keep and bear Arms" applies only to the right of the State to maintain a militia and not to the individual's right to bear arms, there can be no serious claim to any express constitutional right of an individual to possess a firearm. . . .

It is also established that the collective right of the militia is limited to keeping and bearing arms, the possession or use of which "at this time has some reasonable relationship to the preservation or efficiency of a well regulated militia, . . ." *United States v. Miller*, supra, 307 U.S. at 178. See also, *United States v. Johnson*, supra; *Cody v. United States*, 460 F.2d 34, 37 (8th Cir.), cert. denied, 409 U.S. 1010 (1972).

The fact that the defendant Warin, in common with all adult residents and citizens of Ohio, is subject to enrollment in the militia of the State confers upon him no right to possess the submachine gun in question. By statute the State of Ohio exempts "members of . . . the organized militia of this or any other state . . ." (emphasis added) from the provision, "No person shall knowingly acquire, have, carry, or use any dangerous ordnance." Ohio Revised Code §2923.17. "Dangerous ordnance" is defined to include any automatic firearm. O.R.C. §2923.11. There is no such exemption for members of the "sedentary militia." Furthermore, there is absolutely no evidence that a submachine gun in the hands of an individual "sedentary militia" member would have any, much less a "reasonable relationship to the preservation or efficiency of a well regulated militia." *Miller*, supra, 307 U.S. at 178. Thus we conclude that the defendant has no private right to keep and bear arms under the Second Amendment which would bar his prosecution and conviction for violating 26 U.S.C. §5861(d).

Even where the Second Amendment is applicable, it does not constitute an absolute barrier to the congressional regulation of firearms. After considering several arguments the Third Circuit in *United States v. Tot*, supra, stated that it decided the case on the "broader ground" that "weapon bearing was never treated as anything like an absolute right by the common law. It was regulated by statute as to time and place as far back as the Statute of Northampton in 1328 and on many occasions since." 131 F.2d at 266 (footnote omitted). In *Stevens v. United States*, supra, this court discussed the broad power of Congress in relying on the commerce clause of the Constitution to deal with the changing needs of the nation. 440 F.2d at 150-52. . . .

We also agree with the disposition by the district court of defendant's contention that the statute under which he was charged and convicted violates the Ninth Amendment to the Constitution. We simply do not conceive of the possession of an unregistered submachine gun as one of those "additional fundamental rights, protected from governmental infringement, which exist alongside those fundamental rights specifically mentioned in the first eight constitutional amendments." *Griswold v. Connecticut*, 381 U.S. 479, 488 (1965) (concurring opinion of Goldberg, J.).

It would unduly extend this opinion to attempt to deal with every argument made by defendant and amicus curiae, Second Amendment Foundation, all of which are based on the erroneous supposition that the Second Amendment is concerned with the rights of individuals rather than those of the States or that defendant's automatic membership in the "sedentary militia" of Ohio brings him within the reach of its guarantees.

The judgment of the district court is affirmed.

NOTES & QUESTIONS

1. Does the *Warin* court follow the Supreme Court's decision in *Miller* (Chapter 7)? What do you make of the following passage: "Agreeing as we do with the

conclusion in *Cases v. United States, supra,* that the Supreme Court did not lay down a general rule in *Miller,* we consider the present case on its own facts and in light of applicable authoritative decisions"? Assuming it is appropriate to follow *Cases,* are any parts of the *Miller* opinion itself still relevant to the question in *Warin*?

2.   The 1328 English Statute of Northampton (Chapter 2) restricted weapons-carrying, and certainly supports the *Warin* court's proposition that the right to arms was not an "absolute right." How much does evidence that a right is not absolute prove? Does it support the proposition that any curtailment of the right, even complete elimination of it, is allowable?

3.   The *Warin* decision does not mention the definition of militia presented in *Miller.* The district court referred instead to a state constitutional provision. Is the definition of militia in *Miller* relevant to the question in *Warin*?

4.   Consider the policy implications if the *Warin* decision had gone the other way. Would those results be consistent with your understanding of *Miller*? Was the plaintiff's argument a plausible reading of *Miller*? Were Second Amendment advocates trying to do too much in *Warin* by attempting to get a court to enforce an individual right *and* to make that right applicable to a submachine gun? Were they bringing a case that carefully fit within what *Miller* had indicated was the scope of the right?

5.   In the lower federal court cases following *Miller,* the characterization of the Second Amendment varied. Sometimes, as in *Warin,* the right was deemed a "collective" one. Other cases call it a "state's right." Still other cases appeared to recognize an individual right, but one that applies, at most, to persons serving in the National Guard. It was common for federal courts to favorably cite these cases with no apparent acknowledgment of any conflict—for example, a "collective right" court citing a prior "state's right" decision or an individual-National-Guard-only decision as authority for the collective right view. Are such citations examples of sloppy jurisprudence? Or are they defensible, since all the cases shared the conclusion that ordinary citizens had no private right to arms? For more on the different "models" of the right protected by the Second Amendment, see *Silveira v. Lockyer, infra, United States v. Emerson, infra,* and *http://Firearm regulation.org.*

Other widely cited collective, state's rights, or militia-only interpretations of *Miller* include: *United States v. Oakes,* 564 F.2d 384 (10th Cir. 1977) (to apply the Second Amendment to permit defendant to keep a machine gun without complying with the National Firearms Act of 1934, merely because he is technically a member of the Kansas militia, would be unjustifiable in terms of either logic or policy), and *Quilici v. Morton Grove,* 695 F.2d 261 (7th Cir. 1982), cert. denied, 464 U.S. 863 (1983) (a municipal handgun ban does not violate the Second Amendment because the Amendment does not apply to the states and because "the right to keep and bear handguns is not guaranteed by the Second Amendment"). The *Morton Grove* case attracted national attention. When the Supreme Court denied certiorari, gun control groups claimed an important victory, and a vindication of their view of the Second Amendment. Ironically, the Morton Grove handgun ban was the prime engine behind the NRA's successful effort to convince many state legislatures to enact preemption laws prohibiting municipal gun bans. A few weeks after *Heller* (Chapter 9) was decided, the Morton Grove ban was repealed. Morton Grove is a good illustration of how, in the American political and legal conflict over gun control, a small jurisdiction can have a great national impact. Can you think of other constitutional issues in which a small town or suburb has shaped the national debate?

In *Cases*, 131 F.2d at 923 (Chapter 7), the court used a state of mind test to explain why the defendant failed to show a militia connection. Cases, said the court, possessed the gun, "simply on a frolic of his own and without any thought or intention of contributing to the efficiency of a well regulated militia." Would it have made a difference if *Cases* had offered evidence of an explicit intention to contribute to the maintenance of the militia as *Warin* actually did? The next case engages that argument.

United States v. Hale
978 F.2d 1016 (8th Cir. 1992)

JOHN R. GIBSON, Circuit Judge.

Wilbur Hale appeals his conviction of thirteen counts of possession of a machine gun pursuant to 18 U.S.C.A. §922(o) (West Supp. 1992) and three counts of possession of unregistered firearms pursuant to 26 U.S.C. §5861(d) (1988). . . .

Hale next argues that the indictment violates his Second Amendment rights: . . . Hale argues that the Second Amendment bars the federal government from regulating the particular weapons seized because the weapons are susceptible to military use and are therefore, by definition, related to the existence of "a well regulated militia". . . .

Hale wants to find in *Miller* the rule that individual possession of true military weapons is protected under the Second Amendment. When the Second Amendment was ratified in 1791, the state militias functioned as both the principal units of military organization and as an implicit check on federal power. See generally Keith A. Ehrman & Dennis A. Henigan, The Second Amendment in the Twentieth Century: Have You Seen Your Militia Lately?, 15 U. Dayton L. Rev. 5 (1989). These militias were comprised of ordinary citizens who typically were required to provide their own equipment and arms. The Second Amendment prevented federal laws that would infringe upon the possession of arms by individuals and thus render the state militias impotent. Over the next 200 years, state militias first faded out of existence and then later reemerged as more organized, semi-professional military units. The state provided the arms and the equipment of the militia members, and these were stored centrally in armories. With the passage of the Dick Act in 1903, the state militias were organized into the National Guard structure, which remains in place today. Id.

More recently, the Supreme Court in *Perpich v. U.S. Department of Defense*, 496 U.S. 334 (1990), has analyzed the early history of the militia, including the Act of 1792 which required militia members to provide themselves "with a good musket or firelock," as well as cartridges and other equipment. The Court observed that these requirements were virtually ignored for more than a century. Id. at 341. *Perpich* discusses in detail the relationship between the militia and the National Guard and recognizes that the "Federal Government provides virtually all of the funding, the materiel, and the leadership for the State Guard units." Id. at 351. While *Perpich* does not deal with the Second Amendment issue present here, its discussion of the militia gives further dimension to our analysis.

Considering this history, we cannot conclude that the Second Amendment protects the individual possession of military weapons. In *Miller*, the Court simply recognized this historical residue. The rule emerging from *Miller* is that, absent a showing that the possession of a certain weapon has "some reasonable relationship to the preservation or efficiency of a well-regulated militia," the Second Amendment does not guarantee the right to possess the weapon. *Miller*, 307 U.S. at 178. *Miller* simply "did not hold . . . that the Second Amendment is an absolute prohibition against all regulation of the manufacture, transfer and possession of any instrument capable of being used in military action." *Warin*, 530 F.2d at 106. . . .

The Supreme Court has not addressed a Second Amendment issue since the *Miller* decision. *Cases v. United States*, 131 F.2d 916 (1st Cir. 1942), cert. denied, 319 U.S. 770 (1943) remains one of the most illuminating circuit opinions on the subject of "military" weapons and the Second Amendment. *Cases* states that "under the Second Amendment, the federal government can limit the keeping and bearing of arms by a single individual, as well as by a group of individuals, but it cannot prohibit the possession or use of any weapon which has any reasonable relationship to the preservation or efficiency of a well-regulated militia." Id. at 922. After carefully examining the principles and implications of the then recent *Miller* decision, the First Circuit concluded that the existence of any "reasonable relationship to the preservation of a well regulated militia" was best determined from the facts of each individual case. Id. Thus, it is not sufficient to prove that the weapon in question was susceptible to military use. Indeed, as recognized in *Cases*, most any lethal weapon has a potential military use. Id. Rather, the claimant of Second Amendment protection must prove that his or her possession of the weapon was reasonably related to a well regulated militia. See id. at 923. Where such a claimant presented no evidence either that he was a member of a military organization or that his use of the weapon was "in preparation for a military career," the Second Amendment did not protect the possession of the weapon. Id.

Since the *Miller* decision, no federal court has found any individual's possession of a military weapon to be "reasonably related to a well regulated militia." "Technical" membership in a state militia (e.g., membership in an "unorganized" state militia) or membership in a non-governmental military organization is not sufficient to satisfy the "reasonable relationship" test. *Oakes*, 564 F.2d at 387. Membership in a hypothetical or "sedentary" militia is likewise insufficient. See *Warin*, 530 F.2d 103.

Applying these principles to the present case, we conclude that Hale's possession of the weapons in question was not reasonably related to the preservation of a well regulated militia. The allegation by Hale that these weapons are susceptible to military use is insufficient to establish such a relationship. Hale introduced no evidence and made no claim of even the most tenuous relationship between his possession of the weapons and the preservation of a well regulated militia.

Citing dicta from *United States v. Verdugo-Urquidez*, 494 U.S. 259 (1990), Hale argues that the Second Amendment protections apply to individuals and not to states or collective entities like militias. This argument is inapplicable to this case. The purpose of the Second Amendment is to restrain the federal government from regulating the possession of arms where such regulation would interfere with the preservation or efficiency of the militia. . . .

NOTES & QUESTIONS

1. The *Hale* decision seems to dispense with almost any claim based on membership in the unorganized militia through its conclusion that the militia has devolved into the National Guard. Judge Hastings in the *McCutcheon* case took the same position but with less elaboration. Is this view consistent with *Miller*? Is it consistent with the definitions of militia and National Guard in 10 U.S.C. §311?

    §311. Militia: composition and classes
        (a) The militia of the United States consists of all able-bodied males at least 17 years of age and, except as provided in section 313 of title 32, under 45 years of age who are, or who have made a declaration of intention to become, citizens of the United States and of female citizens of the United States who are members of the National Guard.
        (b) The classes of the militia are—
            (1) the organized militia, which consists of the National Guard and the Naval Militia; and
            (2) the unorganized militia, which consists of the members of the militia who are not members of the National Guard or the Naval Militia.

2. The 1989 Ehrman and Henigan article cited in *Hale* is one of the most influential scholarly articles ever written about the Second Amendment. Most of the legal scholarship on the Second Amendment during the 1980s was in support of the broad individual right, which is today known as "the Standard Model." This article was the first significant reply. (Dennis Henigan was, and still is, the head lawyer for the Brady Campaign to Prevent Gun Violence, which in 1989 was known as "Handgun Control, Inc.") Notably, the article does not argue against an individual right *per se*, but argues for what was later called the "narrow individual right" or the "sophisticated collective right." By whatever name, the theory is that the Second Amendment is an individual right, but one that pertains solely to militia service. By the time *Heller* was decided in 2008, this was the most serious intellectual competitor to the broad individual right. While the Scalia majority argued for the broad individual right, the Stevens dissent argued for the narrow individual right. Justice Stevens dismissed any notion

that the Court had ever viewed the Second Amendment right as non-individual. The Ehrman-Henigan thesis was greatly elaborated by later scholars, most notably Saul Cornell. CQ: Assuming that Ehrman, Henigan, Cornell, and Justice Stevens are correct, what accounts for the popularity of the simple "collective rights" or "state's rights" theory in federal court jurisprudence in the late twentieth century? Why was Second Amendment legal scholarship, as of 1989, in such a primitive state that a single article could cause such a paradigm shift? For more on Henigan's influence, see Section C of this chapter.

3. Regarding the post-*Miller* cases, and the Supreme Court's refusal to grant certiorari in any of those cases, Professor Kopel wrote, "One may reasonably draw two conclusions from the inaction. First, in that 'Qui tacet consentit' [silence implies consent], a majority of the Court was probably content with allowing the lower courts to do the work of eliminating the Second Amendment as a meaningful part of the American Constitution. Second, the Court was unwilling to do the job itself." David B. Kopel, *The Right to Arms in the Living Constitution*, 2009 Cardozo L. Rev. De Novo 99, 116. Do you agree with this interpretation? Consider whether the Supreme Court cases in Section B that briefly mention the Second Amendment support Kopel's theory.

B. Six Decades of Cryptic Supreme Court References to the Second Amendment

The Supreme Court issued no direct rulings on the Second Amendment between 1939 and 2008. But the Court was not entirely silent on the issue. Following *Miller* (Chapter 7), the Court rendered relevant decisions in two categories. First, in a variety of cases, the Court and individual Justices made reference to or reasoned from particular views of the Second Amendment. These cases prefigure the Court's treatment of the Second Amendment in *Heller* (Chapter 9) and also suggest how future panels might treat some of the many questions that still remain open. In a second category of cases, the Court heard challenges to legislation regulating firearms. Those cases have continuing but unsettled application post-*Heller*.

Many of the examples in the first category were notable simply because the Court had said *something*, typically in dicta, about the Second Amendment. In several cases, the treatment was not even in the majority opinion. For example, in *Adamson v. California*, 332 U.S. 46 (1947), the majority adhered to early twentieth-century case law that most provisions of the Bill of Rights, including the Fifth Amendment privilege against self-incrimination, were not binding on the states. In a dissenting opinion, Justices Black and Douglas detailed the legislative history of the Fourteenth Amendment to argue that it was intended to incorporate the Bill of Rights, including an individual right to arms. Douglas offered evidence that part of the debate surrounding passage of the Fourteenth Amendment was whether to "guarantee the negro . . . a right to defend himself. . . . To bear arms."

Justice Black pressed the point again in a concurring opinion in *Duncan v. Louisiana*, 391 U.S. 145 (1968). Expanding upon the majority's decision that the Sixth Amendment right to jury trial applied to the states through the Fourteenth Amendment, Justice Black stressed that the "personal rights guaranteed and secured by the first eight amendments of the Constitution [include] . . . the freedom of speech and of the press; the right of the people peaceably to assemble and petition the Government for redress of grievances, a right appertaining to each and all the people; the right to keep and bear arms. . . ."

Chapter 6 contains some of the historical materials about the Fourteenth Amendment on which Justice Black relied. Chapter 9 examines the 2010 case that finally addressed Justice Black's claim that the Fourteenth Amendment makes the Second Amendment enforceable against the states, *McDonald v. Chicago*.

A direct Second Amendment analogy appears in *Johnson v. Eisentrager*, 339 U.S. 736 (1950), where a group of Germans were arrested and tried in China for violation of the laws of war (spying after Germany's unconditional surrender). While imprisoned in Germany, they filed a writ of habeas corpus claiming that their trial and imprisonment violated the United States Constitution. The Court dismissed the petitions. Writing for the Court, Justice Jackson reasoned that extending constitutional rights to enemy aliens would demand the absurd result of granting them "freedoms of speech, press and assembly as in the First Amendment, right to bear arms as in the Second. . . ." *Id.* at 763. *Eisentrager* was later limited in *Hamdan v. Rumsfeld*, 548 U.S. 557 (2006) (holding that sometimes even "enemy combatants" may have habeas corpus rights).

In *Konigsberg v. State Bar of California*, 366 U.S. 36, 49 n.10 (1961), Justice Harlan stated that Second Amendment rights are not absolute. *Konigsberg* involved a challenge to a law that required California Bar applicants to disclose membership in the Communist Party. The Court held that the petitioner's First Amendment rights were not violated. The Court rejected the contention that the First Amendment conferred an absolute right (listing exceptions such as libel, slander, perjury, etc.), and drew a comparison to the Second Amendment: "In this connection also compare the equally unqualified command of the Second Amendment: 'the right of the people to keep and bear arms shall not be infringed.' And see *United States v. Miller*, 307 U.S. 174." Justice Black, in dissent, argued that many rights are absolute. For example, a newspaper editorialist has an absolute right to urge that readers vote against a politician during an election. Justice Black elaborated his argument in a famous speech at New York University Law School. Hugo L. Black, *The Bill of Rights*, 35 N.Y.U. L. Rev. 865 (1960). In the speech, Justice Black said that the Second Amendment right was absolute, within the boundaries of its application, which had been construed by *Miller*.

The only Supreme Court case in this period that actually involved a Second Amendment challenge to a gun control law was *Burton v. Sills*, 394 U.S. 812 (1969), where the plaintiffs challenged New Jersey's recently enacted gun licensing statute. The state supreme court, relying on *Presser* (Chapter 6), said that the Second Amendment did not apply to state governments. In 1969, litigants dissatisfied with a state supreme court ruling would file a direct appeal to the Supreme Court, rather than a petition for certiorari. So when the Supreme Court refused to hear Burton's appeal, the rejection was styled as "dismissed for want of a substantial federal question," rather than "certiorari denied."

Dismissal for want of a substantial federal question is theoretically supposed to have national precedential effect, although the precise character of that "precedent" is disputed. In practice, twenty-first-century courts treat "dismissed for want of a substantial federal question" the same as "certiorari denied," which is to say that the Supreme Court decision not to hear the case provides no practical guidance on the merits. None of the parties in the *McDonald* (Chapter 9) case relied on *Burton v. Sills*, even though *McDonald* directly addressed the issue of Second Amendment applicability to the states.

As this summary shows, the Supreme Court was not entirely silent on the gun issue during the modern era. The cases excerpted in subsections 1 though 4 below contain even stronger suggestions about the meaning of the Second Amendment.

1. The Right to Arms as a Liberty Interest?

One of the most widely invoked Supreme Court references to the Second Amendment appears in one of the most influential dissenting opinions. The reference is merely suggestive because the controversy before the Court was not a firearms case. However, keep this reference in mind when you evaluate the *Heller* and *McDonald* decisions in the next chapter.

Poe v. Ullman was a predecessor to *Griswold v. Connecticut,* asserting an unenumerated right of married couples to use artificial contraception. The *Poe* majority dismissed the case for lack of a case or controversy, but Justice John Marshall Harlan II (grandson of the first Justice Harlan, the lone dissenter in *Plessy v. Ferguson,* 163 U.S. 537 (1896)) disagreed, and explained why he would have ruled in favor of the right to birth control. His dissent in *Poe* would be cited in many future cases as a compelling rationale for recognizing unenumerated rights.

Poe v. Ullman
367 U.S. 497 (1961)

MR. JUSTICE FRANKFURTER announced the judgment of the Court. . . .

These appeals challenge the constitutionality, under the Fourteenth Amendment, of Connecticut statutes which, as authoritatively construed by the Connecticut Supreme Court of Errors, prohibit the use of contraceptive devices and the giving of medical advice in the use of such devices. . . .

It is clear that the mere existence of a state penal statute would constitute insufficient grounds to support a federal court's adjudication of its constitutionality in proceedings brought against the State's prosecuting officials if real threat of enforcement is wanting. See *Ex parte La Prade,* 289 U.S. 444, 458. If the prosecutor expressly agrees not to prosecute, a suit against him for declaratory and injunctive relief is not such an adversary case as will be reviewed here. *C. I. O. v. McAdory,* 325 U.S. 472, 475. . . .

Dismissed. . . .

MR. JUSTICE HARLAN, dissenting. . . .

Due process has not been reduced to any formula; its content cannot be determined by reference to any code. The best that can be said is that through the course of this Court's decisions it has represented the balance which our Nation, built upon postulates of respect for the liberty of the individual, has struck between that liberty and the demands of organized society. If the supplying of content to this Constitutional concept has of necessity been a rational process, it certainly has not been one where judges have felt free to roam where unguided speculation might take them. The balance of which I speak is the balance struck by this country, having regard to what history teaches are the traditions from which it developed as well as the traditions from which it broke. That tradition is a living thing. A decision of this Court which radically departs from it could not long survive, while a decision which builds on what has survived is likely to be sound. No formula could serve as a substitute, in this area, for judgment and restraint.

It is this outlook which has led the Court continuingly to perceive distinctions in the imperative character of Constitutional provisions, since that character must be discerned from a particular provision's larger context. And inasmuch as this context is one not of words, but of history and purposes, the full scope of the liberty guaranteed by the Due Process Clause cannot be found in or limited by the precise terms of the specific guarantees elsewhere provided in the Constitution. This "liberty" is not a series of isolated points pricked out in terms of the taking of property; the freedom of speech, press, and religion; the right to keep and bear arms; the freedom from unreasonable searches and seizures; and so on. It is a rational continuum which, broadly speaking, includes a freedom from all substantial arbitrary impositions and purposeless restraints, see *Allgeyer v. Louisiana*, 165 U.S. 578; *Holden v. Hardy*, 169 U.S. 366; *Booth v. Illinois*, 184 U.S. 425; *Nebbia v. New York*, 291 U.S. 502; *Skinner v. Oklahoma*, 316 U.S. 535, 544 (concurring opinion); *Schware v. Board of Bar Examiners*, 353 U.S. 232, and which also recognizes, what a reasonable and sensitive judgment must, that certain interests require particularly careful scrutiny of the state needs asserted to justify their abridgment. Cf. *Skinner v. Oklahoma*, supra; *Bolling v. Sharpe*, supra. . . .

I would reverse the judgment in each of these cases.

NOTES & QUESTIONS

1. Justice Harlan's dissent in *Poe* has been cited in many cases. For example, Justice Souter's concurring opinion in *Glucksburg v. Washington*, 521 U.S. 702 (1997), is a paean to the Harlan dissent. Also notable is Justice White's concurring opinion in *Moore v. East Cleveland*, 431 U.S. 494 (1977) (striking down a zoning ordinance that prohibited extended family members from living in the same house). Like Justice Jackson's concurrence in the *Steel Seizure* case, 343 U.S. 759 (1952), or Justice Brandeis's dissent in *Olmstead v. United States*, 278 U.S. 438 (1928), the Harlan dissent in *Poe* has been far more influential than the majority opinion in the case. Based on the text of the dissent itself, what made the *Poe* dissent so enduring?

2. Advocates of a broad individual Second Amendment right have often cited Harlan's dissent in *Poe* and the numerous subsequent cases that quote *Poe*'s

reference to the Second Amendment. Does Harlan's language in *Poe* treat the Second Amendment as an individual right, enjoyed by ordinary American citizens?

3. The Harlan dissent in *Poe* figured prominently in the Court's later reproductive rights cases. *See, e.g., Planned Parenthood v. Casey,* 505 U.S. 833 (1992) (plurality op.); *Roe v. Wade,* 410 U.S. 113 (1973) (Stewart, J., concurring). Professor Johnson has argued that there are many shared rationales between abortion rights and right to arms claims. *See* Nicholas J. Johnson, *Principles and Passions, The Intersection of Abortion and Gun Rights,* 50 Rutgers L. Rev. 97 (1997), and *Supply Restrictions at the Margins of Heller and the Abortion Analogue: Stenberg Principles, Assault Weapons and the Attitudinalist Critique,* 60 Hastings L.J. 1285 (2009). What are the similarities and differences between the right to own and use a gun for self-defense and the right to use birth control? The right to an abortion? CQ: *Nordyke v. King,* 699 F.3d 776 (9th Cir. 2011) (Chapter 11) also analogizes Second Amendment rights to abortion rights.

2.   Defining Terms Used in the Second Amendment

Before the Supreme Court's decision in *Heller* (Chapter 9), some scholars argued that the Second Amendment protected only a state right or a collective right. *See, e.g.,* The Second Amendment in Law and History: Historians and Constitutional Scholars on the Right to Bear Arms (Carl T. Bogus ed., 2001). In *United States v. Verdugo-Urquidez,* the Court elucidated the term "people" in the Bill of Rights. The case was widely cited by scholars who took the individual-right view, as well as by a few adhering to the collective-right view. The case involved a Fourth Amendment challenge by a Mexican drug lord, Rene Martin Verdugo-Urquidez, who, with the cooperation of Mexican authorities, had been captured in Mexico and brought to the United States for prosecution. Some of the evidence against him was obtained in a U.S. government search of his home in Mexico. The Supreme Court held that the Fourth Amendment did not apply to Verdugo-Urquidez with respect to the search of his property in Mexico.

United States v. Verdugo-Urquidez
494 U.S. 259 (1990)

CHIEF JUSTICE REHNQUIST delivered the opinion of the Court. . . .

[The text of the Fourth Amendment], by contrast with the Fifth and Sixth Amendments, extends its reach only to "the people." "The people" seems to have been a term of art employed in select parts of the Constitution. The Preamble declares that the Constitution is ordained and established by "the People of the United States." The Second Amendment protects "the right of the people to keep and bear Arms," and the Ninth and Tenth Amendments provide that certain rights and powers are retained by and reserved to "the people." See also U.S. Const., amend. 1 ("Congress shall make no law . . . abridging . . . the right of the people peaceably to assemble"); Art. I, §2, cl. 1 ("The House of Representatives shall be composed of Members chosen every second Year by the

People of the several States"). While this textual exegesis is by no means conclusive, it suggests that "the people" protected by the Fourth Amendment, and
by the First and Second Amendments, and to whom rights and powers are
reserved in the Ninth and Tenth Amendments, refers to a class of persons
who are part of a national community or who have otherwise developed sufficient connection with this country to be considered part of that community.
See *United States ex rel. Turner v. Williams*, 194 U.S. 279, 292 (1904) (excludable
alien is not entitled to First Amendment rights, because "he does not become
one of the people to whom these things are secured by our Constitution by an
attempt to enter forbidden by law"). The language of these Amendments contrasts with the words "person" and "accused" used in the Fifth and Sixth
Amendments regulating procedure in criminal cases.

NOTES & QUESTIONS

1. Consider the language "class of persons who are part of a national community." In the context of the Second Amendment "right of the people to keep
   and bear arms," is this more consistent with a collective right, a state's right,
   or an individual right?

2. What, if anything, does *Verdugo* suggest about the purpose for which a right
   of the people to keep and bear arms may be employed?

3. Justice William Brennan, joined by Justice Thurgood Marshall, dissented in
   Verdugo. He argued that Fourth Amendment rights, like other constitutional
   rights, are not granted by governments, but are inherent and predate the
   Constitution:

   > In drafting both the Constitution and the Bill of Rights, the Framers strove to
   > create a form of Government decidedly different from their British heritage.
   > Whereas the British Parliament was unconstrained, the Framers intended to
   > create a Government of limited powers. See B. Bailyn, The Ideological Origins
   > of the American Revolution 182 (1967); 1 The Complete Anti-Federalist 65 (H.
   > Storing ed. 1981). The colonists considered the British government danger-
   > ously omnipotent. After all, the British declaration of rights in 1688 had been
   > enacted not by the people, but by Parliament. The Federalist No. 84, p. 439 (M.
   > Beloff ed. 1987). Americans vehemently attacked the notion that rights were
   > matters of "'favor and grace,'" given to the people from the Government. B.
   > Bailyn, supra, at 187 (quoting John Dickinson).
   >   Thus, the Framers of the Bill of Rights did not purport to "create" rights.
   > Rather, they designed the Bill of Rights to prohibit our Government from
   > infringing rights and liberties presumed to be pre-existing. See, e.g., U.S.
   > Const., Amdt. 9 ("The enumeration in the Constitution of certain rights,
   > shall not be construed to deny or disparage others retained by the people").
   > The Fourth Amendment, for example, does not create a new right of security
   > against unreasonable searches and seizures. It states that "[t]he right of the
   > people to be secure in their persons, houses, papers, and effects, against unrea-
   > sonable searches and seizures, shall not be violated. . . ."

   494 U.S. at 287 (Brennan, J., dissenting).

Do you agree with Justice Brennan's argument that individual rights preexisted the Bill of Rights? CQ: How does Justice Brennan's view comport with the understanding of the Second Amendment in *Cruikshank* (Chapter 6)? Keep the issue in mind as you evaluate Justice Scalia's claim in *Heller* (Chapter 9) that the motivation for codifying the right to keep and bear arms (maintenance of a well regulated militia) should not limit the scope of the preexisting right.

As Chief Justice Rehnquist's opinion in *Verdugo-Urquidez* discussing the meaning of "people" was noticed by Second Amendment scholars, Justice Ginsburg's dissent in *Muscarello v. United States* was likewise noticed, this time almost uniquely by individual-right scholars, for its discussion of the meaning of "bear."

Muscarello v. United States
524 U.S. 125 (1998)

[Police officers found a handgun locked in the glove compartment of petitioner Muscarello's truck, which he was using to transport marijuana for sale. His sentence was enhanced based on 18 U.S.C. §924(c)(1), which subjects anyone who "carries a firearm" during a drug-trafficking crime to a minimum five-year prison term. The Court held that "carries a firearm" applies to a person who knowingly possesses and conveys firearms in a vehicle. Justice Ginsburg disagreed.]

JUSTICE GINSBURG, with whom THE CHIEF JUSTICE [REHNQUIST], JUSTICE SCALIA, and JUSTICE SOUTER join, dissenting. . . .

It is uncontested that §924(c)(1) applies when the defendant bears a firearm, i.e., carries the weapon on or about his person "for the purpose of being armed and ready for offensive or defensive action in case of a conflict." Black's Law Dictionary 214 (6th ed. 1990) (defining the phrase "carry arms or weapons"); see ante, at 5. The Court holds that, in addition, "carries a firearm," in the context of §924(c)(1), means personally transporting, possessing, or keeping a firearm in a vehicle, anyplace in a vehicle.

Without doubt, "carries" is a word of many meanings, definable to mean or include carting about in a vehicle. But that encompassing definition is not a ubiquitously necessary one. Nor, in my judgment, is it a proper construction of "carries" as the term appears in §924(c)(1). In line with *Bailey* and the principle of lenity the Court has long followed, I would confine "carries a firearm," for §924(c)(1) purposes, to the undoubted meaning of that expression in the relevant context. I would read the words to indicate not merely keeping arms on one's premises or in one's vehicle, but bearing them in such manner as to be ready for use as a weapon. . . .

Unlike the Court, I do not think dictionaries, surveys of press reports, or the Bible tell us, dispositively, what "carries" means embedded in §924(c)(1). On definitions, "carry" in legal formulations could mean, inter alia, transport, possess, have in stock, prolong (carry over), be infectious, or wear or bear on one's person. At issue here is not "carries" at large but "carries a firearm." The Court's computer search of newspapers is revealing in this light. Carrying guns in a car showed up as the meaning "perhaps more than one third" of the time. Ante, at 4. One is left to wonder what meaning showed up some two thirds of the time. Surely a most familiar meaning is, as the Constitution's Second Amendment ("keep and *bear* Arms") (emphasis added) and Black's Law Dictionary, at 214, indicate: "wear, bear, or carry . . . upon the person or in the clothing or in a pocket, for the purpose . . . of being armed and ready for offensive or defensive action in a case of conflict with another person." . . .

NOTES & QUESTIONS

1. Some supporters of the individual rights view of the Second Amendment considered Justice Ginsburg's reference to the Second Amendment tacit support for their position. Do you read Justice Ginsburg's reference to bear arms in the Second Amendment as an endorsement of an individual right? A collective right? Is it neutral on the scope of the right?

2. CQ: As you read the opinions in *Heller* (Chapter 9), consider the ways that you might reconcile Justice Ginsburg's Second Amendment reference in *Muscarello* with her vote in *Heller*.

3. CQ: One question that remains open after the affirmation of the individual right to arms in *Heller* is the meaning and scope of the right to *bear* arms. In *Heller,* the dissenters argued that bear arms had an exclusively military connotation. As illustrated in Chapter 11, several lower courts have held that *Heller* affirmed only a right to keep arms for self-defense in the home and have declined to conclude that the Second Amendment protects a right to carry firearms outside the home. When you read those decisions, consider whether they conflict with Justice Ginsburg's Second Amendment reference in *Muscarello.*

3.   Gun Control and the Limits of Federal Power

Since the early twentieth century, the Interstate Commerce Clause, U.S. Const., art. I, §8, cl. 3, has been a major source of congressional power. As common and easily transported articles of commerce, guns have been subjected to much federal regulation adopted pursuant to the commerce power. One of the early challenges to the 1968 Gun Control Act was raised by a defendant who was prosecuted under the provision that banned all gun possession by convicted felons. In *United States v. Bass*, 404 U.S. 336 (1971), a convicted felon argued that prosecutors failed to show a nexus between his possession of a firearm and interstate commerce. The *Bass* Court held that this burden could be met simply by showing that the firearm had once traveled in interstate commerce. *Bass* was a statutory construction case that did not raise any constitutional questions.

It remains good law today, and has been generally viewed as expressing the Supreme Court's view of the scope of the commerce power.

Years later, in *Scarborough v. United States*, the Court held that Congress had only intended to require a minimal nexus with interstate commerce. As long as the gun had crossed state lines, even if the crossing were years before the felon's conviction, and even if the felon had nothing to do with the interstate crossing, the GCA of 1968 still applied. 431 U.S. 563 (1977). *Scarborough* was purely a statutory construction case, and the defendant apparently never raised the issue of whether the government's interpretation of the GCA of 1968 would mean that the GCA exceeded congressional powers over interstate commerce.

However, two more recent cases were not entirely sympathetic to broad use of the Interstate Commerce Clause as rationale for intrastate federal gun control.

United States v. Lopez
514 U.S. 549 (1995)

CHIEF JUSTICE REHNQUIST delivered the opinion of the Court.

In the Gun-Free School Zones Act of 1990, Congress made it a federal offense "for any individual knowingly to possess a firearm at a place that the individual knows, or has reasonable cause to believe, is a school zone." 18 U.S.C. §922(q)(1)(A). The Act neither regulates a commercial activity nor contains a requirement that the possession be connected in any way to interstate commerce. We hold that the Act exceeds the authority of Congress "to regulate Commerce . . . among the several States. . . ." U.S. Const., Art. I, §8, cl. 3.

On March 10, 1992, respondent, who was then a 12th-grade student, arrived at Edison High School in San Antonio, Texas, carrying a concealed .38 caliber handgun and five bullets. Acting upon an anonymous tip, school authorities confronted respondent, who admitted that he was carrying the weapon. He was arrested and charged under Texas law with firearm possession on school premises. See Tex. Penal Code Ann. §46.03(a)(1). The next day, the state charges were dismissed after federal agents charged respondent by complaint with violating the Gun-Free School Zones Act of 1990. 18 U.S.C. §922(q)(1)(A). . . .

On appeal, respondent challenged his conviction based on his claim that §922(q) exceeded Congress' power to legislate under the Commerce Clause. The Court of Appeals for the Fifth Circuit agreed and reversed respondent's conviction. . . .

We start with first principles. The Constitution creates a Federal Government of enumerated powers. See Art. I, §8. As James Madison wrote, "the powers delegated by the proposed Constitution to the federal government are few and defined. Those which are to remain in the State governments are numerous and indefinite." The Federalist No. 45, pp. 292-293 (C. Rossiter ed. 1961). This constitutionally mandated division of authority "was adopted by the Framers to ensure protection of our fundamental liberties." *Gregory v. Ashcroft*, 501 U.S. 452, 458 (1991) (internal quotation marks omitted). "Just as the separation and independence of the coordinate branches of the Federal Government serve to prevent the accumulation of excessive power in any one branch, a healthy balance of power between the States and the Federal Government will reduce the risk of tyranny and abuse from either front." *Id.*

The Constitution delegates to Congress the power "to regulate Commerce with foreign Nations, and among the several States, and with the Indian Tribes." Art. I, §8, cl. 3. . . .

[W]e have identified three broad categories of activity that Congress may regulate under its commerce power. . . . First, Congress may regulate the use of the channels of interstate commerce. . . . Second, Congress is empowered to regulate and protect the instrumentalities of interstate commerce, or persons or things in interstate commerce, even though the threat may come only from intrastate activities. . . . Finally, Congress' commerce authority includes the power to regulate those activities having a substantial relation to interstate commerce, *Jones & Laughlin Steel*, 301 U.S. at 37. . . .

Within this final category, admittedly, our case law has not been clear whether an activity must "affect" or "substantially affect" interstate commerce in order to be within Congress' power to regulate it under the Commerce Clause. Compare *Preseault v. ICC*, 494 U.S. 1, 17 (1990), with *Wirtz*, supra, at 196, n. 27 (the Court has never declared that "Congress may use a relatively trivial impact on commerce as an excuse for broad general regulation of state or private activities"). We conclude, consistent with the great weight of our case law, that the proper test requires an analysis of whether the regulated activity "substantially affects" interstate commerce.

We now turn to consider the power of Congress, in the light of this framework, to enact §922(q). The first two categories of authority may be quickly disposed of: §922(q) is not a regulation of the use of the channels of interstate commerce, nor is it an attempt to prohibit the interstate transportation of a commodity through the channels of commerce; nor can §922(q) be justified as a regulation by which Congress has sought to protect an instrumentality of interstate commerce or a thing in interstate commerce. Thus, if §922(q) is to be sustained, it must be under the third category as a regulation of an activity that substantially affects interstate commerce. . . .

Section 922(q) is a criminal statute that by its terms has nothing to do with "commerce" or any sort of economic enterprise, however broadly one might define those terms. Section 922(q) is not an essential part of a larger regulation of economic activity, in which the regulatory scheme could be undercut unless the intrastate activity were regulated. It cannot, therefore, be sustained under our cases upholding regulations of activities that arise out of or are connected with a commercial transaction, which viewed in the aggregate, substantially affects interstate commerce.

Second, §922(q) contains no jurisdictional element which would ensure, through case-by-case inquiry, that the firearm possession in question affects interstate commerce. For example, in *United States v. Bass*, 404 U.S. 336 (1971), the Court interpreted former 18 U.S.C. §1202(a), which made it a crime for a felon to "receive, posses[s], or transport in commerce or affecting commerce . . . any firearm." 404 U.S. at 337. The Court interpreted the possession component of §1202(a) to require an additional nexus to interstate commerce both because the statute was ambiguous and because "unless Congress conveys its purpose clearly, it will not be deemed to have significantly changed the federal-state balance." Id. at 349. The Bass Court set aside the conviction because although the Government had demonstrated that Bass had possessed a firearm, it had failed "to show the requisite nexus with interstate commerce." Id. at 347. The Court thus interpreted the statute to reserve the constitutional question whether Congress could regulate, without more, the "mere possession" of firearms. See Id. at 339, n. 4. . . . Unlike the statute in *Bass*, §922(q) has no express jurisdictional element which might limit its reach to a discrete set of firearm possessions that additionally have an explicit connection with or effect on interstate commerce.

Although as part of our independent evaluation of constitutionality under the Commerce Clause we of course consider legislative findings, and indeed even congressional committee findings, regarding effect on interstate commerce, see, e.g., *Preseault v. ICC*, 494 U.S. at 17, the Government concedes that "neither the statute nor its legislative history contain[s] express congressional findings regarding the effects upon interstate commerce of gun possession in a school zone." Brief for United States 5-6. We agree with the Government that Congress normally is not required to make formal findings as to the substantial burdens that an activity has on interstate commerce. . . . But to the extent that congressional findings would enable us to evaluate the legislative judgment that the activity in question substantially affected interstate commerce, even though no such substantial effect was visible to the naked eye, they are lacking here.

The Government's essential contention, in fine, is that we may determine here that §922(q) is valid because possession of a firearm in a local school zone does indeed substantially affect interstate commerce. Brief for United States 17. The Government argues that possession of a firearm in a school zone may result in violent crime and that violent crime can be expected to affect the functioning of the national economy in two ways. First, the costs of violent crime are substantial, and, through the mechanism of insurance, those costs are spread throughout the population. See *United States v. Evans*, 928 F.2d 858, 862 (CA9 1991). Second, violent crime reduces the willingness of individuals to travel to areas within the country that are perceived to be unsafe. Cf. *Heart of Atlanta Motel*, 379 U.S. at 253. The Government also argues that the presence of guns in schools poses a substantial threat to the educational process by threatening the learning environment. A handicapped educational process, in turn, will result in a less productive citizenry. That, in turn, would have an adverse effect on the Nation's economic well-being. As a result, the Government argues that Congress could rationally have concluded that §922(q) substantially affects interstate commerce.

We pause to consider the implications of the Government's arguments. The Government admits, under its "costs of crime" reasoning, that Congress could regulate not only all violent crime, but all activities that might lead to violent crime, regardless of how tenuously they relate to interstate commerce. See Tr. of Oral Arg. 8-9. Similarly, under the Government's "national productivity" reasoning, Congress could regulate any activity that it found was related to the economic productivity of individual citizens: family law (including marriage, divorce, and child custody), for example. Under the theories that the Government presents in support of §922(q), it is difficult to perceive any limitation on federal power, even in areas such as criminal law enforcement or education where States historically have been sovereign. Thus, if we were to accept the

Government's arguments, we are hard pressed to posit any activity by an individual that Congress is without power to regulate.

Although Justice Breyer argues that acceptance of the Government's rationales would not authorize a general federal police power, he is unable to identify any activity that the States may regulate but Congress may not. Justice Breyer posits that there might be some limitations on Congress' commerce power, such as family law or certain aspects of education. Post, at 624. These suggested limitations, when viewed in light of the dissent's expansive analysis, are devoid of substance.

Justice Breyer focuses, for the most part, on the threat that firearm possession in and near schools poses to the educational process and the potential economic consequences flowing from that threat. Post, at 619-624. Specifically, the dissent reasons that (1) gun-related violence is a serious problem; (2) that problem, in turn, has an adverse effect on classroom learning; and (3) that adverse effect on classroom learning, in turn, represents a substantial threat to trade and commerce. Post, at 623. This analysis would be equally applicable, if not more so, to subjects such as family law and direct regulation of education.

For instance, if Congress can, pursuant to its Commerce Clause power, regulate activities that adversely affect the learning environment, then, a fortiori, it also can regulate the educational process directly. Congress could determine that a school's curriculum has a "significant" effect on the extent of classroom learning. As a result, Congress could mandate a federal curriculum for local elementary and secondary schools because what is taught in local schools has a significant "effect on classroom learning," cf. Id. and that, in turn, has a substantial effect on interstate commerce. . . .

Admittedly, a determination whether an intrastate activity is commercial or noncommercial may in some cases result in legal uncertainty. But, so long as Congress' authority is limited to those powers enumerated in the Constitution, and so long as those enumerated powers are interpreted as having judicially enforceable outer limits, congressional legislation under the Commerce Clause always will engender "legal uncertainty." Post, at 630. As Chief Justice Marshall stated in *McCulloch v. Maryland*, 17 U.S. 316 (1819):

> "The [federal] government is acknowledged by all to be one of enumerated powers. The principle, that it can exercise only the powers granted to it . . . is now universally admitted. But the question respecting the extent of the powers actually granted, is perpetually arising, and will probably continue to arise, as long as our system shall exist." Id. at 405.

See also *Gibbons v. Ogden*, 9 Wheat., at 195 ("The enumeration presupposes something not enumerated"). The Constitution mandates this uncertainty by withholding from Congress a plenary police power that would authorize enactment of every type of legislation. See Art. I, §8. Congress has operated within this framework of legal uncertainty ever since this Court determined that it was the Judiciary's duty "to say what the law is." *Marbury v. Madison*, 5 U.S. 137 (1803) (Marshall, C. J.). Any possible benefit from eliminating this "legal uncertainty" would be at the expense of the Constitution's system of enumerated powers. . . .

These are not precise formulations, and in the nature of things they cannot be. But we think they point the way to a correct decision of this case. The possession of a gun in a local school zone is in no sense an economic activity that might, through repetition elsewhere, substantially affect any sort of interstate commerce. Respondent was a local student at a local school; there is no indication that he had recently moved in interstate commerce, and there is no requirement that his possession of the firearm have any concrete tie to interstate commerce.

To uphold the Government's contentions here, we would have to pile inference upon inference in a manner that would bid fair to convert congressional authority under the Commerce Clause to a general police power of the sort retained by the States. Admittedly, some of our prior cases have taken long steps down that road, giving great deference to congressional action. See supra, at 556-558. The broad language in these opinions has suggested the possibility of additional expansion, but we decline here to proceed any further. To do so would require us to conclude that the Constitution's enumeration of powers does not presuppose something not enumerated, cf. *Gibbons v. Ogden*, supra, at 195, and that there never will be a distinction between what is truly national and what is truly local, cf. *Jones & Laughlin Steel*, supra, at 30. This we are unwilling to do.

For the foregoing reasons the judgment of the Court of Appeals is Affirmed.

NOTES & QUESTIONS

1. In response to the holding in *Lopez*, Congress enacted a revised version of the Gun Free School Zones Act that included extensive findings and declarations about the interstate commerce impact of possession of firearms in a school zone. 18 U.S.C. §922(q)(1)(A)-(I). Moreover, the new version includes a "jurisdictional hook" similar to some other federal regulatory statutes. Instead of simply prohibiting possession of firearms in a school zone (as the version of the statute struck down in *Lopez* did), the new version prohibits possession of "a firearm that has moved in or that otherwise affects interstate or foreign commerce" in "a place that the individual knows, or has reasonable cause to believe, is a school zone." 18 U.S.C. §922(q)(2)(A).

    Do these changes make the Act constitutional? Some lower federal courts have concluded that they do, and have upheld the revised Act against claims that it exceeds the limits of the federal commerce power as construed in *Lopez*. See, e.g., *United States v. Dorsey*, 418 F.3d 1038 (9th Cir. 2005). The effect of the revisions to the statute appears to be similar to the effect of the predicate mentioned in *Bass*. The Act would apply to a gun that had once been moved in interstate commerce — such as a gun that was manufactured in Massachusetts in 1985, sold to a Texas retailer and then to a Texas customer in 1986, never left the state thereafter, and was brought into a federal Gun Free School Zone in 2010. For a critique of the argument that one passage in interstate commerce should be deemed sufficient to forever subject an item to congressional control, see David E. Engdahl, *The Necessary and Proper Clause as an Intrinsic Restraint on Federal Lawmaking Power*, 22 Harv. J.L. & Pub. Pol'y 107 (1998) (criticizing "the herpes theory" of interstate commerce); David B. Kopel & Glenn H. Reynolds, *Taking Federalism Seriously:* Lopez *and the Partial Birth Abortion Ban Act,* 30 Conn. L. Rev. 59 (1997) (arguing that the statute in *Bass* exceeds the legitimate scope of the interstate commerce power).

2. The school zone where guns are prohibited extends 1,000 feet from the legal boundaries of the school. Given the number of schools distributed throughout the country, the 1,000-foot radius of the overlapping "school zones" encompasses almost every portion of every city or town in the United States. The Act creates exceptions for unloaded guns in locked containers, guns on private property, guns locked in a rack in a vehicle, and an exception for individuals with state firearms licenses, which has been interpreted to include a license to carry a concealed handgun. *United States v. Tait,* 54 F. Supp. 2d 1100 (S.D. Ala. 1999), *aff'd,* 202 F.3d 1320 (11th Cir. 2000). Is it a legitimate exercise of federal power for Congress to declare most of the inhabited portion of the United States to be a "gun-free zone" except for licensed handgun carry permit holders, and certain other exceptions?

3. In *United States v. Morrison,* 529 U.S. 598 (2000), the Court ruled that part of the federal Violence Against Women Act of 1994 (VAWA) exceeded congressional power under the Interstate Commerce Clause. The challenged provision of VAWA allowed victims of violent crimes based on gender animus to bring civil suits in federal courts against their attackers. In invalidating this civil remedy provision, the Court (by the same 5-4 majority) underscored the requirements of *Lopez,* that the interstate commerce power is limited to power is limited to activities that are both economic and sufficiently connected to interstate commerce. *Id.* at 610. The VAWA, said the Court, "has nothing to do with 'commerce' or any sort of economic enterprise."

Lopez and its progeny sketch the limits of the commerce power. Assertions of federal power also have been deemed illegitimate on the basis of the Tenth Amendment. In the following case, another federal attempt to regulate firearms, interim legislation under the Brady Act, was overturned as a violation of the Tenth Amendment.

‖ Printz v. United States
521 U.S 898 (1997)

JUSTICE SCALIA delivered the opinion of the Court.

The question presented in these cases is whether certain interim provisions of the Brady Handgun Violence Prevention Act, Pub. L. 103-159, 107 Stat. 1536, commanding state and local law enforcement officers to conduct background checks on prospective handgun purchasers and to perform certain related tasks, violate the Constitution.

I

The Gun Control Act of 1968 (GCA), 18 U.S.C. §921 et seq., establishes a detailed federal scheme governing the distribution of firearms. It prohibits firearms dealers from transferring handguns to any person under 21, not resident in the dealer's State, or prohibited by state or local law from purchasing or possessing firearms, §922(b). It also forbids possession of a firearm by, and transfer of a firearm to, convicted felons, fugitives from justice, unlawful users of controlled substances, persons adjudicated as mentally defective or committed to mental institutions, aliens unlawfully present in the United States, persons dishonorably discharged from the Armed Forces, persons who have renounced their citizenship, and persons who have been subjected to certain restraining orders or been convicted of a misdemeanor offense involving domestic violence. §§922(d) and (g).

In 1993, Congress amended the GCA by enacting the Brady Act. The Act requires the Attorney General to establish a national instant background check system by November 30, 1998, Pub. L. 103-159, as amended, Pub. L. 103-322, 103 Stat. 2074, note following 18 U.S.C. §922, and immediately puts in place certain interim provisions until that system becomes operative. Under the interim provisions, a firearms dealer who proposes to transfer a handgun must first: (1) receive from the transferee a statement (the Brady Form), §922(s)(1)(A)(i)(I), containing the name, address and date of birth of the proposed transferee along with a sworn statement that the transferee is not among any of the classes of prohibited purchasers, §922(s)(3); (2) verify the identity of the transferee by examining an identification document, §922(s)(1)(A)(i)(II); and (3) provide the "chief law enforcement officer" (CLEO) of the transferee's residence with notice of the contents (and a copy) of the Brady Form, §§922(s)(1)(A)(i)(III) and (IV). With some exceptions, the dealer must then wait five business days before consummating the sale, unless the CLEO earlier notifies the dealer that he has no reason to believe the transfer would be illegal. §922(s)(1)(A)(ii).

The Brady Act creates two significant alternatives to the foregoing scheme. A dealer may sell a handgun immediately if the purchaser possesses a state handgun permit issued after a background check, §922(s)(1)(C), or if state law provides for an instant background check, §922(s)(1)(D). In States that have not rendered one of these alternatives applicable to all gun purchasers, CLEOs are required to perform certain duties. When a CLEO receives the required notice of a proposed transfer from the firearms dealer, the CLEO must "make a reasonable effort to ascertain within 5 business days whether receipt or possession would be in violation of the law, including research in whatever State and local recordkeeping systems are available and in a national system designated by the Attorney General." §922(s)(2). The Act does not require the CLEO to take any particular action if he determines that a pending transaction would be unlawful; he may notify the firearms dealer to that effect, but is not required to do so. If, however, the CLEO notifies a gun dealer that a prospective purchaser is ineligible to receive a handgun, he must, upon request, provide the would-be purchaser with a written statement of the reasons for that determination. §922(s)(6)(C). Moreover, if the CLEO does not discover any basis for objecting to the sale, he must destroy any records in his possession relating to the transfer, including his copy of the Brady Form. §922(s)(6)(B)(i).

Under a separate provision of the GCA, any person who "knowingly violates [the section of the GCA amended by the Brady Act] shall be fined under this title, imprisoned for no more than 1 year, or both." §924(a)(5).

Petitioners Jay Printz and Richard Mack, the CLEOs for Ravalli County, Montana, and Graham County, Arizona, respectively, filed separate actions challenging the constitutionality of the Brady Act's interim provisions. In each case, the District Court held that the provision requiring CLEOs to perform background checks was unconstitutional, but concluded that that provision was severable from the remainder of the Act, effectively leaving a voluntary background-check system in place. 856 F. Supp. 1372 (Ariz. 1994), 854 F. Supp. 1503 (Mont. 1994). A divided panel of the Court of Appeals for the Ninth Circuit reversed, finding none of the Brady Act's interim provisions to be unconstitutional. 66 F.3d 1025 (1995). We granted certiorari. 135 L. Ed. 2d 1046, 116 S. Ct. 2521. (1996).

II

From the description set forth above, it is apparent that the Brady Act purports to direct state law enforcement officers to participate, albeit only temporarily, in the administration of a federally enacted regulatory scheme. Regulated firearms dealers are required to forward Brady Forms not to a federal officer or employee, but to the CLEOs, whose obligation to accept those forms is implicit in the duty imposed upon them to make "reasonable efforts" within five days to determine whether the sales reflected in the forms are lawful. While the CLEOs are subjected to no federal requirement that they prevent the sales determined to be unlawful (it is perhaps assumed that their state-law duties will require prevention or apprehension), they are empowered to grant, in effect, waivers of the federally prescribed 5-day waiting period for handgun purchases by notifying the gun dealers that they have no reason to believe the transactions would be illegal.

The petitioners here object to being pressed into federal service, and contend that congressional action compelling state officers to execute federal laws is unconstitutional. . . .

To complete the historical record, we must note that there is not only an absence of executive-commandeering statutes in the early Congresses, but there is an absence of them in our later history as well, at least until very recent years. . . .

III

. . . We turn next to consideration of the structure of the Constitution, to see if we can discern among its "essential postulates," *Principality of Monaco v. Mississippi*, 292 U.S. 313, 322 (1934), a principle that controls the present cases.

A

The Framers' experience under the Articles of Confederation had persuaded them that using the States as the instruments of federal governance was both ineffectual and provocative of federal-state conflict. See The Federalist No. 15. Preservation of the States as independent political entities being the price of union, and "the practicality of making laws, with coercive sanctions, for the States as political bodies" having been, in Madison's words, "exploded on all hands," 2 Records of the Federal Convention of 1787, p. 9 (M. Farrand ed. 1911), the Framers rejected the concept of a central government that would act upon and through the States, and instead designed a system in which the state and federal governments would exercise concurrent authority over the people — who were, in Hamilton's words, "the only proper objects of government," The Federalist No. 15, at 109. We have set forth the historical record in more detail elsewhere, see New York v. United States, 505 U.S. at 161-166, and need not repeat it here. It suffices to repeat the conclusion: "The Framers explicitly chose a Constitution that confers upon Congress the power to regulate individuals, not States." . . .

B . . .

The Constitution does not leave to speculation who is to administer the laws enacted by Congress; the President, it says, "shall take Care that the Laws be faithfully executed," Art. II, §3, personally and through officers whom he appoints (save for such inferior officers as Congress may authorize to be appointed by the "Courts of Law" or by "the Heads of Departments" who are themselves presidential appointees), Art. II, §2. The Brady Act effectively transfers this responsibility to thousands of CLEOs in the 50 States, who are left to implement the program without meaningful Presidential control (if indeed meaningful Presidential control is possible without the power to appoint and remove). . . .

C

The dissent of course resorts to the last, best hope of those who defend ultra vires congressional action, the Necessary and Proper Clause. It reasons, post, at 3-5, that the power to regulate the sale of handguns under the Commerce Clause, coupled with the power to "make all Laws which shall be necessary and proper for carrying into Execution the foregoing Powers," Art. I, §8, conclusively establishes the Brady Act's constitutional validity, because the Tenth Amendment imposes no limitations on the exercise of delegated powers but merely prohibits the exercise of powers "not delegated to the United States." What destroys the dissent's Necessary and Proper Clause argument, however, is not the Tenth Amendment but the Necessary and Proper Clause itself. When a "Law . . . for carrying into Execution" the Commerce Clause violates the principle of state sovereignty reflected in the various constitutional provisions we mentioned earlier, supra, at 19-20, it is not a "Law . . . proper for carrying into Execution the Commerce Clause," and is thus, in the words of The Federalist, "merely [an] act of usurpation" which "deserves to be treated as such." The Federalist No. 33, at 204 (A. Hamilton). See Lawson & Granger, The

"Proper" Scope of Federal Power: A Jurisdictional Interpretation of the Sweeping Clause, 43 Duke L. J. 267, 297-326, 330-33 (1993). We in fact answered the dissent's Necessary and Proper Clause argument in *New York*: "Even where Congress has the authority under the Constitution to pass laws requiring or prohibiting certain acts, it lacks the power directly to compel the States to require or prohibit those acts. . . . The Commerce Clause, for example, authorizes Congress to regulate interstate commerce directly; it does not authorize Congress to regulate state governments' regulation of interstate commerce." 505 U.S. at 166. . . .

IV

Finally, and most conclusively in the present litigation, we turn to the prior jurisprudence of this Court. Federal commandeering of state governments is such a novel phenomenon that this Court's first experience with it did not occur until the 1970's, when the Environmental Protection Agency promulgated regulations requiring States to prescribe auto emissions testing, monitoring and retrofit programs, and to designate preferential bus and carpool lanes. The Courts of Appeals for the Fourth and Ninth Circuits invalidated the regulations on statutory grounds in order to avoid what they perceived to be grave constitutional issues, see *Maryland v. EPA*, 530 F.2d 215, 226 (4th Cir. 1975); *Brown v. EPA*, 521 F.2d 827, 838-842 (9th Cir. 1975); and the District of Columbia Circuit invalidated the regulations on both constitutional and statutory grounds, see *District of Columbia v. Train*, 521 F.2d 971, 994 (D.C. Cir. 1975). . . .

[L]ater opinions of ours have made clear that the Federal Government may not compel the States to implement, by legislation or executive action, federal regulatory programs. In *Hodel v. Virginia Surface Mining & Reclamation Assn., Inc.*, 452 U.S. 264 (1981), and *FERC v. Mississippi*, 456 U.S. 742 (1982), we sustained statutes against constitutional challenge only after assuring ourselves that they did not require the States to enforce federal law. . . .

When we were at last confronted squarely with a federal statute that unambiguously required the States to enact or administer a federal regulatory program, our decision should have come as no surprise. At issue in *New York v. United States*, 505 U.S. 144 (1992), were the so-called "take title" provisions of the Low-Level Radioactive Waste Policy Amendments Act of 1985, which required States either to enact legislation providing for the disposal of radioactive waste generated within their borders, or to take title to, and possession of the waste — effectively requiring the States either to legislate pursuant to Congress's directions, or to implement an administrative solution. 505 U.S. 144 at 175-76. We concluded that Congress could constitutionally require the States to do neither. Id. at 176. "The Federal Government," we held, "may not compel the States to enact or administer a federal regulatory program." Id. at 188. . . .

Finally, the Government puts forward a cluster of arguments that can be grouped under the heading: "The Brady Act serves very important purposes, is most efficiently administered by CLEOs during the interim period, and places a minimal and only temporary burden upon state officers." There is considerable disagreement over the extent of the burden, but we need not pause over that detail. Assuming all the mentioned factors were true, they might be relevant if we were evaluating whether the incidental application to the States of a federal law of general applicability excessively interfered with the functioning of state governments. See, e.g., *Fry v. United States,* 421 U.S. 542, 548 (1975); *National League of Cities v. Usery,* 426 U.S. 833, 853 (1976) (overruled by *Garcia v. San Antonio Metropolitan Transit Authority,* 469 U.S. 528 (1985)); *South Carolina v. Baker,* 485 U.S. 505, 529 (1988) (Rehnquist, C. J., concurring in judgment). But where, as here, it is the whole object of the law to direct the functioning of the state executive, and hence to compromise the structural framework of dual sovereignty, such a "balancing" analysis is inappropriate. It is the very principle of separate state sovereignty that such a law offends, and no comparative assessment of the various interests can overcome that fundamental defect. Cf. *Bowsher,* 478 U.S., at 736 (declining to subject principle of separation of powers to a balancing test); *Chadha,* 462 U.S. at 944-946 (same); *Plaut v. Spendthrift Farm, Inc.,* 514 U.S. 211, 239-40 (1995) (holding legislated invalidation of final judgments to be categorically unconstitutional). We expressly rejected such an approach in New York, and what we said bears repeating:

> "Much of the Constitution is concerned with setting forth the form of our government, and the courts have traditionally invalidated measures deviating from that form. The result may appear 'formalistic' in a given case to partisans of the measure at issue, because such measures are typically the product of the era's perceived necessity. But the Constitution protects us from our own best intentions: It divides power among sovereigns and among branches of government precisely so that we may resist the temptation to concentrate power in one location as an expedient solution to the crisis of the day." 505 U.S. 144 at 187.

We adhere to that principle today, and conclude categorically, as we concluded categorically in *New York*: "The Federal Government may not compel the States to enact or administer a federal regulatory program." Id. at 188. The mandatory obligation imposed on CLEOs to perform background checks on prospective handgun purchasers plainly runs afoul of that rule. . . .

V

What we have said makes it clear enough that the central obligation imposed upon CLEOs by the interim provisions of the Brady Act — the obligation to "make a reasonable effort to ascertain within 5 business days whether receipt or possession [of a handgun] would be in violation of the law, including research in whatever State and local recordkeeping systems are available and in a national system designated by the Attorney General," 18 U.S.C. §922(s)(2) — is unconstitutional. Extinguished with it, of course, is the duty implicit in the background-check requirement that the CLEO accept notice of the contents of, and a copy of, the completed Brady Form, which the firearms dealer is required to provide to him, §§922(s)(1)(A)(i)(III) and (IV). . . .

We held in *New York* that Congress cannot compel the States to enact or enforce a federal regulatory program. Today we hold that Congress cannot circumvent that prohibition by conscripting the State's officers directly. The

Federal Government may neither issue directives requiring the States to address particular problems, nor command the States' officers, or those of their political subdivisions, to administer or enforce a federal regulatory program. It matters not whether policymaking is involved, and no case-by-case weighing of the burdens or benefits is necessary; such commands are fundamentally incompatible with our constitutional system of dual sovereignty. Accordingly, the judgment of the Court of Appeals for the Ninth Circuit is reversed. . . .

JUSTICE THOMAS, concurring. . . .

Even if we construe Congress' authority to regulate interstate commerce to encompass those intrastate transactions that "substantially affect" interstate commerce, I question whether Congress can regulate the particular transactions at issue here. The Constitution, in addition to delegating certain enumerated powers to Congress, places whole areas outside the reach of Congress' regulatory authority. The First Amendment, for example, is fittingly celebrated for preventing Congress from "prohibiting the free exercise" of religion or "abridging the freedom of speech." The Second Amendment similarly appears to contain an express limitation on the government's authority. That Amendment provides: "[a] well regulated Militia, being necessary to the security of a free State, the right of the people to keep and bear arms, shall not be infringed." This Court has not had recent occasion to consider the nature of the substantive right safeguarded by the Second Amendment.[2] If, however, the Second Amendment is read to confer a personal right to "keep and bear arms," a colorable argument exists that the Federal Government's regulatory scheme, at least as it pertains to the purely intrastate sale or possession of firearms, runs afoul of that Amendment's protections.[3] As the parties did not raise this argument, however, we

---

2. Our most recent treatment of the Second Amendment occurred in *United States v. Miller*, 307 U.S. 174 (1939), in which we reversed the District Court's invalidation of the National Firearms Act, enacted in 1934. In *Miller*, we determined that the Second Amendment did not guarantee a citizen's right to possess a sawed-off shotgun because that weapon had not been shown to be "ordinary military equipment" that could "contribute to the common defense." Id. at 178. The Court did not, however, attempt to define, or otherwise construe, the substantive right protected by the Second Amendment.

3. Marshaling an impressive array of historical evidence, a growing body of scholarly commentary indicates that the "right to keep and bear arms" is, as the Amendment's text suggests, a personal right. See, e.g., J. Malcolm, To Keep and Bear Arms: The Origins of an Anglo-American Right 162 (1994); S. Halbrook, That Every Man Be Armed, The Evolution of a Constitutional Right (1984); Van Alstyne, The Second Amendment and the Personal Right to Arms, 43 Duke L. J. 1236 (1994); Amar, The Bill of Rights and the Fourteenth Amendment, 101 Yale L. J. 1193 (1992); Cottrol & Diamond, The Second Amendment: Toward an Afro-Americanist Reconsideration, 80 Geo. L. J. 309 (1991); Levinson, The Embarrassing Second Amendment, 99 Yale L. J. 637 (1989); Kates, Handgun Prohibition and the Original Meaning of the Second Amendment, 82 Mich. L. Rev. 204 (1983). Other scholars, however, argue that the Second Amendment does not secure a personal right to keep or to bear arms. See, e.g., Bogus, Race, Riots, and Guns, 66 S. Cal. L. Rev. 1365 (1993); Williams, Civic Republicanism and the Citizen Militia: The Terrifying Second Amendment, 101 Yale L. J. 551 (1991); Brown, Guns, Cowboys, Philadelphia Mayors, and Civic Republicanism: On Sanford Levinson's The Embarrassing Second Amendment, 99 Yale L. J. 661 (1989); Cress, An Armed Community: The Origins and Meaning of the Right to Bear Arms, 71 J. Am. Hist. 22 (1984). Although somewhat overlooked in our jurisprudence, the Amendment has certainly engendered considerable academic, as well as public, debate.

need not consider it here. Perhaps, at some future date, this Court will have the opportunity to determine whether Justice Story was correct when he wrote that the right to bear arms "has justly been considered, as the palladium of the liberties of a republic." 3 J. Story, Commentaries §1890, p. 746 (1833). In the meantime, I join the Court's opinion striking down the challenged provisions of the Brady Act as inconsistent with the Tenth Amendment.

NOTES & QUESTIONS

1. The introductory paragraphs of *Printz* provide a useful history of the Brady Act Amendments to the GCA, implementing the current instant check system. As the Court explained, the waiting period and local background check were interim measures that expired when the electronic National Instant Check System (NICS) came online. Note that some state statutes continue to enforce waiting periods independent of federal law. *See, e.g.*, Cal. Penal Code §§12071, 12072; Haw. Rev. Stat. Ann. §134-2; Md. Code Ann., Pub. Safety §§5-123, 5-124. One justification for this has been that the wait is a cooling off period.

2. What is your assessment of a mandatory cooling off period? Would you apply it to people who already own guns? How would you respond to an exemption for holders of licenses to carry concealed firearms (now issued in most states)? Would you extend the same treatment to holders of a Firearms Owner Identification Card, a type of license required in some states? *See, e.g.*, 430 Ill. Comp. Stat. 65.

EXERCISE: THE FIREARMS FREEDOM ACTS

Justice Thomas's concurrence in *Printz* was another in the string of post-*Miller* hints about the Justices' views of the Second Amendment. Consider Justice Thomas's suggestion that federal regulation of purely intrastate sales might be unconstitutional. Does this suggest that Thomas would uphold the "Firearms Freedom Acts" (FFAs) recently enacted in Alaska, Arizona, Idaho, Montana, South Dakota, Tennessee, Utah, and Wyoming? Examine the text of the Montana legislation below.

AN ACT EXEMPTING FROM FEDERAL REGULATION UNDER THE COMMERCE CLAUSE OF THE CONSTITUTION OF THE UNITED STATES A FIREARM, A FIREARM ACCESSORY, OR AMMUNITION MANUFACTURED AND RETAINED IN MONTANA; AND PROVIDING AN APPLICABILITY DATE

Section 1. Short title. [Sections 1 through 6] may be cited as the "Montana Firearms Freedom Act."

Section 2. Legislative declarations of authority. The legislature declares that the authority for [sections 1 through 6] is the following:

(1) The 10th amendment to the United States constitution guarantees to the states and their people all powers not granted to the federal government elsewhere in the constitution and reserves to the state and people of Montana certain powers

as they were understood at the time that Montana was admitted to statehood in 1889. The guaranty of those powers is a matter of contract between the state and people of Montana and the United States as of the time that the compact with the United States was agreed upon and adopted by Montana and the United States in 1889.

(2) The ninth amendment to the United States constitution guarantees to the people rights not granted in the constitution and reserves to the people of Montana certain rights as they were understood at the time that Montana was admitted to statehood in 1889. The guaranty of those rights is a matter of contract between the state and people of Montana and the United States as of the time that the compact with the United States was agreed upon and adopted by Montana and the United States in 1889.

(3) The regulation of intrastate commerce is vested in the states under the 9th and 10th amendments to the United States constitution, particularly if not expressly preempted by federal law. Congress has not expressly preempted state regulation of intrastate commerce pertaining to the manufacture on an intrastate basis of firearms, firearms accessories, and ammunition.

(4) The second amendment to the United States constitution reserves to the people the right to keep and bear arms as that right was understood at the time that Montana was admitted to statehood in 1889, and the guaranty of the right is a matter of contract between the state and people of Montana and the United States as of the time that the compact with the United States was agreed upon and adopted by Montana and the United States in 1889.

(5) Article II, section 12, of the Montana constitution clearly secures to Montana citizens, and prohibits government interference with, the right of individual Montana citizens to keep and bear arms. This constitutional protection is unchanged from the 1889 Montana constitution, which was approved by congress and the people of Montana, and the right exists as it was understood at the time that the compact with the United States was agreed upon and adopted by Montana and the United States in 1889.

Section 3. Definitions. As used in [sections 1 through 6], the following definitions apply:

(1) "Borders of Montana" means the boundaries of Montana described in Article I, section 1, of the 1889 Montana constitution.

(2) "Firearms accessories" means items that are used in conjunction with or mounted upon a firearm but are not essential to the basic function of a firearm, including but not limited to telescopic or laser sights, magazines, flash or sound suppressors, folding or aftermarket stocks and grips, speedloaders, ammunition carriers, and lights for target illumination.

(3) "Generic and insignificant parts" includes but is not limited to springs, screws, nuts, and pins.

(4) "Manufactured" means that a firearm, a firearm accessory, or ammunition has been created from basic materials for functional usefulness, including but not limited to forging, casting, machining, or other processes for working materials.

Section 4. Prohibitions. A personal firearm, a firearm accessory, or ammunition that is manufactured commercially or privately in Montana and that remains within the borders of Montana is not subject to federal law or federal regulation, including registration, under the authority of congress to regulate interstate commerce. It is declared by the legislature that those items have not traveled in interstate commerce. This section applies to a firearm, a firearm accessory, or ammunition that is manufactured in Montana from basic materials and that can be manufactured without the inclusion of any significant parts imported from another state. Generic and insignificant parts that have other manufacturing or consumer product applications are not firearms, firearms accessories, or ammunition, and their importation into Montana and incorporation into a firearm, a firearm accessory, or ammunition manufactured in Montana does not subject the firearm, firearm accessory, or ammunition to federal regulation. It is declared by the legislature that basic materials, such as unmachined steel and unshaped wood, are not firearms, firearms accessories, or ammunition and are not subject to congressional authority to regulate firearms, firearms accessories, and ammunition under interstate commerce as if they were actually firearms, firearms accessories, or ammunition. The authority of congress to regulate interstate commerce in basic materials does not include authority to regulate firearms, firearms accessories, and ammunition made in Montana from those materials. Firearms accessories that are imported into Montana from another state and that are subject to federal regulation as being in interstate commerce do not subject a firearm to federal regulation under interstate commerce because they are attached to or used in conjunction with a firearm in Montana.

Section 5. Exceptions. [Section 4] does not apply to:

(1) a firearm that cannot be carried and used by one person;

(2) a firearm that has a bore diameter greater than 1 1/2 inches and that uses smokeless powder, not black powder, as a propellant;

(3) ammunition with a projectile that explodes using an explosion of chemical energy after the projectile leaves the firearm; or

(4) a firearm that discharges two or more projectiles with one activation of the trigger or other firing device.

Section 6. Marketing of firearms. A firearm manufactured or sold in Montana under [sections 1 through 6] must have the words "Made in Montana" clearly stamped on a central metallic part, such as the receiver or frame.

The state Firearms Freedom Acts attempt to track the *Bass* Court's interpretation of the jurisdictional predicate in the federal Gun Control Act. They exempt from federal regulation common types of guns manufactured within the state, as long as those guns never leave the state. In light of *Lopez, Bass,* and other Commerce Clause cases you have studied, are the FFAs constitutionally sound? Consider particularly *Gonzales v. Raich,* 545 U.S. 1 (2005), which allowed federal criminal prosecution for the noncommercial cultivation of marijuana for personal medical consumption in compliance with state law. The *Raich* majority reasoned that the federal prohibition of personal cultivation was necessary to control the interstate market in illegal marijuana. Are the FFAs on a collision course with *Raich? See Montana Shooting Sports Ass'n v. Holder,* 2010 WL 3926029 (D. Mont. Aug. 31, 2010) (rejecting lawsuit by plaintiffs who sought a declaration that Congress lacks constitutional power to regulate "Made in Montana" firearms manufactured pursuant to the Montana Firearms Freedom Act; concluding that under *Raich,* "Congress' power under the Commerce Clause is almost unlimited where the prohibited product has significant economic value such as with drugs or guns," and that this is even true "as applied to the purely intrastate manufacture and sale of firearms contemplated by the [Firearms Freedom Act]").

Imagine now that the Supreme Court had taken a purely state's rights interpretation of the Second Amendment. Would that interpretation bolster the argument for the FFA? What if a state legislature designates all FFA arms state militia arms, which the owners are expected to bring to duty whenever summoned to state militia service?

CQ: Consider these questions again after you have evaluated the decision in *Heller.* Try to determine what *Heller* (Chapter 9) says about the militia interest. Are the individual right and militia interest compatible? How does that affect your thinking about the questions above?

4. Felons and the Right to Arms

One of the least controversial things about gun control is the proposition that violent felons should be prohibited from possessing firearms. The following case turns on a provision of the 1968 Gun Control Act that enforces this proposition. The case is a good general introduction to modern federal gun regulation. It also contains in dicta a very different view about the Second Amendment than Justice Thomas expressed above. The defendant had been convicted of a crime. His conviction was invalid, in the sense that he had not been provided with counsel. *See Gideon v. Wainwright,* 372 U.S. 335 (1963) (retroactively invalidating felony, and some misdemeanor, convictions in which the defendant had not been provided with an attorney). The case addresses whether the federal ban on gun possession applies only to constitutionally valid convictions.

Lewis v. United States
445 U.S. 55 (1980)

MR. JUSTICE BLACKMUN delivered the opinion of the Court. . . .

I

In 1961, petitioner George Calvin Lewis, Jr., upon his plea of guilty, was convicted in a Florida state court of a felony for breaking and entering with intent to commit a misdemeanor. He served a term of imprisonment. That conviction has never been overturned, nor has petitioner ever received a qualifying pardon or permission from the Secretary of the Treasury to possess a firearm.

In January 1977, Lewis, on probable cause, was arrested in Virginia, and later was charged by indictment with having knowingly received and possessed at that time a specified firearm, in violation of 18 U.S.C. App. §1202(a)(1). . . .

Shortly before the trial, petitioner's counsel informed the court that he had been advised that Lewis was not represented by counsel in the 1961 Florida proceeding. He claimed that under *Gideon v. Wainwright* a violation of §1202(a)(1) could not be predicated on a prior conviction obtained in violation of petitioner's Sixth and Fourteenth Amendment rights. The court rejected that claim. . . .

On appeal, the United States Court of Appeals for the Fourth Circuit, by a divided vote, affirmed. . . .

III

... The statutory language is sweeping, and its plain meaning is that the fact of a felony conviction imposes a firearm disability until the conviction is vacated or the felon is relieved of his disability by some affirmative action, such as a qualifying pardon or a consent from the Secretary of the Treasury. The obvious breadth of the language may well reflect the expansive legislative approach revealed by Congress' express findings and declarations, in 18 U.S.C. App. §1201, concerning the problem of firearm abuse by felons and certain specifically described persons.

Other provisions of the statute demonstrate and reinforce its broad sweep. . . . In addition, §1202(c)(2) defines "felony" to exclude certain state crimes punishable by no more than two years' imprisonment. No exception, however, is made for a person whose outstanding felony conviction ultimately might turn out to be invalid for any reason. On its face, therefore, §1202(a)(1) contains nothing by way of restrictive language. It thus stands in contrast with other federal statutes that explicitly permit a defendant to challenge, by way of defense, the validity or constitutionality of the predicate felony. . . .

It is not without significance, furthermore, that Title VII, as well as Title IV of the Omnibus Act, was enacted in response to the precipitous rise in political assassinations, riots, and other violent crimes involving firearms, that occurred in this country in the 1960's. . . . This Court, accordingly, has observed:

> "The legislative history [of Title VII] in its entirety, while brief, further supports the view that Congress sought to rule broadly—to keep guns out of the hands of those who have demonstrated that 'they may not be trusted to possess a firearm without becoming a threat to society.'" *Scarborough v. United States*, 431 U.S., at 572. . . .

IV

The firearm regulatory scheme at issue here is consonant with the concept of equal protection embodied in the Due Process Clause of the Fifth Amendment if there is "some 'rational basis' for the statutory distinctions made . . . or . . . they 'have some relevance to the purpose for which the classification is made.'" *Marshall v. United States*, 414 U.S. 417, 422 (1974). . . .[8]

Section 1202(a)(1) clearly meets that test. Congress, as its expressed purpose in enacting Title VII reveals, 18 U.S.C. App. §1201, was concerned

---

8. These legislative restrictions on the use of firearms are neither based upon constitutionally suspect criteria, nor do they trench upon any constitutionally protected liberties. *See United States v. Miller*, 307 U.S. 174, 178 (1939) (the Second Amendment guarantees no right to keep and bear a firearm that does not have "some reasonable relationship to the preservation or efficiency of a well regulated militia"); *United States v. Three Winchester 30-30 Caliber Lever Action Carbines*, 504 F.2d 1288, 1290, n. 5 (7th Cir. 1974); *United States v. Johnson*, 497 F.2d 548 (4th Cir. 1974); *Cody v. United States*, 460 F.2d 34 (8th Cir.) [earlier in this chapter], cert. denied, 409 U.S. 1010 (1972) (the latter three cases holding, respectively, that §1202(a)(1), §922(g), and §922(a)(6) do not violate the Second Amendment).

that the receipt and possession of a firearm by a felon constitutes a threat, among other things, to the continued and effective operation of the Government of the United States. The legislative history of the gun control laws discloses Congress' worry about the easy availability of firearms, especially to those persons who pose a threat to community peace. And Congress focused on the nexus between violent crime and the possession of a firearm by any person with a criminal record. 114 Cong. Rec. 13220 (1968) (remarks of Sen. Tydings); Id. at 16298 (remarks of Rep. Pollock). Congress could rationally conclude that any felony conviction, even an allegedly invalid one, is a sufficient basis on which to prohibit the possession of a firearm. See, e.g., *United States v. Ransom*, 515 F.2d 885, 891-92 (5th Cir. 1975), cert. denied, 424 U.S. 944 (1976). This Court has recognized repeatedly that a legislature constitutionally may prohibit a convicted felon from engaging in activities far more fundamental than the possession of a firearm. See *Richardson v. Ramirez*, 418 U.S. 24 (1974) (disenfranchisement); *De Veau v. Braisted*, 363 U.S. 144 (1960) (proscription against holding office in a waterfront labor organization); *Hawker v. New York*, 170 U.S. 189 (1898) (prohibition against the practice of medicine). . . .

Congress' judgment that a convicted felon, even one whose conviction was allegedly uncounseled, is among the class of persons who should be disabled from dealing in or possessing firearms because of potential dangerousness is rational.

The judgment of the Court of Appeals is affirmed.

NOTES & QUESTIONS

1. The 1968 Gun Control Act, as amended, requires that people who buy guns from federally licensed firearms dealers complete a form (ATF Form 4473) declaring that they do not fall into the classes of persons prohibited from possessing firearms. The prohibited classes are anyone:

    > (1) who has been convicted in any court of, a crime punishable by imprisonment for a term exceeding one year;
    > (2) who is a fugitive from justice;
    > (3) who is an unlawful user of or addicted to any controlled substance (as defined in section 102 of the Controlled Substances Act (21 U.S.C. 802));
    > (4) who has been adjudicated as a mental defective or who has been committed to a mental institution;
    > (5) who, being an alien—
    >   (A) is illegally or unlawfully in the United States; or
    >   (B) except as provided in subsection (y)(2), has been admitted to the United States under a nonimmigrant visa (as that term is defined in section 101(a)(26) of the Immigration and Nationality Act (8 U.S.C. 1101(a)(26)));
    > (6) who has been discharged from the Armed Forces under dishonorable conditions;
    > (7) who, having been a citizen of the United States, has renounced his citizenship;
    > (8) who is subject to a court order that—
    >   (A) was issued after a hearing of which such person received actual notice, and at which such person had an opportunity to participate;

(B) restrains such person from harassing, stalking, or threatening an intimate partner of such person or child of such intimate partner or person, or engaging in other conduct that would place an intimate partner in reasonable fear of bodily injury to the partner or child; and

(C)(i) includes a finding that such person represents a credible threat to the physical safety of such intimate partner or child; or (ii) by its terms explicitly prohibits the use, attempted use, or threatened use of physical force against such intimate partner or child that would reasonably be expected to cause bodily injury; or

(9) who has been convicted in any court of a misdemeanor crime of domestic violence[.]

If the right to arms is constitutionally protected, should that limit the government's power to restrict access to firearms by any of these people?

2. In footnote 8, the *Lewis* Court states, "These legislative restrictions on the use of firearms are neither based upon constitutionally suspect criteria, nor do they trench upon any constitutionally protected liberties." From 1980 through 2008, this was the fundamental proof-text of gun control advocates, demonstrating that the modern Supreme Court shared their reading of *Miller.* CQ: In *Heller* (Chapter 9), Justice Stevens's dissent points to *Lewis* as a modern confirmation of the militia-only understanding of the Second Amendment. Justice Scalia's majority opinion in *Heller* responds that the Second Amendment had not even been briefed in *Lewis,* and that the *Lewis* footnote was gratuitous dicta on an unbriefed issue. Should the 2008 Court in *Heller* have treated *Lewis* as binding precedent?

3. The Gun Control Act defines "felon" to exclude people convicted of certain business crimes and state misdemeanors that are subject to a sentence of less than two years. *See* 18 U.S.C. §921(a)(20). It also allows people who are disqualified from possessing firearms to petition for restoration of the right. 18 U.S.C. §921(a)(20). The restoration petition was intended as a safety valve for persons with old convictions who pose no current danger to society. However, Congress has removed the funding for ATF's consideration of these "rights restoration petitions." So there is currently no viable process for having the right to arms restored. *United States v. Bean,* 537 U.S. 71 (2002); *see also Beecham v. United States,* 511 U.S. 368 (1994) (restoration of rights under state law does not extinguish conviction under federal law); *Logan v. United States,* 552 U.S. 23 (2007) (an offender whose state criminal conviction did not result in a loss of his civil rights, including his right to arms, cannot have his rights "restored" under section 925(c), even though the state conviction results in a lifetime federal ban on gun possession). CQ: Does the Supreme Court recognition of a fundamental individual right to arms in *Heller* and *McDonald* (Chapter 9) suggest that there must be a viable rights restoration mechanism for prohibited persons? Does *Heller*'s specific approval of bans on possession by "convicted felons" preclude any constitutional argument for rights restoration? For a broad assessment of such questions, see Alan Brownstein, *The Constitutionalization of Self-Defense in Tort and Criminal Law,* 60 Hastings L.J. 1203 (2009).

C. *The Social and Political History of the Right to Arms Between* Miller *and* Heller

The period between *Miller* (Chapter 7) and *Heller* (Chapter 9) produced an unparalleled level of legislation and litigation concerning firearms rights and regulation. This is in part a social and political story. As background to the material in Section D and context for the material in the remainder of the book, this section provides an overview of shifting social and political views about firearms regulation over the last half-century. This history highlights the organizations that played large roles in that history, particularly the National Rifle Association. Whatever one thinks of the organization, telling the story of the Second Amendment without acknowledging the NRA would be like discussing the Equal Protection Clause without mentioning the NAACP, or the First Amendment without crediting the ACLU. Each championed broad interpretation of a constitutional provision on which the fortunes of its constituency rested. As counterpoint, this history also discusses the work of organizations that pressed the argument against NRA, particularly, Handgun Control Inc. (now known as the Brady Campaign), which became the most effective advocate for stringent gun control.

Prior to 1968, direct federal regulation of firearms had three major components. A 1927 statute prohibited concealable firearms from being shipped through the mail. 18 U.S.C. §1715(o). The National Firearms Act of 1934 (Chapter 7; later codified as Title II of the Gun Control Act, 26 U.S.C. §§5801 et seq.) imposed what was hoped to be near-prohibitive tax and registration requirements on a small category of guns (machine guns, short shotguns, and short rifles). Enacted as a restriction on "gangster" weapons the NFA was the statute the defendant violated in *United States v. Miller.* Finally, the Federal Firearms Act of 1938 (Chapter 7) required persons engaged in the interstate business of selling or repairing firearms to obtain a one-dollar license before shipping or receiving any firearm in interstate or foreign commerce. Licensed dealers were required to keep a record of firearms sales and were prohibited from shipping guns in interstate commerce to anyone indicted for or convicted of a violent crime or to anyone who was prohibited from owning firearms under state law. *See generally* Alfred M. Ascione, *The Federal Firearms Act,* 13 St. John's L. Rev. 437 (1939).

1. The Calm Before the Storm

Since its founding in 1871, the National Rifle Association has always been political, in the sense that it pressed for government support of rifle marksmanship among the American public. In the early twentieth century, NRA lobbying led to the establishment of a federal program to promote civilian marksmanship, and to sell surplus military rifles to the public, with the NRA the designated intermediary between the U.S. military and the civilian population. *See* Chapter 4.F. The NRA's first venture into the broader political world came in the 1920s when a fledgling handgun prohibition movement emerged out of the Northeast, upper-class, urban establishment. That movement did not have a wide following and was quickly beat back by the NRA (Chapter 7). The next major effort surrounded the National Firearms Act, which the NRA ultimately supported after handguns were excluded from NFA regulation. The NRA also defeated Attorney General Cummings' proposal for national gun registration, supported the Federal Firearms Act of 1938, and ensured that the Property Requisition Act of 1941 would not be used to confiscate or register guns. *See* Chapter 7.E. On all these issues, the NRA succeeded by mobilizing its membership through the association's magazine, *The American Rifleman*. NRA members in turn carried the gun rights message to their representatives in congress through letters, calls, and personal appeals.

After the United States entered World War II, the NRA helped with wartime mobilization and training, earning a post-war letter of thanks from President Truman. Letter from Harry S. Truman National Rifle Association (Nov. 14, 1945), *reprinted in* Federal Firearms Act: Hearings Before the Subcomm. to Investigate Juvenile Delinquency, S. Comm. on the Judiciary, 90th Cong. 484 (1967) (NRA's "small-arms training aids, the nation-wide pre-induction training program, the recruiting of experienced small-arms instructors for all branches of the armed services, and technical advice and assistance to the Government civilian agencies . . . have materially aided our war effort.").

With a few exceptions, the 1940s and 1950s presented little for the NRA to contest politically. Starting in the 1920s, the NRA did attempt to repeal New York's Sullivan Act (requiring licensing for handguns, and very restrictive licensing for handgun carry, Chapter 7) but failed. Generally speaking, the NRA found federal firearms policy unobjectionable and enjoyed good relations with federal officials. General Dwight Eisenhower, formerly the Supreme Commander of the Allied Forces in Europe during World War II, was the keynote speaker at the NRA 1946 Annual Meeting, and as President sent the NRA laudatory letters from time to time. But during President Eisenhower's second term, in 1957, the Alcohol and Tobacco Tax Division of the Internal Revenue Service proposed new regulations under the NFA and FFA, such as mandating that firearm dealers keep permanent records on all handgun ammunition purchasers. 22 Fed. Reg. 3153 (May 3, 1957). (The ATTD is an ancestor of the Bureau of Alcohol, Tobacco, Firearms and Explosives, which was upgraded to a Bureau in 1969, and which became part of the Department of Justice in 2002.) Led by Representative John Dingell (D-Mich.), many congressmen objected, and the final regulations fixed the provisions considered most objectionable by the NRA. 23 Fed. Reg. 343 (Jan. 18, 1958); James B. Trefethen, Americans and Their Guns 295 (1967). (Dingell was first elected in 1954, and is still a U.S. Representative.)

From here, gun regulation returned to its somnolent state. Nobody was proposing gun control, and nobody was raising Second Amendment objections to gun control. Absent controversy, legal scholars paid little attention to the Second Amendment. The NFA had been held constitutional in *United States v. Miller*, and the FFA was considered constitutional even by gun enthusiasts (Chapter 7).

This was the state of things until the late 1950s and early 1960s, when the gun issue rose to prominence in tandem with broader social unrest.

2.   Racial Tensions

As discussed in previous chapters, overtly racist firearms laws and racist enforcement of technically neutral firearms restrictions have a long history in America. Despite these pressures, there has been a strong tradition of arms ownership in the Black community. In practice and philosophically, many in the community endorsed firearms ownership and armed self-defense against private threats. This tradition was embraced by countless Blacks at the grassroots and Black leaders including Frederick Douglass, Henry Highland Garnett, W.E.B Du Bois, Ida B. Wells-Barnett, James Meredith, Robert Moton, A. Phillip Randolph, Daisy Bates, Fannie Lou Hamer, Medgar and Charles Evers, James Farmer and Floyd McKissick. This tradition of arms had roots in the culture of the rural South and drew a sharp distinction between private self-defense and foolhardy political violence. See Nicholas J. Johnson, Firearms and the Black Community (forthcoming), (manuscript *available at* http://firearmsregulation.org).

In the 1950s, a new civil rights movement began in the South. White supremacist tactics were just as violent as they had been during Reconstruction. Over one hundred civil rights workers were murdered during that era, and especially in the early days, the U.S. Department of Justice refused to prosecute the suspects or to protect civil rights workers adequately. State and local governments were widely hostile to the movement and sometimes directly affiliated with the Klan or other terrorist organizations.

Many Blacks and civil rights workers armed for self-defense. Daisy Bates, the leader of the Arkansas NAACP and publisher of the *Arkansas State Press* during the Little Rock High School desegregation case, recalls that three crosses were burned on her lawn and gunshots fired into her home. Her husband, L.C. Bates, stayed up to guard their house with a .45 semi-automatic pistol. Some of their friends organized a volunteer patrol.

Based in local churches, the Deacons for Defense and Justice set up armed patrol car systems in cities such as Bogalusa and Jonesboro, Louisiana, and within their spheres of operations succeeded in deterring Klan and other attacks on civil rights workers and black residents. Lance Hill, The Deacons for Defense: Armed Resistance and the Civil Rights Movement (2004).

In the 1950s, Dr. Martin Luther King, Jr., had been so well-armed that visitors remembered his house as a small arsenal. Later, King became a pacifist. Adam Winkler, Gunfight 253 (2011). The civil rights movement as a whole was brilliant in using King's Americanized version of Mohandas Gandhi's tactics of active, non-violent resistance.

In the "Freedom Summer" campaign of 1964, university students from the North spent the summer registering black voters in Mississippi. Pacifists during public confrontations, many of the civil rights workers from the North, and their Southern allies, were well armed in the cars and in their homes. Among them was a Yale Law School student named Don Kates, whose personal experience with armed self-defense that summer would have important consequences for the Second Amendment.

Birmingham native and former Secretary of State Condoleezza Rice recalls the night in 1963 when a bomb was hurled through the window of a house down the block from her home. Her family fled temporarily to the home of friends in a neighboring town. When they returned home late that night,

Daddy [Reverend Rice] didn't say anything more about the bomb. He just went outside and sat on the porch in the springtime heat with his gun on his lap. He sat there all night looking for white night riders. . . . Eventually Daddy and the men of the neighborhood formed a watch. They would take shifts at the head of the two entrances to our streets. There was a formal schedule, and Daddy would move among them to pray with them and keep their spirits up. Occasionally they would fire a gun into the air to scare off intruders, but they never actually shot anyone.

Condoleezza Rice, Extraordinary Ordinary People: A Memoir of Family 93 (2010).

The black tradition in arms was undermined beginning in the 1960s as black radicals increasingly challenged the line between political violence and legitimate self-defense. These developments are illustrated by the controversy surrounding NAACP Executive Secretary Roy Wilkins's dismissal of North Carolina activist and chapter president Robert Williams. On the courthouse steps, following trials in which two white men were acquitted of allegedly attacking black women, Williams called for violent retribution: "[I]f it's necessary to stop lynching with lynching, then we must be willing to resort to that method."

In the debate over whether Williams's threat to answer lynching with lynching had pushed over the line into advocacy of political violence, there was widespread agreement about the legitimacy and value of firearms for self-defense. Even Martin Luther King endorsed the community's traditional support for armed self-defense.

In a widely reprinted exchange of essays with Williams, King articulated three distinct categories of response to violent attacks and political oppression. The first, pure non-violence, is difficult, King said. It "cannot readily or easily attract large masses, for it requires extraordinary discipline and courage." Edited versions of the essays appear in Eyes on the Prize Civil Rights Reader 110-13 (Clayborn Carson et al. eds., 1991). *See also* Robert F. Williams, Negroes with Guns (1998) (quoting Martin Luther King). The second response, said King, was implicit in the freedom struggle and should not discourage outsiders from supporting the movement:

> Violence exercised merely in self-defense, all societies, from the most primitive to the most cultured and civilized, accept as moral and legal. The principle of self-defense, even involving weapons and bloodshed, has never been condemned, even by Gandhi . . . . When the Negro uses force in self-defense, he does not forfeit support[—]he even win it, by the courage and self respect it reflects.

King, *supra.*

The third approach, Williams's approach, said King, advocated "violence as a tool of advancement, organization as in warfare . . . [and posed] incalculable perils." Political goals, King argued, were best achieved by non-violent, "socially organized masses on the march." *Id.*

With debate raging, and many at the grass roots supporting Williams, Roy Wilkins defended the dismissal of Williams in a pamphlet entitled *The Single Issue in the Robert Williams Case.* Wilkins argued, "There is no issue of self-defense. . . . The charges are based on his call for aggressive, premeditated violence. Lynching is never defensive." Roy Wilkins, *The Single Issue in the Robert Williams Case*, box A333, group 3, NAACP Papers, Library of Congress. Wilkins was articulating the same philosophy as Frederick Douglass, who had argued that blacks could not obtain social justice through violence, and who also knew that laws like the Fugitive Slave Act could have devastating personal consequences. For Blacks facing imminent personal threats, Douglass candidly advised, "A good revolver, a steady hand and a determination to shoot down any man attempting to kidnap." Frederick Douglass, *The True Remedy for the Fugitive Slave Bill, in* 5 The Life and Writings of Frederick Douglass 326 (Philip S. Foner ed., 1955).

At a June 1959 fundraising dinner in Chicago, Roy Wilkins made clear that his dismissal of Williams was not a rejection of the tradition of self-defense in the black community. "Of course, we must defend ourselves when attacked. This is our right under all known laws." Address of Roy Wilkins, Freedom Fund Dinner of the Chicago Branch, Morrison Hotel, Chicago, Illinois, June 12, 1959, 7:00 P.M. 10 Group KKK, series A, box 303, NAACP Papers.

Wilkins's statement reflected the general sense of the organization. Williams appealed his dismissal at the 1959 annual convention. The representatives upheld the suspension but with an important caveat: "We do not deny but reaffirm the right of an individual and collective self-defense against unlawful assaults." The report of the Resolutions Committee that brought the issue to the floor noted in its Preamble the NAACP's long support of the right of self-defense, "by defending those who have exercised the right of self-defense, particularly in the Arkansas Riot Case, The Sweet case in Detroit, the Columbia, Tenn., Riot cases and the Ingram case in Georgia." For full text of the resolutions, see Gloster B. Current, *Fiftieth Annual Convention*, Crisis, August-September 1959, at 400-10.

By the mid-1960s, many radicals were urging aggressive violence. Wilkins, however, reiterated the community's traditional support of private self-defense, and emphasized the distinction between legitimate self-defense and foolhardy political violence. At the NAACP's 1966 Annual Convention, Wilkins contrasted traditional black support for armed self-defense with the radical new calls for "black power":

> One organization which has been meeting in Baltimore has passed a resolution declaring for defense of themselves by Negro citizens if they are attacked. This is not new as far as the NAACP is concerned. Historically our association has defended in court those persons who have defended themselves and their homes with firearms. . . . But the more serious division in the civil rights movement is the one posed by a word formulation that implies clearly a difference in goals. No matter how endlessly they try to explain it, the term "black power" means anti-white power. . . . It has to mean separatism. . . . It is a reverse Mississippi, a reverse Hitler, a reverse Ku Klux Klan. . . .
>
> We of the NAACP will have none of this.

Roy Wilkins, *Whither Black Power*, Crisis, August-September, 1966 at 353, 354, *available at* http://books.google.com/books?id = 51cEAAAAMBAJ&pg = PA353& lpg = PA353&dq = roy+wilkins+keynote+address.

As riots engulfed black neighborhoods, Wilkins and NAACP resisted calls for discriminatory disarmament of Blacks. Wilkins was asked, "Would you be in favor of a massive effort to disarm the Negroes in the ghettoes, just to try to prevent these open-shooting wars such as occurred in Newark last night?" He flatly rejected the idea of discriminatory regulations. "I wouldn't disarm the Negroes and leave them helpless prey to the people who wanted to go in and shoot them up. . . . Every American wants to own a rifle. Why shouldn't the Negroes own rifles?" *See* "Meet the Press," July 16, 1967, Tr. at 9.

While Wilkins clearly rejected gun restrictions targeted exclusively at Blacks, he showed sympathy for more sweeping measures. In his initial response to the question Wilkins stated, "I would be in favor of disarming everybody, not just the Negroes." *Id.* It is unclear whether Wilkins was referring to nationwide disarmament or disarming everyone in riot torn cities. What is clear is that in general, black and progressive leadership was beginning to support stringent gun control.

As black communities withered under waves of rioting, pressure on the tradition of armed self-defense grew. The substantially rural and Southern tradition of arms was wilting under the heat and backlash against untethered urban violence. At the same time, the modern gun control movement emerged, and was embraced by many of the liberals who had been instrumental in advancing black civil rights goals. Soon, a new wave of black elected officials and appointees had adopted gun control as their own. While some might have worried over the evidence that the 1968 federal Gun Control Act (*infra*) was driven substantially by a desire to control black violence, see Robert Sherrill, The Saturday Night Special 283-95 (1973), many black politicians were fed up with the shocking rates of gun crime in black communities, and now viewed the proliferation of firearms as a serious threat.

By the mid 1970s, the black political establishment was firmly allied with the gun control movement. Maynard Jackson (the first black mayor of Atlanta) became the chairman of the National Coalition to Ban Handguns. A succession of black mayors endorsed stringent gun control and gun bans. The Congressional Black Caucus reliably supported stringent federal gun control proposals. Representative Major Owens (D-Brooklyn, NY) persistently introduced bills to repeal the Second Amendment. By the time the Supreme Court took up *Heller* (Chapter 9) in 2008, it was entirely predictable that the NAACP would file an amicus brief, urging the Court to reject the individual rights view of the Second Amendment and to uphold the Washington, D.C., handgun ban.

3. Comprehensive National Gun Control

Even into the early 1960s, war surplus guns were plentiful and long guns could be ordered by mail. But the thriving culture of gun trading, collecting, and shooting sports would be rocked by the next major federal gun control act. Gun control supporter and historian Robert Sherrill characterized the period this way:

> There had been gun-control bills eddying around the backwashes of Congress for years. The big emotional tidal wave that set them going was President Kennedy's death; the momentum was perpetuated by the assassinations of Robert

Kennedy and Martin Luther King, Jr., and by the massacre of fourteen people by Charles Whitman, shooting from the top of the University of Texas tower. Also, from Watts to Newark, rioters did a good job during the 1960s of suggesting that maybe everybody should disarm before a few nuts triggered a race war.

Sherill, *supra* at 70.

In the early 1960s, the only significant gun control proposal in Congress was being pushed by Connecticut Senator Thomas Dodd, a protectionist measure to shield U.S. gun manufacturers from foreign competition, particularly the surplus WWII bolt-action rifles coming in from Europe. The "Gun Valley" along New England's Connecticut River had been the heart of the American firearms industry, since 1777 when the Springfield Armory was created to manufacture arms and ammunition for the Patriots. New firearms companies often set up nearby, such as Colt in Connecticut and Smith & Wesson in Massachusetts in the nineteenth century. Friendly relations with New England's firearms industry were probably one reason why Massachusetts Senator, and then President, John F. Kennedy was a member of the NRA.

Kennedy's assassination in November 1963 by Lee Harvey Oswald (who purchased the rifle used to kill Kennedy by mail order from Klein's Sporting Goods in Chicago for $21.45) had little immediate effect on the gun issue, although Oswald had used an imported Italian rifle, precisely the type of gun that Dodd was trying to block from import.

But by 1966, things were changing drastically. Blacks in the Watts neighborhood of Los Angeles rioted in 1965, in response to allegations of police brutality. In the summers of 1966, 1967, and 1968, black rioting occurred in big cities across the country. At the same time, crime was rising sharply. Crime and riots led many whites (and blacks) to arm for self-defense, which was derided as "white backlash" by some of the media. The media gave enormous coverage to self-proclaimed militant, extremist, and pro-violence black leaders such as Stokely Carmichael and H. Rap Brown. Whether they ever had much of a real following is debatable, but they terrified many Americans.

Significantly adding to public disquiet were the Black Panthers, who called themselves a social justice organization, but who perpetrated many homicides against the police and in factional fighting among the extreme left. The Panthers discovered that California had no law against openly carrying loaded rifles and shotguns in public, and they started to do so, toting loaded guns into the state capitol in Sacramento. The California legislature speedily passed, and Governor Ronald Reagan signed, a bill to outlaw loaded open carry in most circumstances. Cynthia Deitle Leonardatos, California's Attempts to Disarm the Black Panthers, 36 San Diego L. Rev. 947 (1999). Many cities and states followed suit.

By the mid 1960s, violence and social upheaval was fueling new and stronger calls for gun control. The first major law came from Illinois in 1966, requiring a license from the state police (the "Firearms Identification Card") for gun ownership. Having controlled handguns since the 1911 Sullivan Act, New York City imposed long gun registration in 1967. The next year, the New Jersey legislature took up and expanded the Illinois system, requiring licensing for all gun owners, registration for all guns, and police permission required for each handgun purchase.

The idea that civilian gun ownership should be entirely prohibited moved from the fringe into the mainstream of public debate. Gun advocates, now on the defensive, tended to emphasize innocent sporting uses of guns, rather than justify gun ownership for self-defense or resistance to tyranny.

The March 1968 assassination of Martin Luther King, Jr., set off another round of race riots. The final straw was the June 5, 1968 assassination of New York Senator Robert Kennedy, in the kitchen of the Ambassador Hotel in Los Angeles. Kennedy had just delivered his victory speech after winning the California Democratic presidential primary. The assassin, a Palestinian angered by Kennedy's strong support for Israel, used a small, cheap, imported pistol.

Almost immediately, the U.S. Senate Judiciary Committee — traditionally the bulwark against federal gun control — reported out a gun control bill. The National Emergency Committee for Gun Control was created, with its primary objective a federal bill. President Lyndon Johnson, himself a hunter, gave a speech endorsing national gun registration on June 24.

Gun control advocates acknowledged that gun bans were not yet politically viable. So the prime immediate goal was national gun registration. Conversely, gun rights advocates, aware that gun registration lists originally compiled by democratic governments had been used for gun confiscation by Nazis and Communists in Europe, were terrified of registration.

Another spate of riots occurred in August at the Democratic National Convention in Chicago. This time, the riots were led by radical leftists such as Abbie Hoffman and Jerry Rubin of the "Chicago Seven," who were intent on sparking revolution, and who succeeded in hijacking planned peaceful protests against the Vietnam War. The Chicago Seven were perversely aided in their objectives by Chicago Mayor Richard Daley. Daley authorized what amounted to a counter-riot by the Chicago police, who indiscriminately beat rioters, peaceful protestors, and even reporters.

Amid scenes of a nation coming apart, Congress passed the Gun Control Act of 1968 in September 1968. The Act required gun dealers to keep a federal form (now known as Form 4473) detailing the information for each sale (such as the gun's model and serial number, the buyer's name, address, age, race, and so on). The forms would be available for government inspection and for criminal investigations, but the forms would not be collected in a centralized registration list. In addition, mail-order sales of long guns were banned, as were all interstate gun sales to consumers (except where states enacted legislation allowing purchase of long guns in contiguous states).

The GCA also banned all gun possession by enumerated prohibited persons, such as convicted felons, illegal aliens, and illegal drug users. Buyers had to certify on Form 4473 that they were not in a prohibited category.

Gun imports were banned, except for the guns determined by the Treasury Secretary to be "particularly suitable for sporting purposes." As implemented, this prohibited small, inexpensive foreign handguns, and surplus WWII rifles, but allowed almost all other gun imports. While the relationship between American gun manufacturers and Dodd had soured several years earlier, as successive versions of the Dodd bill focused more and more on domestic gun control, the manufacturers still tended to support the new import restrictions.

The 1968 Act also made some changes to the National Firearms Act, such as adding the amorphous category "any other weapon," which by ATF interpretation would expand unpredictably over time. *See* Chapter 7.C. While the "AOW" boundaries are very clouded, it is clear that the category includes disguised firearms, such as a cane and belt buckle guns. *See* 26 U.S.C. §5845(a)(5); Stephen Halbrook, Firearms Law Deskbook 631-35 (2011). The GCA preamble disclaimed any intention to interfere with sporting gun use, gun collecting, or self-protection.

With national registration removed, the NRA made a political compromise. Although it would not endorse the Gun Control Act, it also would not mark GCA votes on the legislative report card where it graded members of Congress A through F on their support of gun rights. This grading was and is one of the NRA's most efficient tools for enabling political action by the membership.

Still, the GCA was opposed by many in Congress. Not one member of the Texas House delegation voted for it, with the exception of a freshman Republican from Houston named George H.W. Bush. Bush called the GCA a positive step, but added that "much more" needed to be done. In 1972, Bush won the Republican nomination for U.S. Senate, but was defeated by Democrat Lloyd Bentsen, who exploited Bush's very unpopular (in Texas) support for gun control.

The more immediately influential political effects were in the 1970 Senate races. The NRA claimed that reaction against the GCA helped to defeat Dodd, liberal New York Republican Charles Goodell, Tennessee's Albert Gore, Sr. (father of the future Vice-President), and Maryland's Joseph Tydings. The claim was least plausible for Senator Dodd, a widely rumored alcoholic, who was likely headed for defeat after being censured for corruption in 1967. Gore lost by 4 percent, within the margin where NRA votes could swing the result. Goodell had the misfortune of splitting the liberal New York vote with Democrat Richard Ottinger and lost to James Buckley (brother of *National Review* publisher William F. Buckley). Buckley ran as the Conservative party nominee, garnering 38 percent of the vote, and his 2 percent margin of victory was also partly thanks to the gun vote.

The biggest political impact, however, came from the narrow defeat of Maryland Democrat Tydings. He had sponsored legislation for national gun licensing and gun control, and had also alienated civil libertarians by shepherding federal wiretap legislation into law. His loss was widely attributed to backlash from gun owners and civil libertarians.

For more on the political and social history of this period, see Robert Sherrill, The Saturday Night Special (1973); Nicholas J. Johnson, *A Second Amendment Moment: The Constitutional Politics of Gun Control*, 71 Brook. L. Rev. 715 (2005).

4. The Rise of the Modern Gun Control Movement and the Revolt at the NRA

With comprehensive gun control now part of federal law, the Alcohol, Tobacco, and Firearms Division of the Treasury Department was upgraded into a Bureau, and given primary responsibility for the enforcement of the GCA. The new bureau was known as BATF, although in the late 1980s, the Bureau would adopt the three-letter moniker "ATF," to emulate the better-respected FBI and DEA.

Gun control advocates in Congress saw a domestic ban on "Saturday Night Specials" as the logical next step. Several times in the 1970s they passed bills out of committee, or through one house of Congress. The high-water mark was a 1973 Senate vote, by a wide margin, to ban about one-third of all handguns. But the Saturday Night Special ban never passed both houses. The Nixon White House repeatedly warned the NRA that it had better cut the best deal it could on an SNS ban, and many in the American gun industry were ready to accept some sort of ban.

The relatively new trade association for the firearms industry, the National Shooting Sports Foundation (founded in 1961) was dominated by long gun manufacturers. The NSSF reflected their discomfort with making handguns and self-defense the dominant themes of gun ownership in America. If an SNS ban was going to be stopped in Congress, the fight would not come from industry. The battle would be fought, if at all, by grassroots and "hard corps" activists under the banner of the NRA.

NRA Executive Vice-President (the day-to-day chief operating officer of the association) Franklin Orth supported a SNS ban, as long as it was not a cover for a more sweeping ban on all handguns. A 1968 issue of *The American Rifleman* contained Orth's scathing denunciation of the poor-quality, dirt cheap, unreliable Saturday Night Special. Orth also judged the 1968 Gun Control Act pretty good, overall.

Other voices within the NRA strongly disagreed. Led by former U.S. Border Patrol head Harlon Carter, they insisted that there was no such thing as a bad gun, only bad gun owners. In the internal battles at the NRA's Washington headquarters, the hard-liners gained control of the lobbying operation and the magazine, while the "Old Guard" held on to general operations. The two sides waged fierce internecine battles.

When Congress created the Consumer Product Safety Commission in 1972 and gave it extremely broad powers to outlaw any consumer product it deemed to impose unwarranted risks, the NRA defeated an amendment giving the CPSC authority to ban firearms. After the new Commission claimed that it nonetheless had authority to ban *ammunition,* freshman Republican Senator James McClure of Idaho secured a large majority to add a specific prohibition on CPSC action against firearms or ammunition. 90 Stat. 504 (1976); Dennis B. Wilson, *What You Can't Have Won't Hurt You! The Real Safety Objective of the Firearms Safety and Consumer Protection Act,* 53 Clev. St. L. Rev. 225 (2005-2006). Still, the impulse for gun control was growing and gun rights victories consisted mostly of defense against proposed new laws.

During the 1960s and 1970s, a tremendous cultural shift took place among American elites. In 1960, it was unexceptional that a liberal Northeastern Democrat, such as John F. Kennedy, would join the NRA. But by the early 1970s, gun ownership itself was reviled by much of the urban intelligentsia. The prominent historian Richard Hofstadter spoke for many when he complained that "Americans cling with pathetic stubbornness" to "the supposed 'right' to bear arms," and refused to adopt European-style gun control laws. Richard Hofstadter, *Gun Culture,* American Heritage, Oct. 1970. While some of the intelligentsia might concede a limited place for sporting guns, guns for self-defense came to represent an insult to a well-ordered society. Barry Bruce-Briggs, *The Great American Gun War*, The Public Interest 37 (Fall 1976).

As for the Second Amendment, the winning entry in the 1965 American Bar Association student paper competition is instructive. Written by Robert Sprecher and published in the ABA Journal, it was titled "The Lost Amendment." Sprecher's historical analysis endorsed the individual-rights view that would later be known as the Standard Model. But in his view, the Amendment was "lost" in the sense that few people paid attention to it, and it was neglected by courts and scholars. Robert Sprecher, *The Lost Amendment*, 51 ABA J. 554, 664 (June-July 1965) (two-part article).

The as-yet-unnamed "Standard Model" (the Second Amendment is a normal individual right, but bounded by permissible controls) remained the dominant view among the general public. But elite opinion mostly considered the Second Amendment as purely a "collective right" or a "state's right." This meant that whatever the Amendment's positive content, it was no barrier to gun prohibition. To the extent that anyone needed proof, there was an often-cited article from the *Northwestern Law Review.* Peter Buck Feller & Karl L. Gotting, *The Second Amendment: A Second Look*, 61 Nw. U. L. Rev. 46 (1966). The conclusion was further supported by the gun control task force of President Johnson's commission on violence. The task force was led by the energetic young scholar Franklin Zimring, whose work would influence the gun debate for years to come. George P. Newton & Franklin Zimring, Firearms and Violence in American Life, Task Force Report to the National Commission on the Causes and Prevention of Violence (1969).

While supported by much of the media, and endorsed by numerous prestigious and powerful individuals and organizations, gun control lacked its own version of the NRA—an organization whose primary purpose was advance the cause. That changed in 1974 with the founding of the National Coalition to Control Handguns. (The group would later change its name to Handgun Control, Inc., and later still to the Brady Campaign.) The NCCH soon found a chairman to build it into an institution. Business executive Nelson "Pete" Shields's son had been murdered in San Francisco by the Zebra killers, a Black Muslim cult that over several years committed random torture murders of non-blacks in the Bay Area. Shields accepted the chairmanship and explained his long-term plan:

> The first problem is to slow down the number of handguns being produced and sold in this country. The second problem is to get handguns registered. The final problem is to make possession of all handguns and all handgun ammunition— except for the military, police, licensed security guards, licensed sporting clubs, and licensed gun collectors—totally illegal.

Richard Harris, *A Reporter at Large: Handguns*, New Yorker, July 26, 1976, at 58.

At the time, the NCCH was a member organization of another new gun control group, the National Council to Ban Handguns. (That group later changed its name to the Coalition to Stop Gun Violence.) For both the NCCH and the NCBH, the initial focus was solely on handguns. As Shields put it in his book, "our organization, Handgun Control, Inc., does not propose further controls on rifles and shotguns. Rifles and shotguns are not the problem;

they are not concealable." Pete Shields, Guns Don't Die, People Do 47-48 (1981). Later, both groups would broaden their focus to include restrictions or prohibitions on all types of firearms.

Meanwhile, the battles within the NRA were continuing. The legislative office was upgraded to the Institute for Legislative Action (ILA) in 1974, but ILA was often under siege by the NRA's Old Guard, who still ran general operations, and who opposed ILA's Second Amendment zealotry. Meanwhile, NRA membership had changed significantly. By the early 1970s, a remarkable 25 percent of NRA members were what the NRA calls "non-shooting constitutionalists" — that is, persons who did not even own a gun, but who joined the NRA in order to defend gun rights. Sherill, *supra*, at 188.

Things came to a head when the NRA leadership announced plans to abandon politics, sell the D.C. headquarters building, move the Association to Colorado Springs, and transform the NRA into purely a hunting and sporting association. The Old Guard had Harlon Carter fired from NRA. Undeterred, Carter organized a faction of members determined to keep the NRA in the political fight. They feared that political compromise by the NRA would unleash a wave of stringent gun controls and prohibitions. The showdown came at the 1977 Annual Meeting of the Members in Cincinnati. Armed with walkie-talkies and skilled in parliamentary procedure, Carter's "Committee for the NRA" won vote after vote and changed the NRA's by-laws.

This triumph became known as the "Revolt at Cincinnati." At 4 A.M., Harlon Carter was elected Executive Vice-President. The next year, Carter appointed Neal Knox as head of the NRA's Institute for Legislative Action. Joseph P. Tartaro, Revolt at Cincinnati (1981).

Knox was a gun periodical editor, and had been national shotgun champion a decade before. Knox's fervor on the gun issue stemmed from his early experience serving in the Texas National Guard where he met a Belgian-American Guardsman named Charley Duer. In gun-rights lore, Duer became known as "the Belgian Corporal." He told Knox how the conquering Nazis had seized the Belgian government's gun registration lists, and demanded the immediate surrender of all registered firearms. One family in town was ordered to produce an old handgun that had been a relic from World War I, a quarter-century before:

> The officer told the father that he had exactly fifteen minutes to produce the weapon. The family turned their home upside down. No pistol. They returned to the SS officer empty-handed.
>
> The officer gave an order and soldiers herded the family outside while other troops called the entire town out into the square. There on the town square the SS machine-gunned the entire family: father, mother, Charley's two friends, their older brother and a baby sister.
>
> I will never forget the moment. We were sitting on the bunk on a Saturday afternoon and Charley was crying, huge tears rolling down his cheeks, making silver dollar size splotches on the dusty barracks floor.

Chris Knox, Neal Knox: The Gun Rights War 16 (2009).

Carter, Knox, and their allies began formulating a detailed political agenda. One of their first priorities was reform of the 1968 Gun Control Act, which they argued was being abusively enforced by ATF. The new approach seemed popular; NRA membership, which was about a million just before the Revolt, grew to 2.6 million by 1983 (and would eventually pass the 4-million mark in the early twenty-first century).

The growing grassroots gun rights movement was also sufficient to engender the birth of two new gun rights organizations, the Second Amendment Foundation in 1974 and Gun Owners of America in 1975. Both organizations continue to play an influential role in firearms policy.

5.   Handgun Prohibition

The mid-1970s witnessed important advances for gun prohibition. Having just been granted home rule by Congress, the newly empowered District of Columbia city government enacted a ban on handguns, which became effective in early 1976.[1] (It would be overturned in *District of Columbia v. Heller* (Chapter 9), 32 years later.) The ban passed the city council 12-1, with some supporters stating that the law probably would have no effect in the District, but hopefully would spur movement toward a national handgun ban.

The NRA sued to overturn the D.C. ban on numerous grounds. Notably, this challenge did not assert that the D.C. law violated the Second Amendment. The NRA won in district court, but lost in the District of Columbia Court of Appeals, the city's equivalent to a state supreme court. *McIntosh v. Washington*, 395 A.2d 744 (D.C. 1978).

The idea of a national handgun ban was gaining momentum. President Ford endorsed a ban on the sale of Saturday Night Specials. His Attorney General Edward Levi floated the idea of a national handgun ban, applicable only to large cities with crime rates above a certain threshold. The proposal stalled, partly because of the obvious impracticality of preventing guns from nearby areas from being brought into the particular cities.

The first serious chance for the D.C. ban to spread nationally came in a 1976 Massachusetts election. The "People vs. Handguns" initiative proposed to confiscate all private handguns in the state. It was supported by Governor Michael Dukakis, and "by much of the state's press." *Bets, Bottles and Bullets*, Time, Nov. 15, 1976. Yet on election day, 69 percent of the state's voters rejected it, at least some of them because of the cost of compensating owners for confiscated guns.

The next major initiative came in California in 1982. To avoid the problem of compensating gun owners for confiscated property, the initiative proposed a "handgun freeze." Current owners could keep their handguns but future sales would be banned. The idea of a "nuclear freeze" was on its way to becoming a mainstream Democratic position, so proponents hoped to gain some ancillary support by calling their idea a "handgun freeze." The California initiative was defeated by a vote of 63 to 37 percent. Opposition to the freeze brought so many

---

1. The District of Columbia had for almost all of its history been ruled by the House and Senate Committees on the District of Columbia. The District of Columbia Home Rule Act was enacted in 1973. 87 Stat. 777 (1973).

additional voters to the polls that they carried Republican George Deukmejian to a 1 percent victory over Tom Bradley in the governor's race.

The first jurisdiction outside D.C. to successfully install a handgun ban was the Chicago suburb of Morton Grove in 1981. Chicago itself would follow suit in 1983, and the suburbs of Evanston, Oak Park, and Wilmette would also enact bans in the next several years.

The Morton Grove ordinance prompted the first big case. The NRA opposed it in state court, under the Illinois Constitution's right to arms guarantee. The state case was suspended when attorney Victor Quilici filed suit in federal district court, alleging a Second Amendment violation. *Quilici v. Morton Grove* attracted extensive national attention.

The loss in federal district court was predictable, because the district judge had already told a television interviewer that he thought the ban was constitutional. The Seventh Circuit upheld the ban 2-1. Quilici v. Morton Grove, 695 F.2d 261 (7th Cir. 1982). Dissenting Judge Coffey based his argument for a right to own a defensive handgun in the home not the Second Amendment, but on the privacy rights protected by the liberty clauses of the Fifth and Fourteenth Amendments.

The NRA sought relief in the United States Supreme Court, which issued one of its most highly publicized denials of a petition for a writ of certiorari in June 1983. 464 U.S. 863 (1983). When the Illinois Supreme Court finally decided the state constitutional law case, it upheld the *Morton Grove* ban 4-3. *Kalodimos v. Morton Grove*, 470 N.E.2d 266 (Ill. 1984).

The *Morton Grove* cases were an important setback for gun rights in the courts. But there was a silver lining for gun advocates. Handgun bans were now a hot button political issue. The growing movement to ban handguns energized gun owners. For NRA lobbyists in the state legislatures, the Illinois bans were the horror story used to convince state legislators that gun bans were a genuine threat. In response, state after state enacted preemption laws forbidding some or all local gun regulation. The impact of these preemption efforts was evident when California's preemption statute was successfully invoked to overturn ordinances banning handguns in San Francisco. *Fiscal v. San Francisco*, 158 Cal. App. 4th 895, 70 Cal. Rptr. 3d 324 (Cal. App. 2008); *Doe v. San Francisco*, 136 Cal. App. 3d 509, 186 Cal. Rptr. 380 (1982).

By the early 1990s, local handgun bans were blocked by state preemption laws almost everywhere in the United States. One of the few states without a preemption law was Wisconsin, which bordered the one state where handgun bans existed. Proposals for handgun bans were put on the ballot in three left-leaning Wisconsin cities. In 1993, voters in Madison rejected a handgun ban by 51 percent. In 1994, handgun bans were voted down by 67 percent in Milwaukee and 73 percent in Kenosha.

The Wisconsin handgun ban initiatives had unintended consequences. The backlash led to passage of a preemption law in 1995. And by 1998, the legislature put a state constitutional right to arms amendment on the ballot. On election day, 73 percent of voters approved the addition of a right to arms guarantee to the state constitution. Wisconsin is one of 17 states that added or strengthened a state right to arms guarantee since the 1960s. (See the appendix to Chapter 1 for all state constitutional provisions and revisions of the right to arms.)

The handgun prohibition surge that began in the 1970s had stalled. Ultimately, D.C. was entirely alone in forbidding the use of a gun for self-defense in the home. This political result prefigured the ultimate constitutional assessment. Professor Jack Balkin observes that the Supreme Court tends to be more likely to find violations in laws that are national outliers. *See* Jack M. Balkin, *Framework Originalism and the Living Constitution*, 103 Nw. U. L. Rev. 549 (2009). While it is impossible to know for sure, it is plausible that the outcome of *Heller* (Chapter 9) and *McDonald* (Chapter 9) is partly attributable to the fact that handgun prohibition remained very rare in the United States, and that no jurisdiction copied D.C.'s ban on home self-defense with a lawfully owned firearm.

6. The NRA Counteroffensive, and the Growing Sophistication of the Gun Control Lobby

After the 1977 Revolt at Cincinnati, the new NRA leaders in Washington soon won an easy victory. The Bureau of Alcohol, Tobacco and Firearms proposed new rules mandating collection of gun sales records from federally licensed firearms dealers, and development of a national registry of guns and gun owners. The ATF said that the program would cost about $5 million, which could be funded out of its existing budget. The congressional response was swift. In 1978, the House of Representatives voted 314 to 80 to block the ATF gun registration plan and amended the Gun Control Act to explicitly forbid ATF from compiling any information beyond that "expressly" required by statute. 18 U.S.C. §923(g)(1)(A). They also sliced ATF's appropriation by $5 million.

The NRA's major legislative initiative, passage of the Firearms Owners Protection Act (FOPA), took far longer. The NRA, an early master of the art of "direct mail," sent millions of mailings in support of Ronald Reagan during the 1980 election. While Reagan's landslide victory was attributable mainly to broad public dissatisfaction with President Jimmy Carter's leadership, the NRA probably helped put Reagan over the top in some close states such as Pennsylvania and Michigan.

Reagan had endorsed the Firearms Owners Protection Act, which was conceived in the late 1970s and early 1980s, as congressional committees recorded horror stories of abusive ATF prosecutions. Many lawmakers found ATF's explanations unconvincing. Ancillary to the ATF hearings, the Senate Subcommittee on the Constitution, a part of the Judiciary Committee, adopted a detailed report in 1982 finding that the Second Amendment was an individual right. The report was published by the Government Printing Office, and sold at GPO bookstores nationally. The Right to Keep and Bear Arms, Report of the Subcommittee on the Constitution of the United States Senate, 97th Cong., 2d Sess. (1982) (also finding that "75 percent of BATF gun prosecutions were aimed at ordinary citizens who had neither criminal intent nor knowledge, but were enticed by agents into unknowing technical violations").

After the election, the new Reagan administration bluntly informed the NRA that the economy was the top priority, and that gun law reforms would have to wait. Indeed, the NRA found itself opposing one of the administration's first relevant proposals. As part of the budget cuts of 1981, there was a proposal to abolish ATF and give its functions to the prestigious and politically influential Secret Service. The NRA opposed the change, on the view that ATF was a weaker political opponent whose suspect practices underscored the need for FOPA.

On March 30, 1981, John Hinckley attempted to assassinate President Reagan, using a cheap handgun. Reagan survived, but his press secretary James Brady was permanently disabled by a shot to the head. Because Hinckley's gun was a classic Saturday Night Special (SNS), gun control advocates in Congress seemed to have momentum to pass Senator Ted Kennedy's (D-Mass.) SNS ban. The momentum fizzled on June 18, with Reagan's first press conference after his release from the hospital. Asked about the Kennedy bill, he replied: "[M]y concern about gun control is that it's taking our eyes off what might be the real answers to crime; it's diverting our attention. There are, today, more than 20,000 gun-control laws in effect — federal, state and local — in the United States.[2] Indeed, some of the stiffest gun-control laws in the nation are right here in the district and they didn't seem to prevent a fellow, a few weeks ago, from carrying one down by the Hilton Hotel." In 1983, Reagan became the first sitting President to address the NRA Annual Meeting.

The advocates of SNS bans continued to lose battles in Congress. Congress essentially accepted the same rationale adopted by the D.C. district court that dismissed James Brady's lawsuit against the maker of Hinckley's gun. Rejecting the label that inexpensive guns are "ghetto" guns, the court wrote that "while blighted areas may be some of the breeding places of crime, not all residents [] are so engaged, and indeed, most persons who live there are law abiding but have no other choice of location . . . it is highly unlikely that they would have the resources or worth to buy an expensive handgun for self-defense. To remove cheap weapons from the community may very well remove a form of protection assuming that all citizens are entitled to possess guns for defense." *Delahanty v. Hinckley*, 686 F. Supp. 920 (D.D.C. 1986), *aff'd*, 900 F.2d 368 (D.C. Cir. 1990).

Advocates of the SNS ban did achieve success in the long term. The 1968 Gun Control Act had shut off imports, and product liability suits over the next several decades, brought under unconventional product liability theories, drove the domestic SNS manufacturers out of the market by the end of the twentieth century. Today there are many small handguns for sale, but they are high-quality, relatively higher-priced models from respected manufacturers.

Handgun prohibition, though, turned out to be much more difficult to achieve than Pete Shields had imagined in 1977. Rather than giving up, Handgun Control, Inc. learned how to make effective use of ancillary issues.

The first of these was the "cop-killer bullet." The bullets were formally known as KTW bullets, the name derived from the developers, Dr. Paul Kopsch and two police officers named Turcus and Ward. While ordinary bullets have a lead core, KTW bullets used brass or iron. The KTW bullet has a conical shape, and was designed for shooting through glass or a car door. The bullets were developed for police special weapons teams and had not been available for sale

---

2. The 20,000 figure apparently traces back to 1965 congressional testimony by Rep. John Dingell (D-Mich.). To be accurate, the figure would probably need to count various subsections of a given statute or ordinance as separate laws. Considering the decimation of local gun control ordinances by statewide preemption statutes during the last three decades, the total quantity of American gun control laws has likely been significantly reduced.

to the general public since the 1960s. They were sometimes called "Teflon bullets," but that name reflected misunderstanding. A Teflon coating reduces a bullet's abrasion in the gun barrel and keeps the barrel cleaner, it also prevents it from ricocheting off a hard target. Teflon has nothing to do with a bullet's penetrability.

The "cop-killer bullet" bill introduced by Rep. Mario Biaggi (D-N.Y.) went far beyond the KTW bullet. It would have outlawed most of the centerfire rifle ammunition in the United States. (For an explanation of centerfire vs. rimfire ammunition, see online Chapter 15.) Despite the apparent legislative overreach, the NRA was boxed in. Its arguments against the ban depended on the technical details of ammunition ballistics. While those arguments were sufficient to block the ban in Congress, at the more general level of public debate, the NRA was tagged with supporting "cop-killer bullets." This did lasting damage to the traditional connection between the NRA and law enforcement.

After the failure of the 1982 California handgun freeze, gun control advocates realized that one of their problems was that many police were gun owners and enthusiasts who strongly opposed the freeze. Many rank and file police supported self-defense by law-abiding citizens, and viewed gun bans as an unrealistic ideal. The "cop-killer bullet" issue was different and was quite effective at driving a wedge between the NRA and its traditional law enforcement allies. For some groups, such as the Fraternal Order of Police (the largest rank and file police organization in the United States), the rift was not fully healed until the twenty-first century.

While Biaggi's ammunition ban would not pass, it did have the effect of blocking progress on the NRA's own flagship bill, the Firearms Owners Protection Act (FOPA), a wide-ranging set of reforms to the 1968 Gun Control Act. Finally, the NRA decided to work with Biaggi on a compromise bill. As enacted, the compromise bill banned a category of ammunition that was no longer being produced for the retail market. The bill passed Congress almost unanimously. Biaggi proclaimed the bill accomplished everything he had wanted.

In 1982, NRA Executive Vice-President Harlon Carter fired Neal Knox as head of NRA-ILA. Knox had refused Carter's order to negotiate with the White House over FOPA, believing that Reagan's 1980 endorsement of FOPA meant that the White House should not attempt to weaken or change it. Knox was also unhappy about what he saw as the NRA misinforming its membership about the compromises on the ammunition bill.

No one had ever been better than Knox at appealing to the hard core of gun rights activists. After his dismissal Knox registered as an independent lobbyist, and started his own newsletter, the "Hard Corps Report." Thereafter, Knox, as well as Gun Owners of America, would define their space in the gun issue by criticizing the NRA for what they saw as an endless series of weak-kneed compromises.

Getting the cop-killer bullet issue off the table cleared the path for FOPA. It passed the Senate 79-15 in 1985, and passed the House 292-130 in 1986, with a majority of Democrats voting in favor. Sponsor Harold Volkmer (D-Mo.) used a discharge petition (requiring a signature of the majority of House members) to spring the bill out of the Judiciary Committee, where Chairman Peter Rodino (D-N.J.) had pronounced it "dead on arrival."

FOPA curtailed ATF's powers of forfeiture, and search and seizure; created due process rules for dealer licensing or license revocation; explicitly outlawed federal gun registration; and declared the Second Amendment to be an individual right. The best in-depth explication of FOPA is David T. Hardy,

Firearms Owners Protection Act: A Historical and Legal Perspective 17 Cumb. L. Rev. 585 (1986) (cited by the Supreme Court, and almost every federal Court of Appeals).

Because of an amendment added on the floor of the House, FOPA also banned the sale of new machine guns (manufactured after the date that FOPA became law, May 19, 1986) for sale to the public. The NRA successfully challenged the ban in district court, but lost in the Eleventh Circuit, and the Supreme Court denied certiorari. *Farmer v. Higgins*, 907 F.2d 1041 (11th Cir. 1990), *cert. denied*, 498 U.S. 1047 (1991). (The challenge had asked that language allowing the sale of new machine guns "under the authority of the United States" be construed to allow sales that complied with the federal National Firearms Act of 1934.)

Although defeated on FOPA, Handgun Control, Inc. (HCI) was becoming more effective politically. The organization had a long-standing practice of calling the victims of notorious gun crimes, or their relatives, and asking them to join the organization as gun control advocates. They approached Sarah Brady, the wife of Reagan's well-liked press secretary. Brady threw herself into the movement that her husband would later join as well. Eventually, the organization would bear her name. Gregg Lee Carter, The Gun Control Movement 95 (1997). HCI renamed its waiting period proposal for the Bradys. As Republican insiders, the Bradys offered the possibility of taking the gun control message to the Republican establishment.

HCI found another effective issue in the "plastic gun." Today, handguns made in part from plastic polymers are common. They are much more durable, and their light weight makes them popular for defensive carry. But polymer guns were novel when Austria's Gaston Glock introduced his eponymous pistol to the U.S. market. Gun control groups dubbed the Glocks "terrorist specials," claiming that they were invisible to metal detectors. Sen. Howard Metzenbaum (D-Ohio) introduced an "undetectable" firearms ban. Ironically, Metzenbaum's bill would not have banned Glocks because they contain enough metal to be easily detectable. But the bill would have banned many small all-metal firearms.

In early 1988, the Reagan White House was on the verge of endorsing the Metzenbaum bill, at the behest of Attorney General Edwin Meese. The endorsement ultimately was withheld in order to accommodate Vice-President George H.W. Bush, who was running for President. Bush had run into trouble on the gun issue not only in 1972, but also in 1980, when he and Ronald Reagan emerged as the leading candidates for the Republican presidential nomination. Reagan gained among gun owners then by highlighting Bush's support for a Saturday Night Special ban. Bush had just bought a NRA Life Membership, was courting the gun vote, and sought to avoid connection with another provocative gun ban.

Even without White House support, the Metzenbaum bill lost by only two votes in the Senate. Again, the NRA compromised, and almost everyone in Congress voted for the compromise. As enacted, the law banned no existing firearm, and did nothing to stop the use of polymers to build firearms. It did require that all new handguns contain at least four ounces of metal, with the profile of a handgun. After winning the Republican presidential nomination in 1988, George Bush wrote a public letter to the NRA promising his opposition to waiting periods, gun bans, gun registration, and other forms of gun control.

Bush's opponent in the 1988 race was Massachusetts Democratic Governor Michael Dukakis. Dukakis had a solid record on gun control. He had supported

Massachusetts's 1976 handgun confiscation initiative, proclaimed a "Domestic Disarmament Day" in which he urged handgun owners to turn over their fire-arms to police, endorsed what he called "stiff federal gun control," and signed a proclamation that the Second Amendment is not an individual right.

As governor, Dukakis had granted a pardon to a man named Sylvester Lindsey. Lindsey had been sentenced to a year in state prison under a new state law imposing the mandatory sentence for any unlicensed possession or carrying of guns or ammunition. Lindsey was caught carrying a handgun after a co-worker, a convicted felon, tried to kill him with a knife, threatened to try again, and then assaulted Lindsey a second time. *Commonwealth v. Lindsey*, 489 N.E.2d 666 (Mass. 1986). While granting the pardon, on June 16, 1986, Governor Dukakis stated: "You know I don't believe in people owning guns, only the police and military. And I'm going to do everything I can to disarm this state."

Gun Week (owned by the Second Amendment Foundation) reported the statement shortly after the 1988 Democratic National Convention, and the NRA put the words on the front cover of its magazines. The NRA also spent a then-record $6 million publicizing Dukakis's record. In Pennsylvania, and in many states to the south and west, the effect was devastating. Dukakis went from a small lead in Texas to a landslide loss. He also lost California, Michigan, and some of the Rocky Mountain states in part because of the gun issue.

After the election, the Democratic Vice-Presidential nominee, Texas Sena-tor Lloyd Bentsen, noted the "incredible effect of gun control," and observed "we lost a lot of Democrats on peripheral issues like gun control and the pledge." Adam Winkler, Gunfight: The Battle over the Right to Bear Arms in America 112 (2011); Ernest B. Furgurson, *Bentsen and Mitchell, Democrats*, Balt. Sun., Dec. 2, 1988. (George H.W. Bush had vociferously criticized Dukakis for opposing Massachusetts legislation to have the Pledge of Allegiance recited in public schools.)

Even normally Democratic Maryland went for Bush due to extra gun owner turnout related to a gun control initiative on the state ballot that year. Maryland was, however, a net win for gun control advocates. A few years earlier, the state supreme court had voted to impose strict liability on the manufacturers and retailers of Saturday Night Specials. *Kelley v. R.G. Industries*, 497 A.2d 1143 (Md. 1985). This was the one major win for the plaintiffs' attorneys who had brought strict product liability suits against handgun manufacturers since the early 1970s (and who had spurred a legislative response in about a third of the states out-lawing such suits). In 1988, the Maryland legislature responded by abolishing strict liability for handguns, but at the same time setting up a Maryland Handgun Roster Board, whose approval would be required for the sale of any new models of handguns in Maryland. Md. Ann. Code art. 27 §36-I(h). A NRA-led initiative to overturn the law failed by a vote of 58 to 42 percent.

7.   George H.W. Bush

As President, George Bush was more the Bush of 1968-80 than the candidate of 1988. Shortly after Bush was inaugurated in January 1989, a repeat violent felon with severe mental problems used a Kalashnikov-style semi-automatic rifle to murder five children at a schoolyard in Stockton, California. "Assault weapons" were suddenly a major national issue.

The previous year, the communications director of the National Coalition to Ban Handguns, Josh Sugarmann, had written a public strategy memo. He pointed out that the media had grown tired of the handgun issue, but "assault weapons" would be novel to them. Further:

> The semiautomatic weapons' menacing looks, coupled with the public's confusion over fully automatic machine guns versus semiautomatic assault weapons—anything that looks like a machine gun is assumed to be a machine gun—can only increase the chance of public support for restrictions on these weapons.

Assault Weapons and Accessories in America (Educ. Fund to End Handgun Violence and New Right Watch, Sept. 1988), at 26. Sugarmann was exactly right.

President Bush's Drug "Czar" William Bennett convinced the Treasury Department to impose a temporary ban on the import of "assault weapons," pursuant to its Gun Control Act authority to block import of non-sporting arms. That authority generally had been used only to block handgun imports. A few weeks later the import ban was expanded. The NRA protested that FOPA had specifically mandated the import of firearms "generally recognized as particularly suitable for or readily adaptable to sporting purposes, excluding surplus military firearms." 18 U.S.C. §925(d)(3). They argued that almost all the banned guns were suitable for and often used at rifle target competitions, such as the federally sponsored National Matches (Chapter 4). Almost all the guns were lawful for hunting in almost every state, when equipped with a hunting capacity ammunition magazine (typically five rounds). Unconvinced, the Treasury Department made the import bans final a few months later.

More significantly, proposals for "assault weapon" restrictions cropped up in Congress, in most state legislatures, and in many municipalities. The NRA's top lobbyist, James J. Baker, told gun owners that there were simply too many fronts for the NRA to fight all at once, and local gun owners would have to organize and fight the bans on their own. Many elected officials who had previously been pro-gun stalwarts could not understand why anyone would want to own what President Bush called "automated attack weapons." (Mar. 7, 1989, press conference, 25 Weekly Comp. Pres. Docs. 294.) Senator Dennis DeConcini (D-Ariz.) had been one of the NRA's best friends in Congress, but introduced his own ban. DeConcini considered his proposal a moderate measure, since it would ban fewer guns than some competing bills. Antidrug, Assault Weapons Limitation Act of 1989, S.747, 101st Cong. (1989).

Prohibition laws passed in California and several cities. Over the next several years, New Jersey, New York, and Massachusetts would pass bans, while Maryland and Hawaii would ban "assault pistols." In Congress, the DeConcini bill passed the Senate by one vote, as an amendment to a comprehensive crime bill sponsored by Senator Joe Biden (D-Del.). The ban was defeated in the House by the substitution of "the Unsoeld Amendment" from Rep. Jolene Unsoeld (D-Wash.). That amendment ratified the Bush import ban by prohibiting the domestic assembly from foreign parts of a non-importable "assault weapon." 18 U.S.C. §922(r).

Along with "assault weapons," the other major item on HCI's agenda was a waiting period for handgun purchases. As with "assault weapons," HCI was not initially successful at passing its bills through Congress, but it did force the NRA to fall back. For several years, HCI had been pushing a national 15-day waiting period for all handgun purchases. HCI almost passed the bill through the House in September 1988 by cutting the wait down to 7 days, and by limiting its application to retail sales by licensed dealers (exempting private sales between individuals).

The "Brady Bill," as HCI now called it, was stopped only by an alternative offered by Rep. Bill McCollum (R-Fla.) to study the creation of a national instant check system for handgun sales. In 1989, Virginia became the first state to actually implement an instant check.

Throughout the Bush administration, the NRA managed to defend against HCI's major bills. But the NRA was clearly on its heels. The Bush administration refused to endorse a domestic ban on "assault weapons," but did propose a ban on ammunition magazines holding more than 15 rounds. The White House offered to sign the Brady Bill and a domestic ban on new semi-automatics (plus a registration requirement for grandfathered guns) if the gun control laws were included in a crime bill that the White House wanted. Gun rights advocates were shut out of the White House. Even with President Bush polling poorly against Bill Clinton in the late summer of 1992, the Bush administration refused any overtures from the gun lobby. The NRA declined to endorse Bush for reelection.

HCI endorsed Clinton. Ross Perot made the best showing of any third-party candidate since Theodore Roosevelt in 1912. Conventional wisdom is that he helped Clinton win, by attracting voters who were dissatisfied with Bush, but unwilling to vote for Clinton. Clinton won the election handily.

8. The Clinton Era

In the mid-1960s, South Carolina repealed its 1903 ban on handgun sales but enacted a new law limiting purchasers to one handgun a month. Three decades later, HCI picked up the idea, advanced it as a national goal, and concentrated on lobbying Virginia to enact it. HCI argued that gun traffickers purchased Virginia guns and resold them illegally in New York City. This claim was disputed, but many acknowledged that the trafficking issue was hurting Virginia's national reputation. The producers of Batman comics even published a special issue, "Seduction of the Gun," highlighting the claims about Virginia guns in "Gotham City," procured for the gangster "Chaka Zulu."

One-gun laws did not get national traction but they did eventually pass in Virginia in 1993, California in 1999, Maryland in 2003, and New Jersey in 2009. Inside the Beltway, the developments in Virginia and Maryland garnered close attention. HCI's success in normally pro-gun Virginia was seen by many in Washington as a sign of a changing national mood about firearms.

In the fall of 1993, the Brady Act easily passed Congress. The NRA put up a token effort to stop it, but focused primarily on influencing the final law through amendments. This yielded several important changes, including requirements that background check records of sales to lawful purchasers be destroyed and that the Brady handgun waiting period would sunset within five years, to be replaced by the National Instant Check System for retail sales of both handguns and long guns. HCI had already conceded the superiority of the instant check, so the primary issue was whether Attorney General Janet Reno would have to implement the instant check by a particular date.

As HCI grew more sophisticated politically, it abandoned the ambition of handgun prohibition. Despite protests from its old allies in the prohibition movement, HCI judged that public opinion did not support prohibition. HCI also concluded that many people were put off by the phrase "gun control," so the group transitioned to "gun safety" as its central theme. HCI's public education campaign began to emphasize injuries and deaths of children by gunshot, and the need to impose "gun safety" laws. During this period, HCI was successful at winning many state laws restricting gun possession by minors, and won unanimous support in the Senate for a federal statute restricting handgun possession by anyone under 18. 18 U.S.C. §922(x).

Violent crime, having declined during the early 1980s, started rising sharply late in the decade. By 1993-94, public and political concern over crime was at a level not seen since the late 1960s. HCI's "assault weapon" strategy keyed directly into this concern.

HCI gave its "assault weapon" ban proposal the oddly positive sounding title "Recreational Firearms Protection Act." The bill — which banned 19 guns by name, and about 200 by generic definition — included an appendix listing over 600 rifles and shotguns that were explicitly *not* banned. New ammunition magazines holding over 10 rounds also were banned. Along the way the bill picked up support through the addition of a 10-year sunset clause and provision for a federal study of the effectiveness of the ban.

The bill passed the Senate 56-43 in November 1993, and the stage was set for a showdown in the House, for which the NRA had been marshaling its resources. President Clinton committed his full resources to passing a gun control bill. With both sides all-in, the "assault weapon" ban passed the House by a single vote in May 1994.

The ban was part of a comprehensive crime bill, intended to be the signature achievement of the new President, given that his efforts toward a comprehensive health care law were foundering in Congress. After months of hard politicking, the Clinton crime bill became law in September 1994. The ban included a variety of distinctions that illustrate the demands of politics. For example, included in the "recreational" guns explicitly exempted from the ban was the Ruger Mini-14. The Ruger was functionally identical to banned guns like the AR-15. But at the time, it had a much larger base of owners than any other "assault weapon."

Also included in the crime bill was a measure that the NRA had not resisted. Senator Paul Wellstone (D-Minn.) successfully proposed a ban on gun possession by anyone under a domestic violence restraining order. Unlike the 1968 bans on gun possession by felons, alcoholics, etc., the Wellstone ban made no exception for the police or military. (The Wellstone ban would be the issue in *United States v. Emerson, infra,* the first modern federal case to provide a detailed exposition of the Second Amendment as an individual right.)

On close inspection, the "assault weapon" ban was mostly about appearances. The generic definition focused on accessories such as bayonet lugs and adjustable stocks. So manufacturers simply removed the prohibited features, renamed the guns, and were soon selling firearms that in internal operation were identical to the banned guns.

On the other hand, the ban on new magazines over ten rounds was real. For some guns of recent vintage, the price of grandfathered high capacity magazines increased tenfold. However, for many of the older model guns on the list, like the AR-15 (in production since the 1960s), the world-wide inventory of ammunition magazines was in the tens or even hundreds of millions.

Whatever the ban's practical impact, it had substantial political resonance. *Washington Post* columnist Charles Krauthammer, a gun prohibition advocate, expressed the view of knowledgeable people on both sides: The ban was "purely symbolic. . . . Its only real justification is not to reduce crime but to desensitize the public to the regulation of weapons in preparation for their ultimate confiscation." Charles Krauthammer, *Disarm the Citizenry. But Not Yet,* Wash. Post, Apr. 5, 1996 at A19.

There was large backlash by gun owners against the assault weapon ban in particular, and the Clinton gun control agenda in general. The 1994 elections were a catastrophe for Democratic gun control advocates. Democrats lost the Senate, and they also lost the House for the first time since 1953. President Clinton said several weeks later that "the NRA is the reason the Republicans control the House." Cleveland *Plain-Dealer,* Jan. 14, 1995. All of the Democratic congressional incumbents endorsed by the NRA retained their seats. A study of U.S. House races in 1994 and 1996 concluded that NRA endorsement could shift between 1 percent and 5 percent of the vote, depending on the number of NRA members in a district. NRA influence was most significant for endorsements of non-incumbents. Christopher B. Kenny, Michael McBurnett & David J. Bordua, *Does the National Rifle Association Influence Federal Elections?,* Independence Institute Issue Paper no. 8-2006. Dec. 2006.

In 1995, Clinton made a public appearance with former New Jersey Governor James Florio, who had been defeated for re-election in 1993, and whose Democratic party had lost control of both houses in the New Jersey legislature, in part because of the "assault weapon" ban in that state. Florio had given up the governorship in order to ban "assault weapons," said Clinton, and Clinton declared himself ready to lose his presidency over the same issue. Susan Page, *Prez Hits the Road, Assails GOP as He Launches Re-Election Bid,* Newsday, June 23, 1995 at A21.

As it turned out, Clinton's commitment would not be tested. For the next several years, Washington was stalemated over guns, and the only new enactments were appropriations riders inserted into spending bills. The 1994 elections did end any hopes of passing "Brady II," HCI's bill for mandatory national licensing of handgun owners, registration of all guns, and warrantless police inspections of the homes with "arsenals" (defined as 20 or more guns or as little as $50 worth of ammunition). H.R. 1321 and S. 631 (1995 Cong.).

The 1994 elections led to tremendous changes in state gun laws. State after state enacted Shall Issue licensing for handgun carry permits, preemption laws to eliminate local gun control, instant checks to replace state-level waiting periods for handgun purchases, range protection bills to prevent noise nuisance suits against shooting ranges, and other gun rights measures.

At the NRA, Neal Knox was working his way back from his 1984 exile, and some of his allies were winning spots on the board of directors. Knox even challenged Wayne LaPierre for Executive Vice-President, but lost. LaPierre countermaneuvered to help the actor Charlton Heston win election to the board, and within a few years, to win three consecutive terms as NRA President. Heston was a popular actor who had marched on Washington with Martin Luther King and was an outspoken advocate for civil rights when many in Hollywood stayed on the sidelines. He was a powerful public face for the NRA.

Knox believed that the NRA could succeed through the power of gun owners to vote politicians in or out of office. While LaPierre and Heston acknowledged the importance of grassroots voters, they considered the electoral anxiety of politicians an incomplete, limited tool. LaPierre and Heston saw the broader fight as a contest for the hearts and minds of the American people. In the long run, they believed, the NRA needed a broad base of public support from citizens who saw the NRA as it sees itself — a civic organization dedicated to mainstream American values.

Gun control advocates sniffed that Heston was merely putting a sunny face on the same old gun rights zealotry. But Heston and LaPierre achieved a measurable success, casting the NRA in a fashion where polling shows that it now enjoys the approval of the majority of Americans. *E.g.*, Lydia Saad, *NRA Viewed Favorably by Most Americans*, Gallup.com, Apr. 15, 2005 (60 percent favorable, 34 percent unfavorable).

9. The Re-emergence of the Second Amendment

In 1974, a Ph.D. candidate attempting to study the Second Amendment began his thesis: "Anyone undertaking research on the origins of the Second Amendment to the Constitution is bound to be impressed by the paucity of published materials on the subject." Charles J. Asbury, The Right to Keep and Bear Arms in America: The Origins and Application of the Second Amendment to the Constitution, at v. (Ph.D. dissertation in History, University of Michigan, 1974). To the chagrin of some and the delight of others, the Second Amendment by the mid-1990s had become a topic of serious academic debate.

Considered inconsequential by many courts and scholars, the Second Amendment now attracted a growing number of scholars who thought that the individual right view might be right after all. One of the first to reexamine the Second Amendment in a serious way was Don Kates. After his armed sojourn in Mississippi as a Yale law student during Freedom Summer in 1964, Kates went to work for the radical New York City lawyer William Kunstler, and eventually went to teach at St. Louis University Law School. Kates's pro-abortion stance was incompatible with his employer's Catholic mission and ultimately cost him his job. Kates left for private practice and continued his life as a scholar. He became a prolific legal commentator, focusing primarily on gun policy. One of his early works, a collection of pro-gun articles that he edited, Restricting Handguns: The Liberal Skeptics Speak Out (1979), featured a foreword by the very liberal Senator Frank Church (D-Idaho).

The late 1970s also saw the first legal scholarship from Stephen Halbrook, a philosophy professor at Howard University, who left academia for private law practice. Halbrook and Kates were unabashed gun-rights advocates, and Halbrook would later represent the NRA as its outside counsel. Halbrook and Kates both agreed that the Second Amendment prohibited gun bans, but Kates readily conceded the constitutionality of many forms of nonprohibitory controls, even though he considered some of them unwise in terms of criminology. Halbrook was a relentless miner of original sources. Kates's work tended toward interdisciplinary synthesis.

In 1983, the *Michigan Law Review* published Kates's *Handgun Prohibition and the Original Meaning of the Second Amendment*, 82 Mich. L. Rev. 204 (1983). It was only the third time in history that a top-ten law review had published a serious article on the Second Amendment. (The previous two were Feller & Gotting's 1966 *Northwestern* article, stating that the Second Amendment is only for the National Guard; and one from retired Maine Supreme Judicial Court Chief Justice Lucilius Emery, *The Constitutional Right to Keep and Bear Arms*, 28 Harv. L. Rev. 473 (1915), arguing that the Second Amendment is for the entire militia, but only for them, and therefore the Amendment poses no barrier to disarming women, children, the elderly, or the disabled.) The Michigan Law Review was prominent but the NRA took no chances. It bought reprints and mailed them to every constitutional law professor in the United States.

The ultimate impact within the legal academy was dramatic. Professor William Van Alstyne later recounted that "this pipsqueak Kates" convinced many of the leading constitutional law professors that the Second Amendment really was an individual right. Still, except for Yale's Akhil Amar, few law professors followed up on paradigm-shifting arguments in Kates's Michigan article.

The reason is difficult to know for sure. Professor Sanford Levinson later suggested that "the best explanation for the absence of the Second Amendment from the legal consciousness of the elite bar, including that component found in the legal academy, is derived from a mixture of sheer opposition to the idea of private ownership of guns and the perhaps subconscious fear that altogether plausible, perhaps even 'winning,' interpretations of the Second Amendment would present real hurdles to those of us supporting prohibitory regulation." Sanford Levinson, *The Embarrassing Second Amendment*, 99 Yale L.J. 637 (1989). Levinson's eminence as a legal scholar and credentials as a political liberal are unquestioned. So when he acknowledged that the individual rights view was probably correct, and that the legal academy had been avoiding the issue for fear of what it would find, it spurred law professors to begin to engage the Second Amendment.

The trickle started by Kates and Halbrook became a flood as successive scholars engaged the material and concluded that the Second Amendment really was an individual right. Even Harvard's Lawrence Tribe reevaluated and endorsed the individual rights view. Tribe's *American Constitutional Law* treatise defined liberal constitutionalism for a generation. Between the second edition (1987) and the third (1999), Tribe assessed the new scholarship and the third edition endorsed what was now called "the Standard Model" (a term Professor Glenn Reynolds borrowed from physics). The Standard Model understood the Second Amendment as an individual right of law-abiding people, including the right to own and carry handguns for defense. The Standard Model also accepted that many non-prohibitory controls were constitutionally permissible. Glenn Harlan Reynolds, *A Critical Guide to the Second Amendment*, 62 Tenn. L. Rev. 461 (1995).

By the mid-1990s, the growing acceptance of the Standard Model sent gun prohibition advocates in search of an alternative. Essayist Garry Wills, having previously described gun owners as "traitors" and homosexuals, declared in the *New York Review of Books* that only "crazy professors" believed in the individual right. The truth, according to Wills, was that the Second Amendment had no legal meaning, but was in fact a "clever trick" by James Madison. Garry Wills, *Why We Have No Right to Bear Arms*, N.Y. Rev. of Books, Sept. 21, 1995, at 62.[3] More sedately, the American Bar Association adhered to its 1975 position: "It is doubtful that the founding fathers had any intent in mind with regard to the meaning of this amendment." Ben R. Miller, *The Legal Basis for Firearms Controls*, 100 Ann. Rep. A.B.A. 1052, 1078 (1975).

The Wills/ABA view of a nihilist Second Amendment would soon be displaced by something far more plausible. The new path already had been cut by Dennis Henigan, who ranks with Halbrook and Kates as one of the most influential Second Amendment lawyers in the period between *Miller* and *Heller*.

Henigan had been a young corporate law partner in D.C. when he followed his ideals and went to work for the litigation arm of Handgun Control, Inc. Before Henigan, HCI had received pro bono help from some of the best liberal D.C. corporate law firms. Henigan developed this into an impressive network of pro bono support from corporate law firms all over United States.

It was Henigan who masterminded the wave of municipal government lawsuits against handgun manufacturers in the late 1990s, bringing in tobacco lawsuit plaintiffs' lawyers to run the litigation. Peter J. Boyer, *Big Guns*, New Yorker, May 17, 1999, p. 54. (The suits are detailed *infra*.) The suits nearly pushed major handgun manufacturers to capitulation in 2000. Although the strategy failed in the end, the lawsuits were the closest thing to a knockout punch ever devised by the gun control lobby.

But most important in the historical development of Second Amendment scholarship was Henigan's pivot away from the "collective right" or the "state's right" view of the Amendment. These terms were still commonly used in the lower federal courts in the 1990s, with little definition or purpose other than to perfunctorily dismiss individual right claims.

To close observers, the ground was shifting. The Supreme Court's 1989 *Verdugo-Urquidez* decision, *supra*, said that "people" was a term of art in the Bill of Rights; that it was used similarly in the First, Second, and Fourth Amendments to connote a class of individual persons. This made it difficult to claim that the right of the people in the Second Amendment was transformed by the prefatory militia clause into a right of the states.

So Henigan acknowledged an individual right: "It may well be that the right to keep and bear arms is individual in the sense that it may be asserted by an individual. But it is a narrow right indeed, for it is violated only by laws that, by regulating the individual's access to firearms, adversely affect the state's interest

---

3. Not the same publication as the *New York Times'* weekly Book Review section. The *New York Review of Books* was for decades the flagship publication of New York's left intelligentsia. For Wills's previous remarks on gun owners, see Garry Wills, *John Lennon's War*, Chi. Sun-Times, Dec. 12, 1980, at 56 (people who own guns for self-defense are "traitors"); Garry Wills, *Gun Rules . . . or Worldwide Gun Control?*, Phil. Inq., May 17, 1981, 15 8E ("the sordid race of gunsels") (literally, a "gunsel" is the passive partner in male homosexual intercourse).

in a strong militia." Further, Henigan suggested that the long list of collective rights and state's right cases should actually be considered narrow individual rights cases; those decisions were really endorsing a narrow individual right that existed for the state or collective purpose of the militia. Keith A. Ehrman & Dennis A. Henigan, *The Second Amendment in the Twentieth Century: Have You Seen Your Militia Lately?*, 15 U. Dayton L. Rev. 5 (1989).

Over the coming years, this theory was called various things, including "sophisticated collective right" (a backhanded admission that the older cases were simplistic). The most straightforward and precise name was "Narrow Individual Right."

Towards the end of the 1990s, scholars sympathetic to gun control took Henigan's thesis and elaborated it in considerable depth. Most prominent among these was the prolific Ohio State (and later, Fordham) history professor Saul Cornell, whose research is encapsulated in his book, A Well-Regulated Militia: The Founding Fathers and the Origins of Gun Control in America (2006). The theory is well presented in H. Richard Uviller & William G. Merkel, The Militia and the Right to Arms, or, How the Second Amendment Fell Silent (2002).

From the late 1990s until *Heller*, the proponents of the Standard Model and the Narrow Individual Right fought it out in journals and books. In what would have been a surprise to a law professor from 1970, the debate was conducted almost entirely on originalist grounds. The *Heller* decision showed that advocates on both sides of the issue, including Halbrook, Kates, and Henigan, all of whom filed briefs in *Heller*, had succeeded in their own ways. Halbrook and Kates had succeeded by pushing the Second Amendment back into the realm of respectable discussion about the Constitution, explaining the original understanding of the Constitution, and constructing the foundation for the Standard Model.

Henigan succeeded in offering a coherent but tightly bounded theory of the Second Amendment that would appeal to one wing of the Supreme Court. The Narrow Individual Right enjoyed the advantage that militia issues, not individual self-defense issues, were a major concern at the state ratifying conventions that asked for a federal bill of rights, and thereby set in motion the movement toward enactment of the Second Amendment. The Narrow Individual Right won four votes in *Heller*, led by Justice Stevens in dissent. Had John Kerry been elected President in 2004, different appointments probably would have resulted in a 6-3 win for the Stevens and Henigan view of the Second Amendment.

In contrast to the 5-4 split on standard vs. narrow individual right, the states/collective right that long dominated lower federal court decisions would be rejected 9-0 by the Court. Justice Stevens said that the Court had always considered the Second Amendment "[s]urely . . . a right that can be enforced by individuals." The only dispute was over the scope. The dissenters' arguments and the 9-0 rejection of states/collective rights are a direct outgrowth of the intellectual foundation constructed by Dennis Henigan. It is a rare advocate who is wise enough to see that his consistently winning arguments require major reformulation. Dennis Henigan was such an advocate.

From the primitive scholarship of the mid-twentieth century, the Second Amendment had developed into two serious schools of thought, each with some historical support. For the Supreme Court, this scholarship gave both the majority and the dissent an arsenal of arguments and counterarguments. But ultimately the full explanation for the Court's affirmation of the right to keep and bear arms lies not in originalism but in living constitutionalism.

10.   Columbine and the 2000 Election

At the federal level, gun control in 1995-98 was less of an issue than it had been in the previous several years. One side had the Presidency, the other had the Congress. Neither side could enact more than minor items on its agenda. The Clinton administration began pushing harder once the 1996 election was over, and accomplished what it could through regulations, such as the import ban on 58 more long gun models in 1998. *See Springfield, Inc. v. Buckles*, 292 F.3d 813 (D.C. Cir. 2002) (upholding the import ban by relying on deference to ATF's definition that "sporting" includes only what hunting guides recommend for their clients).

The Columbine High School murders in April 1999 changed everything. Twelve students and one teacher were murdered by two students who had planned their crime for over a year. There had been school mass murders as early as 1927, when a disgruntled school board member used explosives to murder 44 people in Bath, Michigan. But nothing shocked the nation like Columbine.

One change that resulted from Columbine was police tactics. Although the Columbine murders began while a school security officer was on the campus, and another officer arrived almost instantly, neither officer entered the school building to pursue the killers. Most of the killing happened in the school library, where students were methodically murdered while dozens of police officers were just a few yards away and could have entered from a door that opened to the outside. Post-Columbine, police tactics changed to emphasize immediate action against "active shooters," rather than waiting for a SWAT team to assemble and then clearing rooms one at time.[4]

Columbine prompted California to pass a one-gun-a-month law, but other than that, legal changes at the state level were few. Colorado Governor Bill Owens (R) proposed a five-point gun control program that was rejected by the state legislature the next year. Colorado and Oregon (where a school shooting had taken place in 1998) both passed initiatives requiring private sellers to conduct background checks on buyers at gun shows.

Three of the four Columbine murder weapons had been obtained by another student, acting as a straw purchaser for the killers. She had bought them at a gun show. This transformed gun shows into a major national issue. A few weeks after Columbine, Vice-President Al Gore cast the tie-breaking vote in the U.S. Senate for a bill that would have given the ATF the administrative power to shut down any or all gun shows in the United States.

---

4. The new tactical approach did not become universal; in July 2011, a man spent 90 minutes murdering young people at a youth camp on an island in Norway. Local police, rather than acting immediately, waited for the arrival of a special police team from Oslo, 45 miles away. The killer surrendered the moment he saw a police officer.

"It doesn't take the NRA long to reload," warned Rep. Anthony Weiner (D-N.Y.), who objected to the House waiting a few weeks before taking up gun control legislation. What eventually passed the House was a bill (similar to the Colorado and Oregon laws) requiring background checks on all gun show sales, not just sales by licensed dealers. The bill also would have repealed the D.C. handgun ban.

None of the bills passed. The House and Senate negotiators could not agree about what should happen when the National Instant Check System failed to produce a prompt approval or denial of a proposed private sale. The Republican leadership and the NRA wanted to let the sale go ahead after 24 hours. The Clinton administration and HCI insisted on delaying the sale for up to three days, by which point the gun show (almost all are held on weekends) would be over, and the sale would never take place. Ultimately, gun rights advocates in Congress did not want any new laws and gun control advocates wanted much more than Congress was willing to pass. For the Clinton administration, this kept the issue active for the upcoming 2000 election.

On Mother's Day 2000, over a hundred thousand people participated in a gun-control rally at the National Mall in Washington. Many others participated in smaller rallies around the country. This "Million Mom March" was organized by Donna Dees-Thomases, a former Democratic Senate staffer who was the sister-in-law of Hillary Clinton's best friend. The Office of the First Lady provided substantial support to the organizers. The hope was that angry mothers would change the politics of gun control in the United States. Their most prominent supporter was television show host Rosie O'Donnell, who had thrown herself into gun-control advocacy after Columbine, urging that all guns be banned, and anyone who possessed a gun serve a mandatory sentence. O'Donnell later observed that she had probably hurt her cause by being too "shrill."

The 2000 presidential election promised to be the great showdown on gun control. In the Democratic primaries, former Senator Bill Bradley (D-N.J.) attempted to ride the issue by proposing gun controls that went beyond what Vice-President Gore supported. Gore countered effectively by emphasizing to his own record in support of gun control, bolstered by a photograph of him in the embrace of Sarah Brady.

But by the fall, gun control no longer looked like a winning issue. The million mom movement had fizzled, and a few years later would simply be absorbed into HCI. Gore's running mate, Connecticut Senator Joe Lieberman, tried to convince crowds that "Al Gore and I respect the Second Amendment right to bear arms." Cosmo Macero, Jr., Campaign 2000; *Gore Dependent on Strong Turnout by Pennsylvanians*, Boston Herald, Nov. 3, 2000 at 5.

When *Emerson, infra,* was being argued in the Fifth Circuit in the spring of 2000, the Clinton Department of Justice told the judges that the Second Amendment protected *no* individual right (not even for a National Guardsman on active duty). In response to a letter from a concerned citizen, Solicitor General Seth Waxman articulated the DOJ's position that "the Second Amendment does not extend an individual right to keep and bear arms." Quoting the citizen's letter, Waxman concurred that the government believes that it "could 'take guns away from the public,' and 'restrict ownership of rifles, pistols and shotguns from all people.'" Letter from Seth Waxman, Aug. 22, 2000. The NRA put Waxman's "take guns" quote on billboards in swing states.

George W. Bush won Florida by a few hundred votes, and thus the election by a single electoral vote. If not for the gun issue, the election would not have been close. The gun issue cost Gore Missouri, West Virginia (voting Republican in a close election for the first time in a century), Gore's home state of Tennessee, Clinton's home state of Arkansas, and Florida. President Clinton later wrote that the NRA had been the decisive reason that Gore had lost. Bill Clinton, My Life 928 (2004).

11. The Great American Gun War Winds Down

For the next decade, very little went right for gun control advocates. Had Gore been President on September 11, 2001, his version of the PATRIOT Act might have included many gun control measures. President Bush's PATRIOT Act did not. Attorney General John Ashcroft repudiated the Johnson-Nixon era DOJ position on the Second Amendment, and accepted the Standard Model. *See* Memorandum for the Attorney General from Steven G. Bradbury, Principal Deputy Assistant Attorney General, Office of Legal Counsel, Howard C. Nielson, Jr., Deputy Assistant Attorney General, Office of Legal Counsel, and C. Kevin Marshall, Acting Deputy Assistant Attorney General, Office of Legal Counsel, Re: Whether the Second Amendment Secures an Individual Right (Aug. 24, 2004); Memorandum for All United States' Attorneys from the Attorney General, Re: United States v. Emerson (Nov. 9, 2001).

The Clinton administration had been working for years with many allies at the United Nations toward an international gun control treaty. But the July 2001 U.N. gun control conference ended with only a non-binding Programme of Action. Even that was watered down at the insistence of the U.S. delegation, including John Bolton, the Undersecretary of State for Arms Control and International Security. The absolute red line for the U.S. delegation was insistence that the document not delegitimize the transfer of arms to "non-state actors" (e.g., rebel groups, such as the Kurds fighting Saddam Hussein, or, in earlier times, anti-Nazi partisans, or the American Revolutionaries). (For more on the U.N. Programme of Action, see online Chapter 13.)

September 11 led to wave of gun-buying by Americans, as did the inept government response to Hurricane Katrina in 2005. "Shall issue" concealed carry laws continued to advance state by state. In the early 1990s, gun control advocates had planned "to do to handguns" what other advocates "ha[d] done to cigarettes . . . turn gun ownership from a personal-choice issue to a repulsive, antisocial health hazard." Harold Henderson, *Guns 'n' Poses*, Chicago Reader, Dec. 16, 1994, at 8, 24 (interview with gun-control advocate Dr. Robert Tanz). Now, the Shall Issue laws were making it routine for Americans to be around guns when they went to a shopping mall, a public park, or almost anywhere else.

One reason for the proliferation of Shall Issue laws in particular, and of the political success of the gun rights movement in general, was its success in the communications and organization contest. Ever since gun control became an important national issue in the 1960s, gun control advocates had enjoyed strong support in what is today called "the mainstream media" (MSM). Not all MSM stories were biased, but when there was bias, it almost always tilted pro-control. Gun rights advocates felt that it was difficult to get their side of the story out to the general public. But hostile media coverage also had the unintended

consequence of increasing NRA membership, as Second Amendment suppor-
ters turned to the one group that they felt spoke for their interests. Brian Anse
Patrick, The National Rifle Association and the Media: The Motivating Effects of
Negative Coverage (2002).

In the late 1960s and early 1970s, the NRA was one of the first major organizations to successfully use direct mail. Although direct mail techniques are
now well developed, the NRA blazed trails in the use of mass mailings to encourage supporters to take particular political actions and to make donations for
special legislative projects. Eventually, almost every interest group in the United
States developed effective direct mail programs, but for a while, the NRA's
sophisticated program made it unusually effective when compared to other
interest groups.

By the early 1990s, the proliferation of fax machines and computer modems
provided a vast boost to local gun rights groups. In the days before the Worldwide
Web and e-mail became the primary means of high-speed communication, local
gun activists used computer bulletin boards and other text-based electronic communications to mobilize supporters. Later in the 1990s, the national and local gun
groups moved quickly to utilize websites and e-mail. There was, of course, no
reason why gun control groups could not do the same, and eventually they did.
But for every new technology — from fax machines to Facebook — they tended to
trail the gun rights organizations in the exploitation of new technology.

There are several possible explanations for the gap in the communications
race: The first is simple necessity, in the sense that gun rights groups had a
communications problem to solve, whereas gun control groups could rely on
a usually sympathetic MSM. Second, the gun control groups had a much larger
base of activists. This meant that they had more to gain from enhancing communications with their membership; increased the possibility of there being
sheer numbers of technologically adept people within the group. Third, the
personality type that is often attracted to gun rights — the individualist interested in proficiency with tools (e.g., guns) — may be a type more willing to learn
how to use new tools.

Whatever the underlying reasons, the growing ability of gun rights activists
to end-run the MSM, and to disseminate their own information and viewpoint, is
one important reason for their political success. Brian Anse Patrick, Rise of the
Anti-Media: Informing America's Concealed Weapon Carry Movement (2009);
The National Rifle Association, *supra*.

Gun ownership itself continued to grow, nearly tripling from about one gun
per three persons after World War II, to about one gun per person in the twenty-
first century. (See table on next page.)

By 2004, the federal "assault weapon" ban expired pursuant to its own
terms. HCI changed its name to "the Brady Campaign," eliminating the grating
connotations of "control," and emphasizing its popular public spokescouple.
But the political slide continued. "We've hit rock bottom," Sarah Brady told a
friendly interviewer. Arnold Grossman, One Nation Under Guns 48 (2006).

The 2004 Democratic presidential nominee, John Kerry (Mass.), had a
strong record of supporting gun control, but he was pretty good at shooting
clay pigeons with a shotgun. Despite claiming to be a friend of the Second
Amendment, he too ran into trouble on gun control. When union supporters
presented him with a rifle at a West Virginia rally in September, the gun turned

Year	Total U.S. Civilian Guns	U.S. Population (in thousands)	Guns per Capita
1948	53,203,031	146,091	0.36
1949	55,406,460	148,666	0.37
1950	57,902,081	151,871	0.38
1951	59,988,664	153,970	0.39
1952	61,946,315	156,369	0.40
1953	63,945,235	158,946	0.40
1954	65,558,052	161,881	0.40
1955	67,387,135	165,058	0.41
1956	69,435,933	168,078	0.41
1957	71,416,509	171,178	0.42
1958	73,163,450	174,153	0.42
1959	75,338,188	177,136	0.43
1960	77,501,065	179,972	0.43
1961	79,536,616	182,976	0.43
1962	81,602,984	185,739	0.44
1963	83,834,808	188,434	0.44
1964	86,357,701	191,085	0.45
1965	89,478,922	193,457	0.46
1966	93,000,989	195,499	0.48
1967	97,087,751	197,375	0.49
1968	102,302,251	199,312	0.51
1969	107,111,820	201,298	0.53
1970	111,917,733	203,798.7	0.55
1971	116,928,781	206,817.5	0.57
1972	122,304,980	209,274.9	0.58
1973	128,016,673	211,349.2	0.61
1974	134,587,281	213,333.6	0.63
1975	139,915,125	215,456.6	0.65
1976	145,650,789	217,553.9	0.67
1977	150,748,000	219,760.9	0.69
1978	156,164,518	222,098.2	0.70
1979	161,888,861	224,568.6	0.72
1980	167,681,587	227,224.7	0.74
1981	173,262,755	229,465.7	0.76
1982	178,218,890	231,664.4	0.77
1983	182,273,263	233,792.0	0.78
1984	186,683,867	235,824.9	0.79
1985	190,658,136	237,923.7	0.80
1986	194,182,072	240,132.8	0.81
1987	198,526,508	242,288.9	0.82
1988	203,306,821	244,499.0	0.83
1989	208,489,609	246,819.2	0.84
1990	212,823,547	249,438.7	0.85
1991	216,695,946	252,127.4	0.86
1992	222,067,343	254,994.5	0.87
1993	228,660,966	257,746.1	0.89
1994	235,604,001	260,289.2	0.91
1995	240,770,928	262,764.9	0.92
1996	245,379,137	265,189.8	0.93
1997	249,748,101	267,743.6	0.93
1998	254,199,406	270,248.0	0.94
1999	257,991,026	272,690.8	0.95

Year	Total U.S. Civilian Guns	U.S. Population (in thousands)	Guns per Capita
2000	261,592,676	281,421.9	0.93
2001	264,360,377	285,317.6	0.93
2002	267,556,289	287,973.9	0.93
2003	270,695,992	290,809.8	0.93
2004	273,643,000	293,655.4	0.93
2005	278,796,487	295,516.6	0.94
2006	284,514,812	298,379.9	0.95
2007	290,976,636	301,231.2	0.97
2008	297,853,478	304,094.0	0.98
2009	306,822,660	306,771.5	1.00

Sources: Gary Kleck, Targeting Guns: Firearms and Their Control 96-97 (1997), and Bureau of Alcohol, Tobacco, Firearms and Explosives, *Annual Firearms Manufacture and Export Report, available at* http://www.atf.gov/firearms/stats/index.htm.

out to be one that Kerry had voted to ban. The NRA chided Kerry in ads featuring an exquisitely coiffed French poodle and the headline "This dog won't hunt." In smaller text, the ads detailed Kerry's gun votes as a Senator. The poodle mockery attacked Kerry's gun control record, but was also a culture war slap at the Boston Brahmin, married to a billionaire heiress, who told the press that for relaxation, he wrote French poetry. That President Bush, rather than President Kerry, appointed the Justices to replace William Rehnquist and Sandra Day O'Connor turned out to make all the difference a few years later in *Heller* (Chapter 9).

The last of the municipal lawsuits against gun manufacturers were shut down by the 2006 Protection of Lawful Commerce in Arms Act, which passed in significant part due to the hard work of Senate Minority Leader Harry Reid (D-Nev.). Senator Charles Schumer, who in 1994 masterminded House passage of the "assault weapon" ban, later said that he believed the Second Amendment was an individual right. Senator Hillary Clinton said the same during the 2008 presidential primaries: "You know, I believe in the Second Amendment. People have a right to bear arms." Campaigning in Pennsylvania, she fondly recalled her father teaching her to use a shotgun on family vacations, and her mailers warned voters about Senator Barack Obama's anti-gun views. Obama, for his part, insisted that he also believed the Second Amendment to be an individual right.

None of this is to say that Schumer, Clinton, or Obama believed that the Second Amendment prevented the various gun control proposals that they supported. But it was quite a change from 1988 when the Democratic Party could nominate a candidate who would forthrightly declare that there was no individual right.

By the time *Heller* arrived at the Supreme Court, the great gun control wars of the late twentieth century were receding into history. The 1976 D.C. handgun ban was no longer the hopeful beginning of national trend. Now it was a vestigial oddity, out of step with a national consensus. Politically, gun control had evolved to mean something entirely different from gun prohibition. The public had rejected the choice between Neal Knox's hard corps and the National Coalition to Ban Handguns. The American wanted gun rights *and* gun control. And that is what the political system had provided, and what the Supreme Court in *Heller* and *McDonald* would affirm. *See* Adam Winkler, Gunfight (2011) (*Heller* as the triumph of the majority's belief that gun rights and gun control can co-exist).

See also Cass R. Sunstein, *Second Amendment Minimalism:* Heller *as* Griswold, 122 Harv. L. Rev. 246 (2008) (*Heller* as comparable to *Brown v. Board of Education*, in that it was the product of a mature social movement that had already won the hearts and minds of most of the majority; comparable to *Griswold* in that the case involved a law that was an extreme outlier compared to the rest of the nation); Reva B. Siegel, *Dead or Alive: Originalism as Popular Constitutionalism in* Heller, 122 Harv. L. Rev. 191 (2008) (*Heller* as the result of a successful social movement); David B. Kopel, *The Right to Arms in the Living Constitution*, 2009 Cardozo L. Rev. De Novo 99 (applying the living constitutionalism theories of Jack Balkin and Bruce Ackerman to post-ratification history of the Second Amendment).

The graph below shows changing public answers to the Gallup Poll question, "Do you think there should or should not be a law that would ban the possession of handguns, except by the police and other authorized persons?" When Gallup first asked the question, in 1959, prohibition enjoyed a nearly 2:1 advantage; by 2011, prohibition was opposed by almost 3:1. All the data are available on http://Gallup.com.

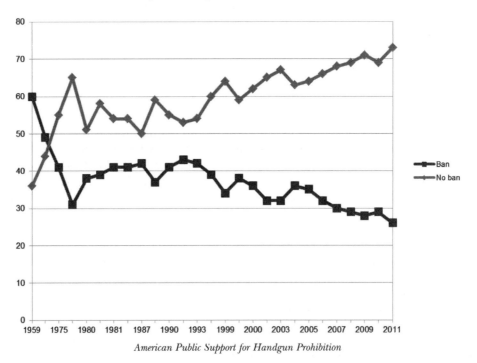

American Public Support for Handgun Prohibition

D. *Federal Regulation of Firearms in the Modern Era*

In this section, we detail the federal gun law that developed between *Miller* (Chapter 7) in 1939 and *Heller* (Chapter 9) in 2008 under the federal Gun Control Act. Most of the cases involve the Gun Control Act of 1968, which remains the major federal statute on gun control. This section examines the details of these various legislative and regulatory measures. This treatment is divided into the following eight subsections:

Section 1:   The Challenge of Defining Specially Regulated Firearms
Section 2:   Regulation of Retail Sales of Ordinary Firearms
               a. Regulation of Buyers
               b. Regulation of Sellers
Section 3:   Private Sales and Private Manufacturers: The Secondary Market and Gun Shows
Section 4:   "Sporting Use" as a Marker of Legitimate Firearms
Section 5:   Policing Illegal Guns
Section 6:   Regulation by Litigation: Suing the Gun Industry and the Legislative Response
Section 7:   "Assault Weapons" Restrictions
Section 8:   Interstate Transportation of Firearms

1. The Challenge of Defining Specially Regulated Firearms

What is a firearm? If someone sells a replacement barrel, or new grips for a pistol, has he sold a "firearm"? Under federal law, the answer is "no." According to federal law, a "firearm" is the frame or receiver. As online Chapter 15 details, the frame or receiver is the part of the gun that contains the "action," which is the collection of parts that cause the ammunition to load, fire, and unload. By regulation, the frame/receiver (and thus, for regulatory purposes, the firearm) is defined as "[t]hat part of a firearm which provides housing for the hammer, bolt or breechblock, and firing mechanism, and which is usually threaded at its forward portion to receive the barrel." 27 CFR §478.11. Under federal law, a serial number must be stamped or engraved onto the frame or receiver.

Gun parts separated from the receiver are not regulated by the GCA. Purchase or sale of a gun barrel, or a stock, or trigger, for example, is not controlled by the GCA. If you have a receiver without a barrel, stock, or trigger, you do not have a usable gun. But you do have a "firearm" according to the GCA. Conversely, you can buy and sell barrels or triggers without ever coming within the ambit of the GCA.

For most guns, deciding what constitutes the "receiver" is easy. However, because firearms are manufactured in a variety of configurations, deciding what to designate as the regulated receiver can sometimes be complicated. For example, one of the most popular contemporary firearms is the AR-15 semi-automatic rifle — the civilian nonautomatic counterpoint of the M-4 and M-16 rifles used by the U.S. military — and its many variants. It has both an upper receiver (which houses the bolt assembly and firing pin and connects to the barrel) and a lower receiver (which houses the hammer and trigger assembly). For this gun, the ATF considers the lower receiver to be the regulated firearm.

On the other hand, the less common FNC rifle (created by Fabrique Nationale, in Belgium) also has an upper receiver (which connects to the barrel and houses the bolt assembly and firing pin) and a lower receiver (which houses the hammer and firing mechanism). For the FNC rifle, the ATF considers the *upper* receiver to be the regulated firearm. ATF ruling 2008-1. So for the FNC, the serial number will appear on the upper receiver, which constitutes the "gun" for regulatory purposes. For AR-15 type rifles, the serial number will be on the lower receiver and the lower receiver constitutes the regulated firearm.

Another important distinction is between ordinary civilian firearms and guns regulated under the more stringent provisions of the NFA. Here, things get much more complicated.

Assume you have a "stripped" receiver for a .22 caliber firearm. Your stripped receiver does not have a barrel, trigger, hammer, or bolt, and in this condition performs none of the functions of a gun. Still, your receiver is a "firearm" under the Gun Control Act.

Also assume you have various parts that are made to fit your stripped receiver, including two barrels. One barrel is 6 inches long, the other barrel is 20 inches long. Finally, assume you have two parts that allow you to handle the gun. One of them is a pistol grip. The other is a shoulder stock.

If you assemble the 6-inch barrel and the pistol grip onto the receiver, you have just made a handgun, according to federal law. If you are not otherwise prohibited from owning a firearm, you have not violated any federal law. (It is legal, under federal law, to manufacture or assemble firearms for personal use. A federal license is required to manufacture them for commercial sale.)

If instead you assemble the 20-inch barrel and the shoulder stock to the receiver, according to federal law, you have just made a rifle. Again, if you are permitted to own a firearm, your actions are perfectly legal under federal law.

Now assume you assemble the 6-inch barrel and the shoulder stock to the receiver. Suddenly, you are in serious trouble. You have just made a NFA short rifle. If you do not have a NFA manufacturing license, you have just committed a felony. By federal law, the shoulder stock makes the gun into a rifle. If a rifle's barrel is less than 16 inches, then it is a short barreled rifle, regulated under the NFA. You are permitted to own or assemble such a rifle only if you have complied with the NFA tax and registration provisions.

Let's try one more. Suppose you do not attach anything to your stripped receiver. You simply *own* the receiver as well as various parts with which you *could* assemble a NFA short rifle — namely, the shoulder stock and the 6-inch barrel. Does the mere fact that you possess these unassembled components mean that you must obtain a NFA license? If a company sells components that *could* be used to build ordinary rifles or handguns, *but also* could be assembled to build NFA short rifles, must the company sell only to persons who have gone through the tax and registration paperwork to own NFA short rifles? That is the question the Supreme Court decided in *United States v. Thompson/Center Arms Company*, excerpted below.

A similar question arose in *United States v. Drasen*, 665 F. Supp. 598 (N.D. Ill. 1987), *rev'd*, 845 F.2d 731 (7th Cir. 1988), where the defendant owned a receiver and various unassembled components including a barrel slightly shorter than the 16 inches necessary to avoid classification as a NFA short barrel. If he assembled the barrel to the receiver, he would have had a NFA short rifle, which would be illegal because he had not paid the NFA tax or filled out the NFA registration form. The defendant also owned a "flash suppressor" (a device that is attached to the muzzle end of the barrel to reduce the flash caused by powder that does not fully burn in the barrel). If he permanently attached the flash suppressor to the barrel, then it would be long enough to avoid classification as a short-barreled rifle and the NFA would not apply. The question is how the law should treat the case where one possesses these parts but has not assembled them into a functional rifle with a less-than-16-inch barrel. Does the possession of these components constitute the felony of possessing a NFA short rifle without the necessary tax and registration? The *Drasen* case is discussed by the Supreme Court in *Thompson/Center.*

United States v. Thompson/Center Arms Company
504 U.S. 505 (1992)

Justice Souter announced the judgment of the Court and delivered an opinion, in which The Chief Justice and Justice O'Connor join.

Section 5821 of the National Firearms Act (NFA or Act), see 26 U.S.C. §5849, levies a tax of $200 per unit upon anyone "making" a "firearm" as that term is defined in the Act. Neither pistols nor rifles with barrels 16 inches long or longer are firearms within the NFA definition, but rifles with barrels less than 16 inches long, known as short-barreled rifles, are. §5845(a)(3). This case presents the question whether a gun manufacturer "makes" a short-barreled rifle when it packages as a unit a pistol together with a kit containing a shoulder stock and a 21-inch barrel, permitting the pistol's conversion into an unregulated long-barreled rifle,[1] or, if the pistol's barrel is left on the gun, a short-barreled rifle that is regulated. We hold that the statutory language may not be construed to require payment of the tax under these facts.

I

The word "firearm" is used as a term of art in the NFA. It means, among other things, "a rifle having a barrel or barrels of less than 16 inches in length. . . ." §5845(a)(3). "The term 'rifle' means a weapon designed or redesigned, made or remade, and intended to be fired from the shoulder and designed or redesigned and made or remade to use the energy of the explosive in a fixed cartridge to fire only a single projectile through a rifled bore for each single pull of the trigger, and shall include any such weapon which may be readily restored to fire a fixed cartridge." §5845(c).

The consequences of being the maker of a firearm are serious. Section 5821(a) imposes a tax of $200 "for each firearm made," which "shall be paid by the person making the firearm," §5821(b). Before one may make a firearm, one must obtain the approval of the Secretary of the Treasury, §5822, and §5841 requires that the "manufacturer, importer, and maker . . . register each firearm he manufactures, imports, or makes" in a central registry maintained by the Secretary of the Treasury. A maker who fails to comply with the NFA's provisions

---

1. Unregulated, that is, under the NFA. [The normal GCA laws would still apply. — Eds.]

is subject to criminal penalties of up to 10 years' imprisonment and a fine of up to $10,000, or both, which may be imposed without proof of willfulness or knowledge. §5871.

Respondent Thompson/Center Arms Company manufactures a single-shot pistol called the "Contender," designed so that its handle and barrel can be removed from its "receiver," the metal frame housing the trigger, hammer, and firing mechanism. See 27 CFR §179.11 (1991) (definition of frame or receiver). For a short time in 1985, Thompson/Center also manufactured a carbine-conversion kit consisting of a 21-inch barrel, a rifle stock, and a wooden fore-end. If one joins the receiver with the conversion kit's rifle stock, the 21-inch barrel, and the rifle fore-end, the product is a carbine rifle with a 21-inch barrel. If, however, the shorter, pistol length barrel is not removed from the receiver when the rifle stock is added, one is left with a 10-inch or "short-barreled" carbine rifle. The entire conversion, from pistol to long-barreled rifle takes only a few minutes; conversion to a short-barreled rifle takes even less time.

In 1985, the Bureau of Alcohol, Tobacco and Firearms advised Thompson/Center that when its conversion kit was possessed or distributed together with the Contender pistol, the unit constituted a firearm subject to the NFA. Thompson/Center responded by paying the $200 tax for a single such firearm, and submitting an application for permission under 26 U.S.C. §5822 "to make, use, and segregate as a single unit" a package consisting of a serially numbered pistol, together with an attachable shoulder stock and a 21-inch barrel. Thompson/Center then filed a refund claim. After more than six months had elapsed without action on it, the company brought this suit in the United States Claims Court under the Tucker Act, 28 U.S.C. §1491, arguing that the unit registered was not a firearm within the meaning of the NFA because Thompson/Center had not assembled a short-barreled rifle from its components. The Claims Court entered summary judgment for the Government, concluding that the Contender pistol together with its conversion kit is a firearm within the meaning of the NFA. 19 Cl. Ct. 725 (1990).

The Court of Appeals for the Federal Circuit reversed, holding that a short-barreled rifle "actually must be assembled" in order to be "made" within the meaning of the NFA. 924 F.2d 1041, 1043 (1991). The Court of Appeals expressly declined to follow the decision of the Court of Appeals for the Seventh Circuit in *United States v. Drasen*, 845 F.2d 731, cert. denied, 488 U.S. 909 (1988), which had held that an unassembled "complete parts kit" for a short-barreled rifle was in fact a short-barreled rifle for purposes of the NFA. We granted certiorari to resolve this conflict. 502 U.S. 807 (1991).

II

The NFA provides that "the term 'make,' and the various derivatives of such word, shall include manufacturing. . . ." But the provision does not expressly address the question whether a short-barreled rifle can be "made" by the aggregation of finished parts that can readily be assembled into one. The Government contends that assembly is not necessary; Thompson/Center argues that it is.

A

The Government urges us to view the shipment of the pistol with the kit just as we would the shipment of a bicycle that requires some home assembly. "The fact that a short-barrel rifle, or any other 'firearm,' is possessed or sold in a partially unassembled state does not remove it from regulation under the Act." Brief for United States 6.

The Government's analogy of the partially assembled bicycle to the packaged pistol and conversion kit is not, of course, exact. While each example includes some unassembled parts, the crated bicycle parts can be assembled into nothing but a bicycle, whereas the contents of Thompson/Center's package can constitute a pistol, a long-barreled rifle, or a short-barreled version. These distinctions, however, do define the issues raised by the Government's argument, the first of which is whether the aggregation and segregation of separate parts that can be assembled only into a short-barreled rifle and are sufficient for that purpose amount to "making" that firearm, or whether the firearm is not "made" until the moment of final assembly. This is the issue on which the Federal and Seventh Circuits are divided.

We think the language of the statute provides a clear answer on this point. The definition of "make" includes not only "putting together," but also "manufacturing . . . or otherwise producing a firearm." If as Thompson/Center submits, a firearm were only made at the time of final assembly (the moment the firearm was "put together"), the additional language would be redundant. Congress must, then, have understood "making" to cover more than final assembly, and some disassembled aggregation of parts must be included. Since the narrowest example of a combination of parts that might be included is a set of parts that could be used to make nothing but a short-barreled rifle, the aggregation of such a set of parts, at the very least, must fall within the definition of "making" such a rifle.

This is consistent with the holdings of every Court of Appeals, except the court below, to consider a combination of parts that could only be assembled into an NFA-regulated firearm, either under the definition of rifle at issue here or under similar statutory language. See *United States v. Drasen*, supra; *United States v. Endicott*, 803 F.2d 506, 508-09 (9th Cir. 1986) (unassembled silencer is a silencer); *United States v. Luce*, 726 F.2d 47, 48-49 (1st Cir. 1984) (same); *United States v. Lauchli*, 371 F.2d 303, 311-13 (7th Cir. 1966) (unassembled machineguns are machineguns).[3] We thus reject the broad language of the Court of Appeals for the Federal Circuit to the extent that it would mean that a disassembled complete short-barreled rifle kit must be assembled before it has been "made" into a short-barreled rifle. The fact that the statute would serve almost no purpose if this were the rule only confirms the reading we have given it.

We also think that a firearm is "made" on facts one step removed from the paradigm of the aggregated parts that can be used for nothing except

---

3. In *Drasen*, a complete-parts kit was sold with a flash suppressor, which, if affixed to the rifle barrel, would have extended it beyond the regulated length. See *Drasen*, 845 F.2d at 737. Because the *Drasen* court concluded that such a flash suppressor was not a part of the rifle's barrel . . . its holding is consistent with ours.

assembling a firearm. Two courts to our knowledge have dealt in some way with claims that when a gun other than a firearm was placed together with a further part or parts that would have had no use in association with the gun except to convert it into a firearm, a firearm was produced. See *United States v. Kokin*, 365 F.2d 595, 596 (3rd Cir. 1966) (carbine together with all parts necessary to convert it into a machinegun is a machinegun), cert. denied, 385 U.S. 987 (1966); see also *United States v. Zeidman*, 444 F.2d 1051, 1053 (7th Cir. 1971) (pistol and attachable shoulder stock found "in different drawers of the same dresser" constitute a short-barreled rifle). Here it is true, of course, that some of the parts could be used without ever assembling a firearm, but the likelihood of that is belied by the utter uselessness of placing the converting parts with the others except for just such a conversion. Where the evidence in a given case supports a finding of such uselessness, the case falls within the fair intendment of "otherwise producing a firearm." See 26 U.S.C. §5845(i).

Here, however, we are not dealing with an aggregation of parts that can serve no useful purpose except the assembly of a firearm, or with an aggregation having no ostensible utility except to convert a gun into such a weapon. There is, to be sure, one resemblance to the latter example in the sale of the Contender with the converter kit, for packaging the two has no apparent object except to convert the pistol into something else at some point. But the resemblance ends with the fact that the unregulated Contender pistol can be converted not only into a short-barreled rifle, which is a regulated firearm, but also into a long-barreled rifle, which is not. The packaging of pistol and kit has an obvious utility for those who want both a pistol and a regular rifle, and the question is whether the mere possibility of their use to assemble a regulated firearm is enough to place their combined packaging within the scope of "making" one.

1

Neither the statute's language nor its structure provides any definitive guidance. Thompson/Center suggests guidance may be found in some subsections of the statute governing other types of weapons by language that expressly covers combinations of parts. The definition of "machinegun," for example, was amended by the Gun Control Act of 1968 to read that "the term shall also include . . . any combination of parts from which a machinegun can be assembled if such parts are in the possession or under the control of a person." 26 U.S.C. §5845(b). In 1986, the definition of "silencer" was amended by the Firearms Owners' Protection Act to "include any combination of parts, designed or redesigned, and intended for use in assembling or fabricating a firearm silencer. . . ." See 26 U.S.C. §5845(a)(7); 18 U.S.C. §921(a)(24).

Thompson/Center stresses the contrast between these references to "any combination of parts" and the silence about parts in the definition of rifle in arguing that no aggregation of parts can suffice to make the regulated rifle. This argument is subject to a number of answers, however. First, it sweeps so broadly as to conflict with the statutory definition of "make," applicable to all firearms, which implies that a firearm may be "made" even where not fully "put together." If this were all, of course, the conflict might well be resolved in Thompson/Center's favor. We do not, however, read the machinegun and silencer definitions as contrasting with the definition of rifle in such a way as to raise a conflict with the broad concept of "making."

The definition of "silencer" is now included in the NFA only by reference, see 26 U.S.C. §5845(a)(7), whereas its text appears only at 18 U.S.C. §921(a)(24), in a statute that itself contains no definition of "make." Prior to 1986 the definition of "firearm" in the NFA included "a muffler or a silencer for any firearm whether or not such firearm is included within this definition." 26 U.S.C. §5845(a)(7) (1982 ed.). Two Courts of Appeals held this language to include unassembled silencers that could be readily and easily assembled. See *United States v. Endicott*, 803 F.2d at 508-509; *United States v. Luce*, 726 F.2d at 48-49.

In 1986, Congress replaced that language with "any silencer (as defined in section 921 of title 18, United States Code)." Pub. L. 99-308, §109(b), 100 Stat. 460. The language defining silencer that was added to 18 U.S.C. §921 at that same time reads: "The terms 'firearm silencer' and 'firearm muffler' mean any device for silencing, muffling, or diminishing the report of a portable firearm, including any combination of parts, designed or redesigned, and intended for use in assembling or fabricating a firearm silencer or firearm muffler, and any part intended only for use in such assembly or fabrication." Pub. L. 99-308, §101, 100 Stat. 451.

Thompson/Center argues that if, even before the amendment, a combination of parts was already "made" into a firearm, the "any combination of parts" language would be redundant. While such a conclusion of redundancy could suggest that Congress assumed that "make" in the NFA did not cover unassembled parts, the suggestion (and the implied conflict with our reading of "make") is proven false by evidence that Congress actually understood redundancy to result from its new silencer definition. Congress apparently assumed that the statute reached complete-parts kits even without the "combination" language and understood the net effect of the new definition as expanding the coverage of the Act beyond complete-parts kits. "The definition of silencer is amended to include any part designed or redesigned and intended to be used as a silencer for a firearm. This will help to control the sale of incomplete silencer kits that now circumvent the prohibition on selling complete kits." H. R. Rep. No. 99-495, p. 21 (1986). Because the addition of the "combination of parts" language to the definition of silencer does not, therefore, bear the implication Thompson/Center would put on it, that definition cannot give us much guidance in answering the question before us. . . .

2

Thompson/Center also looks for the answer in the purpose and history of the NFA, arguing that the congressional purpose behind the NFA, of regulating weapons useful for criminal purposes, should caution against drawing the line in such a way as to apply the Act to the Contender pistol and carbine kit. See H. R. Rep. No. 1337, 83d Cong., 2d Sess., A395 (1954) (the adoption of the original definition of rifle was intended to preclude coverage of antique guns held by collectors, "in pursuance of the clearly indicated congressional intent to cover under the National Firearms Act only such modern and lethal weapons, except pistols and revolvers, as could be used readily and efficiently by criminals or gangsters").

It is of course clear from the face of the Act that the NFA's object was to regulate certain weapons likely to be used for criminal purposes, just as the regulation of short-barreled rifles, for example, addresses a concealable weapon likely to be so used. But when Thompson/Center urges us to recognize that "the Contender pistol and carbine kit is not a criminal-type weapon," Brief for Respondent 20, it does not really address the issue of where the line should be drawn in deciding what combinations of parts are "made" into short-barreled rifles. Its argument goes to the quite different issue whether the single-shot Contender should be treated as a firearm within the meaning of the Act even when assembled with a rifle stock. . . .

III

After applying the ordinary rules of statutory construction, then, we are left with an ambiguous statute. The key to resolving the ambiguity lies in recognizing that although it is a tax statute that we construe now in a civil setting, the NFA has criminal applications that carry no additional requirement of willfulness. Cf. *Cheek v. United States*, 498 U.S. 192, 200 (1991) ("Congress has . . . softened the impact of the common-law presumption [that ignorance of the law is no defense to criminal prosecution] by making specific intent to violate the law an element of certain federal criminal tax offenses"); 26 U.S.C. §§7201, 7203 (criminalizing willful evasion of taxes and willful failure to file a return). Making a firearm without approval may be subject to criminal sanction, as is possession of an unregistered firearm and failure to pay the tax on one, 26 U.S.C. §§5861, 5871. It is proper, therefore, to apply the rule of lenity and resolve the ambiguity in Thompson/Center's favor. See *Crandon v. United States*, 494 U.S. 152, 168 (1990) (applying lenity in interpreting a criminal statute invoked in a civil action); *Commissioner v. Acker*, 361 U.S. 87, 91 (1959). Accordingly, we conclude that the Contender pistol and carbine kit when packaged together by Thompson/Center have not been "made" into a short-barreled rifle for purposes of the NFA. The judgment of the Court of Appeals is therefore

Affirmed.

NOTES & QUESTIONS

1. Note in the first paragraph the Court's explanation that the NFA does not apply to pistols, or to rifles with barrels longer than 16 inches. This is an indirect way of saying that ordinary guns, like rifles with barrels longer than 16 inches, are regulated under the less stringent provisions of Title I of the 1968 GCA.

2. Some guns once sold as ordinary GCA firearms have subsequently been deemed NFA firearms by ATF rulings. For example, USAS-12 and Striker-12 shotguns were originally sold as ordinary, non-NFA firearms. These

shotguns had magazines with a 12-round capacity—whereas most other shotguns can hold no more than 8 rounds. The National Firearms Act gives the ATF discretion to classify as "destructive devices" guns having a barrel (bore hole width) of 0.5 inches or greater, including shotguns if the shotgun is determined to lack a sporting purpose. Almost all modern shotguns, except for the diminutive .410 have a barrel over 0.5 inches in diameter. So, the ATF declared the 12 gauge Striker and USAS guns to be "destructive devices." This meant that they were NFA "firearms," and all owners had to register them.

3. *ATF Rulings 94-1 and 94-2.* From 1994 through 2001, the ATF permitted owners of the USAS-12 and Striker-12 to register them. The ATF closed the registration period on May 1, 2001. After that date, "[p]ersons in possession of unregistered NFA firearms are subject to all applicable penalties. . . ." ATF Ruling 2001-1, 66 Fed. Reg. 9748 (Feb. 9, 2001). The O.F. Mossberg company makes a variety of standard-capacity 12 gauge pump-action shotguns for home defense. Unlike many other shotguns, some of the Mossberg guns are advertised primarily for their utility for home defense, rather than for the shooting sports. In the same petition that led to the reclassification of the USAS and Striker guns, Handgun Control, Inc. (now known as the Brady Campaign) also asked the ATF to classify the Mossberg guns as "destructive devices." The ATF declined to do so. What are the arguments for or against the ATF's different treatment of the Mossberg shotguns and the USAS/Striker shotguns?

4. As *Thompson/Center* noted, federal law is clear that owning all the components that *could* be assembled to make a machine gun or a silencer is legally the same as actually owning a machine gun or silencer. *See also United States v. Leavell*, 386 F.2d 776 (4th Cir. 1967) (machine gun parts that can be assembled to make an operational machine gun constitute taxable firearms). What are the arguments for and against such a rule?

2. Regulation of Retail Sales of Ordinary Firearms

The vast majority of the estimated 300 million privately held guns in the United States are ordinary firearms regulated under Title I of the Gun Control Act. The GCA does not apply to firearms manufactured before 1899, or to later replicas of certain pre-1899 guns. Nor does the GCA apply to muzzleloading guns. (See online Chapter 15 for an explanation of muzzleloaders, which are a type of gun from the nineteenth century and before.) Likewise, the GCA does not apply to air guns, which are fueled by compressed air rather than gunpowder. A few states, however, apply their gun control laws to antiques, muzzleloaders, or air guns.

The Gun Control Act regulates the purchase and sale of firearms by imposing a variety of restrictions and obligations on licensed dealers of ordinary firearms, and on their customers. These detailed requirements are complex enough to generate many interesting and difficult questions.

Persons in the business of selling ordinary firearms must obtain a Federal Firearms License (FFL). These sellers are designated "dealers" (or "licensees") under the Act. 18 U.S.C.A §921(a)(11); 18 U.S.C. §923 (licensing procedures and rules for licensees). Colloquially, the term "FFL" is also used to refer to the license itself. Dealers of NFA "firearms" must obtain a separate Class III dealer's license. 26 U.S.C. §5822.

The 1968 GCA defined "dealer" as someone "engaged in the business of selling firearms." This was sufficiently vague that it supported prosecutions for selling guns without a license of people who made small numbers of sales from their individual collections. *See, e.g., United States v. Huffman*, 518 F.2d 80 (4th Cir. 1975) (evidence supported conviction of gun owner who made "more than a dozen transactions in the course of a few months"). These types of prosecutions were one impetus for enactment of the Firearms Owners Protection Act (FOPA). *See generally* David T. Hardy, *The Firearms Owners Protection Act: A Historical and Legal Perspective*, 17 Cumb. L. Rev. 585 (1986). FOPA explicitly defines "engaged in business" to mean that the seller is dealing in firearms "with the principal objective of livelihood and profit through the repetitive purchase and resale of firearms." 18 U.S.C. §921(a)(21)(C). The definition makes clear that people who make occasional sales and purchases to enhance their personal collection or for a hobby are not dealing in firearms and therefore are not required to obtain an FFL. *Id.*

a. Regulation of Buyers

The Gun Control Act explicitly identifies certain classes of people who are prohibited from receiving or possessing firearms, 18 U.S.C. §922(d), and makes it unlawful for any person to transfer any firearm or ammunition to any person knowing or having reasonable cause to believe that such person

(1) is under indictment for, or has been convicted in any court of, a crime punishable by imprisonment for a term exceeding one year;

(2) is a fugitive from justice;

(3) is an unlawful user of or addicted to any controlled substance (as defined in section 102 of the Controlled Substances Act (21 U.S.C. 802));

(4) has been adjudicated as a mental defective or has been committed to any mental institution;

(5) who, being an alien —

(A) is illegally or unlawfully in the United States; or

(B) except as provided in subsection (y)(2), has been admitted to the United States under a nonimmigrant visa (as that term is defined in section 101(a)(26) of the Immigration and Nationality Act (8 U.S.C. 1101(a)(26)));

(6) has been discharged from the Armed Forces under dishonorable conditions;

(7) who, having been a citizen of the United States, has renounced his citizenship;

(8) is subject to a court order that restrains such person from harassing, stalking, or threatening an intimate partner of such person or child of such intimate partner or person, or engaging in other conduct that would place an intimate

partner in reasonable fear of bodily injury to the partner or child, except that this
paragraph shall only apply to a court order that —
>   (A) was issued after a hearing of which such person received actual notice,
and at which such person had the opportunity to participate; and
>   (B) (i) includes a finding that such person represents a credible threat to
the physical safety of such intimate partner or child; or
>   (ii) by its terms explicitly prohibits the use, attempted use, or threatened
use of physical force against such intimate partner or child that would reasonably
be expected to cause bodily injury; or
>   (9) has been convicted in any court of a misdemeanor crime of domestic
violence.

18 U.S.C. §922(d). Subsection (g) bans possession by such people.

Buyers of firearms from licensed dealers are required to prove their identity
to the FFL (usually by providing a photo ID) and then complete ATF Form 4473
attesting that they do not fall into any of the prohibited categories. For an
example of this form, see ATF Forms at http://www.atf.gov/forms/firearms.
The penalty for providing a false statement on this form is up to ten years'
imprisonment. 18 U.S.C.A. §924(a)(2). Next, the buyer's representations on
Form 4473 are verified through the National Instant Check System. 18 U.S.C.
§922(t).

Handgun Control, Inc. had originally pushed for a permanent waiting
period for all handgun transfers, partly for the purpose of giving law enforcement time to check on the buyer. The NRA countered by proposing an "instant
check" system, where dealers could contact law enforcement by telephone and
have the check completed on the spot (similar to a credit card verification). As a
compromise, Congress enacted the Brady waiting period, but mandated that it
would sunset after five years, to be replaced by the Instant Check.

Recall that the *Printz* case, *supra*, invalidated the federal mandate that local
law enforcement officials conduct the interim manual background check. Once
the National Instant Check System became operational in 1998 (conducted by
FBI offices in West Virginia), federal employees handled the checks. However,
some states exercise the option of having the instant check conducted by a state
agency rather than by the FBI.

Under the Instant Check System, the dealer may not transfer the firearm to
the purchaser until the dealer submits the purchaser's information (typically by
telephone or computer) to the NICS. Then the buyer is screened against the
national database of persons who are ineligible to buy guns because they have a
felony conviction, a misdemeanor domestic violence conviction, a dishonorable
discharge from the military, and so on. If the buyer is approved, the dealer
receives a purchase authorization number, which he records to verify compliance with the instant check requirement. Buyers deemed ineligible to purchase
a firearm may request a written explanation and may supply information to
correct any errors in the NICS database. For example, a database might record
that a person has a conviction, but might not reflect that the conviction was
overturned on appeal. Often, the instant check is not really instant. A buyer may
have to wait hours or in rare cases several days for the state agency or the FBI to
issue the approval number.

One of the political controversies surrounding both paper and electronic
screening systems is what happens to the data collected. Gun rights activists

worry that the information might be used to develop a system of firearms reg-istration, which they see as a dangerous precursor to firearms confiscation. *See* Nicholas J. Johnson, *Imagining Gun Control in America*, 43 Wake Forest L. Rev. 837 (2008) (assessing the argument that confiscation cannot work unless preceded by registration, and the post-*Heller* variations on that argument).

Accordingly, when Congress enacted the Instant Check System, it required that if the buyer is approved, "the system shall . . . destroy all records of the system with respect to the call (other than the identifying number and the date the number was assigned) and all records of the system relating to the person or the transfer." 18 U.S.C. §922(t)(2). This requirement reinforces a provision of the 1986 Firearms Owners Protection Act that outlaws the creation of a national gun registry. The next case illustrates how different administrations charged with enforcement of the Act have approached the obligation to destroy the records of lawful purchases.

National Rifle Ass'n of America Inc. v. Reno
216 F.3d 122 (D.C. Cir. 2000)

TATEL, Circuit Judge:

The National Rifle Association challenges a Justice Department regulation providing for temporary retention of data generated during background checks of prospective firearms purchasers, as required by the Brady Handgun Violence Prevention Act. According to the NRA, the Brady Act requires immediate destruction of personal information relating to lawful firearm transactions. The Attorney General interprets the statute differently, arguing that temporary retention of data for at most six months is necessary to audit the background check system to ensure both its accuracy and privacy. Finding nothing in the Brady Act that unambiguously prohibits temporary retention of information about lawful transactions, and finding that the Attorney General has reasonably interpreted the Act to permit retention of such information for audit purposes, we affirm the district court's dismissal of the complaint.

I.

The Gun Control Act of 1968 makes it unlawful for certain individuals, including convicted felons, fugitives from justice, and illegal aliens, to possess firearms. *See* 18 U.S.C. §922(g). The Brady Handgun Violence Prevention Act of 1993 required the Attorney General to establish a "national instant criminal background check system," known as the NICS, to search the backgrounds of prospective gun purchasers for criminal or other information that would dis-qualify them from possessing firearms. *See* §103(b), Pub. L. No. 103-59, 107 Stat. 1536. A computerized system operated by the FBI, the NICS searches for dis-qualifying information in three separate databases: (1) the "NICS Index," con-taining records on persons known to be disqualified from possessing firearms under federal law; (2) the "National Crime Information Center," containing records on protective orders, deported felons, and fugitives from justice; and (3) the "Interstate Identification Index," containing criminal history records. 28 C.F.R. §25.6(c)(1)(iii).

Before selling a weapon, firearm dealers must submit the prospective purchaser's name, sex, race, date of birth, and state of residence to the NICS operations center at the FBI. *Id.* §25.7(a). If the firearm dealer is in a state that has elected to serve as a "point of contact" for NICS queries, the dealer must submit the inquiry to the relevant state agency. *Id.* §25.6(d). Upon receiving such an inquiry, the FBI or state agency must immediately provide the gun dealer with one of three responses: (1) "proceed," if no information in the system indicates that a firearm transfer would be unlawful; (2) "denied," if the prospective purchaser may not legally possess a firearm; or (3) "delayed," if further research is necessary. *Id.* §25.6(c)(1)(iv); Brady Act §103(b), 107 Stat. at 1541.

Justice Department regulation requires the FBI to retain records of all NICS background searches — including names and other identifying information about prospective gun purchasers — in an automated "Audit Log." 28 C.F.R. §25.9(b). According to the regulation, the Audit Log is "a chronological record of system (computer) activities that enables the reconstruction and examination of the sequence of events and/or changes in an event." *Id.* §25.2. The regulation's preamble describes the purpose of the Audit Log[.]

By auditing the system, the FBI can identify instances in which the NICS is used for unauthorized purposes, such as running checks of people other than actual gun transferees, and protect against the invasions of privacy that would result from such misuse. Audits can also determine whether potential handgun purchasers or [gun dealers] have stolen the identity of innocent and unsuspecting individuals or otherwise submitted false identification information, in order to thwart the name check system. . . .

The regulation restricts use of the Audit Log. Information "pertaining to allowed transfers may only be used by the FBI for the purpose of conducting audits of the use and performance of the NICS." 28 C.F.R. §25.9(b)(2). . . .

On the day the NICS regulation became effective, the National Rifle Association of America, joined by the Law Enforcement Alliance of America, Inc., and four John and Jane Does, filed suit in the U.S. District Court for the District of Columbia, arguing that temporary retention of NICS records of allowed transfers violates three provisions of the Brady Act: section 922(t)(2)(C), requiring that the system "destroy" records of allowed transactions; section 103(i)(1), prohibiting the government from "requiring that any [NICS] record . . . be recorded at or transferred to a [government] facility"; and section 103(i)(2), prohibiting the government from "using the [NICS] system . . . to establish any system for the registration of firearms." 107 Stat. at 1540, 1542.

The Attorney General interpreted the Act differently, arguing that neither section 922(t)(2)(C) nor section 103(i)(1) prohibits temporary retention of NICS records, and that the Audit Log is not a "system for . . . registration" within the meaning of section 103(i)(2). For authority to create the Audit Log, the Attorney General relied on her statutory obligations to establish a system capable of providing accurate information on the lawfulness of firearm transactions, see Brady Act, §103(b), 107 Stat. at 1541, and to protect the privacy and security of the NICS. See Brady Act, §103(h), 107 Stat. at 1542.

The district court, finding nothing in the Brady Act to require immediate destruction and the Attorney General's construction of the statute reasonable, dismissed the complaint. . . .

II.

Because the NRA challenges a statute administered by a government agency, we proceed in accordance with the familiar two-part test of *Chevron U.S.A. Inc. v. Natural Resources Defense Council, Inc.*, 467 U.S. 837 (1984). We ask first "whether Congress has directly spoken to the precise question at issue," for if it has, "that is the end of the matter; for the court, as well as the agency, must give effect to the unambiguously expressed intent of Congress." *Id.* at 842-43. If we find the statute silent or ambiguous with respect to the precise question at issue, we proceed to the second step of *Chevron* analysis, asking "whether the agency's answer is based on a permissible construction of the statute." *Id.* at 843. At this point in our review, we afford substantial deference to the agency's interpretation of statutory language. *See id.* at 844.

We begin with the NRA's *Chevron* one argument that three provisions of the Brady Act unambiguously prohibit the Attorney General from retaining information about allowed transactions for any purpose, including auditing. . . .

According to the NRA, when the statute says "destroy all records" it means "destroy all records immediately," not within six months. That is certainly one possible interpretation of section 922(t)(2)(C). At *Chevron* step one, however, the question is whether the statute unambiguously requires immediate destruction. We think the answer is no.

To begin with, section 922(t)(2)(C) does not say "destroy immediately"; it says only "destroy." . . .

The parties debate the significance of subsequent legislative developments. An appropriations rider, expressly responding to the proposed Audit Log, would have conditioned NICS funding on the "immediate destruction of all information" relating to persons eligible to possess firearms. *See* 144 Cong. Rec. S8680 (daily ed. July 21, 1998) (proposed amendment no. 3233). As in the case of the Brady Act itself, the word "immediately" was deleted from the final act. See Omnibus Consolidated and Emergency Supplemental Appropriations Act of 1999 §621(2), Pub. L. No. 105-277; *see also* An Act Making Consolidated Appropriations For the Fiscal Year Ending September 30, 2000, and For Other Purposes §619(2), Pub. L. No. 106-113 (using the same language). Also, two bills that would have imposed criminal penalties on government employees who retain NICS records for more than twenty-four hours were introduced but never passed. *See* No Gun Tax Act of 1998, H.R. 3949, 105th Cong.; Firearms Owner Privacy Act of 1998, S. 2175, 105th Cong. §2. Heeding the Supreme Court's recent warning, "we do not rely on Congress' failure to act" as dispositive evidence of congressional intent. *Brown & Williamson*, 120 S. Ct. at 1312. At the same time, this post-Brady Act legislative activity reflects no unambiguous congressional intent to require immediate destruction of NICS records. Indeed, the effort to require immediate destruction goes on: A bill now pending in the Senate once again calls for records of allowed transfers to be destroyed immediately. See Right to Bear Arms Privacy and Protection Act of 2000, S. 2270, 106th Cong. §5(b). . . .

The NRA contends that the Audit Log represents a "clear violation" of subsection (1) because the Log "constitutes 'any record or portion thereof generated by' NICS, and it is 'recorded at or transferred to' a federal facility." Several considerations persuade us that subsection (1) is not so clear. To begin with, the statute's prohibition against "recording" a "record" is inherently ambiguous. What is a "record," when has it been "recorded," and what kind of "record" cannot be "recorded"? When a NICS operator enters the name of a prospective purchaser into the system, is that a "record"? Has it been "recorded"? If not, when does it become a "record" that cannot be "recorded"?

In addition to the inherent ambiguity of these words, section 922(t)(2)(C) speaks of "destroying all records" relating to allowed transfers, apparently assuming that records may be created. Asked about this at oral argument, NRA counsel conceded that records could lawfully be kept for three business days while research is undertaken following a "delayed" response. See 18 U.S.C. §922(t)(ii); 28 C.F.R. §25.6(c)(1)(iv)(B). If the NRA's answer is correct—we think it is—then subsection (1) cannot categorically prohibit the government from making records of NICS information. . . .

This brings us to subsection (2), which forbids the government from "using the [NICS] system . . . to establish any system for the registration of firearms, firearm owners, or firearm transactions or dispositions." According to the NRA, the Audit Log regulation violates this subsection because the Audit Log is itself a "form of registration." Appellants' Br. at 15. But subsection (2) does not prohibit all forms of registration. It prohibits only "systems for the registration of firearms, firearm owners, or firearm transactions or dispositions." The Audit Log is not such a system. As designed by the Attorney General, it functions as a system for protecting the privacy of the NICS and for quality control. The Audit Log regulation expressly provides that "information in the Audit Log pertaining to allowed transfers may only be used by the FBI for the purpose of conducting audits of the use and performance of the NICS." 28 C.F.R. §25.9(b)(2). To enforce this restriction, "the Audit Log will be monitored and reviewed on a regular basis to detect any possible misuse of the NICS data." Id.

The Audit Log, moreover, contains no information about "firearms" or "firearm transactions or dispositions." Nor does it contain a comprehensive list of "firearm owners."

To illustrate the difference between the Audit Log and a firearms registry, the Attorney General calls our attention to the central registry of machine guns established by the National Firearms Act. See 26 U.S.C. §5841. The machine gun registry contains information on all machine guns not possessed by the United States, including data on the weapons themselves, dates of registration, and the names and addresses of persons entitled to posses them. Id. §5841(a)(1)-(3). Far less comprehensive, the Audit Log includes no addresses of persons approved to buy firearms, nor any information on specific weapons, nor even whether approved gun purchasers actually completed a transaction. And unlike the machine gun registry, information in the Audit Log is routinely purged after six months. The Audit Log therefore represents only a tiny fraction of the universe of firearm owners. . . .

III.

Having found nothing in either section 922(t)(2)(C) or section 103(i) that unambiguously prohibits temporary retention of NICS records of allowed transactions for audit purposes, we turn to an examination of the affirmative grants of authority on which the Attorney General relies. . . .

So long as the agency's interpretation is reasonable, we uphold it "regardless whether there may be other reasonable, or even more reasonable, views." *Allied Local and Regional Manufacturers Caucus v. EPA*, 215 F.3d 61 (D.C. Cir. 2000) (internal quotation marks omitted). . . .

The first Brady Act provision on which the Attorney General relies is section 103(b): "The Attorney General shall establish a national instant criminal background check system that any [gun dealer] may contact . . . for information, to be supplied immediately, on whether receipt of a firearm by a prospective transferee would [be unlawful]." Brady Act §103(b), 107 Stat. at 1541. According to the Attorney General, "Congress would not have ordered her to establish the NICS without being able to ensure that the system [is] working," i.e., performing as Congress intended. Appellee's Br. at 18. . . .

We think the Attorney General's position represents a reasonable interpretation of section 103(b)'s requirement that the NICS provide "information" on whether firearm transfers would be unlawful. . . .

Our conclusion that the Audit Log regulation represents a reasonable interpretation of section 103(b) finds support from the fact that auditing is not unusual for computerized systems like the NICS. For example, Justice Department regulations require audits of another computerized database, the Criminal History Record Information System, in order to "verify adherence" to applicable law. 28 C.F.R. §20.21(e). . . .

The Attorney General also relies on section 103(h): "The Attorney General shall prescribe regulations to ensure the privacy and security of the information of the system. . . ." Brady Act §103(h), 107 Stat. at 1542. . . . During the debates on the Brady bill, Senator Leahy put the concern this way:

> I am concerned about giving every gun dealer in the country access to people's private lives. . . . My concerns are that access to the background check system may be abused. . . . Somebody is a neighbor and says, "I really don't care too much for those people who moved down the street. Check them out for me." I find that a little bit unsettling. . . .

. . . Here, the Attorney General, the official responsible for establishing and managing a nationwide database of personal information, has determined that auditing is necessary to ensure that the system is not used for unauthorized purposes. Absent evidence that this concern is misplaced, we have no basis for second guessing the Attorney General's judgment. . . .

To sum up, keeping in mind *Chevron* two's highly deferential standard, we find that the Audit Log regulation represents a "permissible construction" of sections 103(b) and 103(h). *Chevron*, 467 U.S. at 843. We think it "common sense" — *Brown & Williamson*'s *Chevron* one words that seem equally applicable at *Chevron* two — that Congress, having directed the Attorney General to establish a system for preventing disqualified persons from purchasing firearms, would expect the Attorney General to ensure that the system produces accurate information and guards against misuse. Indeed, by limiting retention of NICS information to "the minimum reasonable period for performing audits on the system," the Attorney General has obeyed the "destroy" command of section 922(t)(2)(C) while fulfilling her section 103(b) and 103(h) responsibilities. NICS Regulation, 63 Fed. Reg. 58304.

IV.

[In Part IV, the court upholds the Attorney General's determination that the record destruction requirement does not apply to state and local agencies that act as points of contact for processing NICS queries and gather and retain NICS information pursuant to state law.]

The judgment of the district court is affirmed.

NOTES & QUESTIONS

1. The administrations of Presidents Bill Clinton and George W. Bush took different views on the disposition of NICS information. On January 24, 2001, President Bush ordered all pending Clinton administration regulations withdrawn from the Federal Register "for review and approval." "In defiance of this order, two days later the Federal Register published under the authority of Janet Reno (who was no longer Attorney General) a [final Audit Log Rule]." Attorney General Ashcroft delayed implementation of this rule, was sued by the Violence Policy Center for unlawful suspension of the rule, and then declared the rule effective. Stephen P. Halbrook, Firearms Law Deskbook, 2008-2009, at 326-28. Following that, Attorney General Ashcroft proposed a new regulation that required information about lawful transfers to be destroyed within 24 hours. 28 CFR §25.9(b)(iii) now reads: "In cases of NICS Audit Log records relating to allowed transactions, all identifying information submitted by or on behalf of the transferee will be destroyed within 24 hours after the FFL receives communication of the determination that the transfer may proceed."

2. Note the court's description of the registration system under the National Firearms Act (Chapter 7). Would you favor a similar system for all firearms?

3. Registration has been a significant point of controversy in the gun control debate. What is the objection to registration? What is the argument in favor of registration? Is there a constitutional objection to the government keeping records of what books a person purchases, what Internet sites she visits, what type of birth control or abortion she receives, or what organizations she belongs to? How are these similar or dissimilar to gun registration? Is gun registration comparable to automobile registration, or the registration of attorneys? *See* Nicholas J. Johnson, *Imagining Gun Control in America: Understanding the Remainder Problem*, 43 Wake Forest L. Rev. 837 (2008);

David B. Kopel, *Treating Guns Like Consumer Products*, 148 U. Pa. L. Rev. 1213 (2000).

4. When licensed gun dealers go out of business, they are required to submit the records of their transfers to the ATF within 30 days. 18 U.S.C. §923(g)(4) and 27 CFR §478.127. "The NTC receives an average of 1.2 million out-of-business records per month and is the only repository for these records within the United States." Bureau of Alcohol, Tobacco, Firearms and Explosives, ATF Online, Discontinue Being a Federal Firearms Licensee (FFL), *available at* http://www.atf.gov/firearms/how-to/discontinue-being-an-ffl.html. Can you frame the argument that the ATF's putting these records into a searchable database constitutes federal gun registration in violation of FOPA? That it is permissible?

5. Although the interim federal waiting period expired, a few states impose their own waiting periods for the purchase of handguns or all firearms. *See, e.g.,* Cal. Penal Code §§12071(b)(3)(A), 12072(c)(1) (15 days for all firearms). In other states, laws that require a permit for the acquisition of any gun operate as a de facto waiting period. N.J. Stat. Ann. §§2C:58-2(a)(5)(a), 2C:58-3(f). What are the advantages and disadvantages of waiting periods?

6. When state or federal laws make distinctions among types of guns, handguns are usually controlled more stringently than long guns. For example, the Gun Control Act of 1968 allows 18-year-olds to buy long guns from licensed dealers, but sets 21 as the age for handguns. The Brady Act interim provisions attempted to mandate background checks for handguns but not for long guns. A 1994 federal law bans handgun ownership by persons under 18, but not long gun ownership. Some states have waiting periods, registration, or special licensing laws for handguns but not for long guns. What justifies these distinctions? Are these justification sound?

7. "Nonlicensees" (i.e., persons who are not federally licensed firearms dealers) are prohibited from buying handguns outside their state of residence. 18 U.S.C. §922(a)(3). This means, for example, that a buyer who wants to purchase a handgun from a gun shop while he is away from home in another state must have the gun shipped by the seller to another licensed dealer in the buyer's home state. When the handgun is received by the dealer in the buyer's home state, that dealer must require the buyer to complete Form 4473 and submit to a NICS background check. In contrast, long guns may be purchased out of state, as long as the seller is a federally licensed firearms dealer, and the purchase is legal in both the state of purchase and the buyer's home state.

Since passage of the GCA, retail buyers of firearms have been required to complete Form 4473. The form includes a long checklist requiring buyers to aver that they are not legally ineligible to purchase a firearm. Making material false statements on the form is unlawful and punishable by fines and imprisonment. A knowing violation is punishable by up to ten years' imprisonment. 18 U.S.C. §924(a)(2). Sometimes, people who are legally prohibited from purchasing firearms send someone with a clean record to buy a gun for them. This is called a "straw purchase," and is specifically outlawed by the Firearms Owners Protection Act of 1986. The ATF conducts a joint program with the National Shooting Sports Foundation (the trade association for the gun industry) called "Don't Lie for the Other Guy." The program educates consumers that making a straw purchase is a serious crime, and also provides training to gun store employees in detecting straw purchases. The next case illustrates the legislative and regulatory response to straw purchases and raises an interesting policy question.

United States v. Moore
109 F.3d 1456 (9th Cir. 1997) (en banc)

TROTT, Circuit Judge.

Mary Peggy Moore ("Mrs. Moore") and Lee Roy Wiley ("Wiley") appeal their respective convictions for conspiracy and for making a material false statement in connection with the purchase of a firearm. Wiley allegedly bought a firearm as a "straw man" on behalf of Mrs. Moore's fourteen-year-old son, Bobby Moore ("Bobby"). Mrs. Moore allegedly was liable as Wiley's aider and abettor and coconspirator in his making of the false statement. . . .

[W]e affirm the district court. . . .

On September 2, 1993, fourteen-year-old Bobby Moore saw a .25 caliber handgun in a pawnshop which had a federal license to sell firearms. When he showed interest in the weapon, a clerk shooed him off the premises because his age rendered him ineligible under federal law to buy it. Undaunted, Bobby set out to find a way to acquire the handgun for himself. He approached his mother to buy it for him, but she turned him down. Bobby's friend Jason Marks witnessed this discussion. Jason's unchallenged testimony about the discussion established not only that Mrs. Moore refused to buy the gun on behalf of her son, but that she explicitly told him he would have to "get someone else" to get it for him because she "didn't want her name on the papers": . . .

Q. Okay, and tell us what else was said. . . .
A. Yeah, and Bob's mom said she didn't want to do it because she didn't want her name on the papers and he could hurt somebody and she didn't think he needed a gun. But Bob has a way of talking people into things, and so he kind of threw a tantrum and got all mad, and finally his mom said that she would do it.
Q. Said she would do what?
A. Pawn the CD player.
Q. Did she say she would pawn the CD player for the gun, or just pawn the CD player?
A. *Just pawn the CD player and he would have to figure out a different way of getting the gun because she didn't want her name on the papers* . . . (emphasis added).

Mrs. Moore then pawned Bobby's CD player and gave him the cash she received from the transaction. She did so knowing that he intended to use it to purchase a firearm.

The next day, Bobby went looking for someone else to help him acquire the weapon, as suggested by his mother. He took the cash to Wiley's residence to see if Wiley would assist him. The neighborhood knew Wiley as "Grandpa," and he frequently did favors for the neighborhood children. The record reflects that Wiley is a man of limited intelligence. Wiley was neither Bobby's parent nor guardian, nor was he related to him in any respect whatsoever.

Wiley balked at first, but Bobby persisted; and with the promise of money as a sweetener, Wiley relented and agreed to purchase the gun on Bobby's behalf.

Mrs. Moore then drove Wiley, Bobby, and Jason to the pawnshop. During this trip, Wiley asked Mrs. Moore if the purchase of the gun was all right with her, to which she replied that it was fine.

When the group arrived at the pawnshop, Mrs. Moore waited in the car while Wiley, Bobby, and Jason went inside. Wiley asked the clerk to see the handgun Bobby had spotted on his earlier visit. Because the two boys were present, the clerk inquired for whom Wiley wanted to purchase the gun. Wiley responded that the gun was for Bobby, but that he Wiley was Bobby's grandfather, and that he was going to hold it for Bobby until Bobby was 21 years of age. Both of these statements were false and were intended to facilitate the transaction. On cross-examination, Wiley conceded that the only reason he was in the pawnshop was "to stand in for Bobby to get that gun."

The clerk responded to Wiley's representations with an inquiry about Bobby's parents and whether they knew about this purchase. Bobby said that his mother was outside, and he went to get her. In short order, Mrs. Moore appeared briefly in the doorway and, without prompting by Wiley, said to the clerk, "His grandfather is buying a gun for him. He's going to hold it until he's 21, and everything is fine with me."

Satisfied by Mrs. Moore's representations, the clerk had Wiley sign BATF Form 4473 as the "transferee (buyer)," accepted the cash Bobby had given to Wiley for the transaction, and turned the gun over to Wiley. Back in the car, and contrary to the intentions he expressed to the clerk, Wiley gave the gun to Mrs. Moore, expecting that it would go to Bobby. As Bobby intended from the start, he then took the firearm as his own possession.

Mrs. Moore's reluctance to buy this weapon for her son and to put her name on the papers was well founded, and her worry about Bobby hurting someone with it was prescient. On January 20, 1994, Bobby used it to shoot Ronald Wade Feldner, a New Plymouth, Idaho police officer, in the face. Officer Feldner died, leaving behind a wife and minor children.

B. THE FALSE STATEMENT

In 18 U.S.C. §922(a)(6), Congress made it a federal offense for any person in connection with the acquisition or attempted acquisition of any firearm or ammunition from a licensed importer, licensed manufacturer, licensed dealer, or licensed collector, knowingly to make any false or fictitious oral or written statement or to furnish or exhibit any false, fictitious, or misrepresented identification, intended or likely to deceive such importer, manufacturer, dealer, or collector with respect to any fact material to the lawfulness of the sale or other disposition of such firearm or ammunition under the provisions of this chapter.

In the same statute, Congress also rendered it illegal for a licensed firearms dealer to sell or deliver "any firearm or ammunition to any individual who the licensee knows or has reasonable cause to believe is less than eighteen years of age," or to sell or deliver a handgun to anyone less than twenty-one years of age. 18 U.S.C. §922(b)(1). Thus, federal law made Bobby Moore ineligible to purchase a firearm from a federally-licensed dealer.

The government's theory of its case against Wiley, and against Mrs. Moore as an aider and abettor and coconspirator, is straightforward and simple. As charged in the indictment and as explained to the jurors in the jury instructions, the government alleges that the true buyer of the .25 caliber handgun was the ineligible Bobby Moore, and that Wiley acted merely as his disguised agent — in the parlance, as a "straw man" purchaser. Thus, goes the government's argument, when Wiley the straw man agent signed his name on Form 4473 as the "transferee (buyer)," he made a false statement because the buyer was not Wiley, but Bobby himself. The manifest materiality of this false statement, says the government, stems from the law's prohibition against Bobby buying a firearm.

The appellants, on the other hand, contend that Mrs. Moore consented to the acquisition of this firearm by Wiley on behalf of her son. They argue here, as they did to the trial court and to the jury, that such consent rendered the sale lawful per se, and accordingly, that any false statements that Wiley and Mrs. Moore made to the clerk were flatly immaterial. To support this argument, the appellants assert that, at the time of sale, transferring firearms to minors was legal in Idaho, so long as the minor's parents gave consent.[2] . . .

C. THE STRAW MAN DOCTRINE

The straw man doctrine, which is nothing more than a long-standing construction of the relevant statutes, holds that a person violates section 922(a)(6) by acting as an intermediary or agent of someone who is ineligible to obtain a firearm from a licensed dealer and making a false statement that enables the ineligible principal to obtain a firearm. . . . In *Lawrence,* for example, the Sixth Circuit found determinative of straw man status that, like Wiley, the transferee (1) acted under the direction and control of the ineligible buyer, (2) purchased weapons selected by the ineligible buyer with the buyer's money, (3) took a commission that showed agency, and (4) had no intention of keeping the gun for himself. 680 F.2d at 1128. . . . In this context, it is a construction of the statute that directly serves the primary purpose of the Gun Control Act, which is "'to make it possible to keep firearms out of the hands of those not legally entitled to possess them because of age, criminal background, or

---

2. At the time this firearm was purchased, Idaho law did not prohibit the sale of a firearm to a minor so long as the minor had the consent of a parent or a guardian. Idaho Code §18-3302A (1990). Since these events, the Idaho Legislature amended section 18-3302A to require the written permission of a parent or a guardian. The Gun Control Act has also been amended to make it illegal for a juvenile to possess a handgun without a parent's or guardian's written consent. 18 U.S.C. §§922(x)(1)(A), 922(x)(3)(A)(iii) (1994).

incompetency.'" *Barrett v. United States*, 423 U.S. 212, 220 (1976) (quoting S. Rep. No. 1501, 90th Cong., 2d Sess. 22 (1968))....

In the instant case, the uncontested facts presented to the jury did not as a matter of law establish a defense to the straw man doctrine. Nothing in the statute, the case law, or the rules of statutory construction suggests that a parent can either (1) render an unlawful straw man purchase legal by consenting to it, or (2) override the clear prohibition against making material false statements in a firearms transaction. Appellants ignore the specific rules that apply when someone purchases a firearm from a federally licensed dealer. Their suggestion that Idaho Code §18-3302A "empowers" a parent to arm a child is misleading and a non sequitur. The fact that Idaho law permits a weapons transfer to a minor under 16 years of age with parental consent does not "empower" a juvenile to purchase a firearm from a federal dealer through an intermediary who falsely identifies himself as the buyer. The gravamen of the charge against Mrs. Moore and Wiley was the allegation that they made a material false statement....

Wiley's involvement in the transaction is the smoking gun that proves both the illegality of this purchase and the existence of the conspiracy. Under the circumstances and given the jury's verdict, Mrs. Moore's words spoken in the pawnshop in support of the grandfather ruse serve primarily to connect her both to the false statement offense and to the conspiracy, rather than to provide the appellants with a defense. In her cameo appearance in the pawnshop's doorway, she did not reveal what was actually happening. Instead, she lied about the transaction in progress, and by so doing, purposefully enabled Wiley to make a material false statement on BATF Form 4473 and thereby consummate an illegal purchase. Her precise misrepresentation about Wiley's status as Bobby's grandfather and about who was going to control the weapon can hardly be called "consent." What the record demonstrates that she said and did does not square with the appellants' characterization of it. Thus, the appellants' argument that the evidence is insufficient to sustain these verdicts is demonstrably without merit....

Affirmed.

TASHIMA, Circuit Judge, with whom PREGERSON and REINHARDT, Circuit Judges, join, dissenting: ...

The majority's ... error is to ignore Mrs. Moore's consent and, thus, the central issue in this case — the scope of the parental consent exception. The majority ignores Mrs. Moore's consent to the sale because it does not want to deal with the consequences of recognizing it.

Even the Bureau of Alcohol, Tobacco and Firearms ("BATF") agrees that Congress intended that guns purchased for juveniles by their parents be excepted from the Gun Control Act's ("GCA") prohibition, and has administered the GCA to recognize such an exception.[4] However, the BATF would limit

---

4. No party has cited and the court has not found any reported case in which a straw purchaser has been prosecuted for buying a firearm for a juvenile where the straw purchaser is a parent or other close relative of the juvenile.

that exception to transactions in which the parent herself or himself is the purchaser — the "Transferee (Buyer)."

As the panel opinion makes clear, there is no justification in the legislative history to construe the parental consent exception as narrowly as does the BATF, particularly when construing a criminal statute. For the reasons stated in Parts III and IV of the panel opinion, *Moore I*, 84 F.3d at 1571-73, the majority errs in failing to recognize Congress' intent that under the GCA, a parent may validly consent to the purchase of a gun for her minor child without being the physical purchaser.

Congress simply did not intend to criminalize acquisition of firearms by minors where the parent knows of and consents to the purchase.

The report of the Senate Judiciary Committee on the GCA listed among the serious national problems addressed by the legislation the acquisition of fire-arms by "juveniles *without the knowledge and consent of their parents or guardians.* . . ." S. Rep. No. 1097, 90th Cong., 2nd Sess. (1968), *reprinted in* 1968 U.S.C.C.A.N., 2112, 2114 (emphasis added). The report elaborated:

> The *clandestine* acquisition of firearms by juveniles and minors is a most serious problem facing law enforcement and the citizens of this country. The controls proposed in the title are designed to meet this problem and to substantially curtail it.

Id. at 2167 (emphasis added).

The committee report made clear that Congress did not intend to frustrate all gun acquisitions by minors:

> Under the title, a minor or juvenile would not be restricted from owning or learning the proper usage of the firearm, since any firearm which his parent or guardian desired him to have could be obtained for the minor or juvenile by the parent or guardian.

Id.

There is no indication that Congress intended to limit the exception for the purchase of a firearm for a minor exclusively to purchases made by the parent himself or herself. What the legislative history indicates is that Congress considered parental permission sufficient to allow a third party to purchase the firearm on behalf of a minor. The Senate Judiciary Committee's report clearly indicates that Congress' purpose was only to prohibit those acquisitions of firearms by minors that are "clandestine" or made "without the knowledge and consent of their parents." *Moore I*, 84 F.3d at 1571-72. . . .

According to the government's theory of the case, the only material false statement made was made by Wiley when he signed the BATF form stating that he was the "transferee (buyer)." This statement was false, according to the government, because Bobby was the "true" purchaser and Wiley was a "straw man." However, even under this theory, under the BATF's own interpretation of what its own forms and regulations require, Wiley was *required* to state that he was the "transferee (buyer)."

According to the testimony of BATF Special Agent Sterling Nixon, when a parent purchases a gun for her child, even with the child's own money, she is *required* to list her own name as the "transferee (buyer)."[7] BATF Form 4473 simply is not designed to accommodate a straw purchase, whether or not it is lawful.[8] There was no place on the form where Wiley could have disclosed that he intended immediately to transfer the gun to Mrs. Moore, for eventual transfer to Bobby. Wiley did not make a false statement. He was, in fact, the "transferee (buyer)" and listed himself as such. Because he fully complied with the requirements of the BATF form and the form nowhere required disclosure of the "straw" aspect of the transaction, Wiley did not make a false statement by listing himself as the "transferee (buyer)," unless that action were criminalized by the "straw man" doctrine, discussed below.

Further analysis of the BATF's design and administration of its Form 4473 demonstrates the "Catch 22" in which straw purchasers are placed. According to BATF Agent Nixon's testimony, straw purchasers are required to list themselves as the "transferee (buyer)," even though they are standing in for the "true" purchaser, *e.g.*, where a parent is purchasing a firearm for her child. Thus, in the BATF's view, straw purchasers are required to make a false statement. The BATF then, in its discretion, determines whether or not that false statement is material, *i.e.*, whether or not Congress intended that transaction to be exempted from the BATF's "true" purchaser requirement. Whatever the merits of such an administration of the GCA for regulatory purposes, it is hardly a fair way to administer the criminal law. . . .

This court should not default to the BATF, or any other Executive Branch agency, the power to construe our criminal laws in derogation of the intent of Congress. Congress did not intend to criminalize the sale of a firearm to a minor, where the sale is made with the consent of the minor's parent. If, as it should be, the underlying transaction is seen as one within the parental consent exception, then the sale was lawful and any false statement made to facilitate it could not have been of "any fact material to the lawfulness of the sale," within the meaning of 18 U.S.C. §922(a)(6).

For these reasons, I would reverse the convictions. I respectfully dissent.

NOTES & QUESTIONS

1. In many parts of the country, it is not unusual for minors to have guns of their own or easy access to guns owned by the family. Based on the statutory provisions, Idaho is one of those places. What is your assessment of the Idaho statute? Under federal law and in many states, guns are not registered to particular owners in the fashion of automobiles. Absent that sort of formal system, what does it mean to "own" a firearm? What if the parent says that the firearm belongs to the minor, but keeps the gun locked away except when accompanying the minor to shoot the gun? The question of what it

---

7. Agent Nixon further testified that this required listing of the parent's name as transferee (buyer) would be true even if the parent intended immediately to transfer the firearm to her child, and that it would not be a false statement.

8. As noted in the panel opinion, not all straw transactions are illegal. *Moore I*, 84 F.3d at 1570. The paradigmatic straw transaction is, of course, the legal stand-in of a parent for her or his minor child.

means to own or possess a gun in a family situation where several people have access arises again in the context of rules that prohibit gun possession by felons or other disqualified individuals. For a preview of that question, consider the arguments you would make in a situation where the parent of a juvenile felon purchases a firearm and brings to his home, where the juvenile felon resides. *See, e.g., United States v. Stine,* 458 F. Supp. 366 (E.D. Pa. 1978). Licensed dealers also can violate the prohibition on straw sales. *See* Enforcement: Crime Gun Trace Reports (1999) (Nov. 2000). 42, *available at* http://www.atf.gov/publications/download/ycgii/1999/ycgii-report-1999-enforcement.pdf. For an analysis of the incentives that restrain off-the-books sales by licensed dealers, see Nicholas J. Johnson, *Imagining Gun Control in America: Understanding the Remainder Problem,* 43 Wake Forest L. Rev. 837 (2008).

2. In 1993, Congress banned the possession of handguns by juveniles with specific exceptions designated below.

> (3) This subsection does not apply to —
>
>   (A) a temporary transfer of a handgun or ammunition to a juvenile or to the possession or use of a handgun or ammunition by a juvenile if the handgun and ammunition are possessed and used by the juvenile —
>
>   (i) in the course of employment, in the course of ranching or farming related to activities at the residence of the juvenile (or on property used for ranching or farming at which the juvenile, with the permission of the property owner or lessee, is performing activities related to the operation of the farm or ranch), target practice, hunting, or a course of instruction . . .
>
>   (ii) with the prior written consent of the juvenile's parent or guardian who is not prohibited by Federal, State, or local law from possessing a firearm, except —
>
>   (I) during transportation by the juvenile of an unloaded handgun in a locked container directly from the place of transfer to a place at which an activity described in clause (i) is to take place and transportation by the juvenile of that handgun, unloaded and in a locked container, directly from the place at which such an activity took place to the transferor; or
>
>   (II) with respect to ranching or farming activities as described in clause (i), a juvenile may possess and use a handgun or ammunition with the prior written approval of the juvenile's parent or legal guardian and at the direction of an adult who is not prohibited by Federal, State or local law from possessing a firearm;
>
>   (iii) the juvenile has the prior written consent in the juvenile's possession at all times when a handgun is in the possession of the juvenile; and
>
>   (iv) in accordance with State and local law;
>
>   (B) a juvenile who is a member of the Armed Forces of the United States or the National Guard who possesses or is armed with a handgun in the line of duty;
>
>   (C) a transfer by inheritance of title (but not possession) of a handgun or ammunition to a juvenile; or
>
>   (D) the possession of a handgun or ammunition by a juvenile taken in defense of the juvenile or other persons against an intruder into the residence of the juvenile or a residence in which the juvenile is an invited guest.

18 U.S.C.A. §922(x)(3). Are these exceptions proper accommodations of rural or sporting practices and culture? Bobby Moore lived in the rural state of Idaho and his mother could have approved his possession and use of the handgun he used to shoot Officer Feldner. Is it appropriate that minors who use handguns in the context of ranching, farming, target shooting, or hunting must always carry written consent from a parent? Should minors be prohibited the use of pistols regardless of their environment or purpose?

b. *Regulation of Sellers*

In addition to the licensing requirements and the obligation to perform background checks on firearms purchasers discussed above, federally licensed firearms dealers (FFLs) have many other obligations. Among the most important are that dealers must (1) keep an acquisitions and dispositions log recording the details of every purchase and sale (including the identity of the buyer or seller and the make, model, and serial number of the gun); (2) retain all Forms 4473 completed by purchasers; (3) complete and retain Form 3310.4, reports of multiple sales of pistols and revolvers to the ATF; and (4) complete and retain all Form 3301.11 reports of theft or loss of a firearm to the ATF.

Dealers also are required to comply with a variety of general restrictions. For example, dealers may freely ship firearms in interstate commerce between themselves, but may not ship or transport a firearm in interstate commerce to a non-licensee. 18 U.S.C. §922(a)(3). This means that customers cannot buy a gun directly from a dealer over the Internet or through any other non–face-to-face transaction. All transactions must take place face to face at the dealer's place of business (a storefront or a home office) or at a gun show. To purchase a gun remotely, the buyer must arrange for the licensed seller to ship the gun to another licensed dealer in the buyer's location. The buyer takes delivery from that local dealer, after providing a photo ID, completing a Form 4473, and passing the NICS background check. If the seller is a private individual in a different state, the seller must ship the gun to a licensed dealer in the buyer's state where the standard purchasing procedure will occur.

Dealers are also subject to on-premises inspection of their records and inventory, raising a Fourth Amendment question that was addressed by the Supreme Court in the case below.

United States v. Biswell
406 U.S. 311 (1972)

[Biswell held a Federal Firearms License that entitled him to sell guns at his pawn shop. Local and federal agents visited his shop, identified themselves, and asked to enter and inspect his locked gun storage room. Biswell asked if they had a warrant. The agents showed him the provisions of the 1968 Act that permitted warrantless searches, and he consented to the search. During the inspection, agents found two guns covered under the 1934 National Firearms Act (the same statute violated by the defendants in *United States v. Miller*, discussed in

Chapter 7.). Neither gun had the tax stamp required under the '34 Act. Biswell was indicted and convicted. The Fourth Circuit reversed on the grounds that the provision in the 1968 Act for warrantless searches violated the Fourth Amendment. The Supreme Court reversed, and upheld provisions of the 1968 Act that permit unannounced warrantless searches of the premises of dealers who hold Federal Firearms Licenses. *See* 18 U.S.C. §923(g).]

MR. JUSTICE WHITE delivered the opinion of the Court. . . .

. . . Federal regulation of the interstate traffic in firearms . . . is undeniably of central importance to federal efforts to prevent violent crime and to assist the States in regulating the firearms traffic within their borders. See Congressional Findings and Declaration, Note preceding 18 U.S.C. §922. Large interests are at stake, and inspection is a crucial part of the regulatory scheme, since it assures that weapons are distributed through regular channels and in a traceable manner and makes possible the prevention of sales to undesirable customers and the detection of the origin of particular firearms.

It is also apparent that if the law is to be properly enforced and inspection made effective, inspections without warrant must be deemed reasonable official conduct under the Fourth Amendment. . . . Here, if inspection is to be effective and serve as a credible deterrent, unannounced, even frequent inspections are essential. . . .

We have little difficulty in concluding that where, as here, regulatory inspections further urgent federal interest, and the possibilities of abuse and the threat to privacy are not of impressive dimensions, the inspection may proceed without a warrant where specifically authorized by statute. The seizure of respondent's sawed off rifles was not unreasonable under the Fourth Amendment. . . .

NOTES & QUESTIONS

1. *Biswell* is a leading administrative law case for the principle that regulated businesses can be subjected to warrantless inspections. Do you agree with the Court's Fourth Amendment analysis?

2. Consider Justice White's statement that the GCA makes weapons traceable. Where might his reasoning break down?

3. The 1968 Act also raised the question of who precisely was required to obtain a license to sell firearms. It did not prohibit individuals from selling their privately owned firearms. But how many guns can a private person sell before being deemed to be in the business of selling firearms, which requires a FFL? In 1986, Congress passed FOPA, partly in response to concerns about aggressive prosecutions of private collectors and traders in cases like *Mandina v. United States*, 472 F.2d 1110 (8th Cir. 1973); *United States v. Ruisi*, 460 F.2d 153 (2d Cir. 1972) (sale of 11 guns at a gun show; "the question of why the government chose to prosecute these cases inevitably arises"); *United States v. Huffman*, 518 F.2d 80 (4th Cir. 1975) (government must show profit motive and a greater degree of activity than occasional sales

by a hobbyist). Private or secondary sales are at the heart of the questions examined in the next section.

3. Private Sales and Private Manufacturers: The Secondary Market and Gun Shows

Not all sellers of firearms are licensed dealers. Recall that in the previous treatment of what constitutes dealing in firearms, Congress did not require all sellers of firearms to obtain a federal license, only persons "engaged in the business." "Secondary" or "private" sales by non-dealer individuals constitute up to 40 percent of gun sales, by one estimate. National Research Council of the National Academies, Firearms and Violence: A Critical Review p. 74 (National Academies Press 2004). Federal law restricts but does not bar these private transfers. All secondary sales are of used guns, since firearms manufacturers and wholesalers of new guns only sell to FFLs.

A nonlicensee (i.e., private seller) is prohibited from selling a firearm to another non-licensee if the seller "has reasonable cause to believe the buyer resides in another state." However, private transfers of firearms between residents of the same state are permitted. But even then, the private sale is unlawful if the seller knows or has reasonable cause to believe that the buyer is disqualified from purchasing a firearm for any of the reasons designated on Form 4473. 18 U.S.C. §922(d). A few states, such as California, bar private sales, by requiring that all secondary transfers, except among close family members, be routed through a licensed firearms dealer.

Private or secondary sales are at the heart of debate and complaints about what has been called the "Gun Show Loophole." *E.g.*, Violence Policy Center, Closing the Gun Show Loophole (2001), *available at* http://www.vpc.org/studies/gun-loop.htm. Strictly speaking, the label is inaccurate, though one might speak instead of a "Private Sale Loophole." Current law does allow licensed dealers to sell guns at gun shows, but they must comply with the same requirements that would apply to a sale made at their business premises: The buyer must provide proper identification, complete the Form 4473, and pass NICS scrutiny. 18 U.S.C. §923(j). Likewise, the laws regulating secondary sales between private individuals at gun shows are exactly the same as for secondary sales anywhere else, like a hunting club meeting, or at one's home. The Internet has made it easier for would-be secondary sellers and purchasers to find each other. Many firearms enthusiast sites on the Internet contain classified sections where residents of the same state can communicate to purchase or sell used firearms.

Gun shows are usually one- or two-day weekend events where scores and sometimes hundreds of licensed dealers gather to display and sell a portion of their inventory. The gun show is open to members of the public who pay a fee to enter and get access to the inventory of many dealers in one location. Members of the public also may bring their private firearms to sell or trade. People who do not hold FFLs will sometimes rent a table at a gun show to display items for sale. At a typical gun show, there are many products for display other than firearms — such as books, videos, ammunition, accessories such as slings or scopes, outdoor gear, and even beef jerky. Local gun rights groups and politicians like to rent tables to distribute literature, taking advantage of the opportunity for contact with hundreds or thousands of potential customers or supporters.

Federal law generally permits secondary sales between people who are otherwise permitted to own firearms, so long as they reside in the same state. However, some states have imposed additional regulations on secondary sales. Colorado, Oregon, and New York have imposed special restrictions on secondary sales at gun shows, but not on secondary sales elsewhere. (In New York State, but not in New York City, secondary sales of long guns are generally lawful.) As the next case illustrates, regulation of sales at gun shows has raised constitutional questions that go beyond the Second Amendment.

Scope v. Pataki
386 F. Supp. 2d 184 (W.D.N.Y. 2005)

SIRAGUSA, District Judge.

INTRODUCTION

Plaintiffs are challenging a statute enacted by the New York Legislature pertaining to the sale of guns and the creation of a State database for guns sold in New York. Before the Court are defendants' motion for judgment on the pleadings, or motion to dismiss, pursuant to Federal Rules of Civil Procedure 12(c) and 12(b), and plaintiffs' cross-motion, also pursuant to Rule 12(c), for "partial summary judgment" and injunctive relief. For the reasons stated below, the Court partially grants and partially denies both motions.

BACKGROUND

The issues raised in the parties' applications can be resolved at this juncture by examination of the complaint and referenced statute. As to the identity of the plaintiffs, the complaint, filed on April 23, 2004, asserts that the Shooter's Committee on Political Education, Inc. ("SCOPE") is a New York not-for-profit corporation devoted to preserving the legal possession and use of handguns, rifles and shotguns. . . .

The first four causes of action in the complaint pertain to New York General Business Law sections 895, 896 and 897, all enacted as Article 39-DD — Sale of Fire-arms, Rifles, or Shotguns at Gun Shows (McKinney 2000). L. 2000, c. 189, §5, eff. Aug. 8, 2000. Those statutes state in relevant part as follows:

§895. Definitions
   For the purposes of this article:
   1. "Gun show" means an event sponsored, whether for profit or not, by an individual, national, state or local organization, association or other entity devoted to the collection, competitive use, sporting use, or any other legal use of firearms, rifles or shotguns, or an event at which (a) twenty percent or more of the total number of exhibitors are firearm exhibitors or (b) ten or more firearm exhibitors are participating or (c) a total of twenty-five or more pistols or revolvers are offered

for sale or transfer or (d) a total of fifty or more firearms, rifles or shotguns are offered for sale or transfer. The term gun show shall include any building, structure or facility where firearms, rifles or shotguns are offered for sale or transfer and any grounds used in connection with the event.

§896. Operation of a gun show
   1. A gun show operator shall:
       (a) at all times during such show conspicuously post and maintain signs stating "A National Instant Criminal Background Check must be completed prior to all firearm sales or transfers, including sales or transfers of rifles or shotguns." Signs must be posted at all entrances to the gun show, at all places where admission tickets to the gun show are sold and not less than four additional locations within the grounds of the gun show;
       (b) notify all firearm exhibitors in writing that a national instant criminal background check must be completed prior to all firearm sales or transfers, including sales or transfers of rifles or shotguns; and
       (c) provide access at the gun show to a firearm dealer licensed under federal law who is authorized to perform a national instant criminal background check where the seller or transferor of a firearm, rifle or shotgun is not authorized to conduct such a check by (i) requiring firearm exhibitors who are firearm dealers licensed under federal law and who are authorized to conduct a national instant criminal background check to provide such a check at cost or (ii) designating a specific location at the gun show where a firearm dealer licensed under federal law who is authorized to conduct a national instant criminal background check will be present to perform such a check at cost. Any firearm dealer licensed under federal law who performs a national instant criminal background check pursuant to this paragraph shall provide the seller or transferor of the firearm, rifle or shotgun with a copy of the United States Department of Treasury, Bureau of Alcohol, Tobacco and Firearms Form ATF F 4473 and such dealer shall maintain such form and make such form available for inspection by law enforcement agencies for a period of ten years thereafter.
   2. Whenever the attorney general shall believe from evidence satisfactory to him or her that a gun show operator has violated any of the provisions of this section, the attorney general may bring an action or special proceeding in the supreme court for a judgment enjoining the continuance of such violation and for a civil penalty in an amount not to exceed ten thousand dollars. If it shall appear to the satisfaction of the court or justice that the defendant has violated any provisions of this section, no proof shall be required that any person has been injured thereby nor that the defendant intentionally violated such provision. In such action preliminary relief may be granted under article sixty-three of the civil practice law and rules. In connection with any such proposed application, the attorney general is authorized to take proof, issue subpoenas and administer oaths in the manner provided in the civil practice law and rules.

§897. Sale of a firearm, rifle or shotgun at a gun show
   1. A national instant criminal background check shall be conducted and no person shall sell or transfer a firearm, rifle or shotgun at a gun show, except in accordance with the provisions of 18 U.S.C. 922(t).
   2. No person shall offer or agree to sell or transfer a firearm, rifle or shotgun to another person at a gun show and transfer or deliver such firearm, rifle or shotgun to such person or person acting on his or her behalf thereafter at a location other than the gun show for the purpose of evading or avoiding compliance with 18 U.S.C. 922(t).

3. Any person who knowingly violates any of the provisions of this section shall be guilty of a class A misdemeanor punishable as provided for in the penal law.

N.Y. Genl. Bus. Law §§895(1), 896, 897 (McKinney's 2000). . . .

First Four Causes of Action

In the First cause of action, plaintiffs claim that New York General Business Law section 895 "is capable of sweeping and improper interpretation [and that] it violates the Due Process clause of the Fourteenth Amendment." . . .

In the Second cause of action, plaintiffs assert that New York General Business Law section 895(1) "infringes upon constitutionally protected privacy interests because it purports to regulate conduct of conservation members and those attending events sponsored by the plaintiffs which is purely private in nature and which bears no relationship to any substantial interest of the State of New York." . . .

The Third cause of action also pertains to New York General Business Law section 895, and alleges that, "if the purpose of [the statute] in so far as it designates 'events' sponsored by '[persons] devoted to the collection, competitive use, sporting use, or any other legal use of firearms, rifles or shotguns' as a 'gun show,' is to declare any assembly of gun owners anywhere for any purpose a 'gun show,' it is over broad and infringes upon the right of free speech, right to lawfully assemble, and the right to peacefully petition guaranteed by the First Amendment of the Bill of Rights." . . .

The Fourth cause of action states that, "General Business Law Sections 895, 896, and 897 imposes [sic] special obligations upon associations of gun owners and persons interested in gun ownership imposed upon no other 'event' sponsored by any other association of like minded persons. It violates equal protection of the law because it serves no compelling or substantial state interest by seeking to regulate 'private sales' of guns at 'events' totally unrelated to the sale or distribution of guns on the basis of the thoughts and beliefs of those who sponsor those events." . . .

DISCUSSION

Plaintiffs have alleged that the statutory definition of "gun show" is unconstitutionally vague, overbroad, violative of the Due Process clause, gives too much discretion to police and violates plaintiffs' rights to free speech, assembly and petition.

"Gun Show" Definition Not Vague

Plaintiffs' First cause of action claims that the statute is so vague as to be violative of the Due Process Clause of the Fourteenth Amendment. The Court disagrees. "It is settled that the fair-warning requirement embodied in the Due Process Clause prohibits the States from holding an individual 'criminally responsible for conduct which he could not reasonably understand to be proscribed.'" *Rose v. Locke*, 423 U.S. 48, 49 (1975) (quoting *United States v. Harris*, 347 U.S. 612, 617 (1954)). The Court does not agree that the statute is vague.

General Business Law section 895(1) defines a gun show as either "an event sponsored, whether for profit or not, by an individual, national, state or local organization, association or other entity devoted to the collection, competitive use, sporting use, or any other legal use of firearms, rifles or shotguns" or "an event at which (a) twenty percent or more of the total number of exhibitors are firearm exhibitors or (b) ten or more firearm exhibitors are participating or (c) a total of twenty-five or more pistols or revolvers are offered for sale or transfer or (d) a total of fifty or more firearms, rifles or shotguns are offered for sale or transfer."

While the second portion of the "gun show" definition clearly defines objective criteria by which to measure whether the event is considered by the statute a gun show, the first portion does not. However, this does not render that aspect of the definition of "gun show" vague. To the contrary, an event sponsored by plaintiffs at which no gun sales take place could, by the plain meaning of the terms used in the statute, be construed by the New York Attorney General to be a "gun show." This is important to plaintiffs since gun shows trigger the requirements of section 896, which includes the requirement to post signs and make a federal licensed dealer available to run national instant criminal background checks. Of course, if no gun sales take place at the sponsored event, then the requirements of section 896 would be inapplicable. Plaintiffs' concern is that a pig roast sponsored by them could be deemed by the statute to be a gun show, requiring the posting of signs and availability of criminal background checks, if any informal discussion pertaining to the purchase of a firearm takes place at the sponsored event, and is then consummated by a later private sale. (See Compl. P44.)

Defendants respond that since the statute is in an Article entitled, "Sale of Firearms, Rifles, or Shotguns at Gun Shows," there is no possibility of mistaking a pig roast for a gun show under the terms of the statute. However, defendants cite no limiting State court opinion to that effect. . . .

. . . Here the Court agrees with plaintiffs' position. It is indeed conceivable that plaintiffs could sponsor a pig roast at which two individuals discuss the private sale of a gun, and the sale is later consummated, and that plaintiffs could then be found in violation of the statute for not having followed the requirements imposed by section 896 on gun show operators. That section gives the Attorney General great discretion:

> Whenever the attorney general shall believe from evidence satisfactory to him or her that a gun show operator has violated any of the provisions of this section, the attorney general may bring an action or special proceeding in the supreme court for a judgment enjoining the continuance of such violation and for a civil penalty in an amount not to exceed ten thousand dollars. . . .

N.Y. Genl. Bus. Law §896(2). On this point, in support of its determination, the Court refers to defense counsel's exchange with the Court at oral argument:

> The Court: If I'm at the pancake breakfast sponsored by a gun club and I say to you, gee, I heard you have this nifty gun, that it is for sale. Yeah, it's in the trunk here. Why wouldn't that apply?

Defense Counsel: At the risk of taxing the Court's patience, because we say it doesn't. Because we are not going to prosecute (seek) civil actions or enforcement under that situation. In our wisdom, we have reviewed the legislature, the title and concluded these criteria set forth by Mr. Nocenti apply and I'm sorry if the Court feels that procedurally that is beyond the scope of what it can consider, but I think it's important to consider that.

. . . With due respect to the defense, it is not the wisdom of the Attorney General that controls, but the plain text of the statute.

Additionally, citing to *Brotherhood of R.R. Trainmen v. Baltimore & O. R. Co.*, 331 U.S. 519, 528-29 (1947), defendants argue that the Court must construe the meaning of the definition by considering the title of the statute as well as the statute itself. *Id.* Defendants maintain that, in the Attorney General's opinion, when viewed in context with the title, "the law regulates only events sponsored by gun organizations where guns are displayed for sale *or where arrangements for the sale of said weapons are made.*" . . . However, *Brotherhood of R.R. Trainmen* included the following language pertaining to a court's use of the heading or title of a statute to interpret its provisions:

> . . . [T]he title of a statute and the heading of a section cannot limit the plain meaning of the text. . . . For interpretative purposes, they are of use only when they shed light on some ambiguous word or phrase. They are but tools available for the resolution of a doubt. But they cannot undo or limit that which the text makes plain. . . .

Brotherhood of R.R. Trainmen, 331 U.S. at 528-29 (1947).

The statute is not vague. Quite the contrary, the statute is clear in its plain language. Any event sponsored by a gun club would constitute a gun show under the definition of the statute. Consequently, defendants' motion to dismiss the First cause of action (claiming a violation of the Due Process Clause of the Fourteenth Amendment on the grounds of vagueness), must be granted. . . .

"GUN SHOW" DEFINITION OVERBROAD

Plaintiff's Third cause of action alleges that section 895(1) is so broad that it essentially declares any assembly of gun owners for any purpose a "gun show" and infringes on plaintiffs' right to lawfully assemble, right to free speech and right to petition the government. The Court agrees that the statute is overbroad. . . .

"Facial overbreadth has not been invoked when a limiting construction has been or could be placed on the challenged statute." *Broadrick v. Oklahoma*, 413 U.S. 601, 613 (1973). The Supreme Court wrote that to invalidate a state statute that regulates harmful, or constitutionally unprotected conduct, "the overbreadth of a statute must not only be real, but substantial as well, judged in relation to the statute's plainly legitimate sweep." *Broadrick v. Oklahoma*, 413 U.S. 601, 615 (1973). "Where a statute's literal scope, unaided by a narrowing state court interpretation, is capable of reaching expression sheltered by the First Amendment, the doctrine demands a greater degree of specificity than in other contexts." *Smith v. Goguen*, 415 U.S. 566, 573 (1974) (footnote omitted). . . .

As the Supreme Court wrote in *Keyishian v. Board of Regents*, 385 U.S. 589, 602 (1967) (quoting Shelton v. Tucker, 364 U.S. 479, 488), "'even though the governmental purpose be legitimate and substantial, that purpose cannot be pursued by means that broadly stifle fundamental personal liberties when the end can be more narrowly achieved.'"

As indicated above, the Court determines that the plain meaning of the first clause of section 895(1) defines any gathering of a gun club to be a "gun show." Since the Court is unaided by a narrowing State court interpretation, it is not persuaded by defendants' argument that by relying on the title of Article 39-DD, the first clause of section 895(1) can be interpreted in a manner that passes constitutional muster. Here, unaided by a narrowing State court interpretation, the Court finds that the first clause in the definition of a "gun show" in New York General Business Law section 895(1) is overbroad and infringes on the gun club plaintiffs' constitutionally protected rights to free speech, assembly and petition. Therefore, the Court grants plaintiffs' motion for judgment on the pleadings with respect to the Third cause of action.

EQUAL PROTECTION

In their Fourth cause of action, plaintiffs allege that New York General Business Law sections 895, 896 and 897 violate their rights to equal protection of the laws. They argue that the statutes make any assembly of a gun club a "gun show," subject to the requirements and penalties of section 896, whereas a similar assembly of an organization not described in section 895(1) would not be subject to those requirements or penalties. The Court agrees.

As the Supreme Court explained in *Massachusetts Bd. of Retirement v. Murgia*, 427 U.S. 307 (1976), its decision in "*San Antonio School District v. Rodriguez*, 411 U.S. 1, 16 (1973), reaffirmed that Equal Protection analysis requires strict scrutiny of a legislative classification only when the classification impermissibly interferes with the exercise of a fundamental right or operates to the peculiar disadvantage of a suspect class." *Mass. Bd. of Retirement*, 427 U.S. at 312 (footnote omitted). The rights guaranteed by the First Amendment are fundamental. Id. at 312 n.3 (citing *Williams v. Rhodes*, 393 U.S. 23 (1968)). To justify treating all gun club assemblies as "gun shows," New York must show that the unequal treatment is "premised upon some compelling state interest." *San Antonio Sch. Dist.*, 411 U.S. at 16. Because the Court has not converted the Federal Rule of Civil Procedure 12(c) motion to one for summary judgment, and since the issue cannot be decided solely on the allegations contained in the pleadings, the Court denies judgment to either side under Rule 12(c) on this cause of action, and additionally denies defendants' application for dismissal under Rule 12(b)(6). . . .

Ordered, that judgment be entered for plaintiffs on the Third cause of action as it pertains to the following language in New York General Business Law section 895(1) . . . which the Court determines is unconstitutional as an overbroad restriction on plaintiff gun clubs' First Amendment rights to free speech, assembly and petition; and it is further

Ordered, that defendants are enjoined from enforcing the following clause of New York General Business Law section 895(1). . . .

As discussed above, federal law permits private transfers of firearms within the limits discussed above. 18 U.S.C.A. §922(d). Some state laws impose additional requirements. The following case illustrates the Maryland approach and its application.

Chow v. Maryland
903 A.2d 388 (Md. 2006)

CATHELL, J.

This case concerns whether the temporary gratuitous exchange or loan of a regulated firearm[1] between two adult individuals, who were otherwise permitted to own and obtain a handgun, constitutes an illegal transfer of a firearm in violation of Maryland Code (1957, 1996 Repl. Vol., 2002 Supp.), Art. 27, §442.[2] The particular issue before us is the contextual meaning of the word "transfer," as it is used in §442(d), "A person who is not a regulated firearms dealer may not sell, rent, *transfer*, or purchase any regulated firearm. . . ." (Emphasis added). Thus, we must decide whether a temporary gratuitous exchange or loan of a regulated firearm constitutes a "transfer" under §442(d). . . .

. . . [W]e hold that the plain language and legislative history of the "Regulated Firearms" subheading indicates that the word "transfer," as used in §442(d), is used in an ownership context and does not apply to the situation extant in the case *sub judice*— that of a gratuitous temporary exchange or loan between two adults who are otherwise permitted to own and obtain regulated firearms. . . .

---

1. Maryland Code (1957, 1996 Repl. Vol., 2002 Supp.), Art. 27, §441(r) defines "Regulated Firearm":

> "Regulated firearm. — 'Regulated firearm' means:
> (1) Any handgun as defined in this section; or
> (2) Any assault weapon as defined in this section."

2. Maryland Code (1957, 1996 Repl. Vol., 2002 Supp.), Art. 27, §§441 et seq. composes the "Regulated Firearms" subheading. Section 442 states in pertinent part:

> "(d) Sale by other than regulated firearms dealer. — (1) A person who is not a regulated firearms dealer may not sell, rent, transfer, or purchase any regulated firearm until after 7 days shall have elapsed from the time an application to purchase or transfer shall have been executed by the prospective purchaser or transferee, in triplicate, and the original copy is forwarded by a regulated firearms dealer to the Secretary." . . .

I. Facts

We adopt, in part, the facts as stated by the Court of Special Appeals in its opinion below:

"[Petitioner's] friend, Man Nguyen, was the State's main witness at trial. Nguyen testified that, while driving his car on April 1, 2003, he was stopped by the Prince George's County Police Department for a broken taillight. At that time, the police searched Nguyen's vehicle, and discovered a Glock semi-automatic pistol (not the weapon that is the subject of this appeal). The pistol was properly registered in Nguyen's name, but he did not have a permit to carry it. The police confiscated it in connection with their investigation of a recent murder of one of Nguyen's friends.

"The following day, Nguyen contacted [petitioner]. Nguyen explained to [petitioner] that this gun and other guns at his home had been confiscated by the police, and he was 'anxious' to buy another gun. He told [petitioner] that he needed to purchase a gun for protection, by which he meant '[h]ome security,' '[s]o, [petitioner] offered me his gun.'

"The two men arranged to meet later that day for lunch at a restaurant in Bowie, Maryland. Sometime during this meeting, [petitioner] gave Nguyen a nine millimeter, semi-automatic handgun that he had owned since 1996.

"Nguyen told [petitioner] that he wanted to test fire the weapon before purchasing it. The pair got into Nguyen's vehicle and headed to a firing range in Upper Marlboro. En route, Nguyen received a business call on his cellular telephone, requiring that he abort the trip to the firing range. Nguyen drove [petitioner] back to the restaurant where [petitioner's] car was parked and dropped him off. [Petitioner's] weapon remained in Nguyen's car. No money was exchanged between Nguyen and [petitioner].

"Soon thereafter, Nguyen contacted [petitioner] by telephone. Nguyen testified: 'I was interested in buying it and I called him, and, you know, I told him I'd give it back to him but he said, that's cool, just keep it in the house and he'll pick it up.' Nguyen further testified that he anticipated the weapon would be returned to appellant 'as soon as possible.'

"Detective Donnie Judd testified as a State's witness. He reported that, on April 4, 2003, he and other members of the Prince George's County Police Department stopped Nguyen on a warrant to arrest him for having illegally carried the gun that was found in his car three days earlier. In the ensuing search of Nguyen's car, the police discovered [petitioner's] loaded handgun in the car's center console. Detective Judd ran an NCIC check and determined that the handgun had not been reported stolen. The gun was test fired and determined to be operable.

"Nguyen was arrested and taken to the police station, where he gave a four-page statement. The first paragraph of the statement addressed how he had obtained [petitioner's] handgun, and that portion of the statement was admitted into evidence. It varied from Nguyen's trial testimony. Nguyen wrote:

I know [sic] [petitioner] for 2-3 [years]. I was detain [sic] on 4-1-03 and PGPD took all my guns. Next [d]ay, I called [petitioner] and asked him if I could hold on to his gun until I can get my guns back in a week or two because I felt uncomfortable without a gun[.] We then met at Olive Garden att [sic] 4pm in Bowie and had lunch and after that he give [sic] me his 9mm, out of a bag in the front Passengers [sic] seat[.]

"Sergeant William Szimanski, of the State Police Licensing Division, Firearms Registration Section, performs background checks on persons purchasing regulated firearms in Maryland and deals with records concerning firearms purchases. He testified that the records related to [petitioner's] handgun reflect that [petitioner] bought the handgun in November 1996, and it was formally transferred to him on the 27th of that month, after completion of the weapon registration process. The records show no subsequent transfer of the handgun, and no application for a transfer of the gun from [petitioner] to Nguyen.

"Sergeant Guillermo Rivera, of the Office of Internal Affairs of the District of Columbia Metropolitan Police Department, also testified. He stated that appellant had not filed a stolen weapon report between November 17, 2001 and November 17, 2003.

"At the close of the State's case, [petitioner] made a motion for judgment of acquittal. [Petitioner] argued that §442(d) does not cover his conduct, which was simply a temporary exchange of the handgun. In the alternative, [petitioner] argued that he did not 'knowingly' violate the statute, as required by §449(f), because the State did not prove that he knew the transferee, Nguyen, had not filed the application required by §442(d).

"The State countered that [petitioner's] leaving the gun with Nguyen was a 'transfer' of it, and therefore was covered by §442(d). The State further argued that [petitioner] was aware of the requirements for transferring a handgun, because he had fulfilled those requirements himself when he purchased the gun in 1996. The State finally argued that the 'plain meaning' of transfer does not necessarily include the conveyance of title, and encompasses a mere loan.

"After hearing from counsel on both issues, the [Circuit Court for Prince George's County] denied the motion. [Petitioner] then rested without putting on any evidence, and the court issued its ruling."

Chow, 881 A.2d at 1151-52 (some footnotes omitted).

The trial court judge then found petitioner guilty and sentenced him to sixty (60) days — with the sentence suspended — and a fine of two hundred dollars ($200). In doing so, the trial judge stated: "And the reason why I'm giving you the disposition is *I believe that it was a temporary transfer,* it was illegal, but, what the transferee did with it [the regulated firearm] was not within your control, and he clearly stated on the record that you told him to put it in the house, and he chose not to." [Emphasis added].

Petitioner timely noted an appeal to the Court of Special Appeals. On June 2, 2005, The Court of Special Appeals filed its opinion. The court affirmed the decision of the Circuit Court. Specifically, in reference to the interpretation of the word "transfer," the court stated:

"[W]e hold that plainly included within the meaning of 'transfer' of a regulated firearm, in §442(d), is lending a firearm. The plain construction of the term is confirmed by an examination of the general purpose of the regulated firearms [subheading], and by the rule that the remedial portions of a statute are to be liberally construed. Therefore, a person violates §442(d) by lending a regulated firearm to another person without there first being compliance with the application process and seven-day waiting period set forth in that section." . . .

III. DISCUSSION

A. THE MEANING OF "TRANSFER" IN THE CONTEXT OF §442(D)

Section 442(d) of the Regulated Firearms subheading governs the sale or "transfer" of regulated firearms by an individual that is not a regulated firearms dealer. As stated *supra*, the statute states, in pertinent part:

> "(d) *Sale by other than regulated firearms dealer.* — (1) A person who is not a regulated firearms dealer may not sell, rent, *transfer*, or purchase any regulated firearm until after 7 days shall have elapsed from the time an application to purchase or transfer shall have been executed by the prospective purchaser or transferee, in triplicate, and the original copy is forwarded by a regulated firearms dealer to the Secretary."

§442(d)(1) (emphasis added).

Petitioner contends that the legislative intent of using the term "transfer," as found in §442(d), was to mean a permanent exchange of title or possession of a regulated firearm, as in a gift or bequeathment, rather than a mere loan or temporary exchange of such firearm. The State, in opposition, argues that §442(d) prohibits *all* exchanges of regulated firearms, temporary or permanent, whether by sale, rental, gift, loan, exchange or otherwise and no matter how temporary. . . .

The Court of Special Appeals found that an interpretation of "transfer" as suggestive only of a permanent exchange of title or possession "would run afoul of the rule that '[o]rdinary and popular understanding of the English language dictates interpretation of terminology within legislation.'" *Chow*, 881 A.2d at 1154 (citing *Deville*, 858 A.2d 484). The court, however, provides no support for this conclusion other than what can be inferred from its discussion of the two dictionary definitions it provided, *supra*, which arguably supported both the petitioner's and the State's arguments. Analyzing "transfer" in light of the definitions in effect at the time of the legislative enactment of §442(d), we do not find petitioner's interpretation of "transfer" to run afoul of the ordinary and popular understanding of the English language.

Words can have multiple meanings and often do. And the numerous meanings of a particular word may each satisfy the ordinary and popular understanding of that word. In order to interpret a word's specific meaning in a particular statute we look to the context in which the word is used. As we stated *supra*, "The plain language of a provision is not interpreted in isolation. Rather, we analyze the statutory scheme as a whole and attempt to harmonize provisions dealing with the same subject so that each may be given effect. *Deville*, 858 A.2d at 487; *Navarro-Monzo v. Washington Adventist*, 844 A.2d 406, 411 (2004)." *Kushell*, 870 A.2d at 193.

2. "Transfer" in the Context of the Regulated
   Firearms Subheading

While the Regulated Firearms subheading does not specifically define the term "transfer," it does use the term several times throughout its various sections. Section 441 provides the definitions for the subheading. In particular,

§441 (f) states that: "'Dealer' means any person who is engaged in the *business* of: (1) Selling, renting, or *transferring* firearms at wholesale or retail." (Emphasis added). Transfer, as used in this section, obviously concerns transfers for consideration ("wholesale" and "retail" are business terms). Section 441 (t) states that: "'Rent' means the *temporary transfer* of a regulated firearm *for consideration* where the firearm is taken from the firearm owner's property." (Emphasis added). Finally, §441 (w) states that: "'Straw purchase' means any sale of a regulated firearm where the individual uses another person (the straw purchaser) to complete the application to purchase a regulated firearm, take initial possession of that firearm, and subsequently *transfer* that firearm to the individual." (Emphasis added). This section also obviously concerns transfers for consideration. In all of the above instances (except where "Rent" is specifically defined and delineated as a temporary transfer for consideration) the word "transfer" is used in the sense of a permanent exchange of title or possession of the regulated firearm for consideration. . . .

It is evident that the application, referenced by §442(b)(3)(i), to purchase or transfer regulated firearms was only designed for permanent "transfers" of such firearms. In fact, the only options available, as indicated at the top of the second page of the application, are for "Dealer Sale," "Secondary Sale," "Gift," and "Voluntary Registration." With the exception of "Voluntary Registration," each option evinces a permanent exchange of title or possession between two individuals. "Voluntary Registration" is indicative of an individual already in possession of a regulated firearm, not of any type of exchange.

Section 442(d)(2) states: "As an alternative to completing a secondary sale of a regulated firearm through a regulated fire arms dealer, the prospective seller or transferor and the prospective purchaser or transferee may complete the transaction through a designated law enforcement agency." This section provides an alternative to §442(d), the pertinent section in the case *sub judice*. The use of "transfer" in §442(d)(2) distinctly refers to a permanent exchange. This is evident through the introductory language of the section, "As an alternative to completing a secondary *sale*. . . ." §442(d)(2) (emphasis added). Transferor (in conjunction with seller) and transferee (in conjunction with purchaser) in this context is concerned with completing a secondary *sale* (permanent exchange) of a regulated firearm through a designated law enforcement agency rather than through a regulated firearms dealer.

Section 443, entitled "Regulated firearm dealer's license," states in subsection (a), that "[n]o person shall engage in the *business* of selling, renting, or *transferring* regulated firearms unless he lawfully possesses and conspicuously displays at his place of business, in addition to any other license required by law, a regulated firearms dealer's license issued by the Secretary." (Emphasis added). Again, similar to §441(f), the use of "transfer" in the context of a person engaging in the firearms business provides a connotation of permanent exchange of title or possession generally for consideration. . . .

IV. CONCLUSION

We find that the temporary gratuitous exchange or loan of a regulated handgun between two adult individuals, who are otherwise permitted to own and obtain a regulated handgun, does not constitute an illegal "transfer" of a firearm in violation of Maryland Code (1957, 1996 Repl. Vol., 2002 Supp.), Art. 27, §442, in particular, subsection (d). The plain language of §442(d), when construed in harmony with the rest of the subheading, reveals that "transfer" can only refer to a *permanent* exchange of title or possession and does not include gratuitous temporary exchanges or loans. Legislative history further supports our interpretation. We also conclude that the inclusion of the term "knowingly" in §449(f) creates a specific intent *mens rea* for violations of that subsection. Thus, in order to be in violation of §449(f), a person must know that the activity they are engaging in is illegal. This ruling does not place any undue burden on the State. "Rather, as in any other criminal prosecution requiring *mens rea*, the [State] may prove by reference to facts and circumstances surrounding the case that [the defendant] knew that his conduct was unauthorized or illegal." *Liparota*, 471 U.S. at 434 (footnote omitted).

JUDGMENT OF THE COURT OF SPECIAL APPEALS REVERSED. COSTS IN THIS COURT AND IN THE COURT OF SPECIAL APPEALS TO BE PAID BY THE RESPONDENT.

NOTES & QUESTIONS

1. Assume you live in Maryland. Your uncle, also a resident of Maryland, wants to sell you his favorite shotgun. You hand him $300 and take delivery. Have you violated the Maryland law discussed above? Note the definition of firearms subject to the Maryland restriction on secondary sales. Does your answer depend on the type of shotgun transferred?

2. Beyond the limited federal restrictions on secondary sales in 18 U.S.C. §922(d), another provision that we already have discussed is relevant. Recall the definition of dealers who are required to obtain a Federal Firearms License. Consider three scenarios: First, a private seller who brings a single gun to a gun show and sells it to a private buyer in the aisle or to a dealer at a table. Second, a private seller who takes 50 of his guns to a gun show, rents a table to display, sell, and trade them. He does this at gun shows 15 times per year and at the end of the year generally has upgraded his collection or made a profit. Third, siblings inherit their father's lifetime collection of 50 guns and sell them off at a series of gun shows over the course of several years. As a prosecutor, would you charge any of these sellers with dealing firearms without a license?

3. In addition to licensing the trade of NFA firearms and retail sales of ordinary firearms, the ATF issues a third type of license, called a "Curios and Relics" (C&R) license. This license is available to collectors of antique and collectible firearms placed by the ATF on a list of "Curios and Relics." Federal law does not require that gun collectors obtain a C&R license, but the license does provide some benefits. Curios and Relics are guns that have special value to collectors because of "qualities beyond ordinary sporting use or protection." They must meet one of the following criteria: (1) be

manufactured at least 50 years prior to the current date — newer replicas do not count; (2) be certified as curios or relics of museum interest by the curator of a municipal, state, or federal museum that exhibits firearms; or (3) derive a substantial part of their monetary value from the fact that they are novel, rare, bizarre, or from the fact of their association with some historical figure, period, or event. 27 CFR §478.11. Qualifying guns are in the "Firearms Curios or Relics List" (ATF Pub. 5300.11).

Anyone who is eligible to purchase a firearm can obtain a C&R license, so long as it is permitted by local law. The primary advantage of the license is that licensees can buy, sell, and ship firearms in interstate commerce directly with dealers and between themselves. This privilege only applies to guns designated as Curios and Relics. 27 CFR §478.41(c).

4. Under very narrow circumstances, a private person may ship and receive a firearm in interstate commerce. He must ship it to a licensed dealer, gunsmith, or manufacturer. If it is shipped for repair or replacement, it may be shipped back to him directly. 18 U.S.C. §924(a)(1)(d). However, as discussed above, a buyer may not purchase and have shipped to him a firearm in a nonface-to-face transaction.

Federal law also regulates the manufacturing and importation of firearms under separate licensing regimes. 27 CFR §478.41-58. This does not prohibit private parties from manufacturing their own firearms. With certain exceptions, private persons are not required to have a license to build their own guns, so long as the guns are not offered for sale and the private builder is not prohibited from possessing firearms.

However, a 1989 statute does prohibit the manufacture of "nonsporting semi-automatic rifles or non-sporting shotguns" from imported parts. 18 U.S.C. §922(r). The ATF defines "manufacture" to include assembly. So adding some foreign accessories or replacement parts (e.g., a new barrel) to an existing gun can be illegal under certain circumstances. The law against manufacture/assembly from foreign parts applies equally to U.S. firearms manufacturers, importers, and private individuals. 18 U.S.C. §922(r).

5. By far the most common form of home firearms manufacture is of modern replicas of antique guns. For example, a person might build a replica of an old-fashioned flintlock rifle from a kit. Since the GCA does not apply to muzzleloading guns, the flintlock builder is free to give his gun to a friend, or to sell it.

Antique kits aside, it is possible for a person with moderate competence to build a crude, single-shot firearm. Home manufacture of a gun comparable to the quality of what can be purchased in a gun store requires a higher level of skills, and is best done with sophisticated machine tools.

6. What is your assessment of the private manufacturing rules? Try to frame a rule that would improve the current regulation of private manufacturing and then discuss its viability and benefits and anticipate the objections it will raise. Consider what if any unintended consequences and costs and risks it might generate.

4. Sporting Use as a Marker of Legitimate Firearms

A major, long-standing issue in the modern gun control debate is whether a firearm is suitable for sporting use. Many persons argue that only sporting fire-arms should be legal. Some gun control laws, such as the Gun Control Act's criterion for what kinds of firearms may be imported, are explicitly based on the gun's suitability for sporting purposes. While suitability for sporting use is widely employed in the general debate, its statutory function is more limited, as the next case shows.

Gilbert v. Higgins
709 F. Supp. 1071 (S.D. Ala. 1989)

[The district court adopted the opinion of the magistrate judge, which follows.]

WILLIAM E. CASSADY, United States Magistrate.

This case is before the Magistrate for report and recommendation pursuant to 28 U.S.C. §636(b)(1)(B) on cross-motions for summary judgment. Upon consideration of the administrative record and all pertinent materials contained in this file, the Magistrate makes the following recommendation.

FACTS

In 1986, Gilbert Equipment Company, a licensed importer of firearms, applied to the Bureau of Alcohol, Tobacco and Firearms (hereinafter "ATF") for a permit to import the USAS-12 shotgun. . . . The USAS-12 is a highly advanced magazine-fed semiautomatic 12-gauge shotgun manufactured by Daewoo Precision Industries in Korea. (Para. 5 of Complaint). Soon after applying for the permit, Gilbert submitted information to the Bureau in an attempt to demonstrate that the USAS-12 "is generally recognized as particularly suitable for or readily adaptable to sporting purposes" and is thus importable under 18 U.S.C. Section 925(d)(3). . . . After several meetings between the parties and testing and evaluation by the Bureau, ATF, by letter dated December 16, 1986 from the office of William T. Drake, ATF Deputy Director, denied permission to Gilbert to import the USAS-12 inasmuch as "due to the weight, size, bulk, designed magazine capacity, configuration and other factors, the USAS-12 semiautomatic shotgun is not particularly suitable for or readily adaptable to sporting purposes." . . . On February 19, 1988, Gilbert sought ATF's permission to import five hundred (500) USAS-12 shotguns and accompanied its application with extensive memoranda, exhibits, and a videotape in support of a sporting use determination (Para. 14 of Complaint). By letter dated March 1, 1988, William E. Earle, Chief of the Firearms and Explosives Division, denied the application stating that ATF's position remained unchanged. . . . On March 24, 1988, plaintiff filed in this Court a complaint seeking: (1) mandamus relief; (2) a determination by this Court that defendant's actions were arbitrary, capricious, and an abuse of discretion; (3) a determination by the Court that defendant's conclusions were unwarranted by the facts and were not based on any facts; (4) a determination by this Court that the defendant violated its rights to due process of law and equal protection of the laws, rights which are guaranteed by the Fifth Amendment; and (5) a determination by this Court that defendant violated plaintiff's Second Amendment right to keep and bear arms. The parties' summary judgment memoranda have addressed all of the forms of relief requested and thus, a determination by this Court on the cross motions will make unnecessary a trial of this cause.

STATUTORY HISTORY

In 1968, Congress enacted the Gun Control Act which was designed to keep firearms out of the hands of those not legally entitled to possess them because of age, criminal background, or incompetency, and to assist law enforcement authorities in the states and their subdivisions in combating the ever increasing prevalence of crime in the United States. 1968 U.S. Code Cong. & Admin. News 2112, 2113-2114.[2] In 1968, Section 925(d) of the Act provided in pertinent part as follows:

> The Secretary *may* authorize a firearm or ammunition to be imported or brought into the United States or any possession thereof if *the person importing or bringing in the firearm or ammunition establishes to the satisfaction of the Secretary that the firearm or ammunition* . . .
>
> (3) is of a type that does not fall within the definition of a firearm as defined in Section 5845(a) of the Internal Revenue Code of 1954 [the National Firearms Act] and is generally recognized as particularly suitable for or readily adaptable to sporting purposes, excluding surplus military firearms.

18 U.S.C. §925(d)(3) (emphasis added).

The clear intent of Section 925(d)(3) was to "curb the flow of surplus military and other firearms being brought into the United States which are not particularly suitable for target shooting or hunting." 1968 U.S. Code Cong. & Admin. News 2112, 2167.[4] As Senator William [sic, Thomas] Dodd, sponsor of the legislation, emphasized,

> Title IV prohibits importation of arms which the Secretary determines are not suitable for research, sport, or as museum pieces. . . .
>
> The entire intent of the importation section is to get at those kinds of weapons that are used by criminals and that have no sporting purpose.

114 Cong. Rec. S 5556 Col. 3, S 5582 Col. 1, S 5585 Col. 2 (May 14, 1968) (statement of Senator Dodd). The determination of a weapon's suitability for sporting

---

2. The Gun Control Act of 1968, as amended, 18 U.S.C. §§921-29, along with the National Firearms Act of 1934, as amended, 26 U.S.C. Chapter 53, regulate the importation of firearms.

4. However, Section 925(d) of the Act was not meant to interfere with the bringing in of "currently produced firearms, such as rifles, shotguns, pistols or revolvers of recognized quality which are used for hunting and for recreational purposes, or for personal protection." Id. (emphasis added).

purposes was entrusted to the Secretary of the Treasury. 114 Cong. Rec. 27465, Col. 2 (Sept. 18, 1968) (statement of Sen. Murphy). As noted in one of the Senate Reports,

> The difficulty of defining weapons characteristics to meet this target [of eliminating importation of weapons used in crime], without discriminating against sporting quality firearms, was a major reason why the Secretary of the Treasury has been given fairly broad discretion in defining and administering the import prohibition. . . .

S. Rep. No. 1501, 90th Cong. 2d Sess. 38 (Sept. 6, 1968).

To assist the Secretary in exercising his discretion, Congress "recommended that the Secretary establish a council that would provide guidance and assistance to him in determining those firearms which meet the criteria for importation into the United States. . . ." S. Rep. No. 1501, 90th Cong. 2d Sess. 38 (Sept. 6, 1968). Immediately following enactment of the Gun Control Act, the Secretary of the Treasury appointed a Firearms Evaluation Panel to establish guidelines for implementation of the "sporting purposes" test of Section 925(d)(3), said panel being composed of representatives from the military, law enforcement, and firearms industries. While the panel did not propose specific criteria for evaluating shotguns[8] the apparent general criteria relied upon by the advisory panel and ATF from 1968 through 1986 for determining what is "generally recognized" as a sporting firearm is as follows:

> The Director may compile an Importation List of firearms and ammunition which he determines to be generally recognized as particularly suitable for or readily adaptable to sporting purposes. . . . No firearm shall be placed on the Importation List unless it is found that:
> (1) the caliber or gauge of the firearm is suitable for use in a recognized shooting sport,
> (2) the type of firearm is generally recognized as particularly suitable or readily adaptable to such use, and
> (3) the use of the firearm in a recognized shooting sport will not endanger the person using it due to deterioration through such use or because of workmanship, materials or design.

Specifically, with regard to shotguns, the two factors panel members were concerned with were the lack of easy convertability to full automatic and the barrel and overall length of the weapon (18-inch barrel length and 26-inch overall length for shotguns).

---

8. The panel did, however, recommend the adoption of factoring criteria to evaluate the various types of handguns based upon such considerations as overall length of the firearm, caliber, safety features, et cetera, and an evaluation sheet (ATF Form 4590) was thereafter developed and used for the purpose of evaluating handguns pursuant to Section 925(d)(3). The development of a specific evaluation sheet for handguns emphasizes the concern of many in the late 1960's of the proliferation of the cheaply manufactured Saturday Night Specials.

In 1986, Section 925(d) of the Gun Control Act was amended by the Firearms Owner's Protection Act to read in pertinent part as follows:

> The Secretary *shall* authorize a firearm or ammunition to be imported or brought into the United States or any possession thereof if the firearm or ammunition. . . .
>
> (3) is of a type that does not fall within the definition of a firearm as defined in *Section 5845(a) of the Internal Revenue Code of 1954* and is generally recognized as particularly suitable for or readily adaptable to sporting purposes, excluding surplus military firearms, *except in any case where the Secretary has not authorized the importation of the firearm pursuant to this paragraph, it shall be unlawful to import any frame, receiver, or barrel of such firearm which would be prohibited if assembled.*

18 U.S.C. §925(d)(3) (emphasis added).

The amendments to the Statute provide that the Secretary shall (instead of "may") authorize the importation of firearms generally recognized as particularly suitable for or readily adaptable to sporting purposes. Additionally, the amendments whittled away at the Secretary's discretion by eliminating the requirement that the importer of firearms establish to the satisfaction of the Secretary that the particular firearm sought to be imported is generally recognized as particularly suitable for or readily adaptable to sporting purposes. Regardless of the changes made, the firearm must meet the sporting purposes test and it remains the Secretary's obligation to determine whether specific firearms satisfy this test. The Senate Report on the 1986 amendments S. Rep. No. 583, 98th Cong. 1st Sess, August 8, 1984, stated that "it is anticipated that in the vast majority of cases, [the substitution of 'shall' for 'may' in the authorization section] will not result in any change in current practice." However, opponents of the amendments viewed the changes as liberalizing and opening up of the importation of firearms into the United States "by mandating the Secretary to authorize importation of a firearm if there is a sporting purpose and eliminating the requirement that the importer has the burden of satisfying the Secretary of the sporting purpose." Firearms Owners' Protection Act, 100 Stat. 1340 (1986) (amending §925 of the Gun Control Act of 1968, 18 U.S.C. §§921-929 (1986)).

DISCUSSION

I. WAS ATF'S DETERMINATION THAT THE USAS-12 SHOTGUN IS NOT A "SPORTING" WEAPON ARBITRARY OR CAPRICIOUS?

A. *The Scope and Standard of Review.* As the Magistrate has noted previously, plaintiff has alleged that ATF's determination that the USAS-12 is not a "sporting" weapon was "arbitrary, capricious, an abuse of discretion, in excess of statutory authority, and otherwise not in accordance with law." . . .

B. *"Sporting Purposes" Test.* The statute establishes that a "sporting" firearm is a weapon which is generally recognized as particularly suitable or readily adaptable to sporting purposes. 18 U.S.C. §925(d)(3). The Bureau claims that in making a sporting determination it attempts to determine whether the firearm is of a type traditionally used in recognized sporting activities or is as suitable for recognized sporting activities as firearms traditionally used for such activities. . . . ATF views the "generally recognized" qualification to require both that the firearm itself or the "type" of firearm to which the subject firearm is being compared have attained general recognition as being particularly suitable for or readily adaptable to sporting purposes, and that a particular use of a firearm have attained general recognition as being a "sporting purpose," or that an event have attained general recognition as being a "sport," before those uses and/or events can be "sporting purposes" or "sports" under Section 925(d)(3).[15] . . .

Additionally, ATF contends that given the fact that the word "particularly" modifies the word "suitable" a firearm which might be recognized as "suitable" for use in traditional sports would not meet the statutory criteria unless it were recognized as particularly suitable for such use.[16] Finally, ATF argues that the drafters of the legislation did not intend for "sports" to include every available type of activity or competition which might employ a firearm inasmuch as a "sporting purpose" could be advanced for every firearm sought to be imported.

C. *Application of the "Sporting Purposes" Test By ATF to the USAS-12.* As this Court has heretofore stated, ATF, after testing and examining the USAS-12, concluded that due to the weight, size, bulk, designed magazine capacity, configuration, and other factors, Gilbert's semiautomatic shotgun is not particularly suitable for or readily adaptable to sporting purposes; rather, ATF is of the opinion that the weapon is a semiautomatic version of a selective fire military type assault shotgun. . . . The Bureau argues that the aforementioned factors or characteristics provide a rational basis for its determination denying Gilbert permission to import the USAS-12 into the United States. Since the curt administrative denial of Gilbert's application to import the USAS-12 and the mere reaffirmation of that decision in late March, 1988, . . . ATF has provided this Court with further elucidation of its reasons for denying Gilbert's application for a permit to import the firearm, as follows:

1. The weight of the weapon, 12.4 pounds, makes it much heavier than traditional 12-gauge sporting shotguns and thus makes it awkward to carry for extended periods, as is required in hunting, and cumbersome to lift repeatedly to fire at multiple small moving targets as used in skeet and trap shooting.

2. The width of the USAS-12 with drum magazine (approximately 6 inches) and the depth with box magazine (in excess of 11 inches) far exceed that of traditional sporting shotguns which do not exceed three inches in width or four inches in depth. The Bureau argues that because of the large size and bulk of the USAS-12, the firearm is extremely difficult to maneuver quickly enough to

---

15. Thus, ATF argues that while hunting, and trap and skeet shooting have been recognized shotgun "sports" for centuries, and target shooting a recognized handgun and rifle "sport," events such as police combat competitions only recently have generated interest outside the military and law enforcement arena and may or may not attain general recognition as "sports." . . .

16. Senator Dodd pointed out that the intent of the legislation was to "[regulate] the importation of firearms by excluding surplus military handguns, and rifles, and shotguns that are not truly suitable for sporting purposes." 114 Cong. Rec. S 5586, Col. 2 (May 15, 1968) (Statement of Sen. Dodd).

engage in moving targets as is necessary in most types of hunting, and in skeet and trap shooting.

3. The detachable box (12-cartridge capacity) and the drum magazine (28-cartridge capacity) have larger capacities than those of traditional repeating sporting shotguns which contain tubular magazines with a capacity of three to five cartridges. Additionally, detachable magazines permit more rapid reloading than do tubular magazines. Finally, the few manually operated 12-gauge shotguns which incorporate detachable box magazines are supplied with two (2) cartridge capacity magazines; those 12-gauge semiautomatic and fully automatic shotguns which employ larger capacity detachable magazines are specially designed combat weapons or conventional shotguns modified for law enforcement and military use.

4. The combat style pistol grip (located on the bottom of the receiver forward of the buttstock), the barrel-to-buttstock configuration, the bayonet lug, and the overall appearance and general shape of the gun are radically different from traditional sporting shotguns and strikingly similar to shotguns designed specifically for or modified for combat and law enforcement use. Specifically, the pistol grip facilitates the handling of the weapon when fired from positions other than the shoulder and also facilitates control of the weapon with one hand while traditional shotgun sports generally involve firing from the shoulder. Additionally, the bayonet is a distinct military feature which has no sporting application.

In addition to giving further explanation of the specific reasons for denying to Gilbert a permit to import the USAS-12, ATF spokesman Edward M. Owen has stated that ATF relied in part on Gilbert's own marketing and advertising literature, which listed the various combat uses of the weapon (but listed no recognizable sporting uses), in determining that the USAS-12 was not a sporting shotgun. The Bureau argues that the representations, concerning the weapon, made by Gilbert in its advertising literature, together with the physical characteristics of the firearm, indicate that its determination to deny the application to import the weapon was rational, based on relevant factors, and was not a clear error in judgment.

Finally, ATF was wholly unimpressed with the evidence Gilbert submitted with its February 17, 1988 letter requesting reconsideration of the agency's decision specifically finding: (1) that the tape demonstrating the firearm's uses did not provide comparisons of the USAS-12 with conventional sporting shotguns to demonstrate that it was of a type generally recognized as particularly suitable for or readily adaptable to the traditional shotgun sports of hunting and trap or skeet shooting; (2) that comparisons cannot be made between the USAS-12 and rifles or handguns because they are distinctly different weapons and thus it is immaterial that some of the handguns, rifles and "combination" rifle/shotguns the agency has allowed importation of share one or more features with the USAS-12 which the agency now finds objectionable; (3) although the agency has allowed importation of several military-style 12-gauge shotguns (*e.g.*, the Benelli Scope-90, the Benelli VM, and the Benelli 212-M1), these shotguns maintain the basic features of traditional sporting shotguns; (4) the SPAS-12 is a traditional sporting shotgun adapted for military and law enforcement use and was approved for importation in 1982 based upon an agency policy (a policy which recognized police combat competition as a sport) which has been subsequently reversed;[23] (5) the survey of state game commissions was directed to the legality of the use of the USAS-12 for hunting rather than to its suitability for sporting purposes; and (6) the evaluations made by Edward B. Crossman and Robert Sears did not address the salient physical features of the firearm which served as the basis of ATF's December 11, 1986 determination and neither stated that the USAS-12 is a shotgun "of a type" generally recognized as sporting or that the "sports" for which it is suitable are "generally recognized" sports.

D. *Decision.* It is clear to this Magistrate that the 1986 amendments to Section 925(d)(3) of the Gun Control Act were meant not only to liberalize importation of firearms but also to ease the burden on importers by eliminating the requirement that the importer satisfy the Secretary that the firearm sought to be imported is particularly suitable or readily adaptable to sporting purposes. Nevertheless, there is left the basic and undeniable requirement that the particular firearm sought to be imported must be particularly suitable or readily adaptable to sporting purposes.

As this Court has heretofore noted, the Bureau of Alcohol, Tobacco and Firearms determined that due to the weight, size, bulk, designed magazine capacity, configuration and other factors, the USAS-12 semiautomatic shotgun is not particularly suitable for or readily adaptable to sporting purposes. Although the factors relied upon by ATF, to the Court's knowledge, have never been previously cited by ATF as factors determinative of the sporting purposes test, they are characteristic of all firearms and thus, the Magistrate opines that they are logical characteristics for ATF to consider in determining whether a particular firearm is particularly suitable for or readily adaptable to sporting purposes. Given the narrow standard by which this Court must judge agency decisions, *see, e.g., Volpe, supra,* 401 U.S. at 416, the undersigned Magistrate cannot determine that the Bureau's decision to deny permission to Gilbert to import the USAS-12 is arbitrary and capricious. The administrative record supports the agency's determination that the overall appearance and design of the weapon (especially the detachable box magazine and the pistol grip) is that of a combat weapon and not a sporting weapon. In fact, the USAS-12 was specifically marketed by Gilbert as a military and law enforcement weapon. Accordingly, the Magistrate finds that there was a rational relationship between the facts and the decision made by the Bureau not to allow the importation of the USAS-12, and therefore, the Court does not find the decision to be arbitrary or capricious. It is of no moment that the administrative record might also support the opposite conclusion that the USAS-12 is suitable for use as a sporting weapon. This Court need only decide that a rational basis exists for the agency's

---

23. In 1982, ATF determined that a police combat competition could be considered a "sport" under Section 925(d)(3) and found the Franchi SPAS-12 shotgun to be particularly suitable for that sport. . . . However, in 1984, ATF reversed that position and refused to classify the Striker-12 as a "sporting" weapon. . . . The Bureau maintains that the policy change was made in 1984 because police combat competitions had not by 1984 — and still have not — gained general recognition as "sports." ATF claims that due to administrative oversight, the importers of the Franchi SPAS-12 have continued to receive agency permission to import that firearm. However, on December 8, 1988, just one day prior to oral argument in this cause on the cross-motions for summary judgment, ATF sent a letter to the importers of the SPAS-12 informing them that future applications for importation of that firearm will be considered on a case-by-case basis.

decision and having done so, the Magistrate turns to Gilbert's remaining arguments. . . .

III. CONSTITUTIONAL CLAIMS . . .

B. *Second Amendment.* The Second Amendment to the United States Constitution guarantees to all Americans the right "to keep and bear arms" and further provides that this right "shall not be infringed." U.S. Const. Amend. II. Plaintiff alleges that the right to keep and bear arms includes the right to manufacture, import, sell and purchase firearms and to the extent that 18 U.S.C. §925(d)(3) allows ATF not to authorize importation of the USAS-12 on the ground that it is not a sporting shotgun, said code section infringes upon the right of the people to keep arms and is thus unconstitutionally void. In the context of this case, the Magistrate is concerned with whether the Second Amendment's right to keep arms necessarily involves the right to import firearms. The plaintiff, of course, desires to bootstrap the right to import firearms to the right to keep and bear arms. However, Gilbert has cited this Court to no authority, and the Court finds none, where it has been found that the right to keep and bear arms necessarily involves, or extends to, the right to import arms. . . .

CONCLUSION

Considering the foregoing discussion, the Magistrate recommends that the defendant's motion for summary judgment be granted and that plaintiff's cross-motion for summary judgment be denied.

NOTES & QUESTIONS

1. CQ: In light of the explicit constitutional protection extended to handguns commonly used for self-defense in *Heller* (Chapter 9), is the sporting use filter now irrelevant? Unconstitutional? Could a firearm like the USAS-12 shotgun be subject to regulation or prohibition on a different basis, such as that it is a type of "dangerous and unusual weapon" that is not in common use today by law-abiding citizens for self-defense or other purposes?

2. If there is a right to own certain items — such as books, printing presses, contraceptives, or guns — is there a correlative right to import them? Can the government ban the importation of a particular item, even if the government could not constitutionally prohibit its domestic sale or possession? In Chapter 6, *Andrews v. State*, 50 Tenn. (3 Heisk.) 165 (1871), suggested that the right to keep arms includes the right to buy arms. Does this extend to imports? What about heavy taxes on imported items (such as guns, or books) if the tax is intended as a protectionist measure to boost the domestic industry? In the Early Republic, tariff policies were protectionist, with the objective of encouraging the growth of domestic American industries, including the firearms

industry. *See* Stephen Halbrook & David B. Kopel, *Tench Coxe and the Right to Keep and Bear Arms in the Early Republic*, 7 Wm. & Mary Bill Rights J. 347 (1999). The early Presidents who implemented the protectionist import tax on firearms were all "pro-Second Amendment." Madison wrote the Amendment and was a proficient marksman, while Washington and Jefferson were avid gun collectors and shooters. Adams supported gun ownership for personal defense. If we presume that these Presidents supported an individual right to arms, is it reasonable to conclude that federal taxes on gun imports, such as a 10 percent tariff, do not violate the Second Amendment? Although the *Gilbert* opinion does not say so, one of the important reasons for the 1968 GCA's import bans was pure protectionism for U.S. gun manufacturers. Does this motive make the import restrictions more or less legitimate, from a Second Amendment viewpoint?

5.   Policing Illegal Guns

How should police deal with people they believe may be carrying guns illegally? In 1968, the Court rendered a decision on this point in *Terry v. Ohio*, permitting police under particular circumstances to stop and frisk individuals for concealed weapons. *Terry* is an important Fourth Amendment case, with tremendous practical importance to day-to-day police activities.

Terry v. Ohio
392 U.S. 1 (1968)

MR. CHIEF JUSTICE WARREN delivered the opinion of the Court. . . .

Petitioner Terry was convicted of carrying a concealed weapon and sentenced to the statutorily prescribed term of one to three years in the penitentiary. Following the denial of a pretrial motion to suppress, the prosecution introduced in evidence two revolvers and a number of bullets seized from Terry and a codefendant, Richard Chilton, by Cleveland Police Detective Martin McFadden. At the hearing on the motion to suppress this evidence, Officer McFadden testified that while he was patrolling in plain clothes in downtown Cleveland at approximately 2:30 in the afternoon of October 31, 1963, his attention was attracted by two men, Chilton and Terry, standing on the corner of Huron Road and Euclid Avenue. He had never seen the two men before, and he was unable to say precisely what first drew his eye to them. However, he testified that he had been a policeman for 39 years and a detective for 35 and that he had been assigned to patrol this vicinity of downtown Cleveland for shoplifters and pickpockets for 30 years. He explained that he had developed routine habits of observation over the years and that he would "stand and watch people or walk and watch people at many intervals of the day." He added: "Now, in this case when I looked over they didn't look right to me at the time."

[After extended observation,] he suspected the two men of "casing a job, a stick-up," and that he considered it his duty as a police officer to investigate further. He added that he feared "they may have a gun." . . . Deciding that the situation was ripe for direct action, Officer McFadden approached the three men, identified himself as a police officer and asked for their names. . . . When the men "mumbled something" in response to his inquiries, Officer McFadden grabbed petitioner Terry, spun him around so that they were facing the other two, with Terry between McFadden and the others, and patted down the outside of his clothing. In the left breast pocket of Terry's overcoat Officer McFadden felt a pistol. He reached inside the overcoat pocket, but was unable to remove the gun. At this point, keeping Terry between himself and the others, the officer ordered all three men to enter Zucker's store. As they went in, he removed Terry's overcoat completely, removed a .38-caliber revolver from the pocket and ordered all three men to face the wall with their hands raised. Officer McFadden proceeded to pat down the outer clothing of Chilton and the third man, Katz. He discovered another revolver in the outer pocket of Chilton's overcoat, but no weapons were found on Katz. . . .

We would be less than candid if we did not acknowledge that this question thrusts to the fore difficult and troublesome issues regarding a sensitive area of police activity—issues which have never before been squarely presented to this Court. Reflective of the tensions involved are the practical and constitutional arguments pressed with great vigor on both sides of the public debate over the power of the police to "stop and frisk"—as it is sometimes euphemistically termed—suspicious persons.

The crux of this case, however, is not the propriety of Officer McFadden's taking steps to investigate petitioner's suspicious behavior, but rather, whether there was justification for McFadden's invasion of Terry's personal security by searching him for weapons in the course of that investigation. We are now concerned with more than the governmental interest in investigating crime; in addition, there is the more immediate interest of the police officer in taking steps to assure himself that the person with whom he is dealing is not armed with a weapon that could unexpectedly and fatally be used against him. Certainly it would be unreasonable to require that police officers take unnecessary risks in the performance of their duties. American criminals have a long tradition of armed violence, and every year in this country many law enforcement officers are killed in the line of duty, and thousands more are wounded. Virtually all of these deaths and a substantial portion of the injuries are inflicted with guns and knives.[21]

Our evaluation of the proper balance that has to be struck in this type of case leads us to conclude that there must be a narrowly drawn authority to permit a reasonable search for weapons for the protection of the police officer, where he has reason to believe that he is dealing with an armed and dangerous

---

21. Fifty-seven law enforcement officers were killed in the line of duty in this country in 1966, bringing the total to 335 for the seven-year period beginning with 1960. Also in 1966, there were 23,851 assaults on police officers, 9,113 of which resulted in injuries to the policemen. Fifty-five of the 57 officers killed in 1966 died from gunshot wounds, 41 of them inflicted by handguns easily secreted about the person. The remaining two murders were perpetrated by knives. See Federal Bureau of Investigation, Uniform Crime Reports for the United States—1966, at 45-48, 152 and Table 51. The easy availability of firearms to potential criminals in this country is well known and has provoked much debate. See, e.g., President's Commission on Law Enforcement and Administration of Justice, The Challenge of Crime in a Free Society 239-243 (1967). Whatever the merits of gun-control proposals, this fact is relevant to an assessment of the need for some form of self-protective search power.

individual, regardless of whether he has probable cause to arrest the individual for a crime. The officer need not be absolutely certain that the individual is armed; the issue is whether a reasonably prudent man in the circumstances would be warranted in the belief that his safety or that of others was in danger. Cf. *Beck v. Ohio*, 379 U.S. 89, 91 (1964); *Brinegar v. United States*, 338 U.S. 160, 174-176 (1949); *Stacey v. Emery*, 97 U.S. 642, 645 (1878). And in determining whether the officer acted reasonably in such circumstances, due weight must be given, not to his inchoate and unparticularized suspicion or "hunch," but to the specific reasonable inferences which he is entitled to draw from the facts in light of his experience. Cf. *Brinegar v. United States* supra. . . .

When Officer McFadden approached the three men gathered before the display window at Zucker's store he had observed enough to make it quite reasonable to fear that they were armed; and nothing in their response to his hailing them, identifying himself as a police officer, and asking their names served to dispel that reasonable belief. We cannot say his decision at that point to seize Terry and pat his clothing for weapons was the product of a volatile or inventive imagination, or was undertaken simply as an act of harassment; the record evidences the tempered act of a policeman who in the course of an investigation had to make a quick decision as to how to protect himself and others from possible danger, and took limited steps to do so.

In view of these facts, we cannot blind ourselves to the need for law enforcement officers to protect themselves and other prospective victims of violence in situations where they may lack probable cause for an arrest. When an officer is justified in believing that the individual whose suspicious behavior he is investigating at close range is armed and presently dangerous to the officer or to others, it would appear to be clearly unreasonable to deny the officer the power to take necessary measures to determine whether the person is in fact carrying a weapon and to neutralize the threat of physical harm. . . .

We merely hold today that where a police officer observes unusual conduct which leads him reasonably to conclude in light of his experience that criminal activity may be afoot and that the persons with whom he is dealing may be armed and presently dangerous, where in the course of investigating this behavior he identifies himself as a policeman and makes reasonable inquiries, and where nothing in the initial stages of the encounter serves to dispel his reasonable fear for his own or others' safety, he is entitled for the protection of himself and others in the area to conduct a carefully limited search of the outer clothing of such persons in an attempt to discover weapons which might be used to assault him. Such a search is a reasonable search under the Fourth Amendment, and any weapons seized may properly be introduced in evidence against the person from whom they were taken.

Affirmed.

NOTES & QUESTIONS

1. Social scientist James Q. Wilson has argued for increased use of the stop and frisk to combat carrying of illegal guns. Wilson acknowledges "innocent people will be stopped. Young Black and Hispanic men will probably be stopped more often than older white Anglo males or women of any

race." James Q. Wilson, *Just Take Away Their Guns*, N.Y. Times Magazine, Mar. 20, 1994, at 47. Adina Schwartz criticizes Wilson's prescription and the *Terry* decision for concluding that racial impacts are irrelevant to delineating the proper scope of the stop and frisk power. *See* Adina Schwartz, *"Just Take Away Their Guns": The Hidden Racism of* Terry v. Ohio, 23 Fordham Urb. L.J. 317 (1996).

2. In April 2010, the *New York Times* reported that police in New York City conducted 575,000 *Terry*-style stop and frisks, recovering 762 guns, meaning 0.13 percent of such searches resulted in the recovery of a gun. The most commonly listed reason for the stops was "furtive movements." The Center for Constitutional Rights argued that use of stop and frisks is racially driven. Nearly 490,000 blacks and Latinos were stopped compared with 53,000 whites. But once stopped, arrest rates were virtually the same. "Whites were arrested in slightly more than 6 percent of the stops, blacks in slightly fewer than 6 percent." About 1.7 percent of whites had a weapon and 1.1 percent of Blacks. Police administrators argue *Terry* stops are a cornerstone of the effort to suppress crime. *See* Al Baker, *New York Minorities More Likely to Be Frisked*, N.Y. Times, May 13, 2010, at A1.

3. Young Black men are disproportionately victims and perpetrators of gun violence. *See generally* Michael B. de Leeuw, District of Columbia v. Heller *and Communities of Color*, 25 Harv. BlackLetter L.J. 133 (2009). Do you think police consider this in identifying targets for *Terry* frisks? Would you prohibit police from considering such information? How would you enforce the prohibition?

4. Since the decision in *Terry*, most states have enacted shall issue concealed carry laws. This increases the chances in many jurisdictions that police will encounter people who are carrying concealed guns lawfully. How does this fact affect the operation of *Terry* frisks? Assume you are City Attorney for a large city in a state that has passed a concealed carry law. How would you advise the police department to respond in situations where they suspect a private citizen is armed?

5. Criticism of *Terry* reflects a common theme in the gun control debate. In the *McDonald* case, Justice Thomas (concurring) describes the racist Black Codes enacted in the aftermath of the Civil War with the aim of disarming freedmen. *See also* Robert J. Cottrol & Raymond T. Diamond, *"Never Intended to Be Applied to the White Population": Firearms Regulation and Racial Disparity — The Redeemed South's Legacy to a National Jurisprudence?*, 70 Chi.-Kent L. Rev. 1307 (1995). Additionally, some recent scholarly evaluations of the civil rights movement emphasize the role that armed self-defense played in the freedom struggle. *See, e.g.*, Lance Hill, The Deacons for Defense: Armed Resistance and the Civil Rights Movement (2004); Christopher B. Strain, Pure Fire: Self-Defense as Activism in the Civil Rights Era (2005).

6. In a decision that eased the state's burden in firearms prosecutions, the Supreme Court ruled in *Smith v. United States*, 508 U.S. 223 (1993), that

"using" a firearm for purposes of mandatory sentencing in drug/gun indict-ments did not require using the gun as a weapon. However, in *Bailey v. United States*, 516 U.S. 137 (1995), the Court ruled that mere ownership or posses-sion of a gun while committing a crime was not sufficient for a person to be convicted of the separate offense of using a gun in a violent or drug-trafficking crime. Before *Bailey*, for example, if a college student selling drugs had an unloaded rifle in an upstairs closet, while selling marijuana in his downstairs living room, federal prosecutors could charge the individual not only with drug dealing but also with using a weapon in the commission of a crime. Of course, if the drug dealer were already a con-victed felon, he could be charged for the felony of illegally owning the gun. In 1998, Congress enacted the "Bailey Fix." 18 U.S.C. §924(c) now reads:

> any person who, during and in relation to any crime of violence or drug traf-ficking crime (including a crime of violence or drug trafficking crime that provides for an enhanced punishment if committed by the use of a deadly or dangerous weapon or device) for which the person may be prosecuted in a court of the United States, uses or carries a firearm, or who, in furtherance of any such crime, possesses a firearm, shall, in addition to the punishment provided for such crime of violence or drug trafficking crime[.]

Thus, a criminal can be federally convicted of a separate offense not only for using or carrying the gun in the course of a crime, but also for gun posses-sion, if the possession was "in furtherance of" the underlying crime.

7. In many criminal gun law prosecutions, intent is easy to infer. If a person is found with a gun in his pocket, a judge or jury may readily infer that he intended to carry a gun. But there are some gray areas of intent. For example, what if a person knows that he owns a gun, but does not know that the gun has features that make it illegal?

The next case, *Staples v. United States*, involved precisely such an issue. To understand *Staples*, it may be helpful to review some material from Chapter 1, which explains that semi-automatic guns fire one time for each pull of the trigger while fully automatic "machine guns" continue to fire until the trigger is released. There are between 100,000 and 200,000 non-government-owned machine guns in the United States. *See* Gary Kleck, Targeting Guns: Firearms and Their Control 108 (1997). In contrast, approximately 60 percent of U.S. gun owners own some type of semi-automatic firearm. David Hemenway & Elizabeth Richardson, *Characteristics of Automatic or Semiautomatic Firearm Ownership in the United States*, 87 Am. J. Pub. Health 286, 287 (1997). (Confusingly, some semi-automatic guns are colloquially referred to as automatics—for example, the Colt 1911 ".45 automatic" is a semi-automatic handgun.)

As detailed above, it is lawful to own semi-automatic or fully automatic weapons. However, owning an automatic requires compliance with the more stringent provisions of the NFA. Also, the only automatics that may be legally owned are those manufactured and registered before May 19, 1986.

Federal law defines a NFA "automatic" broadly: A gun qualifies if it fires two or more rounds with the single press of the trigger. Sometimes, a worn semi-automatic firearm will malfunction, and will fire two shots with a single trigger press; this is called "doubling." Sometimes a gun will double only when certain brands or types of ammunition are used.

If you or someone you know has a gun that doubles, stop using it and have it repaired immediately. Doubling is the result of an internal defect in the gun that could cause other problems. It may also cause legal problems, as the next case shows.

Staples v. United States
511 U.S. 600 (1994)

JUSTICE THOMAS delivered the opinion of the Court.

The National Firearms Act makes it unlawful for any person to possess a machinegun that is not properly registered with the Federal Government. Petitioner contends that, to convict him under the Act, the Government should have been required to prove beyond a reasonable doubt that he knew the weapon he possessed had the characteristics that brought it within the statutory definition of a machinegun. We agree and accordingly reverse the judgment of the Court of Appeals.

I

The National Firearms Act (Act), 26 U.S.C. §§5801-5872, imposes strict registration requirements on statutorily defined "firearms." The Act includes within the term "firearm" a machinegun, §5845(a)(6), and further defines a machinegun as "any weapon which shoots, . . . or can be readily restored to shoot, automatically more than one shot, without manual reloading, by a single function of the trigger," §5845(b). Thus, any fully automatic weapon is a "firearm" within the meaning of the Act.[1] Under the Act, all firearms must be registered in the National Firearms Registration and Transfer Record maintained by the Secretary of the Treasury. §5841. Section 5861(d) makes it a crime, punishable by up to 10 years in prison, see §5871, for any person to possess a firearm that is not properly registered.

Upon executing a search warrant at petitioner's home, local police and agents of the Bureau of Alcohol, Tobacco and Firearms (BATF) recovered, among other things, an AR-15 rifle. The AR-15 is the semiautomatic, civilian version of the military's M-16 rifle. The M-16, in contrast, is a selective fire rifle that allows the operator, by rotating a selector switch, to choose semiautomatic

---

1. As used here, the terms "automatic" and "fully automatic" refer to a weapon that fires repeatedly with a single pull of the trigger. That is, once its trigger is depressed, the weapon will automatically continue to fire until its trigger is released or the ammunition is exhausted. Such weapons are "machineguns" within the meaning of the Act. We use the term "semiautomatic" to designate a weapon that fires only one shot with each pull of the trigger, and which requires no manual manipulation by the operator to place another round in the chamber after each round is fired.

or automatic fire. Many M-16 parts are interchangeable with those in the AR-15 and can be used to convert the AR-15 into an automatic weapon. To inhibit such conversions, the AR-15 is manufactured with a metal stop on its receiver that will prevent an M-16 selector switch, if installed, from rotating to the fully automatic position. The metal stop on petitioner's rifle, however, had been filed away, and the rifle had been assembled with an M-16 selector switch and several other M-16 internal parts, including a hammer, disconnector, and trigger. Suspecting that the AR-15 had been modified to be capable of fully automatic fire, BATF agents seized the weapon. Petitioner subsequently was indicted for unlawful possession of an unregistered machinegun in violation of §5861(d).

At trial, BATF agents testified that when the AR-15 was tested, it fired more than one shot with a single pull of the trigger. It was undisputed that the weapon was not registered as required by §5861(d). Petitioner testified that the rifle had never fired automatically when it was in his possession. He insisted that the AR-15 had operated only semiautomatically, and even then imperfectly, often requiring manual ejection of the spent casing and chambering of the next round. According to petitioner, his alleged ignorance of any automatic firing capability should have shielded him from criminal liability for his failure to register the weapon. He requested the District Court to instruct the jury that, to establish a violation of §5861(d), the Government must prove beyond a reasonable doubt that the defendant "knew that the gun would fire fully automatically."

The District Court rejected petitioner's proposed instruction and instead charged the jury as follows:

> "The Government need not prove the defendant knows he's dealing with a weapon possessing every last characteristic [which subjects it] to the regulation. It would be enough to prove he knows that he is dealing with a dangerous device of a type as would alert one to the likelihood of regulation."

Petitioner was convicted and sentenced to five years' probation and a $5,000 fine.

The Court of Appeals affirmed. . . . We granted certiorari. . . .

The language of the statute, the starting place in our inquiry, see *Connecticut Nat. Bank v. Germain*, 503 U.S. 249, 253-54, provides little explicit guidance in this case. Section 5861(d) is silent concerning the *mens rea* required for a violation. It states simply that "it shall be unlawful for any person . . . to receive or possess a firearm which is not registered to him in the National Firearms Registration and Transfer Record." 26 U.S.C. §5861(d). Nevertheless, silence on this point by itself does not necessarily suggest that Congress intended to dispense with a conventional *mens rea* element, which would require that the defendant know the facts that make his conduct illegal. See *Balint, supra*, at 251 (stating that traditionally, *"scienter"* was a necessary element in every crime). . . . On the contrary, we must construe the statute in light of the background rules of the common law, see *United States v. United States Gypsum Co.*, 438 U.S. 422, 436-37 (1978), in which the requirement of some *mens rea* for a crime is firmly embedded. . . .

According to the Government, however, the nature and purpose of the Act suggest that the presumption favoring *mens rea* does not apply to this case.

The Government argues that Congress intended the Act to regulate and restrict the circulation of dangerous weapons. Consequently, in the Government's view, this case fits in a line of precedent concerning what we have termed "public welfare" or "regulatory" offenses, in which we have understood Congress to impose a form of strict criminal liability through statutes that do not require the defendant to know the facts that make his conduct illegal. In construing such statutes, we have inferred from silence that Congress did not intend to require proof of *mens rea* to establish an offense. . . .

Such public welfare offenses have been created by Congress, and recognized by this Court, in "limited circumstances." *United States Gypsum,* supra, at 437. Typically, our cases recognizing such offenses involve statutes that regulate potentially harmful or injurious items. Cf. *United States v. International Minerals & Chemical Corp.,* 402 U.S. 558, 564-65 (1971) (characterizing *Balint* and similar cases as involving statutes regulating "dangerous or deleterious devices or products or obnoxious waste materials"). In such situations, we have reasoned that as long as a defendant knows that he is dealing with a dangerous device of a character that places him "in responsible relation to a public danger," *Dotterweich, supra,* at 281, he should be alerted to the probability of strict regulation, and we have assumed that in such cases Congress intended to place the burden on the defendant to "ascertain at his peril whether [his conduct] comes within the inhibition of the statute." *Balint, supra,* at 254. . . .

B

The Government argues that §5861(d) defines precisely the sort of regulatory offense described in *Balint.* In this view, all guns, whether or not they are statutory "firearms," are dangerous devices that put gun owners on notice that they must determine at their hazard whether their weapons come within the scope of the Act. On this understanding, the District Court's instruction in this case was correct, because a conviction can rest simply on proof that a defendant knew he possessed a "firearm" in the ordinary sense of the term.

The Government seeks support for its position from our decision in *United States v. Freed,* 401 U.S. 601 (1971), which involved a prosecution for possession of unregistered grenades under §5861(d).[4] The defendant knew that the items in his possession were grenades, and we concluded that §5861(d) did not require the Government to prove the defendant also knew that the grenades were unregistered. *Id.* at 609. To be sure, in deciding that *mens rea* was not required with respect to that element of the offense, we suggested that the Act "is a regulatory measure in the interest of the public safety, which may well be premised on the theory that one would hardly be surprised to learn that possession of hand grenades is not an innocent act." *Id.* Grenades, we explained, "are highly dangerous offensive weapons, no less dangerous than the narcotics involved in *United States v. Balint.*" *Id.* But that reasoning provides little support for dispensing with *mens rea* in this case.

---

4. A grenade is a "firearm" under the Act. 26 U.S.C. §§5845(a)(8), 5845(f)(1)(B).

. . . [T]he Government urges that *Freed*'s logic applies because guns, no less than grenades, are highly dangerous devices that should alert their owners to the probability of regulation. But the gap between *Freed* and this case is too wide to bridge. In glossing over the distinction between grenades and guns, the Government ignores the particular care we have taken to avoid construing a statute to dispense with *mens rea* where doing so would "criminalize a broad range of apparently innocent conduct." *Liparota*, 471 U.S. at 426. In *Liparota*, we considered a statute that made unlawful the unauthorized acquisition or possession of food stamps. We determined that the statute required proof that the defendant knew his possession of food stamps was unauthorized, largely because dispensing with such a *mens rea* requirement would have resulted in reading the statute to outlaw a number of apparently innocent acts. *Id.* Our conclusion that the statute should not be treated as defining a public welfare offense rested on the commonsense distinction that a "food stamp can hardly be compared to a hand grenade." *Id.* at 433.

Neither, in our view, can all guns be compared to hand grenades. Although the contrast is certainly not as stark as that presented in *Liparota*, the fact remains that there is a long tradition of widespread lawful gun ownership by private individuals in this country. Such a tradition did not apply to the possession of hand grenades in *Freed* or to the selling of dangerous drugs that we considered in *Balint*. See also *International Minerals*, 402 U.S. at 563-65; *Balint*, 258 U.S. at 254. In fact, in *Freed* we construed §5861(d) under the assumption that "one would hardly be surprised to learn that possession of hand grenades is not an innocent act." *Freed, supra*, at 609. Here, the Government essentially suggests that we should interpret the section under the altogether different assumption that "one would hardly be surprised to learn that owning a gun is not an innocent act." That proposition is simply not supported by common experience. Guns in general are not "deleterious devices or products or obnoxious waste materials," *International Minerals*, supra, 402 U.S. at 565, that put their owners on notice that they stand "in responsible relation to a public danger," *Dotterweich*, 320 U.S. at 281.

The Government protests that guns, unlike food stamps, but like grenades and narcotics, are potentially harmful devices. Under this view, it seems that *Liparota*'s concern for criminalizing ostensibly innocuous conduct is inapplicable whenever an item is sufficiently dangerous — that is, dangerousness alone should alert an individual to probable regulation and justify treating a statute that regulates the dangerous device as dispensing with *mens rea*. But that an item is "dangerous," in some general sense, does not necessarily suggest, as the Government seems to assume, that it is not also entirely innocent. Even dangerous items can, in some cases, be so commonplace and generally available that we would not consider them to alert individuals to the likelihood of strict regulation. As suggested above, despite their potential for harm, guns generally can be owned in perfect innocence. Of course, we might surely classify certain categories of guns — no doubt including the machineguns, sawed-off shotguns, and artillery pieces that Congress has subjected to regulation — as items the ownership of which would have the same quasi-suspect character we attributed to owning hand grenades in *Freed*. But precisely because guns falling outside those categories traditionally have been widely accepted as lawful possessions, their destructive potential, while perhaps even greater than that of some items we would classify along with narcotics and hand grenades, cannot be said to put gun owners sufficiently on notice of the likelihood of regulation to justify interpreting §5861(d) as not requiring proof of knowledge of a weapon's characteristics.

On a slightly different tack, the Government suggests that guns are subject to an array of regulations at the federal, state, and local levels that put gun owners on notice that they must determine the characteristics of their weapons and comply with all legal requirements. But regulation in itself is not sufficient to place gun ownership in the category of the sale of narcotics in *Balint*. The food stamps at issue in *Liparota* were subject to comprehensive regulations, yet we did not understand the statute there to dispense with a *mens rea* requirement. Moreover, despite the overlay of legal restrictions on gun ownership, we question whether regulations on guns are sufficiently intrusive that they impinge upon the common experience that owning a gun is usually licit and blameless conduct. Roughly 50 percent of American homes contain at least one firearm of some sort, and in the vast majority of States, buying a shotgun or rifle is a simple transaction that would not alert a person to regulation any more than would buying a car.

If we were to accept as a general rule the Government's suggestion that dangerous and regulated items place their owners under an obligation to inquire at their peril into compliance with regulations, we would undoubtedly reach some untoward results. Automobiles, for example, might also be termed "dangerous" devices and are highly regulated at both the state and federal levels. Congress might see fit to criminalize the violation of certain regulations concerning automobiles, and thus might make it a crime to operate a vehicle without a properly functioning emission control system. But we probably would hesitate to conclude on the basis of silence that Congress intended a prison term to apply to a car owner whose vehicle's emissions levels, wholly unbeknownst to him, began to exceed legal limits between regular inspection dates.

Here, there can be little doubt that, as in *Liparota*, the Government's construction of the statute potentially would impose criminal sanctions on a class of persons whose mental state — ignorance of the characteristics of weapons in their possession — makes their actions entirely innocent. The Government does not dispute the contention that virtually any semiautomatic weapon may be converted, either by internal modification or, in some cases, simply by wear and tear, into a machinegun within the meaning of the Act. Cf. *United States v. Anderson*, 885 F.2d 1248, 1251, 1253-54 (5th Cir. 1989) (en banc). Such a gun may give no externally visible indication that it is fully automatic. See *United States v. Herbert*, 698 F.2d 981, 986 (9th Cir.), cert. denied, 464 U.S. 821 (1983). But in the Government's view, any person who has purchased what he believes to be a semiautomatic rifle or handgun, or who simply has inherited a gun from a relative and left it untouched in an attic or basement, can be subject to imprisonment, despite absolute ignorance of the gun's firing capabilities, if the gun turns out to be an automatic.

We concur in the Fifth Circuit's conclusion on this point: "It is unthinkable to us that Congress intended to subject such law-abiding, well-intentioned citizens to a possible ten-year term of imprisonment if . . . what they genuinely and reasonably believed was a conventional semi-automatic [weapon] turns out to have worn down into or been secretly modified to be a fully automatic weapon." *Anderson, supra*, at 1254. . . .

In short, we conclude that the background rule of the common law favoring *mens rea* should govern interpretation of §5861(d) in this case. Silence does not suggest that Congress dispensed with *mens rea* for the element of §5861(d) at issue here. Thus, to obtain a conviction, the Government should have been required to prove that petitioner knew of the features of his AR-15 that brought it within the scope of the Act.

We emphasize that our holding is a narrow one. As in our prior cases, our reasoning depends upon a commonsense evaluation of the nature of the particular device or substance Congress has subjected to regulation and the expectations that individuals may legitimately have in dealing with the regulated items. In addition, we think that the penalty attached to §5861(d) suggests that Congress did not intend to eliminate a *mens rea* requirement for violation of the section. As we noted in *Morissette*: "Neither this Court nor, so far as we are aware, any other has undertaken to delineate a precise line or set forth comprehensive criteria for distinguishing between crimes that require a mental element and crimes that do not." 342 U.S. at 260. We attempt no definition here, either. We note only that our holding depends critically on our view that if Congress had intended to make outlaws of gun owners who were wholly ignorant of the offending characteristics of their weapons, and to subject them to lengthy prison terms, it would have spoken more clearly to that effect. Cf. *United States v. Harris*, 959 F.2d 246, 261 (D.C. Cir.), cert. denied, 506 U.S. 932 (1992).

For the foregoing reasons, the judgment of the Court of Appeals is reversed, and the case is remanded for further proceedings consistent with this opinion. . . .

JUSTICE GINSBURG, with whom JUSTICE O'CONNOR joins, concurring in the judgment. [After performing an analysis, Justice Ginsburg concludes that "conviction under §5861(d) requires proof that the defendant knew he possessed not simply a gun, but a machinegun. The indictment in this case, but not the jury instruction, properly described this knowledge requirement. I therefore concur in the Court's judgment."]

JUSTICE STEVENS, with whom JUSTICE BLACKMUN joins, dissenting.

To avoid a slight possibility of injustice to unsophisticated owners of machineguns and sawed-off shotguns, the Court has substituted its views of sound policy for the judgment Congress made when it enacted the National Firearms Act (or Act). Because the Court's addition to the text of 26 U.S.C. §5861(d) is foreclosed by both the statute and our precedent, I respectfully dissent.

The Court is preoccupied with guns that "generally can be owned in perfect innocence." . . . This case, however, involves a semiautomatic weapon that was readily convertible into a machinegun — a weapon that the jury found to be "a dangerous device of a type as would alert one to the likelihood of regulation." These are not guns "of some sort" that can be found in almost "50 percent of American homes." They are particularly dangerous — indeed, a substantial percentage of the unregistered machineguns now in circulation are converted semiautomatic weapons.

The question presented is whether the National Firearms Act imposed on the Government the burden of proving beyond a reasonable doubt not only that the defendant knew he possessed a dangerous device sufficient to alert him to regulation, but also that he knew it had all the characteristics of a "firearm" as defined in the statute. Three unambiguous guideposts direct us to the correct answer to that question: the text and structure of the Act, our cases construing both this Act and similar regulatory legislation, and the Act's history and interpretation. . . .

The National Firearms Act unquestionably is a public welfare statute. *United States v. Freed*, 401 U.S. 601, 609 (1971) (holding that this statute "is a regulatory measure in the interest of the public safety"). Congress fashioned a legislative scheme to regulate the commerce and possession of certain types of dangerous devices, including specific kinds of weapons, to protect the health and welfare of the citizenry. To enforce this scheme, Congress created criminal penalties for certain acts and omissions. The text of some of these offenses — including the one at issue here — contains no knowledge requirement. . . .

We thus have read a knowledge requirement into public welfare crimes, but not a requirement that the defendant know all the facts that make his conduct illegal. Although the Court acknowledges this standard, it nevertheless concludes that a gun is not the type of dangerous device that would alert one to the possibility of regulation.

Both the Court and Justice Ginsburg erroneously rely upon the "tradition[al]" innocence of gun ownership to find that Congress must have intended the Government to prove knowledge of all the characteristics that make a weapon a statutory "firearm." . . . We held in *Freed*, however, that a §5861(d) offense may be committed by one with no awareness of either wrongdoing or of all the facts that constitute the offense. 401 U.S. at 607-610. Nevertheless, the Court, asserting that the Government "gloss[es] over the distinction between grenades and guns," determines that "the gap between *Freed* and this case is too wide to bridge." . . . As such, the Court instead reaches the rather surprising conclusion that guns are more analogous to food stamps than to hand grenades. Even if one accepts that dubious proposition, the Court founds it upon a faulty premise: its mischaracterization of the Government's submission as one contending that "*all guns* . . . are dangerous devices that put gun owners on notice. . . ." . . . Accurately identified, the Government's position presents the question whether guns such as the one possessed by petitioner "are highly dangerous offensive weapons, no less dangerous than the narcotics" in *Balint* or the hand grenades in *Freed*. . . .

Thus, even assuming that the Court is correct that the mere possession of an ordinary rifle or pistol does not entail sufficient danger to alert one to the possibility of regulation, that conclusion does not resolve this case. Petitioner knowingly possessed a semiautomatic weapon that was readily convertible into a machinegun. The "'character and nature'" of such a weapon is sufficiently hazardous to place the possessor on notice of the possibility of regulation. *See Posters 'N' Things, Ltd. v. United States*, 511 U.S. 513, 525 (1994) (citation omitted). No significant difference exists between imposing upon the possessor a duty to determine whether such a weapon is registered, *Freed*, 401 U.S. at 607-610, and imposing a duty to determine whether that weapon has been converted into a machinegun.

Cases arise, of course, in which a defendant would not know that a device was dangerous unless he knew that it was a "firearm" as defined in the Act. *Freed* was such a case; unless the defendant knew that the device in question was a hand grenade, he would not necessarily have known that it was dangerous. But given the text and nature of the statute, it would be utterly implausible to suggest that Congress intended the owner of a sawed-off shotgun to be criminally liable if he knew its barrel was 17.5 inches long but not if he mistakenly believed the same gun had an 18-inch barrel. Yet the Court's holding today assumes that Congress intended that bizarre result.

The enforcement of public welfare offenses always entails some possibility of injustice. Congress nevertheless has repeatedly decided that an overriding public interest in health or safety may outweigh that risk when a person is dealing with products that are sufficiently dangerous or deleterious to make it reasonable to presume that he either knows, or should know, whether those products conform to special regulatory requirements. The dangerous character of the product is reasonably presumed to provide sufficient notice of the probability of regulation to justify strict enforcement against those who are merely guilty of negligent, rather than willful, misconduct. . . .

IV

On the premise that the purpose of the *mens rea* requirement is to avoid punishing people "for apparently innocent activity," Justice Ginsburg concludes that proof of knowledge that a weapon is "a dangerous device of a type as would alert one to the likelihood of regulation" is not an adequate *mens rea* requirement, but that proof of knowledge that the weapon possesses "every last characteristic" that subjects it to regulation is. . . .

Assuming that "innocent activity" describes conduct without any consciousness of wrongdoing, the risk of punishing such activity can be avoided only by reading into the statute the common-law concept of *mens rea*: "an evil purpose or mental culpability." *Morissette*, 342 U.S. at 252. But even petitioner does not contend that the Government must prove guilty intent or intentional wrongdoing. Instead, the *"mens rea"* issue in this case is simply what knowledge requirement, if any, Congress implicitly included in this offense. There are at least five such possible knowledge requirements, four of which entail the risk that a completely innocent mistake will subject a defendant to punishment.

First, a defendant may know that he possesses a weapon with all of the characteristics that make it a "firearm" within the meaning of the statute and also know that it has never been registered, but be ignorant of the federal registration requirement. In such a case, we presume knowledge of the law even if we know the defendant is "innocent" in the sense that Justice Ginsburg uses the word. Second, a defendant may know that he possesses a weapon with all of the characteristics of a statutory firearm and also know that the law requires that it be registered, but mistakenly believe that it is in fact registered. *Freed* squarely holds that this defendant's "innocence" is not a defense. Third, a defendant may know only that he possesses a weapon with all of the characteristics of a statutory firearm. Neither ignorance of the registration requirement nor ignorance of the fact that the weapon is unregistered protects this "innocent" defendant. Fourth, a defendant may know that he possesses a weapon that is sufficiently dangerous to likely be regulated, but not know that it has all the characteristics of a statutory firearm. Petitioner asserts that he is an example of this "innocent" defendant. Fifth, a defendant may know that he possesses an ordinary gun and, being aware of the widespread lawful gun ownership in the country, reasonably assume that there is no need "to inquire about the need for registration." . . . That, of course, is not this case. . . .[26]

Justice Ginsburg treats the first, second, and third alternatives differently from the fourth and fifth. Her acceptance of knowledge of the characteristics of a statutory "firearm" as a sufficient predicate for criminal liability—despite ignorance of either the duty to register or the fact of nonregistration, or both—must rest on the premise that such knowledge would alert the owner to the likelihood of regulation, thereby depriving the conduct of its "apparent innocen[ce]." Yet in the fourth alternative, a jury determines just such knowledge: that the characteristics of the weapon known to the defendant would alert the owner to the likelihood of regulation. . . .

This case presents no dispute about the dangerous character of machineguns and sawed-off shotguns. Anyone in possession of such a weapon is "standing in responsible relation to a public danger." See *Dotterweich*, 320 U.S. at 281 (citation omitted). In the National Firearms Act, Congress determined that the serious threat to health and safety posed by the private ownership of such firearms warranted the imposition of a duty on the owners of dangerous weapons to determine whether their possession is lawful. Semiautomatic weapons that are readily convertible into machineguns are sufficiently dangerous to alert persons who knowingly possess them to the probability of stringent public regulation. The jury's finding that petitioner knowingly possessed "a dangerous device of a type as would alert one to the likelihood of regulation" adequately supports the conviction.

Accordingly, I would affirm the judgment of the Court of Appeals.

NOTES & QUESTIONS

1. The question presented by the certiorari grant could have been framed as "Are guns like grenades?" Faced with statutes that were equally silent as to *mens rea*, the Court had previously been willing to allow strict liability for possession of an unregistered hand grenade. *United States v. Freed*, 401 U.S. 601 (1971). But it refused to assume that Congress meant to criminalize the mere possession of illegally diverted food stamps, without proof the owner knew they were illegal. *Liparota v. United States*, 471 U.S. 419. *Liparota* reasoned that food stamps are generally innocent, nonharmful items whose possession does not suggest the likelihood of strict regulation, unlike the grenades in *Freed*. Interestingly, *Staples* holds that the possession of a semiautomatic gun like Staples's AR-15 falls on the same side of the line as food stamps: "[D]espite their potential for harm, guns generally can be owned in

---

26. Although I disagree with the assumption that "widespread lawful gun ownership" provides a sufficient reason for believing that there is no need to register guns (there is also widespread lawful automobile ownership), acceptance of that assumption neither justifies the majority's holding nor contradicts my conclusion on the facts of this case.

perfect innocence," writes Justice Thomas for a majority of the Court. Thus, the Court declined to assume that Congress meant to impose strict criminal liability for possession of a semi-automatic model of gun that fired fully automatically, if the owner did not know the gun could fire automatically. In your view, which side in *Staples* had the better statutory argument?

CQ: Is an AR-15 a firearm in common use protected under the Second Amendment according to *District of Columbia v. Heller* (Chapter 9)? Does the answer affect the legal analysis of the *Staples* issue? Professor O'Shea argues that *Staples* is best understood as a "shadow Second Amendment case." In his view, the majority's discussion of the "long tradition of widespread lawful gun ownership" in America, and its refusal to impose strict liability for possession of a malfunctioning AR-15 that "doubles," suggests that (unlike grenades), the AR-15 and similar semi-automatic rifles are not the kind of "dangerous and unusual weapons" that are excluded from Second Amendment protection under *Heller*. *See* Michael P. O'Shea, *The Right to Defensive Arms After* District of Columbia v. Heller, 111 W. Va. L. Rev. 349, 390-91 (2009). Is this argument persuasive? Or is it an over-reading of an opinion that does not explicitly discuss the Constitution, but instead deals with a question of statutory interpretation?

2. The AR-15 style rifle discussed in *Staples* was classified as an assault weapon by the now-expired 1994 Public Safety and Recreational Firearms Use Protection Act and by similar statutes in several states. Those regulations are discussed later in this chapter.

3. Panic buying and fear of embargo pricing increased the demand for firearms dramatically following President Obama's victory in 2008. Demand for guns like the AR-15 was especially high. Over the past several years, these guns have been among the fastest selling firearms in the country. CQ: When you read *Heller* (Chapter 9), consider how the number of AR-15s in the civilian inventory might impact legislative efforts to ban it.

4. Justice Stevens argues in dissent that the AR-15 rifle is an unusual gun and unlike an ordinary rifle or pistol, its "character and nature . . . is sufficiently hazardous to place the possessor on notice of the possibility of regulation" (internal quotation marks omitted). Is he correct? Would it make a difference to Justice Stevens's analysis that the number of AR-15-style guns in civilian hands has grown from a few hundred thousand before the 1994 ban, to several million and that this rifle type has been the best selling long gun in America for several years running?

6. Regulation by Litigation: Suing the Gun Industry and the Legislative Response

As long as there have been product liability suits, gun manufacturers have faced civil claims by plaintiffs alleging damages from design or manufacturing defects or breach of warranty. Traditionally, those claims alleged that the firearm was defective in the sense that it did not perform as advertised. For example, a gun might fail to fire. Or the barrel might explode because the quality of the metal was inadequate. The product liability suits filed in these cases pushed substandard manufacturers out of the business, and caused other manufacturers to ensure production of properly functioning firearms.

In the 1970s, a new type of lawsuit began to appear: product liability design defect suits that alleged that a properly functioning handgun had a design defect. Some claimed that the handgun was too small, and therefore easy for criminals to conceal. Others alleged that the handgun was not very good for target shooting or hunting and therefore was made for criminal use. Other claims alleged that particular handguns were too powerful. Somewhat more conventional versions of the design defect suits pointed out that the gun lacked a particular safety feature — although most of these safety features had trade-offs (e.g., making the gun more difficult to use in a sudden emergency) that made them undesirable to many consumers.

Generally speaking, the innovative product liability suits were unsuccessful. Most courts viewed them as attempts to eliminate types of handguns that legislatures had decided should remain legal. Many legislatures took the same view, and enacted statutes specifically prohibiting product liability suits against properly functioning firearms.

The one success of the product liability cases was in Maryland, where the state supreme court in 1988 ruled that manufacturers of "Saturday Night Specials" were strictly liable for injuries suffered by crime victims. The Maryland legislature promptly changed the state's liability law to nullify this decision, but the legislature also created a Handgun Roster Board to approve the sale of new models of handguns in Maryland. So the Maryland lawsuit did have some utility in advancing gun control.

Beginning in the mid-1990s, private plaintiffs, often with the assistance of gun control organizations, began moving beyond product liability to bring suits on a wide variety of innovative tort theories. *See, e.g., Hamilton v. ACCU-TEK*, 62 F. Supp. 2d 802 (E.D.N.Y. 1999), *vacated sub nom. Hamilton v. Beretta*, 264 F.3d 21 (2d Cir. 2001) (claiming that defendants' distribution practices created an underground market that gave criminals easy access to handguns); *Merrill v. Navegar*, 89 Cal. Rptr. 2d 146 (Cal. App. 1999), *rev'd* 28 P.3d 116 (Cal. 2001) ("The record includes evidence Navegar deliberately targeted the marketing of the TEC-9 to people attracted to or associated with violence."); *McCarthy v. Olin Corp.*, 119 F.3d 148, 155 (2d Cir. 1997) (alleging that the "Black Talon" bullet was defectively designed because it "results in enhanced injuries beyond ordinary bullets"). Several claimants obtained favorable jury verdicts that were overturned by appellate decisions holding that manufacturers were not liable for the criminal misuse of their products. *See, e.g., Merrill* (California statute barred tort claim against manufacturers where injury was caused by criminal use of product); *Hamilton* (gun manufacturers' connection to victims of criminal gun violence too "remote" to establish a duty of care).

In the late 1990s, the litigation dynamic changed as big city mayors joined the ranks of plaintiffs against the gun industry. Backed by public resources and political clout, over two dozen large municipalities and New York State raised the stakes of litigation against the handgun industry. The Clinton administration, under the leadership of Housing and Urban Development Secretary Andrew Cuomo, also participated in the suits. The suits were designed by Handgun Control, Inc., working together with anti-tobacco lawyers and other top plaintiffs' attorneys. Because state statutes resulting from the previous round of litigation had made product liability claims so difficult, the municipal lawsuits tried new theories, like the argument that "oversupplying" handguns to a particular market constituted negligence or public nuisance. *See, e.g., Archer v. Arms Tech., Inc.*, No. 99-912658 NZ, slip op. (Mich. Cir. Ct. May 16, 2000); *City of Gary v. Smith & Wesson*, 801 N.E.2d 1222, 1228 (Ind. 2003); Rachana Bhowmik, *Aiming for Accountability: How City Lawsuits Can Help Reform an Irresponsible Gun Industry*, 11 J.L. & Pol'y 67 (2002).

As Ed Rendell, then mayor of Philadelphia, explained at an American Bar Association public meeting, the municipal suits were designed to be resistant to consolidation, and to stretch the ability of the handgun manufacturers to pay for legal defense in dozens of jurisdictions at once. (The entire American firearms industry, if consolidated into a single company, would not be among the Fortune 500.)

The ultimate goal of the lawsuits was a voluntary settlement by the firearms industry. In the summer of 2000, there was progress toward that goal. Smith & Wesson, at the orders of its British parent corporation, signed a consent decree that imposed a host of new restrictions on its gun sales, and put its future business operations under the supervision of a committee consisting mainly of gun control advocates. In exchange, the lawsuits against Smith & Wesson would be terminated. *See* U.S. Dep't of Treasury, Press Room, Clinton Administration and State and Local Governments Reach Breakthrough Gun Safety Agreement with Smith & Wesson, *available at* http://www.treas.gov/press/releases/ls474.htm.

For a few days, it appeared that the rest of the American handgun manufacturers might fall in line. But a consumer boycott of Smith & Wesson began to spread the moment that Smith & Wesson settled, and the rest of the industry apparently decided that a settlement might create its own set of problems.

When New Orleans and Chicago filed the first suits in late 1998, the National Shooting Sports Foundation (the trade association for gun manufacturers) and the National Rifle Association began to push back. Building on the existing state laws against product liability gun suits, the NSSF and the NRA now sought bans on any tort lawsuit involving a properly functioning gun. Over 30 states enacted some type of legislation limiting or banning the new lawsuits. More and more states enacted lawsuit bans, and most of the remaining suits lost in state courts. Even Boston — the city that had brought Smith & Wesson to its knees — recognized the trend, and asked for dismissal of the proposed consent decree, which had never gone into effect.

Finally, on October 26, 2005, President Bush signed the bill that had passed by large margins in both houses of Congress: the Protection of Lawful Commerce in Arms Act. 15 U.S.C. §§7901-7903. With a very few exceptions (e.g., breach of contract, violation of a criminal law), the PLCAA retroactively bans civil suits in any federal or state court against manufacturers, or sellers of properly functioning firearms. The Act's application is contested in the case below.

City of New York v. Beretta U.S.A. Corp.
524 F.3d 384 (2d Cir. 2008)

MINER, Circuit Judge:

Defendants-appellants-cross-appellees, manufacturers and wholesale sellers of firearms ("Firearms Suppliers"), appeal from so much of an order entered in the United States District Court for the Eastern District of New York (Weinstein, J.) as denies their motion, grounded on the claim restriction provisions of the Protection of Lawful Commerce in Arms Act, for dismissal of the complaint. In the complaint, plaintiff-appellee-cross-appellant, the City of New York (the "City"), seeks injunctive relief to inhibit the diversion of firearms into illegal markets. The District Court determined that the Act did not violate the United States Constitution, and that the Act's statutory exception for claims based on the violation of a state statute applicable to the sale or marketing of firearms is met by New York's criminal nuisance statute. The City cross appeals from so much of the above-described order as rejects, in accordance with the position taken by intervenor United States of America, various constitutional challenges to the Act raised by the City. Because we conclude that the PLCAA (1) bars the instant action and (2) represents a permissible exercise of Congress's power under the Commerce Clause, we affirm the order of the District Court in part and reverse in part.

BACKGROUND

I. INTRODUCTION

The action giving rise to this appeal was commenced on June 20, 2000, when the City filed a complaint against the Firearms Suppliers seeking injunctive relief and abatement of the alleged public nuisance caused by the Firearms Suppliers' distribution practices. The City claimed that the Firearms Suppliers market guns to legitimate buyers with the knowledge that those guns will be diverted through various mechanisms into illegal markets. The City also claimed that the Firearms Suppliers fail to take reasonable steps to inhibit the flow of firearms into illegal markets. On October 2, 2001, the action was stayed due to issues arising from the September 11, 2001 attacks on the World Trade Center. The initial stay of sixty days was continued pending the outcome of an appeal proceeding in state court involving the same claims for relief sought by the State of New York against most of the defendants in this action. *See Spitzer v. Sturm, Ruger & Co.*, 309 A.D.2d 91, *leave to appeal denied*, 801 N.E.2d 421 (2003) (affirming dismissal of the state's common law public nuisance claim). After the stay was lifted, the City filed a Second Amended Complaint ("Amended Complaint") on January 27, 2004.

On October 26, 2005, the Protection of Lawful Commerce in Arms Act, Pub. L. No. 109-92, 119 Stat. 2095 (codified at 15 U.S.C. §§7901-03) (the "PLCAA" or the "Act") became federal law. The PLCAA provides that any "qualified civil liability action that is pending on October 26, 2005, shall be immediately dismissed by the court in which the action was brought or is currently pending." 15 U.S.C. §7902(b). A "qualified civil liability action" is a civil action or proceeding . . . brought by any person against a manufacturer or seller of a [firearm distributed in interstate or foreign commerce] . . . for damages, punitive damages, injunctive or declaratory relief, abatement, restitution, fines, or penalties, or other relief, resulting from the criminal or unlawful misuse of a [firearm distributed in interstate or foreign commerce] by the person or a third party.

15 U.S.C. §7903(5)(A).

On the day the PLCAA was enacted, the Firearms Suppliers moved to dismiss the Amended Complaint pursuant to section 7902(b). In its opposition to the Firearms Suppliers' motion to dismiss, the City argued that the Act did not bar its causes of action because this case fell within an exception to the forbidden qualified civil liability actions. Pursuant to an exception written into the Act, a suit may proceed when a plaintiff adequately alleges that a "manufacturer or seller of [firearms transported in interstate or foreign commerce] knowingly violated a State or Federal statute applicable to the sale or marketing of [firearms], and the violation was the proximate cause of the harm for which relief is sought." 15 U.S.C. §7903(5)(A)(iii). This provision has been called the "predicate exception," which appellation we adopt. For purposes of this opinion, a statute upon which a case is brought under the predicate exception is referred to as a "predicate statute." The predicate statute at issue in this case is New York Penal Law §240.45, Criminal Nuisance in the Second Degree.[1] The Firearms Suppliers claimed that New York Penal Law §240.45 may not serve as a predicate statute because the predicate exception is meant to apply to statutes that are expressly and specifically applicable to the sale and marketing of firearms, and not to statutes of general applicability, such as section 240.45. The City also challenged the constitutionality of the Act on various grounds. The United States intervened to defend the constitutionality of the PLCAA, taking no position on the PLCAA's effect, if any, on the litigation.

On December 2, 2005, the United States District Court for the Eastern District of New York (Weinstein, J.) denied the Firearms Suppliers' motion to dismiss, finding that the claim restriction provisions of the PLCAA did not require dismissal of the case at bar. *City of New York v. Beretta U.S.A. Corp.*, 401 F. Supp. 2d 244 (E.D.N.Y. 2005). The District Court held that, "[b]y its plain meaning, New York [Penal Law §] 240.45 satisfies the language of the predicate exception requiring a 'statute applicable to the sale or marketing of [a firearm].'" *Id.* at 261. The District Court also found that if the Act did operate to bar the City's claims, it would be constitutional. *Id.* at 251.

The District Court certified its December 2, 2005 order for immediate appeal to this Court, pursuant to 28 U.S.C. §1292(b). *Id.* at 298 ("There is a substantial ground for disagreement about a controlling issue of law — the applicability of the Act to the present litigation — and an immediate appeal may substantially advance the ultimate termination of the litigation."). The

---

1. N.Y. Penal Law §240.45 provides, in pertinent part:

A person is guilty of criminal nuisance in the second degree when . . .

By conduct either unlawful in itself or unreasonable under all the circumstances, he knowingly or recklessly creates or maintains a condition which endangers the safety or health of a considerable number of persons. . . .

Firearms Suppliers appeal from the District Court's denial of their motion to dismiss, and the City cross appeals from the District Court's holding that the PLCAA is constitutional.

For the reasons that follow, we conclude that the City's claim, predicated on New York Penal Law §240.45, does not fall within an exception to the claim restricting provisions of the Act because that statute does not fall within the contours of the Act's predicate exception. We also hold that the PLCAA is a valid exercise of the powers granted to Congress pursuant to the Commerce Clause and that the PLCAA does not violate the doctrine of separation of powers or otherwise offend the Constitution in any manner alleged by the City.

II. The City's Allegations

The factual bases for the City's complaint are set forth in painstaking detail in *NAACP v. Acusport*, 271 F. Supp. 2d 435 (E.D.N.Y. 2003), and *City of New York v. Beretta U.S.A. Corp.*, 315 F. Supp. 2d 256 (E.D.N.Y. 2004) (denying motion to dismiss). Accordingly, our factual summary is brief. The City seeks "injunctive relief and abatement of the public nuisance that defendants cause, contribute to and maintain by their marketing and distribution practices." ... The City alleges that the Firearms Suppliers know that firearms distributed to legitimate retailers are diverted into illegal markets and that the Firearms Suppliers "could, but do not, monitor, supervise or regulate the sale and distribution of their guns by their downstream distributors or dealer-customers"; "could, but do not, monitor, supervise or train distributors or dealers to avoid sales that feed the illegal secondary market"; and "make no effort to determine those distributors and dealers whose sales disproportionately supply the illegal secondary market." ... In spite of New York City's strict controls on gun possession,

> thousands of guns manufactured or distributed by defendants were used to commit crimes in the City of New York. This number includes only guns that were recovered in the course of a crime. The actual number of defendants' 'crime guns' used in New York City over the last five years is vastly higher. [...]

According to the City, among the mechanisms that serve to facilitate the movement of legally distributed handguns into illegal markets are: (i) gun shows, at which non-licensed persons can sell to other private citizens; (ii) private sales from "non-stocking" or "kitchen table" sellers, who are not required to conduct background checks or to maintain records that Federal Firearms Licensees ("FFL") are required to maintain; (iii) "straw purchases," in which persons qualified to purchase handguns make purchases on behalf of those who are not so qualified; (iv) "multiple sales," in which a purchaser buys more than one gun at the same time or during a limited period of time for the purpose of transferring the guns to unqualified purchasers; (v) intentional illegal trafficking by corrupt FFLs; (vi) thefts from FFLs with poor security, as well as false reports of theft by corrupt FFLs; and [(vii)] oversupplying of markets where gun regulations are lax. The City seeks injunctive relief requiring the Firearms Suppliers to take assorted measures that would effectively inhibit the flow of firearms into illegal markets.

DISCUSSION . . .

[The City challenged the constitutionality of the PLCAA on four grounds: (1) impermissible exercise of commerce power; (2) violation of separation of powers by dictating the outcome of pending cases; (3) violation of the Tenth Amendment by dictating which branch of states' governments may authoritatively pronounce state law; and (4) violation of the First Amendment's guarantee of the right to petition the government to redress grievances through access to the courts. The Court rejected each of these arguments and agreed with the District Court that the statute is constitutional.]

IV. DOES THE **PLCAA** REQUIRE DISMISSAL OF THE CITY'S ACTION?

A. PREDICATE EXCEPTION TO QUALIFIED CIVIL LIABILITY ACTIONS

The Firearms Suppliers maintain that the PLCAA requires immediate dismissal of this suit, which is a qualified civil liability action under the statute. The PLCAA defines "qualified civil liability action" as

> a civil action or proceeding or an administrative proceeding brought by any person against a manufacturer or seller of a qualified product [i.e., a firearm that has been shipped or transported in interstate or foreign commerce] or a trade association, for damages, punitive damages, injunctive or declaratory relief, abatement, restitution, fines, or penalties, or other relief, resulting from the criminal or unlawful misuse of a qualified product by the person or a third party.

15 U.S.C. §7903(5)(A).

The PLCAA bars the commencement or the prosecution of qualified civil liability actions by providing as follows:

> (a) In general
> A qualified civil liability action may not be brought in any Federal or State court.
> (b) Dismissal of pending actions
> A qualified civil liability action that is pending on October 26, 2005, shall be immediately dismissed by the court in which the action was brought or is currently pending.

15 U.S.C. §7902. The Act also sets forth certain exceptions to the definition of qualified civil liability action, allowing suits to proceed that meet any of the following criteria:

> (iii) an action in which a manufacturer or seller of a qualified product [i.e., a firearm that has been shipped or transported through interstate or foreign commerce] knowingly violated a State or Federal statute applicable to the sale or marketing of the product, and the violation was a proximate cause of the harm for which relief is sought, including —
> (I) any case in which the manufacturer or seller knowingly made any false entry in, or failed to make appropriate entry in, any record required to be kept

under Federal or State law with respect to the qualified product, or aided, abetted, or conspired with any person in making any false or fictitious oral or written statement with respect to any fact material to the lawfulness of the sale or other disposition of a qualified product; or

(II) any case in which the manufacturer or seller aided, abetted, or conspired with any other person to sell or otherwise dispose of a qualified product, knowing, or having reasonable cause to believe, that the actual buyer of the qualified product was prohibited from possessing or receiving a firearm or ammunition under subsection (g) or (n) of section 922 of Title 18; . . .

15 U.S.C. §7903(5)(A)(iii) (emphasis added).

The City has predicated its claims in this case on the Firearms Suppliers' alleged violation of New York Penal Law §240.45, Criminal Nuisance in the Second Degree, which provides:

A person is guilty of criminal nuisance in the second degree when:

1. By conduct either unlawful in itself or unreasonable under all the circumstances, he knowingly or recklessly creates or maintains a condition which endangers the safety or health of a considerable number of persons; or
2. He knowingly conducts or maintains any premises, place or resort where persons gather for purposes of engaging in unlawful conduct.

The City claims that its suit falls within the exception set forth in section 7903(5)(A)(iii) because New York Penal Law §240.45 is a statute "applicable to the sale or marketing of [firearms]." The Firearms Suppliers disagree, arguing that the predicate exception was intended to include statutes that specifically and expressly regulate the firearms industry. The District Court agreed with the City, finding that, "[b]y its plain meaning, New York [Penal Law §] 240.45 satisfies the language of the predicate exception requiring a 'statute applicable to the sale or marketing of [a firearm].'" *Beretta*, 401 F. Supp. 2d at 261. It is not disputed that New York Penal Law §240.45 is a statute of general applicability that has never been applied to firearms suppliers for conduct like that complained of by the City.

B. Is New York Penal Law §240.45 "Applicable" to the Sale of Firearms?

Central to the issue under examination is what Congress meant by the phrase "applicable to the sale or marketing of [firearms]." The core of the question is what Congress meant by the term "applicable."

We conclude, for the reasons set forth in subsection "1" below, that the meaning of the term "applicable" must be determined in the context of the statute. We find nothing in the statute that requires any express language regarding firearms to be included in a statute in order for that statute to fall within the predicate exception. We decline to foreclose the possibility that, under certain circumstances, state courts may apply a statute of general applicability to the type of conduct that the City complains of, in which case such a statute might qualify as a predicate statute. Accordingly, while the mere absence in New York Penal Law §240.45 of any express reference to firearms does not, in and of itself, preclude that statute's eligibility to serve as a predicate statute under the PLCAA, New York Penal Law §240.45 is a statute of general applicability that does not encompass the conduct of firearms manufacturers of which the City complains. It therefore does not fall within the predicate exception to the claim restricting provisions of the PLCAA.

1. "Applicable" in Context

The City relies on the dictionary definition of "applicable," which is, simply, "capable of being applied."

On the other hand, the Firearms Suppliers contend that the phrase "statute applicable to the sale or marketing of [a firearm]" in the context of the language in the entire statute limits the predicate exception to statutes specifically and expressly regulating the manner in which a firearm is sold or marketed — statutes specifying when, where, how, and to whom a firearm may be sold or marketed. We agree that the examples of state and federal statutory violations in the predicate exception itself refer to state and federal laws that specifically and expressly govern firearms. See 15 U.S.C. §7903(5)(A)(iii)(I)-(II). We also agree with the District Court's rejection of the Firearms Suppliers' argument that the predicate exception is necessarily limited to statutes that expressly regulate the firearms industry. However, for the reasons set forth below, we disagree with the District Court's adoption of the out-of-context "plain meaning" of the term "applicable" and its conclusion that the dictionary definition of the term "applicable" accurately reflects the intent of Congress.

The meaning of the term "applicable" must be determined here by reading that term in the context of the surrounding language and of the statute as a whole. . . . Adhering to this principle, we have held that "fundamental to any task of interpretation is the principle that text must yield to context." *Time Warner Cable, Inc. v. DIRECTV, Inc.*, 497 F.3d 144, 157 (2d Cir. 2007).

Viewed in this light, the term "applicable" must be examined in context. The PLCAA provides that predicate statutes are those that are "applicable to the sale or marketing of [firearms]." 15 U.S.C. §7903(5)(A)(iii). The universe of predicate statutes is further defined as "including" the examples set forth in subsections (I) and (II). As stated, we agree with the Firearms Suppliers that these examples refer to statutes that specifically regulate the firearms industry. Yet, as also stated, we do not agree that the PLCAA requires that a predicate statute expressly refer to the firearms industry. Thus the contours of the universe of predicate statutes — i.e., those statutes that are "applicable" to sale or marketing of firearms — are undefined and we can only conclude that the term "applicable" requires a contextual definition.

Moreover, because both the City and the Firearms Suppliers "rely on a reasonable meaning" of the term "applicable," we must look "to the canons of statutory interpretation to help resolve the ambiguity." . . .

2. Canons of Statutory Construction

We have previously observed that "[t]he meaning of one term may be determined by reference to the terms it is associated with, and [that] where specific words follow a general word, the specific words restrict application of the general term to things that are similar to those enumerated." *Gen. Elec. Co. v. Occupational Safety and Health Review Comm'n*, 583 F.2d 61, 65 (2d Cir. 1978). We have also determined that "[w]here . . . examination of [a] statute as a whole demonstrates that a party's interpretation would lead to 'absurd or futile results . . . plainly at variance with the policy of the legislation as a whole,' that interpretation should be rejected." *Yerdon v. Henry*, 91 F.3d 370, 376 (2d Cir. 1996) (quoting *EEOC v. Commercial Office Prods. Co.*, 486 U.S. 107, 120 (1988) (ellipsis in original)). Defendants contend that their view of the relevant exception "is bolstered by [both of these] settled principles of statutory interpretation."

a. Other Associated Terms

As we noted in *United States v. Dauray*, 215 F.3d 257 (2d Cir. 2000), "the meaning of doubtful terms or phrases may be determined by reference to their relationship with other associated words or phrases (noscitur a sociis)." *Id.* at 262. In addition, "where general words" are accompanied by "a specific enumeration of persons or things, the general words should be limited to persons or things similar to those specifically enumerated (ejusdem generis)." *Id.* (internal quotation marks omitted).

Section 7903(5)(A)(iii) states that the exception set out therein "includ[es]":

> (I) any case in which the manufacturer or seller knowingly made any false entry in, or failed to make appropriate entry in, any record required to be kept under Federal or State law with respect to the [firearm], or aided, abetted, or conspired with any person in making any false or fictitious oral or written statement with respect to any fact material to the lawfulness of the sale or other disposition of a [firearm]; or
>
> (II) any case in which the manufacturer or seller aided, abetted, or conspired with any other person to sell or otherwise dispose of a [firearm], knowing, or having reasonable cause to believe, that the actual buyer of the [firearm] was prohibited from possessing or receiving a firearm or ammunition under subsection (g) or (n) of section 922 of Title 18. . . .

The general language contained in section 7903(5)(A)(iii) (providing that predicate statutes are those "applicable to" the sale or marketing of firearms) is followed by the more specific language referring to statutes imposing record-keeping requirements on the firearms industry, 15 U.S.C. §7903(5)(A)(iii)(I), and statutes prohibiting firearms suppliers from conspiring with or aiding and abetting others in selling firearms directly to prohibited purchasers, U.S.C. §7903(5)(A)(iii)(II). Statutes applicable to the sale and marketing of firearms are said to include statutes regulating record-keeping and those prohibiting participation in direct illegal sales. Thus, the general term — "applicable to" — is to be "construed to embrace only objects similar to those enumerated by" sections 7903(5)(A)(iii)(I) and (II). *See Keffeler*, 537 U.S. at 384. We accordingly conclude that construing the term "applicable to" to mean statutes that clearly can be said to regulate the firearms industry more accurately reflects the intent of Congress. *Cf. Jarecki v. G.D. Searle & Co.*, 367 U.S. 303, 307 (1961) ("The maxim *noscitur a sociis* . . . is often wisely applied where a word is capable of many meanings in order to avoid the giving of unintended breadth to the Acts of Congress").

b. Avoiding Absurdity

The declared purposes of the statute include:

> To prohibit causes of action against manufacturers, distributors, dealers, and importers of firearms or ammunition products, and their trade associations, for the harm solely caused by the criminal or unlawful misuse of firearms products or ammunition products by others when the product functioned as designed and intended.

15 U.S.C. §7901(b)(1). In drafting the PLCAA, Congress found:

> Businesses in the United States that are engaged in interstate and foreign commerce through the lawful design, manufacture, marketing, distribution, importation, or sale to the public of firearms or ammunition products that have been shipped or transported in interstate or foreign commerce are not, and should not, be liable for the harm caused by those who criminally or unlawfully misuse firearm products or ammunition products that function as designed and intended[.]

15 U.S.C. §7901(a)(5). We think Congress clearly intended to protect from vicarious liability members of the firearms industry who engage in the "lawful design, manufacture, marketing, distribution, importation, or sale" of firearms. Preceding subsection (a)(5), Congress stated that it had found that "[t]he manufacture, importation, possession, sale, and use of firearms and ammunition in the United States are heavily regulated by Federal, State, and local laws. Such Federal laws include the Gun Control Act of 1968, the National Firearms Act, and the Arms Export Control Act." 15 U.S.C. §7901(a)(4). We think the juxtaposition of these two subsections demonstrates that Congress meant that "lawful design, manufacture, marketing, distribution, importation, or sale" of firearms means such activities having been done in compliance with statutes like those described in subsection (a)(4).

This conclusion is supported by the "interpretive principle that statutory exceptions are to be construed 'narrowly in order to preserve the primary operation of the [general rule].'" *Nussle v. Willette*, 224 F.3d 95, 99 (2d Cir. 2000) (quoting *Commissioner v. Clark*, 489 U.S. 726, 739 (1989)), *overruled on other grounds by Porter v. Nussle*, 534 U.S. 516 (2002). In the "broader context of the statute as a whole," *Robinson*, 519 U.S. at 341, resort to the dictionary definition of "applicable" — i.e. capable of being applied — leads to a far too-broad reading of the predicate exception. Such a result would allow the predicate exception to swallow the statute, which was intended to shield the firearms industry from vicarious liability for harm caused by firearms that were lawfully distributed into primary markets.

3. Legislative History

We are mindful that "[c]ontemporaneous remarks of a sponsor of legislation are by no means controlling in the analysis of legislative history." *Berger v. Heckler*,

771 F.2d 1556, 1574 (2d Cir. 1985). Nevertheless, we find that the legislative history of the statute supports the Firearms Suppliers' proffered interpretation of the term "applicable." United States Senator Larry E. Craig, a sponsor of the PLCAA, named the case at bar as an "example . . . of exactly the type of . . . lawsuit this bill will eliminate." *See* 151 Cong. Rec. S9374-01, 9394 (2005) (statement of Sen. Craig). United States Representative Clifford B. Stearns, the sponsor of H.R. 800, the House version of the PLCAA, inserted similar comments into the PLCAA's legislative history so that the "Congressional Record [would] clearly reflect some specific examples of the type of . . . lawsuit" the PLCAA would preclude. 151 Cong. Rec. E2162-03 (2005) (statement of Rep. Stearns).

Indeed, the Central District of California found in a strikingly similar case, *Ileto v. Glock*, 421 F. Supp. 2d 1274 (C.D. Cal. 2006), that comments by the bill's proponents consistently referred to firearms-specific statutes when discussing the scope of the predicate exception. For example, Senator Craig stated:

> Let me again say, as I said, if in any way they violate State or Federal law or alter or fail to keep records that are appropriate as it relates to their inventories, they are in violation of law. This bill does not shield them, as some would argue. Quite the contrary. If they have violated existing law, they violated the law, and I am referring to the Federal firearms laws that govern a licensed firearm dealer and that govern our manufacturers today.

Id. at 1292 (quoting 151 Cong. Rec. S9087-01 (statement of Sen. Craig)) (alterations omitted). United States Senator Jefferson B. Sessions stated: "This bill allows lawsuits for violation of contract, for negligence, in not following the rules and regulations and for violating any law or regulation that is part of the complex rules that control sellers and manufacturers of firearms." 151 Cong. Rec. S9374-01, S9378 (daily ed. July 29, 2005).

The *Ileto* court also noted the defeat of attempts to expand the predicate exception to include laws of general applicability. For example, when United States Senator Carl M. Levin sought to include cases in which a firearms supplier's gross negligence or recklessness is a proximate cause of injury or death, *Ileto*, 421 F. Supp. 2d at 1294 (citing 151 Cong. Rec. S9087-01 (statement of Sen. Levin)), the bill's proponents "attacked this amendment, primarily because they believed that it would effectively 'gut' the Act." *Ileto*, 421 F. Supp. 2d at 1294 (citing, e.g., 151 Cong. Rec. S9374-01 (statement of U.S. Sen. John R. Thune)). Recognizing the limited weight owed to such statements, we think that the statements nevertheless support the view that the predicate exception was meant to apply only to statutes that actually regulate the firearms industry, in light of the statements' consistency amongst each other and with the general language of the statute itself. Cf. *Murphy v. Empire of Am., FSA*, 746 F.2d 931, 935 (2d Cir. 1984) (explaining that "isolated remarks, particularly when unclear or conflicting, are entitled to little or no weight"). In sum, we hold that the exception created by 15 U.S.C. §7903(5)(A)(iii): (1) does not encompass New York Penal Law §240.45; (2) does encompass statutes (a) that expressly regulate firearms, or (b) that courts have applied to the sale and marketing of firearms; and (3) does encompass statutes that do not expressly regulate firearms but that clearly can be said to implicate the purchase and sale of firearms.

CONCLUSION

For the foregoing reasons, the judgment of the District Court denying the Firearms Suppliers' motion to dismiss based on the claim restricting provisions of the PLCAA is REVERSED. The judgment of the District Court with respect to the constitutionality of the PLCAA is AFFIRMED. The case is remanded to the District Court with instructions to enter judgment dismissing the case as barred by the PLCAA.

NOTES & QUESTIONS

1. The cities' litigation strategy generated some predictable criticisms. *See, e.g.,* NRA-ILA, Protection of Lawful Commerce in Arms Act (Apr. 1, 2010), *available at* http://www.nraila.org/Issues/FactSheets/ (arguing that the suits were a "shameless attempt to bankrupt the American firearms industry"). But some criticisms came from more surprising sources. *See* Robert B. Reich, *Smoking Guns,* Am. Prospect, Jan. 17, 2000, at 64 ("the goal of [the litigation] efforts is to threaten the industries with the risk of such large penalties that they'll agree to deal. . . . But the way to fix everything isn't to turn our backs on the democratic process and pursue litigation."). *See also When Lawsuits Make Policy,* Economist, Nov. 21, 1998, at 17.

    Does Robert Reich's criticism apply equally to municipal and private lawsuits? Prior to the passage of the PLCAA, litigants and scholars advanced a variety of theories on which the gun industry might be held civilly liable for criminal misuse of their products. *See, e.g.,* Jon S. Vernick & Stephen P. Teret, *A Public Health Approach to Regulating Firearms as Consumer Products,* 148 U. Pa. L. Rev. 1193 (2000); Andrew J. McClurg, *The Tortious Marketing of Handguns: Strict Liability Is Dead, Long Live Negligence,* 19 Seton Hall Legis. J. 777 (1995); Anne Giddings Kimball & Sarah L. Olson, *Municipal Firearms Litigation: Ill Conceived from Any Angle,* 32 Conn. L. Rev. 1277 (2000).

    Some have argued that the price of firearms does not reflect the full costs that they impose on society. Do you agree? Would you apply that reasoning across the board to alcohol or products that impose environmental costs?

2. Some argued that the city plaintiffs also had contributed to the problem they complained about by selling or trading in used police guns at below-market prices. *See, e.g.,* Vanessa O'Connell, *Unloading Old Police Guns: More Cities Ban Trade-ins and Resales,* Wall St. J., Nov. 10, 1999, at B1 (discussing the decisions of New Orleans, Miami, St. Louis, and Bridgeport, Connecticut to abandon trading in old police side arms that end up in the civilian market).

3. The federal power to regulate "commerce . . . among the several states" was originally envisioned as mainly empowering Congress to act against state government interference with interstate commerce, such as state tariffs on the interstate transport of goods. Is the PLCAA a legitimate application of the interstate commerce power?

4. Section 5 of the Fourteenth Amendment empowers Congress to enact "appropriate legislation" enforcing "privilege or immunities of citizens of the United States" and against state deprivation of "life, liberty, or property, without due process of law." The Due Process Clause has been interpreted to make most of the Bill of Rights enforceable against the states. Is the PLCAA a legitimate use of Section 5 of the Fourteenth Amendment?

5. Supporters of the PLCAA included the United States Department of Defense, which wrote a letter to Congress stating that a healthy firearms industry is vital to the defense needs of the United States. Is the PLCAA a legitimate application of congressional military and war power?

6. The lone "pro-gun" Congressperson to vote against the PLCAA was Representative Ron Paul (R-Tex.). He said that he considered the municipal lawsuits to be completely wrong, but that under the Tenth Amendment, Congress had no authority to interfere with state court cases. Do you agree?

7. Assault Weapons Restrictions

Legislation banning "assault weapons" was first enacted in California in 1989. Several other states and municipalities also have enacted bans. A federal ban on assault weapons was enacted in 1994, effective for ten years, and expired in September 2004. This federal ban was preceded by a 1990 prohibition on domestic assembly from imported parts of semi-automatic firearms that could not be imported. 18 U.S.C. §922(r). This import restriction is still in place.

Regulation of assault weapons is complicated by controversies about defining them and discussion of the issue is complicated by public confusion about these definitions. According to the Department of Defense, an "assault rifle" is a relatively light, compact rifle that fires an intermediate power cartridge, and that has a selector switch so that the gun can fire fully automatically or semi-automatically. Small Arms Identification and Operations Guide—Eurasian Communist Countries 105 (4th ed. 1980). Under federal law, such a gun is a "machine gun," which has been strictly regulated ever since the National Firearms Act of 1934.

While "assault rifle" has a precise military definition, "assault weapon" is much more amorphous. In common parlance, the term "assault weapon" may refer to anything that looks like an assault rifle, and any other gun that looks futuristic or especially dangerous.

In a functional sense, almost all the guns that have been labeled "assault weapons" are purely semi-automatic firearms, which is to say that they are functionally identical to all other semi-automatic firearms. As noted in Chapter 1, semi-automatics are the largest category of American handguns, and a very large category of rifles; they first appeared on the market in the late nineteenth century. In appearance, however, some assault weapons do look like machine guns, and this contributes to confusion about the scope and aims of assault weapon legislation.

Assault weapons have been defined various ways in different legislation. But generally, the laws try to capture semi-automatic rifles and shotguns that accept a detachable ammunition feeding device (a detachable box magazine) and have aggressive-looking features like pistol grips, bayonet lugs, or folding/collapsing stocks that give them a military appearance. This definition is not wholly complete because some assault weapon legislation has banned guns that have tubular or other types of feeding devices. It is further complicated because many "assault weapon" bans track the 1989 California ban, which was created by legislative aides looking through a picture book of guns, and outlawing guns based on appearance. The result was a ban on some single-shot guns (the gun could only hold a single round), as well as a ban on nonexistent guns based on typographical and other errors in the picture book.

More coherently, the expired federal assault weapons law banned 19 firearms by name, and about 200 more by defining generic characteristics. The law also outlawed ammunition magazines holding more than 10 rounds. The federal ban did not apply to anything manufactured before the ban's September 1994 effective date, so pre-ban weapons and magazines remained legal.

Ultimately, "assault weapon" is less a technical term than a regulatory vehicle, which means that assault weapons may be defined in a variety of different and sometimes problematic ways. The next case examines some of those problems.

Springfield Armory, Inc. v. City of Columbus
29 F.3d 250 (6th Cir. 1994)

MERRITT, Chief Judge.

Two manufacturers, a dealer and two potential purchasers of weapons challenge the constitutionality of a Columbus city ordinance that bans assault weapons. The ordinance defines "assault weapon" as any one of thirty-four specific rifles, three specific shotguns and nine specific pistols, or "other models by the same manufacturer with the same action design that have slight modifications or enhancements. . . ." The weapons are specified by brand name and model, not generically or by defined categories.

Plaintiffs challenge the ordinance as an unconstitutional bill of attainder because it constrains only the named manufacturers while other manufacturers are free to make and sell similar products. Plaintiffs also contend that the ordinance is unconstitutionally vague. No equal protection claim is raised. The district court rejected the bill of attainder claim on a motion for summary judgment. It did not address the issue of facial validity but found it vague as applied to two of the weapons in question. We find the ordinance unconstitutionally vague on its face and therefore do not reach the bill of attainder issue.

The Supreme Court has stated very general standards for evaluating whether a statute is unconstitutionally vague:

> Vague laws offend several important values. First, because we assume that man is free to steer between lawful and unlawful conduct, we insist that laws give the person of ordinary intelligence a reasonable opportunity to know what is prohibited, so that he may act accordingly. Vague laws may trap the innocent by not providing fair warning. Second, if arbitrary and discriminatory enforcement is to be prevented, laws must provide explicit standards for those who apply them.

Grayned v. Rockford, 408 U.S. 104 (1972) (footnotes omitted). In addition, "the requirement that government articulate its aims with a reasonable degree of clarity ensures that state power will be exercised only on behalf of policies reflecting an authoritative choice among competing social values . . . and permits meaningful judicial review," *Roberts v. United States Jaycees*, 468 U.S. 609, 629 (1984), but the Court has also said that a statute is void only if it is so vague that "no standard of conduct is specified at all." *Coates v. Cincinnati*, 402 U.S. 611, 614 (1971).

At times the Court has suggested that a statute that does not run the risk of chilling constitutional freedoms is void on its face only if it is impermissibly vague in all its applications, *Hoffman Estates v. Flipside, Hoffman Estates, Inc.*, 455 U.S. 489, 495 (1982), but at other times it has suggested that a criminal statute may be facially invalid even if it has some conceivable application. *Kolender v. Lawson*, 461 U.S. 352, 358-59 n.8 (1983); *Colautti v. Franklin*, 439 U.S. 379 (1979). "The degree of vagueness that the Constitution tolerates — as well as the relative importance of fair notice and fair enforcement — depends in part on the nature of the enactment." *Hoffman Estates*, 455 U.S. at 498. When criminal penalties are at stake, as they are in the present case, a relatively strict test is warranted. *Id.* at 499.

In the present case, the ordinance is fundamentally irrational and impossible to apply consistently by the buying public, the sportsman, the law enforcement officer, the prosecutor or the judge. The Columbus ordinance outlaws assault weapons only by outlawing certain brand names without including within the prohibition similar assault weapons of the same type, function or capability. The ordinance does not achieve the stated goal of the local legislature — to get assault weapons off the street. The ordinance purports to ban "assault weapons" but in fact it bans only an arbitrary and ill-defined subset of these weapons without providing any explanation for its selections. Many assault weapons remain on the market and the consumer is without a reasoned basis for determining which firearms are prohibited. The ordinance permits the sale and possession of weapons which are virtually identical to those listed if they are produced by a manufacturer that is not listed. Thus, the Springfield SAR-48 is banned but equivalent designs sold by Browning Arms Company, Paragon Sales and Armscorp are not. The Springfield BM59 is banned but the equivalent Beretta BM59 and BM62 are not banned. The Colt AR-15 Sporter is banned but not identical weapons sold by Bushmaster, SGW/Olympic Arms, Pac West Arms, Eagle Arms, Inc., Holmes Firearms, Frankford Arsenal and Essential Arms Company. The Ruger Mini-14 rifle, which shoots .223 caliber cartridges from a detachable box magazine just like the Colt AR-15 Sporter, is not prohibited. . . .

The ordinance defines "assault weapon" simply by naming forty-six individual models of rifles, shotguns and pistols, listed by model name and manufacturer, and then adds within the prohibition

> other models by the same manufacturer with the same action design that have slight modifications or enhancements of fire-arms listed . . . provided the caliber exceeds .22 rimfire.

Columbus City Codes §2323.01(I). No statement of purpose is added to the ordinance explaining the reason for outlawing some but not all assault weapons of the same type. Nor is there an explanation for drafting the ordinance in terms of brand name rather than generic type or category of weapon. Nor does the ordinance define "same action design" or "slight modifications." We do not know whether a "model by the same manufacturer" that fires twice as fast or twice as many bullets, or half as fast with half as many bullets, or some other combination of changes is a "slight modification" of the "same action design."[1]

Plaintiffs, gun manufacturers and dealers, say that they are unable to comprehend the meaning of the "slight modifications" provision or the purpose of the ordinance and hence cannot know in advance which sales the ordinance purports to prohibit. They argue that the ordinance does not adequately notify the citizenry regarding what conduct is prohibited and will necessarily give rise to arbitrary enforcement. The only clear restriction on the range of modifications which may be considered slight is that the caliber of a modified weapon must exceed .22. Does this mean that any other change in caliber is necessarily slight? What about the range of fire and the magazine capacity of a weapon? Is a doubling, tripling or halving of these measurements a slight modification? Because there is no discernable purpose underlying the slight modifications requirement, the reach of the provision defies definition.

How is the ordinary consumer to determine which changes may be considered slight? A weapon's accuracy, magazine capacity, velocity, size and shape and the caliber of ammunition it takes can all be altered. For example, the Colt Sporter Lightweight is a 5.56 mm caliber weapon equipped with a 16 inch barrel, a 5-round magazine capacity, a 14.5 inch sight radius and weighs 6.7 lbs. . . . If Colt modifies this weapon so that it takes a 9mm cartridge, has a 20 inch barrel, a 20-round magazine capacity, a 19.75 inch sight radius and weighs 10 lbs., would this new weapon be a slight modification? Or if these changes increase the weapon's range and accuracy so that it can shoot at twice the distance, or if a new trigger pull allows the operator to shoot twice as fast, or if Colt doubles the caliber of ammunition but halves the velocity at which the weapon fires the bullet, or if it modifies the gun so that it cannot accept a magazine capacity over 5 rounds? Suppose Colt changes so many of the external features of the weapon — adding a bipod, changing the pistol grip, the stock material, the color, the length and weight — that a person of ordinary intelligence would not, by merely looking at the weapon, be able to recognize any relationship between this modification and the original weapon. Would these changes be considered slight? We see no reasoned basis for making a determination one way or the other.

Even if the term "slight" did not render this provision void, the ordinance's "modifications" requirement would. In order for a difference to constitute a "modification" the weapon in question must have been developed from one of the listed firearms. A copy-cat weapon is only outlawed if it is developed from a listed weapon by a listed manufacturer. As the district court recognized, ordinary consumers cannot be expected to know the developmental history of a particular weapon:

---

1. There are several types of manual actions, such as the bolt and lever designs, which require some manual action to discharge the spent shell and reload a new one into the weapon's chamber. A semi-automatic weapon loads a new shell automatically. It requires a separate pull of the trigger for each shot fired and uses the energy of the discharge to reload. In contrast, a fully automatic weapon fires continuously until the magazine is emptied or the trigger is released. A selective fire weapon is capable of both semi-automatic and full automatic fire. Glossary of the Association of Firearm and Toolmark Examiners 1-2 (1980).

> Neither the M1 nor the M1A were developed from the BM59. Hence, neither . . .
> could be said to represent firearms with "slight modifications or enhancements of
> the firearms listed," in this instance, the Springfield BM59. . . . The actions of
> these firearms are in many respects identical. Nevertheless, persons of ordinary
> intelligence would not know whether the subject ordinance bans the M1 or M1A.
> Only a person with knowledge of the history of these firearms would know that the
> M1 and M1A are not covered by the ordinance. . . .

Nothing in the ordinance provides sufficient information to enable a person of
average intelligence to determine whether a weapon they wish to purchase has a
design history of the sort which would bring it within this ordinance's coverage.
See Robertson v. Denver, No. 93 SA91, 1994 WL 160556, at *7-8 (Colo. Supreme
Court, May 2, 1994) (holding similar provision invalid because "ascertaining the
design history and action design of a pistol is not something that can be
expected of a person of common intelligence.") The record indicates that
the average gun owner knows very little about how his gun operates or its design
features.

These vagueness problems are not difficult to remedy. The subject matter
does allow for more exactness. It is not a case in which greater specificity would
interfere with practical administration. *See Kolender*, 461 U.S. at 361. To the
contrary, Columbus has many options for effectively pursuing its stated goals
without running afoul of due process. Other gun control laws which seek to
outlaw assault weapons provide a general definition of the type of weapon
banned, and the Columbus city council can do the same. *See, e.g.,* Cleveland
Ordinance No. 415-89 §628.02 (banning semi-automatic rifles and pistols that
accept a detachable magazine with capacity of 20 rounds or more and semi-
automatic shotguns with a magazine capacity of more than 6 rounds); H.R.
4296 103rd Cong., 2nd Sess., §2 (1994) (banning semi-automatic rifles, pistols
and shotguns that can accept magazines of more than five rounds and that have
at least two of a number of listed features).

Thus we conclude that the ordinance at issue is invalid on its face. The
district court erred in failing to consider the facial validity of this ordinance and
instead examined only the question of whether the ordinance was vague as
applied to a number of specific weapons. In order to restrict its inquiry, the
court relied on the Supreme Court's statement that "vagueness challenges to
statutes which do not involve First Amendment freedoms must be examined in
the light of the facts of the case at hand," *United States v. Mazurie*, 419 U.S. 544
(1975). Nothing in *Mazurie* indicates that a facial challenge cannot succeed
simply because constitutionally-protected activity is not imperiled. To the
contrary, the Supreme Court has expressly stated that the question of whether
or not a statute impinges on constitutionally-protected activity is but the first
inquiry in a court's examination of a statute challenged on vagueness grounds.
Hoffman Estates, 455 U.S. at 494. A court must also inquire whether the law has
any valid application. *Id.* at 494-95. The district court never considered the
question of whether or not a person of ordinary intelligence could make
sense of this provision. Instead, it requested that plaintiffs produce the
"other firearms" which they believed might be covered and evaluated the ordinance as applied to those weapons. After conducting an evidentiary hearing, the
court found the ordinance void as applied to certain firearms and valid as

applied to others, with no consideration of plaintiff's facial challenge. This was an erroneous way to approach the vagueness problem in this case.

The final issue is the question of severability. The legislation does not include a severability clause. We have no way to know whether the local legislature would have enacted the assault weapons ban without the "slight modifications" provision. 2 Sutherland, Statutory Construction, §44.03 (5th ed. 1992); *Williams v. Standard Oil Co. of Louisiana*, 278 U.S. 235 (1929); *City of New Haven, Connecticut v. United States*, 634 F. Supp. 1449, 1453-59 (D.D.C. 1986). Apparently the city council simply copied the ordinance from a California ordinance. Here, the catch-all phrase is the only element that brings any generality to the measure. The provision seems integral to the ordinance since without it manufacturers could circumvent the ban by merely changing the names of the listed weapons. In view of the arbitrary nature of the ordinance and the historical presumption of inseverability in the absence of a severability clause, we conclude that we should not try to save the assault weapon portion of the ordinance but rather that we should leave it to the local legislature to draft another ordinance that does not suffer from the same defects as this one. 2 Sutherland, Statutory Construction, §§44.08, 44.09 (5th ed. 1992); *Williams v. Standard Oil*, 278 U.S. 235 (1929); *Carter v. Carter Coal Co.*, 298 U.S. 238 (1936). Thus we hold the assault weapon provisions of the ordinance (§§1 and 2 of Ordinance No. 1226-89) invalid. The remaining provisions relating to large capacity magazines, weapons transactions and explosive devices remain unaffected by our decision.

Accordingly the judgment of the district court is reversed.

NOTES & QUESTIONS

1. In *Robertson v. City and County of Denver*, 874 P.2d 325 (Colo. 1994), the Colorado Supreme Court found the following definition of assault weapon unconstitutionally vague: "[a]ll semiautomatic pistols that are modifications of rifles having the same make, caliber and action design but a shorter barrel and no rear stock or modifications of automatic weapons originally designed to accept magazines with a capacity of twenty-one (21) or more rounds."

2. While the 1994 assault weapon ban expired in 1994, a 1990 restriction on importation of specific firearms remains in place. 18 U.S.C.A. §922(r). The 1990 import ban was actually supported by the NRA, which successfully pushed for codification of an earlier import restriction in order to defeat a proposed federal statute against domestic manufacture and possession. The regulatory implementation of this standard restricts assembly or modification of these guns into pre-ban configuration. The guns still can be owned in pre-ban configuration as long as the requisite imported parts are replaced with parts made in the United States. Examine the regulatory language below that implements this requirement. How do you expect manufacturers and gun owners have responded to these restrictions?

Assembly of semiautomatic rifles or shotguns.
(a) No person shall assemble a semiautomatic rifle or any shotgun using more than 10 of the imported parts listed in paragraph (c) of this section if the

assembled firearm is prohibited from importation under section 925(d)(3) as not being particularly suitable for or readily adaptable to sporting purposes.

(b) The provisions of this section shall not apply to:

(1) The assembly of such rifle or shotgun for sale or distribution by a licensed manufacturer to the United States or any department or agency thereof or to any State or any department, agency, or political subdivision thereof; or

(2) The assembly of such rifle or shotgun for the purposes of testing or experimentation authorized by the Director under the provisions of §478.151; or

(3) The repair of any rifle or shotgun which had been imported into or assembled in the United States prior to November 30, 1990, or the replacement of any part of such firearm.

(c) For purposes of this section, the term imported parts are:

(1) Frames, receivers, receiver castings, forgings or stampings
(2) Barrels
(3) Barrel extensions
(4) Mounting blocks (trunions)
(5) Muzzle attachments
(6) Bolts
(7) Bolt carriers
(8) Operating rods
(9) Gas pistons
(10) Trigger housings
(11) Triggers
(12) Hammers
(13) Sears
(14) Disconnectors
(15) Buttstocks
(16) Pistol grips
(17) Forearms, handguards
(18) Magazine bodies
(19) Followers
(20) Floorplates.

27 CFR §478.39.

3. State bans on assault weapons (or any gun restrictions for that matter) raise questions for interstate travelers. Assume you own a gun that is banned by a neighboring state and wish to travel with the gun through the jurisdiction where it is banned. The next section addresses that question.

8. Interstate Transportation of Firearms

Federal law provides a uniform floor of firearms regulation. State laws may supplement the federal rules and impose a variety of additional and often more stringent restrictions on firearms possession and use. Some states also are more liberal, extending, for example, the privilege of carrying concealed firearms within their boundaries. Currently, 38 states have laws providing for the nondiscretionary issue of licenses to carry firearms. Two states (Connecticut and

Alabama) have liberally administered discretionary systems. Four states (Alaska, Arizona, Vermont, and Wyoming) also permit individuals who are qualified to possess firearms, to carry them concealed without a license (all of the four, except Vermont, will issue optional licenses so that residents can carry in other jurisdictions that respect sister-state licenses). In contrast, carry permits are rarely or never issued in 9 states. Also, some jurisdictions have banned particular types of guns entirely. The handgun bans challenged in *Heller* (Chapter 9), and *McDonald v. Chicago*, 130 S. Ct. 3020 (2010) (Chapter 9), were prominent examples of more stringent local laws. Restrictive local and state laws raise issues for interstate travelers. One goal of FOPA was to address these problems. The cases below highlight some of the practical implications of these FOPA provisions.

Revell v. Port Authority of New York and New Jersey
598 F.3d 128 (3d Cir. 2010)

JORDAN, Circuit Judge.

Gregg C. Revell appeals from the dismissal of his claims, brought pursuant to 42 U.S.C. §1983, seeking to impose liability upon the Port Authority of New York and New Jersey ("Port Authority") and Port Authority Police Officer Scott Erickson for arresting him under New Jersey's gun laws and seizing his firearm and ammunition. According to Revell, his arrest was unlawful because he was in compliance with a provision of the Firearm Owners' Protection Act ("FOPA"), 18 U.S.C. §926A, which allows gun owners licensed in one state to carry firearms through another state under certain circumstances. Because we conclude that, at the time of his arrest, Revell's conduct did not bring him within the protection of that statute, we will affirm both the dismissal of his §926A-based claim and the grant of summary judgment to the Port Authority and Erickson on Revell's closely related Fourth Amendment claim. We will likewise affirm the grant of summary judgment against Revell on his due process claim under the Fourteenth Amendment.

I. BACKGROUND

A. REVELL'S ARREST

On March 31, 2005, Revell, a resident of Utah, embarked on a flight from Salt Lake City to Allentown, Pennsylvania, via Minneapolis/St. Paul and Newark, New Jersey. When he arrived at the Northwest Airlines counter in the Salt Lake City Airport, he checked his luggage through to his final destination and declared that, in the luggage, he was carrying an unloaded firearm contained in a locked hard case and ammunition in a separate locked hard case. He signed an orange firearm declaration tag, which was placed inside the locked hard case containing the firearm. That was apparently the last thing on the trip that went as expected. The several mishaps that followed ultimately relate to the accessibility of the firearm and ammunition and are thus key to this dispute.

Because his flight into Newark was late, Revell missed his connection from Newark to Allentown. He booked the next flight to Allentown, which was scheduled to leave Newark at 8 P.M. that evening, but, after the airline changed arrangements, the passengers scheduled for that flight were asked to board a bus, instead of a plane, headed for Allentown. Revell got on the bus; however, when he learned that his luggage was not on board, he got off to locate it.[2] By the time he retrieved his luggage, he had missed the bus, and no other connections to Allentown were available. He then went directly to the Newark Airport Sheraton Hotel in a hotel shuttle, taking his luggage with him. The driver of the shuttle van placed Revell's luggage, which contained the locked hard case containers, in the rear storage area of the van, which was not immediately accessible from the passenger compartment where Revell was seated. Revell stayed at the hotel overnight but did not open either of the locked containers during his stay.

The next morning, he took the hotel's airport shuttle back to the Newark Airport and, again, his luggage was placed out of his reach in the rear of the shuttle. Upon arriving at the airport around 8:30 A.M., he proceeded to the ticket counter to check his luggage and declared that he was carrying an unloaded firearm in a locked hard case and ammunition in a separate locked hard case. Revell was told to take his luggage to the Transportation Security Administration ("TSA") area so that it could be x-rayed. After the luggage went through the x-ray machine, the TSA agent at the other end of the machine took the hard cases out and asked Revell for the key to them, which Revell provided. The TSA agent opened the cases using Revell's key and removed the firearm and ammunition. The orange declaration sheet from Salt Lake City was still in the case with the firearm.

About twenty minutes later, several Port Authority officers, including Officer Erickson, escorted Revell to an area away from other passengers where they questioned him about the firearm and ammunition. Revell explained that he had declared his weapon and ammunition, and that he was merely passing through New Jersey en route to Allentown, Pennsylvania. He also showed the officers his Utah concealed firearm permit and his driver's license. When Erickson questioned Revell about why he had the firearm, Revell explained that he was traveling to Pennsylvania to pick up a car to bring back to Utah and that "he was going to need the weapon for protection" as he drove the car home. . . . Revell also informed Erickson that, upon missing his flight the day before, he had taken possession of his bag with the firearm in it and had gone to a hotel in Newark to stay for the night. Erickson asked Revell whether he had authority to carry the firearm in Pennsylvania, but Revell did not respond.[3]

Erickson arrested Revell for possession of a handgun without a permit in violation of N.J. Stat. Ann. §2C:39-5(b) and for possession of hollow-point ammunition in violation of N.J. Stat. Ann. §2C:39-3(f). Revell was handcuffed, held overnight at the Port Authority jail, and then transferred to the Essex County, New Jersey, Jail, where he was incarcerated for three days until he was released on bond. Four months later, on August 2, 2005, the Essex County

---

2. In a triple-whammy for Revell, not only had the airline made him miss his connection and then put him on a bus instead of a plane, a Northwest employee had mistakenly checked his luggage to Newark, instead of Allentown, as his final destination.

3. At his deposition, Revell stated that he did not check to make sure that he could carry his firearm in Pennsylvania prior to traveling there, but believed that it was legal for him to carry a weapon there because the instructor for his concealed firearm permit class did not mention that he could not do so.

prosecutor administratively dismissed all of the charges against him. However, Revell's firearm, ammunition, holster, locks, and hard cases, which were seized at the time of his arrest, were not returned until July 24, 2008, more than two years after the ill-fated trip and approximately a year after he filed his amended complaint in this action.

B. REVELL'S COMPLAINT

Understandably troubled about his and his property's treatment, Revell brought the present §1983 case, alleging that the Port Authority and Erickson had violated his rights under §926A of FOPA. In essence, §926A allows a person to transport a firearm and ammunition from one state through a second state to a third state, without regard to the second state's gun laws, provided that the traveler is licensed to carry a firearm in both the state of origin and the state of destination and that the firearm is not readily accessible during the transportation. 18 U.S.C. §926A. Revell also alleged that the appellees violated his Fourteenth Amendment rights by retaining his firearm, holster, locks, containers and ammunition, thereby depriving him of his property without due process. He sought damages and an injunction requiring the Port Authority to return his property. . . .

III. DISCUSSION . . .

A. SECTION 926A AND THE FOURTH AMENDMENT

Revell challenges both the District Court's dismissal of his §926A claim and the Court's grant of summary judgment on his Fourth Amendment claim. He asserts that he never should have been required to re-frame his §926A claim in terms of the Fourth Amendment, since, as he sees it, §926A provides a federal right that may be remedied by way of §1983, independent of the Fourth Amendment. As to his Fourth Amendment claim, Revell asserts that the District Court erred in concluding that probable cause existed for his arrest. More specifically, and returning to the same §926A theme, he says that the District Court incorrectly determined that he did not fall within the protection provided by that statute. Revell does not dispute that his conduct violated New Jersey law but instead claims that he was not subject to arrest because he complied with §926A and that §926A preempts New Jersey's gun laws under the circumstances presented here. He also challenges the District Court's conclusion that Erickson was entitled to qualified immunity against the Fourth Amendment claim.

In order for Revell to prevail either on the theory that he had a right under §926A that can be remedied through §1983 or on the theory that the Fourth Amendment should have protected him from arrest because §926A gave him a right to transport his gun, he must first establish that he complied with the conditions set forth in §926A so as to be entitled to its protection. Accordingly, we begin our analysis with the question of whether Revell was in compliance with §926A when he was arrested in New Jersey.

Section 926A of FOPA, entitled "Interstate transportation of firearms," provides:

Notwithstanding any other provision of any law or any rule or regulation of a State or any political subdivision thereof, any person who is not otherwise prohibited by this chapter from transporting, shipping, or receiving a firearm shall be entitled to transport a firearm for any lawful purpose from any place where he may lawfully possess and carry such firearm to any other place where he may lawfully possess and carry such firearm if, during such transportation the firearm is unloaded, and neither the firearm nor any ammunition being transported is readily accessible or is directly accessible from the passenger compartment of such transporting vehicle: Provided, That in the case of a vehicle without a compartment separate from the driver's compartment the firearm or ammunition shall be contained in a locked container other than the glove compartment or console.

18 U.S.C. §926A. It is clear from the statute that a person transporting a firearm across state lines must ensure that the firearm and any ammunition being transported is not "readily accessible or . . . directly accessible from the passenger compartment of [the] transporting vehicle." Id. Looking solely at the allegations of Revell's original complaint, it is also clear that what happened here does not fall within §926A's scope because his firearm and ammunition were readily accessible to him during his overnight stay in New Jersey.

Revell attempts to invoke the protection of the statute by alleging that "[d]uring the transportation of the firearm, neither the firearm nor the ammunition were readily accessible or directly accessible from the passenger compartment of the aircraft or the bus [that he took to the hotel]." . . . But only the most strained reading of the statute could lead to the conclusion that having the firearm and ammunition inaccessible while in a vehicle means that, during the owner's travels, they can be freely accessible for hours at a time as long as they are not in a vehicle. The complaint reveals that Revell's luggage containing the firearm was, in fact, available to him while he was at the hotel. He alleged that, "[a]fter retrieving his bag, because there were no more connections to Allentown until 9:45 A.M. the following morning . . . , [he] went directly to, and stayed the night at, the Airport Sheraton Hotel." . . . He further alleged that he returned with his luggage directly to the airport the next day and that a TSA agent, after x-raying the luggage, opened it with a key that Revell gave him. Taking those facts as true, it is clear that the gun and ammunition were readily accessible to Revell during his stay in New Jersey and, thus, by the allegations of his own complaint, he was not within the scope of §926A. Dismissal of the §926A claim was therefore proper.

Turning to the summary judgment motion on Revell's Fourth Amendment claim, the depositions filed in support of that motion serve to confirm the conclusion that Revell had access to his gun and ammunition, contrary to §926A's requirement. Erickson testified that, under questioning, Revell said he had been forced to stay overnight at a hotel in Newark because he had missed his flight. Erickson also testified that Revell acknowledged he "had the firearm with him when he left for Newark, that he had picked up the bag and taken it with him." . . . Revell's own deposition further confirms that, upon missing his flight to Allentown, he retrieved his luggage, took a shuttle to a nearby hotel, and then returned to the airport the following morning with his bags.

Revell thus had access to his firearm and ammunition during his stay at the New Jersey hotel, whether or not he in fact accessed them and regardless of whether they were accessible while he was traveling by plane or van. That crucial fact takes Revell outside the scope of §926A's protection, as the District Court correctly noted.[15] . . . Accordingly, Revell was subject to arrest for violating New Jersey's gun laws. We will therefore affirm the District Court's grant of summary judgment on his Fourth Amendment claim.

Although we conclude that Revell fell outside of §926A's protection during his stay in New Jersey, we recognize that he had been placed in a difficult predicament through no fault of his own. However, Section 926 clearly requires the traveler to part ways with his weapon and ammunition during travel; it does not address this type of interrupted journey or what the traveler is to do in this situation. Stranded gun owners like Revell have the option of going to law enforcement representatives at an airport or to airport personnel before they retrieve their luggage. The careful owner will do so and explain his situation, requesting that his firearm and ammunition be held for him overnight. While this no doubt adds to the inconvenience imposed upon the unfortunate traveler when his transportation plans go awry, it offers a reasonable means for a responsible gun owner to maintain the protection of Section 926 and prevent unexpected exposure to state and local gun regulations. . . .

IV. CONCLUSION

Section 926A does not apply to Revell because his firearm and ammunition were readily accessible to him during his stay in New Jersey. That conclusion is fatal to his §926A claim and the associated Fourth Amendment claim. We accordingly affirm the District Court's dismissal and grant of summary judgment, respectively, on those claims. We also affirm the District Court's grant

---

15. With regard to whether probable cause existed for his arrest, Revell attempts to raise factual disputes concerning what Erickson knew at the time he arrested Revell, arguing that Erickson did not know what Revell did with his bag when he went to the hotel and that Erickson did not know whether he stayed overnight. First, Revell mischaracterizes the record, as Revell himself testified that he told the officers that he "had been forced to stay in the hotel." . . . Second, even if Erickson were required to consider §926A's impact in his probable cause analysis, an issue on which we express no holding, Revell told Erickson that he had picked up his luggage from the airport and went to a hotel for the night. A reasonable officer would be entitled to infer from Revell's statements that he had access to his firearm and ammunition while at the New Jersey hotel. Whether Revell in fact accessed them is irrelevant. Given our conclusion that Revell was not protected by §926A when he was arrested in New Jersey, we need not address the interrelation between §926A and probable cause. We do, however, note our concern with the implications of Revell's argument that §926A requires an officer to "investigate the laws of the jurisdiction from which the traveler was traveling and the laws of the jurisdiction to which the traveler was going" prior to making an arrest. (Appellant's Reply Br. at 13.) It seems doubtful that, in passing §926A, Congress intended to impose upon police officers such a potentially burdensome requirement. See *Torraco v. Port Auth. of N.Y. & N.J.*, 539 F. Supp. 2d 632, 644 (E.D.N.Y. 2008) ("[I]t is simply too much to read into §926A a Congressional intent to require local police to have on-the-spot knowledge of the firearms laws of all 50 States.").

of summary judgment on Revell's due process claim because he did not take advantage of state procedures available to him for the return of his property.

NOTES & QUESTIONS

1. In *Russo v. Port Authority*, 2008 U.S. Dist. LEXIS 79032 (E.D.N.Y. Sept. 30, 2008), a similar but more violent exchange took place. The plaintiff attempted to check firearms at LaGuardia Airport for a flight to Florida. Yonkers police were called and the plaintiff was arrested. The charges later were dropped. The plaintiff then filed a civil action complaining that he was treated roughly and injured during the arrest. The court dismissed his false imprisonment, malicious prosecution, and excessive force claims on summary judgment.

The following case provides a useful illustration of the wide diversity of approaches to gun regulation in different states and raises a right to travel claim that may be more complicated post-*Heller* (Chapter 9).

Torraco v. Port Authority of New York & New Jersey
539 F. Supp. 2d 632 (E.D.N.Y. 2008) *aff'd* 615 F.3d 129 (2d Cir. 2010)

COGAN, District Judge. . . .

The case is before me on defendants' motion for summary judgment. For the reasons set forth below, the motion is granted.

BACKGROUND

I. JOHN TORRACO

Mr. Torraco is a resident of Florida, an attorney licensed there and in the District of Columbia, and the owner of an Astra pistol. On October 15, 2004, he flew from Florida to La Guardia Airport with his then-wife. He went from LaGuardia to stay with his mother in Franklin Lakes, New Jersey. He owns a different property in Franklin Lakes, which he leases to his father, and his pistol was left there while he was in Franklin Lakes. Two days later, on October 17, 2004, Mr. Torraco's mother drove him and his wife back to Queens, intending to make a stop at a friend's house in Queens before going on to LaGuardia. However, after arriving at the friend's house, they apparently decided to have Mr. Torraco's friend drive them to the airport after their brief visit, which he did, instead of Mr. Torraco's mother. The unloaded pistol was transported during the trip from New Jersey to the friend's house, and then to LaGuardia, in a carrying case.

Upon check-in at the airport, Mr. Torraco advised the airline ticket agent that he was carrying a pistol in a case and wanted to check it through with his luggage. He had previously researched the procedure for transporting firearms under federal law and believed he was in compliance. The airline ticket agent tagged the firearm with an orange firearms declaration tag and checked it through. She also advised him that it was standard operating procedure to notify the Port Authority Police when a passenger declares a weapon, which she did.

Defendant Police Officer Anthony Espinal arrived at the scene and inquired as to whether Mr. Torraco had a New York license for the firearm. Mr. Torraco, specifically identifying 18 U.S.C. §926A, explained that federal law preempted any local licensing requirements, and allowed him to transport the firearm. Officer Espinal was unfamiliar with the statute. He therefore called his superior, defendant Sgt. Lawrence Goldberg.

Sgt. Goldberg testified at deposition that upon arriving on scene, he asked Mr. Torraco and his wife which of them possessed the gun, but that neither of them responded, which he considered to be evasive. He asked them two or three more times, finally telling them that if one of them did not acknowledge possession, he would take them both in for further investigation. Mr. Torraco then acknowledged that the firearm was his. Sgt. Goldberg asked if he had a New York permit, to which Mr. Torraco explained that under 18 U.S.C. §926A, he didn't need one. Sgt. Goldberg asked if he had any documentation showing that he was lawfully in possession of the gun. Mr. Torraco continued to assert that he needed no such documentation to transport the weapon through New York under federal law.

At some point prior to or during this conversation, a Transportation Security Administration ("TSA") Supervisor, Melvin Birch, arrived at the scene. He took the position that Mr. Torraco was correct, and that under federal law, Mr. Torraco was permitted to transport the weapon without regard to local law. Sgt. Goldberg understood the agent to be saying that the weapon was properly packaged in accordance with federal regulations, but that was irrelevant to him. Sgt. Goldberg stated that unless Mr. Torraco could establish legal possession, the federal statute did not override New York State law prohibiting the carrying of firearms. Thus, notwithstanding Agent Birch's position, Sgt. Goldberg and Officer Espinal arrested Mr. Torraco and his wife for a violation of New York Penal Law §265.01(1), Possession of a Firearm in the Fourth Degree: "A person is guilty of criminal possession of a weapon in the fourth degree when . . . [h]e possesses any firearm." . . .

Mr. Torraco was held until the next day, when he was arraigned in Queens County Criminal Court on the charge. (The record does not show what happened to Mr. Torraco's former wife, but since she is not a plaintiff here, it does not appear to be material.) He was apparently released on bail or recognizance. His attorney moved to dismiss on the ground of federal preemption. The motion was carried to April 6, 2005; the District Attorney failed to respond to the motion, although he cross-moved to dismiss in the interests of justice. The Court denied the District Attorney's motion and granted Mr. Torraco's motion, finding that the failure to respond to Mr. Torraco's motion was a concession on the merits.

II. WILLIAM WINSTANLEY

Mr. Winstanley resides in Westchester. He owns three firearms (at least) for which he has permits. On April 1, 2005, he went to JFK Airport to board a flight for Phoenix. He declared the guns to the ticket agent, and again as per standard operating procedure, she called Port Authority Police. Defendant Officer Paulson arrived at the scene and requested, and was shown, the permits for the weapons and Mr. Winstanley's driver's license. He asked Mr. Winstanley if he had an Arizona permit. Mr. Winstanley advised Officer Paulsen that he did not need a permit to openly carry a weapon in Arizona, but that he did have a Florida permit, which permitted him to carry a concealed weapon in Arizona. Officer Paulsen disagreed, and Mr. Winstanley asked to speak to Officer Paulsen's supervisor. Officer Paulsen told Mr. Winstanley that if he persisted in asking to speak to a supervisor, he (Officer Paulsen) would place Mr. Winstanley under arrest. He said that Mr. Winstanley would not be permitted to board the aircraft with the firearms.

Mr. Winstanley changed his flight to the next day, apparently anticipating that the delay in getting approval to board with the firearms would cause him to miss his scheduled flight, and there were no other flights on his ticketed airline that day. He then made his way to the Port Authority Police Headquarters at JFK, and spoke to an unidentified Lieutenant. After some discussion and delay, the Lieutenant agreed with Mr. Winstanley that he did not need a permit in Arizona, but by that time, Mr. Winstanley had indeed missed his flight.

The next day, Mr. Winstanley returned to the airport to try to get another flight. He was told by another officer (who is unidentified) the he had the wrong type of carrying case, although it was one that Mr. Winstanley had used for years. He bought a compliant gun case from the airline without delay, and apparently would have made that flight, but the flight was canceled due to weather and there were again no other flights on his ticketed airline going out that day. The next day, after making some unsuccessful telephone calls to the Port Authority police at JFK to try to pre-clear his transport of the firearms, he returned to JFK, and was permitted to board the flight to Arizona, checking through his pistols upon producing his New York permit and driver's license.

III. THE COMPLAINT . . .

Plaintiffs' legal theories are not entirely clear. For Mr. Winstanley, who only missed his flight, the claim appears to be that (a) his right to travel was infringed; and (b) §926A creates an independent right to transport firearms, which was also infringed. Mr. Winstanley contends that both of these rights are enforceable by an action for damages under §1983. For Mr. Torraco, who was arrested, the claim is either or both that Sgt. Goldberg violated: (a) his Fourth Amendment right to be free from unreasonable search and seizure; and (b) his independent right to carry firearms under §926A. Again, Mr. Torraco seeks to enforce one or both of these rights under §1983.

DISCUSSION

B. FIREARM OWNERS PROTECTION ACT (FOPA), 18 U.S.C. §926A ET SEQ.

Section 926A of FOPA, entitled "Interstate Transportation of Firearms," . . . which was passed in 1986, consisted of a series of amendments, of which §926A was one, to the Gun Control Act of 1968, 18 U.S.C. §921 *et seq.* . . . .

. . . In the instant case, because of the statute's allowance for the transport of firearms "for any lawful purpose from any place where he may lawfully possess and carry such firearm to any other place where he may lawfully possess and carry such firearm," . . . practical problems abound. Although the statute is easily applied to accomplish one goal — preventing conviction under local gun laws for citizens who legally transport firearms between two states (and it in fact accomplished that goal with regard to Mr. Torraco) — its application in the field, to permit real-time transfer of legal firearms interstate in the fast-moving context of trains, planes, and automobiles, without judicial involvement, has, to say the least, severe practical difficulties.

In the instant case, plaintiffs vehemently condemn the lack of training with which the Port Authority provided its police force with respect to §926A. But that was only the smaller part of the reason why Mr. Torraco was arrested and Mr. Winstanley missed his flight. The more elemental reason was that the officers in the field were not familiar with New Jersey, Florida, and Arizona law with respect to possessing and carrying firearms. Even if they had familiarity with §926A, that statute alone would not have answered the question of whether plaintiffs were entitled to rely upon it. They had to know the law of the places to which plaintiffs had traveled and were traveling to determine if §926A applied.

Yet it is simply too much to read into §926A a Congressional intent to require local police to have on-the-spot knowledge of the firearms laws of all 50 States. I say "50 States" because, although it might be tempting to focus on the jurisdictions involved here, since New Jersey is within the Port Authority's jurisdiction and Florida and Arizona are on heavily used flight paths from New York, the logical extension of plaintiffs' theory would require familiarity with the gun laws of every State. Some of those States have few firearms restrictions; some have many. Most require permits to purchase; some permit home or business possession; some require licensing to carry. In many states, either by statute or regulation, different kinds of firearms are regulated in different ways, e.g., by caliber, or barrel length, or even age (of either the firearms or the owner, or both). In addition, many states have varying regulations within the State, either by county or municipality (as does New York). Moreover, since we are of course covering 50 jurisdictions (plus Puerto Rico and the District of Columbia), the certainty of legislative and regulatory amendments and updates would also have to be part of police officers' apparently endless training under plaintiffs' view of §926A. Indeed, although the title of the section shows that its focus is on interstate transport, its language more broadly addresses transport between "places" from and to which the firearm may be lawfully transported, not States, raising the possibility, under plaintiffs' theory, that officers in the field would have to know foreign country law as well multi-state law to determine whether §926A applies.

There is yet an additional problem that stems from the multi-jurisdictional coverage attempted by §926A. It is not enough, as plaintiffs' argument seems to suggest, if the transporter simply tells an officer that he is in the compliance with either §926A or the laws of his departure and destination states. "I haven't done anything wrong" accompanied by a facially plausible explanation is a common enough response in many encounters between the police and suspects. Indeed, Sgt. Goldberg testified that he makes about 50 firearms arrests a year at LaGuardia, and in about half of those, the suspects assert some claim of legal entitlement (although he is not in a position to learn of the disposition of those cases). The statute would make no sense at all if it required an officer to simply accept the oral representation of the suspect without having the legal knowledge base to evaluate the assertion. Yet the practical impossibility of maintaining that knowledge base makes it infeasible to have the officer answer in damages if a gun carrier's assertion turns out to have been correct.

Nothing could better illustrate the difficulty imposed by plaintiffs' strict liability view of the statute than the parties' passionate disagreement concerning whether Mr. Torraco was in compliance with New Jersey law when he left New Jersey for New York with his firearm in tow.[8] Citing the New Jersey Code of Criminal Justice, N.J.S.A. 2C:39-5, which allows a gun owner to keep or carry a firearm at his "business" or "residence," defendants argue that because Mr. Torraco took the gun from his father's house in New Jersey, which Mr. Torraco owned, to his mother's house in New Jersey, which he did not own, he was in violation of State law, and hence not entitled to the protection accorded interstate transport under §926A. Plaintiffs fire back that there is no evidence that Mr. Torraco brought the gun from his father's house to his mother's house (although I do not see how the gun wound up at LaGuardia without making the stop with Mr. Torraco at his mother's house in New Jersey on the way to LaGuardia). Plaintiffs also argue that because New Jersey law allows portage of the firearm "between one place of business or residence and another *when moving*," N.J.S.A. 2C:39-6(e) (emphasis added), Mr. Torraco was in compliance, because he was "moving" to Florida and the New Jersey statute, according to plaintiffs, is intended to have extraterritorial effect to enable that out-of-state move (although it is curious that Mr. Torraco already owned a house in Florida, had been living there, and was domiciled there). He also relies on subsection (g) of that statute, which allows, in the course of such a move, "such deviations as are reasonably necessary under the circumstances." N.J.S.A. 2C:39-6(g).

Of course, Mr. Torraco disclosed none of his prior intrastate movements, either in New Jersey or New York, to Sgt. Goldberg or Officer Espinal. This is probably just as well, as I am not sure how an officer in the field could be expected to make a decision concerning a legal issue upon which the parties here so strongly, and in good faith, disagree. Multiply the fluidity of that scenario by 50 jurisdictions (putting aside issues that might arise as a result of international travel with interim domestic stopovers), and nearly a billion

---

8. I will note, however, that Mr. Torraco was not entitled to the protection of §926A for at least one reason that he did not disclose to Sgt. Goldberg — his stop at his friend's house in Queens before going on to the airport. Plaintiff characterizes the visit as "brief," but §926A does not allow a diversion to visit a friend on the way to the airport while carrying a gun any more than it allows a short shopping trip to Bloomingdale's on the way to the airport while carrying a gun. There may be "necessary" interim stops in transporting a firearm to its ultimate destination, like staying over in an airport hotel to make an early morning flight, which would fall within §926A by implication, cf. N.J.S.A. 2C:39-6(g) (expressly providing for "deviations as are reasonably necessary" in carrying a firearm between two authorized points), but that was not Mr. Torraco's situation when he chose to make a social call.

passengers moving through U.S. airports per year, and it becomes apparent that providing a damage remedy under §1983 for a failure to adequately apply §926A would be unworkable. . . .

II. MR. TORRACO'S FOURTH AMENDMENT CLAIMS

To the extent Mr. Torraco is claiming violation of his Fourth Amendment rights against unreasonable search and seizure under §1983, as opposed to an action under §1983 to enforce independent rights under §926A, the individual defendants have invoked the defense of qualified immunity.

Consideration of the qualified immunity defense is a two-step inquiry. First, the Court must consider the facts in the light most favorable to the plaintiff, and determine whether the officer's conduct violated the plaintiff's Constitutional rights. Only if the answer to that question is in the affirmative does the Court proceed to the second level of inquiry, namely: (a) was the right clearly established at the time of the defendant's actions; or (b) even if the right was clearly established, was the officer objectively reasonable in believing in the lawfulness of his actions? *See Walczyk v. Rio*, 496 F.3d 139, 154 (2d Cir. 2007); *Connecticut v. Crotty*, 346 F.3d 84 (2003).

A. VIOLATION OF CONSTITUTIONAL RIGHTS

Proceeding to the first issue, whether Sgt. Goldberg violated Mr. Torraco's right against unreasonable arrest, the issue is not whether Mr. Torraco was in fact guilty of the crime for which he was arrested. Rather, the issue of whether his rights were violated turns on whether there was probable cause to believe that a crime had been committed. . . .

Probable cause exists if a police officer has "knowledge or reasonably trust-worthy information of facts and circumstances that are sufficient to warrant a person of reasonable caution in the belief that the person to be arrested has committed or is committing a crime." . . .

Although the parties dispute the tone of the conversation between Mr. Torraco and Sgt. Goldberg, there is no dispute about the material facts known to Sgt. Goldberg when he determined to make the arrest. He knew that (a) Mr. Torraco had advised the ticket agent that he had a gun that he wished to check through, which was properly packaged pursuant to TSA regulations; (b) Mr. Torraco could produce no documentation showing his lawful ownership of the gun; (c) Mr. Torraco offered an explanation of federal and state law in an effort to persuade Sgt. Goldberg that his possession was lawful; and (d) Agent Birch supported Mr. Torraco's explanation. . . .

. . . [P]laintiffs assume that any reasonable officer would be familiar with §926A. Considering the narrowly targeted scope of the statute, the extremely limited authority under it despite more than 20 years since its enactment, and the difficulty of its application in the field described above, there is no justification for that assumption. It is particularly inappropriate to presume universal knowledge of the statute because, as plaintiffs acknowledge, the statute does not effect field preemption, but conflict preemption. This means that only if a particular set of facts exist will the federal statute come into play at all. State and local firearms laws, such as N.Y. Penal L. §265.01(1), remain valid, and will in most circumstances be the only relevant authority upon which a local officer needs to be informed in determining whether to make a gun arrest.

... [A]s discussed above, a police officer who finds someone carrying a gun in New York City, with no documentation, is not legally obligated to simply take the suspect's word that his possession is legal when New York law says that it is not. If the suspect can offer nothing to confirm his defense to what appears to be a clear violation of New York law, the officer is entitled to make the arrest and allow a judge or jury to determine the sufficiency of the suspect's story. ...

Like the instant case, *Krause v. Bennett*, 887 F.2d 362, 372 (2d Cir. 1989), also involved an officer's refusal to accept a suspect's story at face value. A State Trooper spotted what appeared to be a County traffic sign hanging in the suspect's garage. He questioned the suspect about it, who advised him that it had been given to him by a friend in exchange for some plumbing work he had done. He gave the Trooper the name of the friend who had given him the sign. The Trooper inspected the sign, confirmed that it was County property, and without making any effort to locate the friend, obtained a warrant to arrest the plaintiff for intentional possession of stolen property. The charge was dismissed. ...

A gun in the possession of someone who is about to get on a plane presents a potentially much more serious situation than one involving a potentially purloined traffic sign. There is no genuine dispute that Sgt. Goldberg did take some action to try to evaluate Mr. Torraco's defense by asking for some documentation concerning the gun, but Mr. Torraco could give him nothing other than his say-so. A reasonable officer, even one aware of §926A, would be fully justified in not accepting plaintiff's explanation at face value. This is because §926A itself does not answer the question; it requires confirmation of a particular set of facts, which a police officer is not obligated to accept from the mouth of the suspect. ...

IV. MR. WINSTANLEY'S RIGHT TO TRAVEL

Relying on *Saenz v. Roe*, 526 U.S. 489 (1999), and *U.S. v. Guest*, 383 U.S. 745 (1966), Mr. Winstanley argues that because Officer Paulsen would not allow him to board the aircraft with his firearm, his Constitutional right to travel interstate without undue interference was infringed.

The right to travel interstate and intrastate is firmly established. The Second Circuit has referred to it as "virtually unqualified." *Karpova v. Snow*, 497 F.3d 262, 272 (2d Cir. 2007). Most of the cases considering the right to travel involve the denial of crucial benefits to new residents, or the concurrent deprivation of other firmly established Constitutional rights. See e.g., *Saenz* (1-year residency requirement for welfare benefits); *Guest* (denial of public facilities used in interstate travel on the basis of race); *Memorial Hospital v. Maricopa County*, 415 U.S. 250 (1974) (1-year residency requirement for receiving medical treatment violates right to travel and equal protection). As can be seen from these and other cases enforcing the right to travel, its infringement by state actors always involves a material interference with a person's freedom of movement.

It follows that not every interference with an attempt to travel violates the Constitutional right. . . .

Officer Paulsen did not prohibit Mr. Winstanley from getting on his plane. He prohibited him from getting on his plane with his firearms. Although it is true, as the cases cited above indicate, that interference with as well as prohibition of travel may be actionable, refusal to allow the transport of a firearm is not sufficiently material to infringe upon that right. It does not rise to the level of receiving medical care, see *Memorial Hospital*; or subsistence benefits, *see Saenz*; or earning a living, *see Connecticut v. Crotty*, 346 F.3d 84 (2d Cir. 2003). There was thus no infringement of the right to travel. . . .

CONCLUSION

Defendants' motion for summary judgment is granted, and the case is dismissed. The Clerk is directed to enter judgment.

NOTES & QUESTIONS

1. The court hints at the complexity of state firearms laws. What accounts for the wide differences in gun regulation from state to state? Population density? The prevalence or absence of open space? Rural hunting culture? Urban crime problems?

2. In 2009, the U.S. Senate considered a proposal for national concealed handgun license reciprocity. The proposal attracted 58 votes in favor, which was not enough to break the filibuster. The House passed a revised version of the proposal in 2011. Under the proposal, a concealed handgun carry license issued to a resident of one state would be considered valid in every other state that issues licences. The license would not be valid in Illinois or D.C., which are the only jurisdictions that have no statutes authorizing the issuance of concealed handgun licenses. Currently, 40 states issue concealed handgun carry permits to any adult who meets the standard licensing requirements. Most of these states allow someone who has a permit from another state to carry in their own state. (Similarly, all states allow someone with a driver's license in a different state to drive within their borders.)

   Eight states issue carry permits on a discretionary basis. In some of those eight states, a persistent applicant can usually obtain a permit (Delaware, rural California, much of rural New York). In other states, a permit is essentially impossible to obtain (New Jersey) or available only to persons with strong political influence (New York City, most of California). Several states, including Florida, Maine, Connecticut, Arizona, New Hampshire, Washington, and Utah, issue carry permits to nonresidents.

   The national carry reciprocity law would have permitted people who obtain a home-state carry permit to carry in 48 states. Vermont does not require a license to carry, and has no procedure to issue licenses, so Vermont residents would not benefit from the bill. Illinois prohibits carry.

Is it appropriate for Congress to federalize the issue of interstate hand-gun-carrying? Does Congress have the legitimate power to do so in order to protect the constitutional right to travel? The constitutional right to arms?

The Family Research Council has warned that GOProud (a group of pro-gay-rights conservative Republicans) is supporting national carry reciprocity in order to promote national marriage reciprocity (i.e., a federal law that would require Alabama to legally recognize a gay marriage contracted in Massachusetts). Do you agree that national carry reciprocity would set the stage for marriage reciprocity? In what ways are the issues similar or different, in a policy sense and in a constitutional sense?

E.   On the Threshold of an Individual Right to Arms: Full Engagement of the Second Amendment by the Fifth and Ninth Circuits

Section A of this chapter covered some of the post-*Miller* decisions from the lower federal courts. It highlighted criticisms of the generally cursory analysis in those decisions. The two cases in this section provide a stark contrast to those early decisions. They are exhaustively researched and reasoned evaluations of the meaning of the Second Amendment. They also come to opposite conclusions about the nature of the constitutional right to arms. But in a broader sense, the cases are very similar. Both of them involved an in-depth engagement with historical sources, case law, and scholarship. Both agreed that the Second Amendment was an important issue worthy of sustained judicial analysis. Both cases represented a rejection of the many post-*Miller* (Chapter 7) lower federal court decisions that had brusquely rejected the notion that the Second Amendment might have legal significance. Within a decade of these decisions, the issues and arguments they raised would form the core of the Supreme Court's first direct consideration of the Second Amendment since 1939.

United States v. Emerson
270 F.3d 203 (5th Cir. 2001)

GARWOOD, Circuit Judge:

The United States appeals the district court's dismissal of the indictment of Defendant-Appellee Dr. Timothy Joe Emerson (Emerson) for violating 18 U.S.C. §922(g)(8)(C)(ii). The district court held that section 922(g)(8)(C)(ii) was unconstitutional on its face under the Second Amendment and as applied to Emerson under the Due Process Clause of the Fifth Amendment. We reverse and remand.

FACTS AND PROCEEDINGS BELOW

On August 28, 1998, Sacha Emerson, Emerson's wife, filed a petition for divorce in the 119th District Court of Tom Green County, Texas. The petition also requested, *inter alia*, a temporary injunction enjoining Emerson from engaging in any of twenty-nine enumerated acts. On September 4, 1998, Judge Sutton held a temporary orders evidentiary hearing. Sacha Emerson was represented by counsel while Emerson appeared *pro se*. Almost all of Sacha Emerson's direct testimony concerned financial matters, but the following relevant exchange took place on direct examination by her attorney:

Q. You are here today asking the Court for temporary orders regarding yourself and your daughter; is that correct?
A. Yes.
Q. You have asked in these restraining orders regarding Mr. Emerson[] that he not communicate with you in an obscene, vulgar, profane, indecent manner, in a coarse or offensive manner?
A. Yes.
Q. He has previous to today threatened to kill you; is that correct?
A. He hasn't threatened to kill me. He's threatened to kill a friend of mine.
Q. Okay. And he has threatened — he has made some phone calls to you about that?
A. Yes.[1]

Emerson declined an opportunity to cross-examine Sacha and presented no evidence tending to refute any of her above quoted testimony or to explain his conduct in that respect. In his testimony he stated in another connection, among other things, that he was suffering from "anxiety" and was not "mentally in a good state of mind."

On September 14, 1998, Judge Sutton issued a temporary order that included a "Temporary Injunction" which stated that Emerson "is enjoined from" engaging in any of twenty-two enumerated acts. . . .

The order provides that it "shall continue in force until the signing of the final decree of divorce or until further order of this court." The September 14, 1998 order did not include any express finding that Emerson posed a future danger to Sacha or to his daughter Logan.

On December 8, 1998, the grand jury for the Northern District of Texas, San Angelo division, returned a five-count indictment against Emerson. The government moved to dismiss counts 2 through 5, which motion the district court subsequently granted. Count 1, the only remaining count and the count here at issue, alleged that Emerson on November 16, 1998, unlawfully possessed "in and affecting interstate commerce" a firearm, a Beretta pistol, while subject to the above mentioned September 14, 1998 order, in violation of 18 U.S.C.

---

1. The district court's opinion observes that "during the [September 4, 1998] hearing, Mrs. Emerson alleged that her husband threatened over the telephone to kill the man with whom Mrs. Emerson had been having an "adulterous affair." *United States v. Emerson*, 46 F. Supp. 2d 598, 599 (N.D. Tex. 1999).

§922(g)(8). It appears that Emerson had purchased the pistol on October 10, 1997, in San Angelo, Texas, from a licensed firearms dealer.

Emerson moved pretrial to dismiss the indictment, asserting that section 922(g)(8), facially and as applied to him, violates the Second Amendment and the Due Process Clause of the Fifth Amendment. He also moved to dismiss on the basis that section 922(g)(8) was an improper exertion of federal power under the Commerce Clause and that, in any case, the law unconstitutionally usurps powers reserved to the states by the Tenth Amendment.

The district court granted Emerson's motions to dismiss. Subsequently, the district court issued an amended memorandum opinion reported at 46 F. Supp. 2d 598 (N.D. Tex. 1999). The district court held that dismissal of the indictment was proper on Second or Fifth Amendment grounds, but rejected Emerson's Tenth Amendment and Commerce Clause arguments.

The government appealed. . . .

DISCUSSION

[Section 922(g)(8) of the Gun Control Act, known as the Lautenberg Amendment, prohibits those who are the subject of a protective order for domestic abuse from possessing a firearm that has traveled in interstate commerce. In Part I of the decision, the court dispenses with Emerson's argument that the statute should be construed to require an explicit finding that the person enjoined posed a credible threat of violence to his spouse or child. In Parts II through IV, the Court rejects Emerson's Fifth Amendment Due Process, Commerce Clause, and Tenth Amendment claims, respectively.]

V. SECOND AMENDMENT . . .

A. INTRODUCTION AND OVERVIEW OF SECOND AMENDMENT MODELS

The district court held that the Second Amendment recognizes the right of individual citizens to own and possess firearms, and declared that section 922(g)(8) was unconstitutional on its face because it requires that a citizen be disarmed merely because of being subject to a "boilerplate [domestic relations injunctive] order with no particularized findings." *Emerson,* 46 F. Supp. 2d at 611. The government opines that stare decisis requires us to reverse the district court's embrace of the individual rights model.

In the last few decades, courts and commentators have offered what may fairly be characterized as three different basic interpretations of the Second Amendment. The first is that the Second Amendment does not apply to individuals; rather, it merely recognizes the right of a state to arm its militia. This "states' rights" or "collective rights" interpretation of the Second Amendment has been embraced by several of our sister circuits. The government commended the states' rights view of the Second Amendment to the district court, urging that the Second Amendment does not apply to individual citizens.

Proponents of the next model admit that the Second Amendment recognizes some limited species of individual right. However, this supposedly "individual" right to bear arms can only be exercised by members of a functioning, organized state militia who bear the arms while and as a part of actively participating in the organized militia's activities. The "individual" right to keep arms only applies to members of such a militia, and then only if the federal and state governments fail to provide the firearms necessary for such militia service. At present, virtually the only such organized and actively functioning militia is the National Guard, and this has been the case for many years. Currently, the federal government provides the necessary implements of warfare, including firearms, to the National Guard, and this likewise has long been the case. Thus, under this model, the Second Amendment poses no obstacle to the wholesale disarmament of the American people. A number of our sister circuits have accepted this model, sometimes referred to by commentators as the sophisticated collective rights model. On appeal the government has abandoned the states' rights model and now advocates the sophisticated collective rights model.

The third model is simply that the Second Amendment recognizes the right of individuals to keep and bear arms. This is the view advanced by Emerson and adopted by the district court. None of our sister circuits has subscribed to this model, known by commentators as the individual rights model or the standard model. The individual rights view has enjoyed considerable academic endorsement, especially in the last two decades.

We now turn to the question of whether the district court erred in adopting an individual rights or standard model as the basis of its construction of the Second Amendment.

B. STARE DECISIS AND UNITED STATES V. MILLER . . .

Only in *United States v. Miller* has the Supreme Court rendered any holding respecting the Second Amendment as applied to the federal government. . . .

The government's Supreme Court brief [in *Miller*] "preliminarily" points out that:

> ". . . the National Firearms Act does not apply to all firearms but only to a limited class of firearms. The term 'firearm' is defined in Section 1 of the Act . . . to refer only to 'a shotgun or rifle having a barrel of less than 18 inches in length, or any other weapon, except a pistol or revolver, from which a shot is discharged by an explosive if such weapon is capable of being concealed on the person, or a machine gun, and includes a muffler or silencer for any firearm whether or not such firearm is included within the foregoing definition.'" . . .

In this connection the brief goes on to assert that it is "indisputable that Congress was striking not at weapons intended for legitimate use but at weapons which form the arsenal of the gangster and the desperado" . . . and that the National Firearms Act restricts interstate transportation "of only those weapons which are the tools of the criminal". . . .

The government's brief thereafter makes essentially *two* legal arguments.

First, it contends that the right secured by the Second Amendment is "only one which exists where the arms are borne in the militia or some other military

organization provided for by law and intended for the protection of the state."
Id. at 15. This, in essence, is the sophisticated collective rights model.

The *second* of the government's two arguments in *Miller* is reflected by the
following passage from its brief:

> "While some courts have said that the right to bear arms includes the right of the
> individual to have them for the protection of his person and property as well as the
> right of the people to bear them collectively (*People v. Brown*, 253 Mich. 537, 235
> N.W. 245; *State v. Duke*, 42 Tex. 455), the cases are unanimous in holding that the
> term "arms" as used in constitutional provisions refers only to those weapons
> which are ordinarily used for military or public defense purposes and does not
> relate to those weapons which are commonly used by criminals. Thus in *Aymette v.*
> *State* [2 Humph., Tenn. 154 (1840)], *supra*, it was said (p. 158):
>
>> 'As the object for which the right to keep and bear arms is secured, is of
>> general and public nature, to be exercised by the people in a body, for their
>> *common defence*, so the *arms*, the right to keep which is secured, are such as are
>> usually employed in civilized warfare, and that constitute the ordinary
>> military equipment. If the citizens have these arms in their hands, they are
>> prepared in the best possible manner to repel any encroachments upon their
>> rights by those in authority. They need not, for such a purpose, the use of
>> those weapons which are usually employed in private broils, and which are
>> efficient only in the hands of the robber and the assassin. These weapons
>> would be useless in war. They could not be employed advantageously in the
>> common defence of the citizens. The right to keep and bear them, is not,
>> therefore, secured by the constitution.'" . . .

The government's *Miller* brief then proceeds . . . to cite various other state cases,
and *Robertson v. Baldwin*, 165 U.S. 275 (1897), in support of its *second* argument,
and states:

> "That the foregoing cases conclusively establish that the *Second Amendment* has
> relation only to the right of the people to keep and bear arms for lawful purposes
> and does not conceivably relate to weapons of the type referred to in the National
> Firearms Act cannot be doubted. Sawed-off shotguns, sawed-off rifles and machine
> guns are clearly weapons which can have no legitimate use in the hands of private
> individuals."

Thereafter, the government's brief in its "conclusion" states: ". . . we
respectfully submit that Section 11 of the National Firearms Act does not
infringe 'the right of the people to keep and bear arms' secured by the Second
Amendment."

Miller reversed the decision of the district court and "remanded for further
proceedings." *Id.* at 820. We believe it is entirely clear that the Supreme Court
decided *Miller* on the basis of the government's *second* argument — that a
"shotgun having a barrel of less than eighteen inches in length" as stated in
the National Firearms Act is not (or cannot merely be assumed to be) one of the
"Arms" which the Second Amendment prohibits infringement of the right of
the people to keep and bear — and *not* on the basis of the government's *first*
argument (that the *Second Amendment* protects the right of the people to keep
and bear *no* character of "arms" when not borne in actual, active service in the

militia or some other military organization provided for by law"). *Miller* expresses its holding as follows:

> "In the absence of any evidence tending to show that possession or use of a 'shotgun having a barrel of less than eighteen inches in length' at this time has some reasonable relationship to the preservation or efficiency of a well regulated militia, we cannot say that the Second Amendment guarantees the right to keep and bear *such an* instrument. Certainly it is not within judicial notice that this weapon is any part of the ordinary military equipment or that its use could contribute to the common defense. *Aymette v. State of Tennessee,* 2 Humph., Tenn. 154, 158." 59 S. Ct. at 818 (emphasis added).

Note that the cited page of *Aymette* (p. 158) is the page from which the government's brief quoted in support of its *second* argument. . . .

Nowhere in the Court's *Miller* opinion is there any reference to the fact that the indictment does not remotely suggest that either of the two defendants was ever a member of any organized, active militia, such as the National Guard, much less that either was engaged (or about to be engaged) in any actual military service or training of such a militia unit when transporting the sawed-off shotgun from Oklahoma into Arkansas. Had the lack of such membership or engagement been a ground of the decision in *Miller,* the Court's opinion would obviously have made mention of it. But it did not.

Nor do we believe that any other portion of the *Miller* opinion supports the sophisticated collective rights model.

Just after the above quoted portion of its opinion, the *Miller* court continued in a separate paragraph initially quoting the militia clauses of article 1, §8 (clauses 15 and 16) and concluding:

> "With obvious purpose to assure the continuation and render possible the effectiveness of such forces [militia] the declaration and guarantee of the Second Amendment were made. It must be interpreted and applied with that end in view." 59 S. Ct. at 818.

Miller then proceeds to discuss what was meant by the term "militia," stating in part:

> "The signification attributed to the term Militia appears from the debates in the Convention, the history and legislation of Colonies and States, and the writings of approved commentators. These show plainly enough that *the Militia comprised all males physically capable of acting in concert for the common defense. . . .* [O]rdinarily when called for service these men were expected to appear *bearing arms supplied by themselves* and of the kind in common use at the time. . . ."

These passages from *Miller* suggest that the militia, the assurance of whose continuation and the rendering possible of whose effectiveness *Miller* says were purposes of the Second Amendment, referred to the generality of the civilian male inhabitants throughout their lives from teenage years until old age and to their personally keeping their own arms, and not merely to individuals during the time (if any) they might be actively engaged in actual military service or only to those who were members of special or select units.

We conclude that *Miller* does not support the government's collective rights or sophisticated collective rights approach to the Second Amendment. Indeed, to the extent that *Miller* sheds light on the matter it cuts against the government's position. Nor does the government cite any other authority binding on this panel which mandates acceptance of its position in this respect. However, we do not proceed on the assumption that *Miller* actually accepted an individual rights, as opposed to a collective or sophisticated collective rights, interpretation of the Second Amendment. Thus, *Miller* itself does not resolve that issue. We turn, therefore, to an analysis of history and wording of the Second Amendment for guidance. In undertaking this analysis, we are mindful that almost all of our sister circuits have rejected any individual rights view of the Second Amendment. However, it respectfully appears to us that all or almost all of these opinions seem to have done so either on the erroneous assumption that *Miller* resolved that issue or without sufficient articulated examination of the history and text of the Second Amendment.

C. TEXT

We begin construing the Second Amendment by examining its text: "[a] well regulated Militia, being necessary to the security of a free State, the right of the people to keep and bear Arms, shall not be infringed." U.S. CONST. amend. II.

1. Substantive Guarantee

a. "People"

The states rights model requires the word "people" to be read as though it were "States" or "States respectively." This would also require a corresponding change in the balance of the text to something like "to provide for the militia to keep and bear arms." That is not only far removed from the actual wording of the Second Amendment, but also would be in substantial tension with Art. 1, §8, Cl. 16 (Congress has the power "To provide for . . . arming . . . the militia . . ."). For the sophisticated collective rights model to be viable, the word "people" must be read as the words "members of a select militia."[23] The individual rights model, of course, does not require that any special or unique meaning be attributed to the word "people." It gives the same meaning to the words "the people" as used in the Second Amendment phrase "the right of the people" as when used in the exact same phrase in the contemporaneously submitted and ratified First and Fourth Amendments.

There is no evidence in the text of the Second Amendment, or any other part of the Constitution, that the words "the people" have a different connotation within the Second Amendment than when employed elsewhere in the

---

23. As noted below in our discussion of the history of the Second Amendment, many Americans at this time not only feared a standing army but also a select *militia, a militia comprised of only a relatively few selected individuals* (perhaps the youngest and fittest) who were more frequently and better trained and equipped than the general, unorganized militia. Such a select militia would be analogous to today's National Guard.

Constitution. In fact, the text of the Constitution, as a whole, strongly suggests that the words "the people" have precisely the same meaning within the Second Amendment as without. And, as used throughout the Constitution, "the people" have "rights" and "powers," but federal and state governments only have "powers" or "authority," never "rights." Moreover, the Constitution's text likewise recognizes not only the difference between the "militia" and "the people" but also between the "militia" which has not been "called forth" and "the militia, when in actual service."

Our view of the meaning of "the people," as used in the Constitution, is in harmony with the United States Supreme Court's pronouncement in *United States v. Verdugo-Urquidez*, 494 U.S. 259 (1990). . . .

Several other Supreme Court opinions speak of the Second Amendment in a manner plainly indicating that the right which it secures to "the people" is an individual or personal, not a collective or quasi-collective, right in the same sense that the rights secured to "the people" in the First and Fourth Amendments, and the rights secured by the other provisions of the first eight amendments, are individual or personal, and not collective or quasi-collective, rights. *See, e.g., Planned Parenthood v. Casey*, 505 U.S. 833 (1992); *Moore v. City of East Cleveland*, 431 U.S. 494 (1977);[26] *Robertson v. Baldwin, supra* . . . ; *Scott v. Sandford*, 60 U.S. (19 How.) 393 (1856). *See also* Justice Black's concurring opinion in *Duncan v. Louisiana*, 391 U.S. 145, (1968).[27]

It appears clear that "the people," as used in the Constitution, including the Second Amendment, refers to individual Americans.

b.   "Bear Arms" . . .

The best evidence that "bear arms" was primarily used to refer to military situations comes from *Aymette v. State*, 2 Humph., Tenn. 154 (1840), a prosecution for carrying a concealed bowie knife. . . .

---

26.   The cited portions of *Casey* and *Moore* quote with approval from Justice Harlan's dissenting opinion in *Poe v. Ullman*, 367 U.S. 497 (1961), the following passage (among others), viz:

> "'The full scope of the liberty guaranteed by the Due Process Clause cannot be found in or limited by the precise terms of the specific guarantees elsewhere provided in the Constitution. This "liberty" is not a series of isolated points pricked out in terms of the taking of property; the freedom of speech, press, and religion; the right to keep and bear arms; the freedom from unreasonable searches and seizures; and so on.'"

The same language is quoted with approval in Justice White's *Moore* dissent. *Id.* 97 S. Ct. at 1957-58. An earlier portion of the *Casey* opinion speaks of rejecting the notion that Fourteenth Amendment "liberty encompasses no more than those rights already guaranteed to the individual against federal interference by the express provisions of the first eight Amendments." *Id.* at 2804-05 (emphasis added).

27.   Justice Black's concurring opinion in *Duncan* quotes with approval a portion of the remarks of Senator Howard on introducing the Fourteenth Amendment for passage in the Senate, stating that its privileges and immunities clause should include:

> ". . . the personal rights guaranteed and secured by the first eight amendments of the Constitution. [. . .]"

Unlike the Tennessee constitution at issue in *Aymette*, the Second Amendment has no "for their common defence" language and the United States Constitution contains no provision comparable to section 28 of the Tennessee constitution on which the *Aymette* court relied.

Amici supporting the government also cite other examples of state constitutional provisions allowing a conscientious objector to be excused from the duty of bearing arms if he pays an equivalent so that another can serve in his place.

However, there are numerous instances of the phrase "bear arms" being used to describe a civilian's carrying of arms. Early constitutional provisions or declarations of rights in at least some ten different states speak of the right of the "people" [or "citizen" or "citizens"] "to bear arms in defense of themselves [or 'himself'] and the state," or equivalent words, thus indisputably reflecting that under common usage "bear arms" was in no sense restricted to bearing arms in military service. And such provisions were enforced on the basis that the right to bear arms was *not* restricted to bearing arms during actual military service. *See Bliss v. Commonwealth*, 12 Ky. 90 (Ky. 1822).

We also note that a minority of the delegates to the Pennsylvania ratification convention proposed the following amendment to the Constitution. . . . This is yet another example of "bear arms" being used to refer to the carrying of arms by civilians for non-military purposes. Also revealing is a bill drafted by Thomas Jefferson and proposed to the Virginia legislature by James Madison (the author of the *Second Amendment*) on October 31, 1785, that would impose penalties upon those who violated hunting laws if they "shall bear a gun out of his [the violator's] inclosed ground, unless whilst performing military duty." 2 The Papers of Thomas Jefferson 443-44 (J.P. Boyd, ed. 1950). A similar indication that "bear arms" was a general description of the carrying of arms by anyone is found in the 1828 edition of Webster's American Dictionary of the English Language; where the third definition of *bear* reads: "to wear; to bear as a mark of authority or distinction, as, to bear a sword, a badge, a name; to bear arms in a coat."

We conclude that the phrase "bear arms" refers generally to the carrying or wearing of arms.

c. "Keep . . . Arms"

Neither the government nor amici argue that "keep . . . Arms" commands a military connotation. The plain meaning of the right of the people to keep arms is that it is an individual, rather than a collective, right and is not limited to keeping arms while engaged in active military service or as a member of a select militia such as the National Guard.

d. Substantive Guarantee as a Whole

Taken as a whole, the text of the Second Amendment's substantive guarantee is not suggestive of a collective rights or sophisticated collective rights interpretation, and the implausibility of either such interpretation is enhanced by consideration of the guarantee's placement within the Bill of Rights and the wording of the other articles thereof and of the original Constitution as a whole.

2. Effect of Preamble

We turn now to the Second Amendment's preamble: "A well-regulated Militia, being necessary to the security of a free State." And, we ask ourselves whether this preamble suffices to mandate what would be an otherwise implausible collective rights or sophisticated collective rights interpretation of the amendment. We conclude that it does not.

Certainly, the preamble implies that the substantive guarantee is one which tends to enable, promote or further the existence, continuation or effectiveness of that "well-regulated Militia" which is "necessary to the security of a free State." As the Court said in *Miller*, immediately after quoting the militia clauses of Article I, §8 (cl. 15 and 16), "with obvious purpose to assure the continuation and render possible the effectiveness of such forces the declaration and guarantee of the Second Amendment were made." *Id.*, 59 S. Ct. at 818. We conclude that the Second Amendment's substantive guarantee, read as guaranteeing individual rights, may as so read reasonably be understood as being a guarantee which tends to enable, promote or further the existence, continuation or effectiveness of that "well-regulated Militia" which is "necessary to the security of a free State." Accordingly, the preamble does not support an interpretation of the amendment's substantive guarantee in accordance with the collective rights or sophisticated collective rights model, as such an interpretation is contrary to the plain meaning of the text of the guarantee, its placement within the Bill of Rights and the wording of the other articles thereof and of the original Constitution as a whole.[32]

As observed in *Miller*, "the Militia comprised all males physically capable of acting in concert for the common defense" and "that ordinarily when called for service these men were expected to appear bearing arms supplied by themselves." *Id.*, 59 S. Ct. at 818. *Miller* further notes that "'in all the colonies . . . the militia systems . . . implied the general obligation of all adult male inhabitants to possess arms.'" *Id.* (citation omitted). There are frequent contemporaneous references to "a well-regulated militia" being "composed of the body of the people, trained in arms." Plainly, then, "a well-regulated Militia" refers *not* to a special or select subset or group taken out of the militia as a whole but rather to

---

32. It seems clear under longstanding and generally accepted principles of statutory construction, that, at least where the preamble and the operative portion of the statute may reasonably be read consistently with each other, the preamble may not properly support a reading of the operative portion which would plainly be at odds with what otherwise would be its clear meaning. *See, e.g.*, Dwarris, A General Treatise On Statutes, 268, 269 (Wm. Gould & Sons, 1871). . . .

We also observe the various particular provisions of the bill of rights of many early state constitutions contained introductory justification clauses, usually in the form of a general statement of political or governmental philosophy. Examples are given in [Eugene Volokh, *The Commonplace Second Amendment*, 73 N.Y.U. L. Rev. 793, 794-95, 814-21 (1998)]. One such example is the provision of the New Hampshire Constitution of 1784 (pt. 1, art. XVII) stating: "in criminal prosecutions, the trial of facts in the vicinity where they happen is so essential to the security of the life, liberty and estate of the citizen, that no crime or offence ought to be tried in any other county than that in which it is committed. . . ." It would be absurd to construe this provision to apply only when a judge agrees with the defendant that trial of the case in another county would likely jeopardize that particular defendant's life, liberty or estate.

the condition of the militia as a whole, namely being well disciplined and trained. And, "Militia," just like "well-regulated Militia," likewise was understood to be composed of the people generally possessed of arms which they knew how to use, rather than to refer to some formal military group separate and distinct from the people at large. Madison also plainly shared these views, as is reflected in his Federalist No. 46 where he argued that power of Congress under the proposed constitution "to raise and support Armies" (art. 1, §8, cl.12) posed no threat to liberty because any such army, if misused, "would be opposed [by] a militia amounting to near half a million of citizens with arms in their hands" and then noting "the advantage of being armed, which the Americans possess over the people of almost every other nation," in contrast to "the several kingdoms of Europe" where "the governments are afraid to trust the people with arms." The Federalist Papers at 299 (Rossiter, New American Library). Plainly, Madison saw an armed people as a foundation of the militia which would provide security for a "free" state, one which, like America but unlike the "kingdoms of Europe," was not afraid to trust its people to have their own arms. The militia consisted of the people bearing their own arms when called to active service, arms which they kept and hence knew how to use. If the people were disarmed there could be no militia (well-regulated or otherwise) as it was then understood. That expresses the proper understanding of the relationship between the Second Amendment's preamble and its substantive guarantee. As stated in Kates, *Handgun Prohibition and the Original Meaning of the Second Amendment*, [82 Mich. L. Rev. 204 (1983)], "the [second] amendment's wording, so opaque to us, made perfect sense to the Framers: believing that a militia (composed of the entire people possessed of their individually owned arms) was necessary for the protection of a free state, they guaranteed the people's right to possess those arms." *Id.* at 217-18. Similarly, Cooley, General Principles of Constitutional Law (Little, Brown, 1880; 1981 Rothman & Co. reprint) rejects, as "not warranted by the intent," an interpretation of the Second Amendment "that the right to keep and bear arms was only guaranteed to the Militia," and states "the meaning of the provision undoubtedly is, that the people, from whom the militia must be taken, shall have the right to keep and bear arms; and they need no permission or regulation of law for the purpose. But this enables the government to have a well-regulated militia; for to bear arms implies something more than the mere keeping; it implies the learning to handle and use them in a way that makes those who keep them ready for their efficient use." *Id.* at 271. Much the same thought was expressed more than one hundred years later in the following passage from Tribe, American Constitutional Law (3d ed. 2000):

> "Perhaps the most accurate conclusion one can reach with any confidence is that the core meaning of the Second Amendment is a populist/republican/federalism one: Its central object is to arm "We the People" so that ordinary citizens can participate in the collective defense of their community and their state. But it does so not through directly protecting a right on the part of states or other collectivities, assertable by them against the federal government, to arm the populace as they see fit. Rather, the amendment achieves its central purpose by assuring that the federal government may not disarm individual citizens without some unusually strong justification consistent with the authority of the states to organize

their own militias. That assurance in turn is provided through recognizing a right (admittedly of uncertain scope) on the part of individuals to possess and use firearms in the defense of themselves and their homes . . . a right that directly limits action by Congress or by the Executive Branch. . . ." *Id.* Vol. 1, n.221 at 902.

In sum, to give the Second Amendment's preamble its full and proper due there is no need to torture the meaning of its substantive guarantee into the collective rights or sophisticated collective rights model which is so plainly inconsistent with the substantive guarantee's text, its placement within the Bill of Rights and the wording of the other articles thereof and of the original Constitution as a whole.

D. HISTORY

[In this section, the court provides a heavily footnoted treatment with numerous references to a separate appendix of historical analysis at the end of the case.]

VI. APPLICATION TO EMERSON

The district court held that section 922(g)(8) was unconstitutionally overbroad because it allows second amendment rights to be infringed absent any express judicial finding that the person subject to the order posed a future danger. In other words, the section 922(g)(8) threshold for deprivation of the fundamental right to keep and bear arms is too low.

Although, as we have held, the Second Amendment does protect individual rights, that does not mean that those rights may never be made subject to any limited, narrowly tailored specific exceptions or restrictions for particular cases that are reasonable and not inconsistent with the right of Americans generally to individually keep and bear their private arms as historically understood in this country. Indeed, Emerson does not contend, and the district court did not hold, otherwise. As we have previously noted, it is clear that felons, infants and those of unsound mind may be prohibited from possessing firearms. Emerson's argument that his Second Amendment rights have been violated is grounded on the propositions that the September 14, 1998 order contains no express finding that he represents a credible threat to the physical safety of his wife (or child), that the evidence before the court issuing the order would not sustain such a finding and that the provisions of the order bringing it within clause (C)(ii) of section 922(g)(8) were no more than uncontested boiler-plate. . . .

We conclude that Congress in enacting section 922(g)(8)(C)(ii) proceeded on the assumption that the laws of the several states were such that court orders, issued after notice and hearing, should not embrace the prohibitions of paragraph (C)(ii) unless such either were not contested or evidence credited by the court reflected a real threat or danger of injury to the protected party by the party enjoined. . . .

In any event, it is clear to us that Texas law meets these general minimum standards. See, e.g., *Texas Indus. Gas v. Phoenix Metallurgical*, 828 S.W.2d 529, 532 (Tex. App.-Hou. [1st Dist.] 1992). . . .

We remand the case for further proceedings not inconsistent herewith.

[Following the main opinion, the court provided a voluminous appendix of references supporting the individual rights view, with the following section headings: 1. Anti-Federalists want a bill of rights; 2. Federalists say bill of rights not needed because federal government given no power to infringe fundamental rights; 3. Federalists argue that bill of rights may imply federal government has power to infringe those rights not mentioned; 4. Federalists argue bill of rights not needed as Americans, used to freedom, would not allow infringement of rights; 5. Federalists argue that federal power to maintain a standing army should not be feared because the American people are armed and hence could resist an oppressive standing army; 6. Federalists argue that federal militia powers obviated the need for and minimized the likelihood of there being a large standing army.]

Silveira v. Lockyer
312 F.3d 1052 (9th Cir. 2002)

REINHARDT, Circuit Judge.

In 1999, the State of California enacted amendments to its gun control laws that significantly strengthened the state's restrictions on the possession, use, and transfer of the semi-automatic weapons popularly known as "assault weapons." Plaintiffs, California residents who either own assault weapons, seek to acquire such weapons, or both, brought this challenge to the gun control statute, asserting that the law, as amended, violates the Second Amendment, the Equal Protection Clause, and a host of other constitutional provisions. The district court dismissed all of the plaintiffs' claims. Because the Second Amendment does not confer an individual right to own or possess arms, we affirm the dismissal of all claims brought pursuant to that constitutional provision. . . .

I. INTRODUCTION . . .

As originally enacted, the AWCA authorized specified law enforcement agencies to purchase and possess assault weapons, and permitted individual sworn members of those agencies to possess and use the weapons in the course of their official duties. Two additional provisions relating to peace officers were added by the 1999 amendments. First, the legislature provided that the peace officers permitted to possess and use assault weapons in the discharge of their official duties were permitted to do so "for law enforcement purposes, whether on or off duty." §12280(g). Second, the amendments added an exception for retired peace officers. The exception provides that "the sale or transfer of assault weapons by an entity [. . .] to a person, upon retirement, who retired as a sworn officer from that entity" is permissible, and that the general restrictions on possession and use of assault weapons do not apply to a retired peace officer who receives the weapon upon retirement from his official duties. §12280(h)-(i). In sum, then, the statute as amended may fairly be characterized as constituting a ban on the possession of assault weapons by private individuals; with a grandfather clause permitting the retention of previously-owned weapons by their purchasers, provided the owners register them with the state; and with a statutory exception allowing the possession of assault weapons by retired peace officers who acquire them from their employers at the time of their retirement.

Plaintiffs who seek to purchase weapons that may no longer lawfully be purchased in California also attack the ban on assault weapon sales as being contrary to their rights under that Amendment. Additionally, plaintiffs who are not active or retired California peace officers challenge on Fourteenth Amendment Equal Protection grounds two provisions of the AWCA: one that allows active peace officers to possess assault weapons while off-duty, and one that permits retired peace officers to possess assault weapons they acquire from their department at the time of their retirement. After a hearing, the district judge granted the defendants' motion in all respects, and dismissed the case. Plaintiffs appeal, and we affirm on all claims but one.

II. Discussion

A. Background and Precedent

A robust constitutional debate is currently taking place in this nation regarding the scope of the Second Amendment, a debate that has gained intensity over the last several years. Until recently, this relatively obscure constitutional provision attracted little judicial or scholarly attention. There are three principal schools of thought that form the basis for the debate. The first, which we will refer to as the "traditional individual rights" model, holds that the Second Amendment guarantees to individual private citizens a fundamental right to possess and use firearms for any purpose at all, subject only to limited government regulation. This view, urged by the NRA and other firearms enthusiasts, as well as by a prolific cadre of fervent supporters in the legal academy, had never been adopted by any court until the recent Fifth Circuit decision in *United States v. Emerson*, 270 F.3d 203, 227 (5th Cir. 2001), *cert. denied*, 536 U.S. 907 (2002). The second view, a variant of the first, we will refer to as the "limited individual rights" model. Under that view, individuals maintain a constitutional right to possess firearms insofar as such possession bears a reasonable relationship to militia service. The third, a wholly contrary view, commonly called the "collective rights" model, asserts that the Second Amendment right to "bear arms" guarantees the right of the people to maintain effective state militias, but does not provide any type of individual right to own or possess weapons. Under this theory of the amendment, the federal and state governments have the full authority to enact prohibitions and restrictions on the use and possession of firearms, subject only to generally applicable constitutional constraints, such as due process, equal protection, and the like. Long the dominant view of the Second Amendment, and widely accepted by the federal courts, the collective rights model has recently come under strong criticism from individual rights advocates. After conducting a full analysis of the amendment, its history, and its purpose, we reaffirm our conclusion in *Hickman v. Block*, 81 F.3d 98 (9th Cir. 1996), that it is this collective rights model which provides the best interpretation of the Second Amendment.

Our court, like every other federal court of appeals to reach the issue except for the Fifth Circuit, has interpreted *Miller* as rejecting the traditional individual rights view. In *Hickman v. Block*, we held that "the Second Amendment guarantees a collective rather than an individual right." 81 F.3d at 102 (citation and quotation marks omitted). Like the other courts, we reached our conclusion regarding the Second Amendment's scope largely on the basis of the rather cursory discussion in *Miller*, and touched only briefly on the merits of the debate over the force of the amendment. *See id.*

Appellants contend that we misread *Miller* in *Hickman*. They point out that, as we have already noted, *Miller*, like most other cases that address the Second Amendment, fails to provide much reasoning in support of its conclusion. We agree that our determination in *Hickman* that *Miller* endorsed the collective rights position is open to serious debate. We also agree that the entire subject of the meaning of the Second Amendment deserves more consideration than we, or the Supreme Court, have thus far been able (or willing) to give it. This is particularly so because, since *Hickman* was decided, there have been a number of important developments with respect to the interpretation of the highly controversial provision: First, as we have noted, there is the recent *Emerson* decision in which the Fifth Circuit, after analyzing the opinion at length, concluded that the Supreme Court's decision in *Miller* does not resolve the issue of the Amendment's meaning. The *Emerson* court then canvassed the pertinent scholarship and historical materials, and held that the Second Amendment does establish an individual right to possess arms — the first federal court of appeals ever to have so decided. Second, the current leadership of the United States Department of Justice recently reversed the decades-old position of the government on the Second Amendment, and adopted the view of the Fifth Circuit. Now, for the first time, the United States government contends that the Second Amendment establishes an individual right to possess arms. The Solicitor General has advised the Supreme Court that "the current position of the United States . . . is that the Second Amendment more broadly protects the rights of individuals, including persons who are not members of any militia or engaged in active military service or training, to possess and bear their own firearms, subject to reasonable restrictions. . . ." Opposition to Petition for Certiorari in *United States v. Emerson*, No. 01-8780, at 19 n.3. In doing so, the Solicitor General transmitted to the Court a memorandum from Attorney General John Ashcroft to all United States Attorneys adopting the Fifth Circuit's view and emphasizing that the *Emerson* court "undertook a scholarly and comprehensive review of the pertinent legal materials . . . ," although the Attorney General was as vague as the Fifth Circuit with respect both to the types of weapons that he believes to be protected by the Second Amendment, and the basis for making such determinations. Id. app. A.

The reversal of position by the Justice Department has caused some turmoil in the lower courts, and has led to a number of challenges to federal statutes relating to weapons sales, transport, and possession, including a heavy volume in the district courts of this circuit. *See, e.g., United States v. Stepney*, 2002 WL 1460258 (N.D. Cal. July 1, 2002); Jason Hoppin, *No Free Ride For Gun Argument*, The Recorder, July 25, 2002 (discussing Second Amendment defenses raised by criminal defendants in Northern District of California cases). Similar Second Amendment defenses have been raised by criminal defendants throughout the nation as a result of the Justice Department's new position on the amendment.

See Adam Liptak, *Revised View of Second Amendment Is Cited As Defense in Gun Cases*, N.Y. Times, July 23, 2002, at A1.

Given the dearth of both reasoned and definitive judicial authority, a particularly active academic debate has developed over the scope of the Second Amendment.

In light of the United States government's recent change in position on the meaning of the amendment, the resultant flood of Second Amendment challenges in the district courts, the Fifth Circuit's extensive study and analysis of the amendment and its conclusion that *Miller* does not mean what we and other courts have assumed it to mean, the proliferation of gun control statutes both state and federal, and the active scholarly debate that is being waged across this nation, we believe it prudent to explore Appellants' Second Amendment arguments in some depth, and to address the merits of the issue, even though this circuit's position on the scope and effect of the amendment was established in *Hickman*. Having engaged in that exploration, we determine that the conclusion we reached in *Hickman* was correct.

B.   APPELLANTS LACK STANDING TO CHALLENGE THE ASSAULT WEAPONS CONTROL ACT ON SECOND AMENDMENT GROUNDS

Appellants contend that the California Assault Weapons Control Act and its 1999 revisions violate their Second Amendment rights. We unequivocally reject this contention. We conclude that although the text and structure of the amendment, standing alone, do not conclusively resolve the question of its meaning, when we give the text its most plausible reading and consider the amendment in light of the historical context and circumstances surrounding its enactment we are compelled to reaffirm the collective rights view we adopted in *Hickman*: The amendment protects the people's right to maintain an effective state militia, and does not establish an individual right to own or possess firearms for personal or other use. This conclusion is reinforced in part by *Miller*'s implicit rejection of the traditional individual rights position. Because we hold that the Second Amendment does not provide an individual right to own or possess guns or other firearms, plaintiffs lack standing to challenge the AWCA.

1.   The Text and Structure of the Second Amendment Demonstrate That the Amendment's Purpose Is to Preserve Effective State Militias; That Purpose Helps Shape the Content of the Amendment

. . . As commentators on all sides of the debate regarding the amendment's meaning have acknowledged, the language of the amendment alone does not conclusively resolve the question of its scope. . . . What renders the language and structure of the amendment particularly striking is the existence of a prefatory clause, a syntactical device that is absent from all other provisions of the Constitution, including the nine other provisions of the Bill of Rights. Our analysis thus must address not only the meaning of each of the two clauses of the amendment but the unique relationship that exists between them.

a. The Meaning of the Amendment's First Clause: "A Well-Regulated Militia Being Necessary to the Security of a Free State" . . .

We agree that the interpretation of the first clause and the extent to which that clause shapes the content of the second depends in large part on the meaning of the term "militia." If militia refers, as the Fifth Circuit suggests, to all persons in a state, rather than to the state military entity, the first clause would have one meaning — a meaning that would support the concept of traditional individual rights. If the term refers instead, as we believe, to the entity ordinarily identified by that designation, the state-created and -organized military force, it would likely be necessary to attribute a considerably different meaning to the first clause of the Second Amendment and ultimately to the amendment as a whole.

We believe the answer to the definitional question is the one that most persons would expect: "militia" refers to a state military force. We reach our conclusion not only because that is the ordinary meaning of the word, but because contemporaneously enacted provisions of the Constitution that contain the word "militia" consistently use the term to refer to a state military entity, not to the people of the state as a whole. We look to such contemporaneously enacted provisions for an understanding of words used in the Second Amendment in part because this is an interpretive principle recently explicated by the Supreme Court in a case involving another word that appears in that amendment — the word "people." That same interpretive principle is unquestionably applicable when we construe the word "militia."

"Militia" appears repeatedly in the first and second Articles of the Constitution. From its use in those sections, it is apparent that the drafters were referring in the Constitution to the second of two government-established and -controlled military forces. Those forces were, first, the national army and navy, which were subject to civilian control shared by the president and Congress, and, second, the *state militias*, which were to be "essentially organized and under control of the states, but subject to regulation by Congress and to 'federalization' at the command of the president." Paul Finkelman, *"A Well Regulated Militia": The Second Amendment in Historical Perspective*, 76 Chi.-Kent L. Rev. 195, 204 (2000).

Article I also provides that the militia, which is essentially a state military entity, may on occasion be federalized; Congress may "provide for calling forth the Militia to execute the Laws of the Union, suppress Insurrections and repel Invasions." U.S. Const. art. I, §8, cl. 15. The fact that the militias may be "called forth" by the federal government only in appropriate circumstances underscores their status as state institutions. Article II also demonstrates that the militia were conceived of as state military entities; it provides that the President is to be "Commander in Chief of the Army and Navy of the United States, and of the *Militia of the several States*, when called into the actual Service of the United States." *Id.* art. II, §2, cl. 1 (emphasis added). Like the Second Amendment, not all of the provisions in Articles I and II refer specifically to the militia as "the state militia." Nevertheless, the contexts in which the term is used demonstrate that even without the prefatory word, "militia" refers to state military organizations and not to their members or potential members throughout these two Articles.

Our conclusion that "militia" refers to a state entity, a state fighting force, is also supported by the use of that term in another of the provisions of the Bill of Rights. The Fifth Amendment, enacted by the First Congress at the same time as the Second Amendment, provides that a criminal defendant has a right to an indictment or a presentment "except in cases arising in the land or naval forces, or in the Militia, when in actual service in time of War or public danger. . . ." U.S. Const. amend. V. The inclusion of separate references to the "land or naval forces" and "the Militia," both of which may be in "actual service" to the nation's defense, indicates that the framers conceived of two formal military forces that would be active in times of war—one being the national army and navy, and the other the federalized state militia. Certainly, the use of "militia" in this provision of the Bill of Rights is most reasonably understood as referring to a state entity, and not to the collection of individuals who may participate in it.

Not only did the drafters of the Constitution use "militia" to refer to state military entities, so too did the drafters of the Constitution's predecessor document, the Articles of Confederation. . . . The Articles of Confederation art. 6 (1777), *in* Documents of American History 112 (Henry Steele Commager ed., 7th ed. 1963). . . .

To determine that "militia" in the Second Amendment is something different from the state entity referred to whenever that word is employed in the rest of the Constitution would be to apply contradictory interpretive methods to words in the same provision. The interpretation urged by those advocating the traditional individual rights view would conflict directly with *Verdugo-Urquidez*. If the term "the people" in the latter half of the Second Amendment must have the same meaning throughout the Constitution, so too must the phrase "militia."

Our reading of the term "militia" as referring to a state military force is also supported by the fact that in the amendment's first clause the militia is described as "necessary to the security of a free State." This choice of language was far from accidental: Madison's first draft of the amendment stated that a well-regulated militia was "the best security of a free country." Anti-Federalist Elbridge Gerry explained that changing the language to "necessary to the security of a free State" emphasized the primacy of the state militia over the federal standing army: "A well-regulated militia being the best security of a free state, admitted an idea that a standing army was a secondary one." [David Yassky, *The Second Amendment: Structure, History and Constitutional Change*, 99 Mich. L. Rev. 588, 610 (2000)] (quoting The Congressional Register, August 17, 1789). In any event, as we will explain *infra* at 32, 45-47, 53-55, it is clear that the drafters believed the militia that provides the best security for a free state to be the permanent state militia, not some amorphous body of the people as a whole, or whatever random and informal collection of armed individuals may from time to time appear on the scene for one purpose or another.

Finally, our definition of "militia" is supported by the inclusion of the modifier "well regulated." As an historian of the Founding Era has noted, the inclusion of that phrase "further shows that the Amendment does not apply to just any-one." Finkelman, *supra*, at 234. The Second Amendment was enacted soon after the August 1786–February 1787 uprising of farmers in Western Massachusetts known as Shays's Rebellion. What the drafters of the amendment thought "necessary to the security of a free State" was not an "unregulated" mob of armed individuals such as Shays's band of farmers, the modern-day privately organized Michigan Militia, the type of extremist "militia" associated with Timothy McVeigh and other militants with similar anti-government views, groups of white supremacists or other racial or religious bigots, or indeed any other private collection of individuals. To the contrary, "well regulated" confirms that "militia" can only reasonably be construed as referring to a military force established and controlled by a governmental entity.

After examining each of the significant words or phrases in the Second Amendment's first clause, we conclude that the clause declares the importance of state militias to the security of the various free states within the confines of their newly structured constitutional relationship. With that understanding, the reason for and purpose of the Second Amendment becomes clearer. . . .

2. The Historical Context of the Second Amendment and the Debates Relevant to Its Adoption Demonstrate That the Founders Sought to Protect the Survival of Free States by Ensuring the Existence of Effective State Militias, Not by Establishing an Individual Right to Possess Firearms

An examination of the historical context surrounding the enactment of the Second Amendment leaves us with little doubt that the proper reading of the amendment is that embodied in the collective rights model. We note at the outset that the interpretation of the Second Amendment lends itself particularly to historical analysis. The content of the amendment is restricted to a narrow, specific subject that is itself defined in narrow, specific terms. Only one other provision of the Bill of Rights is similarly composed — the almost never-used Third Amendment. The other eight amendments all employ broad and general terms, such as "no law respecting" (the Free Exercise Clause), "unreasonable" (searches and seizures), "due process of law" (for deprivations of life, liberty, and property), "cruel and unusual" (punishments). Even the Ninth and Tenth Amendments speak vaguely of "other" rights or unenumerated "reserved" rights. The use of narrow, specific language of limited applicability renders the task of construing the Second Amendment somewhat different from that which we ordinarily undertake when we interpret the other portions of the Bill of Rights.

What our historical inquiry reveals is that the Second Amendment was enacted in order to assuage the fears of Anti-Federalists that the new federal government would cause the state militias to atrophy by refusing to exercise its prerogative of arming the state fighting forces, and that the states would, in the absence of the amendment, be without the authority to provide them with the necessary arms. Thus, they feared, the people would be stripped of their ability to defend themselves against a powerful, over-reaching federal government. The debates of the founding era demonstrate that the second of the first ten amendments to the Constitution was included in order to preserve the efficacy of the state militias for the people's defense — not to ensure an individual right to possess weapons. Specifically, the amendment was enacted to guarantee that the people would be able to maintain an effective state fighting force — that they would have the right to bear arms in the service of the state.

a.   The Problem of Military Power in the Colonies and Confederation

A significant motivation for the American colonists' break from Britain was a distrust of the standing army maintained by the Crown on American shores. Dorf, *supra*, at 308. Indeed, one of the principal complaints listed in the Declaration of the Independence was that King George III "has kept among us, in times of peace, Standing Armies without the Consent of our legislatures. He has affected to render "the Military independent of and superior to the Civil power." The Declaration of Independence para. 2 (U.S. 1776). Standing armies in the colonial era were looked on with great skepticism. . . .

Nevertheless, many other newly independent Americans expressed the need to strengthen the federal fighting force, even in peacetime. During the brief period in which the Articles of Confederation were in effect, from 1781-1789, relatively weak federal authority existed, particularly as related to military matters. The bulwark of the national defense was the state militias, which bodies the states could voluntarily contribute to the services of the Confederation. The states retained the sole power to arm and otherwise to maintain their respective militias. The Articles of Confederation specifically granted that power (and obligation) to the states: "Every state shall always keep up a well regulated and disciplined militia, sufficiently armed and accoutered, and shall provide and constantly have ready for use, in public stores, a due number of field pieces and tents, and a proper quantity of arms, ammunition and camp equipage." The Articles of Confederation, *supra*, art. 6. It is highly significant that prior to the enactment of the Constitution, the prevailing understanding as expressed in the governing charter then in effect was that the responsibility of arming their militias belonged to the states, not the federal government and not the individual militiamen. It was this function of the states, albeit no longer an exclusive one after the Constitution was adopted, that the Anti-Federalists attempted to preserve, through the enactment of the Second Amendment, in order to ensure that the militias would be effective.

Many leaders of the Revolution expressed concern that as the Continental Army disbanded following the cessation of hostilities with England, the various state militias were inadequate to provide for the common defense due to their poor training and equipment. The establishment of a national armed force was one of the primary reasons that the Constitutional Convention in 1787 was convened. The issue pervaded the convention's debates. . . . The compromise that the convention eventually reached, which granted the federal government the dominant control over the national defense, led ultimately to the enactment of the counter-balancing Second Amendment.

b.   The Constitutional Convention and the Compromise of the Army and Militia Clauses

The minutes of the proceedings of the Constitutional Convention reveal that the delegates to the convention devoted substantial efforts to determining the proper balance between state and federal control of military matters. . . .

c. Anti-Federalist Objections and the Ratification Debates

The Anti-Federalists sought to ensure that the people of the several states would enjoy the protection of effective state militias so that their new-found liberties would be preserved. To accomplish this purpose, they sought to change, or at the least, to clarify, the nature of the proposed balance of military power between the state and federal governments. Despite the arguments advanced by Hamilton, Madison, and others, federal control over state militias remained one of the central objections to the new charter on the part of Anti-Federalists. In particular, if the federal Congress were permitted to "organize, arm, and discipline" the militia, opponents of the Constitution contended, then Congress would have the implied power to *disarm* the state militias and thus the people as well. . . . The Anti-Federalists viewed the state militias as providing the only true opportunity for the people to bear arms. . . . The Anti-Federalist concern was that if Congress possessed exclusive power to arm the militia, the people would be incapable of resisting federal tyranny. Although Federalists, like Madison, responded that "the power [to arm the militia] is concurrent, and not exclusive," [The Complete Bill of Rights: The Drafts, Debates, Sources, and Origins 195 (Neil H. Cogan ed., 1997)], the Anti-Federalists remained adamant. From the perspective of history, the Anti-Federalists' worries that the new national government would permit the state militia to atrophy through neglect may seem to be inconsequential, because we have become so accustomed to the provision of defense being essentially a federal function, and so few of us remain concerned with any right of the people to take up arms against the federal government. Nevertheless, such arguments were central to the Anti-Federalist critique of the proposed new government.

Despite the Anti-Federalist arguments regarding the dangers of the distribution of powers with respect to state militias, and the effect upon the people's ability to provide for their own defense, it soon became clear that the requisite number of states would ratify the new Constitution. Once it became apparent that ratification was likely, Anti-Federalists shifted their efforts from defeating the Constitution to securing amendments, to be adopted almost simultaneously, that would render the new system more to their liking. Six of the state ratifying conventions adopted petitions urging that the newly established federal government enact a series of constitutional amendments, many of which became a part of the Bill of Rights. Four of those six state conventions included proposed amendments related to the militia power. . . . Ratification debates from those states demonstrate that the proposed amendments had nothing to do with an individual right to possess arms, whether for personal or other use. Indeed, the ratification debates were almost entirely — but not completely — devoid of any mention of an individual right to own weapons. . . .

In short, to the extent that the ratification debates concerned firearms at all, the discussion related to the importance of ensuring that effective state militias be maintained, such militias being considered essential to the preservation of the people's freedom. Those who deemed the Constitution inadequate for this purpose, absent some amendment, emphasized the importance of the states' being afforded the right to arm their own militias, thus ensuring the people's right to maintain a military force for their self-defense.

There were only a few isolated voices that sought to establish an individual right to possess arms, and alone among the 13 colonies, New Hampshire, by a majority vote of the delegates to its ratifying convention, recommended a proposed amendment to the Constitution explicitly establishing a personal right to possess arms. . . .

d. The First Congress and the Second Amendment

By the conclusion of the process by which the Constitution was ratified, there were already countless proposals for altering the new governing charter; the Virginia convention alone offered forty. Finkelman, *supra*, at 216. Madison, who was responsible for many of the compromises reached at the Constitutional Convention, as well as for many of The Federalist Papers, represented Virginia in the First Congress, which met in New York in April, 1789. . . . The amendments Madison proposed sought to eliminate ambiguities in the document that had been ratified, or to enumerate principles that he believed were implicit within it. *Id.*

The debates of the First Congress regarding Madison's proposed Second Amendment, like the debates at the Constitution's ratifying conventions, support the view that the amendment was designed to ensure that the people retained the right to maintain effective state militias, the members of which could be armed by the states as well as by the federal government. Otherwise, the anti-Federalists feared, the federal government could, by inaction, disarm the state militias (and thus deprive the people of the right to bear arms). No one in the First Congress was concerned, however, that federal marshals might go house-to-house taking away muskets and swords from the man on the street or on the farm. Notably, *there is not a single statement in the congressional debate about the proposed amendment that indicates that any congressman contemplated that it would establish an individual right to possess a weapon. See* [Jack N. Rakove, *The Second Amendment: The Highest Stage of Originalism*, 76 Chi.-Kent L. Rev. 103, 210-11 (2000)]. Moreover, in other public fora, some of the framers explicitly disparaged the idea of creating an individual right to personal arms. For instance, in a highly influential treatise, John Adams ridiculed the concept of such a right, asserting that the general availability of arms would "demolish every constitution, and lay the laws prostrate, so that liberty can be enjoyed by no man — it is a dissolution of the government." 3 John Adams, A Defence of the Constitutions of Government of the United States 475 (1787).[51] [For the rest of the Adams quote, see Chapter 4.E.]

---

51. We differ with the Fifth Circuit's reading of the historical record in this respect. The *Emerson* court cites a number of general statements, both in the congressional record and outside of it, by "prominent Americans" that the first twelve proposed amendments, ten of which were ratified as the Bill of Rights, relate to individual rights. 270 F.3d at 245-55. It is of course true that the amendments primarily establish individual rights; however, it cannot be disputed that certain portions of the proposed amendments related to other matters. The Tenth Amendment, for instance, relates primarily to the balance of power between the state and federal governments. Additionally, the provision that was recently ratified as the Twenty-Seventh Amendment, but was originally promulgated with the original twelve amendments, relates to Congressional compensation, not individual rights. Thus, we find unconvincing the argument that because some legislators and public figures generally discussed the group of proposed amendments, as establishing individual rights, the Second Amendment establishes a private right to own or possess firearms.

Equally important, almost all of the discussion in the First Congress about the proposed amendment related to the conscientious objector provision, which, as we noted earlier, was ultimately removed. . . . The fact that the overwhelming majority of the debate regarding the proposed Second Amendment related to the conscientious objector provision demonstrates that the congressmen who adopted the amendment understood that it was concerned with the subject of state militias. . . .

In sum, our review of the historical record regarding the enactment of the Second Amendment reveals that the amendment was adopted to ensure that effective state militias would be maintained, thus preserving the people's right to bear arms. The militias, in turn, were viewed as critical to preserving the integrity of the states within the newly structured national government as well as to ensuring the freedom of the people from federal tyranny. Properly read, the historical record relating to the Second Amendment leaves little doubt as to its intended scope and effect.

3.   Text, History, and Precedent All Support the Collective Rights View of the Amendment . . .

. . . Our review of the debates during the Constitutional Convention, the state ratifying conventions, and the First Congress, as well as the other historical materials we have discussed, confirmed what the text strongly suggested: that the amendment was adopted in order to protect the people from the threat of federal tyranny by preserving the right of the states to arm their militias. The proponents of the Second Amendment believed that only if the states retained that power could the existence of effective state militias — in which the people could exercise their right to "bear arms" — be ensured. The historical record makes it equally plain that the amendment was not adopted in order to afford rights to individuals with respect to private gun ownership or possession. Accordingly, we are persuaded that we were correct in *Hickman* that the collective rights view, rather than the individual rights models, reflects the proper interpretation of the Second Amendment. Thus, we hold that the Second Amendment imposes no limitation on California's ability to enact legislation regulating or prohibiting the possession or use of firearms, including dangerous weapons such as assault weapons. Plaintiffs lack standing to assert a Second Amendment claim, and their challenge to the Assault Weapons Control Act fails. . . .

NOTES & QUESTIONS

1.   Between *Emerson* and *Silveira*, which decision do you find more convincing? Why? Note that the treatment of the legislative history, ratification, and public debate in *Emerson* takes up far more space than its counterpart in *Silveira*, so those sections have simply been summarized here. Each court is firmly convinced that the history supports its view. Compare the full texts of *Emerson* (including the appendix) and *Silveira*. See if this changes your view about which decision is more convincing.

2. *Silveira* concluded that plaintiffs lacked standing because the Second Amendment does not provide an individual right to own or possess guns or other firearms. CQ: After you read *Heller* in the next chapter, consider whether Justice Stevens would agree with the *Silveira* court on the standing question. Consider what, if anything, distinguishes the view of the *Silveira* court from Justice Stevens's dissent in *Heller*. Compare Justice Breyer's view. What does it say about the nonindividual rights constructions of the Second Amendment that there have been so many variations of it? Variations in the conception of the nonindividual rights view have prompted criticism that these different views have no independent substances but are make-weights in the enterprise of denying individual rights claims. For an exercise exploring what the state's rights Second Amendment might mean in modern practice, see Nicholas J. Johnson, *Testing the States' Rights Second Amendment for Content: A Showdown Between Federal Environmental Closure of Firing Ranges and Protective State Legislation*, 38 Ind. L. Rev. 689 (2005); Randy E. Barnett & Don B. Kates, *Under Fire: The New Consensus on the Second Amendment*, 45 Emory L.J. 1139 (1996).

3. Consider again the Firearms Freedom Act legislation discussed earlier in this chapter. How would you draft a Firearms Freedom Act to capitalize on the view of the Second Amendment advanced in *Silveira*?

4. The *Emerson* and *Silveira* opinions disagree over the meaning of "bear arms." Which view is stronger? The two cases also disagree over the meaning of "keep." Which view is stronger? What precisely is the view of the *Silveira* decision about the meaning of "keep"?

5. Both *Emerson* and *Silveira* refer to Professor Tribe's *Constitutional Law* treatise in support of their views. Review the *Emerson* decision's reference to Professor Tribe. Notice how *Silveira* presents Tribe's evolving view of the Second Amendment in footnote 22.

> Even the learned Professor Tribe has appeared stymied by the task of construing the Second Amendment. In the first two editions of his treatise on constitutional law, he advocated the collective rights position. *See, e.g.*, Laurence H. Tribe, American Constitutional Law 299 n.6 (2d ed. 1988) ("The sole concern of the Second Amendment's framers was to prevent such federal interferences with the state militia as would permit the establishment of a standing national army and the consequent destruction of local autonomy. Thus the inapplicability of the Second Amendment to purely private conduct . . . comports with the narrowly limited aim of the amendment as merely ancillary to other constitutional guarantees of state sovereignty."). However, in the treatise's third edition Professor Tribe tentatively concluded that the amendment provides "a right (admittedly of uncertain scope) on the part of individuals," although he left unresolved many of the more difficult questions regarding the amendment's practical effect, concluding unhelpfully that "the Second Amendment provides fertile ground in which to till the soil of federalism and to unearth its relationship with individual as well as collective notions of rights." Laurence H. Tribe, 1 American Constitutional Law 902 n.221 (3d ed. 2000). Soon after the third edition of the treatise was

sent to press, Professor Tribe, in concert with another equally puzzled law school professor, appeared to equivocate even further regarding the scope of the amendment's protections. The two professors abandoned constitutional analysis almost entirely and retreated to a wholly pragmatic and political, though overly optimistic, discussion of how the two sides to the bitter Second Amendment debate could live happily ever after by reaching reasonable practical accommodations of their sharply conflicting constitutional views. Laurence H. Tribe & Akhil Reed Amar, *Well-Regulated Militias, and More*, N.Y. Times, Oct. 28, 1999, at A31.

6.   In both *Emerson* and *Silveira*, concurring judges agreed with the result, but found the extensive Second Amendment discussion "unnecessary." In *Silveira*, Judge McGill objected that the claim could and should have been dismissed on standing grounds. In *Emerson*, Judge Parker objected that under any view of the Second Amendment, the Gun Control Act was not infirm as to Dr. Emerson. Do you agree that the Second Amendment discussions in the cases are unnecessary dicta?

7.   Section A of this chapter mentioned that some of the early cursory dismissals of individual rights claims might be explained by the arguably frivolous nature of the claims brought by criminal defendants. Are the plaintiffs in *Emerson* and *Silveira* more sympathetic? Were their Second Amendment claims more credible and deserving of deeper analysis than the claims in the cases from Section A?

8.   Note the references in footnotes 26 and 27 of the *Emerson* decision to modern Supreme Court cases that briefly mentioned the Second Amendment or the right to arms. What is your assessment of these references? Are they endorsements of the individual rights view of the Second Amendment? Can you explain them in a way that is consistent with a collective or state's rights view? With the narrow individual right view?

9

The Supreme Court Affirms an Individual Right to Arms

In 1939, the Supreme Court partially interpreted the Second Amendment in *United States v. Miller*, 307 U.S. 174 (1939) (Chapter 7). The Court then waited 69 years before addressing the right to keep and bear arms again. In 2008, the Court settled part of the debate about the meaning of the Second Amendment in *District of Columbia v. Heller, infra,* ruling that the District's handgun ban violated the right to keep and bear arms. Because the District of Columbia is a federal enclave, *Heller* only established that the *federal* government was prohibited from banning private handguns. Whether the Second Amendment right applied to the states via the Fourteenth Amendment was left unresolved. That question would be answered in *McDonald v. Chicago, infra.*

This chapter is devoted to *Heller* and *McDonald.* Their implications are wide-ranging. These two cases are the foundation for a new jurisprudence of the Second Amendment. The many issues regarding existing firearms legislation designated in previous chapters as *connection questions* (with the notation "CQ:") are impacted by these cases. In addition, as discussed in Chapter 11, *Heller* and *McDonald* raise a variety of entirely new questions for lawyers, judges, and legislatures.

A. The Supreme Court Affirms an Individual Right to Keep and Bear Arms Against Federal Infringement

In 2002, Robert Levy, an adjunct law professor at Georgetown, and a Senior Fellow at the Cato Institute (a libertarian think tank), began the process that would ultimately lead the Supreme Court to affirm that the Second Amendment protects an individual right to bear arms. Levy modeled his approach on the strategy of former Chief Counsel to the National Association for the Advancement of Colored People (NAACP), Thurgood Marshall, that culminated in *Brown v. Board of Education,* 347 U.S. 483 (1954). Levy started by selecting a diverse group of plaintiffs who had no obvious negative characteristics (like criminal records) and who desired to own a handgun for self-defense.

In 2003, a lawsuit was filed in United States District Court for the District of Columbia on behalf of six plaintiffs, none of whom had a connection to a military body, challenging the District's laws banning the possession of handguns. The district court dismissed the case on the ground that the Second Amendment did not protect an individual right to bear arms unconnected with militia service. *Parker v. District of Columbia*, 311 F. Supp. 2d 103 (D.D.C. 2004). The plaintiffs appealed. The U.S. Court of Appeals for the District of Columbia Circuit, after dismissing five plaintiffs' claims on standing grounds, reversed the district court and struck down the district's handgun ban. *Parker v. District of Columbia*, 478 F.3d 370 (D.C. Cir. 2007). The Supreme Court granted certiorari.

District of Columbia v. Heller
554 U.S. 570 (2008)

JUSTICE SCALIA delivered the opinion of the Court.

We consider whether a District of Columbia prohibition on the possession of usable handguns in the home violates the Second Amendment to the Constitution.

I

The District of Columbia generally prohibits the possession of handguns. . . . [It] also requires residents to keep their lawfully owned firearms, such as registered long guns, "unloaded and dissembled or bound by a trigger lock or similar device" unless they are located in a place of business or are being used for lawful recreational activities. . . .

II

We turn first to the meaning of the Second Amendment.

A

The Second Amendment provides: "A well regulated Militia, being necessary to the security of a free State, the right of the people to keep and bear Arms, shall not be infringed." . . .

. . . The two sides in this case have set out very different interpretations of the Amendment. Petitioners and today's dissenting Justices believe that it protects only the right to possess and carry a firearm in connection with militia service. Respondent argues that it protects an individual right to possess a firearm unconnected with service in a militia, and to use that arm for traditionally lawful purposes, such as self-defense within the home.

The Second Amendment is naturally divided into two parts: its prefatory clause and its operative clause. The former does not limit the latter grammatically, but rather announces a purpose. The Amendment could be rephrased, "Because a well regulated Militia is necessary to the security of a free State, the right of the people to keep and bear Arms shall not be infringed." See J. Tiffany, A Treatise on Government and Constitutional Law §585, p. 394 (1867). Although this structure of the Second Amendment is unique in our Constitution, other legal documents of the founding era, particularly individual-rights provisions of state constitutions, commonly included a prefatory statement of purpose. *See generally* Volokh, The Commonplace Second Amendment, 73 N.Y.U. L. Rev. 793, 814-21 (1998).

Logic demands that there be a link between the stated purpose and the command. The Second Amendment would be nonsensical if it read, "A well regulated Militia, being necessary to the security of a free State, the right of the people to petition for redress of grievances shall not be infringed." That requirement of logical connection may cause a prefatory clause to resolve an ambiguity in the operative clause ("The separation of church and state being an important objective, the teachings of canons shall have no place in our jurisprudence." The preface makes clear that the operative clause refers not to canons of interpretation but to clergymen.) But apart from that clarifying function, a prefatory clause does not limit or expand the scope of the operative clause. . . . Therefore, while we will begin our textual analysis with the operative clause, we will return to the prefatory clause to ensure that our reading of the operative clause is consistent with the announced purpose. . . .

Operative Clause

a. "Right of the People"

The first salient feature of the operative clause is that it codifies a "right of the people." The unamended Constitution and the Bill of Rights use the phrase "right of the people" two other times, in the First Amendment's Assembly-and-Petition Clause and in the Fourth Amendment's Search-and-Seizure Clause. The Ninth Amendment uses very similar terminology. . . . All three of these instances unambiguously refer to individual rights, not "collective" rights, or rights that may be exercised only through participation in some corporate body. . . . Nowhere else in the Constitution does a "right" attributed to "the people" refer to anything other than an individual right.

What is more, in all six other provisions of the Constitution that mention "the people," the term unambiguously refers to all members of the political community, not an unspecified subset. As we said in *United States v. Verdugo-Urquidez*, 494 U.S. 259 (1990):

> "'[T]he people' seems to have been a term of art employed in select parts of the Constitution. . . . [Its uses] sugges[t] that 'the people' protected by the Fourth Amendment, and by the First and Second Amendments, and to whom rights and powers are reserved in the Ninth and Tenth Amendments, refers to a class of persons who are part of a national community or who have otherwise developed sufficient connection with this country to be considered part of that community."

This contrasts markedly with the phrase "the militia" in the prefatory clause. As we will describe below, the "militia" in colonial America consisted of a subset of "the people" — those who were male, able bodied, and within a certain age range. Reading the Second Amendment as protecting only the right to "keep and bear Arms" in an organized militia therefore fits poorly with the operative clause's description of the holder of that right as "the people."

We start therefore with a strong presumption that the Second Amendment right is exercised individually and belongs to all Americans.

b. "Keep and Bear Arms"

We move now from the holder of the right — "the people" — to the substance of the right: "to keep and bear Arms."

Before addressing the verbs "keep" and "bear," we interpret their object: "Arms." The 18th-century meaning is no different from the meaning today. The 1773 edition of Samuel Johnson's dictionary defined "arms" as "weapons of offence, or armour of defence." 1 Dictionary of the English Language 107 (4th ed.) (hereinafter Johnson). . . . The term was applied, then as now, to weapons that were not specifically designed for military use and were not employed in a military capacity. . . . Although one founding-era thesaurus limited "arms" (as opposed to "weapons") to "instruments of offence *generally* made use of in war," even that source stated that all firearms constituted "arms." 1 J. Trusler, The Distinction Between Words Esteemed Synonymous in the English Language 37 (1794) (emphasis added).

Some have made the argument, bordering on the frivolous, that only those arms in existence in the 18th century are protected by the Second Amendment. We do not interpret constitutional rights that way. Just as the First Amendment protects modern forms of communications, e.g., *Reno v. American Civil Liberties Union*, 521 U.S. 844 (1997), and the Fourth Amendment applies to modern forms of search, e.g., *Kyllo v. United States*, 533 U.S. 27 (2001), the Second Amendment extends, prima facie, to all instruments that constitute bearable arms, even those that were not in existence at the time of the founding.

We turn to the phrases "keep arms" and "bear arms." [One early dictionary] defined "keep" as, most relevantly, "[t]o retain; not to lose," and "[t]o have in custody." Johnson 1095. Webster defined it as "[t]o hold; to retain in one's power or possession." No party has apprised us of an idiomatic meaning of "keep Arms." Thus, the most natural reading of "keep Arms" in the Second Amendment is to "have weapons."

The phrase "keep arms" was not prevalent in the written documents of the founding period that we have found, but there are a few examples, all of which favor viewing the right to "keep Arms" as an individual right unconnected with militia service. William Blackstone, for example, wrote that Catholics convicted of not attending service in the Church of England suffered certain penalties, one of which was that they were not permitted to "keep arms in their houses." 4 Commentaries on the Laws of England 55 (1769) (hereinafter Blackstone). . . . Petitioners point to militia laws of the founding period that required militia members to "keep" arms in connection with militia service, and they conclude from this that the phrase "keep Arms" has a militia-related connotation. This is rather like saying that, since there are many statutes that authorize aggrieved employees to "file complaints" with federal agencies, the phrase "file complaints" has an employment-related connotation. "Keep arms" was simply a common way of referring to possessing arms, for militiamen *and everyone else.*

At the time of the founding, as now, to "bear" meant to "carry." When used with "arms," however, the term has a meaning that refers to carrying for a particular purpose — confrontation. In *Muscarello v. United States*, 524 U.S. 125 (1998), in the course of analyzing the meaning of "carries a firearm" in a federal criminal statute, Justice Ginsburg wrote that "[s]urely a most familiar meaning is, as the Constitution's Second Amendment . . . indicate[s]: 'wear, bear, or carry . . . upon the person or in the clothing or in a pocket, for the purpose . . . of being armed and ready for offensive or defensive action in a case of conflict with another person.'" We think that Justice Ginsburg accurately captured the natural meaning of "bear arms." Although the phrase implies that the carrying of the weapon is for the purpose of "offensive or defensive action," it in no way connotes participation in a structured military organization.

From our review of founding-era sources, we conclude that this natural meaning was also the meaning that "bear arms" had in the 18th century. In numerous instances, "bear arms" was unambiguously used to refer to the carrying of weapons outside of an organized militia. The most prominent examples are those most relevant to the Second Amendment: Nine state constitutional provisions written in the 18th century or the first two decades of the 19th, which enshrined a right of citizens to "bear arms in defense of themselves and the state" or "bear arms in defense of himself and the state." It is clear from those formulations that "bear arms" did not refer only to carrying a weapon in an organized military unit. Justice James Wilson interpreted the Pennsylvania Constitution's arms-bearing right, for example, as a recognition of the natural right of defense "of one's person or house" — what he called the law of "self preservation." 2 Collected Works of James Wilson 1142, and n. x (K. Hall & M. Hall eds. 2007) (citing Pa. Const., Art. IX, §21 (1790)). . . . That was also the interpretation of those state constitutional provisions adopted by pre-Civil War state courts.[9] These provisions demonstrate — again, in the most analogous linguistic context — that "bear arms" was not limited to the carrying of arms in a militia.

The phrase "bear Arms" also had at the time of the founding an idiomatic meaning that was significantly different from its natural meaning: "to serve as a soldier, do military service, fight" or "to wage war." But it unequivocally bore that idiomatic meaning only when followed by the preposition "against," which was in turn followed by the target of the hostilities. 2 Oxford English Dictionary 21 (2d ed. 1989) (hereinafter Oxford). (That is how . . . our Declaration of Independence ¶ 28, used the phrase: "He has constrained our fellow Citizens taken Captive on the high Seas to bear Arms against their Country . . . ."). . . .

In any event, the meaning of "bear arms" that petitioners and Justice Stevens propose is not even the (sometimes) idiomatic meaning. Rather, they manufacture a hybrid definition, whereby "bear arms" connotes the actual carrying of arms (and therefore is not really an idiom) but only in the service of an

---

9. See *Bliss v. Commonwealth*, 12 Ky. 90 (1822); *State v. Reid*, 1 Ala. 612, 616-617 (1840); *State v. Schoultz*, 25 Mo. 128, 155 (1857). . . .

organized militia. No dictionary has ever adopted that definition, and we have been apprised of no source that indicates that it carried that meaning at the time of the founding. But it is easy to see why petitioners and the dissent are driven to the hybrid definition. Giving "bear Arms" its idiomatic meaning would cause the protected right to consist of the right to be a soldier or to wage war — an absurdity that no commentator has ever endorsed. . . . Worse still, the phrase "keep and bear Arms" would be incoherent. The word "Arms" would have two different meanings at once: "weapons" (as the object of "keep") and (as the object of "bear") one-half of an idiom. . . .

Petitioners justify their limitation of "bear arms" to the military context by pointing out the unremarkable fact that it was often used in that context — the same mistake they made with respect to "keep arms." It is especially unremarkable that the phrase was often used in a military context in the federal legal sources (such as records of congressional debate) that have been the focus of petitioners' inquiry. Those sources would have had little occasion to use it except in discussions about the standing army and the militia. And the phrases used primarily in those military discussions include not only "bear arms" but also "carry arms," "possess arms," and "have arms" — though no one thinks that those other phrases also had special military meanings. . . . The common references to those "fit to bear arms" in congressional discussions about the militia are matched by use of the same phrase in the few nonmilitary federal contexts where the concept would be relevant. See, e.g., 30 Journals of Continental Congress 349-351 (J. Fitzpatrick ed. 1934). Other legal sources frequently used "bear arms" in nonmilitary contexts. Cunningham's legal dictionary . . . gave as an example of its usage a sentence unrelated to military affairs ("Servants and labourers shall use bows and arrows on Sundays, & c. and not bear other arms"). And if one looks beyond legal sources, "bear arms" was frequently used in nonmilitary contexts. . . .

Justice Stevens points to a study by amici supposedly showing that the phrase "bear arms" was most frequently used in the military context. Of course, as we have said, the fact that the phrase was commonly used in a particular context does not show that it is limited to that context, and, in any event, we have given many sources where the phrase was used in nonmilitary contexts. Moreover, the study's collection appears to include (who knows how many times) the idiomatic phrase "bear arms against," which is irrelevant. The amici also dismiss examples such as "'bear arms . . . for the purpose of killing game'" because those uses are "expressly qualified." . . . That analysis is faulty. A purposive qualifying phrase that contradicts the word or phrase it modifies is unknown this side of the looking glass (except, apparently, in some courses on Linguistics). If "bear arms" means, as we think, simply the carrying of arms, a modifier can limit the purpose of the carriage ("for the purpose of self-defense" or "to make war against the King"). But if "bear arms" means, as the petitioners and the dissent think, the carrying of arms only for military purposes, one simply cannot add "for the purpose of killing game." The right "to carry arms in the militia for the purpose of killing game" is worthy of the mad hatter. Thus, these purposive qualifying phrases positively establish that "to bear arms" is not limited to military use.

Justice Stevens places great weight on James Madison's inclusion of a conscientious-objector clause in his original draft of the Second Amendment: "but no person religiously scrupulous of bearing arms, shall be compelled to render military service in person." . . . He argues that this clause establishes that the drafters of the Second Amendment intended "bear Arms" to refer only to military service. It is always perilous to derive the meaning of an adopted provision from another provision deleted in the drafting process. In any case, what Justice Stevens would conclude from the deleted provision does not follow. It was not meant to exempt from military service those who objected to going to war but had no scruples about personal gunfights. Quakers opposed the use of arms not just for militia service, but for any violent purpose whatsoever — so much so that Quaker frontiersmen were forbidden to use arms to defend their families, even though "[i]n such circumstances the temptation to seize a hunting rifle or knife in self-defense . . . must sometimes have been almost overwhelming." P. Brock, Pacifism in the United States 359 (1968). . . . The Pennsylvania Militia Act of 1757 exempted from service those "*scrupling the use of arms*" — a phrase that no one contends had an idiomatic meaning. See 5 Stat. at Large of Pa. 613 (J. Mitchell & H. Flanders eds. 1898) (emphasis added). Thus, the most natural interpretation of Madison's deleted text is that those opposed to carrying weapons for potential violent confrontation would not be "compelled to render military service," in which such carrying would be required.

Finally, Justice Stevens suggests that "keep and bear Arms" was some sort of term of art, presumably akin to "hue and cry" or "cease and desist." (This suggestion usefully evades the problem that there is no evidence whatsoever to support a military reading of "keep arms.") Justice Stevens believes that the unitary meaning of "keep and bear Arms" is established by the Second Amendment's calling it a "right" (singular) rather than "rights" (plural). There is nothing to this. State constitutions of the founding period routinely grouped multiple (related) guarantees under a singular "right," and the First Amendment protects the "right [singular] of the people peaceably to assemble, and to petition the Government for a redress of grievances." And even if "keep and bear Arms" were a unitary phrase, we find no evidence that it bore a military meaning. Although the phrase was not at all common (which would be unusual for a term of art), we have found instances of its use with a clearly nonmilitary connotation. In a 1780 debate in the House of Lords, for example, Lord Richmond described an order to disarm private citizens (not militia members) as "a violation of the constitutional right of Protestant subjects to keep and bear arms for their own defense." 49 The London Magazine or Gentlemans Monthly Intelligencer 467 (1780). In response, another member of Parliament referred to "the right of bearing arms for personal defence," making clear that no special military meaning for "keep and bear arms" was intended in the discussion. *Id.* at 467-68.

c. Meaning of the Operative Clause

Putting all of these textual elements together, we find that they guarantee the individual right to possess and carry weapons in case of confrontation. This meaning is strongly confirmed by the historical background of the Second Amendment. We look to this because it has always been widely understood that the Second Amendment, like the First and Fourth Amendments, codified a pre-existing right. The very text of the Second Amendment implicitly recognizes the pre-existence of the right and declares only that it "shall not be infringed." As we said in *United States v. Cruikshank* (1876), "[t]his is not a right granted by the Constitution. Neither is it in any manner dependent upon that instrument for its existence. The Second amendment declares that it shall not be infringed. . . ."

Between the Restoration and the Glorious Revolution, the Stuart Kings Charles II and James II succeeded in using select militias loyal to them to suppress political dissidents, in part by disarming their opponents. See J. Malcolm, To Keep and Bear Arms 31-53 (1994) (hereinafter Malcolm); L. Schwoerer, The Declaration of Rights, 1689, p. 76 (1981). Under the auspices of the 1671 Game Act, for example, the Catholic James II had ordered general disarmaments of regions home to his Protestant enemies. See Malcolm 103-06. These experiences caused Englishmen to be extremely wary of concentrated military forces run by the state and to be jealous of their arms. They accordingly obtained an assurance from William and Mary, in the [English Bill of Rights] that Protestants would never be disarmed: "That the subjects which are Protestants may have arms for their defense suitable to their conditions and as allowed by law." 1 W. & M., c. 2, §7, in 3 Eng. Stat. at Large 441 (1689). This right has long been understood to be the predecessor to our Second Amendment. See E. Dumbauld, The Bill of Rights and What It Means Today 51 (1957); W. Rawle, A View of the Constitution of the United States of America 122 (1825) (hereinafter Rawle). It was clearly an individual right, having nothing whatever to do with service in a militia. To be sure, it was an individual right not available to the whole population, given that it was restricted to Protestants, and like all written English rights it was held only against the Crown, not Parliament. . . .

By the time of the founding, the right to have arms had become fundamental for English subjects. . . . Blackstone . . . cited the arms provision of the Bill of Rights as one of the fundamental rights of Englishmen. See 1 Blackstone 136, 139-40 (1765). His description of it cannot possibly be thought to tie it to militia or military service. It was, he said, "the natural right of resistance and self-preservation," *id.* at 139, and "the right of having and using arms for self-preservation and defence," *id.*, at 140. . . . Other contemporary authorities concurred. . . . Thus, the right secured in 1689 as a result of the Stuarts' abuses was by the time of the founding understood to be an individual right protecting against both public and private violence.

And, of course, what the Stuarts had tried to do to their political enemies, George III had tried to do to the colonists. In the tumultuous decades of the 1760's and 1770's, the Crown began to disarm the inhabitants of the most rebellious areas. That provoked polemical reactions by Americans invoking their rights as Englishmen to keep arms. A New York article of April 1769 said that "[i]t is a natural right which the people have reserved to themselves, confirmed by the Bill of Rights, to keep arms for their own defence." A Journal of the Times: Mar. 17, New York Journal, Supp. 1, Apr. 13, 1769, in Boston Under Military Rule 79 (O. Dickerson ed. 1936). . . . They understood the right to enable individuals to defend themselves. As the most important early American edition of Blackstone's Commentaries (by the law professor and former Anti-federalist St. George Tucker) made clear in the notes to the description of the arms right, Americans understood the "right of self-preservation" as permitting a citizen to "repe[l] force by force" when "the intervention of society in his behalf, may be too late to prevent an injury." 1 Blackstone's Commentaries 145-46, n.42 (1803) (hereinafter Tucker's Blackstone).

There seems to us no doubt, on the basis of both text and history, that the Second Amendment conferred an individual right to keep and bear arms. Of course the right was not unlimited, just as the First Amendment's right of free speech was not, see, e.g., *United States v. Williams*, 553 U.S. 285 (2008). Thus, we do not read the Second Amendment to protect the right of citizens to carry arms for any sort of confrontation, just as we do not read the First Amendment to protect the right of citizens to speak for any purpose. Before turning to limitations upon the individual right, however, we must determine whether the prefatory clause of the Second Amendment comports with our interpretation of the operative clause.

1.   Prefatory Clause

The prefatory clause reads: "A well regulated Militia, being necessary to the security of a free State. . . ."

a.   "Well-Regulated Militia"

In *United States v. Miller*, 307 U.S. 174 (1939), we explained [examining Founding Era sources] that "the Militia comprised all males physically capable of acting in concert for the common defense."

Petitioners take a seemingly narrower view of the militia, stating that "[m]ilitias are the state- and congressionally-regulated military forces described in the Militia Clauses (art. I, §8, cls. 15-16)." Although we agree with petitioners' interpretive assumption that "militia" means the same thing in Article I and the Second Amendment, we believe that petitioners identify the wrong thing, namely, the organized militia. Unlike armies and navies, which Congress is given the power to create ("to raise . . . Armies"; "to provide . . . a Navy," Art. I, §8, cls. 12-13), the militia is assumed by Article I already to be in existence. Congress is given the power to "provide for calling forth the militia," §8, cl. 15; and the power not to create, but to "organiz[e]" it — and not to organize "a" militia, which is what one would expect if the militia were to be a federal creation, but to organize "the" militia, connoting a body already in existence, *id.*, cl. 16. This is fully consistent with the ordinary definition of the militia as all able-bodied men. From that pool, Congress has plenary power to organize the units that will make up an effective fighting force. That is what Congress did in the first militia Act, which specified that "each and every free able-bodied white male citizen of the respective states, resident therein, who is or shall be of the age of eighteen years, and under the age of forty-five years (except as is herein after excepted) shall severally and respectively be enrolled in the militia." 1 Stat. 271. To be sure, Congress need not conscript every able-bodied man into the militia, because nothing in Article I suggests that in exercising its power to organize, discipline, and arm the militia, Congress must focus upon the entire body. Although the militia consists of all able-bodied men, the federally organized militia may consist of a subset of them.

Finally, the adjective "well-regulated" implies nothing more than the imposition of proper discipline and training. See Johnson 1619 ("Regulate": "To adjust by rule or method"); Rawle 121-22. . . .

b. "Security of a Free State"

The phrase "security of a free state" meant "security of a free polity," not security of each of the several States. . . . It is true that the term "State" elsewhere in the Constitution refers to individual States, but the phrase "security of a free state" and close variations seem to have been terms of art in 18th-century political discourse, meaning a "'free country'" or free polity. See Volokh, "Necessary to the Security of a Free State," 83 Notre Dame L. Rev. 1, 5 (2007); see, e.g., 4 Blackstone 151 (1769); Brutus Essay III (Nov. 15, 1787), in The Essential Antifederalist 251, 253 (W. Allen & G. Lloyd eds., 2d ed. 2002). Moreover, the other instances of "state" in the Constitution are typically accompanied by modifiers making clear that the reference is to the several States — "each state," "several states," "any state," "that state," "particular states," "one state," "no state." And the presence of the term "foreign state" in Article I and Article III shows that the word "state" did not have a single meaning in the Constitution.

There are many reasons why the militia was thought to be "necessary to the security of a free state." . . . First, of course, it is useful in repelling invasions and suppressing insurrections. Second, it renders large standing armies unnecessary — an argument that Alexander Hamilton made in favor of federal control over the militia. The Federalist No. 29, pp. 226, 227 (B. Wright ed. 1961) (A. Hamilton). Third, when the able-bodied men of a nation are trained in arms and organized, they are better able to resist tyranny.

2. Relationship Between Prefatory Clause and Operative Clause

We reach the question, then: Does the preface fit with an operative clause that creates an individual right to keep and bear arms? It fits perfectly, once one knows the history that the founding generation knew and that we have described above. That history showed that the way tyrants had eliminated a militia consisting of all the able-bodied men was not by banning the militia but simply by taking away the people's arms, enabling a select militia or standing army to suppress political opponents. This is what had occurred in England that prompted codification of the right to have arms in the English Bill of Rights.

The debate with respect to the right to keep and bear arms, as with other guarantees in the Bill of Rights, was not over whether it was desirable (all agreed that it was) but over whether it needed to be codified in the Constitution. During the 1788 ratification debates, the fear that the federal government would disarm the people in order to impose rule through a standing army or select militia was pervasive in Antifederalist rhetoric. See, e.g., Letters from The Federal Farmer III (Oct. 10, 1787), in 2 The Complete Anti-Federalist 234, 242 (H. Storing ed. 1981). . . . Federalists responded that because Congress was given no power to abridge the ancient right of individuals to keep and bear arms, such a force could never oppress the people. See, e.g., A Pennsylvanian III (Feb. 20, 1788), in The Origin of the Second Amendment 275, 276 (D. Young ed., 2d ed.

2001) (hereinafter Young). . . . It was understood across the political spectrum that the right helped to secure the ideal of a citizen militia, which might be necessary to oppose an oppressive military force if the constitutional order broke down.

It is therefore entirely sensible that the Second Amendment's prefatory clause announces the purpose for which the right was codified: to prevent elimination of the militia. The prefatory clause does not suggest that preserving the militia was the only reason Americans valued the ancient right; most undoubtedly thought it even more important for self-defense and hunting. But the threat that the new Federal Government would destroy the citizens' militia by taking away their arms was the reason that right — unlike some other English rights — was codified in a written Constitution. Justice Breyer's assertion that individual self-defense is merely a "subsidiary interest" of the right to keep and bear arms is profoundly mistaken. He bases that assertion solely upon the prologue — but that can only show that self-defense had little to do with the right's codification; it was the central component of the right itself.

Besides ignoring the historical reality that the Second Amendment was not intended to lay down a "novel principl[e]" but rather codified a right "inherited from our English ancestors," *Robertson v. Baldwin*, 165 U.S. 275, 281 (1897), petitioners' interpretation does not even achieve the narrower purpose that prompted codification of the right. If, as they believe, the Second Amendment right is no more than the right to keep and use weapons as a member of an organized militia . . . it does not assure the existence of a "citizens' militia" as a safeguard against tyranny. For Congress retains plenary authority to organize the militia, which must include the authority to say who will belong to the organized force. . . . Thus, if petitioners are correct, the Second Amendment protects citizens' right to use a gun in an organization from which Congress has plenary authority to exclude them. It guarantees a select militia of the sort the Stuart kings found useful, but not the people's militia that was the concern of the founding generation.

B

Our interpretation is confirmed by analogous arms-bearing rights in state constitutions that preceded and immediately followed adoption of the Second Amendment. Four States adopted analogues to the Federal Second Amendment in the period between independence and the ratification of the Bill of Rights. Two of them — Pennsylvania and Vermont — clearly adopted individual rights unconnected to militia service. Pennsylvania's Declaration of Rights of 1776 said: "That the people have a right to bear arms for the defence of themselves, and the state. . . ." . . . In 1777, Vermont adopted [a substantively] identical provision. . . .

North Carolina also codified a right to bear arms in 1776: "That the people have a right to bear arms, for the defence of the State. . . ." This could plausibly be read to support only a right to bear arms in a militia — but that is a peculiar way to make the point in a constitution that elsewhere repeatedly mentions the militia explicitly. Many colonial statutes required individual arms-bearing for public-safety reasons — such as the 1770 Georgia law that "for the security and *defence of this province* from internal dangers and insurrections" required those men who qualified for militia duty individually "to carry fire arms" "to places of public worship." 19 Colonial Records of the State of Georgia 137-39 (A. Candler ed. 1911 (pt. 2)) (emphasis added). That broad public-safety understanding was the connotation given to the North Carolina right by that State's Supreme Court in 1843. See *State v. Huntly*, 3 Ired. 418, 422-23.

The 1780 Massachusetts Constitution presented another variation on the theme: "The people have a right to keep and to bear arms for the common defence . . . ." Once again, if one gives narrow meaning to the phrase "common defence" this can be thought to limit the right to the bearing of arms in a state-organized military force. But once again the State's highest court thought otherwise. Writing for the court in an 1825 libel case, Chief Justice Parker wrote: "The liberty of the press was to be unrestrained, but he who used it was to be responsible in cases of its abuse; like the right to keep fire arms, which does not protect him who uses them for annoyance or destruction." *Commonwealth v. Blanding*, 20 Mass. 304, 313-14 (1825). The analogy makes no sense if firearms could not be used for any individual purpose at all. . . .

We therefore believe that the most likely reading of all four of these pre-Second Amendment state constitutional provisions is that they secured an individual right to bear arms for defensive purposes. . . .

Between 1789 and 1820, nine States adopted Second Amendment analogues. Four of them — Kentucky, Ohio, Indiana, and Missouri — referred to the right of the people to "bear arms in defence of themselves and the State." Another three States — Mississippi, Connecticut, and Alabama — used the even more individualistic phrasing that each citizen has the "right to bear arms in defence of himself and the State." Finally, two States — Tennessee and Maine — used the "common defence" language of Massachusetts. That of the nine state constitutional protections for the right to bear arms enacted immediately after 1789 at least seven unequivocally protected an individual citizen's right to self-defense is strong evidence that that is how the founding generation conceived of the right. . . .

The historical narrative that petitioners must endorse would thus treat the Federal Second Amendment as an odd outlier, protecting a right unknown in state constitutions or at English common law, based on little more than an overreading of the prefatory clause.

c

Justice Stevens relies on the drafting history of the Second Amendment — the various proposals in the state conventions and the debates in Congress. It is dubious to rely on such history to interpret a text that was widely understood to codify a pre-existing right, rather than to fashion a new one. But even assuming that this legislative history is relevant, Justice Stevens flatly misreads the historical record.

It is true, as Justice Stevens says, that there was concern that the Federal Government would abolish the institution of the state militia. That concern found expression, however, not in the various Second Amendment precursors proposed in the State conventions, but in separate structural provisions that

would have given the States concurrent and seemingly nonpreemptible authority to organize, discipline, and arm the militia when the Federal Government
failed to do so. . . . The Second Amendment precursors, by contrast, referred to
the individual English right already codified in two (and probably four) State
constitutions. The Federalist-dominated first Congress chose to reject virtually
all major structural revisions favored by the Antifederalists, including the proposed militia amendments. Rather, it adopted primarily the popular and uncontroversial (though, in the Federalists' view, unnecessary) individual-rights
amendments. The Second Amendment right, protecting only individuals' liberty to keep and carry arms, did nothing to assuage Antifederalists' concerns
about federal control of the militia. See, e.g., Centinel, Revived, No. XXIX,
Philadelphia Independent Gazetteer, Sept. 9, 1789, in Young 711, 712.

   Justice Stevens thinks it significant that the Virginia, New York, and North
Carolina Second Amendment proposals were "embedded . . . within a group of
principles that are distinctly military in meaning," such as statements about the
danger of standing armies. . . . But so was the highly influential minority proposal in Pennsylvania, yet that proposal, with its reference to hunting, plainly
referred to an individual right. . . .

   D

   We now address how the Second Amendment was interpreted from
immediately after its ratification through the end of the 19th century. . . .

1. Post-ratification Commentary

   Three important founding-era legal scholars interpreted the Second
Amendment in published writings. All three understood it to protect an
individual right unconnected with militia service.

   St. George Tucker's version of Blackstone's Commentaries, as we explained
above, conceived of the Blackstonian arms right as necessary for self-defense. He
equated that right, absent the religious and class-based restrictions, with the
Second Amendment. See 2 Tucker's Blackstone 143. In Note D, entitled,
"View of the Constitution of the United States," Tucker elaborated on the
Second Amendment: "This may be considered as the true palladium of
liberty. . . . The right to self-defence is the first law of nature: in most governments it has been the study of rulers to confine the right within the narrowest
limits possible. Wherever standing armies are kept up, and the right of the
people to keep and bear arms is, under any colour or pretext whatsoever, prohibited, liberty, if not already annihilated, is on the brink of destruction." 1 *id.*,
at App. 300 (ellipsis in original). He believed that the English game laws had
abridged the right by prohibiting "keeping a gun or other engine for the
destruction of game." *Id.* . . . He later grouped the right with some of the
individual rights included in the First Amendment and said that if "a law be
passed by congress, prohibiting" any of those rights, it would "be the province of
the judiciary to pronounce whether any such act were constitutional, or not; and
if not, to acquit the accused. . . ." . . .

In 1825, William Rawle, a prominent lawyer who had been a member of the Pennsylvania Assembly that ratified the Bill of Rights, published an influential treatise, which analyzed the Second Amendment as follows:

> "The first [principle] is a declaration that a well regulated militia is necessary to the security of a free state; a proposition from which few will dissent. . . .
> "The corollary, from the first position is, that the right of the people to keep and bear arms shall not be infringed.
> "The prohibition is general. No clause in the constitution could by any rule of construction be conceived to give to congress a power to disarm the people. Such a flagitious attempt could only be made under some general pretence by a state legislature. But if in any blind pursuit of inordinate power, either should attempt it, this amendment may be appealed to as a restraint on both." Rawle 121-22.

Like Tucker, Rawle regarded the English game laws as violating the right codified in the Second Amendment. See *id.* at 122-23. Rawle clearly differentiated between the people's right to bear arms and their service in a militia: "In a people permitted and accustomed to bear arms, we have the rudiments of a militia, which properly consists of armed citizens, divided into military bands, and instructed at least in part, in the use of arms for the purposes of war." *Id.* at 140. Rawle further said that the Second Amendment right ought not "be abused to the disturbance of the public peace," such as by assembling with other armed individuals "for an unlawful purpose" — statements that make no sense if the right does not extend to any individual purpose.

Joseph Story published his famous Commentaries on the Constitution of the United States in 1833 . . . [and] equated the English right with the Second Amendment:

> "§1891. A similar provision [to the Second Amendment] in favour of protestants (for to them it is confined) is to be found in the bill of rights of 1688, it being declared, 'that the subjects, which are protestants, may have arms for their defence suitable to their condition, and as allowed by law.' But under various pretences the effect of this provision has been greatly narrowed; and it is at present in England more nominal than real, as a defensive privilege." (Footnotes omitted.)

This comparison to the Declaration of Right would not make sense if the Second Amendment right was the right to use a gun in a militia, which was plainly not what the English right protected. As the Tennessee Supreme Court recognized 38 years after Story wrote his Commentaries, "[t]he passage from Story, shows clearly that this right was intended . . . and was guaranteed to, and to be exercised and enjoyed by the citizen as such, and not by him as a soldier, or in defense solely of his political rights." *Andrews v. State*, 50 Tenn. 165, 183 (1871). . . .

Antislavery advocates routinely invoked the right to bear arms for self-defense. . . . In his famous Senate speech about the 1856 "Bleeding Kansas" conflict, Charles Sumner proclaimed:

> "The rifle has ever been the companion of the pioneer and, under God, his tutelary protector against the red man and the beast of the forest. Never was this efficient weapon more needed in just self-defence, than now in Kansas, and at least

one article in our National Constitution must be blotted out, before the complete right to it can in any way be impeached. And yet such is the madness of the hour, that, in defiance of the solemn guarantee, embodied in the Amendments to the Constitution, that 'the right of the people to keep and bear arms shall not be infringed,' the people of Kansas have been arraigned for keeping and bearing them, and the Senator from South Carolina has had the face to say openly, on this floor, that they should be disarmed — of course, that the fanatics of Slavery, his allies and constituents, may meet no impediment." The Crime Against Kansas, May 19-20, 1856, in American Speeches: Political Oratory from the Revolution to the Civil War 553, 606-607 (2006).

We have found only one early 19th-century commentator who clearly conditioned the right to keep and bear arms upon service in the militia — and he recognized that the prevailing view was to the contrary. "The provision of the constitution, declaring the right of the people to keep and bear arms, & c. was probably intended to apply to the right of the people to bear arms for such [militia-related] purposes only, and not to prevent congress or the legislatures of the different states from enacting laws to prevent the citizens from always going armed. A different construction however has been given to it." B. Oliver, The Rights of an American Citizen 177 (1832).[1]

2. Pre-Civil War Case Law

The 19th-century cases that interpreted the Second Amendment universally support an individual right unconnected to militia service. In *Houston v. Moore*, 18 U.S. (5 Wheat.) 1, 24 (1820), this Court held that States have concurrent power over the militia, at least where not pre-empted by Congress. Agreeing in dissent that States could "organize, discipline, and arm" the militia in the absence of conflicting federal regulation, Justice Story said that the Second Amendment "may not, perhaps, be thought to have any important bearing on this point. If it have, it confirms and illustrates, rather than impugns the reasoning already suggested." Of course, if the Amendment simply "protect[ed] the right of the people of each of the several States to maintain a well-regulated militia," it would have enormous and obvious bearing on the point. But the Court and Story derived the States' power over the militia from the nonexclusive nature of federal power, not from the Second Amendment, whose preamble merely "confirms and illustrates" the importance of the militia. Even clearer was Justice Baldwin. In the famous fugitive-slave case of *Johnson v. Tompkins*, 13 F. Cas. 840 (CC Pa. 1833), Baldwin, sitting as a circuit judge, cited both the Second Amendment and the Pennsylvania analogue for his conclusion that a citizen has "a right to carry arms in defence of his property or person, and to use them, if either were assailed with such force, numbers or violence as made it necessary for the protection or safety of either."

---

1. [Benjamin Oliver made his first appearance in modern Second Amendment scholarship when he was discussed in David B. Kopel, *The Second Amendment in the Nineteenth Century*, 1998 BYU L. Rev. 1359. After more than a decade of scholarly attention to this obscure author, no one has yet found a reported nineteenth-century case which cites any part of his book. — EDS.]

Many early 19th-century state cases indicated that the Second Amendment right to bear arms was an individual right unconnected to militia service, though subject to certain restrictions. . . .

In *Nunn v. State*, 1 Ga. 243, 251 (1846), the Georgia Supreme Court construed the Second Amendment as protecting the "natural right of self-defence" and therefore struck down a ban on carrying pistols openly. Its opinion perfectly captured the way in which the operative clause of the Second Amendment furthers the purpose announced in the prefatory clause, in continuity with the English right:

> "The right of the whole people, old and young, men, women and boys, and not militia only, to keep and bear arms of every description, and not such merely as are used by the militia, shall not be infringed, curtailed, or broken in upon, in the smallest degree; and all this for the important end to be attained: the rearing up and qualifying a well-regulated militia, so vitally necessary to the security of a free State. [. . .]"

Likewise, in *State v. Chandler*, 5 La. Ann. 489, 490 (1850), the Louisiana Supreme Court held that citizens had a right to carry arms openly: "This is the right guaranteed by the Constitution of the United States, and which is calculated to incite men to a manly and noble defence of themselves, if necessary, and of their country, without any tendency to secret advantages and unmanly assassinations."

Those who believe that the Second Amendment preserves only a militia-centered right place great reliance on the Tennessee Supreme Court's 1840 decision in *Aymette v. State*, 21 Tenn. 154. The case does not stand for that broad proposition; in fact, the case does not mention the word "militia" at all, except in its quoting of the Second Amendment. *Aymette* held that the state constitutional guarantee of the right to "bear" arms did not prohibit the banning of concealed weapons. The opinion first recognized that both the state right and the federal right were descendents of the 1689 English right, but (erroneously, and contrary to virtually all other authorities) read that right to refer only to "protect[ion of] the public liberty" and "keep[ing] in awe those in power," *id.*, at 158. The court then adopted a sort of middle position, whereby citizens were permitted to carry arms openly, unconnected with any service in a formal militia, but were given the right to use them only for the military purpose of banding together to oppose tyranny. This odd reading of the right is, to be sure, not the one we adopt—but it is not petitioners' reading either. More importantly, seven years earlier the Tennessee Supreme Court had treated the state constitutional provision as conferring a right "of all the free citizens of the State to keep and bear arms for their defence," *Simpson v. State*, 5 Yer., at 360; and [31] years later the court held that the "keep" portion of the state constitutional right included the right to personal self-defense: "[T]he right to keep arms involves, necessarily, the right to use such arms for all the ordinary purposes, and in all the ordinary modes usual in the country, and to which arms are adapted, limited by the duties of a good citizen in times of peace." *Andrews*, 50 Tenn., at 178; see also *id.* (equating state provision with Second Amendment).

3. Post-Civil War Legislation

In the aftermath of the Civil War, there was an outpouring of discussion of the Second Amendment in Congress and in public discourse, as people debated whether and how to secure constitutional rights for newly free slaves. See generally S. Halbrook, Freedmen, the Fourteenth Amendment, and the Right to Bear Arms, 1866-1876 (1998) (hereinafter Halbrook). . . .

Blacks were routinely disarmed by Southern States after the Civil War. Those who opposed these injustices frequently stated that they infringed blacks' constitutional right to keep and bear arms. Needless to say, the claim was not that blacks were being prohibited from carrying arms in an organized state militia. A Report of the Commission of the Freedmen's Bureau in 1866 stated plainly: "[T]he civil law [of Kentucky] prohibits the colored man from bearing arms. . . . Their arms are taken from them by the civil authorities. . . . Thus, the right of the people to keep and bear arms as provided in the Constitution is infringed." H.R. Exec. Doc. No. 70, 39th Cong., 1st Sess., 233, 236. A joint congressional Report decried:

> "in some parts of [South Carolina], armed parties are, without proper authority, engaged in seizing all fire-arms found in the hands of the freemen. Such conduct is in clear and direct violation of their personal rights as guaranteed by the Constitution of the United States, which declares that 'the right of the people to keep and bear arms shall not be infringed.' The freedmen of South Carolina have shown by their peaceful and orderly conduct that they can safely be trusted with fire-arms, and they need them to kill game for subsistence, and to protect their crops from destruction by birds and animals." Joint Comm. on Reconstruction, H.R. Rep. No. 30, 39th Cong., 1st Sess., pt. 2, p. 229 (1866) (Proposed Circular of Brigadier General R. Saxton). . . .

Congress enacted the Freedmen's Bureau Act on July 16, 1866. Section 14 stated:

> "[T]he right . . . to have full and equal benefit of all laws and proceedings concerning personal liberty, personal security, and the acquisition, enjoyment, and disposition of estate, real and personal, including the constitutional right to bear arms, shall be secured to and enjoyed by all the citizens . . . without respect to race or color, or previous condition of slavery. . . ." 14 Stat. 176-177.

The understanding that the Second Amendment gave freed blacks the right to keep and bear arms was reflected in congressional discussion of the bill, with even an opponent of it saying that the founding generation "were for every man bearing his arms about him and keeping them in his house, his castle, for his own defense." Cong. Globe, 39th Cong., 1st Sess., 362, 371 (1866) (Sen. Davis). . . .

It was plainly the understanding in the post-Civil War Congress that the Second Amendment protected an individual right to use arms for self-defense.

4. Post-Civil War Commentators

Every late-19th-century legal scholar that we have read interpreted the Second Amendment to secure an individual right unconnected with militia service. The most famous was the judge and professor Thomas Cooley. . . .

... [I]n his 1880 work, General Principles of Constitutional Law[, t]he Second Amendment, he said, "was adopted with some modification and enlargement from the English Bill of Rights of 1688, where it stood as a protest against arbitrary action of the overturned dynasty in disarming the people." *Id.* at 270. In a section entitled "The Right in General," he continued:

> "It might be supposed from the phraseology of this provision that the right to keep and bear arms was only guaranteed to the militia; but this would be an interpretation not warranted by the intent. The militia, as has been elsewhere explained, consists of those persons who, under the law, are liable to the performance of military duty, and are officered and enrolled for service when called upon. But the law may make provision for the enrolment of all who are fit to perform military duty, or of a small number only, or it may wholly omit to make any provision at all; and if the right were limited to those enrolled, the purpose of this guaranty might be defeated altogether by the action or neglect to act of the government it was meant to hold in check. The meaning of the provision undoubtedly is, that the people, from whom the militia must be taken, shall have the right to keep and bear arms; and they need no permission or regulation of law for the purpose. But this enables government to have a well-regulated militia; for to bear arms implies something more than the mere keeping; it implies the learning to handle and use them in a way that makes those who keep them ready for their efficient use; in other words, it implies the right to meet for voluntary discipline in arms, observing in doing so the laws of public order." *Id.* at 271.

All other post-Civil War 19th-century sources we have found concurred with Cooley. . . .

E

We now ask whether any of our precedents forecloses the conclusions we have reached about the meaning of the Second Amendment.

United States v. Cruikshank, 92 U.S. 542 (1876), in the course of vacating the convictions of members of a white mob for depriving blacks of their right to keep and bear arms, held that the Second Amendment does not by its own force apply to anyone other than the Federal Government. The opinion explained that the right "is not a right granted by the Constitution [or] in any manner dependent upon that instrument for its existence. The second amendment . . . means no more than that it shall not be infringed by Congress." 92 U.S. at 553. States, we said, were free to restrict or protect the right under their police powers. The limited discussion of the Second Amendment in *Cruikshank* supports, if anything, the individual-rights interpretation. There was no claim in *Cruikshank* that the victims had been deprived of their right to carry arms in a militia. . . . We described the right protected by the Second Amendment as "'bearing arms for a lawful purpose'" and said that "the people [must] look for their protection against any violation by their fellow-citizens of the rights it recognizes" to the States' police power. 92 U.S. at 553. That discussion makes little sense if it is only a right to bear arms in a state militia.

Presser v. Illinois, 116 U.S. 252 (1886), held that the right to keep and bear arms was not violated by a law that forbade "bodies of men to associate together as military organizations, or to drill or parade with arms in cities and towns unless authorized by law." This does not refute the individual-rights interpretation of the Amendment; no one supporting that interpretation has contended that States may not ban such groups. . . .

Justice Stevens places overwhelming reliance upon this Court's decision in *United States v. Miller*, 307 U.S. 174 (1939). . . . Justice Stevens [asserts that *Miller* held that] the Second Amendment "protects the right to keep and bear arms for certain military purposes, but that it does not curtail the legislature's power to regulate the nonmilitary use and ownership of weapons."

[*Miller*'s] basis for saying that the Second Amendment did not apply was not that the defendants were [bearing arms for a nonmilitary purpose]. Rather, it was that the *type of weapon at issue* was not eligible for Second Amendment protection: "In the absence of any evidence tending to show that the possession or use of a [short-barreled shotgun] at this time has some reasonable relationship to the preservation or efficiency of a well regulated militia, we cannot say that the Second Amendment guarantees the right to keep and bear *such an instrument*." "Certainly," the Court continued, "it is not within judicial notice that this weapon is any part of the ordinary military equipment or that its use could contribute to the common defense." . . .

This holding is not only consistent with, but positively suggests, that the Second Amendment confers an individual right to keep and bear arms (though only arms that "have some reasonable relationship to the preservation or efficiency of a well regulated militia"). Had the Court believed that the Second Amendment protects only those serving in the militia, it would have been odd to examine the character of the weapon rather than simply note that the two crooks were not militiamen. . . .

. . . *Miller* . . . did not even purport to be a thorough examination of the Second Amendment. . . .[24]

We may as well consider at this point (for we will have to consider eventually) what types of weapons *Miller* permits. Read in isolation, *Miller*'s phrase "part of ordinary military equipment" could mean that only those weapons useful in warfare are protected. That would be a startling reading of the opinion, since it would mean that the National Firearms Act's restrictions on machineguns (not challenged in *Miller*) might be unconstitutional, machineguns being useful in warfare in 1939. We think that *Miller*'s "ordinary military equipment" language must be read in tandem with what comes after: "[O]rdinarily when called for [militia] service [able-bodied] men were expected to appear bearing arms supplied by themselves and of the kind in common use at the time." 307 U.S. at 179. The traditional militia was formed from a pool of men bringing arms "in common use at the time" for lawful purposes like self-defense. "In the colonial and revolutionary war era, [small-arms] weapons used by militiamen and

---

24. As for the "hundreds of judges," . . . who have relied on the view of the Second Amendment Justice Stevens claims we endorsed in *Miller*. If so, they overread *Miller*. And their erroneous reliance upon an uncontested and virtually unreasoned case cannot nullify the reliance of millions of Americans (as our historical analysis has shown) upon the true meaning of the right to keep and bear arms. In any event, it should not be thought that the cases decided by these judges would necessarily have come out differently under a proper interpretation of the right.

weapons used in defense of person and home were one and the same." *State v. Kessler*, 614 P.2d 94, 98 (1980) (citing G. Neumann, Swords and Blades of the American Revolution 6-15, 252-54 (1973)). Indeed, that is precisely the way in which the Second Amendment's operative clause furthers the purpose announced in its preface. We therefore read *Miller* to say only that the Second Amendment does not protect those weapons not typically possessed by law-abiding citizens for lawful purposes, such as short-barreled shotguns. That accords with the historical understanding of the scope of the right. . . .

We conclude that nothing in our precedents forecloses our adoption of the original understanding of the Second Amendment. It should be unsurprising that such a significant matter has been for so long judicially unresolved. For most of our history, the Bill of Rights was not thought applicable to the States, and the Federal Government did not significantly regulate the possession of firearms by law-abiding citizens. Other provisions of the Bill of Rights have similarly remained unilluminated for lengthy periods. . . .

III

Like most rights, the right secured by the Second Amendment is not unlimited. . . . Although we do not undertake an exhaustive historical analysis today of the full scope of the Second Amendment, nothing in our opinion should be taken to cast doubt on longstanding prohibitions on the possession of firearms by felons and the mentally ill, or laws forbidding the carrying of firearms in sensitive places such as schools and government buildings, or laws imposing conditions and qualifications on the commercial sale of arms.[26]

We also recognize another important limitation on the right to keep and carry arms. *Miller* said, as we have explained, that the sorts of weapons protected were those "in common use at the time." 307 U.S. at 179. We think that limitation is fairly supported by the historical tradition of prohibiting the carrying of "dangerous and unusual weapons." See 4 Blackstone 148-149 (1769). . . .

It may be objected that if weapons that are most useful in military service — M-16 rifles and the like — may be banned, then the Second Amendment right is completely detached from the prefatory clause. But as we have said, the conception of the militia at the time of the Second Amendment's ratification was the body of all citizens capable of military service, who would bring the sorts of lawful weapons that they possessed at home to militia duty. It may well be true today that a militia, to be as effective as militias in the 18th century, would require sophisticated arms that are highly unusual in society at large. Indeed, it may be true that no amount of small arms could be useful against modern-day bombers and tanks. But the fact that modern developments have limited the degree of fit between the prefatory clause and the protected right cannot change our interpretation of the right.

---

26. We identify these presumptively lawful regulatory measures only as examples; our list does not purport to be exhaustive.

IV

We turn finally to the law at issue here. As we have said, the law totally bans handgun possession in the home. It also requires that any lawful firearm in the home be disassembled or bound by a trigger lock at all times, rendering it inoperable.

As the quotations earlier in this opinion demonstrate, the inherent right of self-defense has been central to the Second Amendment right. The handgun ban amounts to a prohibition of an entire class of "arms" that is overwhelmingly chosen by American society for that lawful purpose. The prohibition extends, moreover, to the home, where the need for defense of self, family, and property is most acute. Under any of the standards of scrutiny that we have applied to enumerated constitutional rights, banning from the home the most preferred firearm in the nation to "keep" and use for protection of one's home and family, would fail constitutional muster.

Few laws in the history of our Nation have come close to the severe restriction of the District's handgun ban. And some of those few have been struck down. In *Nunn v. State*, the Georgia Supreme Court struck down a prohibition on carrying pistols openly (even though it upheld a prohibition on carrying concealed weapons). See 1 Ga. at 251. In *Andrews v. State*, the Tennessee Supreme Court likewise held that a statute that forbade openly carrying a pistol "publicly or privately, without regard to time or place, or circumstances," 50 Tenn. at 187, violated the state constitutional provision (which the court equated with the Second Amendment). That was so even though the statute did not restrict the carrying of long guns. *Id.* See also *State v. Reid*, 1 Ala. 612, 616-17 (1840) ("A statute which, under the pretence of regulating, amounts to a destruction of the right, or which requires arms to be so borne as to render them wholly useless for the purpose of defence, would be clearly unconstitutional").

It is no answer to say, as petitioners do, that it is permissible to ban the possession of handguns so long as the possession of other firearms (i.e., long guns) is allowed. It is enough to note, as we have observed, that the American people have considered the handgun to be the quintessential self-defense weapon. There are many reasons that a citizen may prefer a handgun for home defense: It is easier to store in a location that is readily accessible in an emergency; it cannot easily be redirected or wrestled away by an attacker; it is easier to use for those without the upper-body strength to lift and aim a long gun; it can be pointed at a burglar with one hand while the other hand dials the police. Whatever the reason, handguns are the most popular weapon chosen by Americans for self-defense in the home, and a complete prohibition of their use is invalid.

We must also address the District's requirement (as applied to respondent's handgun) that firearms in the home be rendered and kept inoperable at all times. This makes it impossible for citizens to use them for the core lawful purpose of self-defense and is hence unconstitutional. The District argues that we should interpret this element of the statute to contain an exception for self-defense. But we think that is precluded by the unequivocal text, and by the presence of certain other enumerated exceptions: "Except for law enforcement personnel ..., each registrant shall keep any firearm in his possession unloaded and disassembled or bound by a trigger lock or similar device unless such firearm is kept at his place of business, or while being used for lawful recreational purposes within the District of Columbia." The nonexistence of a self-defense exception is also suggested by the D.C. Court of Appeals' statement that the statute forbids residents to use firearms to stop intruders, see *McIntosh v. Washington*, 395 A.2d 744, 755-56 (1978).

Justice Breyer has devoted most of his separate dissent to the handgun ban. He says that, even assuming the Second Amendment is a personal guarantee of the right to bear arms, the District's prohibition is valid. He first tries to establish this by founding-era historical precedent, pointing to various restrictive laws in the colonial period. These demonstrate, in his view, that the District's law "imposes a burden upon gun owners that seems proportionately no greater than restrictions in existence at the time the Second Amendment was adopted." Of the laws he cites, only one offers even marginal support for his assertion. A 1783 Massachusetts law forbade the residents of Boston to "take into" or "receive into" "any Dwelling House, Stable, Barn, Out-house, Ware-house, Store, Shop or other Building" loaded firearms, and permitted the seizure of any loaded firearms that "shall be found" there. Act of Mar. 1, 1783, ch. 13, 1783 Mass. Acts p. 218. That statute's text and its prologue, which makes clear that the purpose of the prohibition was to eliminate the danger to firefighters posed by the "depositing of loaded Arms" in buildings, give reason to doubt that colonial Boston authorities would have enforced that general prohibition against someone who temporarily loaded a firearm to confront an intruder (despite the law's application in that case). In any case, we would not stake our interpretation of the Second Amendment upon a single law, in effect in a single city, that contradicts the overwhelming weight of other evidence regarding the right to keep and bear arms for defense of the home. The other laws Justice Breyer cites are gunpowder-storage laws that he concedes did not clearly prohibit loaded weapons, but required only that excess gunpowder be kept in a special container or on the top floor of the home. Nothing about those fire-safety laws . . . remotely burden the right of self-defense as much as an absolute ban on handguns. Nor, correspondingly, does our analysis suggest the invalidity of laws regulating the storage of firearms to prevent accidents.

Justice Breyer points to other founding-era laws that he says "restricted the firing of guns within the city limits to at least some degree" in Boston, Philadelphia and New York. . . . Those laws provide no support for the severe restriction in the present case. The New York law levied a fine of 20 shillings on anyone who fired a gun in certain places (including houses) on New Year's Eve and the first two days of January, and was aimed at preventing the "great Damages . . . frequently done on [those days] by persons going House to House, with Guns and other Firearms and being often intoxicated with Liquor." 5 Colonial Laws of New York 244-246 (1894). It is inconceivable that this law would have been enforced against a person exercising his right to self-defense on New Year's Day against such drunken hooligans. The Pennsylvania law to which Justice Breyer refers levied a fine of 5 shillings on one who fired a gun or set off fireworks in Philadelphia without first obtaining a license from the governor. See Act of Aug. 26, 1721, §4, in 3 Stat. at Large 253-54. Given Justice Wilson's explanation that the right to self-defense with arms was protected by the Pennsylvania Constitution, it is unlikely that this law (which in any event amounted to at most a licensing regime) would have been enforced against a person who used firearms for self-defense. . . .

A broader point about the laws that Justice Breyer cites: All of them punished the discharge (or loading) of guns with a small fine and forfeiture of the weapon (or in a few cases a very brief stay in the local jail), not with significant criminal penalties. They are akin to modern penalties for minor public-safety infractions like speeding or jaywalking. And although such public-safety laws may not contain exceptions for self-defense, it is inconceivable that the threat of a jaywalking ticket would deter someone from disregarding a "Do Not Walk" sign in order to flee an attacker, or that the Government would enforce those laws under such circumstances. Likewise, we do not think that a law imposing a 5-shilling fine and forfeiture of the gun would have prevented a person in the founding era from using a gun to protect himself or his family from violence, or that if he did so the law would be enforced against him. The District law, by contrast, far from imposing a minor fine, threatens citizens with a year in prison (five years for a second violation) for even obtaining a gun in the first place.

Justice Breyer moves on to make a broad jurisprudential point: He criticizes us for declining to establish a level of scrutiny for evaluating Second Amendment restrictions. He proposes, explicitly at least, none of the traditionally expressed levels (strict scrutiny, intermediate scrutiny, rational basis), but rather a judge-empowering "interest-balancing inquiry" that "asks whether the statute burdens a protected interest in a way or to an extent that is out of proportion to the statute's salutary effects upon other important governmental interests." After an exhaustive discussion of the arguments for and against gun control, Justice Breyer arrives at his interest-balanced answer: because handgun violence is a problem, because the law is limited to an urban area, and because there were somewhat similar restrictions in the founding period (a false proposition that we have already discussed), the interest-balancing inquiry results in the constitutionality of the handgun ban. QED.

We know of no other enumerated constitutional right whose core protection has been subjected to a freestanding "interest-balancing" approach. The very enumeration of the right takes out of the hands of government — even the Third Branch of Government — the power to decide on a case-by-case basis whether the right is really worth insisting upon. A constitutional guarantee subject to future judges' assessments of its usefulness is no constitutional guarantee at all. Constitutional rights are enshrined with the scope they were understood to have when the people adopted them, whether or not future legislatures or (yes) even future judges think that scope too broad. We would not apply an "interest-balancing" approach to the prohibition of a peaceful neo-Nazi march through Skokie. See *National Socialist Party of America v. Skokie*, 432 U.S. 43 (1977) (*per curiam*). The First Amendment contains the freedom-of-speech guarantee that the people ratified, which included exceptions for obscenity, libel, and disclosure of state secrets, but not for the expression of extremely unpopular and wrong-headed views. The Second Amendment is no different. Like the First, it is the very product of an interest-balancing by the people — which Justice Breyer would now conduct for them anew. And whatever else it leaves to future evaluation, it surely elevates above all other interests the right of law-abiding, responsible citizens to use arms in defense of hearth and home. . . .

In sum, we hold that the District's ban on handgun possession in the home violates the Second Amendment, as does its prohibition against rendering any lawful firearm in the home operable for the purpose of immediate self-defense. Assuming that Heller is not disqualified from the exercise of Second Amendment rights, the District must permit him to register his handgun and must issue him a license to carry it in the home. . . .

We affirm the judgment of the Court of Appeals.

It is so ordered.

JUSTICE STEVENS, with whom JUSTICE SOUTER, JUSTICE GINSBURG, and JUSTICE BREYER join, dissenting.

The question presented by this case is not whether the Second Amendment protects a "collective right" or an "individual right." Surely it protects a right that can be enforced by individuals. But a conclusion that the Second Amendment protects an individual right does not tell us anything about the scope of that right.

[Whether the Second Amendment] protects the right to possess and use guns for nonmilitary purposes like hunting and personal self-defense is the question presented by this case. The text of the Amendment, its history, and our decision in *United States v. Miller*, 307 U.S. 174 (1939), provide a clear answer to that question.

The Second Amendment was adopted to protect the right of the people of each of the several States to maintain a well-regulated militia. It was a response to concerns raised during the ratification of the Constitution that the power of Congress to disarm the state militias and create a national standing army posed an intolerable threat to the sovereignty of the several States. . . .

In 1934, Congress enacted the National Firearms Act, the first major federal firearms law. Upholding a conviction under that Act, this Court held that, "[i]n the absence of any evidence tending to show that possession or use of a 'shotgun having a barrel of less than eighteen inches in length' at this time has some reasonable relationship to the preservation or efficiency of a well regulated militia, we cannot say that the Second Amendment guarantees the right to keep and bear such an instrument." *Miller*, 307 U.S. at 178. The view of the Amendment we took in *Miller*—that it protects the right to keep and bear arms for certain military purposes, but that it does not curtail the Legislature's power to regulate the nonmilitary use and ownership of weapons—is both the most natural reading of the Amendment's text and the interpretation most faithful to the history of its adoption.

Since our decision in *Miller*, hundreds of judges have relied on the view of the Amendment we endorsed there.[2] . . . [A] review of the drafting history of

---

2. Until the Fifth Circuit's decision in *United States v. Emerson*, 270 F.3d 203 (2001), every Court of Appeals to consider the question had understood *Miller* to hold that the Second Amendment does not protect the right to possess and use guns for purely private, civilian purposes. *See, e.g., United States v. Haney*, 264 F.3d 1161, 1164-66 (10th Cir. 2001); *United States v. Napier*, 233 F.3d 394, 402-04 (6th Cir. 2000); *Gillespie v. Indianapolis*, 185 F.3d 693, 710-11 (7th Cir. 1999); *United States v. Scanio*, No. 97-1584, 1998 WL 802060, *2 (2nd Cir., Nov. 12, 1998) (unpublished opinion); *United States v. Wright*, 117 F.3d 1265, 1271-74 (11th Cir. 1997); *United States v. Rybar*, 103 F.3d 273, 285-86 (3d Cir. 1996); *Hickman v. Block*, 81 F.3d

the Amendment demonstrates that its Framers rejected proposals that would have broadened its coverage to include such uses. . . .

Even if the textual and historical arguments on both sides of the issue were evenly balanced, respect for the well-settled views of all of our predecessors on this Court, and for the rule of law itself, see *Mitchell v. W.T. Grant Co.* (1974) (Stewart, J., dissenting), would prevent most jurists from endorsing such a dramatic upheaval in the law. . . .

I

. . . Three portions of [the Second Amendment's] text merit special focus: the introductory language defining the Amendment's purpose, the class of persons encompassed within its reach, and the unitary nature of the right that it protects.

"A well regulated Militia, being necessary to the security of a free State"

The preamble to the Second Amendment makes three important points. It identifies the preservation of the militia as the Amendment's purpose; it explains that the militia is necessary to the security of a free State; and it recognizes that the militia must be "well regulated." In all three respects it is comparable to provisions in several State Declarations of Rights that were adopted roughly contemporaneously with the Declaration of Independence.[2] Those state provisions highlight the importance members of the founding generation attached to the maintenance of state militias; they also underscore the profound fear shared by many in that era of the dangers posed by standing armies.[6] While the need for state militias has not been a matter of significant public interest for almost two centuries, that fact should not obscure the contemporary concerns that animated the Framers.

98, 100-03 (9th Cir. 1996); *United States v. Hale*, 978 F.2d 1016, 1018-20 (8th Cir. 1992); *Thomas v. City Council of Portland*, 730 F.2d 41, 42 (1st Cir. 1984) (per curiam); *United States v. Johnson*, 497 F.2d 548, 550 (4th Cir. 1974) (per curiam); *United States v. Johnson*, 441 F.2d 1134, 1136 (5th Cir. 1971); see also *Sandidge v. United States*, 520 A.2d 1057, 1058-59 (DC App. 1987). And a number of courts have remained firm in their prior positions, even after considering *Emerson*. See, *e.g.*, *United States v. Lippman*, 369 F.3d 1039, 1043-45 (8th Cir. 2004); *United States v. Parker*, 362 F.3d 1279, 1282-84 (10th Cir. 2004); *United States v. Jackubowski*, 63 Fed. Appx. 959, 961 (7th Cir. 2003) (unpublished opinion); *Silveira v. Lockyer*, 312 F.3d 1052, 1060-66 (9th Cir. 2002); *United States v. Milheron*, 231 F. Supp. 2d 376, 378 (D. Me. 2002); *Bach v. Pataki*, 289 F. Supp. 2d 217, 224-26 (N.D.N.Y. 2003); *United States v. Smith*, 56 M. J. 711, 716 (C. A. Armed Forces 2001).

2.   [See the state constitution appendix to Chapter 1. — EDS.]

6.   The language of the Amendment's preamble also closely tracks the language of a number of contemporaneous state militia statutes, many of which began with nearly identical statements. Georgia's 1778 militia statute, for example, began, "[w]hereas a well ordered and disciplined Militia, is essentially necessary, to the Safety, peace and prosperity, of this State." Act of Nov. 15, 1778, 19 Colonial Records of the State of Georgia 103 (Candler ed. 1911 (pt. 2)). . . .

The parallels between the Second Amendment and these state declarations, and the Second Amendment's omission of any statement of purpose related to the right to use firearms for hunting or personal self-defense, is especially striking in light of the fact that the Declarations of Rights of Pennsylvania and Vermont did expressly protect such civilian uses at the time. Article XIII of Pennsylvania's 1776 Declaration of Rights announced that "the people have a right to bear arms for the defence of themselves and the state" . . . ; §43 of the Declaration assured that "the inhabitants of this state shall have the liberty to fowl and hunt in seasonable times on the lands they hold, and on all other lands therein not inclosed." . . . And Article XV of the 1777 Vermont Declaration of Rights guaranteed "[t]hat the people have a right to bear arms for the defence of themselves and the State." . . . The contrast between those two declarations and the Second Amendment reinforces the clear statement of purpose announced in the Amendment's preamble. It confirms that the Framers' single-minded focus in crafting the constitutional guarantee "to keep and bear arms" was on military uses of firearms, which they viewed in the context of service in state militias.

The preamble thus both sets forth the object of the Amendment and informs the meaning of the remainder of its text. Such text should not be treated as mere surplusage, for "[i]t cannot be presumed that any clause in the constitution is intended to be without effect." *Marbury v. Madison*, 5 U.S. (1 Cranch) 137, 174 (1803).

. . . [A] prefatory clause may resolve an ambiguity in the text. Without identifying any language in the text that even mentions civilian uses of firearms, the Court proceeds to "find" its preferred reading in what is at best an ambiguous text, and then concludes that its reading is not foreclosed by the preamble. . . .

"The right of the people"

The centerpiece of the Court's textual argument is its insistence that the words "the people" as used in the Second Amendment must have the same meaning, and protect the same class of individuals, as when they are used in the First and Fourth Amendments. According to the Court, in all three provisions — as well as the Constitution's preamble, section 2 of Article I, and the Tenth Amendment — "the term unambiguously refers to all members of the political community, not an unspecified subset." But the Court itself reads the Second Amendment to protect a "subset" significantly narrower than the class of persons protected by the First and Fourth Amendments; when it finally drills down on the substantive meaning of the Second Amendment, the Court limits the protected class to "law-abiding, responsible citizens." But the class of persons protected by the First and Fourth Amendments is not so limited; for even felons (and presumably irresponsible citizens as well) may invoke the protections of those constitutional provisions. The Court offers no way to harmonize its conflicting pronouncements.

The Court also overlooks the significance of the way the Framers used the phrase "the people" in these constitutional provisions. In the First Amendment, no words define the class of individuals entitled to speak, to publish, or to worship; in that Amendment it is only the right peaceably to assemble, and to petition the Government for a redress of grievances, that is described as a right of "the people." These rights contemplate collective action. While the right peaceably to assemble protects the individual rights of those persons participating in the assembly, its concern is with action engaged in by members of a group, rather than any single individual. Likewise, although the act of petitioning the Government is a right that can be exercised by individuals, it is primarily collective in nature. For if they are to be effective, petitions must involve groups of individuals acting in concert.

Similarly, the words "the people" in the Second Amendment refer back to the object announced in the Amendment's preamble. They remind us that it is the collective action of individuals having a duty to serve in the militia that the text directly protects and, perhaps more importantly, that the ultimate purpose of the Amendment was to protect the States' share of the divided sovereignty created by the Constitution.

As used in the Fourth Amendment, "the people" describes the class of persons protected from unreasonable searches and seizures by Government officials. It is true that the Fourth Amendment describes a right that need not be exercised in any collective sense. But that observation does not settle the meaning of the phrase "the people" when used in the Second Amendment. For, as we have seen, the phrase means something quite different in the Petition and Assembly Clauses of the First Amendment. Although the abstract definition of the phrase "the people" could carry the same meaning in the Second Amendment as in the Fourth Amendment, the preamble of the Second Amendment suggests that the uses of the phrase in the First and Second Amendments are the same in referring to a collective activity. By way of contrast, the Fourth Amendment describes a right against governmental interference rather than an affirmative right to engage in protected conduct, and so refers to a right to protect a purely individual interest. As used in the Second Amendment, the words "the people" do not enlarge the right to keep and bear arms to encompass use or ownership of weapons outside the context of service in a well-regulated militia.

"To keep and bear Arms"

Although the Court's discussion of these words treats them as two "phrases" — as if they read "to keep" and "to bear" — they describe a unitary right: to possess arms if needed for military purposes and to use them in conjunction with military activities. . . .

The term "bear arms" is a familiar idiom; when used unadorned by any additional words, its meaning is "to serve as a soldier, do military service, fight." 1 Oxford English Dictionary 634 (2d ed. 1989). It is derived from the Latin arma ferre, which, translated literally, means "to bear [ferre] war equipment [arma]." One 18th-century dictionary defined "arms" as "weapons of offence, or armour of defence," 1 S. Johnson, A Dictionary of the English Language (1755), and another contemporaneous source explained that "[b]y arms, we understand those instruments of offence generally made use of in war; such as firearms, swords, & c. By weapons, we more particularly mean instruments of other kinds (exclusive of fire-arms), made use of as offensive, on special occasions." 1 J. Trusler, The Distinction Between Words Esteemed Synonymous in the English Language 37 (1794). Had the Framers wished to expand the meaning of the phrase "bear arms" to encompass civilian possession and use, they could have done so by the addition of phrases such as "for the defense of themselves," as was done in the Pennsylvania and Vermont Declarations of Rights. The unmodified use of "bear arms," by contrast, refers most naturally to a military purpose, as evidenced by its use in literally dozens of contemporary texts. The absence of any reference to civilian uses of weapons tailors the text of the Amendment to the purpose identified in its preamble.[10] But when discussing these words, the Court simply ignores the preamble.

The Court argues that a "qualifying phrase that contradicts the word or phrase it modifies is unknown this side of the looking glass." . . . But this fundamentally fails to grasp the point. The stand-alone phrase "bear arms" most naturally conveys a military meaning unless the addition of a qualifying phrase signals that a different meaning is intended. When, as in this case, there is no such qualifier, the most natural meaning is the military one; and, in the absence of any qualifier, it is all the more appropriate to look to the preamble to confirm the natural meaning of the text. The Court's objection is particularly puzzling in light of its own contention that the addition of the modifier "against" changes the meaning of "bear arms." . . .

The Amendment's use of the term "keep" in no way contradicts the military meaning conveyed by the phrase "bear arms" and the Amendment's preamble. To the contrary, a number of state militia laws in effect at the time of the Second Amendment's drafting used the term "keep" to describe the requirement that militia members store their arms at their homes, ready to be used for service when necessary. The Virginia military law, for example, ordered that "every one of the said officers, non-commissioned officers, and privates, shall constantly keep the aforesaid arms, accoutrements, and ammunition, ready to be produced whenever called for by his commanding officer." Act for Regulating and Disciplining the Militia, 1785 Va. Acts ch. 1, §3, p. 2 (emphasis added). "[K]eep and bear arms" thus perfectly describes the responsibilities of a framing-era militia member.

This reading is confirmed by the fact that the clause protects only one right, rather than two. It does not describe a right "to keep arms" and a separate right "to bear arms." Rather, the single right that it does describe is both a duty and a right to have arms available and ready for military service, and to use them for military purposes when necessary. Different language surely would have been

---

10. *Aymette v. State*, 21 Tenn. 154, 156 (1840), a case we cited in *Miller*, further confirms this reading of the phrase. In *Aymette*, the Tennessee Supreme Court construed the guarantee in Tennessee's 1834 Constitution that "'the free white men of this State, have a right to keep and bear arms for their common defence.'" Explaining that the provision was adopted with the same goals as the Federal Constitution's Second Amendment, the court wrote: "The words 'bear arms' . . . have reference to their military use, and were not employed to mean wearing them about the person as part of the dress. As the object for which the right to keep and bear arms is secured, is of general and public nature, to be exercised by the people in a body, for their common defence, so the arms, the right to keep which is secured, are such as are usually employed in civilized warfare, and that constitute the ordinary military equipment." 21 Tenn. at 158. The court elaborated: "[W]e may remark, that the phrase *'bear arms'* is used in the Kentucky Constitution as well as our own, and implies, as has already been suggested, their military use. . . . A man in the pursuit of deer, elk, and buffaloes, might carry his rifle every day, for forty years, and, yet, it would never be said of him, that he had *borne arms*, much less could it be said, that a private citizen *bears arms*, because he has a dirk or pistol concealed under his clothes, or a spear in a cane." *Id.* at 161.

used to protect nonmilitary use and possession of weapons from regulation if such an intent had played any role in the drafting of the Amendment. . . .

II

The proper allocation of military power in the new Nation was an issue of central concern for the Framers. . . .

Two themes relevant to our current interpretive task ran through the debates on the original Constitution. "On the one hand, there was a widespread fear that a national standing Army posed an intolerable threat to individual liberty and to the sovereignty of the separate States." *Perpich v. Department of Defense*, 496 U.S. 334, 340 (1990). . . . On the other hand, the Framers recognized the dangers inherent in relying on inadequately trained militia members "as the primary means of providing for the common defense," *Perpich*, 496 U.S. at 340. . . . In order to respond to those twin concerns, a compromise was reached: Congress would be authorized to raise and support a national Army and Navy, and also to organize, arm, discipline, and provide for the calling forth of "the Militia." U.S. Const., Art. I, §8, cls. 12-16. The President, at the same time, was empowered as the "Commander in Chief of the Army and Navy of the United States, and of the Militia of the several States, when called into the actual Service of the United States." Art. II, §2. But, with respect to the militia, a significant reservation was made to the States: Although Congress would have the power to call forth, organize, arm, and discipline the militia, as well as to govern "such Part of them as may be employed in the Service of the United States," the States respectively would retain the right to appoint the officers and to train the militia in accordance with the discipline prescribed by Congress. Art. I, §8, cl. 16.

But the original Constitution's retention of the militia and its creation of divided authority over that body did not prove sufficient to allay fears about the dangers posed by a standing army. For it was perceived by some that Article I contained a significant gap: While it empowered Congress to organize, arm, and discipline the militia, it did not prevent Congress from providing for the militia's disarmament. . . .

This sentiment was echoed at a number of state ratification conventions; indeed, it was one of the primary objections to the original Constitution voiced by its opponents. The Anti-Federalists were ultimately unsuccessful in persuading state ratification conventions to condition their approval of the Constitution upon the eventual inclusion of any particular amendment. But a number of States did propose to the first Federal Congress amendments reflecting a desire to ensure that the institution of the militia would remain protected under the new Government. The proposed amendments sent by the States of Virginia, North Carolina, and New York focused on the importance of preserving the state militias and reiterated the dangers posed by standing armies. New Hampshire sent a proposal that differed significantly from the others; while also invoking the dangers of a standing army, it suggested that the Constitution should more broadly protect the use and possession of weapons, without tying such a guarantee expressly to the maintenance of the militia. The States of Maryland, Pennsylvania, and Massachusetts sent no relevant proposed amendments to

Congress, but in each of those States a minority of the delegates advocated related amendments. While the Maryland minority proposals were exclusively concerned with standing armies and conscientious objectors, the unsuccessful proposals in both Massachusetts and Pennsylvania would have protected a more broadly worded right, less clearly tied to service in a state militia. Faced with all of these options, it is telling that James Madison chose to craft the Second Amendment as he did.

[One of t]he relevant proposals sent by the Virginia Ratifying Convention read as follows:

> "17th, That the people have a right to keep and bear arms; that a well regulated Militia composed of the body of the people trained to arms is the proper, natural and safe defence of a free State. That standing armies are dangerous to liberty, and therefore ought to be avoided, as far as the circumstances and protection of the Community will admit; and that in all cases the military should be under strict subordination to and be governed by the civil power." 3 J. Elliot, Debates in the Several State Conventions on the Adoption of the Federal Constitution 659 (2d ed. 1863) (hereinafter Elliot).
>
> "19th, That any person religiously scrupulous of bearing arms ought to be exempted, upon payment of an equivalent to employ another to bear arms in his stead." *Id.* . . .

Madison, charged with the task of assembling the proposals for amendments sent by the ratifying States, was the principal draftsman of the Second Amendment. He had before him, or at the very least would have been aware of, all of these proposed formulations. . . .

With all of these sources upon which to draw, it is strikingly significant that Madison's first draft omitted any mention of nonmilitary use or possession of weapons. Rather, his original draft repeated the essence of the two proposed amendments sent by Virginia, combining the substance of the two provisions succinctly into one, which read: "The right of the people to keep and bear arms shall not be infringed; a well armed, and well regulated militia being the best security of a free country; but no person religiously scrupulous of bearing arms, shall be compelled to render military service in person." . . .

Madison's decision to model the Second Amendment on the distinctly military Virginia proposal is therefore revealing, since it is clear that he considered and rejected formulations that would have unambiguously protected civilian uses of firearms. When Madison prepared his first draft, and when that draft was debated and modified, it is reasonable to assume that all participants in the drafting process were fully aware of the other formulations that would have protected civilian use and possession of weapons and that their choice to craft the Amendment as they did represented a rejection of those alternative formulations.

Madison's initial inclusion of an exemption for conscientious objectors sheds revelatory light on the purpose of the Amendment. It confirms an intent to describe a duty as well as a right, and it unequivocally identifies the military character of both. The objections voiced to the conscientious-objector clause only confirm the central meaning of the text. Although records of the debate in the Senate, which is where the conscientious-objector clause was removed, do not survive, the arguments raised in the House illuminate the perceived problems with the clause: Specifically, there was concern that Congress "can declare who are those religiously scrupulous, and prevent them from bearing arms." The ultimate removal of the clause, therefore, only serves to confirm the purpose of the Amendment—to protect against congressional disarmament, by whatever means, of the States' militias.

The Court also contends that because "Quakers opposed the use of arms not just for militia service, but for any violent purpose whatsoever," the inclusion of a conscientious-objector clause in the original draft of the Amendment does not support the conclusion that the phrase "bear arms" was military in meaning. But . . . both Virginia and North Carolina included the following language: "That any person religiously scrupulous of bearing arms ought to be exempted, upon payment of an equivalent to employ another to bear arms in his stead" (emphasis added). There is no plausible argument that the use of "bear arms" in those provisions was not unequivocally and exclusively military: The State simply does not compel its citizens to carry arms for the purpose of private "confrontation," or for self-defense.

The history of the adoption of the Amendment thus describes an overriding concern about the potential threat to state sovereignty that a federal standing army would pose, and a desire to protect the States' militias as the means by which to guard against that danger. But state militias could not effectively check the prospect of a federal standing army so long as Congress retained the power to disarm them, and so a guarantee against such disarmament was needed. As we explained in *Miller*: "With obvious purpose to assure the continuation and render possible the effectiveness of such forces the declaration and guarantee of the Second Amendment were made. It must be interpreted and applied with that end in view." 307 U.S. at 178. The evidence plainly refutes the claim that the Amendment was motivated by the Framers' fears that Congress might act to regulate any civilian uses of weapons. And even if the historical record were genuinely ambiguous, the burden would remain on the parties advocating a change in the law to introduce facts or arguments "'newly ascertained,'" *Vasquez*, 474 U.S. at 266; the Court is unable to identify any such facts or arguments.

III

Although it gives short shrift to the drafting history of the Second Amendment the Court dwells at length on four other sources: the 17th-century English Bill of Rights; Blackstone's Commentaries on the Laws of England; postenactment commentary on the Second Amendment; and post-Civil War legislative history. All of these sources shed only indirect light on the question before us, and in any event offer little support for the Court's conclusion.

The English Bill of Rights

The Court's reliance on Article VII of the 1689 English Bill of Rights . . . is misguided both because Article VII was enacted in response to different concerns from those that motivated the Framers of the Second Amendment, and because the guarantees of the two provisions were by no means coextensive.

Moreover, the English text contained no preamble or other provision identifying a narrow, militia-related purpose.

The English Bill of Rights responded to abuses by the Stuart monarchs; among the grievances set forth in the Bill of Rights was that the King had violated the law "[b]y causing several good Subjects being Protestants to be disarmed at the same time when Papists were both armed and Employed contrary to Law." Article VII of the Bill of Rights was a response to that selective disarmament; it guaranteed that "the Subjects which are Protestants may have Armes for their defence, Suitable to their condition and as allowed by Law." L. Schwoerer, The Declaration of Rights, 1689 (App. 1, pp. 295, 297) (1981). This grant did not establish a general right of all persons, or even of all Protestants, to possess weapons. Rather, the right was qualified in two distinct ways: First, it was restricted to those of adequate social and economic status ("suitable to their Condition"); second, it was only available subject to regulation by Parliament ("as allowed by Law").

The Court may well be correct that the English Bill of Rights protected the right of some English subjects to use some arms for personal self-defense free from restrictions by the Crown (but not Parliament). But that right — adopted in a different historical and political context and framed in markedly different language — tells us little about the meaning of the Second Amendment.

Blackstone's Commentaries

The Court's reliance on Blackstone's Commentaries on the Laws of England is unpersuasive for the same reason as its reliance on the English Bill of Rights. Blackstone's invocation of "'the natural right of resistance and self-preservation,'" and "'the right of having and using arms for self-preservation and defence'" *id.*, referred specifically to Article VII in the English Bill of Rights. The excerpt from Blackstone offered by the Court, therefore, is, like Article VII itself, of limited use in interpreting the very differently worded, and differently historically situated, Second Amendment. . . .

Postenactment Commentary

The Court also excerpts, without any real analysis, commentary by a number of additional scholars, some near in time to the framing and others post-dating it by close to a century. Those scholars are for the most part of limited relevance in construing the guarantee of the Second Amendment: Their views are not altogether clear, they tended to collapse the Second Amendment with Article VII of the English Bill of Rights, and they appear to have been unfamiliar with the drafting history of the Second Amendment.

The most significant of these commentators was Joseph Story. Contrary to the Court's assertions, however, Story actually supports the view that the Amendment was designed to protect the right of each of the States to maintain a well-regulated militia[, and this is the context in which he used the term "palladium"]:

> "The importance of [the Second Amendment] will scarcely be doubted by any persons who have duly reflected upon the subject. The militia is the natural defence of a free country against sudden foreign invasions, domestic insurrections,

and domestic usurpations of power by rulers. [. . .] The right of the citizens to keep and bear arms has justly been considered as the palladium of the liberties of a republic, since it offers a strong moral check against the usurpation and arbitrary power of rulers, and will generally, even if these are successful in the first instance, enable the people to resist and triumph over them. [. . .]" 2 J. Story, Commentaries on the Constitution of the United States §1897, pp. 620-621 (4th ed. 1873) (footnote omitted).

. . . There is not so much as a whisper in the passage above that Story believed that the right secured by the Amendment bore any relation to private use or possession of weapons for activities like hunting or personal self-defense.

After extolling the virtues of the militia as a bulwark against tyranny, Story went on to decry the "growing indifference to any system of militia discipline." *Id.* at 621. When he wrote, "[h]ow it is practicable to keep the people duly armed without some organization it is difficult to see," *id.*, he underscored the degree to which he viewed the arming of the people and the militia as indissolubly linked. Story warned that the "growing indifference" he perceived would "gradually undermine all the protection intended by this clause of our national bill of rights," *id.* In his view, the importance of the Amendment was directly related to the continuing vitality of an institution in the process of apparently becoming obsolete.

. . . Story's characterization in no way suggests that he believed that the [Second Amendment and Article VII of the English Declaration of Right] had the same scope. To the contrary, Story's exclusive focus on the militia in his discussion of the Second Amendment confirms his understanding of the right protected by the Second Amendment as limited to military uses of arms.

Story's writings as a Justice of this Court, to the extent that they shed light on this question, only confirm that Justice Story did not view the Amendment as conferring upon individuals any "self-defense" right disconnected from service in a state militia. Justice Story dissented from the Court's decision in *Houston v. Moore*, 18 U.S. (5 Wheat.) 1, 24 (1820), which held that a state court "had a concurrent jurisdiction" with the federal courts "to try a militia man who had disobeyed the call of the President, and to enforce the laws of Congress against such delinquent." *Id.* at 31-32. Justice Story believed that Congress' power to provide for the organizing, arming, and disciplining of the militia was, when Congress acted, plenary; but he explained that in the absence of congressional action, "I am certainly not prepared to deny the legitimacy of such an exercise of [state] authority." *Id.* at 52. As to the Second Amendment, he wrote that it "may not, perhaps, be thought to have any important bearing on this point. If it have, it confirms and illustrates, rather than impugns the reasoning already suggested." *Id.* at 52-53. The Court contends that had Justice Story understood the Amendment to have a militia purpose, the Amendment would have had "enormous and obvious bearing on the point." But the Court has it quite backwards: If Story had believed that the purpose of the Amendment was to permit civilians to keep firearms for activities like personal self-defense, what "confirm[ation] and illustrat[ion]," *Houston*, 18 U.S. (5 Wheat.) at 53, could the Amendment possibly have provided for the point that States retained the power to organize, arm, and discipline their own militias?

Post-Civil War Legislative History

The Court suggests that by the post-Civil War period, the Second Amendment was understood to secure a right to firearm use and ownership for purely private purposes like personal self-defense. While it is true that some of the legislative history on which the Court relies supports that contention, such sources are entitled to limited, if any, weight. All of the statements the Court cites were made long after the framing of the Amendment and cannot possibly supply any insight into the intent of the Framers; and all were made during pitched political debates, so that they are better characterized as advocacy than good-faith attempts at constitutional interpretation.

What is more, much of the evidence the Court offers is decidedly less clear than its discussion allows. The Court notes that "[b]lacks were routinely disarmed by Southern States after the Civil War. Those who opposed these injustices frequently stated that they infringed blacks' constitutional right to keep and bear arms." The Court hastily concludes that "[n]eedless to say, the claim was not that blacks were being prohibited from carrying arms in an organized state militia[.]" But some of the claims of the sort the Court cites may have been just that. In some Southern States, Reconstruction-era Republican governments created state militias in which both blacks and whites were permitted to serve. Because "[t]he decision to allow blacks to serve alongside whites meant that most southerners refused to join the new militia," the bodies were dubbed "Negro militia[s]," S. Cornell, A Well-Regulated Militia 176-77 (2006). . . .

IV

The brilliance of the debates that resulted in the Second Amendment faded into oblivion during the ensuing years, for the concerns about Article I's Militia Clauses that generated such pitched debate during the ratification process and led to the adoption of the Second Amendment were short lived.

In 1792, the year after the Amendment was ratified, Congress passed a statute that purported to establish "an Uniform Militia throughout the United States." 1 Stat. 271. The statute commanded every able-bodied white male citizen between the ages of 18 and 45 to be enrolled therein and to "provide himself with a good musket or firelock" and other specified weaponry. *Id.* The statute is significant, for it confirmed the way those in the founding generation viewed firearm ownership: as a duty linked to military service. . . .

The postratification history of the Second Amendment is strikingly similar. The Amendment played little role in any legislative debate about the civilian use of firearms for most of the 19th century, and it made few appearances in the decisions of this Court. Two 19th-century cases, however, bear mentioning.

In *United States v. Cruikshank*, 92 U.S. 542 (1876), the Court sustained a challenge to respondents' convictions under the Enforcement Act of 1870 for conspiring to deprive any individual of "'any right or privilege granted or secured to him by the constitution or laws of the United States.'" *Id.* at 548. The Court wrote, as to counts 2 and 10 of respondents' indictment:

> "The right there specified is that of 'bearing arms for a lawful purpose.' This is not a right granted by the Constitution. Neither is it in any manner dependent on that instrument for its existence. The second amendment declares that it shall not be infringed; but this, as has been seen, means no more than that it shall not be infringed by Congress. This is one of the amendments that has no other effect than to restrict the powers of the national government." *Id.* at 553.

The majority's assertion that the Court in *Cruikshank* "described the right protected by the Second Amendment as 'bearing arms for a lawful purpose,'" (quoting *Cruikshank*, 92 U.S. at 553), is not accurate. The *Cruikshank* Court explained that the defective indictment contained such language, but the Court did not itself describe the right, or endorse the indictment's description of the right.

Moreover, it is entirely possible that the basis for the indictment's counts 2 and 10, which charged respondents with depriving the victims of rights secured by the Second Amendment, was the prosecutor's belief that the victims — members of a group of citizens, mostly black but also white, who were rounded up by the Sheriff, sworn in as a posse to defend the local courthouse, and attacked by a white mob — bore sufficient resemblance to members of a state militia that they were brought within the reach of the Second Amendment. . . .

Only one other 19th-century case in this Court, *Presser v. Illinois*, 116 U.S. 252 (1886), engaged in any significant discussion of the Second Amendment. The petitioner in *Presser* was convicted of violating a state statute that prohibited organizations other than the Illinois National Guard from associating together as military companies or parading with arms. Presser challenged his conviction, asserting, as relevant, that the statute violated both the Second and the Fourteenth Amendments. With respect to the Second Amendment, the Court wrote:

> "We think it clear that the sections under consideration, which only forbid bodies of men to associate together as military organizations, or to drill or parade with arms in cities and towns unless authorized by law, do not infringe the right of the people to keep and bear arms. But a conclusive answer to the contention that this amendment prohibits the legislation in question lies in the fact that the amendment is a limitation only upon the power of Congress and the National government, and not upon that of the States." *Id.* at 264-65.

And in discussing the Fourteenth Amendment, the Court explained:

> "The plaintiff in error was not a member of the organized volunteer militia of the State of Illinois, nor did he belong to the troops of the United States or to any organization under the militia law of the United States. On the contrary, the fact that he did not belong to the organized militia or the troops of the United States was an ingredient in the offence for which he was convicted and sentenced. The question is, therefore, had he a right as a citizen of the United States, in disobedience of the State law, to associate with others as a military company, and to drill and parade with arms in the towns and cities of the State? If the plaintiff in error

has any such privilege he must be able to point to the provision of the Constitution or statutes of the United States by which it is conferred." *Id.* at 266.

Presser, therefore, both affirmed *Cruikshank*'s holding that the Second Amendment posed no obstacle to regulation by state governments, and suggested that in any event nothing in the Constitution protected the use of arms outside the context of a militia "authorized by law" and organized by the State or Federal Government.

In 1901 the President revitalized the militia by creating "'the National Guard of the several States,'" *Perpich*, 496 U.S. at 341, & nn.9-10; meanwhile, the dominant understanding of the Second Amendment's inapplicability to private gun ownership continued well into the 20th century. The first two federal laws directly restricting civilian use and possession of firearms — the 1927 Act prohibiting mail delivery of "pistols, revolvers, and other firearms capable of being concealed on the person," Ch. 75, 44 Stat. 1059, and the 1934 Act prohibiting the possession of sawed-off shotguns and machine guns — were enacted over minor Second Amendment objections dismissed by the vast majority of the legislators who participated in the debates. Members of Congress clashed over the wisdom and efficacy of such laws as crime-control measures. But since the statutes did not infringe upon the military use or possession of weapons, for most legislators they did not even raise the specter of possible conflict with the Second Amendment. . . .

The key to [*Miller*] did not . . . turn on the difference between muskets and sawed-off shotguns; it turned, rather, on the basic difference between the military and nonmilitary use and possession of guns. Indeed, if the Second Amendment were not limited in its coverage to military uses of weapons, why should the Court in *Miller* have suggested that some weapons but not others were eligible for Second Amendment protection? If use for self-defense were the relevant standard, why did the Court not inquire into the suitability of a particular weapon for self-defense purposes?

Perhaps in recognition of the weakness of its attempt to distinguish *Miller*, the Court argues in the alternative that *Miller* should be discounted because of its decisional history. It is true that the appellee in *Miller* did not file a brief or make an appearance, although the court below had held that the relevant provision of the National Firearms Act violated the Second Amendment (albeit without any reasoned opinion). But, as our decision in *Marbury v. Madison*, 5 U.S. (1 Cranch) 137 (1803), in which only one side appeared and presented arguments, demonstrates, the absence of adversarial presentation alone is not a basis for refusing to accord *stare decisis* effect to a decision of this Court. . . . Of course, if it can be demonstrated that new evidence or arguments were genuinely not available to an earlier Court, that fact should be given special weight as we consider whether to overrule a prior case. But the Court does not make that claim, because it cannot. Although it is true that the drafting history of the Amendment was not discussed in the Government's brief, it is certainly not the drafting history that the Court's decision today turns on. And those sources upon which the Court today relies most heavily were available to the *Miller* Court. . . .

The Court is simply wrong when it intones that *Miller* contained "not a word" about the Amendment's history. The Court plainly looked to history to construe the term "Militia," and, on the best reading of *Miller*, the entire guarantee of the

Second Amendment. After noting the original Constitution's grant of power to Congress and to the States over the militia, the Court explained:

> "With obvious purpose to assure the continuation and render possible the effectiveness of such forces the declaration and guarantee of the Second Amendment were made. It must be interpreted and applied with that end in view.
>
> "The Militia which the States were expected to maintain and train is set in contrast with Troops which they were forbidden to keep without the consent of Congress. The sentiment of the time strongly disfavored standing armies; the common view was that adequate defense of country and laws could be secured through the Militia-civilians primarily, soldiers on occasion.
>
> "The signification attributed to the term Militia appears from the debates in the Convention, the history and legislation of Colonies and States, and the writings of approved commentators." *Miller*, 307 U.S. at 178-79.

The majority cannot seriously believe that the *Miller* Court did not consider any relevant evidence; the majority simply does not approve of the conclusion the *Miller* Court reached on that evidence. Standing alone, that is insufficient reason to disregard a unanimous opinion of this Court, upon which substantial reliance has been placed by legislators and citizens for nearly 70 years.

V

The Court concludes its opinion by declaring that it is not the proper role of this Court to change the meaning of rights "enshrine[d]" in the Constitution. But the right the Court announces was not "enshrined" in the Second Amendment by the Framers; it is the product of today's law-changing decision. The majority's exegesis has utterly failed to establish that as a matter of text or history, "the right of law-abiding, responsible citizens to use arms in defense of hearth and home" is "elevate[d] above all other interests" by the Second Amendment. . . .

The Court properly disclaims any interest in evaluating the wisdom of the specific policy choice challenged in this case, but it fails to pay heed to a far more important policy choice — the choice made by the Framers themselves. The Court would have us believe that over 200 years ago, the Framers made a choice to limit the tools available to elected officials wishing to regulate civilian uses of weapons, and to authorize this Court to use the common-law process of case-by-case judicial lawmaking to define the contours of acceptable gun control policy. . . .

For these reasons, I respectfully dissent.

JUSTICE BREYER, with whom JUSTICE STEVENS, JUSTICE SOUTER, and JUSTICE GINSBURG join, dissenting. . . .

I

The majority's conclusion is wrong for two independent reasons. The first reason is that set forth by Justice Stevens — . . . self-defense alone, detached from any militia-related objective, is not the Amendment's concern.

The second independent reason is that the protection the Amendment provides is not absolute. The Amendment permits government to regulate the interests that it serves. Thus, irrespective of what those interests are — whether they do or do not include an independent interest in self-defense — the majority's view cannot be correct unless it can show that the District's regulation is unreasonable or inappropriate in Second Amendment terms. This the majority cannot do.

. . . I shall show that the District's law is consistent with the Second Amendment even if that Amendment is interpreted as protecting a wholly separate interest in individual self-defense. That is so because the District's regulation, which focuses upon the presence of handguns in high-crime urban areas, represents a permissible legislative response to a serious, indeed life-threatening, problem.

Thus I here assume that one objective (but, as the majority concedes, not the primary objective) of those who wrote the Second Amendment was to help assure citizens that they would have arms available for purposes of self-defense. Even so, a legislature could reasonably conclude that the law will advance goals of great public importance, namely, saving lives, preventing injury, and reducing crime. The law is tailored to the urban crime problem in that it is local in scope and thus affects only a geographic area both limited in size and entirely urban; the law concerns handguns, which are specially linked to urban gun deaths and injuries, and which are the overwhelmingly favorite weapon of armed criminals; and at the same time, the law imposes a burden upon gun owners that seems proportionately no greater than restrictions in existence at the time the Second Amendment was adopted. In these circumstances, the District's law falls within the zone that the Second Amendment leaves open to regulation by legislatures.

II

. . . I take as a starting point the following four propositions, based on our precedent and today's opinions, to which I believe the entire Court subscribes:

(1) The Amendment protects an "individual" right — i.e., one that is separately possessed, and may be separately enforced, by each person on whom it is conferred.

(2) As evidenced by its preamble, the Amendment was adopted "[w]ith obvious purpose to assure the continuation and render possible the effectiveness of [militia] forces." *United States v. Miller*, 307 U.S. 174, 178 (1939).

(3) The Amendment "must be interpreted and applied with that end in view." *Miller, supra*, at 178.

(4) The right protected by the Second Amendment is not absolute, but instead is subject to government regulation. See *Robertson v. Baldwin*, 165 U.S. 275, 281-82 (1897). . . .

Although I adopt for present purposes the majority's position that the Second Amendment embodies a general concern about self-defense, I shall not assume that the Amendment contains a specific untouchable right to keep guns in the house to shoot burglars. . . .

To the contrary, colonial history itself offers important examples of the kinds of gun regulation that citizens would then have thought compatible with the "right to keep and bear arms," whether embodied in Federal or State Constitutions, or the background common law. And those examples include substantial regulation of firearms in urban areas, including regulations that imposed obstacles to the use of firearms for the protection of the home.

Boston, Philadelphia, and New York City, the three largest cities in America during that period, all restricted the firing of guns within city limits to at least some degree. . . . Boston in 1746 had a law prohibiting the "discharge" of "any Gun or Pistol charged with Shot or Ball in the Town" on penalty of 40 shillings, a law that was later revived in 1778. . . . Philadelphia prohibited, on penalty of 5 shillings (or two days in jail if the fine were not paid), firing a gun or setting off fireworks in Philadelphia without a "governor's special license." . . . And New York City banned, on penalty of a 20-shilling fine, the firing of guns (even in houses) for the three days surrounding New Year's Day. . . .

Furthermore, several towns and cities (including Philadelphia, New York, and Boston) regulated, for fire-safety reasons, the storage of gunpowder, a necessary component of an operational firearm. See Cornell & DeDino, A Well Regulated Right, 73 Fordham L. Rev. 487, 510-12 (2004). Boston's law in particular impacted the use of firearms in the home very much as the District's law does today. Boston's gunpowder law imposed a £10 fine upon "any Person" who "shall take into any Dwelling-House, Stable, Barn, Out-house, Ware-house, Store, Shop, or other Building, within the Town of Boston, any . . . Fire-Arm, loaded with, or having Gun-Powder." . . . Even assuming, as the majority does, that this law included an implicit self-defense exception, it would nevertheless have prevented a homeowner from keeping in his home a gun that he could immediately pick up and use against an intruder. Rather, the homeowner would have had to get the gunpowder and load it into the gun, an operation that would have taken a fair amount of time to perform. . . .

Moreover, the law would, as a practical matter, have prohibited the carrying of loaded firearms anywhere in the city, unless the carrier had no plans to enter any building or was willing to unload or discard his weapons before going inside. And Massachusetts residents must have believed this kind of law compatible with the provision in the Massachusetts Constitution that granted "the people . . . a right to keep and to bear arms for the common defence" — a provision that the majority says was interpreted as "secur[ing] an individual right to bear arms for defensive purposes." . . .

The New York City law, which required that gunpowder in the home be stored in certain sorts of containers, and laws in certain Pennsylvania towns, which required that gunpowder be stored on the highest story of the home, could well have presented similar obstacles to in-home use of firearms. . . . Although it is unclear whether these laws, like the Boston law, would have prohibited the storage of gunpowder inside a firearm, they would at the very least have made it difficult to reload the gun to fire a second shot unless the homeowner happened to be in the portion of the house where the extra gunpowder was required to be kept. . . . And Pennsylvania, like Massachusetts, had at the time one of the self-defense-guaranteeing state constitutional provisions on which the majority relies.

The majority criticizes my citation of these colonial laws. But, as much as it tries, it cannot ignore their existence. I suppose it is possible that, as the majority suggests, they all in practice contained self-defense exceptions. But none of them expressly provided one, and the majority's assumption that such exceptions existed relies largely on the preambles to these acts—an interpretive methodology that it elsewhere roundly derides. And in any event, as I have shown, the gunpowder-storage laws would have burdened armed self-defense, even if they did not completely prohibit it.

This historical evidence demonstrates that a self-defense assumption is the beginning, rather than the end, of any constitutional inquiry. That the District law impacts self-defense merely raises questions about the law's constitutionality. But . . . to see whether the statute is unconstitutional requires us to focus on practicalities, the statute's rationale, the problems that called it into being, its relation to those objectives. . . .

III

I therefore begin by asking a process-based question: How is a court to determine whether a particular firearm regulation (here, the District's restriction on handguns) is consistent with the Second Amendment? What kind of constitutional standard should the court use? How high a protective hurdle does the Amendment erect?

The question matters. The majority is wrong when it says that the District's law is unconstitutional "[u]nder any of the standards of scrutiny that we have applied to enumerated constitutional rights." How could that be? It certainly would not be unconstitutional under, for example, a "rational basis" standard, which requires a court to uphold regulation so long as it bears a "rational relationship" to a "legitimate governmental purpose." *Heller v. Doe*, 509 U.S. 312, 320 (1993). The law at issue here, which in part seeks to prevent gun-related accidents, at least bears a "rational relationship" to that "legitimate" life-saving objective. And nothing in the three 19th-century state cases [*Andrews v. State, Nunn v. State*, and *State v. Reid*] to which the majority turns for support mandates the conclusion that the present District law must fall. . . . These cases . . . involve laws much less narrowly tailored that the one before us. . . .

Respondent proposes that the Court adopt a "strict scrutiny" test, which would require reviewing with care each gun law to determine whether it is "narrowly tailored to achieve a compelling governmental interest." *Abrams v. Johnson*, 521 U.S. 74 (1997). But the majority implicitly, and appropriately, rejects that suggestion by broadly approving a set of laws—prohibitions on concealed weapons, forfeiture by criminals of the Second Amendment right, prohibitions on firearms in certain locales, and governmental regulation of commercial firearm sales—whose constitutionality under a strict scrutiny standard would be far from clear.

Indeed, adoption of a true strict-scrutiny standard for evaluating gun regulations would be impossible. That is because almost every gun-control regulation will seek to advance (as the one here does) a "primary concern of every government — a concern for the safety and indeed the lives of its citizens." *United States v. Salerno*, 481 U.S. 739, 755 (1987). The Court has deemed that interest, as well as "the Government's general interest in preventing crime," to be "compelling," see *id.* at 750, 754, and the Court has in a wide variety of constitutional contexts found such public-safety concerns sufficiently forceful to justify restrictions on individual liberties., see e.g., *Brandenburg v. Ohio*, 395 U.S. 444, 447 (1969) (per curiam) (First Amendment free speech rights); *Sherbert v. Verner*, 374 U.S. 398, 403 (1963) (First Amendment religious rights); *Brigham City v. Stuart*, 547 U.S. 398, 403-04 (2006) (Fourth Amendment protection of the home); *New York v. Quarles*, 467 U.S. 649, 655 (1984) (Fifth Amendment rights under *Miranda v. Arizona*, 384 U.S. 436 (1966)); *Salerno*, supra, at 755 (Eighth Amendment bail rights). Thus, any attempt *in theory* to apply strict scrutiny to gun regulations will *in practice* turn into an interest-balancing inquiry, with the interests protected by the Second Amendment on one side and the governmental public-safety concerns on the other, the only question being whether the regulation at issue impermissibly burdens the former in the course of advancing the latter.

I would simply adopt such an interest-balancing inquiry explicitly. The fact that important interests lie on both sides of the constitutional equation suggests that review of gun-control regulation is not a context in which a court should effectively presume either constitutionality (as in rational-basis review) or unconstitutionality (as in strict scrutiny). Rather, "where a law significantly implicates competing constitutionally protected interests in complex ways," the Court generally asks whether the statute burdens a protected interest in a way or to an extent that is out of proportion to the statute's salutary effects upon other important governmental interests. See *Nixon v. Shrink Missouri Government PAC*, 528 U.S. 377, 402 (2000) (Breyer, J., concurring). Any answer would take account both of the statute's effects upon the competing interests and the existence of any clearly superior less restrictive alternative. See *id.* Contrary to the majority's unsupported suggestion that this sort of "proportionality" approach is unprecedented, the Court has applied it in various constitutional contexts, including election-law cases, speech cases, and due process cases. See 528 U.S. at 403 (citing examples where the Court has taken such an approach); see also, e.g., *Thompson v. Western States Medical Center*, 535 U.S. 357, 388 (2002) (Breyer, J., dissenting) (commercial speech); *Burdick v. Takushi*, 504 U.S. 428, 433 (1992) (election regulation); *Mathews v. Eldridge*, 424 U.S. 319, 339-49 (1976) (procedural due process); *Pickering v. Board of Ed. of Township High School Dist. 205, Will Cty.*, 391 U.S. 563, 568 (1968) (government employee speech).

In applying this kind of standard the Court normally defers to a legislature's empirical judgment in matters where a legislature is likely to have greater expertise and greater institutional factfinding capacity. See *Turner Broadcasting System, Inc. v. FCC*, 520 U.S. 180, 195-96 (1997). . . . Nonetheless, a court, not a legislature, must make the ultimate constitutional conclusion, exercising its "independent judicial judgment" in light of the whole record to determine whether a law exceeds constitutional boundaries. *Randall v. Sorrell*, 548 U.S. 230, 249 (2006) (opinion of Breyer, J.) (citing *Bose Corp. v. Consumers Union of United States, Inc.*, 466 U.S. 485, 499 (1984)). . . .

IV

. . . The second District restriction requires that the lawful owner of a firearm keep his weapon "unloaded and disassembled or bound by a trigger lock or similar device" unless it is kept at his place of business or being used for lawful recreational purposes. . . . [B]ecause I see nothing in the District law that would preclude the existence of a background common-law self-defense exception, I would avoid the constitutional question by interpreting the statute to include it. See *Ashwander v. TVA*, 297 U.S. 288, 348 (1936) (Brandeis, J., concurring).

I am puzzled by the majority's unwillingness to adopt a similar approach. It readily reads unspoken self-defense exceptions into every colonial law, but it refuses to accept the District's concession that this law has one. The one District case it cites to support that refusal, *McIntosh v. Washington*, 395 A.2d 744, 755-56 (1978), merely concludes that the District Legislature had a rational basis for applying the trigger-lock law in homes but not in places of business. Nowhere does that case say that the statute precludes a self-defense exception of the sort that I have just described. And even if it did, we are not bound by a lower court's interpretation of federal law.

The third District restriction prohibits (in most cases) the registration of a handgun within the District. . . . Because registration is a prerequisite to firearm possession . . . the effect of this provision is generally to prevent people in the District from possessing handguns. In determining whether this regulation violates the Second Amendment, I shall ask how the statute seeks to further the governmental interests that it serves, how the statute burdens the interests that the Second Amendment seeks to protect, and whether there are practical less burdensome ways of furthering those interests. The ultimate question is whether the statute imposes burdens that, when viewed in light of the statute's legitimate objectives, are disproportionate. See *Nixon*, 528 U.S. at 402 (Breyer, J., concurring).

A

No one doubts the constitutional importance of the statute's basic objective, saving lives. See, e.g., *Salerno*, 481 U.S. at 755. . . .

1

First, consider the facts as the legislature saw them when it adopted the District statute. As stated by the local council committee that recommended its adoption, the major substantive goal of the District's handgun restriction is "to reduce the potentiality for gun-related crimes and gun-related deaths from occurring within the District of Columbia." . . .

The committee informed the Council that guns were [responsible for 25,000 deaths and 200,000 injuries annually nationwide, including 3,000 accidental deaths, of which a quarter were minors; that] "[f]or every intruder stopped by a homeowner with a firearm, there are 4 gun-related accidents within the home"; [that there were a record 285 murders in the District during 1974;

and that guns are more likely to hurt or kill family members and acquaintances than strangers in accidents or heat-of-passion crimes].

The committee report furthermore presented statistics strongly correlating handguns with crime. . . . The committee furthermore presented statistics regarding the availability of handguns in the United States, . . . and noted that they had "become easy for juveniles to obtain," even despite then-current District laws prohibiting juveniles from possessing them. . . .

In the committee's view, the current District firearms laws were unable [to adequately deal with the problems of gun violence in an urban environment and recommended that the Council ban handguns in the city].

The District's special focus on handguns thus reflects the fact that the committee report found them to have a particularly strong link to undesirable activities in the District's exclusively urban environment. . . . The District did not seek to prohibit possession of other sorts of weapons deemed more suitable for an "urban area." . . .

2

Next, consider the facts as a court must consider them looking at the matter as of today. See, e.g., *Turner*, 520 U.S. at 195 (discussing role of court as factfinder in a constitutional case). Petitioners, and their amici, have presented us with more recent statistics that tell much the same story that the committee report told 30 years ago. . . .

[Justice Breyer here recites a number of statistics suggesting a national and local state of affairs similar to that presented to the D.C. Council, discussed above, before it passed the handgun ban: many gun deaths and injuries, including accidents, injuries to family members and acquaintances, the disproportionate use of handguns in violent crime, and the special problems urban areas face with respect to handgun-related gun violence.]

3

Respondent and his many amici for the most part do not disagree about the figures set forth in the preceding subsection, but they do disagree strongly with the District's predictive judgment that a ban on handguns will help solve the crime and accident problems that those figures disclose. In particular, they disagree with the District Council's assessment that "freezing the pistol . . . population within the District," will reduce crime, accidents, and deaths related to guns. And they provide facts and figures designed to show that it has not done so in the past, and hence will not do so in the future[, that] firearm ownership does have a beneficial self-defense effect [both in and out of the home, and] that laws criminalizing gun possession . . . will have the effect only of restricting law-abiding citizens, but not criminals, from acquiring guns. . . . In the view of respondent's amici, this evidence shows that other remedies — such as less restriction on gun ownership, or liberal authorization of law-abiding citizens to carry concealed weapons — better fit the problem [and that] the District fails to show that its remedy, the gun ban, bears a reasonable relation to the crime and accident problems that the District seeks to solve.

These empirically based arguments may have proved strong enough to convince many legislatures, as a matter of legislative policy, not to adopt total handgun bans. But the question here is whether they are strong enough to destroy judicial confidence in the reasonableness of a legislature that rejects them. And that they are not. For one thing, they can lead us more deeply into the uncertainties that surround any effort to reduce crime, but they cannot prove either that handgun possession diminishes crime or that handgun bans are ineffective. The statistics do show a soaring District crime rate. And the District's crime rate went up after the District adopted its handgun ban. But, as students of elementary logic know, after it does not mean because of it. What would the District's crime rate have looked like without the ban? Higher? Lower? The same? Experts differ; and we, as judges, cannot say. . . .

Further, suppose that respondent's amici are right when they say that householders' possession of loaded handguns help to frighten away intruders. On that assumption, one must still ask whether that benefit is worth the potential death-related cost. And that is a question without a directly provable answer.

Finally, consider the claim of respondent's amici that handgun bans cannot work; there are simply too many illegal guns already in existence for a ban on legal guns to make a difference. In a word, they claim that, given the urban sea of pre-existing legal guns, criminals can readily find arms regardless. Nonetheless, a legislature might respond, we want to make an effort to try to dry up that urban sea, drop by drop. And none of the studies can show that effort is not worthwhile.

In a word, the studies to which respondent's amici point raise policy-related questions. They succeed in proving that the District's predictive judgments are controversial. But they do not by themselves show that those judgments are incorrect; nor do they demonstrate a consensus, academic or otherwise, supporting that conclusion. . . .

In particular this Court, in First Amendment cases applying intermediate scrutiny, has said that our "sole obligation" in reviewing a legislature's "predictive judgments" is "to assure that, in formulating its judgments," the legislature "has drawn reasonable inferences based on substantial evidence." *Turner*, 520 U.S. at 195 (internal quotation marks omitted). And judges, looking at the evidence before us, should agree that the District legislature's predictive judgments satisfy that legal standard. That is to say, the District's judgment, while open to question, is nevertheless supported by "substantial evidence."

. . . [D]eference to legislative judgment seems particularly appropriate here, where the judgment has been made by a local legislature, with particular knowledge of local problems and insight into appropriate local solutions. See *Los Angeles v. Alameda Books, Inc.*, 535 U.S. 425, 440 (2002) (plurality opinion) ("[W]e must acknowledge that the Los Angeles City Council is in a better position than the Judiciary to gather an evaluate data on local problems"). . . . Different localities may seek to solve similar problems in different ways, and a "city must be allowed a reasonable opportunity to experiment with solutions to admittedly serious problems." *Renton v. Playtime Theatres, Inc.*, 475 U.S. 41, 52 (1986) (internal quotation marks omitted). "The Framers recognized that the most effective democracy occurs at local levels of government, where people with firsthand knowledge of local problems have more ready access to public officials responsible for dealing with them." *Garcia v. San Antonio Metropolitan*

Transit Authority, 469 U.S. 528, 575, n.18 (1985) (Powell, J., dissenting) (citing The Federalist No. 17, p. 107 (J. Cooke ed. 1961) (A. Hamilton)). We owe that democratic process some substantial weight in the constitutional calculus.

For these reasons, I conclude that the District's statute properly seeks to further the sort of life-preserving and public-safety interests that the Court has called "compelling." *Salerno*, 481 U.S. at 750, 754.

B

I next assess the extent to which the District's law burdens the interests that the Second Amendment seeks to protect. Respondent and his amici, as well as the majority, suggest that those interests include: (1) the preservation of a "well regulated Militia"; (2) safeguarding the use of firearms for sporting purposes, e.g., hunting and marksmanship; and (3) assuring the use of firearms for self-defense. For argument's sake, I shall consider all three of those interests here.

1

The District's statute burdens the Amendment's first and primary objective hardly at all. . . .

To begin with, the present case has nothing to do with actual military service. The question presented presumes that respondent is "not affiliated with any state-regulated militia." 552 U.S. 1035 (2007) (emphasis added). I am aware of no indication that the District either now or in the recent past has called up its citizenry to serve in a militia, that it has any inkling of doing so anytime in the foreseeable future, or that this law must be construed to prevent the use of handguns during legitimate militia activities. Moreover, even if the District were to call up its militia, respondent would not be among the citizens whose service would be requested. The District does not consider him, at 66 years of age, to be a member of its militia. See D.C. Code §49-401 (2001) (militia includes only male residents ages 18 to 45). . . .

Nonetheless, as some amici claim, the statute might interfere with training in the use of weapons, training useful for military purposes. . . .

Regardless, to consider the military-training objective a modern counterpart to a similar militia-related colonial objective and to treat that objective as falling within the Amendment's primary purposes makes no difference here. That is because the District's law does not seriously affect military training interests. The law permits residents to engage in activities that will increase their familiarity with firearms. They may register (and thus possess in their homes) weapons other than handguns, such as rifles and shotguns. And they may operate those weapons within the District "for lawful recreational purposes." These permissible recreations plainly include actually using and firing the weapons, as evidenced by a specific D.C. Code provision contemplating the existence of local firing ranges.

And while the District law prevents citizens from training with handguns within the District, the District consists of only 61.4 square miles of urban area. . . . The adjacent States do permit the use of handguns for target practice, and those States are only a brief subway ride away. . . .

... I conclude that the District's law burdens the Second Amendment's primary objective little, or not at all.

2

The majority briefly suggests that the "right to keep and bear Arms" might encompass an interest in hunting. But in enacting the present provisions, the District sought "to take nothing away from sportsmen." DC Rep., at 33. And any inability of District residents to hunt near where they live has much to do with the jurisdiction's exclusively urban character and little to do with the District's firearm laws. For reasons similar to those I discussed in the preceding subsection — that the District's law does not prohibit possession of rifles or shotguns, and the presence of opportunities for sporting activities in nearby States — I reach a similar conclusion, namely, that the District's law burdens any sports-related or hunting-related objectives that the Amendment may protect little, or not at all.

3

The District's law does prevent a resident from keeping a loaded handgun in his home. And it consequently makes it more difficult for the householder to use the handgun for self-defense in the home against intruders, such as burglars. As the Court of Appeals noted, statistics suggest that handguns are the most popular weapon for self defense. See 478 F.3d at 400 (citing Kleck & Gertz, 86 J. Crim. L. & C., at 182-83). And there are some legitimate reasons why that would be the case: Amici suggest (with some empirical support) that handguns are easier to hold and control (particularly for persons with physical infirmities), easier to carry, easier to maneuver in enclosed spaces, and that a person using one will still have a hand free to dial 911. . . . To that extent the law burdens to some degree an interest in self-defense that for present purposes I have assumed the Amendment seeks to further.

C

In weighing needs and burdens, we must take account of the possibility that there are reasonable, but less restrictive alternatives. Are there other potential measures that might similarly promote the same goals while imposing lesser restrictions? See *Nixon*, 528 U.S. at 402 (Breyer, J., concurring) ("existence of a clearly superior, less restrictive alternative" can be a factor in determining whether a law is constitutionally proportionate). Here I see none.

The reason there is no clearly superior, less restrictive alternative to the District's handgun ban is that the ban's very objective is to reduce significantly the number of handguns in the District, say, for example, by allowing a law enforcement officer immediately to assume that any handgun he sees is an illegal handgun. And there is no plausible way to achieve that objective other than to ban the guns.

It does not help respondent's case to describe the District's objective more generally as an "effort to diminish the dangers associated with guns." That is because the very attributes that make handguns particularly useful for self-defense are also what make them particularly dangerous. That they are easy to hold and control means that they are easier for children to use. That they are maneuverable and permit a free hand likely contributes to the fact that they are by far the firearm of choice for crimes such as rape and robbery. . . . That they are small and light makes them easy to steal and concealable.

This symmetry suggests that any measure less restrictive in respect to the use of handguns for self-defense will, to that same extent, prove less effective in preventing the use of handguns for illicit purposes. If a resident has a handgun in the home that he can use for self-defense, then he has a handgun in the home that he can use to commit suicide or engage in acts of domestic violence. If it is indeed the case, as the District believes, that the number of guns contributes to the number of gun-related crimes, accidents, and deaths, then, although there may be less restrictive, less effective substitutes for an outright ban, there is no less restrictive equivalent of an outright ban.

Licensing restrictions would not similarly reduce the handgun population, and the District may reasonably fear that even if guns are initially restricted to law-abiding citizens, they might be stolen and thereby placed in the hands of criminals. Permitting certain types of handguns, but not others, would affect the commercial market for handguns, but not their availability. And requiring safety devices such as trigger locks, or imposing safe-storage requirements would interfere with any self-defense interest while simultaneously leaving operable weapons in the hands of owners (or others capable of acquiring the weapon and disabling the safety device) who might use them for domestic violence or other crimes.

The absence of equally effective alternatives to a complete prohibition finds support in the empirical fact that other States and urban centers prohibit particular types of weapons. Chicago has a law very similar to the District's, and many of its suburbs also ban handgun possession under most circumstances. . . . Toledo bans certain types of handguns. . . . And San Francisco in 2005 enacted by popular referendum a ban on most handgun possession by city residents; it has been precluded from enforcing that prohibition, however, by state-court decisions deeming it pre-empted by state law. See *Fiscal v. City and County of San Francisco*, 70 Cal. Rptr. 3d 324, 326-28 (2008). . . .

In addition, at least six States and Puerto Rico impose general bans on certain types of weapons, in particular assault weapons or semiautomatic weapons. . . . These bans, too, suggest that there may be no substitute to an outright prohibition in cases where a governmental body has deemed a particular type of weapon especially dangerous.

D

The upshot is that the District's objectives are compelling; its predictive judgments as to its law's tendency to achieve those objectives are adequately supported; the law does impose a burden upon any self-defense interest that the Amendment seeks to secure; and there is no clear less restrictive alternative.

I turn now to the final portion of the "permissible regulation" question: Does the District's law disproportionately burden Amendment-protected interests? Several considerations, taken together, convince me that it does not.

First, the District law is tailored to the life-threatening problems it attempts to address. The law concerns one class of weapons, handguns, leaving residents free to possess shotguns and rifles, along with ammunition. The area that falls within its scope is totally urban. Cf. *Lorillard Tobacco Co. v. Reilly*, 533 U.S. 525, 563 (2001) (varied effect of statewide speech restriction in "rural, urban, or suburban" locales "demonstrates a lack of narrow tailoring"). That urban area suffers from a serious handgun-fatality problem. The District's law directly aims at that compelling problem. And there is no less restrictive way to achieve the problem-related benefits that it seeks.

Second, the self-defense interest in maintaining loaded handguns in the home to shoot intruders is not the primary interest, but at most a subsidiary interest, that the Second Amendment seeks to serve. The Second Amendment's language, while speaking of a "Militia," says nothing of "self-defense." As Justice Stevens points out, the Second Amendment's drafting history shows that the language reflects the Framers' primary, if not exclusive, objective. And the majority itself says that "the threat that the new Federal Government would destroy the citizens' militia by taking away their arms was the reason that right . . . was codified in a written Constitution." The way in which the Amendment's operative clause seeks to promote that interest — by protecting a right "to keep and bear Arms" — may in fact help further an interest in self-defense. But a factual connection falls far short of a primary objective. The Amendment itself tells us that militia preservation was first and foremost in the Framers' minds. See *Miller*, 307 U.S. at 178 ("With obvious purpose to assure the continuation and render possible the effectiveness of [militia] forces the declaration and guarantee of the Second Amendment were made," and the amendment "must be interpreted and applied with that end in view").

Further, any self-defense interest at the time of the Framing could not have focused exclusively upon urban-crime related dangers. Two hundred years ago, most Americans, many living on the frontier, would likely have thought of self-defense primarily in terms of outbreaks of fighting with Indian tribes, rebellions such as Shays' Rebellion, marauders, and crime-related dangers to travelers on the roads, on footpaths, or along waterways. . . . Insofar as the Framers focused at all on the tiny fraction of the population living in large cities, they would have been aware that these city dwellers were subject to firearm restrictions that their rural counterparts were not. See *supra*. They are unlikely then to have thought of a right to keep loaded handguns in homes to confront intruders in urban settings as central. And the subsequent development of modern urban police departments, by diminishing the need to keep loaded guns nearby in case of intruders, would have moved any such right even further away from the heart of the amendment's more basic protective ends. See, e.g., Sklansky, *The Private Police*, 46 UCLA L. Rev. 1165, 1206-07 (1999) (professional urban police departments did not develop until roughly the mid-19th century).

Nor, for that matter, am I aware of any evidence that handguns in particular were central to the Framers' conception of the Second Amendment. The lists of militia-related weapons in the late 18th-century state statutes appear primarily to refer to other sorts of weapons, muskets in particular. See *Miller*, 307 U.S. at

180-82 (reproducing colonial militia laws). Respondent points out in his brief that the Federal Government and two States at the time of the founding had enacted statutes that listed handguns as "acceptable" militia weapons. But these statutes apparently found them "acceptable" only for certain special militiamen (generally, certain soldiers on horseback), while requiring muskets or rifles for the general infantry. . . .

Third, irrespective of what the Framers could have thought, we know what they did think. Samuel Adams, who lived in Boston, advocated a constitutional amendment that would have precluded the Constitution from ever being "construed" to "prevent the people of the United States, who are peaceable citizens, from keeping their own arms." 6 Documentary History of the Ratification of the Constitution 1453 (J. Kaminski & G. Saladino eds. 2000). Samuel Adams doubtless knew that the Massachusetts Constitution contained somewhat similar protection. And he doubtless knew that Massachusetts law prohibited Bostonians from keeping loaded guns in the house. So how could Samuel Adams have advocated such protection unless he thought that the protection was consistent with local regulation that seriously impeded urban residents from using their arms against intruders? It seems unlikely that he meant to deprive the Federal Government of power (to enact Boston-type weapons regulation) that he know Boston had and (as far as we know) he would have thought constitutional under the Massachusetts Constitution. Indeed, since the District of Columbia (the subject of the Seat of Government Clause, U.S. Const., Art. I, §8, cl. 17) was the only urban area under direct federal control, it seems unlikely that the Framers thought about urban gun control at all. Cf. *Palmore v. United States*, 411 U.S. 389, 397-98 (1973) (Congress can "legislate for the District in a manner with respect to subjects that would exceed its powers, or at least would be very unusual, in the context of national legislation enacted under other powers delegated to it").

Of course the District's law and the colonial Boston law are not identical. But the Boston law disabled an even wider class of weapons (indeed, all firearms). And its existence shows at the least that local legislatures could impose (as here) serious restrictions on the right to use firearms. Moreover, as I have said, Boston's law, though highly analogous to the District's, was not the only colonial law that could have impeded a homeowner's ability to shoot a burglar. . . . I cannot agree with the majority that these laws are largely uninformative because the penalty for violating them was civil, rather than criminal. The Court has long recognized that the exercise of a constitutional right can be burdened by penalties far short of jail time. See, e.g., *Murdock v. Pennsylvania*, 319 U.S. 105 (1943) (invalidating $7 per week solicitation fee as applied to religious group); see also *Forsyth County v. Nationalist Movement*, 505 U.S. 123, 136 (1992) ("A tax based on the content of speech does not become more constitutional because it is a small tax").

Regardless, why would the majority require a precise colonial regulatory analogue in order to save a modern gun regulation from constitutional challenge? After all, insofar as we look to history to discover how we can constitutionally regulate a right to self-defense, we must look, not to what 18th-century legislatures actually did enact, but to what they would have thought they could enact. There are innumerable policy-related reasons why a legislature might not act on a particular matter, despite having the power to do so. This Court has "frequently cautioned that it is at best treacherous to find in congressional silence alone the adoption of a controlling rule of law." *United States v. Wells*, 519 U.S. 482, 496 (1997). It is similarly "treacherous" to reason from the fact that colonial legislatures did not enact certain kinds of legislation an unalterable constitutional limitation on the power of a modern legislature cannot do so. The question should not be whether a modern restriction on a right to self-defense duplicates a past one, but whether that restriction, when compared with restrictions originally thought possible, enjoys a similarly strong justification. At a minimum that similarly strong justification is what the District's modern law, compared with Boston's colonial law, reveals.

Fourth, a contrary view, as embodied in today's decision, will have unfortunate consequences. The decision will encourage legal challenges to gun regulation throughout the Nation. Because it says little about the standards used to evaluate regulatory decisions, it will leave the Nation without clear standards for resolving those challenges. And litigation over the course of many years, or the mere specter of such litigation, threatens to leave cities without effective protection against gun violence and accidents during that time.

... The majority says that it leaves the District "a variety of tools for combating" such problems. It fails to list even one seemingly adequate replacement for the law it strikes down. I can understand how reasonable individuals can disagree about the merits of strict gun control as a crime-control measure, even in a totally urbanized area. But I cannot understand how one can take from the elected branches of government the right to decide whether to insist upon a handgun-free urban populace in a city now facing a serious crime problem and which, in the future, could well face environmental or other emergencies that threaten the breakdown of law and order.

V

The majority derides my approach as "judge-empowering." I take this criticism seriously, but I do not think it accurate. As I have previously explained, this is an approach that the Court has taken in other areas of constitutional law. Application of such an approach, of course, requires judgment, but the very nature of the approach — requiring careful identification of the relevant interests and evaluating the law's effect upon them — limits the judge's choices; and the method's necessary transparency lays bare the judge's reasoning for all to see and to criticize.

The majority's methodology is, in my view, substantially less transparent than mine. At a minimum, I find it difficult to understand the reasoning that seems to underlie certain conclusions that it reaches.

The majority spends the first 54 pages of its opinion attempting to rebut Justice Stevens' evidence that the Amendment was enacted with a purely militia-related purpose. In the majority's view, the Amendment also protects an interest in armed personal self-defense, at least to some degree. But the majority does not tell us precisely what that interest is. "Putting all of [the Second Amendment's] textual elements together," the majority says, "we find that they guarantee the individual right to possess and carry weapons in case of confrontation." Then, three pages later, it says that "we do not read the Second

Amendment to permit citizens to carry arms for any sort of confrontation." Yet, with one critical exception, it does not explain which confrontations count. It simply leaves that question unanswered.

The majority does, however, point to one type of confrontation that counts, for it describes the Amendment as "elevat[ing] above all other interests the right of law-abiding, responsible citizens to use arms in defense of hearth and home." What is its basis for finding that to be the core of the Second Amendment right? The only historical sources identified by the majority that even appear to touch upon that specific matter consist of an 1866 newspaper editorial discussing the Freedmen's Bureau Act, two quotations from that 1866 Act's legislative history, and a 1980 state court opinion saying that in colonial times the same were used to defend the home as to maintain the militia. How can citations such as these support the far-reaching proposition that the Second Amendment's primary concern is not its stated concern about the militia, but rather a right to keep loaded weapons at one's bedside to shoot intruders?

Nor is it at all clear to me how the majority decides which loaded "arms" a homeowner may keep. The majority says that that Amendment protects those weapons "typically possessed by law-abiding citizens for lawful purposes." This definition conveniently excludes machineguns, but permits handguns, which the majority describes as "the most popular weapon chosen by Americans for self-defense in the home." But what sense does this approach make? According to the majority's reasoning, if Congress and the States lift restrictions on the possession and use of machineguns, and people buy machineguns to protect their homes, the Court will have to reverse course and find that the Second Amendment does, in fact, protect the individual self-defense-related right to possess a machinegun. On the majority's reasoning, if tomorrow someone invents a particularly useful, highly dangerous self-defense weapon, Congress and the States had better ban it immediately, for once it becomes popular Congress will no longer possess the constitutional authority to do so. In essence, the majority determines what regulations are permissible by looking to see what existing regulations permit. There is no basis for believing that the Framers intended such circular reasoning.

I am similarly puzzled by the majority's list, in Part III of its opinion, of provisions that in its view would survive Second Amendment scrutiny. These consist of (1) "prohibitions on carrying concealed weapons"; (2) "prohibitions on the possession of firearms by felons"; (3) "prohibitions on the possession of firearms by . . . the mentally ill"; (4) "laws forbidding the carrying of firearms in sensitive places such as schools and government buildings"; and (5) government "conditions and qualifications" attached "to the commercial sale of arms." Why these? Is it that similar restrictions existed in the late 18th century? The majority fails to cite any colonial analogues. And even were it possible to find analogous colonial laws in respect to all these restrictions, why should these colonial laws count, while the Boston loaded-gun restriction (along with the other laws I have identified) apparently does not count?

At the same time the majority ignores a more important question: Given the purposes for which the Framers enacted the Second Amendment, how should it be applied to modern-day circumstances that they could not have anticipated? Assume, for argument's sake, that the Framers did intend the Amendment to offer a degree of self-defense protection. Does that mean that the Framers also intended to guarantee a right to possess a loaded gun near swimming pools, parks, and playgrounds? That they would not have cared about the children who might pick up a loaded gun on their parents' bedside table? That they (who certainly showed concern for the risk of fire) would have lacked concern for the risk of accidental deaths or suicides that readily accessible loaded handguns in urban areas might bring? Unless we believe that they intended future generations to ignore such matters, answering questions such as the questions in this case requires judgment—judicial judgment exercised within a framework for constitutional analysis that guides that judgment and which makes its exercise transparent. One cannot answer those questions by combining inconclusive historical research with judicial *ipse dixit.*

The argument about method, however, is by far the less important argument surrounding today's decision. Far more important are the unfortunate consequences that today's decision is likely to spawn. Not least of these, as I have said, is the fact that the decision threatens to throw into doubt the constitutionality of gun laws throughout the United States. I can find no sound legal basis for launching the courts on so formidable and potentially dangerous a mission. In my view, there simply is no untouchable constitutional right guaranteed by the Second Amendment to keep loaded handguns in the house in crime-ridden urban areas.

VI

For these reasons, I conclude that the District's measure is a proportionate, not a disproportionate, response to the compelling concerns that led the District to adopt it. And, for these reasons as well as the independently sufficient reasons set forth by Justice Stevens, I would find the District's measure consistent with the Second Amendment's demands.

With respect, I dissent.

NOTES & QUESTIONS

1. The Court says "[t]he Constitution was written to be understood by the voters; its words and phrases were used in their normal and ordinary as distinguished from technical meaning." How do you think ordinary voters understand the text of the Second Amendment? Over the next week, ask some of your relatives and friends for their impressions of the language of the Second Amendment. Compare your results with those of your classmates.

2. The Court explains that the prefatory militia clause of the Second Amendment does not "limit or expand the scope of the operative clause." Can you propose a reading of the Second Amendment that recognizes a right of "the people" (not only the militia), and in which the prefatory clause affects the scope of the right in the main clause? Which term is broader, "militia" or "people"? Examine the statutory definition of the militia at 10 U.S.C. §311. Do the gender and age distinctions in the definition affect your analysis?

3. The Court says that interpreting the Second Amendment to protect only those arms in existence in the eighteenth century is an argument that "border[s] on the frivolous." If you take this argument seriously, would you recognize a right only to guns *literally* in existence or the *type* of gun in existence? If a theory that the Second Amendment, or another part of the Bill of Rights, includes only technologies in existence at the time of the Framing, should the theory allow a technological update from 1791 to 1868, since the Second Amendment, like most of the Bill of Rights, was made applicable to the states through the Fourteenth Amendment, which was ratified in 1868? Note that, by the late 1860s, technologies like repeating firearms were already in existence: six-shot revolvers had been popular since the 1830s; and seven-shot lever-action rifles played a significant role on the battlefields of the Civil War.

4. Note the Court's explanation that "arms" in the Second Amendment includes not only weapons, but also, in the words of Samuel Johnson's dictionary, "armour of defence." Does this suggest that it would be unconstitutional to outlaw the possession of bullet-resistant vests? What other types of defensive gear might be protected by the Second Amendment?

5. The Court wrote that "the Second Amendment extends, prima facie, to all instruments that constitute bearable arms." Does this mean that the Second Amendment protects only things that can be worn or carried, and does not extend to things that are fixed in place (e.g., a home burglar alarm), or that cannot be carried (e.g., a heavy wheeled cannon), or that themselves bear people (e.g., a tank, a battleship)?

6. The majority opinion cites several cases, such as *Nunn v. State*, 1 Ga. 243 (1846) and *State v. Chandler*, 5 La. Ann. 489 (1850), which the Court says expressed the correct view of the Second Amendment. The Court also points to *Aymette v. State*, 21 Tenn. (2 Hump.) 154 (1840) as expressing the incorrect view (all of these cases appear in Chapter 5). Beyond the specific language quoted in *Heller*, can other portions of these cases be cited as expressing the correct (or incorrect) approach to Second Amendment analysis?

7. The Court's reference to Justice Ginsburg's explanation of "bear" in *Muscarello v. United States*, 524 U.S. 125 (1998) as the ordinary nonmilitary carrying of arms, is one of the cryptic comments covered in Chapter 8. In *Muscarello*, Justice Ginsburg seemed to view "bear arms" in the Second Amendment to mean the ordinary carrying of a firearm. But in *Heller*, she joined Justice Stevens's dissent, arguing that "bear arms" has a special military connotation. Later, she expressed her hope that either of the dissents in *Heller* would one day be the majority. Speech at Harvard Club, Washington, D.C., Dec. 17, 2009. Do you think she changed her mind? What else might account for her *Muscarello* opinion? Did some people just over-read *Muscarello*?

8. The majority argues that the military construction of "bear" would denote a right to be a soldier or to wage war. This, says the majority, is "an absurdity that no commentator has ever endorsed." To avoid this result, says the

majority, Justice Stevens "manufactures a hybrid definition whereby 'bear arms' connotes the actually carrying of arms but only in the service of the organized militia." What is the difference between Stevens's conception of the right and the "absurd" version that Scalia criticizes? Is military or militia service properly conceived of as a *right* or as a *duty*? What difference does this make? For more on the different "models" of the right protected by the Second Amendment, see *Silveira v. Lockyer*, 312 F.3d 1052 (9th Cir. 2002) (Chapter 8), *United States v. Emerson*, 270 F.3d 203 (5th Cir. 2001) (Chapter 8), and http://firearmregulation.com.

9. The dissenters agree with the majority that the Second Amendment is an individual right. What exactly is the scope of the individual right, according to the dissenters? While the dissenters are clear about what the Second Amendment is *not* (not the nonmilitia right to own a handgun), do they ever say what the Second Amendment right *is*? Why might the dissenters fail to elaborate their affirmative version of the Second Amendment?

10. The "collective right" interpretation of the Second Amendment (that the right belongs collectively to the People as a whole, but cannot be legally invoked by any individual) was very popular in academia and the lower federal courts, especially in the 1970s and 1980s. An amicus brief by former Attorney General Janet Reno, future Attorney General Eric Holder, and other former Department of Justice officials argued that the collective right was the correct interpretation of the Second Amendment. Why do you think both the majority and the dissent barely mentioned the collective right theory?

11. The majority and the Stevens dissent briefly mentioned some of the cases upholding federal plenary authority over the militia, notwithstanding state objections. Among the cases affirming federal militia supremacy are *Perpich v. Dep't of Defense*, 496 U.S. 334-54 (1990) (militias may be called into federal service and sent outside the United States for training despite the state governor's objection); *Selective Draft Law Cases*, 245 U.S. 366 (1918) (Congress has the authority to effectively abolish a state militia by conscripting all its members into the federal army); *Martin v. Mott*, 25 U.S. 19 (1827) (President's decision that circumstances exist to call the militia from state control into federal service is not judicially reviewable and over-rides any governor's view to the contrary); and *Houston v. Moore*, 18 U.S. (5 Wheat.) 1 (1820) (federal militia legislation preempts even state legislation that copies federal law verbatim). Can these cases be reconciled with the theory that the Second Amendment protects a "state right"? A "collective right"? An individual right to serve in the militia? A right that can be invoked by militiamen when they are actually serving in a state militia?

12. The Court argues that the Second Amendment "like the First and Fourth Amendments, codified a pre-existing right." Besides the authorities mentioned in the *Heller* opinions, what other authorities, from previous chapters of this book, shed light on the issue? Consider, for example, Justice Brennan's preexisting rights argument in his dissent to *United States v. Verdugo-Urquidez*, 494 U.S. 259 (Chapter 8).

13. The Court dismissed the argument that the militia clause is a limitation on the right to arms. "[T]he prologue . . . can only show that self-defense had little to do with the right's codification; it was the central component of the right itself." If so, then why was the militia clause included? Consider again Justice Brennan's preexisting rights argument, in his dissent to *Verdugo-Urquidez* (Chapter 8).

14. Consider the historical sources that the majority and the dissenters argue about, such as the English right to arms (Chapter 2), James Madison (Chapter 4), Justice Joseph Story (Chapter 5), and Congress during Reconstruction (Chapter 6). Which side more accurately reflects the views of those sources?

15. The idea that constitutional rights are preexisting and extend beyond those things specifically enumerated is affirmed by the Ninth Amendment. The Ninth Amendment was a direct response to criticisms that an enumerated bill of rights would imply that no other rights existed. See Chapter 4. Assume the Bill of Rights did not exist. How would you decide whether the Constitution protected an individual right to arms, or a free press? Justice Stevens's dissent in *McDonald, infra*, will address this question at length.

16. The Court's survey of nineteenth-century commentators includes William Rawle's 1825 constitutional treatise. Rawle wrote that "[n]o clause in the constitution could by any rule of construction be conceived to give to congress a power to disarm the people. Such a flagitious attempt could only be made under some general pretence by a state legislature. But if any blind pursuit of inordinate power, either should attempt it, this amendment may be appealed to as a restraint on both." How do you explain the difference between Rawle's conception of congressional power and the modern view? Does this difference help explain how views of the Second Amendment might shift over time? Professor Johnson argues that conceptions of rights and powers are intertwined and that recognition of a right to arms depends on a commitment to limited federal power. Nicholas J. Johnson, *Plenary Power and Constitutional Outcasts: Federal Power, Critical Race Theory, and the Second, Ninth, and Tenth Amendments*, 57 Ohio St. L.J. 1555 (1996).

17. William Rawle was one of the ratifiers of the Bill of Rights, so his 1825 elaboration of the Second Amendment might be considered a source of original understanding of the Second Amendment. But the Court's opinion goes well beyond the immediate time frame of the Second Amendment's ratification. Instead, *Heller* devotes much attention to interpretations of the Second Amendment throughout the antebellum nineteenth century. Professor Lund has criticized the opinion as an embarrassment to originalism. Nelson Lund, *The Second Amendment, Heller, and Originalist Jurisprudence*, 56 UCLA L. Rev. 1343 (2009). Other criticisms of *Heller*'s version of originalism include Lawrence B. Solum, District of Columbia v. Heller *and Originalism*, 103 Nw. U. L. Rev. 923 (2009). Is this use of nineteenth-century sources bad originalism? Is it living constitutionalism? A form of traditionalism? As Professor Michael O'Shea writes:

> [D]espite [its] self-conscious modern originalism, the *Heller* opinion is at least equally effective if it is viewed instead as an example of an older, less formalized type of historical inquiry into legal meaning. This older approach is Burkean: it allows *tradition*, the aggregated perspectives of successive periods of time, to claim weight in settling the meaning of the [constitutional] text.

Michael P. O'Shea, *The Right to Defensive Arms After* District of Columbia v. Heller, 111 W. Va. L. Rev. 349, 371-72 (2009); *see also id.* at 372 (*Heller* "recognizes a nineteenth-century right to arms"). Does consistent understanding for decades following ratification provide evidence of original meaning? Note that these sources will figure prominently in the assessment of whether the Fourteenth Amendment protects an individual right to arms addressed in *McDonald v. Chicago, infra.*

18. Suppose a government, either by statute or case law, prohibited ordinary citizens from engaging in self-defense against criminal violence by police, even under circumstances that ordinarily would trigger the right. Would such a law violate the Second Amendment? Is the answer affected by whether the right to arms is construed as a bulwark against tyranny, for more prosaic self-defense, or for both? For exploration of this issue, see Darrell A.H. Miller, *Retail Rebellion and the Second Amendment*, 86 Ind. L.J. 939 (2011).

19. Consider the Court's interpretation of *United States v. Miller*, 307 U.S. 174 (1939) (Chapter 7). Compare this interpretation to your own understanding of *Miller*. Compare these with the interpretations of lower federal courts in *Cases* (Chapter 7), *Tot* (Chapter 7), and the decisions in Chapter 8.A. How many distinct interpretations of the Second Amendment can you identify in these sources?

20. In footnote 24, the Court criticizes lower courts for over-reading *United States v. Miller*. Recall from Chapter 8 that *Silveira v. Lockyer*, 312 F.3d 1052 (9th Cir. 2002), criticized lower federal cases that failed to develop or explain the collective rights view of the Second Amendment. Would it have been more difficult for the *Heller* Court to advance the individual right if there had been strong positive content to the collective right view?

21. Justice Stevens's dissent emphasized the broad reliance on what he described as a settled understanding of *Miller*. He cited 19 lower court cases in particular. Half of those cases adopted the "collective right," which all 9 of the *Heller* Justices rejected. Does this undercut Justice Stevens's reliance argument? In what sense did those lower court collective right cases rely on *Miller*?

    Responding to the judicial reliance argument, Justice Scalia commented that the lower court judges had over-read *Miller*, and that most of the cases would have come out the same way under the *Heller* majority's reading of the Second Amendment (e.g., that prohibiting guns to felons or banning machine guns is constitutional). Justice Scalia also wrote that erroneous judicial reliance "cannot nullify the reliance of millions of Americans (as our historical analysis has shown) upon the true meaning of the right to keep and bear arms." Empirically, Justice Scalia was correct that, even pre-*Heller*, large majorities of the American public believed that they had an individual Second Amendment right to arms, unconnected to militia service. *See* David B. Kopel, *The Second Amendment in the Living Constitution*, 2009 Cardozo L. Rev. 99 (opinion polls from 1970s to the present). To what extent, if any, should courts consider societal reliance on a particular understanding of personal rights? In *Planned Parenthood v. Casey*, the plurality opinion of Justices Sandra Day O'Connor, David Souter, and Anthony Kennedy acknowledged that *Roe v. Wade* might have been wrongly decided, but declined to overturn *Roe*, in part because of societal reliance: "[F]or two decades of economic and social developments, people have organized intimate relationships and made choices that define their views of themselves and their places in society, in reliance on the availability of abortion in the event that contraception should fail." 505 U.S. 833, 856 (1992). What are the similarities and differences between the public's reliance on a right to abortion, and a right to own and carry firearms? In which ways is *Heller*'s treatment of social reliance similar to or different from *Casey*'s? CQ: *Nordyke v. King*, 644 F.3d 776 (9th Cir. 2011), (Chapter 11) applies the abortion-rights standard of review to the Second Amendment.

22. Consider the Court's assessment of the suggestion in *United States v. Miller* that the Second Amendment primarily protects "ordinary military equipment." This, said Justice Scalia, would produce a "startling reading of the opinion, since it would mean that . . . restrictions on machine guns might be unconstitutional. . . ." Compare this assessment to the argument in *Cases v. United States*, 131 F.2d 916 (1st Cir. 1942) (Chapter 7), that literal application of *Miller* is unpalatable "because of the well known fact that in the so called 'Commando Units' some sort of military use seems to have been found for almost any modern lethal weapon." What is the jurisprudential justification for the *Heller* Court's dismissal of *Miller*'s suggestion about the type of arms protected by the Second Amendment?

23. The Court argues that *Miller*'s ostensible protection of "ordinary military equipment" is moderated by what comes after: "Ordinarily when called for militia service able-bodied men were expected to appear bearing arms supplied by themselves and of the kind in common use at the time." From this the *Heller* Court concludes: "The traditional militia was formed from a pool of men bringing arms [that were] 'in common use at the time' for lawful purposes like self defense." Does this adequately reconcile the two clauses of the Second Amendment? Might this "common use" standard also generate worrisome practical results? What if Americans are gripped with a perception that they must stockpile the most lethal types of weapons lawfully available, causing those weapons to become widely possessed by private citizens? Would this automatically render those guns constitutionally protected under the "common use" standard? Does this formula invite a spiraling arms race?

24. The inverse of the common use standard is *Heller*'s statement that the Second Amendment "does not protect those weapons not typically possessed by law-abiding citizens for lawful purposes." How exactly should we determine what is typically possessed for law-abiding purposes, and what is not? Some scholars have attempted to add structure to the common use test and predict its consequences. *See, e.g.*, Nicholas J. Johnson, *The Second Amendment in the States and the Limits of the Common Use Standard*, 4 Harv. L. & Pol'y Rev. Online, Apr. 8, 2010, *available at* http://hlpronline.com/2010/04/johnson_commonuse/ (courts should apply a "functional commonality" approach, in which guns are protected if they are similar in ballistic energy, ammunition feeding mechanism, and similar criteria to other guns that are considered protected); Michael O'Shea, *The Right to Defensive Arms After* District of Columbia v. Heller, 111 W. Va. L. Rev. 349, 384-93 (2009) (courts should use readily verifiable, objective standards, such as which types of defensive weapons are, in fact, most commonly purchased by law-abiding individuals and/or police departments).

25. In Part III, the Court states that nothing in the opinion should cast doubt on longstanding prohibitions on firearms possession by felons, the mentally ill, etc. Complaining that the Court offers no standard for deciding future cases, Justice Breyer criticizes: "Why these? Is it that similar restrictions existed in the late 18th century? The Majority fails to cite any colonial analogues." Professor Lund also has criticized the list of permissible controls as particularly poor originalism. Lund, *supra*. While prohibitions on recently released violent felons possessing handguns became common in the 1930s, lifetime firearms prohibition for all felonies dates back only to the federal Gun Control Act of 1968. *See* Kevin C. Marshall, *Why Can't Martha Stewart Have a Gun?*, 32 Harv. J.L. & Pub. Pol'y 695 (2009). What sort of constitutional methodology sustains the lifetime ban on gun possession by felons? The Comment at the end of this chapter suggests a variety of interpretive methodologies that seem to be at work in *Heller*. Read the Comment and then consider whether the classification of the lifetime ban for felons as presumptively permissible is just a policy-oriented and loose version of living constitutionalism. Or of the tradition and history approach? Of Justice Kennedy's "emerging awareness" approach *infra*? Or can lifetime bans on felons be justified through modern analogies to Founding Era practices of disarming persons who were considered potentially dangerous, such as slaves or Tories? For an argument in favor of the latter theory, see Adam Winkler, Gunfight (2011).

26. In Part IV, the Court focuses on the particular utility of handguns for self-defense. Justice Breyer's dissent highlights that most gun crime is committed with handguns. Professor Johnson argues that the portability and other characteristics that make the handgun a good tool for self-defense are the same things that make it useful for committing crimes. Depending on the standard the Court adopts for resolving close cases, this "regulatory paradox" may impose significant limitations on the power to regulate firearms. *See* Nicholas J. Johnson, *Supply Restrictions at the Margins of* Heller *and the*

Abortion Analogue: Stenberg *Principles, Assault Weapons, and the Attitudinalist Critique,* 60 Hastings L.J. 1285 (2009).

To conserve space, we have omitted the Justices' discussion of the social science about guns and gun control. Justice Breyer addressed these issues at length, concluding that because there were studies in support of both sides of the issue the Court should defer to the D.C. City Council's judgment. Chapters 10 and 11 address social science, and online Chapter 12 examines it in depth.

27. The majority criticizes Justice Breyer's interest-balancing approach, which seemingly would permit jurisdictions to decide that handguns were too dangerous to tolerate: "We know of no other enumerated constitutional right whose core protection has been subjected to a freestanding interest balancing approach." Is this accurate? Do the strict scrutiny and rational basis standards applied in other contexts involve interest balancing? *See* Joseph Blocher, *Categoricalism and Balancing in First and Second Amendment Analysis,* 84 N.Y.U. L. Rev. 375, 439 (2009). Is Justice Breyer's interest balancing just another way of denying Second Amendment protection to handguns? Is there any sort of gun or type of gun ownership that his standard would protect against a legislative judgment that prohibition is the best policy?

28. *Heller* has been criticized for leaving many questions unanswered. The majority argues that the same was true when the first free-exercise-of-religion case was decided under the First Amendment in 1879. How powerful is the criticism that *Heller* leaves many things unsettled? Would statements beyond those necessary to resolve the case be properly construed as dicta? Compare your assessment with your answer to the same question about the lower court opinions (elaborating on *Miller*) discussed in Chapter 8.A.

29. In the district and circuit court, the *Heller* case was designated *Parker v. District of Columbia,* 478 F.3d 370 (2007); 311 F. Supp. 2d 103. Shelly Parker is a black woman who was threatened and besieged by local drug dealers and users in retaliation for her community activism (calling police and organizing block watches). *See* Robert A. Levy, *A Woman's Right: One Woman's Fight to Bear Arms,* Nat'l Rev. Online, http://old.nationalreview.com/comment/comment-levy042403.asp Apr. 24, 2003. Another plaintiff, Tom Palmer, was a Cato Institute scholar who, when living in California, had used a firearm to save himself from a murderous gay-bashing gang of attackers. The plaintiff in *McDonald v. Chicago, infra,* was a 76-year-old black army veteran. The neighborhood where he bought a home in 1970 had declined and became dominated by drug dealers and gangs. Otis McDonald expressed his desire for a handgun this way: "I'm 76 years old. Yes, I own long guns . . . but how long do you think it will take me to get up, get out of bed, and get my hands on a shotgun if someone is breaking in through the bedroom window?" Massad Ayoob, *Meet Otis McDonald* Backwoods Home Magazine (Mar. 17, 2010), http://backwoodshome.com/blogs/MassadAyoob/2010/03/17/meet-otis-mcdonald; Colleen Mastony, *The Public Face of Gun Rights,* Chi. Trib., Jan. 30, 2010, at 1. Do you think

Otis McDonald, Tom Palmer, and Shelly Parker represent the views of most members of their communities on this issue? Should they? Do their "communities" consist of people who share the same race or sexual orientation?

30. The Court says "[t]he phrase 'security of a free state' meant 'security of a free polity,' not security of each of the several States." Do you find this argument convincing? Hypothesize that the Second Amendment's objective of "a free State" meant "a state which belongs to the Union." How would the different meaning of "state" change the legal effect of the Second Amendment? Can a state government be "secure" or "free" government if the federal government prohibits the state's citizens from using firearms for self-defense? From owning handguns? What if the prohibition were imposed by the state government? The argument that "a free state" means "a state of the Union" was offered by the dissenting opinion in *Parker v. District of Columbia* (D.C. Cir. 2007), *supra*, which became *Heller* on appeal. Responding to the dissent, Professor Eugene Volokh argues that in usage of the Founding Era, "a free state" meant a free society. Eugene Volokh, "*Necessary to the Security of a Free State*," 83 Notre Dame L. Rev. 1 (2007).

31. Justice Stevens states that *Presser* confirmed that "nothing in the Constitution protected the use of arms outside the context of a militia 'authorized by law' and organized by the State or Federal Government." Does this necessarily mean that private firearms can be banned? Might even a militia-centric understanding of the Second Amendment protect arms ownership by persons who are not part of an "organized" militia but who are defined by law as belonging to the unorganized militia? Consider, for example, 10 U.S.C. §311, defining the unorganized militia to include most able-bodied males aged 18 to 45. Consider also the many state constitutions and statutes that define state militias to include most able-bodied adult males.

32. Is Justice Breyer correct that the District's laws imposed no significant burden on militia-related firearms use, since a D.C. resident can travel to a shooting range in Virginia or Maryland, and rent a gun there to shoot at the range? Is militia-related firearms use "significantly burdened" by effective prohibition on homebound activities like cleaning, disassembly, and "dry firing" (practice with an unloaded gun)?

33. Justice Breyer argues, "[B]ecause I see nothing in the District law that would preclude the existence of a background common-law self-defense exception, I would avoid the constitutional question by interpreting the statute to include it." This is contrary to pre-*Heller* enforcement of the law, which did not allow a self-defense exception. *See* Joint Appendix at 70a, 86a-90a District of Columbia v. Heller, 554 U.S. 570 (2008) (No. 07-290) (District of Columbia affirming that "Defendants prohibit the possession of lawfully owned firearms for self-defense within the home, even in instances when self-defense would be lawful by other means under District

of Columbia law."); *see also McIntosh v. Washington*, 395 A.2d 744, 754-56 (D.C. 1978) (holding that it was not an equal protection violation to allow business owners to use registered guns for self-defense, while banning self-defense in the home).

34. At oral argument, Chief Justice John Roberts stated that mandatory trigger locks made self-defense impractical, since removing a lock at night during a home invasion would be difficult and time consuming. Do you agree? How would one test this? Is it appropriate for judges to rely on their own common sense and experience in addressing factual questions like this, or should they insist on formal empirical testing?

35. Justice Breyer states that "subsequent development of modern urban police departments, by diminishing the need to keep loaded guns nearby in case of intruders, would have moved any such right even further away from the heart of the amendment's more basic protective ends." Does this adequately account for the fact that police do not have an obligation to protect any given individual from criminal harm? *DeShaney v. Winnebago County*, 489 U.S. 189 (1989) (government inaction in rescuing child who was known to be severely abused, and was later murdered); *Riss v. City of New York*, 240 N.E.2d 860 (N.Y. 1958) (stalker who attacked and disfigured his victim; dissent notes that Miss Riss was prevented from carrying a gun in public by New York law).

    Would you favor imposing an affirmative obligation on state and local governments to provide police protection? Would you favor holding governments liable for injuries to victims when police failed to protect? Is it reasonable to expect police to interdict most violent crime? Are police now so effective that private firearms are unneeded? Does your answer require assumptions about the utility of private firearms?

36. If, as *Heller* says, "bear arms" really means "carry," does it imply that carrying a handgun must be legal everywhere except in the "sensitive places" described by the Court? Are "sensitive places" the exception that proves the rule, in the same way that gun bans for felons are the exception to the general right to own guns?

37. At the time of the Framing, there were no laws that generally prohibited either the open or concealed carrying of firearms in public places. The majority opinion approvingly cites several nineteenth-century state court cases affirming a right to open carry, but not concealed carry. The opinion also lists bans on concealed carry as among the presumptively constitutional gun controls. How would a right to carry derived from *Heller* mesh with current practices in most states — where licensed concealed carry is common, and open carry is rare? Can a state comply with the Second Amendment right to "bear" arms by banning open carry, while allowing licensed concealed carry or vice versa?

    Review the comment on methods of constitutional interpretation at the end of this chapter. Does the right-to-bear-arms question demand assessment of the Second Amendment as part of a "living Constitution," in which "traditions" about the approved method of carry are malleable? What else about the Second Amendment could change from one century to another? What current trends in state gun laws might become part of the "tradition" or "emerging awareness" of the Second Amendment?

38. What does the Court mean when it describes some gun controls as "presumptively lawful regulatory measures"? Does this mean that such measures are presumed to be constitutional, but a particular litigant might provide sufficient evidence to overcome the presumption? Does "presumptively lawful" really mean "conclusively lawful," and therefore all such laws are necessarily constitutional? Chapter 11 shows how lower courts have addressed this question, with many of them taking the "conclusively lawful" approach.

39. What might account for the Court granting certiorari in *Heller*, but not in *Emerson* (Chapter 8) or *Silveira* (Chapter 8)? Cass Sunstein suggests it is essentially the same reason the Court tackled K-12 school segregation in 1954, rather than in 1945 or 1933: *Brown v. Board of Education* and *District of Columbia v. Heller* were both the products of a mature movement that had over decades of work convinced the national majority (and the national elites) of the justice of their cause, and the legitimacy of their constitutional vision. Cass Sunstein, *Second Amendment Minimalism:* Heller *as* Griswold, 122 Harv. L. Rev. 248 (2008). Sunstein suggests that this is one way in which *Heller* can be considered more of an expression of living constitutionalism than of originalism.

40. CQ: The *Heller* majority did not explicitly articulate a standard of review. But is the case entirely devoid of guidance about the standard of review? Can courts take a leaf from First Amendment jurisprudence and apply strict scrutiny to some laws (e.g., for the First Amendment, most restrictions on the content of speech), and intermediate scrutiny for others (e.g., "time, place, and manner" controls on speech in public places). What types of Second Amendment laws should trigger strict scrutiny, and which should be subject to intermediate scrutiny? This is the approach of the Seventh Circuit's decision in *Ezell v. City of Chicago*, 651 F.3d 684 (7th Cir. 2011) (Chapter 11).

B. The Supreme Court Incorporates the Right to Keep and Bear Arms Against the States

Heller decided that the Second Amendment established an individual right to arms that restrained the federal government. It did not decide whether the right also applied to the states. That question would require a challenge to a state or local gun ban.

Two lawsuits challenging the City of Chicago's handgun ban were filed within 48 hours of the Supreme Court's decision in *District of Columbia v. Heller*. The first suit was brought by Alan Gura, the winning attorney from *Heller*, on behalf of Otis McDonald, two other individuals, the Second Amendment Foundation, and the Illinois State Rifle Association. The National Rifle Association (NRA) also sued Chicago and sued or threatened to sue all five of the Chicago suburbs that had enacted handgun bans. All of the suburbs except Oak Park repealed their bans in 2008. In the Seventh Circuit, all the cases were consolidated, and the Seventh Circuit ruled 3-0 in favor of Chicago and Oak Park.

The Chicago litigation was entirely predictable. The cleanest test of whether the Second Amendment applied to the states would be a challenge to a *Heller*-style gun ban. Chicago was one of the few places in the country that banned handguns. No states and no municipalities beyond Chicagoland imposed gun restrictions similar to the overturned Washington, D.C. law. This was partly because of preemption in 49 states. These preemption laws typically mandate uniform state gun laws and prohibit separate municipal gun controls. A minority of preemption laws leave some room for local gun controls, but none of them allow bans on any of three major classes of firearms: handguns, rifles, and shotguns. These preemption laws became especially popular after the U.S. Supreme Court denied certiorari in *Quilici v. Morton Grove*, 695 F.2d 261 (7th Cir. 1982), where the Seventh Circuit ruled that Morton Grove's handgun ban did not violate the Second Amendment.

Illinois statewide preemption laws are among the very weakest, and do not outlaw local gun bans. In the 1980s, Chicago and five of its suburbs enacted handgun bans very similar to the one overturned in *Heller*. When plaintiffs filed lawsuits challenging these local laws, four of the suburbs decided to repeal their gun bans rather than litigate. But the City of Chicago and its suburb of Oak Park chose to fight all the way to the Supreme Court.

The NRA and Alan Gura petitioned separately for certiorari, emphasizing different theories for applying the Second Amendment to the states. Gura relied mainly on the Privileges or Immunities Clause of the Fourteenth Amendment, while briefly arguing in the alternative for Due Process incorporation. The NRA relied mainly on the now-standard methodology of selective incorporation via the Due Process Clause of the Fourteenth Amendment, and made the Privileges or Immunities argument in the alternative. The Court granted certiorari in *McDonald v. Chicago*, 130 S. Ct. 48 (2009), asking for briefing on both the Privileges or Immunities and Due Process arguments. The Court then admitted the NRA and Oak Park into the case. As a result, both the NRA and Oak Park gained the right to file briefs as parties, rather than as amici. Oak Park participated in the filing of a joint brief with Chicago. The NRA briefed separately. It asked for, and was granted, 10 minutes of Gura's 30-minute oral argument time, in order to present its own argument.

In June of 2010 the Court handed down the decision in *McDonald v. City of Chicago*, which held that the Fourteenth Amendment extends the individual Second Amendment right to arms to prohibit *state* as well as federal infringement. As with almost all Fourteenth Amendment rights, the standards applicable to states apply equally to local governments.

Fourteenth Amendment Background

If you have not previously taken a course that discusses how the Fourteenth Amendment has been used to make most of the Bill of Rights applicable to the states, the material below will help you follow the discussion in *McDonald*.

As detailed in Chapter 6, there were, at the least, many congressmen who intended that putting the Fourteenth Amendment in the Constitution would make the Second Amendment, and the rest of the Bill of Rights, applicable to the states (and therefore to local governments, since local governments derive their power from their states). The clause that was intended to effectuate provides that "[n]o State shall make or enforce any law which shall abridge the privileges or immunities of citizens of the United States."

However, the *Slaughter-House Cases*, 83 U.S. 36 (1873), and *United States v. Cruikshank*, 92 U.S. 542 (1876) (Chapter 6), soon reduced the Privileges or Immunities Clause to a practical nullity. Subsequent cases repeatedly ruled that various parts of the Bill of Rights were not protected by the Privileges or Immunities Clause.

But by the time of *McDonald v. Chicago*, the Supreme Court had developed an entirely different approach to applying portions of the Bill of Rights to the states. Immediately following the Privilege or Immunities Clause, the Fourteenth Amendment provides that "nor shall any State deprive any person of life, liberty, or property, without due process of law." The Court has used this clause for "selective incorporation" of particular provisions of the Bill of Rights. The Court decides whether a particular enumerated right is "fundamental" to the American system of liberty. If so, the right is fully enforceable against the states. E.g., *Duncan v. Louisiana*, 391 U.S. 145 (1968).

In *McDonald*, the four-member plurality led by Justice Alito applies the standard doctrinal tools for selective incorporation, and rules that the Second Amendment is enforceable against the states. Three dissenters, led by Justice Breyer, argue against selective incorporation of the Second Amendment.

Justice Thomas, in a concurring opinion, argues for incorporation via the Privileges or Immunities Clause. He does not join the portion of the plurality opinion that relies on due-process selective incorporation.

Justice Stevens's dissent, which was his final opinion as a Supreme Court Justice, argues for an entirely different approach. He argues that the whole notion of incorporation is mistaken. Instead, the correct approach is for the Court to decide whether any particular aspect of freedom should be directly protected by the Fourteenth Amendment as a form of "liberty." In other words, the reason that states must respect free speech is not because the Fourteenth Amendment makes the First Amendment "freedom of speech" applicable to the states. Rather, free speech is inherently a fundamental right that is inherent in Fourteenth Amendment liberty, and would be protected by the Fourteenth Amendment even if the First Amendment had never been written.

Similarly, suggests Justice Stevens, Fourteenth Amendment liberty may include self-defense and a right to arms for self-defense, even if there had never been a Second Amendment. However, as you will read, Justice Stevens's vision of these liberties is sufficiently flexible to uphold the Chicago handgun ban.

Justice Stevens also argues for return to an approach that the Court often used in the 1940s and 1950s, but which has been almost entirely abandoned since the 1960s: partial incorporation of a right. The lone example of this approach that is valid in current law is the Sixth Amendment right to jury trial. The Court has ruled that states must give jury trials to criminal defendants for all of the same types of prosecutions for which a defendant would be entitled to a jury trial in federal court. However, the Sixth Amendment, as interpreted by the Supreme Court, requires that a conviction in federal court be by a unanimous 12-member jury. Yet for state criminal cases, the Court allows smaller juries, or nonunanimous verdicts of 10-2 or 11-1.

The Court never used partial incorporation for any parts of the First Amendment, but did use partial incorporation for some of the criminal-investigation and prosecution Amendments. During the 1960s, the Court adopted "jot-for-jot" complete incorporation of all rights, so that the right would impose identical constraints on the federal and state governments (except for Sixth Amendment jury trials).

Thus, the *McDonald* opinions, besides being important as constitutional analysis of the right to arms, are also quite important to the general doctrine of the Fourteenth Amendment, illustrating the standard modern approach, and also providing two quite different alternative approaches.

McDonald v. City of Chicago
130 S. Ct. 3020 (2010)

JUSTICE ALITO announced the judgment of the Court and delivered the opinion of the Court with respect to Parts I, II-A, II-B, II-D, III-A, and III-B, in which THE CHIEF JUSTICE, JUSTICE SCALIA, JUSTICE KENNEDY, and JUSTICE THOMAS join, and an opinion with respect to Parts II-C, IV, and V, in which THE CHIEF JUSTICE, JUSTICE SCALIA, and JUSTICE KENNEDY join.

Two years ago, in *District of Columbia v. Heller*, 128 S. Ct. 2873 (2008), we held that the Second Amendment protects the right to keep and bear arms for the purpose of self-defense, and we struck down a District of Columbia law that banned the possession of handguns in the home. The city of Chicago (City) and the village of Oak Park, a Chicago suburb, have laws that are similar to the District of Columbia's, but Chicago and Oak Park argue that their laws are constitutional because the Second Amendment has no application to the States. . . . Applying the standard that is well established in our case law, we hold that the Second Amendment right is fully applicable to the States.

I

[Petitioner] Chicago residents . . . would like to keep handguns in their homes for self-defense but are prohibited from doing so by Chicago's firearms laws. A City ordinance provides that "[n]o person shall . . . possess . . . any firearm unless such person is the holder of a valid registration certificate for such firearm." . . . The Code then prohibits registration of most handguns, thus effectively banning handgun possession by almost all private citizens. . . . Like Chicago, Oak Park makes it "unlawful for any person to possess . . . any fire-arm," a term that includes "pistols, revolvers, guns and small arms . . . commonly known as handguns." . . .

Chicago enacted its handgun ban to protect its residents "from the loss of property and injury or death from firearms." . . . The Chicago petitioners and their *amici,* however, argue that the handgun ban has left them vulnerable to criminals. Chicago Police Department statistics, we are told, reveal that the City's handgun murder rate has actually increased since the ban was enacted and that Chicago residents now face one of the highest murder rates in the country and rates of other violent crimes that exceed the average in comparable cities.

Several of the Chicago petitioners have been the targets of threats and violence. For instance, Otis McDonald . . . is a community activist involved with alternative policing strategies, and his efforts to improve his neighborhood have subjected him to violent threats from drug dealers. . . .

The District Court rejected plaintiffs' argument that the Chicago and Oak Park laws are unconstitutional. . . .

The Seventh Circuit affirmed, relying on three 19th-century cases — *United States v. Cruikshank,* 92 U.S. 542 (1876), *Presser v. Illinois,* 116 U.S. 252 (1886), and *Miller v. Texas,* 153 U.S. 535 (1894) — that were decided in the wake of this Court's interpretation of the Privileges or Immunities Clause of the Fourteenth Amendment in the *Slaughter-House Cases,* 83 U.S. (16 Wall.) 36 (1873). The Seventh Circuit described the rationale of those cases as "defunct" and recognized that they did not consider the question whether the Fourteenth Amendment's Due Process Clause incorporates the Second Amendment right to keep and bear arms. *NRA, Inc. v. Chicago,* 567 F.3d 856, 857, 858 (2009). Nevertheless, the Seventh Circuit observed that it was obligated to follow Supreme Court precedents that have "direct application," and it declined to predict how the Second Amendment would fare under this Court's modern "selective incorporation" approach. *Id.* at 857-58 (internal quotation marks omitted).

We granted certiorari. . . .

II

A

Petitioners argue that the Chicago and Oak Park laws violate the right to keep and bear arms for two reasons. Petitioners' primary submission is that this right is among the "privileges or immunities of citizens of the United States" and that the narrow interpretation of the Privileges or Immunities Clause adopted in the *Slaughter-House Cases, supra,* should now be rejected. As a secondary argument, petitioners contend that the Fourteenth Amendment's Due Process Clause "incorporates" the Second Amendment right.

Chicago and Oak Park (municipal respondents) maintain that a right set out in the Bill of Rights applies to the States only if that right is an indispensable attribute of *any* "'civilized'" legal system. If it is possible to imagine a civilized country that does not recognize the right, the municipal respondents tell us, then that right is not protected by due process. And since there are civilized countries that ban or strictly regulate the private possession of handguns, the municipal respondents maintain that due process does not preclude such measures. . . .

B

The Bill of Rights, including the Second Amendment, originally applied only to the Federal Government. [*Barron ex rel. Tiernan v. Mayor of Baltimore,* 32 U.S. (7 Pet.) 243 (1833).] . . .

The constitutional Amendments adopted in the aftermath of the Civil War fundamentally altered our country's federal system. The provision at issue in this case, §1 of the Fourteenth Amendment, provides, among other things, that a State may not abridge "the privileges or immunities of citizens of the United States" or deprive "any person of life, liberty, or property, without due process of law."

Four years after the adoption of the Fourteenth Amendment, this Court was asked to interpret the Amendment's reference to "the privileges or immunities of citizens of the United States." The *Slaughter-House Cases, supra,* involved challenges to a Louisiana law permitting the creation of a state-sanctioned monopoly on the butchering of animals within the city of New Orleans. Justice Samuel Miller's opinion for the Court concluded that the Privileges or Immunities Clause protects only those rights "which owe their existence to the Federal government, its National character, its Constitution, or its laws." *Id.* at 79. The Court held that other fundamental rights — rights that predated the creation of the Federal Government and that "the State governments were created to establish and secure" — were not protected by the Clause. *Id.* at 76.

In drawing a sharp distinction between the rights of federal and state citizenship, the Court [held that] . . .

. . . the Privileges or Immunities Clause protects such things as the right

"to come to the seat of government to assert any claim [a citizen] may have upon that government, to transact any business he may have with it, to seek its protection, to share its offices, to engage in administering its functions . . . [and to] become a citizen of any State of the Union by a *bonafide* residence therein, with the same rights as other citizens of that State." *Id.* at 79-80 (internal quotation marks omitted).

Finding no constitutional protection against state intrusion of the kind envisioned by the Louisiana statute, the Court upheld the statute. Four Justices dissented. Justice Field, joined by Chief Justice Chase and Justices Swayne and Bradley, criticized the majority for reducing the Fourteenth Amendment's Privileges or Immunities Clause to "a vain and idle enactment, which accomplished nothing, and most unnecessarily excited Congress and the people on its passage." *Id.* at 96. . . .

C

. . . We see no need to reconsider [*Slaughter-House Cases'*] interpretation here. For many decades, the question of the rights protected by the Fourteenth

Amendment against state infringement has been analyzed under the Due Process Clause of that Amendment. . . .

At the same time, however, this Court's decisions in *Cruikshank, Presser,* and *Miller* do not preclude us from considering whether the Due Process Clause of the Fourteenth Amendment makes the Second Amendment right binding on the States. . . . *Cruikshank, Presser,* and *Miller* all preceded the era in which the Court began the process of "selective incorporation" under the Due Process Clause, and we have never previously addressed the question whether the right to keep and bear arms applies to the States under that theory.

Indeed, *Cruikshank* has not prevented us from holding that other rights that were at issue in that case are binding on the States through the Due Process Clause. In *Cruikshank,* the Court held that the general "right of the people peaceably to assemble for lawful purposes," which is protected by the First Amendment, applied only against the Federal Government and not against the States. See 92 U.S. at 551-52. Nonetheless, over 60 years later the Court held that the right of peaceful assembly was a "fundamental righ[t] . . . safeguarded by the due process clause of the Fourteenth Amendment." *De Jonge v. Oregon,* 299 U.S. 353, 364 (1937). We follow the same path here and thus consider whether the right to keep and bear arms applies to the States under the Due Process Clause.

D

1

In the late 19th century, the Court began to consider whether the Due Process Clause prohibits the States from infringing rights set out in the Bill of Rights. See *Hurtado v. California,* 110 U.S. 516 (1884) (due process does not require grand jury indictment); *Chicago, B. & Q.R. Co. v. Chicago,* 166 U.S. 226 (1897) (due process prohibits States from taking of private property for public use without just compensation). Five features of the approach taken during the ensuing era should be noted.

First, the Court viewed the due process question as entirely separate from the question whether a right was a privilege or immunity of national citizenship. See *Twining v. New Jersey,* 211 U.S. 78, 99 (1908).

Second, the Court explained that the only rights protected against state infringement by the Due Process Clause were those rights "of such a nature that they are included in the conception of due process of law." . . . While it was "possible that some of the personal rights safeguarded by the first eight Amendments against National action [might] also be safeguarded against state action," the Court stated, this was "not because those rights are enumerated in the first eight Amendments." *Twining, supra,* at 99.

The Court used different formulations in describing the boundaries of due process. For example, in *Twining,* the Court referred to "immutable principles of justice which inhere in the very idea of free government which no member of the Union may disregard." 211 U.S. at 102 (internal quotation marks omitted). In *Snyder v. Massachusetts,* 291 U.S. 97, 105 (1934), the Court spoke of rights that are "so rooted in the traditions and conscience of our people as to be ranked as fundamental." And in *Palko v. Connecticut,* the Court famously said that due process protects those rights that are "the very essence of a scheme of ordered liberty" and essential to "a fair and enlightened system of justice." 302 U.S. 319, 325 (1937).

Third, in some cases decided during this era the Court "can be seen as having asked, when inquiring into whether some particular procedural safeguard was required of a State, if a civilized system could be imagined that would not accord the particular protection." *Duncan v. Louisiana,* 391 U.S. 145, 149, n.14 (1968). . . .

Fourth, the Court during this era was not hesitant to hold that a right set out in the Bill of Rights failed to meet the test for inclusion within the protection of the Due Process Clause. The Court found that some such rights qualified. See, *e.g., Gitlow v. New York,* 268 U.S. 652, 666 (1925) (freedom of speech and press); . . . *Powell, supra* (assistance of counsel in capital cases); *De Jonge, supra* (freedom of assembly); *Cantwell v. Connecticut,* 310 U.S. 296 (1940) (free exercise of religion). But others did not. See, *e.g., Hurtado, supra* (grand jury indictment requirement); *Twining, supra* (privilege against self-incrimination).

Finally, even when a right set out in the Bill of Rights was held to fall within the conception of due process, the protection or remedies afforded against state infringement sometimes differed from the protection or remedies provided against abridgment by the Federal Government. . . .

2

An alternative theory regarding the relationship between the Bill of Rights and §1 of the Fourteenth Amendment was championed by Justice Black. This theory held that §1 of the Fourteenth Amendment totally incorporated all of the provisions of the Bill of Rights. See, *e.g., Adamson, supra,* at 71-72 (Black, J., dissenting); *Duncan, supra,* at 166 (Black, J., concurring). As Justice Black noted, the chief congressional proponents of the Fourteenth Amendment espoused the view that the Amendment made the Bill of Rights applicable to the States and, in so doing, overruled this Court's decision in *Barron.*[9] *Adamson,*

---

9. Senator Jacob Howard, who spoke on behalf of the Joint Committee on Reconstruction and sponsored the Amendment in the Senate, stated that the Amendment protected all of "the personal rights guarantied and secured by the first eight amendments of the Constitution." Cong. Globe, 39th Cong., 1st Sess., 2765 (1866) (hereinafter 39th Cong. Globe). Representative John Bingham, the principal author of the text of §1, said that the Amendment would "arm the Congress . . . with the power to enforce the bill of rights as it stands in the Constitution today." *Id.* at 1088; see also *id.,* at 1089-90; A. Amar, The Bill of Rights: Creation and Reconstruction 183 (1998) (hereinafter Amar, Bill of Rights). After ratification of the Amendment, Bingham maintained the view that the rights guaranteed by §1 of the Fourteenth Amendment "are chiefly defined in the first eight amendments to the Constitution of the United States." Cong. Globe, 42d Cong., 1st Sess., App. 84 (1871). Finally, Representative Thaddeus Stevens, the political leader of the House and acting chairman of the Joint Committee on Reconstruction, stated during the debates on the Amendment that "the Constitution limits only the action of Congress, and is not a limitation on the States. This amendment supplies that defect, and allows Congress to correct the unjust legislation of the States." 39th Cong. Globe 2459; see also M. Curtis, No State Shall Abridge: The Fourteenth Amendment and the Bill of Rights 112 (1986) (counting at least 30 statements during the debates in Congress interpreting §1 to incorporate the Bill of Rights); Brief for Constitutional Law Professors as Amici Curiae 20 (collecting authorities and stating that

332 U.S. at 72 (dissenting opinion). Nonetheless, the Court never has embraced Justice Black's "total incorporation" theory.

3

While Justice Black's theory was never adopted, the Court eventually moved in that direction by initiating what has been called a process of "selective incorporation," *i.e.*, the Court began to hold that the Due Process Clause fully incorporates particular rights contained in the first eight Amendments. . . .

The decisions during this time abandoned three of the previously noted characteristics of the earlier period. The Court made it clear that the governing standard is . . . fundamental to *our* scheme of ordered liberty and system of justice. *Id.* at 149 and n.14. . . .

The Court also shed any reluctance to hold that rights guaranteed by the Bill of Rights met the requirements for protection under the Due Process Clause. The Court eventually incorporated almost all of the provisions of the Bill of Rights.[12] Only a handful of the Bill of Rights protections remain unincorporated.[13]

"[n]ot a single senator or representative disputed [the incorporationist] understanding" of the Fourteenth Amendment).

12. With respect to the First Amendment, see *Everson v. Board of Ed. of Ewing*, 330 U.S. 1 (1947) (Establishment Clause); *Cantwell v. Connecticut*, 310 U.S. 296 (1940) (Free Exercise Clause); *De Jonge v. Oregon*, 299 U.S. 353 (1937) (freedom of assembly); *Gitlow v. New York*, 268 U.S. 652 (1925) (free speech); *Near v. Minnesota ex rel. Olson*, 283 U.S. 697 (1931) (freedom of the press).

With respect to the Fourth Amendment, see *Aguilar v. Texas*, 378 U.S. 108 (1964) (warrant requirement); *Mapp v. Ohio*, 367 U.S. 643 (1961) (exclusionary rule); *Wolf v. Colorado*, 338 U.S. 25 (1949) (freedom from unreasonable searches and seizures).

With respect to the Fifth Amendment, see *Benton v. Maryland*, 395 U.S. 784 (1969) (Double Jeopardy Clause); *Malloy v. Hogan*, 378 U.S. 1 (1964) (privilege against self-incrimination); *Chicago, B. & Q.R. Co. v. Chicago*, 166 U.S. 226 (1897) (Just Compensation Clause).

With respect to the Sixth Amendment, see *Duncan v. Louisiana*, 391 U.S. 145 (1968) (trial by jury in criminal cases); *Washington v. Texas*, 388 U.S. 14 (1967) (compulsory process); *Klopfer v. North Carolina*, 386 U.S. 213 (1967) (speedy trial); *Pointer v. Texas*, 380 U.S. 400 (1965) (right to confront adverse witness); *Gideon v. Wainwright*, 372 U.S. 335 (1963) (assistance of counsel); *In re Oliver*, 333 U.S. 257 (1948) (right to a public trial).

With respect to the Eighth Amendment, see *Robinson v. California*, 370 U.S. 660 (1962) (cruel and unusual punishment); *Schilb v. Kuebel*, 404 U.S. 357 (1971) (prohibition against excessive bail).

13. In addition to the right to keep and bear arms (and the Sixth Amendment right to a unanimous jury verdict . . .), the only rights not fully incorporated are (1) the Third Amendment's protection against quartering of soldiers; (2) the Fifth Amendment's grand jury indictment requirement; (3) the Seventh Amendment right to a jury trial in civil cases; and (4) the Eighth Amendment's prohibition on excessive fines.

We never have decided whether the Third Amendment or the Eighth Amendment's prohibition of excessive fines applies to the States through the Due Process Clause. See Browning-Ferris Industries of Vt., Inc. v. Kelco Disposal, Inc., 492 U.S. 257, 276, n.22 (1989) (declining to decide whether the excessive-fines protection applies to the States); see also Engblom v. Carey, 677 F.2d 957, 961 (2d Cir. 1982) (holding as a matter of first impression that the "Third Amendment is incorporated into the Fourteenth Amendment for application to the states").

Our governing decisions regarding the Grand Jury Clause of the Fifth Amendment and the Seventh Amendment's civil jury requirement long predate the era of selective incorporation.

Finally, the Court abandoned "the notion that the Fourteenth Amendment applies to the States only a watered-down, subjective version of the individual guarantees of the Bill of Rights," stating that it would be "incongruous" to apply different standards "depending on whether the claim was asserted in a state or federal court." *Malloy,* 378 U.S. at 10-11 (internal quotation marks omitted). . . .

III

With this framework in mind, we now turn directly to the question whether the Second Amendment right to keep and bear arms is incorporated in the concept of due process. In answering that question, as just explained, we must decide whether the right to keep and bear arms is fundamental to *our* scheme of ordered liberty, *Duncan,* 391 U.S. at 149, or as we have said in a related context, whether this right is "deeply rooted in this Nation's history and tradition," *Washington v. Glucksberg,* 521 U.S. 702, 721 (1997) (internal quotation marks omitted).

A

Our decision in *Heller* points unmistakably to the answer. Self-defense is a basic right, recognized by many legal systems from ancient times to the present day, and in *Heller,* we held that individual self-defense is "the *central component*" of the Second Amendment right. 128 S. Ct. at 2801-02. . . .

Heller makes it clear that this right is "deeply rooted in this Nation's history and tradition." *Glucksberg, supra,* at 721 (internal quotation marks omitted). . . .

The right to keep and bear arms was considered . . . fundamental by those who drafted and ratified the Bill of Rights. "During the 1788 ratification debates, the fear that the federal government would disarm the people in order to impose rule through a standing army or select militia was pervasive in Anti-federalist rhetoric." . . . Federalists responded, not by arguing that the right was insufficiently important to warrant protection but by contending that the right was adequately protected by the Constitution's assignment of only limited powers to the Federal Government. *Heller,* 128 S. Ct. at 2801-02. . . . Thus, Anti-federalists and Federalists alike agreed that the right to bear arms was fundamental to the newly formed system of government. . . . But those who were fearful that the new Federal Government would infringe traditional rights such as the right to keep and bear arms insisted on the adoption of the Bill of Rights as a condition for ratification of the Constitution. This is surely powerful evidence that the right was regarded as fundamental in the sense relevant here.

This understanding persisted in the years immediately following the ratification of the Bill of Rights. In addition to the four States that had adopted Second Amendment analogues before ratification, nine more States adopted state constitutional provisions protecting an individual right to keep and bear arms between 1789 and 1820. *Heller,* 128 S. Ct. at 2802-04. Founding-era legal commentators confirmed the importance of the right to early Americans. St. George Tucker, for example, described the right to keep and bear arms as "the true palladium of liberty" and explained that prohibitions on the right would place liberty "on the brink of destruction." 1 Blackstone's Commentaries, Editor's App. 300 (S. Tucker ed. 1803). . . .

B

1

By the 1850's, the perceived threat that had prompted the inclusion of the Second Amendment in the Bill of Rights—the fear that the National Government would disarm the universal militia—had largely faded as a popular concern, but the right to keep and bear arms was highly valued for purposes of self-defense. . . . Abolitionist authors wrote in support of the right. . . . And when attempts were made to disarm "Free-Soilers" in "Bloody Kansas," Senator Charles Sumner, who later played a leading role in the adoption of the Fourteenth Amendment, proclaimed that "[n]ever was [the rifle] more needed in just self-defense than now in Kansas." The Crime Against Kansas: The Apologies for the Crime: The True Remedy, Speech of Hon. Charles Sumner in the Senate of the United States 64-65 (1856). Indeed, the 1856 Republican Party Platform protested that in Kansas the constitutional rights of the people had been "fraudulently and violently taken from them" and the "right of the people to keep and bear arms" had been "infringed." National Party Platforms 1840-1972, p. 27 (5th ed. 1973).

After the Civil War, many of the over 180,000 African Americans who served in the Union Army returned to the States of the old Confederacy, where systematic efforts were made to disarm them and other blacks. See *Heller*, 128 S. Ct. at 2810. . . . The laws of some States formally prohibited African Americans from possessing firearms. For example, a Mississippi law provided that "no freedman, free negro or mulatto, not in the military service of the United States government, and not licensed so to do by the board of police of his or her county, shall keep or carry fire-arms of any kind, or any ammunition, dirk or bowie knife." Certain Offenses of Freedmen, 1865 Miss. Laws p. 165, §1, in 1 Documentary History of Reconstruction 289 (W. Fleming ed. 1950). . . .

Throughout the South, armed parties, often consisting of ex-Confederate soldiers serving in the state militias, forcibly took firearms from newly freed slaves. . . .

Union Army commanders took steps to secure the right of all citizens to keep and bear arms, but the 39th Congress concluded that legislative action was necessary. Its efforts to safeguard the right to keep and bear arms demonstrate that the right was still recognized to be fundamental.

The most explicit evidence of Congress' aim appears in §14 of the Freedmen's Bureau Act of 1866, which provided that "the right . . . to have full and equal benefit of all laws and proceedings concerning personal liberty, personal security, and the acquisition, enjoyment, and disposition of estate, real and personal, *including the constitutional right to bear arms,* shall be secured to and enjoyed by all the citizens . . . without respect to race or color, or previous condition of slavery." 14 Stat. 176-77 (emphasis added). Section 14 thus explicitly guaranteed that "all the citizens," black and white, would have "the constitutional right to bear arms."

The Civil Rights Act of 1866, 14 Stat. 27, which was considered at the same time as the Freedmen's Bureau Act, similarly sought to protect the right of all citizens to keep and bear arms. Section 1 of the Civil Rights Act guaranteed the "full and equal benefit of all laws and proceedings for the security of person and property, as is enjoyed by white citizens." *Id.* This language was virtually identical to language in §14 of the Freedmen's Bureau Act, 14 Stat. 176-77 ("the right . . . to have full and equal benefit of all laws and proceedings concerning personal liberty, personal security, and the acquisition, enjoyment, and disposition of estate, real and personal"). And as noted, the latter provision went on to explain that one of the "laws and proceedings concerning personal liberty, personal security, and the acquisition, enjoyment, and disposition of estate, real and personal" was "the constitutional right to bear arms." *Id.* Representative Bingham believed that the Civil Rights Act protected the same rights as enumerated in the Freedmen's Bureau bill, which of course explicitly mentioned the right to keep and bear arms. 39th Cong. Globe 1292. The unavoidable conclusion is that the Civil Rights Act, like the Freedmen's Bureau Act, aimed to protect "the constitutional right to bear arms" and not simply to prohibit discrimination. . . .

Congress, however, ultimately deemed these legislative remedies insufficient. Southern resistance, Presidential vetoes, and this Court's pre-Civil War precedent persuaded Congress that a constitutional amendment was necessary to provide full protection for the rights of blacks. Today, it is generally accepted that the Fourteenth Amendment was understood to provide a constitutional basis for protecting the rights set out in the Civil Rights Act of 1866. *See General Building Contractors Assn., Inc. v. Pennsylvania,* 458 U.S. 375, 389 (1982). . . .

In debating the Fourteenth Amendment, the 39th Congress referred to the right to keep and bear arms as a fundamental right deserving of protection. Senator Samuel Pomeroy described three "indispensable" "safeguards of liberty under our form of Government." 39th Cong. Globe 1182. One of these, he said, was the right to keep and bear arms:

> "Every man . . . should have the right to bear arms for the defense of himself and family and his homestead. And if the cabin door of the freedman is broken open and the intruder enters for purposes as vile as were known to slavery, then should a well-loaded musket be in the hand of the occupant to send the polluted wretch to another world, where his wretchedness will forever remain complete." *Id.*

Even those who thought the Fourteenth Amendment unnecessary believed that blacks, as citizens, "have equal right to protection, and to keep and bear arms for self-defense." *Id.* at 1073 (Sen. James Nye). . . .[25]

---

25. Other Members of the 39th Congress stressed the importance of the right to keep and bear arms in discussing other measures. In speaking generally on reconstruction, Representative Roswell Hart listed the "'right of the people to keep and bear arms'" as among those rights necessary to a "republican form of government." 39th Cong. Globe 1629. Similarly, in objecting to a bill designed to disarm southern militias, Senator Willard Saulsbury argued that such a measure would violate the Second Amendment. Id. at 914-15. Indeed, the bill "ultimately passed in a form that disbanded militias but maintained the right of individuals to their private firearms." Cramer, "This Right is Not Allowed by Governments That Are Afraid of The People": The Public Meaning of the Second Amendment When the Fourteenth Amendment was Ratified, 17 Geo. Mason L. Rev. 823, 858 (2010).

Evidence from the period immediately following the ratification of the Fourteenth Amendment only confirms that the right to keep and bear arms was considered fundamental. In an 1868 speech addressing the disarmament of freedmen, Representative Stevens emphasized the necessity of the right: "Disarm a community and you rob them of the means of defending life. Take away their weapons of defense and you take away the inalienable right of defending liberty." "The fourteenth amendment, now so happily adopted, settles the whole question." Cong. Globe, 40th Cong., 2d Sess., 1967. And in debating the Civil Rights Act of 1871, Congress routinely referred to the right to keep and bear arms and decried the continued disarmament of blacks in the South. S. Halbrook, Freedmen, The Fourteenth Amendment, and The Right to Bear Arms, 1866-1876, pp. 120-21 (1998). Finally, legal commentators from the period emphasized the fundamental nature of the right. See, e.g., T. Farrar, Manual of the Constitution of the United States of America §118, p. 145 (1867) (reprint 1993); J. Pomeroy, An Introduction to the Constitutional Law of the United States §239, pp. 152-53 (3d ed. 1875).

The right to keep and bear arms was also widely protected by state constitutions at the time when the Fourteenth Amendment was ratified. In 1868, 22 of the 37 States in the Union had state constitutional provisions explicitly protecting the right to keep and bear arms. [*See* Chapter 6.F.] Quite a few of these state constitutional guarantees, moreover, explicitly protected the right to keep and bear arms as an individual right to self-defense. [*See* Chapter 6.F.] What is more, state constitutions adopted during the Reconstruction era by former Confederate States included a right to keep and bear arms. [*See* Chapter 6.F.] A clear majority of the States in 1868, therefore, recognized the right to keep and bear arms as being among the foundational rights necessary to our system of Government.

In sum, it is clear that the Framers and ratifiers of the Fourteenth Amendment counted the right to keep and bear arms among those fundamental rights necessary to our system of ordered liberty.

2

Despite all this evidence, municipal respondents contend that Congress, in the years immediately following the Civil War, merely sought to outlaw "discriminatory measures taken against freedmen, which it addressed by adopting a non-discrimination principle" and that even an outright ban on the possession of firearms was regarded as acceptable, "so long as it was not done in a discriminatory manner." . . .

First, while §1 of the Fourteenth Amendment contains "an antidiscrimination rule," namely, the Equal Protection Clause, municipal respondents can hardly mean that §1 does no more than prohibit discrimination. If that were so, then the First Amendment, as applied to the States, would not prohibit nondiscriminatory abridgments of the rights to freedom of speech or freedom of religion; the Fourth Amendment, as applied to the States, would not prohibit all unreasonable searches and seizures but only discriminatory searches and seizures — and so on. We assume that this is not municipal respondents' view, so what they must mean is that the Second Amendment should be singled out for special — and specially unfavorable — treatment. We reject that suggestion.

Second, municipal respondents' argument ignores the clear terms of the Freedmen's Bureau Act of 1866, which acknowledged the existence of the right to bear arms. [It] speaks of and protects "the constitutional right to bear arms," an unmistakable reference to the right protected by the Second Amendment. . . .

Third, if the 39th Congress had outlawed only those laws that discriminate on the basis of race or previous condition of servitude, African Americans in the South would likely have remained vulnerable to attack by many of their worst abusers: the state militia and state peace officers. In the years immediately following the Civil War, a law banning the possession of guns by all private citizens would have been nondiscriminatory only in the formal sense. Any such law — like the Chicago and Oak Park ordinances challenged here — presumably would have permitted the possession of guns by those acting under the authority of the State and would thus have left firearms in the hands of the militia and local peace officers. And . . . those groups were widely involved in harassing blacks in the South. . . .

IV

Municipal respondents' remaining arguments are at war with our central holding in *Heller*: that the Second Amendment protects a personal right to keep and bear arms for lawful purposes, most notably for self-defense within the home. . . .

Municipal respondents' main argument is nothing less than a plea to disregard 50 years of incorporation precedent and return (presumably for this case only) to a bygone era. Municipal respondents submit that the Due Process Clause protects only those rights "'recognized by all temperate and civilized governments, from a deep and universal sense of [their] justice.'" According to municipal respondents, if it is possible to imagine *any* civilized legal system that does not recognize a particular right, then the Due Process Clause does not make that right binding on the States. Therefore, the municipal respondents continue, because such countries as England, Canada, Australia, Japan, Denmark, Finland, Luxembourg, and New Zealand either ban or severely limit handgun ownership, it must follow that no right to possess such weapons is protected by the Fourteenth Amendment.

This line of argument is, of course, inconsistent with the long-established standard we apply in incorporation cases. See *Duncan,* 391 U.S. at 149, and n.14. And the present-day implications of municipal respondents' argument are stunning. For example, many of the rights that our Bill of Rights provides for persons accused of criminal offenses are virtually unique to this country. If *our* understanding of the right to a jury trial, the right against self-incrimination, and the right to counsel were necessary attributes of *any* civilized country, it would follow that the United States is the only civilized Nation in the world. . . .

Municipal respondents maintain that the Second Amendment differs from all of the other provisions of the Bill of Rights because it concerns the right to possess a deadly implement and thus has implications for public safety. And they note that there is intense disagreement on the question whether the private possession of guns in the home increases or decreases gun deaths and injuries.

The right to keep and bear arms, however, is not the only constitutional right that has controversial public safety implications. All of the constitutional provisions that impose restrictions on law enforcement and on the prosecution of crimes fall into the same category. *See, e.g., Hudson v. Michigan,* 547 U.S. 586, 591 (2006) ("The exclusionary rule generates 'substantial social costs,' *United States v. Leon,* 468 U.S. 897, 907 (1984), which sometimes include setting the guilty free and the dangerous at large"); *Barker v. Wingo,* 407 U.S. 514, 522 (1972) (reflecting on the serious consequences of dismissal for a speedy trial violation, which means "a defendant who may be guilty of a serious crime will go free"); *Miranda v. Arizona,* 384 U.S. 436, 517 (1966) (Harlan, J., dissenting); *id.* at 542 (White, J., dissenting) (objecting that the Court's rule "[i]n some unknown number of cases . . . will return a killer, a rapist or other criminal to the streets . . . to repeat his crime"); *Mapp,* 367 U.S., at 659. Municipal respondents cite no case in which we have refrained from holding that a provision of the Bill of Rights is binding on the States on the ground that the right at issue has disputed public safety implications.

We likewise reject municipal respondents' argument that we should depart from our established incorporation methodology on the ground that making the Second Amendment binding on the States and their subdivisions is inconsistent with principles of federalism and will stifle experimentation. Municipal respondents point out — quite correctly — that conditions and problems differ from locality to locality and that citizens in different jurisdictions have divergent views on the issue of gun control. . . .

There is nothing new in the argument that, in order to respect federalism and allow useful state experimentation, a federal constitutional right should not be fully binding on the States. This argument was made repeatedly and eloquently by Members of this Court who rejected the concept of incorporation and urged retention of the two-track approach to incorporation. . . .

Time and again, however, those pleas failed. Unless we turn back the clock or adopt a special incorporation test applicable only to the Second Amendment, municipal respondents' argument must be rejected. Under our precedents, if a Bill of Rights guarantee is fundamental from an American perspective, then, unless *stare decisis* counsels otherwise, that guarantee is fully binding on the States and thus *limits* (but by no means eliminates) their ability to devise solutions to social problems that suit local needs and values. As noted by the 38 States that have appeared in this case as *amici* supporting petitioners, "[s]tate and local experimentation with reasonable firearms regulations will continue under the Second Amendment." . . .

Municipal respondents assert that, although most state constitutions protect firearms rights, state courts have held that these rights are subject to "interest-balancing" and have sustained a variety of restrictions. In *Heller,* however, we expressly rejected the argument that the scope of the Second Amendment right should be determined by judicial interest balancing, 128 S. Ct. at 2820-21, and this Court decades ago abandoned "the notion that the Fourteenth Amendment applies to the States only a watered-down, subjective version of the individual guarantees of the Bill of Rights," *Malloy, supra,* at 10-11 (internal quotation marks omitted).

. . . It is important to keep in mind that *Heller,* while striking down a law that prohibited the possession of handguns in the home, recognized that the right to keep and bear arms is not "a right to keep and carry any weapon whatsoever in any manner whatsoever and for whatever purpose." 128 S. Ct. at 2816. . . . We repeat those assurances here. Despite municipal respondents' doomsday proclamations, incorporation does not imperil every law regulating firearms.

Municipal respondents argue, finally, that the right to keep and bear arms is unique among the rights set out in the first eight Amendments "because the reason for codifying the Second Amendment (to protect the militia) differs from the purpose (primarily, to use firearms to engage in self-defense) that is claimed to make the right implicit in the concept of ordered liberty." Municipal respondents suggest that the Second Amendment right differs from the rights heretofore incorporated because the latter were "valued for [their] own sake." But we have never previously suggested that incorporation of a right turns on whether it has intrinsic as opposed to instrumental value, and quite a few of the rights previously held to be incorporated — for example the right to counsel and the right to confront and subpoena witnesses — are clearly instrumental by any measure. Moreover, this contention repackages one of the chief arguments that we rejected in *Heller, i.e.,* that the scope of the Second Amendment right is defined by the immediate threat that led to the inclusion of that right in the Bill of Rights. In *Heller,* we recognized that the codification of this right was prompted by fear that the Federal Government would disarm and thus disable the militias, but we rejected the suggestion that the right was valued only as a means of preserving the militias. 128 S. Ct. at 2801-02. On the contrary, we stressed that the right was also valued because the possession of firearms was thought to be essential for self-defense. As we put it, self-defense was "the *central component* of the right itself." *Id.*

V . . .

B

Justice Breyer's dissent makes several points to which we briefly respond. To begin, while there is certainly room for disagreement about *Heller*'s analysis of the history of the right to keep and bear arms, nothing written since *Heller* persuades us to reopen the question there decided. Few other questions of original meaning have been as thoroughly explored.

Justice Breyer's conclusion that the Fourteenth Amendment does not incorporate the right to keep and bear arms appears to rest primarily on four factors: First, "there is no popular consensus" that the right is fundamental; second, the right does not protect minorities or persons neglected by those holding political power; third, incorporation of the Second Amendment right would "amount to a significant incursion on a traditional and important area of state concern, altering the constitutional relationship between the States and the Federal Government" and preventing local variations; and fourth, determining the scope of the Second Amendment right in cases involving state and local laws will force judges to answer difficult empirical questions regarding matters that are outside their area of expertise. Even if we believed that these factors were relevant to the incorporation inquiry, none of these factors undermines the case for incorporation of the right to keep and bear arms for self-defense.

First, we have never held that a provision of the Bill of Rights applies to the States only if there is a "popular consensus" that the right is fundamental, and we see no basis for such a rule. But in this case, as it turns out, there is evidence of such a consensus. An *amicus* brief submitted by 58 Members of the Senate and 251 Members of the House of Representatives urges us to hold that the right to keep and bear arms is fundamental. Another brief submitted by 38 States takes the same position.

Second, petitioners and many others who live in high-crime areas dispute the proposition that the Second Amendment right does not protect minorities and those lacking political clout. The plight of Chicagoans living in high-crime areas was recently highlighted when two Illinois legislators representing Chicago districts called on the Governor to deploy the Illinois National Guard to patrol the City's streets. The legislators noted that the number of Chicago homicide victims during the current year equaled the number of American soldiers killed during that same period in Afghanistan and Iraq and that 80% of the Chicago victims were black. *Amici* supporting incorporation of the right to keep and bear arms contend that the right is especially important for women and members of other groups that may be especially vulnerable to violent crime. If, as petitioners believe, their safety and the safety of other law-abiding members of the community would be enhanced by the possession of handguns in the home for self-defense, then the Second Amendment right protects the rights of minorities and other residents of high-crime areas whose needs are not being met by elected public officials.

Third, Justice Breyer is correct that incorporation of the Second Amendment right will to some extent limit the legislative freedom of the States, but this is always true when a Bill of Rights provision is incorporated. . . .

Finally, Justice Breyer is incorrect that incorporation will require judges to assess the costs and benefits of firearms restrictions and thus to make difficult empirical judgments in an area in which they lack expertise. As we have noted, while his opinion in *Heller* recommended an interest-balancing test, the Court specifically rejected that suggestion. . . .

* * *

. . . Unless considerations of *stare decisis* counsel otherwise, a provision of the Bill of Rights that protects a right that is fundamental from an American perspective applies equally to the Federal Government and the States. See *Duncan,* 391 U.S. at 149, and n.14. We therefore hold that the Due Process Clause of the Fourteenth Amendment incorporates the Second Amendment right recognized in *Heller.* . . .

It is so ordered.

JUSTICE SCALIA, concurring.

I join the Court's opinion. Despite my misgivings about Substantive Due Process as an original matter, I have acquiesced in the Court's incorporation of certain guarantees in the Bill of Rights "because it is both long established and narrowly limited." *Albright v. Oliver,* 510 U.S. 266, 275 (1994) (Scalia, J., concurring). This case does not require me to reconsider that view, since straightforward application of settled doctrine suffices to decide it. . . .

II

. . . [Justice Stevens] offers several reasons for concluding that the Second Amendment right to keep and bear arms is not fundamental enough to be applied against the States. None is persuasive. . . .

Justice Stevens begins with the odd assertion that "firearms have a fundamentally ambivalent relationship to liberty," since sometimes they are used to cause (or sometimes accidentally produce) injury to others. The source of the rule that only nonambivalent liberties deserve Due Process protection is never explained. . . . Surely Justice Stevens does not mean that the Clause covers only rights that have *zero* harmful effect on *anyone*. Otherwise even the First Amendment is out. Maybe what he means is that the right to keep and bear arms imposes *too great* a risk to others' physical well-being. But as the plurality explains, other rights we have already held incorporated pose similarly substantial risks to public safety. . . .

Justice Stevens next suggests that the Second Amendment right is not fundamental because it is "different in kind" from other rights we have recognized. In one respect, of course, the right to keep and bear arms *is* different from some other rights we have held the Clause protects and he would recognize: It is deeply grounded in our nation's history and tradition. But Justice Stevens has a different distinction in mind: Even though he does "not doubt for a moment that many Americans . . . see [firearms] as critical to their way of life as well as to their security," he pronounces that owning a handgun is not "critical to leading a life of autonomy, dignity, or political equality." Who says? . . .

No determination of what rights the Constitution of the United States covers would be complete, of course, without a survey of what *other* countries do. When it comes to guns, Justice Stevens explains, our Nation is *already* an outlier among "advanced democracies"; not even our "oldest allies" protect as robust a right as we do, and we should not widen the gap. Never mind that he explains neither which countries qualify as "advanced democracies" nor why others are irrelevant. . . . [T]his follow-the-foreign-crowd requirement would foreclose rights that we have held . . . incorporated, but that other "advanced" nations do not recognize — from the exclusionary rule to the Establishment Clause. . . .

Justice Stevens also argues that since the right to keep and bear arms was *codified* for the purpose of "prevent[ing] elimination of the militia," it should be viewed as "'a federalism provision'" logically incapable of incorporation (quoting *Elk Grove Unified School Dist. v. Newdow,* 542 U.S. 1, 45 (2004) (Thomas, J., concurring in judgment); [(]some internal quotation marks omitted). . . . The opinion Justice Stevens quotes for the "federalism provision" principle, Justice Thomas's concurrence in *Newdow,* argued that incorporation of the Establishment Clause "makes little sense" because that Clause was originally understood as a limit on congressional interference with state establishments of religion. *Id.* at 49-51. Justice Stevens, of course, has no problem with applying the Establishment Clause to the States. . . . While he insists *that* Clause is not a "federalism provision," he does not explain why *it* is not, but the right to keep and bear arms *is* (even though only the latter refers to a "right of the people"). The "federalism" argument prevents the incorporation of only *certain* rights.

Justice Stevens next argues that even if the right to keep and bear arms is "deeply rooted in some important senses," the roots of States' efforts to regulate guns run just as deep. But this too is true of other rights we have held incorporated. No fundamental right — not even the First Amendment — is absolute. The traditional restrictions go to show the scope of the right, not its lack of fundamental character. . . .

Assuming that there is a "plausible constitutional basis" for holding that the right to keep and bear arms is incorporated, [Justice Stevens] asserts that we ought not to do so *for prudential reasons.* Even if we had the authority to withhold rights that are within the Constitution's command (and we assuredly do not), two of the reasons Justice Stevens gives for abstention show just how much power he would hand to judges. The States' "right to experiment" with solutions to the problem of gun violence, he says, is at its apex here because "the best solution is far from clear." That is true of most serious social problems — whether, for example, "the best solution" for rampant crime is to admit confessions unless they are affirmatively shown to have been coerced, but see *Miranda v. Arizona,* 384 U.S. 436, 444-45 (1966), or to permit jurors to impose the death penalty without a requirement that they be free to consider "any relevant mitigating factor," see *Eddings v. Oklahoma,* 455 U.S. 104, 112 (1982), which in turn leads to the conclusion that defense counsel has provided inadequate defense if he has not conducted a "reasonable investigation" into potentially mitigating factors, *see, e.g., Wiggins v. Smith,* 539 U.S. 510, 534 (2003), inquiry into which question tends to destroy any prospect of prompt justice, *see, e.g., Wong v. Belmontes,* 130 S. Ct. 383 (2009) (*per curiam*) (reversing grant of habeas relief for sentencing on a crime committed in 1981). The obviousness of the optimal answer is in the eye of the beholder. The implication of Justice Stevens' call for abstention is that if We The Court conclude that They The People's answers to a problem are silly, we are free to "interven[e]," but if we too are uncertain of the right answer, or merely think the States may be on to something, we can loosen the leash.

A second reason Justice Stevens says we should abstain is that the States have shown they are "capable" of protecting the right at issue, and if anything have protected it too much. That reflects an assumption that judges can distinguish between a *proper* democratic decision to leave things alone (which we should honor), and a case of democratic market failure (which we should step in to correct). I would not — and no judge should — presume to have that sort of omniscience, which seems to me far more "arrogant," than confining courts' focus to our own national heritage. . . .

JUSTICE THOMAS, concurring in part and concurring in the judgment.

I agree with the Court that the Fourteenth Amendment makes the right to keep and bear arms set forth in the Second Amendment "fully applicable to the States." I write separately because I believe there is a more straightforward path to this conclusion, one that is more faithful to the Fourteenth Amendment's text and history.

Applying what is now a well-settled test, the plurality opinion concludes that the right to keep and bear arms applies to the States through the Fourteenth

Amendment's Due Process Clause because it is "fundamental" to the American "scheme of ordered liberty," . . . and "'deeply rooted in this Nation's history and tradition,'". . . . I agree with that description of the right. But I cannot agree that it is enforceable against the States through a clause that speaks only to "process." Instead, the right to keep and bear arms is a privilege of American citizenship that applies to the States through the Fourteenth Amendment's Privileges or Immunities Clause.

I

In *District of Columbia v. Heller,* 128 S. Ct. 2783 (2008), this Court held that the Second Amendment protects an individual right to keep and bear arms for the purpose of self-defense, striking down a District of Columbia ordinance that banned the possession of handguns in the home. *Id.* at 2821-22. The question in this case is whether the Constitution protects that right against abridgment by the States.

As the Court explains, if this case were litigated before the Fourteenth Amendment's adoption in 1868, the answer to that question would be simple. In *Barron ex rel. Tiernan v. Mayor of Baltimore,* 32 U.S. (7 Pet.) 243 (1833), this Court held that the Bill of Rights applied only to the Federal Government. Writing for the Court, Chief Justice Marshall recalled that the founding generation added the first eight Amendments to the Constitution in response to Antifederalist concerns regarding the extent of federal—not state—power, and held that if "the framers of these amendments [had] intended them to be limitations on the powers of the state governments," "they would have declared this purpose in plain and intelligible language." *Id.* at 250. . . .

Nearly three decades after *Barron,* the Nation was splintered by a civil war fought principally over the question of slavery. As was evident to many throughout our Nation's early history, slavery, and the measures designed to protect it, were irreconcilable with the principles of equality, government by consent, and inalienable rights proclaimed by the Declaration of Independence and embedded in our constitutional structure. . . .

After the war, a series of constitutional amendments were adopted to repair the Nation from the damage slavery had caused. The provision at issue here, §1 of the Fourteenth Amendment, significantly altered our system of government. The first sentence of that section provides that "[a]ll persons born or naturalized in the United States and subject to the jurisdiction thereof, are citizens of the United States and of the State wherein they reside." This unambiguously overruled this Court's contrary holding in *Dred Scott v. Sandford,* 60 U.S. (19 How.) 393 (1857), that the Constitution did not recognize black Americans as citizens of the United States or their own State. *Id.* at 405-06.

The meaning of §1's next sentence has divided this Court for many years. That sentence begins with the command that "[n]o State shall make or enforce any law which shall abridge the privileges or immunities of citizens of the United States." On its face, this appears to grant the persons just made United States citizens a certain collection of rights—*i.e.,* privileges or immunities— attributable to that status.

This Court's precedents accept that point, but define the relevant collection of rights quite narrowly. In the *Slaughter-House* Cases, 83 U.S. (16 Wall.) 36 (1873), decided just five years after the Fourteenth Amendment's adoption, the Court interpreted this text . . . for the first time. In a closely divided decision, the Court drew a sharp distinction between the privileges and immunities of state citizenship and those of federal citizenship, and held that the Privileges or Immunities Clause protected only the latter category of rights from state abridgment. *Id.* at 78. The Court defined that category to include only those rights "which owe their existence to the Federal government, its National character, its Constitution, or its laws." *Id.* at 79. This arguably left open the possibility that certain individual rights enumerated in the Constitution could be considered privileges or immunities of federal citizenship. See *id.* (listing "[t]he right to peaceably assemble" and "the privilege of the writ of *habeas corpus*" as rights potentially protected by the Privileges or Immunities Clause). But the Court soon rejected that proposition, interpreting the Privileges or Immunities Clause even more narrowly in its later cases.

Chief among those cases is *United States v. Cruikshank*, 92 U.S. 542 (1876). There, the Court held that members of a white militia who had brutally murdered as many as 165 black Louisianians congregating outside a courthouse had not deprived the victims of their privileges as American citizens to peaceably assemble or to keep and bear arms. *Id.;* see L. Keith, The Colfax Massacre 109 (2008). According to the Court, the right to peaceably assemble codified in the First Amendment was not a privilege of United States citizenship because "[t]he right . . . existed long *before* the adoption of the Constitution." 92 U.S. at 551 (emphasis added). Similarly, the Court held that the right to keep and bear arms was not a privilege of United States citizenship because it was not "in any manner dependent upon that instrument for its existence." *Id.* at 553. In other words, the reason the Framers codified the right to bear arms in the Second Amendment—its nature as an inalienable right that pre-existed the Constitution's adoption—was the very reason citizens could not enforce it against States through the Fourteenth.

That circular reasoning effectively has been the Court's last word on the Privileges or Immunities Clause.[1] In the intervening years, the Court has held that the Clause prevents state abridgment of only a handful of rights, such as the right to travel, see *Saenz v. Roe*, 526 U.S. 489, 503 (1999), that are not readily described as essential to liberty. . . .

While this Court has at times concluded that a right gains "fundamental" status [required for incorporation under the Due Process Clause] only if it is essential to the American "scheme of ordered liberty" or "'deeply rooted in this Nation's history and tradition,'" (plurality opinion) (quoting *Glucksberg*, 521 U.S. at 721), the Court has just as often held that a right warrants Due Process Clause protection if it satisfies a far less measurable range of criteria, see *Lawrence v. Texas*, 539 U.S. 558, 562 (2003) (concluding that the Due Process Clause protects "liberty of the person both in its spatial and in its more

---

1. In the two decades after *United States v. Cruikshank*, 92 U.S. 542 (1876), was decided, this Court twice reaffirmed its holding that the Privileges or Immunities Clause does not apply the Second Amendment to the States. *Presser v. Illinois*, 116 U.S. 252, 266-67 (1886); *Miller v. Texas*, 153 U.S. 535 (1894).

transcendent dimensions"). Using the latter approach, the Court has determined that the Due Process Clause applies rights against the States that are not mentioned in the Constitution at all, even without seriously arguing that the Clause was originally understood to protect such rights. *See, e.g., Lochner v. New York,* 198 U.S. 45 (1905); *Roe v. Wade,* 410 U.S. 113 (1973); *Lawrence,* supra.

All of this is a legal fiction. The notion that a constitutional provision that guarantees only "process" before a person is deprived of life, liberty, or property could define the substance of those rights strains credulity for even the most casual user of words. Moreover, this fiction is a particularly dangerous one. The one theme that links the Court's substantive due process precedents together is their lack of a guiding principle to distinguish "fundamental" rights that warrant protection from nonfundamental rights that do not. Today's decision illustrates the point. Replaying a debate that has endured from the inception of the Court's substantive due process jurisprudence, the dissents laud the "flexibility" in this Court's substantive due process doctrine while the plurality makes yet another effort to impose principled restraints on its exercise. But neither side argues that the meaning they attribute to the Due Process Clause was consistent with public understanding at the time of its ratification. . . .

I cannot accept a theory of constitutional interpretation that rests on such tenuous footing. This Court's substantive due process framework fails to account for both the text of the Fourteenth Amendment and the history that led to its adoption, filling that gap with a jurisprudence devoid of a guiding principle. I believe the original meaning of the Fourteenth Amendment offers a superior alternative, and that a return to that meaning would allow this Court to enforce the rights the Fourteenth Amendment is designed to protect with greater clarity and predictability than the substantive due process framework has so far managed.

I acknowledge the volume of precedents that have been built upon the substantive due process framework, and I further acknowledge the importance of *stare decisis* to the stability of our Nation's legal system. But *stare decisis* is only an "adjunct" of our duty as judges to decide by our best lights what the Constitution means. *Planned Parenthood of Southeastern Pa. v. Casey,* 505 U.S. 833, 963 (1992) (Rehnquist, C. J., concurring in judgment in part and dissenting in part). It is not "an inexorable command." *Lawrence,* supra, at 577. Moreover, as judges, we interpret the Constitution one case or controversy at a time. The question presented in this case is not whether our entire Fourteenth Amendment jurisprudence must be preserved or revised, but only whether, and to what extent, a particular clause in the Constitution protects the particular right at issue here. With the inquiry appropriately narrowed, I believe this case presents an opportunity to reexamine, and begin the process of restoring, the meaning of the Fourteenth Amendment agreed upon by those who ratified it.

II

"It cannot be presumed that any clause in the constitution is intended to be without effect." *Marbury v. Madison,* 1 Cranch 137, 174 (1803) (Marshall, C. J.). Because the Court's Privileges or Immunities Clause precedents have presumed just that, I set them aside for the moment and begin with the text.

The Privileges or Immunities Clause of the Fourteenth Amendment declares that "[n]o State . . . shall abridge the privileges or immunities of citizens of the United States." In interpreting this language, it is important to recall that constitutional provisions are "'written to be understood by the voters.'" *Heller,* 128 S. Ct. at 2788 (quoting *United States v. Sprague,* 282 U.S. 716, 731 (1931)). Thus, the objective of this inquiry is to discern what "ordinary citizens" at the time of ratification would have understood the Privileges or Immunities Clause to mean. 128 S. Ct. at 2788.

A

1

At the time of Reconstruction, the terms "privileges" and "immunities" had an established meaning as synonyms for "rights." The two words, standing alone or paired together, were used interchangeably with the words "rights," "liberties," and "freedoms," and had been since the time of Blackstone. See 1 W. Blackstone, Commentaries *129 (describing the "rights and liberties" of Englishmen as "private immunities" and "civil privileges"). A number of antebellum judicial decisions used the terms in this manner. *See, e.g., Magill v. Brown,* 16 F. Cas. 408, 428 (No. 8,952) (CC ED Pa. 1833) (Baldwin, J.) ("The words 'privileges and immunities' relate to the rights of persons, place or property; a privilege is a peculiar right, a private law, conceded to particular persons or places"). In addition, dictionary definitions confirm that the public shared this understanding. *See, e.g.,* N. Webster, An American Dictionary of the English Language 1039 (C. Goodrich & N. Porter rev. 1865) (defining "privilege" as "a right or immunity not enjoyed by others or by all" and listing among its synonyms the words "immunity," "franchise," "right," and "liberty"); *id.* at 661 (defining "immunity" as "[f]reedom from an obligation" or "particular privilege"); *id.* at 1140 (defining "right" as "[p]rivilege or immunity granted by authority").

The fact that a particular interest was designated as a "privilege" or "immunity," rather than a "right," "liberty," or "freedom," revealed little about its substance. Blackstone, for example, used the terms "privileges" and "immunities" to describe both the inalienable rights of individuals and the positive-law rights of corporations. See 1 Commentaries, at *129 (describing "private immunities" as a "*residuum* of natural liberty," and "civil privileges" as those "which society has engaged to provide, in lieu of the natural liberties so given up by individuals" (footnote omitted)); *id.* at *468 (stating that a corporate charter enables a corporation to "establish rules and orders" that serve as "the privileges and immunities . . . of the corporation"). . . .

2

The group of rights-bearers to whom the Privileges or Immunities Clause applies is, of course, "citizens." By the time of Reconstruction, it had long been established that both the States and the Federal Government existed to preserve their citizens' inalienable rights, and that these rights were considered "privileges" or "immunities" of citizenship.

This tradition begins with our country's English roots. Parliament declared the basic liberties of English citizens in a series of documents ranging from the Magna Carta to the Petition of Right and the English Bill of Rights. See 1 B. Schwartz, The Bill of Rights: A Documentary History 8-16, 19-21, 41-46 (1971) (hereinafter Schwartz). These fundamental rights, according to the English tradition, belonged to all people but became legally enforceable only when recognized in legal texts, including acts of Parliament and the decisions of common-law judges. See B. Bailyn, The Ideological Origins of the American Revolution 77-79 (1967). These rights included many that later would be set forth in our Federal Bill of Rights, such as the right to petition for redress of grievances, the right to a jury trial, and the right of "Protestants" to "have arms for their defence." English Bill of Rights (1689), reprinted in 1 Schwartz 41, 43.

As English subjects, the colonists considered themselves to be vested with the same fundamental rights as other Englishmen. They consistently claimed the rights of English citizenship in their founding documents, repeatedly referring to these rights as "privileges" and "immunities." For example, a Maryland law provided that

"[A]ll the Inhabitants of this Province being Christians (Slaves excepted) Shall have and enjoy all such *rights liberties immunities priviledges and free customs* within this Province as any natural born subject of England hath or ought to have or enjoy in the Realm of England. . . ." Md. Act for the Liberties of the People (1639), in *id.* at 68 (emphasis added).

As tensions between England and the Colonies increased, the colonists adopted protest resolutions reasserting their claim to the inalienable rights of Englishmen. Again, they used the terms "privileges" and "immunities" to describe these rights. As the Massachusetts Resolves declared:

"*Resolved,* That there are certain essential Rights of the *British* Constitution of Government, which are founded in the Law of God and Nature, and are the common Rights of Mankind — Therefore. . . .

"*Resolved,* That no Man can justly take the Property of another without his Consent: And that upon this *original* Principle the Right of Representation . . . is evidently founded. . . . *Resolved,* That this *inherent* Right, together with all other, essential *Rights, Liberties, Privileges and Immunities* of the People of *Great Britain,* have been fully confirmed to them by *Magna Charta.*" The Massachusetts Resolves (Oct. 29, 1765), reprinted in Prologue to Revolution: Sources and Documents on the Stamp Act Crisis, 1764-1766, p. 56 (E. Morgan ed. 1959) (some emphasis added).

In keeping with this practice, the First Continental Congress declared in 1774 that the King had wrongfully denied the colonists "the rights, liberties, and immunities of free and natural-born subjects . . . within the realm of England." 1 Journals of the Continental Congress 1774-1789, p. 68 (1904). In an address delivered to the inhabitants of Quebec that same year, the Congress described those rights as including the "great" "right[s]" of "trial by jury," "Habeas Corpus," and "freedom of the press." Address of the Continental Congress to the Inhabitants of Quebec (1774), reprinted in 1 Schwartz 221-23.

After declaring their independence, the newly formed States replaced their colonial charters with constitutions and state bills of rights, almost all of which guaranteed the same fundamental rights that the former colonists previously had claimed by virtue of their English heritage. [See the appendix to Chapter 1.]

Several years later, the Founders amended the Constitution to expressly protect many of the same fundamental rights against interference by the Federal Government. Consistent with their English heritage, the founding generation generally did not consider many of the rights identified in these amendments as new entitlements, but as inalienable rights of all men, given legal effect by their codification in the Constitution's text. *See, e.g.,* 1 Annals of Cong. 431-32, 436-37, 440-42 (1834) (statement of Rep. Madison) (proposing Bill of Rights in the first Congress); The Federalist No. 84, pp. 531-33 (B. Wright ed. 1961) (A. Hamilton); see also *Heller,* 128 S. Ct. at 2797 ("[I]t has always been widely understood that the Second Amendment, like the First and Fourth Amendments, codified a *pre-existing* right"). The Court's subsequent decision in *Barron,* however, made plain that the codification of these rights in the Bill made them legally enforceable only against the Federal Government, not the States. See 32 U.S. (7 Pet.) at 247.

3

Even though the Bill of Rights did not apply to the States, other provisions of the Constitution did limit state interference with individual rights. Article IV, §2, cl. 1 provides that "[t]he Citizens of each State shall be entitled to all Privileges and Immunities of Citizens in the several States." The text of this provision resembles the Privileges or Immunities Clause, and it can be assumed that the public's understanding of the latter was informed by its understanding of the former.

Article IV, §2 was derived from a similar clause in the Articles of Confederation, and reflects the dual citizenship the Constitution provided to all Americans after replacing that "league" of separate sovereign States. *Gibbons v. Ogden,* 22 U.S. (9 Wheat.) 1, 187 (1824). . . . By virtue of a person's citizenship in a particular State, he was guaranteed whatever rights and liberties that State's constitution and laws made available. Article IV, §2 vested citizens of each State with an additional right: the assurance that they would be afforded the "privileges and immunities" of citizenship in any of the several States in the Union to which they might travel.

What were the "Privileges and Immunities of Citizens in the several States"? That question was answered perhaps most famously by Justice Bushrod Washington sitting as Circuit Justice in *Corfield v. Coryell,* 6 F. Cas. 546, 551-52 (No. 3,230) (CC ED Pa. 1825). In that case, a Pennsylvania citizen claimed that a New Jersey law prohibiting nonresidents from harvesting oysters from the State's waters violated Article IV, §2 because it deprived him, as an out-of-state citizen, of a right New Jersey availed to its own citizens. *Id.* at 550. Justice Washington rejected that argument, refusing to "accede to the proposition" that Article IV, §2 entitled "citizens of the several states . . . to participate in *all* the rights which belong exclusively to the citizens of any other particular state." *Id.* at 552 (emphasis added). In his view, Article IV, §2 did not guarantee equal access to all public benefits a State might choose to make available to its citizens. See *id.* at 552. Instead, it applied only to those rights "which are, in their nature, *fundamental*, which belong, of right, to the citizens of all free governments." *Id.* at 551 (emphasis added). . . .

When describing those "fundamental" rights, Justice Washington thought it "would perhaps be more tedious than difficult to enumerate" them all, but suggested that they could "be all comprehended under" a broad list of "general heads," such as "[p]rotection by the government," "the enjoyment of life and liberty, with the right to acquire and possess property of every kind," "the benefit of the writ of habeas corpus," and the right of access to "the courts of the state," among others.[6] *Corfield, supra,* at 551-52.

Notably, Justice Washington did not indicate whether Article IV, §2 *required* States to recognize these fundamental rights in their own citizens and thus in sojourning citizens alike, or whether the Clause simply prohibited the States from discriminating against sojourning citizens with respect to whatever fundamental rights state law happened to recognize. On this question, the weight of legal authorities at the time of Reconstruction indicated that Article IV, §2 prohibited States from discriminating against sojourning citizens when recognizing fundamental rights, but did not require States to recognize those rights and did not prescribe their content. . . . This Court adopted the same conclusion in a unanimous opinion just one year after the Fourteenth Amendment was ratified. See *Paul v. Virginia,* 75 U.S. (8 Wall.) 168, 180 (1869).

* * *

The text examined so far demonstrates three points about the meaning of the Privileges or Immunities Clause in §1. First, "privileges" and "immunities" were synonyms for "rights." Second, both the States and the Federal Government had long recognized the inalienable rights of their citizens. Third, Article IV, §2 of the Constitution protected traveling citizens against state discrimination with respect to the fundamental rights of state citizenship.

Two questions still remain, both provoked by the textual similarity between §1's Privileges or Immunities Clause and Article IV, §2. The first involves the nature of the rights at stake: Are the privileges or immunities of "citizens of the United States" recognized by §1 the same as the privileges and immunities of "citizens in the several States" to which Article IV, §2 refers? The second involves the restriction imposed on the States: Does §1, like Article IV, §2, prohibit only discrimination with respect to certain rights *if* the State chooses to recognize

---

6. Justice Washington's complete list was as follows:

"Protection by the government; the enjoyment of life and liberty, with the right to acquire and possess property of every kind, and to pursue and obtain happiness and safety; subject nevertheless to such restraints as the government may justly prescribe for the general good of the whole. The right of a citizen of one state to pass through, or to reside in any other state, for purposes of trade, agriculture, professional pursuits, or otherwise; to claim the benefit of the writ of habeas corpus; to institute and maintain actions of any kind in the courts of the state; to take, hold and dispose of property, either real or personal; and an exemption from higher taxes or impositions than are paid by the other citizens of the state; may be mentioned as some of the particular privileges and immunities of citizens, which are clearly embraced by the general description of privileges deemed to be fundamental: to which may be added, the elective franchise, as regulated and established by the laws or constitution of the state in which it is to be exercised." 6 Fed. Cas. at 551-552.

them, or does it require States to recognize those rights? I address each question in turn.

B

I start with the nature of the rights that §1's Privileges or Immunities Clause protects. Section 1 overruled *Dred Scott*'s holding that blacks were not citizens of either the United States or their own State and, thus, did not enjoy "the privileges and immunities of citizens" embodied in the Constitution. 60 U.S. (19 How.) at 417. The Court in *Dred Scott* did not distinguish between privileges and immunities of citizens of the United States and citizens in the several States, instead referring to the rights of citizens generally. It did, however, give examples of what the rights of citizens were — the constitutionally enumerated rights of "the full liberty of speech" and the right "to keep and carry arms." *Id.*

Section 1 protects the rights of citizens "of the United States" specifically. The evidence overwhelmingly demonstrates that the privileges and immunities of such citizens included individual rights enumerated in the Constitution, including the right to keep and bear arms.

1

Nineteenth-century treaties through which the United States acquired territory from other sovereigns routinely promised inhabitants of the newly acquired territories that they would enjoy all of the "rights," "privileges," and "immunities" of United States citizens. *See, e.g.,* Treaty of Amity, Settlement, and Limits, Art. 6, Feb. 22, 1819, 8 Stat. 256-58 (entered into force Feb. 19, 1821) (cession of Florida) ("The inhabitants of the territories which his Catholic Majesty cedes to the United States, by this Treaty, shall be incorporated in the Union of the United States, as soon as may be consistent with the principles of the Federal Constitution, and admitted to the enjoyment of *all the privileges, rights, and immunities, of the citizens of the United States*" (emphasis added)).

Commentators of the time explained that the rights and immunities of "citizens of the United States" recognized in these treaties "undoubtedly mean[t] those privileges that are common to all citizens of this republic." Marcus, An Examination of the Expediency and Constitutionality of Prohibiting Slavery in the State of Missouri 17 (1819). It is therefore altogether unsurprising that several of these treaties identify liberties enumerated in the Constitution as privileges and immunities common to all United States citizens.

For example, the Louisiana Cession Act of 1803, which codified a treaty between the United States and France culminating in the Louisiana Purchase, provided that

> "The inhabitants of the ceded territory shall be incorporated in the Union of the United States, and admitted as soon as possible, according to the principles of the Federal constitution, to the enjoyments of *all the rights, advantages and immunities of citizens of the United States;* and in the mean time they shall be maintained and protected in *the free enjoyment of their liberty, property and the religion which they profess.*" Treaty Between the United States of America and the French Republic, Art. III, Apr. 30, 1803, 8 Stat. 202 (emphasis added).

The Louisiana Cession Act reveals even more about the privileges and immunities of United States citizenship because it provoked an extensive public debate on the meaning of that term. In 1820, when the Missouri Territory (which the United States acquired through the Cession Act) sought to enter the Union as a new State, a debate ensued over whether to prohibit slavery within Missouri as a condition of its admission. Some congressmen argued that prohibiting slavery in Missouri would deprive its inhabitants of the "privileges and immunities" they had been promised by the Cession Act. *See, e.g.,* 35 Annals of Cong. 1083 (1855) (remarks of Kentucky Rep. Hardin). But those who opposed slavery in Missouri argued that the right to hold slaves was merely a matter of state property law, not one of the privileges and immunities of United States citizenship guaranteed by the Act.

Daniel Webster was among the leading proponents of the antislavery position. In his "Memorial to Congress," Webster argued that "[t]he rights, advantages and immunities here spoken of [in the Cession Act] must . . . be such as are recognized or communicated by the Constitution of the United States," not the "rights, advantages and immunities, derived exclusively from the *State* governments. . . ." D. Webster, A Memorial to the Congress of the United States on the Subject of Restraining the Increase of Slavery in New States to be Admitted into the Union 15 (Dec. 15, 1819) (emphasis added). "The obvious meaning" of the Act, in Webster's view, was that "*the rights derived under the federal Constitution* shall be enjoyed by the inhabitants of [the territory]." *Id.* at 15-16 (emphasis added). In other words, Webster articulated a distinction between the rights of United States citizenship and the rights of state citizenship, and argued that the former included those rights "recognized or communicated by the Constitution." Since the right to hold slaves was not mentioned in the Constitution, it was not a right of federal citizenship. . . .

2

Evidence from the political branches in the years leading to the Fourteenth Amendment's adoption demonstrates broad public understanding that the privileges and immunities of United States citizenship included rights set forth in the Constitution, just as Webster and his allies had argued. In 1868, President Andrew Johnson issued a proclamation granting amnesty to former Confederates, guaranteeing "to all and to every person who directly or indirectly participated in the late insurrection or rebellion, a full pardon and amnesty for the offence of treason . . . with restoration of *all rights, privileges, and immunities under the Constitution* and the laws which have been made in pursuance thereof." 15 Stat. 712.

Records from the 39th Congress further support this understanding.

A

After the Civil War, Congress established the Joint Committee on Reconstruction to investigate circumstances in the Southern States and to determine whether, and on what conditions, those States should be readmitted to the Union. See Cong. Globe, 39th Cong., 1st Sess., 6, 30 (1865) (hereinafter 39th

Cong. Globe); M. Curtis, No State Shall Abridge: The Fourteenth Amendment and the Bill of Rights 57 (1986) (hereinafter Curtis). That Committee would ultimately recommend the adoption of the Fourteenth Amendment, justifying its recommendation by submitting a report to Congress that extensively catalogued the abuses of civil rights in the former slave States and argued that "adequate security for future peace and safety . . . can only be found in such changes of the organic law as shall determine the civil rights and privileges of all citizens in all parts of the republic." See Report of the Joint Committee on Reconstruction, S. Rep. No. 112, 39th Cong., 1st Sess., p. 15 (1866); H. R. Rep. No. 30, 39th Cong., 1st Sess., p. XXI (1866).

As the Court notes, the Committee's Report "was widely reprinted in the press and distributed by members of the 39th Congress to their constituents." . . . In addition, newspaper coverage suggests that the wider public was aware of the Committee's work even before the Report was issued. For example, the Fort Wayne Daily Democrat (which appears to have been unsupportive of the Committee's work) paraphrased a motion instructing the Committee to

> "enquire into [the] expediency of amending the Constitution of the United States so as to declare with greater certainty the power of Congress to enforce and determine by appropriate legislation all the guarantees contained in *that instrument.*" The Nigger Congress!, Fort Wayne Daily Democrat, Feb. 1, 1866, p. 4 (emphasis added).

B

Statements made by Members of Congress leading up to, and during, the debates on the Fourteenth Amendment point in the same direction. . . . Before considering that record here, it is important to clarify its relevance. When interpreting constitutional text, the goal is to discern the most likely public understanding of a particular provision at the time it was adopted. Statements by legislators can assist in this process to the extent they demonstrate the manner in which the public used or understood a particular word or phrase. They can further assist to the extent there is evidence that these statements were disseminated to the public. In other words, this evidence is useful not because it demonstrates what the draftsmen of the text may have been thinking, but only insofar as it illuminates what the public understood the words chosen by the draftsmen to mean.

(1)

Three speeches stand out as particularly significant. Representative John Bingham, the principal draftsman of §1, delivered a speech on the floor of the House in February 1866 introducing his first draft of the provision. Bingham began by discussing *Barron* and its holding that the Bill of Rights did not apply to the States. He then argued that a constitutional amendment was necessary to provide "an express grant of power in Congress to enforce by penal enactment these great canons of the supreme law, securing to all the citizens in every State all the privileges and immunities of citizens, and to all the people all the sacred rights of person." 39th Cong. Globe 1089-90 (1866). Bingham emphasized that §1 was designed "to arm the Congress of the United States, by the consent of the people of the United States, with the power to enforce the bill of rights as it stands in the Constitution today. It 'hath that extent — no more.'" *Id.* at 1088.

Bingham's speech was printed in pamphlet form and broadly distributed in 1866 under the title, "One Country, One Constitution, and One People," and the subtitle, "In Support of the Proposed Amendment to Enforce the Bill of Rights." Newspapers also reported his proposal, with the New York Times providing particularly extensive coverage, including a full reproduction of Bingham's first draft of §1 and his remarks that a constitutional amendment to "enforc[e]" the "immortal bill of rights" was "absolutely essential to American nationality." N.Y. Times, Feb. 27, 1866, p. 8.

Bingham's first draft of §1 was different from the version ultimately adopted. Of particular importance, the first draft granted Congress the "power to make all laws . . . necessary and proper to secure" the "citizens of each State all privileges and immunities of citizens in the several States," rather than restricting state power to "abridge" the privileges or immunities of citizens of the United States. 39th Cong. Globe 1088.

That draft was met with objections, which the Times covered extensively. A front-page article hailed the "Clear and Forcible Speech" by Representative Robert Hale against the draft, explaining — and endorsing — Hale's view that Bingham's proposal would "confer upon Congress all the rights and power of legislation now reserved to the States" and would "in effect utterly obliterate State rights and State authority over their own internal affairs." N.Y. Times, Feb. 28, 1866, p. 1.

Critically, Hale did *not* object to the draft insofar as it purported to protect constitutional liberties against state interference. Indeed, Hale stated that he believed (incorrectly in light of *Barron*) that individual rights enumerated in the Constitution were already enforceable against the States. See 39th Cong. Globe 1064 ("I have, somehow or other, gone along with the impression that there is that sort of protection thrown over us in some way, whether with or without the sanction of a judicial decision that we are so protected"). . . .

Bingham's draft was tabled for several months. In the interim, he delivered a second well-publicized speech, again arguing that a constitutional amendment was required to give Congress the power to enforce the Bill of Rights against the States. That speech was printed in pamphlet form, see Speech of Hon. John A. Bingham, of Ohio, on the Civil Rights Bill, Mar. 9, 1866 (Cong. Globe); see 39th Cong. Globe 1837 (remarks of Rep. Lawrence) (noting that the speech was "extensively published"), and the New York Times covered the speech on its front page. Thirty-Ninth Congress, N.Y. Times, Mar. 10, 1866, p. 1.

By the time the debates on the Fourteenth Amendment resumed, Bingham had amended his draft of §1 to include the text of the Privileges or Immunities Clause that was ultimately adopted. Senator Jacob Howard introduced the new draft on the floor of the Senate in the third speech relevant here. Howard explained that the Constitution recognized "a mass of privileges, immunities, and rights, some of them secured by the second section of the fourth article of the Constitution, . . . some by the first eight amendments of the Constitution," and that "there is no power given in the Constitution to enforce and to carry out any of these guarantees" against the States. 39th Cong. Globe 2765. Howard then stated that "the great object" of §1 was to "restrain the power of the States and compel them at all times to respect these great fundamental guarantees." *Id.* at 2766. Section 1, he indicated, imposed "a general prohibition upon all the States, as such, from abridging the privileges and immunities of the citizens of the United States." *Id.* at 2765.

In describing these rights, Howard explained that they included "the privileges and immunities spoken of" in Article IV, §2. *Id.* at 2765. Although he did not catalogue the precise "nature" or "extent" of those rights, he thought "Corfield v. Coryell" provided a useful description. Howard then submitted that

> "[t]o these privileges and immunities, whatever they may be—... should be added *the personal rights guarantied and secured by the first eight amendments of the Constitution*; such as the freedom of speech and of the press; the right of the people peaceably to assemble and petition the Government for a redress of grievances, [and] ... *the right to keep and to bear arms.*" *Id.* (emphasis added).

News of Howard's speech was carried in major newspapers across the country, including the New York Herald, see N.Y. Herald, May 24, 1866, p. 1, which was the best-selling paper in the Nation at that time. . . .

As a whole, these well-circulated speeches indicate that §1 was understood to enforce constitutionally declared rights against the States, and they provide no suggestion that any language in the section other than the Privileges or Immunities Clause would accomplish that task.

(2)

When read against this backdrop, the civil rights legislation adopted by the 39th Congress in 1866 further supports this view. Between passing the Thirteenth Amendment—which outlawed slavery alone—and the Fourteenth Amendment, Congress passed two significant pieces of legislation. The first was the Civil Rights Act of 1866, which provided that "all persons born in the United States" were "citizens of the United States" and that "such citizens, of every race and color, . . . shall have the same right" to, among other things, "full and equal benefit of all laws and proceedings for the security of person and property, as is enjoyed by white citizens." Ch. 31, §1, 14 Stat. 27.

Both proponents and opponents of this Act described it as providing the "privileges" of citizenship to freedmen, and defined those privileges to include constitutional rights, such as the right to keep and bear arms. See 39th Cong. Globe 474 (remarks of Sen. Trumbull) (stating that the "the late slaveholding States" had enacted laws "depriving persons of African descent of privileges which are essential to freemen," including "prohibit[ing] any negro or mulatto from having fire-arms" and stating that "[t]he purpose of the bill under consideration is to destroy all these discriminations"); *id.* at 1266-67 (remarks of Rep. Raymond) (opposing the Act, but recognizing that to "[m]ake a colored man a citizen of the United States" would guarantee to him, *inter alia,* "a defined *status* . . . a right to defend himself and his wife and children; a right to bear arms").

Three months later, Congress passed the Freedmen's Bureau Act, which also entitled all citizens to the "full and equal benefit of all laws and proceedings concerning personal liberty" and "personal security." Act of July 16, 1866, ch. 200, §14, 14 Stat. 176. The Act stated expressly that the rights of personal liberty and security protected by the Act "includ[ed] the constitutional right to bear arms." *Id.*

(3)

There is much else in the legislative record. Many statements by Members of Congress corroborate the view that the Privileges or Immunities Clause enforced constitutionally enumerated rights against the States. . . . I am not aware of any statement that directly refutes that proposition. That said, the record of the debates — like most legislative history — is less than crystal clear. In particular, much ambiguity derives from the fact that at least several Members described §1 as protecting the privileges and immunities of citizens "in the several States," harkening back to Article IV, §2. These statements can be read to support the view that the Privileges or Immunities Clause protects some or all the fundamental rights of "citizens" described in *Corfield*. They can also be read to support the view that the Privileges or Immunities Clause, like Article IV, §2, prohibits only state discrimination with respect to those rights it covers, but does not deprive States of the power to deny those rights to all citizens equally.

I examine the rest of the historical record with this understanding. But for purposes of discerning what the public most likely thought the Privileges or Immunities Clause to mean, it is significant that the most widely publicized statements by the legislators who voted on §1 — Bingham, Howard, and even Hale — point unambiguously toward the conclusion that the Privileges or Immunities Clause enforces at least those fundamental rights enumerated in the Constitution against the States, including the Second Amendment right to keep and bear arms.

3

Interpretations of the Fourteenth Amendment in the period immediately following its ratification help to establish the public understanding of the text at the time of its adoption.

Some of these interpretations come from Members of Congress. During an 1871 debate on a bill to enforce the Fourteenth Amendment, Representative Henry Dawes listed the Constitution's first eight Amendments, including "the right to keep and bear arms," before explaining that after the Civil War, the country "gave the most grand of all these rights, privileges, and immunities, by one single amendment to the Constitution, to four millions of American citizens" who formerly were slaves. Cong. Globe, 42d Cong., 1st Sess., 475-76 (1871). . . . Even opponents of Fourteenth Amendment enforcement legislation acknowledged that the Privileges or Immunities Clause protected constitutionally enumerated individual rights. See 2 Cong. Rec. 384-85 (1874) (remarks of Rep. Mills) (opposing enforcement law, but acknowledging, in referring to the Bill of Rights, that "[t]hese first amendments and some provisions of the Constitution of like import embrace the 'privileges and immunities' of citizenship as set forth in article 4, section 2 of the Constitution *and in the fourteenth amendment*" (emphasis added)). . . .

Legislation passed in furtherance of the Fourteenth Amendment demonstrates even more clearly this understanding. For example, Congress enacted the Civil Rights Act of 1871, 17 Stat. 13, which was titled in pertinent part "An Act to enforce the Provisions of the Fourteenth Amendment to the Constitution of the United States," and which is codified in the still-existing 42 U.S.C. §1983. That statute prohibits state officials from depriving citizens of "any rights, privileges, or immunities *secured by the Constitution.*" 42 U.S.C. §1983 (emphasis added). . . . [T]his Court has come to interpret the statute, unremarkably in light of its text, as protecting constitutionally enumerated rights. *Monroe v. Pape,* 365 U.S. 167, 171 (1961).

A Federal Court of Appeals decision written by a future Justice of this Court adopted the same understanding of the Privileges or Immunities Clause. *See, e.g., United States v. Hall,* 26 F. Cas. 79, 82 (No. 15,282) (CC SD Ala. 1871) (Woods, J.) ("We think, therefore, that the . . . rights enumerated in the first eight articles of amendment to the constitution of the United States, are the privileges and immunities of citizens of the United States"). In addition, two of the era's major constitutional treatises reflected the understanding that §1 would protect constitutionally enumerated rights from state abridgment.[14] A third such treatise unambiguously indicates that the Privileges or Immunities Clause accomplished this task. G. Paschal, The Constitution of the United States 290 (1868) (explaining that the rights listed in §1 had "already been guarantied" by Article IV and the Bill of Rights, but that "[t]he new feature declared" by §1 was that these rights, "which had been construed to apply only to the national government, are thus imposed upon the States").

Another example of public understanding comes from United States Attorney Daniel Corbin's statement in an 1871 Ku Klux Klan prosecution. Corbin cited *Barron* and declared:

> "[T]he fourteenth amendment changes all that theory, and lays the same restriction upon the States that before lay upon the Congress of the United States — that, as Congress heretofore could not interfere with the right of the citizen to keep and bear arms, now, after the adoption of the fourteenth amendment, the State cannot interfere with the right of the citizen to keep and bear arms. The right to keep and bear arms is included in the fourteenth amendment, under 'privileges and immunities.'" Proceedings in the Ku Klux Trials at Columbia, S. C., in the United States Circuit Court, November Term, 1871, p. 147 (1872).

* * *

---

14. See J. Pomeroy, An Introduction to the Constitutional Law of the United States 155-56 (E. Bennett ed. 1886) (describing §1, which the country was then still considering, as a "needed" "remedy" for *Barron ex rel. Tiernan* v. *Mayor of Baltimore,* 32 U.S. (7 Pet.) 243 (1833), which held that the Bill of Rights was not enforceable against the States); T. Farrar, Manual of the Constitution of the United States of America 58-59, 145-46, 395-97 (1867) (reprint 1993); *id.* at 546 (3d ed. 1872) (describing the Fourteenth Amendment as having "swept away" the "decisions of many courts" that "the popular rights guaranteed by the Constitution are secured only against [the federal] government").

This evidence plainly shows that the ratifying public understood the Privileges or Immunities Clause to protect constitutionally enumerated rights, including the right to keep and bear arms. As the Court demonstrates, there can be no doubt that §1 was understood to enforce the Second Amendment against the States. In my view, this is because the right to keep and bear arms was understood to be a privilege of American citizenship guaranteed by the Privileges or Immunities Clause.

C

The next question is whether the Privileges or Immunities Clause merely prohibits States from discriminating among citizens if they recognize the Second Amendment's right to keep and bear arms, or whether the Clause requires States to recognize the right. The municipal respondents, Chicago and Oak Park, argue for the former interpretation. They contend that the Second Amendment, as applied to the States through the Fourteenth, authorizes a State to impose an outright ban on handgun possession such as the ones at issue here so long as a State applies it to all citizens equally. The Court explains why this antidiscrimination-only reading of §1 as a whole is "implausible." I agree, but because I think it is the Privileges or Immunities Clause that applies this right to the States, I must explain why this Clause in particular protects against more than just state discrimination, and in fact establishes a minimum baseline of rights for all American citizens.

1

I begin, again, with the text. The Privileges or Immunities Clause opens with the command that "*No State shall*" abridge the privileges or immunities of citizens of the United States. Amdt. 14, §1 (emphasis added). The very same phrase opens Article I, §10 of the Constitution, which prohibits the States from "pass[ing] any Bill of Attainder" or "ex post facto Law," among other things. Article I, §10 is one of the few constitutional provisions that limits state authority. In *Barron,* when Chief Justice Marshall interpreted the Bill of Rights as lacking "plain and intelligible language" restricting state power to infringe upon individual liberties, he pointed to Article I, §10 as an example of text that would have accomplished that task. 32 U.S. (7 Pet.) at 250. Indeed, Chief Justice Marshall would later describe Article I, §10 as "a bill of rights for the people of each state." *Fletcher v. Peck,* 10 U.S. (6 Cranch) 87, 138 (1810). Thus, the fact that the Privileges or Immunities Clause uses the command "[n]o State shall" — which Article IV, §2 does not — strongly suggests that the former imposes a greater restriction on state power than the latter.

This interpretation is strengthened when one considers that the Privileges or Immunities Clause uses the verb "abridge," rather than "discriminate," to describe the limit it imposes on state authority. The Webster's dictionary in use at the time of Reconstruction defines the word "abridge" to mean "[t]o deprive; to cut off; . . . as, to *abridge* one of his rights." Webster, An American Dictionary of the English Language, at 6. The Clause is thus best understood to impose a limitation on state power to infringe upon pre-existing substantive rights. It raises no indication that the Framers of the Clause used the word "abridge" to prohibit only discrimination.

This most natural textual reading is underscored by a well-publicized revision to the Fourteenth Amendment that the Reconstruction Congress rejected. After several Southern States refused to ratify the Amendment, President Johnson met with their Governors to draft a compromise. N.Y. Times, Feb. 5, 1867, p. 5. Their proposal eliminated Congress' power to enforce the Amendment (granted in §5), and replaced the Privileges or Immunities Clause in §1 with the following:

> "All persons born or naturalized in the United States, and subject to the jurisdiction thereof, are citizens of the United States, and of the States in which they reside, and the Citizens of each State shall be entitled to all *the privileges and immunities of citizens in the several States.*" Draft reprinted in 1 Documentary History of Reconstruction 240 (W. Fleming ed. 1950) (hereinafter Fleming).

Significantly, this proposal removed the "[n]o State shall" directive and the verb "abridge" from §1, and also changed the class of rights to be protected from those belonging to "citizens of the United States" to those of the "citizens in the several States." This phrasing is materially indistinguishable from Article IV, §2, which generally was understood as an antidiscrimination provision alone. The proposal thus strongly indicates that at least the President of the United States and several southern Governors thought that the Privileges or Immunities Clause, which they unsuccessfully tried to revise, prohibited more than just state-sponsored discrimination.

2

The argument that the Privileges or Immunities Clause prohibits no more than discrimination often is followed by a claim that public discussion of the Clause, and of §1 generally, was not extensive. Because of this, the argument goes, §1 must not have been understood to accomplish such a significant task as subjecting States to federal enforcement of a minimum baseline of rights. That argument overlooks critical aspects of the Nation's history that underscored the need for, and wide agreement upon, federal enforcement of constitutionally enumerated rights against the States, including the right to keep and bear arms.

a

I turn first to public debate at the time of ratification. It is true that the congressional debates over §1 were relatively brief. It is also true that there is little evidence of extensive debate in the States. Many state legislatures did not keep records of their debates, and the few records that do exist reveal only modest discussion. . . .

First, however consequential we consider the question today, the nationalization of constitutional rights was not the most controversial aspect of the Fourteenth Amendment at the time of its ratification. The Nation had just endured a tumultuous civil war, and §§2, 3, and 4 — which reduced the representation of States that denied voting rights to blacks, deprived most former

Confederate officers of the power to hold elective office, and required States to disavow Confederate war debts — were far more polarizing and consumed far more political attention. . . .

Second, the congressional debates on the Fourteenth Amendment reveal that many representatives, and probably many citizens, believed that the Thirteenth Amendment, the 1866 Civil Rights legislation, or some combination of the two, had already enforced constitutional rights against the States. Justice Black's dissent in *Adamson* chronicles this point in detail. 332 U.S. at 107-08 (Appendix to dissenting opinion). Regardless of whether that understanding was accurate as a matter of constitutional law, it helps to explain why Congressmen had little to say during the debates about §1. See *id.*

Third, while *Barron* made plain that the Bill of Rights was not legally enforceable against the States, . . . the significance of that holding should not be overstated. Like the Framers, . . . many 19th-century Americans understood the Bill of Rights to declare inalienable rights that pre-existed all government. Thus, even though the Bill of Rights technically applied only to the Federal Government, many believed that it declared rights that no legitimate government could abridge.

Chief Justice Henry Lumpkin's decision for the Georgia Supreme Court in *Nunn v. State*, 1 Ga. 243 (1846), illustrates this view. In assessing state power to regulate firearm possession, Lumpkin wrote that he was "aware that it has been decided, that [the Second Amendment], like other amendments adopted at the same time, is a restriction upon the government of the United States, and does not extend to the individual States." *Id.* at 250. But he still considered the right to keep and bear arms as "an unalienable right, which lies at the bottom of every free government," and thus found the States bound to honor it. *Id.* Other state courts adopted similar positions with respect to the right to keep and bear arms and other enumerated rights. Some [state] courts even suggested that the protections in the Bill of Rights were legally enforceable against the States, *Barron* notwithstanding. A prominent treatise of the era took the same position. W. Rawle, A View of the Constitution of the United States of America 124-25 (2d ed. 1829) (reprint 2009) (arguing that certain of the first eight Amendments "appl[y] to the state legislatures" because those Amendments "form parts of the declared rights of the people, of which neither the state powers nor those of the Union can ever deprive them"); *id.* at 125-26 (describing the Second Amendment "right of the people to keep and bear arms" as "a restraint on both" Congress and the States). . . . Certain abolitionist leaders adhered to this view as well. Lysander Spooner championed the popular abolitionist argument that slavery was inconsistent with constitutional principles, citing as evidence the fact that it deprived black Americans of the "natural right of all men 'to keep and bear arms' for their personal defence," which he believed the Constitution "prohibit[ed] both Congress and the State governments from infringing." L. Spooner, The Unconstitutionality of Slavery 98 (1860).

In sum, some appear to have believed that the Bill of Rights *did* apply to the States, even though this Court had squarely rejected that theory. . . . Many others believed that the liberties codified in the Bill of Rights were ones that no State *should* abridge, even though they understood that the Bill technically did not apply to States. These beliefs, combined with the fact that most state constitutions recognized many, if not all, of the individual rights enumerated in the Bill of Rights, made the need for federal enforcement of constitutional liberties against the States an afterthought. . . . That changed with the national conflict over slavery.

b

In the contentious years leading up to the Civil War, those who sought to retain the institution of slavery found that to do so, it was necessary to eliminate more and more of the basic liberties of slaves, free blacks, and white abolitionists. Congressman Tobias Plants explained that slaveholders "could not hold [slaves] safely where dissent was permitted," so they decided that "all dissent must be suppressed by the strong hand of power." 39th Cong. Globe 1013. The measures they used were ruthless, repressed virtually every right recognized in the Constitution, and demonstrated that preventing only discriminatory state firearms restrictions would have been a hollow assurance for liberty. Public reaction indicates that the American people understood this point.

The overarching goal of pro-slavery forces was to repress the spread of abolitionist thought and the concomitant risk of a slave rebellion. Indeed, it is difficult to overstate the extent to which fear of a slave uprising gripped slaveholders and dictated the acts of Southern legislatures. Slaves and free blacks represented a substantial percentage of the population and posed a severe threat to Southern order if they were not kept in their place. According to the 1860 Census, slaves represented one quarter or more of the population in 11 of the 15 slave States, nearly half the population in Alabama, Florida, Georgia, and Louisiana, and *more* than 50% of the population in Mississippi and South Carolina. Statistics of the United States (Including Mortality, Property, &c.,) in 1860, The Eighth Census 336-50 (1866).

The Southern fear of slave rebellion was not unfounded. Although there were others, two particularly notable slave uprisings heavily influenced slaveholders in the South. In 1822, a group of free blacks and slaves led by Denmark Vesey planned a rebellion in which they would slay their masters and flee to Haiti. H. Aptheker, American Negro Slave Revolts 268-270 (1983). The plan was foiled, leading to the swift arrest of 130 blacks, and the execution of 37, including Vesey. *Id.* at 271. Still, slave owners took notice — it was reportedly feared that as many as 6,600 to 9,000 slaves and free blacks were involved in the plot. *Id.* at 272. A few years later, the fear of rebellion was realized. An uprising led by Nat Turner took the lives of at least 57 whites before it was suppressed. *Id.* at 300-02.

The fear generated by these and other rebellions led Southern legislatures to take particularly vicious aim at the rights of free blacks and slaves to speak or to keep and bear arms for their defense. Teaching slaves to read (even the Bible) was a criminal offense punished severely in some States. See K. Stampp, The Peculiar Institution: Slavery in the Ante-bellum South 208, 211 (1956). Virginia made it a crime for a member of an "abolition" society to enter the State and argue "that the owners of slaves have no property in the same, or advocate or advise the abolition of slavery." 1835-1836 Va. Acts ch. 66, p. 44. Other States prohibited the circulation of literature denying a master's right to property in his slaves and passed laws requiring postmasters to inspect the mails in search of such material. C. Eaton, The Freedom-of-Thought Struggle in the Old South 118-43, 199-200 (1964).

Many legislatures amended their laws prohibiting slaves from carrying firearms to apply the prohibition to free blacks as well. See, *e.g.,* Act of Dec. 23, 1833, §7, 1833 Ga. Acts pp. 226, 228 (declaring that "it shall not be lawful for any free person of colour in this state, to own, use, or carry fire arms of any description whatever"). . . . Florida made it the "duty" of white citizen "patrol[s] to search negro houses or other suspected places, for fire arms." Act of Feb. 17, 1833, ch. 671, 1833 Fla. Acts pp. 26, 30. If they found any firearms, the patrols were to take the offending slave or free black "to the nearest justice of the peace," whereupon he would be "severely punished" by "whipping on the bare back, not exceeding thirty-nine lashes," unless he could give a "plain and satisfactory" explanation of how he came to possess the gun. *Id.*

Southern blacks were not alone in facing threats to their personal liberty and security during the antebellum era. Mob violence in many Northern cities presented dangers as well. Cottrol & Diamond, The Second Amendment: Toward an Afro-Americanist Reconsideration, 80 Geo. L.J. 309, 340 (1991). . . .

c

After the Civil War, Southern anxiety about an uprising among the newly freed slaves peaked. As Representative Thaddeus Stevens is reported to have said, "[w]hen it was first proposed to free the slaves, and arm the blacks, did not half the nation tremble? The prim conservatives, the snobs, and the male waiting-maids in Congress, were in hysterics." K. Stampp, The Era of Reconstruction, 1865-1877, p. 104 (1965) (hereinafter Era of Reconstruction).

As the Court explains, this fear led to "systematic efforts" in the "old Confederacy" to disarm the more than 180,000 freedmen who had served in the Union Army, as well as other free blacks. Some States formally prohibited blacks from possessing firearms. Others enacted legislation prohibiting blacks from carrying firearms without a license, a restriction not imposed on whites. Additionally, "[t]hroughout the South, armed parties, often consisting of ex-Confederate soldiers serving in the state militias, forcibly took firearms from newly freed slaves."

As the Court makes crystal clear, if the Fourteenth Amendment "had outlawed only those laws that discriminate on the basis of race or previous condition of servitude, African-Americans in the South would likely have remained vulnerable to attack by many of their worst abusers: the state militia and state peace officers." In the years following the Civil War, a law banning firearm possession outright "would have been nondiscriminatory only in the formal sense," for it would have "left firearms in the hands of the militia and local peace officers."

Evidence suggests that the public understood this at the time the Fourteenth Amendment was ratified. The publicly circulated Report of the Joint Committee on Reconstruction extensively detailed these abuses, and statements by citizens indicate that they looked to the Committee to provide a federal solution to this problem. . . .

One way in which the Federal Government responded was to issue military orders countermanding Southern arms legislation. *See, e.g.,* Jan. 17, 1866, order from Major General D.E. Sickles, reprinted in E. McPherson, The Political History of the United States of America During the Period of Reconstruction 37 (1871) ("The constitutional rights of all loyal and well-disposed inhabitants to bear arms will not be infringed"). The significance of these steps was not lost on those they were designed to protect. After one such order was issued, The Christian Recorder, published by the African Methodist Episcopal Church, published the following editorial:

> "'We have several times alluded to the fact that the Constitution of the United States, guaranties to every citizen the right to keep and bear arms. . . . All men, without the distinction of color, have the right to keep arms to defend their homes, families, or themselves.'
> "We are glad to learn that [the] Commissioner for this State . . . has given freedmen to understand that they have as good a right to keep fire arms as any other citizens. The Constitution of the United States is the supreme law of the land, and we will be governed by that at present." Right to Bear Arms, Christian Recorder (Phila.), Feb. 24, 1866, pp. 29-30.

The same month, The Loyal Georgian carried a letter to the editor asking "Have colored persons a right to own and carry fire arms? — A Colored Citizen." The editors responded as follows:

> "Almost every day, we are asked questions similar to the above. We answer *certainly* you have the *same* right to own and carry fire arms that *other* citizens have. You are not only free but citizens of the United States and, as such, entitled to the same privileges granted to other citizens by the Constitution of the United States. . . .
> ". . . Article II, of the amendments to the Constitution of the United States, gives the people the right to bear arms and states that this right shall not be infringed. . . . All men, without distinction of color, have the right to keep arms to defend their homes, families or themselves." Letter to the Editor, Loyal Georgian (Augusta), Feb. 3, 1866, p. 3.

These statements are consistent with the arguments of abolitionists during the antebellum era that slavery, and the slave States' efforts to retain it, violated the constitutional rights of individuals — rights the abolitionists described as among the privileges and immunities of citizenship. . . . The problem abolitionists sought to remedy was that, under *Dred Scott,* blacks were not entitled to the privileges and immunities of citizens under the Federal Constitution and that, in many States, whatever inalienable rights state law recognized did not apply to blacks. See, e.g., *Cooper v. Savannah,* 4 Ga. 68, 72 (1848) (deciding, just two years after Chief Justice Lumpkin's opinion in *Nunn* recognizing the right to keep and bear arms . . . that "[f]ree persons of color have never been recognized here as citizens; they are not entitled to bear arms").

Section 1 guaranteed the rights of citizenship in the United States and in the several States without regard to race. But it was understood that liberty would be assured little protection if §1 left each State to decide which privileges or immunities of United States citizenship it would protect. As Frederick Douglass explained before §1's adoption, "the Legislatures of the South can take from him the right to keep and bear arms, as they can — they would not allow a negro to walk with a cane where I came from, they would not allow five of them to assemble together." In What New Skin Will the Old Snake Come Forth? An Address Delivered in New York, New York, May 10, 1865, reprinted in 4 The Frederick Douglass Papers 79, 83-84 (J. Blassingame & J. McKivigan eds., 1991) (footnote omitted). "Notwithstanding the provision in the Constitution of the United States, that the right to keep and bear arms shall not be abridged," Douglass explained that "the black man has never had the right either to keep or bear arms." *Id.* at 84. Absent a constitutional amendment to enforce that right against the States, he insisted that "the work of the Abolitionists [wa]s not finished." *Id.*

This history confirms what the text of the Privileges or Immunities Clause most naturally suggests: Consistent with its command that "[n]o State shall . . . abridge" the rights of United States citizens, the Clause establishes a minimum baseline of federal rights, and the constitutional right to keep and bear arms plainly was among them.[19]

III

My conclusion is contrary to this Court's precedents, which hold that the Second Amendment right to keep and bear arms is not a privilege of United States citizenship. See *Cruikshank*, 92 U.S. at 548-49, 551-53. I must, therefore, consider whether *stare decisis* requires retention of those precedents. As mentioned at the outset, my inquiry is limited to the right at issue here. Thus, I do not endeavor to decide in this case whether, or to what extent, the Privileges or Immunities Clause applies any other rights enumerated in the Constitution against the States. Nor do I suggest that the *stare decisis* considerations surrounding the application of the right to keep and bear arms against the States would be the same as those surrounding another right protected by the Privileges or Immunities Clause. I consider *stare decisis* only as it applies to the question presented here.

A

This inquiry begins with the *Slaughter-House Cases*. There, this Court upheld a Louisiana statute granting a monopoly on livestock butchering in and around the city of New Orleans to a newly incorporated company. 83 U.S. (16 Wall.) 36. Butchers excluded by the monopoly sued, claiming that the statute violated the Privileges or Immunities Clause because it interfered with their right to pursue and "exercise their trade." *Id.* at 60. This Court rejected the butchers' claim,

---

19. I conclude that the right to keep and bear arms applies to the States through the Privileges or Immunities Clause, which recognizes the rights of United States "citizens." The plurality concludes that the right applies to the States through the Due Process Clause, which covers all "person[s]." Because this case does not involve a claim brought by a noncitizen, I express no view on the difference, if any, between my conclusion and the plurality's with respect to the extent to which the States may regulate firearm possession by noncitizens.

holding that their asserted right was not a privilege or immunity of American citizenship, but one governed by the States alone. The Court held that the Privileges or Immunities Clause protected only rights of *federal* citizenship — those "which owe their existence to the Federal government, its National character, its Constitution, or its laws," *id.* at 79 — and did not protect *any* of the rights of state citizenship, *id.* at 74. In other words, the Court defined the two sets of rights as mutually exclusive.

After separating these two sets of rights, the Court defined the rights of state citizenship as "embrac[ing] nearly every civil right for the establishment and protection of which organized government is instituted" — that is, all those rights listed in *Corfield.* 83 U.S. (16 Wall.) at 76 (referring to "those rights" that "Judge Washington" described). That left very few rights of federal citizenship for the Privileges or Immunities Clause to protect. The Court suggested a handful of possibilities, such as the "right of free access to [federal] seaports," protection of the Federal Government while traveling "on the high seas," and even two rights listed in the Constitution. *Id.* at 79 (noting "[t]he right to peaceably assemble" and "the privilege of the writ of *habeas corpus*"). But its decision to interpret the rights of state and federal citizenship as mutually exclusive led the Court in future cases to conclude that constitutionally enumerated rights were excluded from the Privileges or Immunities Clause's scope. See *Cruikshank, supra.*

I reject that understanding. There was no reason to interpret the Privileges or Immunities Clause as putting the Court to the extreme choice of interpreting the "privileges and immunities" of federal citizenship to mean either all those rights listed in *Corfield,* or almost no rights at all. 83 U.S. (16 Wall.) at 76. The record is scant that the public understood the Clause to make the Federal Government "a perpetual censor upon all legislation of the States" as the *Slaughter-House* majority feared. *Id.* at 78. For one thing, *Corfield* listed the "elective franchise" as one of the privileges and immunities of "citizens of the several states," 6 F. Cas. at 552, yet Congress and the States still found it necessary to adopt the Fifteenth Amendment — which protects "[t]he right of citizens of the United States to vote" — two years after the Fourteenth Amendment's passage. If the Privileges or Immunities Clause were understood to protect every conceivable civil right from state abridgment, the Fifteenth Amendment would have been redundant.

The better view, in light of the States and Federal Government's shared history of recognizing certain inalienable rights in their citizens, is that the privileges and immunities of state and federal citizenship overlap. This is not to say that the privileges and immunities of state and federal citizenship are the same. At the time of the Fourteenth Amendment's ratification, States performed many more functions than the Federal Government, and it is unlikely that, simply by referring to "privileges or immunities," the Framers of §1 meant to transfer every right mentioned in *Corfield* to congressional oversight. As discussed, "privileges" and "immunities" were understood only as synonyms for "rights." It was their attachment to a particular group that gave them content, and the text and history recounted here indicate that the rights of United States citizens were not perfectly identical to the rights of citizens "in the several States." Justice Swayne, one of the dissenters in *Slaughter-House,* made the point clear:

"The citizen of a State has the *same* fundamental rights as a citizen of the United States, *and also certain others,* local in their character, arising from his relation to the State, and in addition, those which belong to the citizen of the United States, he being in that relation also. There may thus be a double citizenship, each having some rights peculiar to itself. It is only over those which belong to the citizen of the United States that the category here in question throws the shield of its protection." 83 U.S. (16 Wall.) at 126 (emphasis added).

Because the privileges and immunities of American citizenship include rights enumerated in the Constitution, they overlap to at least some extent with the privileges and immunities traditionally recognized in citizens in the several States. . . .

B

Three years after *Slaughter-House,* the Court in *Cruikshank* squarely held that the right to keep and bear arms was not a privilege of American citizenship, thereby overturning the convictions of militia members responsible for the brutal Colfax Massacre. *Cruikshank* is not a precedent entitled to any respect. The flaws in its interpretation of the Privileges or Immunities Clause are made evident by the preceding evidence of its original meaning, and I would reject the holding on that basis alone. But, the consequences of *Cruikshank* warrant mention as well.

Cruikshank's holding that blacks could look only to state governments for protection of their right to keep and bear arms enabled private forces, often with the assistance of local governments, to subjugate the newly freed slaves and their descendants through a wave of private violence designed to drive blacks from the voting booth and force them into peonage, an effective return to slavery. Without federal enforcement of the inalienable right to keep and bear arms, these militias and mobs were tragically successful in waging a campaign of terror against the very people the Fourteenth Amendment had just made citizens.

Take, for example, the Hamburg Massacre of 1876. There, a white citizen militia sought out and murdered a troop of black militiamen for no other reason than that they had dared to conduct a celebratory Fourth of July parade through their mostly black town. The white militia commander, "Pitchfork" Ben Tillman,[3] later described this massacre with pride: "[T]he leading white men of Edgefield" had decided "to seize the first opportunity that the negroes might offer them to provoke a riot and teach the negroes a lesson by having the whites demonstrate their superiority by killing as many of them as was justifiable." S. Kantrowitz, Ben Tillman & the Reconstruction of White Supremacy 67 (2000) (ellipsis, brackets, and internal quotation marks omitted). None of the perpetrators of the Hamburg murders was ever brought to justice.

---

3.   [Tillman was a notoriously violent racist even by the standards of his time. He was elected Governor of South Carolina, and then United States Senator. He is most well-known today for "The Tillman Act," the first federal law forbidding corporate contributions to federal candidates. — EDS.]

Organized terrorism like that perpetuated by Tillman and his cohorts pro-liferated in the absence of federal enforcement of constitutional rights . . . for decades.

The use of firearms for self-defense was often the only way black citizens could protect themselves from mob violence. . . . Sometimes . . . self-defense did not succeed. . . . But at other times, the use of firearms allowed targets of mob violence to survive. One man recalled the night during his childhood when his father stood armed at a jail until morning to ward off lynchers. See Cottrol, 354. The experience left him with a sense, "not 'of powerlessness, but of the "possibilities of salvation"'" that came from standing up to intimida-tion. *Id.*

In my view, the record makes plain that the Framers of the Privileges or Immunities Clause and the ratifying-era public understood—just as the Fra-mers of the Second Amendment did—that the right to keep and bear arms was essential to the preservation of liberty. The record makes equally plain that they deemed this right necessary to include in the minimum baseline of federal rights that the Privileges or Immunities Clause established in the wake of the War over slavery. There is nothing about *Cruikshank*'s contrary holding that warrants its retention.

* * *

I agree with the Court that the Second Amendment is fully applicable to the States. I do so because the right to keep and bear arms is guaranteed by the Fourteenth Amendment as a privilege of American citizenship.

JUSTICE STEVENS, dissenting.

In *District of Columbia v. Heller*, 128 S. Ct. 2783, 2788 (2008), the Court answered the question whether a federal enclave's "prohibition on the posses-sion of usable handguns in the home violates the Second Amendment to the Constitution." The question we should be answering in this case is whether the Constitution "guarantees individuals a fundamental right," enforceable against the States, "to possess a functional, personal firearm, including a handgun, within the home." That is a different—and more difficult—inquiry than asking if the Fourteenth Amendment "incorporates" the Second Amendment. The so-called incorporation question was squarely and, in my view, correctly resolved in the late 19th century.

Before the District Court, petitioners focused their pleadings on the special considerations raised by domestic possession, which they identified as the core of their asserted right. In support of their claim that the city of Chicago's hand-gun ban violates the Constitution, they now rely primarily on the Privileges or Immunities Clause of the Fourteenth Amendment. They rely secondarily on the Due Process Clause of that Amendment. Neither submission requires the Court to express an opinion on whether the Fourteenth Amendment places any limit on the power of States to regulate possession, use, or carriage of firearms outside the home.

I agree with the plurality's refusal to accept petitioners' primary submission. Their briefs marshal an impressive amount of historical evidence for their argu-ment that the Court interpreted the Privileges or Immunities Clause too narrowly in the *Slaughter-House* Cases, 83 U.S. (16 Wall.) 36 (1873). But the original meaning of the Clause is not as clear as they suggest — and not nearly as clear as it would need to be to dislodge 137 years of precedent. The burden is severe for those who seek radical change in such an established body of constitutional doctrine. . . .

I further agree with the plurality that there are weighty arguments supporting petitioners' second submission, insofar as it concerns the possession of firearms for lawful self-defense in the home. But these arguments are less compelling than the plurality suggests; they are much less compelling when applied outside the home; and their validity does not depend on the Court's holding in *Heller*. For that holding sheds no light on the meaning of the Due Process Clause of the Fourteenth Amendment. Our decisions construing that Clause to render various procedural guarantees in the Bill of Rights enforceable against the States likewise tell us little about the meaning of the word "liberty" in the Clause or about the scope of its protection of nonprocedural rights.

This is a substantive due process case.

I

Section 1 of the Fourteenth Amendment decrees that no State shall "deprive any person of life, liberty, or property, without due process of law." The Court has filled thousands of pages expounding that spare text. As I read the vast corpus of substantive due process opinions, they confirm several important principles that ought to guide our resolution of this case. The principal opinion's lengthy summary of our "incorporation" doctrine, and its implicit (and untenable) effort to wall off that doctrine from the rest of our substantive due process jurisprudence, invite a fresh survey of this old terrain.

Substantive Content

The first, and most basic, principle established by our cases is that the rights protected by the Due Process Clause are not merely procedural in nature. . . . Procedural guarantees are hollow unless linked to substantive interests; and no amount of process can legitimize some deprivations.

I have yet to see a persuasive argument that the Framers of the Fourteenth Amendment thought otherwise. To the contrary, the historical evidence suggests that, at least by the time of the Civil War if not much earlier, the phrase "due process of law" had acquired substantive content as a term of art within the legal community. This understanding is consonant with the venerable "notion that governmental authority has implied limits which preserve private autonomy," a notion which predates the founding and which finds reinforcement in the Constitution's Ninth Amendment, see *Griswold v. Connecticut*, 381 U.S. 479, 486-93 (1965) (Goldberg, J., concurring).[7] The Due Process Clause cannot claim to be the source of our basic freedoms — no legal document ever

---

7. The Ninth Amendment provides: "The enumeration in the Constitution, of certain rights, shall not be construed to deny or disparage others retained by the people."

could, see *Meachum v. Fano,* 427 U.S. 215, 230 (1976) (Stevens, J., dissenting) — but it stands as one of their foundational guarantors in our law.

If text and history are inconclusive on this point, our precedent leaves no doubt: It has been "settled" for well over a century that the Due Process Clause "applies to matters of substantive law as well as to matters of procedure." *Whitney v. California,* 274 U.S. 357, 373 (1927) (Brandeis, J., concurring). . . .

Liberty

The second principle woven through our cases is that substantive due process is fundamentally a matter of personal liberty. For it is the liberty clause of the Fourteenth Amendment that grounds our most important holdings in this field. It is the liberty clause that enacts the Constitution's "promise" that a measure of dignity and self-rule will be afforded to all persons. *Planned Parenthood of Southeastern Pa. v. Casey,* 505 U.S. 833, 847 (1992). It is the liberty clause that reflects and renews "the origins of the American heritage of freedom [and] the abiding interest in individual liberty that makes certain state intrusions on the citizen's right to decide how he will live his own life intolerable." *Fitzgerald v. Porter Memorial Hospital,* 523 F.2d 716, 720 (7th Cir. 1975) (Stevens, J.). Our substantive due process cases have episodically invoked values such as privacy and equality as well, values that in certain contexts may intersect with or complement a subject's liberty interests in profound ways. But as I have observed on numerous occasions, "most of the significant [twentieth-century] cases raising Bill of Rights issues have, in the final analysis, actually interpreted the word 'liberty' in the Fourteenth Amendment."

It follows that the term "incorporation," like the term "unenumerated rights," is something of a misnomer. Whether an asserted substantive due process interest is explicitly named in one of the first eight Amendments to the Constitution or is not mentioned, the underlying inquiry is the same: We must ask whether the interest is "comprised within the term liberty." *Whitney,* 274 U.S. at 373 (Brandeis, J., concurring). As the second Justice Harlan has shown, ever since the Court began considering the applicability of the Bill of Rights to the States, "the Court's usual approach has been to ground the prohibitions against state action squarely on due process, without intermediate reliance on any of the first eight Amendments." *Malloy v. Hogan,* 378 U.S. 1, 24 (1964) (dissenting opinion). . . . In the pathmarking case of *Gitlow v. New York,* 268 U.S. 652, 666 (1925), for example, both the majority and dissent evaluated petitioner's free speech claim not under the First Amendment but as an aspect of "the fundamental personal rights and 'liberties' protected by the due process clause of the Fourteenth Amendment from impairment by the States."[9]

In his own classic opinion in *Griswold,* 381 U.S. at 500 (concurring in judgment), Justice Harlan memorably distilled these precedents' lesson: "While the relevant inquiry may be aided by resort to one or more of the provisions of the

---

9. See also *Gitlow,* 268 U.S. at 672 (Holmes, J., dissenting) ("The general principle of free speech, it seems to me, must be taken to be included in the Fourteenth Amendment, in view of the scope that has been given to the word 'liberty' as there used, although perhaps it may be accepted with a somewhat larger latitude of interpretation than is allowed to Congress by the sweeping language that governs or ought to govern the laws of the United States"). . . .

Bill of Rights, it is not dependent on them or any of their radiations. The Due Process Clause of the Fourteenth Amendment stands . . . on its own bottom." Inclusion in the Bill of Rights is neither necessary nor sufficient for an interest to be judicially enforceable under the Fourteenth Amendment. This Court's "'selective incorporation'" doctrine is not simply "related" to substantive due process; it is a subset thereof.

Federal/State Divergence

The third precept to emerge from our case law flows from the second: The rights protected against state infringement by the Fourteenth Amendment's Due Process Clause need not be identical in shape or scope to the rights protected against Federal Government infringement by the various provisions of the Bill of Rights. As drafted, the Bill of Rights directly constrained only the Federal Government. See *Barron ex rel. Tiernan v. Mayor of Baltimore*, 32 U.S. (7 Pet.) 243 (1833). Although the enactment of the Fourteenth Amendment profoundly altered our legal order, it "did not unstitch the basic federalist pattern woven into our constitutional fabric." *Williams v. Florida*, 399 U.S. 78, 133 (1970) (Harlan, J., concurring in result). Nor, for that matter, did it expressly alter the Bill of Rights. The Constitution still envisions a system of divided sovereignty, still "establishes a federal republic where local differences are to be cherished as elements of liberty" in the vast run of cases, *National Rifle Assn. of Am. Inc. v. Chicago*, 567 F.3d 856, 860 (7th Cir. 2009) (Easterbrook, C. J.), still allocates a general "police power . . . to the States and the States alone," *United States v. Comstock*, 130 S. Ct. 1949, 1967 (2010) (Kennedy, J., concurring in judgment). Elementary considerations of constitutional text and structure suggest there may be legitimate reasons to hold state governments to different standards than the Federal Government in certain areas.

It is true, as the Court emphasizes, that we have made numerous provisions of the Bill of Rights fully applicable to the States. . . . But we have never accepted a "total incorporation" theory of the Fourteenth Amendment, whereby the Amendment is deemed to subsume the provisions of the Bill of Rights en masse. And we have declined to apply several provisions to the States in any measure. See, e.g., *Minneapolis & St. Louis R. Co. v. Bombolis*, 241 U.S. 211 (1916) (Seventh Amendment); *Hurtado v. California*, 110 U.S. 516 (1884) (Grand Jury Clause). We have, moreover, resisted a uniform approach to the Sixth Amendment's criminal jury guarantee, demanding 12-member panels and unanimous verdicts in federal trials, yet not in state trials. See *Apodaca v. Oregon*, 406 U.S. 404 (1972) (plurality opinion). . . .

It is true, as well, that during the 1960's the Court decided a number of cases involving procedural rights in which it treated the Due Process Clause as if it transplanted language from the Bill of Rights into the Fourteenth Amendment. See, e.g., *Benton v. Maryland*, 395 U.S. 784, 795 (1969) (Double Jeopardy Clause); *Pointer v. Texas*, 380 U.S. 400, 406 (1965) (Confrontation Clause). "Jot-for-jot" incorporation was the norm in this expansionary era. Yet at least one subsequent opinion suggests that these precedents require perfect state/federal congruence only on matters "'at the core'" of the relevant constitutional guarantee. *Crist v. Bretz*, 437 U.S. 28, 37 (1978). . . . In my judgment, this line of cases is best understood as having concluded that, to ensure a criminal trial satisfies essential standards of fairness, some procedures should be the same in state and federal courts: The need for certainty and uniformity is more pressing, and the margin for error slimmer, when criminal justice is at issue. That principle has little relevance to the question whether a *non*procedural rule set forth in the Bill of Rights qualifies as an aspect of the liberty protected by the Fourteenth Amendment.

Notwithstanding some overheated dicta in *Malloy*, 378 U.S. at 10-11, it is therefore an overstatement to say that the Court has "abandoned" a "two-track approach to incorporation." The Court moved away from that approach in the area of criminal procedure. But the Second Amendment differs in fundamental respects from its neighboring provisions in the Bill of Rights, as I shall explain in Part V, *infra*; and if some 1960's opinions purported to establish a general method of incorporation, that hardly binds us in this case. The Court has not hesitated to cut back on perceived Warren Court excesses in more areas than I can count.

I do not mean to deny that there can be significant practical, as well as esthetic, benefits from treating rights symmetrically with regard to the State and Federal Governments. Jot-for-jot incorporation of a provision may entail greater protection of the right at issue and therefore greater freedom for those who hold it; jot-for-jot incorporation may also yield greater clarity about the contours of the legal rule. . . . In a federalist system such as ours, however, this approach can carry substantial costs. When a federal court insists that state and local authorities follow its dictates on a matter not critical to personal liberty or procedural justice, the latter may be prevented from engaging in the kind of beneficent "experimentation in things social and economic" that ultimately redounds to the benefit of all Americans. *New State Ice Co. v. Liebmann*, 285 U.S. 262, 311 (1932) (Brandeis, J., dissenting). The costs of federal courts' imposing a uniform national standard may be especially high when the relevant regulatory interests vary significantly across localities, and when the ruling implicates the States' core police powers.

Furthermore, there is a real risk that, by demanding the provisions of the Bill of Rights apply identically to the States, federal courts will cause those provisions to "be watered down in the needless pursuit of uniformity." *Duncan v. Louisiana*, 391 U.S. 145, 182 n.21 (1968) (Harlan, J., dissenting). When one legal standard must prevail across dozens of jurisdictions with disparate needs and customs, courts will often settle on a relaxed standard. This watering-down risk is particularly acute when we move beyond the narrow realm of criminal procedure and into the relatively vast domain of substantive rights. So long as the requirements of fundamental fairness are always and everywhere respected, it is not clear that greater liberty results from the jot-for-jot application of a provision of the Bill of Rights to the States. Indeed, it is far from clear that proponents of an individual right to keep and bear arms ought to celebrate today's decision.[13]

---

13. The vast majority of States already recognize a right to keep and bear arms in their own constitutions, see Volokh, State Constitutional Rights to Keep and Bear Arms, 11 Tex. Rev. L. & Pol. 191 (2006) (cataloguing provisions). . . .

II

So far, I have explained that substantive due process analysis generally requires us to consider the term "liberty" in the Fourteenth Amendment, and that this inquiry may be informed by but does not depend upon the content of the Bill of Rights. How should a court go about the analysis, then? Our precedents have established, not an exact methodology, but rather a framework for decisionmaking. In this respect, too, the Court's narrative fails to capture the continuity and flexibility in our doctrine.

The basic inquiry was described by Justice Cardozo more than 70 years ago. When confronted with a substantive due process claim, we must ask whether the allegedly unlawful practice violates values "implicit in the concept of ordered liberty." *Palko v. Connecticut*, 302 U.S. 319, 325 (1937). If the practice in question lacks any "oppressive and arbitrary" character, if judicial enforcement of the asserted right would not materially contribute to "a fair and enlightened system of justice," then the claim is unsuitable for substantive due process protection. *Id.* at 327, 325. Implicit in Justice Cardozo's test is a recognition that the postulates of liberty have a universal character. Liberty claims that are inseparable from the customs that prevail in a certain region, the idiosyncratic expectations of a certain group, or the personal preferences of their champions, may be valid claims in some sense; but they are not of constitutional stature. . . .

Justice Cardozo's test undeniably requires judges to apply their own reasoned judgment, but that does not mean it involves an exercise in abstract philosophy. In addition to other constraints I will soon discuss, see Part III, *infra*, historical and empirical data of various kinds ground the analysis. Textual commitments laid down elsewhere in the Constitution, judicial precedents, English common law, legislative and social facts, scientific and professional developments, practices of other civilized societies, and, above all else, the "'traditions and conscience of our people,'" *Palko*, 302 U.S. at 325 (quoting *Snyder v. Massachusetts*, 291 U.S. 97, 105 (1934)), are critical variables. They can provide evidence about which rights really are vital to ordered liberty, as well as a spur to judicial action.

The Court errs both in its interpretation of *Palko* and in its suggestion that later cases rendered *Palko*'s methodology defunct. Echoing *Duncan*, the Court advises that Justice Cardozo's test will not be satisfied "'if a civilized system could be imagined that would not accord the particular protection.'" (quoting 391 U.S. at 149 n.14). *Palko* does contain some language that could be read to set an inordinate bar to substantive due process recognition, reserving it for practices without which "neither liberty nor justice would exist." 302 U.S. at 326. But in view of Justice Cardozo's broader analysis, as well as the numerous cases that have upheld liberty claims under the *Palko* standard, such readings are plainly overreadings. We have never applied *Palko* in such a draconian manner.

Nor, as the Court intimates, did *Duncan* mark an irreparable break from *Palko*, swapping out liberty for history. *Duncan* limited its discussion to "particular procedural safeguard[s]" in the Bill of Rights relating to "criminal processes," 391 U.S. at 149 n.14; it did not purport to set a standard for other types of liberty interests. Even with regard to procedural safeguards, *Duncan* did not jettison the *Palko* test so much as refine it: The judge is still tasked with evaluating whether a practice "is fundamental ... to ordered liberty," within the context of the "Anglo-American" system. *Duncan,* 391 U.S. at 149-50 n.14. . . .

The Court's flight from *Palko* leaves its analysis, careful and scholarly though it is, much too narrow to provide a satisfying answer to this case. The Court hinges its entire decision on one mode of intellectual history, culling selected pronouncements and enactments from the 18th and 19th centuries to ascertain what Americans thought about firearms. Relying on *Duncan* and *Glucksberg,* the plurality suggests that only interests that have proved "fundamental from an American perspective," or "'deeply rooted in this Nation's history and tradition,'" (quoting *Glucksberg,* 521 U.S. at 721), to the Court's satisfaction, may qualify for incorporation into the Fourteenth Amendment. To the extent the Court's opinion could be read to imply that the historical pedigree of a right is the exclusive or dispositive determinant of its status under the Due Process Clause, the opinion is seriously mistaken.

A rigid historical test is inappropriate in this case, most basically, because our substantive due process doctrine has never evaluated substantive rights in purely, or even predominantly, historical terms. When the Court applied many of the *procedural* guarantees in the Bill of Rights to the States in the 1960's, it often asked whether the guarantee in question was "fundamental in the context of the criminal processes maintained by the American States." *Duncan,* 391 U.S. at 150 n.14. That inquiry could extend back through time, but it was focused not so much on historical conceptions of the guarantee as on its functional significance within the States' regimes. This contextualized approach made sense, as the choice to employ any given trial-type procedure means little in the abstract. It is only by inquiring into how that procedure intermeshes with other procedures and practices in a criminal justice system that its relationship to "liberty" and "due process" can be determined.

Yet when the Court has used the Due Process Clause to recognize rights distinct from the trial context — rights relating to the primary conduct of free individuals — Justice Cardozo's test has been our guide. The right to free speech, for instance, has been safeguarded from state infringement not because the States have always honored it, but because it is "essential to free government" and "to the maintenance of democratic institutions" — that is, because the right to free speech is implicit in the concept of ordered liberty. *Thornhill v. Alabama,* 310 U.S. 88, 95, 96 (1940). . . . While the verbal formula has varied, the Court has largely been consistent in its liberty-based approach to substantive interests outside of the adjudicatory system. As the question before us indisputably concerns such an interest, the answer cannot be found in a granular inspection of state constitutions or congressional debates.

More fundamentally, a rigid historical methodology is unfaithful to the Constitution's command. For if it were really the case that the Fourteenth Amendment's guarantee of liberty embraces only those rights "so rooted in our history, tradition, and practice as to require special protection," *Glucksberg,* 521 U.S. at 721 n.17, then the guarantee would serve little function, save to ratify those rights that state actors have *already* been according the most extensive protection. Cf. *Duncan,* 391 U.S. at 183 (Harlan, J., dissenting) (critiquing "circular[ity]" of historicized test for incorporation). That approach is unfaithful to the expansive principle Americans laid down when they ratified the Fourteenth

Amendment and to the level of generality they chose when they crafted its language; it promises an objectivity it cannot deliver and masks the value judgments that pervade any analysis of what customs, defined in what manner, are sufficiently "'rooted'"; it countenances the most revolting injustices in the name of continuity, for we must never forget that not only slavery but also the subjugation of women and other rank forms of discrimination are part of our history; and it effaces this Court's distinctive role in saying what the law is, leaving the development and safekeeping of liberty to majoritarian political processes. It is judicial abdication in the guise of judicial modesty.

No, the liberty safeguarded by the Fourteenth Amendment is not merely preservative in nature but rather is a "dynamic concept." Stevens, The Bill of Rights: A Century of Progress, 59 U. Chi. L. Rev. 13, 38 (1972). Its dynamism provides a central means through which the Framers enabled the Constitution to "endure for ages to come," *McCulloch v. Maryland*, 17 U.S. (4 Wheat.) 316, 415 (1819), a central example of how they "wisely spoke in general language and left to succeeding generations the task of applying that language to the unceasingly changing environment in which they would live," Rehnquist, The Notion of a Living Constitution, 54 Tex. L. Rev. 693, 694 (1976). . . .

III

At this point a difficult question arises. In considering such a majestic term as "liberty" and applying it to present circumstances, how are we to do justice to its urgent call and its open texture — and to the grant of interpretive discretion the latter embodies — without injecting excessive subjectivity or unduly restricting the States' "broad latitude in experimenting with possible solutions to problems of vital local concern," *Whalen v. Roe*, 429 U.S. 589, 597 (1977)? . . .

Yet while "the 'liberty' specially protected by the Fourteenth Amendment" is "perhaps not capable of being fully clarified," *Glucksberg*, 521 U.S. at 722, it is capable of being refined and delimited. . . .

Rather than seek a categorical understanding of the liberty clause, our precedents have thus elucidated a conceptual core. The clause safeguards, most basically, "the ability independently to define one's identity," *Roberts v. United States Jaycees*, 468 U.S. 609, 619 (1984), "the individual's right to make certain unusually important decisions that will affect his own, or his family's, destiny," *Fitzgerald*, 523 F.2d at 719, and the right to be respected as a human being. Self-determination, bodily integrity, freedom of conscience, intimate relationships, political equality, dignity and respect — these are the central values we have found implicit in the concept of ordered liberty.

Another key constraint on substantive due process analysis is respect for the democratic process. If a particular liberty interest is already being given careful consideration in, and subjected to ongoing calibration by, the States, judicial enforcement may not be appropriate. When the Court declined to establish a general right to physician-assisted suicide, for example, it did so in part because "the States [were] currently engaged in serious, thoughtful examinations of physician-assisted suicide and other similar issues," rendering judicial intervention both less necessary and potentially more disruptive. *Glucksberg*, 521 U.S. at 719, 735. Conversely, we have long appreciated that more "searching" judicial

review may be justified when the rights of "discrete and insular minorities" —
groups that may face systematic barriers in the political system — are at stake.
United States v. Carolene Products Co., 304 U.S. 144, 153 n.4 (1938). Courts have a
"comparative . . . advantage" over the elected branches on a limited . . . range
of legal matters.

Recognizing a new liberty right is a momentous step. It takes that right, to a
considerable extent, "outside the arena of public debate and legislative action."
Glucksberg, 521 U.S. at 720. Sometimes that momentous step must be taken;
some fundamental aspects of personhood, dignity, and the like do not vary
from State to State, and demand a baseline level of protection. But sensitivity
to the interaction between the intrinsic aspects of liberty and the practical real-
ities of contemporary society provides an important tool for guiding judicial
discretion.

This sensitivity is an aspect of a deeper principle: the need to approach our
work with humility and caution. . . .

Several rules of the judicial process help enforce such restraint. In the substantive due process field as in others, the Court has applied both the doctrine of
stare decisis — adhering to precedents, respecting reliance interests, prizing stability and order in the law — and the common-law method — taking cases and controversies as they present themselves, proceeding slowly and incrementally,
building on what came before. This restrained methodology was evident even
in the heyday of "incorporation" during the 1960's. Although it would have
been much easier for the Court simply to declare certain Amendments in the
Bill of Rights applicable to the States *in toto,* the Court took care to parse each
Amendment into its component guarantees, evaluating them one by one. This
piecemeal approach allowed the Court to scrutinize more closely the right at issue
in any given dispute, reducing both the risk and the cost of error.

Relatedly, rather than evaluate liberty claims on an abstract plane, the
Court has "required in substantive-due-process cases a 'careful description' of
the asserted fundamental liberty interest." *Glucksberg,* 521 U.S. at 721. . . . And
just as we have required such careful description from the litigants, we have
required of ourselves that we "focus on the allegations in the complaint to
determine how petitioner describes the constitutional right at stake." *Collins,*
503 U.S. at 125. . . .

Our holdings should be similarly tailored. Even if the most expansive formulation of a claim does not qualify for substantive due process recognition,
particular components of the claim might. Just because there may not be a
categorical right to physician-assisted suicide, for example, does not "'foreclose
the possibility that an individual plaintiff seeking to hasten her death, or a
doctor whose assistance was sought, could prevail in a more particularized
challenge.'" *Glucksberg,* 521 U.S. at 735 n.24. . . . Even if a State's interest in
regulating a certain matter must be permitted, in the general course, to
trump the individual's countervailing liberty interest, there may still be situations in which the latter "is entitled to constitutional protection." *Glucksberg,* 521
U.S. at 742 (Stevens, J., concurring in judgments).

As this discussion reflects, to acknowledge that the task of construing the
liberty clause requires judgment is not to say that it is a license for unbridled
judicial lawmaking. To the contrary, only an honest reckoning with our discretion allows for honest argumentation and meaningful accountability.

IV

The question in this case, then, is not whether the Second Amendment right to keep and bear arms (whatever that right's precise contours) applies to the States because the Amendment has been incorporated into the Fourteenth Amendment. It has not been. The question, rather, is whether the particular right asserted by petitioners applies to the States because of the Fourteenth Amendment itself, standing on its own bottom. And to answer that question, we need to determine, first, the nature of the right that has been asserted and, second, whether that right is an aspect of Fourteenth Amendment "liberty." Even accepting the Court's holding in *Heller,* it remains entirely possible that the right to keep and bear arms identified in that opinion is not judicially enforceable against the States, or that only part of the right is so enforceable. It is likewise possible for the Court to find in this case that some part of the *Heller* right applies to the States, and then to find in later cases that other parts of the right also apply, or apply on different terms.

As noted at the outset, the liberty interest petitioners have asserted is the "right to possess a functional, personal firearm, including a handgun, within the home." The city of Chicago allows residents to keep functional firearms, so long as they are registered, but it generally prohibits the possession of handguns, sawed-off shotguns, machine guns, and short-barreled rifles. See Chicago, Ill., Municipal Code §8-20-050 (2009). Petitioners' complaint centered on their desire to keep a handgun at their domicile — it references the "home" in nearly every paragraph — as did their supporting declarations. Petitioners now frame the question that confronts us as "[w]hether the Second Amendment right to keep and bear arms is incorporated as against the States by the Fourteenth Amendment's Privileges or Immunities or Due Process Clauses." But it is our duty "to focus on the allegations in the complaint to determine how petitioner describes the constitutional right at stake," *Collins,* 503 U.S. at 125, and the gravamen of this complaint is plainly an appeal to keep a handgun or other firearm of one's choosing in the home.

Petitioners' framing of their complaint tracks the Court's ruling in *Heller.* The majority opinion contained some dicta suggesting the possibility of a more expansive arms-bearing right, one that would travel with the individual to an extent into public places, as "in case of confrontation." 128 S. Ct. at 2797-98. But the *Heller* plaintiff sought only dispensation to keep an operable firearm in his home for lawful self-defense, see *id.* at 2788 & n.2, and the Court's opinion was bookended by reminders that its holding was limited to that one issue, *id.* at 2788, 2821-22. The distinction between the liberty right these petitioners have asserted and the Second Amendment right identified in *Heller* is therefore evanescent. Both are rooted to the home. Moreover, even if both rights have the logical potential to extend further, upon "future evaluation," *Heller,* 128 S. Ct. at 2821, it is incumbent upon us, as federal judges contemplating a novel rule that would bind all 50 States, to proceed cautiously and to decide only what must be decided.

Understood as a plea to keep their preferred type of firearm in the home, petitioners' argument has real force. The decision to keep a loaded handgun in the house is often motivated by the desire to protect life, liberty, and property. It is comparable, in some ways, to decisions about the education and upbringing of

one's children. For it is the kind of decision that may have profound consequences for every member of the family, and for the world beyond.
In considering whether to keep a handgun, heads of households must ask themselves whether the desired safety benefits outweigh the risks of deliberate or
accidental misuse that may result in death or serious injury, not only to residents
of the home but to others as well. Millions of Americans have answered this
question in the affirmative, not infrequently because they believe they have an
inalienable right to do so — because they consider it an aspect of "the supreme
human dignity of being master of one's fate rather than a ward of the State,"
Indiana v. Edwards, 554 U.S. 164, 186 (2008) (Scalia, J., dissenting). Many such
decisions have been based, in part, on family traditions and deeply held beliefs
that are an aspect of individual autonomy the government may not control.

Bolstering petitioners' claim, our law has long recognized that the home
provides a kind of special sanctuary in modern life. *See, e.g.,* U.S. Const., Amdts.
3, 4; *Lawrence,* 539 U.S. at 562, 567; *Payton v. New York,* 445 U.S. 573, 585-90
(1980); *Stanley v. Georgia,* 394 U.S. 557, 565-68 (1969); *Griswold,* 381 U.S. at 484-
85. Consequently, we have long accorded special deference to the privacy of the
home, whether a humble cottage or a magnificent manse. This veneration of the
domestic harkens back to the common law. William Blackstone recognized a
"right of habitation," 4 Commentaries *223, and opined that "every man's
house is looked upon by the law to be his castle of defence and asylum," 3 *id.*
at *288. *Heller* carried forward this legacy, observing that "the need for defense
of self, family, and property is most acute" in one's abode, and celebrating "the
right of law-abiding, responsible citizens to use arms in defense of hearth and
home." 128 S. Ct. at 2817, 2821.

While the individual's interest in firearm possession is thus heightened in
the home, the State's corresponding interest in regulation is somewhat weaker.
The State generally has a lesser basis for regulating private as compared to public
acts, and firearms kept inside the home generally pose a lesser threat to public
welfare as compared to firearms taken outside. The historical case for regulation
is likewise stronger outside the home, as many States have for many years
imposed stricter, and less controversial, restrictions on the carriage of arms
than on their domestic possession. . . .

In their briefs to this Court, several *amici* have sought to bolster petitioners'
claim still further by invoking a right to individual self-defense. As petitioners
note, the *Heller* majority discussed this subject extensively and remarked that
"[t]he inherent right of self-defense has been central to the Second Amendment right." 128 S. Ct. at 2817. And it is true that if a State were to try to deprive
its residents of any reasonable means of defending themselves from imminent
physical threats, or to deny persons any ability to assert self-defense in response
to criminal prosecution, that might pose a significant constitutional problem.
The argument that there is a substantive due process right to be spared such
untenable dilemmas is a serious one.

But that is not the case before us. Petitioners have not asked that we establish a constitutional right to individual self-defense; neither their pleadings in
the District Court nor their filings in this Court make any such request. Nor do
petitioners contend that the city of Chicago — which, recall, allows its residents
to keep most rifles and shotguns, and to keep them loaded — has unduly burdened any such right. What petitioners have asked is that we "incorporate" the

Second Amendment and thereby establish a constitutional entitlement, enforceable against the States, to keep a handgun in the home.

Of course, owning a handgun may be useful for practicing self-defense. But the right to take a certain type of action is analytically distinct from the right to acquire and utilize specific instrumentalities in furtherance of that action. . . . It is a very long way from the proposition that the Fourteenth Amendment protects a basic individual right of self-defense to the conclusion that a city may not ban handguns.

In short, while the utility of firearms, and handguns in particular, to the defense of hearth and home is certainly relevant to an assessment of petitioners' asserted right, there is no freestanding self-defense claim in this case. The question we must decide is whether the interest in keeping in the home a fire-arm of one's choosing — a handgun, for petitioners — is one that is "comprised within the term liberty" in the Fourteenth Amendment. *Whitney,* 274 U.S. at 373 (Brandeis, J., concurring).

V

While I agree with the Court that our substantive due process cases offer a principled basis for holding that petitioners have a constitutional right to pos-sess a usable firearm in the home, I am ultimately persuaded that a better reading of our case law supports the city of Chicago. I would not foreclose the possibility that a particular plaintiff — say, an elderly widow who lives in a dangerous neighborhood and does not have the strength to operate a long gun — may have a cognizable liberty interest in possessing a handgun. But I cannot accept petitioners' broader submission. A number of factors, taken together, lead me to this conclusion.

First, firearms have a fundamentally ambivalent relationship to liberty. Just as they can help homeowners defend their families and property from intruders, they can help thugs and insurrectionists murder innocent victims. The threat that firearms will be misused is far from hypothetical, for gun crime has devas-tated many of our communities. *Amici* calculate that approximately one million Americans have been wounded or killed by gunfire in the last decade. Urban areas such as Chicago suffer disproportionately from this epidemic of violence. Handguns contribute disproportionately to it. Just as some homeowners may prefer handguns because of their small size, light weight, and ease of operation, some criminals will value them for the same reasons. See *Heller,* 128 S. Ct. at 2864-65 (Breyer, J., dissenting). In recent years, handguns were reportedly used in more than four-fifths of firearm murders and more than half of all murders nationwide.

Hence, in evaluating an asserted right to be free from particular gun-control regulations, liberty is on both sides of the equation. Guns may be useful for self-defense, as well as for hunting and sport, but they also have a unique potential to facilitate death and destruction and thereby to destabilize ordered liberty. *Your* interest in keeping and bearing a certain firearm may diminish *my* interest in being and feeling safe from armed violence. And while granting you the right to own a handgun might make you safer on any given day — assuming the handgun's marginal contribution to self-defense outweighs its marginal contribution to the risk of accident, suicide, and criminal mischief—it may make you and the community you live in less safe overall, owing to the increased number of handguns in circulation. It is at least reasonable for a democratically elected legislature to take such concerns into account in considering what sorts of regulations would best serve the public welfare.

The practical impact of various gun-control measures may be highly controversial, but this basic insight should not be. The idea that deadly weapons pose a distinctive threat to the social order—and that reasonable restrictions on their usage therefore impose an acceptable burden on one's personal liberty—is as old as the Republic. As The Chief Justice observed just the other day, it is a foundational premise of modern government that the State holds a monopoly on legitimate violence: "A basic step in organizing a civilized society is to take [the] sword out of private hands and turn it over to an organized government, acting on behalf of all the people." *Robertson v. United States ex rel. Watson*, 130 S. Ct. 2184 (dissenting opinion). The same holds true for the handgun. The power a man has in the state of nature "of doing whatsoever he thought fit for the preservation of himself and the rest of mankind, he gives up," to a significant extent, "to be regulated by laws made by the society." J. Locke, Second Treatise of Civil Government §129, p. 64 (J. Gough ed. 1947).

Limiting the federal constitutional right to keep and bear arms to the home complicates the analysis but does not dislodge this conclusion. Even though the Court has long afforded special solicitude for the privacy of the home, we have never understood that principle to "infring[e] upon" the authority of the States to proscribe certain inherently dangerous items, for "[i]n such cases, compelling reasons may exist for overriding the right of the individual to possess those materials." *Stanley*, 394 U.S. at 568 n.11. And, of course, guns that start out in the home may not stay in the home. Even if the government has a weaker basis for restricting domestic possession of firearms as compared to public carriage—and even if a blanket, statewide prohibition on domestic possession might therefore be unconstitutional—the line between the two is a porous one. A state or local legislature may determine that a prophylactic ban on an especially portable weapon is necessary to police that line.

Second, the right to possess a firearm of one's choosing is different in kind from the liberty interests we have recognized under the Due Process Clause. Despite the plethora of substantive due process cases that have been decided in the post-*Lochner* century, I have found none that holds, states, or even suggests that the term "liberty" encompasses either the common-law right of self-defense or a right to keep and bear arms. I do not doubt for a moment that many Americans feel deeply passionate about firearms, and see them as critical to their way of life as well as to their security. Nevertheless, it does not appear to be the case that the ability to own a handgun, or any particular type of firearm, is critical to leading a life of autonomy, dignity, or political equality: The marketplace offers many tools for self-defense, even if they are imperfect substitutes, and neither petitioners nor their *amici* make such a contention. Petitioners' claim is not the kind of substantive interest, accordingly, on which a uniform, judicially enforced national standard is presumptively appropriate.

Indeed, in some respects the substantive right at issue may be better viewed as a property right. Petitioners wish to *acquire* certain types of firearms, or to *keep* certain firearms they have previously acquired. Interests in the possession of chattels have traditionally been viewed as property interests subject to definition and regulation by the States. Cf. *Stop the Beach Renourishment, Inc. v. Florida Dept. of Environmental Protection*, 130 S. Ct. 2592 (2010) (opinion of Scalia, J.) ("Generally speaking, state law defines property interests"). Under that tradition, Chicago's ordinance is unexceptional.

The liberty interest asserted by petitioners is also dissimilar from those we have recognized in its capacity to undermine the security of others. To be sure, some of the Bill of Rights' procedural guarantees may place "restrictions on law enforcement" that have "controversial public safety implications." (plurality opinion); see also (opinion of Scalia, J.). But those implications are generally quite attenuated. . . . The handgun is itself a tool for crime; the handgun's bullets *are* the violence.

Similarly, it is undeniable that some may take profound offense at a remark made by the soapbox speaker, the practices of another religion, or a gay couple's choice to have intimate relations. But that offense is moral, psychological, or theological in nature; the actions taken by the rights-bearers do not actually threaten the physical safety of any other person. Firearms may be used to kill another person. If a legislature's response to dangerous weapons ends up impinging upon the liberty of any individuals in pursuit of the greater good, it invariably does so on the basis of more than the majority's "'own moral code,'" *Lawrence*, 539 U.S. at 571 (quoting *Casey*, 505 U.S. at 850). While specific policies may of course be misguided, gun control is an area in which it "is quite wrong . . . to assume that regulation and liberty occupy mutually exclusive zones — that as one expands, the other must contract." Stevens, 41 U. Miami L. Rev. at 280.

Third, the experience of other advanced democracies, including those that share our British heritage, undercuts the notion that an expansive right to keep and bear arms is intrinsic to ordered liberty. Many of these countries place restrictions on the possession, use, and carriage of firearms far more onerous than the restrictions found in this Nation. That the United States is an international outlier in the permissiveness of its approach to guns does not suggest that our laws are bad laws. It does suggest that this Court may not need to assume responsibility for making our laws still more permissive.

Admittedly, these other countries differ from ours in many relevant respects, including their problems with violent crime and the traditional role that firearms have played in their societies. But they are not so different from the United States that we ought to dismiss their experience entirely. Cf. (plurality opinion); (opinion of Scalia, J.). The fact that our oldest allies have almost uniformly found it appropriate to regulate firearms extensively tends to weaken petitioners' submission that the right to possess a gun of one's choosing is fundamental to a life of liberty. While the "American perspective" must always be our focus, (plurality opinion), it is silly — indeed, arrogant — to think we have nothing to learn about liberty from the billions of people beyond our borders.

Fourth, the Second Amendment differs in kind from the Amendments that surround it, with the consequence that its inclusion in the Bill of Rights is not merely unhelpful but positively harmful to petitioners' claim. Generally, the inclusion of a liberty interest in the Bill of Rights points toward the conclusion that it is of fundamental significance and ought to be enforceable against the

States. But the Second Amendment plays a peculiar role within the Bill, as announced by its peculiar opening clause. Even accepting the *Heller* Court's view that the Amendment protects an individual right to keep and bear arms disconnected from militia service, it remains undeniable that "the purpose for which the right was codified" was "to prevent elimination of the militia." *Heller,* 128 S. Ct. at 2801; see also *United States v. Miller,* 307 U.S. 174, 178 (1939) (Second Amendment was enacted "[w]ith obvious purpose to assure the continuation and render possible the effectiveness of [militia] forces"). It was the States, not private persons, on whose immediate behalf the Second Amendment was adopted. Notwithstanding the *Heller* Court's efforts to write the Second Amendment's preamble out of the Constitution, the Amendment still serves the structural function of protecting the States from encroachment by an overreaching Federal Government.

The Second Amendment, in other words, "is a federalism provision," *Elk Grove Unified School Dist. v. Newdow,* 542 U.S. 1, 45 (2004) (Thomas, J., concurring in judgment). It is directed at preserving the autonomy of the sovereign States, and its logic therefore "resists" incorporation by a federal court *against* the States. *Id.* No one suggests that the Tenth Amendment, which provides that powers not given to the Federal Government remain with "the States," applies to the States; such a reading would border on incoherent, given that the Tenth Amendment exists (in significant part) to safeguard the vitality of state governance. The Second Amendment is no different.

The Court is surely correct that Americans' conceptions of the Second Amendment right evolved over time in a more individualistic direction; that Members of the Reconstruction Congress were urgently concerned about the safety of the newly freed slaves; and that some Members believed that, following ratification of the Fourteenth Amendment, the Second Amendment would apply to the States. But it is a giant leap from these data points to the conclusion that the Fourteenth Amendment "incorporated" the Second Amendment as a matter of original meaning or postenactment interpretation. Consider, for example, that the text of the Fourteenth Amendment says nothing about the Second Amendment or firearms; that there is substantial evidence to suggest that, when the Reconstruction Congress enacted measures to ensure newly freed slaves and Union sympathizers in the South enjoyed the right to possess firearms, it was motivated by antidiscrimination and equality concerns rather than arms-bearing concerns *per se;* that many contemporaneous courts and commentators did not understand the Fourteenth Amendment to have had an "incorporating" effect; and that the States heavily regulated the right to keep and bear arms both before and after the Amendment's passage. The Court's narrative largely elides these facts. The complications they raise show why even the most dogged historical inquiry into the "fundamentality" of the Second Amendment right (or any other) necessarily entails judicial judgment — and therefore judicial discretion — every step of the way.

I accept that the evolution in Americans' understanding of the Second Amendment may help shed light on the question whether a right to keep and bear arms is comprised within Fourteenth Amendment "liberty." But the reasons that motivated the Framers to protect the ability of militiamen to keep muskets available for military use when our Nation was in its infancy, or that motivated the Reconstruction Congress to extend full citizenship to the freedmen in the wake of the Civil War, have only a limited bearing on the question that confronts the homeowner in a crime-infested metropolis today. The many episodes of brutal violence against African-Americans that blight our Nation's history, see (majority opinion); (Thomas, J., concurring in part and concurring in judgment), do not suggest that every American must be allowed to own whatever type of firearm he or she desires—just that no group of Americans should be systematically and discriminatorily disarmed and left to the mercy of racial terrorists. And the fact that some Americans may have thought or hoped that the Fourteenth Amendment would nationalize the Second Amendment hardly suffices to justify the conclusion that it did.

Fifth, although it may be true that Americans' interest in firearm possession and state-law recognition of that interest are "deeply rooted" in some important senses, it is equally true that the States have a long and unbroken history of regulating firearms. The idea that States may place substantial restrictions on the right to keep and bear arms short of complete disarmament is, in fact, far more entrenched than the notion that the Federal Constitution protects any such right. Federalism is a far "older and more deeply rooted tradition than is a right to carry," or to own, "any particular kind of weapon." *National Rifle Assn. of Am. Inc.*, 567 F.3d at 860.

From the early days of the Republic, through the Reconstruction era, to the present day, States and municipalities have placed extensive licensing requirements on firearm acquisition, restricted the public carriage of weapons, and banned altogether the possession of especially dangerous weapons, including handguns. See *Heller*, 128 S. Ct. at 2848-50 (Breyer, J., dissenting) (reviewing colonial laws). . . . After the 1860's just as before, the state courts almost uniformly upheld these measures: Apart from making clear that all regulations had to be constructed and applied in a nondiscriminatory manner, the Fourteenth Amendment hardly made a dent. And let us not forget that this Court did not recognize *any* non-militia-related interests under the Second Amendment until two Terms ago, in *Heller*. Petitioners do not dispute the city of Chicago's observation that "[n]o other substantive Bill of Rights protection has been regulated nearly as intrusively" as the right to keep and bear arms.

This history of intrusive regulation is not surprising given that the very text of the Second Amendment calls out for regulation, and the ability to respond to the social ills associated with dangerous weapons goes to the very core of the States' police powers. Our precedent is crystal-clear on this latter point. *See, e.g., Gonzales v. Oregon*, 546 U.S. 243, 270 (2006) ("[T]he structure and limitations of federalism . . . allow the States great latitude under their police powers to legislate as to the protection of the lives, limbs, health, comfort, and quiet of all persons" (internal quotation marks omitted)); *United States v. Morrison*, 529 U.S. 598, 618 (2000) ("[W]e can think of no better example of the police power, which the Founders denied the National Government and reposed in the States, than the suppression of violent crime and vindication of its victims"); *Kelley v. Johnson*, 425 U.S. 238, 247 (1976) ("The promotion of safety of persons and property is unquestionably at the core of the State's police power"); *Automobile Workers v. Wisconsin Employment Relations Bd.*, 351 U.S. 266, 274 (1956) ("The dominant interest of the State in preventing violence and property damage cannot be questioned. It is a matter of genuine local concern"). Compared with today's ruling, most if not all of this Court's decisions requiring the States to comply with other provisions in the Bill of Rights did not exact nearly so heavy a toll in terms of state sovereignty.

Finally, even apart from the States' long history of firearms regulation and its location at the core of their police powers, this is a quintessential area in which federalism ought to be allowed to flourish without this Court's meddling. Whether or not we *can* assert a plausible constitutional basis for intervening, there are powerful reasons why we *should not* do so.

Across the Nation, States and localities vary significantly in the patterns and problems of gun violence they face, as well as in the traditions and cultures of lawful gun use they claim. . . .

Given that relevant background conditions diverge so much across jurisdictions, the Court ought to pay particular heed to state and local legislatures' "right to experiment." *New State Ice,* 285 U.S., at 311 (Brandeis, J., dissenting). So long as the regulatory measures they have chosen are not "arbitrary, capricious, or unreasonable," we should be allowing them to "try novel social and economic" policies. *Id.* It "is more in keeping . . . with our status as a court in a federal system," under these circumstances, "to avoid imposing a single solution . . . from the top down." *Smith v. Robbins,* 528 U.S. 259, 275 (2000).

It is all the more unwise for this Court to limit experimentation in an area "where the best solution is far from clear." *United States v. Lopez,* 514 U.S. 549, 581 (1995) (Kennedy, J., concurring). Few issues of public policy are subject to such intensive and rapidly developing empirical controversy as gun control. See *Heller,* 128 S. Ct. at 2857-60 (Breyer, J., dissenting). Chicago's handgun ban, in itself, has divided researchers. Of course, on some matters the Constitution requires that we ignore such pragmatic considerations. But the Constitution's text, history, and structure are not so clear on the matter before us — as evidenced by the groundbreaking nature of today's fractured decision — and this Court lacks both the technical capacity and the localized expertise to assess "the wisdom, need, and propriety" of most gun-control measures. *Griswold,* 381 U.S. at 482.

Nor will the Court's intervention bring any clarity to this enormously complex area of law. Quite to the contrary, today's decision invites an avalanche of litigation. . . .

Furthermore, and critically, the Court's imposition of a national standard is still more unwise because the elected branches have shown themselves to be perfectly capable of safeguarding the interest in keeping and bearing arms. The strength of a liberty claim must be assessed in connection with its status in the democratic process. And in this case, no one disputes "that opponents of [gun] control have considerable political power and do not seem to be at a systematic disadvantage in the democratic process," or that "the widespread commitment to an individual right to own guns . . . operates as a safeguard against excessive or unjustified gun control laws." Sunstein, Second Amendment Minimalism: *Heller* as *Griswold,* 122 Harv. L. Rev. 246, 260 (2008). Indeed, there is a good deal of evidence to suggest that, if anything, American lawmakers tend to *under*-regulate guns, relative to the policy views expressed by majorities in opinion polls. See K. Goss, Disarmed: The Missing Movement for Gun Control in America 6 (2006). If a particular State or locality has enacted some "improvident" gun-control measures, as petitioners believe Chicago has done, there is no apparent reason to infer that the mistake will not "eventually be rectified by the democratic process." *Vance v. Bradley,* 440 U.S. 93, 97 (1979).

This is not a case, then, that involves a "special condition" that "may call for a correspondingly more searching judicial inquiry." *Carolene Products,* 304 U.S. at 153 n.4. Neither petitioners nor those most zealously committed to their views represent a group or a claim that is liable to receive unfair treatment at the hands of the majority. On the contrary, petitioners' views are supported by powerful participants in the legislative process. Petitioners have given us no reason to believe that the interest in keeping and bearing arms entails any special need for judicial lawmaking, or that federal judges are more qualified to craft appropriate rules than the people's elected representatives. Having failed to show why their asserted interest is intrinsic to the concept of ordered liberty or vulnerable to maltreatment in the political arena, they have failed to show why "the word liberty in the Fourteenth Amendment" should be "held to prevent the natural outcome of a dominant opinion" about how to deal with the problem of handgun violence in the city of Chicago. *Lochner,* 198 U.S. at 76 (Holmes, J., dissenting). . . .

VII

The fact that the right to keep and bear arms appears in the Constitution should not obscure the novelty of the Court's decision to enforce that right against the States. By its terms, the Second Amendment does not apply to the States; read properly, it does not even apply to individuals outside of the militia context. The Second Amendment was adopted to protect the *States* from federal encroachment. And the Fourteenth Amendment has never been understood by the Court to have "incorporated" the entire Bill of Rights. There was nothing foreordained about today's outcome.

Although the Court's decision in this case might be seen as a mere adjunct to its decision in *Heller,* the consequences could prove far more destructive — quite literally — to our Nation's communities and to our constitutional structure. Thankfully, the Second Amendment right identified in *Heller* and its newly minted Fourteenth Amendment analogue are limited, at least for now, to the home. But neither the "assurances" provided by the plurality, nor the many historical sources cited in its opinion should obscure the reality that today's ruling marks a dramatic change in our law — or that the Justices who have joined it have brought to bear an awesome amount of discretion in resolving the legal question presented by this case.

I would proceed more cautiously. For the reasons set out at length above, I cannot accept either the methodology the Court employs or the conclusions it draws. Although impressively argued, the majority's decision to overturn more than a century of Supreme Court precedent and to unsettle a much longer tradition of state practice is not, in my judgment, built "upon respect for the teachings of history, solid recognition of the basic values that underlie our society, and wise appreciation of the great roles that the doctrines of federalism and separation of powers have played in establishing and preserving American freedoms." *Griswold,* 381 U.S. at 501 (Harlan, J., concurring in judgment).

Accordingly, I respectfully dissent.

JUSTICE BREYER, with whom JUSTICE GINSBURG and JUSTICE SOTOMAYOR join, dissenting.

In my view, Justice Stevens has demonstrated that the Fourteenth Amendment's guarantee of "substantive due process" does not include a general right to keep and bear firearms for purposes of private self-defense. As he argues, the Framers did not write the Second Amendment with this objective in view. See (dissenting opinion). Unlike other forms of substantive liberty, the carrying of arms for that purpose often puts others' lives at risk. And the use of arms for private self-defense does not warrant federal constitutional protection from state regulation.

The Court, however, does not expressly rest its opinion upon "substantive due process" concerns. Rather, it directs its attention to this Court's "incorporation" precedents and asks whether the Second Amendment right to private self-defense is "fundamental" so that it applies to the States through the Fourteenth Amendment.

I shall therefore separately consider the question of "incorporation." I can find nothing in the Second Amendment's text, history, or underlying rationale that could warrant characterizing it as "fundamental" insofar as it seeks to protect the keeping and bearing of arms for private self-defense purposes. Nor can I find any justification for interpreting the Constitution as transferring ultimate regulatory authority over the private uses of firearms from democratically elected legislatures to courts or from the States to the Federal Government. I therefore conclude that the Fourteenth Amendment does not "incorporate" the Second Amendment's right "to keep and bear Arms." And I consequently dissent.

I

The Second Amendment says: "A well regulated Militia, being necessary to the security of a free State, the right of the people to keep and bear Arms, shall not be infringed." Two years ago, in *District of Columbia v. Heller,* 128 S. Ct. 2783 (2008), the Court rejected the pre-existing judicial consensus that the Second Amendment was primarily concerned with the need to maintain a "well regulated Militia." *See id.* at 2823 & n.2, 2842-46 (Stevens, J., dissenting); *United States v. Miller,* 307 U.S. 174, 178 (1939). Although the Court acknowledged that "the threat that the new Federal Government would destroy the citizens' militia by taking away their arms *was the reason* that right . . . was codified in a written Constitution," the Court asserted that "individual self defense . . . was the *central component* of the right itself." *Heller,* 128 S. Ct. at 2801 (first emphasis added). The Court went on to hold that the Second Amendment restricted Congress' power to regulate handguns used for self-defense, and the Court found unconstitutional the District of Columbia's ban on the possession of handguns in the home. *Id.* at 2821-22.

The Court based its conclusions almost exclusively upon its reading of history. But the relevant history in *Heller* was far from clear: Four dissenting Justices disagreed with the majority's historical analysis. And subsequent scholarly writing reveals why disputed history provides treacherous ground on which to build decisions written by judges who are not expert at history.

Since *Heller,* historians, scholars, and judges have continued to express the view that the Court's historical account was flawed. . . .

Consider as an example of these critiques an *amici* brief filed in this case by historians who specialize in the study of the English Civil Wars. They tell us that *Heller* misunderstood a key historical point. *Heller*'s conclusion that "individual self-defense" was "the *central component*" of the Second Amendment's right "to keep and bear Arms" rested upon its view that the Amendment "codified a *pre-existing* right" that had "nothing whatever to do with service in a militia." 128 S. Ct. at 2797, 2801-02. That view in turn rested in significant part upon Blackstone having described the right as "'the right of having and using arms for self-preservation and defence,'" which reflected the provision in the English Declaration of Right of 1689 that gave the King's Protestant "'subjects'" the right to "'have Arms for their defence suitable to their Conditions, and as allowed by law.'" *Id.* at 2798 (quoting 1 W. Blackstone, Commentaries on the Laws of England 140 (1765) (hereinafter Blackstone) and 1 W. & M., c. 2, §7, in 3 Eng. Stat. at Large 441 (1689)). The Framers, said the majority, understood that right "as permitting a citizen to 'repe[l] force by force' when 'the intervention of society in his behalf, may be too late to prevent an injury.'" 128 S. Ct. at 2799 (quoting St. George Tucker, 1 Blackstone's Commentaries 145-46, n.42 (1803)).

The historians now tell us, however, that the right to which Blackstone referred had, not *nothing,* but *everything,* to do with the militia. As properly understood at the time of the English Civil Wars, the historians claim, the right to bear arms "ensured that *Parliament* had the power" to arm the citizenry: "to defend the realm" in the case of a foreign enemy, and to "secure the right of 'self-preservation,'" or "self-defense," should "*the sovereign* usurp the English Constitution." Thus, the Declaration of Right says that private persons can possess guns only "as allowed by law." Moreover, when Blackstone referred to "'the right of having and using arms for self-preservation and defence,'" he was referring to the right of the people "*to take part in the militia* to defend their political liberties," and *to the right of Parliament* (which represented the people) to *raise a militia* even when the King sought to deny it that power. Nor can the historians find any convincing reason to believe that the Framers had something different in mind than what Blackstone himself meant. The historians concede that at least one historian takes a different position, but the Court, they imply, would lose a poll taken among professional historians of this period, say, by a vote of 8 to 1.

If history, and history alone, is what matters, why would the Court not now reconsider *Heller* in light of these more recently published historical views? . . . At the least, where *Heller*'s historical foundations are so uncertain, why extend its applicability?

My aim in referring to this history is to illustrate the reefs and shoals that lie in wait for those nonexpert judges who place virtually determinative weight upon historical considerations. In my own view, the Court should not look to history alone but to other factors as well — above all, in cases where the history is so unclear that the experts themselves strongly disagree. It should, for example, consider the basic values that underlie a constitutional provision and their contemporary significance. And it should examine as well the relevant consequences and practical justifications that might, or might not, warrant removing an important question from the democratic decisionmaking process. See (Stevens, J., dissenting) (discussing shortcomings of an exclusively historical approach).

II

A

In my view, taking *Heller* as a given, the Fourteenth Amendment does not incorporate the Second Amendment right to keep and bear arms for purposes of private self-defense. Under this Court's precedents, to incorporate the private self-defense right the majority must show that the right is, *e.g.*, "fundamental to the American scheme of justice," *Duncan v. Louisiana*, 391 U.S. 145, 149 (1968). . . . And this it fails to do.

The majority here, like that in *Heller*, relies almost exclusively upon history to make the necessary showing. But to do so for incorporation purposes is both wrong and dangerous. As Justice Stevens points out, our society has historically made mistakes — for example, when considering certain 18th- and 19th-century property rights to be fundamental. And in the incorporation context, as elsewhere, history often is unclear about the answers. *See* Part I, *supra;* Part III, *infra.*

Accordingly, this Court, in considering an incorporation question, has never stated that the historical status of a right is the only relevant consideration. Rather, the Court has either explicitly or implicitly made clear in its opinions that the right in question has remained fundamental over time. *See, e.g., Apodaca v. Oregon*, 406 U.S. 404, 410 (1972) (plurality opinion) (stating that the incorporation "inquiry must focus upon the function served" by the right in question in "*contemporary society*" (emphasis added)); *Duncan v. Louisiana*, 391 U.S. 145, 154 (1968) (noting that the right in question "continues to receive strong support"); *Klopfer v. North Carolina*, 386 U.S. 213, 226 (1967) (same). And, indeed, neither of the parties before us in this case has asked us to employ the majority's history-constrained approach.

I thus think it proper, above all where history provides no clear answer, to look to other factors in considering whether a right is sufficiently "fundamental" to remove it from the political process in every State. I would include among those factors the nature of the right; any contemporary disagreement about whether the right is fundamental; the extent to which incorporation will further other, perhaps more basic, constitutional aims; and the extent to which incorporation will advance or hinder the Constitution's structural aims, including its division of powers among different governmental institutions (and the people as well). Is incorporation needed, for example, to further the Constitution's effort to ensure that the government treats each individual with equal respect? Will it help maintain the democratic form of government that the Constitution foresees? In a word, will incorporation prove consistent, or inconsistent, with the Constitution's efforts to create governmental institutions well suited to the carrying out of its constitutional promises?

Finally, I would take account of the Framers' basic reason for believing the Court ought to have the power of judicial review. Alexander Hamilton feared granting that power to Congress alone, for he feared that Congress, acting as judges, would not overturn as unconstitutional a popular statute that it had recently enacted, as legislators. The Federalist No. 78, p. 405 (G. Carey & J. McClellan eds. 2001) (A. Hamilton) ("This independence of the judges is equally requisite to guard the constitution and the rights of individuals from the effects of those ill humours, which" can, at times, lead to "serious oppressions of the minor part in the community"). Judges, he thought, may find it easier to resist popular pressure to suppress the basic rights of an unpopular minority. See *United States v. Carolene Products Co.,* 304 U.S. 144, 152, n.4 (1938). That being so, it makes sense to ask whether that particular comparative judicial advantage is relevant to the case at hand. . . .

B

How do these considerations apply here? For one thing, I would apply them only to the private self-defense right directly at issue. After all, the Amendment's militia-related purpose is primarily to protect *States* from *federal* regulation, not to protect individuals from militia-related regulation. *Heller,* 128 S. Ct. at 2801-02; see also *Miller,* 307 U.S. at 178. Moreover, the Civil War Amendments, the electoral process, the courts, and numerous other institutions today help to safeguard the States and the people from any serious threat of federal tyranny. How are state militias additionally necessary? It is difficult to see how a right that, as the majority concedes, has "largely faded as a popular concern" could possibly be so fundamental that it would warrant incorporation through the Fourteenth Amendment. Hence, the incorporation of the Second Amendment cannot be based on the militia-related aspect of what *Heller* found to be more extensive Second Amendment rights.

For another thing, as *Heller* concedes, the private self-defense right that the Court would incorporate has nothing to do with "the *reason*" the Framers "codified" the right to keep and bear arms "in a written Constitution." 128 S. Ct. at 2801-02 (emphasis added). *Heller* immediately adds that the self-defense right was nonetheless "the *central component* of the right." *Id.* In my view, this is the historical equivalent of a claim that water runs uphill. But, taking it as valid, the Framers' basic *reasons* for including language in the Constitution would nonetheless seem more pertinent (in deciding about the contemporary *importance* of a right) than the particular *scope* 17th- or 18th-century listeners would have then assigned to the words they used. And examination of the Framers' motivation tells us they did not think the private armed self-defense right was of paramount importance. See Amar, The Bill of Rights as a Constitution, 100 Yale L.J. 1131, 1164 (1991) ("[T]o see the [Second] Amendment as primarily concerned with an individual right to hunt, or protect one's home," would be "like viewing the heart of the speech and assembly clauses as the right of persons to meet to play bridge"). . . .

Further, there is no popular consensus that the private self-defense right described in *Heller* is fundamental. The plurality suggests that two *amici* briefs filed in the case show such a consensus, but, of course, numerous *amici* briefs have been filed opposing incorporation as well. Moreover, every State regulates firearms extensively, and public opinion is sharply divided on the appropriate level of regulation. Much of this disagreement rests upon empirical considerations. One side believes the right essential to protect the lives of those attacked in the home; the other side believes it essential to regulate the right in order to protect the lives of others attacked with guns. It seems unlikely that definitive evidence will develop one way or the other. And the appropriate level of firearm regulation has thus long been, and continues to be, a hotly contested matter of political debate. . . .

Moreover, there is no reason here to believe that incorporation of the private self-defense right will further any other or broader constitutional objective. We are aware of no argument that gun-control regulations target or are passed with the purpose of targeting "discrete and insular minorities." *Carolene Products Co., supra,* at 153, n.4. . . . Nor will incorporation help to assure equal respect for individuals. Unlike the First Amendment's rights of free speech, free press, assembly, and petition, the private self-defense right does not comprise a necessary part of the democratic process that the Constitution seeks to establish. *See, e.g., Whitney v. California,* 274 U.S. 357, 377 (1927) (Brandeis, J., concurring). Unlike the First Amendment's religious protections, the Fourth Amendment's protection against unreasonable searches and seizures, the Fifth and Sixth Amendments' insistence upon fair criminal procedure, and the Eighth Amendment's protection against cruel and unusual punishments, the private self-defense right does not significantly seek to protect individuals who might otherwise suffer unfair or inhumane treatment at the hands of a majority. Unlike the protections offered by many of these same Amendments, it does not involve matters as to which judges possess a comparative expertise, by virtue of their close familiarity with the justice system and its operation. And, unlike the Fifth Amendment's insistence on just compensation, it does not involve a matter where a majority might unfairly seize for itself property belonging to a minority.

Finally, incorporation of the right *will* work a significant disruption in the constitutional allocation of decisionmaking authority, thereby interfering with the Constitution's ability to further its objectives.

First, on any reasonable accounting, the incorporation of the right recognized in *Heller* would amount to a significant incursion on a traditional and important area of state concern, altering the constitutional relationship between the States and the Federal Government. Private gun regulation is the quintessential exercise of a State's "police power" — *i.e.,* the power to "protec[t] . . . the lives, limbs, health, comfort, and quiet of all persons, and the protection of all property within the State," by enacting "all kinds of restraints and burdens" on both "persons and property." *Slaughter-House Cases,* 83 U.S. (16 Wall.) 36, 62 (1873) (internal quotation marks omitted). The Court has long recognized that the Constitution grants the States special authority to enact laws pursuant to this power. *See, e.g., Medtronic, Inc. v. Lohr,* 518 U.S. 470, 475 (1996) (noting that States have "great latitude" to use their police powers (internal quotation marks omitted)); *Metropolitan Life Ins. Co. v. Massachusetts,* 471 U.S. 724, 756 (1985). A decade ago, we wrote that there is "no better example of the police power" than "the suppression of violent crime." *United States v. Morrison,* 529 U.S. 598, 618 (2000). And examples in which the Court has deferred to state legislative judgments in respect to the exercise of the police power are legion. *See, e.g., Gonzales v. Oregon,* 546 U.S. 243, 270 (2006) (assisted suicide); *Washington v. Glucksberg,* 521 U.S. 702, 721 (1997) (same); *Berman v. Parker,* 348 U.S. 26, 32 (1954) ("We deal, in other words, with what traditionally has been known as the police power. An attempt to define its reach or trace its outer limits is fruitless . . .").

Second, determining the constitutionality of a particular state gun law requires finding answers to complex empirically based questions of a kind that legislatures are better able than courts to make. *See, e.g., Los Angeles v. Alameda Books, Inc.,* 535 U.S. 425, 440 (2002) (plurality opinion); *Turner Broadcasting System, Inc. v. FCC,* 520 U.S. 180, 195-96 (1997). And it may require this kind of analysis in virtually every case.

Government regulation of the right to bear arms normally embodies a judgment that the regulation will help save lives. The determination whether a gun regulation is constitutional would thus almost always require the weighing of the constitutional right to bear arms against the "primary concern of every government—a concern for the safety and indeed the lives of its citizens." *United States v. Salerno,* 481 U.S. 739, 755 (1987). With respect to other incorporated rights, this sort of inquiry is *sometimes* present. *See, e.g., Brandenburg v. Ohio,* 395 U.S. 444, 447 (1969) (*per curiam*) (free speech); *Sherbert v. Verner,* 374 U.S. 398, 403 (1963) (religion); *Brigham City v. Stuart,* 547 U.S. 398, 403-04 (2006) (Fourth Amendment); *New York v. Quarles,* 467 U.S. 649, 655 (1984) (Fifth Amendment); *Salerno, supra,* at 755 (bail). But here, this inquiry— calling for the fine tuning of protective rules—is likely to be part of a daily judicial diet. . . .

Consider too that countless gun regulations of many shapes and sizes are in place in every State and in many local communities. Does the right to possess weapons for self-defense extend outside the home? To the car? To work? What sort of guns are necessary for self-defense? Handguns? Rifles? Semiautomatic weapons? When is a gun semi-automatic? Where are different kinds of weapons likely needed? Does time-of-day matter? Does the presence of a child in the house matter? Does the presence of a convicted felon in the house matter? Do police need special rules permitting patdowns designed to find guns? When do registration requirements become severe to the point that they amount to an unconstitutional ban? Who can possess guns and of what kind? Aliens? Prior drug offenders? Prior alcohol abusers? How would the right interact with a state or local government's ability to take special measures during, say, national security emergencies? As the questions suggest, state and local gun regulation can become highly complex, and these "are only a few uncertainties that quickly come to mind." *Caperton v. A.T. Massey Coal Co.,* 129 S. Ct. 2252, 2261 (2009) (Roberts, C.J., dissenting). . . .

In answering such questions judges cannot simply refer to judicial homilies, such as Blackstone's 18th-century perception that a man's home is his castle. See 4 Blackstone 223. Nor can the plurality so simply reject, by mere assertion, the fact that "incorporation will require judges to assess the costs and benefits of firearms restrictions." How can the Court assess the strength of the government's regulatory interests without addressing issues of empirical fact? How can the Court determine if a regulation is appropriately tailored without considering its impact? And how can the Court determine if there are less restrictive alternatives without considering what will happen if those alternatives are implemented? . . .

In *New State Ice Co. v. Liebmann,* 285 U.S. 262, 310-11 (1932), Justice Brandeis stated in dissent:

> "Some people assert that our present plight is due, in part, to the limitations set by courts upon experimentation in the fields of social and economic science; and to the discouragement to which proposals for betterment there have been subjected otherwise. There must be power in the States and the Nation to remould, through experimentation, our economic practices and institutions to meet changing social and economic needs. I cannot believe that the framers of the Fourteenth Amendment, or the States which ratified it, intended to deprive us of the power to correct [the social problems we face]."

There are 50 state legislatures. The fact that this Court may already have refused to take this wise advice with respect to Congress in *Heller* is no reason to make matters worse here.

Third, the ability of States to reflect local preferences and conditions — both key virtues of federalism — here has particular importance. The incidence of gun ownership varies substantially as between crowded cities and uncongested rural communities, as well as among the different geographic regions of the country. . . .

The nature of gun violence also varies as between rural communities and cities. . . .

It is thus unsurprising that States and local communities have historically differed about the need for gun regulation as well as about its proper level. Nor is it surprising that "primarily, and historically," the law has treated the exercise of police powers, including gun control, as "matter[s] of local concern." *Medtronic,* 518 U.S. at 475 (internal quotation marks omitted).

Fourth, although incorporation of any right removes decisions from the democratic process, the incorporation of this particular right does so without strong offsetting justification — as the example of Oak Park's handgun ban helps to show. . . . Oak Park decided to ban handguns in 1983, after a local attorney was shot to death with a handgun that his assailant had smuggled into a courtroom in a blanket. A citizens committee spent months gathering information about handguns. It secured 6,000 signatures from community residents in support of a ban. And the village board enacted a ban into law.

Subsequently, at the urging of ban opponents the Board held a community referendum on the matter. The citizens committee argued strongly in favor of the ban. It pointed out that most guns owned in Oak Park were handguns and that handguns were misused more often than citizens used them in self-defense. The ban opponents argued just as strongly to the contrary. The public decided to keep the ban by a vote of 8,031 to 6,368. And since that time, Oak Park now tells us, crime has decreased and the community has seen no accidental handgun deaths.

Given the empirical and local value-laden nature of the questions that lie at the heart of the issue, why, in a Nation whose Constitution foresees democratic decisionmaking, is it so *fundamental* a matter as to require taking that power from the people? What is it here that the people did not know? What is it that a judge knows better?

* * *

In sum, the police power, the superiority of legislative decisionmaking, the need for local decisionmaking, the comparative desirability of democratic decisionmaking, the lack of a manageable judicial standard, and the life-threatening harm that may flow from striking down regulations all argue against incorporation. Where the incorporation of other rights has been at issue, *some* of these problems have arisen. But in this instance *all* these problems are present, *all* at the same time, and *all* are likely to be present in most, perhaps nearly all, of the cases in which the constitutionality of a gun regulation is at issue. At the same time, the important factors that favor incorporation in other instances — *e.g.,* the protection of broader constitutional objectives — are not present here. The upshot is that all factors militate against incorporation — with the possible exception of historical factors.

III

I must, then, return to history. The plurality, in seeking to justify incorporation, asks whether the interests the Second Amendment protects are "'deeply rooted in this Nation's history and tradition.'" (quoting *Glucksberg,* 521 U.S. at 721; internal quotation marks omitted). It looks to selected portions of the Nation's history for the answer. And it finds an affirmative reply.

As I have made clear, I do not believe history is the only pertinent consideration. Nor would I read history as broadly as the majority does. In particular, since we here are evaluating a more particular right — namely, the right to bear arms for purposes of private self-defense — general historical references to the "right to keep and bear arms" are not always helpful. Depending upon context, early historical sources may mean to refer to a militia-based right — a matter of considerable importance 200 years ago — which has, as the majority points out, "largely faded as a popular concern." There is no reason to believe that matters of such little contemporary importance should play a significant role in answering the incorporation question. See *Apodaca,* 406 U.S. at 410 (incorporation "inquiry must focus upon the function served" by the right in question in "contemporary society"); *Wolf v. Colorado,* 338 U.S. 25, 27 (1949) (incorporation must take into account "the movements of a free society" and "the gradual and empiric process of inclusion and exclusion" (internal quotation marks omitted)); cf. U.S. Const., Art. I, §9 (prohibiting federal officeholders from accepting a "Title, of any kind whatever, from [a] foreign State" — presumably a matter of considerable importance 200 years ago).

That said, I can find much in the historical record that shows that some Americans in some places at certain times thought it important to keep and bear arms for private self-defense. For instance, the reader will see that many States have constitutional provisions protecting gun possession. But, as far as I can tell, those provisions typically do no more than guarantee that a gun regulation will be a *reasonable* police power regulation. See Winkler, Scrutinizing the Second Amendment, 105 Mich. L. Rev. 683, 686, 716-17 (2007) (the "courts of every state to consider the question apply a deferential 'reasonable regulation' standard") (hereinafter Winkler, Scrutinizing). . . . It is thus altogether unclear whether such provisions would prohibit cities such as Chicago from enacting laws, such as the law before us, banning handguns. See *id.* at 723. The majority, however, would incorporate a right that is likely *inconsistent* with Chicago's law; and the majority would almost certainly *strike down* that law. Cf. *Heller,* 128 S. Ct. at 2818-22 (striking down the District of Columbia's handgun ban).

Thus, the specific question before us is not whether there are references to the right to bear arms for self-defense throughout this Nation's history—of course there are—or even whether the Court should incorporate a simple constitutional requirement that firearms regulations not unreasonably burden the right to keep and bear arms, but rather whether there is a consensus that *so substantial* a private self-defense right as the one described in *Heller* applies to the States. *See, e.g., Glucksberg,* supra, at 721 (requiring "a careful description" of the right at issue when deciding whether it is "deeply rooted in this Nation's history and tradition" (internal quotation marks omitted)). On this question, the reader will have to make up his or her own mind about the historical record that I describe in part below. In my view, that record is insufficient to say that the right to bear arms for private self-defense, as explicated by *Heller,* is fundamental in the sense relevant to the incorporation inquiry. . . .

I thus cannot find a historical consensus with respect to whether the right described by *Heller* is "fundamental" as our incorporation cases use that term. Nor can I find sufficient historical support for the majority's conclusion that that right is "deeply rooted in this Nation's history and tradition." Instead, I find no more than ambiguity and uncertainty that perhaps even expert historians would find difficult to penetrate. And a historical record that is so ambiguous cannot itself provide an adequate basis for incorporating a private right of self-defense and applying it against the States.

The Eighteenth Century

The opinions in *Heller* collect much of the relevant 18th-century evidence. See 128 S. Ct. at 2790-05; *id.* at 2824-38 (Stevens, J., dissenting); *id.* at 2848-50 (Breyer, J., dissenting). In respect to the relevant question—the "deeply rooted nature" of a right to keep and bear arms for purposes of private self-defense—that evidence is inconclusive, particularly when augmented as follows:

First, as I have noted earlier in this opinion, and Justice Stevens argued in dissent, the history discussed in *Heller* shows that the Second Amendment was enacted primarily for the purpose of protecting militia-related rights. See *Heller,* 128 S. Ct. at 2790-05. Many of the scholars and historians who have written on the subject apparently agree.

Second, historians now tell us that the right to which Blackstone referred, an important link in the *Heller* majority's historical argument, concerned the right of Parliament (representing the people) to form a militia to oppose a tyrant (the King) threatening to deprive the people of their traditional liberties (which did not include an unregulated right to possess guns). Thus, 18th-century language referring to a "right to keep and bear arms" does not *ipso facto* refer to a private right of self-defense—certainly not unambiguously so.

Third, scholarly articles indicate that firearms were heavily regulated at the time of the framing—perhaps more heavily regulated than the Court in *Heller* believed. For example, one scholar writes that "[h]undreds of individual statutes regulated the possession and use of guns in colonial and early national

America." Churchill, Gun Regulation, the Police Power, and the Right to Keep Arms, 25 Law & Hist. Rev. 139, 143 (2007). Among these statutes was a ban on the private firing of weapons in Boston, as well as comprehensive restrictions on similar conduct in Philadelphia and New York. See Acts and Laws of Massachusetts, p. 208 (1746); 5 J. Mitchell, & H. Flanders, Statutes at Large of Pennsylvania From 1682 to 1801, pp. 108-109 (1898); 4 Colonial Laws of New York ch. 1233, p. 748 (1894). . . .

Fourth, after the Constitution was adopted, several States continued to regulate firearms possession by, for example, adopting rules that would have prevented the carrying of loaded firearms in the city, *Heller,* 128 S. Ct. at 2848-50 (Breyer, J., dissenting). . . . Scholars have thus concluded that the primary Revolutionary era limitation on a State's police power to regulate guns appears to be only that regulations were "aimed at a legitimate public purpose" and "consistent with reason." Cornell, Early American Gun Regulation and the Second Amendment, 25 Law & Hist. Rev. 197, 198 (2007).

The Pre-Civil War Nineteenth Century

I would also augment the majority's account of this period as follows:

First, additional States began to regulate the discharge of firearms in public places. *See, e.g.,* Act of Feb. 17, 1831, §6, reprinted in 3 Statutes of Ohio and the Northwestern Territory 1740 (S. Chase ed. 1835); Act of Dec. 3, 1825, ch. CCXCII, §3, 1825 Tenn. Priv. Acts 306.

Second, States began to regulate the possession of concealed weapons, which were both popular and dangerous. *See, e.g.,* C. Cramer, Concealed Weapon Laws of the Early Republic 143-152 (1999) (collecting examples). . . .

State courts repeatedly upheld the validity of such laws, finding that, even when the state constitution granted a right to bear arms, the legislature was permitted to, *e.g.,* "abolish" these small, inexpensive, "most dangerous weapons entirely from use," even in self-defense. *Day v. State,* 37 Tenn. 496, 500 (1857). . . .

The Post-Civil War Nineteenth Century

It is important to read the majority's account with the following considerations in mind:

First, the Court today properly declines to revisit our interpretation of the Privileges or Immunities Clause. The Court's case for incorporation must thus rest on the conclusion that the right to bear arms is "fundamental." But the very evidence that it advances in support of the conclusion that Reconstruction-era Americans strongly supported a private self-defense right shows with equal force that Americans wanted African-American citizens to have the *same* rights to possess guns as did white citizens. Here, for example is what Congress said when it enacted a Fourteenth Amendment predecessor, the Second Freedmen's Bureau Act. It wrote that the statute, in order to secure "the constitutional right to bear arms . . . for all citizens," would assure that each citizen:

> "shall have . . . *full and equal benefit* of all laws and proceedings concerning personal liberty, personal security, and the acquisition, enjoyment, and disposition of estate, real and personal, including the constitutional right to bear arms, [by

securing] . . . to . . . all the citizens of [every] . . . State or district without *respect to race or color, or previous condition of slavery.*" §14, 14 Stat. 176-77 (emphasis added).

This sounds like an *antidiscrimination* provision. See Rosenthal, The New Originalism Meets the Fourteenth Amendment: Original Public Meaning and the Problem of Incorporation, 18 J. Contemp. Legal Issues 361, 383-84 (2009) (discussing evidence that the Freedmen's Bureau was focused on discrimination).

Another Fourteenth Amendment predecessor, the Civil Rights Act of 1866, also took aim at *discrimination.* See §1, 14 Stat. 27 (citizens of "every race and color, without regard to any previous condition of slavery or involuntary servitude . . . shall have the same right [to engage in various activities] and to full and equal benefit of all laws . . . as is enjoyed by white citizens"). And, of course, the Fourteenth Amendment itself insists that all States guarantee their citizens the "equal protection of the laws."

There is thus every reason to believe that the *fundamental* concern of the Reconstruction Congress was the eradication of discrimination, not the provision of a new substantive right to bear arms free from reasonable state police power regulation. Indeed, why would those who wrote the Fourteenth Amendment have wanted to give such a right to Southerners who had so recently waged war against the North, and who continued to disarm and oppress recently freed African-American citizens? Cf. Act of Mar. 2, 1867, §6, 14 Stat. 487 (disbanding Southern militias because they were, *inter alia,* disarming the freedmen).

Second, firearms regulation in the later part of the 19th century was common. The majority is correct that the Freedmen's Bureau points to a right to bear arms, and it stands to reason, as the majority points out, that "[i]t would have been nonsensical for Congress to guarantee the . . . equal benefit of a . . . right that does not exist." But the majority points to no evidence that there existed during this period a fundamental right to bear arms for private self-defense immune to the reasonable exercise of the state police power. See Emberton, The Limits of Incorporation: Violence, Gun Rights, and Gun Regulation in the Reconstruction South, 17 Stan. L. & Pol'y Rev. 615, 621-22 (2006) (noting that history shows that "nineteenth-century Americans" were "not opposed to the idea that the state should be able to control the use of firearms").

To the contrary, in the latter half of the 19th century, a number of state constitutions adopted or amended after the Civil War explicitly recognized the legislature's general ability to limit the right to bear arms. [See the appendix to Chapter 1.] And numerous other state constitutional provisions adopted during this period explicitly granted the legislature various types of regulatory power over firearms.

Moreover, four States largely banned the possession of all nonmilitary handguns during this period. . . . Fifteen States banned the concealed carry of pistols and other deadly weapons. And individual municipalities enacted stringent gun controls, often in response to local conditions—Dodge City, Kansas, for example, joined many western cattle towns in banning the carrying of pistols and other dangerous weapons in response to violence accompanying western cattle drives. . . .

Further, much as they had during the period before the Civil War, state courts routinely upheld such restrictions. *See, e.g., English v. State,* 35 Tex. 473

(1871); *Hill v. State,* 53 Ga. 472, 475 (1874); *Fife v. State,* 31 Ark. 455, 461 (1876); *State v. Workman,* 14 S.E. 9 (1891). The Tennessee Supreme Court, in upholding a ban on possession of nonmilitary handguns and certain other weapons, summarized the Reconstruction understanding of the states' police power to regulate firearms:

> "Admitting the right of self-defense in its broadest sense, still on sound principle every good citizen is bound to yield his preference as to the means to be used, to the demands of the public good; *and where certain weapons are forbidden to be kept or used by the law of the land,* in order to the prevention of *[sic]* crime — a great public end — *no man can be permitted to disregard this general end, and demand of the community the right, in order to gratify his whim or willful desire to use a particular weapon in his particular self-defense.* The law allows ample means of self-defense, without the use of the weapons which we have held may be rightfully prescribed by this statute. The object being to banish these weapons from the community by an absolute prohibition for the prevention of crime, no man's particular safety, if such case could exist, ought to be allowed to defeat this end." *Andrews v. State,* 50 Tenn. 165, 188-89 (1871) (emphasis added).

The Twentieth and Twenty-First Centuries

Although the majority does not discuss 20th- or 21st-century evidence concerning the Second Amendment at any length, I think that it is essential to consider the recent history of the right to bear arms for private self-defense when considering whether the right is "fundamental." To that end, many States now provide state constitutional protection for an individual's right to keep and bear arms. See Volokh, State Constitutional Rights to Keep and Bear Arms, 11 Tex. Rev. L. & Pol. 191, 205 (2006) (identifying over 40 States). In determining the importance of this fact, we should keep the following considerations in mind:

First, by the end of the 20th century, in every State and many local communities, highly detailed and complicated regulatory schemes governed (and continue to govern) nearly every aspect of firearm ownership: Who may sell guns and how they must be sold; who may purchase guns and what type of guns may be purchased; how firearms must be stored and where they may be used; and so on. See generally Legal Community Against Violence, Regulating Guns In America (2008), available at http://www.lcav.org/publications-briefs/regulating_guns.asp (detailing various arms regulations in every State).

Of particular relevance here, some municipalities ban handguns, even in States that constitutionally protect the right to bear arms. . . . Moreover, at least seven States and Puerto Rico ban assault weapons or semiautomatic weapons. . . .

Thirteen municipalities do the same. . . . And two States, Maryland and Hawaii, ban assault pistols. . . .

Second, as I stated earlier, state courts in States with constitutions that provide gun rights have almost uniformly interpreted those rights as providing protection only against *unreasonable* regulation of guns. See, e.g., Winkler, Scrutinizing 686 (the "courts of every state to consider" a gun regulation apply the "'reasonable regulation'" approach); *State v. McAdams,* 714 P.2d

1236, 1238 (Wyo. 1986); *Robertson v. City & County of Denver,* 874 P.2d 325, 328 (Colo. 1994).

When determining reasonableness those courts have normally adopted a highly deferential attitude towards legislative determinations. See Winkler, Scrutinizing 723 (identifying only six cases in the 60 years before the article's publication striking down gun control laws: three that banned "the transportation of any firearms for any purpose whatsoever," a single "permitting law," and two as-applied challenges in "unusual circumstances"). Hence, as evidenced by the breadth of existing regulations, States and local governments maintain substantial flexibility to regulate firearms — much as they seemingly have throughout the Nation's history — even in those States with an arms right in their constitutions.

Although one scholar implies that state courts are less willing to permit total gun prohibitions, see Volokh, Implementing the Right to Keep and Bear Arms for Self-Defense: An Analytical Framework and a Research Agenda, 56 UCLA L. Rev. 1443, 1458 (2009), I am aware of no instances in the past 50 years in which a state court has struck down as unconstitutional a law banning a particular class of firearms, see Winkler, Scrutinizing 723.

Indeed, state courts have specifically upheld as constitutional (under their state constitutions) firearms regulations that have included handgun bans. See *Kalodimos v. Village of Morton Grove,* 470 N.E.2d 266, 273 (1984) (upholding a handgun ban because the arms right is merely a right "to possess some form of weapon suitable for self-defense or recreation"); *Cleveland v. Turner,* No. 36126, 1977 WL 201393, *5 (Ohio Ct. App., Aug. 4, 1977) (handgun ban "does not absolutely interfere with the right of the people to bear arms, but rather proscribes possession of a specifically defined category of handguns"); *State v. Bolin,* 662 S.E.2d 38, 39 (2008) (ban on handgun possession by persons under 21 did not infringe arms right because they can "posses[s] other types of guns"). Thus, the majority's decision to incorporate the private self-defense right recognized in *Heller* threatens to alter state regulatory regimes, at least as they pertain to handguns.

Third, the plurality correctly points out that *only a few* state courts, a "paucity" of state courts, have specifically upheld handgun bans. But which state courts have struck them down? The absence of supporting information does not help the majority find support. . . . Silence does not show or tend to show a consensus that a private self-defense right (strong enough to strike down a handgun ban) is "deeply rooted in this Nation's history and tradition."

* * *

In sum, the Framers did not write the Second Amendment in order to protect a private right of armed self-defense. There has been, and is, no consensus that the right is, or was, "fundamental." No broader constitutional interest or principle supports legal treatment of that right as fundamental. To the contrary, broader constitutional concerns of an institutional nature argue strongly against that treatment.

Moreover, nothing in 18th-, 19th-, 20th-, or 21st-century history shows a consensus that the right to private armed self-defense, as described in *Heller,* is "deeply rooted in this Nation's history or tradition" or is otherwise "fundamental." Indeed, incorporating the right recognized in *Heller* may change the law in many of the 50 States. Read in the majority's favor, the historical evidence is at most ambiguous. And, in the absence of any other support for its conclusion, ambiguous history cannot show that the Fourteenth Amendment incorporates a private right of self-defense against the States.

With respect, I dissent.

NOTES & QUESTIONS

1. What is your assessment of the immediate practical impact of *Heller* and *McDonald*? Prior to these decisions, there were handgun bans in the District of Columbia, and Chicago and a few of its surrounding suburbs. Preemption laws ensured that, in most states, no bans would be enacted. The only city that attempted to enact a handgun ban notwithstanding a preemption statute was San Francisco, and that ban was quickly declared void. *See Fiscal v. City and County of San Francisco*, 70 Cal. Rptr. 3d 324, 341 (Cal. Ct. App. 2008) (holding that recently enacted San Francisco handgun ban was invalid as a violation of California's preemption statute); Cal. Penal Code §12026 (2000); Cal. Gov't Code §53071 (1997) (expressing state's intent to occupy the field of firearms and ammunition regulation).

    Wisconsin had no preemption law until 1995. In 1993 and 1994, voters in three Wisconsin towns were asked to ban handguns. The bans were defeated in Madison (51%), Milwaukee (67%), and Kenosha (73%). The backlash against the handgun ban proposals led to a preemption statute in 1995 and voter adoption of a state constitutional right to arms by 1998.

    State-wide gun ban proposals have been placed on the ballot on two other occasions. A handgun confiscation initiative was rejected by 69 percent of Massachusetts voters in 1976. A handgun "freeze" (no sales of new handguns) was rejected by 63 percent of California voters in 1982.

2. What is the scope of the right to keep and bear arms after *Heller* and *McDonald*? Is the Second Amendment solely a right to handguns for home defense? The dissents in *McDonald* seem to suggest so. Are the *Heller* and the *McDonald* majorities consistent with this view? Do they describe home defense as the only purpose of the Second Amendment, or instead as the leading purpose?

    Does *McDonald* clarify the meaning of the Second Amendment right described in *Heller*? Does *McDonald* describe self-defense in the home as the most important Second Amendment activity, or as the only Second Amendment activity?

3. The *McDonald* opinions spend much time debating the proper method for deciding whether a right should be incorporated against the states. What issues are raised by each method?

4. In *Heller*, the Court stated that "the enshrinement of constitutional rights necessarily takes certain policy choices off the table," including a total

handgun ban. But in *McDonald*, both the majority and Justice Breyer discuss the *effectiveness* of Chicago's ban. Similarly, Justice Thomas discusses the "consequences of *Cruikshank*." To what degree should courts base decisions about the constitutional right to arms on empirical assessments of the costs and benefits of an armed citizenry? What if those empirical assessments are disputed? How should courts decide what empirical claims to credit?

5. Justice Stevens argued that even if the Second Amendment were to be incorporated, the full scope of the Amendment should not be applied "jot for jot." At oral argument, Chief Justice Roberts rejected the notion of creating a "shadow" version of the Second Amendment to apply to the states. If only part of the Second Amendment were to be applied to states, what parts would be most appropriate to apply? Consider the view of the *Heller* dissenters that the Second Amendment individual right was originally intended solely to prevent the federal government from destroying state militias. Now integrate the evidence that the enactors of the Fourteenth Amendment intended to secure the Second Amendment right to keep and bear arms for personal self-defense, especially against Klansmen and similar racial terrorists.

6. The plurality opinion lists the provisions of the Bill of Rights that have and have not been incorporated against the states. If you were framing a list of fundamental rights, would those incorporated rights be on it? What about the remaining unincorporated rights (quartering of soldiers, grand jury indictment, jury right in civil cases, excessive fines)?

7. The First Amendment text says nothing about a right of association. However, the Supreme Court has determined it to be implicit, and necessary to the exercise of the enumerated First Amendment rights. The first right-of-association case was *NAACP v. Alabama*, 357 U.S. 449 (1958). Since then, the right of association has grown into a robust right that will be recognized even where it is unconnected to the textual guarantees of the First Amendment. *E.g., Boy Scouts of America v. Dale*, 530 U.S. 640 (2000). In light of *Heller* and *McDonald*, is self-defense a Second Amendment right? Can a government constitutionally outlaw forcible self-defense? If a government outlawed the use of firearms for self-defense, could the government then outlaw firearms? Chief Judge Easterbrook's opinion for the Seventh Circuit suggested that this would be lawful. *See National Rifle Ass'n of America, Inc. v. Chicago*, 567 F.3d 856 (7th Cir. 2009), *cert. granted sub nom. McDonald v. Chicago*, 130 S. Ct. 48 (2009). For an argument that even without the Second Amendment, self-defense is a universal human right, see David B. Kopel, Paul Gallant & Joanne D. Eisen, *The Human Right of Self-Defense*, 22 BYU J. Pub. L. 43 (2007) (arguing that an overwhelming consensus of past and present legal authorities, from all over the world, recognize self-defense as a foundational human right).

8. Assume that the assessment of the Privileges or Immunities Clause in the *Slaughter-House Cases* is correct. Can you make a case that the right to keep and bear arms is one of those privileges or immunities? For an argument

that *Slaughter-House* (but not *Cruikshank*) can be read to protect an individual right to arms because federal militia membership is a privilege or immunity of U.S. citizenship that is created by the Constitution, see Kenneth Kulokowski, *Citizen Gun Rights: Incorporating the Second Amendment Through the Privileges or Immunities Clause*, 39 N.M. L. Rev. 195 (2009).

9. In the 1939 case of *Hague v. CIO*, 307 U.S. 496, the Supreme Court applied part of the First Amendment to overturn Jersey City, New Jersey, Mayor Frank Hague's policy of forbidding all political meetings and pamphlet distribution (especially by labor organizers) which contradicted his own agenda. Three Justices did so on the basis of the Due Process Clause. Two based their decision on the Privileges or Immunities Clause. Today, *Hague* is a foundational case for First Amendment law, but its brief revival of Privileges or Immunities has been forgotten (mostly because in subsequent cases, all Justices fell in line with the Due Process approach).

10. The Fourteenth Amendment's Due Process Clause has been interpreted to protect a wide variety of unenumerated rights, in addition to those described in the Bill of Rights. These include the right to teach children a foreign language (*Meyer v. Nebraska*, 262 U.S. 390 (1923)), the right to attend a nongovernment school, such as a Catholic or Lutheran School (*Pierce v. Society of Sisters*, 268 U.S. 510 (1925)), the right to use birth control (*Griswold v. Connecticut*, 381 U.S. 479 (1965), and *Eisenstadt v. Baird*, 405 U.S. 438 (1972)), the right to intimate sexual relations (*Lawrence v. Texas*, 539 U.S. 558 (2003)), and, most controversially, the right to abortion (*Roe v. Wade*, 410 U.S. 113 (1973), and *Planned Parenthood v. Casey*, 505 U.S. 833 (1992)). An excellent summary of the Court's jurisprudence on unenumerated rights, from the nineteenth century to the present, is provided by Justice Souter's concurrence in *Washington v. Glucksberg*, 521 U.S. 702 (1997). The modern, and generally followed, standard for recognition of additional unenumerated rights is that such proposed right must be "deeply rooted in this nation's history and tradition." *Id.* at 703. *Lawrence*, however, uses a standard of "emerging awareness" and speaks broadly about the individual's right to realize his full human potential. 539 U.S. at 559. Do either the *Glucksberg* or the *Lawrence* standards have the potential to protect a right to arms or self-defense beyond what is protected by the Second Amendment? If there were no Second Amendment, would the *Gluckberg* or the *Lawrence* principle support arms rights or self-defense rights?

11. While a diverse majority of modern legal scholars agree that the Privileges or Immunities Clause was intended to make the Bill of Rights applicable to the states, scholars disagree about whether the clause was also intended to protect unenumerated rights. If the Privileges or Immunities Clause were interpreted to protect unenumerated rights, and in a manner that did not merely duplicate the unenumerated rights jurisprudence of the Due Process Clause, what might some of those rights be? For examination of how the Privileges or Immunities Clause might be used for judicial enforcement/creation of many important new rights, see The Constitution in

2020 (Jack M. Balkin & Reva B. Siegel eds., 2009). Other than the rights guaranteed by the Second Amendment, are there privileges or immunities of citizens of the United States regarding arms or defense?

12. Consider the Ninth Amendment, which reads: "The enumeration in the Constitution, of certain rights, shall not be construed to deny or disparage others retained by the people." When Senator Jacob Howard gave his "great fundamental guarantees" speech introducing the Fourteenth Amendment in the Senate, he referred specifically to the "first eight amendments of the Constitution." Cong. Globe, 39th Cong., 1st Sess. 2765-66 (1866). Is there any reason that the Framers of the Fourteenth Amendment might not have wanted to have the Ninth Amendment applied to the states? In Senator Howard's case, it appears that he considered privileges or immunities to include unenumerated rights as well, citing *Corfield v. Coryell*, 6 Fed. Cas. 546 (C.C. E.D. Pa. 1823), in the same speech. (*Corfield* was an influential case describing the "Privileges and Immunities in Article IV of the Constitution." One possible answer is that the Ninth and Tenth Amendments were both considered to be rules of construction. *See* Michael W. McConnell, *The Ninth Amendment in Light of Text and History*, 2010 Cato Sup. Ct. Rev. 13 (arguing that the Ninth Amendment means that courts should construe laws so as not to infringe liberty, unless legislative intent is unmistakable); Kurt Lash, The Lost History of the Ninth Amendment (2009); Burt Neuborne, *"The House Was Quiet and the World Was Calm The Reader Became The Book": Reading the Bill of Rights as a Poem: An Essay in Honor of the Fiftieth Anniversary of* Brown v. Board of Education, 57 Vand. L. Rev. 2007 (2004) (arguing that the Ninth Amendment means that rights should be construed broadly while the Tenth Amendment means that federal powers should be construed narrowly).

13. Consider the competing assessments by Justice Alito and Justice Stevens of the impact that the individual right to arms will have on constitutional provisions restricting police and prosecutors. Which view do you find more convincing? Why? For some specific law enforcement perspectives, see the amicus briefs in *Heller* and *McDonald* (available on Westlaw via links at the end of each case and at http://DCguncase.org and http://chicagoguncase.org) filed by various law enforcement organizations, police executives, and district attorneys on both sides of the cases.

14. Do you agree with the municipal respondents that the right to bear arms has no intrinsic value — that arms possession is not a good in itself, but is, at most, a means to some genuine good (such as saving lives)? Assume that guns have only instrumental value. Should that matter in determining the scope of the right to bear arms? What do you think of the claim that the defensive or sporting use of firearms has the same kind of intrinsic value often attributed to reading, religion, or political activity?

15. If the intended beneficiary of the Second Amendment is the states, does it make sense to incorporate it as a limitation on state action? Do the amicus briefs of 38 state attorneys general asking for incorporation, and three

attorneys general opposing it affect the answer? (All the *McDonald* briefs are available at http://www.chicagoguncase.org.) In 2011, the Supreme Court unanimously ruled that an individual could, in certain circumstances, have standing to challenge a federal law that allegedly violated the Tenth Amendment. The Court reasoned that federalism is not only a protection for state sovereignty, but also a protector of individual rights, because "[b]y denying any one government complete jurisdiction over all aspects of public life, federalism protects the liberty of the individual from arbitrary power." *Bond v. United States*, 131 S. Ct. 2355, 2364 (2011).

16. Do you agree with Justices Stevens and Breyer that armed self-defense does not protect minorities, or other groups at a disadvantage in the political process, or the democratic process itself? Compare the discussion of the racial and ethnic aspects of gun control in American history (Chapters 3, 5, and 6) with your sense of modern America.

17. How should the practical effectiveness of a contested constitutional right affect the Court's decision to recognize or enforce it? What time frame should the Court use to determine the "current" importance of a right?

18. Justice Breyer's dissent suggests that one reason Second Amendment rights should not be incorporated is that gun owners generally have been successful in protecting their rights in the political arena. Should this matter? Should judicial intervention be reserved only for politically powerless groups? Should courts be more active in policing alleged constitutional violations in areas such as New York City, the District of Columbia, Chicago, or New Jersey, where gun owners are an unusually small percentage of the population (relative to American norms), are politically weak, and many gun owners are "in the closet" because of social pressures?

19. Is the right to bear arms properly analyzed as a purely "liberty" interest, as Justice Stevens suggests? Might firearms owners argue that gun bans impair a constitutionally protected property interest? When would that claim be strongest? Does the claim in *McDonald* also implicate "life" interests?

20. Both dissenters imply that they might support Fourteenth Amendment enforcement of a self-defense right under certain circumstances. What circumstances would qualify?

21. What reasons does Justice Stevens give for concluding that the Court should not recognize a firearms right outside the home? For commentary advocating a right of self-defense in the home but a heavily limited right outside the home, see Darrell A.H. Miller, *Guns as Smut: Defending the Home-Bound Second Amendment*, 109 Colum. L. Rev. 1278 (2009) (analogizing firearms to obscenity, and *Heller* to *Stanley v. Georgia*, 394 U.S. 557 (1969), which held that possession of obscenity in the home could not

be criminalized, even though the sale and production, and possession of obscenity can be criminalized, as can possession or use outside the home). In a reply article, Eugene Volokh argues that the obscenity analogy is inapt, since there is no constitutional right to obscenity, but there is an explicit constitutional right to arms. Eugene Volokh, *The First and Second Amendments*, 109 Colum. L. Rev. Sidebar 97 (2009).

22. Do "firearms have a fundamentally ambivalent relationship to liberty"? Justice Stevens states that "liberty is on both sides of the equation" because victims of gun violence have a liberty interest in "being and feeling safe from armed violence." Can you think of other contexts in which a similar analysis occurs? Should *feeling* safe be considered separately from *being* safe?

23. Justice Stevens argues that the public safety implications of other Bill of Rights liberties are comparatively "quite attenuated." Is this an empirical assessment? What if empirical studies show that *Miranda* warnings, the exclusionary rule, or the requirement for unanimous jury verdicts resulted in thousands of criminals being set free, and that those thousands of criminals committed thousands of subsequent crimes? Are the public safety *benefits* of the Bill of Rights equally "attenuated"? How attenuated are the public safety benefits of the right to arms? To what extent should judges consider such issues in deciding the scope of constitutional rights?

24. Justice Breyer argues that because "other advanced democracies, including those that share our British heritage," do not constitutionally protect "an expansive right to keep and bear arms," such a right should not be protected by the U.S. Supreme Court. Does it matter that the Second Amendment was apparently intended by James Madison to protect the right to arms more expansively than Great Britain did? (Chapter 4) Discuss with your classmates what you know about the government practices in other advanced democracies, such as those with British heritage, about the scope of the rights to free exercise of religion, non-establishment of religion, freedom from warrantless searches, the exclusionary rule, grand juries, criminal or civil juries, privacy, and abortion. Which of those might make good constitutional models for the United States? Are any of these modern versions of practices the United States consciously broke from in the American Revolution?

25. Do you agree with Justice Steven's theory that "'[a] basic step in organizing a civilized society is to take [the] sword out of private hands and turn it over to an organized government, acting on behalf of all the people'"? See Chapters 2 through 4; *State v. Buzzard*, 4 Ark. 18 (1842) (Chapter 5; compare the three opinions); George A. Mocsary, *Monopoly of Violence*, Claremont Rev. of Books, Summer 2010, at 46. Consider that it is generally, though by no means universally, recognized that self-defense against imminent threats is a necessary exception to state monopoly of violence. *See, e.g.*, George P. Fletcher, Rethinking Criminal Law §10.5.4 (2000). Are firearms

a necessary part of this accommodation? Can the self-defense interest be adequately respected without recognizing a right to arms?

26. Quoting the Seventh Circuit decision under review, Justice Breyer writes that "[f]ederalism is a far 'older and more deeply rooted tradition than is a right to carry,' or to own, 'any particular kind of weapon.'" Presumably if the "particular kind of weapon" is defined precisely, such as "Glock 26 pistol," the statement is indisputable, since modern firearms are based on inventions from the nineteenth century or afterwards. But is federalism older than the right of self-defense? The right to own a firearm for legitimate purposes? The right to own a handgun for such purposes? Does *Cruikshank* (1876) (Chapter 6) suggest an answer?

27. Does the Second Amendment, as construed in *McDonald* and *Heller*, retain the tyranny-control purpose that so occupied the Framers? (Chapter 4) Consider the list of concerns the Court said were driving the enactment of the Fourteenth Amendment. Is defense from a tyrannical government a subcategory of self-defense? (Chapters 2-4). Do the conditions that led to the Fourteenth Amendment (Chapter 6) suggest that resisting tyranny can include resisting local criminals, such as the Ku Klux Klan? What about *Heller*'s observation that "when the able-bodied men of a nation are trained in arms and organized, they are better able to resist tyranny"?

28. Justice Breyer argues that "determining the constitutionality of a particular state gun law requires finding answers to complex empirically based questions of a kind that legislatures are better able than courts to make." Under what circumstances should the complexity of the problem cause a court to defer to the legislature? If a regulation goes to the basic existence of a constitutional right, should the court defer? Is Justice Breyer's argument for deference more convincing in the context of a specific restriction on a particular type of gun? Is it just as convincing in the context of a ban on all guns? On all guns of a certain type? How much should legislatures and executive agencies incorporate constitutional assessments into development and administration of firearms laws? If you were counsel to an urban mayor, how would you advise her to deal with state firearms legislation you deemed unconstitutional?

29. Consider Justice Breyer's litany of questions:

> Does the right to possess weapons for self-defense extend outside the home? To the car? To work? What sort of guns are necessary for self-defense? Handguns? Rifles? Semiautomatic weapons? When is a gun semi-automatic? Where are different kinds of weapons likely needed? Does time-of-day matter? Does the presence of a child in the house matter? Does the presence of a convicted felon in the house matter? Do police need special rules permitting patdowns designed to find guns? When do registration requirements become severe to the point that they amount to an unconstitutional ban? Who can possess guns and of what kind? Aliens? Prior drug offenders? Prior alcohol abusers? How would the right interact with a state or local government's ability to take special measures during, say, national security emergencies?

Have any of these questions already been answered by *Heller* and *McDonald*? Are there easy answers to any of the other questions? Which questions are uniquely difficult compared to questions posed by other provisions of the Bill of Rights?

30. Justice Breyer writes, "Compared with today's ruling, most if not all of this Court's decisions requiring the States to comply with other provisions in the Bill of Rights did not exact nearly so heavy a toll in terms of state sovereignty." What state or local laws in your state might be unconstitutional under *McDonald* and *Heller*? What other U.S. Supreme Court decisions exact a toll on state sovereignty? What about decisions that control the operation of state courts? Or Fourteenth Amendment decisions controlling the size and boundaries of election districts for state and federal officials?

31. Justice Stevens states that he has found no case that "holds, states, or even suggests that the term 'liberty' encompasses either the common-law right of self-defense or a right to keep and bear arms." What about the *Self-Defense Cases* (Chapter 6.G)? Why do you think that *none* of the opinions mention these cases?

32. As Justice Breyer points out, the Second Amendment right has often been controversial, and remains so today. As he also points out, over the course of American history, some states have enacted strong restrictions on the right to arms, and many courts have upheld those restrictions. Many of the restrictions were based on legislative and judicial determinations regarding public safety. If the Breyer standard for incorporation is that a right should not be incorporated if it is controversial today, and if there has been a history of some states sharply restricting the right, then were some previous Supreme Court decisions on incorporation of other rights incorrect? Which incorporated parts of the Bill of Rights would pass the Breyer test of being non-controversial, and of having no history of significant restrictions by some states?

33. In *McDonald,* Justice Thomas uses an originalist approach. Justices Stevens and Breyer adopt an approach that gives flexibility to discern and apply their understanding of important constitutional values. What method does Justice Alito employ? Justice Scalia (who joined the Alito opinion) once described himself as a "faint-hearted originalist" — meaning that he sought guidance from original meaning, but was cautious about overturning major precedents. Is the Alito plurality in *McDonald* an example of faint-hearted originalism? Notably, the plurality opinion never asserts that Justice Thomas's historical exposition of the Privileges or Immunities Clause is incorrect. Why do you think the plurality chose not to argue the issue? When should *stare decisis* be dispositive?

34. The values-based approach of Justices Stevens and Breyer is a form of "living constitutionalism." Should living constitutionalism direct Justices to do what they think is best, or is living constitutionalism something that

must be guided by the expressed constitutional values of the American people? If the latter, is it relevant that amicus briefs in support of *McDonald* were filed by majorities of both houses of Congress, and by 38 state Attorneys General? (Similar numbers of congresspersons and attorneys general also filed amicus briefs in *Heller*.) This was the first time in history that a Supreme Court amicus brief was filed on behalf of majorities of both houses, and the first time that such a supermajority of Attorneys General filed a brief asking the Supreme Court to incorporate a right against state and local governments. Were the Attorneys General representing the interest of the States? Of the People of the States?

COMMENT: MODES OF CONSTITUTIONAL INTERPRETATION

Both *Heller* and *McDonald* are excellent cases for studying the variety of methods currently used in constitutional interpretation. So we will briefly summarize the leading methods. No Justice relies on a single method in all cases, but Justices do differ in which methods they prefer to use most. These methods are not necessarily mutually exclusive.

Textualism. This method bases constitutional decisions on the actual words of the Constitution itself. To some degree, using this method at least part of the time is inescapable. *Heller* features an extensive textual argument between Justice Scalia's majority and Justice Stevens's dissent about the right way to construe the relationship between the first and second clauses of the Second Amendment.

Originalism. The judge attempts to discern the intent of those who created a constitutional provision ("original intent") or the intent of the People who ratified it, as judged by how a well-informed citizen did (or would have) understood the provision ("original public meaning"). When originalism returned in the 1970s as an important theory of constitutional interpretation, the emphasis tended to be on original intent, while today original public meaning is more commonly used. Some originalist scholars, however, adhere to original intent, or to a combination of original intent and meaning. Originalist scholars generally agree that while originalism and textualism can resolve many constitutional questions, they cannot resolve everything. There is considerable scholarly disagreement about what to do when original meaning or intent do not provide an answer.

On the current Court, Justices Thomas and Scalia are the leading proponents of originalism, although Justice Scalia is more reluctant than Justice Thomas to overrule precedents he considers contrary to originalism. Some form of originalism has always been part of the judicial toolkit, but it is considerably more influential in the Roberts and Rehnquist Courts than it was during the Warren and Burger Courts.

Heller is in some sense a triumph of originalism in that all nine Justices present their arguments primarily in originalist terms. The Scalia majority relies mainly on original public meaning, while the Stevens dissent is based on inferences of original intent. In *McDonald*, Justice Thomas's concurrence is founded on Fourteenth Amendment originalism, while all the other opinions include at least some originalist analysis.

Tradition and History. *Washington v. Glucksberg, supra,* declares that the Court should recognize unenumerated rights that are "deeply rooted in this Nation's history and tradition." 521 U.S. at 721. History and tradition can also be used to define the contours of enumerated rights. The *Heller* majority presents an extensive recitation of the history and tradition of the Second Amendment in the nineteenth century. The earliest citations of this history might be considered a form of originalism, in that the early authorities (such as St. George Tucker's 1802 treatise, which reprised his 1791-92 lectures at William & Mary) are so close to the Founding (the Second Amendment was ratified in 1791) that they may be considered strong evidence of original meaning. However, as the nineteenth century progresses, the citations from later in the nineteenth century become less pertinent to originalism, and more relevant as proof of a continuing history and tradition.

Perhaps the most influential affirmation of tradition as a source of constitutional authority is Justice John Marshall Harlan's famous dissent in *Poe v. Ullman,* an unsuccessful challenge to Connecticut's criminalization of birth control even for married couples.

> Due process has not been reduced to any formula; its content cannot be determined by reference to any code. The best that can be said is that through the course of this Court's decisions it has represented the balance which our Nation, built upon postulates of respect for the liberty of the individual, has struck between that liberty and the demands of organized society. If the supplying of content to this Constitutional concept has of necessity been a rational process, it certainly has not been one where judges have felt free to roam where unguided speculation might take them. The balance of which I speak is the balance struck by this country, having regard to what history teaches are the traditions from which it developed as well as the traditions from which it broke. That tradition is a living thing. A decision of this Court which radically departs from it could not long survive, while a decision which builds on what has survived is likely to be sound. No formula could serve as a substitute, in this area, for judgment and restraint.

367 U.S. 497, 542 (1961) (Harlan, J., dissenting). Harlan's *Poe* dissent was later reprised as a concurrence in *Griswold v. Connecticut,* which invalidated the Connecticut statute. *Griswold v. Connecticut,* 348 U.S. 479, 599 (1965) (Harlan, J., concurring). However, the *Poe* dissent remains the iconic and oft-cited affirmation of traditionalism.

In the *Poe* dissent, Justice Harlan declared that "tradition is a living thing." In the particular context of *Poe,* Justice Harlan seemed to be saying that even if the authors/ratifiers of the Fourteenth Amendment (1866-68) had no objection to criminalizing birth control, by 1961 it was anathema to the American tradition of liberty. Indeed, Connecticut was the only state in the Union to outlaw contraceptive use by married couples.

In a Second Amendment context, living traditionalism would maintain that, however militia-centric the original Second Amendment might have been, by the early nineteenth century the American people thought that the Second Amendment guaranteed their right to keep and bear arms for self-defense, hunting, and all of the lawful purposes, and have thought so ever since.

The Scalia majority in *Heller* and the Alito plurality in *McDonald* present this viewpoint, while the Stevens dissent in *Heller* and *McDonald* and (especially) the Breyer dissent in *McDonald* contest it. "Tradition is a living thing" could be considered an example of "the living Constitution," a term that is sometimes presented as the opposite of originalism and textualism. However, "living constitutionalism" is a name loosely given to extremely broad and diverse theories of constitutional law, including the claim that judges can make up whatever results they want — regardless of text, original understanding, or tradition — based on the judges' perceptions of good policy. Professor Kopel calls that theory "dead constitutionalism," arguing that if judges can make up whatever they want, then a written constitution is meaningless.

"Tradition is a living thing," might best be characterized as "Strict Living Constitutionalism." This recognizes that the Constitution can change over time, and imposes the restraint that changes in understanding must be longstanding, and accepted by a supermajority of the American people. Neither the Scalia majority in *Heller* nor the Alito plurality in *McDonald* describes their work in these terms, but you may perhaps find some living traditionalism in both opinions.

Emerging Awareness. This term comes from Justice Kennedy's majority opinion in *Lawrence v. Texas, supra,* holding that it was unconstitutional to criminalize homosexual oral and anal sex (or, by extension, such acts between heterosexual adults). The record of history and tradition could not possibly support the majority's result, since the acts had traditionally been criminalized (even between married couples). However, Justice Kennedy pointed to an "emerging awareness" of the right to make intimate decisions, starting with the Model Penal Code in the late 1950s, and ending with modern state laws. By 2003, only four state laws penalized "deviate sex" when committed by homosexuals, and nine states penalized it regardless of sexual orientation. All of these laws were rarely enforced. In the *Lawrence* analysis, 37 states had statutorily recognized the right of intimate choice, and the other 13 had tacitly chosen not to contest the right through nonenforcement of their deviate sex statutes. Emerging awareness plays no formal role in *Heller* and *McDonald.* Yet practically speaking, it can be considered the heart of the decision. In 1965, the American Bar Association awarded a prize for "The Forgotten Second Amendment," a two-part student article arguing that even though text, originalism, tradition, and history all pointed toward a meaningful Second Amendment right, the Amendment had been forgotten by the legal mandarinate of judges and law professors. Yet by the late 1990s, no one could say the Amendment had been forgotten. Legal scholarship on the Second Amendment had fought its way in from the margins in the 1970s to the mainstream. The Second Amendment had been a crucial rallying point for the end of nearly a half-century of Democratic control of House of Representatives in 1994, and for the defeat of the Democratic presidential candidates in 2000 and 2004. The Democratic retaking of Congress in 2008 was made possible by the victories of many "pro-gun" Democratic candidates. Whatever the Second Amendment had meant in 1789-91, the control of depended on the assent of a large constituency who believed that their inalienable Second Amendment rights guaranteed their right to own and carry guns for any nonaggressive purpose. (For more on the social and political history leading to *Heller,* see Chapter 8.)

Stare Decisis. Under this theory, the Court should rule according to whatever its previous decisions would tend to suggest, even if they were not controlling on the precise question before the Court. The second Justice Harlan often advocated this approach, and dutifully followed precedents even from cases in which he had dissented. The *McDonald* dissenters, in contrast, show no deference to the *Heller* precedent; in *Heller* itself, the Scalia and Stevens opinions both claim to follow *United States v. Miller,* although they disagree about what *Miller* means. In *McDonald,* all of the Justices except Justice Thomas are deferential to the old (but oft-criticized) precedents of the *Slaughter-House Cases* (Chapter 6) and *Cruikshank* (Chapter 6).

Values. In the nineteenth century, a common mode of constitutional analysis was to announce the true "purpose" of a constitutional provision, and to interpret the constitutional provision consistent with that purpose. Today, "purposivism" endures under the name of "values." That is, the judge describes the values that are said to underlie a constitutional provision, and then interprets the provision so as to protect those values, against other interests. On the current Court, Justice Breyer has been most explicit in advocating a values-based approach. Stephen Breyer, Making Our Democracy Work: A Judge's View (2010). His *Heller* dissent is founded on the value of a militia. More expansively, Justice Stevens's dissent in *McDonald* invokes a host of constitutional values for interpreting the Fourteenth Amendment. In contrast, the Scalia concurrence in *McDonald* criticizes Stevens for providing so many goalposts that the judge can go in any direction he wishes.

Liberty. Under this theory, the purpose of the Constitution, and of any legitimate government, is to protect the inalienable, natural, and inherent rights of life, liberty, and the pursuit of happiness, as expressed in the Declaration of Independence. During his confirmation hearings, Justice Kennedy explained he was not a pure originalist, and that in his view, the Constitution should be interpreted to protect liberty.

Popular Constitutionalism. This is not a theory of how judges should decide cases; it is a political science theory that suggests that in the long run, the Constitution is what the public wishes it to be, especially when public opinion on an issue is strong and sustained. Popular constitutionalism is one explanation for the Supreme Court's ultimate acquiescence in the tremendous expansion of federal regulatory powers of the economy that took place during the New Deal. It is illuminating to consider whether popular constitutionalism is at work in *Heller* and *McDonald.* Note the majority's statement in *Heller* that "nothing in our opinion should be taken to cast doubt on longstanding" modern regulations aimed to keep guns away from the untrustworthy. In dissent, Justice Breyer chides, "Why these? Is it that similar restrictions existed in the late eighteenth century? The majority fails to cite any colonial analogues."

Good Policy Results. No current Justice on the Supreme Court would claim that Justices should simply pick which result they favor on policy grounds, and then start looking for supporting legal rationales. Some previous Justices, however, were not shy about such an approach. *See* Laura Ray, *The Legacy of a*

Supreme Court Clerkship: Stephen Breyer and Arthur Goldberg, 115 Penn. St. L. Rev. 83, 90-102 (2010) (Goldberg as unabashedly results-oriented). Justice Thurgood Marshall famously explained his judicial philosophy: "You do what you think is right and let the law catch up." Deborah L. Rhode, *Letting the Law Catch Up*, 44 Stan. L. Rev. 1259, 1259 (1992).

    Judicial Activism and Judicial Restraint. In the public discourse of the early twenty-first century, these words have almost no practical meaning. "Judicial activism" is little more than a fancy epithet for "a result I do not like." Historically, judicial restraint was a theory, advocated by progressives like Harvard law professor and Supreme Court Justice Felix Frankfurter, that courts should almost never overturn the actions of the other two branches, except where clearly unconstitutional. "Judicial activism" was a term invented in 1949 by the eminent liberal historian Arthur M. Schlesinger, Jr. He used it to describe (with approval) the approach of "activist" Justices, such as Hugo Black and William O. Douglas, in protecting individual rights from majoritarian abuses. Arthur M. Schlesinger, Jr., *The Supreme Court 1947*, Fortune, Jan. 1947, at 73 (admiringly describing Justices Black, Douglas, Murphy, and Rutledge as "Judicial Activists"). During the Warren Court, "judicial activism" became a term of derision for Justices who were allegedly using the Constitution as a pretext for imposing their personal agendas.

    Today, many claim to favor "judicial restraint" and to oppose "judicial activism." But the terms have been forced to accommodate a variety of outcomes by people of very different persuasions. For example, "judicial restraint" could mean "nearly unlimited deference to majorities" (the Frankfurter model), or it could mean "strictly enforced originalism" (since originalism constrains judicial choices), or it could mean "judges using their own wisdom to decide when courts should be active and when they should be passive" (the Stevens approach in *McDonald*). In public debate, *Heller* and *McDonald* have prompted plenty of arguments about judicial restraint and judicial activism.

EXERCISE: HARM IN THE SPEECH CONTEXT

    Imagine that it is the end of your first semester in a public law school and you and your classmates are about to take your first exam in constitutional law. The class is graded on a curve, and has been very competitive all semester, especially between two of your classmates, John and Jane, who are gunning (pun intended) for the only A+ that can be awarded in the class. A few minutes before the exam is about to start, John announces to the class something about Jane's past life that most people would consider private and confidential, but that is completely true. Jane immediately turns red and begins to sweat. During the exam, you hear her sobbing in her seat behind you. She does very poorly on the exam and John winds up getting the A+. Because the facts revealed by John contained some reference to matters of public significance, John's actions are protected by the First Amendment, as incorporated against the states, thus barring a chain of intentional infliction of emotional distress claim by Jane. *See Florida Star v. B.J.F.*, 491 U.S. 524 (1989); *Smith v. Daily Mail Publishing Co.*, 443 U.S. 97 (1979).

Should John's actions be protected?

Now consider the arms-bearing context. Assume that the presence of a pistol in the home increases the risk of intentional shootings by family members or domestic partners. Is this fact a reason to ban pistols? Can you think of other methods of preventing such shootings? *Should* such methods be implemented? What would be the costs and benefits of implementing such methods?

More generally, under what circumstances is the potential for harm great enough or direct enough to warrant the reining in of a constitutional right? Should the method and extent of the curtailment matter?

John's statement before the exam added very little to civic discourse, but the firearm in the home could save lives. Do the potential benefits of exercise of the right matter? Should the risks of curtailment be abstracted? That is, silencing John's statement might impose only a trivial loss to free speech, but a law that allowed him to be silenced could severely limit speech. Are there parallels in the Second Amendment context?

EXERCISE: CONSTITUTIONAL DRAFTING

Assume that you are the framer of a constitutional amendment and you *do not* want your original intent for enacting it to control future courts. Instead, you want societal change to determine the contours and limits of your enactment. How would you draft such a provision? Why would you want to frame an amendment in such a way?

Now attempt the converse. Draft a foolproof amendment that can never be interpreted to protect activities that you are certain you never want protected, and that will compel protection of what you do want to protect.

‖10‖

Firearms Policy and Status: Race, Gender, Age, Disability, and Sexual Orientation

Firearms policy debates are complicated by the special concerns of different groups in American society. This chapter examines disparate views about the costs and benefits of firearms in the context of race, gender, age, disability, and sexual orientation.

Previous chapters have primarily focused on judicial decisions, and legislative and historical material. The content here is different. This chapter presents the views and special perspectives of advocates and organizations who filed amicus briefs in *District of Columbia v. Heller*, 554 U.S. 570 (2008) (Chapter 9). These briefs illustrate the special concerns of various communities. They also illustrate disagreement within those communities. Groups raising special concerns of race, gender, age, sexual orientation, and disability filed amicus briefs on both sides in *Heller*. The selections below present those viewpoints as well as competing empirical claims and policy prescriptions.

A. Firearms Policy and the Black Community

‖ **Brief for NAACP Legal Defense and Educational Fund, Inc. as Amicus Curiae Supporting Petitioner, District of Columbia v. Heller, 554 U.S. 570 (2008)**

. . . In densely populated urban centers like the District of Columbia . . . gun violence deprives many residents of an equal opportunity to live, much less succeed.

SUMMARY OF ARGUMENT

. . . Although the type, use, cultural significance and regulations on the purchase, possession, and use of firearms vary from community to community, handguns—because they are portable and easy to conceal—are uniquely lethal instruments, which are involved in the vast majority of firearm violence in America. Handgun violence in the District exacts a particularly high toll on the District's African-American residents. Multiple municipalities, including the District, have placed significant restrictions on the possession and use of handguns, while permitting the registration of other weapons such as shotguns and rifles. . . .

ARGUMENT . . .

B.   THE CLEAR AND ESTABLISHED UNDERSTANDING OF THE SECOND AMENDMENT SHOULD NOT BE DISTURBED

1.   Abandoning the Clear and Established Understanding of the Second Amendment Would Produce Substantial Upheaval in the Manner in Which Firearms Have Been Regulated Nationwide . . .

. . . The principal characteristic of the District's firearms legislation that is being challenged in this case — a rule that prohibits handguns while permitting shotguns and rifles[—]was enacted over 30 years ago, in 1976, after the District Council received substantial evidence that handguns were disproportionately linked to violent and deadly crime, and posed unique risks in an urban setting. In sum, the District's handgun regulations are reasonable, passed by a legislature, in line with long-standing historical practices and Supreme Court precedents, and recognize[] the unique circumstances posed by the link between the District's high crime rate and the prevalence of handguns. . . .

2.   Abandoning the Clear and Established Understanding of the Second Amendment Unduly Limits the Ability of States and Municipalities Struggling to Address the Problem of Gun Violence, a Problem of Particular Interest to This Nation's African-American Community

Firearm regulations like those of the District are one piece of a much larger puzzle — how to address the unacceptable levels of injuries and fatalities from gun violence in many communities across the nation. The fact that local firearm regulations alone do not solve this puzzle does not mean that such regulations have no place at all in the fight to ensure the safety of our nation's residents. States and localities must have flexibility to assess their public health and safety needs, and to determine the best means of achieving them. Accordingly, the degree of gun regulation may vary from place to place. Under these circumstances, the lower court's radical departure from this Court's clear and established Second Amendment jurisprudence should be reversed.

Legislatures enact firearm regulations to reduce crime and save lives threatened by the vexing problem of gun violence. African Americans, especially those who are young, are at a much greater risk of sustaining injuries or dying from gunshot wounds. The number of African-American children and teenagers killed by gunfire since 1979 is more than ten times the number of African-American citizens of all ages lynched throughout American history. *See* Children's Defense Fund, *Protect Children, Not Guns* 1 (2007). . . . Firearm homicide is the leading cause of death for fifteen to thirty-four year-old African Americans. *See* The Centers for Disease Control and Prevention, *WISQARS, Leading Causes of Death Reports (1999-2004),* http://webappa.cdc.gov/sasweb/ncipc/leadcauses.html. Although African Americans comprise only thirteen percent of the United States population, African Americans suffered almost twenty-five percent of all firearm deaths and fifty-three percent of all firearm homicides during the years 1999 to 2004. *See The Centers for Disease Control, WISQARS Injury Mortality Reports (1999-2004),* http://webappa.cdc.gov/sasweb/ncipc/mortrate10_sy.html.

With respect to handguns specifically, African Americans again suffer disproportionately. From 1987 to 1992, African-American males were victims of handgun crimes at a rate of 14.2 per 1,000 persons compared to a rate of 3.7 per 1,000 for white males. *See* U.S. Dep't of Justice, Bureau of Justice Statistics, Crime Data Brief, *Guns and Crime: Handgun Victimization, Firearm Self-Defense, and Firearm Theft* (Apr. 1994). . . . During the same period, African-American women were victims of gun violence at a rate nearly four times higher than white women. *See id.* Overall, African-American males between sixteen and nineteen years old had the highest rate of handgun crime victimization, at a rate of forty per 1,000 persons, or four times that of their white counterparts. *See id.*

Gun violence also adds significant direct and indirect costs to America's criminal justice and health care systems, while reducing the nation's overall life expectancy. *See generally* Philip Cook & Jens Ludwig, *Gun Violence: The Real Costs* (Oxford Univ. Press 2002) (estimating medical expenditures relating to gun violence, with costs borne by the American public because many gun victims are uninsured and cannot pay for their medical care); Linda Gunderson, *The Financial Costs of Gun Violence,* 131 Annals of Internal Medicine 483 (1999) (noting that the American public paid about eighty-five percent of the medical costs relating to gun violence); Jean Lemaire, *The Cost of Firearm Deaths in the United States: Reduced Life Expectancies and Increased Insurance Costs* (2005).

Although African Americans suffer from a disproportionate share of gun violence nationally, these disparities are significantly larger in the District. In 2004 alone, all but two of the 137 firearm homicide victims in the District were African-American, most of them between the ages of fifteen and twenty-nine years old. *See* CDC, *WISQARS, Injury Mortality Reports (2004), supra.* African Americans make up approximately sixty percent of the District's population, but comprise ninety-four percent of its homicide victims. *See* D.C. Dep't of Health, Center for Policy, Planning, and Epidemiology, State Center for Health Statistics, Research and Analysis Division, *Homicide in the District of Columbia, 1995-2004* 5 (Feb. 1, 2007). Between 1999 and 2004, African Americans in the District died from firearm use at a rate 10.6 times higher than did whites, and suffered from firearm homicide at a rate 16.7 times higher than did whites. *See* CDC, *WISQARS, Injury Mortality Reports (1999-2004), supra.* The vast majority of these deaths were the result of handgun violence. *See* Nat'l Public Radio (NPR), *D.C. Mayor Addresses Blow to Handgun Ban* (Mar. 13, 2007).

Given the prevalence of gun violence in the District and the devastating impact on its residents, the District Council had sound reasons to conclude that its handgun regulations would constitute a wise policy. Ultimately, the overall effectiveness of the District's handgun prohibition is not relevant to the Court, given the applicable legal standard as discussed above. However, we submit that, although the District's prohibition may not be a complete solution, especially because the absence of regional regulations permits guns to continue to flow into the District from neighboring jurisdictions, local efforts to reduce the number of handguns on the District's streets should be considered one piece of a larger solution. Indeed, the enactment of the handgun ban in the District thirty years ago was accompanied by an abrupt decline in firearm-caused homicides in the District, but not elsewhere in the Metropolitan area. *See* Petitioners' Br. 52. . . . These trends underscore the importance of the District's efforts and certainly do not counsel in favor of an unwarranted jurisprudential break that could drastically limit or foreclose such efforts. This Court's settled precedents provide the necessary latitude for the District to best protect its citizens by making the policy decision that fewer handguns, not more, promote public health and safety. . . .

3. Abandoning the Clear and Established Understanding of the Second Amendment Would Not Address Racial Discrimination in the Administration of Criminal Justice in General or the Administration of Firearm Restrictions in Particular

Concerns about this nation's past or present-day problems with racial discrimination do not provide a basis for invalidating the District's handgun regulations. The solution to discriminatory enforcement of firearm laws is not to reinterpret the Second Amendment to protect an individual right to "keep and bear Arms" for purely private purposes, but rather to employ, as necessary, this Court's traditional vehicle for rooting out racial discrimination: the Equal Protection Clause of the Fourteenth Amendment, or, where the actions of the federal government are at issue, the Due Process Clause of the Fifth Amendment. *See United States v. Armstrong*, 517 U.S. 456, 464-65 (1996) (administration of a criminal law may be "directed so exclusively against a particular class of persons . . . with a mind so unequal and oppressive" that the system of enforcement and prosecution amounts to "a practical denial" of equal protection of the laws) (*quoting Yick Wo v. Hopkins*, 118 U.S. 356, 373 (1886)); *see also Vasquez v. Hillery*, 474 U.S. 254 (1986) (racial discrimination in the selection of the grand jury violates Equal Protection); *Batson v. Kentucky*, 476 U.S. 79 (1986) (invalidating the use of race as a factor in the exercise of peremptory challenges). To the extent the history surrounding the adoption of early gun control laws, or even the Second Amendment itself, is tainted by racial discrimination, *see* Carl T. Bogus, *The Hidden History of the Second Amendment*, 31 U.C. Davis L. Rev. 309 (1998) (arguing that a major function of the "well regulated militia" of the Second Amendment during colonial and post-revolutionary times was the maintenance of slavery in the South and the suppression of slave rebellion); Robert J. Cottrol & Raymond T. Diamond, *The Second Amendment: Toward an Afro-Americanist Reconsideration*, 80 Geo. L.J. 309 (1991) (tracing the discriminatory intent of early firearms restrictions), then the Fourteenth Amendment is the appropriate vehicle for that bias to be ferreted out and eliminated.

Contrary to the assertions of some, the modern firearm regulations at issue in this case should not be confused with the Black Codes, other discriminatory laws that the Fourteenth Amendment invalidated, or more recent cases where Fourteenth Amendment protections have been implicated. The Fourteenth Amendment's protections rightly extend in the face of a colorable assertion that the District's firearm regulations (or those of any other jurisdiction) are racially discriminatory in origin or application, but such a showing has not been made here or even alleged by Respondents.

Brief for Congress of Racial Equality as Amicus Curiae Supporting Respondent, District of Columbia v. Heller, 554 U.S. 570 (2008)

. . . The Congress of Racial Equality, Inc. ("CORE") is a New York not-for-profit corporation founded in 1942, with national headquarters in Harlem, New York City. CORE is a nationwide civil rights organization, with consultative status at the United Nations, which is primarily interested in the welfare of the black community, and the protection of the civil rights of all citizens.

SUMMARY OF ARGUMENT

The history of gun control in America has been one of discrimination, disenfranchisement and oppression of racial and ethnic minorities, immigrants, and other "undesirable" groups. Robert Cottrol and Raymond Diamond, *Never Intended to be Applied to the White Population: Firearms Regulation and Racial Disparity-The Redeemed South's Legacy to a National Jurisprudence?*, 70 Chi. Kent L. Rev. 1307-1335 (1995); Robert Cottrol and Raymond Diamond, *The Second Amendment: Toward an Afro-Americanist Reconsideration*, 80 Georgetown L.J. 309-361 (1991); Raymond Kessler, *Gun Control and Political Power*, 5 Law & Pol'y Q. 381 (1983); Stefan Tahmassebi, *Gun Control and Racism*, 2 Geo. Mason U. Civ. Rts. L.J. 67. Gun control laws were often specifically enacted to disarm and facilitate repressive action against these groups. Id.

More recently, facially neutral gun control laws have been enacted for the alleged purpose of controlling crime. Often, however, the actual purpose or the actual effect of such laws has been to discriminate or oppress certain groups. Id.; *Ex Parte Lavinder*, 88 W.Va. 713, 108 S.E. 428 (1921) (striking down martial law regulation inhibiting possession and carrying of arms). As Justice Buford of the Florida Supreme Court noted in his concurring opinion narrowly construing a Florida gun control statute:

> I know something of the history of this legislation. The original Act of 1893 was passed when there was a great influx of negro laborers in this State drawn here for the purpose of working in turpentine and lumber camps. The same condition existed when the Act was amended in 1901 and the Act was passed for the purpose of disarming the negro laborers. . . . The statute was never intended to be applied to the white population and in practice has never been so applied. . . . [T]here has never been, within my knowledge, any effort to enforce the provisions of this statute as to white people, because it has been

generally conceded to be in contravention of the Constitution and nonenforce-able if contested.

Watson v. Stone, 4 So. 2d 700, 703 (1941) (Buford, J., concurring).

The worst abuses at present occur under the mantle of facially neutral laws that are, however, enforced in a discriminatory manner. Even those laws that are passed with the intent that they be applied to all, are often enforced in a discriminatory fashion and have a disparate impact upon blacks, the poor and other minorities. Present day enforcement of gun laws frequently targets minorities and the poor, and often results in illegal searches and seizures.

ARGUMENT

I. Gun Control Measures Have Been and Are Used to Disarm and Oppress Blacks and Other Minorities . . .

E. Gun Control in the Twentieth Century . . .

Most of the American handgun ownership restrictions adopted between 1901 and 1934 followed on the heels of highly publicized incidents involving the incipient black civil rights movement, foreign-born radicals, or labor agitators. In 1934, Hawaii, and in 1930 Oregon, passed gun control statutes in response to labor organizing efforts in the Port of Honolulu and the Oregon lumber mills. A Missouri permit law was enacted in the aftermath of a highly publicized St. Louis race riot. Michigan's version of the Sullivan law was enacted in the aftermath of the trial of Dr. Ossian Sweet, a black civil rights leader. Dr. Sweet had moved into an all white neighborhood and had been indicted for murder for shooting one of a white mob that had attacked his house while Detroit police looked on. [Don B. Kates, *Toward A History of Handgun Prohibition in the United States in* Restricting Handguns: The Liberal Skeptics Speak 18-19 (D.B. Kates ed., 1979)].

In its opening statement, in the NAACP's lawsuit against the firearms indus-try, the NAACP admitted the importance of the constitutional right:

> Certainly the NAACP of all organizations in this country understands and respects the constitutional right to bear arms. Upon the NAACP's founding in 1909 in New York City, soon thereafter it took up its first criminal law case [i]n Ossien, Michigan, where a black male, Mr. Sweet, was charged with killing a white suprem-acist along with several accomplices. The court, to rule out Mr. Sweet and his family to be pushed out of their home in Michigan, it was in that case that the presiding judge, to uphold Mr. Sweet's right to be with his family, coined the popular phrase "a man's home is his castle."

NAACP et al. v. Acusport, Inc. et al., Trial Tr. at 103. (The incident actually occurred in Detroit — not "Ossien" — Michigan in 1926. The NAACP and Clarence Darrow came to the defense of Dr. Ossian Sweet who had fatally shot a person in a white mob which was attacking his home because Dr. Sweet had moved into an all-white neighborhood. Furthermore, the phrase "a man's home is his castle," while certainly relevant to the Sweet case, first appears in an English 1499 case.)

After World War I, a generation of young blacks, often led by veterans familiar with firearms and willing to fight for the equal treatment that they had received in other lands, began to assert their civil rights. In response, the Klan again became a major force in the South in the 1910s and 1920s. Often public authorities stood by while murders, beatings, and lynchings were openly perpetrated upon helpless black citizens. And once again, gun control laws made sure that the victims of the Klan's violence were unarmed and did not possess the ability to defend themselves, while at the same time cloaking the often specially deputized Klansmen in the safety of their monopoly of arms. Id. at 19.

The Klan was also present in force in southern New Jersey, Illinois, Indiana, Michigan and Oregon. Between 1913 and 1934, these states enacted either handgun permit laws or laws barring alien handgun possession. The Klan targeted not only blacks, but also Catholics, Jews, labor radicals, and the foreign born; and these people also ran the risk of falling victim to lynch mobs or other more clandestine attacks, often after the victims had been disarmed by state or local authorities. Id. at 19-20.

II. Current Gun Control Efforts: A Legacy of Racism

Behind current gun control efforts often lurks the remnant of an old prejudice, that the lower classes and minorities, especially blacks, are not to be trusted with firearms. Today, the thought remains among gun control advocates; if the poor or blacks are allowed to have firearms, they will commit crimes with them. Even noted gun control activists have admitted this. Gun control proponent and journalist Robert Sherrill frankly admitted that the Gun Control Act of 1968 was "passed not to control guns but to control Blacks." Robert Sherrill, *The Saturday Night Special* 280 (1972). "It is difficult to escape the conclusion that the 'Saturday night special' is emphasized because it is cheap and it is being sold to a particular class of people. The name is sufficient evidence — the reference is to 'nigger-town Saturday night.'" Barry Bruce-Briggs, *The Great American Gun War*, The Public Interest, Fall 1976 at 37.

The worst abuses at present occur under the mantle of facially neutral laws that are, however, enforced in a discriminatory manner. Even those laws that are passed with the intent that they be applied to all, are often enforced in a discriminatory fashion and have a disparate impact upon blacks, the poor, and other minorities. In many jurisdictions which require a discretionary gun permit, licensing authorities have wide discretion in issuing a permit, and those jurisdictions unfavorable to gun ownership, or to the race, politics, or appearance of a particular applicant frequently maximize obstructions to such persons while favored individuals and groups experience no difficulty in the granting of a permit. Hardy and Chotiner, "The Potential for Civil Liberties Violations in the Enforcement of Handgun Prohibitions" in *Restricting Handguns: the Liberal Skeptics Speak Out*, supra, at 209-10; William Tonso, *Gun Control: White Man's Law*, Reason, Dec. 1985, at 24. In St. Louis, permits are automatically denied . . . to wives who don't have their husband's permission, homosexuals, and non-voters . . . As one of my students recently learned, a personal "interview" is now required for every St. Louis application. After many delays, he finally got to see the sheriff who looked at him only long enough to see that he wasn't black, yelled "he's alright" to the permit secretary, and left.

Don Kates, *On Reducing Violence or Liberty,* 1976 Civ. Liberties Rev. 44, 56.

New York's infamous Sullivan Law, originally enacted to disarm Southern and Eastern European immigrants who were considered racially inferior and religiously and ideologically suspect, continues to be enforced in a racist and elitist fashion "as the police seldom grant hand gun permits to any but the wealthy or politically influential." Tonso, supra, at 24.

New York City permits are issued only to the very wealthy, the politically powerful, and the socially elite. Permits are also issued to: private guard services employed by the very wealthy, the banks, and the great corporations; to ward heelers and political influence peddlers; . . .

Kates, "Introduction," in *Restricting Handguns: the Liberal Skeptics Speak Out,* supra, at 5.

A.   BY PROHIBITING THE POSSESSION OF FIREARMS, THE STATE DISCRIMINATES AGAINST MINORITY AND POOR CITIZENS

The obvious effect of gun prohibitions is to deny law-abiding citizens access to firearms for the defense of themselves and their families. That effect is doubly discriminatory because the poor, and especially the black poor, are the primary victims of crime and in many areas lack the necessary police protection.

African Americans, especially poor blacks, are disproportionately the victims of crime, and the situation for households headed by black women is particularly difficult. In 1977, more than half of black families had a woman head of household. A 1983 report by the U.S. Department of Labor states that:

among families maintained by a woman, the poverty rate for blacks was 51%, compared with 24% for their white counterparts in 1977. . . . Families maintained by a woman with no husband present have compromised an increasing proportion of both black families and white families in poverty; however, families maintained by a woman have become an overwhelming majority only among poor black families. . . . About 60% of the 7.7 million blacks below the poverty line in 1977 were living in families maintained by a black woman.

U.S. Dept. of Labor, *Time of Change: 1983 Handbook on Women Workers* 118 Bull. 298 (1983).

The problems of these women are far more than merely economic. National figures indicate that a black female in the median female age range of 25-34 is about twice as likely to be robbed or raped as her white counterpart. She is also three times as likely to be the victim of an aggravated assault. Id. at 90. *See* United States Census Bureau, *U.S. Statistical Abstract* (1983). A 1991 DOJ study concluded that "[b]lack women were significantly more likely to be raped than white women." Caroline Wolf Harlow, U.S. Dept. of Justice, *Female Victims of Violent Crime* 8 (1991). "Blacks are eight times more likely to be victims of homicide and two and one-half times more likely to be rape victims. For robbery, the black victimization rate is three times that for whites. . . ." Paula McClain, *Firearms Ownership, Gun Control Attitudes, and Neighborhood Environments*, 5 Law & Pol'y Q. 299, 301 (1983).

The need for the ability to defend oneself, family, and property is much more critical in the poor and minority neighborhoods ravaged by crime and without adequate police protection. Id.; Don Kates, *Handgun Control: Prohibition Revisited*, Inquiry, Dec. 1977, at 21. However, citizens have no right to demand or even expect police protection. Courts have consistently ruled "that there is no constitutional right to be protected by the state against being murdered by criminals or madmen." *Bowers v. DeVito*, 686 F.2d 616, 618 (7th Cir. 1982). Furthermore, courts have ruled that the police have no duty to protect the individual citizen. *DeShaney v. Winnebago County Dep't of Social Serv.*, 109 S. Ct. 998, 1004 (1989); *South v. Maryland*, 59 U.S. 396 (1855); *Morgan v. District of Columbia*, 468 A.2d 1306 (D.C. App. 1983) (en banc); *Warren v. District of Columbia*, 444 A.2d 1 (D.C. App. 1981) (en banc); *Ashburn v. Anne Arundel County*, 360 Md. 617 (1986).

The fundamental civil rights regarding the enjoyment of life, liberty and property, the right of self-defense and the right to keep and bear arms, are merely empty promises if a legislature is allowed to restrict the means by which one can protect oneself and one's family. This constitutional deprivation discriminates against the poor and minority citizen who is more exposed to the acts of criminal violence and who is less protected by the state.

Reducing gun ownership among law-abiding citizens may significantly reduce the proven deterrent effect of widespread civilian gun ownership on criminals, particularly in regard to such crimes as residential burglaries and commercial robberies. Of course, this effect will be most widely felt among the poor and minority citizens who live in crime-ridden areas without adequate police protection.

B. THE ENFORCEMENT OF GUN PROHIBITIONS SPUR INCREASED CIVIL LIBERTIES VIOLATIONS, ESPECIALLY IN REGARD TO MINORITIES AND THE POOR

Constitutional protections, other than those afforded by the right to keep and bear arms, have been and are threatened by the enforcement of restrictive firearms laws. The enforcement of present firearms controls account for a large number of citizen and police interactions, particularly in those jurisdictions in which the purchase or possession of certain firearms are prohibited. Between 1989 and 1998, arrests for weapons carrying and possession numbered between 136,049 and 224,395 annually. FBI Uniform Crime Reports, *Crime in the United States Annual Reports (1989-1998)* Table: Total Arrests, Distribution by Age.

The most common and, perhaps, the primary means of enforcing present firearms laws are illegal searches by the police. A former Ohio prosecutor has stated that in his opinion 50% to 75% of all weapon arrests resulted from questionable, if not clearly illegal, searches. *Federal Firearms Legislation: Hearings Before the Subcomm. on Crime of the House Judiciary Committee*, 94th Cong. 1589 (1975) [hereinafter House Hearings]. A study of Detroit criminal cases found that 85% of concealed weapons carrying cases that were dismissed, were dismissed due to the illegality of the search. This number far exceeded even the 57% percent for narcotics dismissals, in which illegal searches are frequent. Note, *Some Observations on the Disposition of CCW Cases in Detroit*, 74 Mich. L. Rev. 614, 620-21 (1976). A study of Chicago criminal cases found that motions to suppress for illegal evidence were filed in 36% of all weapons charges; 62% of such motions were granted by the court. Critique, *On the Limitations of Empirical Evaluation of the Exclusionary Rule*, 69 N.W. U. L. Rev. 740, 750 (1974). A Chicago judge presiding over a court devoted solely to gun law violations has stated:

> The primary area of contest in most gun cases is in the area of search and seizure. . . . Constitutional search and seizure issues are probably more regularly argued in this court than anywhere in America. . . . More than half these contested cases begin with the motion to suppress . . . these arguments dispose of more contested matters than any other.

House Hearings, supra, at 508 (testimony of Judge D. Shields).

These suppression hearing figures represent only a tiny fraction of the actual number of illegal searches that take place in the enforcement of current gun laws, as they do not include the statistics for illegal searches that do not produce a firearm or in which the citizen is not charged with an offense. The ACLU has noted that the St. Louis police department, in the mid-1970s, made more than 25,000 illegal searches "on the theory that any black, driving a late model car has an illegal gun." However, these searches produced only 117 firearms. Kates, *Handgun Control: Prohibition Revisited*, supra, at 23.

In light of these facts, many of the proponents of gun control have commented on the need to restrict other constitutionally-guaranteed rights in order to enforce gun control or prohibition laws. A federal appellate judge urged the abandonment of the exclusionary rule in order to better enforce gun control laws. Malcolm Wilkey, *Why Suppress Valid Evidence?*, Wall Street J., Oct. 7, 1977, at 14. A police inspector called for a "reinterpretation" of the Fourth Amendment to allow police to assault strategically located streets, round up pedestrians en masse, and herd them through portable, airport-type gun detection machines. Detroit Free Press, Jan. 26, 1977, at 4. Prominent gun control advocates have flatly stated that "there can be no right to privacy in regard to armament." Norville Morris and Gordon Hawkins, *The Honest Politician's Guide to Crime Control* 69 (1970).

Florida v. J.L. involved a defendant who had been stopped, searched, and arrested by Miami police after an anonymous telephone caller claimed that one of three black males fitting the defendant's description was in possession of a firearm. Amongst other arguments, the State asked the Court to carve out a gun exception to the Fourth Amendment. The Supreme Court unanimously declined to create such an exception to the Fourth Amendment. *Florida v. J.L.*, 120 S. Ct. 1375 (2000).

Statistics and past history show that many millions of otherwise law-abiding Americans would not heed any gun ban. One should consider America's past experience with liquor prohibition. Furthermore, in many urban neighborhoods, especially those of poor blacks and other minorities, the possession of a firearm for self-defense is often viewed as a necessity in light of inadequate police protection.

Federal and state authorities in 1975 estimated that there were two million illegal handguns among the population of New York City. Selwyn Raab, *2 Million Illegal Pistols Believed Within the City*, N.Y. Times, Mar. 2, 1975, at 1 (estimate by BATF); N.Y. Post, Oct. 7, 1975, at 5, col. 3 (estimate by Manhattan District Attorney). In a 1975 national poll, some 92% of the respondents estimated that 50% or more of handgun owners would defy a confiscation law. 121 Cong. Rec. S189, 1 (daily ed. Dec. 19, 1975).

Even registration laws, as opposed to outright bans, measure a high percentage of non-compliance among the citizenry. In regard to Illinois' firearm owner registration law, Chicago Police estimated the rate of non-compliance at over two thirds, while statewide non-compliance was estimated at three fourths. In 1976, Cleveland city authorities estimated the rate of compliance with Cleveland's handgun registration law at less than 12%. Kates, supra, *Handgun Control: Prohibition Revisited*, at 20 n.1. In regard to citizens' compliance with Cleveland's "assault gun" ban, a Cleveland Police Lieutenant stated: "To the best of our knowledge, no assault weapon was voluntarily turned over to the Cleveland Police Department . . . considering the value that these weapons have, it certainly was doubtful individuals would willingly relinquish one." Associated Press, *Cleveland Reports No Assault Guns Turned In*, Gun Week, Aug. 10, 1990, at 2.

In response to New Jersey's "assault weapon" ban, as of the required registration date, only 88 of the 300,000 or more affected weapons in New Jersey had been registered, none had been surrendered to the police and only 7 had been rendered inoperable. Masters, *Assault Gun Compliance Law*, Asbury Park Press, Dec. 1, 1990, at 1. As of November 28, 1990, only 5,150 guns of the estimated 300,000 semiautomatic firearms banned by the May 1989 California "Assault Gun" law had been registered as required. Jill Walker, *Few Californians Register Assault Guns*, Washington Post, Nov. 29, 1990, at A27.

These results suggest that the majority of otherwise law-abiding citizens will not obey a gun prohibition law; much less criminals, who will disregard such laws anyway. It is ludicrous to believe that those who will rob, rape and murder will turn in their firearms or any other weapons they may possess to the police, or that they would be deterred from possessing them or using them by the addition of yet another gun control law to the more than twenty thousand gun laws that are already on the books in the U.S. James Wright, Peter Rossi and Kathleen Daly, *Under the Gun: Weapons, Crime and Violence in America* 244 (1983).

A serious attempt to enforce a gun prohibition would require an immense number of searches of residential premises. Furthermore, the bulk of these intrusions will, no doubt, be directed against racial minorities, whose possession of arms the enforcing authorities may view as far more dangerous than illegal arms possession by other groups.

As civil liberties attorney Kates has observed, when laws are difficult to enforce, "enforcement becomes progressively haphazard until at last the laws are used only against those who are unpopular with the police." Of course minorities, especially minorities who don't "know their place," aren't likely to be popular with the police, and those very minorities, in the face of police indifference or perhaps even antagonism, may be the most inclined to look to guns for protection — guns that they can't acquire legally and that place them in jeopardy if possessed illegally. While the intent of such laws may not be racist, their effect most certainly is.

Tonso, supra, at 25. . . .

NOTES & QUESTIONS

1. After reading the competing arguments from the NAACP and the CORE, which do you find most convincing?

2. Imagine you are a legislator and have just reviewed the arguments and empirical claims in these two briefs. What questions would you ask representatives of CORE and the NAACP?

3. Do the two briefs reveal any common ground?

4. As a matter of policy, which view seems to offer the most practical pathway to public safety? What about individual safety? Are public safety measures and individual safety measures incompatible?

5. The *Heller* (Chapter 9) and *McDonald v. City of Chicago*, 130 S. Ct. 3020 (2010) (Chapter 9) decisions make gun ownership legal for people who are not disqualified by nature of criminal activity and who satisfy reasonable local and state requirements. What is the nature of the threat posed by legal handguns in the possession of people who have no criminal records or other disqualifying characteristics?

6. Michael de Leeuw, who headed the NAACP's amicus submission in *Heller*, argues that the modern civil rights agenda should include weakening *Heller* so as to permit local governments to ban handguns. Such exceptions would permit revival of Washington, D.C.'s overturned gun ban, which de Leeuw argues should be respected as an exercise of black community autonomy. See Michael B. de Leeuw et al., *Ready Aim Fire?* District of Columbia v. Heller *and Communities of Color*, 25 Harv. BlackLetter L.J. 133 (2009). Professor Nicholas Johnson takes a different view, arguing that (1) stringent gun control requires a level of trust in the competence and benevolence of government that is difficult to square with the black experience in America; (2) historically, armed self-defense in the face of state failure has been a crucial private resource for blacks; (3) as a matter of practice and philosophy, blacks from the leadership to the grass roots have supported armed self-defense by maintaining a distinction between counterproductive political violence and indispensible self-defense against imminent threats; and (4) isolated gun bans cannot work in a nation already saturated with guns. *See* Nicholas J. Johnson, Firearms and the Black Community: An Assessment of the Modern Orthodoxy (forthcoming) (manuscript available at firearmregulation.org).

B.   Gender

Brief for National Network to End Domestic Violence et al. as Amici Curiae Supporting Petitioner, District of Columbia v. Heller, 554 U.S. 570 (2008)

SUMMARY OF ARGUMENT

Domestic violence is a pervasive societal problem that affects a significant number of women and children each year. Correctly recognized as a national crisis, domestic violence accounts for a significant portion of all violence against women and children. The effect of such violence on the lives of its victims shocks the conscience. Domestic violence victims are battered and killed. They are terrorized and traumatized. They are unable to function as normal citizens because they live under the constant threat of harassment, injury, and violence. And these are just the more obvious effects. Other wounds exist beneath the surface — injuries that are not so easily recognizable as a bruise or a broken bone, but that affect victims' lives just the same. For example, victims often miss work due to their injuries, and must struggle with the prospect of losing their jobs, resulting in significant financial and emotional burdens. Lacking safe outlets for escape or legal recourse, these victims persevere.

One particularly ominous statistic stands out in its relevance here: domestic violence accounts for between one-third and almost one-half of the female murders in the United States. These murders are most often committed by intimate partners with handguns. And while murder is the most serious crime that an abuser with a gun can commit, it is not the only crime; short of murder, batterers also use handguns to threaten, intimidate, and coerce victims. Handguns empower batterers and provide them with deadly capabilities, exacerbating an already pervasive problem.

This crisis has not gone unaddressed; Congress and numerous states have attempted to limit the access that batterers have to handguns. Chief among the Congressional statutes is 18 U.S.C. §922(g)(9), which addresses the lethal and widespread connection between domestic violence and access to firearms by prohibiting those convicted of domestic violence crimes from possessing guns. Many states also have laws addressing the nexus between domestic violence and firearms. For example, faced with a record of handgun violence in its urban environment, including domestic gun violence, the District of Columbia ("the District") enacted comprehensive legislation regulating handgun possession in D.C. Code §§7-2502.02(a)(4), 22-4504(a), and 7-2507.02. The D.C. Council had ample empirical justifications for determining that such laws were the best method for reducing gun violence in the District. Important government interests support statutes and regulations intended to reduce the number of domestic violence incidents that turn deadly; such statutes should be given substantial deference. . . .

ARGUMENT

Women are killed by intimate partners — husbands, lovers, ex-husbands, or ex-lovers — more often than by any other category of killer. It is the leading cause of death for African-American women aged 15-45 and the seventh leading cause of premature death for U.S. women overall. Intimate partner homicides make up 40 to 50 percent of all murders of women in the United States, [and that number excludes ex-lovers, which account for as much as 11 percent of intimate partner homicides of women]. . . . When a gun [is] in the house, an abused woman [is] 6 times more likely than other abused women to be killed. Jacquelyn C. Campbell et al., *Assessing Risk Factors for Intimate Partner Homicide,* NIJ Journal, Nov. 2003, at 15, 16, 18 [hereinafter *Risk Factors*].

I.   DOMESTIC VIOLENCE IS A SERIOUS CRIME THAT LEAVES MILLIONS OF WOMEN AND CHILDREN NATIONWIDE SCARRED BOTH PHYSICALLY AND EMOTIONALLY

. . . Experts in the field of domestic violence have come to understand domestic violence as a pattern of coercive controls broader than the acts recognized by the legal definition, including a range of emotional, psychological, and financial tactics and harms batterers perpetrate against victims. Regardless of the definition applied, domestic violence is a profound social problem with far-reaching consequences throughout the United States. Between 2001 and 2005, intimate partner violence constituted, on average, 22% of violent crime against women. In the United States, intimate partner violence results each year in almost two million injuries and over half a million hospital emergency room visits. About 22% of women, and seven percent of men, report having been physically assaulted by an intimate partner. According to one study of crimes reported by police in 18 states and the District, family violence accounted for 33% of all violent crimes; 53% of those crimes were between spouses.

Domestic violence has severe and devastating effects. Injuries such as broken bones, bruises, burns, and death, are physical manifestations of its consequences. But there are also emotional and societal impacts. Domestic violence is characterized by a pattern of terror, domination, and control — it thus obstructs victims' efforts to escape abuse and achieve safety. Victims of domestic violence often have difficulty establishing independent lives due to poor credit, rental, and employment histories resulting from their abuse. Similarly, victims often miss work due to their injuries and can ultimately lose their jobs as a result of the violence against them. Moreover, the injuries that domestic violence causes go beyond the immediate injury. Chronic domestic violence is associated with poor health, and can manifest itself as stress-related mental and physical health problems for as long as a year after the abuse.

Above all, incidents of abuse often turn deadly. American women who die by homicide are most often killed by their intimate partners — according to various studies, at least one-third, Callie Marie Rennison, Bureau of Justice Stat., *Intimate Partner Violence, 1993-2001,* NCJ 197838 at 1 (Feb. 2003) and perhaps up to one-half of female murder victims, are killed by an intimate partner. Jacquelyn C. Campbell et al., *Assessing Risk Factors for Intimate Partner*

Homicide, NIJ Journal, Nov. 2003, at 18. A study based on the Federal Bureau of Investigation's Supplementary Homicide Report found that female murder victims were more than 12 times as likely to have been killed by a man they knew than by a male stranger. Violence Policy Center, *When Men Murder Women: An Analysis of 2005 Homicide Data*, at 3 (Sept. 2007) [hereinafter *When Men Murder Women*]. Of murder victims who knew their offenders, 62% were killed by their husband or intimate acquaintance. Id.

Although victims bear the primary physical and emotional brunt of domestic violence, society pays an economic price. Victims require significant medical attention. The Centers for Disease Control and Prevention reports that the health-related costs of domestic violence approach $4.1 billion every year. Gun-related injuries account for a large portion of that cost. Combined increased healthcare costs and lost productivity cost the United States over $5.8 billion each year. Domestic violence also accounts for a substantial portion of criminal justice system activity. For example, according to a study assessing the economic impact of domestic violence in Tennessee, the state of Tennessee spends about $49.9 million annually in domestic violence court processing fees. . . .

II.   Firearms Exacerbate an Already Deadly Crisis

Domestic violence perpetrators use firearms in their attacks with alarming frequency. Of every 1,000 U.S. women, 16 have been threatened with a gun, and seven have had a gun used against them by an intimate partner. *See* [Kathleen A. Vittes & Susan B. Sorenson, *Are Temporary Restraining Orders More Likely to Be Issued When Applications Mention Firearms?*, 30 Evaluation Rev. 266, 277 (2006).] (one in six victims of domestic violence who filed for a restraining order at the Los Angeles County Bar Association's Barrister's Domestic Violence Project clinic between May 2003 and January 2004 reported being threatened or harmed by a firearm). "American women who are killed by their intimate partners are more likely to be killed with guns than by all other methods combined. In fact, each year from 1980 to 2000, 60% to 70% of batterers who killed their female intimate partners used firearms to do so." Emily F. Rothman et al., *Batterers' Use of Guns to Threaten Intimate Partners*, 60 J. Am. Med. Women's Ass'n 62, 62 (2005) (noting also that "[f]our percent to 5% of women who have experienced nonlethal intimate partner violence . . . have reported that partners threatened them with guns at some point in their lives"). *See* [Susan B. Sorenson, *Firearm Use in Intimate Partner Violence*, 30 Evaluation Rev. 229, 232 (2006)]. ("Women are more than twice as likely to be shot by their male intimates as they are to be shot, stabbed, strangled, bludgeoned, or killed in any other way by a stranger.") (citation omitted); Susan B. Sorenson, *Taking Guns From Batterers*, 30 Evaluation Rev. 361, 362 (2006) (between 1976 to 2002, women in the United States were 2.2 times more likely to die of a gunshot wound inflicted by a male intimate partner than from any form of assault by a stranger); *When Men Murder Women*, *supra* [], at 3 (in 2005, "more female homicides were committed with firearms (52 percent) than with any other weapon"); Vittes & Sorenson, *supra* [], at 267 (55% of intimate partner homicides in 2002 were committed with a firearm).

Thus, every year, 700-800 women are shot and killed by their spouses or intimate partners, and handguns are the weapon of choice. For example, according to the Violence Policy Center, "[i]n 2000, in homicides where the weapon was known, 50 percent (1,342 of 2,701) of female homicide victims were killed with a firearm. Of those female firearm homicides, 1,009 women (75 percent) were killed with a handgun." The number remains relatively consistent. In 2004, 72% of women killed by firearms were killed by handguns. *When Men Murder Women, supra* [], at 3.

The mere presence of or access to a firearm increases fatality rates in instances of abuse. A person intent on committing violence will naturally reach for the deadliest weapon available. Accordingly, the presence of a gun in an already violent home acts as a catalyst, increasing the likelihood that domestic violence will result in severe injury or death. *See, e.g.,* [Kathryn E. Moracco et al., *Preventing Firearm Violence Among Victims of Intimate Partner Violence: An Evaluation of a New North Carolina Law,* at 1 (2006)]; Jacquelyn C. Campbell et al., *Risk Factors for Femicide in Abusive Relationships: Results From a Multisite Case Control Study,* 93 Am. J. of Pub. Health 1089, 1090 (2003) (the intimate partner's access to a gun is strongly associated with intimate partner homicide). Estimates of the increased likelihood of death when a firearm is present vary. *Compare When Men Murder Women, supra* [], at 2 (three times more likely), *with Risk Factors, supra* [], at 16 (six times more likely). When domestic violence incidents involve a firearm, the victim is 12 times more likely to die as compared to incidents not involving a firearm. Shannon Frattaroli & Jon S. Vernick, *Separating Batterers and Guns,* 30 Evaluation Rev. 296, 297 (2006).

Even when he does not actually fire his weapon, a batterer may use a gun as a tool to "threaten, intimidate, and coerce." Vittes & Sorenson, *supra* [], at 267. For example, batterers make threats with their firearm by pointing it at the victim; cleaning it; shooting it outside; threatening to harm people, pets, or others about whom the victim cares; or threatening suicide. Such threats do not leave physical marks, but they can result in emotional problems, such as post-traumatic stress disorder. Thus, a firearm is a constant lethal threat, and its presence may inhibit a victim of abuse from seeking help or from attempting to leave the relationship.

The statistics reveal a stark reality — guns exacerbate the already pervasive problem of domestic violence. The use of firearms intensifies the severity of the violence and increases the likelihood that domestic violence victims will be killed by their intimate partners.

▌ Brief for 126 Women State Legislators and Academics as Amici Curiae Supporting Respondent, District of Columbia v. Heller, 554 U.S. 570 (2008)

SUMMARY OF ARGUMENT

This case provides the Court an opportunity to advance the ability of women to free themselves from being subject to another's ill will and to counter the commonly-held prejudice that women are "easier targets" simply because of their gender characteristics. Violence against women in the United States is endemic, often deadly, and most frequently committed by men superior in physical strength to their female victims.

The District's current prohibition against handguns and immediately service-able firearms in the home effectively eliminates a woman's ability to defend her very life and those of her children against violent attack. Women are simply less likely to be able to thwart violence using means currently permitted under D.C. law. Women are generally less physically strong, making it less likely that most physical confrontations will end favorably for women. Women with access to immediately disabling means, however, have been proven to benefit from the equalization of strength differential a handgun provides. Women's ability to own such serviceable firearms is indeed of even greater importance given the holdings of both federal and state courts that there is no individual right to police protection.

Washington, D.C.'s current firearms regulations are facially gender-neutral, and according to Petitioners, were intended to decrease the incidents of fire-arms violence equally among both men and women. . . . What the District's current firearms laws do is manifest "gross indifference" to the self-defense needs of women. Effectively banning the possession of handguns ignores biological differences between men and women, and in fact allows gender-inspired violence free rein. . . .

ARGUMENT

I. The Time Has Long Passed When Social Conditions Mandated That All Women Equally Depend Upon the Protection of Men for Their Physical Security

For centuries the concept of women's self-defense was as nonexistent as the idea that women were to, and could, provide their own means of financial support. That women themselves could possibly have some responsibility for their own fates was not only not a topic for debate, but would have been deemed a foolish absurdity.

A. The Defense of Women as Men's Sole Prerogative and Responsibility

Such paternalism reflected widely-accepted views of men's physical prowess vis-à-vis women generally and the roles women were expected to play in society. Few women expected to leave the confines of their families before marriage. . . .

B. Changing Demographics Heighten the Need for Many Women to Provide Their Own Physical Security

Throughout history, family and household demographics reinforced the expectation that men would be available to provide protection to women and chil-dren. Extended families were the norm across all cultural backgrounds, providing women the immediately available support of fathers, brothers, and husbands. In 1900, only 5% of households in the United States consisted of people living alone, while nearly half the population lived in households of six or more individuals.

Widespread demographic changes now make it far less likely that women will live in households with an adult male present to provide the traditionally-expected protection. In 2000, slightly more than 25 percent of individuals lived in households consisting only of themselves. Between 1970 and 2000, the proportion of women aged 20 to 24 who had never married increased from 36 to 73 percent; for women aged 30 to 34, that proportion tripled from 6 to 22 percent. While these statistics do not reflect the increasing percentage of women who choose to cohabit without marriage, it should be noted that these percentages of women living alone are likely higher in metropolitan areas of the Northeast and Mid-Atlantic.

These statistics do not emphasize the rapidly increasing number of single mothers in the District. According to a 2005 survey, there are over 46,000 single mothers living within Washington, D.C. Of those single mothers, almost half live in poverty. These women are the most immediate and often sole source of protection of their children against abusive ex-husbands, ex-boyfriends, or unknown criminals who prey on the District's most vulnerable households. Many do not have the resources to choose neighborhoods in which their children face few threats or to install expensive monitoring systems and alarms. Moreover, many will not have the knowledge or social network to access those violence prevention services available. An inexpensive handgun, properly stored to prevent access to children, could therefore very well be the sole means available for these women to protect themselves and their children. *See* also Brief of *Amici Curiae* International Law Enforcement Educators and Trainers Association, *et al.*, in Support of Respondent ("Int'l L. Enf. Educ. & Trainers Assoc. Br.") at section II.D. (discussing the increasingly rare incidents of gun accidents).

In addition to young women and those who are single mothers, there is an increasing number of elderly women who live alone and feel highly vulnerable to violent crime. Greater improvements in female than in male mortality rates have increased the percentage of women aged 65 and older who live alone. From 1960 to 2000, women aged 65 and over accounted for a single digit percentage of the total population but more than 30 percent of households consisting of only one person. This population of older women living alone will only increase as baby boomers age and fewer children are capable of caring for aging parents. Some 40 percent of elderly and mid-life women have below-median incomes, leaving them with little or no choice of neighborhoods and expensive security measures. Edward R. Roybal, *The Quality of Life for Older Women: Older Women Living Alone*, H.R. Rep. No. 100-693, at 1 (2d Sess. 1989). . . .

II.   EQUAL PROTECTION IN WASHINGTON, D.C. NOW MEANS THAT WOMEN ARE EQUALLY FREE TO DEFEND THEMSELVES FROM PHYSICAL ASSAULT WITHOUT THE MOST EFFECTIVE MEANS TO TRULY EQUALIZE GENDER-BASED PHYSICAL DIFFERENCES

. . . Violence against women is predominately gender-based, most often perpetrated by men against the women in their lives. Men who react with violence against women in the domestic sphere often seek to reassert their control over those whom the men believe should be held as subordinates. Since 1976, approximately 30% of all U.S. female murder victims have been killed by their male, intimate partners. . . .

A.   VIOLENCE AGAINST WOMEN IN THE DISTRICT OF COLUMBIA
AND THE DISTRICT'S RESPONSE

In 2005, the Metropolitan Police Department (MPD) received over 11,000 calls reporting a domestic violence crime or about 30 calls per day. There were 51 murders attributed to domestic violence between 2001 and 2004, counting only those cases in which the so-called victim-offender relation could be proven. These statistics of course cannot convey the number of women who live in perpetual fear that an abuser will return and escalate the violence already experienced. As to those women who are able to report domestic violence-related crimes or who choose to do so, the MPD is often simply unable to take any proactive measures to protect their safety. In 2004, the MPD's Civil Protection and Temporary Protection Unit was able to locate and serve only 49.6% of those against whom a protection order had been issued.

Such statistics are even more alarming when it is understood that domestic batterers who ultimately take the lives of women are repeat offenders, most likely those with both a criminal background and repeated assaults against the women they eventually murder. Murray A. Straus, Ph.D., *Domestic Violence and Homicide Antecedents*, 62 Bull. N.Y. Acad. Med. 457 (No. 5 June 1986). These are not men who inexplicably react violently one day and then never again present a threat. One study found that a history of domestic violence was present in 95.8% of the intra-family homicides studied. In 2004, the District's Police Department reported that of the 7,449 homes from which domestic violence was reported, almost 13% had three or more calls that year alone. These numbers cannot account for the violence that is never reported, or for which only some incidents are reported.

Women who eventually face life-threatening dangers from a domestic abuser or stalker are therefore well aware of the specific threat presented. In fact, Petitioners' *Amici* may well be correct in their claim that "female murder victims were more than 12 times as likely to have been killed by a man they knew than by a male stranger" and that "[o]f murder victims who their knew their offenders, 62% were killed by their husband or intimate acquaintance." Brief of *Amici Curiae* National Network to End Domestic Violence, *et al.*, in Support of Petitioners at 23 ("Pets' Network Br."). Such knowledge of an individualized threat should allow women to more easily prepare the best defenses they can employ, using their ability to weigh the threat against their ability to protect themselves should the threat ever become one of serious bodily injury or death. Current D.C. gun restrictions on handguns and serviceable firearms in the home simply eliminate that option for women altogether.

Those women who are attacked by strangers or whose children are in danger should also be provided the option of choosing a firearm if they would feel safer having one in their home. Other women who live alone, particularly the elderly who are more likely to be of lower incomes, may not have choices as to where they must live, nor the ability to relocate if stalked. These women too should be able to weigh the threat of an unknown assailant against their ability to defend themselves should they ever be attacked in the privacy of their own homes.

Without the freedom to have a readily available firearm in the home, a woman is at a tremendous disadvantage when attempting to deter or stop an assailant should her attacker allow her no other option. Reflecting upon one of the most notorious tragedies of domestic abuse turned murder, Andrea Dworkin stated directly the stakes involved:

> Though the legal system has mostly consoled and protected batterers, when a woman is being beaten, it's the batterer who has to be stopped; as Malcolm X used to say, "by any means necessary" — a principle women, all women, had better learn. A woman has a right to her own bed, a home she can't be thrown out of, and for her body not to be ransacked and broken into. She has a right to safe refuge, to expect her family and friends to stop the batterer — by law or force — before she's dead. She has a constitutional right to a gun and a legal right to kill if she believes she's going to be killed. And a batterer's repeated assaults should lawfully be taken as intent to kill.

It must be added, however, that it is not just the physical cost of violence against women that must be considered. A woman who feels helpless in her own home is simply not an autonomous individual, controlling her own fate and able to "participate fully in political life." While possessing a handgun or a serviceable long gun in the home will of course not erase all incidents of sex-based violence against women, denying women the right to choose such an option for themselves does nothing but prevent the independent governance women must be afforded.

Self-defense classes, particularly those involving training women to use handguns, often help to provide women the sense of self-worth necessary for them to feel equals in civil society. *See* Martha McCaughey, *Real Knockouts: The Physical Feminism of Women's Self-Defense* (N.Y. Univ. Press 1997). Women who take such classes no longer see themselves as powerless potential victims, but as individuals who may demand that their rights be respected. There is some evidence that men recognize this transformation and alter their conduct toward those women. As one study noted, "[t]he knowledge that one can defend oneself — and that the self is valuable enough to merit defending — changes everything." Jocelyn A. Hollander, *"I Can Take Care of Myself": The Impact of Self-Defense Training on Women's Lives*, 10 *Violence Against Women* 205, at 226-27 (2004). Therefore, even if women are never placed in a position to defend themselves with a firearm or their own bodies, there are less material but no less compelling justifications for allowing them that ability. *E.g.*, Mary Zeiss Stange, *From Domestic Terrorism to Armed Revolution: Women's Right to Self-Defense as an Essential Human Right*, 2 J. L. Econ. & Pol'y 385-91 (2006).

B.   THE BENEFITS OF HANDGUNS FOR WOMEN FACING GRAVE THREAT

For years women were advised not to fight back and to attempt to sympathize with their attackers while looking for the first opportunity to escape. Well meaning women's advocates counseled that such passivity would result in fewer and less serious injuries than if a woman attempted to defend herself and angered the perpetrator. More recent, empirical studies indicate, however, that owning a firearm is one of the best means a woman can have for preventing crime against her. The National Crime Victimization Survey ("NCVS") indicates that allowing a woman to have a gun has a "much greater effect" on her ability to defend herself against crime than providing that same gun to a man. In fact, the NCVS and researchers have concluded that women who offer no resistance are 2.5 times more likely to be seriously injured than women who resist their attackers with a gun. While the overall injury rate for both men and women was 30.2%, only 12.8% of those using a firearm for self-protection were injured. Subjective data from the 1994 NCVS reveals that 65 percent of victims felt that self-defense improved their situation, while only 9 percent thought that fighting back caused them greater harm.

Studies of the effects of concealed carry legislation offer additional proof. Although the case now before the Court involves keeping a firearm only in the home, studies looking specifically at women granted concealed carry handgun permits have shown that each additional woman carrying a concealed handgun reduces women's murder rate by between three to four times more than an additional man carrying a concealed handgun reduces the male murder rate. John Lott, Jr., *More Guns, Less Crime*, 62, 161 (2d ed., Univ. of Chicago, 2000) (1998). Providing women handguns simply increases their ability to defend themselves far more than does providing handguns to generally more physically able men. *See also* Paxton Quigley, *Armed and Female* (E.P. Dutton 1989).

Given relative size disparities, men who threaten women and children can easily cause serious bodily injury or death using another type of weapon or no weapon at all. Between 1990 and 2005, 10% of wives and 14% of girlfriends who fell victim to homicide were murdered by men using only the men's "force" and no weapon of any type. It should also be noted that a violent man turning a gun on a woman or child announces his intent to do them harm. A woman using a gun in self-defense does so rarely with the intent to cause death to her attacker. Instead, a woman in such a situation has the intent only to sufficiently stop the assault and to gain control of the situation in order to summon assistance. This simple brandishing of a weapon often results in the assailant choosing to discontinue the crime without a shot having been fired. *See also* Gary Kleck & Marc Gertz, *Armed Resistance to Crime: The Prevalence and Nature of Self-Defense with a Gun*, 86 J. Crim. L. & Crimon. 150 (1995); Gary Kleck, *Policy Lessons From Recent Gun Control Research*, 49 Law and Contemporary Problems 35, 44 (No. 1 Winter 1986) (noting that only a small minority, 8.3% of defensive gun uses, resulted in the assailant's injury or death).

The value of widespread handgun ownership lies not only in the individual instances in which a violent criminal is thwarted while attempting to harm someone, but in the general deterrent effects created by criminals' knowledge of firearms ownership among potential victims. Women alarmed by a series of savage rapes in Orlando, Florida in 1966 rushed local gun stores to arm themselves in self-defense. In a widely publicized campaign, the Orlando Police Department trained approximately 3,000 in firearms safety. According to the FBI Uniform Crime Report for 1967, the city then experienced over an 88% reduction in rapes, while rape throughout Florida continued to increase by 5% and nationwide by 7%. Similar crime reduction efforts involving well-publicized firearms ownership in other U.S. cities saw comparable reductions in the rates of armed robbery and residential burglaries. *See also* Don B. Kates, Jr., *The Value of Civilian Handgun Possession as a Deterrent to Crime or a Defense Against Crime*, 18 Am. J. of Crim. L. 113, 153-56 (1991) (describing the deterrent effects handguns create for crimes requiring direct confrontation with a victim such as rape and robbery and for non-confrontational crime such as car theft and the burglary of unoccupied locations); Int'l L. Enf. Educ. & Trainers Assoc. Br. at sections I.B., I.G. (discussing the crime deterrence value of victim armament).

Violent criminals who may view women as easy targets find their jobs far less taxing in communities such as Washington, D.C. Researchers conducting the [National] Institute of Justice Felon Survey confirm the common-sense notion that those wishing to do harm often think closely before confronting an individual who may be armed. According to this survey, some 56% of the felons agreed that "[a] criminal is not going to mess around with a victim he knows is armed with a gun." Over 80% agreed that "[a] smart criminal always tries to find out if his potential victim is armed," while 57% admitted that "[m]ost criminals are more worried about meeting an armed victim than they are about running into the police." Some 39% said they personally had been deterred from committing at least one crime because they believed the intended victim was armed, and 8% said they had done so "many" times. Almost three-quarters stated that "[o]ne reason burglars avoid houses when people are at home is that they fear being shot during the crime." James D. Wright and Peter H. Rossi, 145 *Armed and Considered Dangerous, a Survey of Felons and Their Firearms* (Aldine de Gruyter, 1986). Some 34% said they had been "scared off, shot at, wounded, or captured by an armed victim" at some point in their criminal careers, while almost 70% had at least one acquaintance who had a similar previous experience. *Id.* at 154-55.

Stalkers and abusive boyfriends, spouses, or ex-spouses may be even more significantly deterred than the hardened, career felons participating in this survey. Under current Washington, D.C. gun regulations, stalkers and violent intimate partners may be confident that their female victims have not armed themselves since the threats or violence began. Many of these men have already been emboldened by women's failure to report such threats and previous violence, or by the oftentimes inadequate resources available to help such women. Allowing women the option to purchase a serviceable handgun will not deter all stalkers and abusive intimate partners willing to sacrifice their own lives. However, the fact that men inclined toward violence will know that women have that choice and may well have exercised it will no doubt inhibit those less willing to pay that price.

The District would like to restrict women's choice of firearm to those it gauges most appropriate rather than to allow rational women the ability to decide whether a handgun is more suited to their needs. Petitioner's Brief cites two articles from firearms magazines in which a shotgun is mentioned as appropriate for home defense. Pet. Br. at 54-55. An assembled shotgun is certainly better than nothing and could provide deterrence benefits provided it is accessible to a woman. However, most women are best served by a handgun, lighter in weight, lighter in recoil, far less unwieldy for women with shorter arm spans, and far more easily carried around the home than a shotgun or rifle. Moreover, women who are holding a handgun are able to phone for assistance, while any type of long gun requires two hands to keep the firearm pointed at an assailant. *See also* Int'l L. Enf. Educ. & Trainers Assoc. Br. at section III. The fact that two articles in firearms magazines suggest a long gun for home defense should not impinge upon the constitutional right for a woman to select the firearm she feels most meets her needs.

Petitioner's *Amici* claims that allowing firearms in the home will only increase women's risk of being murdered. In fact, Petitioners' *Amici Curiae* opens its argument by stating that, when a gun is in the home, an abused woman is "6 times more likely" to be killed than other abused women. Pets' Network Br. at 20. However, this statistic has some verifiable basis only when particular adjustments for other risk factors are weighed. Most importantly, any validity that statistic holds is only for battered women who live with abusers who have guns. The odds for an abused woman living apart from her abuser, when she herself has a firearm, are only 0.22, far below the 2.0 level required for statistical significance. The presence of a firearm is simply negligible compared to obvious forewarnings such as the man's previous rape of the woman, previous threats with a weapon, and threats to kill the woman. Moreover, the "most important demographic risk factor for acts of intimate partner femicide" is the male's unemployment. Jacquelyn C. Campbell, Ph.D., RN, *et al., Risk Factors for Femicide in Abusive Relationships: Results from a Multisite Case Control Study* in 93 Am. J. Pub. Health 1090-92 (No. 7 July 2003). Programs that help women leave an already terribly violent situation and that decrease unemployment should therefore be keys to the abatement of femicide, not laws that serve only to disarm potential victims.

It must also be noted that allowing women handguns will not increase the type of random, violent crime that causes such uneasiness among District residents. Women are far less likely to commit murder than are men. Despite being roughly half of the U.S. population, women comprised only 10% of murder offenders in 2006 and 2004, only 7% in 2005. Even more important to note are the circumstances under which women kill. Some estimates indicate that between 85% and 90% of women who commit homicides do so against men who have battered them for years. Allison Bass, *Women Far Less Likely to Kill than Men; No One Sure Why*, Boston Globe, February 24, 1992, at 27. *See also* Int'l L. Enf. Educ. & Trainers Assoc. Br. at Section II.A. One 1992 study by the Georgia Department of Corrections reported that of the 235 women serving jail time for murder or manslaughter in Georgia, 102 were deemed domestic killings. Almost half those women claimed that their male partners had regularly beaten them. The vast majority of those who claimed previous beatings had repeatedly reported the domestic violence to law enforcement. Kathleen O'Shea, *Women on Death Row* in *Women Prisoners: A Forgotten Population* 85 (Beverly Fletcher *et al.* eds., Praeger, 1993). *See also* Angela Browne, *Assault and Homicide at Home: When Battered Women Kill*, in 3 Advances in Applied Soc. Psych. 61 (Michael Saks & Leonard Saxe, eds., 1986) (including FBI data that 4.8% of all U.S. homicides are women who have killed an intimate partner in self-defense.) While these deaths are of course tragic, their occurrences do not indicate that women with access to handguns will commit the random acts of violence law-abiding residents most fear.

Men and women with a history of aggression, domestic violence, and mental disturbance are already prohibited from possessing firearms under both federal and District of Columbia law. Federal law bars possession to any individual who has been convicted of a "crime punishable by imprisonment for a term exceeding one year," who is an "unlawful user of or addicted to any controlled substance," who has been "adjudicated as a mental defective or who has been committed to a mental institution," who is under an active restraining order, or who has been "convicted in any court of a misdemeanor crime of domestic violence." 18 U.S.C. §§922(g)(1), (3), (4), (8), (9)[.] Washington, D.C. law contains similar provisions, but adds as prohibited persons chronic alcoholics and those who have been "adjudicated negligent in a firearm mishap causing death or serious injury to another human being." D.C. Code §§7-2502.03(a)(5), (a)(8). Rigorous enforcement of existing law should therefore minimize the risk that both men and women with histories of violence, mental instability, or negligence with a firearm will have a firearm in their homes.

C. WOMEN MAY NOT DEPEND UPON THE DISTRICT'S LAW ENFORCEMENT SERVICES

The situation now in Washington, D.C. is that women can no longer depend upon the men in their lives to provide protection against violent crime, nor do women themselves have access to handguns that equalize the inherent biological differences between a woman victim and her most likely male attacker. The traditional emphasis of men's duty to protect women not only increases this defenselessness, but in fact has proved of less worth as increasingly more women live alone. Women in the District have therefore been compelled to rely upon the protections of a government-provided police force.

Courts have found that such reliance is unfounded. *See,* Licia A. Esposito Eaton, Annotation, *Liability of Municipality or Other Governmental Unit for Failure to Provide Police Protection from Crime,* 90 A.L.R.5th 273 (2001). Despite women's expectations, courts across the nation have ruled that the Due Process Clause does not "requir[e] the State to protect the life, liberty, and property of its citizens against invasion by private actors." *DeShaney v. Winnebago County Soc. Servs.,* 489 U.S. 189, 194 (1989). Women simply have no legal right to law enforcement protection unless they are able to prove special and highly narrow circumstances. Just how special and highly narrow those circumstances are were proven in this Court's *Castle Rock v. Gonzales* decision. 545 U.S. 748 (2005). In *Castle Rock,* the Court found that a temporary restraining order, a mandatory arrest statute passed with the clear legislative intent of ensuring enforcement of domestic abuse restraining orders, and Jessica Gonzalez's repeated pleas for help were insufficient for her to demand protection. *Castle Rock* therefore left open the question of just what a woman and a well-meaning legislature would have to do to create such a right to expect police protection from a known and specific threat.

There is no case that better illustrates both how little individual citizens may demand of their local police forces and the utility of a serviceable firearm than Washington, D.C.'s own *Warren v. District of Columbia,* 444 A.2d 1 (D.C. 1981). One morning two men broke down the door and climbed to the second floor of a home where a mother and her four-year-old daughter were sleeping. The men raped and sodomized the mother. Her screams awoke two women living upstairs, who phoned 911 and were assured that help would soon arrive. The neighbors then waited upon an adjoining roof while one policeman simply drove past the residence and another departed after receiving no response to his knock on the door. Believing the two men had fled, the women climbed back into the home and again heard their neighbor's screams. Again they called the police. This second call was never even dispatched to officers.

After hearing no further screams, the two women trusted that police had indeed arrived and called down to their neighbor. Then alerted to the presence of two other victims nearby, the men proceeded to rape, beat, and compel all three women to sodomize each other for the next fourteen hours. Upon their seeking some compensation from the District for its indifference, the women were reminded that a government providing law enforcement services "assumes a duty only to the public at large and not to individual members of the community." *Id.* at 4. The District thus simultaneously makes it impossible for women to protect themselves with a firearm while refusing to accept responsibility for their protection.

D.   CONGRESS SPEAKS: THE VIOLENCE AGAINST WOMEN ACT OF 1994

The Congressional history behind the passage of the 1994 Violence Against Women Act shows the introduction of study after study showing the prevalence of gender-based violence and its human toll. Pub. L. No. 103-322, 108 Stat. 1796 (1994)[.] Eleanor Smeal, representative of the Fund for the Feminist Majority, testified that Title III of the Act was to "provide women federal civil remedies to compensate in part for the inefficient, ineffective, and often unsympathetic police response at state and local levels." *Violence Against Women Act: Hearing on H.B. 3355 before the Subcommittee on Civil and Constitutional Rights of the Committee on the Judiciary House of Representatives*, 103 Cong. 51 (November 16, 1993) (Testimony by Eleanor Smeal, President, Fund for the Feminist Majority). The creation of these federal civil remedies indicates one of Congress' first and most powerful acknowledgments that, at least within the goals of the 1994 VAWA, women should be given some greater legal protection because of their gender.

Although the Act was expanded in 2006 to include male victims of sexual assault and domestic violence, the title of the original act and its text make evident that Congress was originally concerned only with the special dangers facing women and so offered federal protection only to them. Rather than viewing any existing bias or discrimination in state and local courts as a matter to erode over time, Congress deemed it necessary to guarantee equal protection of the laws to women disadvantaged under existing law. The Court should view this legislative precedent not as justification to find constitutional the District's firearms laws as applied to all but women, but as the judgment of a coequal branch that the disparities between male and female should not be overlooked.

III.   GENDER CHARACTERISTICS SHOULD AT LEAST BE CONSIDERED BEFORE BARRING LAW-ABIDING WOMEN HANDGUNS, THE MOST SUITABLE MEANS FOR THEIR SELF-PROTECTION

Women are at a severe disadvantage when confronting a likely stronger male assailant. In general, women simply do not have the upper body strength and testosterone-driven speed to effectively defend themselves without help.

A firearm, particularly an easily manipulable handgun, equalizes this strength differential and thereby provides women the best chance they have of thwarting an attacker. Even more statistically likely, a firearm in the hands of a threatened woman offers the deterrence empty hands and an often unavailing 911 call do not. *E.g.*, Int'l L. Enf. Educ. & Trainers Assoc. Br. at section I.E. (noting that in 2003, Washington, D.C.'s average police response time for the highest-priority emergency calls was almost 8 and a half minutes). Even in cases in which a 911 response would be effective, an attacker in control of the situation will not allow a woman to pick up the phone to make that call.

Women have made such advances in equality under the law that it is altogether too easy to disregard the innate gender-based biological inequality when it comes to self-defense. Television provides countless examples of strong women standing toe-to-toe against male evildoers and emerging with only minor cuts and bruises. Our invariably gorgeous heroines manage to successfully defend themselves without so much as smudging their make-up or breaking a heel off their stilettos. Women with children are commonly depicted imploring their children to be silent until a caravan of police cars arrives with sirens blaring to finally arrest the assailant. Such images do not conform with most people's experiences and do nothing to decrease the level of violence actual women often suffer.

Advocates of women's reproductive choice commonly argue that pregnancy disproportionately affects women due to their innate gender-based characteristics. Thus, they argue, courts failing to recognize the right to terminate a pregnancy therefore discriminate against women and bar their ability to participate as equal and full members of civil society. While choices about pregnancy no doubt impact a woman's ability to determine the course of part of her life, it is not clear why such a right should be due greater protection than a woman's ability to defend her very existence. A woman who is murdered, a woman who is so badly injured that she may never recover emotionally and/or physically, and a woman who feels constantly helpless faces even greater barriers to her ability to function as an equal member of society.

Amicae therefore contend that depriving women of the right to possess a handgun in the privacy of their own homes reflects at best an insensitivity to women's unique needs created by their inherent gender characteristics. A handgun simply is the best means of self-defense for those who generally lack the upper body strength to successfully wield a shotgun or other long gun. To therefore deny half the population a handgun, as the District and the Office of the Solicitor General urge, evinces the "blindness or indifference" to women that only perpetuates women's vulnerability to physical subordination.

NOTES & QUESTIONS

1. Although there is considerable overlap between the two assessments of the risks and dangers faced by women in our society, the briefs take very different views about how to combat those dangers. What explains the different assessments? Do these competing assessments simply reflect different estimates about the risks and utilities of firearms? If so, can this disagreement be resolved empirically? *See* Exercise: Empirical Assessments, Personal Risk Assessments, and Public Policy, *infra.*

2. Assume that the empirical case were convincing one way or the other. Is there a difference between measurements of the past and expectations about future events? Do you generally find empirical evidence convincing when making decisions about the future?

3. Assume you are a woman living in a high-crime neighborhood and are considering obtaining a firearm for self-protection. How much of your decision will be based on data about the risks and utilities of firearms? What other factors might influence your decision? What are the factors that *should* influence a personal decision to obtain a firearm? Are those the same factors that should influence public officials who set firearms policy?

4. Robin West argues that the failure of state and social institutions justifies the right to abortion. "To whatever degree we fail to create the minimal conditions for a just society, we also have a right, individually and fundamentally to be shielded from the most dire or simply the most damaging consequences of that failure. . . . We must have the right to opt out of an unjust patriarchal world that visits unequal but unparalleled harms upon women . . . with unwanted pregnancies." Robin L. West, *The Nature of the Right to an Abortion*, 45 Hastings L.J. 961, 964, 965 (1994). Does that argument also support a woman's claim of right to own a firearm for self-defense?

5. There is no doubt that an abused woman is at substantially greater risk if her abuser has a gun, as pointed out in the National Network brief. However, as noted in the Legislature's Women and Academics brief, research shows no statistically significant heightened risk to an abuse victim who both lives apart from her abuser and has her own gun. Living with armed abuser results in 7.59 odds ratio for increased risk of femicide, an odds ratio so high as to almost certainly be statistically valid. (In other words, a woman who lives with an armed abuser is about 750 percent more likely to be murdered than is a woman who lives with an unarmed abuser.) Jacquelyn Campbell et al., *Risk Factors for Femicide in Abusive Relationships*, 93 Am. J. Pub. Health 1089, 1090-92 (2003).

6. The brief of the Women State Legislators and Academics disclaims the position that *only* women should have a constitutional right to a handgun. However, could you construct an argument for such a position, using the data in the two briefs above? Laws that discriminate on the basis of sex are generally subject to intermediate scrutiny under the Equal Protection Clause of the Fourteenth Amendment. (This review sometimes comes close to strict scrutiny in practice. *See United States v. Virginia*, 518 U.S. 515, 531 (1996) (striking down a state military college's single-sex admissions policy, and holding that an "exceedingly persuasive justification" was required before "gender-based government action" could be upheld).) If *Heller* had not recognized a right of individuals to own handguns, would it be constitutional for a city or state to enact a law prohibiting men, but not women, from owning handguns? Are there any circumstances today where gender-based firearms legislation might be upheld against Second and/or Fourteenth Amendment challenge? Where it might be appropriate?

C. Age and Physical Disability

People who are physically weaker than average may have heightened concerns about their physical security. The two briefs that follow reflect that concern, but take different views about the effectiveness of gun control and the utility of private firearms.

> ## Brief for American Academy of Pediatrics et al. as Amici Curiae Supporting of the Petition for Writ of Certiorari, District of Columbia v. Heller, 552 U.S. 1035 (2007)

American Academy of Pediatrics ("AAP"), the Society for Adolescent Medicine ("SAM"), and the Children's Defense Fund ("CDF"). . . .

These amici share a commitment to the health and well-being of America's children and youth.

Founded in 1930, the American Academy of Pediatrics is a national, not-for-profit organization dedicated to furthering the interests of children's health and the pediatric specialty. Since its inception, the membership of AAP has grown from the original group of 60 physicians specializing in children's health to 60,000 primary care physicians, pediatric medical subspecialists, and pediatric surgical specialists. Over the past 77 years, AAP has become a powerful voice for children's health through education, research, advocacy, and expert advice and has demonstrated a continuing commitment to working with hospitals and clinics, as well as with state and federal governments to protect the well-being of America's children.

The Society for Adolescent Medicine is a multi-disciplinary international non-profit organization of health care professionals who are committed to advancing the health and well-being of adolescents. Over its 39-year history, members of SAM have worked to enhance public and professional awareness of adolescent health issues through education, research, clinical services, and advocacy activities. For over 20 years, SAM has published the *Journal of Adolescent Health*, the pre-eminent, authoritative peer-reviewed journal in the field of adolescent health.

Founded in 1969 as the Washington Research Project, the Children's Defense Fund began work under its new name in 1973 as a national non-profit organization whose mission is to ensure every child a Healthy Start, a Head Start, a Fair Start, a Safe Start, and a Moral Start in life and successful passage to adulthood with the help of caring families and communities. . . .

These amici recognize that firearm-related injury to children is a significant public health problem both in terms of its impact on children's physical and mental health and its impact on and cost to the public health system in America. Because of their historical and continuing commitment to protecting children and youth and their recognition of the particular threat that handguns pose to America's young people, AAP, SAM, and CDF have closely followed and been actively involved in developments in controlling access to and possession of all firearms, including handguns. It is the firm belief of the amici that the absence of handguns from children's homes and communities is the most reliable and effective method to prevent firearm-related injuries to children and adolescents. . . .

ARGUMENT

The United States generally and the District of Columbia in particular face the cruel reality that their children and youth are being slaughtered and maimed by handguns. These readily concealed, easily transferred, and widely available instruments of death are the leading weapons of choice when children or adolescents kill or wound each other or themselves.

In response to this public health epidemic, the District of Columbia carefully considered and then enacted reasonable legislation narrowly tailored to thwart the crisis. The decision of the United States Court of Appeals for the District of Columbia Circuit places that Court in direct conflict with the applicable precedent of this Court and the decisions of no fewer than eight Circuits and the District of Columbia Court of Appeals. Unless the decision is reviewed and reversed, the residents of the District of Columbia, and particularly its children and adolescents, will be placed at direct and immediate increased risk of harm by handgun violence. Nothing in the jurisprudence of this Court, the intention of the Framers of the Constitution, or sound public policy allows for a court to invalidate reasonable public health measures and in their place visit serious harm upon so many.

For the reasons set forth below, these amici urge the Court to grant the Petition for Certiorari.

I. HANDGUNS POSE A UNIQUE DANGER TO CHILDREN AND YOUTH

Handguns pose a danger to all citizens. Handguns are more likely than any other type of gun to be used in interpersonal violence and crime, as well as self-directed injury. Firearm & Inj. Ctr. at Penn, *Firearm Injury in the U.S.*, at 7 (Oct. 2006). Indeed, handguns are used in nearly 70 percent of firearm suicides and 75 percent of firearm homicides in the United States. *See* Garen J. Wintemute et al., *The Choice of Weapons in Firearm Suicides*, 78 Am. J. Pub. Health 824 (1988); Stephen W. Hargarten et al., *Characteristics of Firearms Involved in Fatalities*, 275 JAMA 42 (1996). Handguns account for 77 percent of all traced guns used in crime. Firearm & Inj. Ctr. at Penn, *supra*, at 8.

Handguns, however, pose a particular risk to children and adolescents. When a gun is carried outside the home by a high school-aged youth, it is most likely to be a semiautomatic handgun (50 percent) and next most likely to be a revolver (30 percent). Josh Sugarmann, Every Handgun Is Aimed at You: The Case for Banning Handguns 113 (2001) (citing Joseph F. Sheley & James D. Wright, Nat'l Inst. of Justice, High School Youths, Weapons, and Violence: A National Survey 6 (1998)). Further, there is no way to make guns "safe" for children — gun safety programs have little effect in reducing firearms death and injury. *Id.* at 125. Death and injury to America's children and youth is undeniably linked to the presence and availability of handguns, as discussed further below.

A.   **THE DISTRICT OF COLUMBIA HANDGUN LAW IS A REASONABLE RESTRICTION
     BECAUSE HANDGUNS MAKE SUICIDE MORE LIKELY AND SUICIDE-ATTEMPTS
     MORE INJURIOUS TO CHILDREN AND ADOLESCENTS**

Access to firearms, and handguns in particular, increases the risk that children will die in a firearm-related suicide. In 1997, 1,262 children committed
suicide using a firearm, and 63 percent of all suicides in adolescents 15 through
19 years of age were committed with a firearm. Am. Acad. of Pediatrics, Comm.
on Inj. & Poison Prevention, [*Firearm-Related Injuries Affecting the Pediatric Population*, 105 Pediatrics 888,] 889-90 Fig. 1. In 1996, handguns were involved in
70 percent of teenage suicides in which a firearm was used. *Id.* at 889.

Case studies reveal that suicide by firearm is strongly associated with the
presence of a gun in the home of the victim. *See generally* David A. Brent et al.,
Firearms and Adolescent Suicide, 147 Am. J. of Diseases of Child. 1066 (1993);
Arthur L. Kellermann et al., *Suicide in the Home in Relation to Gun Ownership*,
327 New Eng. J. Med. 467 (1992). In fact, the risk of suicide is five times greater
in households with guns. Brent, *supra*, at 1068. A study on adolescent suicide and
firearms found that while 87.8 percent of suicide victims who lived in a home
with a gun died by firearms, only 18.8 percent of suicide victims that did not have
a gun died by firearms. *Id.* Even more telling is that homes with handguns have a
risk of suicide almost twice as high as that in homes containing only long guns.
Kellermann, *supra*, at 470.

Moreover, statistics reveal that restrictions on access to handguns in the
District of Columbia significantly reduced the incidence of suicide by firearms
and resulted in a substantial reduction in the number of deaths by suicide. Colin
Loftin et al., *Effects of Restrictive Licensing of Handguns on Homicide and Suicide in the
District of Columbia*, 325 New Eng. J. Med. 1615, 1617 (1991). A study by the
Institute of Criminal Justice and Criminology at the University of Maryland
showed a decline of 23 percent in the number of suicides by firearms in the
District of Columbia from 1968 to 1987. *Id.* at 1616 Table 1. Tellingly, the number
of non-firearm-related suicides in the District of Columbia during that same time
frame did not decline; nor did the number of firearm-related suicides in neighboring communities that were not subject to a similar ban on handguns. *Id.* at
1617-18. Additionally, the reduction in the number of suicides by firearms in the
District during this time did not result in a corresponding increase in the incidents of suicides by other means. *See id.* at 1619. Thus, researchers concluded
from the study that "restrictions on access to guns in the District of Columbia
prevented an average of 47 deaths each year after the law was implemented." *Id.*

In addition, between 2000 and 2002, no child under the age of 16 died from
suicide by firearm in the District of Columbia. In contrast, states without handgun
bans (and less restrictive guns laws generally), such as Alaska, Montana and Idaho,
led the country with 14, 15, and 15, respectively, firearm suicide deaths, respectively, in the same population in the same time period. Violence Pol'y Ctr., Press
Release, *New Study Shows District of Columbia's Tough Gun Laws Work to Prevent Youth
Suicide — No Child 16 Years of Age or Younger in DC Was the Victim of Firearm Suicide
According to Most Recent Federal Data* (July 12, 2005). Given that in 2003, the third
leading cause of death nationwide among youth aged ten to twenty-four was
suicide and that the risk of suicide is five times greater in homes with guns,
invalidation of the law will almost certainly increase the number of children

that die from a suicide. *See* U.S. Dep't of Health & Human Servs., Ctrs. for Disease Control & Prevention, Nat'l Vital Statistics Sys., Nat'l Ctr. for Health Statistics, *10 Leading Causes of Death by Age Group, United States–2003.*

B. **THE DISTRICT OF COLUMBIA'S HANDGUN LAW IS A REASONABLE RESTRICTION BECAUSE HANDGUNS INCREASE THE LIKELIHOOD AND DEADLINESS OF ACCIDENTS INVOLVING CHILDREN**

The increased accessibility to handguns that will result if the District of Columbia handgun ban is struck down will increase the number of children who will be harmed in accidents involving firearms. Studies have shown that fewer than half of United States families with both firearms and children secure firearms separate from ammunition. *See, e.g.*, Mark A. Schuster et al., *Firearm Storage Patterns in U.S. Homes with Children*, 90 Am. J. of Pub. Health 588, 590-91 (2000). This practice is especially troubling because children as young as three are able to pull the trigger of most handguns. Am. Acad. of Pediatrics, Comm. on Inj. & Poison Prevention, *supra* n.2, at 890. Approximately 70 percent of all unintentional firearm injuries and deaths are a result of handguns. *Id.* at 888.

Unintentional firearm death disproportionately affects children: In 2004, firearms accounted for 27 percent of the unintentional deaths in 2004 among youth aged 10-19, while accounting for only 22 percent of unintentional deaths among the population as a whole. *See* U.S. Dep't of Health & Human Servs., Ctrs. for Disease Control & Prevention, WISQARS database. Additionally, each year nearly 90 children are killed and approximately 1,400 are treated in hospital emergency rooms for unintentional firearm-related injuries. SAFE KIDS USA, Press Release, *Unintentional Shooting Prompts SAFE KIDS to Issue Warning About Dangers of Guns in the Home* (2003). Most of these deaths occur in or around the home, and most involve guns that are loaded and accessible to children. *Id.*

The more guns a jurisdiction has, the more likely children in that jurisdiction will die from a firearm accident. In a study of accidental firearm deaths that occurred between 1979 and 1999, children aged four and under were 17 times more likely to die from a gun accident in the four states with the most guns versus the four states with the fewest guns. Matthew Miller et al., *Firearm Availability and Unintentional Firearm Deaths*, 333 Accident Analysis & Prevention 477, 481 Table 3 (2001). Thus, if the decision to strike the handgun ban in the District of Columbia is not reversed, the number of children who will die or be injured by handguns accidentally will increase significantly.

C. **THE DISTRICT OF COLUMBIA HANDGUN LAW IS A REASONABLE RESTRICTION BECAUSE FIREARMS AND ESPECIALLY HANDGUNS INCREASE HOMICIDE AND NONFATAL ASSAULT RATES AMONG AMERICA'S YOUTH**

Firearm-related homicides and assaults affect children, adolescents, and young adults in staggering measure. Between 1987 and 1992, adolescents aged 16 to 19 had the highest rate of handgun crime victimization, nearly three times the average rate. Michael R. Rand, U.S. Dep't of Justice, Bureau of Justice Statistics, *Guns and Crime: Handgun Victimization, Firearm Self-Defense, and Firearm Theft,* NCJ 147003 (Apr. 1994, rev. Sept. 2002). Between 1993 and 1997, those aged 19 and younger accounted for 20 percent of firearm homicide victims and 29 percent of victims of nonfatal firearm injury from assault. Marianne W. Zavitz & Kevin J. Strom, U.S. Dep't of Justice, Bureau of Justice Statistics, *Firearm Injury and Death from Crime, 1993-1997,* at 3, NCJ 182993 (Oct. 2000). For the period 1993-2001, of the average 847,000 violent victimizations committed with firearms each year, 87 percent were committed with handguns. Craig Perkins, U.S. Dep't of Justice, Bureau of Justice Statistics, *Nat'l Crime Victimization Survey, 1993-2001: Weapon Use and Violent Crime,* at 3, NCJ 194820 (Sept. 2003). In 2005, 25 percent of the nation's 10,100 firearm homicide victims were under the age of 22. U.S. Dep't of Justice, Fed. Bureau of Investigation, *Crime in the United States, 2005,* at Table 8 (Murder Victims by Age by Weapon, 2005) (2006). Handguns were responsible for 75 percent of those homicides. *Id.* at Table 7 (Murder Victims by Weapon, 2001-2005). Indeed, the number of juvenile handgun homicides is directly correlated to the overall number of juvenile homicides. Sugarmann, *supra,* at 116 Fig. 7-7.

Moreover, nationally, children and young adults are killed by firearms more frequently than almost any other cause of death. In 2004, firearm homicide was the second leading cause of injury death for persons 10 to 24 years of age, second only to motor vehicle crashes. Brady Campaign Publication, *Firearm Facts* (Apr. 2007). Incredibly, in that same year, firearm homicide — not car accidents — was the leading cause of death for African American males between the ages of 15 and 34. *Id.* Children and youth are murdered with handguns more often than all other weapons combined. Violence Pol'y Ctr., *Kids in the Line of Fire: Children, Handguns, and Homicide.* And, for every child killed by a gun, four are wounded. Diane [sic] Degette, *When the Unthinkable Becomes Routine,* 77 Denv. U. L. Rev. 615, 615 n.5 (2000).

Finally, firearms (particularly handguns) represent the leading weapon utilized by both children and adults in the commission of homicide. *See* Fox Butterfield, *Guns Blamed for Rise in Homicides by Youths in the 80's,* N.Y. Times, Dec. 10, 1998, at 29. Between 1985 and 2002, the firearm homicide death rate increased 36 percent for teens aged 15 to 19 nationwide. *See* U.S. Dep't of Health & Human Servs., Ctrs. for Disease Control & Prevention, WISQARS database. Not coincidentally, in each year after 1985, handguns have been the most used homicide weapon by juveniles (those age 17 and under) nationwide. Alfred Blumstein, *Youth, Guns, and Violent Crime,* 12 The Future of Children 39, at Fig. 5 (2002). Scholars note that the dramatic increases in the rate of homicide committed by juveniles are attributable largely to the increases in homicides in which a firearm is used. Alan Lizotte, *Guns & Violence: Patterns of Illegal Gun Carrying Among Young Urban Males,* 31 Val. U. L. Rev. 375, 375 (1998). University of California, Berkeley law professor Frank Zimring has observed, "the most important reason for the sharp escalation in homicide [among offenders 13 to 17] was an escalating volume of fatal attacks with firearms." Franklin E. Zimring, *American Youth Violence* 35-36 (1998).

Handgun bans alleviate the problem of firearm homicide. Researchers at the Institute of Criminal Justice and Criminology at the University of Maryland found that gun-related homicides in the District of Columbia dropped 25 percent after the enactment of the ban. Loftin et al., *supra,* at 1616 Table 1.

In addition, the relatively low incidence of gun-related violence in America's schools proves that gun bans work. Thanks to the absolute prohibition of guns on the nation's elementary and secondary school campuses, fewer than one percent of school-aged homicide victims are killed on or around school grounds or on the way to and from school. Jill F. DeVoe et al., U.S. Dep't of Justice, Bureau of Justice Statistics and U.S. Dep't of Education, Nat'l Ctr. for Ed. Statistics, *Indicators of School Crime and Safety: 2004*, at iii, NCES 2005-002/NCJ 205290 (2005). In each year between 1992 and 2000, children and youth aged five to 19 were at least 70 times more likely to be murdered away from school than at school. *Id.* at 1. College campuses also reflect similarly lower rates for on-campus as compared to off-campus violence, Katrina Baum & Patsy Klaus, U.S. Dep't of Justice, Bureau of Justice Statistics, *Violent Victimization of College Students 1995-2002*, at 1, NCJ 206836 (2005).

II. THE DISTRICT'S HANDGUN LAW IS A REASONABLE RESTRICTION BECAUSE OF THE ECONOMIC, SOCIETAL, AND PSYCHOLOGICAL COSTS OF HANDGUN VIOLENCE UPON CHILDREN

As discussed above, handguns are directly responsible for increasing the number of deaths and injuries to children and families from violent crime, suicide and accidents. The most serious harm resulting from youth violence is caused by firearms; most firearm-related injuries, in turn, involve handguns.

The economic, societal and psychological costs of youth violence also are well established. According to Centers for Disease Control and Prevention statistics, the consequences of youth violence include:

> Direct and indirect costs of youth violence (e.g., medical, lost productivity, quality of life) in excess of $158 billion every year. . . .

> In a nationwide survey of high school students, about six percent reported not going to school on one or more days in the 30 days preceding the survey because they felt unsafe at school or on their way to and from school. . . .

> In addition to causing injury and death, youth violence affects communities by increasing the cost of health care, reducing productivity, decreasing property values, and disrupting social services. . . .

The public bears the majority of these costs. A recent study found that, in 2000, the average cost for each: (i) homicide was $4,906 in medical costs, and $1.3 million in lost productivity; (ii) non-fatal assault resulting in hospitalization was $24,353 in medical costs and $57,209 in lost productivity; (iii) suicide was $2,596 in medical costs and $1 million lost productivity; and (iv) non-fatal self inflicted injury was $7,234 in medical costs and $9,726 in lost productivity. Phaedra S. Corso et al., *Medical Costs and Productivity Losses Due to Interpersonal Violence and Self-Directed Violence*, 32 Am. J. of Preventive Med. 474 (2007). . . .

Economic costs provide, at best, an incomplete measure of the toll of violence and injuries caused by handguns. Children, like all victims of violence, are more likely to experience a broad range of mental and physical health problems not reflected in these estimates from post-traumatic stress disorder to depression, cardiovascular disease, and diabetes. *See generally* Corso et al., *supra;* Carole Goguen, *The Effects of Community Violence on Children and Adolescents,* U.S. Dep't of Veterans Affairs, Nat'l Ctr. for Posttraumatic Stress Disorder.

Brief for Southeastern Legal Foundation, Inc. et al. as Amici Curiae Supporting Respondent, District of Columbia v. Heller, 554 U.S. 570 (2008)

. . . Advocating on behalf of women, the elderly and the physically disabled, the *amici* herein argue the actions of the District of Columbia have harmed the members of society most physically vulnerable to criminal attack. . . .

ARGUMENT

I. THE BRIEF'S STRUCTURE . . .

One anomaly uncovered in approaching this issue from the viewpoint of women, the elderly and the physically disabled is that not all of these groups are equally represented in the literature. Studies referencing women are more prevalent. However, what is apparent from the anecdotal examples presented with this brief are the groups' members' characteristics for this discussion overlap to a great degree. Arguments asserted on behalf of women can be made, by analogy, on behalf of the members of the other two groups. This reinforces the main theme that all three groups' members occupy a physically inferior position relative to their potential attackers and benefit from defensive use of handguns.

II. EMPIRICAL RESEARCH ILLUSTRATES THE USE OF THE INDIVIDUAL RIGHT OF ARMED SELF-DEFENSE EMBODIED IN THE SECOND AMENDMENT FOR THE BENEFIT OF WOMEN, THE ELDERLY AND THE PHYSICALLY DISABLED

A. EMPIRICAL RESEARCH SUPPORTS THE COMMON SENSE ARGUMENT THAT THE USE OF HANDGUNS PROTECTS WOMEN, THE ELDERLY AND THE PHYSICALLY DISABLED FROM GREATER PHYSICAL THREAT

It is well-recognized that the disparity in size and strength between men and women generally provides men with an advantage during physical combat. In her note *Why Annie Can't Get Her Gun: A Feminist Perspective on the Second Amendment,* Inge Anna Larish supported this general statement with the following:

> On average women are weaker than men of comparable height. Muscles form a lower proportion of female body weight than of male body weight (36% and 43%, respectively). Kenneth F. Dyer, *Challenging the Men: The Social Biology of Female Sporting Achievement* 71-72 (1982). Women can develop arm muscles only 75% to 85% the strength of men's muscles. Generally, actual differences in average strength tend to be greater because women do not exercise their upper bodies

adequately to develop their potential strength while men are more likely to engage in vigorous exercise to develop strength closer to their potential. *Id.* Men also have more power available for explosive events than women. *Id.* at 74.

Women are on average smaller than men. The average height of men in the United States ranges from 5′ 7.4″ to 5′ 9.7″ and from 163 to 178 pounds; the average height for women ranges from 5′ 2.2″ to 5′ 4.3″ and from 134 to 150 pounds. Bureau of the Census, U.S. Dep't of Commerce, *Statistical Abstract of the United States* 108 (107th ed. 1987).

Larish, Inge Anna, *Why Annie Can't Get Her Gun: A Feminist Perspective on the Second Amendment*, 1996 U. Ill. L. Rev. 467, 494, fn. 213 (1996).

In light of the differences, Larish concludes the possession of a gun not only serves to "equalize the differences between men . . . ," but also serves to "eliminate the disparity in physical power between the sexes." *Id.* Furthermore, she posits, *"The available information on civilian restriction of gun ownership indicates that one of the groups most harmed by restrictions on private gun ownership will be women." Id.* (emphasis added). Larish further states, "Analysts repeatedly find that guns are the surest and safest method of protection for those who are most vulnerable to 'vicious male predators.' Guns are thus the most effective self-defense tools for women, the elderly, the weak, the infirm and the physically handicapped." *Id. 498* (citing Edgar A. Suter, *Guns in the Medical Literature — A Failure of Peer Review*, 83 J. Med. Ass'n Ga. 133, 140 (1994)). . . .

According to Dr. Kleck's findings, firearms are used defensively 2.2 to 2.5 million times a year, with *handguns accounting for 1.5 to 1.9 million of the instances.* Kleck and Gertz, *Armed Resistance to Crime: The Prevalence and Nature of Self Defense with a Gun*, J. Crim. L. and Criminology, Vol. 86, No. 1, 164 (1995) (emphasis added). Of the sample used to calculate the number of times a gun was used defensively during a year, women made up 46 percent. *Id.* at 178. Of the 2 million defensive gun uses each year, 8.2 percent involved sexual assault. This translates to approximately 205,000 occurrences each year. *Id.* at 185. In addition, overall, with a handgun, the odds in favor of reducing serious injury to the victim increase. Tark and Kleck, *Resisting Crime: The Effects of Victim Action on the Outcomes of Crimes*, Criminology, Vol. 42, No. 4, 861-909, 902 (November, 2004).

The empirical literature is unanimous in portraying defensive handgun use as effective, in the sense that gun-wielding victims are less likely to be injured, lose property, or otherwise have crimes completed against them than victims who either do nothing, resist or who resist without weapons. Kleck and Gertz, *Carrying Guns for Protection: Results from the National Self-Defense Survey,* J. Research in Crime and Delinquency, Vol. 35, No. 2, 193, 194 (May, 1998). . . .

B.   THE *AMICI CURIAE* BRIEF FILED BY VIOLENCE POLICY CENTER IN SUPPORT OF APPELLANTS INCORRECTLY CHARACTERIZES THE VALUE OF THE HANDGUN AS AN EFFECTIVE MEANS OF SELF-DEFENSE

On pages 29-31 of the brief submitted in this case by Violence Policy Center [hereinafter VPC], it argues that handgun use is the least effective method for self-defense and that shotguns and rifles are better suited for this purpose. Brief for Violence Policy Center, *et al.* as *Amici Curiae* Supporting Petitioners at 29-31,

District of Columbia, et al. v. Dick Anthony Heller, No. 07-290 (January 11, 2008). VPC further states that this argument is supported by a "wealth of evidence." *Id.* at 30.

The problem with this contention is VPC fails to cite *any* evidence supporting its proposition. Moreover, for women, the elderly and the physically disabled, VPC's "one-size-fits-all" approach ignores the physical requirements necessary to use shotguns or other long guns. Finally, the argument disregards the obvious: a handgun's compact nature lends itself to easier use by individuals with lesser physical ability, including but not limited to persons who are unable to brandish a shotgun when threatened.

VPC cites to "[f]irearms expert" Chris Bird, quoting from his book *The Concealed Handgun Manual, How to Choose, Carry and Shoot a Gun in Self Defense* in support of its assertion that the "handgun is the least effective firearm for self defense." The absurdity of pretending a book advocating the use of handguns *really* contains the opposite conclusion does not go unnoticed. The quote used by VPC, "a handgun 'is the least effective firearm for self defense' and in almost all situations 'shotguns and rifles are much more effective in stopping a [criminal],'" however will be examined. The quote is drawn from *Chapter 5, Choosing a Handgun: Semi-automatics and Revolvers* and reads in its entirety:

> Like many things in life, a handgun is a compromise. It is the least effective firearm for self-defense. Except at very close quarters — at arm's length — shotguns and rifles are much more effective in stopping a drug-hyped robber or rapist intent on making you pay for his lack of social skills. A handgun is the hardest firearm to shoot accurately, and, even when you hit what you are shooting at, your target does not vaporize in a red mist like on television.

Id. at 114.

Contrary to VPC's assertion, Bird's point is not that handguns are ineffective, but their effectiveness depends on the ammunition's stopping power. He states in the same section:

> In choosing a handgun for self defense, remember that the gun has two functions. In some cases, presentation of the gun, coupled with a shouted order to "STOP, GO AWAY, BACK UP," will be enough, to diffuse the threat. It reminds the potential robber or rapist he has urgent business in another county. . . . While any handgun will do, a large gun with a hole in the business end as big as a howitzer reinforces the seriousness of your intentions.
>
> In cases where the threat is not enough, the gun is a delivery system for those little missiles, scarcely bigger than a cigarette filter, that rip and tear your attacker's anatomy. It is the bullet that stops the attack, not the gun. The size and weight of the bullet depend mostly on the caliber of the gun from which it is fired. So one of your first decisions on picking a gun is deciding on a caliber.

Id. at 115.

None of this material, nor the balance of Bird's book, supports VPC's assertion that handguns are ineffective to deter crime or as a means of self-defense.

Moreover, VPC fails to support its additional argument that handguns are hard to shoot accurately because when characterized correctly, the cited work by noted firearms instructor Massad Ayoob, *In the Gravest Extreme, The Role of the Firearm in Personal Protection,* is contrary to VPC's contention. First, the section of

Ayoob's book to which VPC refers has nothing to do with personal defense of the individual or the homeowner; instead, the quote comes from *Chapter 6, How and When to Use Firearms in Your Store. Id.* at 43. Thus, this section is concerned with the proficiency of handgun use to avoid "wild shots" in order to avoid endangering customers or other persons. *Id.* at 47. Individual defense of the person and deterrence are treated in other chapters. *Id.* at 51, 75.

Second, the "accuracy" argument ignores that a criminal encounter is not a target shoot or practice. Moreover, it ignores a handgun's deterrent effect. Ayoob corrects, qualifies and explains VPC's mischaracterization of his statements in his declaration. He attests that:

> The statements in question in the VPC brief glaringly ignore the well-established fact that the great majority of times when a private citizen draws a gun on a criminal suspect, the very presence of the gun suffices to end hostilities with no shots fired. This simple fact makes marksmanship skill under stress a moot point in the majority of instances when defensive firearms are brought into action by private citizens acting in defense of themselves or others.

See Declaration of Massad F. Ayoob *infra* p. App. 4.

Further, Ayoob observes, from a practical standpoint the use of a handgun, as opposed to a long gun, is superior in that long guns are more easily taken away during defensive use. He states:

> The VPC brief falsely attributes its imputation that rifles and shotguns are superior to handguns for defensive purposes, to me among others. Yet in going through "In the Gravest Extreme" carefully enough to cherry-pick the misleading out-of-context quotes, that brief pointedly ignores my flat statements on Page 100 of the book in question: "High powered rifles are not recommended for self-defense. . . . A major problem with any rifle or shotgun is that it is too awkward to get into action quickly, or to handle in close quarters. A burglar will find it much easier to get a 3 $\frac{1}{2}$ foot weapon away from you, than a pistol you can hold and fire with one hand." This is especially true with regard to any person who may be at a physical disadvantage when contrasted with the physical ability of their attacker, such as a woman, an elderly person or someone who is physically disabled.

Id. at pp. App. 4-5.

In addition, VPC's argument fails to acknowledge the logical proposition that one may dial 911 when holding a handgun, but it is difficult to do so with two hands occupied with a long gun. . . .

IV. ANECDOTAL EVIDENCE AND DECLARATIONS ILLUSTRATE THE CRITICAL IMPORTANCE OF THE INDIVIDUAL RIGHT OF ARMED SELF-DEFENSE EMBODIED IN THE SECOND AMENDMENT FOR WOMEN, THE ELDERLY AND THE PHYSICALLY DISABLED

Although statistics and empirical data are critical to understanding the broad spectrum of what defensive gun use means to society, the actual flesh-and-blood people, who have had to defend themselves or their families with handguns or other firearms, stand behind the data.

A printed compilation of the instances when women, the elderly or physically disabled defensively used guns in the United States would be unwieldy (though compelling), so the efficacy of statistics is obvious. Behind the rows and columns of data analyzed as statistics, however, are the faces of real, frightened and vulnerable people who have reached for their handguns after hearing the sounds of intruders in the night. These individuals, discussed below, avoided injury or death because they resisted their attackers with handguns. But, sadly, the same may not have been true if their homes were in the District of Columbia.

A.   RECENT ANECDOTES EFFECTIVELY ILLUSTRATE THE IMPORTANCE OF THE PERSONAL RIGHT OF ARMED SELF-DEFENSE FOR WOMEN, THE ELDERLY AND THE PHYSICALLY DISABLED

The following includes instances where women, the elderly and the physically disabled defended themselves during home invasions as well as attacks outside the home. The attacks were perpetrated by younger, stronger assailants. Moreover, the victims in some instances protected not only themselves, but also loved ones.

The anecdotes are arranged in reverse chronological order and by type. The home invasions come first, followed by parking lot incidents.

1. Home Invasions

On January 25, 2008 in Atlanta, Georgia, an intruder assaulted a wheelchair-bound homeowner at the homeowner's front door. During the struggle, the homeowner was able to use his handgun to shoot the attacker.

In December 2007, there were numerous instances of home invasion attacks on women and the elderly. On December 14, 2007 in Lexington, Kentucky, two women were inside their home when they heard a man trying to break in. They dialed 911, keeping the dispatcher on the phone while they warned the man to stop. When he would not stop, one of the women shot him. Investigators ruled the shooting self-defense.

On December 8, 2007 at Hialeah Gardens, Florida, four armed men attacked a 74-year-old heart patient, Jorge Leonton, in his driveway. After he withdrew money from an ATM, the four followed him home and choked him after he got out of the car, demanding money. While being choked by one of the attackers, Leonton took out his gun, for which he had a concealed weapon permit, and told the attacker three times he had a heart condition, could not breathe and the assailant was killing him. When the attacker would not let go, Leonton shot him. The other three men fled. Leonton's wife said, "If he wouldn't have been armed, I think he would have been killed." . . .

In November 2007, there were several attacks against all groups' members. On November 27, 2007 in Carthage, Missouri, a 63-year-old grandmother brandishing a handgun caused two burglars to run away after they broke down her back door. Her grandchild was in the house at the time.

Two weeks earlier, on November 16, 2007 in Waynesville, Missouri, a disabled man chased one intruder away and took one prisoner for the police with his handgun. Before breaking into the disabled man's trailer, the two male assailants had broken into a local motel room where they had beaten two people with a baseball bat so severely that one had to be taken by "life flight" to the hospital. Later, the two intruders entered the trailer and confronted the disabled man and his wife. One intruder pulled a pellet gun, but the homeowner pulled a "real gun." The pellet gun-wielding intruder fled while the other was held until the police arrived.

Two days earlier, on November 14, 2007 in Hessville, Indiana, a woman who was being stalked had her door kicked in by a former date. Later, when he returned to her home, she called 911 and was told to lock herself in the bedroom. When she retreated to the bedroom, she found a pistol which had been given to her for protection. She hid in a closet, the stalker opened the door, she told him to stop, but when he advanced toward her, she fired three times. She struck the stalker in the abdomen and he died from his wounds.

On November 5, 2007 in Bartlett, Tennessee, Dorothy "Bobbi" Lovell's charges were dropped after a review of the evidence indicated self-defense in the shooting of her husband. Mrs. Lovell shot her husband with a .357-caliber magnum handgun after he held Mrs. Lovell and her 21-year-old son hostage, threatening their lives.

October 2007 was replete with the defensive use of handguns. On October 27, 2007 in Gainesville, Florida, a 28-year-old male tried to kick down the door of a home owned by Arthur Williams, a 75-year-old, legally blind, retired taxi dispatcher. The homeowner fired on the intruder, striking him in the neck. Local officials praised Williams for defending himself. On October 24, 2007 in Wichita, Kansas, a 76-year-old man shot his 52-year-old live-in girlfriend after she poured bleach on him, sprayed him with mace and beat him with a frying pan. The police called the use of the weapon self-defense. On October 15, 2007 in Kansas City, Missouri, a 69-year-old man thwarted a home invasion by firing a shot from his .40-caliber handgun at his bedroom door when he heard an intruder approaching after his front door had been pried open. The intruder fled without apparent injury.

In July 2007, there were several reported attacks against the elderly and the disabled. On July 30, 2007 in Limestone County, Alabama, a disabled man who collected aluminum cans to supplement his income confronted two men, ages 20 and 24, stealing his cans. He immediately called the sheriff's office. The men thought he had left, walked back onto the property and, when they discovered him in his truck, one of them came toward the homeowner and threatened him. The homeowner told him to stop. When he did not, the homeowner showed his gun and demanded the two men lie on the ground to wait for the sheriff. On July 27, 2007 in El Dorado, Arkansas, a 24-year-old intruder beat 93-year-old Mr. Hill with a soda can, striking him 50 times before he passed out. Covered with blood, the elderly man awoke and retrieved a .38-caliber handgun. The assailant charged at him, forcing Hill to shoot him in the throat. Police arrived and took both Hill and the intruder to the hospital. On July 4, 2007 in Hickory, North Carolina, a 79-year-old man shot a 23-year-old intruder in his bedroom. After the intruder broke into the house, the homeowner's wife escaped to the neighbors and the homeowner shot the intruder. The intruder was expected to survive.

On April 26, 2007 in Augusta, Georgia, an assailant awakened his 57-year-old neighbor, Theresa Wachowiak, putting a knife to her throat. She resisted and managed to grab her .357-caliber handgun, and she shot the intruder in the stomach. The intruder survived. . . .

2006 saw notable examples of defensive gun use. On December 2, 2006 in Zion, Illinois, a 55-year-old wife heard her kitchen doorjamb shatter. She grabbed her pistol and shot the intruder in the chest after he forced his way into her house. The intruder was wearing a black ski mask and gloves.

On October 18, 2006 in Santa Clarita, California, an intruder broke the lock on Nadine Teter's back door and barged into her home. She fled to her back-yard with a gun, but he followed and charged at her. She shot him. The intruder fell, got back up and advanced again, requiring her to shoot him two more times. The attacker then jumped over a fence and ran away. He was later apprehended when the intruder's mother, who was driving the "get-away" car, flagged down law enforcement for medical attention. The intruder survived, and he and his mother were convicted in December 2007 of charges arising out of the attack. With regard to the use of the firearm, Teter said she thinks every woman should carry a gun. She also said:

> Never in a million years, did I think I would use (the gun) — never. And whatever higher power, whatever gave me the strength to pull that trigger. . . . You're looking at him or me. My life or his life. I was not going to get raped. I was not going to get murdered. There was no way — and I didn't.

On April 27, 2006 in Red Bank, Tennessee, at 1:30 A.M., a disabled man saw a masked man crawling through his bedroom window. After he was awakened by the window breaking, David McCutcheon, the disabled homeowner, reached for his .32-caliber revolver and fired four times, forcing the masked man to flee. The intruder was arrested.

2005 saw attacks on the elderly thwarted by defensive handgun use. On May 31, 2005 in Indialantic, Florida, Ms. Judith Kuntz, a 64-year-old widow armed with a .38-caliber revolver shot an intruder in the chest after he broke into her home. She fired at him as he entered her bedroom with a flashlight. She stated, "I'm doing fine under the circumstances. . . . I don't take any joy in somebody being dead. My self-preservation instinct took over." *See* Declaration of Judith Kuntz *infra* pp. App. 19-20. On March 30, 2005 in Kingsport, Tennessee, an 83-year-old woman wrestled with a home intruder. Although he left with her purse, she was able to fire her handgun at him during the struggle, causing him to flee.

Women and the elderly used handguns to stave off assailants in 2004. On March 22, 2004 in Springfield, Ohio, 49-year-old Melanie Yancey shot and killed a 21-year-old intruder when he and an accomplice broke into her home after kicking in her door. She sealed herself in her bedroom, but the two tried to break in. She then fired a shot at them from her .40-caliber handgun and they returned fire. When she heard them go into another unoccupied bedroom, she ran out of the room and fired at them as she ran out of the house. Later, one of the intruders was found lying on a nearby driveway.

On November 4, 2004 in Pensacola, Florida, a 77-year-old retired oil worker, James Workman, shot an intruder who entered the trailer where Workman and his wife, Kathryn, were at home. The intruder advanced toward the trailer despite a warning shot, and Workman struggled with the intruder inside the trailer, shooting him in the process.

2. Parking Lot Incidents

On December 27, 2007 in Orlando, Florida, a 65-year-old man fought off five thugs with a handgun. He was collecting money for parking at a church when a man, accompanied by four other men, put a gun to his head. The victim reached inside his jacket as if to pull out money, but instead, pulled out a handgun and started firing. The men ran away. The elderly man reported he obtained a concealed weapon permit after he was previously attacked by eight teens who tried to rob him with a pipe.

On July 1, 2007 in Dallas, Texas, a 31-year-old man stopped Amor Kerboua, a 79-year-old man, in Kerboua's apartment parking lot. The man put a gun in Kerboua's face and demanded money. Thinking the attacker was joking, Kerboua pushed the gun away. Again, the man put the gun in his face and Kerboua handed him a cup containing $242.50. The assailant then told Kerboua he was going to kill him, pointing the gun at his stomach. Instead, Kerboua, who had a concealed weapon permit, drew his .38-caliber revolver and shot the assailant in the throat. The assailant fell, but maintained his gun aim at Kerboua, forcing Kerboua to fire two more times. The police determined Kerboua acted in self-defense. The assailant survived.

B. NANCY HART AND MINNIE LEE FAULKNER: HISTORICAL AND PRESENT DAY ILLUSTRATIONS OF HOW FIREARMS DETER ASSAILANTS . . .

2. Minnie Lee Faulkner: A Modern Illustration That the Use of a Firearm Deters an Attacker

. . . Mrs. Minnie Lee Faulkner, 88, lives alone in her home in Elbert County, Georgia near the Savannah River. Elbert County is still rural though settled early in the State's history. Faulkner purchased a handgun for personal defense and home protection after the death of her husband in 1993. Faulkner chose a handgun over a rifle or shotgun because it was small, maneuverable and easy to use for home defense by someone of her age, size and strength.

On October 10, 2004, Faulkner's doorbell rang at one o'clock in the morning. From the porch, a voice called, "Minnie Lee, I've got car trouble — open the door." Faulkner replied that she was not going to open the door, and the man on her porch started kicking the door. He split the door and Faulkner called 911.

Faulkner told the man that she had called 911 and he stopped kicking. With pistol in hand, Faulkner then peered out the window and she saw a young man's face with a clear complexion. Faulkner said in a stout voice, "I have my gun and I have it trained right on you." The intruder left. Later, when the front door was examined, it was determined that one more kick would have broken the door. Later that night, the intruder broke into a nearby trailer and attacked an elderly woman while she was in bed. Faulkner believes that the intruder would have tried to kill her had he entered.

Faulkner spoke with the local sheriff's office and was able to provide information for a composite drawing, identifying the intruder as the son of a deceased neighbor. Faulkner specifically noted his clear eyes and good complexion. Using this information and other evidence, the sheriff's office was able to apprehend the intruder. He was convicted of burglary and aggravated assault with intent to rape.

Faulkner was badly frightened by the attack. She believes that her handgun is her only protection, and she is glad she had it the night of the attack. She did not have to shoot the intruder because the mere presence of the weapon scared him away. Faulkner believes people have a right to have a gun for protection and self-defense.

Faulkner's experience poignantly illustrates why the individual right of self-defense through the use of a handgun is so vital to women, the elderly and the physically disabled. Faulkner is from the same county where Nancy Hart stood against the Tories during the War for Independence. As Hart used her intelligence, courage and the Tories' own rifles against them, Faulkner used her courage, fortitude and handgun against an intruder in the night. These women, though separated by two hundred thirty years, have in common the necessity of firearms to deter their bigger, stronger or more numerous assailants. Without firearms, both Nancy Hart and Minnie Lee Faulkner, living on the same land but separated by time, would have been victims. With firearms, they became more than equal to the imminent danger they faced. . . .

DECLARATION OF JUDITH KUNTZ . . .

2. I am a 67-year-old widow and live in Indialantic, Florida.

3. I own a .38-caliber handgun for personal defense. I believe my ownership of the gun and the use of it for personal defense saved my life. I chose a handgun over a rifle or shotgun because it is small, maneuverable and easy to use. I did not choose the rifle or shotgun because they are heavy, unwieldy and difficult to use in a confined space such as my home.

4. On May 31, 2005, I shot an intruder who unlawfully entered my home. I attempted to hide from the intruder in my bedroom, but the intruder proceeded to enter my bedroom while I was in it. I shot the intruder in order to protect myself and my property.

5. I am glad I had my handgun during the incident and that I was able to defend myself and my property, I believe people have a right to own and use a gun for personal defense. . . .

DECLARATION OF THERESA WACHOWIAK . . .

2. I am 57-years-old, and I live in Augusta, Georgia.

3. I own a .357-caliber handgun for personal defense. I believe my ownership of this gun and the use of it for personal defense saved my life. I defer to a handgun over a rifle or shotgun because it is small, maneuverable and easy to use. I did not choose the rifle or shotgun because they are heavy, unwieldy and difficult to use in a confined space such as my home if an intruder actually entered.

4. On April 26, 2007, an intruder gained entrance into my house, in the early morning hours, woke me up, and put a knife to my throat with the intent of doing me bodily harm. He was in my bed and unaware of the handgun I kept in

my bed stand. I protested against his covering my mouth with his hand as he pressed his knife to my throat repeatedly, threatening to kill me as I was struggling to remove his hand. This interaction provided me an opportunity to keep his focus on my resistance while I secured my handgun with his being unaware of my other activities. I appeared to comply finally with his "being in control" and ceased struggling upon securing my weapon. I asked him what did he want. Simultaneously, he realized there were dogs in the room and demanded I "get the dogs out." With him at my back and his knife still ready, we moved off of my bed to the bedroom door. When at the dog gate he demanded the dogs be removed from the room, I unfastened the dog gate and with him preoccupied with their imminent release I pivoted and shot him in the right side of his chest. I did not randomly exercise force, only sufficient force to remove him as a personal threat. He was still mobile and anxious to get away through the now opened dog gate. I called the police and secured medical help for him as I did not expect he could get very far. He did survive his single wound. I was saddened and shocked to find out that the man was a neighbor and a relative of a family I cared about and had known for decades.

5. I am glad I had my handgun that morning and was able to defend myself and my property. I would be no match in a physical contest of strength with my assailant and would have just been another sad statistic. My handgun was the tool I used to preserve my life. . . .

DECLARATION OF JAMES H. WORKMAN, JR. . . .

2. I am 80-years-old, a retired oil industry worker and I live with my wife Kathryn in Pensacola, Florida.

3. I own a .38-caliber handgun for personal defense. I believe my ownership of the gun and the use of it for personal defense saved my wife Kathryn's life and mine. I chose a handgun over a rifle or shotgun because it is small, maneuverable and easy to use. I did not choose the rifle or shotgun because they are heavy, unwieldy and difficult to use in a confined space such my home if an intruder actually entered.

4. On November 4, 2004, I shot an intruder who entered the trailer where my wife and I were staying. We were living in a trailer in front of our home that was damaged by Hurricane Ivan. When the intruder entered our yard at 2:20 A.M., I confronted him. Despite my firing a warning shot into the ground, the intruder advanced toward the trailer. I struggled with him inside the trailer, shooting him in the process

5. I am glad I had my handgun that night and was able to defend my wife, myself and our property. I believe people have a right to own and use a gun for personal defense. . . .

NOTES & QUESTIONS

1. In the previous section, there was significant overlap between the circumstances of the two competing women's organizations. The arguments suggest that women might embrace either gun prohibition or gun possession as a pathway to personal security. Can you say the same thing about the groups represented in this section?

2.   Were you surprised by the data about firearms suicide in the American Academy of Pediatrics brief? Pay particular attention to the data about adolescent suicide with guns. In general, suicide attempts with firearms are far more likely to succeed than attempts involving most other common methods such as drowning, cutting, or asphyxiation. Suicide rates differ widely from state to state. The demographic group most likely to commit suicide, particularly with firearms, is elderly white men. While rural states such as Alaska and Montana tend to have high suicide rates, the District of Columbia has traditionally had one of the lowest suicide rates in the nation. The American data suggest that firearms availability increases the percentage of suicides in which firearms are used, but does not change the overall suicide rate. Gary Klock, Targeting Guns, Firearms and Their Control 275-79 (1997).

International data complicate the picture. Many nations with few privately possessed guns nevertheless have higher suicide rates than the United States. For example, private firearms ownership is almost completely illegal in Japan, and is heavily restricted in Russia, but each of these countries has a per capita suicide rate more than double that of the United States. *See* World Health Organization, Suicide Rates (per 100,000) by Country, Year and Gender (2003), *available at* http://www.who.int/mental_health/prevention/suicide/suiciderates/en/.

If private firearms ownership does make suicide more common among all or some groups, then how should this be taken into account in debates about gun policy? Is suicide as harmful or immoral as unlawful homicide? Are all suicides wrong? Are some worse than others? Is it inappropriate for public policy to make distinctions in this area?

3.   Does advocacy of strict firearms bans give sufficient attention to beneficial gun use like those described in the Southeastern Legal Foundation amicus brief?

4.   What type of laws and regulatory system would eliminate the need for guns in cases like those described in the "Declarations" of Southeastern Legal Foundation brief?

5.   Are the stories in the amicus "Declarations" examples of "good" results? Would disarming people like Judith Kuntz be an acceptable cost of strict gun laws with the expectation of a net benefit to the community overall?

6.   Do these personal episodes affect your view of optimal firearms policy? Do they affect your view about whether to own a firearm? Does the answer to one question influence the other?

7.   As detailed in the American Academy of Pediatrics amicus brief, an article in the New England Journal of Medicine concluded that the ban had significantly reduced homicide and suicide. The conclusion was strongly disputed in an amicus brief of Criminologists and the Claremont Institute:

> Over the five pre-ban years the murder rate fell from 37 to 27 per 100,000 population. . . . In the five post-ban years the murder rate rose to 35. . . .

Averaging the rates over the 40 years surrounding the bans yields a pre-ban DC rate (1960-76) of 24.6 murders. The average for the post-ban years is nearly double: 47.4 murders per 100,000 population. The year before the bans (1976), the District's murder rate was 27 per 100,000 population; after 15 years under the bans it had tripled to 80.22 per 100,000 (1991). . . .

   After the gun prohibitions, the District became known as the "murder capital" of America. Before the challenged prohibitions, the District's murder rate was declining, and by 1976 had fallen to the 15th highest among the 50 largest American cities. . . . After the ban, the District's murder rate fell below what it was in 1976 only one time. . . . In half of the post-ban years, the District was ranked the worst or the second-worst; in four years it was the fourth worst. . . .

Brief for Criminologists, et al. as Amici Curiae Supporting Respondent, District of Columbia v. Heller, 554 U.S. 570, at 7-8 (2008).

   The brief also quoted from a National Academies of Sciences meta-study that surveyed the social science literature on gun control, and concluded that the evidence was not strong enough to support the hypothesis that gun control is beneficial, or the hypothesis that gun ownership is beneficial. Regarding the *New England Journal of Medicine* study of D.C., the National Academies concluded:

> Thus, if Baltimore is used as a control group rather than the suburban areas surrounding DC, the conclusion that the handgun law lowered homicide and suicide rates does not hold. Britt et al. (1996) also found that extending the sample frame an additional two years (1968-1989) eliminated any measured impact of the handgun ban in the District of Columbia. Furthermore, Jones (1981) discusses a number of contemporaneous policy interventions that took place around the time of the Washington, DC, gun ban, which further call into question a causal interpretation of the results. In summary, the District of Columbia handgun ban yields no conclusive evidence with respect to the impact of such bans on crime and violence. The nature of the intervention — limited to a single city, nonexperimental, and accompanied by other changes that could also affect handgun homicide — make it a weak experimental design. Given the sensitivity of the results to alternative specifications, it is difficult to draw any causal inferences.

Charles F. Wellford, John V. Pepper & Carol V. Petrie (eds.), Firearms and Violence: A Critical Review 98 (2005).

   For the academic debate on the NEJM study, see Chester L. Britt, Gary Kleck & David J. Bordua, *A Reassessment of the D.C. Gun Law: Some Cautionary Notes on the Use of Interrupted Time Series Designs for Policy Impact Assessment*, 30 Law & Soc'y Rev. 361 (1996); David McDowall, Colin Loftin & Brian Wiersema, *Using Quasi-Experiments to Evaluate Firearm Laws: Comment on Britt et al.'s Reassessment of the DC Gun Law*, 30 Law & Soc'y Rev. 381 (1996); Chester L. Britt, et al., *Avoidance and Misunderstanding: A Rejoinder to McDowall et al.*, 30 Law & Soc'y Rev. 393 (1996).

   In *Heller*, a collection of 24 professors conducted a new study of the D.C. ban, and reported the results in an amicus brief. Brief for Academics as Amici Curiae Supporting Respondent, District of Columbia v. Heller, 554 U.S. 570 (2008). That study compared the post-ban changes in D.C. homicide rates to the rate in the other 49 largest cities, to Maryland and Virginia, and to the United States as a whole. The data showed that D.C. grew substantially worse in comparison to all of them. *Id.* at 7-10.

Two criminology professors, including David McDowall, who had been a co-author of the NEJM study, filed their own amicus brief. Brief for Professors of Criminal Justice as Amici Curiae Supporting Petitioner, District of Columbia v. Heller, 554 U.S. 570 (2008). That brief argued that post-ban increases in D.C. homicide were the result of a national trend caused by the spread of crack cocaine. *Id.* at 9-11.

Justice Breyer's dissenting opinion in *Heller* (Chapter 9) summarized the D.C. debate, and also the conflicting empirical evidence about gun ownership in general that had been offered by various amici. Because there was supporting evidence on each side, he concluded that the Court should defer to the D.C. City Council's empirical judgment. Do you agree with his position that as long as there is *some* social science research that supports a particular gun control law, then courts should not rule the law unconstitutional? Or should courts try to evaluate the evidence on each side? Should they attempt to evaluate the evidence at all? Does it matter whether the original legislative body, such as the D.C. City Council, actually conducted a serious empirical analysis of its own before enacting the law?

D. Sexual Orientation

People with unconventional sexual orientations have a variety of concerns about unequal treatment in our society and under the law. In the firearms context, that concern manifests as a special worry about physical threats rooted in bigotry and, more subtly, in the form of political exclusion. The brief below elaborates both concerns.

Brief for Pink Pistols et al. as Amici Curiae Supporting Respondent, District of Columbia v. Heller, 554 U.S. 570 (2008)

Pink Pistols is an unincorporated association established in 2000 to advocate on behalf of lesbian, gay, bisexual and transgendered (hereinafter LGBT) firearms owners, with specific emphasis on self-defense issues. There are 51 chapters in 33 states and 3 countries. Membership is open to any person, regardless of sexual orientation, who supports the rights of LGBT firearm owners. Pink Pistols is aware of the long history of hate crimes and violence directed at the LGBT community. More anti-gay hate crimes occur in the home than in any other location, and there are significant practical limitations on the ability of the police to protect individuals against such violence. Thus, the right to keep and bear arms for self-defense in one's home is of paramount importance to Pink Pistols and members of the LGBT community. . . .

SUMMARY OF THE ARGUMENT

Laws that prevent the use of firearms for self-defense in one's own home disproportionately impact those individuals who are targets of hate violence due to their minority status, whether defined by race, religion, sexual orientation, or other characteristic. Even in their homes, LGBT individuals are at risk of murder, aggravated assault and other forms of hate violence because of their sexual orientation. In fact, the home is the most common site of anti-gay violence. Thus, for certain LGBT individuals, the possession of firearms in the home is essential for a sense of personal security—a fact generally lost in the majoritarian debate about restricting individual's access to, and use of, firearms. As shown below, not only do members of the LGBT community have a heightened need to possess firearms for self-protection in their homes, the Second Amendment clearly guarantees this most basic right. This Court should not permit the democratic majority to deprive LGBT individuals of their *essential* and constitutional right to keep and bear arms for self-defense in their own homes. *See Raines v. Byrd*, 521 U.S. 811, 829 (1997) (recognizing "the counter-majoritarian implications of judicial review").

Indeed, Petitioners' arguments seeking to limit the right to keep and bear arms to persons who are actively serving in militias would produce absurd results irreconcilable with the purpose of the Bill of Rights and the plain language of the Second Amendment. Interpreting the Second Amendment as recognizing a right conditioned upon military service, where eligibility for military service is defined by the Government, prevents the Amendment from acting as any constraint on Government action at all. Such a result is contrary not only to the literal text of the Amendment, but to the intentions of the Framers. Further, in light of the current "Don't Ask, Don't Tell" policy, such an interpretation would completely eradicate any Second Amendment right for members of the LGBT community. Petitioners' strained construction should be rejected.

ARGUMENT

I. The Second Amendment Guarantees LGBT Individuals the Right to Keep and Bear Arms to Protect Themselves in Their Homes

Almost five years ago this Court held that the Due Process Clause protects the right of gay men and lesbians to engage in consensual sexual acts within the privacy of their own homes, "without intervention of the government." *Lawrence v. Texas*, 539 U.S. 558, 578 (2003). The exercise of that right, or even the non-sexual act of having a certain "appearance," however, continues to put members of the LGBT community at risk of anti-gay hate violence and even death. Since *Lawrence* was decided, at least 58 members of the LGBT community have been murdered and thousands of others have been assaulted, many in their own homes (the most common site of anti-gay hate crimes), because of their sexual orientation. The question now presented is whether LGBT individuals have a right to keep firearms in their homes to protect themselves from such violence. Because LGBT individuals cannot count on the police to protect them from such violence, their safety depends upon this Court's recognition of their right to possess firearms for self-protection in the home.

A. RECOGNITION OF AN INDIVIDUAL RIGHT TO KEEP AND BEAR ARMS
   IS LITERALLY A MATTER OF LIFE OR DEATH FOR MEMBERS
   OF THE LGBT COMMUNITY

The need for individual self-protection remains and is felt perhaps most pointedly by members of minority groups, such as the LGBT community. Minority and other marginalized groups are disproportionately targeted by violence, and have an enhanced need for personal protection. In 2005 alone, law enforcement agencies reported the occurrence of 7,163 hate crime incidents. Federal Bureau of Investigation, Uniform Crime Report, Hate Crime Statistics, 2005 Edition (2006). Members of the LGBT community are frequent targets of such violence. Indeed, for the years 1995-2005, law enforcement agencies reported more than 13,000 incidents of hate violence resulting from sexual-orientation bias. *See* Federal Bureau of Investigation, Uniform Crime Report, Hate Crime Statistics (1995-2005). The individual stories of brutality underlying those statistics are horrific:

- On April 19, 2005, Adam Bishop was bludgeoned to death with a claw hammer in his home because he was gay. He was hit at least eighteen times in the head and then left face down in a bathtub with the shower running.
- On May 13, 1988, Claudia Brenner and Rebecca Wight were shot eight times—in the neck, the head and the back—and left for dead while hiking the Appalachian Trail, because they were lesbians. Rebecca died.
- On December 31, 1993, Brandon Teena, Lisa Lambert and Philip De Vine were murdered in a farmhouse in rural Richardson County, Nebraska in an act of anti-LGBT violence. Brandon and Lisa were both shot execution style, and Brandon was cut open with a knife.
- On the night of October 6-7, 1998, Matthew Shepard was pistol-whipped, tortured, tied to a fence in a remote area and left to die. He was discovered eighteen hours later, still tied to the fence and in a coma. Matthew suffered a fracture from the back of his head to the front of his right ear. He had severe brain stem damage and multiple lacerations on his head, face and neck. He died days later.
- On February 19, 1999, Billy Jack Gaither was set on fire after having his throat slit and being brutally beaten to death with an ax handle. In his initial police confession, Gaither's murderer explained "I had to 'cause he was a faggot."
- On November 19, 2006, Thalia Sandoval, a 27-year-old transgender Latina woman, was stabbed to death in her home in Antioch, California. The death was reported as a hate crime.

In fact, anti-gay violence is even more prevalent than the FBI statistics indicate. "Extensive empirical evidence shows that, for a number of reasons, anti-lesbian/gay violence is vastly under-reported and largely undocumented." LAMBDA Services Anti-Violence Project (March 7, 1995) at ii. The U.S. Department of Justice estimates that only 49% of violent crimes (rape, robbery, aggravated assault, and simple assault) are reported to the police. Many incidents of anti-lesbian/gay violence are not reported to police because victims fear secondary victimization, hostile police response, public disclosure of their sexual orientation, or physical abuse by police. Further, investigative bias and lack of police training also contribute to underreporting of anti-LGBT hate crimes. — For these reasons, incidents of anti-gay violence reported by the FBI represent a small fraction of those reported to LGBT community antiviolence programs. During 1994, for example, "for every incident classified as anti-lesbian/gay by local law enforcement, community agencies classified 4.67 incidents as such." Similarly, while the FBI reported only 26 anti-gay homicides in the ten-year period 1995-2005, the National Coalition of Anti-Violence Programs reported three times that number in half that time (78 anti-gay homicides in the five year period 2002-2006). *See* National Coalition of Anti-Violence Programs, Anti-Lesbian, Gay, Bisexual and Transgender Violence (2003-2006). Studies have shown that approximately 25% of gay males have experienced an anti-gay physical assault. *See* From Hate Crimes to Human Rights: A Tribute to Matthew Shepard, [Mary E. Swigorski, et al. eds. 2001].

Hate crimes based on sexual orientation are the most violent bias crimes. *See* From Hate Crimes to Human Rights: A Tribute to Matthew Shepard, *supra*, at 2 ("Anti-LGBT crimes are characterized as the most violent bias crimes."). *See also* LAMBDA Services Anti-Violence Project (March 7, 1995) at 20 ("The reported [anti-gay] homicides were marked by an extraordinary and horrific level of violence with 49, or 70%, involving "overkill," including dismemberment, bodily and genital mutilation, multiple weapons, repeated blows from a blunt object, or numerous stab wounds."); Gregory M. Herek & Kevin T. Berrill, Hate Crimes: Confronting Violence Against Lesbians and Gay Men 25 (Diane S. Foster ed., 1992) ("A striking feature . . . is their gruesome, often vicious nature.").

Anti-gay hate crimes are also the most likely to involve multiple assailants. LAMBDA Services Anti-Violence Project (March 7, 1995) at 7 ("[A]nti-lesbian/ gay offenses involve a higher number of offenders per incident than other forms of hate crime."). In 1994 "[n]ationally, 38% of the incidents involved two or more perpetrators." *Id.* "One-quarter involved between two and three offenders, and 12% involved four or more offenders. Nationally, there were at least 1.47 offenders for each victim." *Id.*

While the District of Columbia's gun laws preclude LGBT residents from possessing in their homes firearms that can be used for self-protection, *see* D.C. Code §7-2507.02, the laws do not protect LGBT residents from gun violence. To the contrary, "when a weapon was involved [in an anti-gay attack] in the D.C. area, that weapon was three times more likely to be a gun" than elsewhere in the nation. Gay Men & Lesbians Opposing Violence, *Anti-Gay Violence Climbs 2% in 1997.* "Firearms accounted for 33% of all D.C.-area [anti-gay] assaults involving weapons, compared to 9% nationally." *Id.*

Laws, such as D.C. Code §7-2507.02, that prevent the use of firearms for self-protection in the home are of particular concern to members of the LGBT community, because historically hate crimes based on sexual-orientation bias have most commonly occurred in the home or residence. *See, e.g.,* Federal Bureau of Investigation, Uniform Crime Report, Hate Crime Statistics, 2002 Edition (2003) at 7 ("Incidents associated with a sexual-orientation bias (1,244) most often took place at homes or residences — 30.8 percent. . . ."); Federal Bureau of Investigation, Uniform Crime Report, Hate Crime Statistics, 2003 Edition (2004) at 8 ("Incidents involving bias against a sexual orientation also occurred most often in homes or residences — 30.3 percent of the 1,239 incidents reported in 2003."); Federal Bureau of Investigation, Uniform Crime Report, Hate Crime Statistics, 2001 Edition (2002) at 7 ("The data indicated that of the 1,393 hate crime incidents motivated by sexual-orientation bias, 33.4 percent of the incidents occurred at residences or homes."); Federal Bureau of Investigation, Uniform Crime Report, Hate Crime Statistics, 2005 Edition (2006) at Table 10 (reporting more anti-gay incidents in a home or residence than in any other location). Thus, members of the LGBT community have an acute need for this Court to recognize their right to possess firearms to protect themselves from hate violence in their homes.

B. THE POLICE HAVE NO DUTY TO PROTECT AND DO NOT ADEQUATELY PROTECT LGBT INDIVIDUALS FROM HATE VIOLENCE THAT OCCURS IN THEIR HOMES

Members of the LGBT community often must rely upon themselves for protection against hate violence in their homes. Police are seldom able to respond quickly enough to prevent in-home crimes. Worse, as this Court has held, the police have no mandatory legal duty to provide protection to individuals. *See Town of Castle Rock, Colo. v. Gonzales*, 545 U.S. 748, 760-61 (2005). To the contrary, police officers are granted discretion in determining when and where to exercise their authority:

> A well established tradition of police discretion has long coexisted with apparently mandatory arrest statutes.
> "In each and every state there are longstanding statutes that, by their terms, seem to preclude nonenforcement by the police. . . . However, for a number of reasons, including their legislative history, insufficient resources, and sheer physical impossibility, it has been recognized that such statutes cannot be interpreted literally. . . . [T]hey clearly do not mean that a police officer may not lawfully decline to . . . make an arrest. . . ."
> . . . It is, the [*Chicago v. Morales*, 527 U.S. 41 (1999)] Court proclaimed, simply "common sense that all police officers must use some discretion in deciding when and where to enforce city ordinances." . . .

Moreover, police have historically exercised their discretion in a manner that disfavored the protection of members of the LGBT community. *See* Lillian Faderman, Odd Girls Out and Twilight Lovers: A History of Lesbian Life in Twentieth-Century America 194-95 (Richard D. Mohr, et al., eds. 1991). In fact, in 1997 the National Coalition of Anti-Violence Programs reported that, in anti-gay violence "[t]he number of reported *offenders who were law enforcement officers* increased by 76% nationally, from 266 in 1996 to 468 in 1997." *See* Gay Men & Lesbians Opposing Violence, *Anti-Gay Violence Climbs 2% in 1997. See also* National Coalition of Anti-Violence Programs, Anti-Lesbian, Gay, Bisexual and Transgender Violence in 1998 (April 6, 1999) at 24 ("[T]here were very dramatic increases in 1998 in reports of verbal and/or physical abuse by police in response to victim's attempts to report a bias crime. . . . [O]ne in five victims of an anti-gay bias incident in 1998 who attempted to report it to police were treated to more of the same. Almost one in 14 became victims of actual (and in some cases, further) physical abuse."). As a consequence, members of the LGBT community have a heightened need for this Court to recognize their individual right to possess firearms to protect themselves.

The triple-murder of Brandon Teena and two others in a rural farmhouse in 1993 starkly illustrates this need. Brandon, his girlfriend and a male friend were murdered in an anti-LGBT hate crime, after police failed to arrest the two men who had previously kidnapped, raped and assaulted Brandon:

> On December 31, 1993, John Lotter and Marvin Thomas Nissen murdered Brandon, Lisa Lambert and Philip De Vine in a farmhouse in rural Richardson County, Nebraska. These multiple murders occurred one week after Lotter and Nissen forcibly removed Brandon's pants and made Lana Tisdel, whom Brandon had been dating since moving to Falls City from Lincoln three weeks earlier, look to prove that her boyfriend was "really a woman." Later in the evening of this assault, Lotter and Nissen kidnapped, raped, and assaulted Brandon. Despite threats of reprisal should these crimes be reported, Brandon filed charges with the Falls City Police Department and the Richardson County Sheriff, however, Lotter and Nissen remained free. Lotter and Nissen have [since] both been convicted. . . .

Brandon, Lisa and Philip were home when their anti-gay attackers broke in and shot them execution-style. In D.C. they would have been prevented by law from possessing a firearm in the house that they could have used in self-defense to save their own lives. This Court should not adopt a reading of the Second Amendment that would leave LGBT individuals helpless targets for gay-bashers. *See United States v. Panter*, 688 F.2d 268, 271 (5th Cir. 1982) ("The right to defend oneself from a deadly attack is fundamental."); *United States v. Henry*, 865 F.2d 1260 (4th Cir. 1988) (same).

III.   The Second Amendment Must Recognize an Individual Right of "The People" to Avoid Disqualifying LGBT Individuals from any Enjoyment of That Right

An interpretation of the Second Amendment as a guarantee of an individual, rather than collective right of the states, is required if the Second Amendment is to have any application to LGBT individuals. Because the law effectively prevents members of the LGBT community from offering military service, reading the Second Amendment as Petitioners urge — to confer a collective right to keep and bear arms, based upon the condition of membership in "state and congressionally regulated military forces" (*see* Brief of Petitioners at 8-9, 12-14) — renders that right meaningless to LGBT individuals. Moreover, interpreting the Second Amendment as recognizing a right conditioned upon military service, where eligibility for military service is defined by the Government, prevents the Amendment from acting as a constraint on Government action. Such a result is contrary not only to the literal text of the Amendment, but to the intentions of the framers, who would not have guaranteed the right to possess firearms solely to those eligible for military service, while denying the right to possess firearms, for self-defense, from those groups most in need.

A. IF THE RIGHT RECOGNIZED IN THE SECOND AMENDMENT IS CONDITIONED UPON MEMBERSHIP IN STATE AND CONGRESSIONALLY REGULATED MILITARY FORCES, LGBT INDIVIDUALS, AND OTHERS, ARE EXCLUDED FROM THE RIGHT TO BEAR ARMS

The definition of persons eligible for military service is far narrower than "the People." *See, e.g.*, 10 U.S.C. §311 (1994) (The "Militia Act") (the militia consists of "all able-bodied males at least 17 years of age and . . . under 45 years of age [some National Guard re-enlistees to age 64] who are, or who have made a declaration of intention to become, citizens of the United States and of female citizens of the United States who are members of the National Guard"). *See also* 10 U.S.C. §654 ("Policy Concerning Homosexuality in the Armed Forces") ("A member of the armed forces shall be separated from the armed forces if . . . the member has engaged in . . . a homosexual act or acts" or "the member has stated that he or she is a homosexual or bisexual, or words to that effect" or "the member has married or attempted to marry a person known to be of the same biological sex."). Even if the Court's decisions on sex equality, including *United States v. Virginia*, 518 U.S. 515 (1996) and *Craig v. Boren*, 429 U.S. 190 (1976), are applied to the Militia Act to include able-bodied women between the ages of seventeen and forty-four, individuals of any gender over forty-four years of age, those whose professions exempt them, or open members of the LGBT community remain excluded from eligibility for military service.

While such eligibility restrictions are discriminatory, this Court has made clear its deference to the judgment of Congress on issues of "national defense and military affairs" when applying an apparently relaxed form of rational basis review. *See Rostker v. Goldberg*, 453 U.S. 57, 64 (1981). Indeed, "perhaps in no other area has the Court afforded Congress greater deference." *Id.* at 64-65. The Court has described the "constitutional power of Congress" to "raise and support armies and to make all laws necessary and proper to that end" as "broad and sweeping," (*id.* at 65 (quoting *United States v. O'Brien*, 391 U.S. 367, 377 (1968))), while describing its own "lack of competence" on issues relating to the regulation of the armed forces as "marked." *Id.* at 65-66 (quoting *Gilligan v. Morgan*, 413 U.S. 1, 10 (1973) ("[I]t is difficult to conceive of an area of governmental activity in which the courts have less competence. The complex, subtle, and professional decisions as to the composition, training, equipping, and control of a military force are essentially professional military judgments, subject *always* to civilian control of the Legislative and Executive Branches.")). *See also Parker v. Levy*, 417 U.S. 733, 743 (1974) ("This Court has long recognized that the military is, by necessity, a specialized society separate from civilian society.")

Relying on this Court's decisions and the extreme deference afforded to Congress in a rational basis review of issues related to military regulation, federal courts considering the constitutionality of 10 U.S.C. §654 and its prohibitions on the service of open members of the LGBT community in the military have found those prohibitions constitutional. *See, e.g., Thomasson v. Perry*, 80 F.3d 915, 927 (4th Cir. 1996) (upholding 10 U.S.C. §654 and noting that "'[t]he special status of the military has required, the Constitution has contemplated, Congress has created, and [the Supreme] Court has long recognized' that constitutional challenges to military personnel policies and decisions face heavy burdens," and that "[i]t is with those burdens in mind that we address appellant's particular arguments"); *Able v. United States*, 155 F.3d 628, 632 (2nd Cir. 1998) (upholding 10 U.S.C. §654, emphasizing the "narrow" rational basis review and "great deference" applied to "Congressional judgments affecting the military"); *Richenberg v. Perry*, 97 F.3d 256, 261 (8th Cir. 1996) (upholding 10 U.S.C. §654 and noting the "especially deferential" rational basis review applied to due process challenges of "military policy"); *Selland v. Perry*, 905 F. Supp. 260, 264 (D. Md. 1995) (upholding 10 U.S.C. §654 and noting the "general principle of deference" and thus "relaxed restrictions" of the First Amendment in military settings); *Witt v. United States Dep't of Air Force*, 444 F. Supp. 2d 1138, 1145 (W.D. Wash. 2006) (upholding 10 U.S.C. §654, explaining that "review of Congressional enactments is especially deferential in the military context"); Cook v. Rumsfeld, 429 F. Supp. 2d 385, 397-98 (D. Mass. 2006) (upholding 10 U.S.C. §654 under a rational basis review, noting that "[d]eference to Congressional judgment is of even greater importance in a case such as this one where the legislation challenged was enacted pursuant to Congress' authority over the national military forces"). These cases effectively find, as Congress pronounced in its findings supporting the "Don't Ask, Don't Tell" policy, that "[t]here is no constitutional right to serve in the armed forces." 10 U.S.C. §654(a)(2).

Consequently, under Petitioner's construction of the Second Amendment, which conditions the right to keep and bear arms upon membership in an organized military force, the exclusion of older individuals and openly LGBT individuals from military service would necessarily exclude them from the right to keep and bear arms in their own self-defense. Such an interpretation unacceptably robs from those groups most vulnerable, the means to protect themselves in their own homes.

B. BECAUSE THE GOVERNMENT DEFINES ELIGIBILITY FOR SERVICE IN REGULATED MILITARY FORCES, INTERPRETING THE SECOND AMENDMENT AS A RIGHT CONDITIONED UPON MEMBERSHIP IN A REGULATED MILITARY FORCE, PREVENTS THE AMENDMENT FROM CONSTRAINING GOVERNMENT ACTION

Interpreting the justification clause as a condition on the existence of the right would render the Second Amendment nugatory. The Amendment, specifically its operative clause, is useful only if it provides some meaningful constraint on government action. It fails to provide such constraint if [] the right is conditioned on military service, since, as demonstrated above, the government is permitted to limit eligibility for military service as it sees fit. Indeed, if the scope of the right recognized in the operative clause is limited by the justification clause's reference to the militia, which the government can define, then the Second Amendment provides no meaningful check against government power. Such a reading cannot be squared with the purpose behind the Bill of Rights. While the justification clause may aid interpretation of the operative clause where there are ambiguities, it cannot take away what the operative clause clearly gives. Furthermore, a construction of the right recognized by the Second Amendment which ties that right to eligibility for military service renders the right and the Amendment devoid of any fixed meaning, as military eligibility requirements are ever-changing. Such a construction would also permit modification of the scope of a Constitutional right *via* statute—e.g., 10 U.S.C. §654 ("Policy Concerning Homosexuality in the Armed Forces").

C. CONDITIONING SECOND AMENDMENT RIGHTS UPON MEMBERSHIP IN A REGULATED MILITARY FORCE, WHICH EXCLUDES LGBT AND OTHER INDIVIDUALS FROM ENJOYING THE RIGHT TO SELF-DEFENSE, IS CONTRARY TO THE INTENTIONS OF THE FRAMERS

Construing the Second Amendment to recognize a right of "the People," rather than merely those recognized as eligible for formal military service is consistent with the intentions of the Constitution's framers. The text of the Amendment, itself, indicates that the framers acknowledged the right to inhere in "the People," not just those "militia eligible." Had the framers meant to limit the acknowledged right only to those militia-eligible, they could have easily done so. *See, e.g.*, Militia Act of May 8, 1792, ch. 33, §1, Stat. 271 (repealed 1903) (limiting military service members to white, able-bodied male citizens between the ages of eighteen and forty-five). Rather, the choice not to limit the right to possess firearms, acknowledged in the Second Amendment, to only those "militia eligible" follows logically from the framers' belief that the right to self-preservation and self-defense, through the possession of arms, if necessary, was a right conferred upon each individual by natural, rather than positive, law. *See supra*, §II.B.

To read the Second Amendment as Petitioners insist, as a right which turns solely upon militia eligibility, would mean that the framers guaranteed the right to self-defense through the possession of arms to those who needed such defense the least, while leaving the groups most vulnerable to attack helpless to defend themselves even in their own homes. While Jefferson feared that laws preventing persons from bearing firearms would "serve rather to encourage than to prevent homicides, for an unarmed man may be attacked with greater confidence than an armed man," [The Commonplace Book of Thomas Jefferson 314 (Gilbert Chinard ed. 1926)] reading the Second Amendment as acknowledging a collective right, and upholding the D.C. law at issue, here, accomplishes the same. By effectively preventing LGBT individuals from defending themselves through possession of firearms in their own homes, persons motivated to attack LGBT individuals may do so with the confidence that their intended victims will be unarmed. Such a result not only conflicts with the natural law right of man to act in his own self-defense, as recognized by the framers, but jeopardizes the privacy rights of LGBT individuals recognized by this Court in *Lawrence*, when the exercise of such rights makes one an unarmed target. . . .

NOTES & QUESTIONS

1. Do the concerns about hate crimes inevitably lead to the position advocated by the Pink Pistols? Do these episodes just as easily support arguments for

strict gun control or gun prohibition? Which response promises to be more effective for those concerned about being victims of hate crimes? If, as the Pink Pistols argue, there is a natural law right of self-defense, see Chapter 2, should it matter whether other people think the exercise of the right is wise or not?

2. The Pink Pistols advocate a response to hate crimes that depends on individual initiative. Many would urge a primarily public response to hate crimes that involves combination of tough criminal laws, gun control, and education. What are the strengths and weaknesses of each approach? Are the private and public responses incompatible? Is either response, standing alone, sufficient?

3. Now that *Heller* has taken gun prohibition off the table, what would be your policy advice to groups concerned about hate crimes against the LGBT community?

4. Some leading advocates of gun control have urged victims to eschew self-defense. Pete Shields, the chair of Handgun Control, Inc. (now known as the Brady Campaign) advised: "[P]ut up no defense — give them what they want." Nelson T. "Pete" Shields, Guns Don't Die — People Do, 125 (1981). This advice assumed that theft was the main goal of physical attacks. How would you answer the criticism that this seems to be unsatisfactory in the context of hate crimes?

5. Do the targets of hate crimes face different problems than people who are physically weak, such as the elderly, the disabled, or small-statured women?

EXERCISE: SUBJECTIVITY IN FORMING POLICY VIEWS

The special concerns of the communities surveyed in this chapter have generated views and policy prescriptions on both sides of the gun question. It is difficult to know exactly what factors explain this divide. In many ways, the competing views seem to turn on different assessments of the risks and utilities of firearms. But that raises the further question, what is the basis for those assessments? People might develop a sense of the risks and utilities of private firearms in a number of ways. Ask three people you know the following questions. Once you have collected the responses, compare and discuss the results with your classmates.

1. Do you think that private ownership of firearms in America imposes more costs than benefits or more benefits than costs? Or is the answer uncertain?
2. What is the basis for your assessment of the risks and utilities of private firearms?
3. How much of your assessment is based on an individual sense of your own capabilities and temperament?
4. How much of your assessment is based on your sense of the capabilities and temperament of other people?

5. How much of your assessment is based on data you have seen about the risks and utilities of firearms in the general population? What information specifically comes to mind?
6. How much of your assessment is based on having grown up in an environment where firearms were common or uncommon?
7. Approximately how many private firearms are there in the United States?
8. Approximately how many people die from gunshots in the United States each year?
9. Define "assault weapon."
10. Roughly what percentage of firearms homicides involve black victims? Black perpetrators?
11. What percentage of firearms fatalities involve female victims? Female perpetrators?
12. Roughly how many children (14 and under) are killed in firearms accidents each year?

EXERCISE: EMPIRICAL ASSESSMENTS, PERSONAL RISK ASSESSMENTS, AND PUBLIC POLICY

The gun debate often involves competing empirical claims about the costs and benefits of firearms. There is a strong tendency to propose policy on the assumption that observed trends will continue into the future. Many people find these empirical claims unconvincing. Sometimes we find the data sources untrustworthy. Sometimes the empirical claims seem so different from what we observe or believe that even though we credit the data, we are unwilling to assume that they model the future.

Think about the choices and predictions that you and others make. Consider the dangers of failing to wear seatbelts. Have you ever failed to buckle up? How do you explain that decision? Did you simply choose to flout the empirical assessments showing seatbelts save lives? Was your decision based on personal observations or beliefs that contradict the data about seat belts? Was your decision irrational? Was it non-rational?

Do people make other decisions about their personal safety in similar ways? Have you ever heard someone say that she feels safe because "this is a good neighborhood"? Did she support that claim with statistically sound empirical evidence? Are personal assessments unsupported by sound empirical evidence illegitimate? How much respect do they deserve?

Assume now that you are married with two children, ages 4 and 2. You live in a town bordering a large city in the Northeast. You commute into the city from the train station that is two blocks from your house. Your spouse cares for the children at home. In the last year, your neighborhood has experienced one incident of vandalism (a swastika sprayed on a garage door) and one home invasion daylight armed robbery. Your town is facing budget constraints and has cut its police force by 15 percent. Your spouse wants to purchase a handgun for protection. You are familiar with guns and have a bolt-action deer rifle, inherited from your grandfather, stored in the attic. You and your spouse are both lawyers and always make important decisions after robust debate. What factors will affect your decision to buy a handgun or not? Does your assessment change if you are a same-sex couple? If you are an interracial couple? If your spouse has a physical disability?

Plagued by complaints about a rising crime rate and emerging gang activity, the mayor of your town has assigned his staff to develop a policy response. The mayor's chief of staff suggests an ordinance banning the sale and possession of all semi-automatic handguns, but allowing possession and sale of revolvers. A junior staffer suggests that the mayor establish free firearms training courses at mobile firing ranges set up around town. What factors should influence the mayor's assessment of these proposals? What would you propose? What would you do as mayor?

Compare your decision making as mayor to your decision making as a spouse with a worried partner. Did you consider the same variables in each case? Did you weight them the same way? Is the decision making in the two contexts compatible? Incompatible? In the case of conflict, whose concerns should trump?

‖11‖

Applying the Affirmed Right to Arms

The Supreme Court's decisions in *District of Columbia v. Heller*, 554 U.S. 570 (2008) (Chapter 9), and *McDonald v. Chicago*, 130 S. Ct. 3020 (2010) (Chapter 9), leave many questions open. In both cases, the Court suggested that its ruling should not be read to cast doubt on the validity of many gun control regulations. The full range of state and federal regulation of firearms is tremendously varied. A uniform methodology for deciding close cases has yet to develop, and there is no indication of how strictly the Supreme Court will police lower court interpretations of *Heller* and *McDonald*. (Some material in Chapters 7, and 8 suggested that lower courts adopted a crimped view of *United States v. Miller*, 307 U.S. 174 (1939) (Chapter 7), in the twentieth century, with the tacit acceptance of the Supreme Court. The *Heller* majority likewise suggested that lower courts' "erroneous reliance upon [the] . . . virtually unreasoned [*Miller*] case" in this period might have obscured the "true meaning" of the Second Amendment. 554 U.S. at 624 n.24.)

This chapter treats some of the important questions raised by the Supreme Court's affirmation and incorporation of the individual right to arms. Important cases too recent to be included in this book will be available on this book's website, http://www.firearmregulation.com.

A. The Aftermath of **Heller** in the District of Columbia: Intermediate Scrutiny Versus History and Tradition, and the Common Use Standard

In striking down the District of Columbia handgun ban, home self-defense ban, and ban on carrying a handgun in the home, the Supreme Court found three particular restrictions on firearms unconstitutional. Lower courts generally are engaging the Supreme Court's signal to treat the Second Amendment as an important individual right. Even so, the full boundaries of permissible gun regulation after *Heller* are yet to be determined.

The following case grows out of a challenge to the District's post-*Heller* gun regulations. The lead plaintiff is the same Dick Anthony Heller from the Supreme Court's 2008 decision. As you will see, the majority and the dissent take very different views about both the validity of the District's post-*Heller* gun laws and about the proper methodology for evaluating gun regulations under *Heller*.

Heller v. District of Columbia (*Heller II*)
2011 WL 4551558 (D.C. Cir. Oct. 4, 2011)

GINSBURG, CIRCUIT JUDGE:

In June 2008 the Supreme Court held the District of Columbia laws restricting the possession of firearms in one's home violated the Second Amendment right of individuals to keep and bear arms. *See District of Columbia v. Heller*, 554 U.S. 570. In the wake of that decision, the District adopted the Firearms Registration Amendment Act of 2008 (FRA), D.C. Law 17-372, which amended the Firearms Control Regulations Act of 1975, D.C. Law 1-85. The plaintiffs in the present case challenge, both facially and as applied to them, the provisions of the District's gun laws, new and old, requiring the registration of firearms and prohibiting both the registration of "assault weapons" and the possession of magazines with a capacity of more than ten rounds of ammunition. The plaintiffs argue those provisions (1) are not within the District's congressionally delegated legislative authority or, if they are, then they (2) violate the Second Amendment.

The district court granted summary judgment for the District and the plaintiffs appealed. We hold the District had the authority under D.C. law to promulgate the challenged gun laws, and we uphold as constitutional the prohibitions of assault weapons and of large-capacity magazines and some of the registration requirements. We remand the other registration requirements to the district court for further proceedings because the record is insufficient to inform our resolution of the important constitutional issues presented.

I. BACKGROUND

In *Heller*, the Supreme Court held the Second Amendment protects "an individual right to keep and bear arms," 554 U.S. at 595, but not a right "to keep and carry any weapon whatsoever in any manner whatsoever and for whatever purpose," *id.* at 626. More specifically, the Court held unconstitutional the District's "ban on handgun possession in the home" as well as its "prohibition against rendering any lawful firearm in the home operable for the purpose of immediate self-defense," *id.* at 635, noting "the inherent right of self-defense [is] central to the Second Amendment right," *id.* at 628. Therefore, unless the plaintiff was "disqualified from the exercise of Second Amendment rights" for some reason, such as a felony conviction, the District had to permit him to register his handgun. *Id.* at 635.

Shortly after the Supreme Court issued its decision in *Heller*, the D.C. Council passed emergency legislation in an effort to conform the District's laws to the Supreme Court's holding while it considered permanent legislation.

The Council's Committee on Public Safety and the Judiciary then held three public hearings on the subject. In December 2008, upon the Committee's recommendation, the full Council passed the FRA. 56 D.C. Reg. 3438 (May 1, 2009).

The plaintiffs challenge a host of provisions of the new scheme for regulating firearms. First they object to the general requirement that owners register their firearms. . . . In particular, the plaintiffs challenge the following requirements that apply each time a person applies to the Metropolitan Police Department (MPD) for a registration certificate. Each applicant must:

- Disclose certain information about himself — such as his name, address, and occupation — and about his firearm. . . .
- Submit "for a ballistics identification procedure" each pistol to be registered. . . . Ballistics testing is not required for long guns. . . .
- Appear in person and, at the MPD's request, bring with him the firearm to be registered. . . .
- Register no more than one pistol in a 30-day period. . . .
- Renew each registration certificate "3 years after the date of issuance." . . .

In addition, the plaintiffs challenge five requirements that are more similar to licensing the owner of the firearm than to registering the weapon itself. Specifically, the applicant must:

- Have vision qualifying one for a driver's license. . . .
- Demonstrate knowledge of the District's laws pertaining to firearms "and, in particular, the safe and responsible use, handling, and storage of the same." . . .
- Submit to being fingerprinted and photographed. . . .
- Undergo a background check every six years to confirm his continuing compliance with . . . registration requirements. . . .
- Attend a firearms training or safety course providing "a total of at least one hour of firing training at a firing range and a total of at least 4 hours of classroom instruction." . . .

Second, the plaintiffs challenge the District's prohibitions of "assault weapon[s]," and of magazines holding more than ten rounds of ammunition. . . . The FRA defines "assault weapon" to include certain brands and models of semi-automatic rifles, pistols, and shotguns, such as the Colt AR-15 series of rifles, as well as semi-automatic firearms with certain features, regardless of make and model, such as a semi-automatic rifle with a "pistol grip that protrudes conspicuously beneath the action of the weapon" or a "thumbhole stock." [Most semi-automatic pistols are not prohibited by the statute.] . . . The District also prohibits possession of "any large capacity ammunition feeding device," which includes "a magazine . . . or similar device that has a capacity of . . . more than 10 rounds of ammunition." . . . (hereinafter "large-capacity magazines").

Plaintiffs Mark Snyder and Absalom F. Jordan, Jr. complied with the registration requirements and successfully registered a rifle and a pistol respectively. Plaintiff Jordan, however, was unable to register two additional pistols due to the one-gun-per-30-days limit. Three of the plaintiffs, Dick Anthony Heller, William Carter, and Jordan applied to register semi-automatic rifles, but the MPD denied their applications because it found the firearms were prohibited "assault weapons." Plaintiff Heller was also denied registration of a pistol because the magazine had a capacity of 15 rounds. . . .

II. . . .

B.   THE SECOND AMENDMENT . . .

1. The *Heller* Decision

In *Heller* the Supreme Court explained the Second Amendment "codified a *pre-existing*" individual right to keep and bear arms, 554 U.S. at 592, which was important to Americans not only to maintain the militia, but also for self-defense and hunting, *id.* at 599. Although "self-defense had little to do with the right's *codification*[,] it was the *central component* of the right itself." *Id.*

Still, the Court made clear "the right secured by the Second Amendment is not unlimited," *id.* at 626, and it gave some examples to illustrate the boundaries of that right. For instance, the Court noted "the Second Amendment does not protect those weapons not typically possessed by law-abiding citizens for lawful purposes, such as short-barreled shotguns." *Id.* at 625 (citing *United States v. Miller*, 307 U.S. 174 (1939)). This limitation upon the right to keep and bear arms was "supported by the historical tradition of prohibiting the carrying of dangerous and unusual weapons." *Id.* at 627 (internal quotation marks omitted).

The Court identified other historical limitations upon the scope of the right protected by the Second Amendment. For example, it noted "the majority of the 19th-century courts to consider the question held that prohibitions on carrying concealed weapons were lawful under the Second Amendment or state analogues." *Id.* at 626. It also provided a list of some "presumptively lawful regulatory measures":

> nothing in our opinion should be taken to cast doubt on longstanding prohibitions on the possession of firearms by felons and the mentally ill, or laws forbidding the carrying of firearms in sensitive places such as schools and government buildings, or laws imposing conditions and qualifications on the commercial sale of arms.

Id. at 626-27 & n.26. The Court made clear, however, it was not "undertak[ing] an exhaustive historical analysis today of the full scope of the Second Amendment." *Id.* at 626.

2. The Constitutional Framework

Under *Heller*, therefore, there are certain types of firearms regulations that do not govern conduct within the scope of the Amendment. We accordingly adopt, as have other circuits, a two-step approach to determining the constitutionality of the District's gun laws. *Ezell v. City of Chicago,* 2011 WL 2623511 (7th Cir. July 6, 2011); *United States v. Chester,* 628 F.3d 673 (4th Cir. 2010); *United States v. Reese,* 627 F.3d 792 (10th Cir. 2010); *United States v. Marzzarella,* 614 F.3d 85, 89 (3d Cir. 2010). We ask first whether a particular provision impinges upon a right protected by the Second Amendment; if it does, then we go on to determine whether the provision passes muster under the appropriate level of constitutional scrutiny. *See Ezell,* 2011 WL 2623511, at *12-13; *Chester,* 628 F.3d at 680; *Reese,* 627 F.3d at 800-01; *Marzzarella,* 614 F.3d at 89; *see also Nordyke v. King,* 644 F.3d 776, 786 (9th Cir. 2011) ("only regulations which substantially burden the right to keep and to bear arms trigger heightened scrutiny under the Second Amendment"). As explained below, and again in keeping with other circuits, we think that insofar as the laws at issue here do impinge upon a Second Amendment right, they warrant intermediate rather than strict scrutiny.

With respect to the first step, *Heller* tells us "longstanding" regulations are "presumptively lawful," 554 U.S. at 626-27 & n.26; that is, they are presumed not to burden conduct within the scope of the Second Amendment. *See McDonald v. City of Chicago,* 130 S. Ct. 3020, 3047 (2010) (*Heller* "did not cast doubt on [certain types of] longstanding regulatory measures"); *Chester,* 628 F.3d at 679 (*Heller* "acknowledged that the scope of the Second Amendment is subject to historical limitations"); *Marzzarella,* 614 F.3d at 91 (*Heller* indicates "longstanding limitations are exceptions to the right to bear arms"); *United States v. Rene E.,* 583 F.3d 8, 12 (1st Cir. 2009) (*Heller* "identified limits" of the Second Amendment based upon "various historical restrictions on possessing and carrying weapons"). This is a reasonable presumption because a regulation that is "longstanding," which necessarily means it has long been accepted by the public, is not likely to burden a constitutional right; concomitantly the activities covered by a longstanding regulation are presumptively not protected from regulation by the Second Amendment. A plaintiff may rebut this presumption by showing the regulation does have more than a de minimis effect upon his right. A requirement of newer vintage is not, however, presumed to be valid.

3.   Registration Requirements

To apply this analytical framework, we first consider whether each of the challenged registration requirements impinges upon the right protected by the Second Amendment. We uphold the requirement of mere registration because it is longstanding, hence "presumptively lawful," and the presumption stands unrebutted. Other registration requirements we remand to the district court, as explained below, for further proceedings.

a.   Do the Registration Requirements Impinge upon the Second Amendment Right?

The plaintiffs argue the registration requirements are not longstanding and therefore not presumptively lawful, and in fact impermissibly burden the right protected by the Second Amendment. The District responds that registration requirements have been accepted throughout our history, are not overly burdensome, and therefore do not affect the right protected by the Second Amendment.

i. Basic Registration Requirements

The record supports the view that basic registration of handguns is deeply enough rooted in our history to support the presumption that a registration requirement is constitutional. The Court in *Heller* considered "prohibitions on the possession of firearms by felons" to be "longstanding" although states did not start to enact them until the early 20th century. *See* C. Kevin Marshall, *Why Can't Martha Stewart Have a Gun?*, 32 Harv. J.L. & Pub. Pol'y 695, 708 (2009) (noting "ban on convicts possessing firearms were unknown before World War I" and "compilation of laws in mid-1925 indicated that no State banned posses-sion of long guns based on a prior conviction; that only six banned possession of concealable weapons on such basis; that, except for New York, . . . even those laws dated from 1923 or later"). At just about the same time, states and localities began to require registration of handguns.

Registration typically required that a person provide to the local Govern-ment a modicum of information about the registrant and his firearm. A 1911 New York statute delegated the record keeping function to sellers of concealable firearms, requiring them to "keep a register" recording the "date of sale, name, age, occupation and residence of every purchaser of such a [firearm], together with the calibre, make, model, manufacturer's number or other mark of iden-tification on such [firearm]," which register had to be "open at all reasonable hours for the inspection of any peace officer." Act of May 25, 1911, ch. 195, §2, 1911 N.Y. Laws 444-45. Similar laws had already been enacted by Illinois, Act of Apr. 16, 1881, ¶90, and Georgia, Act of Aug. 12, 1910, No. 432, §2, 1910 Ga. Laws 134, 135 (official who grants license to carry pistol or revolver "shall keep a record of the name of the person taking out such license, the name of the maker of the fire-arm to be carried, and the caliber and number of the same"). Other states were soon to do so. *See* Oregon, Act of Feb. 21, 1917, ch. 377, 1917 Or. Laws 804, 805-06; Michigan, Act of June 2, 1927, No. 372, §9, 1927 Mich. Laws 887, 891 ("any person within this state who owns or has in his pos-session a pistol" must "present such weapon for safety inspection to the com-missioner or chief of police. . . . A certificate of inspection shall thereupon be issued . . . and kept as a permanent official record for a period of six years"). In 1917 California likewise required the purchaser of a concealable firearm to give the seller basic information about himself, including his name, address, occupation, physical description (height and color of skin, eyes, and hair), and about the weapon (caliber, make, model, number). Act of May 4, 1917, ch. 145, §7, 1917 Cal. Laws 221, 222-23. Hawaii did the same in 1927, while still a territory, Small Arms Act, Act 206, §9, 1927 Haw. Laws 209, 211, as did the Congress for the District of Columbia in 1932, *see* Act of July 8, 1932, ch. 465, §8, 47 Stat. 650, 652.

In sum, the basic requirement to register a handgun is longstanding in American law, accepted for a century in diverse states and cities and now appli-cable to more than one fourth of the Nation by population. Therefore, we presume the District's basic registration requirement . . . , including the submis-sion of certain information . . . , does not impinge upon the right protected by the Second Amendment. Further, we find no basis in either the historical record or the record of this case to rebut that presumption. Indeed, basic registration requirements are self-evidently de minimis, for they are similar to other common registration or licensing schemes, such as those for voting or for driving a car, that cannot reasonably be considered onerous. *Cf. Rosario v. Rocke-feller*, 410 U.S. 753, 754-58 (1973) (law "requir[ing] a voter to enroll in the party of his choice at least 30 days before the general election in November in order to vote in the next subsequent party primary" does not violate First and Fourteenth Amendments because "if [the petitioners'] plight [could] be characterized as disenfranchisement at all, it was not caused by [the law], but by their own failure to take timely steps to effect their enrollment"); *id.* at 760 ("the State is certainly justified in imposing some reasonable cutoff point for registration or party enrollment, which citizens must meet in order to participate in the next elec-tion"); *Justice v. Town of Cicero*, 577 F.3d 768, 773-74 (7th Cir. 2009) ("ordinance requiring the registration of all firearms . . . appears to be consistent with the ruling in *Heller*"). These early registration requirements, however, applied with only a few exceptions solely to handguns — that is, pistols and revolvers — and not to long guns. Consequently, we hold the basic registration requirements are constitutional only as applied to handguns. With respect to long guns they are novel, not historic.

ii.   Novel Registration Requirements

Several other of the District's registration requirements are not longstand-ing, including the ballistics-identification provision . . . , the one-pistol-per-30-days rule . . . , and the requirements that applicants appear in person . . . , and re-register each firearm after three years. . . . Certain portions of the law that are more akin to licensing the gun owner than to registering the gun are also novel; these include the requirement that an applicant demonstrate knowledge about firearms . . . , be fingerprinted and photographed . . . , take a firearms training or safety course . . . , meet a vision requirement . . . , and submit to a background check every six years. . . .

The requirements that are not longstanding, which include, in addition to those listed in the prior paragraph, *all* the requirements as applied to long guns, also affect the Second Amendment right because they are not de minimis. All of these requirements, such as the mandatory five hours of firearm training and instruction . . . , make it considerably more difficult for a person lawfully to acquire and keep a firearm, including a handgun, for the purpose of self-defense in the home — the "core lawful purpose" protected by the Second Amendment, *Heller*, 554 U.S. at 630. Because they impinge upon that right, we must determine whether these requirements are constitutional. In order to do that, however, we must first determine the degree of scrutiny to which they are appropriately subject.

b.   Intermediate Scrutiny Is Appropriate

The plaintiffs argue strict scrutiny is the appropriate standard of review because, in holding the Fourteenth Amendment made the Second Amendment applicable to the States, the Court in *McDonald* described the right "to keep and bear arms [as] among those fundamental rights necessary to our system of ordered liberty," 130 S. Ct. at 3042. The District responds that strict scrutiny would be inappropriate because, among other reasons, the right to keep and carry arms has always been heavily regulated; it argues we should adopt a "reasonable-regulation test." The plaintiffs, in turn, contend *Heller* forecloses a "reasonableness" test.

Heller clearly does reject any kind of "rational basis" or reasonableness test, *see* 554 U.S. at 628 n.27, but it leaves open the question what level of scrutiny we are to apply to laws regulating firearms. True, the Supreme Court often applies strict scrutiny to legislation that impinges upon a fundamental right. *See, e.g., Clark v. Jeter*, 486 U.S. 456, 461 (1988) ("classifications affecting fundamental rights are given the most exacting scrutiny" . . .). In applying strict scrutiny, the Court requires the Government to prove its law "furthers a compelling interest and is narrowly tailored to achieve that interest." *Citizens United v. FEC*, 130 S. Ct. 876, 898 (2010). . . . The Court has not said, however, and it does not logically follow, that strict scrutiny is called for whenever a fundamental right is at stake. *See, e.g., Ward v. Rock Against Racism*, 491 U.S. 781, 791 (1989) (applying intermediate scrutiny to restrictions on "time, place, or manner of protected speech"); *Marzzarella*, 614 F.3d at 96 ("Strict scrutiny does not apply automatically any time an enumerated right is involved"); *Chester*, 628 F.3d at 682 ("We do not apply strict scrutiny whenever a law impinges upon a right specifically enumerated in the Bill of Rights"); Adam Winkler, *Scrutinizing the Second Amendment*, 105 Mich. L. Rev. 683, 697-98, 700 (2007) ("mere fact of 'fundamentality' does not answer the question of what would be the appropriate standard of review for the right to bear arms" as "many of the individual rights in the Bill of Rights do not trigger strict scrutiny, including many that are incorporated," and "[e]ven among those incorporated rights that do prompt strict scrutiny, such as the freedom of speech and of religion, strict scrutiny is only occasionally applied"). *Cf. Mills v. Habluetzel*, 456 U.S. 91, 98-99 (1982) (disabilities attendant to illegitimacy are constitutional "to the extent they are substantially related to a legitimate state interest"); *Craig v. Boren*, 429 U.S. 190, 197 (1976) ("classifications by gender must serve important governmental objectives and must be substantially related to achievement of those objectives").

As with the First Amendment, the level of scrutiny applicable under the Second Amendment surely "depends on the nature of the conduct being regulated and the degree to which the challenged law burdens the right." *Chester*, 628 F.3d at 682; *see also Turner Broad. Sys., Inc. v. FCC (Turner I)*, 512 U.S. 622, 642 (1994) ("regulations that are unrelated to the content of speech are subject to an intermediate level of scrutiny because in most cases they pose a less substantial risk of excising certain ideas or viewpoints from the public dialogue" . . .); *Zauderer v. Office of Disciplinary Counsel of Supreme Court of Ohio*, 471 U.S. 626, 651 (1985) ("We recognize that unjustified or unduly burdensome disclosure requirements might offend the First Amendment by chilling protected commercial speech. But we hold that an advertiser's rights are adequately protected as long as disclosure requirements are reasonably related to the State's interest in preventing deception of consumers."); Nelson Lund, *The Second Amendment, Heller, and Originalist Jurisprudence*, 56 UCLA L. Rev. 1343, 1376 (2009) ("The case law dealing with free speech and the free exercise of religion provides a particularly good analogue" for Second Amendment). That is, a regulation that imposes a substantial burden upon the core right of self-defense protected by the Second Amendment must have a strong justification, whereas a regulation that imposes a less substantial burden should be proportionately easier to justify. *See Turner I,* 512 U.S. at 661 ("must-carry provisions do not pose such inherent dangers to free expression . . . as to justify application of the most exacting level of First Amendment scrutiny"; rather, "the appropriate standard . . . is the intermediate level of scrutiny applicable to content-neutral restrictions that impose an incidental burden on speech"); *Board of Trustees of State Univ. of N.Y. v. Fox,* 492 U.S. 469, 477 (1989) ("commercial speech [enjoys] a limited measure of protection, commensurate with its subordinate position in the scale of First Amendment values" (internal quotation marks omitted)); *Buckley v. Valeo,* 424 U.S. 1, 44-45 (1976) ("expenditure limitations" are subject to "exacting scrutiny applicable to limitations on core First Amendment rights of political expression" because they impose a "great burden on basic freedoms"); *Ezell,* 2011 WL 2623511, at 13 (level of scrutiny "will depend on how close the law comes to the core of the Second Amendment right and the severity of the law's burden on the right"); *see also* Eugene Volokh, *Implementing the Right to Keep and Bear Arms for Self-Defense: An Analytical Framework and a Research Agenda,* 56 UCLA L. Rev. 1443, 1471 (2009) ("Ballot access regulations are . . . subject to strict scrutiny if they 'impose a severe burden on associational rights,' but to a much weaker level of scrutiny if they 'impose only modest burdens'" (quoting *Wash. State Grange v. Wash. State Republican Party,* 128 S. Ct. 1184, 1191-92 (2008))); Winkler, *supra,* at 698 ("Strict scrutiny . . . does not apply to fundamental, preferred rights when the courts determine that the underlying burden is only incidental").

As between strict and intermediate scrutiny, we conclude the latter is the more appropriate standard for review of gun registration laws. As the Third Circuit reasoned in *Marzzarella* with regard to a prohibition on possession of a firearm with the serial numbers obliterated, registration requirements "do not severely limit the possession of firearms." 614 F.3d at 97. Indeed, none of the District's registration requirements prevents an individual from possessing a firearm in his home or elsewhere, whether for self-defense or hunting, or any other lawful purpose.

c. Intermediate Scrutiny Requires Remand

As for the novel registration requirements, to pass muster under intermediate scrutiny the District must show they are "substantially related to an important governmental objective." *Clark,* 486 U.S. at 461; *see also United States v. Williams,* 616 F.3d 685, 692-94 (7th Cir. 2010) (prohibition of firearm possession by felons survives intermediate scrutiny). That is, the District must establish a tight "fit" between the registration requirements and an important or substantial governmental interest, a fit "that employs not necessarily the least restrictive means but . . . a means narrowly tailored to achieve the desired objective." *Fox,* 492 U.S. at 480; *see also Ward,* 491 U.S. at 782-83 ("The requirement of narrow tailoring is satisfied so long as the regulation promotes a substantial governmental interest that would be achieved less effectively absent the regulation, and the means chosen are not substantially broader than necessary to achieve that interest"). We think the District has advanced, albeit incompletely—almost cursorily—articulated, two important governmental interests it may have in the registration requirements, *viz.,* to protect police officers and to aid in crime control. *Cf. United States v. Salerno*, 481 U.S. 739, 750 (1987) ("the Government's general interest in preventing crime is compelling"). The Council Committee on Public Safety explained: "Registration is critical because it . . . allows officers to determine in advance whether individuals involved in a call may have firearms . . . [and] assists law enforcement in determining whether registered owners are eligible to possess firearms or have fallen into a prohibited class."* Report on Bill 17-843, at 3-4 (Nov. 25, 2008).

We cannot conclude, however, that the novel registration requirements — or any registration requirement as applied to long guns — survive intermediate scrutiny based upon the record as it stands because the District has not demonstrated a close fit between those requirements and its governmental interests. In support of the registration requirements, the District relies upon the Committee Report on the FRA, along with testimony and written statements submitted to the Committee at public hearings. Even so, the record is inadequate for us confidently to hold the registration requirements are narrowly tailored.

For example, the Committee Report asserts "studies show" that "laws restricting multiple purchases or sales of firearms are designed to reduce the number of guns entering the illegal market and to stem the flow of firearms between states," and that "handguns sold in multiple sales to the same individual purchaser are frequently used in crime." *Id.* at 10. The Report neither identifies the studies relied upon nor claims those studies showed the laws achieved their purpose, nor in any other way attempts to justify requiring a person who registered a pistol to wait 30 days to register another one. The record does include testimony that offers cursory rationales for some other requirements, such as safety training and demonstrating knowledge of gun laws, *see, e.g.,* Testimony of Cathy L. Lanier, Chief of Police, at 2 (Oct. 1, 2008), but the District fails to present any data or other evidence to substantiate its claim that these requirements can reasonably be expected to promote either of the important governmental interests it has invoked (perhaps because it was relying upon the asserted interests we have discounted as circular).

Although we do "accord substantial deference to the predictive judgments" of the legislature, *Turner Broad. Sys., Inc. v. FCC (Turner II)*, 520 U.S. 180, 195 (1997) . . . , the District is not thereby "insulated from meaningful judicial review," *Turner I*, 512 U.S. at 666 (controlling opinion of Kennedy, J.); *see also City of Los Angeles v. Alameda Books, Inc.,* 535 U.S. 425, 440 (2002) (plurality opinion) (citing *Turner I* and "acknowledg[ing] that the Los Angeles City Council is in a better position than the Judiciary to gather and evaluate data on local problems"). Rather, we must "assure that, in formulating its judgments, [the legislature] has drawn reasonable inferences based on substantial

---

* On remand, the District will have an opportunity to explain in greater detail how these governmental interests are served by the novel registration requirements. The Committee also thought registration useful because it "gives law enforcement essential information about firearm ownership, . . . permits officers to charge individuals with a crime if an individual is in possession of an unregistered firearm, and permits officers to seize unregistered weapons." Report on Bill 17-843, at 3-4 (Nov. 25, 2008). These rationales are circular, however, and do not on their own establish either an important interest of the Government or a substantial relationship between the registration of firearms and an important interest.

evidence." *Turner II*, 520 U.S. at 195. . . . Therefore, the District needs to present some meaningful evidence, not mere assertions, to justify its predictive judgments. On the present record, we conclude the District has not supplied evidence adequate to show a substantial relationship between any of the novel registration requirements and an important governmental interest.

Nor, however, do the plaintiffs present more meaningful contrary evidence concerning handguns, and neither the District nor the plaintiffs present any evidence at all concerning application of the registration requirements to long guns. The parties' mutual failure in their briefs to distinguish between handguns and long guns points up a significant deficiency in the present record. The Committee Report implicitly acknowledged the distinction between handguns and long guns only back-handedly, quoting *Heller* to emphasize specifically "the problem of handgun violence in this country" before discussing the proposed FRA. Report on Bill 17-843, at 3 (Nov. 25, 2008). Handguns indeed appear to have been the exclusive subject of the Committee's concern. Nowhere in the Report is there even a single reference to the need for registration of rifles or shotguns. For all the legislative record and the record in this case reveal, the provisions of the FRA that deal specifically with registration of long guns might have been written in invisible ink.

In the light of these evidentiary deficiencies and "the importance of the issues" at stake in this case, taking our cue from the Supreme Court in *Turner I*, we believe the parties should have an opportunity "to develop a more thorough factual record." 512 U.S. at 664-68. . . . In *Turner I*, the Court had determined intermediate scrutiny was appropriate for the First Amendment challenge at issue. "On the state of the record developed [that] far," however, the Government was unable to show the law was narrowly tailored. *Id.* at 665. Rather than invalidate a legislative judgment based upon that shortcoming, the Court remanded the case for development of "a more thorough factual record." *Id.* at 668. We follow suit by remanding the novel registration requirements, and all registration requirements as applied to long guns, to the district court for further evidentiary proceedings.

4. Assault Weapons and Large-Capacity Magazines

Because the plaintiffs fail to present an argument in their briefs questioning the constitutionality of the ban on semi-automatic pistols and shotguns . . . we construe the plaintiffs' challenge to the ban on assault weapons as going only to the prohibition of certain semi-automatic rifles. We are not aware of evidence that prohibitions on either semi-automatic rifles or large-capacity magazines are longstanding and thereby deserving of a presumption of validity. For the court to determine whether these prohibitions are constitutional, therefore, we first must ask whether they impinge upon the right protected by the Second Amendment. That is, prohibiting certain arms might not meaningfully affect "individual self-defense, [which] is 'the *central component*' of the Second Amendment right." *McDonald*, 130 S. Ct. at 3036 (quoting *Heller*, 554 U.S. at 599). Of course, the Court also said the Second Amendment protects the right to keep and bear arms for other "lawful purposes," such as hunting, but self-defense is the "core lawful purpose" protected, *Heller*, 554 U.S. at 630.

The Court in *Heller,* as mentioned above at pages 12-13, recognized yet another "limitation on the right to keep and carry arms," namely that the "sorts of weapons protected" are those "'in common use at the time' for lawful purposes like self-defense." *Id.* at 624, 627. The Court found this limitation "fairly supported by the historical tradition of prohibiting the carrying of 'dangerous and unusual weapons.'" *Id.* at 627. Because the prohibitions at issue, unlike the registration requirements, apply only to particular classes of weapons, we must also ask whether the prohibited weapons are "typically possessed by law-abiding citizens for lawful purposes," *id.* at 625; if not, then they are not the sorts of "Arms" protected by the Second Amendment.

a. Do the Prohibitions Impinge upon the Second Amendment Right?

The plaintiffs contend semi-automatic rifles, in particular the AR variants, are commonly possessed for self-protection in the home as well as for sport. They also argue magazines holding more than ten rounds are commonly possessed for self-defense and for other lawful purposes and that the prohibition of such magazines would impose a burden upon them. Specifically, they point out that without a large-capacity magazine it would be necessary, in a stressful situation, to pause in order to reload the firearm.

The District, by contrast, argues neither assault weapons nor weapons with large-capacity magazines are among the "Arms" protected by the Second Amendment because they are both "dangerous and unusual," *Heller,* 554 U.S. at 627 (internal quotation marks omitted), and because prohibiting them minimally burdens the plaintiffs; hence the District maintains the bans are constitutional. The Committee on Public Safety received evidence that assault weapons are not useful for the purposes of sporting or self-defense, but rather are "military-style" weapons designed for offensive use. *See generally* Testimony of Brian J. Siebel, Brady Center to Prevent Gun Violence (Oct. 1, 2008). The Committee concluded assault weapons "have no legitimate use as self-defense weapons, and would in fact increase the danger to law-abiding users and innocent bystanders if kept in the home or used in self-defense situations." Report on Bill 17-843, at 7 (Nov. 25, 2008).

The District likewise contends magazines holding more than ten rounds are disproportionately involved in the murder of law enforcement officers and in mass shootings, and have little value for self-defense or sport. It cites the Siebel testimony, which relies upon a report of the federal Bureau of Alcohol, Tobacco, Firearms and Explosives (ATF) stating that semi-automatic rifles with large-capacity magazines are not suitable for sporting purposes. The District also reasons that the usefulness of large-capacity magazines for self-defense in rare circumstances does not mean the burden imposed upon the plaintiffs is more than minimal.

We think it clear enough in the record that semi-automatic rifles and magazines holding more than ten rounds are indeed in "common use," as the plaintiffs contend. Approximately 1.6 million AR-15s alone have been manufactured since 1986, and in 2007 this one popular model accounted for 5.5 percent of all firearms, and 14.4 percent of all rifles, produced in the U.S. for the domestic market. As for magazines, fully 18 percent of all firearms owned by civilians in 1994 were equipped with magazines holding more than ten rounds, and approximately 4.7 million more such magazines were imported into the United States between 1995 and 2000. There may well be some capacity above which magazines are not in common use but, if so, the record is devoid of evidence as to what that capacity is; in any event, that capacity surely is not ten.

Nevertheless, based upon the record as it stands, we cannot be certain whether these weapons are commonly used or are useful specifically for self-defense or hunting and therefore whether the prohibitions of certain semi-automatic rifles and magazines holding more than ten rounds meaningfully affect the right to keep and bear arms. We need not resolve that question, however, because even assuming they do impinge upon the right protected by the Second Amendment, we think intermediate scrutiny is the appropriate standard of review and the prohibitions survive that standard.

b.   Intermediate Scrutiny Is Appropriate

As we did in evaluating the constitutionality of certain of the registration requirements, we determine the appropriate standard of review by assessing how severely the prohibitions burden the Second Amendment right. Unlike the law held unconstitutional in *Heller*, the laws at issue here do not prohibit the possession of "the quintessential self-defense weapon," to wit, the handgun. 554 U.S. at 629. Nor does the ban on certain semi-automatic rifles prevent a person from keeping a suitable and commonly used weapon for protection in the home or for hunting, whether a handgun or a non-automatic long gun. *See* Gary Kleck & Marc Gertz, *Armed Resistance to Crime: The Prevalence and Nature of Self-Defense with a Gun*, 86 J. Crim. L. & Criminology 150, 185 (1995) (revolvers and semi-automatic pistols are together used almost 80% of the time in incidents of self-defense with a gun); Dep't of Treasury, *Study on the Sporting Suitability of Modified Semiautomatic Assault Rifles* 38 (1998) (semi-automatic assault rifles studied are "not generally recognized as particularly suitable for or readily adaptable to sporting purposes"). Although we cannot be confident the prohibitions impinge at all upon the core right protected by the Second Amendment, we are reasonably certain the prohibitions do not impose a substantial burden upon that right. As the District points out, the plaintiffs present hardly any evidence that semi-automatic rifles and magazines holding more than ten rounds are well suited to or preferred for the purpose of self-defense or sport. *Cf.* Kleck & Gertz, *supra*, at 177 (finding that of 340,000 to 400,000 instances of defensive gun use in which the defenders believed the use of a gun had saved a life, 240,000 to 300,000 involved handguns). Accordingly, we believe intermediate rather than strict scrutiny is the appropriate standard of review.

In this we agree with the reasoning of the Third Circuit in *Marzzarella*. The court there applied intermediate scrutiny to the prohibition of unmarked firearms in part because it thought the ban was similar to a regulation "of the manner in which . . . speech takes place," a type of regulation subject to intermediate scrutiny "under the time, place, and manner doctrine" of the First Amendment. 614 F.3d at 97. Notably, because the prohibition left a person "free to possess any otherwise lawful firearm," the court reasoned it was "more accurately characterized as a regulation of the manner in which persons may lawfully exercise their Second Amendment rights." *Id.* Here, too, the prohibition of semi-automatic rifles and large-capacity magazines does not effectively disarm individuals or substantially affect their ability to defend themselves. *See* Volokh, *supra*, at 1471 ("where content-neutral speech restrictions are involved, restrictions that impose severe burdens (because they don't leave open ample alternative channels) must be judged under strict scrutiny, but restrictions that impose only modest burdens (because they do leave open ample alternative channels) are judged under a mild form of intermediate scrutiny").

c. The Prohibitions Survive Intermediate Scrutiny

Recall that when subject to intermediate scrutiny the Government has the burden of showing there is a substantial relationship or reasonable "fit" between, on the one hand, the prohibition on assault weapons and magazines holding more than ten rounds and, on the other, its important interests in protecting police officers and controlling crime. The record evidence substantiates that the District's prohibition is substantially related to those ends.

The Committee on Public Safety relied upon a report by the ATF, which described assault weapons as creating "mass produced mayhem." *Assault Weapons Profile* 19 (1994). This description is elaborated in the Siebel testimony for the Brady Center: "the military features of semiautomatic assault weapons are designed to enhance their capacity to shoot multiple human targets very rapidly" and "[p]istol grips on assault rifles . . . help stabilize the weapon during rapid fire and allow the shooter to spray-fire from the hip position." The same source also suggests assault weapons are preferred by criminals and place law enforcement officers "at particular risk . . . because of their high firepower," as does the ATF, *see* Dep't of Treasury, *Study on the Sporting Suitability of Modified Semiautomatic Assault Rifles* 34-35, 38 (1998). *See also* Christopher S. Koper et al., U. Penn. Jerry Lee Ctr. of Criminology, *An Updated Assessment of the Federal Assault Weapons Ban: Impacts on Gun Markets and Gun Violence, 1994-2003*, at 51, 87 (2004) (assault weapons "account for a larger share of guns used in mass murders and murders of police, crimes for which weapons with greater firepower would seem particularly useful," and "criminal use of [assault weapons] . . . declined after" the federal assault weapons ban enacted in 1994 "independently of trends in gun crime"); *id.* at 11 ("AR-15 type rifles are civilian weapons patterned after the U.S. military's M-16 rifle and were the assault rifles most commonly used in crime before the ban" in federal law from 1994 to 2004).

Heller suggests "M-16 rifles and the like" may be banned because they are "dangerous and unusual," *see* 554 U.S. at 627. The Court had previously described the "AR-15" as "the civilian version of the military's M-16 rifle." *Staples v. United States*, 511 U.S. 600, 603 (1994). Although semi-automatic firearms, unlike automatic M-16s, fire "only one shot with each pull of the trigger," *id.* at 602 n.1, semi-automatics still fire almost as rapidly as automatics. *See* Testimony of Brian J. Siebel, Brady Center to Prevent Gun Violence, at 1 (Oct. 1, 2008) ("30-round magazine" of UZI "was emptied in slightly less than two seconds on full automatic, while the same magazine was emptied in just five seconds on semiautomatic"). Indeed, it is difficult to draw meaningful distinctions between the AR-15 and the M-16. *See Staples*, 511 U.S. at 603 ("Many M-16 parts are interchangeable with those in the AR-15 and can be used to convert the AR-15 into an automatic weapon"); Koper, *supra*, at 4 (AR-15 and other federally banned assault weapons "are civilian copies of military weapons and accept ammunition magazines made for those military weapons"). In short, the evidence demonstrates a ban on assault weapons is likely to promote the Government's interest in crime control in the densely populated urban area that is the District of Columbia. *See* Comm. on Pub. Safety, Report on Bill 17-593, at 4 (Nov. 25, 2008) ("The District shares the problem of gun violence with other dense, urban jurisdictions").

The record also supports the limitation on magazine capacity to ten rounds. The Committee relied upon Siebel's testimony that "[t]he threat posed by military-style assault weapons is increased significantly if they can be equipped with high-capacity ammunition magazines" because, "[b]y permitting a shooter to fire more than ten rounds without reloading, they greatly increase the firepower of mass shooters." *See also* Koper, *supra*, at 87 ("guns used in shootings are 17% to 26% more likely to have [magazines holding more than ten rounds] than guns used in gunfire cases resulting in no wounded victims"); *id.* at 97 ("studies . . . suggest that attacks with semiautomatics — including [assault weapons] and other semiautomatics with [magazines holding more than ten rounds] — result in more shots fired, persons wounded, and wounds per victim than do other gun attacks"). The Siebel testimony moreover supports the District's claim that high-capacity magazines are dangerous in self-defense situations because "the tendency is for defenders to keep firing until all bullets have been expended, which poses grave risks to others in the household, passersby, and bystanders." Moreover, the Chief of Police testified the "2 or 3 second pause" during which a criminal reloads his firearm "can be of critical benefit to law enforcement." Overall the evidence demonstrates that large-capacity magazines tend to pose a danger to innocent people and particularly to police officers, which supports the District's claim that a ban on such magazines is likely to promote its important governmental interests.

We conclude the District has carried its burden of showing a substantial relationship between the prohibition of both semi-automatic rifles and magazines holding more than ten rounds and the objectives of protecting police officers and controlling crime. Accordingly, the bans do not violate the plaintiffs' constitutional right to keep and bear arms.

III. CONCLUSION

For the reasons stated above, we affirm the judgment of the district court with respect, first, to the requirement of mere registration as applied to handguns . . . , and second, to the ban on "assault weapons" and large-capacity magazines. . . . With respect to the registration requirements . . . the judgment is vacated and this matter is remanded to the district court for further proceedings consistent with this opinion.

So ordered.

Appendix: Regarding the Dissent

[Here the majority addresses several points raised by Judge Kavanaugh's dissent.]

KAVANAUGH, Circuit Judge, dissenting: ...

In *Heller*, the Court ruled that the District of Columbia's ban on the possession of handguns violated the Second Amendment. 554 U.S. at 635. In the wake of *Heller*, the District of Columbia enacted a new gun law. As relevant here, D.C. bans possession of most semi-automatic rifles and requires registration of all guns possessed in the District of Columbia. ...

In my judgment, both D.C.'s ban on semi-automatic rifles and its gun registration requirement are unconstitutional under *Heller*.

In *Heller*, the Supreme Court held that handguns — the vast majority of which today are semi-automatic — are constitutionally protected because they have not traditionally been banned and are in common use by law-abiding citizens. There is no meaningful or persuasive constitutional distinction between semi-automatic handguns and semi-automatic rifles. Semi-automatic rifles, like semi-automatic handguns, have not traditionally been banned and are in common use by law-abiding citizens for self-defense in the home, hunting, and other lawful uses. Moreover, semi-automatic *handguns* are used in connection with violent crimes far more than semi-automatic *rifles* are. It follows from *Heller*'s protection of semi-automatic handguns that semi-automatic rifles are also constitutionally protected and that D.C.'s ban on them is unconstitutional. (By contrast, fully automatic weapons, also known as machine guns, have traditionally been banned and may continue to be banned after *Heller*.)

D.C.'s registration requirement, which is significantly more stringent than any other federal or state gun law in the United States, is likewise unconstitutional. *Heller* and later *McDonald* said that regulations on the sale, possession, or use of guns are permissible if they are within the class of traditional, "longstanding" gun regulations in the United States. Registration of all lawfully possessed guns — as distinct from licensing of gun owners or mandatory record-keeping by gun sellers — has not traditionally been required in the United States and even today remains highly unusual. Under *Heller's* history- and tradition-based test, D.C.'s registration requirement is therefore unconstitutional.

It bears emphasis that *Heller*, while enormously significant jurisprudentially, was not revolutionary in terms of its immediate real-world effects on American gun regulation. Indeed, *Heller* largely preserved the status quo of gun regulation in the United States. *Heller* established that traditional and common gun laws in the United States remain constitutionally permissible. The Supreme Court simply pushed back against an outlier local law — D.C.'s handgun ban — that went far beyond the traditional line of gun regulation. As *Heller* emphasized: "Few laws in the history of our Nation have come close to the severe restriction of the District's" law. 554 U.S. at 629.[3]

---

3. In that sense, *Heller* was similar in its overarching practical and real-world ramifications to recent Supreme Court decisions such as *Brown v. Entertainment Merchants Ass'n*, 131 S. Ct. 2729 (2011); *Graham v. Florida*, 130 S. Ct. 2011 (2010); *Kennedy v. Louisiana*, 554 U.S. 407 (2008); and *Romer v. Evans*, 517 U.S. 620 (1996). Those decisions disapproved novel or

After *Heller*, however, D.C. seemed not to heed the Supreme Court's message. Instead, D.C. appeared to push the envelope again, with its new ban on semi-automatic rifles and its broad gun registration requirement. D.C.'s public safety motivation in enacting these laws is worthy of great respect. But the means D.C. has chosen are again constitutionally problematic. The D.C. gun provisions at issue here, like the ban at issue in *Heller*, are outliers that are not traditional or common in the United States. As with D.C.'s handgun ban, therefore, holding these D.C. laws unconstitutional would not lead to nationwide tumult. Rather, such a holding would maintain the balance historically and traditionally struck in the United States between public safety and the individual right to keep arms — a history and tradition that *Heller* affirmed and adopted as determining the scope of the Second Amendment right.

I

A key threshold question in this case concerns the constitutional test we should employ to assess the challenged provisions of the D.C. gun law. The *Heller* Court held that the Second Amendment guarantees an individual right to possess guns. But the Court emphasized that the Second Amendment does not protect "a right to keep and carry any weapon whatsoever in any manner whatsoever and for whatever purpose." *District of Columbia v. Heller*, 554 U.S. 570, 626 (2008). "Like most rights, the right secured by the Second Amendment is not unlimited." *Id.*

In light of that limiting language in *Heller*, constitutional analysis of D.C.'s new law raises two main questions. Under *Heller*, what kinds of firearms may the government ban? And what kinds of regulations may the government impose on the sale, possession, or use of firearms?

Put in simple terms, the issue with respect to what test to apply to gun bans and regulations is this: Are gun bans and regulations to be analyzed based on the Second Amendment's text, history, and tradition (as well as by appropriate analogues thereto when dealing with modern weapons and new circumstances, *see infra* Part I.B)? Or may judges re-calibrate the scope of the Second Amendment right based on judicial assessment of whether the law advances a sufficiently compelling or important government interest to override the individual right? And if the latter, is the proper test strict scrutiny or intermediate scrutiny?

As I read *Heller*, the Supreme Court was not silent about the answers to those questions. Rather, the Court set forth fairly precise guidance to govern those issues going forward.

---

uncommon state legislative efforts to regulate beyond traditional boundaries in areas that affected enumerated individual constitutional rights — California's law banning sale of violent video games, Florida's law permitting life without parole for certain juvenile crimes, Louisiana's law permitting the death penalty for certain rapes, and Colorado's law prohibiting gay people from receiving protection from discrimination. Because those laws were outliers, the decisions invalidating them did not cause major repercussions throughout the Nation. *Heller* was a decision in that same vein, in terms of its immediate practical effects in the United States. . . .

A

In my view, *Heller* and *McDonald* leave little doubt that courts are to assess gun bans and regulations based on text, history, and tradition, not by a balancing test such as strict or intermediate scrutiny. To be sure, the Court never said something as succinct as "Courts should not apply strict or intermediate scrutiny but should instead look to text, history, and tradition to define the scope of the right and assess gun bans and regulations." But that is the clear message I take away from the Court's holdings and reasoning in the two cases.

As to bans on categories of guns, the *Heller* Court stated that the government may ban classes of guns that have been banned in our "historical tradition"—namely, guns that are "dangerous and unusual" and thus are not "the sorts of lawful weapons that" citizens typically "possess[] at home." 554 U.S. at 627. The Court said that "dangerous and unusual weapons" are equivalent to those weapons not "in common use," as the latter phrase was used in *United States v. Miller*, 307 U.S. 174, 179 (1939). *Heller*, 554 U.S. at 627. Thus, the "Second Amendment does not protect those weapons not typically possessed by law-abiding citizens for lawful purposes, such as short-barreled shotguns" or automatic "M-16 rifles and the like." *Id.* at 625, 627. That interpretation, the Court explained, "accords with the historical understanding of the scope of the right." *Id.* at 625. "Constitutional rights," the Court said, "are enshrined with the scope they were understood to have when the people adopted them, whether or not future legislatures or (yes) even future judges think that scope too broad." *Id.* at 634-35. The scope of the right is thus determined by "historical justifications." *Id.* at 635. And tradition (that is, post-ratification history) also matters because "examination of a variety of legal and other sources to determine the public understanding of a legal text in the period after its enactment or ratification" is a "critical tool of constitutional interpretation." *Id.* at 605.

Because the D.C. law at issue in *Heller* banned handguns (including semi-automatic handguns), which have not traditionally been banned and are in common use by law-abiding citizens, the Court found that the D.C. ban on handgun possession violated the Second Amendment. Stressing the D.C. law's inconsistency with our "historical tradition," *id.* at 627, the Court stated that "[f]ew laws in the history of our Nation have come close to the severe restriction of the District's" law, *id.* at 629.

As to regulations on the sale, possession, or use of guns, *Heller* similarly said the government may continue to impose regulations that are traditional, "long-standing" regulations in the United States. *Id.* at 626-27. In *McDonald*, the Court reiterated that "longstanding regulatory measures" are permissible. *McDonald v. City of Chicago*, 130 S. Ct. 3020, 3047 (2010). . . . Importantly, the *Heller* Court listed several examples of such longstanding (and therefore constitutionally permissible) regulations, such as laws against concealed carry and laws prohibiting possession of guns by felons. 554 U.S. at 626. The Court stated that analysis of whether other gun regulations are permissible must be based on their "historical justifications." *Id.* at 635.

In disapproving D.C.'s ban on handguns, in approving a ban on machine guns, and in approving longstanding regulations such as concealed-carry and felon-in-possession laws, *Heller* established that the scope of the Second

Amendment right—and thus the constitutionality of gun bans and regulations—is determined by reference to text, history, and tradition. As to the ban on handguns, for example, the Supreme Court in *Heller* never asked whether the law was narrowly tailored to serve a compelling government interest (strict scrutiny) or substantially related to an important government interest (intermediate scrutiny). If the Supreme Court had meant to adopt one of those tests, it could have said so in *Heller* and measured D.C.'s handgun ban against the relevant standard. But the Court did not do so; it instead determined that handguns had not traditionally been banned and were in common use— and thus that D.C.'s handgun ban was unconstitutional.

Moreover, in order for the Court to prospectively approve the constitutionality of several kinds of gun laws—such as machine gun bans, concealed-carry laws, and felon-in-possession laws—the Court obviously had to employ *some* test. Yet the Court made no mention of strict or intermediate scrutiny when approving such laws. Rather, the test the Court relied on—as it indicated by using terms such as "historical tradition" and "longstanding" and "historical justifications"—was one of text, history, and tradition. *Id.* at 626-27, 635; *see* Eugene Volokh, *Implementing the Right to Keep and Bear Arms for Self-Defense: An Analytical Framework and a Research Agenda*, 56 UCLA L. Rev. 1443, 1463 (2009) ("Absent [from *Heller*] is any inquiry into whether the law is necessary to serve a compelling government interest in preventing death and crime, though handgun ban proponents did indeed argue that such bans are necessary to serve those interests and that no less restrictive alternative would do the job."); Joseph Blocher, *Categoricalism and Balancing in First and Second Amendment Analysis*, 84 N.Y.U. L. Rev. 375, 380 (2009) ("Rather than adopting one of the First Amendment's many Frankfurter-inspired balancing approaches, the majority endorsed a categorical test under which some types of 'Arms' and arms-usage are protected absolutely from bans and some types of 'Arms' and people are excluded entirely from constitutional coverage."); *id.* at 405 (*Heller* "neither requires nor permits any balancing beyond that accomplished by the Framers themselves.").[5]

B

Before addressing the majority opinion's contrary analysis of *Heller* and *McDonald*, it is important to underscore two points regarding *Heller*'s focus on text, history, and tradition.

First, just because gun regulations are assessed by reference to history and tradition does not mean that governments lack flexibility or power to enact gun

---

5. The Court's failure to employ strict or intermediate scrutiny appears to have been quite intentional and well-considered. *Cf.* Tr. of Oral Arg. at 44, *Heller*, 554 U.S. 570 (No. 07-290) (Chief Justice Roberts: "Well, these various phrases under the different standards that are proposed, 'compelling interest,' 'significant interest,' 'narrowly tailored,' none of them appear in the Constitution. . . . I mean, these standards that apply in the First Amendment just kind of developed over the years as sort of baggage that the First Amendment picked up.").

regulations. Indeed, governments appear to have *more* flexibility and power to impose gun regulations under a test based on text, history, and tradition than they would under strict scrutiny. After all, history and tradition show that a variety of gun regulations have co-existed with the Second Amendment right and are consistent with that right, as the Court said in *Heller*. By contrast, if courts applied strict scrutiny, then presumably very few gun regulations would be upheld. Indeed, Justice Breyer made this point in his dissent in *Heller* when he noted that the majority opinion had listed certain permissible gun regulations "whose constitutionality under a strict-scrutiny standard would be far from clear." 554 U.S. at 688 (Breyer, J., dissenting).

So the major difference between applying the *Heller* history- and tradition-based approach and applying one of the forms of scrutiny is not necessarily the number of gun regulations that will pass muster. Instead, it is that the *Heller* test will be more determinate and "much less subjective" because "it depends upon a body of evidence susceptible of reasoned analysis rather than a variety of vague ethico-political First Principles whose combined conclusion can be found to point in any direction the judges favor." *McDonald*, 130 S. Ct. at 3058 (Scalia, J., concurring). . . .

Second, when legislatures seek to address new weapons that have not traditionally existed or to impose new gun regulations because of conditions that have not traditionally existed, there obviously will not be a history or tradition of banning such weapons or imposing such regulations. That does not mean the Second Amendment does not apply to those weapons or in those circumstances. Nor does it mean that the government is powerless to address those new weapons or modern circumstances. Rather, in such cases, the proper interpretive approach is to reason by analogy from history and tradition. *See Parker v. District of Columbia,* 478 F.3d 370, 398 (D.C. Cir. 2007) ("[J]ust as the First Amendment free speech clause covers modern communication devices unknown to the founding generation, e.g., radio and television, and the Fourth Amendment protects telephonic conversation from a 'search,' the Second Amendment protects the possession of the *modern-day equivalents* of the colonial pistol.") (emphasis added), *aff'd sub nom. Heller,* 554 U.S. 570; Tr. of Oral Arg. at 77, *Heller,* 554 U.S. 570 (No. 07-290) (Chief Justice Roberts: "[Y]ou would define 'reasonable' in light of the restrictions that existed at the time the amendment was adopted. . . . [Y]ou can't take it into the marketplace was one restriction. So that would be — we are talking about lineal descendents of the arms but presumably there are lineal descendents of the restrictions as well."); *cf. Kyllo v. United States,* 533 U.S. 27, 31-35 (2001) (applying traditional Fourth Amendment standards to novel thermal imaging technology); *California v. Ciraolo,* 476 U.S. 207, 213 (1986) (allowing government to view property from airplanes based on common-law principle that police could look at property when passing by homes on public thoroughfares). . . .

C

The majority opinion here applies intermediate scrutiny and contends that intermediate scrutiny is consistent with *Heller* and *McDonald*. The majority opinion employs history and tradition only as a threshold screen to determine whether the law in question implicates the individual right; if so, the majority opinion then subjects the individual right to balancing under the intermediate scrutiny test. As explained above, I disagree with that approach. I read *Heller* and *McDonald* as setting forth a test based wholly on text, history, and tradition. Deeper examination of the two Supreme Court opinions — and, in particular, how the Court's opinions responded to the dissents in the two cases — buttresses my conclusion.

Turning first to *Heller*. The back and forth between the *Heller* majority opinion and Justice Breyer's dissent underscores that the proper Second Amendment test focuses on text, history, and tradition. In his dissent, Justice Breyer suggested that the Court should follow the lead of certain First Amendment cases, among others, that had applied a form of intermediate-scrutiny interest balancing. . . . *Heller*, 554 U.S. at 689-90, 704-05, 714 (Breyer, J., dissenting).

Justice Breyer expressly rejected strict scrutiny and rational basis review. Instead, he explicitly referred to intermediate scrutiny and relied on cases such as *Turner Broadcasting* that had applied intermediate scrutiny. *See Turner Broadcasting System, Inc. v. FCC*, 520 U.S. 180, 189-225 (1997). And he discussed the strength of the government's interest and the fit between the law and those interests, as the Court does when applying heightened scrutiny. It is thus evident that Justice Breyer's *Heller* dissent advocated a form of intermediate scrutiny.

The Court responded to Justice Breyer by rejecting his "judge-empowering 'interest-balancing inquiry' that 'asks whether the statute burdens a protected interest in a way or to an extent that is out of proportion to the statute's salutary effects upon other important governmental interests.'" *Heller*, 554 U.S. at 634 (quoting *id.* at 689-90 (Breyer, J., dissenting)). The Court stated rather emphatically: "We know of no other enumerated constitutional right whose core protection has been subjected to a freestanding 'interest-balancing' approach. The very enumeration of the right takes out of the hands of government — even the Third Branch of Government — the power to decide on a case-by-case basis whether the right is *really worth* insisting upon. A constitutional guarantee subject to future judges' assessments of its usefulness is no constitutional guarantee at all." *Id.*

In rejecting a judicial interest-balancing approach, the Court explained that the Second Amendment "is the very *product* of an interest balancing by the people" that judges should not "now conduct for them anew." *Id.* at 635. The Court added that judges may not alter the scope of the Amendment because "[c]onstitutional rights are enshrined with the scope they were understood to have when the people adopted them, whether or not future legislatures or (yes) even future judges think that scope too broad." *Id.* at 634-35. The Court emphasized that the scope of the right was determined by "historical justifications." *Id.* at 635. And the Court stated that tradition (that is, post-ratification history) matters because "examination of a variety of legal and other sources to determine the public understanding of a legal text in the period after its enactment or ratification" is a "critical tool of constitutional interpretation." *Id.* at 605 (emphasis omitted).

To be sure, the Court noted in passing that D.C.'s handgun ban would fail under any level of heightened scrutiny or review the Court applied. *Id.* at 628-29. But that was more of a gilding-the-lily observation about the extreme nature of

D.C's law—and appears to have been a pointed comment that the dissenters should have found D.C.'s law unconstitutional even under their own suggested balancing approach—than a statement that courts may or should apply strict or intermediate scrutiny in Second Amendment cases. We know as much because the Court expressly dismissed Justice Breyer's *Turner Broadcasting* intermediate scrutiny approach and went on to demonstrate how courts should consider Second Amendment bans and regulations—by analysis of text, history, and tradition. *Id.* at 626-27, 634-35.

Is it possible, however, that the *Heller* Court was ruling out intermediate scrutiny but leaving open the possibility that strict scrutiny might apply? That seems highly unlikely, for reasons Justice Breyer himself pointed out in dissent:

> Respondent proposes that the Court adopt a "strict scrutiny" test, which would require reviewing with care each gun law to determine whether it is "narrowly tailored to achieve a compelling governmental interest." *Abrams v. Johnson*, 521 U.S. 74, 82 (1997); see Brief for Respondent 54-62. But the majority implicitly, and appropriately, rejects that suggestion by broadly approving a set of laws . . . whose constitutionality under a strict-scrutiny standard would be far from clear.

Id. at 688 (Breyer, J., dissenting) [alteration added].

Justice Breyer thus perceived that the Court's history- and tradition-based approach would likely permit governments to enact *more* gun laws and regulations than a strict scrutiny approach would allow. History and tradition establish that several gun regulations have co-existed with the Second Amendment right and are consistent with that right, as the Court determined in *Heller*. If courts applied strict scrutiny, however, very few gun regulations would presumably be constitutional.

Even more to the point, as Justice Breyer also noted, the Court in *Heller* affirmatively *approved* a slew of gun laws—machine gun bans, concealed-carry laws, felon-in-possession laws, and the like—without analyzing them under strict scrutiny. The Court approved them based on a history- and tradition-based test, not strict scrutiny. Indeed, these laws might not have passed muster under a strict scrutiny analysis.

The Court's later decision in *McDonald* underscores that text, history, and tradition guide analysis of gun laws and regulations. There, the Court again precluded the use of balancing tests; furthermore, it expressly rejected judicial assessment of "the costs and benefits of firearms restrictions" and stated that courts applying the Second Amendment thus would not have to make "difficult empirical judgments" about the efficacy of particular gun regulations. 130 S. Ct. at 3050. . . .

That language from *McDonald* is critically important because strict and intermediate scrutiny obviously require assessment of the "costs and benefits" of government regulations and entail "difficult empirical judgments" about their efficacy—precisely what *McDonald* barred. *McDonald's* rejection of such inquiries, which was even more direct than *Heller's*, is flatly incompatible with a strict or intermediate scrutiny approach to gun regulations.

That conclusion is fortified by a careful examination of the back and forth in *McDonald* between Justice Alito's controlling opinion and Justice Breyer's dissent.

In his *McDonald* dissent, Justice Breyer explained at some length that he was concerned about the practical ramifications of *Heller* and *McDonald* because judges would have great difficulty assessing gun regulations under heightened scrutiny (whether it might be called strict or intermediate or something else on that heightened scrutiny spectrum). He stated that determining the constitutionality of a gun regulation would "almost always require the weighing of the constitutional right to bear arms against the primary concern of every government—a concern for the safety and indeed the lives of its citizens." 130 S. Ct. at 3126. . . . He listed a variety of possible gun laws that would raise such difficult empirical questions, including laws regulating semi-automatic rifles and laws imposing registration requirements. *Id.* Justice Breyer asserted that assessing the constitutionality of those laws under heightened scrutiny would require difficult judicial evaluations of the effectiveness of particular gun laws. . . .

The questions identified by Justice Breyer are of course the kinds of questions that courts ask when applying heightened scrutiny. So how did the Court respond to Justice Breyer? The Court simply rejected the premise of Justice Breyer's criticism. Those kinds of difficult assessments would not need to be made, the Court said, because courts would not be applying that kind of test or scrutiny: "Justice Breyer is incorrect that incorporation will require judges to assess the costs and benefits of firearms restrictions and thus to make difficult empirical judgments in an area in which they lack expertise. As we have noted, while his opinion in *Heller* recommended an interest-balancing test, the Court specifically rejected that suggestion. 'The very enumeration of the right takes out of the hands of government—even the Third Branch of Government—the power to decide on a case-by-case basis whether the right is *really worth* insisting upon.'" *Id.* at 3050. . . . The Court also reiterated that "longstanding" gun regulations were constitutionally permissible. *Id.* at 3047.

The *McDonald* Court's response to Justice Breyer is quite telling for our purposes: The Court dismissed the suggestion that courts in Second Amendment cases would need to assess the strength of the government's regulatory interests, or determine whether the regulation was appropriately tailored, or consider the alternatives. In other words, the Court declined to conduct the kinds of inquiries that would need to be conducted under a form of strict or intermediate scrutiny.

But Justice Breyer then asked: From where did the Court derive the exceptions the Court listed in *Heller* and *McDonald* allowing laws that ban concealed carry, possession by a felon, and the like? Justice Breyer suggested that the Court "simply invented rules that sound sensible." *Id.* at 3127 (Breyer, J., dissenting). But the Court responded that, no, it was not inventing rules but rather was holding that the scope of the right was determined by text, history, and tradition—and that "longstanding regulatory measures" were therefore permissible. *Id.* at 3047 (controlling opinion of Alito, J.). As the Court had explained in *Heller*, the scope of the right was determined by text, history, and tradition, and such longstanding laws were within the historical understanding of the scope of the right. *See also McDonald*, 130 S. Ct. at 3050, 3056 (Scalia, J., concurring) (Court's approach "makes the traditions of our people paramount"; "traditional restrictions" on the right are permissible).

D

Although *Heller* and *McDonald* rejected judicial interest balancing, the majority opinion here applies intermediate scrutiny. The majority opinion does so because it says that heightened scrutiny tests are not actually balancing tests and thus were not precluded by the Supreme Court's rejection of balancing tests. I disagree with the majority opinion's attempt to distinguish *Heller* and *McDonald* in this way.

To begin with, as explained above, the Court in my view went further in *Heller* and *McDonald* than just rejecting the concept of balancing tests. The Court emphasized the role of history and tradition; it rejected not only balancing but also examination of costs and benefits; it disclaimed the need for difficult empirical judgments; it specifically rejected Justice Breyer's approach, which was a form of intermediate scrutiny as applied in *Turner Broadcasting*; and it prospectively blessed certain laws for reasons that could be (and were) explained only by history and tradition, not by analysis under a heightened scrutiny test.

It is ironic, moreover, that Justice Breyer's dissent explicitly advocated an approach based on *Turner Broadcasting*; that the *Heller* majority flatly rejected that *Turner Broadcasting*-based approach; and that the majority opinion here nonetheless turns around and relies expressly and repeatedly on *Turner Broadcasting*. *See Heller*, 554 U.S. at 690, 704-05 (Breyer, J., dissenting) (citing *Turner Broadcasting*, 520 U.S. 180); *Heller*, 554 U.S. at 634-35. . . .

In addition, the premise of the majority opinion's more general point — that *Heller's* rejection of balancing tests does not mean it rejected strict and intermediate scrutiny — is incorrect. Strict and intermediate scrutiny are balancing tests and thus are necessarily encompassed by *Heller's* more general rejection of balancing.

. . . From the beginning, it was recognized that those tests were balancing tests. In *Barenblatt*, for example, one of the early cases applying a form of what we now call strict scrutiny, the Court stated that First Amendment rights may be overcome based on "a balancing by the courts of the competing private and public interests at stake in the particular circumstances shown," and that the "subordinating interest of the State must be compelling in order to overcome the individual constitutional rights at stake." 360 U.S. at 126-27 (internal quotation marks omitted). In [*Konigsberg v. State Bar of California*, 366 U.S. 36 (1961),] the Court similarly explained that laws limiting speech could be justified by "valid governmental interests, a prerequisite to constitutionality which has necessarily involved a weighing of the governmental interest involved." 366 U.S. at 50-51. Writing for the Court, Justice Harlan noted that the test required an "appropriate weighing of the respective interests involved." *Id.* at 51. In dissent, Justice Black objected to a "doctrine that permits constitutionally protected rights to be 'balanced' away whenever a majority of this Court thinks that a State might have interest sufficient to justify abridgment of those freedoms." *Id.* at 61 (Black, J., dissenting).

As in their original formulations, the successor strict and intermediate scrutiny tests applied today remain quintessential balancing inquiries that focus ultimately on whether a particular government interest is sufficiently compelling or important to justify an infringement on the individual right in question. . . .

To be sure, application of the strict and intermediate scrutiny tests yields categorical results and rules over time. And strict scrutiny in particular places a heavy thumb on the scale in favor of the individual right in question, meaning the balance is often struck against the government. But the tests are undoubtedly balancing tests that require a contemporary judicial assessment of the strength of the asserted government interests in imposing a particular regulation. . . .

Of course, as noted above, *Heller* and *McDonald* didn't just reject interest balancing. The Court went much further by expressly rejecting Justice Breyer's intermediate scrutiny approach, disclaiming cost-benefit analysis, and denying the need for empirical inquiry. By doing so, the Court made clear, in my view, that strict and intermediate scrutiny are inappropriate.

. . . The majority opinion here refers to the levels of scrutiny as "familiar." . . . As one commentator has stated, however, "the search for the familiar may be leading courts and commentators astray: The central disagreement in *Heller* was a debate not about strict scrutiny and rational basis review but rather about categoricalism and balancing." Blocher, *Categoricalism and Balancing in First and Second Amendment Analysis*, 84 N.Y.U. L. Rev. at 379. That disagreement in *Heller* was resolved in favor of categoricalism — with the categories defined by text, history, and tradition — and against balancing tests such as strict or intermediate scrutiny or reasonableness. . . .

F

. . . Even if it were appropriate to apply one of the levels of scrutiny after *Heller*, surely it would be strict scrutiny rather than the intermediate scrutiny test adopted by the majority opinion here. *Heller* ruled that the right to possess guns is a core enumerated constitutional right and rejected Justice Breyer's suggested *Turner Broadcasting* intermediate scrutiny approach. And *McDonald* later held that "the right to keep and bear arms" is "among those fundamental rights necessary to our system of ordered liberty." 130 S. Ct. at 3042.

For those fundamental substantive constitutional rights that the Court has subjected to a balancing test and analyzed under one of the levels of scrutiny — for example, the First Amendment freedom of speech and the rights protected by substantive due process — the Court has generally employed strict scrutiny to assess direct infringements on the right. *See, e.g., Citizens United v. FEC*, 130 S. Ct. 876, 898 (2010) (First Amendment strict scrutiny in context of infringement on "political speech"); *Boy Scouts of America v. Dale*, 530 U.S. 640, 648 (2000) (First Amendment strict scrutiny in context of infringement on freedom of association); *United States v. Playboy Entertainment Group, Inc.*, 529 U.S. 803, 813 (2000) (First Amendment strict scrutiny in context of content-based speech regulation); *Washington v. Glucksberg*, 521 U.S. 702, 721 (1997) (substantive due process doctrine "forbids the government to infringe fundamental liberty interests . . . unless the infringement is narrowly tailored to serve a compelling state interest") (internal quotation marks and alteration omitted); *see generally* Richard H. Fallon, Jr., *Strict Judicial Scrutiny*, 54 UCLA L. Rev. 1267, 1271 (2007) ("the Supreme Court adopted the strict scrutiny formula as its generic test for the protection of fundamental rights"). . . .

It is especially inappropriate for the majority opinion here to apply intermediate scrutiny rather than strict scrutiny to D.C.'s ban on semi-automatic rifles. No court of appeals decision since *Heller* has applied intermediate scrutiny to a ban on a class of arms that have not traditionally been banned and are in common use. A ban on a class of arms is not an "incidental" regulation. It is equivalent to a ban on a category of speech. Such restrictions on core enumerated constitutional protections are *not* subjected to mere intermediate scrutiny review. The majority opinion here is in uncharted territory in suggesting that intermediate scrutiny can apply to an outright ban on possession of a class of weapons that have not traditionally been banned. . . .

II

Whether we apply the *Heller* history- and tradition-based approach or strict scrutiny or even intermediate scrutiny, D.C.'s ban on semi-automatic rifles fails to pass constitutional muster. D.C.'s registration requirement is likewise unconstitutional.

A

The first issue concerns D.C.'s ban on most semi-automatic rifles. . . .

The vast majority of handguns today are semi-automatic. In *Heller*, the Supreme Court ruled that D.C.'s law banning handguns, including semi-automatic handguns, was unconstitutional. *District of Columbia v. Heller*, 554 U.S. 570, 628-29 (2008). This case concerns semi-automatic rifles. As with handguns, a significant percentage of rifles are semi-automatic. D.C. asks this Court to find that the Second Amendment protects semi-automatic *handguns* but not semi-automatic *rifles*.

There is no basis in *Heller* for drawing a constitutional distinction between semi-automatic handguns and semi-automatic rifles.

As an initial matter, considering just the public safety rationale invoked by D.C., semi-automatic handguns are more dangerous as a class than semi-automatic rifles because handguns can be concealed. As was noted by the dissent in *Heller*, handguns "are the overwhelmingly favorite weapon of armed criminals." 554 U.S. at 682 (Breyer, J., dissenting); *see also* FBI, Crime in the United States, 2009 tbl.20 (2010). So it would seem a bit backwards — at least from a public safety perspective — to interpret the Second Amendment to protect semi-automatic handguns but not semi-automatic rifles. Indeed, at oral argument, the excellent Solicitor General for D.C. acknowledged that "an argument could be made that the government interest in banning handguns is just as compelling, if not more compelling" than the government interest in banning semi-automatic rifles. . . . He added that "the government's interest may be more compelling with regard to handgun[s]." *Id.* at 36. Counsel's frank acknowledgment highlights the serious hurdle that *Heller* erects in the way of D.C.'s attempt to ban semi-automatic rifles. Put simply, it would strain logic and common sense to conclude that the Second Amendment protects semi-automatic handguns but does not protect semi-automatic rifles.

More to the point for purposes of the *Heller* analysis, the Second Amendment as construed in *Heller* protects weapons that have not traditionally been banned and are in common use by law-abiding citizens. Semi-automatic rifles have not traditionally been banned and are in common use today, and are thus protected under *Heller*.

The first commercially available semi-automatic rifles, the Winchester Models 1903 and 1905 and the Remington Model 8, entered the market between 1903 and 1906. . . . These semi-automatic rifles were designed and marketed primarily for use as hunting rifles, with a small ancillary market among law enforcement officers. . . .

By contrast, full automatics were developed for the battlefield and were never in widespread civilian use in the United States. . . . Within less than a decade, the Tommy gun and other automatic weapons had been subjected to comprehensive federal regulation. National Firearms Act, ch. 757, 48 Stat. 1236 (1934); *see also* 18 U.S.C. §922(o).

Semi-automatic rifles remain in common use today, as even the majority opinion here acknowledges. . . . ("We think it clear enough in the record that semi-automatic rifles . . . are indeed in 'common use,' as the plaintiffs contend."). According to one source, about 40 percent of rifles sold in 2010 were semi-automatic. *See* Nicholas J. Johnson et al., Firearms Law and the Second Amendment: Regulation, Rights, and Policy ch. 1 (forthcoming 2012). The AR-15 is the most popular semi-automatic rifle; since 1986, about two million semi-automatic AR-15 rifles have been manufactured. J.A. 84 (Declaration of Firearms Researcher Mark Overstreet). In 2007, the AR-15 *alone* accounted for 5.5 percent of firearms and 14.4 percent of rifles produced in the United States for the domestic market. *Id.* A brief perusal of the website of a popular American gun seller underscores the point that semi-automatic rifles are quite common in the United States. *See, e.g.*, Cabela's, http://www.cabelas.com. Semi-automatic rifles are commonly used for self-defense in the home, hunting, target shooting, and competitions. J.A. 137 (Declaration of Firearms Expert Harold E. Johnson). And many hunting guns are semi-automatic. *Id.*

Although a few states and municipalities ban some categories of semi-automatic rifles, most of the country does not, and even the bans that exist are significantly narrower than D.C.'s. What the Supreme Court said in *Heller* as to D.C.'s handgun ban thus applies just as well to D.C.'s new semi-automatic rifle ban: "Few laws in the history of our Nation have come close to the severe restriction of the District's" law. 554 U.S. at 629.

What is more, in its 1994 decision in *Staples*, the Supreme Court already stated that semi-automatic weapons "traditionally have been widely accepted as lawful possessions." 511 U.S. at 612. Indeed, the precise weapon at issue in *Staples* was the AR-15. The AR-15 is the quintessential semi-automatic rifle that D.C. seeks to ban here. Yet as the Supreme Court noted in *Staples*, the AR-15 is in common use by law-abiding citizens and has traditionally been lawful to possess. By contrast, as the Court stated in *Staples* and again in *Heller*, short-barreled shotguns and automatic "M-16 rifles and the like" are not in common use and have been permissibly banned by Congress. *Heller*, 554 U.S. at 625, 627; *see also* [*Staples v. United States*, 511 U.S. 600, 611-12 (1994)] ("certain categories of guns — no doubt including the machineguns, sawed-off shotguns, and artillery pieces that Congress has subjected to regulation — . . . have the same quasi-suspect character we attributed to owning hand grenades," but "guns falling outside those categories traditionally have been widely accepted as lawful possessions"); 18 U.S.C. §922(o)(1) ("it shall be unlawful for any person to transfer or possess a machinegun").

The Supreme Court's statement in *Staples* that semi-automatic rifles are traditionally and widely accepted as lawful possessions further demonstrates that such guns are protected under the *Heller* history- and tradition-based test. The government may still ban automatic firearms (that is, machine guns), which traditionally have been banned. But the government may not generally ban semi-automatic guns, whether semi-automatic rifles, shotguns, or handguns.

Even if it were appropriate to apply some kind of balancing test or level of scrutiny to D.C.'s ban on semi-automatic rifles, the proper test would be strict scrutiny, as explained above. *See supra* Part I.F. That is particularly true where, as here, a court is analyzing a ban on a *class* of arms within the scope of Second Amendment protection. If we are to apply strict scrutiny, we must do so in a manner consistent with *Heller's* holding that D.C.'s handgun ban was unconstitutional. But D.C. cannot show a compelling interest in banning semi-automatic rifles because the necessary implication of the decision in *Heller* is that D.C. could not show a sufficiently compelling interest to justify its banning semi-automatic handguns.

For its part, the majority opinion analyzes D.C.'s ban on semi-automatic rifles under an intermediate scrutiny balancing test. Even if the majority opinion were right that intermediate scrutiny is the proper test, the majority opinion's application of intermediate scrutiny here is unconvincing: The fundamental flaw in the majority opinion is that it cannot persuasively explain why semi-automatic handguns are constitutionally protected (as *Heller* held) but semi-automatic rifles are not.

In attempting to distinguish away *Heller's* protection of semi-automatic handguns, the majority opinion suggests that semi-automatic rifles are almost as dangerous as automatic rifles (that is, machine guns) because semi-automatic rifles fire "almost as rapidly." . . . Putting aside that the majority opinion's data indicate that semi-automatics actually fire two-and-a-half times slower than automatics, *id.*, the problem with the comparison is that semi-automatic *rifles* fire at the same general rate as semi-automatic *handguns*. And semi-automatic handguns are constitutionally protected under the Supreme Court's decision in *Heller*. So the majority opinion cannot legitimately distinguish *Heller* on that basis. *See* Eugene Volokh, *Implementing the Right to Keep and Bear Arms for Self-Defense: An Analytical Framework and a Research Agenda*, 56 UCLA L. Rev. 1443, 1484 (2009) ("The laws generally define assault weapons to be a set of semiautomatic weapons (fully automatic weapons have long been heavily regulated, and lawfully owned fully automatics are very rare and very expensive) that are little different from semiautomatic pistols and rifles that are commonly owned by tens of millions of law-abiding citizens. 'Assault weapons' are no more 'high power' than many other pistols and rifles that are not covered by the bans.").[16]

---

16. In passing, the majority opinion here tosses out the possibility that *Heller* might protect handguns that are revolvers but not handguns that are semi-automatic pistols. . . . I find that an utterly implausible reading of *Heller* given the Court's many blanket references to handguns and given that most handguns are semi-automatic.

The majority opinion next contends that semi-automatic handguns are good enough to meet people's needs for self-defense and that they shouldn't need semi-automatic rifles. But that's a bit like saying books can be banned because people can always read newspapers. That is not a persuasive or legitimate way to analyze a law that directly infringes an enumerated constitutional right. Indeed, *Heller* itself specifically rejected this mode of reasoning: "It is no answer to say, as petitioners do, that it is permissible to ban the possession of handguns so long as the possession of other firearms (*i.e.*, long guns) is allowed." 554 U.S. at 629; . . . Furthermore, the majority opinion's assertion does not sufficiently account for the fact that rifles, but typically not handguns, are used for hunting. *Cf. Heller*, 554 U.S. at 599 (most founding-era Americans "undoubtedly" thought right to own firearms "even more important for self-defense and hunting" than for militia service).

In support of its law, D.C. suggests that semi-automatic rifles are "offensive" and not just "defensive." But that is plainly true of semi-automatic handguns as well (after all, handguns are far and away the guns most often used in violent crimes), and yet the Supreme Court held semi-automatic handguns to be constitutionally protected. Moreover, it's hard to see why, if a gun is effective for "offense," it might not also be effective for "defense." If a gun is employed by criminals on the offense who are willing to violate laws and invade homes, for example, their potential victims will presumably want to be armed with similarly effective weapons for their defense. *Cf. Heller*, 554 U.S. at 711 (Breyer, J., dissenting) ("the very attributes that make handguns particularly useful for self-defense are also what make them particularly dangerous"). There is no reason to think that semi-automatic rifles are not effective for self-defense in the home, which *Heller* explained is a core purpose of the Second Amendment right. The offense/defense distinction thus doesn't advance the analysis here, at least in part because it is the person, not the gun, who determines whether use of the gun is offensive or defensive. Perhaps D.C. — by referring to the offense/defense distinction — is simply intending to say that semi-automatic rifles are especially dangerous. But it is difficult to make the case that semi-automatic rifles are significantly more dangerous than semi-automatic handguns, and the Supreme Court has already held semi-automatic handguns to be constitutionally protected.

D.C. repeatedly refers to the guns at issue in this case as "assault weapons." But if we are constrained to use D.C.'s rhetoric, we would have to say that *handguns* are the quintessential "assault weapons" in today's society; they are used far more often than any other kind of gun in violent crimes. *See* Bureau of Justice Statistics, Pub. No. 194820, Weapon Use and Violent Crime 3 (2003) (87% of violent crimes committed with firearms between 1993 and 2001 were committed with handguns). So using the rhetorical term "assault weapon" to refer to semi-automatic rifles does not meaningfully distinguish semi-automatic rifles from semi-automatic handguns. Nor does the rhetorical term "assault weapon" help make the case that semi-automatic rifles may be banned even though semi-automatic handguns are constitutionally protected.

Under intermediate scrutiny, yet another problem with D.C.'s law is its tailoring. The law is not sufficiently tailored even with respect to the category of semi-automatic rifles. It bans certain semi-automatic rifles but not others — with no particular explanation or rationale for why some made the list and some did not. The list appears to be haphazard. It does not reflect the kind of tailoring that is necessary to justify infringement of a fundamental right, even under the more relaxed intermediate scrutiny test.

In short, the majority opinion cannot persuasively explain why semi-automatic handguns are constitutionally protected but semi-automatic rifles are not. In *Heller*, D.C. argued that it could ban handguns because individuals could still own rifles. That argument failed. Here, D.C. contends that it can ban rifles because individuals can still own handguns. D.C.'s at-least-you-can-still-possess-other-kinds-of-guns argument is no more persuasive this time around. Under the *Heller* history- and tradition-based test, or the strict scrutiny test, or even the majority opinion's own intermediate scrutiny test, the D.C. ban on semi-automatic rifles is unconstitutional.

B

The second main issue on appeal concerns D.C.'s gun registration regime. D.C. requires registration of all guns lawfully possessed in D.C. The Supreme Court in *Heller* expressly allowed "*longstanding* prohibitions on the possession of firearms by felons and the mentally ill, or laws forbidding the carrying of fire-arms in sensitive places such as schools and government buildings, or laws imposing conditions and qualifications on the commercial sale of arms." 554 U.S. at 626-27. . . .

The fundamental problem with D.C.'s gun registration law is that registration of lawfully possessed guns is not "longstanding." Registration of all guns lawfully possessed by citizens in the relevant jurisdiction has not been tradition-ally required in the United States and, indeed, remains highly unusual today.

In considering D.C.'s registration requirement, it's initially important to distinguish registration laws from licensing laws. Licensing requirements mandate that gun owners meet certain standards or pass certain tests before owning guns or using them in particular ways. Those laws can advance gun safety by ensuring that owners understand how to handle guns safely, particularly before guns are carried in public. . . . Registration requirements, by contrast, require registration of individual guns and do not meaningfully serve the purpose of ensuring that owners know how to operate guns safely in the way certain licensing requirements can. . . . It is true that registration requirements also provide a hook to convict (and potentially flip) criminals who are suspected of having committed other illegal acts, but as the majority opinion recognizes, that is a "circular" and constitutionally unacceptable rationale for requiring registration with respect to a core enumerated constitutional right. . . .

Likewise, it's also important at the outset to distinguish registration require-ments imposed on gun *owners* from record-keeping requirements imposed on gun *sellers*. Some record-keeping requirements on gun sellers are traditional and common. Thus, the government may constitutionally impose certain record-keeping requirements on the sellers of guns. . . .

The issue here, however, is registration of all guns owned by people in the District of Columbia. As D.C. acknowledges, there is not, and never has been, a "comprehensive federal system of firearm registration." Council Comm. on Pub. Safety & the Judiciary, Comm. Rep. on B. 17-843, at 3 (D.C. 2008). Similarly, the vast majority of states have not traditionally required registration of lawfully possessed guns. The majority opinion cites several state laws that have existed since the beginning of the 20th Century. . . . But those state laws generally required record-keeping by gun *sellers*, not registration of all lawfully possessed guns by gun *owners*. There certainly is no tradition in the United States of gun registration imposed on all guns. . . .

Today, most states require no registration for *any* firearms; only seven states require registration for *some* firearms; and only Hawaii requires registration for *all* firearms. And even Hawaii does not impose all of the onerous requirements associated with registration that D.C. does. Put simply, D.C.'s registration law is the strictest in the Nation, by D.C.'s own admission. *See* Firearms Control: Hearing of the H.C. Comm. on Home Aff. (U.K. 2010) (statement of Peter Nickles, D.C. Att'y Gen.) (acknowledging common view that D.C. has "the strictest gun laws in the United States"). . . .

Because the vast majority of states have not traditionally required and even now do not require registration of lawfully possessed guns, D.C.'s registration law—which is the strictest in the Nation and mandates registration of all guns—does not satisfy the history- and tradition-based test set forth in *Heller* and later *McDonald*. . . .

D.C.'s law requiring registration of all lawfully possessed guns in D.C. is not part of the tradition of gun regulation in the United States; it is the most stringent such law in the Nation; and it is significantly more onerous than traditional licensing requirements or record-keeping requirements imposed only on gun sellers. Registration requirements of the kind enacted by D.C. thus do not satisfy the Supreme Court's history- and tradition-based test.

Even if it were proper to apply strict or intermediate scrutiny to D.C.'s registration law (as the majority opinion does), the registration requirement still would run into serious constitutional problems. If we were applying one of those balancing tests, however, I would remand: The current record is insufficient to render a final evaluation of the registration law under those balancing tests.

To begin with, it would be hard to persuasively say that the government has an interest sufficiently weighty to justify a regulation that infringes constitutionally guaranteed Second Amendment rights if the Federal Government and the states have not traditionally imposed—and even now do not commonly impose—such a regulation. *Cf. Brown v. Entertainment Merchants Ass'n*, 131 S. Ct. 2729, 2736 (2011) (considering First Amendment challenge to ban on sale of violent video games: "California's argument would fare better if there were a *longstanding tradition* in this country of specially restricting children's access to depictions of violence, but there is none.") (emphasis added); *United States v. Stevens*, 130 S. Ct. 1577, 1585 (2010) (considering First Amendment challenge to ban on depictions of animal cruelty: "we are unaware of any . . . tradition excluding depictions of animal cruelty from 'the freedom of speech' codified in the First Amendment") (emphasis omitted). . . .

Moreover, D.C.'s articulated basis for the registration requirement is that police officers, when approaching a house to execute a search or arrest warrant or take other investigative steps, will know whether the residents have guns. But that is at best a Swiss-cheese rationale because police officers obviously will assume the occupants might be armed regardless of what some central registration list might say. So this asserted rationale leaves far too many false negatives to satisfy strict or intermediate scrutiny with respect to burdens on a fundamental individual constitutional right.[19] . . .

In any event, the proper test to apply is *Heller's* history- and tradition-based test. Because most of the Nation has never required — and even now does not require — registration of all lawfully possessed firearms, D.C.'s strict registration law is not "longstanding" in the United States. After *Heller*, some licensing requirements remain permissible, and some record-keeping requirements on gun sellers remain permissible. But D.C.'s registration law violates the Second Amendment as construed by the Supreme Court.

* * *

This is a case where emotions run high on both sides of the policy issue because of the vital public safety interests at stake. As one who was born here, grew up in this community in the late 1960s, 1970s, and 1980s, and has lived and worked in this area almost all of his life, I am acutely aware of the gun, drug, and gang violence that has plagued all of us. As a citizen, I certainly share the goal of Police Chief Cathy Lanier to reduce and hopefully eliminate the senseless violence that has persisted for too long and harmed so many. And I greatly respect the motivation behind the D.C. gun laws at issue in this case. So my view on how to analyze the constitutional question here under the relevant Supreme Court precedents is not to say that I think certain gun registration laws or laws regulating semi-automatic guns are necessarily a bad idea as a matter of policy. If our job were to decree what we think is the best policy, I would carefully consider the issues through that different lens and might well look favorably upon certain regulations of this kind. But our task is to apply the Constitution and the precedents of the Supreme Court, regardless of whether the result is one we agree with as a matter of first principles or policy. *See Texas v. Johnson*, 491 U.S. 397, 420-21 (1989) (Kennedy, J., concurring) ("The hard fact is that sometimes we must make decisions we do not like. We make them because they are right, right in the sense that the law and the Constitution, as we see them, compel the result."). A lower-court judge has a special obligation, moreover, to strictly and faithfully follow the lead of the "one supreme Court" established by our Constitution, regardless of whether the judge agrees or disagrees with the precedent.

D.C. believes that its law will help it fight violent crime. Few government responsibilities are more significant. That said, the Supreme Court has long made clear that the Constitution disables the government from employing

---

19. Moreover, citizens may not be forced to register in order to exercise certain other constitutionally recognized fundamental rights, such as to publish a blog or have an abortion. . . . In concluding that D.C.'s handgun registration requirement might satisfy intermediate scrutiny, the majority opinion notes that the government may require registration for voting. . . . But those laws serve the significant government interest of preventing voter fraud. The majority opinion also cites car registration laws. . . . Of course, there is no enumerated constitutional right to own a car. Perhaps more to the point, those laws help prevent theft and assist recovery of stolen cars. No similar interest justifies gun registration laws.

Oddly, the majority opinion says that a registration requirement is permissible for handguns but might be impermissible for rifles or other long guns. *See id.* That approach gives potentially greater constitutional protection to long guns than to handguns even though *Heller* held that handguns warrant the highest constitutional protection.

certain means to prevent, deter, or detect violent crime. *See, e.g., Mapp v. Ohio,* 367 U.S. 643 (1961); *Miranda v. Arizona,* 384 U.S. 436 (1966); *City of Indianapolis v. Edmond,* 531 U.S. 32 (2000); *Crawford v. Washington,* 541 U.S. 36 (2004); *Kennedy v. Louisiana,* 554 U.S. 407 (2008); *District of Columbia v. Heller,* 554 U.S. 570 (2008). In the words of the Supreme Court, the courts must enforce those constitutional rights even when they have "controversial public safety implications." *McDonald v. City of Chicago,* 130 S. Ct. 3020, 3045 (2010) (controlling opinion of Alito, J.).

As I read the relevant Supreme Court precedents, the D.C. ban on semi-automatic rifles and the D.C. gun registration requirement are unconstitutional and may not be enforced. We should reverse the judgment of the District Court and remand for proceedings consistent with this opinion. I respectfully dissent.

NOTES & QUESTIONS

1. Consider the competing methodologies offered by the majority and the dissent for applying the right to arms as elaborated in *Heller* (Chapter 9) and *McDonald* (Chapter 9). Which approach is most faithful to the Supreme Court's decisions in those cases? Why?

2. The majority decision deploys a conventional form of intermediate scrutiny that also has been adopted by some other lower federal courts. Several other post-*Heller* decisions, including the *Ezell* decision, below, apply a similar standard for some aspects of the right, borrowing from First Amendment jurisprudence. On the other hand, the *Nordyke* case below analogizes the Second Amendment to abortion rights and accordingly applies a burden-based analysis. Judge Kavanaugh argues that embracing the familiar methodologies from these other areas of law is a mistake. He contends that the Supreme Court explicitly rejected the traditional system of strict and intermediate scrutiny, and instead provided a methodology based on history and tradition. Do you agree? Consider Judge Kavanaugh's invocation in footnote 5 of Chief Justice Roberts's statement at oral argument that traditional "tiered" constitutional scrutiny might not be appropriate for the Second Amendment. Is that sentiment reflected in the *Heller* opinion?

3. *Targeted gun bans and intermediate scrutiny.* Note that intermediate scrutiny has different sub-rules depending on which part of the Constitution is at issue. For example, time, place, and manner restrictions on speech protected by the First Amendment are subject to intermediate scrutiny, but Free Speech intermediate scrutiny requires more than just a substantial relationship to an important government interest (which is all that is required for Equal Protection intermediate scrutiny of discrimination based on sex or illegitimacy). First Amendment intermediate scrutiny also requires that the restriction leave "ample alternative channels" available for exercise of the right. *Ward v. Rock Against Racism,* 491 U.S. 781, 791 (1989). Assuming there are distinctive self-defense advantages to handguns, such as light weight and small size (and, of course, being usable with a single hand), could it be argued that a handgun ban fails to leave "ample alternative

channels" for bearing arms in self-defense? This might reconcile the outcome in *Heller* with intermediate scrutiny. What if particular plaintiffs were able to show that because of age, disability, or other factors, certain semiautomatic rifles were the best or only self-defense guns which they could use? For analysis of the particular self-defense benefits of semi-automatic long guns for some people, see David B. Kopel, *Rational Basis of "Assault Weapon" Prohibition*, 20 J. Contemp. L. 381 (1994). Would the state's concerns about the "offensive" capabilities of those guns outweigh those individual concerns and justify a ban?

4. Would a federal law banning all semi-automatic pistols (which comprise over two-thirds of handguns sold in a typical year), but allowing the sale and possession of revolvers, be constitutional or unconstitutional under *Heller*? What about a ban on the magazines that feed ammunition to semiautomatic pistols? If most pistol magazines typically hold at least 12 rounds, and magazines up to 19 rounds are standard for many handgun models, are laws that limit magazine capacity to 10 rounds permissible? What about laws that limit magazine capacity to 5 rounds? One round? How would the majority in *Heller II* make the decision? How would Judge Kavanaugh make the decision? How should courts decide what is a legitimate limitation on magazine capacity?

5. Judge Kavanaugh argues that his approach, rooted in tradition and history, is more predictable and objective than the balancing methodology adopted by the majority. Do you agree? Can you think of subjects for which history and tradition do not provide definitive guidance? What about regulation of firearms technology that has no clear traditional or historical analogue? Imagine, for example, a state law that prohibits sales of any new firearms except those that incorporate "smart gun" technology that (through a palm-print reader on the grip, or other user recognition protocol) attempt to prevent anyone except the authorized user from operating the firearm? How would Judge Kavanaugh evaluate a law that permitted possession of every traditional form of firearm (including semi-automatics) but only if they incorporated "smart gun" technology? For technical background on "smart guns," see Cynthia Leonardatos, David B. Kopel & Paul H. Blackman, *Smart Guns/Foolish Legislators: Finding the Right Public Safety Laws, and Avoiding the Wrong Ones*, 34 Conn. L. Rev. 157 (2001).

6. Evaluate Judge Kavanaugh's argument that the *Heller II* majority effectively adopts the very methodology that was advanced by Justice Breyer's dissent in *Heller* and explicitly rejected by the Supreme Court majority in that case. Do you agree? What, if any, differences can you discern between Justice Breyer's approach and the methodology applied by the majority in *Heller II*?

7. In enacting its post-*Heller* ban on semi-automatic rifles such as the AR-15, the D.C. City Council made a finding that stated that such rifles are "military-style weapons of war, made for offensive military use." However, in addition to being owned by private citizens in most American states today, such rifles are common police equipment, often carried in patrol cars. In fact, the District

of Columbia Metropolitan Police Department itself uses the Colt AR15A3 as its issued "patrol rifle," and did so at the time the ban challenged in *Heller II* was enacted. D.C. Metro. Police Dep't, General Order GO-RAR-901.01, at 3 (June 12, 2008). By the reasoning of the City Council, does this imply that the police department is waging war or engaged in "offensive military" action? Or does it imply something else? In general, consider whether courts should use information about police practices, or patterns of ownership by citizens in other jurisdictions, to evaluate legislative claims about the risks, utilities, and characteristics of particular kinds of weapons. Are standard police firearms, by definition, the type of firearms that are well suited for self-defense and defense of others by law-abiding persons? *See* David B. Kopel, *The Second Amendment in the Nineteenth Century,* 1998 BYU L. Rev. 1359, 1531-35 (nineteenth-century "civilized warfare" test for protected Second Amendment arms should be updated to protect the types of firearms typical for police duty).

8. Judge Kavanaugh argues that semi-automatic handguns impose far more costs than semi-automatic rifles. Given that there is no dispute that most gun crime is handgun crime, what is the strongest argument in favor of the District's ban on semi-automatic rifles? Does one have to conclude that *Heller* only protects handguns in order to uphold the District's rifle ban? Does it make a difference that the District's regulations ban some semi-automatic rifles but not others?

9. Consider Judge Kavanaugh's argument that the distinction between offensive and defensive weapons is illusory. Professor Johnson has called this phenomenon the "regulatory paradox" — observing that the same characteristics that make a firearm especially useful also make it dangerous, rendering the balance between the interest of the individual self-defender and the state a difficult call. *See* Nicholas J. Johnson, *Supply Restrictions at the Margins of* Heller *and the Abortion Analogue,* 60 Hastings L.J. 1285 (2009).

B.   The Aftermath of McDonald *in the City of Chicago: Historical Inquiry, Then Nearly Strict Scrutiny Toward the Core*

║ **Ezell v. City of Chicago**
║ **651 F.3d 684 (7th Cir. 2011)**

Sykes, Circuit Judge.

For nearly three decades, the City of Chicago had several ordinances in place "effectively banning handgun possession by almost all private citizens." *McDonald v. City of Chicago,* 130 S. Ct. 3020, 3026 (2010). In 2008 the Supreme Court struck down a similar District of Columbia law on an original-meaning interpretation of the Second Amendment. *District of Columbia v. Heller,* 554 U.S.

570, 635-36 (2008). *Heller* held that the Amendment secures an individual right to keep and bear arms, the core component of which is the right to possess operable firearms — handguns included — for self-defense, most notably in the home. *Id.* at 592-95, 599, 628-29.

Soon after the Court's decision in *Heller*, Chicago's handgun ban was challenged. *McDonald*, 130 S. Ct. at 3027. The foundational question in that litigation was whether the Second Amendment applies to the States and subsidiary local governments. The Supreme Court gave an affirmative answer: The Second Amendment applies to the States through the Due Process Clause of the Fourteenth Amendment. In the wake of *McDonald*, the Chicago City Council lifted the City's laws banning handgun possession and adopted the Responsible Gun Owners Ordinance in their place.

The plaintiffs here challenge the City Council's treatment of firing ranges. The Ordinance mandates one hour of range training as a prerequisite to lawful gun ownership, *see* Chi. Mun. Code §8-20-120, yet at the same time prohibits all firing ranges in the city, *see id.* §8-20-020. The plaintiffs contend that the Second Amendment protects the right to maintain proficiency in firearm use — including the right to practice marksmanship at a range — and the City's total ban on firing ranges is unconstitutional. They add that the Ordinance severely burdens the core Second Amendment right to possess firearms for self-defense because it conditions possession on range training but simultaneously forbids range training everywhere in the city. Finally, they mount a First Amendment challenge to the Ordinance on the theory that range training is protected expression. The plaintiffs asked for a preliminary injunction, but the district court denied this request.

We reverse. The court's decision turned on several legal errors. To be fair, the standards for evaluating Second Amendment claims are just emerging, and this type of litigation is quite new. Still, the judge's decision reflects misunderstandings about the nature of the plaintiffs' harm, the structure of this kind of constitutional claim, and the proper decision method for evaluating alleged infringements of Second Amendment rights. On the present record, the plaintiffs are entitled to a preliminary injunction against the firing-range ban. The harm to their Second Amendment rights cannot be remedied by damages, their challenge has a strong likelihood of success on the merits, and the City's claimed harm to the public interest is based entirely on speculation.

I. BACKGROUND

A. CHICAGO'S RESPONSIBLE GUN OWNERS ORDINANCE

The day after the Supreme Court decided *McDonald*, the Chicago City Council's Committee on Police and Fire held a hearing to explore possible legislative responses to the decision. A Chicago alderman asked the City's legal counsel what could be done about firearms possession and other gun-related activity in the city, including shooting ranges. The City's Corporation Counsel replied that the Council could "limit what we allow to operate in our city however is reasonable as decided by the City Council."

The Committee quickly convened hearings and took testimony about the problem of gun violence in Chicago. Witnesses included academic experts on the issue of gun violence in general; community organizers and gun-control advocates; and law-enforcement officers, including Jody Weis, then the Superintendent of the Chicago Police Department. Based on these hearings, the Committee made recommendations to the City Council about how it should regulate firearm possession and other firearm-related activity.

The Council immediately took up the Committee's recommendations and, just four days after *McDonald* was decided, repealed the City's laws banning handgun possession and unanimously adopted the Responsible Gun Owners Ordinance. *See Nat'l Rifle Ass'n of Am., Inc. v. City of Chicago, Ill.,* 2011 WL 2150785, at 1 (7th Cir. June 2, 2011). The new Ordinance—a sweeping array of firearm restrictions—took effect on July 12, 2010. To give a sense of its scope: The Ordinance prohibits handgun possession outside the home, Chi. Mun. Code §8-20-020, and the possession of long guns outside the home or the owner's fixed place of business, *id.* §8-20-030. It forbids the sale or other transfer of firearms except through inheritance or between peace officers. *Id.* §8-20-100. A person may have "no more than one firearm in his home assembled and operable." *Id.* §8-20-040. The Ordinance bans certain kinds of firearms, including assault weapons and "unsafe handgun[s]," as well as certain firearm accessories and types of ammunition. *Id.* §§8-20-060, 8-20-085, 8-20-170.

The Ordinance also contains an elaborate permitting regime. It prohibits the possession of any firearm without a Chicago Firearm Permit. Chi. Mun. Code §8-20-110(a). (Certain public-safety and private-security professionals are exempt.) In addition, all firearms must have a registration certificate, and to register a firearm, the owner must have a valid Permit. *Id.* at §8-20-140(a), (b). To apply for a Permit, a person must have an Illinois Firearm Owner's Identification Card. *Id.* §8-20-110(b)(2). Only those 21 years of age or older may apply for a Permit, except that a person between the ages of 18 and 20 may apply with the written consent of a parent or legal guardian if the parent or guardian is not prohibited from having a Permit or a Firearm Owner's Identification Card. *Id.* §8-20-110(b)(1). Persons convicted of certain crimes may not obtain a Permit. *Id.* §8-20-110(b)(3) (disqualifying persons convicted of any violent crime, a second or subsequent drunk-driving offense, or an offense relating to the unlawful use of a firearm). Other lawsuits challenging these and other provisions of the Ordinance are currently pending in the District Court for the Northern District of Illinois. *See, e.g., Second Amendment Arms v. City of Chicago,* No. 10 C 4257 (N.D. Ill. filed July 9, 2010); *Benson v. City of Chicago,* No. 10 C 4184 (N.D. Ill. filed July 6, 2010).

As relevant here, permits are conditioned upon completion of a certified firearm-safety course. Applicants must submit an affidavit signed by a state-certified firearm instructor attesting that the applicant has completed a certified firearm-safety and training course that provides at least four hours of classroom instruction and one hour of range training. Chi. Mun. Code §8-20-120(a)(7). At the same time, however, the Ordinance prohibits all "[s]hooting galleries, firearm ranges, or any other place where firearms are discharged." *Id.* §8-20-280. The Ordinance also prohibits the "discharge [of] any firearm within the city," making no exception for controlled shooting at a firing range — because, of course, firing ranges are banned throughout the city.[4] *Id.* §8-24-010.

Violations are punishable by a fine of $1,000 to $5,000 and incarceration for a term of "not less than 20 days nor more than 90 days," and "[e]ach day that such violation exists shall constitute a separate and distinct offense." Chi. Mun. Code §8-20-300(a), (b). The penalties go up for subsequent convictions. *Id.* §8-20-300(b). . . . The firing-range ban does not apply to governmental agencies. *Id.* §8-20-280. The federal government operates four indoor firing ranges in Chicago, and the Chicago Police Department operates five. Apparently, the City also exempts private security companies; there are two indoor firing ranges operated by private security companies in Chicago.

B. THE LITIGATION

The plaintiffs are three Chicago residents, Rhonda Ezell, William Hespen, and Joseph Brown; and three organizations, Action Target, Inc.; the Second Amendment Foundation, Inc.; and the Illinois State Rifle Association. Action Target designs, builds, and furnishes firing ranges throughout the United States and would like to do so in Chicago. The Second Amendment Foundation and the Illinois Rifle Association are nonprofit associations whose members are fire-arms enthusiasts; among other activities, these organizations advocate for Second Amendment rights and have made arrangements to try to bring a mobile firing range to Chicago.

The plaintiffs sought a temporary restraining order ("TRO"), a preliminary injunction, and a permanent injunction against the City's ban on firing ranges, and corresponding declaratory relief invalidating the ban. The district court twice denied a TRO, finding that the plaintiffs were not irreparably harmed. . . .

The City called two witnesses: Sergeant Daniel Bartoli, a former rangemas-ter for the Chicago Police Department, and Patricia Scudiero, Chicago's Zoning Commissioner. Bartoli testified that firing ranges can carry a risk of injury from unintentional discharge and raised concerns about criminals seeking to steal firearms from range users. He also explained the possible problem of contam-ination from lead residue left on range users' hands after shooting.

Scudiero testified that Chicago's zoning code prohibits all property uses not expressly permitted and contains no provision for gun ranges. If firing ranges were added as a permitted use, she said they should be classified as an "intensive use" under the Code. An "intensive use," she explained, is a use "that could pose a threat to the health, safety and welfare" of city residents and therefore may be located only in a manufacturing district; even then, intensive uses are allowed only by special-use permit, not presumptively. On cross-examination Scudiero admitted she has never been to a firing range. She acknowledged as well that the governmental firing ranges within the city are not limited to man-ufacturing districts; they are located near churches, schools, university

---

4. There are exceptions for discharging a firearm in self-defense or in defense of another, and also for game-bird hunting in certain limited areas of the city. *Id.* §8-24-010.

buildings, residential housing, a county courthouse, retail stores, and parks. She has not received any complaints from the public about these ranges.

The City introduced evidence that there are 14 firing ranges open to the public and located within 50 miles of its borders. Of these, seven are located within 25 miles of the city, and five are located within 5 miles of the city.

C. THE DECISION BELOW

Soon after the hearing, the district court issued a decision denying preliminary injunctive relief because the plaintiffs were neither irreparably harmed nor likely to succeed on the merits. The court's decision is a bit hard to follow; standing and merits inquiries are mixed in with the court's evaluation of irreparable harm. As we will explain, the court made several critical legal errors. To see how the decision got off-track requires that we identify its key holdings.

The judge began by "declin[ing] to adopt the intermediate scrutiny standard" of review, but held in the alternative that "even if" intermediate scrutiny applied, the "[p]laintiffs still fail to meet their burden of demonstrating irreparable harm." The judge said the organizational plaintiffs "do not have the necessary standing to demonstrate their irreparable harm" because "*Heller* and *McDonald* addressed an individual's right to possess a firearm" but "did not address an organization's right." Again, the court purported to enter an alternative holding: "Even if" the organizations had standing to assert a claim under *Heller* and *McDonald*, they "failed to present sufficient evidence . . . that their constituency has been unable to comply with the statute." The court held that none of the plaintiffs were suffering irreparable harm because the injury in question was limited to the minor cost and inconvenience of having to travel outside the city to obtain the range training necessary to qualify for a Permit and money damages would be sufficient to compensate the plaintiffs for this travel-related injury if they ultimately prevailed.

On the plaintiffs' likelihood of success on the merits, the judge was skeptical that the firing-range ban violated anyone's Second Amendment rights: "Suggesting that firing a weapon at a firing range is tantamount to possessing a weapon within one's residence for self-defense would be establishing law that has not yet been expanded to that breadth." If the Second Amendment was implicated at all, the judge characterized the claim as a minor dispute about an inconvenient permit requirement: "[T]he [c]ity's boundaries are merely artificial borders allegedly preventing an individual from obtaining a [firearm] permit. . . ." The court concluded that the City's evidence about "stray bullets," potential theft, and lead contamination was sufficient to show that "the safety of its citizens is at risk when compared to the minimal inconvenience of traveling outside of the [c]ity for a one-hour course."

Finally, the judge concluded that the balance of harms favored the City because the "potential harmful effects of firing ranges" outweighed any inconvenience the plaintiffs might experience from having to travel to ranges outside of Chicago. The court summarily rejected the plaintiffs' First Amendment claim, finding it underdeveloped. Alternatively, the court held that the range ban did not appear to implicate any expressive message.

The plaintiffs appealed.

II. Analysis

We review the court's legal conclusions de novo, its findings of fact for clear error, and its balancing of the injunction factors for an abuse of discretion.

The district court got off on the wrong foot by accepting the City's argument that its ban on firing ranges causes only minimal harm to the plaintiffs — nothing more than the minor expense and inconvenience of traveling to one of 14 firing ranges located within 50 miles of the city limits — and this harm can be adequately compensated by money damages. This characterization of the plaintiffs' injury fundamentally misunderstands the form of this claim and rests on the mistaken premise that range training does not implicate the Second Amendment *at all*, or at most only minimally. The City's confused approach to this case led the district court to make legal errors on several fronts: (1) the organizational plaintiffs' standing; (2) the nature of the plaintiffs' harm; (3) the scope of the Second Amendment right as recognized in *Heller* and applied to the States in *McDonald*; and (4) the structure and standards for judicial review of laws alleged to infringe Second Amendment rights.

A. STANDING

[The court noted that the City did not question the individual plaintiffs' standing.]

Regarding the organizational plaintiffs, however, the City's argument led the district court astray. The City emphasized that the Second Amendment protects an individual right, not an organizational one, and this point led the court to conclude that "the organizations do not have the necessary standing to demonstrate their irreparable harm." This was error. Action Target, as a supplier of firing-range facilities, is harmed by the firing-range ban and is also permitted to "act as [an] advocate of the rights of third parties who seek access to" its services. *See Craig v. Boren*, 429 U.S. 190, 195 (1976). . . . The Second Amendment Foundation and the Illinois Rifle Association have many members who reside in Chicago and easily meet the requirements for associational standing. . . .

The district court held in the alternative that the organizational plaintiffs "failed to present sufficient evidence to support their position that their constituency has been unable to comply with the statute." More specifically, the court held that the plaintiffs failed to produce "evidence of any one resident [of Chicago] who has been unable to travel to . . . a range [or] has been unable to obtain [the] range training" required for a Permit. It's not clear whether these observations were directed at standing or the merits of the motion for a preliminary injunction; this discussion appears in the court's evaluation of irreparable harm. Either way, the point is irrelevant. Nothing depends on this kind of evidence. The availability of range training outside the city neither defeats the organizational plaintiffs' standing nor has anything to do with merits of the claim. The question is not whether or how easily Chicago residents can comply with the range-training requirement by traveling outside the city; the plaintiffs are not seeking an injunction against the range-training requirement. The pertinent question is whether the Second Amendment prevents the City Council from banning firing ranges everywhere in the city; that ranges are present in neighboring jurisdictions has no bearing on this question.

B.   IRREPARABLE HARM AND ADEQUACY OF REMEDY AT LAW

The City's misplaced focus on the availability of firing ranges outside the city also infected the district court's evaluation of irreparable harm. The judge's primary reason for rejecting the plaintiffs' request for a preliminary injunction was that they had "failed to establish the irreparable harm they have suffered by requiring them to travel outside of the [c]ity's borders to obtain their firing[-] range permits." The judge thus framed the relevant harm as strictly limited to incidental travel burdens associated with satisfying the Ordinance's range-training requirement. The judge noted that for at least some — perhaps many — Chicago residents, complying with the range-training requirement did not appear to pose much of a hardship at all. She observed that it might actually be easier for some Chicagoans to travel to a firing range in the suburbs than to one located, say, at the opposite end of the city if ranges were permitted to locate within city limits. The judge thought it significant that none of the individual plaintiffs had "testif[ied] that s/he was unable to travel outside of the [c]ity's borders to obtain the one-hour range training and all three have shown that they are capable of doing so and have done so in the past." The court held that although the Ordinance may force the plaintiffs to travel longer distances to use a firing range, this was a "quantifiable expense that can be easily calculated as damages."

This reasoning assumes that the harm to a constitutional right is measured by the extent to which it can be exercised in another jurisdiction. That's a profoundly mistaken assumption. In the First Amendment context, the Supreme Court long ago made it clear that "'one is not to have the exercise of his liberty of expression in appropriate places abridged on the plea that it may be exercised in some other place.'" *Schad v. Borough of Mt. Ephraim*, 452 U.S. 61, 76-77 (1981). The same principle applies here. It's hard to imagine anyone suggesting that Chicago may prohibit the exercise of a free-speech or religious-liberty right within its borders on the rationale that those rights may be freely enjoyed in the suburbs. That sort of argument should be no less unimaginable in the Second Amendment context.

Focusing on individual travel harms was mistaken for another equally fundamental reason. The plaintiffs have challenged the firing-range ban on its face, not merely as applied in their particular circumstances. In a facial constitutional challenge, individual application facts do not matter. Once standing is established, the plaintiff's personal situation becomes irrelevant. It is enough that "[w]e have only the [statute] itself" and the "statement of basis and purpose that accompanied its promulgation." *Reno v. Flores*, 507 U.S. 292, 300-01 (1993); *see also* Nicholas Quinn Rosenkranz, *The Subjects of the Constitution*, 62 Stan. L. Rev. 1209, 1238 (2010) ("[F]acial challenges are to constitutional law what res ipsa loquitur is to facts — in a facial challenge, *lex ipsa loquitur*: the law speaks for itself."). . . .

Though she did not specifically mention it, the judge might have had the *Salerno* [*United States v. Salerno*, 481 U.S. 739 (1987)] principle in mind when she limited her focus to individual travel harms. Under *Salerno* a law is not facially unconstitutional unless it "is unconstitutional in all of its applications." *Wash. State Grange v. Wash. State Republican Party*, 552 U.S. 442, 449 (2008). Stated differently, "[a] person to whom a statute properly applies can't obtain relief based on arguments that a differently situated person might present." *United States v. Skoien*, 614 F.3d 638, 645 (7th Cir. 2010) (en banc) (citing *Salerno*, 481 U.S. at 745) [*infra*].

Here, the judge zeroed in on the occasional expense and inconvenience of having to travel to a firing range in the suburbs, but that's not the relevant constitutional harm. The plaintiffs contend that the Second Amendment protects the right to maintain proficiency in firearm use—including the right to train at a range—and the City's complete ban on range training violates this right. They also claim that the range ban impermissibly burdens the core Second Amendment right to possess firearms at home for protection because the Ordinance conditions lawful possession on range training but makes it impossible to satisfy this condition anywhere in the city. If they're right, then the range ban was unconstitutional when enacted and violates their Second Amendment rights every day it remains on the books. These are not application-specific harms calling for individual remedies.

In a facial challenge like this one, the claimed constitutional violation inheres in the terms of the statute, not its application. *See* Rosenkranz, *The Subjects of the Constitution*, 62 Stan. L. Rev. at 1229-38. The remedy is necessarily directed at the statute itself and *must* be injunctive and declaratory; a successful facial attack means the statute is wholly invalid and cannot be applied *to anyone*. Chicago's law, if unconstitutional, is unconstitutional *without regard* to its application—or *in all* its applications, as *Salerno* requires. That is, the City Council violated the Second Amendment when it made this law; its very existence stands as a fixed harm to every Chicagoan's Second Amendment right to maintain proficiency in firearm use by training at a range. This kind of constitutional harm is not measured by whether a particular person's gasoline or mass-transit bill is higher because he must travel to a firing range in the suburbs rather than one in the city, as the district court seemed to think.

Beyond this crucial point about the form of the claim, for some kinds of constitutional violations, irreparable harm is presumed. *See* 11A Charles Alan Wright et al., Federal Practice & Procedure §2948.1 (2d ed. 1995) ("When an alleged deprivation of a constitutional right is involved, most courts hold that no further showing of irreparable injury is necessary."). This is particularly true in First Amendment claims. *See, e.g.,* [*Christian Legal Soc'y v. Walker*, 453 F.3d 853, 867 (7th Cir. 2006)]. . . . The loss of a First Amendment right is frequently presumed to cause irreparable harm based on "the intangible nature of the benefits flowing from the exercise of those rights; and the fear that, if those rights are not jealously safeguarded, persons will be deterred, even if imperceptibly, from exercising those rights in the future." *Miles Christi Religious Order v. Twp. of Northville*, 629 F.3d 533, 548 (6th Cir. 2010). . . . The Second Amendment protects similarly intangible and unquantifiable interests. *Heller* held that the Amendment's central component is the right to possess firearms for protection. 554 U.S. at 592-95. Infringements of this right cannot be compensated by damages.

In short, for reasons related to the form of the claim and the substance of the Second Amendment right, the plaintiffs' harm is properly regarded as irreparable and having no adequate remedy at law.

C. LIKELIHOOD OF SUCCESS ON THE MERITS

Having rejected the plaintiffs' claim of irreparable harm, the district court only summarily addressed whether they were likely to succeed on the merits. Early on in her decision, the judge said she would not apply intermediate scrutiny to evaluate the constitutionality of the range ban — and by implication, rejected *any* form of heightened review. When she later returned to the merits, the judge suggested that banning range training might not implicate anyone's Second Amendment rights *at all*. She observed that although Chicago requires range training as a prerequisite to firearm possession, "the City does not have the ability to create a Constitutional right to that training." Instead, the judge thought the key question was "whether the individual's right to possess firearms within his residence expands to the right to train with that same firearm in a firing range located within the [c]ity's borders." This statement of the question ends the court's discussion of the merits.

There are several problems with this analysis. First, it is incomplete. The judge identified but did not evaluate the Second Amendment merits question. More importantly, the court framed the inquiry the wrong way. Finally, it was a mistake to reject heightened scrutiny. The judge was evidently concerned about the novelty of Second Amendment litigation and proceeded from a default position in favor of the City. The concern is understandable, but the default position cannot be reconciled with *Heller*.

1. *Heller, McDonald,* and a Framework for Second Amendment Litigation

It's true that Second Amendment litigation is new, and Chicago's ordinance is unlike any firearms law that has received appellate review since *Heller*. But that doesn't mean we are without a framework for how to proceed. The Supreme Court's approach to deciding *Heller* points in a general direction. Although the critical question in *Heller* — whether the Amendment secures an individual or collective right — was interpretive rather than doctrinal, the Court's decision method is instructive.

With little precedent to synthesize, *Heller* focused almost exclusively on the original public meaning of the Second Amendment, consulting the text and relevant historical materials to determine how the Amendment was understood at the time of ratification. This inquiry led the Court to conclude that the Second Amendment secures a pre-existing natural right to keep and bear arms; that the right is personal and not limited to militia service; and that the "central component of the right" is the right of armed self-defense, most notably in the home. *Heller*, 554 U.S. at 595, 599-600; *see also McDonald*, 130 S. Ct. at 3036-37, 3044. On this understanding the Court invalidated the District of Columbia's ban on handgun possession, as well as its requirement that all firearms in the home be kept inoperable. *Heller,* 554 U.S. at 629-35. The Court said these laws were uncon-stitutional "[u]nder any . . . standard of scrutiny" because "the inherent right of self-defense has been central to the Second Amendment right" and the District's restrictions "extend . . . to the home, where the need for defense of self, family, and property is most acute." *Id.* at 628-29. That was enough to decide the case. The Court resolved the Second Amendment challenge in *Heller* without specifying any doctrinal "test" for resolving future claims.

For our purposes, however, we know that *Heller*'s reference to "any standard of scrutiny" means any *heightened* standard of scrutiny; the Court specifically excluded rational-basis review. *Id.* at 628-29 & n.27 ("If all that was required to overcome the right to keep and bear arms was a rational basis, the Second Amendment would be redundant with the separate constitutional prohibitions on irrational laws, and would have no effect."); *see also Skoien,* 614 F.3d at 641 ("If a rational basis were enough [to justify a firearms law], the Second Amendment would not do anything . . . because a rational basis is essential for legislation in general."). Beyond that, the Court was not explicit about how Second Amend-ment challenges should be adjudicated now that the historic debate about the Amendment's status as an individual-rights guarantee has been settled. *Heller,* 554 U.S. at 635 ("[S]ince this case represents this Court's first in-depth exam-ination of the Second Amendment, one should not expect it to clarify the entire field. . . ."). Instead, the Court concluded that "whatever else [the Second Amendment] leaves to future evaluation, it surely elevates above all other inter-ests the right of law-abiding, responsible citizens to use arms in defense of hearth and home." *Id.*

And in a much-noted passage, the Court carved out some exceptions:

> [N]othing in our opinion should be taken to cast doubt on longstanding prohibi-tions on the possession of firearms by felons and the mentally ill, or laws forbidding the carrying of firearms in sensitive places such as schools and government build-ings, or laws imposing conditions and qualifications on the commercial sale of arms.

Id. at 626-27. The Court added that this list of "presumptively lawful regulatory measures" was illustrative, not exhaustive. *Id.* at 627 n.26; *see also McDonald,* 130 S. Ct. at 3047 (repeating *Heller*'s "assurances" about exceptions).

These now-familiar passages from *Heller* hold several key insights about judicial review of laws alleged to infringe Second Amendment rights. First, the threshold inquiry in some Second Amendment cases will be a "scope" question: Is the restricted activity protected by the Second Amendment in the first place? *See* Eugene Volokh, *Implementing the Right to Keep and Bear Arms for Self-Defense: An Analytical Framework and a Research Agenda,* 56 UCLA L. Rev. 1443, 1449. The answer requires a textual and historical inquiry into original meaning. *Heller,* 554 U.S. at 634-35 ("Constitutional rights are enshrined with the scope they were understood to have when the people adopted them, whether or not future legislatures or (yes) even future judges think that scope too broad."); *McDonald,* 130 S. Ct. at 3047 ("[T]he scope of the Second Amendment right" is determined by textual and historical inquiry, not interest-balancing.).

McDonald confirms that when state- or local-government action is challenged, the focus of the original-meaning inquiry is carried forward in time; the Second

Amendment's scope as a limitation on the States depends on how the right was understood when the Fourteenth Amendment was ratified. *See McDonald*, 130 S. Ct. at 3038-42. Setting aside the ongoing debate about which part of the Fourteenth Amendment does the work of incorporation, and how, *see id.* at 3030-31 (plurality opinion of Alito, J.); *id.* at 3058-80 (Thomas, J., concurring); *id.* at 3089-99 (Stevens, J., dissenting); *id.* at 3120-21 (Breyer, J., dissenting), this wider historical lens is required if we are to follow the Court's lead in resolving questions about the scope of the Second Amendment by consulting its original public meaning as both a starting point and an important constraint on the analysis. *See Heller*, 554 U.S. at 610-19; *McDonald*, 130 S. Ct. at 3038-42.

The Supreme Court's free-speech jurisprudence contains a parallel for this kind of threshold "scope" inquiry. The Court has long recognized that certain "well-defined and narrowly limited classes of speech" — e.g., obscenity, defamation, fraud, incitement — are categorically "outside the reach" of the First Amendment. *United States v. Stevens*, 130 S. Ct. 1577, 1584-85 (2010); *see also Brown v. Entm't Merchants Ass'n*, 2011 WL 2518809, at 3-4 (June 27, 2011). When the Court has "identified categories of speech as fully outside the protection of the First Amendment, it has not been on the basis of a simple cost-benefit analysis." *Stevens*, 130 S. Ct. at 1586. Instead, some categories of speech are unprotected as a matter of history and legal tradition. *Id.* So too with the Second Amendment. *Heller* suggests that some federal gun laws will survive Second Amendment challenge because they regulate activity falling outside the terms of the right as publicly understood when the Bill of Rights was ratified; *McDonald* confirms that if the claim concerns a state or local law, the "scope" question asks how the right was publicly understood when the Fourteenth Amendment was proposed and ratified. *Heller*, 554 U.S. at 625-28; *McDonald*, 130 S. Ct. at 3038-47. Accordingly, if the government can establish that a challenged firearms law regulates activity falling outside the scope of the Second Amendment right as it was understood at the relevant historical moment — 1791 or 1868 — then the analysis can stop there; the regulated activity is categorically unprotected, and the law is not subject to further Second Amendment review.

If the government cannot establish this — if the historical evidence is inconclusive or suggests that the regulated activity is *not* categorically unprotected — then there must be a second inquiry into the strength of the government's justification for restricting or regulating the exercise of Second Amendment rights. *Heller's* reference to "any . . . standard of scrutiny" suggests as much. 554 U.S. at 628-29. *McDonald* emphasized that the Second Amendment "limits[,] but by no means eliminates," governmental discretion to regulate activity falling within the scope of the right. 130 S. Ct. at 3046. . . . Deciding whether the government has transgressed the limits imposed by the Second Amendment — that is, whether it has "infringed" the right to keep and bear arms — requires the court to evaluate the regulatory means the government has chosen and the public-benefits end it seeks to achieve. Borrowing from the Court's First Amendment doctrine, the rigor of this judicial review will depend on how close the law comes to the core of the Second Amendment right and the severity of the law's burden on the right. *See generally*, Volokh, *Implementing the Right to Keep and Bear Arms for Self-Defense*, 56 UCLA L. Rev. at 1454-72 (explaining the scope, burden, and danger-reduction justifications for firearm regulations post-*Heller*); Nelson Lund, *The Second Amendment*, Heller, *and Originalist Jurisprudence*, 56 UCLA

L. Rev. 1343, 1372-75 (2009); Adam Winkler, Heller's *Catch-22*, 56 UCLA L. Rev. 1551, 1571-73 (2009); Lawrence B. Solum, District of Columbia v. Heller *and Originalism*, 103 Nw. U. L. Rev. 923, 979-80 (2009); Glenn H. Reynolds & Brannon P. Denning, Heller's *Future in the Lower Courts*, 102 Nw. U. L. Rev. 2035, 2042-44 (2008).

Both *Heller* and *McDonald* suggest that broadly prohibitory laws restricting the core Second Amendment right—like the handgun bans at issue in those cases, which prohibited handgun possession even in the home—are categorically unconstitutional. *Heller*, 554 U.S. at 628-35 ("We know of no other enumerated constitutional right whose core protection has been subjected to a freestanding 'interest-balancing' approach."); *McDonald*, 130 S. Ct. at 3047-48. For all other cases, however, we are left to choose an appropriate standard of review from among the heightened standards of scrutiny the Court applies to governmental actions alleged to infringe enumerated constitutional rights; the answer to the Second Amendment "infringement" question depends on the government's ability to satisfy whatever standard of means-end scrutiny is held to apply.

The approach outlined here does not undermine *Skoien*, 614 F.3d at 639-43, or *United States v. Williams*, 616 F.3d 685, 691-93 (7th Cir. 2010), both of which touched on the historical "scope" question before applying a form of intermediate scrutiny. And this general framework has been followed by the Third, Fourth, and Tenth Circuits in other Second Amendment cases.[12] *See United States v. Marzzarella*, 614 F.3d 85, 89 (3d Cir. 2010) ("As we read *Heller*, it suggests a two-pronged approach to Second Amendment challenges. First, we ask whether the challenged law imposes a burden on conduct falling within the scope of the Second Amendment's guarantee. . . . If it does not, our inquiry is complete. If it does, we evaluate the law under some form of means-end scrutiny."); *United States v. Chester*, 628 F.3d 673, 680 (4th Cir. 2010) (A "two-part approach to Second Amendment claims seems appropriate under *Heller*, as explained by . . . the now-vacated *Skoien* panel opinion . . . ."); *United States v. Reese*, 627 F.3d 792, 800-01 (10th Cir. 2010) (same). Each of these cases involved a Second Amendment challenge asserted as a defense to a federal prosecution under 18 U.S.C. §922, but we think the same principles apply here. *McDonald* reiterated that the Court has long since "abandoned 'the notion that the *Fourteenth Amendment* applies to the States only a watered-down, subjective version of

---

12. The Ninth Circuit recently adopted a somewhat different framework for Second Amendment claims. In *Nordyke v. King*, a divided panel announced a gatekeeping "substantial burden" test before the court will apply heightened scrutiny. 644 F.3d 716, 783-86 (9th Cir. 2011) (O'Scannlain, J.). Under this approach only laws that substantially burden Second Amendment rights will get some form of heightened judicial review. The *Nordyke* majority specifically deferred judgment on "what type of heightened scrutiny applies to laws that substantially burden Second Amendment rights." Judge Gould, concurring in *Nordyke*, would apply heightened scrutiny "only [to] arms regulations falling within the core purposes of the Second Amendment, that is, regulations aimed at restricting defense of the home, resistance of tyrannous government, and protection of country." All other firearms laws, he said, should be reviewed for reasonableness, although by this he meant the sort of reasonableness review that applies in the First Amendment context, not the deferential rational basis review that applies to all laws.

the individual guarantees of the Bill of Rights.'" 130 S. Ct. at 3035 (quoting *Malloy v. Hogan*, 378 U.S. 1, 10-11 (1964)).

2. Applying the Framework to Chicago's Firing-Range Ban

The plaintiffs challenge only the City's ban on firing ranges, so our first question is whether range training is categorically unprotected by the Second Amendment. *Heller* and *McDonald* suggest to the contrary. The Court emphasized in both cases that the "central component" of the Second Amendment is the right to keep and bear arms for defense of self, family, and home. *Heller*, 554 U.S. at 599; *McDonald*, 130 S. Ct. at 3048. The right to possess firearms for protection implies a corresponding right to acquire and maintain proficiency in their use; the core right wouldn't mean much without the training and practice that make it effective. Several passages in *Heller* support this understanding. Examining post-Civil War legal commentaries to confirm the founding-era "individual right" understanding of the Second Amendment, the Court quoted at length from the "massively popular 1868 Treatise on Constitutional Limitations" by judge and professor Thomas Cooley: "[T]o bear arms implies something more than the mere keeping; it implies the learning to handle and use them . . . ; it implies the right to meet for voluntary discipline in arms, observing in doing so the laws of public order." 554 U.S. at 616, 617-18 (internal quotation marks omitted); *see also id.* at 619 ("'No doubt, a citizen who keeps a gun or pistol under judicious precautions, practices in safe places the use of it, and in due time teaches his sons to do the same, exercises his individual right.'" (quoting Benjamin Vaughan Abbott, Judge and Jury: A Popular Explanation of the Leading Topics in the Law of the Land 333 (1880))).

Indeed, the City considers live firing-range training so critical to responsible firearm ownership that it mandates this training as a condition of lawful firearm possession. At the same time, however, the City insists in this litigation that range training is categorically outside the scope of the Second Amendment and may be completely prohibited. There is an obvious contradiction here, but we will set it aside for the moment and consider the City's support for its categorical position. The City points to a number of founding-era, antebellum, and Reconstruction state and local laws that limited the discharge of firearms in urban environments. As we have noted, the most relevant historical period for questions about the scope of the Second Amendment as applied to the States is the period leading up to and surrounding the ratification of the Fourteenth Amendment. That point aside, most of the statutes cited by the City are not specific to controlled target practice and, in any event, contained significant carveouts and exemptions.

For example, the City cites a 1790 Ohio statute that prohibited the discharge of a firearm before sunrise, after sunset, or within one-quarter of a mile from the nearest building. . . . This statute is not directly related to controlled target practice. A similar 1746 statute limiting the discharge of firearms in Boston provided an exception for target practice: City residents could "fir[e] at a Mark or Target for the Exercise of their Skill and Judgment . . . at the lower End of the Common" if they obtained permission from the "Field Officers of the Regiment in Boston"; they could also "fir[e] at a Mark from the Several Batteries in" Boston with permission from the "Captain General." . . .

The City cites other eighteenth- and nineteenth-century statutes regulating the discharge of firearms in cities, but most of these allowed citizens to obtain a permit or license to engage in firearms practice from the governor or city council. That was the case under the Philadelphia Act of August 26, 1721, §4, one of the very statutes the Supreme Court considered in *Heller* and deemed "a licensing regime." 554 U.S. at 633. In short, these laws were merely *regulatory* measures, distinguishable from the City's absolute *prohibition* on firing ranges. *See id.* at 632, 574 (founding-era statute that "restricted the firing of guns within the city limits to at least some degree" did not support the District of Columbia's "general prohibit[ion] on the possession of handguns"). These "time, place, and manner" regulations do not support the City's position that target practice is categorically unprotected.

To be sure, a few of the eighteenth- and nineteenth-century statutes cited by the City might accurately be described as general prohibitions on discharging firearms within cities. Three of these, however, had clear fire-suppression purposes and do not support the proposition that target practice at a safely sited and properly equipped firing range enjoys no Second Amendment protection whatsoever. Only two—a Baltimore statute from 1826 and an Ohio statute from 1831—flatly prohibited the discharge of firearms based on concerns unrelated to fire suppression, in contrast to the other regulatory laws we have mentioned. *Cf. Heller*, 554 U.S. at 632 ("[W]e would not stake our interpretation of the Second Amendment upon a single law . . . that contradicts the overwhelming weight of other evidence. . . ."). This falls far short of establishing that target practice is wholly outside the Second Amendment as it was understood when incorporated as a limitation on the States.

We proceed, then, to the second inquiry, which asks whether the City's restriction on range training survives Second Amendment scrutiny. As we have explained, this requires us to select an appropriate standard of review. Although the Supreme Court did not do so in either *Heller* or *McDonald*, the Court *did* make it clear that the deferential rational-basis standard is out, and with it the presumption of constitutionality. *Heller*, 554 U.S. at 628 n.27. . . . This necessarily means that the City bears the burden of justifying its action under *some* heightened standard of judicial review.

The district court specifically decided against an intermediate standard of scrutiny but did not settle on any other, then sided with the City "even if" intermediate scrutiny applied. A choice must be made. The City urges us to import the "undue burden" test from the Court's abortion cases, *see, e.g., Planned Parenthood of Se. Pa. v. Casey*, 505 U.S. 833, 876-79 (1992), but we decline the invitation. Both *Heller* and *McDonald* suggest that First Amendment analogues are more appropriate, *see Heller*, 554 U.S. at 582, 595, 635; *McDonald*, 130 S. Ct. at 3045, and on the strength of that suggestion, we and other circuits have already begun to adapt First Amendment doctrine to the Second Amendment context, *see Skoien*, 614 F.3d at 641; *id.* at 649 (Sykes, J., dissenting); *Chester*, 628 F.3d at 682; *Marzzarella*, 614 F.3d at 89 n.4; *see also* Volokh, *Implementing the Right to Keep and Bear Arms for Self-Defense*, 56 UCLA L. Rev. at 1449, 1452, 1454-55; Lund, *The Second Amendment*, Heller, *and Originalist Jurisprudence*, 56 UCLA L. Rev. at 1376; Winkler, Heller*'s Catch-22*, 56 UCLA L. Rev. at 1572.

In free-speech cases, the applicable standard of judicial review depends on the nature and degree of the governmental burden on the *First Amendment* right and sometimes also on the specific iteration of the right. For example, "[c]ontent-based regulations are presumptively invalid," *R.A.V. v. City of St. Paul*, 505 U.S. 377, 382 (1992), and thus get strict scrutiny, which means that the law must be narrowly tailored to serve a compelling governmental interest, *id.* at 395; . . . Likewise, "[l]aws that burden political speech are subject to strict scrutiny." *Citizens United v. Fed. Election Comm'n*, 130 S. Ct. 876, 898 (2010). . . . On the other hand, "time, place, and manner" regulations on speech need only be "reasonable" and "justified without reference to the content of the regulated speech." *Ward v. Rock Against Racism*, 491 U.S. 781, 791 (1989). The Supreme Court also uses a tiered standard of review in its speech-forum doctrine; regulations in a traditional public or designated public forum get strict scrutiny, while regulations in a nonpublic forum "must not discriminate on the basis of viewpoint and 'must be reasonable in light of the forum's purpose.'" *Choose Life Ill., Inc. v. White*, 547 F.3d 853, 864 (7th Cir. 2008) (quoting *Good News Club v. Milford Cent. Sch.*, 533 U.S. 98, 106-07 (2001)).

In election-law cases, regulations affecting the expressive association rights of voters, candidates, and parties are subject to a fluctuating standard of review that varies with the severity of the burden on the right; laws imposing severe burdens get strict scrutiny, while more modest regulatory measures need only be reasonable, politically neutral, and justified by an important governmental interest. *See Crawford v. Marion Cnty. Election Bd.*, 553 U.S. 181, 190-91 (2008). . . . "First Amendment challenges to disclosure requirements in the electoral context" — for example, laws compelling the disclosure of the names of petition signers — are reviewed "under what has been termed 'exacting scrutiny.'" *Doe v. Reed*, 130 S. Ct. 2811, 2818 (2010). This standard of review requires "a substantial relation between the disclosure requirement and a sufficiently important governmental interest," and "the strength of the governmental interest must reflect the seriousness of the actual burden on First Amendment rights." *Id.*

Similarly, restrictions imposed on adult bookstores are reviewed under an intermediate standard of scrutiny that requires the municipality to present "evidence that the restrictions actually have public benefits great enough to justify any curtailment of speech." *Annex Books, Inc. v. City of Indianapolis*, 581 F.3d 460, 462 (7th Cir. 2009) (citing *Los Angeles v. Alameda Books, Inc.*, 535 U.S. 425 (2002), and *Renton v. Playtime Theatres*, Inc., 475 U.S. 41 (1986)). And in commercial-speech cases, the Court applies an intermediate standard of review that accounts for the "subordinate position" that commercial speech occupies "in the scale of First Amendment values." *Bd. of Trs. of State Univ. of N.Y. v. Fox*, 492 U.S. 469, 477 (1989). In this context intermediate scrutiny requires "a fit between the legislature's ends and the means chosen to accomplish those ends, . . . a fit that is not necessarily perfect, but reasonable; that represents not necessarily the single best disposition but one whose scope is in proportion to the interest served." *Id.* at 480. . . .

Labels aside, we can distill this First Amendment doctrine and extrapolate a few general principles to the Second Amendment context. First, a severe burden on the core Second Amendment right of armed self-defense will require an extremely strong public-interest justification and a close fit between the government's means and its end. Second, laws restricting activity lying closer to the margins of the Second Amendment right, laws that merely regulate rather than restrict, and modest burdens on the right may be more easily justified. How much more easily depends on the relative severity of the burden and its proximity to the core of the right.

In *Skoien* we required a "form of strong showing" — a/k/a "intermediate scrutiny" — in a Second Amendment challenge to a prosecution under 18 U.S.C. §922(g)(9), which prohibits the possession of firearms by persons convicted of a domestic-violence misdemeanor. 614 F.3d at 641. We held that "logic and data" established a "substantial relation" between dispossessing domestic-violence misdemeanants and the important governmental goal of "preventing armed mayhem." *Id.* at 642. Intermediate scrutiny was appropriate in *Skoien* because the claim was not made by a "law-abiding, responsible citizen" as in *Heller*, 554 U.S. at 635; nor did the case involve the central self-defense component of the right, *Skoien*, 614 F.3d at 645.

Here, in contrast, the plaintiffs *are* the "law-abiding, responsible citizens" whose Second Amendment rights are entitled to full solicitude under *Heller*, and their claim comes much closer to implicating the core of the Second Amendment right. The City's firing-range ban is not merely regulatory; it *prohibits* the "law-abiding, responsible citizens" of Chicago from engaging in target practice in the controlled environment of a firing range. This is a serious encroachment on the right to maintain proficiency in firearm use, an important corollary to the meaningful exercise of the core right to possess firearms for self-defense. That the City conditions gun possession on range training is an additional reason to closely scrutinize the range ban. All this suggests that a more rigorous showing than that applied in *Skoien* should be required, if not quite "strict scrutiny." To be appropriately respectful of the individual rights at issue in this case, the City bears the burden of establishing a strong public-interest justification for its ban on range training: The City must establish a close fit between the range ban and the actual public interests it serves, and also that the public's interests are strong enough to justify so substantial an encumbrance on individual Second Amendment rights. Stated differently, the City must demonstrate that civilian target practice at a firing range creates such genuine and serious risks to public safety that prohibiting range training throughout the city is justified.

At this stage of the proceedings, the City has not come close to satisfying this standard. In the district court, the City presented no data or expert opinion to support the range ban, so we have no way to evaluate the seriousness of its claimed public-safety concerns. Indeed, on this record those concerns are entirely speculative and, in any event, can be addressed through sensible zoning and other appropriately tailored regulations. That much is apparent from the testimony of the City's own witnesses, particularly Sergeant Bartoli, who testified to several common-sense range safety measures that could be adopted short of a complete ban.

The City maintains that firing ranges create the risk of accidental death or injury and attract thieves wanting to steal firearms. But it produced no evidence to establish that these are realistic concerns, much less that they warrant a total prohibition on firing ranges. In the First Amendment context, the government must supply actual, reliable evidence to justify restricting protected expression based on secondary public-safety effects. *See Alameda Books, Inc.*, 535 U.S. at 438 (A municipality defending zoning restrictions on adult bookstores cannot "get away with shoddy data or reasoning. The municipality's evidence must fairly support the municipality's rationale for its ordinance."); *see also Annex Books,*

Inc. v. City of Indianapolis, 624 F.3d 368, 369 (7th Cir. 2010) (affirming preliminary injunction where a city's "empirical support for [an] ordinance [limiting the hours of operation of an adult bookstore] was too weak"); *New Albany DVD, LLC v. City of New Albany*, 581 F.3d 556, 560-61 (7th Cir. 2009) (affirming preliminary injunction where municipality offered only "anecdotal justifications" for adult zoning regulation and emphasizing the necessity of assessing the seriousness of the municipality's concerns about litter and theft).

By analogy here, the City produced no empirical evidence whatsoever and rested its entire defense of the range ban on speculation about accidents and theft. Much of the focus in the district court was on the possible hazards of mobile firing ranges. The City hypothesized that one cause of range-related injury could be stray bullets, but this seems highly implausible insofar as a properly equipped indoor firing range is concerned. The district court credited the plaintiffs' evidence that "mobile ranges are next to Sam's Clubs and residences and shopping malls and in parking lots, and there's not been any difficulties with them in those places." Commissioner Scudiero acknowledged that the law-enforcement and private-security firing ranges in Chicago are located near schools, churches, parks, and stores, and they operate safely in those locations. And Sergeant Bartoli testified about the availability of straightforward range-design measures that can effectively guard against accidental injury. He mentioned, for example, that ranges should be fenced and should designate appropriate locations for the loading and unloading of firearms. Other precautionary measures might include limiting the concentration of people and firearms in a range's facilities, the times when firearms can be loaded, and the types of ammunition allowed. *See also, e.g.,* NRA Range Source Book (providing "basic and advanced guidance to assist in the planning, design, construction and maintenance of shooting range facilities"), http://www.nrahq.org/shootingrange/sourcebook. asp (last visited June 2, 2011); Fla. Stat. §823.16(6) (2011) (referencing the safety standards of the NRA *Range Source Book*); Kan. Admin. Regs. §115-22-1(b) (2011) (same); Minn. Stat. §87A.02 (2010) (same); Neb. Rev. Stat. §37-1302(4) (2010) (same); Ohio Admin. Code 1501: 31-29-03(D) (2011) (same).

At the preliminary-injunction hearing, the City highlighted an additional public-safety concern also limited to mobile ranges: the risk of contamination from lead residue left on range users' hands after firing a gun. Sergeant Bartoli was asked a series of questions about the importance of hand-washing after shooting; he said that "lucrative amounts of [cold running] water and soap" were required to ensure that lead contaminants were removed. The City argued below that mobile firing ranges might not be sufficiently equipped for this purpose, suggesting that mobile ranges would have inadequate restroom facilities and might have to rely on "port-a-potties." This sparked a discussion about the adequacy of the water supply available at a standard "port-a-potty." The City continued on this topic until the judge cut it short by acknowledging her own familiarity with "port-a-potties." On appeal the City raised but did not dwell on its concern about lead contamination. For good reason: It cannot be taken seriously as a justification for banishing all firing ranges from the city. To raise it at all suggests pretext.

Perhaps the City can muster sufficient evidence to justify banning firing ranges everywhere in the city, though that seems quite unlikely. As the record comes to us at this stage of the proceedings, the firing-range ban is wholly out of proportion to the public interests the City claims it serves. Accordingly, the plaintiffs' Second Amendment claim has a strong likelihood of success on the merits.

D.   BALANCE OF HARMS

The remaining consideration for preliminary injunctive relief is the balance of harms. It should be clear from the foregoing discussion that the harms invoked by the City are entirely speculative and in any event may be addressed by more closely tailored regulatory measures. Properly regulated firing ranges open to the public should not pose significant threats to public health and safety. On the other side of the scale, the plaintiffs have established a strong likelihood that they are suffering violations of their Second Amendment rights every day the range ban is in effect. The balance of harms favors the plaintiffs.

The plaintiffs asked the district court to enjoin the enforcement of Chicago Municipal Code §8-20-280 — the prohibition on "[s]hooting galleries, firearm ranges, or any other place where firearms are discharged." They are entitled to a preliminary injunction to that effect. To be effective, however, the injunction must also prevent the City from enforcing other provisions of the Ordinance that operate indirectly to prohibit range training. The plaintiffs have identified several provisions of the Ordinance that implicate activities integral to range training: Chi. Mun. Code §§8-20-020 (prohibiting the possession of handguns outside the home), 8-20-030 (prohibiting the possession of long guns outside the home or business), 8-20-080 (prohibiting the possession of ammunition without a corresponding permit and registration certificate), 8-20-100 (prohibiting the transfer of firearms and ammunition except through inheritance), 8-24-010 (prohibiting the discharge of firearms except for self-defense, defense of another, or hunting). To the extent that these provisions prohibit law-abiding, responsible citizens from using a firing range in the city, the preliminary injunction should include them as well. Similarly, the injunction should prohibit the City from using its zoning code to exclude firing ranges from locating anywhere in the city.

Finally, because range training is required for the issuance of a Chicago Firearm Permit, a registration certificate, and ultimately, for lawful possession of any firearm, . . . the firing-range ban implicates not only the right to train at a range but also the core Second Amendment right to possess firearms for self-defense. Accordingly, the preliminary injunction should include sections 8-20-110(a) and 8-20-140(a) to the extent that those provisions operate to prohibit otherwise eligible persons from "carry[ing] or possess[ing] a firearm" at a range without a Permit or registration certificate while they are trying to complete the range-training prerequisite for lawful firearm possession.

Those are the bounds of the proposed preliminary injunction, which should be entered upon remand. The City worries that entering an order enjoining the range ban would allow "anyone [to] park a mobile range anywhere, anytime"; shoddy ranges operated by unlicensed instructors and lacking adequate hand-washing facilities could crop up in Chicago's most dangerous neighborhoods. To the contrary, a preliminary injunction against the range ban does not open the door to a parade of firing-range horribles. *Cf. McDonald*, 130 S. Ct. at 3047 ("Despite municipal respondents' doomsday proclamations, incorporation does not imperil every law regulating firearms."). The City may promulgate zoning and safety regulations governing the operation of ranges not inconsistent with the Second Amendment rights of its citizens; the plaintiffs may challenge those regulations, but not based on the terms of this injunction. As for the City's concern about a "regulatory vacuum" between the issuance of the preliminary injunction and the promulgation of firing-range zoning and safety regulations, we note that it faced a similar dilemma after the Supreme Court decided *McDonald*. The sky did not fall. The City Council moved with dispatch and enacted the Ordinance just four days later.

The plaintiffs have established their entitlement to a preliminary injunction based on their Second Amendment claim, so we need not address the alternative argument that range training is protected expression under the First Amendment. Given the strong likelihood of success on the former claim, the latter claim seems like surplusage.

For the foregoing reasons, we Reverse the district court's order denying the plaintiffs' motion for a preliminary injunction and Remand with instructions to enter a preliminary injunction consistent with this opinion.

NOTES & QUESTIONS

1. *A method for Second Amendment decision making.* One of the early criticisms of *Heller* was its refusal to formally announce a standard of review and methodology for resolving subsequent cases. The *Ezell* decision offers a detailed exposition of methodology and standard of review that the court claims to derive mainly from *Heller* (Chapter 9). Do you agree that the framework developed in *Ezell* is fairly derived from *Heller*? Why? Are there any elements of *Ezell* that you think are unsound extrapolations from *Heller*? Can you think of a Second Amendment dispute that will not fit within the methodological framework provided by *Ezell*?

2. Following the Supreme Court's decision in *Miller* (Chapter 7), lower courts interpreted the Second Amendment in a fashion that rejected any meaningful individual right to arms. The Supreme Court was silent on those interpretations for more than 70 years. Many took the Court's silence as acquiescence. Others suggested that those lower court decisions were erroneous interpretations of both the Constitution and of *Miller*. Is *Ezell* analogous to those post-*Miller* decisions or is it different? Why?

3. *The concurrence.* In a separate opinion concurring in the judgment in *Ezell*, Judge Ilana Diamond Rovner notes that the City of Chicago "thumbed a municipal nose at the Supreme Court" with a "too clever by half" ordinance that outlaws one of its own prerequisites for owning a gun. "The City may not condition gun ownership for self-defense in the home on a prerequisite that the City renders impossible to fulfill within the City limits." However, Judge Rovner disagrees with the majority's conclusion that an independent right to "live-range training is so closely allied to 'core' Second Amendment rights that a standard akin to strict scrutiny should be applied." A ban on live training, she argues, does not mean a ban on all training.

. . . There is no ban on training with a simulator and several realistic simulators are commercially available, complete with guns that mimic the recoil of firearms discharging live ammunition. *See e.g.* http://www.virtrasystems.com/law-enforcement-training/virtra-range-le (last visited July 6, 2011); http://www.meggitttrainingsystems.com/main.php?id = 25&name = LE_Virtual_Bluefire_Weapons (last visited June 24, 2011); http://www.ontargetfirearmstraining.com/ simulator.php (last visited July 6, 2011). It is possible that, with simulated training, technology will obviate the need for live-range training. . . .

. . . A right to maintain proficiency in firearms handling is not the same as the right to practice at a live gun range. As such, I cannot agree that "a more rigorous showing than that applied in *Skoien*, should be required, if not quite 'strict scrutiny.'" . . . *Skoien* required the government to demonstrate that the statute at issue served an "important government objective," and that there was a "substantial relationship" between the challenged legislation and that objective. . . .

. . . The majority's analysis of laws in effect during the time period surrounding the adoption of the Second and Fourteenth Amendments helps to prove the point that no scrutiny beyond that described in *Skoien* is necessary. The majority concedes that the City has presented us with "a number of founding-era, antebellum, and Reconstruction state and local laws that limited the discharge of firearms in urban environments."

Ezell, 651 F.3d 684, 712-13 (Rovner, J., concurring). As a practical matter, are any of Judge Rovner's hypothetical alternatives a satisfactory replacement for practicing live fire with one's own firearm? Connecticut requires that pistol-permit applicants take a training class that includes live fire before being issued a permit. State of Connecticut, Dept. of Pub. Safety, Special Licensing and Firearms, Connecticut State Pistol Permit, http://www.ct.gov/dps/cwp/view.asp?a=2158&q = 294502.

Do you agree with Judge Rovner or the majority? Is your conclusion based on originalism, living constitutionalism, or one of the other interpretive methodologies described in Chapter 9? Is it a combination of them? Do any of those labels fully account for your decision-making process?

4. Judge Rovner also complains that the majority under-credits the City's concern about gun range safety. "One need only perform a simple internet search on 'gun range accidents' to see the myriad ways that gun owners manage to shoot themselves and others while practicing in these supposedly safe environments. From dropping a loaded gun in a parking lot to losing control of a strong weapon on recoil, gun owners have caused considerable damage to themselves and others at live gun ranges. To say that the City's concerns for safety are 'entirely speculative' is unfounded." *Id.* at 714.

How would it affect Judge Rovner's analysis if the gun accident rate were higher in the home than at firing ranges? What about data showing that gun accidents account for far fewer accidental deaths and injuries than other common sources? The Centers for Disease Control report the following causes of accidental death for 2007 (the most recent year for which data is available): There were 46,844 transportation accidents in various types of vehicles, 29,846 accidental deaths from poisoning, 22,631 accidental deaths from falling, 3,443 accidental deaths from drowning, 3,286 accidental deaths from fire and smoke, and 613 deaths from accidental discharge of firearms. Center for Disease Control, National Vital Statistics Reports, Vol. 58, No. 19, May 20, 2010, page 44, table 12, *available at* http://www.cdc.gov/nchs/data/nvsr/nvsr58/nvsr58_19.pdf. There is no official compilation of data about accidental deaths at shooting ranges, but they appear to be quite rare.

5. *Scope and historical inquiry.* The *Ezell* decision instructs that when a law is "alleged to infringe Second Amendment rights," there is a two-step inquiry, beginning with the question "Is the restricted activity protected by the Second Amendment in the first place?)."

   To answer the first question, the court directs that we look to original meaning from both 1791 and 1868. In footnote 11, the court cites works it views as providing sound assessments of original public meaning:

   > On this aspect of originalist interpretive method as applied to the Second Amendment, see generally Akhil Reed Amar, The Bill of Rights: Creation and Reconstruction 215-30, 257-67 (1998); Brannon P. Denning & Glenn H. Reynolds, *Five Takes on* McDonald v. Chicago, 26 J.L & Pol. 273, 285-87 (2011); Josh Blackmun [sic, Blackman] & Ilya Shapiro, *Keeping Pandora's Box Sealed: Privileges or Immunities, The Constitution in 2020, and Properly Extending the Right to Keep and Bear Arms to the States*, 8 Geo. J.L. & Pub. Pol'y 1, 51-57 (2010); Clayton E. Cramer, Nicholas J. Johnson & George A. Mocsary, *"This Right Is Not Allowed by Governments That Are Afraid of the People": The Public Meaning of the Second Amendment When the Fourteenth Amendment Was Ratified*, 17 Geo. Mason L. Rev. 823, 824-25 (2010); Steven G. Calabresi & Sarah E. Agudo, *Individual Rights Under State Constitutions When the Fourteenth Amendment Was Ratified in 1868: What Rights Are Deeply Rooted in American History and Tradition?*, 87 Tex. L. Rev. 7, 11-17, 50-54 (2008); Randy E. Barnett, *Was the Right to Keep and Bear Arms Conditioned on Service in an Organized Militia?*, 83 Tex. L. Rev. 237, 266-70 (2004); David B. Kopel, *The Second Amendment in the Nineteenth Century*, 1998 BYU L. Rev. 1359; Stephen P. Halbrook, *Personal Security, Personal Liberty, and "The Constitutional Right to Bear Arms": Visions of the Framers of the Fourteenth Amendment*, 5 Seton Hall Const. L.J. 341 (1995).

6. *1791 versus 1868?* Judge Sykes concludes in *Ezell* that when courts apply the Second Amendment to state or municipal gun regulations, they should ask "how the right was understood when the Fourteenth Amendment was ratified" in 1868.

   Was the right to arms conceived in the same way in 1791 (on the heels of a successful war of revolution) as in 1868 (on the heels of a civil war and failed secession)? Was discussion of the right to arms in the context of the Fourteenth Amendment concerned more with enabling state militias to resist federal tyranny, or with individual self-defense? Is it possible that this balance changed between 1791 (when the Second Amendment was adopted as a limitation on federal power) and 1868 (our reference point for a right applicable to the states via the Fourteenth Amendment)? If so, Judge Sykes's approach might imply that the right to arms can mean different things when raised against the state versus the federal governments.

   But consider the Supreme Court's statements in *McDonald* that the Second Amendment standards that apply to the states are the same as those that apply to the federal government. *E.g., McDonald v. Chicago*, 130 S. Ct. 3020, 3026 (Chapter 9) (holding that "the Second Amendment right is fully applicable to the States"); *id.* at 3035 (approving of prior incorporation decisions that "decisively held that incorporated Bill of Rights protections are all to be enforced against the States under the Fourteenth Amendment according to the same standards that protect those personal rights against federal encroachment"). Do these statements preclude the possibility that the right to arms might mean different things depending on the government against which it is being enforced?

What practical differences might there be between the Second Amendment as it existed in 1791, and in 1868? *Heller* concluded that self-defense was the "core" of the Second Amendment right starting in 1791, and *McDonald* reached the same conclusion about the right in 1868. Was the militia valued in the same way during the two periods?

During the 1940s and 1950s, the Supreme Court sometimes applied a lesser version of a Bill of Rights protection to the states — for example, holding that states could not conduct unconscionable searches, but that the exclusionary rule of the Fourth Amendment did not apply in state courts. The Court abandoned that two-tiered approach in the 1960s. Today, only one part of the Bill of Rights applies in a lesser way to the states. The Sixth Amendment right to a jury trial requires a unanimous verdict by a criminal jury in federal court, but nonunanimous verdicts are allowed in state courts. *Apodaca v. Oregon*, 406 U.S. 404 (1972).

7. Why does *Ezell* hold that laws restricting the core, or near-core, of the Second Amendment get only "not quite strict scrutiny," rather than normal strict scrutiny — that is, "an extremely strong" state interest, rather than a "compelling one"; and "a close fit" rather than "narrowly tailored"? Is it plausible that the panel felt constrained by the Seventh Circuit's earlier *en banc* decision in *United States v. Skoien*, below? Can you think of a gun law that would pass "not quite strict scrutiny," yet would fail strict scrutiny?

8. *Ezell* clearly views the First Amendment as the best analogy for developing Second Amendment doctrine. Consider the arguments favoring this analogy. First Amendment law has been well developed by the Supreme Court in many decisions over the past eight decades. *See* Lucas A. Powe, Jr., *Guns, Words, and Constitutional Interpretation*, 38 Wm. & Mary L. Rev. 1311, 1397 (1997) (describing First Amendment free speech doctrine as "a mature area of the law" compared to the Second Amendment). Another possibility is that the First and Second Amendments are the only parts of the Bill of Rights that guarantee the right to engage in specific activities, as opposed to constraining government processes (criminal investigations and prosecutions, which comprise most of Amendments Four, Five, Six, and Eight and the civil jury trial guarantee in the Seventh Amendment). Yet another possibility is that both the First and Second Amendments seem to preserve very basic aspects of individual autonomy against government suppression. Finally, some might propose the more instrumental reason that judges and other elites tend to have a high regard for the First Amendment freedom of speech, compared to other provisions that might also be likened to the

Second Amendment—for example, the Fourth Amendment's protection against unreasonable search and seizure — or abortion rights, as analogized in *Nordyke v. King*, below.

Do you find the First Amendment a compelling analogy for developing the Second Amendment? What about the difference that individual rights protecting speech, religion, and public assemblies do not pose direct threats to human life?

9. Is it true, as *Ezell* suggests, that a constitutional right to do something necessarily implies the right to learn how to do so, to practice and gain proficiency? One legal maxim states, "When the law grants anything to anyone, all incidents are tacitly granted." (In the original, *Quando lex aliquid alicui concedit, omnia incidentia tacite conceduntur.*) Besides firing range practice, what are the other incidents of the right to arms? The 1871 Tennessee case *Andrews v. State*, 50 Tenn. (3 Heisk.) 165 (Chapter 6), provides a starting point.

C. An Alternative Methodology for Judging Second Amendment Claims: Substantial Burden

First Amendment jurisprudence is not the only possible analogy for developing a Second Amendment methodology. The following case offers an interesting alternative.

Nordyke v. King
644 F.3d 776 (9th Cir. 2011)

O'SCANNLAIN, CIRCUIT JUDGE:

We must decide whether the Second Amendment prohibits a local government from banning gun shows on its property.

I

A

Russell and Sallie Nordyke operate a business that promotes gun shows throughout California. A typical gun show involves the display and sale of thousands of firearms, generally ranging from pistols to rifles. Since 1991, the Nordykes have promoted numerous shows across the state, including one at the public fairgrounds in Alameda County. The Alameda gun shows routinely draw about 4,000 people. In the summer of 1999, the county passed an ordinance making it a misdemeanor to bring onto or to possess a firearm or ammunition on county property. *See* Alameda Code §9.12.120(b) ("the Ordinance"). The Ordinance does not mention gun shows.

The county asserts that it passed the Ordinance in response to a shooting that occurred the previous summer at the annual county fair. The Ordinance's text reflects this, finding that "gunshot fatalities are of epidemic proportions in Alameda County." *Id.* §9.12.120(a). The Nordykes, however, allege that the Ordinance's real purpose is to ban gun shows from county fairgrounds. To support this allegation, the Nordykes note that, shortly before proposing the Ordinance, the former county supervisor, Mary King, sent a memorandum to Richard Winnie, the county counsel, stating that King has "been trying to get rid of gun shows on County property" for "about three years," and asking Winnie to research "the most appropriate way that [King] might proceed." The memorandum also states that, in her efforts to ban gun shows, King has "gotten the run around" from "spineless people hiding behind the Constitution." At a subsequent press conference, the Nordykes assert, King again made clear that the purpose of the Ordinance was to outlaw gun shows on county property.[2]

Whatever the intent of the Ordinance, the Nordykes assert that its effect was to ban gun shows on county property. After the county passed the Ordinance, the manager of the fairgrounds asked the Nordykes to submit a written plan explaining how their next gun show would comply with the Ordinance. Although the Ordinance did not expressly prohibit gun shows or the sale of firearms, the Nordykes insisted then and maintain now that they cannot hold a gun show without guns. Rather than submitting a compliance plan, the Nordykes filed this suit.

B

[Here, the court describes the "long and tangled" procedural history of the case, which has generated four prior opinions, designated *Nordyke I* through *Nordyke IV.*]

II

Because the Supreme Court has yet to articulate a standard of review in Second Amendment cases, that task falls to the courts of appeals and the district courts. It has been suggested that only regulations which substantially burden the right to keep and to bear arms should receive heightened scrutiny. *See United States v. Masciandaro*, 638 F.3d 458, 469-70 (4th Cir. 2011); *United States v. Chester*, 628 F.3d 673, 680-83 (4th Cir. 2010); *United States v. Marzzarella*, 614 F.3d 85, 89 (3d Cir. 2010); *Heller v. District of Columbia*, 698 F. Supp. 2d 179,

---

2. At the press conference, King said that she "finds it ridiculous that the county is participating . . . in the distribution of guns" by hosting gun shows on the county fairgrounds. She found it "strange," that "a facility owned by the residents of this county" is used "to display guns for worship as deities for the collectors who treat them as icons of patriotism." She spoke of her past "efforts . . . to outlaw [gun] shows on county property," and implied that the Ordinance was the fruit of these efforts. King later referred to gun show supporters as "gun worshipers."

188 (D.D.C. 2010). Other courts would apply strict scrutiny to all gun-control regulations. *See United States v. Engstrum*, 609 F. Supp. 2d 1227, 1231-32 (D. Utah 2009).

A

The Supreme Court's reasoning in *Heller* and *McDonald* suggests that heightened scrutiny does not apply unless a regulation substantially burdens the right to keep and to bear arms for self-defense. In *Heller*, the Court distinguished the blanket handgun ban there at issue from apparently permissible gun-control regulations, by examining the extent to which each law burdened the core right to armed self-defense. The Court asserted that "the inherent right of self-defense has been central to the Second Amendment right. The handgun ban amounts to a prohibition of an entire class of arms that is overwhelmingly chosen by American society for that lawful purpose." *Heller*, 554 U.S. at 628. The *Heller* Court proceeded to review several reasons why "a citizen may prefer a handgun for home defense." *Id.* at 629. The Court concluded that, "whatever the reason, handguns are the most popular weapon chosen by Americans for self-defense in the home, and a complete prohibition of their use is invalid." *Id.* "Few laws in the history of our Nation have come close to the severe restriction of the District's handgun ban," the Court added. *Id. Heller* thus reasoned that, because handguns are extremely useful for self-defense, the District's complete handgun ban substantially burdened the core right to armed self-defense, and was therefore unconstitutional. . . . Likewise, *Heller* determined that the District's requirement that firearms in the home be kept inoperable made "it impossible for citizens to use [firearms] for the core lawful purpose of self-defense and is hence unconstitutional." *Id.* at 630. It was the handgun ban's heavy burden on effective self-defense that offended the Second Amendment.

The *Heller* Court contrasted the handgun ban's substantial burden on Second Amendment rights with eighteenth-century gunpowder storage laws, which required that excess gunpowder be kept in a special container or on the top floor of the home. The Court noted that "[n]othing about those fire-safety laws undermines our analysis" because "they do not remotely burden the right of self-defense as much as an absolute ban on handguns." *Id.* at 632. Similarly, in distinguishing the handgun ban from colonial laws that imposed minor fines for unauthorized discharge of weapons, the Court asserted that "[t]hose [colonial] laws provide no support for the severe restriction in the present case." *Id.* In so reasoning, the *Heller* Court again suggested a distinction between remote and severe burdens on the right to keep and to bear arms. . . .

Conversely, applying strict scrutiny to every gun-control regulation would be inconsistent with *Heller*'s reasoning. Under the strict scrutiny approach, a court would have to determine whether each challenged gun-control regulation is narrowly tailored to a compelling governmental interest (presumably, the interest in reducing gun crime). But *Heller* specifically renounced an approach that would base the constitutionality of gun-control regulations on judicial estimations of the extent to which each regulation is likely to reduce such crime.

Indeed, the *Heller* majority rejected Justice Breyer's proposed "interest-balancing" test that would ask "whether the statute burdens a protected interest . . . out of proportion to the statute's salutary effects upon other important governmental interests." *Id.* at 689-90 (Breyer, J., dissenting). The problem with Justice Breyer's test was not that it would require judges to determine the burden that gun-control regulations impose on the right to keep and to bear arms; indeed, as demonstrated above, the *Heller* majority engaged in just that analysis. Rather, the majority rejected such test because it would allow judges to constrict the scope of the Second Amendment in situations where they believe the right is too dangerous. . . . But applying strict scrutiny to every gun-control regulation would require courts routinely to make precisely those types of government interest assessments.

Just as important as what *Heller* said about a government-interest approach is what *Heller* did not say. Nowhere did it suggest that some regulations might be permissible based on the extent to which the regulation furthered the government's interest in preventing crime. Instead, *Heller* sorted such regulations based on the burden they imposed on the right to keep and to bear arms for self-defense.

B

We are satisfied that a substantial burden framework will prove to be far more judicially manageable than an approach that would reflexively apply strict scrutiny to all gun-control laws. As *McDonald* recognized, "assess[ing] the costs and benefits of firearms restrictions" requires "difficult empirical judgments in an area in which [judges] lack expertise." 130 S. Ct. at 3050. Indeed, whether a gun-control regulation serves the government's interest in safety is likely to be a difficult question to answer. *See* Heller, 554 U.S. at 702 (Breyer, J., dissenting) ("[E]mpirically based arguments . . . cannot prove either that handgun possession diminishes crime or that handgun bans are ineffective.") . . .

Applying strict scrutiny to every gun regulation would require courts to assess the effectiveness of a myriad of gun-control laws. Whenever a law is challenged under the Second Amendment, the government is likely to claim that the law serves its interest in reducing crime. . . . Because the Supreme Court has already held that "the Government's general interest in preventing crime" is "compelling," *United States v. Salerno*, 481 U.S. 739, 754 (1987), the question, under strict scrutiny, would be whether the regulation is narrowly tailored to that interest. But courts cannot determine whether a gun-control regulation is narrowly tailored to the prevention of crime without deciding whether the regulation is *likely to be effective* (or, at least, whether less burdensome regulations would be as effective). Sorting gun-control regulations based on their likely effectiveness is a task better fit for the legislature. . . .

By contrast, the substantial burden test, though hardly mechanical, will not produce nearly as many difficult empirical questions as strict scrutiny. *See Volokh, supra,* at 1459-60 (arguing that it is easier to determine whether a law substantially burdens the right to bear arms than to figure out whether a law "will reduce the danger of gun crime"). Indeed, courts make similar determinations in other constitutional contexts. *See, e.g., Planned Parenthood of Se. Pa. v. Casey,* 505 U.S. 833 (1992) (holding that pre-viability abortion regulations are unconstitutional if they impose an "undue burden" on a woman's right to terminate her pregnancy). . . .

c

In their supplemental briefs, the Nordykes and their amici argue that *McDonald* requires this Court to give strict scrutiny to the Ordinance. This is so, the briefs assert, because *McDonald* held that the right to keep and to bear arms is "fundamental." For support, the briefs point to a number of cases noting that laws burdening fundamental rights trigger strict scrutiny. . . .

But, the Supreme Court does not apply strict scrutiny to every law that regulates the exercise of a fundamental right, despite language in some cases suggesting the contrary. Instead, in a variety of contexts, the Court applies mere rational basis scrutiny to laws that regulate, but do not significantly burden, fundamental rights. . . .

For instance, even though the Supreme Court has recognized a constitutional right to obtain an abortion,[8] it has approved a number of regulations that had the "effect of increasing the cost or decreasing the availability" of abortions. *Id.* at 874. These regulations command mere rational basis review so long as they do not pose an "undue burden" on the right to abort a non-viable fetus. *See Gonzales v. Carhart,* 550 U.S. 124, 146 (2007). Similarly, "the government may impose reasonable restrictions on the time, place, or manner of protected speech," provided, inter alia, that the restrictions are not too cumbersome. *See Ward v. Rock Against Racism,* 491 U.S. 781, 791(1989).

And the Court has rejected the proposition that "a law that imposes any burden upon the right to vote [or to associate with others for political purposes] must be subject to strict scrutiny." *Burdick v. Takushi,* 504 U.S. 428, 432 (1992). Thus, rather than strictly scrutinizing every law which burdens these rights, the Supreme Court has held that "the rigorousness of our inquiry into the propriety of a state election law depends upon the extent to which a challenged regulation burdens First and Fourteenth Amendment rights." *Id.* at 434. Election laws trigger strict scrutiny only where the rights to vote and to associate "are subjected to 'severe' restrictions." *Id.* (internal quotation marks and citations omitted); *see also Wash. State Grange v. Wash. State Republican Party,* 552 U.S. 442, 451-52 (2008). Indeed, even though "the right to marry is of fundamental importance," regulations of that right do not trigger strict scrutiny unless they "significantly interfere with [its] exercise." *Zablocki v. Redhail,* 434 U.S. 374 (1978).

Accordingly, we hold that only regulations which substantially burden the right to keep and to bear arms trigger heightened scrutiny under the Second Amendment.

---

8. Admittedly, there is some dispute over whether the right to obtain an abortion still enjoys "fundamental" status. *See Lawrence v. Texas,* 539 U.S. 558, 589-95 (2003) (Scalia, J., dissenting) (arguing that *Roe*'s statement that abortion is a "fundamental right" has been undermined by subsequent cases holding that only rights that are "'deeply rooted in this Nation's history and tradition'" are "fundamental". . .).

III

Having determined the standard of review, the question becomes whether the Nordykes' Proposed Second Amended Complaint sufficiently alleged that the Ordinance substantially burdens their right to keep and to bear arms. The Nordykes only challenge the ordinance as an effective prohibition of gun shows on county fairgrounds. That is, they complain that they cannot display and sell guns on county property; they do not allege that they wish to carry guns on county property for the purpose of defending themselves while on that property. Thus, the proper inquiry is whether a ban on gun shows at the county fairgrounds substantially burdens the right to keep and to bear arms; not whether a county can ban all people from carrying firearms on all of its property for any purpose. . . .

A

Where, as here, government restricts the distribution of a constitutionally protected good or service, courts typically ask whether the restriction leaves open sufficient alternative avenues for obtaining the good or service. For instance, courts reviewing a restriction on the time, place, or manner of protected speech will ask whether the restriction "leave[s] open ample alternative channels for communication of the information." *Ward*, 491 U.S. at 791. Thus, the Supreme Court upheld an ordinance that prohibited "picketing before or about the residence . . . of any individual" because protestors were not barred from residential neighborhoods generally, but rather could "enter such neighborhoods, alone or in groups, even marching," go "door-to-door to proselytize their views," "distribute literature," and "contact residents by telephone." *Frisby v. Schultz*, 487 U.S. 474, 477, 483-84 (1988).

Likewise, the Supreme Court recently held that a ban on one particular method of performing an abortion did not constitute an "undue burden" on the right to an abortion in part because "[a]lternatives [were] available to the prohibited procedure." *Carhart*, 550 U.S. at 164; *see also id.* at 165 ("[T]he Act allows . . . a commonly used and generally accepted [abortion] method, so it does not construct a substantial obstacle to the abortion right.").

Following this lead, when deciding whether a restriction on gun sales substantially burdens Second Amendment rights, we should ask whether the restriction leaves law-abiding citizens with reasonable alternative means for obtaining firearms sufficient for self-defense purposes. *See United States v. Marzzarella*, 595 F. Supp. 2d 596, 606 (W.D. Pa. 2009) (suggesting that a ban on guns with obliterated serial numbers should be judged under a standard comparable to that "applicable to content-neutral time, place and manner restrictions," and upholding the ban partly because it leaves "open ample opportunity for law-abiding citizens to own and possess guns"), *aff'd*, 614 F.3d 85, 95 (3d Cir. 2010).

Similarly, a law does not substantially burden a constitutional right simply because it makes the right more expensive or more difficult to exercise. *See Carhart*, 550 U.S. at 157-58 ("'The fact that a law which serves a valid purpose, one not designed to strike at the right itself, has the incidental effect of making it more difficult or more expensive to procure an abortion cannot be enough to invalidate it.'" . . . ; *Zablocki*, 434 U.S. at 387 n.12 (noting that a law reducing the federal benefits of a couple by twenty dollars on account of their marriage did not "substantial[ly] . . . interfere with the freedom to marry," because it was unlikely to "significantly discourage" any marriage). Thus, regulations of gun sales do not substantially burden Second Amendment rights merely because they make it more difficult to obtain a gun. *Cf. Heller*, 554 U.S. at 626-27 ("[N]othing in our opinion should be taken to cast doubt on . . . laws imposing conditions and qualifications on the commercial sale of arms.").

Finally, a regulation is particularly unlikely to impose a substantial burden on a constitutional right where it simply declines to use government funds or property to facilitate the exercise of that right. For instance, the Supreme Court held that excluding even medically necessary abortions from Medicaid coverage did not constitute an "unduly burdensome interference with [a pregnant women's] freedom to decide whether to terminate her pregnancy." *Harris v. McRae*, 448 U.S. 297, 313(1980). Regulations that simply refuse to provide government subsidies to gun dealers, therefore, do not constitute a substantial burden on the right to keep and to bear arms.

B

Applying the foregoing considerations, we must determine whether the Proposed Second Amended Complaint alleged sufficient facts to suggest plausibly that the Ordinance substantially burdens the Nordykes' right to keep and to bear arms. It does not assert that the Ordinance makes it materially more difficult to obtain firearms. Nor does it allege a shortage of places to purchase guns in or near Alameda County. In any event, the Ordinance does not prohibit gun shows, but merely declines to host them on government premises. The Proposed Second Amended Complaint, therefore, does not allege sufficient facts to state a Second Amendment claim capable of surviving a motion to dismiss. . . .

IV

Judge Gould respectfully disagrees with the substantial burden framework that we adopt today. Instead, he would "subject to heightened scrutiny only arms regulations falling within the core purposes of the Second Amendment." . . . All other gun-control regulations would trigger only "reasonableness review." *Id.* Depending on how one reads Judge Gould's framework, we suggest that it is either equivalent to the approach we adopt today, or inconsistent with the Supreme Court's decisions in *Heller* and *McDonald*.

On one reading, Judge Gould's approach is roughly the same as our own. After all, it is not initially clear how determining whether a regulation "substantially burdens the right to keep and to bear arms" is different from determining whether the regulation "fall[s] within the core purposes of the Second Amendment." Both approaches would require a court to determine the extent to which a regulation interferes with the right to keep and to bear arms, and both would apply heightened scrutiny only to regulations whose interference with the right reaches a certain threshold.

Judge Gould seems to think his "core purposes" test does not require any such degree-of-burden analysis. For instance, he insists that "[l]aws banning handguns are constitutionally suspect not because they 'burden' the Second Amendment right, but because they proscribe the very activity that the Second Amendment protects — armed defense of the home." . . . But a handgun ban does not "proscribe" armed self-defense; it just makes it far more difficult. Thus, in *Heller*, the District of Columbia asserted that "it is permissible to ban the possession of handguns so long as the possession of other firearms (i.e., long guns) is allowed." 554 U.S. at 629. In order to reject this argument, the *Heller* majority had to establish that handguns are extremely useful for self-defense and, therefore, that the handgun ban seriously undermined the right to armed self-defense. *Id.* Given the infinite variety of conceivable gun-control regulations, we suspect that applying Judge Gould's test would require a similar degree-of-burden assessment in order to determine which regulations conflict with the "core purposes" of the Second Amendment and which do not.

Judge Gould's framework could also be read as applying mere rational basis scrutiny to every gun-control regulation that is not a complete ban on handguns. This reading is suggested by Judge Gould's statements that "*reasonableness* should be our guide in the Second Amendment context," . . . and that he "would be deferential to a legislature's reasonable regulations unless they specifically restrict defense of the home, resistance of tyrannous government, or protection of country." . . . But the Supreme Court has rejected an approach that would enforce the Second Amendment wholly, or primarily, through rational basis review. . . .

Appearing to defend this second reading of his approach, Judge Gould asserts that "[i]n the First Amendment context, we do not hold time, place, and manner speech restrictions to be constitutionally suspect when they substantially burden speech." . . . But, even content-neutral time, place, and manner restrictions are suspect if they fail to "leave open ample alternative channels for communication." *Ward*, 491 U.S. at 791. That is just another way of saying that such regulations cannot be too "restrictive," *id.* at 802, or, too burdensome. Accordingly, the Court has struck down content-neutral, time, place, and manner restrictions that are so broad as to burden substantially one's freedom of speech. . . .

Drawing from these cases, we have directed lower courts, when deciding whether a restriction on gun sales substantially burdens Second Amendment rights, to ask whether the restriction leaves law-abiding citizens with reasonable alternative means for obtaining firearms sufficient for self-defense purposes. *See supra* Part III.A. By contrast, Judge Gould would apparently apply rational basis review to every gun sales regulation, even if it made guns nearly impossible to obtain. This is alarming since almost every gun-control regulation — even those amounting to de facto gun bans — is rationally related to the government's legitimate interest in reducing gun crime. . . . The Supreme Court was not exaggerating when it insisted that a Second Amendment backed only by rational basis review would have "no effect." *Heller*, 554 U.S. at 629 n.27.

Finally, Judge Gould asserts that there is a difference between "rational basis review" and "reasonableness review," in that the latter "'focuses on the balance of the interests at stake, rather than merely on whether any conceivable rationale exists.'" ... This interest-balancing test sounds exactly like Justice Breyer's "interest-balancing" test that would ask "whether the statute burdens a protected interest ... out of proportion to the statute's salutary effects upon other important governmental interests." *Heller*, 554 U.S. at 689-90 (Breyer, J., dissenting). We believe the Supreme Court has rejected such an approach in no uncertain terms. ...

V

[Here, the Ninth Circuit panel addresses the Nordykes' appeal from the district court's grant of summary judgment on their First Amendment claim. The County conceded that the gun show is expressive conduct. However, the Ninth Circuit refuses to apply strict scrutiny, rejecting the plaintiffs' claim that the intended purpose of the county ordinance was to prevent members of the "gun culture" from expressing their views about firearms and the Second Amendment. The panel concludes that the statute survives the First Amendment intermediate scrutiny standard set forth in *United States v. O'Brien*, 391 U.S. 367, 377 (1968).]

VI

The Nordykes' final claim alleges a violation of the Equal Protection Clause. This claim revolves around their suspicion that the exception in the Ordinance for certain artistic events, Alameda Code §9.12.120(f)(4), was designed to favor military reenactors over gun show participants, an alleged favoritism resting on the County's disdain for the "gun culture."

Where, as here, an ordinance does not "purposefully operate to the detriment of a suspect class, the only requirement of equal protection is that [the ordinance] be rationally related to a legitimate governmental interest." *Harris*, 448 U.S. at 326. ... Here, the burdened class — be it "gun-owners," or "gun-show promoters and participants" — is not suspect. *See Olympic Arms v. Buckles*, 301 F.3d 384, 388-89 (6th Cir. 2002). And, although the right to keep and to bear arms for self-defense is a fundamental right, *McDonald*, 130 S. Ct. at 3036-43, that right is more appropriately analyzed under the Second Amendment. *Cf. Albright v. Oliver*, 510 U.S. 266, 273 (1994) ("Where a particular Amendment 'provides an explicit textual source of constitutional protection' against a particular sort of government behavior, 'that Amendment, not the more generalized notion of substantive due process, must be the guide for analyzing these claims.'"). ...

Therefore, the Nordykes' equal protection claim will fail so long as the Ordinance's distinction between military reenactments and gun shows is rational. *See Romer*, 517 U.S. at 631. The County could reasonably conclude that gun shows are more dangerous than military reenactments. This is enough to satisfy rational basis scrutiny. *See Williamson v. Lee Optical*, 348 U.S. 483, 489 (1955) ("Evils in the same field may be of different dimensions and proportions, requiring different remedies. Or so the legislature may think.") ...

VII

For the foregoing reasons, we AFFIRM the district court's grant of summary judgment to the County on the Nordykes' First Amendment and equal protection claims. Because the Nordykes may still be able to allege sufficient facts to state a Second Amendment claim, we VACATE the district court's denial of leave to amend the complaint to the extent that the denial was with prejudice, and REMAND for further proceedings.

NOTES & QUESTIONS

1. The *Nordyke* court deemed the standard applied in the Supreme Court's abortion rights cases to be apt for resolving Second Amendment claims. It applied a burden-based style of scrutiny to gun regulations, similar to that governing abortion cases. The *Ezell* court, on the other hand, felt that First Amendment jurisprudence is the proper analogy for Second Amendment scrutiny. Are the concerns raised by the right to arms more like the abortion question, or more like First Amendment questions?

    Is the right to abortion the more persuasive analogy in the sense that the right to arms and the right to abortion impair competing life interests? Put another way, is there a connection in that both rights are constitutional justifications to employ violence in certain circumstances? Is the risk to human life or life interests caused by the First Amendment comparatively more attenuated than in the firearms or abortion context? *See* Chapter 9, Exercise: Harm in the Speech Context.

2. The analogy between abortion and arms rights comports with early scholarly work grounding the right to abortion on the principle of self-defense. *See, e.g.*, Donald H. Regan, *Rewriting* Roe v. Wade, 77 Mich. L. Rev. 1569 (1979) (presenting abortion choice in the context of a spectrum of self-defense scenarios); Judith Jarvis Thomson, *A Defense of Abortion*, 1 Phil. & Pub Aff. 47 (1971) (using the self-defense analogy to support abortion choice as a matter of moral philosophy); *see also* Linda C. McClain, *Inviolability and Privacy: The Castle, the Sanctuary and the Body*, 7 Yale J.L. & Human. 195 (1995) (McClain presents a theory of inviolability aimed "to secure women's sexual autonomy, to achieve reproductive autonomy and to eliminate violence against women." She acknowledges that "[o]ne dimension of the idea of the home as castle is the right of a man or woman to protect the home and persons within it against intrusions or attack by using force.").

3. The abortion analogy in *Nordyke* permits broader comparison of two of the most politically divisive constitutional rights. Between the abortion right and the right to arms, which prompts the greater justification for state interference? Armed self-defense is generally permissible only against imminent threats of death, serious bodily harm, or a violent felony. A person typically forfeits some or all of his or her right to use force in self-defense if she provoked or otherwise helped to create a situation that required the use of force. Is the same true for abortion? Should it be? What is the comparative

responsibility of the mother and the armed self-defender for the problem that prompts the need to destroy a competing life/life interest? How does the duty (if any) of the mother to the fetus compare to the duty (if any) of the self-defender to her attacker? What other comparisons between the two rights can you discern? *See* Nicholas J. Johnson, *Principles and Passions: The Intersection of Abortion and Gun Rights*, 50 Rutgers L. Rev. 97 (1997).

4. How should we assess the burden that the gun and abortion rights impose on competing or collateral life interests? Is it possible to reach a consensus on which right imposes higher costs? Consider the following factors. Abortion does not threaten the life or health of innocent bystanders. In comparison, there are fewer than one thousand accidental firearms deaths annually. Center for Disease Control, National Vital Statistics Reports, *supra* (reporting 613 accidental firearms deaths in 2007). There are roughly 10,000 annual firearms homicides. (Of 14,180 murders in the United States in 2008, 9,484 were committed with firearms, and of those, at least 6,755 were committed with handguns.) Online Chapter 12 presents the social science arguments about what fraction of those homicides might be justifiable but there is broad agreement that the solid majority of the homicides are criminal. By way of comparison, over a million fetuses are destroyed by abortion each year. *See* Guttmacher Institute, Facts on Induced Abortion in the United States, http://www.guttmacher.org/pubs/fb_induced_abortion.html (May 2011). Abortion jurisprudence concludes that the fetus is not a full person, but is a life interest of some value. How does the life interest destroyed by more than one million abortions per year compare to roughly 10,000 gun homicides yearly? Does this comparison advance the issues provoked by the *Nordyke* decision?

5. Which is more constitutionally sound, the version of the right to arms articulated in *Heller* (Chapter 9), or the right to abortion? Or are they on equal footing? Is it relevant that the "right of the people to keep and bear arms" is expressly recognized in the text of the Constitution, while the abortion right is not?

6. The basic idea in *Nordyke*—that the constitutionality of regulations of the right to arms often depends on the degree of burden that they impose upon the conduct protected by the right—also has antecedents in state constitutional law, and these antecedents do not depend upon an analogy to abortion rights. A number of state courts take the view that regulations of the right to bear arms are generally constitutional if they do not "frustrate" the right, "frustrate or impair" its exercise, or similar terms. Regulations that *do* frustrate the right are normally unconstitutional. *See, e.g., State v. Hamdan,* 665 N.W.2d 785 (Wis. 2003) (holding that a law requiring handguns to be carried openly when worn in one's own place of business frustrated the right to bear arms for self-defense under the Wisconsin Constitution, and so was invalid); *City of Tuscon v. Rineer,* 971 P.2d 207 (Ariz. App. 1997) (prohibition on carrying handguns in city park "neither frustrates nor impairs" the right to bear arms); *State ex rel. City of Princeton v. Buckner,* 377 S.E.2d 139 (W. Va. 1988) (holding that discretionary carry permit system was invalid because

it threatened to frustrate the ability to carry a handgun for self-defense); *State v. Kessler*, 614 P.2d 94, 99 (Or. 1980) (observing that courts applying the individual right to bear arms have generally held that "a regulation is valid if the aim of public safety does not frustrate the guarantees of the state constitution"). Is the frustration rule a more, or less, manageable way of applying a burden-based form of scrutiny to Second Amendment claims than the "substantial burden" framework adopted in *Nordyke?* Or are they basically equivalent?

7. Compare the development of abortion rights and gun rights in terms of their foundation in the interpretive methodologies discussed in Chapter 9, Comment: Modes of Constitutional Interpretation.

    What would it take to conclude that the court is correct about the right to abortion but wrong about the right to arms? Does this view require a rejection of originalism and textualism as interpretive methodologies? Now consider the opposite view: that the recognition of the abortion right was wrong, but *Heller* was correctly decided. What would it imply about one's methodological preferences for interpreting the Constitution?

EXERCISE: PRESSING THE EDGES OF THE ABORTION ANALOGY

    How far does the abortion analogy deployed in *Nordyke* extend? What implications does it have for the continuing debate about the right to arms and the right to abortion?

    In 2000, Justice Stephen Breyer wrote the majority opinion in *Stenberg v. Carhart*, 530 U.S. 914 (2000), overturning as unconstitutional a state statute that banned an uncommon abortion procedure known to opponents as "partial-birth abortion," and to supporters and performing physicians as "dilation and extraction." Professor Johnson finds strong parallels between the analysis and issues raised by *Stenberg*, and laws banning semi-automatic "assault weapons." He stipulates that they are similarly aggressive renditions of the respective rights claims. Both are claims that the existence of a constitutional right sometimes implies a right to choose a particular *means* of exercising it. Johnson argues that neutral application of "Stenberg Standards" sustains a right to own an AR-15 more easily than a right to a partial-birth abortion. He posits that under some circumstances, for some people, guns labeled "assault weapons" by opponents might be the best civilian self-defense technology, much as *Stenberg* reasons that for some women, in some circumstances, a "partial-birth" procedure might be the best means of obtaining a safe abortion.

    Consider how the following "Stenberg Standards" for protecting controversial contested abortion methodologies operate in the right to arms context. For the following themes, replace abortion "methodology" with common firearms "technology" and think through the implications.

- *Alternative methodologies.* The *Stenberg* majority rejected the assertion that Nebraska adequately respected the right to abortion even though Nebraska still allowed safe alternative abortion procedures.

- *Never the best methodology.* The state could ban the disputed procedure only if it could show that it was never the best methodology for protecting the life or health of the mother.
- *Rarity of use and need.* "The state cannot prohibit [a useful methodology] simply by pointing out that most people do not need it."
- *Disputed utility.* "Unanimity of [expert] opinion" about the utility of the methodology is not required. Differences of expert opinion about the utility of the methodology will be resolved in favor of the mother in order to avoid "unnecessary risk of tragic health consequences."
- *Regulating the margin as an irrational distinction.* The challenged statute did not really further the state's asserted interest in protecting the fetus because it only affected a rare methodology and because abortion by other methods was still freely available, including in the final trimester. (The "partial-birth abortion" ban applied only to abortions in which the living fetus was partially removed from the womb before being killed; the ban did not affect abortions in which the fetus was dismembered in the womb before being removed.) Justice Stevens's short concurrence stated frankly that the statute was not rational because there was no reason to believe the banned methodology was any "more brutal, more gruesome or less respectful of 'potential life'" than permitted methodologies.

For an assessment of these and other issues, including the implications of the Supreme Court's later, and arguably less protective, treatment of late term abortion methods in *Gonzales v. Carhart*, 550 U.S. 124 (2007), see Nicholas J. Johnson, *Supply Restrictions at the Margins of* Heller *and the Abortion Analogue*, 60 Hastings L.J. 1285 (2009). For a treatment of the ways courts might treat the exercise's connected question of what satisfies *Heller*'s common use standard, see Nicholas J. Johnson, *The Second Amendment in the States and the Limits of the Common Use Standard*, 4 Harv. L. & Pol'y Rev., Online, Apr. 8, 2010, *available at* http://www.hpronline.com/2010/04/Johnson_commonuse/.

Continuing the abortion analogy, Judge J. Harvie Wilkinson argued that *Heller* is essentially a conservative version of *Roe v. Wade*. Judge Wilkinson's article is excerpted below.

J. Harvie Wilkinson, III, Of Guns, Abortions, and the Unraveling Rule of Law
95 Va. L. Rev. 253 (2009)

INTRODUCTION

Conservatives across the nation are celebrating. This past Term, in *District of Columbia v. Heller*, [554 U.S. 570 (Chapter 9),] the Supreme Court held for the first time in the nation's history that the Second Amendment protects an individual right, unrelated to military service, to keep and bear arms.

I am unable to join in the jubilation. *Heller* represents a triumph for conservative lawyers. But it also represents a failure — the Court's failure to adhere to a conservative judicial methodology in reaching its decision. . . .

In this Article, I compare *Heller* to another Supreme Court opinion, *Roe v. Wade*[, 410 U.S. 113 (1973)]. . . . In a number of important ways, the *Roe* and *Heller* Courts are guilty of the same sins.

Both decisions share four major shortcomings: an absence of a commitment to textualism; a willingness to embark on a complex endeavor that will require fine-tuning over many years of litigation; a failure to respect legislative judgments; and a rejection of the principles of federalism. . . .

. . . Law's power to shape human conduct depends on its perceived legitimacy as much as on the threat of force that stands behind its commands. Law is seen as legitimate only if it lays down rules applicable to all, rules that are enforced day-in and day-out, in good times and bad, for conservative and liberal ends, for policies the Justices like and for those they do not. *Roe* and *Heller* do not meet this basic requirement. Each decision discarded the tenets of restraint that alone make the application of neutral principles possible, and *Heller* found the Justices in both camps at odds with positions they had earlier and passionately espoused.

. . . While *Heller* can be hailed as a triumph of originalism, it can just as easily be seen as the opposite — an expose of original intent as a theory no less subject to judicial subjectivity and endless argumentation as any other. *Roe*'s flaw was not just that it was anti-originalist, but that it was inimical to the values of textualism, self-restraint, separation of powers, and federalism as well. . . .

Heller has swept away these counsels of caution. It has left only originalism as the foundation of conservative jurisprudence. A set of reasonable tenets, each providing a separate check on judicial activism, has now been replaced by a singular focus on original understanding. Whereas once legal conservatism demanded that judges justify decisions by reference to a number of restraining principles, *Heller* requires that they only make originalist arguments supporting their preferred view. Yet originalism cannot bear the weight that the *Heller* majority would place upon it. Originalism, though important, is not determinate enough to constrain judges' discretion to decide cases based on outcomes they prefer. . . .

It is astonishing that two decisions supported by such different majorities would share so many of the same infirmities. Part I critiques *Roe* and *Heller* for recognizing a substantive right grounded in an ambiguous constitutional text. Part II argues that *Roe* did, and *Heller* will, lead the Court into a dense political thicket that it would do best to avoid. Part III discusses legislative and judicial competence, and argues that legislatures are better positioned to address the tough issues surrounding gun and abortion rights. Part IV contends that both *Heller* and *Roe* rejected the principles of federalism that conservatives ought to cherish. . . .

I. FASHIONING NOVEL SUBSTANTIVE RIGHTS

Roe and *Heller* share a significant flaw: both cases found judicially enforceable substantive rights only ambiguously rooted in the Constitution's text. I will first document some of the criticisms of *Roe* on this point. I will then show that these same criticisms can be made of the *Heller* decision.

A. *ROE*

In 1973, the Supreme Court in *Roe v. Wade* and *Doe v. Bolton*[, 410 U.S. 179 (1973),] held that a woman's right to end her pregnancy was a fundamental one under the Fourteenth Amendment's Due Process Clause. In doing so, the Court set forth a rigid set of constitutional rules restricting the state's regulation of abortion. . . .

Roe has been criticized because of the absence of any relationship between this newly-discovered right to abortion and the text or structure of the Constitution. While the Court declared a right to personal privacy as the basis of its decision, it is a long trek from the liberty protected by due process to a general right of privacy; a longer journey still from a general privacy right to a specific right to induce an abortion; and a longer distance still from a right to abort a fetus to the elaborate trimester framework set forth in the Court's decision. . . .

The creation of new substantive constitutional rights is one of the biggest steps the Supreme Court can take. Society is a defined balance between individual and community. When rights are enumerated, courts are empowered to strike the balance; when they are not enumerated, or only ambiguously so, the balance is set by democracy. . . .

Quite apart from the Fourteenth Amendment, there is a broader point to be made about the judiciary's creation of substantive rights not explicit, or at best ambiguously indicated, in the constitutional text. Inasmuch as Article III does not provide the judiciary with prescriptive authority in the manner that Article I, Section 8, for example, provides the Congress, it behooves the judiciary to be cautious in creating for itself new substantive — and hence prescriptive — power that the Constitution did not clearly envision. . . .

Remarkably, the criticism continues from all quarters and has not abated with the passage of time. The result in *Roe* remains without any rationale that its defenders could comfortably call home. Even defenders of *Roe* have admitted that the holding should have been reached on a different basis, though on what basis remains unclear. . . .

The stakes of this debate can hardly be overstated. It is no exaggeration to say that *Roe* gave rise to the modern conservative legal movement. The decision came to stand for the worst kind of judicial overreaching; a generation of conservative lawyers came of age in its shadow. Conservatism was all those things that *Roe* was not, the movement's virtues illumined by *Roe*'s vices. . . . So the challenge to conservatism was clearly to transcend the parties or interests or even the results involved, and to lead the way back to a rule of law whose distinct and separate nobility would discredit the stark forays into policy. . . .

B. *HELLER*

There is now a real risk that the Second Amendment will damage conservative judicial philosophy as much as the Due Process Clause damaged its liberal counterpart. . . .

It can, of course, be readily agreed that of the two decisions, *Roe* involved the more brazen assertion of judicial authority. *Heller* differs from *Roe* in important respects. Most strikingly, the text of the Constitution alludes to a right "to keep and bear arms," but it does not so much as mention a right to abortion. . . .

Second, the cases use history in markedly different ways. *Heller* made an extended inquiry into history to determine the "normal meaning" of the amendment as understood by people at the time it was written. In contrast, *Roe* did not look to history to interpret an ambiguous textual phrase. Nor did it look to history for a tradition of protection for abortion — no such history exists. Instead, the Court's discussion of history was mostly spent explaining away ancient, common law and statutory prohibitions on abortion to prove that this history did not preclude finding a constitutional right to abortion.

Next, *Heller* struck down a draconian law, one that completely banned handgun possession at home. That law was one of the strictest in the nation. In contrast, the *Roe* Court struck down Texas's prohibition on abortion and the much more moderate Georgia law that merely regulated abortion. The Court in *Roe* and *Doe* cut a wide swath through all sorts of state laws, while *Heller*, at least initially, cut down only the most extreme variety.

Finally, *Heller*'s actual holding is narrower than *Roe*'s. The rationale of its holding — that the Second Amendment embodies an individual right to bear arms — is sure to call many gun restrictions into question, but the application of that rationale, invalidating a statute forbidding handguns in the home for self-protection, is much narrower. *Roe*, in contrast, established from the start a detailed trimester framework. Unlike *Roe*, no page in *Heller* reads like a statute.

So *Heller* is not *Roe*. But to say that *Heller* was marginally more justified than *Roe* is not saying much. . . .

[D]espite a difference in the magnitude of judicial overreaching, the methodological similarities between *Roe* and *Heller* are large. Both cases interpreted ambiguous constitutional provisions and both claimed to find in them mandates that put to rest an extremely controversial issue of social policy, in the process overturning decisions by popularly elected officials. . . .

When a constitutional question is so close, when conventional interpretive methods do not begin to resolve the issue decisively, the tie for many reasons should go to the side of deference to democratic processes. . . . And the argumentative exchange, even under the guise of an originalist inquiry, came perilously close to recreating *Roe*'s fundamental misapprehension — namely that law is politics pursued by other means.

What is lacking in *Heller* is what was lacking in *Roe*: the sort of firm constitutional foundation from which to announce a novel substantive constitutional right. Consider the text of the Second Amendment. Does the Amendment's prefatory clause limit the scope of the right found in the operative clause, or merely explain its justification? . . .

Is "keep and bear arms" a construction that refers specifically to military uses, or does it mean the personal right to possess and carry firearms? . . . As to pre-enactment history, the two sides went at it again. Each, not surprisingly, found the history to support its own view of the text. . . .

The debate over post-enactment developments was every bit as lively. The majority cited post-enactment commentary on the Second Amendment, post-Civil War legislative history, as well as a number of nineteenth-century cases all suggesting that the Amendment established an individual right to bear arms unconnected to military service. But the very range of sources consulted by the majority carries with it the danger of selectivity, that is, picking and choosing from a vast array of materials those that appear to support the preferred result. . . .

What is a neutral observer left with? Each of the points on which the two sides take issue ends inconclusively. . . . In the face of such equivocal evidence, plausibly supporting both the majority and dissenting positions, the choice before the Court was a discretionary one. *Heller* was wrong because the majority exercised its discretion to assert judicial supremacy in a manner, I will argue, that will place the courts in the same position envisioned by the judicial supremacists in *Roe*. . . .

II. DESCENDING INTO THE POLITICAL THICKET

Heller is similar to *Roe* for another reason: both decisions placed courts in the middle of political thickets. By finding an individual right to bear arms in the Second Amendment, the Court called into question the whole complex maze of federal, state, and local gun control regulations. As courts get drawn farther into the gun control thicket, they will be forced, as they were by *Roe*, to decide contentious questions without clear constitutional guidance. . . .

The dangers of entering such a morass are exceeded only by the difficulties of extrication from it. Repudiating *Roe* at this late date would leave egg on lots of faces. No one breathlessly anticipates the renunciation of decisions and doctrines in which the Justices over time have become deeply invested. But continuing to fine-tune abortion law is not a happy prospect either. . . .

Just as in *Roe*, the Court in *Heller* is now facing a thicket of subsidiary issues that will thoroughly ensnare it if it applies anything but the most deferential standard of review. The Court has invited future challenges by not defining the scope of the right to bear arms, by not providing a standard of review for firearms regulation, and by creating a list of exceptions to the newfound personal Second Amendment right. . . .

The Court did provide some guidance to lower courts by addressing potential limits on the right to bear arms, but what those limits are and what rationale now justifies them remain open — and litigious — questions. . . .

The Court also recognized one important across-the-board limit on the right to bear arms: it only protects the types of weapons that are commonly used for "lawful purposes like self-defense" and allows the prohibition of "dangerous and unusual weapons." This limit was not at issue in *Heller* because it involved a handgun prohibition. The Court reasoned that handguns were clearly within the types of weapons covered by the Second Amendment because they are the "most popular weapon chosen by Americans for self-defense in the home."

Although the limits that the Court announced were not directly at issue in *Heller*, they were quickly tested in the courts — the "avalanche of Second Amendment claims" has already begun. . . .

The cases and motions filed almost immediately after *Heller* may seem to have clear answers. In some, plaintiffs challenged handgun prohibitions that were similar to those at issue in *Heller* and are likely to be struck down. In others, criminal defendants challenged gun control regulations that were explicitly listed as "presumptively lawful" in *Heller* and are likely to be upheld. But even simple cases foreshadow complicated questions. For example, if the Second Amendment only protects a right to bear arms for the purpose of self-defense, what type of proof suffices that someone sought the weapon for some other purpose? What classes of persons may be presumed to possess a weapon for other than self-defensive purposes and what classes of weapons may be presumed non self-protective? Can a municipality that wants strict gun control regulations simply ban the possession of weapons outside the home — for example, in the car? Does the right to bear arms protect the possession of weapons for purposes other than purely self-defense — for recreational pursuits, for the protection of property, or for the protection of others?

Similar issues are raised by the "presumptively lawful" regulations. . . . It is not as if the Justices in *Heller* were not warned. The problems the thicket presents — consuming judicial resources and forcing unending arbitrary decisions outside the realm of judicial competency — came to the forefront in the aftermath of *Roe* as courts got drawn into deciding complex abortion issues. . . .

III.   Ignoring the Legislature's Strengths

In addition to involving courts in complex inquiries best left to the political process, *Heller* and *Roe* are alike for a similar reason: the rights involved in both cases depend on judgments that legislatures are far better equipped than courts to make.

A.   *ROE*

Roe's problems began with how it read: more like a statute than a judicial opinion. In 1973, John Hart Ely called *Roe*'s detailed trimester framework a guideline "one generally associates with a commissioner's regulations." . . . Justice Rehnquist's verdict was succinct. *Roe* was, he said, "judicial legislation."

Later commentators have echoed this critique, noting several unfavorable consequences of *Roe*'s legislative character. First, by usurping the legislative role, the Court ignored the legislature's comparative expertise in assessing empirical claims and adjusting to changes in science and technology. Second, *Roe* shut down the political process by foreclosing legislative compromise and ignoring the lessons of community experience. Finally, the Court's legislative foray has had sociological and institutional effects — emboldening the pro-life movement and radicalizing public positions on abortion, while weakening the Court's legitimacy as an interpretative arbiter on sensitive cultural issues. . . .

Moreover, *Roe* shut down this process of legislative accommodation, polarizing the debate and making future compromise more difficult. . . .

B. *HELLER*

Justice Breyer's dissent in *Heller* sounds familiar. He criticized the majority for acting like a legislature. He noted that courts typically defer to legislatures' empirical judgments, and that legislatures are better than courts at analyzing facts. He acknowledged there is a right at stake, but finds that the D.C. regulation is reasonable. This sounds all too much like Justice Rehnquist in *Roe*, who would have upheld Texas's law as a reasonable regulation of the Fourteenth Amendment's due process right. . . .

1. Separation of Powers and Comparative Expertise

Both *Roe* and *Heller* turn on complicated facts. Under the Court's new *Heller* rule, whether a state regulation passes constitutional muster depends on whether that regulation interferes with the Second Amendment's right to bear arms. Therefore, *Heller* (like *Roe*) has given birth to a balancing test that will force courts into the "conscious weighing of competing factors" [*Roe*, 410 U.S. at 173-74 (Rehnquist, J., dissenting),] as they decide which state interests are sufficiently strong and which regulations unduly burden the new right.

Ironically, Justice Scalia deplores this sort of balancing. In *Heller*, he rebutted Justice Breyer's dissent by chiding that judges cannot balance away the core of an enumerated right. In the Second Amendment context, this core is the "lawful purpose of self-defense." But the Court's dicta on the likely constitutionality of commercial sale regulations and felon possession bans sure looks like balancing. . . . In this way, *Heller* reads like *Roe*, deciding issues not before the Court and making casual empirical assumptions to justify those decisions. . . .

2. Political Process and Compromise

Next, as with abortion, there is no political process problem when it comes to gun control — in fact, debate over guns has been quite vigorous. The National Rifle Association currently has over four million members, and advocacy groups for gun control, such as the Brady Campaign and the Coalition to Stop Gun Violence, are also strong. . . . This issue is clearly one that has engaged the electorate's attention, engendered intense feeling, and spawned muscular interest group participation. There is no reason to remove it from what is plainly a highly energized electorate and place it in the lap of the courts. . . .

Moreover, it is patently wrong to have an issue that will not only affect people's lives, but could literally cost them their lives, decided by courts that are not accountable to them. Some studies suggest that restrictions on handguns reduce violent crime, and that overturning these laws may lead to increased rates of murder and suicide. Absent the clearest sort of textual mandate, we should not entrust courts with such life and death decisions. As noted above, the sheer hubris of unelected and unaccountable judges taking over the legislative function on a sensitive political issue was at the core of conservative criticism of *Roe*. . . .

Finally, given that *Roe* and *Heller* employ such strikingly similar methodologies — relying on contested premises to create a new substantive right and to strike down a legislative act on a sensitive social issue — it is remarkable that no Justice in *Heller* even mentions *Roe*. . . .

IV. DISREGARDING FEDERALISM'S VIRTUES

The Court's impersonation of a legislature in *Heller* was not the decision's final similarity to *Roe*. Both *Roe* and *Heller* also demonstrated a lack of respect for the constitutional division of powers between the federal government and the states. By raising the controversy over guns to the constitutional level, *Heller* continued *Roe*'s troublesome course of arrogating to the Court the power to override laws at the core of the residual police powers the Framers plainly allocated to the states.

A. *ROE*

It is important to remember just how sharp the criticism of *Roe* on federalism grounds actually was. The federalism-based critiques took two basic forms. First, conservatives denounced *Roe* for uprooting traditional state authority over abortion regulations. And second, conservatives faulted *Roe* for improvising a nationwide set of rules for abortions and thus extinguishing the many salutary benefits inherent in our federal structure: adaptation of local policies to local preferences, assimilation of actual experience within the content of the law, the protection of individual liberty through mobility and competition between the states, and the fostering of compromise and unity on divisive policy issues by avoiding a single constitutional approach. . . .

1. Traditional State Authority

Roe drew sharp criticism — and charges of judicial activism — for overriding the traditional police power of the states. . . . [M]ost states had regulated abortions from the mid-nineteenth century onward. And until *Roe* was decided in 1973, the states' authority over abortion regulations remained plenary. . . .

2. The Federal Design . . .

One common critique was that *Roe* neglected an obvious benefit of the Framers' federal design: the states' ability to tailor their policies to local preferences and conditions, thereby tending to please more constituents than could be done with a single national rule. . . .

Roe also generated substantial criticism for ignoring a second "happy incident" of our federal system, recognized famously by Justice Brandeis: experimentation and innovation in the natural laboratories of the states. . . .

Critics went on to fault *Roe* for overlooking a third benefit of federalism with respect to abortion, namely the inherent protection of fundamental liberties within our federal structure . . . by allowing for mobility between the states, our federal system secures a second form of liberty — a democratic or common liberty. This democratic liberty is the familiar right of persons to live, to go to work, and to raise their families in communities that reflect their own deepest moral and personal views. . . .

Roe also was harshly criticized for neglecting a fourth and final benefit of federalism: the ability to achieve compromise, and even national unity, on a divisive issue like abortion. . . . [C]ompromise between stark policy choices can often occur more easily within a legislature than within a court. But federalism fosters a different sort of compromise as well, in which citizens of different states can effectively agree to disagree by achieving their own policy objectives within their own jurisdictions. *Roe* effectively obliterated this possibility. . . .

B. *HELLER*

Several members of the *Heller* majority have been among the most outspoken critics of *Roe*'s abandonment of federalist principles. Yet the *Heller* decision threatens to subvert federalism in precisely the same manner as *Roe*. The Court's nascent Second Amendment jurisprudence will inevitably upset the states' longstanding authority over gun regulations. *Heller*'s renunciation of federalist principles in the context of the Second Amendment is problematic for a number of reasons, not least of which is that gun regulations are so tied to regional preferences and local concerns. Constitutionalizing the issue of firearms regulation will erode the diversity that geography and demography would otherwise produce. And the extent of that erosion will be entirely up to the Court. By contrast, the interventions of the Rehnquist Court marginally curtailed the powers of Congress under the Commerce Clause and Section 5 of the Fourteenth Amendment, but those interventions had the virtue of simultaneously opening up options for the individual states. Put another way, the Rehnquist Court acted to protect the authority of one democratic institution from the overreaching of another. *Heller* cannot claim that advantage. Like *Roe*, *Heller* threatens to restrict both federal and state initiatives, thereby cementing the authority of the Court alone to decide the proper scope of gun restrictions throughout the country. . . .

1. Traditional State Authority

So the shadow is cast over the traditional authority of the states in the same manner that drew such heated criticism in *Roe*. *Heller* acknowledged that the regulation of firearms has historically fallen within the states' police power over public safety. . . .

2. The Federal Design

The Court's apparent willingness to constitutionalize the field of firearms also threatens to sacrifice — as in *Roe* — the many prospective benefits produced by different policies in different places under our federal structure. For one, *Heller* diminished the benefits of decentralized decision-making in adapting gun policies to local opinions and concerns. In particular, establishing a more

uniform national gun policy through the Second Amendment would be particularly improvident because gun regulations are so uniquely tied to the different
views and conditions among regions, individual states, and even smaller units of
government.

It should go without saying that preferences for gun regulations vary widely
among regions within the United States. . . . For example, only seven states currently ban assault weapons: California, Connecticut, Hawaii, Massachusetts,
Maryland, New Jersey, and New York. The regional distribution of those states
is readily apparent. And when the Brady Campaign to Prevent Gun Violence
recently ranked the states based on the overall restrictiveness of their firearm
regulations, the ten most restrictive states exhibited a similarly striking regional
concentration. . . .

The marked differences among gun regulations in individual states also
demonstrate the utility of allowing states to tailor their policies to local preferences. California, for instance, has enacted the following laws, among others:
bans on assault weapons, large capacity ammunition magazines, and fifty caliber
rifles; regulations of ammunition and non-powder guns; waiting periods for gun
purchases; a limit of one handgun purchase per person per month; regulations
of firearm dealers and gun shows; universal background checks for all firearm
transfers; licensing requirements for handguns; and locking device requirements. Montana and Arkansas, on the other hand, have enacted none of
those policies. And North Carolina, for example, operates somewhere in
between: it regulates ammunition, non-powder guns, and gun dealers, and it
also requires licenses for handguns, but it shares none of California's additional
restrictions.

Important distinctions also exist between policies at the statewide and local
levels, suggesting even further benefits of localized decision-making. For
example, no state bans all types of handguns. But some cities have enacted
complete handgun bans. . . . Similarly, nearly every state issues permits to
allow concealed carrying of weapons. But a number of cities . . . restrict concealed carrying much more strictly than their respective states. . . .

Heller also endangers, like *Roe* before it, another fundamental benefit of
federalism: experimentation and innovation in the natural laboratories of the
states. Experimentation among states and cities is critical to producing effective
gun regulations. . . . And state and local governments need the freedom to
improvise and innovate and, in particular, to adapt their solutions to the unique
circumstances in their own community. . . .

Heller threatens to curb this experimentation and its benefits. As with *Roe*,
innovation now faces almost certain litigation. . . . The *Heller* decision also
repeated *Roe*'s mistake of underestimating federalism's inherent capacity to
protect liberty. Like the Court's recognition of a fundamental right to abortion
in *Roe*, the Court's recognition of a robust Second Amendment individual right
appeared to presume that states and cities cannot adequately protect the liberty to keep and bear arms. But that presumption ignored the protection of
liberties in our federal system through diffusion of power, as well as mobility
and competition between the states. Residents of the District who were
unhappy with the handgun ban, for example, remain free to move to other
localities more protective of gun rights. To be sure, moving anywhere is no
small inconvenience, but staying put does not confer the right to have the law

comply with one's own preferences. Under the Court's rigid national rule, moreover, no one will be able to exercise the liberty to live in a city in which handguns are prohibited. . . .

Finally, the *Heller* decision abandoned a fourth benefit of our federal structure: the possibility of state-by-state compromise on the controversial issue of gun control and the fostering of national unity around the positive principle of federalism. Just as *Roe* made the abortion issue significantly more divisive by taking the possibility of its resolution away from the states, *Heller* elevated the review of gun regulations to the national level, "where it is infinitely more difficult to resolve." These efforts will serve only to make the debate over gun laws more intractable. . . .

It is disheartening that Justices who deplored decisions like *Roe* on federalism grounds ignore the constraints of federalism when the substantive terrain shifts to firearms. It is disheartening that the dissenting Justices in *Heller* decline to apply their federalism-based critiques across the board, even on issues like abortion. The shoe must be worn when it pinches as well as when it comforts. Uneven treatment denies dual sovereignty the respect it deserves and will fuel accusations of a policy-driven Court. . . .

NOTES & QUESTIONS

1. Judge Wilkinson's article raises a variety of powerful and provocative points. Nelson Lund and David B. Kopel offer a point-by-point response in *Unraveling Judicial Restraint: Guns, Abortion, and the Faux Conservatism of J. Harvie Wilkinson III*, 25 J.L. & Pol. 1 (2009).

D.   *The Presumptive Legitimacy of Disarming the Untrustworthy: Analogizing from* Heller

Heller II, supra, Ezell, supra, and *Nordyke* each dealt with restrictions that applied generally to everyone. However, not all gun laws function in this way. After *Heller* (Chapter 9), public defenders and other criminal defense lawyers soon raised Second Amendment challenges to the various categories of "prohibited persons" under the federal Gun Control Act. (See Chapter 8 for details on the federal bans on gun possession by certain categories of people.) *Heller* said that bans on gun possession by convicted felons were presumptively constitutional. But what about other categories of prohibited persons? The *Skoien* case below is one of the most prominent appellate cases on the subject. It prompted disagreement between judges on the United States Court of Appeals for the Seventh Circuit about the proper methodology for resolving Second Amendment disputes. Compared to *Ezell* and *Nordyke, Skoien* provides less general methodological guidance to future courts. Note that the dissenting opinion is written by the same Judge Diane Sykes who later penned the decision in *Ezell.* Chief Judge Frank Easterbrook, who writes for the *en banc* majority in *Skoien,* authored the earlier Seventh Circuit decision that the Supreme Court ultimately reversed in *McDonald v. Chicago* (Chapter 9).

United States v. Skoien
614 F.3d 638 (7th Cir. 2010) (en banc)

EASTERBROOK, CHIEF JUDGE.

Steven Skoien has two convictions for "misdemeanor crime[s] of domestic violence" and therefore is forbidden to carry firearms in or affecting interstate commerce. 18 U.S.C. §922(g)(9). Wisconsin informed Skoien about this rule; he signed an acknowledgment of the firearms disability. While he was on probation from the second of his domestic-violence convictions, he was found in possession of three firearms: a pistol, a rifle, and a shotgun. He pleaded guilty to violating §922(g)(9) by possessing the shotgun and was sentenced to two years' imprisonment. His conditional guilty plea, see Fed. R. Crim. P. 11(a)(2), reserves the right to contend that §922(g)(9) violates the Constitution's Second Amendment. We heard this appeal en banc to decide whether §922(g)(9) comports with that amendment, as interpreted in *District of Columbia v. Heller*, 128 S. Ct. 2783 (2008). The eleventh circuit has held that it does. *United States v. White*, 593 F.3d 1199, 1205-06 (11th Cir. 2010). The fourth circuit has implied otherwise, though in a non-precedential order. *United States v. Chester*, 367 Fed. Appx. 392 (4th Cir. 2010).

Heller concludes that the Second Amendment "protects the right to keep and bear arms for the purpose of self-defense" and that a law "that banned the possession of handguns in the home" violates that right. *McDonald v. Chicago*, 130 S. Ct. 3020, 3021 (2010). The United States submits that, before considering how the amendment applies to shotguns and hunting (which is how Skoien contends he used that weapon), we must decide whether Congress is entitled to adopt categorical disqualifications such as §922(g)(9). The prosecutor relies on this passage from *Heller*:

> Like most rights, the right secured by the Second Amendment is not unlimited. . . . Although we do not undertake an exhaustive historical analysis today of the full scope of the Second Amendment, nothing in our opinion should be taken to cast doubt on longstanding prohibitions on the possession of firearms by felons and the mentally ill, or laws forbidding the carrying of firearms in sensitive places such as schools and government buildings, or laws imposing conditions and qualifications on the commercial sale of arms.

128 S. Ct. at 2816-17, reiterated by *McDonald*, at 3063 (plurality opinion). To this Skoien replies that his prior offenses were misdemeanors rather than felonies, and that §922(g)(9) is not a "longstanding" prohibition, having been enacted in 1996. See *United States v. Hayes*, 129 S. Ct. 1079 (2009) (discussing its genesis). The prosecutor rejoins by noting that the Court stated its holding this way:

> [W]e hold that the District's ban on handgun possession in the home violates the Second Amendment, as does its prohibition against rendering any lawful firearm in the home operable for the purpose of immediate self-defense. Assuming that

Heller is not disqualified from the exercise of Second Amendment rights, the District must permit him to register his handgun and must issue him a license to carry it in the home.

128 S. Ct. at 2821-22. The reference to being "disqualified" relates to prior convictions and mental illness. *Id.* at 2819. *Heller* also observes that the Second Amendment "elevates above all other interests the right of law-abiding, responsible citizens to use arms in defense of hearth and home." *Id.* at 2821. People convicted of domestic violence are neither law-abiding nor responsible, the prosecutor contends.

We do not think it profitable to parse these passages of *Heller* as if they contained an answer to the question whether §922(g)(9) is valid. They are precautionary language. Instead of resolving questions such as the one we must confront, the Justices have told us that the matters have been left open. The language we have quoted warns readers not to treat *Heller* as containing broader holdings than the Court set out to establish: that the Second Amendment creates individual rights, one of which is keeping operable handguns at home for self-defense. What other entitlements the Second Amendment creates, and what regulations legislatures may establish, were left open. The opinion is not a comprehensive code; it is just an explanation for the Court's disposition. Judicial opinions must not be confused with statutes, and general expressions must be read in light of the subject under consideration. See *Zenith Radio Corp. v. United States*, 437 U.S. 443, 462 (1978).

Although the passages we have quoted are not dispositive, they are informative. They tell us that statutory prohibitions on the possession of weapons by some persons are proper — and, importantly for current purposes, that the legislative role did not end in 1791. That *some* categorical limits are proper is part of the original meaning, leaving to the people's elected representatives the filling in of details. *Heller* identified, 128 S. Ct. at 2804, as a "highly influential" "precursor" to the Second Amendment the Address and Reasons of Dissent of the Minority of the Convention of the State of Pennsylvania to Their Constituents. . . . The report asserted that citizens have a personal right to bear arms "unless for crimes committed, or real danger of public injury." Many of the states, whose own constitutions entitled their citizens to be armed, did not extend this right to persons convicted of crime. See Stephen P. Halbrook, *The Founders' Second Amendment* 273 (2008) (concluding that this limitation was understood in the eighteenth century even when not stated expressly in the constitutional text); C. Kevin Marshall, *Why Can't Martha Stewart Have a Gun?*, 32 Harv. J.L. & Pub. Policy 695, 700-13 (2009) (surveying the history of state laws limiting convicts' entitlement to possess firearms). . . .

The first federal statute disqualifying felons from possessing firearms was not enacted until 1938; it also disqualified misdemeanants who had been convicted of violent offenses. Federal Firearms Act, c. 850, §2(f), 52 Stat. 1250, 1251. (Technically the crime was "receipt" of a gun that had crossed state lines; the statute treated possession as evidence of receipt.) A 1938 law may be "longstanding" from the perspective of 2008, when *Heller* was decided, but 1938 is 147 years after the states ratified the Second Amendment. The Federal Firearms Act covered only a few violent offenses; the ban on possession by *all* felons was not enacted until 1961. Pub. L. 87-342, 75 Stat. 757 (extending the disqualification to all persons convicted of any "crime punishable by imprisonment for a term exceeding one year," the current federal definition of a "felony"). In 1968 Congress changed the "receipt" element of the 1938 law to "possession," giving 18 U.S.C. §922(g)(1) its current form. If such a recent extension of the disqualification to non-violent felons (embezzlers and tax evaders, for example) is presumptively constitutional, as *Heller* said in note 26, it is difficult to condemn §922(g)(9), which like the 1938 Act is limited to violent crimes. It would be weird to say that §922(g)(9) is unconstitutional in 2010 but will become constitutional by 2043, when it will be as "longstanding" as §922(g)(1) was when the Court decided *Heller*. Moreover, legal limits on the possession of firearms by the mentally ill also are of 20th Century vintage; §922(g)(4), which forbids possession by a person "who has been adjudicated as a mental defective or who has been committed to a mental institution," was not enacted until 1968. Pub. L. 90-618, 82 Stat. 1213, 1220.

So although the Justices have not established that any particular statute is valid, we do take from *Heller* the message that exclusions need not mirror limits that were on the books in 1791. This is the sort of message that, whether or not technically dictum, a court of appeals must respect, given the Supreme Court's entitlement to speak through its opinions as well as through its technical holdings. See *United States v. Bloom*, 149 F.3d 649, 653 (7th Cir. 1998). This means that some categorical disqualifications are permissible: Congress is not limited to case-by-case exclusions of persons who have been shown to be untrustworthy with weapons, nor need these limits be established by evidence presented in court. *Heller* did not suggest that disqualifications would be effective only if the statute's benefits are first established by admissible evidence.

Categorical limits on the possession of firearms would not be a constitutional anomaly. Think of the First Amendment, which has long had categorical limits: obscenity, defamation, incitement to crime, and others. . . .

We do not mean that a categorical limit on the possession of firearms can be justified under the rational-basis test, which deems a law valid if any justification for it may be imagined. E.g., *Vance v. Bradley*, 440 U.S. 93 (1979). If a rational basis were enough, the Second Amendment would not do anything, see *Heller*, 128 S. Ct. at 2817-18 n.27 — because a rational basis is essential for legislation in general. The Court avoided deciding in *Stevens* how great the public interest must be to adopt a new categorical limit on speech — the United States had argued for treating depictions of extreme animal cruelty the same as child pornography — but stated that the showing must be strong. The United States concedes that some form of strong showing ("intermediate scrutiny," many opinions say) is essential, and that §922(g)(9) is valid only if substantially related to an important governmental objective. See *Buckley v. American Constitutional Law Foundation, Inc.*, 525 U.S. 182, 202-04 (1999) (using this formula for some First Amendment questions); *Heckler v. Mathews*, 465 U.S. 728, 744-51 (1984) (using this formula for statutes that affect marriage and child-bearing). The concession is prudent, and we need not get more deeply into the "levels of scrutiny" quagmire, for no one doubts that the goal of §922(g)(9), preventing armed mayhem, is an important governmental objective. Both logic and data establish a substantial relation between §922(g)(9) and this objective. . . .

A "misdemeanor crime of domestic violence" thus is one in which violence (actual or attempted) is an element of the offense; it is not enough if a risky act happens to cause injury. . . .

The belief underpinning §922(g)(9) is that people who have been convicted of violence once — toward a spouse, child, or domestic partner, no less — are likely to use violence again. That's the justification for keeping firearms out of their hands, for guns are about five times more deadly than knives, given that an attack with some kind of weapon has occurred. See Franklin E. Zimring, *Firearms, Violence, and the Potential Impact of Firearms Control*, 32 J.L. Med. & Ethics 34 (2004) (collecting studies).

Hayes, which we mentioned above, held that whether a crime is one of "domestic violence" depends on the identity of the victim rather than the elements of the offense. When describing why §922(g)(9) was enacted, the Court wrote (129 S. Ct. at 1087):

> Existing felon-in-possession laws, Congress recognized, were not keeping firearms out of the hands of domestic abusers, because "many people who engage in serious spousal or child abuse ultimately are not charged with or convicted of felonies." 142 Cong. Rec. 22985 (1996) (statement of Sen. Lautenberg). By extending the federal firearm prohibition to persons convicted of "misdemeanor crime[s] of domestic violence," proponents of §922(g)(9) sought to "close this dangerous loophole." . . .
>
> Construing §922(g)(9) to exclude the domestic abuser convicted under a generic use-of-force statute (one that does not designate a domestic relationship as an element of the offense) would frustrate Congress' manifest purpose. Firearms and domestic strife are a potentially deadly combination nationwide.

There are three propositions in this passage: first that domestic abusers often commit acts that would be charged as felonies if the victim were a stranger, but that are charged as misdemeanors because the victim is a relative (implying that the perpetrators are as dangerous as felons); second that firearms are deadly in domestic strife; and third that persons convicted of domestic violence are likely to offend again, so that keeping the most lethal weapon out of their hands is vital to the safety of their relatives. Data support all three of these propositions.

Start with prosecuting domestic violence as a misdemeanor when similar acts against a stranger would be a felony (a practice often called "undercharging"). Prosecutors face two major obstacles to obtaining felony convictions: some family members are willing to forgive the aggressors in order to restore harmonious relations, while others are so terrified that they doubt the ability of the police to protect their safety. Either way, victims of domestic violence are less willing to cooperate with prosecutors, who may need to reduce charges to obtain even limited cooperation and thus some convictions. See Eve S. Buzawa & Carl G. Buzawa, *Domestic Violence: The Criminal Justice Response* 177-89 (3d ed. 2002). Indeed, either forgiveness or fear induces many victims not to report the attack to begin with. The result is that many aggressors end up with no conviction, or a misdemeanor conviction, when similar violence against a stranger would produce a felony conviction. See, e.g., *Report of the Florida Supreme Court Gender Bias Study Commission*, reprinted in 42 Fla. L. Rev. 803, 859-60 (1990). . . .

That firearms cause injury or death in domestic situations also has been established. Domestic assaults with firearms are approximately twelve times more likely to end in the victim's death than are assaults by knives or fists. Linda E. Saltzman, James A. Mercy, Patrick W. O'Carroll, Mark L. Rosenberg & Philip H. Rhodes, *Weapon Involvement and Injury Outcomes in Family and Intimate Assaults*, 267 J. Am. Medical Ass'n 3043 (1992). Part of this effect stems from the fact that some would-be abusers go buy a gun, see Susan B. Sorenson & Douglas J. Wiebe, *Weapons in the Lives of Battered Women*, 94 Am. J. Pub. Health 1412 (2004), and much from the fact that guns are more lethal than knives and clubs once an attack begins. See Zimring, *Firearms & Violence, supra*. The presence of a gun in the home of a convicted domestic abuser is "strongly and independently associated with an increased risk of homicide." Arthur L. Kellermann, et al., *Gun Ownership as a Risk Factor for Homicide in the Home*, 329 New England J. Medicine 1084, 1087 (1993). . . . And for this purpose the victims include police as well as spouses, children, and intimate partners. Responding to a domestic-disturbance call is among an officer's most risky duties. Approximately 8% of officers' fatalities from illegal conduct during 1999 through 2008 arose from attempts to control domestic disturbances. FBI, Law Enforcement Officers Killed and Assaulted 2008, Table 19 (2009).

Finally, the recidivism rate is high, implying that there are substantial benefits in keeping the most deadly weapons out of the hands of domestic abusers. For example, a study of persons arrested for misdemeanor domestic violence in Cincinnati concluded that 17% of those who remained in the area were arrested again for domestic violence within three years. John Wooldredge & Amy Thistlethwaite, *Reconsidering Domestic Violence Recidivism: Individual and Contextual Effects of Court Dispositions and Stake in Conformity* vi (1999). The full recidivism rate includes violence that does not lead to an arrest. Estimates of this rate come from survey research and range from 40% to 80% "when victims are followed longitudinally and interviewed directly." Carla Smith Stover, *Domestic Violence Research*, 20 J. Interpersonal Violence 448, 450 (2005). . . . Skoien cites, as if it were favorable, a study showing that within three years of conviction 48% of domestic abusers "suspended" their abusive conduct—which means that the other 52% did not, and that even the 48% may have committed new crimes within three years after conviction. John H. Laub & Robert J. Sampson, *Understanding Desistance from Crime*, 28 Crime & Justice 1, 31 (2001). No matter how you slice these numbers, people convicted of domestic violence remain dangerous to their spouses and partners.

By the time this appeal reached oral argument *en banc*, Skoien's principal argument had shifted. Instead of denying the logical and empirical basis of §922(g)(9), he contended that Congress overreached by creating a "perpetual" disqualification for persons convicted of domestic violence. This goes too far, according to Skoien, because the propensity for violence declines with advancing age, and people who are not convicted of additional offenses have demonstrated that they no longer pose risks to other members of their households. Applying §922(g)(9) to older persons who have not been in legal trouble for many years cannot be substantially related to an important governmental objective, the argument concludes.

Although the statute provides that expungement, pardon, or restoration of civil rights means that a conviction no longer disqualifies a person from possessing firearms, see 18 U.S.C. §921(a)(33)(B)(ii), Skoien maintains that, as a practical matter, these routes to restoration are unavailable to domestic-battery misdemeanants in Wisconsin. We have our doubts. As the Supreme Court observed in *Logan v. United States*, 552 U.S. 23 (2007), although Wisconsin does not deprive misdemeanants of the civil rights to vote, serve on a jury, or hold public office — so these rights cannot be "restored" by the passage of time, as felons' rights often are — the state does give misdemeanants an opportunity to seek pardon or expungement. Some of the largest states make expungement available as of right to misdemeanants who have a clean record for a specified time. California, for example, has such a program. Cal. Penal Code §1203.4a. . . . This means that §922(g)(9) in its normal application does not create a perpetual and unjustified disqualification for a person who no longer is apt to attack other members of the household. True, the statute tolerates different outcomes for persons convicted in different states, but this is true of all situations in which a firearms disability (or any other adverse consequence) depends on state law. The Justices held in *Logan* that this variability does not call into question federal firearms limits based on state convictions that have been left in place under the states' widely disparate approaches to restoring civil rights.

But let us assume that the effect of §922(g)(9) should be assessed state by state, rather than for the nation as a whole. The fact remains that Skoien is poorly situated to contend that the statute creates a lifetime ban for someone who does not pose any risk of further offenses. First, Skoien is himself a recidivist, having been convicted twice of domestic battery. The first victim (in 2003) was his wife; after that marriage ended, the second victim (in 2006) was his new fiancee. And Skoien was arrested for possessing multiple guns just one year after that second conviction — while he was still on probation.

A person to whom a statute properly applies can't obtain relief based on arguments that a differently situated person might present. See *United States v. Salerno*, 481 U.S. 739, 745 (1987). Although the *Salerno* principle has been controversial, and the Justices have allowed "overbreadth" arguments when dealing with laws that restrict speech and reach substantially more conduct than the justifications advanced for the statute support, see [*United States v. Stevens*, 130 S. Ct. 1577, 1587 (2010)], the Court has continued to cite *Salerno* favorably in other situations. See, e.g., *Washington State Grange v. Washington State Republican Party*, 552 U.S. 442, 449-50 (2008); cf. *Gonzales v. Carhart*, 550 U.S. 124, 167-68 (2007) (observing that "facial" challenges to statutes generally are restricted to litigation under the First Amendment). If convictions may be used to limit where sex offenders can live (and whether they must register), see *Connecticut Department of Public Safety v. Doe*, 538 U.S. 1 (2003), a disqualification-on-conviction statute such as §922(g)(9) also is generally proper. Whether a misdemeanant who has been law abiding for an extended period must be allowed to carry guns again, even if he cannot satisfy §921(a)(33)(B)(ii), is a question not presented today. There will be time enough to consider that subject when it arises.

Affirmed.

SYKES, CIRCUIT JUDGE, dissenting.

Steven Skoien was indicted under 18 U.S.C. §922(g)(9) for possessing a hunting shotgun after he was convicted of a misdemeanor crime of domestic violence. . . . The government invoked *Heller*'s anticipatory language about certain "presumptively lawful" firearms regulations — specifically, felon-dispossession laws — as a sort of "safe harbor" for analogous prohibitions. . . . This approach fell far short of the legal heavy lifting normally required to justify criminally punishing the exercise of an enumerated constitutional right.

The now-vacated panel opinion rejected the government's argument and instead read *Heller*'s holdings in light of its limiting language about exceptions, distilling a decision method focused first on a textual and historical inquiry into "the terms of the [Second Amendment] right as publicly understood when the Bill of Rights was ratified," and then — if this inquiry didn't resolve the case — an application of a degree of heightened judicial review appropriate to the nature of the challenged law's burden on the right. *United States v. Skoien*, 587 F.3d 803, 809 (7th Cir. 2009). Because the government hadn't argued that domestic-violence misdemeanants were excluded from the scope of the Second Amendment right as a textual-historical matter, we assumed Skoien's Second Amendment rights were intact. Nor had the government tried to establish a strong relationship between the important governmental objective of reducing firearm violence against domestic intimates and §922(g)(9)'s permanent disarmament of domestic-violence misdemeanants like Skoien. So we vacated Skoien's conviction and remanded for application of intermediate scrutiny on an appropriately developed record.

The en banc court now performs the analysis that would have occurred on remand had we not reheard this case. . . .

My colleagues discuss but do not decide the scope question and avoid the standard-of-review "quagmire" by simply accepting the government's "concession" that "some form of strong showing ('intermediate scrutiny,' many opinions say) is essential, and that §922(g)(9) is valid only if substantially related to an important governmental objective." When it comes to applying this standard, they give the government a decisive assist; most of the empirical data cited to sustain §922(g)(9) has been supplied by the court. This is an odd way to put the government to its burden of justifying a law that prohibits the exercise of a constitutional right. . . . The court declines to be explicit about its decision method, sends doctrinal signals that confuse rather than clarify, and develops its own record to support the government's application of §922(g)(9) to this defendant. . . .

The en banc court reads *Heller*'s reference to exceptions as a warning not to apply the opinion too broadly. Fair enough. This "precautionary language" — especially the inclusion of felon-disqualification laws on the list of "presumptively lawful" firearms regulations — is "informative" but not "dispositive," and conveys a message that "whether or not technically dictum, a court of appeals must respect." I agree, and all the more so after *McDonald* . . . reiterat[ed] the presumptive validity of certain "longstanding regulatory measures." But my colleagues are not clear about how this limiting dicta should inform the constitutional analysis. The court thinks it "not . . . profitable to parse these passages of *Heller* as if they contained an answer to the question whether §922(g)(9) is valid," . . . but proceeds to parse the passages anyway. My colleagues read *Heller*'s dicta to mean that "statutory prohibitions on the possession of weapons by some persons are proper — and, importantly for current purposes, that the legislative role did not end in 1791. That *some* categorical limits are proper is part of the original meaning, leaving to the people's elected representatives the filling in of details." . . .

There are several problems with this analysis. First, no one has suggested that the legislative role ended in 1791; the pertinent question is how contemporary gun laws should be evaluated to determine whether they infringe the Second Amendment right. More significantly, that "categorical" disarmament is "proper" as "part of the original meaning" of the Second Amendment has not been established. *Heller* certainly did not say this; its reference to exceptions was — and remains — unexplained. . . .

The court also asserts that "[m]any of the states, whose own constitutions entitled their citizens to be armed, did not extend this right to persons convicted of crime." . . . This is a considerable overstatement. Only four state constitutions had what might be considered Second Amendment analogues in 1791 — Massachusetts, North Carolina, Pennsylvania, and Vermont — and none of these provisions excluded persons convicted of a crime. . . .

Regardless, the court hazards these historical observations but ultimately leaves the matter unresolved, moving on to compare categorical limits on firearms possession to categorical limits on the freedom of speech: "obscenity, defamation, incitement to crime, and others." Adapting First Amendment doctrine to the Second Amendment context is sensible in some cases; indeed, *Heller* expressly approved the comparison of the Second Amendment to the First. . . . But this particular First Amendment analogy doesn't work here. Obscenity, defamation, incitement, and so on are among the few "well-defined and narrowly limited classes of speech, the prevention and punishment of which have never been thought to raise any Constitutional problem." *United States v. Stevens*, 130 S. Ct. 1577 (2010). These "historic and traditional categories [of speech] long familiar to the bar" are "outside the reach of that Amendment altogether — they fall into a 'First Amendment Free Zone.'" *Id.* at 1584-85. . . .

The better approach is to acknowledge the limits of the scope inquiry in a more straightforward way: The historical evidence is inconclusive at best. As noted in the panel opinion, scholars disagree about the extent to which *felons* — let alone misdemeanants — were considered excluded from the right to bear arms during the founding era. . . . We simply cannot say with any certainty that persons convicted of a domestic-violence misdemeanor are wholly excluded from the Second Amendment right as originally understood. Because Skoien is not categorically unprotected, the government's use of §922(g)(9) against him must survive Second Amendment scrutiny.

My colleagues evidently agree; they move on to discuss the standard for determining whether the disarmament of domestic-violence misdemeanants is constitutionally permissible. This inquiry is necessary only if Skoien's Second Amendment rights are intact notwithstanding his domestic-violence conviction. The court properly concludes that some form of heightened judicial scrutiny is required; rational-basis review has been ruled out. . . . The court assumes without deciding that intermediate scrutiny applies, and holds that data establish a substantial relationship between §922(g)(9) and the important governmental objective of "preventing armed mayhem." *Id.* What follows is a discussion of the Supreme Court's decision in *United States v. Hayes*, 129 S. Ct. 1079 (2009) — in particular, its reference to a statement in the congressional record by the principal Senate sponsor of §922(g)(9)—and several pages of social-science research on the criminal-justice system's treatment of domestic-violence cases, firearm violence in the home, and recidivism by domestic-violence offenders. Most of this data, as I have noted, has been supplied by the court.

The court thus accepts that it is the government's burden to make a "strong showing" of the danger-reduction justification for stripping domestic-violence misdemeanants of their Second Amendment rights but in the end makes the case for itself. This relieves the government of its burden and deprives Skoien of the opportunity to review the outcome-determinative evidence, let alone subject it to normal adversarial testing. One obvious peril in this approach: The court's understanding of the research on domestic violence might be mistaken. That is certainly true of my colleagues' conclusion that "domestic abusers often commit acts that would be charged as felonies if the victim were a stranger, but that are charged as misdemeanors because the victim is a relative." . . .

The court also dismisses Skoien's contention that §922(g)(9) is impermissibly overinclusive because it is a permanent disqualification and provides no effective way for an offender to reacquire his Second Amendment rights. It is true, as the court notes, that a pardon, expungement, or restoration of civil rights will lift the federal firearms ban. See 18 U.S.C. §921(a)(33)(B)(ii) (excluding domestic-violence convictions that have been pardoned, expunged, or for which civil rights have been restored *unless* the pardon, expungement, or restoration of rights provides that the person may not possess firearms). But as my colleagues acknowledge, in Wisconsin misdemeanants do not lose their civil rights, and rights not lost cannot be "restored" for purposes of the statutory exception. See *Logan v. United States*, 552 U.S. 23, 36 (2007). The court nonetheless maintains that "the state does give misdemeanants an opportunity to seek pardon or expungement." . . . Pardon, yes; expungement, no—at least not in the typical case. In Wisconsin the expungement remedy is extremely narrow; it applies only to misdemeanants under the age of 21 and must be ordered at the time of sentencing. Wis. Stat. §973.015(1)(a). There is no after-the-fact or generally available opportunity to seek expungement. It is true that the pardon power is very broad, but I doubt that governors—in Wisconsin or elsewhere—pardon domestic-violence misdemeanants with any regularity. So Skoien is right that the §922(g)(9) ban is effectively permanent, at least as to him.

This brings me to the court's final point: that Skoien is "poorly situated" to complain about the perpetual nature of the §922(g)(9) ban because he is a recidivist who was caught with "multiple guns just one year after [his] second conviction—while he was still on probation." Majority Op. at 16. Maybe so. Skoien's status as a recent domestic-violence recidivist certainly diminishes the force of his argument about the permanent feature of §922(g)(9) as the statute has been applied to him. The court properly reserves the question whether application of §922(g)(9) would survive a Second Amendment challenge by "a misdemeanant who has been law abiding for an extended period." Still, I think it highly inappropriate for the court to resolve this challenge to the application of the statute without requiring the government to shoulder its burden—and giving Skoien the opportunity to respond—on remand in the district court. The sort of empirical inquiry normally required by intermediate scrutiny should not be performed by the court of appeals in the first instance.

The court thus short-circuits the usual process and resolves this case on a record of its own creation, prematurely ending Skoien's challenge and leaving markers for the future that will immunize most applications of §922(g)(9) from serious Second Amendment scrutiny. This approach is difficult to reconcile with either the reasoning or the result in *Heller*, though it might be thought consistent with an aggressive reading of the Court's reference to presumptively lawful firearms regulations. Of course there are several ways to understand the Court's analysis in *Heller* in light of its limiting dicta about exceptions. But we cannot read *Heller*'s dicta in a way that swallows its holdings. The government normally has the burden of justifying the application of laws that criminalize the exercise of enumerated constitutional rights. We should follow that norm, not pay lip service to it. I would remand for the government to make its own case for imprisoning Steven Skoien for exercising his Second Amendment rights.

NOTES & QUESTIONS

1. What is the impact of the ruling in *Skoien*? What does it offer as guidance for deciding subsequent cases? Does *Skoien* follow the same methodological model applied in *Ezell*, or a competing method?

2. The *en banc* decision in *Skoien* overturned the panel opinion written by Judge Sykes, *United States v. Skoien*, 587 F.3d 803 (7th Cir 2009). The panel opinion directed the district court to use intermediate scrutiny to review the domestic violence misdemeanor ban, and to reject bare assertions from the government as sufficient to pass intermediate scrutiny. Judge Sykes also wrote the panel opinion in *Ezell*.

3. By its terms, 18 U.S.C. §922(g)(9) creates a nationwide, lifetime prohibition on gun ownership for any person convicted of a single misdemeanor crime of domestic violence against an intimate partner. The prohibition is also retroactive: It applies equally to individuals convicted prior to 1996, when §922(g)(9) was enacted. Should individuals lose a fundamental constitutional right for the rest of their lives because of a single misdemeanor conviction, which is normally a crime punishable by no more than one year's imprisonment? Would a similar lifetime ban be constitutional as applied to other fundamental rights, such as freedom of speech or religion? The right to vote? Is there something peculiar about domestic violence misdemeanors? About the right to arms?

   Might the constitutionality of a lifetime ban on gun possession depend on whether there is a functional system for restoring the right? If so, is the Wisconsin system, as described in Judge Sykes's dissent, functional enough?

   The *Skoien* dissent criticizes the majority for creating its own record on the question of the risk posed by domestic violence misdemeanants. In footnote 13, she observes:

   > On rebriefing before the en banc court, the government cited several reports showing high recidivism rates among domestic-violence offenders. *See* Carla

> Smith Stover, *Domestic Violence Research: What Have We Learned and Where Do We Go From Here?*, 20 J. of Interpersonal Violence 448 (2005); Julia C. Babcock, et al., *Does Batterers' Treatment Work? A Meta-Analytic Review of Domestic Violence Treatment*, 23 Clinical Psychol. Rev. 1023 (2004); John H. Laub & Robert J. Sampson, *Understanding Desistance from Crime*, 28 Crime & Justice 1 (2001); John Wooldredge & Amy Thistlethwaite, *Reconsidering Domestic Violence Recidivism: Individual and Contextual Effects of Court Dispositions and Stake in Conformity*, Project Report Submitted to the Nat'l Inst. of Justice (1999), *available at* http://www.ncjrs.gov/pdffiles1/nij/grants/188509.pdf. On the more precise question of the relationship between ready access to a gun and the risk that a gun will be used against a domestic intimate, the government cited two studies showing a correlation: Jacqueline C. Campbell, et al., *Risk Factors for Femicide in Abusive Relationships: Results from a Multisite Case Control Study*, 93 Am. J. of Pub. Health 1089 (2003), and Arthur L. Kellermann, et al., *Gun Ownership as a Risk Factor for Homicide in the Home*, 329 New Eng. J. Med. 1084 (1993). The most recent of these, however, also establishes that a "prior arrest for domestic violence actually decreased the risk for femicide, suggesting that arrest of abusers protects against future intimate partner femicide risks." Campbell, *supra*, at 1092. Another study cited by the government shows that domestic assaults with a firearm are more likely to result in death than domestic assaults with other types of weapons. *See* Linda E. Saltzman, et al., *Weapon Involvement and Injury Outcomes in Family and Intimate Assaults*, 267 JAMA 3043 (1992).

What accounts for the majority building its own record in this fashion? Is this proper procedure for an appellate court? Has the court simply taken judicial notice of some of the obvious risks of firearms? Are those risks contestable? Recall the debate about the risks and utilities of firearms for women in Chapter 10.

4. The majority concludes that Mr. Skoien is poorly situated to press the boundaries of the Second Amendment, in part because he was in possession of multiple guns just one year after his second domestic battery conviction in three years. The dissent responds:

> Skoien's conviction was based on his possession of the hunting shotgun, which he admitted using to kill a deer on the morning of his arrest. Two other guns were found in his home: a handgun and a hunting rifle. The prosecutor conceded that he could not prove the handgun and rifle were Skoien's. There was evidence suggesting that the handgun belonged to Skoien's wife and the rifle belonged to their roommate. Nonetheless, at sentencing Skoien did not contest constructive possession of the two additional guns for purposes of increasing his base offense level by two levels under U.S.S.G. §2K2.1(b)(1)(A). The parties agreed that the handgun "was maintained for protection of the home" (these are the prosecutor's words), and Skoien told the court at sentencing that there had been several attempted break-ins at his home.

Do these details enhance the strength of Skoien's claim? What changes in the facts would make Skoien better situated to raise a Second Amendment claim?

E.   The Second Amendment and the Gun Control Act of 1968

In a widely cited passage of the *Heller* opinion, the Court stated, without citation of authority, that many traditional limitations on possession of firearms were presumptively constitutional. The following case is a lower court implementation of the *Heller* principle that respecting an individual right to arms does not impair gun control laws aimed at the dangerous—such as persons possessing guns with obliterated serial numbers.

United States v. Marzzarella
595 F. Supp. 2d 596 (W.D. Pa. 2009)

SEAN J. MCLAUGHLIN, DISTRICT J.

Defendant is charged in a one-count indictment with knowingly possessing a firearm with an obliterated serial number, in violation of 18 U.S.C. §922(k). The government alleges that, in April of 2006, officers of the Pennsylvania State Police received information from a confidential informant that the Defendant was involved in gun trafficking in and around Meadville, Pennsylvania and that the Defendant possessed a firearm with an obliterated serial number. According to the government, an undercover Pennsylvania State Trooper accompanied the confidential informant to the Defendant's apartment on April 26, 2006, where the Defendant sold the undercover officer a .25 caliber titan pistol with a partially obliterated serial number. It is alleged that this same undercover officer purchased a second firearm from the Defendant on May 16, 2006, at which time the Defendant informed the officer that the serial number on the second firearm could be obliterated in a similar fashion.

Defendant now moves this Court to dismiss the Indictment on the ground that the charge against him infringes his Second Amendment rights. For the reasons set forth below, Defendant's motion will be denied.

DISCUSSION . . .

In *District of Columbia v. Heller*, 128 S. Ct. 2783 (2008), the Supreme Court clarified that the Second Amendment protects an individual right to possess a firearm unconnected with service in a militia. . . .

Based on *Heller*, Defendant argues that 18 U.S.C. §922(k), as applied to his case, is unconstitutional. He asserts that, under *Heller*, "[t]he core right of the Second Amendment is the private possession of firearms for use in defense of hearth and home" and "[t]he only limitations on the right to keep and bear arms identified by the Court were those limitations in effect at the time of the enactment of the Second Amendment." . . . Because serial numbers had not yet come into use at the time of the Second Amendment's enactment, there were no laws extant in 1787 requiring serial markings on firearms. Defendant thus theorizes that:

> [s]ince possession of a handgun with an obliterated serial number was not proscribed under the common law, and therefore not an exception to the right to keep and bear arms codified by the Second Amendment, §922(k), as applied to this case, purports to outlaw the otherwise lawful possession of a handgun by a citizen in his home. . . .

Defendant further theorizes that the right to possess an unmarked handgun is a fundamental constitutional right, such that any government regulation burdening the right must be subjected to strict scrutiny. In Defendant's view, §922(k) cannot meet the demands of strict scrutiny and, thus, he concludes, the indictment charging him under that statute must be dismissed.

Since the Supreme Court issued its opinion in *Heller* nearly seven months ago, numerous defendants prosecuted under the federal firearms laws have challenged their criminal proceedings on Second Amendment grounds. Notably, Defendant cites no case in which §922(k) — or any other subsection of §922, for that matter — has been found invalid. On the contrary, it appears that every court which has considered a Second Amendment challenge to 18 U.S.C. §922, post-*Heller*, has upheld the statute as constitutional. . . .

I likewise conclude that nothing in *Heller* invalidates the specific provision of §922 that is being challenged in this case. Fundamentally, *Heller* must be viewed in its proper perspective and distinguished from the case before me.

It must be noted at the outset that the regulations which *Heller* struck down were far broader in scope than the restriction imposed by §922(k). As described by the *Heller* Court, the D.C. law "totally ban[ned] handgun possession in the home" and "also require[d] that any lawful firearm in the home be disassembled or bound by a trigger lock at all times, rendering it inoperable." 128 S. Ct. at 2817. The Court noted that "[f]ew laws in the history of our Nation have come close to the severe restriction of the District's hand-gun ban." *Id.* at 2818. The law amounted, in the Court's words, "to a prohibition of an entire class of 'arms' that is overwhelmingly chosen by American society for [the] lawful purpose" of self-defense, *id.* at 2817 — a right which the Court considered "inherent" and "central" to the Second Amendment's protection. *Id.* Moreover, the prohibition extended to the home, where, the Court observed, "the need for defense of self, family, and property is most acute." *Id.* In light of these rather extreme circumstances, the Court concluded that the D.C. law would be unconstitutional "[u]nder any of the standards of scrutiny that we have applied to enumerated constitutional rights." *Id.* . . .

The regulation at issue here imposes a burden on gun ownership that is practically negligible when compared to the District of Columbia's complete ban on operable firearms within the home. In relevant part, §922(k) merely prohibits individuals from possessing a firearm if the individual has knowledge that the firearm's serial number has been obliterated, removed or altered. Since firearms with intact serial numbers are the norm and are readily available in our society through ordinary commercial channels, it cannot be said that §922(k) meaningfully burdens the "core" Second Amendment right recognized in

Heller—i.e., possession of an operable firearm for purposes of self-defense within the home.

Defendant attempts to liken this case to *Heller* by characterizing §922(k) as a "complete ban on possessing a handgun that has an altered or obliterated serial number" . . . , but the comparison is flawed. Firearms lacking serial numbers cannot be equated to "an entire class of 'arms' that is overwhelming chosen by American society for [the] lawful purpose" of self-defense, 128 S. Ct. at 2817. Whereas *Heller* can be read as recognizing a limited constitutional right for individuals to possess handguns, there is no recognized constitutional right, even under *Heller*, to own a handgun with an obliterated serial mark. Thus, the differences in terms of the both the nature and the scope of the regulation at issue here versus the regulation at issue in *Heller* are so fundamental as to make *Heller* factually inapposite to this case.

Heller may also be inapposite for another reason. Defendant claims that he is being prosecuted for engaging in "the very core conduct protected by the Second Amendment" . . . , but the "core" Second Amendment right recognized by *Heller*, as Defendant himself admits, is the right to possess a firearm "for use in defense of hearth and home." . . . Here, the evidence allegedly will show that the Defendant was trafficking in firearms and that he sold the subject firearm to an undercover law enforcement officer. The Defendant's possession of a firearm in connection with its private sale to another is inherently inconsistent with an intention to possess the firearm for defense of the Defendant's home, since the Defendant cannot protect himself with a weapon that he sells away.

As the *Heller* Court made clear, the right to bear arms under the Second Amendment is not unconditional:

> Like most rights, the right secured by the Second Amendment is not unlimited. From Blackstone through the 19th-century cases, commentators and courts routinely explained that the right was not a right to keep and carry any weapon whatsoever in any manner whatsoever and for whatever purpose. . . . For example, the majority of the 19th-century courts to consider the question held that prohibitions on carrying concealed weapons were lawful under the Second Amendment or state analogues. . . . Although we do not undertake an exhaustive historical analysis today of the full scope of the Second Amendment, nothing in our opinion should be taken to cast doubt on longstanding prohibitions on the possession of firearms by felons and the mentally ill, or laws forbidding the carrying of firearms in sensitive places such as schools and government buildings, or laws imposing conditions and qualifications on the commercial sale of arms.

128 S. Ct. at 2816-17. . . . In a follow-up footnote, the Court expressly advised that these "presumptively lawful regulatory measures" were merely exemplary, not exhaustive. *Id.* at 2817 n.26.

Defendant acknowledges that the right to bear arms is not without limits, but he interprets the foregoing language as indicating that the only limitations on Second Amendment rights are those that were in effect at the time of the Second Amendment's enactment. The corollary to this assertion is that any mode or manner of possessing a firearm that was not expressly prohibited in 1787 should be viewed as a fundamental constitutional right and any infringements thereof should be considered presumptively unconstitutional.

In this regard I think the Defendant reads too much into *Heller*. It is clear from the majority's language that it was disavowing any effort to establish definitive boundaries on the scope of the Second Amendment's protection. In addition, the majority made clear in footnote 26 that the "presumptively lawful regulatory" measures which it had identified were merely exemplary and not exhaustive. In my view, the majority's language, cited above, should not be read as implying that all modern-day gun regulations are presumptively unconstitutional. *See Luedtke*, 589 F. Supp. 2d at 1021 ("[N]othing in *Heller* suggests that the Court intended to permit only those precise regulations accepted at the founding. Rather, the Court's examples are best understood as representing the types of regulations that pass constitutional muster.").

In any event, it is worth considering that among the types of regulations which the Court implicitly sanctioned were "laws imposing conditions and qualifications on the commercial sale of arms" and "prohibitions on the possession of firearms by felons and the mentally ill," 128 S. Ct. at 2816-17. The latter type of restriction is directed at "keep[ing] firearms out of the hands of presumptively risky people." *Dickerson v. New Banner Inst., Inc.*, 460 U.S. 103, 112 n.6 (1983) (discussing Congress' intent in enacting 18 U.S.C. §922(g), which codifies similar prohibitions), superseded in non-relevant part by statute, as recognized in *U.S. v. Balascsak*, 873 F.2d 673, 677 (3d Cir. 1989).

Section 922(k) is one aspect of a broad statutory scheme designed both to regulate the commercial sale of firearms and to keep them out of the hands of those individuals who are considered dangerous. The provision, as originally enacted, was part of the Federal Firearms Act of 1938, an Act expressly designed "[t]o regulate commerce in firearms." Pub. L. No. 785, 52 Stat. 1250. By this Act, Congress intended "to prevent the crook and gangster, racketeer and fugitive from justice from being able to purchase or in any way come in contact with firearms of any kind." S. Rep. No. 1189, 75th Cong. 1st, Sess., 33 (1937) (quoted in *Barrett v. United States*, 423 U.S. 212, 220, (1976)). Section 2(i) of the Federal Firearms Act made it unlawful "for any person to transport, ship, or knowingly receive in interstate or foreign commerce any firearm from which the manufacturer's serial number has been removed, obliterated, or altered." *Id.* at §2(i), 52 Stat. 1251.

When Congress enacted the Omnibus Crime Control and Safe Streets Act of 1968, Pub. L. No. 90-351, 82 Stat. 197, the provision was incorporated into Title IV of the Act and codified at 18 U.S.C. §922(i). Within months, Title IV was amended by Congress' enactment of the Gun Control Act of 1968, Pub. L. No. 90-618, 82 Stat. 1213 (1968), which expanded upon Title IV's regulations and re-codified §922(i) at §922(k). *See id.* at §922(k), 82 Stat. 1221.

The goal of the Gun Control Act was "not . . . merely to restrict interstate sales" of firearms but, more broadly, "to keep firearms away from persons Congress classified as potentially irresponsible and dangerous." Barrett v. United States, 423 U.S. 212, 218 (1976). To achieve this goal, Congress put in place "a comprehensive scheme to regulate the movement of firearms." *United States v. Mobley*, 956 F.2d 450, 453 (3d Cir. 1992). Thus,

[c]ommerce in firearms is channeled through federally licensed importers, manufacturers, and dealers in an attempt to halt mail-order and interstate consumer

traffic in these weapons. The principal agent of federal enforcement is the dealer. He is licensed, §§922(a)(1) and 923(a); he is required to keep records of "sale . . . or other disposition," §923(g); and he is subject to a criminal penalty for disposing of a weapon contrary to the provisions of the Act, §924.

See Huddleston v. United States, 415 U.S. 814, 824 (1974). By channeling the sales of firearms through federally licensed dealers, the Act sought to "insure that, in the course of sales or other dispositions by these dealers, weapons could not be obtained by individuals whose possession of them would be contrary to the public interest." *Huddleston*, 415 U.S. at 825.

Section 922(k)'s proscription against dealing in firearms with obliterated serial numbers serves these broad purposes. As our circuit court of appeals has observed:

> the trade in guns is monitored for a reason. Registration and verification procedures are imposed largely to combat crime. It is no secret that a chain of custody for a firearm greatly assists in the difficult process of solving crimes. When a firearm is stolen, determining this chain is difficult and when serial numbers are obliterated, it is virtually impossible. Therefore, stolen or altered firearms in the hands of people recognized as irresponsible pose great dangers. . . .

[*United States v. Mobley*, 956 F.2d 450, 454 (3d Cir. 1992)]. As a matter of common sense, untraceable firearms are of no particular use to the ordinary law-abiding citizen who intends to possess the firearm for common lawful purposes (such as defense of hearth and home). Rather, such weapons hold special value only for those individuals who intend to use them for unlawful activity. *See United States v. Carter*, 421 F.3d 909, 910 (9th Cir. 2005) (noting the district court's observation that weapons which have the appearance of being untraceable "have a greater street value . . . or a greater flexibility to be utilized in (il)licit activities") (discussing and applying the sentencing enhancement at U.S.S.G. §2K2.1(b)(4) relative to possession of firearms with obliterated serial marks) (ellipsis and alteration in the original). Thus, §922(k)'s proscription against transporting, shipping, or receiving, in interstate or foreign commerce, any firearm with an obliterated or altered serial number imposes a particular condition and qualification on the commercial sale of arms which is designed to discourage the use of untraceable firearms and keep them out of the hands of those most likely to use such weaponry for unlawful activity.

Importantly for our purposes, it should be noted that Congress further amended §922(k) in 1990 so as to also make it unlawful for any person knowingly "to possess or receive any firearm which has had the importer's or manufacturer's serial number removed, obliterated, or altered and has, at any time, been shipped or transported in interstate or foreign commerce." Comprehensive Crime Control Act of 1990, Pub. L. 101-647, §2202(b), 104 Stat. 4789 4856. The intent of this amendment was to expand the time frame for establishing interstate movement of the contraband, thereby expanding federal jurisdiction beyond direct interstate trafficking in untraceable weaponry to include intrastate trafficking as well. *See* H.R. Rep. No. 681, 101st Cong., 2d Sess., pt. 1 (1990), *reprinted in* 1990 U.S.C.C.A.N. 6472, 6510 (explaining that the amendment will "expand Federal jurisdiction to permit prosecution for transactions involving . . . firearms missing serial numbers where the firearms have already moved in interstate or foreign commerce" prior to the obliteration of the mark); Comprehensive Violent Crime Control Act of 1989: Hearing on H.R. 2709 Before the Subcomm. on Crime of the House Comm. on the Judiciary, 101st Cong., 2d Sess. 79-80 (1990), comments of Assistant Attorney General Edward Dennis (explaining that the amendment "would expand federal jurisdiction to permit federal prosecution for trafficking in firearms which . . . have had the serial number removed or altered and which have moved in interstate commerce at any time").

Although the *Heller* Court declined to exhaustively define the outer boundaries of the Second Amendment's protection, its implicit sanctioning of laws imposing conditions and qualifications on the commercial sale of arms and laws prohibiting presumptively risky individuals from possessing firearms is significant. Section 922(k) partakes, to some extent, of both characteristics. It is part of a regulatory scheme designed to impose and enforce a specific condition upon the commercial sale of arms — namely, the requirement that all firearms which pass at some time through interstate commerce bear an intact serial number. This requirement, in turn, serves the government's interest in discouraging the availability of untraceable firearms and ensuring that they do not fall into the hands of those individuals who would be inclined to use them for unlawful purposes.[7]

Even if *Heller* cannot be read to implicitly sanction the type of regulation contained in §922(k), it does not follow inexorably from *Heller* that §922(k) must survive strict scrutiny in order to pass constitutional muster. Indeed, the *Heller* Court expressly disavowed any intention of setting a definitive standard of review in Second Amendment cases and instead left that issue to be sorted out in subsequent rulings. *See Heller*, 128 S. Ct. at 2821. Moreover, the Court's willingness to presume the validity of several types of gun regulations is arguably inconsistent with the adoption of a strict scrutiny standard of review. *See* 128 S. Ct. at 2851 (Breyer, J., dissenting) ("[T]he majority implicitly, and appropriately, rejects th[e] suggestion [that strict scrutiny would be the appropriate standard of review] by broadly approving a set of laws — prohibitions on concealed weapons, forfeiture by criminals of the Second Amendment right, prohibitions on firearms in certain locales, and governmental regulation of commercial firearm sales — whose constitutionality under a strict scrutiny standard would be far from clear."). . . .

---

7. Section §922(k), as applied to this case, is no less constitutionally valid simply because the Defendant is not a federally licensed firearms dealer. I do not read the *Heller* majority's sanctioning of "laws imposing conditions and qualifications on the commercial sale of arms," 128 S. Ct. at 2817, as an indication that the government may regulate interstate commerce of firearms only insofar as it occurs through the ordinary channels of licensed dealers. Interpreting the Second Amendment in such a manner would lead to a bizarre result whereby the government would be powerless to regulate the trade of guns which occurs, often illicitly, in private settings and on the streets. I doubt that is what the *Heller* majority had in mind when it granted "presumptively valid" status to laws imposing conditions and qualifications on the commercial sale of arms.

In addition, the fact that the Second Amendment is enumerated in the Bill of Rights does not necessarily mean that strict scrutiny must be applied as a matter of course whenever a law burdens the right to bear arms in any manner. As one constitutional scholar has explained:

> The Court has never purported to apply strict scrutiny in every provision of the Bill of Rights. Of the "first ten amendments" a grand total of two trigger strict scrutiny. Laws invading on First Amendment rights of speech, association, and religious liberty are often subject to strict scrutiny, as are laws that restrict the due process and (invisible) equal protection guarantees of the Fifth Amendment. But strict scrutiny is nowhere to be found in the jurisprudence of the Second Amendment, the Third Amendment, the Fourth Amendment, the Sixth Amendment, the Seventh Amendment, the Eighth Amendment, the Ninth Amendment, or the Tenth Amendment. Two amendments trigger strict scrutiny; eight do not.

See Adam Winkler, *Fundamentally Wrong About Fundamental Rights*, 23 Const. Comment. 227, 229 (Summer 2006); *id.* at 239 ("[T]he old adage about laws infringing fundamental rights being subject to strict scrutiny remains a favorite of scholars, judges, and law students. And it is flatly wrong.").

Given the *Heller* Court's several references to First Amendment jurisprudence in the course of its opinion, Defendant contends that "it is appropriate to look to the Court's free speech jurisprudence to discern how strict scrutiny review should be applied to legislation that burdens the right to keep and bear arms." . . . From there, Defendant likens §922(k) to a content-based regulation of speech which invokes a presumption of unconstitutionality, see *United States v. Playboy Entertainment Group, Inc.*, 529 U.S. 803, 817 (2000), and which requires the government to prove that the regulation in question is narrowly tailored to serve a compelling government interest and that it is the least restrictive means to achieve that interest. *See United States v. Stevens*, 533 F.3d 218, 232 (3d Cir. 2008) (en banc) (citing *Sable Commc'ns of Calif., Inc. v. F.C.C.*, 492 U.S. 115, 126 (1989)).

Assuming for the moment that First Amendment law provides a suitable framework for determining the validity of §922(k), it does not necessarily follow that strict scrutiny is the appropriate standard of review in this case:

> Perhaps the most preferred of all rights is the freedom of speech, the so-called First Freedom. Yet strict scrutiny is not always applied in free speech cases. Traditional speech doctrine distinguishes between regulations that are content-based and those that are content-neutral. The former generally trigger strict scrutiny, but the latter do not. Content-neutral laws that limit the freedom of speech are subject to the much more deferential standard of *United States v. O'Brien* [391 U.S. 367 (1968)], under which laws are regularly upheld. Even content-based speech regulations do not always receive strict scrutiny treatment. If the content regulated is commercial speech, the courts apply a form of intermediate review established in *Central Hudson Gas & Electric Corp. v. Public Service Commission of New York* [447 U.S. 557 (1980)]. A similarly less stringent form of review is applied to content-based regulations when the government is acting as an employer (as compared to a sovereign) under the rule of *Pickering v. Board of Education* [391 U.S. 563 (1968)]. These First Amendment doctrines have led Ashutosh Bhagwat to characterize intermediate scrutiny as the "test that ate everything" in free speech jurisprudence.

Adam Winkler, *supra*, at 237-38 (endnotes omitted). Thus, even in cases involving the infringement of First Amendment rights, it is by no means a given that strict scrutiny will be applied.

In the area of free speech jurisprudence, "laws that by their terms distinguish favored speech from disfavored speech on the basis of the ideas or views expressed" are considered content-based. *Turner Broadcasting Sys., Inc. v. FCC*, 512 U.S. 622, 643 (1994). Such restrictions are presumptively invalid and subject to the most exacting scrutiny because they create the "inherent risk that the Government seeks not to advance a legitimate regulatory goal, but to suppress unpopular ideas or information or manipulate the public debate through coercion rather than persuasion." *Id.* at 641. *See id* at 642; *R.A.V. v. City of St. Paul*, 505 U.S. 377, 382 (1992). Thus, "[t]o justify a content-based restriction, the government must show that the regulation or restriction is necessary to serve a compelling state interest and that it is narrowly drawn to achieve that end." *Startzell v. City of Philadelphia, Pennsylvania*, 533 F.3d 183, 193 (3d Cir. 2008) (citation omitted).

Restrictions on speech that are neutral in terms of viewpoint and subject-matter, on the other hand, "may permissibly regulate the time, place, or manner of expression if they are content neutral, are narrowly tailored to serve a significant government interest, and leave open ample alternative channels of communication." *Startzell*, 533 F.3d at 193. The Third Circuit has explained the concept of content-neutrality as follows:

> To determine if a restriction is content neutral, "(t)he principal inquiry . . . , in speech cases generally and in time, place, or manner cases in particular, is whether the government has adopted a regulation of speech because of disagreement with the message it conveys." *Ward* [*v. Rock Against Racism*], 491 U.S. [781, 791]. It is the government's purpose that controls. *Id.* A regulation is deemed content neutral if it serves purposes unrelated to the content of speech, regardless of whether it incidentally affects certain speakers or messages and not others. *Id.* That is, government regulation of speech is properly regarded as content neutral if it is "justified without reference to the content of the regulated speech." *Id.* (citation and internal quotations omitted) (emphasis in original).

Startzell, 533 F.3d at 197 (ellipsis in the original).

Here, as I have discussed, the restriction imposed by §922(k) does not target any particular "class of 'arms' overwhelmingly chosen by American society" for a lawful purpose, 128 S. Ct. at 2817, nor does it target any particular class of otherwise law-abiding gun owners. The law does not suppress or limit the right of law-abiding citizens to possess firearms generally, but merely regulates the manner in which they may be possessed — requiring, in essence, only that the firearm in question bear, in fact, the manufacturer's or importer's original serial number, which is the norm in the firearms industry. In sum, the burden which §922(k) imposes on the right to bear arms is both incidental and minimal, and it makes no sense to equate §922(k) to a content-based regulation on protected speech.

If this Court were to fashion a standard of review based on principles borrowed from First Amendment jurisprudence, a more appropriate standard of review would be the standard applicable to content-neutral time, place and manner restrictions. Section 922(k), as previously discussed, is designed to discourage the use of untraceable firearms and, in so doing, assist law enforcement in solving crimes and in keeping firearms away from those individuals who are likely to use them toward unlawful ends. As I previously noted, firearms with intact serial numbers are the norm in this society and are readily available to citizens who are otherwise permitted under the law to possess guns. As a practical matter, in the overwhelming majority of cases, the restriction imposed by §922(k) will burden only those individuals who have a particular interest in possessing an untraceable weapon—a characteristic for which this Court is hard-pressed to imagine any legitimate use. Thus, the regulation is narrowly tailored and leaves open ample opportunity for law-abiding citizens to own and possess guns within the parameters recognized by *Heller*. Under this standard of review, §922(k) passes constitutional muster.

CONCLUSION

In sum, I see nothing in the Supreme Court's recent decision in *District of Columbia v. Heller* that would compel the conclusion that 18 U.S.C. §922(k), as applied in this case, is unconstitutional. Defendant cites no other case or source of law which arguably places the validity of §922(k) in question. Accordingly, for the reasons set forth above, the Defendant's motion to dismiss the indictment will be denied. . . .

NOTES & QUESTIONS

1. *Marzzarella* examines the degree of burden that the serial-number requirement imposes on exercise of the right to keep and bear arms, and concludes that the burden is negligible. Should such burden analysis be a required part of Second Amendment scrutiny? *Cf. Nordyke v. King, supra* (constitutionality of a gun control law depends on how much the law burdens exercise of the Second Amendment right).

2. Judge McLaughlin discusses at length what framework should be used to determine whether a provision of the 1968 Gun Control Act violates the Second Amendment. Is there an interpretation of *Heller* (Chapter 9) that would eliminate the need for such a structure? If you interpret *Heller* as simply prohibiting bans on the possession of firearms in common use for self-defense in the home, could you resolve the *Marzzarella* case without redress to levels of scrutiny? There may be cases where levels of scrutiny introduce burdensome complications. Consider that possibility in the following exercise.

EXERCISE: SOLDIERS AND SECOND AMENDMENT SCRUTINY

Assume you settle on a method for assessing Second Amendment questions. Now apply that method to a Second Amendment challenge brought by a United States Army soldier who is disqualified from possessing firearms under §922(g)(9) of the Gun Control Act.

Section 922(g)(9) of the Gun Control Act, also known as the Lautenberg Amendment, retroactively disqualifies anyone convicted of a misdemeanor crime of domestic violence from possessing firearms.

For members of the military, this prohibition will likely render them incapable effectively performing their duty. The Army policy for a soldier subject to §922(g)(9) renders that soldier non-deployable for missions requiring firearms or ammunition, or overseas assignments. The scope of this consequence ultimately affects soldiers of every military occupational specialty from performing their job, and more than likely leads to their discharge. *See* Department of Defense, Instruction No. 6400.06 on Domestic Abuse Involving DoD Military and Civilian Personnel, Aug. 21, 2007 (as modified, Sept. 20, 2011), §6.1.4.5.1.7, *available at* http://www.dtic.mil/whs/directives/corres/pdf/640006p.pdf (Stating, in a section relating to the Lautenberg Amendment, that "[c]onsistent with applicable laws and regulations, the Military Departments may promulgate regulations governing permanent adverse personnel actions, including separation, that may be taken with respect to Service members who have a qualifying conviction.").

A provision of the Gun Control Act known as a "government interest exception" creates an exemption from some GCA disabilities. Today, the "government exception," §925(a)(1), reads as follows:

> The provisions of this chapter [18 USCS §921 et seq.], except for sections 922(d)(9) and 922(g)(9) [18 USCS §922(d)(9) and 922(g)(9)] and provisions relating to firearms subject to the prohibitions of section 922(p) [18 USCS §922(p)], shall not apply with respect to the transportation, shipment, receipt, possession, or importation of any firearm or ammunition imported for, sold or shipped to, or issued for the use of, the United States or any department or agency thereof or any State or any department, agency, or political subdivision thereof.

The Lautenberg Amendment was deliberately excluded from this exception. The effect is counterintuitive. Released *felons* are covered by the "government exemption" so they may still serve in the military. But anyone convicted of a domestic violence *misdemeanor* would not qualify for the "government exemption" and would likely be discharged.

F.   Guns in Common Use and the State Courts

Heller (Chapter 9) suggests that the Second Amendment protects a right to firearms in "common use." The decision signaled strongly that machine guns, which are specially regulated by the National Firearms Act (NFA) (Chapter 7), are not protected under the common use standard. In *Heller II*, the Court of Appeals upheld the District of Columbia's ban on semi-automatic firearms deemed "assault weapons" and rejected the dissent's arguments that some of the banned guns were firearms in common use. The case below introduces a variation on the "assault weapons" theme; the California legislation at issue bans a class of guns by caliber.

People v. James
174 Cal. App. 4th 662 (2009)

SIMS, J.

In this case, we hold that possession of an assault weapon in California remains unlawful and is not protected by the Second Amendment to the federal Constitution as construed by the United States Supreme Court in *District of Columbia v. Heller*, (2008) 554 U.S. 570.

Defendant Michael Eugene James was convicted by jury of three counts of unlawful possession of an assault weapon (Pen. Code, §12280, subd. (b)), one count of unlawful possession of a .50-caliber BMG rifle (§12280, subd. (c)), 10 counts of unlawful possession of a firearm (§12021, subd. (g)(2)), and one count of unlawful possession of a blowgun (§12582). The trial court sentenced defendant to two years in state prison and imposed other orders. On appeal, defendant asserts two claims of instructional error and further asserts that his right to bear arms under the Second Amendment to the United States Constitution has been violated. . . .

FACTUAL AND PROCEDURAL BACKGROUND

In May of 2006, Special Agent John Marsh of the California Department of Justice began investigating defendant for possible firearms violations. Special Agent Marsh discovered that a restraining order had been issued against defendant, expressly prohibiting defendant from possessing firearms. The restraining order further directed defendant to "turn in or sell" all firearms in his possession by a certain date. Upon receiving this information, Marsh consulted the Automated Firearms System (AFS) database and discovered that defendant had roughly 20 firearms registered to his name. Marsh then contacted defendant by phone; defendant explained that all of his firearms had been turned in to the Sacramento Police Department. A comparison of the AFS database with the list of weapons turned in to police revealed 10 outstanding firearms. . . . Notwithstanding the weapons turned in to the Sacramento Police Department, and the five weapons taken by Special Agent Marsh during the two trips to defendant's house, there were still a number of firearms registered to defendant that had not been turned in. Marsh returned two days later with a search warrant. An Armalite AR-50 .50-caliber BMG rifle was found in its original box on a shelf in the garage. An Eagle Arms AR-15 lower receiver, and a DPMS AR-15 lower receiver, were also found in a box in the garage. An Eagle Flight blowgun and darts were found on a shelf in the garage. A 1911 Springfield .45-caliber semiautomatic handgun, and a Remington 12-gauge shotgun, were found next to the front door.

Defendant told Marsh that he did not turn in the .50-caliber BMG because he knew that he did not register it and if he turned it in, then he could get in trouble. Defendant said he thought he had turned all the other guns in.

Defendant was charged with three counts of unlawful possession of an assault weapon (counts 1, 2 & 4), one count of unlawful possession of a .50-caliber BMG rifle (count 3), 10 counts of unlawful possession of a firearm (counts 5-14), and one count of unlawful possession of a blowgun (count 15). He was tried by a jury. . . . Defendant's final contention on appeal is that section 12280, subdivisions (b) and (c), prohibiting possession of an assault weapon or .50-caliber BMG rifle, violated his right to bear arms under the Second Amendment to the United States Constitution. Defendant relies on language in *Heller, supra,* 554 U.S. 570, "indicating that the Second Amendment is a pre-existing right of the individual and that military type weapons were the type originally sought to be protected."[4] Defendant's reading of *Heller* does not withstand scrutiny.

A . . .

Section 12280, subdivision (c), was enacted as part of the .50 Caliber BMG Regulation Act of 2004 (Stats. 2004, ch. 494, §8), and provides in relevant part: "Any person who, within this state, possesses any .50 BMG rifle, except as provided in this chapter, shall be punished by a fine of one thousand dollars ($1,000), imprisonment in a county jail for a period not to exceed one year, or by both that fine and imprisonment."

In section 12275.5, the Legislature codified its findings, declarations, and legislative intent behind the Roberti-Roos Assault Weapons Control Act of 1989 and the .50 Caliber BMG Regulation Act of 2004: . . . (b) The Legislature hereby finds and declares that *the proliferation and use of .50 BMG rifles, as defined in Section 12278, poses a clear and present terrorist threat to the health, safety, and security of all residents of, and visitors to, this state, based upon findings that those firearms have such a high capacity for long distance and highly destructive firepower that they pose an unacceptable risk to the death and serious injury of human beings, destruction or serious damage of vital public and private buildings, civilian, police and military vehicles, power generation and transmission facilities, petrochemical production and storage facilities, and transportation infrastructure.* It is the intent of the Legislature in enacting this chapter to place restrictions on the use of these rifles and to establish a registration and permit procedure for their lawful sale and possession." (Italics added.)

. . . A review of the legislative history of the .50 Caliber BMG Regulation Act of 2004 reveals that the Legislature was not only concerned by the threat to public safety posed by the prospect of .50-caliber BMG rifles being used by criminals, but also by the threat to national security posed by the prospect of these weapons falling into the hands of terrorist organizations.

As expressed by the author of the bill: "[Fifty-caliber BMG] sniper rifles and .50 [caliber] BMG ammunition are armaments designed for military applications

---

4. [D]efendant acknowledges that the Second Amendment has not been held to apply to the states through the Fourteenth Amendment. . . . Since we hold that defendant's right to bear arms was not infringed by section 12280, subdivisions (b) and (c), we do not address the incorporation issue.

involving the destruction of infrastructure and anti-personnel purposes. The military uses these weapons to destroy concrete structures, including bunkers, light armored vehicles, and stationary tactical targets such as fuel storage facilities, aircraft, communications structures and energy transfer stations. . . . [Fifty-caliber BMG] weapons and their ammunition have increasingly been manufactured and marketed to civilians over the past several years. There is increasing evidence of these weapons falling into the hands of political extremists and terrorists, and more recently drug and street gangs. The manufacturers of these weapons have been reducing the weight, enhancing portability and lowering the price to own these weapons, so there is currently an expanding proliferation of these war weapons. The facts indicate that [.50 caliber BMG] sniper weapons and .50 [caliber] BMG ammunition present a clear and present public health and safety danger to California and the nation." . . . "According to the author, '[t]he fifty-caliber sniper rifle is one of the United States military's highest-powered rifles, capable of ripping through armored limousines. It is said to be able to punch holes through military personnel carriers at a distance of 2,000 yards, the length of 20 football fields. It is deadly accurate at up to one mile and effective at more than four miles. . . .'" . . .

The Assembly Committee on Public Safety analysis of the bill contains the following: "The term '.50 BMG' stands for Browning machine gun (one of the earliest firearms to use the ammunition) and is a technical designation for the round used in the weapon. . . . Manufacturers of the rifles claim that the rifle is accurate up to 2,000 yards and effective up to 7,500 yards. . . . The .50 caliber ammunition . . . [is] capable of piercing through body armor. . . . The Violence Policy Center has issued two reports on the .50 caliber sniper rifle. . . . Both reports stated that the unregulated sale of military sniper rifles to civilians creates a danger to national security as the rifles have the ability to shoot down aircraft. The second report also states that at least 25 Barrett .50 caliber sniper rifles were sold to the Al Qaeda network. . . ." . . .

The bill was supported by the Los Angeles County Sheriff's Department, which argued in support of the legislation: "'This weapon, which is readily available on the civilian market, can pierce armored vehicles and concrete structures from one mile away with pinpoint accuracy. In the hands of terrorists, .50 BMG sniper rifles pose a grave threat to airplanes, refineries or other potential targets.'" . . .

In sum, the Legislature enacted the Roberti-Roos Assault Weapons Control Act of 1989 and the .50 Caliber BMG Regulation Act of 2004 in order to address the proliferation and use of unusually dangerous weapons: assault weapons, with an incredibly "high rate of fire and capacity for firepower," which can be used to indiscriminately "kill and injure human beings" (§12275.5, subd. (a)); and .50 caliber BMG rifles, which "have such a high capacity for long distance and highly destructive firepower that they pose an unacceptable risk to the death and serious injury of human beings, destruction or serious damage of vital public and private buildings, civilian, police and military vehicles, power generation and transmission facilities, petrochemical production and storage facilities, and transportation infrastructure" (§12275.5, subd. (b)).

It is against this backdrop that we must analyze *Heller* . . . and determine whether section 12280, subdivisions (b) and (c), violate the right to bear arms guaranteed by the Second Amendment to the United States Constitution.

B

In *Heller* . . . the United States Supreme Court held that "the [District of Columbia's] ban on handgun possession in the home violates the Second Amendment, as does its prohibition against rendering any lawful firearm in the home operable for the purpose of immediate self-defense." . . . In so holding, the court explained that the Second Amendment codified a preexisting right of the individual "to possess and carry weapons in case of confrontation." . . . However, the court was careful to point out that, like the First Amendment's right to freedom of speech, the Second Amendment's right to bear arms is not unlimited: "Thus, we do not read the Second Amendment to protect the right of citizens to carry arms for *any sort* of confrontation, just as we do not read the First Amendment to protect the right of citizens to speak for *any purpose.*" . . .

Nor does the Second Amendment's protection extend to any type of weapon. As the *Heller* court explained, its previous decision in *United States v. Miller* (1939), 307 U.S. 174, held that the Second Amendment did not protect an individual's right to transport an unregistered short-barreled shotgun in interstate commerce. . . . The reason, the court explained, was that "the *type of weapon at issue* was not eligible for Second Amendment protection: 'In the absence of any evidence tending to show that the possession or use of a [short-barreled shotgun] at this time has some reasonable relationship to the preservation or efficiency of a well regulated militia, we cannot say that the Second Amendment guarantees the right to keep and bear such an instrument.'" . . .

The *Heller* court then elaborated on the types of weapons protected by the Second Amendment: "Read in isolation, *Miller*'s phrase 'part of ordinary military equipment' could mean that only those weapons useful in warfare are protected. That would be a startling reading of the opinion, since it would mean that the National Firearms Act's restrictions on machineguns (not challenged in *Miller*) might be unconstitutional, machineguns being useful in warfare in 1939. We think that *Miller*'s 'ordinary military equipment' language must be read in tandem with what comes after: '[O]rdinarily when called for [militia] service [able-bodied] men were expected to appear bearing arms supplied by themselves and of the kind in common use at the time.' The traditional militia was formed from a pool of men bringing arms 'in common use at the time' for lawful purposes like self-defense. 'In the colonial and revolutionary war era, [small-arms] weapons used by militiamen and weapons used in defense of person and home were one and the same.' Indeed, that is precisely the way in which the Second Amendment's operative clause ['the right of the people to keep and bear Arms, shall not be infringed'] furthers the purpose announced in its preface ['[a] well regulated militia, being necessary to the security of a free State']. We therefore read *Miller* to say only that the Second Amendment does not protect those weapons not typically possessed by law-abiding citizens for lawful purposes, such as short-barreled shotguns." . . .

The *Heller* court continued: "It may be objected that if weapons that are most useful in military service — M-16 rifles and the like — may be banned, then the Second Amendment right is completely detached from the prefatory clause. But as we have said, the conception of the militia at the time of the Second Amendment's ratification was the body of all citizens capable of military service, who would bring the sorts of lawful weapons that they possessed at home to militia duty. It may well be true today that a militia, to be as effective as militias in the 18th century, would require sophisticated arms that are highly unusual in society at large. Indeed, it may be true that no amount of small arms could be useful against modern-day bombers and tanks. But the fact that modern developments have limited the degree of fit between the prefatory clause and the protected right cannot change our interpretation of the right." . . .

Accordingly, "the right secured by the Second Amendment is not . . . a right to keep and carry any weapon whatsoever in any manner whatsoever and for whatever purpose." . . . Rather, it is the right to possess and carry weapons typically possessed by law-abiding citizens for lawful purposes such as self-defense. . . . It protects the right to possess a handgun in one's home because handguns are a "class of 'arms' that is overwhelmingly chosen by American society" for the lawful purpose of self-defense. . . .

As the court's discussion makes clear, the Second Amendment right does not protect possession of a military M-16 rifle. . . . Likewise, it does not protect the right to possess assault weapons or .50-caliber BMG rifles. As we have already indicated, in enacting the Roberti-Roos Assault Weapons Control Act of 1989 and the .50 Caliber BMG Regulation Act of 2004, the Legislature was specifically concerned with the unusual and dangerous nature of these weapons. An assault weapon "has such a high rate of fire and capacity for firepower that its function as a legitimate sports or recreational firearm is substantially outweighed by the danger that it can be used to kill and injure human beings." (§12275.5, subd. (a).) The .50-caliber BMG rifle has the capacity to destroy or seriously damage "vital public and private buildings, civilian, police and military vehicles, power generation and transmission facilities, petrochemical production and storage facilities, and transportation infrastructure." (§12275.5, subd. (b).) These are not the types of weapons that are typically possessed by law-abiding citizens for lawful purposes such as sport hunting or self-defense; rather, these are weapons of war.

Our conclusion that *Heller* does not extend Second Amendment protection to assault weapons and .50-caliber BMG rifles is supported by post-*Heller* federal precedent. In *United States v. Fincher*, [], 538 F.3d 868 [8th Cir. 2008] . . . , the Eighth Circuit Court of Appeals held that Fincher's possession of a machine gun was "not protected by the Second Amendment" because "[m]achine guns are not in common use by law-abiding citizens for lawful purposes and therefore fall within the category of dangerous and unusual weapons that the government can prohibit for individual use." (*Fincher, supra,* 538 F.3d at p. 874; see *United States v. Gilbert* [286 Fed. Appx. 383] (9th Cir. 2008) ["Under *Heller,* individuals still do not have the right to possess machineguns or short-barreled rifles."]; *Hamblen v. U.S.* (M.D. Tenn., Dec. 5, 2008, No. 3:08-1034) 2008 WL 5136586 [also holding that *Heller* did not extend Second Amendment protection to machine guns].) While the fully automatic nature of a machine gun renders such a weapon arguably more dangerous and unusual than a semiautomatic assault weapon, that observation does not negate the fact that assault weapons, like machine guns, are not in common use by law-abiding citizens for lawful purposes and likewise fall within the category of dangerous and unusual weapons that the government can prohibit for individual use. Moreover, the .50-caliber BMG rifle has the capacity to take down an aircraft, a fact which arguably makes such a weapon more dangerous and unusual than the average machine gun. In any event, assault weapons and .50-caliber BMG rifles are at least as dangerous and unusual as the short-barreled shotgun at issue in *United States v. Miller, supra,* 307 U.S. 174.

We conclude that section 12280, subdivisions (b) and (c), does not prohibit conduct protected by the Second Amendment to the United States Constitution as defined in *Heller.* . . .

The judgment is affirmed.

NOTES & QUESTIONS

1. Under federal law, .50 caliber rifles are simply regulated as ordinary firearms under the Gun Control Act of 1968. Though rifles such as the AR-50 are large, heavy (often over 30 pounds), and expensive, and therefore fairly uncommon, many commercial gun stores sell them. Rifles *over* .50 caliber are regulated under the more stringent provisions of the National Firearms Act. 26 U.S.C. §5845(f)(3) (defining a rifle with a bore diameter of over .50 as a "destructive device" subject to special registration, taxation, and transfer requirements). Is the longstanding treatment of .50 caliber rifles as ordinary firearms sufficient in itself to sustain the claim that such guns are firearms in common use?

2. Should the common-use standard focus on how many units of a gun have been sold? If so, how many must be sold to qualify? Are there other ways to apply the common-use test? For different proposals on how courts should implement the common use test, see Nicholas J. Johnson, *The Second Amendment in the States and the Limits of the Common Use Standard,* 4 Harv. L. & Pol'y Rev., Online, Apr. 8, 2010, *available at* http://www.hlpronline.com/2010/04/Johnson_commonuse/ (arguing that courts should use a "functional" test that asks whether the prohibited weapons are no more dangerous than other weapons agreed to be in common use); Nicholas J. Johnson, *Administering the Second Amendment: Law, Politics and Taxonomy,* 50 Santa Clara L. Rev. 1263 (2010) (examining some of the problems of classifying weapons for constitutional purposes); Michael P. O'Shea, *The Right to Defensive Arms After* District of Columbia v. Heller, 111 W. Va. L. Rev. 349, 380-93 (2009) (arguing that courts should use an objective, statistical approach that focuses on which types of guns are actually acquired and possessed by private citizens and police departments).

3. The California legislation bans all rifles (semi-automatic or single-shot) chambered for a particular ammunition type, the .50 BMG. This evinces more of a concern about the ammunition than about the particular characteristics of the guns. Other jurisdictions have created special laws for particular types of ammunition. New Jersey, for example, restricts hollow point ammunition. N.J. Stat. Ann. §2C:39-3f(1). What questions would you want answered before deciding whether the New Jersey restrictions are constitutional post-*Heller*? For background on hollow points (which are often superior for self-defense), including their common usage by American police, see Joshua F. Berry, *Hollow Point Bullets: How History Has Hijacked Their Use in Combat and Why It Is Time to Reexamine the 1899 Hague Declaration Concerning Expanding Bullets,* 206 Mil. L. Rev. 88 (2010).

4. Consider again the tyranny-control justifications for the right to arms. Assuming that .50 BMG rifles are too cumbersome for individual self-defense, do they have higher value as instruments of resistance to tyranny? Is that concern still legally salient after *Heller* (Chapter 9)? Is the sporting use of long-distance target-shooting rifles part of the Second Amendment?

5. Recall the Firearms Freedom Act legislation discussed in Chapter 8. Would .50 BMG rifles fall under the protection of the Montana Firearms Freedom Act legislation? Would protection of civilian possession of .50 BMG rifles bc a legitimate exercise of the state's militia interest? Should a court consider whether legislative findings, such as the claim that a .50 BMG rifle using civilian ammunition can take down an airplane, are actually true?

6. Reconsider the distinction in *Heller* between dangerous and unusual firearms and constitutionally protected firearms in common use. Aren't common, constitutionally protected guns still dangerous? If so, what factors should distinguish dangerous and unusual firearms from ordinary, common, but still dangerous firearms?

7. James was also prosecuted for possessing a blowgun. Should blowguns and similar arms (traditional non-powder weapons used by tribal peoples in North America and elsewhere be recognized as Second Amendment arms?

EXERCISE: AMMUNITION-BASED CONTROLS

Shortly after the California ban, Barrett Firearms Manufacturing, the leading maker of .50 BMG rifles, developed and began producing rifles in the new caliber, .416 Barrett. This is a large caliber rifle round that is similar and in some respects superior to the .50 BMG. The .416 Barrett has a higher ballistic coefficient, meaning that the bullet is more aerodynamic and thus flatter shooting. It also produces more destructive energy at 1,000 yards than the .50 BMG (3,341 foot pounds versus 3,230 foot pounds, respectively). In addition to the .416 Barrett, there are many other .40 or greater caliber rifle cartridges and a variety of other .50 caliber cartridges that California has not banned. Based on the ballistics chart below, can you make a case for distinguishing the .50 BMG from the other large caliber rifles listed?

Could California ban the .416 Barrett on the same rationale as the ban of the .50 BMG? Does it make a difference that the variety of projectiles available for the .50 BMG is more varied, and includes some types of ammunition that are only available to the military, namely, anti-material projectiles — for use against equipment — that contain an explosive charge?

As a new, proprietary round, could the .416 Barrett be considered novel and thus uncommon? Would it make a difference if the .416 Barrett were just an improvement of an existing large game cartridge that is many decades old? The .416 Barrett is in fact novel, but a very similar cartridge, the .408 Cheyenne Tactical (a/k/a "CheyTac") is a redesign of the old-fashioned big game .400 Taylor Magnum. How should improvements of long-existing calibers or firearms technologies be evaluated? Should certain rifles or cartridges be considered dangerous and unusual regardless of pedigree? At what point, if any, do long range rifles transform from dangerous and unusual to ordinary and common?

Assume the role of a lawyer arguing each side of the case. After you have developed the competing arguments, shift your perspective to that of a judge who must decide whether to uphold a ban of the .416 Barrett. Integrate into your analysis any of the previous material. Pay particular attention to the competing methodologies for interpreting the right to arms presented earlier in this chapter.

Representative Ballistics

The following table shows a sample of cartridge ballistics. A complete representation of firearms ballistics would fill a book. Many calibers are omitted from this table. Literally hundreds of cartridges fall between the diminutive .22 rimfire and the pistol and large rifle cartridges represented in the table. The handgun calibers in the table are a broad range of common cartridges, while all the rifle cartridges in the table, except .22 and .223 Remington, are high-powered cartridges designed for long distances. The .223 Remington is the cartridge used in M-16 rifles and most AR-15–style rifles. It is also used in many sporting rifles but is generally considered adequate only for shooting smaller animals. Many consider it inadequate for medium game like deer, and some states disallow it for deer hunting out of concern that it tends to wound rather than cleanly kill the animal. *See, e.g.,* Conn. Dep't of Envtl. Prot., Connecticut Hunting and Trapping Guide 4, 9-13 (2009).

A full representation would show many variations within each cartridge type, caused by the use of different weight bullets, different shaped bullets, and different amounts of gunpowder. For example, the .30-06 rifle cartridge comes in at least 10 different bullet weights ranging from 125 grain to 220 grain. The 220 grain is the same diameter (.30 caliber or roughly 30/100ths of an inch) as the 125 grain but is longer and heavier. The different .30-06 cartridges will exhibit very different velocity and energy numbers. Other factors also will affect reported ballistics, including the length of the test barrel. The same bullet shot from a longer barrel will have higher velocity and energy. For example, in a handgun with a three-inch barrel, after the bullet has travelled three inches, it receives no further propulsion from the burning gunpowder. Once the bullet has exited the barrel, the remaining gunpowder energy just dissipates out the muzzle. If the barrel is six inches, the bullet receives more energy from the burning gunpowder.

The Velocity columns show the speed of the bullet in feet per second. This will always be faster at the muzzle of the gun and will slow as the bullet travels.

The Energy columns show the kinetic energy of the bullet at different ranges. This force is a function of the weight of the bullet and the bullet speed. Other factors, including bullet composition and bullet shape, will also affect performance.

The Trajectory columns show the bullet's flight path over a distance. Because gravity immediately begins pulling a bullet downward, shooting at even moderate distances requires the gun to be pointed slightly upward. The bullet does not travel flat, but rather in an arc between the muzzle and the target. Early in its arc, the bullet will hit slightly higher than the point of aim. Later in its arc, the bullet will hit below the point of aim. So to shoot the .450 Dakota at 400 yards, for example, you have to aim 33.8 inches above where you want the bullet to hit. The less that a bullet drops over distance ("the flatter the trajectory"), the erosion it is to shoot accurately at a distance.

Cartridge	Bullet Wgt. (Grns.)	Velocity (feet per second)					Energy (foot-pounds)					Trajectory (inches)			
		Muzzle	100 yds.	200 yds.	300 yds.	400 yds.	Muzzle	100 yds.	200 yds.	300 yds.	400 yds.	100 yds.	200 yds.	300 yds.	400 yds.
.22 LR Rimfire	40	1070	890	n/a	n/a	n/a	93	70	n/a	n/a	n/a	+4.6	n/a	n/a	n/a
.223 Rem. (The M-16/AR-15 cartridge)	55	3240	2748	2305	1906	1556	1282	922	649	444	296	+2.0	-0.2	-9.0	-27.0
.378 Wea. Magnum	270	3180	2976	2781	2594	2415	6062	5308	4635	4034	3495	+2.5	+2.6	-1.8	-11.3
.408 CheyTac	419	2850	2752	2657	2562	2470	7551	7048	6565	6108	5675	-1.02	0.00	-1.9	-4.2
.458 Win Magnum	465	2220	1999	1791	1601	n/a	5088	4127	3312	2646	n/a	+2.5	-2.00	-17.7	n/a
.450 Dakota	500	2450	2235	2030	1838	1658	6663	5544	4576	3748	3051	+2.5	-0.6	-12.0	-33.8
.460 Wea. Magnum	500	2700	2404	2128	1869	1635	8092	6416	5026	3878	2969	+2.5	+0.6	-8.9	-28.0
.495 A Square	600	2280	2050	1833	1635	n/a	6925	5598	4478	3562	n/a	+2.5	-2.0	-17.0	n/a
.500 A Square	707	2250	2040	1841	1567	n/a	7947	6530	5318	4431	n/a	+2.5	-2.0	-17	n/a
.500 Tyrannosaur	750	2400	2141	1898	1675	n/a	9591	7633	5996	4671	n/a	+3.0	0.0	-12.9	n/a
.416 Barrett	450	3025	2757	2629	2504	2383	9141	8356	7594	6905	6267	0.0	-1.2	-6.9	-17.7
.50 BMG	661	2750	2601	2458	2319	2185	9934	8870	7897	7009	6201	0.0	-2.1	-10.0	-24.4

COMPARATIVE HANDGUN BALLISTICS	Bullet Wgt. (Grns.)	Velocity (ft. per sec.)			Energy (ft.-lbs.)		
		Muzzle	50 yds.	100 yds.	Muzzle	50 yds.	100 yds.
.22 LR Rimfire* 6'' Barrel	40	940	n/a	n/a	78	n/a	n/a
.25 auto	50	760	705	660	65	55	50
.32 auto	65	950	890	830	130	115	100
9mm Luger	115	1155	1045	970	340	280	240
.38 special	148	710	635	565	175	160	120
.357 Mag.	150	1235	1105	1015	535	430	360
.40 S&W	155	1140	1026	958	447	362	309
.44 Mag.	250	1250	1148	1070	867	732	635
.45 Auto	230	880	846	816	396	366	340
.45 Colt	225	960	890	830	460	395	345

*When fired from a handgun, the .22 rimfire is generally considered effective only at relatively close range, so ballistics reporting for .22 rimfire from a handgun at 50 and 100 yards is uncommon. Likewise, even when fired from a rifle, the .22 rimfire's effective range is well under 200 yards, so the 200-400 yard rifle data are usually not reported.

n/a means that the cartridge is not typically fired to such a distance.

G. *Child-Access-Prevention Laws*

One of the most-discussed costs of our armed society is the injury or death of children in firearms accidents. *See, e.g.*, Kim Minugh, The Sacramento Bee (2010), Colleagues Shaken by Gun Death of Calif. Deputy's Toddler, *available at* http://www.officer.com/online/article.jsp?siteSection=1&id=51925 (child of a Sacramento, CA police officer picked up her father's loaded handgun and accidentally shot and killed herself). These incidents are relatively rare in comparison to intentional firearms deaths and to other types of fatal accidents. As the National Safety Council explains,

> how many children are killed by guns is a complicated question. If the age range is 0-19 years, and homicide, suicide, and unintentional injuries are included, then the total firearms-related deaths for 2007 is 3,067. This is . . . a figure commonly used by journalists. The 3,067 firearms-related deaths for age group 0-19 breaks down to 138 unintentional, 683 suicides, and 2,161 homicides, 60 for which the intent could not be determined, and 25 due to legal intervention. Viewed by age group, 85 of the total firearms-related deaths were of children under 5-years-old, 313 were children 5-14 years old, and 2,669 were teens and young adults 15-19 years old.

National Safety Council, Injury Facts 2011, at 143 (2011).

While accidental firearms deaths among children under 14 are relatively rare (65 in 2007), these accidents have had an enormous impact on the firearms debate, prompting child-access-prevention (CAP) laws and regulations. These restrictions generally impose liability on gun owners for allowing minors access to a firearm. *See, e.g.*, Rachel Shaffer, *Child Access Prevention Laws: Keeping Guns Out of Our Children's Hands*, 27 Fordham Urb. L.J. 1985 (2000); Erin P. Lynch, *Federal Gun Storage Legislation: Will This Keep Guns Out of the Hands of Our Children?*, 16 J. Contemp. Health L. & Pol'y 211, 221-30 (1999). Specific definitions of prohibited conduct vary widely. In Massachusetts, for example, a gun owner may be found liable under Mass. Gen. Laws ch. 140, §131L for storing his gun in a fashion in which a person under the age of 18 *may potentially* gain access to it. Liability attaches regardless of whether the gun is loaded and regardless of whether the minor actually gains access to the gun or uses it in a crime. Virginia, on the other hand, imposes liability on a gun owner for intentionally providing a loaded firearm to a minor under the age of 14. Va. Code Ann. §18.2-56.2. The laws typically have exceptions for authorized use, such as allowing a minor to have a gun while legally hunting.

Some object that trigger locks and similar devices to delay access to the gun, make the gun more dangerous (for example, low-quality trigger locks can cause an accidental discharge), or diminish its utility for self-defense. *See, e.g.*, Cynthia Leonardatos, Paul H. Blackman & David B. Kopel, *Smart Guns/Foolish Legislators*, 34 Conn. L. Rev. 157 (2001). Recall that *Heller* (Chapter 9) invalidated a D.C. statute that required guns to be kept unloaded and disassembled. The following case upholding a prosecution under Massachusetts's CAP law was decided after *Heller* and before *McDonald* (Chapter 9).

Commonwealth v. Runyan
922 N.E.2d 794 (2010)

GANTS, J.

The defendant was charged in the Lowell Division of the District Court Department with storing or keeping a firearm that was not "secured in a locked container or equipped with a tamper-resistant mechanical lock or other safety device, properly engaged so as to render such weapon inoperable by any person other than the owner of other lawfully authorized user," in violation of G. L. c. 140, §131L(a). On October 15, 2008, a judge dismissed the count against the defendant, explaining that he was "unable to distinguish the provisions of G. L. c. 140, §131L, from those struck down" by the United States Supreme Court in *District of Columbia v. Heller*, 128 S. Ct. 2783, (2008) (*Heller*), as unconstitutionally infringing the right to bear arms under the Second Amendment to the United States Constitution. The Commonwealth filed a timely notice of interlocutory appeal. We granted the Commonwealth's application for direct appellate review. We now reverse the judge's decision and vacate the dismissal of the count.

Background. According to the police report that accompanied the application for criminal complaint, police officers were dispatched to 7 Fernwood Road in Billerica following a report that "BB" pellets were being shot into the window of the house from a neighbor's house at 9 Fernwood Road. When the officers arrived, they observed the side window of 9 Fernwood Road, which faced the house at 7 Fernwood Road, being closed by a young male.

When the police officers went to 9 Fernwood Road, the only person at home was the defendant's eighteen year old son, who appeared to have developmental disabilities. The son admitted to the police officers that he had fired shots at his neighbor's house with a BB rifle that was in his bedroom closet. When the officers asked why he had been shooting at his neighbor's house, the son stated, "I hate him." When the officers asked the son if there were more guns in the house, the son took them to the defendant's bedroom and pointed to two soft carrying cases located under the bed. One case contained a shotgun secured with a trigger lock. The other contained a semiautomatic hunting rifle that had no gun locking device. When the officers asked if there was any ammunition for these firearms, the son opened a dresser drawer that contained rifle rounds and shotgun shells.

The defendant was charged with violating G. L. c. 140, §131L(a), for failing to secure the rifle in a locked container or by means of a trigger lock or comparable safety device. He moved to dismiss the count, arguing that the requirements of G. L. c. 140, §131L(a), mandating the safe storage of firearms, impermissibly infringed his right to bear arms for self-defense under the Second Amendment to the United States Constitution, as articulated in *Heller, supra*. The judge allowed the motion to dismiss.

Discussion. In *Heller*, the Supreme Court held that the District of Columbia's "ban on handgun possession in the home violates the Second Amendment, as does its prohibition against rendering any lawful firearm in the home operable for the purpose of immediate self-defense." *Id.* at 2821-22. In doing so, the Court announced for the first time that the Second Amendment protects a limited, individual right to keep and bear firearms for the purpose of self-defense, not simply a collective right to possess and carry arms for the purpose of maintaining a State militia. See *id.* at 2799, 2803.

The judge's conclusion that the Supreme Court's decision in *Heller* required a dismissal of the count charging a violation of G. L. c. 140, §131L(a), rests on two premises, both of which are in error. First, the decision assumes that the protection of the Second Amendment applies to the States as a matter of substantive due process under the Fourteenth Amendment to the United States Constitution. To reach such a conclusion would require a determination that the right protected under the Second Amendment is among those fundamental rights "implicit in the concept of ordered liberty." *Wolf v. Colorado,* 338 U.S. 25, 27-28 (1949), quoting *Palko v. Connecticut,* 302 U.S. 319, 325-326 (1937) (Fourth Amendment's protection against unreasonable searches incorporated under Fourteenth Amendment's due process clause). See, e.g., *Louisiana ex rel. Francis v. Resweber,* 329 U.S. 459, 463 (1947) (humane tradition of Anglo-American law requires incorporation of Eighth Amendment's prohibition against cruel and unusual punishment under Fourteenth Amendment's due process clause); *Gitlow v. New York,* 268 U.S. 652 (1925) (First Amendment's protections of freedom of speech and press among fundamental personal rights protected by Fourteenth Amendment's due process clause). Based on current Federal law, however, we cannot say that the Second Amendment applies to the States, either through the Fourteenth Amendment's guarantee of substantive due process or otherwise.

In *Heller,* the Supreme Court acknowledged that in *United States v. Cruikshank,* 92 U.S. 542, (1875) (*Cruikshank*), it held that "the Second Amendment does not by its own force apply to anyone other than the Federal Government." *Heller, supra* at 2812. In *Cruikshank, supra* at 553, the Supreme Court explained that the Second Amendment "means no more than that [the right to bear arms] shall not be infringed by Congress. This is one of the amendments that has no other effect than to restrict the powers of the national government. . . ." In *Heller,* when considering whether any of its precedents challenged the conclusion it had reached about the meaning of the Second Amendment, the Court stated that its decisions in *Presser v. Illinois,* 116 U.S. 252 (1886), and *Miller v. Texas,* 153 U.S. 535 (1894), had "reaffirmed" after *Cruikshank* "that the Second Amendment applies only to the Federal Government." *Heller, supra* at 2813 n.23. *Heller* did not overrule these decisions.

We recognize that each of the cited cases limiting the application of the Second Amendment to the Federal government preceded the Supreme Court's selective incorporation of some provisions of the Bill of Rights under the due process clause of the Fourteenth Amendment, and that each was decided without reference to or consideration of the requirements of substantive due process. See *National Rifle Ass'n of Am. v. Chicago,* 567 F.3d 856, 857 (7th Cir.), cert. granted sub nom. *McDonald v. Chicago,* 130 S. Ct. 48 (2009). Nonetheless, these cases are the law of the land until the Supreme Court decides otherwise, and we are therefore bound by them. See *State Oil Co. v. Khan,* 522 U.S. 3, 20 (1997) (Supreme Court alone has prerogative to overrule its own precedents); *Rodriguez de Quijas v. Shearson/American Express, Inc.,* 490 U.S. 477 (1989) ("If a precedent of this Court has direct application in a case, yet appears to rest on reasons rejected in some other line of decisions, [lower courts] should follow the case which directly controls, leaving to this Court the prerogative of overruling its own decisions").

The vast majority of courts considering this question since *Heller* was decided have adopted this principle of deference. See *National Rifle Ass'n of Am. v. Chicago, supra* at 857 (lawsuits dismissed against municipalities that banned possession of most handguns because Second Amendment not applicable to States); *Maloney v. Cuomo*, 554 F.3d 56, 58 (2d Cir. 2009) (per curiam) (settled law that Second Amendment only applies to limitations Federal government seeks to impose on individual right to keep and bear arms); *State v. Turnbull*, 766 N.W.2d 78, 80 (Minn. Ct. App. 2009) (Second Amendment not incorporated in *due process clause* and therefore not enforceable against States); *Crespo v. Crespo*, 408 N.J. Super. 25, 41 (App. Div. 2009) (in announcing individual right under Second Amendment, *Heller* Court did not alter view that Second Amendment poses no limits on States). But see *Nordyke v. King*, 563 F.3d 439, 457 (9th Cir.), reh'g granted, 575 F.3d 890 (9th Cir. 2009) ("Due Process Clause of the Fourteenth Amendment incorporates the Second Amendment and applies it against the states and local governments").

If the Second Amendment is not incorporated under the Fourteenth Amendment's guarantee of substantive due process and therefore does not apply to the States, the defendant's claim that the obligation safely to secure his firearm under G. L. c. 140, §131L(a), unconstitutionally infringes on his right to keep and bear arms in his home for self-defense must fail. Under *Cruikshank*, the Second Amendment imposes no limitations on the ability of the Massachusetts Legislature to regulate the possession of firearms and ammunition.

The judge's second erroneous premise was that the provisions of G. L. c. 140, §131L(a), are indistinguishable from those held unconstitutional by the Supreme Court in *Heller*. General Laws, c. 140, §131L(a), provides:

> "It shall be unlawful to store or keep any firearm, rifle or shotgun . . . unless such weapon is secured in a locked container or equipped with a tamper-resistant mechanical lock or other safety device, properly engaged so as to render such weapon inoperable by any person other than the owner or other lawfully authorized user. For purposes of this section, such weapon shall not be deemed stored or kept if carried by or under the control of the owner or other lawfully authorized user."

Under this provision, an individual with a valid firearms identification card issued under G. L. c. 140, §129C, is not obliged to secure or render inoperable a firearm while the individual carries it or while it remains otherwise under the individual's control. A gun owner may therefore carry or keep a loaded firearm under his or her control in his or her home without securing it with a trigger lock or comparable safety device. The gun owner's obligation to secure the firearm in accordance with the statute arises only when the firearm is stored or otherwise outside the owner's immediate control.[6]

---

6. This statutory obligation owed by one who keeps firearms in the home to secure those firearms safely is separate and distinct from the common-law duty of a home owner to ensure that the firearms stored on the property are properly secured when the home owner "allows unsupervised access to that property by a person known by her to have a history of violence and mental instability." *Jupin v. Kask*, 849 N.E.2d 829 (Mass. 2006).

In contrast, the comparable provision of the District of Columbia Code challenged in *Heller* required:

> "Except for law enforcement personnel described in §7-2502.01(b)(1), each registrant shall keep any firearm in his possession unloaded and disassembled or bound by a trigger lock or similar device unless such firearm is kept at his place of business, or while being used for lawful recreational purposes within the District of Columbia."

D.C. Code §7-2507.02 (2008). Under this provision, a person registered to keep a firearm (apart from law enforcement personnel) was prohibited in any circumstance from carrying or keeping a loaded firearm in his or her home. The ordinance prohibited a registered gun owner from keeping even an unloaded firearm in his or her home unless it was disassembled or rendered inoperable by a trigger lock or similar device. The Supreme Court ruled that the District of Columbia's requirement "that firearms in the home be rendered and kept inoperable at all times" made it "impossible for citizens to use them for the core lawful purpose of self-defense and is hence unconstitutional." *Heller, supra* at 2818. General Law c. 140, §131L(a), does not require that firearms in the home be rendered and kept inoperable at all times and does not prohibit a licensed gun owner from carrying a loaded firearm in the home; the statute therefore does not make it impossible for those persons licensed to possess firearms to rely on them for lawful self-defense.[7]

We conclude that the legal obligation safely to secure firearms in G. L. c. 140, §131L(a), is not unconstitutional, that the motion to dismiss the count charging its violation was allowed in error, and that the defendant may face prosecution on this count.

Conclusion. For the reasons stated above, the order allowing the motion to dismiss is reversed, the dismissal is vacated, and the case is remanded to the District Court for further proceedings consistent with this opinion.

So ordered.

NOTES & QUESTIONS

1. *Runyan* preceded the incorporation of the Second Amendment and its recognition as fundamental in *McDonald* (Chapter 9). Does anything in *McDonald* cast doubt on *Runyan?*

2. Gun rights advocates argue that trigger locks or other devices that limit firearms access could potentially obstruct or delay access at a critical time. Opponents respond that defensive gun uses are rare.

---

7. We note that the Court in *Heller, supra* at 2820, declared that its analysis should not be taken to "suggest the invalidity of laws regulating the storage of firearms to prevent accidents." We do not, however, decide whether the defendant's alleged violation of G. L. c. 140, §131L(a), could survive a motion to dismiss if the Second Amendment were made applicable to the States through incorporation under the Fourteenth Amendment's due process clause.

There have been 13 major surveys regarding the frequency of defensive gun use (DGU) in the modern United States. The surveys range from a low of 760,000 annually to a high of 3 million. In contrast, much lower annual estimates come from the National Crime Victimization Survey (NCVS), a poll using in-person home interviews conducted by the Census Bureau in conjunction with the Department of Justice. The NCVS for 1992-2005 suggests about 97,000 DGUs annually. All the surveys define "defensive gun use" to include instances where an attack is thwarted without discharge of the gun. These non-shooting DGUs constitute the vast majority of the total. *See, e.g.*, Gun Control and Gun Rights: A Reader and Guide 6-33 (Andrew J. McClurg, David B. Kopel & Brannon P. Denning eds., 2002).

Critics say the NCVS figure is too low because the survey never directly asks about DGUs. The NCVS first asks if the respondent has been a "victim" of a crime. Critics charge that this excludes successful DGUs where people do not consider themselves "victims." Additionally, critics charge, the NCVS only asks about some crimes, and not the full range of crimes where a DGU might occur. *See, e.g.*, Gary Kleck, Targeting Guns: Firearms and Their Control 152-54 (1997).

Gary Kleck and Mark Gertz conducted an especially thorough survey in 1993, with stringent safeguards to cull respondents who might mis-describe a DGU story. Kleck and Gertz found a midpoint estimate of 2.5 million DGUs annually. *See* Gary Kleck & Marc Gertz, *Armed Resistance to Crime: The Prevalence and Nature of Self-Defense with a Gun*, 86 J. Crim. L. & Criminology 150 (1995). The Kleck/Gertz survey found that 80 percent of DGUs involved handguns, and that 76 percent did not involve firing the weapon, but merely brandishing it to scare away an attacker. *Id.* at 175.

Marvin Wolfgang, one of the most eminent criminologists of the twentieth century, and an ardent supporter of gun prohibition, reviewed Kleck's findings and wrote:

> I am as strong a gun-control advocate as can be found among the criminologists in this country. . . . I would eliminate all guns from the civilian population and maybe even from the police. I hate guns. . . .
> Nonetheless, the methodological soundness of the current Kleck and Gertz study is clear. . . .
> The Kleck and Gertz study impresses me for the caution the authors exercise and the elaborate nuances they examine methodologically. I do not like their conclusions that having a gun can be useful, but I cannot fault their methodology. They have tried earnestly to meet all objections in advance and have done exceedingly well.

Marvin Wolfgang, *A Tribute to a View I Have Opposed*, 86 J. Crim. L. & Criminology, 188, 191-92 (1995).

Philip Cook of Duke and Jens Ludwig of Georgetown were skeptical of Kleck's results, and conducted their own survey for the Police Foundation. That survey produced an estimate of 1.46 million DGUs per year. Philip Cook & Jens Ludwig, Guns in America: Results of a Comprehensive National Survey of Firearms Ownership and Use 62-63 (1996). Cook and Ludwig argue that their own study produced implausibly high numbers, and they prefer the NCVS estimate. *Id.* at 68-75. For a response to Cook and Ludwig, *see* Gary Kleck, *Has the Gun Deterrence Hypothesis Been Discredited?*, 10 J. on Firearms & Pub. Pol'y 65 (1998).

　　The National Opinion Research Center argues that Kleck's figures are probably too high, and the NCVS too low. It estimates annual DGUs in the range of 256,500 to 1,210,000. Tom Smith, *A Call for a Truce in the DGU War*, 87 J. Crim. L. & Criminology 1462 (1997).

3.　What is your assessment of the constitutionality of CAP laws after *Heller* (Chapter 9), and *McDonald* (Chapter 9)? Should every type of CAP legislation survive *Heller*? Would your answer vary depending on the level of scrutiny applied to the question?

4.　Recall the discussion of laws restricting minors' access to firearms in Chapter 8. The federal Gun Control Act seemed to accommodate differences between rural and urban cultures. Should the evaluation of CAP laws vary by whether the jurisdiction is rural or urban?

5.　For work supporting CAP laws, *see, e.g.*, L. Hepburn, M. Miller, D. Hemenway & D. Azrael, *The U.S. Gun Stock: Results from the 2004 National Firearms Survey*, 13 Injury Prevention 15 (2007); Daniel W. Webster & Marc Starnes, *Reexamining The Association Between Child Access Prevention Gun Laws and Unintentional Shooting Deaths of Children*, 106 Pediatrics 1466 (2000); Andrew J. McClurg, *Child Access Prevention Laws: A Common Sense Approach to Gun Control*, 18 St. Louis U. Pub. L. Rev. 47, 57 (1999); Peter Cummings & Frederick P. Rivara, *State Gun Safe Storage Laws and Child Mortality Due to Firearms*, 278 JAMA 1084 (1997). For a criticism of CAP laws, see Leonardatos, Blackman & Kopel, *supra*.

H.　The Right to Bear Arms and Carrying Handguns for Self-Defense

Heller (Chapter 9) concluded that firearms for self-defense in the home were at the core of the Second Amendment right to keep and bear arms. The main ordinance overturned in *Heller* prohibited the mere possession, the "keeping," of handguns. *Heller* did not directly affect the right to "bear" arms, except in striking down the accompanying ban on rendering one's firearms operational for defensive use within the home, and finding that D.C. could not refuse to grant Heller a license to carry a gun in his own home. (The D.C. law at the time required a license for any carrying, even for moving a gun's storage place from one room to another, and carry permits were almost never granted.)

　　Possession of firearms in the home and carrying firearms in public have obviously different policy implications. There is a long history of hunting and sporting use of firearms in places that are in some sense public, including public lands owned by state or federal governments. We already have seen provisions of the federal 1986 Firearms Owners Protection Act that attempt to accommodate the interstate transportation of firearms but restrict accessibility during transportation. On the other hand, many state and local governments have long imposed various limits on carrying firearms in public. As discussed in Chapters 6 and 7, many of these early laws were overtly race- or class-motivated and enforced in a discriminatory fashion.

Following *Heller* and *McDonald* (Chapter 9), a series of Second Amendment challenges were brought in jurisdictions that heavily restrict the carrying of handguns. These challenges press the question of exactly what is protected by what the *McDonald* majority described as the right to "bear arms for the purpose of self-defense." The large majority of states have laws that allow lawful gun owners to obtain a license to carry a gun in public. But a handful of states generally prohibit most citizens from carrying defensive handguns in public under any circumstances, giving rise to claims that they are violating the Second Amendment right to bear arms. *See* Chapter 8.C.; *infra*. The decision below addresses one of those claims.

Peruta v. County of San Diego
678 F. Supp. 2d 1046 (S.D. Cal. 2010)

IRMA E. GONZALEZ, CHIEF JUDGE.

This is a Section 1983 action, challenging the constitutionality of California's law governing the carrying of concealed weapons, both facially and as applied to Plaintiff. Currently before the Court is Defendant William Gore's ("Gore") Motion to Dismiss pursuant to Fed. R. Civ. P. 12(b)(6). Having considered the parties' arguments, and for the reasons set forth below, the Court DENIES the motion.

BACKGROUND

Plaintiff is a sixty year old United States citizen and a California resident, who "maintains several residences across the United States, including but not limited to a residence in San Diego County." According to Plaintiff, he maintains a permanent mailing address in San Diego, "where he and his wife have a room in which they keep a wardrobe and other personal items." Plaintiff and his wife have made their motor home their "permanent residence," and allegedly stay in San Diego for extended periods of time. For example, Plaintiff claims to have reserved space at Campland on the Bay, in San Diego, from November 15, 2008 through April 15, 2009. He had also reserved spaces at the same place from February 2007 through April 2007. . . .

The present case arises from Plaintiff's attempts to obtain a concealed weapon's permit in San Diego County. Plaintiff alleges that he obtained and provided to the San Diego County Sheriff the required 8 Hour Firearms Safety and Proficiency Certificate in accordance with California Penal Code §12050(a)(1)(E)(i). He also alleges that the Firearms Licensing and Permits Unit of the State of California Department of Justice found him eligible to possess firearms. On November 17, 2008, Plaintiff requested a license to carry a concealed weapon from the San Diego County Sheriff's License Division ("SD License Division"), at which time he was interviewed by a licensing supervisor to determine whether he satisfied the licensing criteria. On February 3, 2009, Plaintiff submitted an application for a license to carry a concealed weapon. Plaintiff alleges he was denied a license to carry a concealed weapon by Defendant Gore's predecessor because the SD License Division made a finding that Plaintiff did not have good cause and was not a resident of San Diego — both of which are requirements under Section 12050.

Plaintiff filed his complaint on October 9, 2009, alleging three causes of action. First, Plaintiff argues Section 12050's requirements of (1) "good cause" beyond the interests of self-defense and (2) durational "residency" violate the Second and Fourteenth Amendments to the U.S. Constitution. Second, Plaintiff alleges that Defendants' subjective application of the "good cause" and "residency" requirements results in an unequal treatment of similarly situated individuals, and therefore violates the Eighth Amendment of the U.S. Constitution. Finally, Plaintiff argues the requirement that individuals reside full time in San Diego County before they can apply for a concealed weapon's permit violates Plaintiff's right to travel under the Fourteenth Amendment to the U.S. Constitution. . . .

LEGAL STANDARD

A motion to dismiss under Rule 12(b)(6) tests the legal sufficiency of the pleadings. A complaint survives a motion to dismiss if it contains "enough facts to state a claim to relief that is plausible on its face." *Bell Atl. Corp. v. Twombly*, 550 U.S. 544, 570 (2007). The court may dismiss a complaint as a matter of law for: (1) "lack of cognizable legal theory," or (2) "insufficient facts under a cognizable legal claim." The court only reviews the contents of the complaint, accepting all factual allegations as true, and drawing all reasonable inferences in favor of the nonmoving party. Despite the deference, the court need not accept "legal conclusions" as true. *Ashcroft v. Iqbal*, 129 S. Ct. 1937, 1949-50 (2009). It is also improper for the court to assume "the [plaintiff] can prove facts that [he or she] has not alleged." On the other hand, "[w]hen there are well-pleaded factual allegations, a court should assume their veracity and then determine whether they plausibly give rise to an entitlement to relief." *Iqbal*, 129 S. Ct. at 1950.

DISCUSSION

The Second Amendment provides: "A well regulated Militia, being necessary to the security of a free State, the right of the people to keep and bear Arms, shall not be infringed." The Supreme Court's landmark decision in *District of Columbia v. Heller*, 128 S. Ct. 2783, (2008), resolved some of the hotly debated issues with regard to the Second Amendment, but left many others lingering for future determination. In *Heller*, after an exhaustive analysis of the text of the Amendment and the founding-era sources of its original public meaning, the Supreme Court stated unequivocally that the Second Amendment guarantees "the individual right to possess and carry weapons in case of confrontation." 128 S. Ct. at 2797. However, like most rights, "the right secured by the Second Amendment is not unlimited." *Id.* at 2816. Thus, the Supreme Court also made it clear that "the right was not a right to keep and carry any weapon whatsoever in any manner whatsoever and for whatever purpose." *Id.* For example, the Supreme Court noted that:

> the majority of the 19th-century courts to consider the question held that prohibitions on carrying concealed weapons were lawful under the Second Amendment or state analogues. Although we do not undertake an exhaustive historical analysis today of the full scope of the Second Amendment, nothing in our opinion should be taken to cast doubt on longstanding prohibitions on the possession of firearms by felons and the mentally ill, or laws forbidding the carrying of firearms in sensitive places such as schools and government buildings, or laws imposing conditions and qualifications on the commercial sale of arms.

Id. at 2816-17 (internal citations omitted). In a footnote immediately following, the Supreme Court explained: "We identify these presumptively lawful regulatory measures only as example; our list does not purport to be exhaustive." *Id.* at 2817 n.26.

In *Heller,* having concluded that the Second Amendment protects an individual right to "keep and bear arms," and noting that "the inherent right of self-defense has been central to the Second Amendment right," the Supreme Court turned to the challenged law before it. *Id.* at 2817-18. Without deciding what level of scrutiny should be applied (except stating that it would have to be more than "rational basis"), the Supreme Court concluded that the District of Columbia's "absolute prohibition of handguns held and used for self-defense in the home" clearly violated the Second Amendment. *Id.* at 2817-22.[2]

I. RIGHT TO BEAR ARMS

A. PARTIES' ARGUMENTS

Plaintiff's first cause of action alleges that Section 12050's requirements of (1) "good cause" beyond the interests of self-defense and (2) durational residency violate the Second and Fourteenth Amendments. Defendant moves to dismiss this cause of action, arguing that the Supreme Court in *Heller,* 128 S. Ct. at 2816-17, expressly stated that the right secured by the Second Amendment is not unlimited, and that it certainly does not prohibit states from regulating the carrying of concealed weapons. Defendant argues that, unlike possession of a gun for protection within a residence—which was the issue in *Heller*—carrying

---

2. Because *Heller* involved a challenge to a District of Columbia statute, the Supreme Court there did not have to decide whether the Second Amendment also applied to the states. *See id.* at 2812-13. No party has raised this issue in the present case either. Accordingly, because it appears that both parties agree that the Second Amendment applies in this case, the Court will proceed on that assumption, without deciding the issue at this time. The Court does note, however, that it is aware of the pre-*Heller* Ninth Circuit case law on this issue, as well as the post-*Heller* trend. . . .

a concealed firearm presents a recognized "'threat to public order.'" . . . (quoting *People v. Hale,* 43 Cal. App. 3d 353, 356 (1974)).

Plaintiff agrees that the constitutional right to "keep and bear arms" is not unlimited, and therefore concedes that some regulations are permissible under the Second Amendment. However, also relying on *Heller,* Plaintiff argues that at the center of the Second Amendment is an individual right "to possess and carry weapons in case of confrontation, self-defense, or other traditionally lawful purposes, unconnected with service in a militia." . . . Thus, to be armed and ready in case of confrontation, Plaintiff argues the Second Amendment requires that a person be allowed to carry a weapon "that is immediately capable of being used for its intended purpose." . . . According to Plaintiff, by imposing the "good cause" requirement, Section 12050 violates the Second Amendment. In the alternative, Plaintiff argues the application of Section 12050's "good cause" and "residency" requirements violates the Second Amendment because law abiding citizens who desire to carry concealed firearms solely for self-defense purposes and/or those that are not full-time residents of San Diego County are deemed by the sheriff not to satisfy the statute's requirements.

B.   ANALYSIS

The Supreme Court's decision in *Heller* made it clear — for the first time — that the Second Amendment guarantees "the individual right to possess and carry weapons in case of confrontation." 128 S. Ct. at 2797. It also made clear that this right is not unlimited. *Id.* at 2816-17. Accordingly, while *Heller* does not preclude Second Amendment challenges to laws regulating firearm possession outside of home, "*Heller*'s *dicta* makes pellucidly clear that the Supreme Court's holding should not be read by lower courts as an invitation to invalidate the existing universe of public weapons regulations." *United States v. Masciandaro,* 648 F. Supp. 2d 779, 788 (E.D. Va. 2009).

In the present case, Plaintiff's complaint challenges constitutionality of Section 12050's requirements of "good cause" and "residency" as they relate to his ability to obtain a concealed weapon's permit. This precise issue was not directly addressed by the Supreme Court in *Heller,* which involved a challenge to District of Columbia's prohibition on the possession of a loaded firearm in the home. 128 S. Ct. at 2817-22. Thus, the Court must determine whether Section 12050's application to Plaintiff's request for a permit withstands the appropriate level of constitutional scrutiny.

1.   Presumptive Constitutionality of Concealed Weapon Bans

As a threshold matter, the Court rejects Defendant's contention that the Supreme Court in *Heller* held that prohibitions on carrying of concealed weapons are presumptively constitutional. First, because this precise question was not before the Supreme Court, any pronouncements to that effect would generally be considered *dicta,* even if persuasive. Moreover, the Supreme Court in *Heller* expressly stated that it was leaving the determination of the scope of "permissible" Second Amendment restrictions for a later time. *Id.* at 2816-18, 2821

("[T]here will be time enough to expound upon the historical justifications for the exceptions we have mentioned if and when those exceptions come before us.").

Finally, a closer examination of the cases and authorities relied upon by the Supreme Court suggests that it did not intend to make *all* concealed weapon bans presumptively constitutional. The Supreme Court's entire pronouncement on the validity of concealed weapon bans was:

> Like most rights, the right secured by the Second Amendment is not unlimited. . . . For example, the majority of the 19th-century courts to consider the question held that prohibitions on carrying concealed weapons were lawful under the Second Amendment or state analogues. . . .

Id. at 2816. Both *Chandler* and *Nunn,* the two cases relied upon by the Supreme Court, concerned prohibitions on carrying of concealed weapons where the affected individuals had alternate ways to exercise their Second Amendment rights — by *openly* carrying those weapons. See [*State v. Chandler,* 5 La. Ann. 489-90 (1850)] (noting that the law against carrying of concealed weapons was "absolutely necessary" and that "[i]t interfered with no man's right to carry arms . . . 'in full view,' which places men upon an equality"); [*Nunn v. State,* 1 Ga., 243, 251 (1846)] ("We are of the opinion, then, that so far as the act of 1837 seeks to suppress the practice of carrying certain weapons *secretly,* that it is valid, inasmuch as it does not deprive the citizen of his *natural* right of self-defence, or of his constitutional right to keep and bear arms. But that so much of it, as contains a prohibition against bearing arms *openly,* is in conflict with the Constitution, and *void.* . . ." (emphases in original)). The applicability of these cases is questionable where, as here, the State expressly *prohibits* individuals such as Plaintiff from openly carrying a loaded firearm in public places. See Cal. Penal Code §12031(a)(1).

The other authorities cited by the Supreme Court further undermine Defendant's position. Thus, in *Commentaries on American Law,* James Kent states that "[t]here has been a great difference of opinion on the question" of whether a prohibition on carrying of concealed weapons was constitutional. 2 Kent, *supra,* at *340 n.(b). Likewise, in *The American Students' Blackstone,* George Chase first notes that "it is generally held that statutes prohibiting the carrying of *concealed* weapons are not in conflict with [the Second Amendment], since they merely prohibit the carrying of arms in a particular manner." The American Students' Blackstone, [] at 84, n.11 [G. Chase ed. 1884]. However, he immediately points out that "[i]n some states . . . a contrary doctrine is maintained." *Id.* These pronouncements are directly at odds with Defendant's contention that *Heller* expressed constitutional approval for *all* concealed weapon bans. . . .

Finally, Defendant's reliance on *Hall,* 2008 WL 3097558, is misplaced. In that case, the district court for the Southern District of West Virginia denied the defendant's second motion to suppress made after the Supreme Court's decision in *Heller. Hall,* 2008 WL 3097558, at *2. In reaffirming its prior ruling, the court noted that "the prohibition, as in West Virginia, on the carrying of a concealed weapon without a permit, continues to be a lawful exercise by the state of its regulatory authority notwithstanding the Second Amendment." *Id.* at *1. However, unlike California, West Virginia is an "open carry" state, and therefore allows individuals to carry weapons openly. See Office of the Att'y

Gen., West Virginia Firearm Laws 1 (October 2009). . . . Thus, just like in *Chandler* and *Nunn*, but unlike California, there is a ready alternative available to the affected individuals — the ability to carry weapons openly if they cannot obtain a concealed weapons permit.

For the foregoing reasons, the Court is convinced the *Heller* decision cannot stand for the broad proposition that *all* concealed weapon bans are presumptively constitutional. Accordingly, the Court will proceed to determine whether Section 12050's application to Plaintiff's request for a permit withstands the appropriate level of constitutional scrutiny.

2. Level of Scrutiny

The Supreme Court in *Heller*, while not designating any specific level of scrutiny for evaluating Second Amendment restrictions, explicitly rejected the "rational basis" test. According to the Supreme Court, the rational basis test "could not be used to evaluate the extent to which a legislature may regulate a specific, enumerated right," such as "the right to keep and bear arms." 128 S. Ct. at 2818 n.27 (citation omitted). "If all that was required to overcome the right to keep and bear arms was a rational basis, the Second Amendment would be redundant with the separate constitutional prohibitions on irrational laws, and would have no effect." *Id.* The *Heller* majority also rejected an "interest-balancing inquiry" suggested by the dissent that "asks whether the statute burdens a protected interest in a way or to an extent that is out of proportion to the statute's salutary effect upon other important governmental interests." *Id.* at 2821. According to the Supreme Court, such a "freestanding" approach, which is subject to future judges' assessments of the constitutional guarantee's usefulness, "is no constitutional guarantee at all." *Id.*

With these standards out, the Court must choose between "strict scrutiny" — typically reserved for laws that restrict certain fundamental rights, see *Reno v. Flores*, 507 U.S. 292, 301-02 (1993) — and some form of "intermediate scrutiny."[9] Following *Heller*, courts have not been uniform in the level of scrutiny that should be applied to Second Amendment restrictions. Some courts have applied strict scrutiny, others have used intermediate scrutiny, and still others have either formulated their own tests or have upheld a challenged regulation without specifying a standard of review.

At this stage of the proceedings, the Court need not decide which heightened level of scrutiny applies because the government has failed to meet its burden even if the Court applies the more lenient standard of "intermediate scrutiny." Under both "strict scrutiny" and "intermediate scrutiny" the burden is on the government to show that the challenged law is constitutional, by demonstrating that the law is either "narrowly tailored to serve a compelling state interest," *Flores*, 507 U.S. at 301-02 (citations omitted), or necessary to further an

---

9. When a fundamental right is recognized, substantive due process forbids infringement of that right "at all, no matter what process is provided, unless the infringement is narrowly tailored to serve a compelling state interest." *Flores*, 507 U.S. at 301-02 (citations omitted) (emphasis in original). On the other hand, intermediate scrutiny allows the State to regulate the right at issue if necessary to further an important governmental interest. See *Sell v. United States*, 539 U.S. 166, 178-80 (2003).

important governmental interest, *Sell*, 539 U.S. at 178-80. In the present case, apart from arguing that Section 12050 is within one of the "presumptively lawful" restrictions recognized in *Heller* and that it passes "rational basis" standard of review, the government has made little effort to defend the statute's constitutionality under either of the heightened levels of scrutiny.

3. Application to Plaintiff's Case

Accordingly, taking Plaintiff's allegations as true, his first cause of action for violation of the Second Amendment appears to state a claim upon which relief can be granted. *Twombly*, 550 U.S. at 570. Plaintiff alleges that he was denied a license to carry a concealed weapon by Defendant Gore's predecessor because the SD License Division made a finding that Plaintiff did not have good cause and was not a resident of San Diego — both of which are requirements under Section 12050. As an initial matter, Plaintiff challenges the "good cause" requirement as violating his Second Amendment right "to possess and carry weapons in case of confrontation." See *Heller*, 128 S. Ct. at 2797. The Supreme Court has explained that the natural meaning of "bear arms" is to "'wear, bear, or carry . . . upon the person or in a pocket, for the purpose . . . of being armed and ready for offensive or defensive action in a case of conflict with another person.'" *Id.* at 2793 (quoting *Muscarello v. United States*, 524 U.S. 125, 143 (1998)). Accordingly, by imposing a "good cause" requirement before a concealed weapon's permit can be issued, the State undoubtedly infringes Plaintiff's right to "possess and carry weapons in case of confrontation." See *id.* at 2797. For such infringement to pass constitutional muster, Defendant must at the very least demonstrate that it is necessary to further an important governmental interest. See *Sell*, 539 U.S. at 178-80. In the present case, Defendant has made very little effort to either identify an "important governmental interest" or demonstrate the required "fit" between the law and the interest served.[13]

---

13. The Court does note that California law provides a number of exceptions, some of which significantly undermine portions of Plaintiff's claims. For example, Section 12026(b) of the Penal Code provides that no permit or license is necessary to possess, keep, or carry, "either openly or concealed, a pistol, revolver, or other firearm capable of being concealed upon the person within the citizen's or legal resident's place of residence, place of business, or on private property owned or lawfully possessed by the citizen or legal resident." Because this exemption also applies to anyone who is "temporarily within this state," nothing prevents Plaintiff from carrying a gun while inside of his motor home. See Cal. Penal Code §12026(b); accord id. §12031(l). . . . Likewise, Section 12031(j) allows carrying of a loaded firearm "by a person who reasonably believes that the person or property of himself or herself or of another is in immediate, grave danger and that the carrying of the weapon is necessary for the preservation of that person or property." However, this exemption is limited to the "brief interval" between the notification of the local law enforcement agency and its arrival for assistance. *Id.* §12031(j).

Plaintiff's first cause of action is broader than any of these exceptions. What Plaintiff seeks is enforcement of what he believes is the right guaranteed by the Second Amendment, as interpreted in *Heller*, to carry a weapon that is "immediately capable of being used for its intended purpose," both in his motor home and while on public property. . . . At least at this stage of the proceedings, even with the above exceptions in mind, the Court cannot say that as a matter of law, Plaintiff's first cause of action either lacks cognizable legal theory, or alleges insufficient facts under a cognizable legal theory. See *SmileCare Dental Group* [V. Delta Dental Pkg of Calif., Inc.], 88 F.3d [780,] 783 [9th Cir. 1996].

Accordingly, Defendant's Motion to Dismiss for failure to state a claim Plaintiff's challenge to the "good cause" requirement of Section 12050 fails. *Cf.* [*United States v. Skoien*, 587 F.3d 803, 814 [7th Cir. 2009)] (vacating and remanding where "the government has made little effort to discharge its burden of demonstrating the relationship between §922(g)(9)'s means and its end").

Plaintiff's challenge to the requirements of Section 12050 as applied by Defendants also survives the Motion to Dismiss. Plaintiff alleges that he satisfies the "good cause" requirement because he needs to carry a gun for self-defense, seeing as he is sixty years old and travels to high crime areas for his job. . . . Plaintiff also alleges that he satisfies the "residency" requirement because he resides in San Diego at least four months out of the year, even though he does so in a motor home. . . . Taking Plaintiff's allegations as true, Defendants' application of Section 12050's requirements appears to infringe upon Plaintiff's right to "possess and carry weapons in case of confrontation." See *Heller*, 128 S. Ct. at 2797. As already noted, for such infringement to be in accord with the Second Amendment, Defendant must at the very least demonstrate that it is necessary to further an important governmental interest. See *Sell*, 539 U.S. at 178-180. Seeing as Defendant has failed to either identify an "important governmental interest" or demonstrate the required "fit" between the law and the interest served, the Motion to Dismiss Plaintiff's challenge to the "good cause" and "residency" requirements as applied by Defendants also fails. *Cf. Skoien*, 587 F.3d at 814-15.

4.   Conclusion

It is important to keep in mind the narrow issue before the Court at this stage of the proceedings. The Court is not asked to, and does not, decide whether Section 12050 is constitutional. Rather, the question is whether Plaintiff's complaint contains "enough facts to state a claim to relief that is plausible on its face." *Twombly*, 550 U.S. at 570. The Court only reviews the contents of the complaint, accepting all factual allegations as true, and drawing all reasonable inferences in favor of the nonmoving party. *al-Kidd*, 580 F.3d at 956 (citation omitted). In the present case, because Plaintiff's complaint alleges sufficient facts to state a claim for relief and because Defendant's Motion to Dismiss does little to identify an "important governmental interest" or to demonstrate the required "fit" between the law and the interest served, the Court DENIES Defendant's Motion to Dismiss as it relates to Plaintiff's first cause of action for violation of the Second Amendment.

II.   EQUAL PROTECTION

A.   PARTIES' ARGUMENTS

Plaintiff's second cause of action alleges that Defendant Gore's application of Section 12050's "good cause" and "residency" requirements violates the Equal Protection Clause of the Fourteenth Amendment. Defendant argues there is no equal protection violation because the government can legitimately treat differently persons dissimilarly situated. Moreover, because no suspect classification or fundamental right is involved, Defendant argues the Court should apply rational basis to Plaintiff's challenge. According to Defendant, Plaintiff's second cause of action should be dismissed because it is both rational and reasonable to deny a permit to an individual, such as Plaintiff, who only occasionally visits San Diego and who voluntarily places himself in dangerous situations and places.

Plaintiff opposes the application of "rational basis" standard of review as contrary to the Supreme Court's decision in *Heller*. According to Plaintiff, with heightened level of scrutiny applied, there is no justification for treating Plaintiff differently than other residents of San Diego County. First, Plaintiff argues that, as used in Section 12050, "residency" refers to something temporary in nature, as opposed to the fixed nature of "domicile." Thus, because he resides full-time in his motor home and rents space at Campland on the Bay for at least four months during the year, Plaintiff alleges he satisfies the "residency" require-ment of Section 12050. (Pl. Opp., at 11-13.) Second, Plaintiff argues he meets the "good cause" requirement because he needs a gun to protect himself and his wife when he travels on business and when they travel to remote areas in their motor home. . . .

B. ANALYSIS . . .

Contrary to Defendant's arguments, the Supreme Court in *Heller* explicitly rejected "rational basis" as the applicable standard of review for Second Amend-ment restrictions. *See* 128 S. Ct. at 2818 n.27. Accordingly, the Court has to apply one of the heightened levels of scrutiny to Plaintiff's challenge to Section 12050. . . . Thus, as long as Plaintiff can demonstrate that he is "similarly situated" to other San Diego County residents and was "treated differently" by Defendants, his second cause of action for violation of the Equal Protection Clause would survive the motion to dismiss.

1. Similarly Situated

Defendant urges the Court to find that Plaintiff is not "similarly situated" to other San Diego County residents because his residence in San Diego is only temporary. . . .

Plaintiff's presence in San Diego appears to be more than "temporary or transitory" even under the definition urged by Defendant. Accordingly, Plaintiff alleged sufficient facts to demonstrate he is a "resident" of San Diego County and therefore is "similarly situated" to other San Diego County residents.

2. Treated Differently

According to Plaintiff, he was denied a license to carry a concealed weapon by Defendant Gore's predecessor because the SD License Division made a find-ing that Plaintiff's need for self-defense was not a "good cause" and because his residency in a motor home did not meet the "residency" requirement. Taking these allegations as true, Plaintiff alleges sufficient facts to demonstrate he was treated differently than other similarly situated individuals.

3. Conclusion

For the foregoing reasons, because Plaintiff's complaint alleges sufficient facts to state a claim for relief and because Defendant's Motion to Dismiss does little to identify an "important governmental interest" or to demonstrate the required "fit" between the law and the interest served, the Court DENIES Defendant's Motion to Dismiss as it relates to Plaintiff's second cause of action for violation of the Equal Protection Clause.

III. RIGHT TO TRAVEL

A. PARTIES' ARGUMENTS

Plaintiff's third cause of action alleges that Defendants' requirement of full-time residence violates his right to travel under the Fourteenth Amendment. Defendant moves to dismiss this cause of action, arguing that Section 12050 does not actually deter the right to travel, impeding travel is not one of its primary objectives, and it does not use any classification which serves to penalize the exercise of that right. On the other hand, Plaintiff argues Defendants' application of the statute does actually deter his right to travel because "San Diego residents, such as Plaintiff, must stay fulltime in San Diego in order to have any sort of opportunity to apply and be granted a concealed carrying weapons permit." . . .

B. ANALYSIS

The constitutional "right to travel"[15] embraces at least three different components: (1) it protects the right of a citizen of one State to enter and to leave another State; (2) the right to be treated as a welcome visitor rather than an unfriendly alien when temporarily present in the second State, and (3) for those travelers who elect to become permanent residents, the right to be treated like other citizens of that State. *Saenz v. Roe*, 526 U.S. 489 (1999). . . .

In all cases, the analysis is informed by the same guiding principle — the right to travel "protects residents of a State from being disadvantaged, or from being treated differently, simply because of the timing of their migration, from other similarly situated residents." *Id.* at 904 (citations omitted). Whenever a state law burdens the right to travel, the court must apply strict scrutiny and ask whether the challenged law is "necessary to further a compelling state interest." . . .

---

15. Although the Supreme Court has made it clear that the "right to travel" exists, it has struggled in identifying the precise constitutional source of that right. See, e.g., *Att'y Gen. of New York v. Soto-Lopez*, 476 U.S. 898, 902-03 (1986) (plurality) (noting that the right has been inferred from federal structure of Government, and found variously in Privileges & Immunities Clause of Article IV, Commerce Clause, and Privileges & Immunities Clause of the Fourteenth Amendment).

In the present case, Defendant has failed either to identify a "compelling state interest" or to demonstrate that the challenged law is "necessary" to further that interest. Accordingly, the Court DENIES Defendant's Motion to Dismiss as it relates to Plaintiff's third cause of action for violation of his right to travel.

CONCLUSION

For the foregoing reasons, because Plaintiff's complaint alleges sufficient facts to state claims for relief that are plausible on their face, the Court DENIES the Motion to Dismiss in its entirety.

NOTES & QUESTIONS

1. In a subsequent ruling on cross-motions for summary judgment in this case, the court held that California law sufficiently protected the right to bear arms. The case was then appealed to the United States Court of Appeals for the Ninth Circuit, where it is still pending at the time of publication of this book. *Peruta v. County of San Diego*, No. 10-56971 (9th Cir.). Under California law, licenses are required for concealed carry, and some jurisdictions, such as San Diego County, refuse to issue license for ordinary citizens to carry for lawful protection. However, until 2011, California allowed open carry without a license, provided that the handgun was not loaded. Ammunition could be carried on the person, such as in magazine pouches on the belt, but not loaded in the gun. Under the old California law, a person could only load the openly carried gun when there was an imminent, particular threat of the type that would justify calling 911. In an amicus brief to the Ninth Circuit, the International Association of Law Enforcement Educators and Trainers Association (a professional organization of police firearms trainers) disputed the claim that unloaded carry is sufficient for self-defense against a sudden attack. The brief argued that loading a pistol or revolver while undergoing a violent attack takes too long (generally several seconds); has too high a risk of error (e.g., forgetting to rack the slide on a semi-automatic handgun), requires two hands to perform (which may be impossible if one hand is needed to fend off a violent attacker), and distracts the victim from paying attention to the environment (e.g., to see if the first attacker is being joined by someone else). Brief for International Law Enforcement Educators and Trainers Association, and the Independence Institute, as Amicus Curiae in Support of Neither Party, Peruta v. County of San Diego, 10-56971 (9th Cir. May 30, 2011) (2011 WL 2180509). Crediting these claims, can you construct an argument that California law as of 2010 was compliant with the Second Amendment? Now that California no longer allows unloaded open carry without a license, is it still constitutional for a California sheriff to generally deny applications for concealed carry licenses?

2. In recent decades, nondiscretionary concealed carry laws have become the norm in the states. In 41 states, people who are permitted to own a handgun

will generally qualify for a license to carry a gun concealed in public. Contrast these laws with discretionary systems in eight states where a sheriff or other official makes a subjective judgment about the applicant's need or suitability. Discretionary systems were sometimes saddled with charges of corruption and cronyism. Those criticisms were one impulse for the rise of nondiscretionary systems. *See, e.g.,* Suzanne Novak, *Why the New York State System for Obtaining a License to Carry a Concealed Weapon Is Unconstitutional,* 26 Fordham Urb. L.J. 121 (1998); Clayton Cramer & David B. Kopel, *"Shall Issue": The New Wave of Concealed Handgun Laws,* 62 Tenn. L. Rev. 679 (1995). One state, Illinois, has no procedure for issuing concealed carry permits, but does allow unlicensed concealed carry in certain statutorily specified circumstances (e.g., on one's own property; while hunting; by elected officials).

3. There is a robust debate about the impact of concealed carry. Initially, opponents claimed that the laws would spark a tremendous increase in shootings. As the laws were implemented, crime and even gun crime actually declined. This led some researchers to conclude that CCW laws were a direct cause of decreases in crime. *See, e.g.,* John R. Lott, More Guns, Less Crime: Understanding Crime and Gun Control Laws (1998). Other scholars, however, have challenged Lott's research, and concluded that there are no statistically significant effects. Ian Ayres & John J. Donohue, III, *Shooting Down the "More Guns, Less Crime" Hypothesis,* 55 Stan. L. Rev. 1193 (2003). Reviewing both John Lott's research and the Ayres-Donohue response, James Q. Wilson concluded, "The direct evidence that shooting sprees occur [because of RTC laws] is non-existent. The indirect evidence as found in papers by . . . Ayers and Donohue is controversial. Indeed, the Ayres and Donohue paper shows that there was a 'statistically significant downward shift in the trend' of the murder rate. This suggests to me that for people interested in RTC laws, the best evidence we have is that they pose no cost and may confer benefits." James Q. Wilson, *Dissent, in* Firearms and Violence: A Critical Review 270 (2004). Wilson dissented from the committee report on RTC laws because the committee subjected Lott's studies to close scrutiny but did not closely scrutinize the studies done by his critics. The committee majority concluded that different authors have reached different conclusions on the impact of RTC laws, and that further research is needed before determining whether the laws have any statistically discernible results on crime rates.

   More recently, a study that reviewed the entire literature on the subject of concealed carry, and that added additional years and variables to the Ayers-Donohue analysis, found that the only statistically significant long-term effect is a reduction in assault. Carlisle E. Moody & Thomas B. Marvell, *The Debate on Shall-Issue Laws,* 5 Econ J. Watch 269 (2008); *but cf.* Ian Ayres & John J. Donohue III, *Yet Another Refutation of the More Guns, Less Crime Hypothesis—With Some Help from Moody and Marvell,* 6 Econ J. Watch 35 (2009) (responding to Moody and Marvell).

4. The argument that concealed carry will reduce crime suggests that criminal many actors respond rationally to incentives that make crime more risky.

What is your assessment of that assumption? Do you credit it in other contexts? Do you think that harsh mandatory prison sentences successfully deter criminals?

A study for the federal National Institute of Justice interviewed felony prisoners in 11 prisons in 10 states. The study took place in the early 1980s, when only about half a dozen states granted concealed carry permits to trustworthy adults. Even then, however, unlicensed carry in one's automobile was lawful in many states, open carry was lawful and tolerated in some jurisdictions, and, of course, some otherwise law-abiding people chose to carry a concealed handgun even though the local police refused to issue permits. The study did not distinguish between defensive use in public and in the home, and (except in the District of Columbia) defensive gun ownership and use in the home was lawful throughout the United States. The study found that:

- 34 percent of the felons reported personally having been "scared off, shot at, wounded or captured by an armed victim."
- 8 percent said the experience had occurred "many times."
- 69 percent reported that the experience had happened to another criminal whom they knew personally.
- 39 percent had personally decided not to commit a crime because they thought the victim might have a gun.
- 56 percent said that a criminal would not attack a potential victim who was known to be armed.
- 74 percent agreed with the statement that "One reason burglars avoid houses where people are at home is that they fear being shot."[1]
- "the highest concern about confronting an armed victim was registered by felons from states with the greatest relative number of privately owned firearms."

---

1. The only national study of how frequently firearms are used against burglars was conducted by the Centers for Disease Control and Prevention (CDC). In 1994, random digit dialing phone calls were made throughout the United States, resulting in 5,238 interviews. The interviewees were asked about use of a firearm in a burglary situation during the previous 12 months. Extrapolating the polling sample to the national population, the researchers estimated that in the previous 12 months, there were approximately 1,896,842 incidents in which a householder retrieved a firearm but did not see an intruder. There were an estimated 503,481 incidents in which the armed householder *did* see the burglar, and 497,646 incidents in which the burglar was scared away by the firearm. Robert M. Ikeda, Linda L. Dahlberg, Jeffrey J. Sacks, James A. Mercy & Kenneth E. Powell, *Estimating Intruder-Related Firearms Retrievals in U.S. Households, 1994*, 12 Violence & Victims 363 (1997). For analysis of whether the high rate of gun ownership, and defensive gun use against burglars is one reason why the United States, compared to other nations, has a much lower rate of burglaries attempted against occupied residences, see David B. Kopel, *Lawyers, Guns, and Burglars*, 43 Ariz. L. Rev. 345 (2001) (collecting all previous research on the topic), and Philip Cook & Jens Ludwig, *Guns & Burglary*, and David B. Kopel, *Comment*, both *in* Evaluating Gun Policy (Jens Ludwig & Philip Cook eds., 2003) (pro/con analysis of the relationship between guns and burglary).

James Wright & Peter Rossi, Armed and Considered Dangerous: A Survey of Felons and Their Firearms 146, 151, 155 (expanded ed. 1994).

5. The following chart shows the changes in state firearm-carry laws from 1986, as measured by the proportion of American citizens living in jurisdictions with different carry laws. "No Issue" refers to jurisdictions where there is no way for a typical private citizen to obtain authority to carry a handgun in public places for self-defense. (As of 2011, this means Illinois and the District of Columbia.) "May Issue" jurisdictions make handgun carry permits available to some citizens, at the discretion of local government officials. "Shall Issue" jurisdictions make carry permits available to all citizens who meet certain objective criteria such as a lack of a serious criminal record or mental illness; many of these jurisdictions also require a class in gun safety and/or self-defense law. (The category includes Connecticut and Alabama, whose statutory language is discretionary, but which in practice function as Shall Issue states.) Finally, "Unrestricted" jurisdictions allow any person who can lawfully own a handgun to carry it concealed for self-defense.

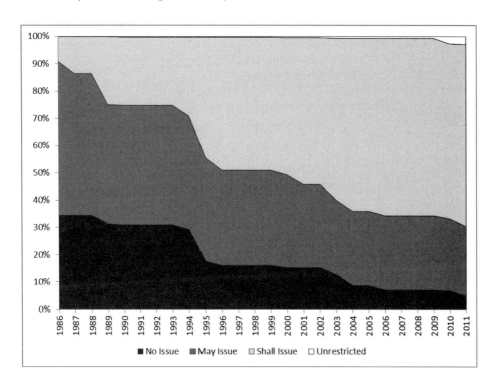

See Posting of John Richardson to http://onlygunsandmoney.blogspot.com/2011/10/every-picture-tells-story.html (Oct. 6, 2011).

Many states' laws are less permissive for nonfirearm weapons. For example, in Colorado, a person can obtain a concealed handgun license, but cannot obtain a license to carry a six-inch bladed knife for self-defense. Why might that be the case?

EXERCISE: IN-STATE CONCEALED CARRY

You are counsel in the office of the Attorney General in a state that does not grant private citizens a permit to carry firearms outside the home for self-defense. As part of the debate about a state concealed carry licensing bill, members of the legislature are threatening litigation charging that the state's blanket prohibition violates the constitutional right to bear arms. Assuming standing and other procedural requirements are satisfied, your assignment is to anticipate and assess the viability of Plaintiffs' claims and frame responses to those claims.

Potentially relevant state legislation currently includes issuance of hunting licenses permitting individuals to bear arms in the field in pursuit of game during specified seasons (or year-round, for some game). The hunting license also allows hunters to transport their unloaded firearms to and from the field. Gun owners also are allowed to transport their unloaded firearms to and from shooting ranges. Farmers and other large landowners may carry loaded guns in vehicles and on their person within the boundaries of their property and while on public roads traveling between adjacent tracts of their property. Citizens can keep firearms in their homes. State law requires that those guns be locked securely when the owner is away from home. However, when the owner is present at his residence, the gun may be kept loaded and may be carried by the owner openly or concealed on his person within the legal boundaries of his property. Open carry within the boundaries of the owner's property may not be done in a fashion that is deemed "menacing" or "threatening" to third parties.

I.   Regulating the "Terror Gap"

Federal law prohibits a variety of people from possessing firearms. People in those categories have a defined status that has been adjudicated or can be documented (e.g., felons, illegal aliens, persons who have been adjudicated mentally ill), or who can be proven to have been recently committing crimes (illegal drug users). Consider now the possibility of denying people access to firearms based on the suspicion that they are untrustworthy. In 2009, Senator Frank Lautenberg of New Jersey introduced a bill entitled Denying Firearms and Explosives to Dangerous Terrorists Act of 2009. Similar legislation was introduced in the 2011 Congress. The professed goal of the bill is to close the "Terror Gap" in the current system of federal gun regulation. The bill would prevent any person on a secret government watch lists from purchasing a firearm or explosive in the United States. The bill would be implemented by incorporating the watch list into the National Instant Criminal Background Check System (NICS) data base (the NICS is discussed in Chapter 8) and would grant the Attorney General power to prohibit the sale to individuals on the list. It would create exceptions for cases where blocking the sale might tip off a suspect under investigation. It would contain an appeal procedure for challenging the denial decision. By the ordinary operation of the "prohibited persons" desig-nation under the Gun Control Act, the bill also would make it a federal felony for any person on the watch list to possess a gun even temporarily, such as firing a friend's gun at a target range.

EXERCISE: THE RIGHT TO BEAR ARMS VS. TERRORISM CONCERNS

Your assignment is to advise on the constitutionality of the bill in light of the *Heller* decision and considering the following additional facts.

In September 2003, the Terrorist Screening Center (TSC) was created. It is managed by the FBI and is charged with administering the Terrorist Screening Database (TSDB). The TSDB is a watch list made available to law enforcement. It is constantly updated with information on known or suspected terrorists, and their associates, or people who may know them. There is no formal protocol to update or remove people from these watch list records, and names could remain on the watch list for an indefinite period of time. The list has contained as many as one million entries. The list includes individuals who are not themselves suspects, but whom the FBI wishes to question, as part of an investigation (e.g., a person who is a relative or neighbor of a suspect).

Civil rights organizations have documented that the list has included pre-sumably innocent individuals, including a liberal United States Senator, the wife of a conservative United States Senator, a black member of the House of Representatives, and a Boy Scout. Having one's name removed from the list can be a cumbersome, time-consuming, and sometimes futile process. Recall that federal law already prohibits an individual from purchasing a weapon unless he is either an American citizen or a legal resident alien. The watch list is largely comprised of illegal aliens and of foreign citizens who are not in the United States.

You may also want to consult the following additional resources:

- American Civil Liberties Union, Small, Focused Watch Lists Are Better for Civil Liberties and for Security, http://www.aclu.org/technology-and-liberty/watch-lists.
- National Rifle Association Institute for Legislative Action, Senate Hear-ing Promotes Anti-American Watchlist Bills, http://www.nraila.org/legislation/read.aspx?id = 5807 (May 7, 2010).
- Office of the Inspector General Audit Division, The Federal Bureau of Investigation's Terrorist Watchlist Nomination Practices, U.S. Dep't of Justice Audit Report (May 2009), *available at* http://www.justice.gov/oig/reports/FBI/a0925/final.pdf.
- David B. Kopel, The New McCarthyism: Restricting Constitutional Rights Based on Mere Suspicion, Independence Institute Issue Back-grounder 2005-B. June 2005, *available at* http://davekopel.org/2A/IB/New-McCarthyism.pdf.

J. Gun Regulation, Local Autonomy, and Urban Violence

Anticipating the decision in *McDonald* (Chapter 9), some commentators urged that local communities be permitted to craft their own more restrictive standards regulating firearms. *See, e.g.*, Michael B. de Leeuw et al., *Ready, Aim, Fire? District of Columbia v. Heller and Communities of Color*, 25 Harv. BlackLetter L.J. 133 (2009). These proposals mirror the approach suggested by Justice Breyer's dissent in *Heller* (Chapter 9), which proposed an interest-balancing approach that would accommodate the special problems faced by urban communities. Under this approach, the Second Amendment seemingly would have no minimum universal content. Rather, the individual right to arms would tolerate different levels of regulation (and even prohibition) in different places. The authors argue that the local community standards approach to identifying obscenity under the Court's First Amendment jurisprudence is an apt analogy. The 1973 Supreme Court case *Miller v. California*, 413 U.S. 15 (1973), allows states to criminalize the dissemination of obscene materials. Part of the test for obscenity is "whether 'the average person, applying contemporary community standards' would find that the work, taken as a whole, appeals to the prurient interest." *Id.* at 24. However, another part of the *Miller* test uses national standards to determine whether "the work, taken as a whole, lacks serious literary, artistic, political or scientific value." *Id.*

The briefing in *Heller*, the dissent of Justice Breyer, and the work of numerous commentators all point to the extensive evidence that poor urban communities suffer disproportionately from gun violence. Half of all homicides occur in America's largest cities, which house only 16 percent of the country's population. A large percentage are committed with handguns, often obtained illegally. Some illegal guns come from straw sales or illegal sales from scofflaw dealers. Approximately 500,000 guns are stolen every year from lawful owners. National Research Council of The National Academies, Firearms and Violence: A Critical Review 74 (2005). Black people are disproportionately victims of gun violence. The leading cause of death for 15- to 34-year-old African-American males is firearm homicide. African Americans are also disproportionately perpetrators of gun crime.

Some researchers tie this disproportionate rate of gun crime and victimization to a "southern subculture of violence," making the problem of Black homicide a subset of the southern subculture (including elements of that culture brought elsewhere by migrants from the South). *See* Robert J. Cottrol, *Submission Is Not the Answer: Lethal Violence, Microcultures of Criminal Violence and the Right to Self-Defense*, 69 U. Colo. L. Rev. 1029, 1050-52 (1998).

Densely populated urban areas with large minority populations generally have some of the nation's most restrictive firearms laws, largely as a response to the scourge of firearm-related violence in those communities. Michael de Leeuw et al. urge that distinguishing *Heller* to permit these communities to implement or continue their more stringent regulation of firearms should be a central part of the civil rights agenda. On the other hand, the Black plaintiffs in *Parker v. District of Columbia*, 478 F.3d 370 (D.C. Cir. 2007), *aff'd sub nom. District of Columbia v. Heller*, 554 U.S. 570 (2008), and *McDonald*, and the Congress of Racial Equality (CORE), which filed amicus briefs in *Heller* and *McDonald*, argue that possession of private firearms will help good people resist the criminal element that is terrorizing their communities.

Gun ownership is "'higher among whites than among blacks, higher among middle-aged people than among young people, higher among married than among unmarried people, higher among richer people than poor;'" — "all these 'patterns are the reverse of the way in which criminal behavior is distributed.'" Don B. Kates & Gary Mauser, *Would Banning Firearms Reduce Murder and Suicide? A Review of International and Some Domestic Evidence*, 30 Harv. J.L. & Pub. Pol'y 649 (2007). Despite a lower rate of gun ownership, the murder rate for blacks is higher than the murder rate for whites. Within the African-American community, rural Blacks own more guns than urban Blacks. Still the firearms murder rate for urban Blacks is much higher than for rural Blacks. *Id.*

EXERCISE: ADAPTING THE RIGHT TO BEAR ARMS TO LOCAL CIRCUMSTANCES

Assume *Heller* has been distinguished by subsequent decisions to allow state and local governments to impose tighter restrictions on the right to keep and bear arms to fit special state and local circumstances. Now evaluate as a matter of policy the proposal of the city of Philadelphia to ban handguns and handgun ammunition.

Incorporate the following factors into your analysis:

- Pennsylvania has a high rate of firearms ownership and a very strong culture of hunting. Pennsylvania has been a "shall issue" right-to-carry state since 1988.
- Pennsylvania is a largely rural state containing two major urban areas, Philadelphia and Pittsburgh. The balance of the state forms a "T" (consisting of the center third and the northern half) where rural and conservative values dominate. There are far more guns and more gun stores but fewer people and far less gun crime in the "T."
- Nothing in federal or state law prohibits Philadelphia residents from buying guns in other Pennsylvania counties.
- As in over half the states, Pennsylvania state law completely preempts local gun control ordinances. (A minority of states have only partial preemption, on particular firearms laws.) Thus, Philadelphia is prohibited from enacting gun laws that are more restrictive than state law. However, for purposes of this exercise, assume that the state does not prohibit Philadelphia from banning firearms possession. Assume also that Philadelphia cannot legally prohibit Philadelphians from buying guns elsewhere in Pennsylvania, but that it can criminalize bringing guns into the city.
- Nationally, approximately 500,000 guns (less than 1 percent of the civilian inventory of approximately 300 million) are stolen each year.
- Both *Heller* (in its District and Circuit Court stages, as *Parker v. District of Columbia*) and *McDonald* involved Black plaintiffs who expressed a desire to possess firearms for protection against a class of young, strong, violent

criminals who terrorized their neighborhoods. The mayor and many members of the Philadelphia City Council are Black.

Incorporate into your assessment the following questions:

- Would the Philadelphia ordinance make people like Otis McDonald (a 70-year-old veteran and pensioner who had never been arrested) better or worse off? In what ways does allowing people like Mr. McDonald to have guns/handguns contribute to the crime problem?
- What percentage of people do you estimate would defy Philadelphia's handgun ban?
- One of the pre-*Heller* complaints in jurisdictions with stringent gun laws or gun bans was that illegal guns were coming in from lax jurisdictions. Would this be a problem for the city of Philadelphia? How would you solve it?
- What changes in assumptions would make the Philadelphia policy more or less promising?

K.   Tyranny Control as a Justification for the Modern Right to Arms

While *Heller* focused mainly on the idea that the Second Amendment protects an individual right to arms for self-defense, it did not reject the proposition that the Amendment also protects the tools of political violence. *Heller* used the anti-tyranny concept to explain why the "militia" referred to in the Second Amendment's prefatory clause could not be the "organized militia," which is currently defined by statute as the National Guard, and which is subject to extensive control by the federal government. *See* Chapter 4.F. If *that* reading were true, the Court reasoned, then the Second Amendment would fail to achieve its intended purpose, because it would fail to "assure the existence of a 'citizens' militia' as a safeguard against tyranny." 554 U.S. at 600. Elsewhere, Justice Scalia's opinion stated that "when the able-bodied men of a nation are trained in arms and organized, they are better able to resist tyranny." *Id.* at 598. These brief affirmations of the anti-tyranny concept fueled criticism that carried over into *McDonald. See, e.g.*, Brief for Educational Fund to Stop Gun Violence as Amicus Curiae Supporting Respondent, McDonald v. Chicago, 130 S. Ct. 3020 (2010) (unsuccessfully urging the *McDonald* Court to "clarify that the right [recognized in *Heller*] does not include an insurrectionary component," and criticizing *Heller*'s references to armed resistance of tyranny).

Ironically, the anti-tyranny aspect of the Second Amendment was, before *Heller*, sometimes vigorously pressed by opponents of strong individual-right self-defense claims (See Chapters 5-6). But on close inspection the idea that the Second Amendment robustly protects the keeping and bearing of arms by the states for resistance to internal tyranny or external attack raises a variety of questions. The excerpt below invites discussion about the tyranny control purpose of the Second Amendment.

Silveira v. Lockyer
328 F.3d 567 (9th Cir. 2003)

KOZINSKI, J., dissenting from denial of rehearing en banc.

Judges know very well how to read the Constitution broadly when they are sympathetic to the right being asserted. We have held, without much ado, that "speech, or . . . the press" also means the Internet, *see Reno v. ACLU,* 521 U.S. 844 (1997), and that "persons, houses, papers, and effects" also means public telephone booths, *see Katz v. United States,* 389 U.S. 347 (1967). When a particular right comports especially well with our notions of good social policy, we build magnificent legal edifices on elliptical constitutional phrases—or even the white spaces between lines of constitutional text. *See, e.g., Compassion in Dying v. Washington,* 79 F.3d 790 (9th Cir. 1996) (en banc), *rev'd sub nom. Washington v. Glucksberg,* 521 U.S. 702 (1997). But, as the panel amply demonstrates, when we're none too keen on a particular constitutional guarantee, we can be equally ingenious in burying language that is incontrovertibly there.

. . . As guardians of the Constitution, we must be consistent in interpreting its provisions. . . .

The majority falls prey to the delusion—popular in some circles—that ordinary people are too careless and stupid to own guns, and we would be far better off leaving all weapons in the hands of professionals on the government payroll. But the simple truth—born of experience—is that tyranny thrives best where government need not fear the wrath of an armed people. Our own sorry history bears this out: Disarmament was the tool of choice for subjugating both slaves and free blacks in the South. In Florida, patrols searched blacks' homes for weapons, confiscated those found and punished their owners without judicial process. *See* Robert J. Cottrol & Raymond T. Diamond, *The Second Amendment: Toward an Afro-Americanist Reconsideration,* 80 Geo. L.J. 309, 338 (1991). In the North, by contrast, blacks exercised their right to bear arms to defend against racial mob violence. *Id.* at 341-42. As Chief Justice Taney well appreciated, the institution of slavery required a class of people who lacked the means to resist. *See Dred Scott v. Sandford,* 60 U.S. (19 How.) 393, 417 (1857) (finding black citizenship unthinkable because it would give blacks the right to "keep and carry arms wherever they went"). A revolt by Nat Turner and a few dozen other armed blacks could be put down without much difficulty; one by four million armed blacks would have meant big trouble.

All too many of the other great tragedies of history—Stalin's atrocities, the killing fields of Cambodia, the Holocaust, to name but a few—were perpetrated by armed troops against unarmed populations. Many could well have been avoided or mitigated, had the perpetrators known their intended victims were equipped with a rifle and twenty bullets apiece, as the Militia Act required here. . . . If a few hundred Jewish fighters in the Warsaw Ghetto could hold off the Wehrmacht for almost a month with only a handful of weapons, six million Jews armed with rifles could not so easily have been herded into cattle cars.

My excellent colleagues have forgotten these bitter lessons of history. The prospect of tyranny may not grab the headlines the way vivid stories of gun crime routinely do. But few saw the Third Reich coming until it was too late. The Second Amendment is a doomsday provision, one designed for those exceptionally rare

circumstances where all other rights have failed — where the government refuses
to stand for reelection and silences those who protest; where courts have lost the
courage to oppose, or can find no one to enforce their decrees. However improb-
able these contingencies may seem today, facing them unprepared is a mistake a
free people get to make only once.

Fortunately, the Framers were wise enough to entrench the right of the
people to keep and bear arms within our constitutional structure. The purpose
and importance of that right was still fresh in their minds, and they spelled it out
clearly so it would not be forgotten. Despite the panel's mighty struggle to erase
these words, they remain, and the people themselves can read what they say
plainly enough:

> A well regulated Militia, being necessary to the security of a free State, *the right of the*
> *people to keep and bear Arms, shall not be infringed.*

The sheer ponderousness of the panel's opinion — the mountain of verbiage it
must deploy to explain away these fourteen short words of constitutional text —
refutes its thesis far more convincingly than anything I might say. The panel's
labored effort to smother the Second Amendment by sheer body weight has all
the grace of a sumo wrestler trying to kill a rattlesnake by sitting on it — and is
just as likely to succeed.

NOTES & QUESTIONS

1. Some have suggested that the Constitution empowers Congress to call forth
    the militia to "suppress Insurrections," and it thus makes no sense that a
    constitutional provision would protect armed resistance to government. *See,*
    e.g., Dennis A. Henigan, *Arms, Anarchy and the Second Amendment*, 26 Val. U. L.
    Rev. 107, 115 (1991). Others counter that the Second Amendment protects
    not "rebellion" or "insurrection" against lawful government, but rather the
    use of force to restore constitutional order from a tyrannical usurpation. *See,*
    e.g., David C. Williams, *The Constitutional Right to "Conservative" Revolution*, 32
    Harv. C.R.-C.L. L. Rev. 413, 428 (1997); Joseph Story, A Familiar Exposition
    of the Constitution of the United States 264-65 (1840) ("The right of the
    citizens to keep and bear arms has justly been considered, as the palladium
    of the liberties of a republic; since it offers a strong moral check against the
    usurpation and arbitrary power of rulers; and it will generally, even if these
    are successful in the first instance, enable the people to resist and triumph
    over them."); *The Federalist* No. 46 (James Madison) (In the unlikely event
    the federal government became tyrannical, the tyranny could not endure,
    because the small federal standing army "would be opposed a militia
    amounting to near half a million of citizens [this figure approximates the
    size of the free adult male population in 1787] with arms in their hands,
    officered by men chosen from among themselves, fighting for their
    common liberties, and united and conducted by governments possessing
    their affections and confidence. It may well be doubted, whether a militia

thus circumstanced could ever be conquered by such a proportion of regular troops.").

Some contend that tyranny control is no longer relevant because government now has weapons against which citizens deploying small arms cannot be effective. Charles J. Dunlap, Jr., *Revolt of the Masses: Armed Civilians and the Insurrectionary Theory of the Second Amendment*, 62 Tenn. L. Rev. 643 (1995). Another argument in this vein contends that fully acknowledging a constitutional right of tyranny control would generate a right to possess bazookas, tanks, and even weapons of mass destruction. *See, e.g.,* Michael C. Dorf, *What Does the Second Amendment Mean Today?*, 76 Chi.-Kent L. Rev. 291, 297 (2000); Saul Cornell, History News Network, *The Right to Bear Bazookas: A New Take on the Second Amendment* (Mar. 19, 2007), http://hnn.us/articles/36531.html. The American Civil Liberties Union's official position prior to *Heller* summed up this view:

> If indeed the Second Amendment provides an absolute, constitutional protection for the right to bear arms in order to preserve the power of the people to resist government tyranny, then it must allow individuals to possess bazookas, torpedoes, SCUD missiles and even nuclear warheads, for they, like handguns, rifles and M-16s, are arms. Moreover, it is hard to imagine any serious resistance to the military without such arms.

American Civil Liberties Union, Gun Control (1996), *available at* http://web.archive.org/web/20020924205016/http://www.aclu.org/library/aaguns.html.

Others, like Judge Kozinski, disagree, citing evidence that even in a world with modern weapons, armed individuals have resisted their oppressors, without necessarily having to possess nuclear weapons, torpedoes, and so on.

2. Is tyranny control an unimportant aspect of the Second Amendment in the modern world? Online chapters 13 and 14 discuss the issue in an international context.

3. Does the Constitution forbid the taking up of arms against the federal or state governments? *See* U.S. Const., art. I, §8, cl. 15 (Congress can call forth the militia to suppress insurrection); U.S. Const., art. I, §9, cl. 2 (writ of Habeas Corpus may be suspended "when in Cases of Rebellion . . . the public safety may require it"); U.S. Const., amend. XIV, §2 (states that deny the vote to males age 21 or older are punished with reduced representation in the House, but states may deny the vote "for participation in rebellion, or other crime"), §3 (prohibiting the holding of any federal or state office by a person who took an oath to support the Constitution of the United States, and who later "engaged in insurrection or rebellion against the same"), §4 (debts "incurred in aid of insurrection or rebellion against the United States" are "illegal and void"). Does the answer depend on whether the purpose is to overthrow, or to restore, constitutional order?

4. Assume *arguendo* that the sophisticated collective right model is correct. (That there is an individual right to arms, solely for service in a well-regulated

militia.) Some argue that because militias as they existed in the Founding Era have essentially disappeared, any individual right associated with it has ceased to exist. *See, e.g.,* Lawrence D. Cress, *An Armed Community: The Origins and Meaning of the Right to Bear Arms,* 71 J. Am. Hist. 22 (1984). Do you find this argument compelling? If the Second Amendment's first clause controls the meaning of the second clause, what meaning should be attached to the statement that the militia is "necessary"?

5. Given that our judicial system often upholds individual rights in the face of oppressive legislative and executive action, is there any real need for a forcible check on tyranny?

Consider the ways in which power is divided in the U.S. constitutional system. The federal government is divided into three branches, the executive, legislative, and judicial. (Some consider the modern administrative state to be a fourth branch. *See* Peter L. Strauss, *The Place of Agencies in Government: Separation of Powers and the Fourth Branch,* 84 Colum. L. Rev. 573 (1984).) The legislature is itself divided into the Senate and House of Representatives. The federal government is counterbalanced by state governments.

With government power so widely dispersed, is an armed populace necessary as an additional check on power? If the Founders thought so, were they wrong? How would such a check operate? Can you imagine any circumstances where that check would be important in the modern era? Does that danger justify the costs that private firearms impose on society?

6. In general, the Federalist/Anti-Federalist conflict during the constitutional ratification debates led to a constitutional structure designed to ensure that states and individuals would not be helpless in the face of attempted federal infringements on liberty *See* Chapter 4. However, James Madison expressed his fear during congressional debates on the Bill of Rights that "there is more danger of . . . powers being abused by the State Governments than by the Government of the United States," and to that end he proposed a constitutional amendment explicitly prohibiting states from violating "the equal rights of conscience, or the freedom of the press, or the trial by jury in criminal cases." 1 Annals of Cong. 452, 458 (Joseph Gales ed., 1834). Can you think of situations where the federal government has infringed on individual liberty and states have not risen to defend their citizens? Consider the internments of Japanese-Americans, German-Americans, and Italian-Americans during World War II. *See Korematsu v. United States,* 323 U.S. 214 (1944) (upholding the internment as constitutional). On the other hand, can you think of situations where states have infringed individual liberties and the federal government has come to the individuals' aid? Consider the 1957 crisis at Central High School in Little Rock, Arkansas, where the governor of Arkansas, citing "states rights," called out the National Guard to prevent nine students from attending the school as per a desegregation plan that implemented *Brown v. Board of Education,* 347 U.S. 483 (1954). In response, President Dwight D. Eisenhower called the Arkansas National Guard into federal service, and sent in federal troops to escort the students into school. Do these episodes raise concerns about state tyranny in the modern era?

7. Assume the Second Amendment was intended to give the people a mechanism for opposing tyranny. How should the people go about defining tyranny as a procedural matter and what government actions should qualify as tyranny? Following the September 11, 2001 attacks on the United States, the USA PATRIOT Act of 2001, Pub. L. No. 107-56, gave the federal government unprecedented new powers of warrantless surveillance. Though passed for the stated purpose of helping authorities prevent further terrorist attacks before they happen, the use of the new powers has been linked to the illegal surveillance of political enemies. *See, e.g.*, Eric Lichtblau, *F.B.I. Watched Activist Groups, New Files Show*, N.Y. Times, Dec. 20, 2005, at A1; Eric Lichtblau & David E. Sanger, *Administration Cites War Vote in Spying Case*, N.Y. Times, Dec. 20, 2005, at A1. The executive branch has also asserted the power to detain American citizens, indefinitely and without habeas corpus rights, if they are deemed "enemy combatants." How should the "People" decide whether such acts constitute tyranny? What if only a few hundred or a few thousand people believe that such acts constitute tyranny?

8. Does the determination to resist tyranny with force properly lie with the state governments? James Madison seemed to suggest so in *Federalist* No. 46. So did Thomas Jefferson, in his 1811 letter to Destutt de Tracy. Jefferson acknowledged that American demagogues could arise, but he was confident that they could not rule for long. While the force of a demagogue "may paralyze the single State in which it happens to be encamped, sixteen other, spread over a country of two thousand miles diameter, rise up on every side, ready organized for deliberation by a constitutional legislature, and for action by their governor, constitutionally, the commander of the militia of the State, that is to say, of every man in it able to bear arms; and that militia, too, regularly formed into regiments and battalions, into infantry, cavalry and artillery, trained under officers general and subordinate, legally appointed, always in readiness, and to whom they are already in habits of obedience." Letter from Thomas Jefferson to Destutt de Tracy (Jan. 26, 1811), *in* 9 The Writings of Thomas Jefferson 308-09 (P. Ford ed., 1898).

   Jefferson thought the republicans fell in France because there were no local centers to resist national control. "But with us, sixteen out of seventeen States rising in mass, under regular organization, and legal commanders, united in object and action by their Congress, or, if that be in duresse, by a special convention, presents such obstacles to an usurper as forever to stifle ambition the first conception of that object." *Id.*

   Recall that article 61 of Magna Charta (Chapter 2) authorized forcible resistance to the monarch when a *majority* of the barons determined that the king was violating Magna Charta. Would armed resistance to federal "tyranny" be similarly legitimate if a majority of state governments determine it to be necessary?

Table of Cases

Principal cases are in italics, as are the page numbers on which the principal case excerpt appears. Significant briefs are cited underneath the case in which they were filed.

Table of Authorities

If an article has no listed author, it is alphabetized by the first word of the title. "A" and "The" are not taken into account in the alphabetization. If there is also no title, it is alphabetized by the name of the periodical. Documents in a collection (such as letters by an individual, or essays from a historical period) are usually listed the writer's name, not by the compilation in which they are found. Some collections of documents are listed by the last name of the editor; some are listed by the compilation's title. Documents in a compilation are often listed without additional text about the compilation; of course the full cite in compilation will be available on the relevant page of the main text.

Cerone, John, Is There a Human Right of Self Defense?, 2 J. of L., Econ & Pol'y (2006), 344

Chandler, Charles, Gun-Making as a Cottage Industry, 3 J. on Firearms & Pub. Pol'y 155 (1990), 65

Chapin, Bradley, Criminals Justice in Colonial America, 1606-1660 (1983), 115

Charles, Patrick J., The Right of Self-Preservation And Resistance: A True Legal and Historical Understanding of the Anglo-American Right to Arms, 2010 Cardozo L. Rev. De Novo 18 (2010), 93

Chase, George ed., The American Students' Blackstone (1884), 904

Children's Defense Fund, Protect Children, Not Guns (2007), 726-27

Chronicle, 53 Niles' National Register 400 (Feb. 17, 1838), 269

Chuang-Tzu, The Complete Works of Chuang Tzu (Burton Watson trans., 1968), 41

Churchill, Robert. H, Gun Regulation, the Police Power, and the Right to Keep Arms in Early America: the Legal Context of the Second Amendment, 25 Law & Hist. Rev. 139 (2007), 364, 706-07

_____, Popular Nullification, Fries's Rebellion, and the Waning of Radical Republicanism, 1798-1801, 67 Penn. Hist. 105 (Winter 2000), 248-49

_____, To Shake Their Guns in the Tyrant's Face: Libertarian Political Violence and the Origins of the Militia Movement (2008), 246

Cicero, Marcus Tullius, On Duties [De Officiis], *in* Cicero's Three Books of Offices and Other Moral Works (Cyrus R. Edmonds trans., 1871), 55-56

_____, Speech in Defence of Titus Annius Milo, *in* Orations of Marcus Tullius Cicero (Charles Duke Yonge trans., Colonial Pr., rev. ed., 1899) (52 B.C.), 55, 118-19

Cleary, Thomas, The Taoist Classics: The Collected Translations of Thomas Cleary (1999), 42-44

Clinton, Bill, My Life (2004), 450

Cobbett, William & John Wright, The Parliamentary History of England (1808), 139

Cogan, Neil H. ed., The Complete Bill Of Rights: The Drafts, Debates, Sources, and Origins (1997), 571

Coke, Edward, Institutes of the Laws of England (Johnson & Warner eds., 1812), 88

Cole, S.W. & Simon Brown eds., The New England Farmer (1851), 228

Coleman, Kenneth, The American Revolution in Georgia, 1763-1789 (1958), 173-74

Coleman-Norton, Paul Robinson & Frank Bourne, Ancient Roman Statutes: A Translation with Introduction, Commentary, Glossary, and Index (Allan Chester Johnson & Clyde Pharr eds., 2003) (1961), 53, 56

Concealed Pistols, (editorial) N.Y. Times (Jan. 27, 1905), 353

Confucius, The Analects of Confucius (Simon Leys trans., 1997), 38

Connecticut Courant (May 8, 1775), 150

Conner, R.D.W., History of North Carolina: The Colonial and Revolutionary Periods, 1584-1783 (1919), 155

Conseil du Patrimoine Privé de la Ville de Paris, Les Acquisitions Immobilières de la Ville de Paris Entre 1940 et 1944 Sont-Elles le Produit de Spoliations? (Nov. 16, 1998), 160

Continental Congress, Address of the Continental Congress to the Inhabitants of Quebec (1774), 661

A Conversation with President Clinton, (Cleveland) Plain-Dealer (Jan. 14, 1995), 443

Cook, Philip J. & Jens Ludwig, Guns in America: Results of a Comprehensive National Survey on Firearms Ownership and Use (1996), 7, 10, 898-99

_____, Gun Violence: The Real Costs (2002), 727

_____, Guns & Burglary, *in* Evaluating Gun Policy (Jens Ludwig & Philip Cook eds., 2003), 912

Cooley, Thomas M., The General Principles of Constitutional Law in the United States of America (1880), 314-18, 561, 593-94

_____, A Treatise on the Constitutional Limitations Which Rest Upon the Legislative Power of the States of the American Union (1868 and later eds.), 314-18, 829

Cooley's Constitutional Limitations, 27 Alb L.J. 300 (1883) (book note), 314

Cooper, Jerry M., The Militia and the National Guard in America Since Colonial Times: A Research Guide (1993), 236, 239, 242

_____, Jerry M., The Rise of the National Guard: The Evolution of the American Militia, 1865-1920 (2002), 147, 164, 167, 236, 239, 242

Cornell, Saul, Early American Gun Regulation and the Second Amendment: A Closer Look at the Evidence, 25 Law & Hist. Rev. 197 (2007), 707

_____, *Heller*, New Originalism, and Law Office History: "Meet the Old Boss, Same as the New Boss," 56 UCLA L. Rev. 1095 (2009), 234

_____, Originalist Methodology: A Critical Comment, 103 Nw. U. L. Rev. Colloquy 406 (2009), 234

_____, History News Network, The Right to Bear Bazookas: A New Take on the Second Amendment (2007), 921

_____, St. George Tucker's Lecture Notes, the Second Amendment, 103 Nw. U. L. Rev. Colloquy 272 (2008)

_____, St. George Tucker and the Second Amendment: Original Understandings and Modern Misunderstandings, 47 Wm. & Mary L. Rev. 1123 (2006), 233-34

_____, A Well-Regulated Militia: The Founding Fathers and the Origins of Gun Control in America (2006), 447, 610

_____ & Nathan DeDino, A Well Regulated Right, 73 Fordham L. Rev. 487 (2004), 615

Corso, Phaedra S. et al., Medical Costs and Productivity Losses Due to Interpersonal Violence and Self-Directed Violence, 32 Am. J. of Preventive Med. 474 (2007), 757

Schuster, Mark A. et al., Firearm Storage Patterns in U.S. Homes with Children, 90 Am. J. Pub. Health 588 (2000), 755

Schwartz, Adina, "Just Take Away Their Guns": The Hidden Racism of Terry v. Ohio, 23 Fordham Urb. L.J. 317 (1996), 507

Schwartz, Bernard, The Bill of Rights: A Documentary History (1971), 661

Schwoerer, Lois G., The Declaration of Rights, 1689 (1981), 584

_____, "No Standing Armies!" The Antiarmy Ideology in Seventeenth-Century England (1974), 91

Scott, S.P., The Civil Law Including The Twelve Tables, The Institutes of Gaius, The Rules of Ulpian, The Opinions of Paulus, The Enactments of Justinian, and The Constitutions of Leo (1932), 53

Scribble-Scrabble, Cumberland Gazette (Portland, Me.) (Dec. 8, 1786), 181

_____, Cumberland Gazette (Portland, Me.) (Jan. 26, 1787), 181

Selsam, J. Paul, The Pennsylvania Constitution of 1776: A Study in Revolutionary Democracy (1936), 171

Seneca, De Beneficiis (A. Golding trans., 1974), 56

Senex, Cumberland Gazette (Portland, Me.) (Jan. 12, 1787), 181

Shaffer, Rachel, Child Access Prevention Laws: Keeping Guns Out of Our Children's Hands, 27 Fordham Urb. L.J. 1985 (2000), 893

Sheehan, Colleen A., & Gary L. McDowell eds., Friends of the Constitution: Writings of the "Other" Federalists 1787-1788 (1998), 212

Sheley, Joseph F. & James D. Wright, High School Youths, Weapons, and Violence: A National Survey (Nat'l Inst. of Justice, 1998), 753

Sherrill, Robert, The Saturday Night Special (1973), 426-27, 429, 731

Shields, Nelson T. "Pete," Guns Don't Die — People Do (1981), 431-32, 779

Sickles, Daniel, Order of Major General D.E. Sickles, in E. McPherson, The Political History of the United States of America During the Period of Reconstruction (1871), 675-76

Sidney, Algernon, Discourses Concerning Government (Thomas G. West ed., 1996) (1698), 41, 63, 89

Siegel, Reva B., Dead Or Alive: Originalism As Popular Constitutionalism in Heller, 122 Harv. L. Rev. 191 (2008), 454

Simon, Jonathan, Gun Rights and the Constitutional Significance of Violent Crime, 12 Wm. & Mary Bill Rts. J. 335 (2004), 221

Singer, Norman J., Sutherland Statutory Construction (5th ed. 1992), 536

Singletary, Otis A., Negro Militia and Reconstruction (1957), 296

Skeen, C. Edward, Citizen Soldiers in the War of 1812 (1999), 250

Sklansky, David A., The Private Police, 46 UCLA L. Rev. 1165 (1999), 624

Skinner, Quentin, The Foundations of Modern Political Thought: The Renaissance (2002), 74

Small Arms Identification and Operations Guide — Eurasian Communist Countries (1980), 531

Small Arms Survey, Small Arms Survey 2007: Guns and the City (2007), 7

Smith, Adam, The Wealth of Nations (1776), 362

Smith, Page, A New Age Now Begins: A People's History of the American Revolution (1976), 150

Smith, Tom, A Call for a Truce in the DGU War, 87 J. Crim. L. & Criminology 1462 (1997), 899

Snyder, Jeffrey R., A Nation of Cowards, 113 Pub. Interest 40 (1993), 24

Solum, Lawrence B., District of Columbia v. Heller and Originalism, 103 Nw. U. L. Rev. 923 (2009), 631, 828

Some Observations on the Disposition of CCW Cases in Detroit, Note, 74 Mich. L. Rev. 614 (1976), 734

Sorenson, Susan B., Taking Guns from Batterers, 30 Evaluation Rev. 361 (2006), 739

_____ & Douglas J. Wiebe, Weapons in the Lives of Battered Women, 94 Am. J. Pub. Health 1412 (2004), 866

Sowatey, Emanuel Addo, Small Arms Proliferation and Regional Security in West Africa: The Ghanian Case, 1 New from the Nordic Afr. Inst. 6 (2005), 65

Spice, Linda, West Allis Judge Says Man Could Carry Gun, Milwaukee Journal-Sentinel (Feb. 17, 2009), 261

Spooner, Lysander, The Unconstitutionality of Slavery (1965) (1860), 278, 673

Sprecher, Robert, The Lost Amendment, 51 ABA J. 554 (June-July 1965), 431, 721

Stampp, Kenneth M., The Era of Reconstruction, 1865-1877 (1965), 674-75

_____, The Peculiar Institution: Slavery in the Ante-bellum South (1956)

Stange, Mary Zeiss, From Domestic Terrorism to Armed Revolution: Women's Right to Self-Defense as an Essential Human Right, 2 J.L. Econ. & Pol'y 385 (2006), 744

Steel, Edward M., Criminality in Jeffersonian America — A Sample, 18 Crime & Delinquency 154 (1972), 275

Stevens, John Paul, The Bill of Rights: A Century of Progress, 59 U. Chi. L. Rev. 13 (1972), 687

_____, The Third Branch of Liberty, 41 U. Miami L. Rev. 277 (1986), 693

Storing, Herbert ed., The Complete Anti-Federalist (1981), 399

Story, Joseph, Commentaries on the Constitution of the United States (1833), 285-86, 414, 590, 608-09

_____, Familiar Exposition of the Constitution of the United States (1842), 73, 285-86, 323-24, 920

Strain, Christopher B., Pure Fire: Self-Defense as Activism in the Civil Rights Era (2005), 507

Stout, Harry S., The New England Soul: Preaching and Religious Culture in Colonial New England (1988), 134

Table of Statutes, Constitutions, and Regulations

The first parts of this Table covers federal materials. The Constitution and other essential national documents come first, followed by the U.S. Code, and then by historical statutes. For some historical statutes that are still in effect, such as the National Firearms Act of 1934, the page cite may be either in the U.S. Code section, or on the Historical Statutes section. Generally speaking, if the page cite involves the interpretation of an current statute, it will be in the U.S. Code section.

After the statutes, there are sections on congressional debates, congressional reports, federal regulations, and other federal materials. Included here are materials from the Bureau of Alcohol, Tobacco, Firearms and Explosives. Note that materials from most other federal offices are in the Table of Authorities, under various subheadings of "United States."

Next are state laws, in order by state. The state constitutions come first, followed by current statutes, then historical statutes, then by city ordinances. If a constitutional provision does not have an explanatory parenthetical, it is for the state right to arms guarantee.

Finally, there are foreign laws. The United Kingdom comes first, then Roman law, and then some miscellaneous foreign laws.

Articles of Confederation (1781-88)

United States Code

*Page entries may also be listed in the Historical Statutes
section, especially for the 1934 National Firearms Act
and the 1968 Gun Control Act*

Historical Federal Statutes, in chronological order

Titles may be a popular or informal name, or a summary of the relevant content.

Bills which were not enacted

Right to Bear Arms Privacy and Protection Act, S. 2270, 106th Cong. (2000), 468-69

Denying Firearms and Explosives to Dangerous Terrorists Act (2009), 914

Congressional Debates, Hearings

For materials from the early 19th and late 18th centuries, see the Table of Authorities. The Annals of Congress listing will have many of them. Materials from the Continental Congress are in the Journals of that Congress.

35 Annals of Cong. 1083 (1855) (Rep. Hardin)

Sumner, Rep. Charles, The Crime Against Kansas (May 19-20, 1856), 590-91, 648

Cong. Globe, 39th Cong., 1st Sess., 6, 30 (1865) (Joint Comm. on Reconstruction, 14th Amend.), 294, 665-66, 675

_____, 14 (1865) (to begin drafting 14th Amend.), 294

_____, 337 (1866) (S.C. Black petition for right to arms), 294

_____, 362 (1866) (Sen. Davis's understanding was that the Second Freedman's Bureau Act protected a right to arms), 593

_____, 914-15 (1866) (Sen. Saulsbury), 649

_____, 1013 (1866) (Rep. Plants), 674

_____, 1064 (1866) (Rep. Hale), 667

_____, 1073 (1866) (Sen. Nye), 649

_____, 1088-89 (1866) (Rep. Bingham), 645, 666-67

_____, 1182 (1866) (Sen. Pomeroy), 649

_____, 1292 (1866) (Rep. Bingham), 649

_____, 1629 (1866) (Rep. Hart), 649

_____, 1838 (1866) (Rep. Lawrence), 667

_____, 1838 (1866) (Ala. Black Code), 292

_____, 2459 (1866) (Rep. Stevens), 645

_____, 2765-66 (1866) (Sen. Howard), 645, 667-68, 714

Cong. Globe, 40th Cong., 2d Sess., 1967 (1868) (Rep. Stevens), 650

Cong. Globe, 42d Cong., 1st Sess., 475-76 (1871) (Rep. Dawes), 669

_____, App. 84 (1871) (Rep. Bingham), 645

2 Cong. Rec. 384-85 (1874) (Rep. Mills), 669

National Firearms Act: Hearings on H.R. 9066 Before the House Comm. on Ways and Means, 73rd Cong. (1934), 360-61

114 Cong. Rec. 13220 (1968) (Sen. Tydings), 419

_____, 16298 (1968) (Rep. Pollock), 419

_____, 27465 (1968) (Sen. Murphy), 498

114 Cong. Rec. S5556, S5582, S5585-86 (1968) (Sen. Dodd), 497, 500

House Judiciary Committee, Federal Firearms Legislation: Hearings Before the Subcomm. on Crime of the House Judiciary Committee, 94th Cong. 1589 (1975), 733-34

Proposed Legislation to Modify the 1968 Gun Control Act: Hearings before the House Judiciary Committee, 99th Cong., 1165 (1987) (ATF Dir. Higgins), 369

Comprehensive Violent Crime Control Act of 1989: Hearing on H.R. 2709 Before the Subcomm. on Crime of the House Comm. on the Judiciary, 101st Cong., 2d Sess. 79-80 (1990) (Asst. A.G. Edward Dennis), 878

Hearing on H.R.2709 Before the Subcomm. on Crime of the House Comm. on the Judiciary, 101st Cong., 2d Sess., Comprehensive Violent Crime Control Act of 1989 (1990) (obliterated serial numbers), 878

Violence Against Women Act: Hearing on H.B. 3355 before the Subcommittee on Civil and Constitutional Rights of the Committee on the Judiciary House of Representatives, 103 Cong. 51 (November 16, 1993), 749

142 Cong. Rec. 22985 (1996) (Sen. Lautenberg), 865, 869-70

144 Cong. Rec. S8680 (July 21, 1998) (instant check records), 468

151 Cong. Rec. E2162-03 (2005) (Rep. Stearns), 529

151 Cong. Rec. S9087-01, S9374-01, 9394 (1995) (Sen. Craig), 529

_____, S9087-01 (1995) (Sen. Levin), 529

_____, S9374-01 (1995) (Sen. Thune), 529

_____, S9374-01, 9378 (2005) (Sen. Sessions), 529

Congressional Reports

Report of the Joint Committee on Reconstruction, S. Rep. No. 112 & H. R. Rep. No. 30, 39th Cong., 1st Sess. (1866), 229, 666

H.R. Exec. Doc. No. 70, 39th Cong., 1st Sess. (1866) (Freedmen's Bureau on disarmament in Kentucky), 593

H.R. Rep. No. 37, 41st Cong., (1871) (Rep. Butler), 304

H.R. Rep. No. 297, 64th Cong., 1st Sess. (1916) (National Guard), 237

S. Rep. No. 1189, 75th Cong. 1st, Sess. (1937) (Federal Firearms Act), 876

H. R. Rep. No. 1337, 83d Cong., 2d Sess., A395 (1954) (NFA short rifles), 461-62

S. Rep. No. 1097. Omnibus Crime Control and Safe Streets Act, 90th Cong., 2d Sess., 1968 U.S.C.C.A.N. 2112 (1968), 418, 477, 497

S. Rep. No. 1501, 90th Cong. 2d Sess. (Sept. 6, 1968) (Gun Control Act), 475-76, 498

U.S. Senate, Subcommittee on the Constitution, The Right to Keep and Bear Arms (1982), 435

S. Rep. No. 583, 98th Cong. 1st Sess. (1984) (Firearms Owner's Protection Act), 499

H. R. Rep. No. 495, 99th Cong. (1986) (National Firearms Act), 461

H.R. Rep. No. 693, 100th Cong. (2d Sess. 1989) (Edward R. Roybal, The Quality of Life for Older Women: Older Women Living Alone), 742

H.R. Rep. No. 681, 101st Cong., 2d Sess., pt. 1, (1990); 1990 U.S.C.C.A.N. 6472, 6510 (obliterated serial numbers), 877-78

Index